Volume 41, Number 4
October 2011

Published by the Association
Special Interest Group on D
An ACM SIGCOMM Publication

COMPUTER COMMUNICATION *review*

Proceedings of
SIGCOMM 2011

&
Best Papers of the Co-Located Workshops

Association for
Computing Machinery

Advancing Computing as a Science & Profession

acm sigcomm

Association for Computing Machinery

Advancing Computing as a Science & Profession

The Association for Computing Machinery
2 Penn Plaza, Suite 701
New York, New York 10121-0701

ISBN: 978-1-4503-0797-0

Additional copies may be ordered prepaid from:

ACM Order Department
PO Box 30777
New York, NY 10087-0777, USA

Phone: 1-800-342-6626 (USA and Canada)
+1-212-626-0500 (Global)
Fax: +1-212-944-1318
E-mail: acmhelp@acm.org
Hours of Operation: 8:30 am – 4:30 pm ET

Printed in the USA

Conference Chairs' Welcome

Welcome to ACM SIGCOMM 2011 in Toronto! As in previous years, SIGCOMM is being organized as a weeklong series of research events: the main conference is both preceded and followed by five workshops on current topics in networking.

We are happy to report that we have not only maintained registration fees at the same level of 2008, the last time SIGCOMM was held in North America. We even reduced the student registration fee compared to 2008. Given the high costs of services and goods in Canada, planning for a budget without compromising the conference experience posed quite a few challenges that were overcome only due to the generous financial help from industrial supporters of the conference. It is our privilege to acknowledge the help from our <u>Diamond supporters</u>: Infosys Corp. and Juniper Networks; <u>Platinum supporters</u>: Cisco Systems and NEC, <u>Gold supporters</u>: AT&T, Google, Riverbed, and Research in Motion; <u>Silver supporters</u>: Akamai, Alcatel-Lucent Bell Labs, HP, Intel, Microsoft Research, and Telefonica; <u>Bronze supporters</u>: Conviva, IBM Research, and Nokia. We would like to especially thank Cisco Systems Canada for their generous support of the network infrastructure during the conference.

SIGCOMM has a long tradition of supporting student participation. We have continued this tradition by keeping the cost of student registrations as low as possible, by organizing a student dinner where students can meet with leaders of the research community, and by continuing to provide liberal student travel grants. We are thankful for student travel support provided by the US National Science Foundation, ACM SIGCOMM, and the ACM Student Research Competition.

Organizing a conference such as SIGCOMM requires the involvement and dedication of a large and enthusiastic group of volunteers. We have enjoyed working with an outstanding group of colleagues who served on the organization committee and have unstintingly contributed their time and energy. The conference would be impossible to run without their volunteer spirit.

We thank all those who contributed to the organization of the technical program of the main conference and the workshops: Program chairs John Byers and Jeff Mogul, Workshop chairs Ellen Zegura and Ken Calvert, the chairs of the five selected workshops, and the chairs of the Demo and Poster program, Lili Qiu and Aditya Akella.

We want to thank the ACM SIGCOMM chair Bruce Davie, and conference coordinator Jaudelice de Oliveira for their active role and help in all stages of preparation of the conference. Last but not the least, we gratefully acknowledge the help from ACM headquarters and Lisa Tolles from Sheridan Printing Company with the preparation of the conference and workshop proceedings.

We hope that you will find SIGCOMM 2011 to be a stimulating and scientifically enriching experience. We also hope that you will find the time to enjoy the hospitable and cosmopolitan atmosphere of the city of Toronto.

Srinivasan Keshav *SIGCOMM 2011 Co-Chair* *University of Waterloo*

Jörg Liebeherr *SIGCOMM 2011 Co-Chair* *University of Toronto*

Message from the Technical Program Committee Chairs

Welcome to the 2011 ACM SIGCOMM Conference in Toronto, Canada. It has been our pleasure to oversee the tremendous efforts volunteered by our technical program committee and other individuals in shaping this year's technical program. We hope that you will find the papers selected for the technical program stimulating and thought-provoking, and that you enjoy the conference!

SIGCOMM 2011 received 223 submissions, and we accepted 32 papers, for an acceptance ratio of 14%. This represents a modest drop over the number of submissions from previous years. We received submissions from authors in at least 36 countries, and the final program reflects the significant geographical diversity across submissions, with authors representing 12 different countries and 44 distinct institutions.

The SIGCOMM 2011 TPC comprised 50 members from academia and industry, reflecting the diversity of our community. The TPC members' research interests span the wide range of topics present in this year's submissions and accepted papers. The members of the TPC wrote at least three first-round reviews for all 223 submissions, as well as three or more second-round reviews for the top 101 papers. Thus, we had at least 6 reviews for each of the 70 papers that we discussed in the TPC meeting. Most second-round papers received significant online discussion between PC members prior to the TPC meeting, and in some cases we solicited additional reviews from external topic experts. In total, the submissions received over 1000 written reviews. Reviewing was double-blind, and was subject to a strict conflict-of-interest policy. PC members with potential conflicts of interest were excluded from all discussions of the relevant papers. Both of the TPC co-chairs were authors of submissions; these reviews were handled entirely outside of the online review system, so as to guarantee reviewer anonymity.

Almost all of the TPC members attended the TPC meeting in Boston in person, for 1.5 days of energetic discussion. Those who were not able to attend in person participated via a telephone conference. We strove, as TPC chairs, to ensure that all 70 papers received full and fair discussion, and we encouraged the TPC to consider prioritizing "appropriately risky" papers over otherwise comparable "correct but boring" papers when there was a choice. Each of the 32 accepted papers was shepherded by a member of the TPC, to help the authors improve their final versions.

Many people contributed to creating the SIGCOMM 2011 technical program. First of all, we would like to thank the authors of all submissions for the significant effort this represents. We also thank the members of the TPC for their hard and careful work in writing reviews and shepherding the accepted papers. (The average member wrote 20 reviews, most of them quite detailed.) In addition, we thank the external reviewers for augmenting our expertise. We received considerable help from the SIGCOMM Technical Steering Committee, and from past SIGCOMM chairs including K.K. Ramakrishnan, Geoff Voelker, and Stefan Savage.

We could never have managed this process without Eddie Kohler's superb HotCRP software, and especially without Eddie's prompt responses to our requests for bug fixes and improvements. We also thank Geoff Voelker for his banal software for checking the format of submitted PDFs, the staff at HP Labs Research Services for providing server support, Boston University graduate student Michel Machado for his helpful support during the PC meeting, and Ellen Grady at BU for her help with PC meeting logistics.

Many people on the SIGCOMM 2011 Organizing Committee allowed us to focus on selecting the papers by relieving us of most other tasks. In particular, we would like to thank Nicolas Christin for his rapid updates to the conference Web site, and Stratis Ioannidis for relieving us of the burden of dealing with many of the tedious details associated with the Proceedings.

Finally, we would like to thank the many industry supporters of SIGCOMM 2011, especially for their support of travel grants for students, post-docs, and junior faculty. The newer members of our community create much of the vibrancy that makes SIGCOMM a uniquely exciting event, and corporate financial support represents an effective investment in the future of our field.

We encourage SIGCOMM attendees to take full advantage of the many opportunities at the conference, including the chance to catch up with old friends and meet new ones, to generate new ideas in hallway discussions, and even to complain to us about the papers you don't like – we hope we took enough risky papers to get some of you upset.

John Byers
Boston University, USA

Jeff Mogul
HP Labs, USA

SIGCOMM 2011 TPC Co-Chairs

Table of Contents

Keynote Address

Session 1: Security
Session Chair: Balachander Krishnamurthy *(AT&T Labs - Research)*

Session 2: Novel Data Center Architectures
Session Chair: Jitendra Padhye *(Microsoft Research)*

Session 3: Bulk Data Transfers
Session Chair: David Clark *(Massachusetts Institute of Technology)*

Session 9: Network Management – Reasoning and Debugging
Session Chair: Sachin Katti *(Stanford University)*

Session 10: ISPs and Wide-Area Networking
Session Chair: Walter Willinger *(AT&T Labs - Research)*

Session 11: Network Measurement II – What's Going On?
Session Chair: Emin Gün Sirer *(Cornell University)*

SIGCOMM 2011 Posters Session 1

SIGCOMM 2011 Demos Session 1

SIGCOMM 2011 Demos Session 2

SIGCOMM 2011 Best Workshop Papers

GreenNet'11 Best Papers

HomeNets'11 Best Papers

ICN'11 Best Papers

W-MUST'11 Best Papers

NetEd'11 Best Papers

SIGCOMM 2011 Conference Organization

General Chairs:	Srinivasan Keshav *(University of Waterloo, Canada)*
	Jörg Liebeherr *(University of Toronto, Canada)*
Program Chairs:	John Byers *(Boston University, USA)*
	Jeffrey Mogul *(HP Labs, USA)*
Local Arrangements Chair:	Yashar Ganjali *(University of Toronto, Canada)*
Finance Chair:	Martin Karsten *(University of Waterloo, Canada)*
Workshop Chairs:	Ken Calvert *(University of Kentucky, USA)*
	Ellen Zegura *(Georgia Institute of Technology, USA)*
Web and Publicity Chair:	Nicolas Christin *(Carnegie Mellon University, USA)*
Poster/Demo Chairs:	Aditya Akella *(University of Wisconsin–Madison)*
	Lili Qiu *(University of Texas–Austin, USA)*
Travel Grant Chairs:	Kenjiro Cho *(IIJ Research Laboratory, Japan)*
	Arun Venkataramani *(University of Massachusetts–Amherst, USA)*
	Giorgio Ventre *(University of Napoli, Italy)*
Publications Chair:	Stratis Ioannidis *(Technicolor, USA)*
Registrations Chair:	Georgios Smaragdakis *(Deutsche Telekom Labs, Germany)*
Outrageous Opinions Session Chair:	Stefan Saroiu *(Microsoft Research, USA)*
SIGCOMM Conference Coordinator:	Jaudelice de Oliveira *(Drexel University, USA)*
SIGCOMM Chair:	Bruce Davie *(Cisco)*
SIGCOMM Conference Technical Steering Committee:	K. K. Ramakrishnan *(AT&T Labs – Research, USA)*, Chair
	Ernst Biersack *(Eurecom, France)*
	Peter Druschel *(Max Planck Institute for Software Systems, Germany)*
	Konstantina Papagiannaki *(Telefonica, Spain)*
	Jennifer Rexford *(Princeton University, USA)*
	Stefan Savage *(University of California, San Diego, USA)*

SIGCOMM 2011 Sponsor and Supporters

Sponsor:

Diamond Supporters:

Platinum Supporters:

Gold Supporters:

Silver Supporters:

Bronze Supporters:  IBM Research

Keynote Address

Reflections on Measurement Research: Crooked Lines, Straight Lines, and Moneyshots

Vern Paxson

University of California and International Computer Science Institute
Berkeley, California, USA

"Recipient of the 2011 SIGCOMM Award"

sigcomm 2011
Toronto

They Can Hear Your Heartbeats: Non-Invasive Security for Implantable Medical Devices

Shyamnath Gollakota [†]   Haitham Hassanieh[†]   Benjamin Ransford[*]   Dina Katabi[†]   Kevin Fu[*]

[†]Massachusetts Institute of Technology
{gshyam, haithamh, dk}@mit.edu

[*]University of Massachusetts, Amherst
{ransford, kevinfu}@cs.umass.edu

ABSTRACT

Wireless communication has become an intrinsic part of modern implantable medical devices (IMDs). Recent work, however, has demonstrated that wireless connectivity can be exploited to compromise the confidentiality of IMDs' transmitted data or to send unauthorized commands to IMDs—even commands that cause the device to deliver an electric shock to the patient. The key challenge in addressing these attacks stems from the difficulty of modifying or replacing already-implanted IMDs. Thus, in this paper, we explore the feasibility of protecting an implantable device from such attacks without modifying the device itself. We present a physical-layer solution that delegates the security of an IMD to a personal base station called the *shield*. The shield uses a novel radio design that can act as a jammer-cum-receiver. This design allows it to jam the IMD's messages, preventing others from decoding them while being able to decode them itself. It also allows the shield to jam unauthorized commands—even those that try to alter the shield's own transmissions. We implement our design in a software radio and evaluate it with commercial IMDs. We find that it effectively provides confidentiality for private data and protects the IMD from unauthorized commands.

Categories and Subject Descriptors C.2.2 [**Computer Systems Organization**]: Computer-Communications Networks

General Terms Algorithms, Design, Performance, Security

Keywords Full-duplex, Implanted Medical Devices, Wireless

1. INTRODUCTION

The past few years have produced innovative health-oriented networking and wireless communication technologies, ranging from low-power medical radios that harvest body energy [27] to wireless sensor networks for in-home monitoring and diagnosis [51, 55]. Today, such wireless systems have become an intrinsic part of many modern medical devices [39]. In particular, implantable medical devices (IMDs), including pacemakers, cardiac defibrillators, insulin pumps, and neurostimulators all feature wireless communication [39]. Adding wireless connectivity to IMDs has enabled remote monitoring of patients' vital signs and improved care providers' ability to deliver timely treatment, leading to a better health care system [31].

Recent work, however, has shown that such wireless connectivity can be exploited to compromise the confidentiality of the IMD's transmitted data or to send the IMD unauthorized commands—even commands that cause the IMD to deliver an electric shock to the patient [21, 22]. In other systems, designers use cryptographic methods to provide confidentiality and prevent unauthorized access. However, adding cryptography *directly* to IMDs themselves is difficult for the following reasons:

- *Inalterability:* In the U.S. alone, there are millions of people who already have wireless IMDs, and about 300,000 such IMDs are implanted every year [58]. Once implanted, an IMD can last up to 10 years [14], and replacing it requires surgery that carries risks of major complications. Incorporating cryptographic mechanims into existing IMDs may be infeasible because of limited device memory and hence can only be achieved by replacing the IMDs. This is not an option for people who have IMDs or may acquire them in the near future.

- *Safety:* It is crucial to ensure that health care professionals always have immediate access to an implanted device. However, if cryptographic methods are embedded in the IMD itself, the device may deny a health care provider access unless she has the right credentials. Yet, credentials might not be available in scenarios where the patient is at a different hospital, the patient is unconscious, or the cryptographic key storage is damaged or unreachable [22, 31]. Inability to temporarily adjust or disable an IMD could prove fatal in emergency situations.[1]

- *Maintainability:* Software bugs are particularly problematic for IMDs because they can lead to device recalls. In the last eight years, about 1.5 million software-based medical devices were recalled [15]. Between 1999 and 2005, the number of recalls of software-based medical devices more than doubled; more than 11% of all medical-device recalls during this time period were attributed to software failures [15]. Such recalls are costly and could require surgery if the model is already implanted. Thus, it is desirable to limit IMDs' software to only medically necessary functions.

This paper explores the feasibility of protecting IMDs *without modifying them* by implementing security mechanisms entirely on an external device. Such an approach enhances the security of IMDs for patients who already have them, empowers medical personnel to access a protected IMD by removing the external device or powering it off, and does not in itself increase the risk of IMD recalls.

---

[1]Note that distributing the credentials widely beyond the patient's primary health care providers increases the probability of the key being leaked and presents a major key revocation problem.

We present a design in which an external device, called the *shield*, is interposed between the IMD and potential counter-parties—e.g., worn on the body near an implanted device. The shield acts as a gateway that relays messages between the IMD and authorized endpoints. It uses a novel physical-layer mechanism to secure its communication with the IMD, and it uses a standard cryptographic channel to communicate with other authorized endpoints.

The shield counters two classes of adversarial actions: passive eavesdropping that threatens the confidentiality of the IMD's transmissions, and active transmission of unauthorized radio commands to the IMD. First, to provide confidentiality for the IMD's transmissions, the shield continuously listens for those transmissions and jams them so that they cannot be decoded by eavesdroppers. The shield uses a novel radio design to simultaneously receive the IMD's signal and transmit a jamming signal. The shield then transmits the IMD's signal to an authorized endpoint using standard cryptographic techniques. Second, to protect the IMD against commands from unauthorized endpoints, the shield listens for unauthorized transmissions addressing the IMD and jams them. As a result of jamming, the IMD cannot decode the adversarial transmissions, and hence the adversary fails to make the IMD execute an unauthorized command.

A key challenge that we had to overcome to realize this architecture is to design a small wearable radio that simultaneously jams the IMD's signal and receives it. We build on prior work in the area of full-duplex radio design, which enables a single node to transmit and receive simultaneously [3, 7]. However, prior work requires large antenna separation and hence yields large devices unsuitable for our application. In particular, the state-of-the-art design for full-duplex radios [3] exploits the property that a signal reverses its phase every half a wavelength; it transmits the same signal from two antennas and puts a receive antenna *exactly* half a wavelength closer to one of the transmit antennas than the other. An antenna separation of half a wavelength, however, is unsuitable for our context: the IMDs we consider operate in the 400 MHz band [13] with a wavelength of about 75 cm. A shield that requires the antennas to be rigidly separated by exactly half a wavelength (37.5 cm) challenges the notion of wearability and therefore patient acceptability.

This paper presents a full-duplex radio that does not impose restrictions on antenna separation or positioning, and hence can be built as a small wearable device. Our design uses two antennas: a jamming antenna and a receive antenna, placed next to each other. The jamming antenna transmits a random signal to prevent eavesdroppers from decoding the IMD's transmissions. However, instead of relying on a particular positioning to cancel the jamming signal at the receive antenna, we connect the receive antenna simultaneously to both a transmit and a receive chain. We then make the transmit chain send an *antidote* signal that cancels the jamming signal at the receive antenna's front end, allowing it to receive the IMD's signal and decode it. We show both analytically and empirically that our design delivers its security goals without antenna separation; hence it can be built as a small wearable radio.

Our design has additional desirable features. Specifically, because the shield can receive while jamming, it can detect adversaries who try to alter the shield's signal to convey unauthorized messages to the IMD. It can also ensure that it stops jamming the medium when an adversarial signal ends, allowing legitimate devices to communicate.

We have implemented a prototype of our design on USRP2 software radios [9]. We use 400 MHz daughterboards for compatibility with the 402–405 MHz Medical Implant Communication Services (MICS) band used by IMDs [13]. We evaluate our prototype shield against two modern IMDs, namely the Medtronic Virtuoso implantable cardiac defibrillator (ICD) [37] and the Concerto cardiac resynchronization therapy device (CRT) [36]. Our evaluation reveals the following:

- When the shield is present, it jams the IMD's messages, causing even nearby (20 cm away) eavesdroppers to experience a bit error rate of nearly 50%, which is no better than a random guess.
- When the shield jams the IMD's packets, it can still reliably decode them (the packet loss rate is 0.2%, which is negligible). We conclude that the shield and the IMD share an information channel that is inaccessible to other parties.
- When the shield is absent, the IMD replies to unauthorized commands, even if the adversary is in a non-line-of-sight location more than 14 m away, and uses a commercial device that operates in the MICS band and adheres to the FCC power limit.
- When the shield is present and has the same transmit power as the adversary, the IMD does not respond to unauthorized commands, even when the adversary is only 20 cm away.
- When the shield is absent and an adversary with 100 times the shield's power transmits unauthorized commands, the IMD responds from distances as large as 27 m. When the shield is present, however, the high-powered adversary's attempts succeed only from distances less than 5 m, and only in line-of-sight locations. The shield always detects high-powered adversarial transmissions and raises an alarm. We conclude that sufficiently high-powered adversaries present an intrinsic limitation to our physical-layer protection mechanism. However, the shield's presence reduces the adversary's success range and informs the patient, raising the bar for the adversary's attempts.

The shield is, to our knowledge, the first system that simultaneously provides confidentiality for IMDs' transmissions and protects IMDs against commands from unauthorized parties *without requiring any modification to the IMDs themselves*. Further, because it affords physical-layer protection, it may also help provide a complementary defense-in-depth solution to devices that feature cryptographic or other application-layer protection mechanisms.

Disclaimer. Operating a jamming device has legal implications that vary by jurisdiction and frequency band. The definition of jamming also depends on both context and intent. Our experiments were conducted in tightly controlled environments where no patients were present. Further, the intent of a shield is never to interfere with communications that do not involve its protected IMD. We recommend that anyone considering deployment of technology based on this research consult with their own legal counsel.

2. IMD COMMUNICATION PRIMER

Wireless communication appears in a wide range of IMDs, including those that treat heart failure, diabetes, and Parkinson's disease. Older models communicated in the 175 KHz band [22]. However, in 1999, the FCC set aside the 402–405 MHz band for medical implant communication services (MICS) [13]. The MICS band was considered well suited for IMDs because of its international availability for this purpose [10], its signal propagation characteristics in the human body, and its range of several meters that allows remote monitoring. Modern IMDs communicate medical information in the MICS band, though devices may use other bands for activation (e.g., 2.4 GHz or 175 KHz) [45]. IMDs share the MICS band with meteorological systems on a secondary basis and should ensure that their usage of it does not interfere with these systems. The FCC divides the MICS band into multiple channels of 300 KHz width [13]. A pair of communicating devices uses one of these channels.

IMDs typically communicate infrequently with a device called an IMD programmer (hereafter, *programmer*). The programmer initiates a session with the IMD during which it either queries the IMD for its data (e.g., patient name, ECG signal) or sends it commands (e.g., a treatment modification). By FCC requirement, the IMD does not normally initiate communications; it transmits *only* in response to a transmission from a programmer [13] or if it detects a life-threatening condition [23].

A programmer and an IMD share the medium with other devices as follows [13]. Before they can use a 300 KHz channel for their session, they must "listen" for a minimum of 10 ms to ensure that the channel is unoccupied. Once they find an unoccupied channel, they establish a session and alternate between the programmer transmitting a query or command, and the IMD responding immediately without sensing the medium [24]. The programmer and IMD can keep using the channel until the end of their session, or until they encounter persistent interference, in which case they listen again to find an unoccupied channel.

3. ASSUMPTIONS AND THREAT MODEL

3.1 Assumptions

We assume that IMDs and authorized programmers are honest and follow the protocols specified by the FCC and their manufacturers. We also assume the availability of a secure channel for transmissions between authorized programmers and the shield; this channel may use the MICS band or other bands. We further assume that the shield is a wearable device located close to the IMD, such as a necklace. Wearable medical devices are common in the medical industry [34, 49]. We also assume that the adversary does not physically try to remove the shield or damage it. We assume that legitimate messages sent to an IMD have a checksum and that the IMD will discard any message that fails the checksum test. This latter assumption is satisfied by all wireless protocols that we are aware of, including the ones used by the IMDs we tested (§9). Finally, we assume that the IMD does not normally initiate transmissions (in accordance with FCC rules [13]); if the IMD initiates a transmission because it detects a life-threatening condition, we make no attempt to protect the confidentiality of that transmission.

3.2 Threat Model

We address two classes of commonly considered radio-equipped adversaries: passive eavesdroppers that threaten the confidentiality of the IMD's transmissions, and active adversaries that attempt to send unauthorized radio commands to the IMD [15, 32].

(a) Passive eavesdropper: Such an adversary eavesdrops on the wireless medium and listens for an IMD's transmissions. Specifically, we consider an adversary with the following properties:

- The adversary may try different decoding strategies. It may consider the jamming signal as noise and try to decode in the presence of jamming. Alternatively, it can implement interference cancellation or joint decoding in an attempt to simultaneously decode the jamming signal and the IMD's transmission. However, basic results in multi-user information theory show that decoding multiple signals is impossible if the total information rate is outside the capacity region [53]. We ensure that the information rate at the eavesdropper exceeds the capacity region by making the shield jam at an excessively high rate; the jamming signal is random and sent without modulation or coding.
- The adversary may use standard or custom-built equipment. It may also use MIMO systems and directional antennas to try to separate the jamming signal from the IMD's signal. MIMO and directional antenna techniques, however, require the two transmitters to be separated by more than half a wavelength (see

Chapter 1 in [26] and Chapter 7 in [53]). The IMDs we consider operate in the 400 MHz band with a wavelength of about 75 cm. Thus, one can defend against a MIMO eavesdropper or an eavesdropper with a directional antenna by ensuring that the shield is located significantly less than half a wavelength from the IMD. For example, if the protected IMD is a pacemaker implanted near the clavicle, the shield may be implemented as a necklace or a brooch, allowing it to sit within a few centimeters of the IMD.

- The adversary may be in any location farther away from the IMD than the shield (e.g., at distances 20 cm and greater).

(b) Active adversary: Such an adversary sends unauthorized radio commands to the IMD. These commands may be intended to modify the IMD's configuration or to trigger the IMD to transmit unnecessarily, depleting its battery. We allow this adversary the following properties:

- The adversary may use one of the following approaches to send commands: it may generate its own unauthorized messages; it may record prior messages from other sources and play them back to the IMD; or it may try to alter an authorized message on the channel, for example, by transmitting at a higher power and causing a capture effect at the IMD [46].
- The adversary may use different types of hardware. The adversary may transmit with a commercial IMD programmer acquired from a hospital or elsewhere. Such an approach does not require the adversary to know the technical specifications of the IMD's communication or to reverse-engineer its protocol. However, an adversary that simply uses an unmodified commercial IMD programmer cannot use a transmit power higher than that allowed by the FCC. Alternatively, a more sophisticated adversary might reverse-engineer the IMD's communication protocol, then modify the IMD programmer's hardware or use his own radio transmitter to send commands. In this case, the adversary can customize the hardware to transmit at a higher power than the FCC allows. Further, the adversary may use MIMO or directional antennas. Analogous to the above, however, MIMO beamforming and directional antennas require the two receivers to be separated by a minimum of half a wavelength (37 cm in the MICS band), and hence can be countered by keeping the shield in close proximity to the IMD.
- The adversary may be in any location farther away from the IMD than the shield.

4. SYSTEM OVERVIEW

To achieve our design goal of protecting an IMD without modifying it, we design a device called the *shield* that sits near the IMD and acts as a proxy. An authorized programmer that wants to communicate with the IMD instead exchanges its messages with the shield, which relays them to the IMD and sends back the IMD's responses, as shown in Fig. 1. We assume the existence of an authenticated, encrypted channel between the shield and the programmer. This channel can be established using either in-band [19] or out-of-band solutions [28].

The shield actively prevents *any* device other than itself from communicating directly with the IMD. It does so by jamming messages sent to and from the IMD. Key to the shield's role is its ability to act as a jammer-cum-receiver, which enables it to jam the IMD's transmissions and prevent others from decoding them, while still being able to decode them itself. It also enables the shield to detect scenarios in which an adversary tries to overpower the shield's own transmissions to create a capture effect on the IMD and deliver an unauthorized message. By proxying IMD communications

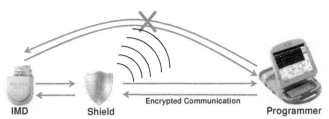

Figure 1—Protecting an IMD without modifying it: The shield jams any direct communication with the IMD. An authorized programmer communicates with the IMD only through the shield, with which it establishes a secure channel.

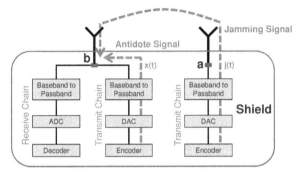

Figure 2—The jammer-cum-receiver design uses two antennas: a jamming antenna that transmits the jamming signal, and a receive antenna. The receive antenna is connected to both a transmit and receive chain. The antidote signal is transmitted from the transmit chain to cancel out the jamming signal in the receive chain.

without requiring patients to interact directly with the shield, our design aligns with IMD industry trends toward wireless, time- and location-independent patient monitoring.

The next sections explain the jammer-cum-receiver's design, implementation, and use against passive and active adversaries.

5. JAMMER-CUM-RECEIVER

A jammer-cum-receiver naturally needs to transmit and receive simultaneously. This section presents a design for such a full-duplex radio. Our design has two key features: First, it imposes no size restrictions and hence can be built as a small wearable device. Second, it cancels the jamming signal only at the device's receive antenna and at no other point in space—a necessary requirement for our application.

Our design, shown in Fig. 2, uses two antennas: a jamming antenna and a receive antenna. The jamming antenna transmits a random jamming signal. The receive antenna is simultaneously connected to both a transmit and a receive chain. The transmit chain sends an antidote signal that cancels the jamming signal at the receive antenna's front end, allowing the receive antenna to receive any signal without disruption from its own jamming signal.

The antidote signal can be computed as follows. Let $j(t)$ be the jamming signal and $x(t)$ be the antidote. Let H_{self} be the self-looping channel on the receive antenna (i.e., the channel from the transmit chain to the receive chain on the same antenna) and $H_{jam \to rec}$ the channel from the jamming antenna to the receive antenna. The signal received by the shield's receive antenna is:

$$y(t) = H_{jam \to rec} \, j(t) + H_{self} \, x(t). \qquad (1)$$

To cancel the jamming signal at the receive antenna, the antidote must satisfy:

$$x(t) = -\frac{H_{jam \to rec}}{H_{self}} \, j(t). \qquad (2)$$

Thus, by transmitting a random signal $j(t)$ on its jamming antenna

and an antidote $x(t)$ on its receive antenna, the shield can receive signals transmitted by other nodes while jamming the medium.

Next, we show that the antidote cancels the jamming signal only at the shield's receive antenna, and no other location. Let $H_{jam \to l}$ and $H_{rec \to l}$ be the channels from the shield's jamming and receive antennas, respectively, to the adversary's location l. An antenna positioned at l receives the combined signal:

$$y(t) = H_{jam \to l} \, j(t) + H_{rec \to l} \, x(t) \qquad (3)$$

$$= \left(H_{jam \to l} - H_{rec \to l} \frac{H_{jam \to rec}}{H_{self}} \right) j(t). \qquad (4)$$

For the jamming signal to be cancelled out at location l, the following must be satisfied:

$$\frac{H_{jam \to l}}{H_{rec \to l}} = \frac{H_{jam \to rec}}{H_{self}}. \qquad (5)$$

Locating the shield's two antennas very close to each other ensures that at any location l the attenuation from the two antennas is comparable, i.e., $\left| \frac{H_{jam \to l}}{H_{rec \to l}} \right| \approx 1$ (see Chapter 7 in [53] for a detailed analysis). In contrast, $\left| \frac{H_{jam \to rec}}{H_{self}} \right| \ll 1$; $|H_{self}|$ is the attenuation on the short wire between the transmit and receive chains in the receive antenna, which is significantly less than the attenuation between the two antennas that additionally have to go on the air [17]. For example, in our USRP2 prototype, the ratio $\left| \frac{H_{jam \to rec}}{H_{self}} \right| \approx -27$ dB. Thus, the above condition is physically infeasible, and cancelling the jamming signal at the shield's receive antenna does not cancel it at any other location.

We note several ancillary properties of our design:

- *Transmit and receive chains connected to the same antenna:* Off-the-shelf radios such as the USRP [9] have both a receive and a transmit chain connected to the same antenna; they can in principle transmit and receive simultaneously on the same antenna. Traditional systems cannot exploit this property, however, because the transmit signal overpowers the receive chain, preventing the antenna from decoding any signal but its own transmission. When the jamming signal and the antidote signal cancel each other, the interference is cancelled and the antenna can receive from other nodes while transmitting.

- *Antenna cancellation vs. analog and digital cancellation:* Cancelling the jamming signal with an antidote is a form of antenna cancellation. Thus, as in the antenna cancellation scheme by Choi et al. [3], one can improve performance using hardware components such as analog cancelers [43]. In this case, the input to the analog canceler will be taken from points **a** and **b** in Fig. 2; the output will be fed to the passband filter in the receive chain.

- *Channel estimation:* Computing the antidote in equation 2 requires knowing the channels H_{self} and $H_{jam \to rec}$. The shield estimates these channels using two methods. First, during a session with the IMD, the shield measures the channels immediately before it transmits to the IMD or jams the IMD's transmission. In the absence of an IMD session the shield periodically (every 200 ms in our prototype) estimates this channel by sending a probe. Since the shield's two antennas are close to each other, the probe can be sent at a low power to allow other nodes to leverage spatial reuse to concurrently access the medium.

- *Wideband channels:* Our discussion has been focused on narrowband channels. However, the same description can be extended to work with wideband channels which exhibit multipath effects. Specifically, such channels use OFDM, which divides the bandwidth into orthogonal subcarriers and treats each of the subcarri-

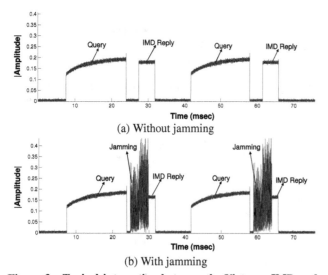

(a) Without jamming

(b) With jamming

Figure 3—Typical interaction between the Virtuoso IMD and its programmer: Without jamming (a), the IMD transmits in response to an interrogation. The bottom graph (b) shows that the IMD transmits within a fixed interval without sensing the medium.

ers as if it was an independent narrowband channel. Our model naturally fits in this context.[2]

6. VERSUS PASSIVE EAVESDROPPERS

To preserve the confidentiality of an IMD's transmissions, the shield jams the IMD's signal on the channel. Since the wireless channel creates linear combinations of concurrently transmitted signals, jamming with a random signal provides a form of one-time pad, where only entities that know the jamming signal can decrypt the IMD's data [50]. The shield leverages its knowledge of the jamming signal and its jammer-cum-receiver capability to receive the IMD's data in the presence of jamming.

To realize our design goal, the shield must ensure that it jams every packet transmitted by the IMD. To this end, the shield leverages two properties of MICS-band IMD communications [13, 24]:

- An IMD does not transmit except in a response to a message from a programmer. The shield can listen for programmer transmissions and anticipate when the IMD may start transmitting.
- An IMD transmits in response to a message from a programmer without sensing the medium. This allows the shield to bound the interval during which the IMD replies after receiving a message.

Fig. 3 shows an example exchange between a Medtronic Virtuoso implantable cardiac defibrillator (ICD) and a programmer (in this case, a USRP). Fig. 3(a) shows that the Virtuoso transmits in response to a programmer's message after a fixed interval (3.5 ms). To check that the Virtuoso indeed does not sense the medium, we made the programmer USRP transmit a message to the Virtuoso and within 1 ms transmit another random message. Fig. 3(b) plots the resulting signal and shows that the Virtuoso still transmitted after the same fixed interval even though the medium was occupied.

Given the above properties, the shield uses the following algorithm to jam the IMD's transmissions. Let T_1 and T_2 be the lower and upper bounds on the time that the IMD takes to respond to a message, and let P be the IMD's maximum packet duration. Whenever the shield sends a message to the IMD, it starts jamming the medium exactly T_1 milliseconds after the end of its transmission.

---

[2]More generally, one could compute the multi-path channel and apply an equalizer [18] on the time-domain antidote signal that inverts the multi-path of the jamming signal.

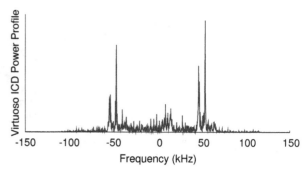

Figure 4—The frequency profile of the FSK signal captured from a Virtuoso cardiac defibrillator shows that most of the energy is concentrated around ±50 KHz.

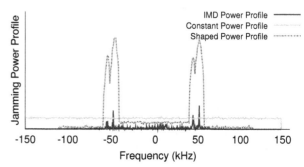

IMD Power Profile ———
Constant Power Profile ·········
Shaped Power Profile ··········

Figure 5—Shaping the jamming signal's profile to match an IMD's allows the shield to focus its jamming power on the frequencies that matter for decoding, as opposed to jamming across the entire 300 KHz channel.

While jamming, the shield receives the signal on the medium using its receive antenna. The shield jams for $(T_2 - T_1) + P$ milliseconds.

Additionally, to deal with scenarios in which the IMD may transmit in response to an unauthorized message, the shield uses its ability to detect active adversaries that might succeed at delivering a message to the IMD (see §7(d)). Whenever such an adversary is detected, the shield uses the same algorithm above, as if the message were sent to the IMD by the shield itself.

We note that each shield should calibrate the above parameters for its own IMD. In particular, for the IMDs tested in this paper, the above parameters are as follows: $T_1 = 2.8$ ms, $T_2 = 3.7$ ms, and $P = 21$ ms.

Our design of the shield sets three sub-goals:

(a) Maximize jamming efficiency for a given power budget: It is important to match the frequency profile of the jamming signal to the frequency profile of the jammed signal [30]. To understand this issue, consider the example of the Virtuoso cardiac defibrillator. This device operates over a channel bandwidth of 300 KHz. However, it uses FSK modulation where a '0' bit is transmitted at one frequency f_0 and a '1' bit is transmitted at a different frequency f_1. Fig. 4 shows the frequency profile of the FSK signal captured from a Virtuoso cardiac defibrillator. A jammer might create a jamming signal over the entire 300 KHz. However, since the frequency-domain representation of the received FSK signal has most of its energy concentrated around f_0 and f_1, an adversary can eliminate most of the jamming signal by applying two band-pass filters centered on f_0 and f_1.

Therefore, an effective jammer should consider the structure of the IMD's signal when crafting the jamming signal, shaping the amount of energy it puts in each frequency according to the frequency profile of the IMD signal. Fig. 5 compares the power profile of a jamming signal that is shaped to fit the signal in Fig. 4 and an oblivious jamming signal that uses a constant power profile. The figure shows that the shaped signal has increased jamming power in frequencies that matter for decoding.

To shape its jamming signal appropriately, the shield generates the jamming signal by taking multiple random white Gaussian noise signals and assigning each of them to a particular frequency bin in the 300 KHz MICS channel. The shield sets the variance of the white Gaussian noise in each frequency bin to match the power profile resulting from the IMD's FSK modulation in that frequency bin. We then take the IFFT of all the Gaussian signals to generate the time-domain jamming signal. This process generates a random jamming signal that has a power profile similar to the power profile generated by IMD modulation. The shield scales the amplitude of the jamming signal to match its hardware's power budget. The shield also compensates for any carrier frequency offset between its RF chain and that of the IMD.

(b) Ensure independence of eavesdropper location: To ensure confidentiality, the shield must maintain a high bit error rate (BER) at the adversary, *independent* of the adversary's location. The BER at the adversary, however, strictly depends on its signal-to-interference-and-noise ratio, $SINR_A$ [17]. To show that the BER at the adversary is independent of its location, we show that the SINR at the adversary is independent of its location.

Suppose the IMD transmits its signal at a power P_i dB and the shield transmits the jamming signal at a power P_j dB. The IMD's signal and the jamming signal will experience a pathloss to the adversary of L_i and L_j, respectively. Thus, the SINR at the adversary can be written in dB as:

$$\text{SINR}_A = (P_i - L_i) - (P_j - L_j) - N_A, \qquad (6)$$

where N_A is the noise in the adversary's hardware. Since equation 6 is written in a logarithmic scale, the pathlosses translate into subtractions.

The pathloss from the IMD to the adversary can be expressed as the sum of the pathloss that the IMD's signal experiences in the body and on the air, i.e., $L_i = L_{body} + L_{air}$ [39]. Since the shield and the IMD are close together, the pathlosses they experience on the air to the adversary are approximately the same—i.e., $L_{air} \approx L_j$ [53]. Thus, we can rewrite equation 6 as:

$$\text{SINR}_A = (P_i - L_{body}) - P_j - N_A. \qquad (7)$$

The above equation shows that SINR_A is independent of the adversary's location and can be controlled by setting the jamming power P_j to an appropriate value. This directly implies that the BER at the adversary is independent of its location.

(c) SINR tradeoff between the shield and the adversary: Similarly to how we computed the SINR of an eavesdropper, we can compute the SINR of the shield (in dB) as:

$$\text{SINR}_S = (P_i - L_{body}) - (P_j - G) - N_G, \qquad (8)$$

where N_G is the thermal noise on the shield and G is the reduction in the jamming signal power at the receive antenna due to the antidote. The above equation simply states that SINR_S is the IMD power after subtracting the pathloss due mainly to in-body propagation, the residual of the jamming power $(P_j - G)$, and the noise.

Note that if one ignores the noise on the shield's receive antenna and the adversary's device (which are negligible in comparison to the other terms), one can express the relation between the two SINRs using a simple equation:

$$\text{SINR}_S = \text{SINR}_A + G. \qquad (9)$$

This simplified view reveals an intrinsic tradeoff between the SINR at the shield and the adversary, and hence their BERs. To increase

the BER at the adversary while maintaining a low BER at the shield, one needs to increase G, which is the amount of jamming power cancelled at the shield's receive antenna. We refer to G as the *SINR gap* between the shield and the adversary.

We show in §10.1 that for the tested IMDs, an SINR gap of $G = 32$ dB suffices to provide a BER of nearly 50% at the adversary (reducing the adversary to guessing) while maintaining reliable packet delivery at the shield.

7. VERSUS ACTIVE ADVERSARIES

Next, we explain our approach for countering active adversaries. At a high level, the shield detects unauthorized packets and jams them. The jamming signal combines linearly with the unauthorized signal, causing random bit flips during decoding. The IMD ignores these packets because they fail its checksum test.

The exact active jamming algorithm follows. Let S_{id} be an *identifying sequence*, i.e., a sequence of m bits that is always used to identify packets destined to the IMD. S_{id} includes the packets' physical-layer preamble and the subsequent header. When the shield is not transmitting, it constantly monitors the medium. If it detects a signal on the medium, it proceeds to decode it. For each newly decoded bit, the shield checks the last m decoded bits against the identifying sequence S_{id}. If the two sequences differ by fewer than a threshold number of bits, b_{thresh}, the shield jams the signal until the signal stops and the medium becomes idle again.

The shield also uses its receive antenna to monitor the medium while transmitting. However, in this case, if it detects a signal concurrent to its transmission, it switches from transmission to jamming and continues jamming until the medium becomes idle again. The reason the shield jams any concurrent signal without checking for S_{id} is to ensure that an adversary cannot successfully alter the shield's own message on the channel in order to send an unauthorized message to the IMD.

We note five subtle design points:

(a) Choosing identifying sequences: Our algorithm relies on the identifying sequence S_{id} in order to identify transmissions destined for the protected IMD. We therefore desire a method of choosing a per-device S_{id} based on unique device characteristics. Fortunately, IMDs already bear unique identifying characteristics. For example, the Medtronic IMDs that we tested (the Virtuoso ICD and the Concerto CRT) use FSK modulation, a known preamble, a header, and the device's ID, i.e., its 10-byte serial number. More generally, each wireless device has an FCC ID, which allows the designer to look up the device in the FCC database and verify its modulation, coding, frequency and power profile [12].[3] One can use these specifications to choose an appropriate identifying sequence. Furthermore, once in a session, the IMD locks on to a unique channel, to receive any future commands. Since other IMD–programmer pairs avoid occupied channels, this channel ID can be used to further specify the target IMD.

(b) Setting the threshold b_{thresh}: If an adversary can transmit a signal and force the shield to experience a bit error rate higher than the IMD's, it may prevent the shield from jamming an unauthorized command that the IMD successfully decodes and executes. However, we argue that such adversarial success is unlikely, for two reasons. First, because the signal goes through body tissue, the IMD experiences an additional pathloss that could be as high as 40 dB [47], and hence it naturally experiences a much weaker signal than the shield. Second, the IMD uses a harder constraint to accept a packet than the constraint the shield uses to jam a packet. Specifically, the IMD requires that all bits be correct to pass a checksum,

---

[3]For example, the FCC ID *LF5MICS* refers to Medtronic IMDs we tested.

while the shield tolerates some differences (up to b_{thresh} bits) between the identifying sequence and the received one. We describe our empirical method of choosing b_{thresh} in §10.1(c).

(c) Customizing for the MICS band: It is important to realize that the shield can listen to the entire 3 MHz MICS band, transmit in all or any subset of the channels in this band, and further continue to listen to the whole band as it is transmitting in any subset of the channels. It is fairly simple to build such a device by making the radio front end as wide as 3 MHz and equipping the device with per-channel filters. This enables the shield process the signals from all channels in the MICS band simultaneously.

The shield uses this capability to monitor the entire 3 MHz MICS band because an adversary can transmit to the IMD on any channel in the band. This monitoring allows the shield to detect and counter adversarial transmissions even if the adversary uses frequency hopping or transmits in multiple channels simultaneously to try to confuse the shield. The shield jams any given 300 KHz channel if the channel contains a signal that matches the constraints described in the active jamming algorithm.

(d) Complying with FCC rules: The shield must adhere to the FCC power limit even when jamming an adversary. However, as explained in §3, a sophisticated adversary may use a transmission power much higher than the FCC limit. In such cases, the adversary will be able to deliver its packet to the IMD despite jamming. However, the shield is still useful because it can detect the high-powered adversary in real time and raise an alarm to attract the attention of the patient or a caregiver. Such alarms may be similar to a cell phone alarm, i.e., the shield may beep or vibrate. It is desirable to have a low false positive rate for such an alarm. To that end, we calibrate the shield with an IMD to find the minimum adversarial transmit power that can trigger a response from the IMD despite jamming. We call this value P_{thresh}. When the shield detects a potentially adversarial transmission, it checks whether the signal power exceeds P_{thresh}, in which case it raises an alarm.

Finally, we note that when the shield detects a high-powered active adversary, it also considers the possibility that the adversary will send a message that triggers the IMD to send its private data. In this case, the shield applies the passive jamming algorithm: in addition to jamming the adversary's high-powered message, it jams the medium afterward as detailed in §6.

(e) Battery life of the shield: Since jamming consumes power, one may wonder how often the shield needs to be charged. In the absence of attacks, the shield jams only the IMD's transmissions, and hence transmits approximately as often as the IMD. IMDs are typically nonrechargeable power-limited devices that do not transmit frequently [11]. Thus, in this mode of operation, we do not expect the battery of the shield to be an issue. When the IMD is under an active attack, the shield will have to transmit as often as the adversary. However, since the shield transmits at the FCC power limit for the MICS band, it can last for a day or longer even if transmitting continuously. For example, wearable heart rate monitors that continuously transmit ECG signals can last 24–48 hours [57].

8. IMPLEMENTATION

We implement a proof-of-concept prototype shield with GNU Radio and USRP2 hardware [9, 16]. The prototype uses the USRP's RFX400 daughterboards, which operate in the MICS band [13]. The USRP2 does not support multiple daughterboards on the same motherboard, so we implement a two-antenna shield with two USRP2 radio boards connected via an external clock [25] so that they act as a single node. The two antennas are placed right next to each other.

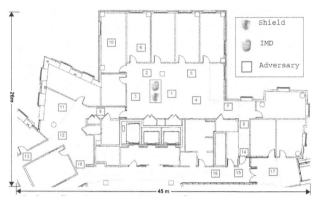

Figure 6—Testbed setup showing shield, IMD, and adversary locations. We experiment with 18 adversary locations, numbered here in descending order of received signal strength at the shield.

Our design for a two-antenna jammer-cum-receiver requires the receive antenna to be always connected to both a transmit and a receive chain. To enable the shield's receive antenna to transmit and receive simultaneously, we turn off the USRP RX/TX switch, which leaves both the transmit and receive chains connected to the antenna all the time. Specifically, we set `atr_txval=MIX_EN` and `atr_rxval=ANT_SW` in the TX chain, and we set `atr_txval=MIX_EN` and `atr_rxval=MIX_EN` in the RX chain, in the USRP2's firmware and FPGA code. Finally, we equip the shield with FSK modulation and demodulation capabilities so that it can communicate with an IMD.

9. TESTING ENVIRONMENT

Our experiments use the following devices:

- Medtronic Virtuoso DR implantable cardiac defibrillators (ICDs) [37].
- A Medtronic Concerto cardiac resynchronization therapy device (CRT) [36].
- A Medtronic Vitatron Carelink 2090 Programmer [35].
- USRP2 software radio boards [9].

In our *in vitro* experiments, the ICD and CRT play the role of the protected IMD. The USRP devices play the roles of the shield, the adversary, and legitimate users of the MICS band. We use the programmer off-line with our active adversary; the adversary records the programmer's transmissions in order to replay them later. Analog replaying of these captured signals doubles their noise, reducing the adversary's probability of success, so the adversary demodulates the programmer's FSK signal into the transmitted bits to remove the channel noise. The adversary then re-modulates the bits to obtain a clean version of the signal to transmit to the IMD.

Fig. 6 depicts the testing setup. To simulate implantation in a human, we followed prior work [22] and implanted each IMD beneath 1 cm of bacon, with 4 cm of 85% lean ground beef packed underneath. We placed the shield next to the IMD on the bacon's surface to simulate a necklace. We varied the adversary's location between 20 cm and 30 m, as shown in the figure.

10. EVALUATION

We evaluate our prototype of a shield against commercially available IMDs. We show that the shield effectively protects the confidentiality of the IMD's messages and defends the IMD against commands from unauthorized parties. We experiment with both the Virtuoso ICD and the Concerto CRT. However, since the two IMDs did not show any significant difference, we combine the experimen-

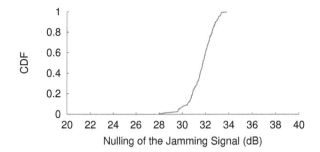

Figure 7—Antenna cancellation: The antidote signal reduces the jamming signal by 32 dB on average.

tal results from both devices and present them together. Our results can be summarized as follows.

- In practice, our antenna cancellation design can cancel about 32 dB of the jamming signal at the receive antenna (§10.1(a)). This result shows that our design achieves similar performance to the antenna cancellation algorithm proposed in prior work [3], but without requiring a large antenna separation.
- Setting the shield's jamming power 20 dB higher than the IMD's received power allows the shield to achieve a high bit error rate at adversarial locations while still being able to reliably decode the IMD's transmissions (§10.1(b)). The shield's increased power still complies with FCC rules in the MICS band since the transmit power of implanted devices is 20 dB less than the transmit power for devices outside the body [40, 41].
- With the above setting, the bit error rate at a passive eavesdropper is nearly 50% at all tested locations—i.e., an eavesdropping adversary's decoding efforts are no more effective than random guessing. Further, even while jamming, the shield can reliably decode the IMD's packets with a packet loss rate less than 0.2%. We conclude that the shield and the IMD share an information channel inaccessible to other parties (§10.2).
- When the shield is present and active, an adversary using off-the-shelf IMD programmers cannot elicit a response from the protected IMD even from distances as small as 20 cm. A more sophisticated adversary that transmits at 100 times the shield's power successfully elicits IMD responses only at distances less than 5 meters, and only in line-of-sight locations. Further, the shield detects these high-powered transmissions and raises an alarm. We conclude that the shield significantly raises the bar for such high-powered adversarial transmissions (§10.3).

10.1 Micro-Benchmark Results

In this section, we calibrate the parameters of the shield and examine the performance of its components.

(a) Antenna cancellation: We first evaluate the performance of the antenna cancellation algorithm in §5, in which the shield sends an antidote signal to cancel the jamming signal on its receive antenna.

In this experiment, the shield transmits a random signal on its jamming antenna and the corresponding antidote on its receive antenna. In each run, it transmits 100 Kb without the antidote, followed by 100 Kb with the antidote. We compute the received power at the receive antenna with and without the antidote. The difference in received power between the two trials is the amount of jamming cancellation resulting from the transmission of the antidote.

Fig. 7 shows the CDF of the amount of cancellation over multiple runs of the experiment. It shows that the average reduction in jamming power is about 32 dB. The figure also shows that the variance of this value is small. This result shows that the antenna cancellation

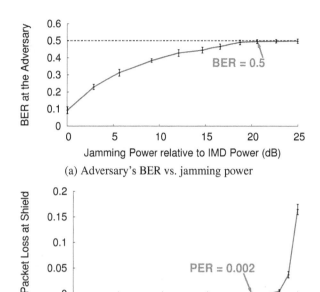

(a) Adversary's BER vs. jamming power

(b) Shield's PER vs. jamming power

Figure 8—Tradeoff between BER at the eavesdropper and reliable decoding at the shield: If the shield sets its jamming power 20 dB higher than the power it receives from the IMD, it can ensure that an eavesdropper sees a BER around 50% (a)—effectively reducing the eavesdropper to guessing—while keeping the packet loss rate (PER) at the shield as low as 0.2% (b).

algorithm introduced in this paper achieves similar performance to the antenna cancellation algorithm proposed by Choi et al. [3], but without requiring a large antenna separation.[4]

(b) Tradeoffs between eavesdropper error and shield error: The aforementioned 32 dB of cancellation at the shield's receive antenna naturally sets an upper bound on the jamming power: if the residual error after jamming cancellation is too high, the shield will fail to decode the IMD's data properly.

To explore the tradeoff between the error at the shield and the error at an eavesdropper, we run the following experiment. We place the IMD and the shield at their marked locations in Fig. 6, and we place a USRP eavesdropper 20 cm away from the IMD at location 1. In each run of the experiment, the shield repeatedly triggers the IMD to transmit the same packet. The shield also uses its jammer-cum-receiver capability to simultaneously jam and decode the IMD's packets. The eavesdropper tries to decode the IMD packets, in the presence of jamming, using an optimal FSK decoder [38].

Fig. 8(a) plots the eavesdropper's BER as a function of the shield's jamming power. Since the required jamming power naturally depends on the power of the jammed IMD's signal, the x-axis reports the shield's jamming power relative to the power of the signal it receives from the IMD. The figure shows that if the shield sets its jamming power 20 dB higher than the power of the signal it receives from the IMD, the BER at an eavesdropper is 50%, which means the eavesdropper's decoding task is no more successful than random guessing.

Next, we check that the above setting allows the shield to reliably decode the IMD's packets. As above, Fig. 8(b) plots the shield's packet loss rate as a function of its jamming power relative to the

---

[4]Choi et al. [3] also combine antenna cancellation with analog and digital cancellation to obtain a total cancellation of 60 dB at the receive antenna. However, we show in §10.2 that for our purposes, a cancellation of 32 dB suffices to achieve our goal of high reliability at the shield and nearly 50% BER at the adversary.

P_{thresh}: Adversary power that elicits IMD response	Minimum	−11.1 dBm
	Average	−4.5 dBm
	Standard Deviation	3.5 dBm

Table 1—Adversarial RSSI that elicits IMD responses despite the shield's jamming.

power of the signal it receives from the IMD. The figure shows that if the shield's jamming power is 20 dB higher than the IMD's power, the packet loss rate is no more than 0.2%. We conclude that this jamming power achieves both a high error rate at the eavesdropper and reliable decoding at the shield.

We note that the shield's increased power, described above, still complies with FCC rules on power usage in the MICS band because the transmit power of implanted devices is 20 dB less than the maximum allowed transmit power for devices outside the body [40, 41].

(c) Setting the jamming parameters: Next we calibrate the jamming parameters for countering active adversaries. The shield must jam unauthorized packets sent to the IMD it protects. It must jam these packets even if it receives them with some bit errors, because they might otherwise be received correctly at the IMD. We therefore empirically estimate an upper bound, b_{thresh}, on the number of bit flips an IMD accepts in an adversary's packet header. The shield uses this upper bound to identify packets that must be jammed.

To estimate b_{thresh}, we perform the following experiment. First, a USRP transmits unauthorized commands to the IMD to trigger it to send patient data. We repeat the experiment for all locations in Fig. 6. The shield stays in its marked location in Fig. 6, but its jamming capability is turned off. However, the shield logs all of the packets transmitted by the IMD as well as the adversarial packets that triggered them. We process these logs offline and, for packets that successfully triggered an IMD response despite containing bit errors, we count the number of bit flips in the packet header. Our results show that it is unlikely that a packet will have bit errors at the shield but still be received correctly by the IMD. Out of 5000 packets, only three packets showed errors at the shield but still triggered a response from an IMD. The maximum number of bit flips in those packets was 2, so we conservatively set $b_{thresh} = 4$.

Next, we measure P_{thresh}, the minimum adversary RSSI at the shield that can elicit a response from the IMD in the presence of jamming. To do so, we fix the location of the IMD and the shield as shown in Fig. 6. Again we use a USRP that repeatedly sends a command to trigger the IMD to transmit. We fix the adversary in location 1 and vary its transmit power. Table 1 reports the minimum and average RSSI at the shield's receive antenna for all packets that succeeded in triggering the IMD to transmit. We set P_{thresh} 3 dB below the minimum RSSI in the table and use that value for all subsequent experiments.

10.2 Protecting from Passive Adversaries

To evaluate the effectiveness of the shield's jamming, we run an experiment in which the shield repeatedly triggers the IMD to transmit the same packet. The shield also uses its jammer-cum-receiver capability to jam the IMD's packets while it decodes them. We set the shield's jamming power as described in §6. In each run, we position an eavesdropper at a different location shown in Fig. 6 and make the IMD send 1000 packets. The eavesdropping adversary attempts to decode the IMD's packets using an optimal FSK decoder [38]. We record the BER at the eavesdropper and the packet loss rate at the shield.

Fig. 9 plots a CDF of the eavesdropper's BER taken over all locations in Fig. 6. The CDF shows that the eavesdropper's BER is nearly 50% in all tested locations. We conclude that our design of the shield achieves the goal of protecting the confidentiality of

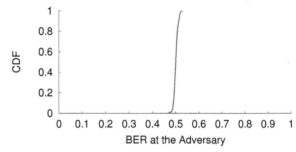

Figure 9—CDF of an eavesdropper's BER over all eavesdropper locations in Fig. 6: At all locations, the eavesdropper's BER is nearly 50%, which makes its decoding task no more successful than random guessing. The low variance in the CDF shows that an eavesdropper's BER is independent of its location.

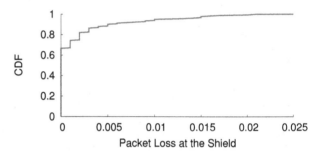

Figure 10—Packet loss at the shield: When the shield is jamming, it experiences an average packet loss rate of only 0.2% when receiving the IMD's packets. We conclude that the shield can reliably decode the IMD's transmissions despite jamming.

IMD's transmissions from an eavesdropper regardless of the eavesdropper's location.

For the same experiment, Fig. 10 plots a CDF of the packet loss rate of IMD-transmitted packets at the shield. Each point on the x-axis refers to the packet loss rate over 1000 IMD packets. The average packet loss rate is about 0.2%, considered low for wireless systems [8]. Such a low loss rate is due to two factors. First, we locate the shield fairly close to the IMD, so it receives the IMD's signal at a relatively high SNR. Second, the jamming cancellation is sufficient to maintain a high SNR that ensures a low packet loss rate. We conclude that the shield can decode the IMD's packets reliably, even while jamming.

10.3 Protecting from Active Adversaries

We distinguish between two scenarios representing different levels of adversarial sophistication. In the first, we consider scenarios in which the adversary uses an off-the-shelf IMD programmer to send unauthorized commands to the IMD. In the second, a more sophisticated adversary reverse-engineers the protocol and uses custom hardware to transmit with much higher power than is possible in the first scenario.

(a) Adversary that uses a commercial IMD programmer: The simplest way an adversary can send unauthorized commands to an IMD is to obtain a standard IMD programmer and use its built-in radio. Since commercial programmers abide by FCC rules, in this scenario, the adversary's transmission power will be comparable to that of the shield.

Using an IMD programmer we obtained via a popular auction website, we play the role of such an active adversary. We use the setup in Fig. 6, fixing the IMD's and shield's locations and transmitting unauthorized commands from all the marked locations. As shown in the figure, we experiment with both line-of-sight and non-

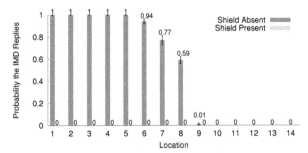

Figure 11—Without the shield, triggering an IMD to transmit and deplete its battery using an off-the-shelf IMD programmer succeeds with high probability. With the shield, such attacks fail.

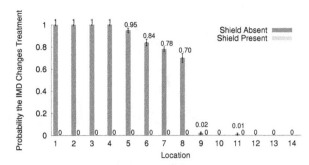

Figure 12—Without the shield, an adversary using an off-the-shelf programmer to send unauthorized commands (in this case, to modify therapy parameters) succeeds with high probability. The shield materially decreases the adversary's ability to control the IMD.

line-of-sight locations as well as nearby (20 cm) and relatively far locations (30 m).

To test whether the shield's jamming is effective against unauthorized commands, regardless of which unauthorized command the adversary chooses to send, we experiment with two types of adversarial commands: those that trigger the IMD to transmit its data with the objective of depleting its battery, and those that change the IMD's therapy parameters. In each location, we play each command 100 times with the shield on and 100 times with the shield off. After each attempt, we check whether the command was successful. To determine whether the first type of command was successful—i.e., whether it elicited a reply—we sandwiched a USRP observer along with the IMD between the two slabs of meat. To allow the USRP observer to easily check whether the IMD transmitted in response to the adversary's command, we configure the shield to jam only the adversary's packets, not the packets transmitted by the IMD. To determine whether a therapy modification command was successful, we use the IMD programmer to read the therapy parameters before and after the attempt.

Fig. 11 and Fig. 12 show the results of these experiments. They plot the probability that adversarial commands succeed with the shield off (absent) and on (present), each as a function of adversary locations. The locations are ordered by decreasing SNR at the USRP observer. The figures show the following:

- When the shield is off, adversaries located up to 14 meters away (location 8) from the IMD—including non-line-of-sight locations—can change the IMD's therapy parameters or cause the IMD to transmit its private data using precious battery energy, in contrast to past work in which the adversarial range is limited to a few centimeters [22]. We attribute this increased adversarial range to recent changes in IMD design that enable longer-range radio communication (MICS band) meant to support remote monitoring and a larger sterile field during surgery.
- When the shield is on, it successfully prevents the IMD from receiving adversarial commands as long as the adversary uses a device that obeys FCC rules on transmission power—even when the adversary is as close as 20 cm.
- There is no statistical difference in success rate between commands that modify the patient's treatment and commands that trigger the IMD to transmit private data and deplete its battery.

(b) High-powered active adversary: Next, we experiment with scenarios in which the adversary uses custom hardware to transmit at 100 times the shield's transmit power. The experimental setup is similar to those discussed above; specifically, we fix the locations of the IMD and the shield and vary the high-powered adversary's position among the numbered locations in Fig. 6. Each run has two phases: one with the shield off and another with the shield on. Since we found no statistical difference in success rate between unautho-

rized commands that trigger the IMD to transmit and those that change its therapy parameters, we show results only for the therapy modification command.

Fig. 13 shows the results of this experiment in terms of the observed probability of adversarial success, with the shield both on and off. It also shows the observed probability that the shield raises an alarm, which is how the shield responds to a high-powered (above P_{thresh}) adversarial transmission. The figure further shows:

- When the shield is off, the adversary's increased transmission power allows it to elicit IMD responses from as far as 27 meters (location 13) and from non-line-of-sight locations.
- When the shield is on, the adversary elicits IMD responses only from nearby, line-of-sight locations. Thus, the shield's presence raises the bar even for high-powered adversaries.
- Whenever the adversary elicits a response from the IMD in the presence of the shield, the shield raises an alarm. The shield also raises an alarm in response to *unsuccessful* adversarial transmissions that are high powered and emanate from nearby locations (e.g., location 6). While this conservative alert results in false positives, we believe it is reasonable to alert the patient that an adversary is nearby and may succeed at controlling the IMD.

11. COEXISTENCE

We investigate how the presence of a shield affects other legitimate users of the medium. As explained in §2, the FCC rules for medical devices in the MICS band require such devices to monitor a candidate channel for 10 ms and avoid using occupied channels. As a result, two pairs of honest medical devices are unlikely to share the same 300 KHz channel. We focus our evaluation on coexistence with the meteorological devices that are the primary users of the MICS band (and hence can transmit even on occupied channels).

In this experiment, we position the IMD and the shield in the locations marked on Fig. 6. We make a USRP board alternate between sending unauthorized commands to the IMD and transmitting cross-traffic unintended for the IMD. The cross-traffic is modeled after the transmissions of meteorological devices, in particular a Vaisala digital radiosonde RS92-AGP [1] that uses GMSK modulation. For each of the adversary positions in Fig 6, we make the USRP alternate between one packet to the IMD and one cross-traffic packet. The shield logs all packets it detects and reports which of them it jammed.

Post-processing of the shield's log showed that the shield did not jam any of the cross-traffic packets, regardless of the transmitter's location. In contrast, the shield jammed all of the packets that it detected were addressed to the IMD; see Table 2. Further, our software radio implementation of the shield takes 270 ± 23 μs after an adversary stops transmitting to turn around and stop its own

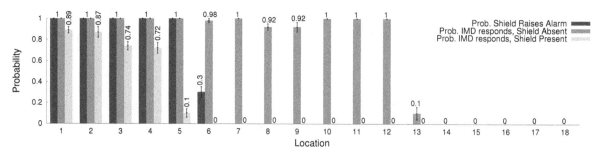

Figure 13—High-powered adversary: Without the shield, an adversary transmitting at 100 times the shield's power can change the IMD's therapy parameters even from non-line-of-sight locations up to 27 m away. With the shield, the adversary is successful only from line-of-sight locations less than 5 m away, and the shield raises an alarm.

Probability of Jamming	Cross-Traffic	0
	Packets that trigger IMD	1
Turn-around Time	Average	270 μs
	Standard Deviation	23 μs

Table 2—Coexistence results: Jamming behavior and turn-around time in the presence of simulated meteorological cross-traffic.

transmissions. This delay is mainly due to the shield's being implemented in software. A hardware implementation would have a more efficient turn-around time of tens of microseconds. (Note, for example, that a 802.11 card can turn around in a SIFS duration of 10 μs.) The low turn-around time shows that the shield does not continuously jam the medium (thereby denying others access to it).

12. RELATED WORK

Recent innovations in health-related communication and networking technologies range from low-power implantable radios that harvest body energy [27] to medical sensor networks for in-home monitoring and diagnosis [51, 55]. Past work has also studied the vulnerabilities of these systems and proposed new designs that could improve their security [21, 22]. Our work builds on this foundation, but it differs from all past works in that it presents the first system that defends existing commercial IMDs against adversaries who eavesdrop on transmissions or send unauthorized commands.

Our design is motivated by the work of Halperin et al., who analyzed the security properties of an implantable cardiac device and demonstrated its vulnerability to adversarial actions that compromise data confidentiality or induce potentially harmful heart rhythms [21, 22]. They also suggested adding passively powered elements to implantable devices to allow them to authenticate their interlocutors. Along similar lines, Denning et al. propose a class of devices called *cloakers* that would share secret keys with IMDs [6]; an IMD would attempt to detect an associated cloaker's presence either periodically or when presented with an unknown programmer. Unlike these three proposals, our technique does not require cryptographic methods and is directly applicable to IMDs that are already implanted.

Other work has focused on the problem of key distribution for cryptographic security. Cherukuri et al. propose using consistent human biometric information to generate identical secret keys at different places on a single body [2]. Schechter suggests that key material could be tattooed onto patients using ultraviolet micro-pigmentation [48].

Our work builds on a rich literature in wireless communication. Specifically, past work on jamming focuses on enabling wireless communication in the presence of adversarial jamming [29, 42]. Some past work, however, has proposed to use friendly jamming to prevent adversarial access to RFID tags, sensor nodes, and IMDs [33, 44, 56]. Our work is complementary to this past work

but differs from it in that our jammer can transmit and receive at the same time; this allows it to decode IMD messages while protecting their confidentiality.

Our work is related to prior work on physical-layer information-theoretic security. Past work in this area has shown that if the channel to the receiver is better than the channel to an eavesdropper, the sender-receiver pair can securely communicate [5, 52, 54]. Also, our prior work proposes iJam, an OFDM-based technique that jams while receiving to prevent unauthorized receivers from obtaining a protected signal [20]. iJam, however, is not applicable to IMDs because it relies on the intrinsic characteristics of OFDM signals, which differ greatly from IMDs' FSK signals. Further, iJam requires changes to both the transmitter and receiver, and hence does not immediately apply to IMDs that are already implanted.

Finally, our work also builds on past work on full-duplex radio [3, 7, 4]. Ours, however, differs from all past works in that it is the first to demonstrate the value of using full-duplex radios for security. Furthermore, we implement a radio where the antennas are placed next to each other so that it can be built as a small device and show both empirically and analytically that our design secures IMDs using only 30 dB cancellation which is significantly less than the 60-80 dB cancellation required by prior work [7, 3].

13. CONCLUSION

The influx of wireless communication in medical devices brings a number of domain-specific problems that require the expertise of both the wireless and security communities. This paper addresses the problem of communication security for implantable medical devices. The key challenge in addressing this problem stems from the difficulty of modifying or replacing implanted devices. We present the design and implementation of a wireless physical-layer solution that delegates the task of protecting IMD communication to an external device called the shield. Our evaluation shows that the shield effectively provides confidentiality for IMDs' transmitted data and shields IMDs from unauthorized commands, both without requiring any changes to the IMDs themselves.

Acknowledgments: We thank Arthur Berger, Ramesh Chandra, Rick Hampton, Steve Hanna, Dr. Daniel Kramer, Swarun Kumar, Nate Kushman, Kate Lin, Hariharan Rahul, Stefan Savage, Keith Winstein, and Nickolai Zeldovich for their insightful comments. The authors acknowledge the financial support of the Interconnect Focus Center, one of the six research centers funded under the Focus Center Research Program, a Semiconductor Research Corporation program. This research is also supported by NFS CNS-0831244, an NSF Graduate Research Fellowship, a Sloan Research Fellowship, the Armstrong Fund for Science, and Cooperative Agreement No. 90TR0003/01 from the Department of Health and Human Services. Its contents are solely the responsibility of the authors and do not necessarily represent the official views of the DHHS or NSF. K. Fu is listed as an inventor on patent applications pertaining to zero-power security and low-power flash memory both with assignee UMass.

14. REFERENCES

[1] J. Åkerberg. State-of-the-art radiosonde telemetry. In *Proc. Symp. Integrated Observing and Assimilation Systems for Atmosphere, Oceans, and Land Surface*. American Meterological Society, 2004.

[2] S. Cherukuri, K. K. Venkatasubramanian, and S. K. S. Gupta. Biosec: A biometric based approach for securing communication in wireless networks of biosensors implanted in the human body. In *International Conference on Parallel Processing Workshops*, 2003.

[3] J. Choi, M. Jain, K. Srinivasan, P. Levis, and S. Katti. Achieving single channel, full duplex wireless communication. In *Proc. ACM MobiCom*, 2010.

[4] J. Choi, M. Jain, K. Srinivasan, P. Levis, and S. Katti. A working single channel, full duplex wireless system. In *Mobicom Demo*, 2010.

[5] I. Csiszar and J. Korner. Broadcast channels with confidential messages. *IEEE Trans. Inf. Theory*, 24(3):339–348, 1978.

[6] T. Denning, K. Fu, and T. Kohno. Absence makes the heart grow fonder: New directions for implantable medical device security. In *Proc. USENIX Workshop on Hot Topics in Security (HotSec)*, 2008.

[7] M. Duarte and A. Sabharwal. Full-duplex wireless communications using off-the-shelf radios: Feasibility and first results. In *Asilomar Conference on Signals, Systems, and Computers*, 2010.

[8] D. Eckhardt and P. Steenkiste. Measurement and analysis of the error characteristics of an in-building wireless network. In *Proc. ACM SIGCOMM*, 1996.

[9] Ettus Inc. Universal Software Radio Peripheral. http://ettus.com/.

[10] European Telecommunications Standard Institute. ETSI EN 301 839-1 V1.3.1, 2009.

[11] C. Falcon. Inside implantable devices. *Medical Design Tech.*, 2004.

[12] Federal Communications Commission. FCC ID number search. http://www.fcc.gov/searchtools.html.

[13] Federal Communications Commission. MICS Medical Implant Communication Services, FCC 47CFR95.601-95.673 Subpart E/I Rules for MedRadio Services.

[14] K. Fu. Inside risks: Reducing the risks of implantable medical devices: A prescription to improve security and privacy of pervasive health care. *Communications of the ACM*, 52(6):25–27, 2009.

[15] K. Fu. Trustworthy medical device software. In *Public Health Effectiveness of the FDA 510(k) Clearance Process: Measuring Postmarket Performance and Other Select Topics: Workshop Report*. IOM (Institute of Medicine), National Academies Press, 2011.

[16] GNU Radio. http://gnuradio.org/.

[17] A. Goldsmith. *Wireless Communications*. Cambridge University Press, 2005.

[18] S. Gollakota, F. Adib, D. Katabi, and S. Seshan. Clearing the RF smog: Making 802.11 robust to cross-technology interference. In *ACM SIGCOMM*, 2011.

[19] S. Gollakota, N. Ahmed, N. Zeldovich, and D. Katabi. Secure in-band wireless pairing. In *USENIX Security Sym.*, 2011.

[20] S. Gollakota and D. Katabi. Physical layer security made fast and channel-independent. In *Proc. IEEE INFOCOM*, 2011.

[21] D. Halperin, T. S. Heydt-Benjamin, K. Fu, T. Kohno, and W. H. Maisel. Security and privacy for implantable medical devices. *IEEE Pervasive Computing*, 7(1), 2008.

[22] D. Halperin, T. S. Heydt-Benjamin, B. Ransford, S. S. Clark, B. Defend, W. Morgan, K. Fu, T. Kohno, and W. H. Maisel. Pacemakers and implantable cardiac defibrillators: Software radio attacks and zero-power defenses. In *Proc. IEEE Symposium on Security and Privacy*, 2008.

[23] Industry Canada. Radio Standards Specification RSS-243: Medical Devices Operating in the 401–406 MHz Frequency Band. Spectrum Management and Telecommunications, 2010.

[24] International Telecommunications Union. ITU-R Recommendation RS.1346: Sharing between the meteorological aids service and medical implant communication systems (MICS) operating in the mobile service in the frequency band 401–406 MHz, 1998.

[25] Jackson Labs. Fury GPSDO. http://www.jackson-labs.com/.

[26] W. C. Jakes. *Microwave Mobile Communications*. Wiley, 1974.

[27] M. Koplow, A. Chen, D. Steingart, P. Wright, and J. Evans. Thick film thermoelectric energy harvesting systems for biomedical applications. In *Proc. Symp. Medical Devices and Biosensors*, 2008.

[28] C. Kuo, J. Walker, and A. Perrig. Low-cost manufacturing, usability and security: An analysis of bluetooth simple pairing and wi-fi protected setup. In *Usable Security Workshop*, 2007.

[29] Y. Liu, P. Ning, H. Dai, and A. Liu. Randomized differential DSSS: Jamming-resistant wireless broadcast communication. In *Proc. IEEE INFOCOM*, 2010.

[30] J. Lopatka. Adaptive generating of the jamming signal. In *Proc. IEEE Military Communications Conference (MILCOM)*, 1995.

[31] W. H. Maisel. Safety issues involving medical devices: Implications of recent implantable cardioverter-defibrillator malfunctions. *Journal of the American Medical Association*, 2005.

[32] W. H. Maisel and T. Kohno. Improving the security and privacy of implantable medical devices. *New England Journal of Medicine*, 362(13):1164–1166, 2010.

[33] I. Martinovic, P. Pichota, and J. Schmitt. Jamming for good: A fresh approach to authentic communication in WSNs. In *Proc. ACM Conf. on Wireless Network Security (WiSec)*, 2009.

[34] Medtronic's Paradigm Veo wireless insulin pump helps prevent hypoglycemia. *MedGadget—Internet Journal for emerging medical technologies*, 2009.

[35] Medtronic Inc. CareLink Programmer. http://www.medtronic.com/.

[36] Medtronic Inc. Concerto II CRT-D digital implantable cardioverter defibrillator with cardiac resynchronization therapy. http://www.medtronic.com/.

[37] Medtronic Inc. Virtuoso DR/VR implantable cardioverter defibrillator systems. http://medtronic.com/.

[38] H. Meyr, M. Moeneclaey, and S. A. Fechtel. *Digital Communication Receivers: Synchronization, Channel Estimation, and Signal Processing*. Wiley, 1998.

[39] D. Panescu. Wireless communication systems for implantable medical devices. *IEEE Eng. in Medicine and Biology Mag.*, 2008.

[40] PCTest Engineering Labs, Inc. Certificate of compliance, fcc part 95 certification, test report number: 95.220719375.1f5, 2002.

[41] PCTest Engineering Labs, Inc. Certificate of compliance, fcc part 95 and en 301 839-2, test report number: 0703090168.med, 2007.

[42] C. Pöpper, M. Strasser, and S. Capkun. Jamming-resistant broadcast communication without shared keys. In *USENIX Security Sym.*, 2009.

[43] B. Radunovic, D. Gunawardena, P. Key, A. Proutiere, N. Singh, H. V. Balan, and G. Dejean. Rethinking indoor wireless: Low power, low frequency, full-duplex. Technical report, Microsoft Research, 2009.

[44] M. Rieback, B. Crispo, and A. Tanenbaum. RFID Guardian: A battery-powered mobile device for RFID privacy management. In *Proc. Australasian Conf. on Information Security and Privacy*, 2005.

[45] D. Sagan. Rf integrated circuits for medical applications: Meeting the challenge of ultra low power communication. Zarlink Semiconductor. http://stf.ucsd.edu/presentations.

[46] N. Santhapuri, R. R. Choudhury, J. Manweiler, S. Nelakuduti, S. Sen, and K. Munagala. Message in message mim: A case for reordering transmissions in wireless networks. In *ACM HotNets-VII*, 2008.

[47] K. Sayrafian-Pour, W. Yang, J. Hagedorn, J. Terrill, K. Yazdandoost, and K. Hamaguchi. Channel models for medical implant communication. *Inter. Journal of Wireless Info. Networks*, 2010.

[48] S. Schechter. Security that is meant to be skin deep: Using ultraviolet micropigmentation to store emergency-access keys for implantable medical devices. In *USENIX Workshop HealthSec*, 2010.

[49] M. Scheffler, E. Hirt, and A. Caduff. Wrist-wearable medical devices: Technologies and applications. *Medical Device Technology*, 2003.

[50] C. E. Shannon. Communication theory of secrecy systems. *Bell System Technical Journal*, 28(4):656–715, 1949.

[51] V. Shnayder, B. Chen, K. Lorincz, T. R. F. Fulford-Jones, and M. Welsh. Sensor networks for medical care. Technical Report TR-08-05, Harvard University, 2005.

[52] M. J. Siavoshani, U. Pulleti, E. Atsan, I. Safaka, C. Fragoulia, K. Argyraki, and S. Diggavi. Exchanging secrets without using cryptography. *arXiv:1105.4991v1*, 2011.

[53] D. Tse and P. Vishwanath. *Fundamentals of Wireless Communications*. Cambridge University Press, 2005.

[54] A. Wyner. The wire-tap channel. *Bell Sys. Technical Journal*, 1975.

[55] S. Xiao, A. Dhamdhere, V. Sivaraman, and A. Burdett. Transmission power control in body area sensor networks for healthcare monitoring. *IEEE Journal on Selected Areas in Comm.*, 2009.

[56] F. Xu, Z. Qin, C. C. Tan, B. Wang, and Q. Li. IMDGuard: Securing implantable medical devices with the external wearable guardian. In *Proc. IEEE INFOCOM*, 2011.

[57] Zephyr Inc. BioHarness BT. http://www.zephyr-technology.com.

[58] C. Zhan, W. B. Baine, A. Sedrakyan, and S. Claudia. Cardiac device implantation in the US from 1997 through 2004: A population-based analysis. *Journal of General Internal Medicine*, 2007.

Let the Market Drive Deployment:
A Strategy for Transitioning to BGP Security

Phillipa Gill
University of Toronto

Michael Schapira
Princeton University

Sharon Goldberg
Boston University

Abstract

With a cryptographic root-of-trust for Internet routing (RPKI [17]) on the horizon, we can finally start planning the deployment of one of the secure interdomain routing protocols proposed over a decade ago (Secure BGP [22], secure origin BGP [37]). However, if experience with IPv6 is any indicator, this will be no easy task. Security concerns alone seem unlikely to provide sufficient local incentive to drive the deployment process forward. Worse yet, the security benefits provided by the S*BGP protocols do not even kick in until a large number of ASes have deployed them.

Instead, we appeal to ISPs' interest in increasing revenue-generating traffic. We propose a strategy that governments and industry groups can use to harness ISPs' local business objectives and drive global S*BGP deployment. We evaluate our deployment strategy using theoretical analysis and large-scale simulations on empirical data. Our results give evidence that the market dynamics created by our proposal can transition the majority of the Internet to S*BGP.

Categories and Subject Descriptors: C.2.2 [Computer-Communication Networks]: Network Protocols

General Terms: Economics, Security

1. INTRODUCTION

The Border Gateway Protocol (BGP), which sets up routes from autonomous systems (ASes) to destinations on the Internet, is amazingly vulnerable to attack [7]. Every few years, a new failure makes the news; ranging from misconfigurations that cause an AS to become unreachable [34, 29], to possible attempts at traffic interception [11]. To remedy this, a number of widely-used stop-gap measures have been developed to *detect* attacks [20, 25]. The next step is to harden the system to a point where attacks can be *prevented*. After many years of effort, we are finally seeing the initial deployment of the Resource Public Key Infrastructure (RPKI) [4, 27], a cryptographic root-of-trust for Internet routing that authoritatively maps ASes to their IP prefixes and public keys. With RPKI on the horizon, we

can now realistically consider deploying the S*BGP protocols, proposed a decade ago, to prevent routing failures by validating AS-level paths: Secure BGP (S-BGP) [22] and Secure Origin BGP (soBGP) [37].

1.1 Economic benefits for S*BGP adoption.

While governments and industry groups may have an interest in S*BGP deployment, ultimately, the Internet lacks a centralized authority that can mandate the deployment of a new secure routing protocol. Thus, a key hurdle for the transition to S*BGP stems from the fact that each AS will make deployment decisions according to its own local business objectives.

Lessons from IPv6? Indeed, we have seen this problem before. While IPv6 has been ready for deployment since around 1998, the lack of tangible local incentive for IPv6 deployment means that we are only now starting to see the seeds of large-scale adoption. Conventional wisdom suggests that S*BGP will suffer from a similar lack of local incentives for deployment. The problem is exacerbated by the fact that an AS cannot validate the correctness of an AS-level path unless all the ASes on the path deployed S*BGP. Thus, the security benefits of S*BGP only apply after a large fraction of ASes have already deployed the protocol.

Economic incentives for adoption. We observe that, unlike IPv6, S*BGP can impact routing of Internet traffic, and that this may be used to drive S*BGP deployment. These crucial observations enable us to avoid the above issues and show that global S*BGP deployment is possible even if local ASes' deployment decisions are *not* motivated by security concerns! To this end, we present a prescriptive strategy for S*BGP deployment that relies solely on Internet Service Providers' (ISPs) local economic incentives to drive global deployment; namely, ISP's interest in attracting revenue-generating traffic to their networks.

Our strategy is prescriptive (Section 2). We propose guidelines for how (a) ASes should deploy S*BGP in their networks, and (b) governments, industry groups, and other interested parties should invest their resources in order to drive S*BGP deployment forward.

1. Break ties in favor of secure paths. First, we require ASes that deploy S*BGP to actually use it to inform route selection. However, rather than requiring security be the first criterion ASes use to select routes, we only require secure ASes to *break ties* between equally-good routes in favor of secure routes. This way, we create incentives for ISPs to deploy S*BGP so they can transit more revenue-generating customer traffic than their insecure competitors.

2. Make it easy for stubs to adopt S*BGP. 85% of ASes in the Internet are *stubs* (*i.e.*, ASes with no customers) [9]. Because stubs earn no revenue from providing Internet service, we argue for driving down their deployment costs by having ISPs sign BGP announcements on their behalf or deploy a simplex (unidirectional) S*BGP [26] on their stub customers. In practice, such a simplex S*BGP must either be extremely lightweight or heavily subsidized.

3. Create market pressure via early adopters. We propose that governments and industry groups concentrate their regulatory efforts, or financial incentives, on convincing a small set of *early adopters* to deploy S*BGP. We show that this set of early adopters can create sufficient market pressure to convince a large fraction of ASes to follow suit.

1.2 Evaluation: Model and simulations.

To evaluate our proposal, we needed a model of the S*BGP deployment process.

Inspiration from social networks? At first glance, it seems that the literature on technology adoption in social networks would be applicable here (*e.g.*, [30, 21] and references therein). However, in social networks models, an entity's decision to adopt a technology depends only on its immediate *neighbors* in the graph; in our setting, this depends on the number of secure *paths*. This complication means that many elegant results from this literature have no analogues in our setting (Section 9).

Our model. In contrast to earlier work that assumes that ASes deploy S*BGP because they are concerned about security [8, 5], our model assumes that ISPs' local deployment decisions are based solely on their interest in increasing customer traffic (Section 3).

We carefully designed our model to capture a few crucial issues, including the fact that (a) traffic transited by an ISP can include flows from any pair of source and destination ASes, (b) a large fraction of Internet traffic originates in a few large content provider ASes [24], and (c) the cost of S*BGP deployment can depend on the size of the ISP's network. The vast array of parameters and empirical data relevant to such a model (Section 8) mean that our analysis is *not* meant to *predict* exactly how the S*BGP deployment process will proceed in practice; instead, our goal was to evaluate the efficacy of our S*BGP deployment strategy.

Theorems, simulations and examples. We explore S*BGP deployment in our model using a combination of theoretical analysis and simulations on empirical AS-level graphs [9, 3] (Sections 5-7). Every example we present comes directly from these simulations. Instead of artificially reducing algorithmic complexity by subsampling [23], we ran our simulations over the full AS graph (Section 4). Thus, our simulations ran in time $O(N^3)$ with $N = 36K$, and we devoted significant effort to developing parallel algorithms that we ran on a 200-node DryadLINQ cluster [38].

1.3 Key insights and recommendations.

Our evaluation indicates that our strategy for S*BGP deployment can drive a transition to S*BGP (Section 5). While we cannot predict exactly how S*BGP deployment will progress, a number of important themes emerge:

1. Market pressure can drive deployment. We found that when S*BGP deployment costs are low, the vast majority of ISPs have incentives to deploy S*BGP in order to dif-

ferentiate themselves from, or keep up with, their competitors (Section 5). Moreover, our results show this holds even if 96% of routing decisions (across all source-destination AS pairs) are *not* influenced by security concerns (Section 6.6).

2. Simplex S*BGP is crucial. When deployment costs are high, deployment is primarily driven by simplex S*BGP (Section 6).

3. Choose a few well-connected early adopters. The set of early adopters cannot be random; it should include well-connected ASes like the Tier 1's and content providers (Section 6). While we prove that it is NP-hard to even *approximate* the *optimal* set of early adopters (Section 6.1), our results show that even 5-10 early adopters suffice when deployment costs are low.

4. Prepare for incentives to disable S*BGP. We show that ISPs can have incentives to *disable* S*BGP (Section 7). Moreover, we prove that there could be deployment oscillations (where ASes endlessly turn S*BGP on and off), and that it is computationally hard to even *determine* whether such oscillations exist.

5. Minimize attacks during partial deployment. Even when S*BGP deployment progressed, there were always some ASes that did not deploy (Section 5, 6). As such, we expect that S*BGP and BGP will coexist in the long term, suggesting that careful engineering is required to ensure that this does not introduce new vulnerabilities into the interdomain routing system.

Paper organization. Section 2 presents our proposed strategy for S*BGP deployment. To evaluate the proposal, we present a model of the deployment process in Section 3. In Section 5-7 we explore this model using theoretical analysis and simulations, and present an in-depth discussion of our modeling assumptions in Section 8. Section 9 presents related work. The full version of this paper [2] contain implementation details for our simulations, proofs of all our theorems, and supplementary data analysis.

2. S*BGP DEPLOYMENT STRATEGY

2.1 S*BGP: Two possible solutions.

With RPKI providing an authoritative mapping from ASes to their cryptographic public keys, two main protocols have been proposed that prevent the propagation of bogus AS path information:

Secure BGP (S-BGP) [22]. S-BGP provides *path validation*, allowing an AS a_1 that receives a BGP announcement $a_1a_2...a_kd$ to validate that every AS a_j actually sent the announcement in the path. With S-BGP, a router must cryptographically sign each routing message it sends, and cryptographically verify each routing message it receives.

Secure Origin BGP (soBGP) [37]. soBGP provides a slightly weaker security guarantee called *topology validation*, that allows an AS to validate that a path it learns physically exists in the network. To do this, soBGP requires neighboring ASes to mutually authenticate a certificate for the existence of a link between them, and validate every path it learns from a BGP announcement against these cryptographic certificates.

Because our study is indifferent to attacks and adversaries, it applies equally to each of these protocols. We refer to them collectively as S*BGP, and an AS that deploys them as *secure*.

2.2 How to standardize S*BGP deployment.

To create local economic incentives for ISPs to deploy S*BGP, we propose that Internet standards should require ASes to deploy S*BGP as follows:

2.2.1 Simplex S*BGP for stubs.

For stubs, Internet access is a cost, rather than a revenue source, and it seems unlikely that security concerns alone will suffice to motivate stubs to undertake a costly S*BGP deployment. However, because stubs propagate only *outgoing* BGP announcements for *their own IP prefixes* we suggest two possible solutions to this problem: (1) allow ISPs to sign on behalf of their stub customers or (2) allow stubs to deploy simplex (unidirectional) S*BGP. Indeed, the latter approach has been proposed by the Internet standards community [26].

Simplex S-BGP. For S-BGP, this means that stubs need only sign outgoing BGP announcements for their own IP prefixes, but not validate incoming BGP announcements for other IP prefixes[1]. Thus, a stub need only store its own public key (rather than obtaining the public keys of each AS on the Internet from the RPKI) and cryptographically sign only a tiny fraction of the BGP announcements it sees. Simplex S-BGP can significantly decrease the computational load on the stub, and can potentially be deployed as a software, rather than hardware, upgrade to its routers.

Simplex soBGP. For soBGP, this means that a stub need only create certificates for its links, but need not need validate the routing announcements it sees. Simplex soBGP is done offline; once a stub certifies his information in the soBGP database, its task is complete and no router upgrade is required.

The objective of simplex S*BGP is to make it easy for stubs to become secure by lowering deployment costs and computational overhead. While we certainly allows for stubs (*e.g.,* banks, universities) with an interest in security to move from simplex S*BGP to full S*BGP, our proposal does not require them to do so.

Impact on security. With simplex S*BGP, a stub lacks the ability to validate paths for prefixes other than its own. Since stubs constitute about 85% of ASes [9], a first glance suggests that simplex S*BGP leads to significantly worse security in the global Internet.

We argue that this is not so. Observe that if a stub s has an immediate provider p that has deployed S*BGP and is correctly validating paths, then no false announcements of fully secure paths can reach s from that provider, unless p *himself* maliciously (or mistakenly) announces false secure paths to s. Thus, in the event that stubs upgrade to simplex S*BGP and all other ASes upgrade to full S*BGP, the only open attack vector is for ISPs to announce false paths to their *own* stub customers. However, we observe the impact of a single misbehaving ISP is small, since 80% of ISPs have less than 7 stub customers, and only about 1% of ISPs have more than 100 stub customers [9]. Compare this to the

insecure status quo, where an arbitrary misbehaving AS can impact about half of the ASes in the Internet (around $15K$ ASes) on average [14].

2.2.2 Break ties in favor of fully secure paths.

In BGP, an AS chooses the path to a given destination AS d based on a *ranking* on the outgoing paths it learns from its neighbors (*e.g.,* Appendix A). Paths are first ranked according to interdomain considerations (local preference, AS path length) and then according to intradomain considerations (*e.g.,* MEDs, hot-potato routing)[2].

Secure paths. We say that a path is secure iff *every* AS on that path is secure. We do this because an AS cannot validate a path unless every AS on the path signed the routing announcement (S-BGP) or issued certificates for the links on the path (soBGP).

Security as part of route selection. The next part of our proposal suggests that once an AS has the ability to validate paths, it should actually use this information to inform its routing decisions. In principle, an AS might even modify its ranking on outgoing paths so that security is its highest priority. Fortunately, we need not go to such lengths. Instead, we only require secure ASes to *break ties* between equally good interdomain paths in favor of secure paths. This empowers secure ISPs to attract customer traffic away from their insecure competitors. To ensure that a newly-secure AS can *regain* lost customer traffic, we require that original tie-break criteria (*e.g.,* intradomain considerations) be employed in the case of equally good, *secure* interdomain paths. Thus, the size of the set of equally-good interdomain paths for a given source-destination pair (which we call the *tiebreak set*) gives a measure of competition in the AS graph.

Route selection at stubs. For stubs running simplex S*BGP, we consider both the case where they break ties in favor of secure paths (*i.e.,* because they trust their providers to verify paths for them) and the case where they ignore security altogether (*i.e.,* because they do not verify paths) (Section 6.7).

Partially secure paths. We do not allow ASes to prefer partially-secure paths over insecure paths, to avoid introducing *new* attack vectors that do exist even without S*BGP (*e.g.,* attack in Appendix B).

We shall show that S*BGP deployment progresses quite effectively even if stubs ignore security and tiebreak sets are very small (Section 6.7-6.6).

2.3 How third parties should drive deployment.

Early adopters. To kick off the process, we suggest that interested third parties (*e.g.,* governments, regulators, industry groups) focus regulation, subsidies, or external financial incentives on convincing a set of *early adopter* ASes to deploy S*BGP. One regulatory mechanism may be for the government to require their network providers to deploy S*BGP first. In the AS graph ([9, 3]), providers to the government include many Tier 1 ISPs who may be difficult or expensive to persuade via other means.

ISPs upgrade their stubs. Next, we suggest that a secure ISP should be responsible for upgrading all its insecure stub customers to simplex S*BGP. To achieve this,

---

[1] A stub may even choose to delegate its cryptographic keys to its ISPs, and have them sign for him; while this might be a good first step on the path to deployment, ceding control of cryptographic keys comes at the cost of reduced security.

[2] For simplicity, we do not model intradomain routing considerations. However, it should be explored in future work.

interested third parties should ensure that simplex S*BGP is engineered to be as lightweight as possible, and potentially provide additional subsidies for ISPs that secure their stubs. (ISPs also have a local incentives to secure stubs, *i.e.,* to transit more revenue-generating traffic for multi-homed stubs (Section 5.1).)

3. MODELING S*BGP DEPLOYMENT

We evaluate our proposal using a model of the S*BGP deployment process. For brevity, we now present only the details of our model. Justification for our modeling decisions and possible extensions are in Section 8.

3.1 The Internetwork and entities.

The AS graph. The interdomain-routing system is modeled with a labeled AS graph $G(V, E)$. Each node $n \in V$ represents an AS, and each edge represents a physical link between ASes. Per Figure 1, edges are annotated with the standard model for business relationships in the Internet [13]: *customer-provider* (where the customer pays the provider), and *peer-to-peer* (where two ASes agree to transit each other's traffic at no cost). Each AS n is also assigned weight w_n, to model the volume of traffic that *originates* at each AS. For simplicity, we assume ASes divide their traffic evenly across all destination ASes. However, our results are robust even when this assumption is relaxed (Section 6.8).

We distinguish three types of ASes:

Content providers. Content providers (CPs) are ASes whose revenue (*e.g.,* advertising) depends on reliably delivering their content to as many users as possible, rather than on providing Internet transit. While a disproportionately large volume of Internet traffic is known to originate at a few CPs, empirical data about Internet traffic volumes remains notoriously elusive. Thus, based on recent research [24, 35] we picked five content providers: Google (AS 15169), Facebook (AS 32934), Microsoft (AS 8075), Akamai (AS 20940), and Limelight (AS 22822). Then, we assigned each CP weight w_{CP}, so that the five CPs originate an x fraction of Internet traffic (equally split between them), with the remaining $1 - x$ split between the remaining ASes.

Stubs. Stubs are ASes that have no customers of their own and are not CPs. Every stub s has unit weight $w_s = 1$. In Figure 1, ASes 34376 and 31420 are stubs.

ISPs. The remaining ASes in the graph (that are not stubs or CPs) are ISPs. ISPs earn revenue by providing Internet service; because ISPs typically provide transit service, rather that originating traffic (content), we assume they have unit weight $w_n = 1$. In Figure 1, ASes 25076, 8866 and 8928 are ISPs.

3.2 The deployment process.

We model S*BGP deployment as an infinite round process. Each round is represented with a state S, capturing the set of ASes that have deployed S*BGP.

Initial state. Initially, the only ASes that are secure are (1) the ASes in the set of early adopters and (2) the direct customers of the early adopter ISPs that are stubs. (The stubs run simplex S*BGP.) All other ASes are insecure. For example, in Figure 1, early adopters ISP 8866 and CP 22822 are secure, and stub 31420 runs simplex S*BGP because its provider is secure.

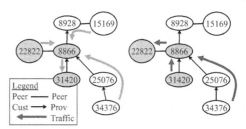

Figure 1: Destinations (left) 31420, (right) 22822.

Each round. In each round, *every* ISP chooses an action (deploy S*BGP or not) that improves its utility relative to the current state. We discuss the myopic best-response strategy that ISPs use to choose their actions in Section 3.3. Once an ISP becomes secure, it deploys simplex S*BGP at *all* its stub customers (Section 2.3). Because CPs do not earn revenues by providing Internet service, some external incentive (*e.g.,* concern for security, subsidies) must motivate them to deploy S*BGP. Thus, in our model, a CP may only deploy S*BGP if it is in the set of early adopters.

Once ASes choose their actions, paths are established from every source AS i to every destination AS d, based on the local BGP *routing policies* of each AS and the state S of the AS graph. We use a standard model of BGP routing policies, based on business relationships and path length (see Appendix A). Per Section 2.3, we also assume that routing policies of secure ASes require them to break ties by preferring fully secure paths over insecure ones, so that the path to a given destination d depends on the state S. Paths to a destination d form a tree rooted at d, and we use the notation $T_n(d, S)$ to represent the subtree of ASes routing through AS n to a destination d when the deployment process is in state S. Figure 1 (right) shows part of the routing tree for destination 22822; notice that $T_{8866}(22822, S)$ contains ASes 31420, 25076, 34376.

Termination. We proceed until we reach a stable state, where no ISP wants to deploy (or disable) S*BGP.

3.3 ISP utility and best response.

We model an ISP's utility as related to the volume of traffic it transits for its customers; this captures the fact that many ISPs either bill their customers directly by volume, or indirectly through flat rates for fixed traffic capacities. Utility is a function of the paths chosen by each AS. Because path selection is a function of routing policies (Appendix A) and the state S, it follows that *the utility of each ISP is completely determined by the AS weights, AS graph topology, and the state S.*

We have two models of ISP utility that capture the ways in which an ISP can transit customer traffic:

Outgoing utility. ISP n can increase its utility by forwarding traffic *to* its customers. Thus, we define outgoing utility as the amount of traffic that ISP n routes to each destination d via a customer edge. Letting $\hat{D}(n)$ be the set of such destinations, we have:

$$u_n(S) = \sum_{\substack{\text{Destns} \\ d \in \hat{D}(n)}} \sum_{\substack{\text{Sources} \\ i \in T_n(d, S)}} w_i \qquad (1)$$

Let's use Figure 1 to find the outgoing utility of ISP $n = 8866$ due to destinations 31420 and 22822. Destination 31420 is in $\hat{D}(n)$ but destination 22822 is not. Thus, two CPs (Google AS 15169 and Limelight 22822), and 3 other ASes (*i.e.*, AS 8928, 25076, 34376) transit traffic through $n = 8866$ to destination $d = 31420$, contributing a $2w_{CP} + 3$ outgoing utility to $n = 8866$.

Incoming utility. An ISP n can increase its utility by forwarding traffic *from* its customers. Thus, we define incoming utility as the amount of traffic that ISP n receives via customer edges for each destination d. We restrict the subtree $T_n(d, S)$ to branches that are incident on n via customer edges to obtain the *customer subtree* $\hat{T}_n(d, S) \subset T_n(d, S)$, we have:

$$u_n(S) = \sum_{\substack{\text{Destns} \\ d}} \sum_{\substack{\text{Sources} \\ i \in \hat{T}_n(d,S)}} w_i \qquad (2)$$

Let's compute outgoing utility of $n = 8866$ due to destinations 31420 and 22822 in Figure 1. For destination 31420, ASes 25076 and 34376 are part of the customer subtree $\hat{T}_n(d, S)$, but 15169, 8928 and 22822 are not. For destination $d = 22822$, ASes 31420, 25076, 34376 are part of the customer subtree. Thus, these ASes contribute $2 + 3$ incoming utility to ISP $n = 8866$.

Realistically, ISP utility is some function of both of these models; to avoid introducing extra parameters into our model, we consider each separately.

Myopic best response. We use a standard game-theoretic update rule known as *myopic best response*, that produces the most favorable outcome for a node in the next round, taking other nodes' strategies as given [16]. Let $(\neg S_n, S_{-n})$ denote the state when n 'flips' to the opposite action (either deploying or undeploying S*BGP) that it used in state S, while other ASes maintain the same action they use in state S. ISP n changes its action in state S iff its *projected utility* $u_n(\neg S_n, S_{-n})$ is sufficiently high, *i.e.*,

$$u_n(\neg S_n, S_{-n}) > (1 + \theta) \cdot u_n(S) \qquad (3)$$

where θ is a threshold denoting the increase in utility an ISP needs to see before it is willing to change its actions. Threshold θ captures the cost of deploying BGP security; *e.g.*, an ISP might deploy S*BGP in a given round if S*BGP deployment costs do not exceed $\theta = 5\%$ of the profit it earns from transiting customer traffic. Since θ is multiplicative, it captures the idea that deployment costs are likely to be higher at ISPs that transit more traffic. The update rule is myopic, because it focuses on increasing ISP n's utility in the next round only. It is best-response because it does *not* require ISP n to speculate on other ASes' actions in future rounds; instead, n takes these actions as given by the current state S.

Discussion. Our update rule requires ASes to predict their future utility. In our model, ASes have full information of S and G, a common approach in game theory, which enables them to project their utility accurately. We discuss the consequences of our update rule, and the impact of partial information in Sections 8.1-8.2.

4. SIMULATION FRAMEWORK

Computing utility $u_n(S)$ and projected utility $u_n(\neg S_n, S_{-n})$ requires us to determine the path from *every* source AS to *every* destination AS, for *every* ISP n's unique projected state $(\neg S_n, S_{-n})$. Thus, our simulations had complexity $O(|V|^3)$ on an AS graph $G(V, E)$. To accurately simulate our model, we chose *not* to 'sample down' the complexity of our simulations:

Projecting utility for each ISP. If we had computed the utility for only a few sampled ISPs, this would reduce the number of available secure paths and artificially prevent S*BGP deployment from progressing.

Simulations over the entire AS graph. Our proposal is specifically designed to leverage the extreme skew in AS connectivity (*i.e.*, many stubs with no customers, few Tier 1s with many customers), to drive S*BGP deployment. To faithfully capture the impact of this skew, we computed utility over traffic from *all* sources to *all* destination ASes. Furthermore, we ran our simulations on the full empirical AS graph [9], rather than a subsampled version [23], or a smaller synthetic topology [28, 39], as in prior work [8, 5]. We used the Cyclops AS graph (with its inferred AS relationships) from Dec 9, 2010 [9], with an additional 16K peering edges discovered at Internet exchange points (IXPs) [3], as well as an additional peering-heavy AS graph described in Section 6.8.

The AS graph $G(V, E)$ had $|V| = 36K$; to run $O(|V|^3)$-simulations at such a scale, we parallelized our algorithms on a 200-node DryadLINQ cluster [38] that could run through a single simulation in 1-12 hours. (Details of our implementation are in the full version.)

5. CASE STUDY: S*BGP DEPLOYMENT

We start by showing that even a small set of early adopters can create enough market pressure to transition the vast majority of ASes to S*BGP.

Case study overview. We focus on a single simulation where the early adopters are the five CPs (Google, Facebook, Microsoft, Limelight, Akamai, see Section 3.1), and the top five Tier 1 ASes in terms of degree (Sprint (1239), Verizon (701), AT&T (7018), Level 3 (3356), Cogent (174)). Every ISP uses an update rule with a relatively low threshold $\theta = 5\%$, that the five CPs originate $x = 10\%$ of the traffic in the Internet, and that stubs *do* break ties in favor of secure routes. We now show how even a small set of ten early adopters (accounting for less that 0.03% of the AS graph) can convince 85% of ASes to deploy S*BGP, and secure 65% of all paths in the AS graph.

5.1 Competition drives deployment.

We start by zooming in on S*BGP deployment at two competing ISPs, in a scenario we call a DIAMOND.

Figure 5: Two ISPs, AS 8359 and AS 13789, compete for traffic from Sprint (AS 1239) to their stub customer, AS 18608. Sprint is an early adopter of S*BGP, and initially the three other ASes are insecure. Both ISPs offer Sprint equally good two-hop customer paths to the stub, and AS 8359 is chosen to carry traffic by winning the tie break. In the first round, AS 13789 computes its projected utility, and realizes it can gain Sprint's traffic by adopting S*BGP and upgrading its stub to simplex S*BGP. (See Section 8.2 for more discussion on how ISPs compute projected utility.) By the fourth round, AS 8359 has lost so much utility (due to traffic lost to ASes like 13789) that he decides to deploy S*BGP.

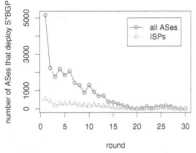

Figure 2: The number of ASes that deploy S*BGP each round.

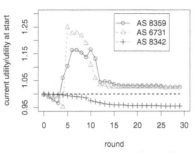

Figure 3: Normalized utility of ISPs in Fig. 5 and 6.

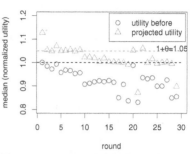

Figure 4: Projected and actual utility before deploying S*BGP normalized by starting utility.

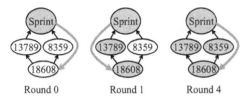

Round 0   Round 1   Round 4

Figure 5: A Diamond: ISPs 13789 and 8359 compete for traffic from Sprint (AS 1239).

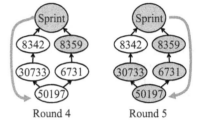

Round 4   Round 5

Figure 6: A newly created four-hop secure path.

Of course, Figure 5 is only a very small snapshot of the competition for traffic destined to a single stub AS 18608; utility for each ISPs is based on customer traffic transited to *all* destinations in the AS graph. Indeed, this DIAMOND scenario is quite common. We counted more than 6.5K instances of the DIAMOND, each involving two ISPs, a stub, and one of our early adopters.

5.2 Global deployment dynamics.

Figure 2:   We show the number of ASes (*i.e.,* stubs, ISPs and CPs) and the number of ISPs that deploy S*BGP at each round. In the first round, 548 ISPs become secure; because each of these ISPs deploy simplex S*BGP in their stubs, we see that over 5K ASes become secure by the end of the first round. In subsequent rounds, hundreds of ISPs deploy S*BGP in each round; however, the number of newly secure stubs drops dramatically, suggesting that many ISPs deploy S*BGP to regain traffic lost when their stubs were secured by competitors. After the 17th iteration, the process tapers off, with fewer than 50 ASes becoming secure in each round. The final surge in deployment occurs in round 25, when a large AS, 6939, suddenly became secure, causing a total of 436 ASes to deploy S*BGP in the remaining six rounds. When the process terminates, 85% of ASes are secure, including 80% of the 6K ISPs in the AS graph.

5.3 Longer secure paths sustain deployment.

In Figure 2 we observed rapid, sustained deployment of S*BGP in the first 17 iterations. This happens because longer secure paths are created as more ASes deploy S*BGP, thus creating incentives for S*BGP at ASes that are far away from the early adopters:

Figure 6:   We once again encounter AS 8359 from Figure 5. We show how AS 8359's decision to deploy S*BGP in round 4 allows a new ISP (AS 6371) to compete for traffic. In round 5 AS 6731 sees a large increase in utility by becoming secure.

This occurs, in part, because AS 6371 can now entice six of the early adopters to route through him on a total of 69 newly-secure paths. Indeed, when AS 6731 becomes secure, he continues the chain reaction set in motion by AS 8359; for instance, in round 7 (not shown), AS 6371's neighbor AS 41209 becomes secure in order to offer Sprint a new, secure four-hop path to one of 41209's own stubs.

5.4 Keeping up with the competition.

Two behaviors drive S*BGP deployment in a DIAMOND. First, an ISP becomes secure to steal traffic from a competitor, and then the competitor becomes secure in order to regain the lost traffic. We can watch this happening for the ISPs from Figure 5 and 6:

Figure 3:   We show the utilities of ISPs 8359, 6731, and 8342 in each round, normalized by *starting utility i.e.,* the utility before the deployment process began (when all ASes, including the early adopters, were still insecure). As we saw in Figure 5, AS 8359 deploys S*BGP in round 4 in order to regain traffic he lost to his secure competitors; here we see that in round 4, AS 8359 has lost 3% of his starting utility. Once AS 8359 deploys S*BGP, his utility jumps up to more than 125% of his starting utility, but these gains in utility are only temporary, disappearing around round 15. The same is true in round 6 for AS 6371 from Figure 6. By round 15, 60% ISPs in the AS graph are already secure (Figure 2), and our ISPs can no longer use security to differentiate themselves, causing their utility to return to within 3% of their starting utility.

This is also true more generally:

Figure 4:   For each round i, we show the median utility and median projected utility for ISPs that become secure in round $i+1$, each normalized by starting utility. (Recall from (3) that these ISPs have projected utility at least $1+\theta$ times their utility in round i.) In the first 9 rounds, ISPs mainly deploy S*BGP to steal traffic from competitors; that is, their projected utility in the round before they deploy S*BGP is at least $1 + \theta = 105\%$ times their starting utility. However, as deployment progresses, ASes increasingly deploy S*BGP in order to recover lost traffic and return to their starting utility; that is, in rounds 10-20 ISP utility drops to at least $\theta = 5\%$ less than starting utility, while projected utility approaches starting utility (y=1).

5.5 Is S*BGP deployment a zero-sum game?

Our model of S*BGP deployment is indeed a zero-sum game; we assume that ISPs compete over a fixed set of customer traffic. Thus, when the vast majority of ASes have deployed S*BGP, ISPs can no longer use security to distinguish themselves their from competitors (Figure 3). At the termination of this case study, only 8% of ISPs have an increase in utility of more than $\theta = 5\%$ over their starting utility. On the other hand, 85% of ASes now benefit from a (mostly) secure Internet. Furthermore, like ASes 8359 and 6731 in Figure 3, many of these secure ASes enjoyed a prolonged period of increased utility that could potentially help defray the costs of deploying S*BGP.

It is better to deploy S*BGP. One might argue that a cynical ISP might preempt the process by *never* deploying S*BGP. However, a closer look shows that its almost always in the ISPs interest to deploy S*BGP. ISPs that deploy S*BGP usually return to their starting utility or slightly above, whereas ISPs that do *not* deploy S*BGP lose traffic in the long term. For instance, AS 8342 in Figure 6 never deploys S*BGP. As shown in Figure 3, when the deployment process terminates, AS 8342 has lost 4% of its starting utility. Indeed, another look at the data (not shown) shows that the ISPs that remain insecure when the process terminates lose on average 13% of their starting utility!

6. CHOOSING EARLY ADOPTERS

Next, we consider choosing the set of ASes that should be targeted to become early adopters of S*BGP.

6.1 It's hard to choose early adopters.

Ideally, we would like to choose the *optimal* set of early adopters that could cause the maximum number of other ASes to deploy S*BGP. We show that this is NP-hard by presenting a reduction to the 'set cover' problem (proof in the full version):

THEOREM 6.1. *For an AS graph $G(V, E)$ and a parameter $1 \leq k \leq |V|$, finding a set of early adopter ASes of size k that maximizes the number of ASes that are secure when the deployment process terminates is NP-hard. Approximating the solution within a constant factor is also NP-hard.*

As such, we use simulations[3] of the deployment process to investigate heuristic approaches for choosing early adopters, including AS degree (*e.g.*, Tier 1s) and volume of traffic originated by an AS (*e.g.*, content providers).

6.2 The parameter space.

We consider how the choice of early adopters is impacted by assumptions on (1) whether or not stubs running simplex

---

[3]Since there is no sampling involved, there is no variability between simulations run with the same set of parameters.

S*BGP break ties based on security, (2) the AS graph, and (3) traffic volumes sourced by CPs.

Outgoing utility. Also, recall that we have two models of ISP utility (Section 3.3). In this section, we dive into the details of the *outgoing utility* model because it has the following very nice property:

THEOREM 6.2. *In the outgoing utility model, a secure node will never have an incentive to turn off S*BGP.*

As a consequence of this theorem (proof in the full version), it immediately follows that (a) every simulation must terminate, and (b) we can significantly reduce compute time by *not* computing projected utility for ISPs that are already secure. (We discuss complications that arise from the incoming utility model in Section 7.)

Deployment threshold θ. Our update rule (3) is such that ISPs change their actions if they can increases utility by at least θ. Thus, to gain insight into how 'difficult' it is to convince ISPs to deploy S*BGP, we assume that each ISP uses the same threshold θ, and sweep through different values of θ (but see also Section 8.2).

6.3 Comparing sets of early adopters.

We next explore the influence of different early adopters:

Figure 7 (top): We show the fraction of ASes that adopt S*BGP for different values of θ. We consider no early adopters, the top 5-200 ISPs in terms of degree, the five CPs, five CPs in combination with the top five ISPs, and 200 random ISPs.

There are incentives to deploy S*BGP. For low values of $\theta < 5\%$, we observe that there is sufficient competition over customer traffic to transition 85% of ASes to S*BGP. Moreover, this holds for almost every set of early adopters we considered. (Note that in the unrealistic case where $\theta = 0$, we see widespread S*BGP deployment even with *no* early adopters, because we assume the stubs break ties in favor of secure paths. But see also Section 6.7.) Furthermore, we find that the five CPs have approximately the same amount of influence as the case where there are no early adopters; we investigate this in more detail in Section 6.8.

Some ISPs always remain insecure. We find 20% of the 6K ISPs in the AS graph [9, 3] never deploy S*BGP, because they are never subject to competition for customer traffic. This highlights two important issues: (1) some ISPs may never become secure (*e.g.*, ASes whose customers are exclusively single-homed) (2) S*BGP and BGP will coexist in the long term.

Choice of early adopters is critical. For higher values of $\theta \geq 10\%$, it becomes important to choose ISPs with high customer degree as early adopters. In fact, Figure 7 shows a set of 200 random ASes has significantly lower influence than a set containing only the five top ASes in terms of degree. For large values of $\theta \geq 30\%$, a larger set of high-degree early adopters is required, with the top 200 ASes in terms of degree causing 53% of the ASes to deploy S*BGP for $\theta = 50\%$. However, to put this observation in some perspective, recall that $\theta = 30\%$ suggests that the cost of S*BGP deployment exceeds 30% of an ISP's profit margin from transiting customer traffic.

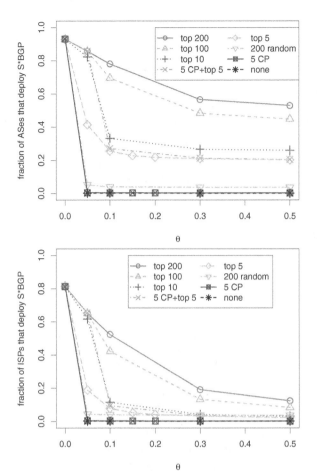

Figure 7: Fraction of ASes (top) and ISPs (bottom) that deploy S*BGP for varying θ and early adopters.

6.4 How much security do we get?

We count the number of secure paths at the end of the deployment process, as a measure of the efficacy of S*BGP deployment. (Of course, this is *not* a perfect measure of the AS graph's resiliency to attack; quantifying this requires approaches similar to [14, 8], an important direction for future work.) We find that the fraction of secure path is only slightly lower than f^2, where f is the fraction of ASes that have deployed S*BGP (figure in the full version). (The f^2 follows from the fact that for a path to be secure, both its source AS and its destination AS must be secure.)

6.5 Market pressure vs. simplex S*BGP

The cause of for global S*BGP deployment differs for low and high values of the deployment threshold θ:

Figure 7 (bottom): We show the fraction of ISPs (not ASes) that deploy S*BGP for the early adopter sets and varying values of θ. For low values of θ, market pressure drives a large fraction of ISPs to deploy S*BGP. In contrast, for higher values of θ very few ISPs deploy S*BGP, even for large sets of well-connected early adopters. In these cases, most of the deployment is driven by ISPs upgrading their stub customers to simplex S*BGP. For example, for the top 200 ISPs, when $\theta = 50\%$, only a small fraction of secure ASes (4%) deploy S*BGP because of market pressure, the vast majority (96%) are stubs running simplex S*BGP.

6.6 The source of competition: tie break sets.

Recall that the *tiebreak set* is the set of paths on which an AS employs the security criterion to select paths to a destination AS (Section 2.2.2). A tiebreak set with multiple paths presents opportunities for ISPs to compete over traffic from the source AS.

We observe that tiebreak sets are typically very small in the AS graph under the routing policies of Appendix A (figure in the full version). Moreover, only 20% tiebreak sets contain more than a single path.

This striking observation suggests that even a very limited amount of competition suffices to drive S*BGP deployment for low θ.

6.7 Stubs don't need to break ties on security.

So far, we have focused on the case where secure stubs break ties in favor of secure paths. Indeed, given that stubs typically make up the majority of secure ASes, one might expect that their routing decisions can have a major impact of the success of the S*BGP deployment process. Surprisingly, we find that this is not the case. Indeed, our results are insensitive to this assumption, for $\theta > 0$ and regardless of the choice of early adopter (Figure shown in full version). We explain this by observing that stubs both (a) have small tiebreak sets, and (b) transit no traffic.

Security need only effect a fraction of routing decisions! Thus, only 15% of ASes (*i.e.*, the ISPs) need to break ties in favor of secure routes, and only 23% of ISP tiebreak sets contain more than one path. Combining these observations, we find that S*BGP deployment can progress even if only $0.15 \times 0.23 = 3.5\%$ of routing decisions are effected by security considerations!

6.8 Robustness to traffic and connectivity

6.8.1 Varying parameters.

To understand the sensitivity of our results we varied the following parameters:

1. Originated traffic volumes. We swept through different values $x = \{10\%, 20\%, 33\%, 50\%\}$ for the fraction of traffic originated by the five CPs (Section 3.1); recent work suggests a reasonable range is $x = 10\text{-}20\%$ [24] .

2. Traffic destinations. Initially, we assume ASes uniformly spread their traffic across all potential destinations. We test the robustness of our results to this assumption by modeling traffic locality. We model locality by assuming ASes send traffic proportional to $1/k$ to destination ASes that are k hops away.

3. Connectivity of content providers. Published AS-level topologies are known to have poor visibility into peering links at the edge of the AS-level topology [31]. This is particularly problematic for CPs, who in recent years, have shifted towards peering with many other ASes to cut down content delivery costs [12] . Indeed, while the CPs known to have short path lengths [32], their average path length in our AS graph (with routing policies as in Appendix A) was 2.7 hops or more. Thus, for sensitivity analysis, we created a peering-heavy AS graph with 19.7K artificial peering edges from the five CPs to 80% of ASes found to be present at IXPs [3]. In our augmented AS graph, the average path length of the CPs dropped to about 2, and their degree increased to be as high as the largest Tier 1 ISPs.

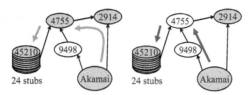

Figure 8: AS 4755 incentives turn off S*BGP.

6.8.2 Impact of traffic volumes and connectivity

We now present an overview of our model's robustness (additional detail in the full version):

1. Originated traffic volumes vs. degree. Surprisingly, when the five CPs source $x = 10\%$ of traffic, they are much less effective as early adopters than the top five Tier 1 ASes. Even though in the augmented topology the Tier 1s and CPs have about equal degree, the dominant factor here is traffic; even though the CPs *originate* 10% of traffic, the Tier 1s still *transit* 2-9X times more traffic.

2. Localized interdomain traffic. We validate that our results are robust to localized interdomain traffic using the 5 CP and top 5 as early adopters. For both the original and augmented topology, our results are robust even when ASes direct most of their traffic to nearby destinations.

3. Impact of peering-heavy structure on simplex S*BGP. Even in the augmented topology, where the CPs peer with large number of ASes, the Tier 1s consistently out perform the CPs by immediately upgrading their *stub customers* to simplex S*BGP. This suggests that having CPs to upgrade their *stub peers* to simplex S*BGP could potentially drive S*BGP deployment further.

6.9 Summary and recommendations.

We make two key observations regarding selection of early adopters. First, only a small number of ISPs suffice as early adopters when deployment thresholds θ are small. Second, to withstand high θ, Tier 1 ASes should be targeted. This is due to the high volumes of traffic they transit and the many stubs they upgrade to simplex S*BGP. Finally, we note that our results hold even if more than 96% of routing decisions are insensitive to security considerations!

7. OTHER COMPLICATIONS

Intuition suggests that a secure ISP will observe increased utility because secure ASes transit traffic through it. While this is true in the *outgoing utility* model (Theorem 6.2), it turns out that this is *not* the case for the *incoming utility* model. We now discuss complications that might arise because we require S*BGP to play a role in route selection.

7.1 Buyer's Remorse: Turning off S*BGP.

We present an example of a severe obstacle to S*BGP deployment: an secure ISP that has incentive to turn *off* S*BGP. The idea here is that when an ISP n becomes secure, some of n's incoming traffic might change its path, and enter n's network along peer/provider edges instead of customer edges, thus reducing n's utility. This causes the secure ISP's utility to satisfy Equation 3, resulting in the ISP opting to undeploy S*BGP.

Figure 8: We show that AS 4755, a Telecom provider in India, has an incentive to turn off S*BGP in its network. We assume content providers have $w_{CP} = 821$ which corre-

sponds to 10% of Internet traffic originating at the big five CPs (including Akamai's AS 20940).

In the state S on the left, Akamai, AS 4755, and NTT (AS 2914) are secure, the stub customers of these two secure ISPs run simplex S*BGP, and all other ASes are insecure. Here, AS 4755 transits traffic sourced by Akamai from his provider NTT AS 2914, to a collection of twenty-four of its stub customers (including AS 45210). Akamai's traffic does *not* increase AS 4755's utility because it arrives at AS 4755 along a provider edge.

In the state $(\neg S_{4755}, S_{-4755})$ on the right, AS 4755 turns S*BGP off. If we assume that stubs running simplex S*BGP do *not* break ties based on security, then the only ASes that could potentially change their routes are the secure ASes 20940 and 2914. Notice that when AS 4755 turns S*BGP off, Akamai's AS 20940 has *no secure route* to AS 4755's stub customers (including AS 45210). As such, Akamai will run his usual tie break algorithms, which in our simulation came up in favor of AS 9498, a customer of AS 4755. Because Akamai's traffic is now enters AS 4755 on customer edges, AS 4755's incoming utility *increases* by a factor of 205% per each of the 24 stub destinations.

Turning off the entire network. Our simulations confirmed that, apart from Akamai changing its chosen path these twenty-four stubs, all other ASes use the same routes in state S and state $(\neg S_{4755}, S_{-4755})$. This means that AS 4755 has an incentive to turn off S*BGP in his *entire network*; no routes other than those ones Akamai uses to reach the twenty-four stubs are impacted by his decision. Indeed, we found that the utility of AS 4755 increase by a total of 0.5% (over all destinations) when he turns off S*BGP!

Turning off a destination. AS 4775 could just as well turn off S*BGP on a *per destination* basis, *i.e.,* by refusing to propagate S*BGP announcements for the twenty-four stubs in Figure 8, and sending insecure BGP messages for these destinations instead.

7.2 Turning off S*BGP can cause oscillations.

To underscore the seriousness of an ISP turning off S*BGP in his entire network, we now argue that a group of ISPs could *oscillate*, alternating between turning S*BGP on and off, and never arriving at a stable state. In the full version, we exhibit an example AS graph and state S that proves that oscillations could exist. Worse yet, we show that it is hard to even *determine* whether or not the deployment process will oscillate!

THEOREM 7.1. *Given an AS graph and state S, it is PSPACE-complete to decide if the deployment process will terminate at a stable state in the* incoming utility *model.*

Our proof, in the full version is by reduction to the PSPACE-complete problem of determining whether a space-bounded Turing Machine will halt for a given input string. The complexity class PSPACE consists of all decisions problems that can be solved using only polynomial *space*, but in unbounded *time*. PSPACE-complete problems (intuitively, the hardest problems in PSPACE) are at least as hard as the NP-complete problems, and widely believed to be even harder.

7.3 How common are these examples?

At this point, the reader may be wondering how often an AS might have incentives to turn off S*BGP.

Turning off an entire network? Figure 8 proves that cases where an ISP has an incentive to turn off S*BGP in its *entire network* do exist in realistic AS-level topologies [9]. However, we speculate that such examples will occur infrequently in practice. While we cannot provide any concrete evidence of this, our speculation follows from the fact that an ISP n obtains utility from many destinations. Thus, even if n has increased its utility by turning OFF S*BGP for destinations that are part of subgraphs like Figure 8, he will usually obtain higher utility by turning ON S*BGP for the other destinations that are not part of such subgraphs. (In Figure 8, this does not happen because the state S is such that only a very small group of ASes are secure; thus, no routes other than the ones pictured are effected by AS 4755's decision to turn off S*BGP.)

Turning off a destination is likely. On the other hand, it is quite easy to find examples of *specific destinations* for which an ISP might want to turn off S*BGP. Indeed, a search through the AS graph found that at least 10% of the 5,992 ISPs could find themselves in a state where they have incentives to turn off S*BGP for at least one destination!

8. DISCUSSION OF OUR MODEL

The wide range of parameters involved in modeling S*BGP deployment means that our model (Section 3) cannot be *predictive* of S*BGP deployment in practice. Instead, our model was designed to (a) capture a few of the most crucial issues that might drive S*BGP deployment, while (b) taking the approach that simplicity is preferable to complexity.

8.1 Myopic best response.

For simplicity, we used a *myopic best-response* update rule that is standard in the game-theory literature [16]. In Section 5.5, we discussed the consequences of the fact that ISPs only act to improve their utility in the next round, rather than in long run. Another potential issue is that our update rule ignores the possibility that *multiple* ASes could deploy S*BGP in the transition from a round i to round $i + 1$, resulting in the gap between the projected utility, and the actual utility in the subsequent round. Fortunately, our simulations show projected utility $u_n(\neg S_n, S_{-n})$ is usually an excellent estimate of actual utility in the subsequent round. For example, in the case study of Section 5, 80% of ISPs overestimate their utility by less than 2%, 90% of ISPs overestimate by less than 6.7%. In the full version, we present additional results that the show that this observation also holds more generally across simulations.

8.2 Computing utility locally.

Because we lack information about interdomain traffic flows in the Internet, our model uses weighted counts of the subtrees of ASes routing through ISP n as a stand-in for traffic volumes, and thus ISP utility. While computing these subtrees in our model requires *global* information that would be unavailable to the average ISP (*e.g.*, the state S, the AS graph topology, routing policies), in practice, an ISP can just compute its utility by locally observing traffic flows through its network.

Computing projected utility. Computing projected utility $u_n(\neg S_n, S_{-n})$ in practice is significantly more complex. While projected utility gives an accurate estimate of actual utility when it is computed using global informa-

tion, ISPs may inaccurately estimate their projected utility when using only local information. Our model can accommodate these inaccuracies by rolling them into the deployment threshold θ. (That is, if projected utility is off by a factor of $\pm\epsilon$, model this with threshold $\theta \pm \epsilon$.) Thus, while our approach was to sweep through a common value of θ for every ISP (Section 6.2), extensions might capture inaccurate estimates of projected utility by randomizing θ, or even by systematically modeling an ISP's estimation process to obtain a measure for how it impacts θ.

Practical mechanisms for projecting future traffic patterns. Because S*BGP deployment can impact route selection, it is crucial to develop mechanisms that allow ISPs predict how security will impact traffic patterns through it's network. Moreover, if ISPs could use such mechanisms to estimate projected utility, they would also be an important driver for S*BGP deployment. For example, an ISP might set up a router that listens to S*BGP messages from neighboring ASes, and then use these message to predict how becoming secure might impact its neighbors' route selections. A more sophisticated mechanism could use extended "shadow configurations" with neighboring ASes [1] to gain visibility into how traffic flows might change.

8.3 Alternate routing policies and actions.

Routing policies. Because our model of ISP utility depends on traffic volumes (Section 3.3), we need to a model for how traffic flows in the Internet. In practice, traffic flow is determined by the local routing policies used by each AS, which are arbitrary and not publicly known. Thus, we use a standard model of routing policies (Appendix A) based on business relationship and path length [14, 6].

Routing policies are likely to impact our results by determining (a) AS path lengths (longer AS paths mean it is harder to secure routes), and (b) tiebreak set size (Section 6.6). For example, we speculate that considering shortest path routing policy would lead to overly optimistic results; shortest-path routing certainly leads to shorter AS paths, and possibly also to larger tiebreak sets. On the other hand, if a large fraction of multihomed ASes always use one provider as primary and the other as backup (irrespective of the AS path lengths *etc.*) then our current analysis is likely to be overly optimistic. (Of course, modeling this is difficult given a dearth of empirical data on backup paths).

Choosing routing policies. An AS might cleverly choose its routing policies to maximize utility. However, the following suggests that this is intractable:

THEOREM 8.1. *When all other ASes' routing policies are as in Appendix A, it is NP hard for any AS n to find the routing policy that maximizes its utility (in both the incoming and outgoing utility models). Moreover, approximating the optimal routing policy within any constant factor is also NP hard.*

The proof (in the full version) shows that this is NP-hard even if n has a single route to the destination, and must only choose the set of neighbors to which it announces the route. (Thus, the problem is tractable when the node's neighbors set is of constant size.)

Lying and cheating. While it is well known that an AS can increase the amount of traffic it transits by manipulating its BGP messages [7], we avoided this issue because our focus is on technology adoption by economically-motivated ASes, not BGP manipulations by malicious or misconfigured ASes.

9. RELATED WORK

Social networks. The diffusion of new technologies in social networks has been well studied in economics and game theory (*e.g.,* [30, 21] and references therein). The idea that players will myopically best-respond if their utility exceeds a threshold is standard in this literature (*cf.,* our update rule (3)). However, in a social network, a player's utility depends only on its immediate *neighbors*, while in our setting it depends on the set of secure *paths*. Thus, while [21] finds approximation algorithms for choosing an optimal set of early adopters, this is NP-hard in our setting (Theorem 6.1).

Protocol adoption in the Internet. The idea that competition over customer traffic can drive technology adoption in the Internet has appeared in many places in the literature [10, 33]. Ratnasamy *et al.* [33] suggest using competition for customer traffic to drive protocol deployment (*e.g.,* IPv6) at ISPs by creating new mechanisms for directing traffic to ASes with IPv6. Leveraging competition is much simpler with S*BGP, since it directly influences routing decisions without requiring adoption of new mechanisms.

Multiple studies [19, 18, 36] consider the role of converters (*e.g.,* IPv4-IPv6 gateways) on protocol deployment. While S*BGP must certainly be backwards compatible with BGP, the fact that security guarantees only hold for fully-secure paths (Section 2.2.2) means that there is no reason to convert BGP messages to S*BGP messages. Thus, we do not expect converters to drive S*BGP deployment.

S*BGP adoption. Perhaps most relevant is Chang *et al.*'s comparative study on the adoptability of secure inter-domain routing protocols [8]. Like [8], we also consider how early adopters create local incentives for other ASes to deploy S*BGP. However, our study focuses on how S*BGP deployment can be driven by (a) simplex S*BGP deployment at stubs, and (b) the requirement that security plays a role in routing decisions. Furthermore, in [8] ISP utility depends on the security benefits offered by the partially-deployed protocol. Thus, the utility function in [8] depends on possible attacker strategies (*i.e.,* path shortening attacks) and attacker location (*i.e.,* random, or biased towards small ISPs). In contrast, our model of utility is based solely on economics (*i.e.,* customer traffic transited). Thus, we show that global S*BGP deployment is possible even if ISPs' local deployment decisions are *not* driven by security concerns. Also, complementary to our work is [5]'s forward-looking proposal that argues that extra mechanisms (*e.g.,* secure data-plane monitoring) can be added to S*BGP to get around the problem of partially-secure paths (Appendix B). Finally, we note both our work and [5, 8] find that ensuring that Tier 1 ASes deploy S*BGP is crucial, a fact that is not surprising in light of the highly-skewed degree distribution of the AS graph.

10. CONCLUSION

Our results indicate that there is hope for S*BGP deployment. We have argued for (1) simplex S*BGP to secure stubs, (2) convincing but a small, but influential, set of ASes to be early adopters of S*BGP, and (3) ensuring that S*BGP influences traffic by requiring ASes to (at minimum) break ties between equally-good paths based on security.

We have shown that, if deployment cost θ is low, our proposal can successfully transition a majority of ASes to S*BGP. The transition is driven by market pressure created when ISPs deploy S*BGP in order draw revenue-generating traffic into their networks. We also pointed out unexplored challenges that result from S*BGP's influence of route selection (*e.g.,* ISPs may have incentives to disable S*BGP).

We hope that this work motivates the standardization and research communities to devote their efforts along three key lines. First, effort should be spent to engineer a lightweight simplex S*BGP. Second, with security impacting route selection, ISPs will need tools to forecast how S*BGP deployment will impact traffic patterns (*e.g.,* using "shadow configurations", inspired by [1], with cooperative neighboring ASes) so they can provision their networks appropriately. Finally, our results suggest that S*BGP and BGP will coexist in the long term. Thus, effort should be devoted to ensure that S*BGP and BGP can coexist without introducing new vulnerabilities into the interdomain routing system.

Acknowledgments

This project was motivated by discussions with the members of the DHS S&T CSD Secure Routing project. We especially thank the group for the ideas about simplex S*BGP, and Steve Bellovin for the example in Appendix B.

We are extremely grateful to Mihai Budiu, Frank McSherry and the rest of the group at Microsoft Research SVC for helping us get our code running on DryadLINQ. We also thank Edwin Guarin and Bill Wilder for helping us get our code running on Azure, and the Microsoft Research New England lab for supporting us on this project. We thank Azer Bestavros, John Byers, Mark Crovella, Jef Guarente, Vatche Ishakian, Isaac Keslassy, Eric Keller, Leo Reyzin, Jennifer Rexford, Rick Skowyra, Renata Texiera, Walter Willinger and Minlan Yu for comments on drafts of this work. This project was supported by NSF Grant S-1017907 and a gift from Cisco.

11. REFERENCES

[1] R. Alimi, Y. Wang, and Y. R. Yang. Shadow configuration as a network management primitive. In *Sigcomm*, 2008.

[2] Anonymized. Let the market drive deployment: A strategy for transitioning to bgp security. Full version. Technical report, 2011.

[3] B. Augustin, B. Krishnamurthy, and W. Willinger. IXPs: Mapped? In *IMC*, 2009.

[4] R. Austein, G. Huston, S. Kent, and M. Lepinski. Secure inter-domain routing: Manifests for the resource public key infrastructure. draft-ietf-sidr-rpki-manifests-09.txt, 2010.

[5] I. Avramopoulos, M. Suchara, and J. Rexford. How small groups can secure interdomain routing. Technical report, Princeton University Comp. Sci., 2007.

[6] H. Ballani, P. Francis, and X. Zhang. A study of prefix hijacking and interception in the Internet. In *SIGCOMM*, 2007.

[7] K. Butler, T. Farley, P. McDaniel, and J. Rexford. A survey of BGP security issues and solutions. *Proceedings of the IEEE*, 2010.

[8] H. Chang, D. Dash, A. Perrig, and H. Zhang. Modeling adoptability of secure BGP protocol. In *SIGCOMM*, 2006.

[9] Y.-J. Chi, R. Oliveira, and L. Zhang. Cyclops: The Internet AS-level observatory. *ACM SIGCOMM CCR*, 2008.

[10] D. D. Clark, J. Wroclawski, K. R. Sollins, and R. Braden. Tussle in cyberspace: defining tomorrow's Internet. *Trans. on Networking*, 2005.

[11] J. Cowie. Rensys blog: China's 18-minute mystery. http://www.renesys.com/blog/2010/11/chinas-18-minute-mystery.shtml.

[12] A. Dhamdhere and C. Dovrolis. The internet is flat: Modeling the transition from a transit hierarchy to a peering mesh. In *CoNEXT*, 2010.

[13] L. Gao and J. Rexford. Stable Internet routing without global coordination. *Trans. on Networking*, 2001.

[14] S. Goldberg, M. Schapira, P. Hummon, and J. Rexford. How secure are secure interdomain routing protocols. In *Sigcomm*, 2010.

[15] T. Griffin, F. B. Shepherd, and G. Wilfong. The stable paths problem and interdomain routing. *Trans. on Networking*, 2002.

[16] S. Hart. Adaptive heuristics. *Econometrica*, 2005.

[17] IETF. Secure interdomain routing (SIDR) working group. http://datatracker.ietf.org/wg/sidr/charter/.

[18] Y. Jin, S. Sen, R. Guerin, K. Hosanagar, and Z. Zhang. Dynamics of competition between incumbent and emerging network technologies. In *NetEcon*, 2008.

[19] D. Joseph, N. Shetty, J. Chuang, and I. Stoica. Modeling the adoption of new network architectures. In *CoNEXT*, 2007.

[20] J. Karlin, S. Forrest, and J. Rexford. Autonomous security for autonomous systems. *Computer Networks*, oct 2008.

[21] D. Kempe, J. Kleinberg, and E. Tardos. Maximizing the spread of influence through a social network. In *ACM SIGKDD*, 2003.

[22] S. Kent, C. Lynn, and K. Seo. Secure border gateway protocol (S-BGP). *JSAC*, 2000.

[23] V. Krishnamurthy, M. Faloutsos, M. Chrobak, L. Lao, J.-H. Cui, and A. G. Percus. Sampling large internet topologies for simulation purposes. *Computer Networks (Elsevier)*, 51(15):4284–4302, 2007.

[24] C. Labovitz, S. Iekel-Johnson, D. McPherson, J. Oberheide, and F. Jahanian. Internet inter-domain traffic. In *SIGCOMM*, 2010.

[25] M. Lad, D. Massey, D. Pei, Y. Wu, B. Zhang, and L. Shang. Phas: Prefix hijack alert system. In *Usenix Security*, 2006.

[26] M. Lepinski and S. Turner. Bgpsec protocol specification, 2011. http://tools.ietf.org/html/draft-lepinski-bgpsec-overview-00.

[27] C. D. Marsan. U.S. plots major upgrade to Internet router security. *Network World*, 2009.

[28] A. Medina, A. Lakhina, I. Matta, and J. Byers. BRITE: an approach to universal topology generation. In *MASCOTS*, 2001.

[29] S. Misel. "Wow, AS7007!". Merit NANOG Archive, apr 1997. http://www.merit.edu/mail.archives/nanog/1997-04/msg00340.html.

[30] S. Morris. Contagion. *Review of Economics Studies*, 2003.

[31] R. Oliveira, D. Pei, W. Willinger, B. Zhang, and L. Zhang. Quantifying the completeness of the observed internet AS-level structure. *UCLA Computer Science Department - Techical Report TR-080026-2008*, Sept 2008.

[32] F. Orbit. http://www.fixedorbit.com/metrics.htm.

[33] S. Ratnasamy, S. Shenker, and S. McCanne. Towards an evolvable Internet architecture. In *SIGCOMM*, 2005.

[34] Rensys Blog. Pakistan hijacks YouTube. http://www.renesys.com/blog/2008/02/pakistan_hijacks_youtube_1.shtml.

[35] Sandvine. Fall 2010 global internet phenomena, 2010.

[36] S. Sen, Y. Jin, R. Guerin, and K. Hosanagar. Modeling the dynamics of network technology adoption and the role of converters. *Trans. on Networking*, 2010.

[37] R. White. Deployment considerations for secure origin BGP (soBGP). draft-white-sobgp-bgp-deployment-01.txt, June 2003, expired.

[38] Y. Yu, M. Isard, D. Fetterly, M. Budiu, U. Erlingsson, P. K. Gunda, and J. Currey. Dryadlinq: a system for

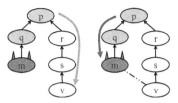

Figure 9: A new attack vector.

general-purpose distributed data-parallel computing using a high-level language. In *Usenix OSDI*, 2008.

[39] E. Zegura, K. Calvert, and S. Bhattarcharjee. How to model an internetwork. In *Infocom*, 1996.

APPENDIX

A. A MODEL OF ROUTING WITH BGP.

We follow [15] by assuming that each AS a computes paths to a given destination AS d based a *ranking* on outgoing paths, and an *export policy* specifying the set of neighbors to which a given path should be announced.

Rankings. AS a selects a path to d from the set of simple paths it learns from its neighbors as follows:

LP Local Preference. Paths are ranked based on their next hop: customer is chosen over peer which is chosen over provider.

SP Shortest Paths. Among the paths with the highest local preference, prefer the shortest ones.

SecP Secure Paths. If there are multiple such paths, and node a is secure, then prefer the secure paths.

TB Tie Break. If there are multiple such paths, node a breaks ties: if b is the next hop on the path, choose the path where hash, $H(a, b)$ is the lowest.[4]

This standard model of local preference [13] captures the idea that an AS has incentives to prefer routing through a customer (that pays it) over a peer (no money is exchanged) over a provider (that it must pay).

Export Policies. This standard model of export policies captures the idea that an AS will only load its network with transit traffic if its customer pays it to do so [13]:

GR2 AS b announces a path via AS c to AS a iff at least one of a and c are customers of b.

B. ATTACKS ON PARTIALLY SECURE PATHS

We show how preferring partially secure paths over insecure paths can introduce *new* attack vectors that do not exist even without S*BGP:

Figure 9: Suppose that only ASes p and q are secure, and that malicious AS m falsely announces the path (m, v), and suppose that p's tiebreak algorithm prefers paths through r over paths through q. Then, p has a choice between two paths; a partially-secure false path (p, q, m, v), and and insecure true path (p, r, s, v). If no AS used S*BGP, p would have chosen the true path (per his tiebreak algorithm); if p prefers partially secure paths, he will be fooled into routing to AS m.

---

[4]In practice, this is done using the distance between routers and router IDs. Since we do not incorporate this information in our model we use a randomized tie break which prevents certain ASes from "always winning".

Finding Protocol Manipulation Attacks

Nupur Kothari
USC

Ratul Mahajan
Microsoft Research

Todd Millstein
UCLA

Ramesh Govindan
USC

Madanlal Musuvathi
Microsoft Research

ABSTRACT

We develop a method to help discover manipulation attacks in protocol implementations. In these attacks, adversaries induce honest nodes to exhibit undesirable behaviors by misrepresenting their intent or network conditions. Our method is based on a novel combination of static analysis with symbolic execution and dynamic analysis with concrete execution. The former finds code paths that are likely vulnerable, and the latter emulates adversarial actions that lead to effective attacks. Our method is precise (i.e., no false positives) and we show that it scales to complex protocol implementations. We apply it to four diverse protocols, including TCP, the 802.11 MAC, ECN, and SCTP, and show that it is able to find all manipulation attacks that have been previously reported for these protocols. We also find a previously unreported attack for SCTP. This attack is a variant of a TCP attack but must be mounted differently in SCTP because of subtle semantic differences between the two protocols.

Categories and Subject Descriptors

C.2.2 [Computer communication networks]: Network protocols–protocol verification

General Terms

Security, Reliability

1. INTRODUCTION

That network protocols can be vulnerable to attacks is well-known. By sending unexpected or malformed messages that exploit bugs or inadequate defenses (e.g., buffer overflows) in protocol implementations, adversaries can crash or hijack victims. Over time, research has led to a good understanding of such attacks and developed general tools and techniques to detect and mitigate them [4, 16, 20, 22]. Examples include automatically generating vulnerability signatures to filter malicious inputs and tracking the influence of tainted inputs on critical segments of the code.

In this paper, we consider a different and a more subtle class of attacks that we call *manipulation attacks*. In these attacks, the goal of the adversaries is not to crash or hijack the honest participants but to induce other behaviors that benefit the adversaries or harm the honest participants. Such attacks have been identified in several common protocols. Savage et al. found three different ways (e.g., by acknowledging packets even before they are received) in which an adversarial TCP receiver can manipulate the sender into send-ing at a rate faster than that dictated by congestion control dynamics [24]. Ely et al. showed that an ECN (Explicit Congestion Notification) receiver can manipulate the sender into ignoring congestion by simply flipping a bit in the packet headers [11]. Manipulation attacks that starve the honest participants have been identified for the 802.11 MAC protocol as well [1].

Instead of relying (only) on implementation bugs in protocols, manipulation attacks leverage the fact that individual participants do not have complete knowledge of network conditions (e.g., degree of congestion) or other participants' intent. Adversaries can exploit this incomplete knowledge by misrepresenting network conditions or their own intent in their messages to honest participants and can thus induce undesirable behavior in them. The induced behavior may be valid in certain circumstances but incorrect under current circumstances; for instance, increasing the sending rate is desirable when there is no congestion but undesirable otherwise. Often, adversaries may need to repeat such manipulations several times in order to achieve their goals such as performance gains for themselves or starving the honest participants.

Our long-term goal is to make protocols robust to manipulation attacks. In this paper, we focus on developing a method to help developers (and researchers) (a) identify whether a protocol implementation is susceptible to manipulation attacks, and (b) compute the sequence of messages that can be used to mount the attack. To our knowledge, these capabilities do not exist today; all manipulation attacks mentioned above were discovered through manual inspection of protocols by researchers. Techniques developed for other kinds of protocol vulnerabilities are unsuitable for detecting manipulation attacks. For instance, vulnerability signatures for detecting manipulating messages are hard to develop because such messages can be valid under certain circumstances.

Discovering manipulation attacks is challenging. Whether a single packet is successful in manipulating the honest participant towards a goal (e.g., increasing connection throughput) depends upon the goal itself, the network topology and traffic, and the internal protocol state (e.g., connection state, number of outstanding packets) at the honest participant. A brute force search of the entire space of packets, goals, topologies, traffic, and protocol states is clearly intractable. Even worse, successful attacks may require repeated manipulations where each input packet must leave honest participants in a valid state to continue execution, yet steer them towards the adversary's goal. This requirement significantly increases the search space.

To reduce the search space, we assume that developers specify goals as well as topologies and traffic. We posit that developers can provide these inputs based on their expertise and intuition. For instance, specifying the goal involves identifying a resource that may be vulnerable to manipulation (e.g., bandwidth) and protocol actions at honest participants related to that resource (e.g., sending a packet). Developers can iteratively explore many possible goals with varying topologies and traffic.

```
1   void ack_received(char *buffer){          1   void pkt_received(char *buffer)
2     int num_pkts_to_send;                   2     int ecn_bit = ((packet *)buffer)->ecn_bit;
3     if(num_pkts_in_flight == 0)  return;    3     packet *ack_buffer;
4     num_pkts_in_flight--;                    4     num_pkts_rcvd++;
5     num_pkts_sent++;                         5     ack_buffer = create_ack(buffer);
6     int ecn_bit = ((packet *)buffer)->ecn_bit; 6
7                                              7     //if the ecnbit is non-zero,
8     //if ecn bit is zero, send two           8     //set it in the ack header
9     //packets in response else send none     9     if (ecn_bit != 0) {
10    if (ecn_bit == 0)                        10      ack_buffer->ecn_bit = ecn_bit;
11      num_pkts_to_send = 2;                  11    }
12    else                                     12
13      num_pkts_to_send = 0;                  13    //send the ACK to the sender
14    if(num_pkts_to_send > 0)                 14    send_ack(ack_buffer,
15      send_pkts();                           15      ((packet *)buffer)->src);
16  }                                          16  }
```

(a) ECN Sender   **(b)** ECN Receiver

Figure 1: Code for a simplified version of the ECN protocol

Even with these inputs from developers, the space of possible manipulation attacks, defined by the space of possible messages and internal protocol state, is too large to allow for an exhaustive, blind search. To explore this space in a scalable and precise manner, we leverage two complementary program-analysis techniques.

The first is symbolic execution [15], a general method for static analysis of code, which we use to infer conditions on an incoming message and on the current state that may lead an honest participant to execute actions consistent with the adversaries' goals.

Because static analysis of complex code is inevitably imprecise, we combine it with a form of concrete, system-level testing. We run the protocol implementation and, based on information from symbolic execution, modify messages such that the honest participant is repeatedly induced to exhibit the identified behaviors. By comparing protocol runs with and without modifications, developers can determine if manipulation attacks can succeed. Additionally, the sequence of modifications provides information on how the attack was mounted and can guide the development of fixes.

While other researchers have used one or both of these techniques to find software bugs [6, 13, 28, 30], current approaches aim to identify a single bad input. We combine these techniques in a qualitatively different way, using symbolic execution to approximate single inputs that can manipulate the honest participant in its current state, and then using concrete execution to search for a sequence of inputs that constitutes an effective attack. Further, we adapt these techniques, sometimes using domain-specific optimizations and appropriately managing the trade-off between precision and scalability, to be able to handle full-fledged implementations of complex protocols such as TCP and SCTP [25].

We implement our method in a tool called MAX (Manipulation Attack eXplorer) and demonstrate its efficacy by applying it to implementations of TCP, the 802.11 MAC, ECN, and SCTP. For the first three protocols, we show that MAX is able to find and quantify the impact of all the manipulation attacks that researchers have discovered manually. We show that SCTP too is vulnerable to a manipulation attack, a finding that we believe has not been previously reported in the literature. While this attack is similar to one of the attacks on TCP, the way it is mounted in SCTP is different because of different receiver window semantics in the two protocols. MAX's analysis recognizes these semantic differences and infers the correct manipulation method for each protocol. We also show how MAX can not only find manipulation attacks but can also help developers gain confidence that their implementations are robust to certain attacks or that their protective measures are effective.

While these results are promising, our work represents only a first step towards a general tool for finding manipulation attacks. In the future, we plan to investigate the generality of MAX and its techniques by applying it to other, less well-explored protocols. Such an investigation will also help understand the prevalence of vulnerabilities to manipulation attacks in protocol implementations.

2. DEFINING MANIPULATION ATTACKS

Consider a protocol with two or more participants. The honest participants correctly follow the protocol, but adversarial participants may deviate arbitrarily. A manipulation attack has the following two characteristics:

1. Adversaries induce the honest participants to change behavior in a way that benefits adversaries or harms the honest participants.

2. The induced behavior is actually protocol-compliant under some circumstances and network conditions.

These characteristics rule out attacks where, for example, a rogue wireless node unilaterally jams the medium or where crashes are induced in honest participants. These attacks are important as well but are not the focus of our work; techniques exist to detect and mitigate them (e.g., [4, 6, 20, 22]).

Because they are subtle and indirect, most manipulation attacks have a third characteristic:

3. A single manipulative act is insufficient to mount an effective attack. Instead, the manipulation must be repeated many times in order to have a noticeable impact.

We use the ECN protocol as a running example in this paper, to illustrate a simple manipulation attack and the conceptual ideas behind our approach. ECN enables the network to notify the senders of congestion. When a packet encounters congestion, the congested router sets the ECN bit in the header of the packet. The receiver copies the ECN bit into the acknowledgment packet that it sends out. The sender becomes aware of the congestion when it receives an acknowledgment with the ECN bit set, and it can react by reducing its sending rate.

Figure 1 shows snippets of code for a simplified version of ECN that we wrote for illustrative purposes. The sender (Figure 1a), on receiving an acknowledgment from the receiver, checks the ECN bit in the header. If it is set, the sender does not send out any new packets. If the ECN bit is not set, which indicates that there is no congestion in the network, the sender sends two new packets to the receiver. The receiver (Figure 1b), on getting a packet from the sender, obediently reflects the ECN bit from the packet header into the acknowledgment packet that it sends back to the sender.

Ely *et al.* [11] report a manipulation attack on ECN in which the receiver is adversarial, while the sender is honest. The adversarial receiver never sets the ECN bit, irrespective of what it receives from the routers, thus manipulating the sender into believing that the network is not congested (even if it is). As a result, the sender sends two new packets upon receiving each acknowledgment. This behavior results in increased throughput for the receiver at the expense of other flows traversing the congested router.

The attack above exhibits all three characteristics of a manipulation attack. The adversarial ECN receiver manipulates the behavior of the honest sender for its own benefit. Further, this manipulated behavior is protocol-compliant under some circumstances, namely when there is no congestion. For this reason, the attack is hard for the ECN sender to detect. Finally, the manipulation must be repetitively performed to have a noticeable impact on throughput. Modifying a single message only causes two extra messages to be sent, which will not improve the receiver's throughput by much.

A number of manipulation attacks have been manually discovered in other widely used network protocols as well. For example, an adversarial TCP receiver can manipulate an honest sender into sending faster and obtain an unfair share of bandwidth, by sending duplicate acknowledgments (DupACK spoofing), by acknowledging individual bytes rather than whole packets (ACK division), or by acknowledging packets before they are received (Optimistic ACKs) [24]. 802.11 implementations have been found to be vulnerable to manipulation attacks that prevent honest nodes from gaining access to the channel and thus starve them, by setting large values in the `duration` field in packet headers [1].

3. FINDING MANIPULATION ATTACKS

Our goal is to enable systematic exploration of manipulation attacks in protocol implementations. Although analyzing abstract protocol specifications is easier, we analyze real implementations because inadvertent programming errors can produce vulnerable implementations even if specifications are robust. Further, specifications of complex protocols are typically imprecise and, because different implementations make different design choices, each may have a different set of potential vulnerabilities. For instance, not all manipulation attacks for TCP [24] were successful for all implementations. Analyzing implementations allows us to uncover both vulnerabilities in a protocol's specification and vulnerabilities created by specific implementation choices.

3.1 Challenges and Approach

A tool that only takes the protocol implementation as input, and automatically outputs all possible manipulation attacks on it, would need to search a very large space. This space includes all possible goals of manipulation (e.g., starving honest participants or inducing them to send more traffic), all possible network configurations (i.e., topology and traffic workload) as well as all possible combinations of message contents and internal protocol state (because the protocol behavior is a function of both these factors).

We reduce this search space in two ways. First, we require the tool's user (a developer or a researcher) to specify the manipulation goal. This involves specifying a protocol action (e.g., sending a packet, in the ECN example) whose repeated execution could lead to a manipulation attack. Second, we require the user to specify the network configurations under which the potential for a manipulation attack should be explored. While it may be possible to

automate the search of goals and network configurations, we leave this to future work. Our approach leverages the intuition and understanding that developers have of the likely protocol actions that can be exploited and the likely network conditions under which manipulations can succeed.

With these inputs, we are left with the problem of exploring the space of possible packet inputs and protocol internal states. This problem poses two challenges. The primary one is scalability—the space of possible manipulations is huge. Adversaries interact with honest participants by sending packets, and there are in principle 2^{12000} possible ways of crafting a 1500-byte packet. Even if we focus only on protocol headers, there are 2^{160} possibilities for a 20-byte header. Further, the exact contents of a packet that successfully manipulates an honest participant may depend on the (dynamically varying) state of the participant.

This intractably large space of possibilities implies that blind exhaustive or random search is unlikely to be effective. We thus leverage program semantics to efficiently search the space. In particular, we use symbolic execution, a static program analysis technique, of the protocol implementation to determine the set of packets that may induce honest participants to execute actions of interest, as a function of their current state. This set is determined statically, without actually running the protocol, and is represented in a concise, symbolic form. Packets that are not in the set are not considered further in our approach, allowing us to dramatically reduce the search space for manipulation attacks.

The second challenge is precision. In principle, symbolic execution alone can identify manipulation attacks. In practice, however, static analysis of complex code can be imprecise. Real protocol implementations can contain tens of thousands of lines of code with many low-level constructs. For instance, the Linux implementation of TCP that we analyze is over 14K lines of C code with many pointers and loops that are hard for static analysis to handle precisely. Imprecision in the analysis can lead, for instance, to false positives (i.e., attack strategies that do not work in practice) that may render the tool unusable. Further, unlike crash attacks, being able to reach an action of interest once does not imply that an effective manipulation attack exists. Instead, the adversary may need to repeatedly drive honest participants to execute certain actions. That ability depends on complex, dynamic factors (e.g., network congestion) that are hard to capture statically. Finally, even if a manipulation can be successfully repeated, it may or may not have a significant enough impact compared to an honest run of the protocol to be considered a success. It is difficult for static analysis to quantify the impact of an attack.

We address the limitations of symbolic execution above by combining it with *adversarial concrete execution*. We run the protocol implementation and use information from symbolic execution about possible packet manipulations, along with information about the current execution state, to perform manipulations that induce honest participants to execute actions of interest repeatedly. This produces an end-to-end demonstration of manipulation attacks, a catalog of one or more sequences of packet manipulations that led to the attack, and a quantification of the impact of these attacks. Furthermore, concrete execution ensures that no false positives are reported. However, as we discuss later, there can be false negatives.

3.2 Method Overview

We now describe our method for systematically exploring manipulation attacks. We focus on its conceptual elements and leave to §4 the details of a tool that embodies our ideas.

We assume that one or more adversaries manipulate an honest participant, called the *target*, through their protocol messages.

While we allow for multiple (possibly colluding) adversaries, we currently allow only one target and leave to future work extensions to handle multiple targets. There can be other (non-target) honest participants in the network.

We also assume that the attack is launched by repeated manipulations of individual messages. To our knowledge, this is true of all manipulation attacks that have been uncovered to date. In theory, however, more complicated manipulation attacks are possible. For instance, they may require a specific sequence of distinct manipulations or may require that a manipulation occur at a specific time. We leave the exploration of these variants to future work.

The main input that we require from the users of our tool is a set of *vulnerable statements* representing the actions of interest for achieving a manipulation goal. Our approach is agnostic to the specific actions represented by these statements. We expect that users would typically first identify a resource (e.g., memory, network bandwidth, etc.) whose vulnerability they are interested in exploring and then use code points where these resources are allocated as vulnerable statements. For example, if manipulation of memory allocation is of interest, statements that allocate memory would be deemed vulnerable. Similarly, for network bandwidth, statements where packets are transmitted or where variables that control the sending rate are updated would be deemed vulnerable. The vulnerable statements are by themselves benign and are likely executed frequently even in the absence of attacks. Thus, unlike assertion failures, their mere reachability does not signify the possibility of a successful attack.

We test if adversaries can repeatedly drive the target to these vulnerable statements and if that significantly impacts the protocol performance compared to scenarios without manipulation. To quantify the impact of an manipulation attack, users specify a set of metrics defined on the resource of interest. For a resource like network bandwidth, this may simply be the number of times the vulnerable statement (that transmits a packet) is executed. For a resource like memory, this may be the cumulative number of bytes allocated during the execution.

We accomplish our goal of finding manipulation attacks by using the two analysis techniques discussed earlier, in a way that exploits the strengths of each. Symbolic execution prunes the search space dramatically by providing a set of constraints on network messages and the target's state that must be satisfied to reach the vulnerable statements. Adversarial concrete execution exploits knowledge of the target's current state to repeatedly solve these constraints and observe if an effective manipulation attack can be mounted. We describe our use of these techniques in more detail below.

3.2.1 Path exploration using symbolic execution

Symbolic execution [15] simulates the execution of code using a symbolic value σ_x to represent the value of each variable x. As the symbolic executor runs, it updates the symbolic store that maintains information about program variables. For example, after the assignment y = 2*x the symbolic executor does not know the exact value of y but has learned that $\sigma_y = 2\sigma_x$. At branches, symbolic execution uses a constraint solver to determine the value of the guard expression, given the information in the symbolic store. The symbolic executor only explores the branch corresponding to the guard's value as returned by the constraint solver, ensuring that infeasible paths are ignored. If there is insufficient information to determine the guard's value, both branches are explored. In this way, a tree of possible program execution paths is produced. Each path is summarized by a *path condition* that is the conjunction of branch choices made to go down that path.

We use symbolic execution on the target's implementation to explore possible paths that lead from message reception to vulnerable statements. Consider the ECN sender code in Figure 1a and assume that statement `send_pkts()` at line 16 is the sole vulnerable statement. Of all the possible paths through this code, symbolic execution determines that there is only one feasible path that reaches this statement, with the following associated path condition:

$$\sigma_{\texttt{num\_pkts\_in\_flight}} \neq 0 \ \& \ \sigma_{\texttt{ecn\_bit}} = 0 \ \& \ \sigma_{\texttt{num\_pkts\_to\_send}} > 0$$

This path is the one that takes the `else` branch at line 3, the `then` branch at line 11, and the `then` branch at line 15. All other paths either can never lead to the vulnerable statement (e.g., the `then` branch at line 3) or are infeasible. For example, the `else` branch at line 11 sets num_pkts_to_send to 0, which prevents the `then` branch at line 15 from being taken.

We convert each path condition into an *input constraint*, a predicate on symbolic values (i.e., on the incoming protocol message and internal protocol state) that is sufficient for execution to go down that path. This conversion is straightforward given the symbolic store. For the path condition described above for the ECN example, the input constraint is:

$$\sigma_{\texttt{num\_pkts\_in\_flight}} \neq 0 \ \& \ \sigma_{\texttt{buffer->ecn\_bit}} = 0$$

3.2.2 Attack emulation using concrete execution

We use the input constraints derived above to emulate manipulation attacks using concrete execution of the protocol implementation on a network configuration specified by the user. During this execution, we intercept each protocol message from an adversary that is directed to the target. An *adversarial module* then attempts to modify the message so as to drive the target to execute a vulnerable statement. We use a constraint solver to find concrete values for the message fields that, given the current internal protocol state of the target, satisfy one of the input constraints.

Per the input constraint above for ECN, whenever the sender's internal state has a nonzero value for `num_pkts_in_flight`, setting `buffer->ecn_bit` to 0 will drive the sender to execute the vulnerable statement. The adversarial module performs this modification and passes it to the target's message handling function. The control is then transferred to the protocol implementation to process this message.

By intercepting every message from the adversary to the target and using the adversarial module to modify it, our concrete execution attempts to repeatedly drive execution to a vulnerable statement. The user can determine, using the output values of the specified impact metrics and by comparing with a non-adversarial run, whether the implementation is vulnerable to a manipulation attack.

4. MAX DESIGN AND IMPLEMENTATION

We now describe our tool, called MAX, which uses the approach above to find manipulation attacks in protocol implementations written in C. Program analysis in C is challenging since the language has many low-level constructs, but we choose it because it is widely used in real-world protocol implementations.

MAX consists of three main components (Figure 2). The *path explorer* uses static analysis to find feasible paths and constraints that lead to vulnerable statements. The *adversarial module generator* uses the results from the *path explorer* to generate an adversarial module, which mimics the behavior of an adversary attempting to launch a manipulation attack. The *attack emulator* runs the protocol implementation using the adversarial module.

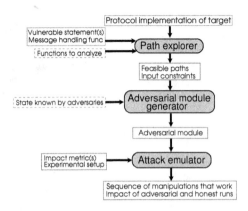

Figure 2: Overview of MAX. The dashed inputs are optional.

4.1 Path Explorer

The path explorer takes as input the protocol implementation of the target and along with the vulnerable statements and the function(s) that represents the starting point for handling incoming messages. Protocol implementations typically have a few, easily recognizable places where the processing of incoming messages begins (e.g., the `message_rcv()` function in our TCP implementation). An optional input is a set of functions in the protocol implementation that should be explored. This input can be used to focus the analysis on a subset of the code when the user is interested in (faster) exploration of specific aspects of the protocol. The default is to consider the entire implementation.

The path explorer operates in three steps. First, it parses the source code and build a control flow graph (CFG) for each function; nodes in a CFG are statements, and edges represent the order of execution of statements. From these individual CFGs, it builds a composite CFG, rooted at the protocol's message reception function, where there is an edge from a statement in one CFG to the root of another CFG if that statement calls the function corresponding to the target CFG. We use the CIL infrastructure for C program analysis [21] for this task. Second, to reduce the complexity of symbolic execution and improve scalability, the path explorer uses a standard reachability analysis to identify and remove nodes that do not reach vulnerable statements. Finally, it uses our symbolic execution engine (described below) on the pruned CFG. Whenever one of the vulnerable statements is reached during this execution, we convert the associated path condition into an input constraint. After we store this information, execution continues, until the entire CFG has been explored.

4.1.1 Symbolic execution engine

We implement our own symbolic execution engine rather than using an existing one [5, 30] in order to manage the tradeoff between precision and scalability, which is critical for handling real protocol implementations. Further, most existing engines work only on whole programs, while we wanted the flexibility of analyzing a subset of the implementation if desired by the user.

MAX's symbolic execution engine is implemented as an interprocedural analysis in CIL and uses the Z3 constraint solver [10]. It is multi-threaded, to take advantage of multi-core architectures.

As mentioned previously, symbolic execution converts program statements into relationships (or constraints) among symbolic values. Much of this processing is fairly standard except for some types of program constructs that we describe below.

Function calls: We first check if the body of the function being called is included in the user's set of functions to explore and if it is

part of the pruned CFG for the implementation. If both conditions are true, the function needs to be analyzed. For such functions, the symbolic executor adds its formal parameters to the symbolic store, mapping them to the arguments specified in the function call, and starts traversing the function body.

If the function need not be analyzed, the symbolic executor assigns fresh symbolic values to variables that might be modified by the call and continues with the statement following the function call. This approach is conservative, essentially assuming that the variables can take on any value after the call, and it can cause the tool to treat some infeasible paths as possibly feasible. However, our attack emulation step weeds out any such false positives, thus maintaining precision.

Loops: A naive treatment of loops would require the symbolic execution engine to consider an unbounded number of paths, since the actual number of loop iterations cannot always be known statically. To address this problem, the symbolic execution engine partitions the possible paths through a loop into two cases: *i*) when the loop guard is false and the body is never entered; and *ii*) when the loop body in entered at least once [12]. We invoke Z3 (constraint solver) to evaluate the loop guard, and if the guard is known to be false, we consider only the first case. If the guard is known to be true, we consider only the second case. Otherwise, we consider both cases.

For the false case, the loop body is simply skipped and simulation continues at the subsequent statement. For the true case, the engine conservatively simulates the effect of an arbitrary number of iterations of the loop. It first invalidates information in the symbolic store about any variable that may be modified by the loop body, similar to what is done for calls to un-analyzed functions. Then, the loop body is symbolically executed once. Finally, the loop guard is assumed to be false, its negation is added to the path condition, and symbolic execution continues after the loop.

Low-level constructs: Network protocol implementations make heavy use of features such as pointer manipulation, type casting, and arrays. One option for handling such features uniformly is to model all variables as byte arrays [5]. While highly precise, this approach dramatically increases the complexity (and thus reduces scalability) of symbolic execution. Instead, we use a single symbolic value for most variables. For compound types like structs and arrays, we use a symbolic value per field and introduce these symbolic values lazily as each field is encountered.

In order to retain precision, we employ domain knowledge about how network protocols use low-level features in order to devise precise ways of simulating their execution. For example, consider a statement of the form `x = (struct_b *)y`, where `y` is of type `struct_a *`. In general, it is difficult to deduce the relationship between the two struct types, which is necessary to transfer any knowledge in the symbolic store about `y` and its fields to `x`. We leverage the fact that when these structs represent packet headers, typically one of the two structs is embedded as a field of the other. We thus search for such an embedding in the struct definitions. If found, it is straightforward to update the symbolic store with information about `x`. If we cannot determine the relationship between the two structs, we conservatively learn nothing about `x` and its fields.

We use a few other simple heuristics to improve the precision of symbolic execution in the presence of other low-level features. For example, when trying to resolve a function pointer, we only consider functions having the same signature as the function pointer, whose addresses were stored somewhere in the protocol code.

In the implementations that we study, we find that symbolic execution retains precision for 75-80% of the analyzed statements that update state. Because our analysis approach is conservative, most of the imprecision leads to false positives (which are later eliminated). However, there is one source of imprecision that may lead to false negatives. We are sometimes unable to link header fields of an incoming message to the corresponding variables in the target. For instance, bits 33-64 in the TCP header correspond to the sequence number. The target may parse these bits to obtain the value of a variable called seqno. If the complexity of the parsing code prevents us from correctly determining how the value of seqno is instantiated, we would not be able to analyze the impact of an adversary manipulating the sequence number field. In our experiments, we find that this is not a significant limitation because for all attacks that we study, we are able to link the relevant header fields to internal variables. To accommodate implementations where this does not hold, our analysis can be extended to accept this linkage as an input.

4.1.2 Emulation-driven optimization

For highly complex protocols, the path explorer may need to explore an extremely large number of paths (on the order of billions). Inspired by symbolic execution engines that use a mix of symbolic and concrete execution [13], we handle this challenge by introducing a profiling step before path exploration. We run an instrumented version of the protocol implementation on the network configuration that is used during attack emulation (see below) and automatically record the set of internal states encountered at the target. We seed the path explorer with this information, which explores only paths consistent with at least one of these concrete states and deems other paths as infeasible. In this way, the path explorer focuses on the network conditions likely to be encountered during concrete execution, improving scalability without sacrificing precision.

4.2 Adversarial Module Generator

The adversarial module generator analyzes input constraints for the paths discovered by the path explorer to generate an adversarial module. As mentioned in §3, this module computes message contents that, when received by the target in it's current state, are likely to cause it to execute a vulnerable statement.

By default, we assume that the adversary knows the values of all internal state variables of the target and can use them for crafting messages that lead to vulnerable statements. This adversary model ensures that MAX can find manipulation attacks that might be possible with an omniscient adversary that can infer all state variables through inference based on protocol dynamics or out-of-band information. However, users can explore weaker adversary models by specifying the subset of state variables that are known and a subset of message fields that can be manipulated.

The adversarial module resides at the target, where it intercepts and modifies incoming messages from adversaries. It is compiled with the protocol implementation and includes a function for modifying messages. A call to this function is inserted in the protocol code where message handling begins, enabling interception. This function first reads the current (visible) state of the target and then invokes the Z3 constraint solver to find an assignment of values for message fields that satisfy an input constraint provided by the path explorer. The message is then overwritten by these values and returned. From the target's perspective, it appears that the adversary itself had crafted and sent this message.

Given input constraints for multiple feasible paths and multiple satisfying assignments for the same input constraint (and thus possibly multiple ways to modify the message), there are many ways to explore the space of adversarial executions. Our current strategy is quite simple. We consider input constraints in an arbitrary order and use the first satisfiable one. To reduce the time spent searching for a satisfiable constraint, we cache this satisfiable constraint and,

for future messages, first check if it still satisfiable. We use the default solution returned by the solver for the satisfiable constraint, rather than explore all feasible solutions.

The strategy above can in theory lead MAX to miss some manipulation attacks (i.e., a false negative). For instance, we would miss an attack that relied on sending the target down paths P1, P2, P3 in that order if we emulated a different order. We would also miss attacks that required a different assignment of values than the one returned by Z3 for the same input constraint. In practice, however, we find that this simple strategy is quite effective (§5) at finding manipulation attacks (perhaps because such attacks do not require a high degree of sophistication). In the future, we will extend the adversarial module with more exhaustive search strategies of the type used by model checking tools [14, 19, 31].

We find that in some cases the attack goals are more conveniently expressed not as vulnerable statements, towards which emulation should be driven, but as "not-vulnerable" statements, which should be avoided (§5.5). For example, it may be useful to explore manipulations of TCP that work by avoiding statements that reduce the congestion window. We thus allow users to specify such statements. The path explorer treats them just as vulnerable statements and generates input constraints for them. However, the adversarial module solves for the negation of those constraints.

4.3 Attack Emulator

The goal of the attack emulator is to find a sequence of manipulations that constitute an effective manipulation attack. The inputs to the emulator include the impact metrics and network configuration. The user specifies impact metrics using variables in the target whose values capture the impact of the manipulation attack. If such variables do not already exist, users can instrument the code to introduce new variables. One instrumentation that we provide by default is a variable that counts the number of times vulnerable statements are executed. In many cases, this instrumentation measures the cumulative resource usage for the resource of interest (e.g., when bandwidth is the resource and send_pkt() is a vulnerable statement). In our current implementation, the user is required to manually configure the network topology and traffic to be used for emulation. It is, however, straightforward to automate this process by having users specify the desired topology and traffic in a configuration file, which we can use to configure the emulation experiment.

The attack emulator runs unmodified protocol implementations for all participants except the target. For the target, it uses the protocol implementation, compiled with the adversarial module, so that the incoming messages can be intercepted and modified.

The attack emulator performs two sets of runs: an adversarial run in which messages from adversaries to the target are modified and an honest one in which the messages are not modified. For complex protocols with many paths, interception of messages can introduce noticeable delay in message processing, which can slow protocol dynamics. For instance, for TCP this delay translates to participants observing higher round trip times and thus slower growth in sending rate. For a fair comparison between the two runs, the adversarial module is executed for the honest run as well, but without the modification step, to introduce comparable delays. For multi-party protocols, messages received by the target from non-adversaries are delayed similarly (during both adversarial and honest runs).

After completing the runs, the emulator outputs the impact metrics for both runs, a trace of the manipulations used by the adversarial module, their success in reaching the vulnerable statements, and symbolic constraints on the selected paths. The impact metrics let users determine whether the manipulation attack was effective. The

	LoC (K)	Paths explored (K)	Feasible paths (K)	Avg. path length (#conds)	Avg. compute time / path (s)
TCP	14.2	7,747	6,163	83	0.59
SCTP	12.5	2,124	359	134	10.11
802.11	11.0	7,288	237	63	15.26
ECN	7.6	2	1	28	0.58

Table 1: Complexity of the protocols that we analyze

other pieces of information can be used to infer the attack method. This process currently requires manual inspection of the constraints and manipulations. In theory, this inspection can be tedious. For the attacks that we find in §5, however, even though the attack emulator chooses multiple different paths to reach the vulnerable statements, the paths have similar constraints on the inputs (header fields) and protocol state variables. In such cases, manual inspection sufficed for inferring the header manipulations needed for mounting the attack. We emphasize that this inspection is not required to establish whether or not the manipulation attack was successful, but only to find the manipulations required to recreate the attack. Developing tools to help with the inference of attack strategy from emulator traces is an interesting avenue for future work.

5. EVALUATION

We use MAX to analyze implementations of four diverse protocols: TCP, 802.11, ECN, and SCTP. Before describing its efficacy in finding manipulation attacks in these protocols, we quantify their complexity and the performance of MAX when analyzing them.

5.1 Benchmarks

Table 1 shows different measures of protocol complexity. Each implementation has thousands of lines of C code. These lines represent the core protocol logic and do not include header files.

The statistics related to paths are based on running the path explorer for each of these protocols. While the symbolic execution ran to completion for ECN, for the other protocols, we ran it for two weeks before collecting these statistics. We used the emulation-driven optimization (§4.1.2) only for TCP. We see that for each protocol, over 2K distinct paths are explored, with over 7.7M paths being examined for TCP. Handling such complex code is challenging for any software analysis tool.

Scaling benefits of symbolic execution. Two measures shed light on the value of static analysis in our method. The first is the fraction paths that it can recognize as infeasible, so that they need not be analyzed further. Table 1 shows that this fraction ranges from 21-97%. This fraction is exceptionally low for the case of TCP (21%) because a large number of infeasible paths were pruned out before symbolic execution by using emulation-driven optimization.

Another measure stems from contrasting with a strategy proposed in prior work [29] for finding similar attacks without symbolic execution. This work proposes that, rather than exploring all possible bit patterns in the header, users restrict the search to header fields that likely impact the resource being manipulated, based on expert knowledge of the protocol. For example, in TCP, restricting the exploration to the sequence number field may suffice, which would yield 2^{32} possible inputs instead of $2^{40 \times 8}$. Even if we ignore the error prone nature of manually identifying important fields, the value of symbolic execution is impressive. For TCP, we get 6M feasible paths, which is over three orders of magnitude lower than blindly manipulating the 32-bit sequence number. The scaling for SCTP is even better, where the number of feasible paths is $359K$, but the attacks we find below require manipulating two

header fields with 32 bits each. Even if we assume that these two fields can be independently explored [29], this represents a scaling factor of over five orders of magnitude ($\frac{359K}{2 \times 2^{32}}$).

The scaling benefits computed above are an underestimate because a packet's ability to manipulate and reach the vulnerable statement depends on not only the header values but also the internal state of the target. While a blind search would have to explore all possible internal states, MAX compactly represents each path predicate in terms of the header values and internal state needed to traverse the path. A single packet from this set, sent when the internal state has the appropriate values, suffices to exercise this path.

Computational complexity of symbolic execution. Table 1 also shows the average time taken to compute a feasible path for all protocols. This time ranges from 0.6 seconds for ECN and TCP, to 10-15 seconds for SCTP and 802.11. This disparity arises for different reasons for ECN and TCP. Firstly, ECN is a much simpler protocol, and the average number of conditions that need to be solved (path length in Table 1) is much lower than that for other protocols. In TCP, since a large number of infeasible paths have already been pruned by emulation-driven optimization, the number of paths that need to be explored before finding a feasible path is much lower. Using emulation-driven optimization for SCTP and 802.11 would have likely lowered their computation time as well.

5.2 Case Study I: TCP

We now report on what MAX finds for each protocol, starting with TCP, which is one of the most complex network protocols and thus represents a good stress test. Our TCP implementation is Daytona [23], a user-space port from the Linux 2.3.29 kernel.[1] As shown above, it has 14K lines of code and over 7M paths. We wanted to check if, in this complex implementation, MAX can find attacks that have been previously discovered using manual inspection. We show that it is not only able to find vulnerabilities that exist but also helped confirm robustness to those that do not.

Finding the Optimistic ACK attack. In this attack, an adversarial TCP receiver sends ACKs with sequence numbers for packets that it is yet to receive. These Optimistic ACKs fool the sender into believing that more packets have been received and thus sending faster than with honest ACKs. If the traffic goes over a shared bottleneck, such an adversary would receive better performance at the expense of others. For this attack to work, however, the ACK numbers need to be within a range that represents the current window of unacknowledged sequence numbers.

In this experiment, we used a topology consisting of one target and one adversary communicating on the same LAN. We emulated a shared bottleneck by setting up background TCP traffic. The sender was deemed as the target. The relevant sender-side state variable that determines when new packets should be sent is the number of outstanding bytes (sent but not acknowledged). We specify as vulnerable statements places in code that decrease this variable, and thereby increase transmission opportunities. We ran the attack emulator for two hours and used the number of bytes transmitted (throughput) as the impact metric.

MAX successfully discovered the Optimistic ACK attack on the TCP sender by modifying the ACK sequence numbers. In particular, it automatically inferred the range of sequence numbers for which an ACK would reduce the number of outstanding packets. Even when a packet was dropped and a duplicate ACK was sent, MAX was able to automatically modify it such that its sequence

---

[1] We picked a user-space implementation for ease of experimentation. MAX can be applied to kernel-space protocols as well.

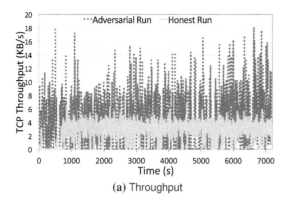

(a) Throughput

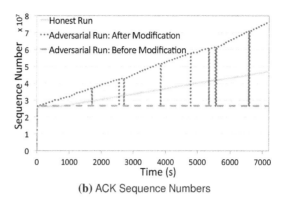

(b) ACK Sequence Numbers

Figure 3: TCP behavior for the adversarial and honest runs for the Optimistic ACK attack.

number was in the queue of outstanding packets. MAX's modifications did not result in connection termination (§6).

Studying MAX's behavior in more detail, we see that it successfully manipulated the sender into executing the vulnerable statements for all but 22 times out of 11,480 packets. The 22 packets were received when the number of outstanding packets was zero, so MAX (correctly) found no feasible path that led to the vulnerable statement. This ability to determine if modifications would lead to vulnerable statements and compute the correct modifications when they can exemplifies the precision of MAX's analysis techniques.

Figures 3a depicts the impact of the attack by plotting the throughput for the adversarial and honest runs of the attack emulator. The average throughput in the honest run is 2.9 KBps. Manipulation increases it to 4.1 KBps, for a gain of over 40%.

Figure 3b illustrates the progression of the ACK sequence numbers. The middle curve shows a slow increase for the honest run. The other two curves show the sequence numbers before and after modification by the adversarial module. We see that modifications causes a faster growth than the honest run, which fools the sender into sending more packets. The sharp decrease in the sequence number in certain places is for the ACKs that were not modified.

Confirming robustness to attacks. Two other manipulation attacks have been reported earlier for TCP. These involve inducing the sender into quickly increasing the congestion window by acknowledging individual bytes instead of whole packets and by sending duplicate ACKs [24]. Fooling the sender into increasing the congestion window will give the receiver more throughput. These attacks do not work for all TCP implementations.

To determine if our implementation is vulnerable, we conducted an experiment similar to the Optimistic ACK attack above except that we specified statements that increase the congestion window as vulnerable. In this case, MAX was unable to repeatedly force the sender into executing the vulnerable statements. Sporadic manipulations of the congestion window did occur but did not lead to a noticeable increase in the adversary's throughput.

Manual inspection confirmed that the Daytona implementation indeed has safeguards [24] against these attacks. Because it is highly error-prone, manual inspection by itself is a weak indicator that an implementation is robust to certain attacks. The more systematic exploration of MAX provides a stronger safeguard.

5.3 Case Study II: SCTP

SCTP is a new transport protocol designed for reliable delivery and targets multi-homed environments [25]. To our knowledge, no manipulation attacks have been reported for SCTP [27]. We show

that SCTP is vulnerable to attacks that are similar to those in TCP, though the exact mechanics of the attacks differ.

SCTP supports multiple independent streams within a connection and ensures sequenced, reliable delivery with each stream. This makes SCTP headers different (and richer) that those of TCP and some of the fields have different semantics. For instance, SCTP has two sequence numbers, the stream sequence number (SSN) used for ordering messages in a stream, and the transmission sequence number (TSN) used for reliable delivery. Given such differences, it was unclear to us if SCTP had vulnerabilities similar to TCP.

In these experiments, we used a complete user-level implementation of SCTP [26], with over 12K lines of code. The setup was similar to the one for the Optimistic ACK attack in TCP. That is, we deemed as vulnerable statements that decrease the number of outstanding bytes.

During attack emulation, MAX manipulated the SCTP sender into executing the vulnerable statement by modifying the cumulative TSN ACK field in all ACKs received at the target. This field represents the largest TSN of a packet received at the receiver, such that all packets before it have been successfully received. MAX increased the value of this field such that it was always less than or equal to the TSN for the last packet sent by the target (Figure 4a). This manipulated the SCTP sender into reducing the number of outstanding bytes and into sending faster than the honest run, for nearly 200s. (We explain the period after 200s below.) Within this time, this manipulation enabled the adversarial receiver to obtain almost 5 times more throughput than the honest receiver. (Figure 4b). Thus, for moderate sized transfers at least, we find that SCTP is susceptible to a manipulation attack in which the receiver optimistically increases the TSN ACK field. While such an attack has been reported previously for TCP, that SCTP is also vulnerable was not previously known.

However, for longer flows, SCTP's vulnerability to manipulating the number of outstanding bytes appears reduced, as shown in Figure 4b. Within a stream, when a data packet is lost (around 200s mark), subsequent packets are buffered at the receiver and the receiver window decreases significantly, preventing the sender from sending more packets. This loss is never recovered because MAX manipulates the TSN ACK to cover the lost sequence number and the situation persists. Because of the vulnerable statement that we use, which does not directly control the resource of network throughput and is not impacted by the receiver window, MAX does not infer that this window can limit network usage.

To evaluate if SCTP is vulnerable to longer-term Optimistic ACK manipulations, we experimented with specifying as vulnerable state-

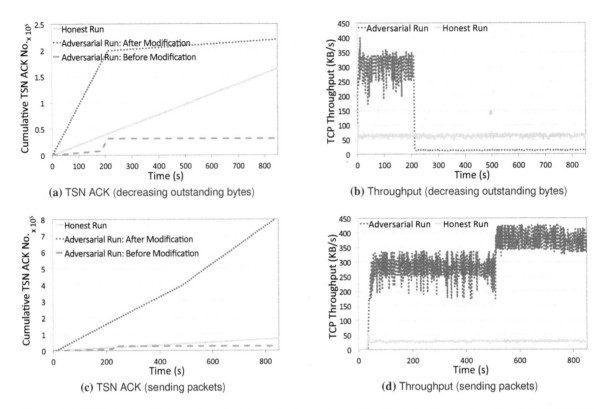

(a) TSN ACK (decreasing outstanding bytes)

(b) Throughput (decreasing outstanding bytes)

(c) TSN ACK (sending packets)

(d) Throughput (sending packets)

Figure 4: SCTP behavior with two vulnerable statements: decreasing outstanding bytes (top) and sending packets (bottom)

ments that send packets, which directly impacts network usage. We found that MAX now manipulates both the cumulative TSN ACK field as well as the receiver window, correctly inferring the values that lead to packet transmissions. Figures 4c and 4d show the results for the TSN ACK field and the throughput obtained. The impact of manipulating both fields is that even after a packet is dropped (around the 250s mark), the adversary is still able to obtain a higher throughput than the honest receiver, unlike in the previous experiment. This occurs because MAX increases the receiver window values as well, which are very low prior to the manipulation. Overall, the adversarial run achieves a 10x throughput over the honest case. (We do not fully understand the reasons behind the jump in throughput around the 500s mark, which was present in each of the many trials that we conducted to rule out experimental and measurement artifacts. This jump is consistent with the faster growth rate of the TSN ACK field around the same time. It may stem from constants in the SCTP implementation that trigger faster transmissions under certain conditions.)

Thus, SCTP is susceptible to the Optimistic ACK attack for long flows as well, but both the receiver window and cumulative ACK fields must be manipulated. This behavior differs from TCP, for which we confirmed that the receiver window modification is not required, because of a subtle difference in the receiver window semantics between the two protocols. In TCP, packets received outside the sequence number space demarcated by the advertised window are dropped. Thus, during the Optimistic ACK attack the receiver window is always open and the adversary does not need to manipulate it. In SCTP, however, receivers store any received packet and discard packets only when there is no available buffer space—this behavior is necessary to support multiple streams in a

connection. The adversary cannot mount a sustained attack without also manipulating the receiver window.

Finally, MAX was able to highlight a different vulnerability in our SCTP implementation. This implementation does not check that the cumulative TSN ACK value is less than or equal to the largest TSN transmitted. In the absence of this check, if a buggy proxy or a man-in-the-middle attacker sends a high TSN ACK value, inconsistent state will occur between the sender and receiver. (The ACK should contain the correct verification tag [25] for the connection to be accepted by the sender.) There is no recovery when that happens and the connection will eventually terminate. The experiments above use a version of SCTP with this bug fixed.

5.4 Case Study III: 802.11 MAC

We next used MAX on the 802.11 MAC protocol, which differs significantly from TCP and SCTP. It is a link-layer protocol and is broadcast-based. As for TCP, manipulation attacks have been reported for the 802.11 MAC [1]. By deeming as vulnerable statements that impact how a node uses air-time, the primary resource in 802.11, we show that MAX succeeds in finding these attacks.

We used the 802.11 MAC implementation in the Qualnet simulator. Qualnet is implemented in C++, but the core of the 802.11 code is written using the C idiom. We were able to analyze this code after removing bindings to the Qualnet scheduler and redefining a few C++-specific data structures. Our ability to focus program analysis on a relevant subset was a key enabler. Symbolic execution engines that perform whole program analysis would not have been able to do a similar analysis of the 802.11 code.

Finding the NAV attack. In this attack the adversary sets an abnormally high value in the duration field of the 802.11 header. The receiving nodes use this field to compute the Network Allocation

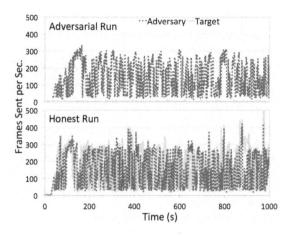

Figure 5: Impact of the NAV attack in the 802.11 MAC.

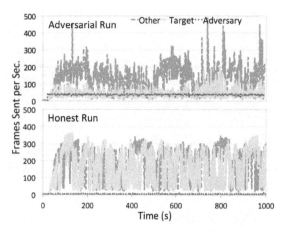

Figure 6: Impact of the RTS attack in the 802.11 MAC.

Vector (NAV) which dictates how long they should consider the medium as busy before they can transmit they own packets. High duration field values can starve honest participants and enable adversaries to gain an unfair share of the medium.

In this experiment, we considered the statement that sets the state of the 802.11 protocol to `WF_NAV` (*i.e.,,* waiting for the Network Allocation Vector value to expire) as vulnerable. A node cannot transmit any data while the NAV value has not expired, so forcing the NAV value to not expire can potentially induce a DoS attack.

We used as network configuration a simple topology with one access point (AP), one target client, and one adversarial client, with each client sending an infinite demand flow to the AP. We also included five other honest participants, to see if the use of MAX in a broadcast setting creates side-effects that hinder its abilities (§6). We used the number of frames transmitted as the impact metric and allowed the modification of all header fields except for `FrameType`. Modifying this field leads to another attack (see below).

We found that MAX successfully finds the NAV attack by repeatedly setting an abnormally high value in the `duration` field of the packet sent by the adversary, resulting in the the target using this high value to compute its NAV. Figure 5 shows the impact of this attack. It plots the frames sent by the nodes in the adversarial and honest runs. We see a dramatic difference; the target is shut out almost completely in the adversarial run.

Finding the RTS attack. In this attack, the adversary sends an RTS frame to the target with a high `duration` field value. The target responds with a CTS frame with a high `duration` value. Any node that hears either the RTS or the CTS frame updates its NAV value and stays silent for a long time. The target too stays silent, awaiting a (long) data to arrive. Thus, by sending a single packet, the adversary can impact multiple participants, some of them not even within its broadcast range. This attack is akin to virtual jamming, since the sender effectively prevents others from using the channel without sending at a high rate itself.

In this experiment, we considered statements that set a sleep timer as vulnerable. By sleeping, the target is deprived of bandwidth, which makes it vulnerable to the attack above. We used an ad-hoc network, which enables nodes to transmit to each other without an AP, with eight nodes: one adversary, one target, and six other honest participants. There was a flow from the adversary to the target that transmits a low rate of one packet per second. We also instantiated an infinite demand flow from the target to an honest participant and another between two honest participants. We allowed modification of all fields in the header.

We found that MAX can successfully discover the RTS attack. The frames sent by the adversary are modified in two ways: the `FrameType` is set to RTS and the `duration` is set to a large value. Figure 6 shows the impact of this attack. It plots the frame rate the adversary (configured to be low), the target, and another honest participant. We see that the adversary succeeds in reducing the rate for both of the other participants, with a bigger impact on the target.

During analysis, we also found an interesting bug in Qualnet. In a few places in the code, there is no verification for sleep timer values being non-negative. Therefore, the input constraints that MAX creates for paths to those timer settings do not require non-negative values. During emulation, MAX sometimes chose a negative value, which caused Qualnet to crash. Thus, MAX's techniques may also help find implementation bugs that cause crashes.

5.5 Case Study IV: ECN

While ECN is logically a rather simple protocol, it is unique from an implementation perspective. Bits relevant to the protocol are carried in both the network layer (IP) and the transport layers (TCP). We show that this does not prevent MAX from finding the manipulation attack in ECN that we mentioned earlier (§2). We also illustrate the utility of MAX as a design tool by patching the implementation using a known fix and then using MAX to check that the patched implementation is indeed robust. Due to space constraints, we omit detailed impact graphs in this section.

Finding the manipulation attack. We used the ECN-enabled TCP implementation in Qualnet. Because the value of the received ECN bit directly determines if the TCP congestion window should be reduced, we deem as "not vulnerable" (§4.2) any statement that reduces the congestion window. Intuitively, an adversary can increase its throughput by continually forcing the target to avoid reducing the congestion window.

MAX correctly deduces that in order to avoid reducing the congestion window, the adversary should not reflect the ECN bit in its ACKs when the bit is set.

Confirming the robustness of the patch. We modified the Qualnet ECN implementation to protect against this attack using nonces [11]. The sender inserts a randomly-generated nonce in its packets, and congested routers delete the nonce to indicate congestion. When the sender receives an ACK, it reduces the congestion window if the nonce is deleted or differs from the original. To fool the sender that there was no congestion along a congested path, the adversarial receiver needs to guess the deleted nonce correctly, which is difficult to do often enough to substantially alter protocol behavior.

We used MAX on this modified version of ECN, after hiding the nonce state at the target to emulate an adversary that does not know the nonce values. The path explorer found the same code paths as before. However, during emulation, MAX was unable to reliably force execution down these paths because it could not reconstruct the nonce value. The honest and adversarial runs yielded similar throughputs. Hence the attack was not successful, and MAX was able confirm that the fix and its implementation are effective.

6. DISCUSSION AND FUTURE WORK

Our work represents a first effort to build a practical tool for finding manipulation attacks. It opens avenues for future investigation towards improving MAX and mitigating such attacks.

Extending MAX. The current design of MAX has several limitations that we plan to address in the future. These include extending it to handle multiple targets, incorporating a more exhaustive search over feasible paths, and allowing an adversary to send multiple messages or no message at all when an honest participant would have sent a single message.

Another limitation involves protocol implementations where the vulnerable actions are not executed immediately after receiving a manipulated message, but at a later point in time. For instance, imagine a protocol where manipulated messages update a data structure at the target, and later when a timer fires, this data structure is read and the vulnerable statement is executed. Such a programming paradigm makes it hard to link an incoming message to vulnerable actions. We are exploring if such behaviors can be handled by using taint analysis to infer that link.

In MAX, we place the adversarial module at the target, which has two advantages that we plan to exploit in the future. This placement can assess the worst-case effects of an attack because it gives access to the target's exact internal state. It can also accommodate multiple adversaries, allowing us to explore collusion between adversaries.

However, two mismatches occur due to this placement. First, it does not naturally handle link-layer broadcast protocols, in which a manipulation message from an adversary is visible to other participants. Our approach instead (logically) allows an adversary to send a manipulated message to the target while hiding the manipulation from others. Second, it introduces a possible mismatch between the protocol state at the target and the adversaries. The target assumes that the modified messages come from the adversary and updates its state accordingly, when in reality the adversary's implementation never sent the message. In our experiments thus far, we have not experienced significant side effects from these mismatches (even though we analyze broadcast-based 802.11 MAC), but we plan to explore methods that place the adversarial module at the adversary.

Finally, we plan to explore mechanisms that can reduce the amount of input required from the user. For instance, we may be able to use program analysis to automatically identify vulnerable statements from high-level descriptions of resources (e.g., throughput, memory, etc.); and we may be able to find most manipulation attacks by running the protocol over a set of common network topology and traffic configurations.

Mitigating Manipulation Attacks. While this paper focuses on finding manipulation attacks, our eventual goal is to make protocols robust to these attacks. We conjecture, however, that it is impossible to completely prevent all manipulations unless we can enforce correct protocol execution by all participants (e.g., using trusted hardware). The main reason is not code complexity (as for buffer overflow vulnerabilities) but partial information—each participant has a partial view of the state of the network (e.g., presence of congestion) or of other participants (e.g., if it received a packet). If all participants had complete knowledge, they would not need to exchange any information in the protocol headers. The need for information exchange opens the door to manipulation. (The role of MAX is to help identify which information can be exploited and how.)

While we cannot prevent all manipulations, we can certainly mitigate their impact. One approach is to verify received information and take protective action if discrepancies are detected. Sometimes, verification can be done by simply retaining historical information. For instance, ACK division in TCP can be detected by remembering where packet boundaries occurred in the byte stream. In protocols with more than two participants, verification can be done by comparing information from different participants (e.g., OSPF nodes check if link-state reports from the two ends of a link are consistent). It may also be possible to verify information by observing a participant's future behavior. For instance, NAV manipulations in 802.11 MAC can be detected post-facto by observing if nodes actually occupy the medium for the claimed duration.

Verification may be infeasible in some cases, however (e.g., verifying if a participant received a packet). Here, a second approach that relies on explicitly considering adversaries' incentives can help. In particular, we can modify the protocol exchange such that adversaries can only hurt themselves by manipulation. Examples are the use of nonces in ECN or anonymous packets in Catch to prevent wireless relays from dropping packets [17].

7. RELATED WORK

While we adapt and combine symbolic and concrete execution in a novel way, we build on work that uses these general techniques to detect other kinds of software vulnerabilities. The inspiration for MAX comes from the work of Stanojevic et al. [29], who defined the notion of protocol *gullibility* that is similar to, but broader than, our notion of manipulation attacks. They also present a preliminary tool to detect protocol gullibility based on concrete execution alone. To reduce the search space they require the user to input a set of attack strategies (e.g., only manipulate certain header fields). This tool could find the gullibility in a simplified version of the ECN protocol. In contrast, by using symbolic execution as well, we do not require that users input attack strategies and can also scale to complex protocol implementations.

Other relevant prior work can be divided into three categories. The first category uses static analysis alone to protect against (other types of) network attacks. For example, SAFER [7] uses taint analysis to identify inputs that can cause DoS attacks; and Elcano [4] uses symbolic execution to generate signatures that filter out inputs known to exploit protocol vulnerabilities, given an initial exploit that exposes the vulnerability.

To eliminate or reduce false positives inherent in this first category, the second category combines static analysis with concrete test generation [13, 28, 30]. For example, EXE [6] generates "inputs of death" that cause a program to crash, Brumley et al. present a technique to automatically generate exploits from software patches that target input validation vulnerabilities [3], and Bouncer [9] uses a combination of static and dynamic analysis to create filters that block bad inputs during program execution. These approaches aim to identify a single bad input. However, a single input is insufficient to mount an effective manipulation attack, which requires the ability to repeatedly induce honest participants into performing certain actions. Further, for manipulation attacks, a "bad" input can be perfectly valid under different conditions, which renders input filtering invalid. MAX thus first uses symbolic execution to approximate single inputs that can manipulate the target in a given state and then uses adversarial concrete execution to search for a sequence of inputs that constitutes an effective attack.

The third category uses concrete execution alone and is exemplified by several model checking systems. For example, CMC [18, 19] identifies generic errors and invariant violations in protocol implementations, and MaceMC detects violations of liveness properties for protocols [14]. More recently, CrystalBall [31] adapted model checking to an online setting by check-pointing a running system and using the checkpoints as the starting point for the model checker. Unlike the first two categories, model checking can find errors triggered by a sequence of events. However, model checking aims to identify errors in a setting where participants run the protocol implementation faithfully. In manipulation attacks adversaries can arbitrarily deviate from the protocol implementation in order to induce undesirable behavior. This possibility leads to a dramatically larger search space which makes a concrete execution-only approach intractable. MAX uses information from symbolic execution to help steer its adversarial concrete execution towards code paths that are likely lead to manipulation attacks.

Finally, Bethea *et al.* [2] recently described an approach and associated tool to perform online verification that a sequence of inputs received at the server could have been generated by an honest client. Like MAX, their tool combines the results of symbolic execution with state information derived from concrete execution. However, their tool cannot be used to detect manipulation attacks, because the sequence of inputs generated by an adversarial client may be perfectly valid under the right network conditions.

8. CONCLUSIONS

We presented a method and a tool to find manipulation attacks in which adversaries induce honest participants into undesirable behaviors. A novel combination of symbolic and concrete execution, and their adaptation to network protocol code, allows our tool to scalably and precisely analyze complex protocol implementations and find a diverse set of attacks.

We believe this combination is useful beyond finding manipulation attacks and opens the door to other forms of semantic analysis of protocols. For instance, a similar approach may be able to analyze how state flows across a network, with symbolic execution inferring what parts of a node's internal state are carried in outgoing messages and concrete execution observing how messages flow between nodes. The resulting analysis could enable, among other things, an automatic quantification of protocol complexity [8].

Acknowledgements

We thank the SIGCOMM '11 reviewers and our shepherd, Brad Karp, for feedback on this paper. This work is supported by the National Science Foundation award CNS-0725354.

References

[1] J. Bellardo and S. Savage. 802.11 denial-of-service attacks: real vulnerabilities and practical solutions. In *USENIX Security*, 2003.

[2] D. Bethea, R. Cochran, and M. K. Reiter. Server-side Verification of Client Behavior in Online Games. In *NDSS*, 2010.

[3] D. Brumley, P. Poosankam, D. X. Song, and J. Zheng. Automatic patch-based exploit generation is possible: Techniques and implications. In *Security and Privacy*, 2008.

[4] J. Caballero, Z. Liang, P. Poosankam, and D. Song. Towards generating high coverage vulnerability-based signatures with protocol-level constraint-guided exploration. In *RAID*, 2009.

[5] C. Cadar, D. Dunbar, and D. Engler. Klee: Unassisted and automatic generation of high-coverage tests for complex systems programs. In *OSDI*, 2008.

[6] C. Cadar, P. Twohey, V. Ganesh, and D. Engler. Exe: A system for automatically generating inputs of death using symbolic execution. In *CCS*, 2006.

[7] R. Chang, G. Jiang, F. Ivancic, S. Sankaranarayanan, and V. Shmatikov. Inputs of coma: Static detection of denial-of-service vulnerabilities. In *IEEE Computer Security Foundations Symp.*, 2009.

[8] B.-G. Chun, S. Ratnasamy, and E. Kohler. Netcomplex: A complexity metric for networked system designs. In *NSDI*, 2008.

[9] M. Costa, M. C. L. Zhou, L. Zhang, and M. Peinado. Bouncer: securing software by blocking bad input. In *SOSP*, 2007.

[10] L. M. de Moura and N. Bjørner. Z3: An efficient SMT solver. In *TACAS*, 2008.

[11] D. Ely, N. Spring, D. Wetherall, S. Savage, and T. Anderson. Robust congestion signaling. In *ICNP*, 2001.

[12] C. Flanagan, K. R. M. Leino, M. Lillibridge, G. Nelson, J. B. Saxe, and R. Stata. Extended static checking for Java. In *PLDI*, 2002.

[13] P. Godefroid, N. Klarlund, and K. Sen. DART: directed automated random testing. In *PLDI*, 2005.

[14] C. E. Killian, J. W. Anderson, R. Jhala, and A. Vahdat. Life, death, and the critical transition: Finding liveness bugs in systems code. In *NSDI*, 2007.

[15] J. C. King. Symbolic execution and program testing. *Commun. ACM*, 19(7), 1976.

[16] R. Mahajan, S. M. Bellovin, S. Floyd, J. Ioannidis, V. Paxson, and S. Shenker. Controlling high bandwidth aggregates in the network. *SIGCOMM CCR*, 32(3), 2002.

[17] R. Mahajan, M. Rodrig, D. Wetherall, and J. Zahorjan. Sustaining cooperation in multi-hop wireless networks. In *NSDI*, 2005.

[18] M. Musuvathi and D. R. Engler. Model checking large network protocol implementations. In *NSDI*, 2004.

[19] M. Musuvathi, D. Y. W. Park, A. Chou, D. R. Engler, and D. L. Dill. CMC: A programatic approach to model checking real code. In *OSDI*, 2002.

[20] V. Navda, A. Bohra, and S. Ganguly. Using channel hopping to increase 802.11 resilience to jamming attacks. In *IEEE Infocom Mini Symp.*, 2007.

[21] G. C. Necula, S. McPeak, S. Rahul, and W. Weimer. CIL: Intermediate language and tools for analysis and transformation of C programs. In *CCC*, 2002.

[22] J. Newsome and D. Song. Dynamic taint analysis for automatic detection, analysis, and signature generation of exploits on commodity software. In *NDSS*, 2005.

[23] P. Pradhan, S. Kandula, W. Xu, A. Shaikh, and E. Nahum. Daytona: A user-level TCP stack. http://nms.lcs.mit.edu/~kandula/data/daytona.pdf.

[24] S. Savage, N. Cardwell, D. Wetherall, and T. Anderson. TCP congestion control with a misbehaving receiver. *SIGCOMM CCR*, 29(5), 1999.

[25] Stream control transmission protocol. IETF RFC 2960, 2000.

[26] Stream control transmission protocol (SCTP). http://sctp.de/sctp.html.

[27] Security attacks found against the stream control transmission protocol (SCTP) and current countermeasures. IETF RFC 5062, 2007.

[28] K. Sen, D. Marinov, and G. Agha. CUTE: A concolic unit testing engine for C. *SIGSOFT Softw. Eng. Notes*, 30(5), 2005.

[29] M. Stanojevic, R. Mahajan, T. Millstein, and M. Musuvathi. Can you fool me? towards automatically checking protocol gullibility. In *HotNets*, 2008.

[30] N. Tillmann and J. de Halleux. Pex: White box test generation for .NET. In *Tests and Proofs*, LNCS. 2008.

[31] M. Yabandeh, N. Knezevic, D. Kostic, and V. Kuncak. Crystalball: predicting and preventing inconsistencies in deployed distributed systems. In *NSDI*, 2009.

Augmenting Data Center Networks with Multi-Gigabit Wireless Links

Daniel Halperin*†, Srikanth Kandula†, Jitendra Padhye†, Paramvir Bahl†, and David Wetherall*
Microsoft Research† and University of Washington*

Abstract – The 60 GHz wireless technology that is now emerging has the potential to provide dense and extremely fast connectivity at low cost. In this paper, we explore its use to relieve hotspots in oversubscribed data center (DC) networks. By experimenting with prototype equipment, we show that the DC environment is well suited to a deployment of 60 GHz links contrary to concerns about interference and link reliability. Using directional antennas, many wireless links can run concurrently at multi-Gbps rates on top-of-rack (ToR) switches. The wired DC network can be used to sidestep several common wireless problems. By analyzing production traces of DC traffic for four real applications, we show that adding a small amount of network capacity in the form of *wireless flyways* to the wired DC network can improve performance. However, to be of significant value, we find that one hop indirect routing is needed. Informed by our 60 GHz experiments and DC traffic analysis, we present a design that uses DC traffic levels to select and adds flyways to the wired DC network. Trace-driven evaluations show that network-limited DC applications with predictable traffic workloads running on a 1:2 oversubscribed network can be sped up by 45% in 95% of the cases, with just one wireless device per ToR switch. With two devices, in 40% of the cases, the performance is identical to that of a non-oversubscribed network.

Categories and Subject Descriptors

C.2.1 [**Computer-Communication Networks**]: Network Architecture and Design—Wireless Communication

General Terms

Design, Experimentation, Measurement, Performance

1. INTRODUCTION

Millimeter wavelength wireless technology is rapidly being developed. Spectrum between 57–64 GHz, colloquially known as the 60 GHz band, is available world-wide for unlicensed use. The band contains over 80 times the bandwidth available for 802.11b/g at 2.4 GHz, and supports devices with multi-Gbps data rates. Furthermore, 60 GHz devices with directional antennas can be deployed densely, because the signal attenuates rapidly due to the high frequency. The VLSI technology has now matured to the point where 60 GHz radio hardware can be built using CMOS technology, and companies like SiBeam [26] promise to deliver 60 GHz devices at less than $10 per unit at OEM quantities. In summary, 60 GHz technology can lead to dense, high-bandwidth wireless connectivity at low cost.

To date, 60 GHz technology has been explored for isolated point-to-point links. A common scenario is home entertainment, e.g., a Blu-Ray player that communicates wirelessly with a nearby television instead of using bulky HDMI cables.

In this paper, we consider the novel possibility of using 60 GHz links in a data center (DC), to augment the wired network. This is a promising approach to explore for several reasons. First, we note that the machines in a DC are densely packed, so wireless devices that provide high bandwidth over short ranges are a natural fit. Second, the radio environment is largely static since people and equipment move around infrequently, minimizing fluctuations in wireless link quality. Third, line-of-sight communication is achievable by mounting 60 GHz radios on top of racks. Finally, the wired DC network is available as a reliable channel for coordinating wireless devices, thereby simplifying many traditional wireless problems such as aligning directional senders and receivers, and interference avoidance.

Traditional, wired DC networks are tree-structured and oversubscribed to keep costs down [15]. For example, a typical DC rack comprises 40 machines connected to a top-of-the-rack (ToR) switch with 1 Gbps links. The ToR is connected to an aggregation switch (to network with other racks) with 10 Gbps links. Thus, the link from the ToR to the aggregation switch can be oversubscribed with a ratio of 1:4. However, each oversubscribed link is a potential hotspot that hinders some DC application. Recent research tackles this problem by combining many more links and switches with variants of multipath routing so that the core of the network is no longer oversubscribed [1, 8, 9]. Of course, this benefit comes with large material cost and implementation complexity [15]. Some designs require so many wires that cabling becomes a challenge [1], and most require "fork lift" [5] upgrades to the entire infrastructure.

In prior work [15], we argued instead for a more modest addition of links to relieve hotspots and boost application performance. The links, called *flyways*, add extra capacity to the base network to alleviate hotspots. When the traffic matrix is sparse (i.e. only a few ToR switches are hot), a small number of flyways can significantly improve performance, without the cost of building a fully non-oversubscribed network.

The basic design of a DC network with 60 GHz flyways is as follows. The *base wired network* is provisioned for the average case and can be oversubscribed. Each top-of-rack (ToR) switch is equipped with one or more 60 GHz wireless devices, with electronically steerable directional antennas. A central controller monitors DC traffic patterns, and switches the beams of the wireless devices to set up flyways between ToR switches that provide added bandwidth as needed.

Other researchers have explored use of fiber optic cables and MEMS switches [7, 30] for creating flyways. We believe that 60 GHz flyways are an attractive choice because wireless devices simplify DC upgrades, as no wiring changes are needed. Furthermore, 60 GHz technology is likely to become inexpensive as it is commoditized by consumer applications, while optical switches are not. Wireless devices can introduce additional issues as well—for example, with dynamic topology, the network management may become more

Figure 1: Narrow-beam (left) and wide-beam (right) horn antennas for 60 GHz. Note the small size.

Figure 2: HXI device, paired with a horn antenna.

complicated. However, before cost or management considerations come into play, we need to first understand whether 60 GHz wireless will perform well in the DC environment despite the challenges of interference and reliability. Answering this question is the primary focus of this paper.

We make three contributions. First, we report experiments with prototype 60 GHz devices and measurement-based simulations that show the feasibility of 60 GHz networks in the DC. To our knowledge, we are the first to report such results. Second, we show by analyzing four DC traffic traces that real workloads have few hotspots even when they lack predictable elephant flows. This implies that flyways can provide substantial benefits to real applications at low cost. Prior work [7, 30] has used synthetic workloads. Third, we present the design of a 60 GHz wireless flyway system motivated by our measurements. It differs from previous work on flyways [7, 30] in its use of indirect routing to obtain good gains from flyways. A trace-driven evaluation shows that in a 73-rack cluster with a 1:2 oversubscribed network, and just one wireless device per TOR, our system improves performance of a network-limited DC application by 45% in 95% of the cases. With two devices per ToR, the performance is identical to that of a non-oversubscribed network in 40% of the cases.

The rest of the paper proceeds as follows. We give background on 60 GHz in §2. Then, using experiments and simulations, we show that of 60 GHz data center deployments are feasible (§3). We then analyze DC traffic traces for different applications to understand what flyway characteristics are needed (§4). We present the design of our system (§5) followed by evaluation results (§6). We wrap up with a discussion (§7), related work (§8) and our conclusions (§9).

2. 60 GHz TECHNOLOGY

Recent advances in CMOS technology have reduced the cost of 60 GHz devices significantly, leading to commercial interest in indoor applications. This differs from initial, limited uses of 60 GHz for outdoor, point-to-point infrastructure [16, 29]. This section gives a brief primer on the 60 GHz physical layer and ongoing research and standardization efforts.

The nature of 60 GHz radio waves leads to significant challenges for operating high rate links. All other factors being equal, a 60 GHz link is roughly 55 dB (a factor of 300,000× worse) than a 2.4 GHz link in terms of the signal-to-noise ratio (SNR) that determines packet delivery. This is due to three factors. First, the free-space path loss is higher due to the small 5 mm wavelength (Friis' law [23]). Second, the channels are 100 times wider and thus 20 dB noisier [10, 32] to enable high multi-Gbps bit-rates. Third, most commercial equipment uses only 10 mW transmit power (compared to 802.11's typical 50 mW) in order to meet regulations and energy budgets. To compensate for these losses, indoor 60 GHz technologies such as 802.11ad [10] target a *short range* of 10 meters, and 60 GHz links use *highly directional antennas*.

Directionality represents the primary novel aspect of 60 GHz tech-

nology and is the key to enable a dense indoor deployment of 60 GHz links. With directional antennas, 60 GHz links can support multi-Gbps rates over distances of several meters [31, 32]. Directional antenna effectiveness is inversely proportional to the square of the radio wavelength, and so the short wavelength of 60 GHz leads to compact antennas. For fixed links, such as long range outdoor deployments, physically directional antennas (e.g., pyramidal gain horns such as in Figure 1) are used. For dynamic links, such as indoor Wireless HDTV [32], phased array antennas are used. Phased array antennas can rapidly change their directional radiation pattern electronically, i.e. with no moving parts.

WirelessHD [32] and IEEE 802.11ad/WiGig [10, 31] are the two main ongoing efforts to standardize the PHY and MAC of the 60 GHz band. WirelessHD standardizes streaming media traffic in home entertainment systems. It was explicitly not intended for general data communication [32] and is a poor fit for our goals. IEEE 802.11ad enhances 802.11 for 60 GHz. It operates like standard Wi-Fi, with changes to the 802.11 PHY and MAC that support higher data rates that range from 385 Mbps to 6.76 Gbps. We use 802.11ad as the starting point for our flyways system.

3. 60 GHz LINKS IN THE DATA CENTER

The goal of this section is to find out whether 60 GHz links perform well in a DC environment. This primarily means that the links must offer steady, high throughput, even when deployed in a dense manner. We first measure 60 GHz propagation, link stability, and spatial reuse using prototype 60 GHz hardware. We then use these measurements to simulate dense collections of 60 GHz links in the DC. The results from this section guide our system design (§5).

3.1 Hardware

Our results are based on the device shown in Figure 2, built by HXI. It provides a full duplex, 60 GHz Gigabit Ethernet data link. It has a 1000BASE-SX fiber interface, and directly modulates the 1.25 Gbps line rate Ethernet protocol onto a 60 GHz carrier wave using On-Off-Keying (OOK). Rather than use any MAC protocol, this hardware employs frequency division to support the full duplex links: a paired set of devices operates on center frequencies that are 3.7 GHz apart sharing a single antenna per node. An SNMP management interface to the device provides continuous estimates of signal quality in the form of RSSI with 0.1 dB resolution.

This device interfaces with a removable antenna using the standard 60 GHz WR-15 waveguide. We use two physical directional antennas: a wide-beam horn antenna, marketed as a 10 dBi (60°) gain antenna, and a narrow-beam horn antenna, marketed as a 23 dBi (15°) gain antenna. Figure 1 shows how small these antennas are. We measured their radiation patterns in a large, free-space environment; unsurprisingly, the actual gain values (Figure 3) differ slightly from manufacturer claims. We will refer to these two antennas as wide-beam (WB) and narrow-beam (NB), respectively.

The measurement results in this paper use these fixed-beam directional antennas. However, we envision the use of electronically steerable phased array antennas that can change their radiation pat-

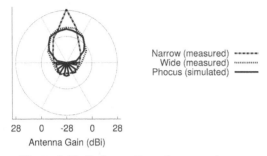

Figure 3: Radiation patterns for our antennas.

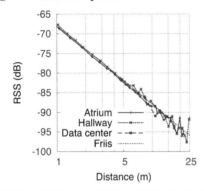

Figure 4: RSS vs Distance. RSS is relative to the transmitter power level, and fits the Friis model with exponent 2. The signal degrades by around 88 dB at 10 meters.

tern rapidly and with no moving parts. Phased arrays can be significantly more powerful than fixed-beam antennas, as they can generate patterns of variable beam width, control the amount and angle of side lobes, and can be used in more advanced ways to, e.g., null-form away from specific interferers [20]. As 60 GHz arrays are not yet available, we instead simulated the radiation pattern from the Geo-fencing project [25] that uses the commercially available Phocus phased array which operates at 2.4 GHz. Lacking real phased arrays for 60 GHz, we do not speculate on antenna properties, such as steering time. However, prior work [17, 19] shows that such antennas can be steered in hundreds of microseconds. Further details about the simulated Phocus array pattern and our assumptions about the 60 GHz phased arrays are in Appendix A.

Note that the Phocus pattern actually has smaller back and side lobes than our measured directional antennas (Figure 3). This is because, in our measurements with the NB and WB antennas, we conservatively assumed that any angle at which we measured no signal strength (e.g., sender facing directly away from the receiver) is in fact a received signal with strength just below the noise floor.

3.2 Signal propagation

We studied 60 GHz propagation in multiple environments. First, the atrium of our building, which resembles a free-space environment with no walls closer than 40 m from either end of the link. Second, a 1.5 m wide interior hallway, where multiple paths and physical obstructions exist. We chose line-of-sight environments as they come closest to the space on top of racks in our data centers. Finally, we measured propagation across the tops of rows of racks in a production data center, similar to the way in which wireless flyways could be deployed. As real data centers do, this production environment has a low ceiling, rows of racks (Figure 9), pipes for cabling as well as to and from the cooling systems and metal cages. In each scenario, we set up one sender and one receiver and varied the distance between the two, measuring the signal strength at the receiver at each step.

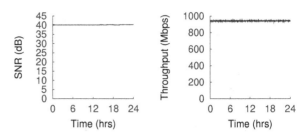

Figure 5: SNR and TCP are stable for 24 h in a data center.

The results are shown in Figure 4. We see that signal strength degrades rapidly with distance. The path exponent is 2, reflecting near-perfect Friis free-space propagation. Prior studies show that line-of-sight links in multi-path environments (waves in the 900–2400 MHz frequency with omni-directional antennas) have path exponents between 1.6–1.8 [23]. Thus, we believe that our directional antennas effectively mitigate the impact of multi-path. In fact, even at distances of 25 m, the signal variation (likely due to multi-path) is no more than 3 dB in the atrium and 5 dB in the hallway. This conclusion is supported by prior 60 GHz measurements [18] that showed that directionality at just one side of the link greatly reduced indoor multi-path effects.

These results show that the Friis model is appropriate for indoor line-of-sight 60 GHz links when the endpoints use narrow directional antennas.

3.3 Link stability

The adjective "flaky" is often associated with performance of wireless links, and is a potential concern for using wireless links in the DC. However, the performance variability seen in typical WLAN/Wi-Fi deployments comes from device mobility, environmental movement (people, doors opening and closing), temperature changes, and interference. The data center offers a stable, temperature-controlled environment, with infrequent movement of equipment, people, or doors. With devices mounted on top of racks and using directional antennas, the impact of these movements is even less. There is also no external interference in the 60 GHz band due to high attenuation by atmospheric oxygen and by walls. Thus, we expect individual links to be extremely stable.

To verify link stability, we set up a 60 GHz link in our data center using HXI devices with NB antennas. We deployed the devices atop two racks, facing each other across an aisle. We ran a long-lived TCP flow (using `iperf`) for 24 hours across two normal workdays, measuring throughput and SNR information every second. During the last five minutes of the measurement, one of the authors repeatedly walked under the link.

Figure 5 shows the link SNR and TCP throughput over the 24 hour period. TCP throughput achieves the full 1 Gbps rate, with almost no variation. In fact, none of the 1 s RSSI samples was off the average by more than 0.1 dB. The throughput curve shows that all the end-to-end components, not just the wireless link, are stable as perceived by the application. Even in the last five minutes, there is no variation in the throughput.

To provide a counterpoint, we set up a link with the same hardware, but at 3 feet above the ground. We then walked across it. Figure 6 shows the resulting variation due to line-of-sight obstruction.

These results show that in a typical DC, line-of-sight 60 GHz links set up at rack height provide stable performance.

3.4 Interference (Spatial reuse)

So far, we have studied wireless link properties in isolation. However, our system will require multiple flyways to be active simulta-

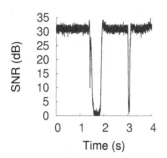

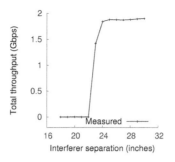

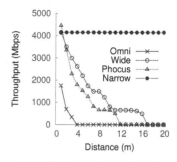

Figure 6: SNR fluctuates wildly when people walk (left) or wave hands (right) across the line-of-sight path.

Figure 7: Interference experiment results

Figure 8: TCP throughput at various distances when sender and receiver both use directional antennas of various gains.

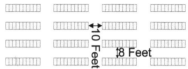

Figure 9: Partial top view of data center of a large search provider. Each row has ten 24x48 inch racks. The aisles are 10 and 8 feet wide, as shown. Overall area is roughly 14 m x 14 m.

neously. Interference between flyways must be mitigated for good performance. This can be accomplished in a number of ways: by using multiple channels, by using directional antennas at both the sender and the receiver, and by carefully controlling which flyways are activated. We use all these techniques in our system design, but the bulk of interference mitigation happens due to directional antennas.

We now devise an experiment to see how directionality impacts spatial reuse. We configured two parallel links using HXI devices equipped with NB antennas. Recall that these links use frequency division to support bidirectional communication; we configured the links so that nodes facing in the same direction used the same frequency to maximize interference. We separated source and destination by a fixed 85 inches to mimic the width of an aisle, and varied the separation between the links in small increments. At each position, each source sends a greedy TCP flow to its destination. The cumulative throughput, shown in Figure 7, indicates whether the two links interfere with each other. Note that this prototype hardware has no MAC and uses no physical- or link-layer backoff, so the links interfere completely or not at all. We see that parallel links closer than 24 inches interfere, but directional antennas enable them to coexist perfectly with slightly more separation. Note that 24 inches is about 1 rack wide, and with 3 available 802.11ad channels, a large number of flyways can operate simultaneously.

These results show that directional antennas can isolate links and enable spatial reuse.

Later in this section, we will study the impact of interference with more links, and at various data rates, using simulations.

3.5 TCP throughput

In §3.3, we saw that a 60 GHz link set up over an aisle can provide stable 1 Gbps throughput. That throughput, however, was limited by the capabilities of HXI equipment. To get a better idea of what TCP throughput a full-fledged 802.11ad link can support, we rely on packet-level simulations. The simulations are done using the ns-3 simulator [21], which we have extensively modified to model 60 GHz propagation, 802.11ad MAC, directional antennas and data center layouts. For more details on the changes we made to the simulator, see Appendix B.

We simulate the TCP throughput obtained over a 60 GHz link at various distances for the four antenna models. Note that these simulations account for overheads such as headers and various MAC overheads. The results are shown in Figure 8 and underscore the need for directional antennas. Omni-directional antennas provide no throughput at under 4 m, but modestly directional WB antennas can provide nearly 1 Gbps of throughput between nodes that are 15 m apart. With NB antennas, the TCP performance barely degrades with distance because the RSSI is sufficient to use the highest encoding rate of 6.76 Gbps even at 20 m. The performance

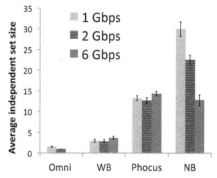

Figure 10: Number of flyways that can operate concurrently on one channel. Mean and standard deviation over 100 runs.

of the Phocus array is comparable to that of the WB antenna. Arrays with more elements (e.g., 30 as opposed to the 8 used here which we derived from [25]) should perform comparable to the NB antennas.

These results show that directional antennas are necessary to achieve high throughputs over links more than 1 m long.

Note that there is a gap between the maximum TCP throughput achieved ($\approx$ 4 Gbps) and the highest link transmission rate (6.76 Gbps). This gap is due to various wireless MAC and TCP overheads. In Appendix C, we describe some ideas on how to reduce these overheads by exploiting the unique hybrid nature of a wired data center network enhanced with wireless flyways.

3.6 Dense deployment of links

In §3.4, we showed that two high-rate 60 GHz links can coexist in close proximity. Using simulations, we now investigate the number of 60 GHz links that can operate simultaneously in a typical data center while still offering reasonable performance. We simulate the data center layout shown in Figure 9. This layout is based on an operational data center of a large search provider. We consider the case of a number of racks (160) connected to a single aggregation switch. We assume that each top-of-rack (ToR) switch is equipped with a single 60 GHz device, connected to a steerable antenna with a specified gain. All devices operate on the same channel and so may interfere.

Name	# Servers	Description
Cosmos	O(1K)	Map-Reduce
IndexSrv	O(10K)	Index lookup
Neon	O(100)	Car Simulation: HPC
3Cars	O(100)	Car Simulation: HPC

Table 1: Datasets

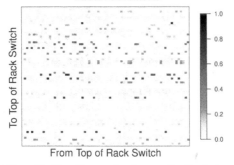

Figure 11: Traffic Demands (normalized) between ToR Switches.

We use the Monte-Carlo method to find maximal independent sets of flyway links [12]. Given n devices, note that $n \cdot (n-1)$ links are potentially feasible. A set of links is deemed independent if every link in the set provides some minimal throughput, even when all links in the set are active concurrently. The set is maximal if no other links can be added to it without violating the independence property. To test for independence, we simulate running long-lived TCP flows across the links. To limit the complexity of the simulation, we allow each device to participate in only one link at a time.

For a given DC layout, the average size of the maximal independent set tells us how many flyways may be set up at the same time. It depends on the antenna used, and the minimum throughput required from each link. Figure 10 shows the average size and one standard deviation over 100 randomly generated maximal independent sets for various antenna gains and minimum throughputs. Since each ToR can participate in only one flyway, and we have 160 ToRs, the set size cannot exceed 80.

With a Phocus antenna array or NB antennas, the number of flyways that can operate together increases dramatically. If the ToRs are equipped with NB antennas, the average size of the independent set is more than 30 for 1 Gbps links. Note that this is with just one channel; the set size increases linearly with more channels. We shall see later in the paper that for our workloads, these numbers suffice to provide significant performance gains.

In summary, these results give us confidence that in a typical data center, a large number of 60 GHz links can operate while delivering desired performance.

4. ANALYZING DATA CENTER TRAFFIC

We now examine traffic from four real applications in the data center to understand how much value flyways can add.

4.1 Datasets

Table 1 summarizes the analyzed datasets. Together, these logs represent over 76 hours worth of traces, and over 114 terabytes of traffic. The Cosmos dataset was measured on a pre-production cluster with O(1K) servers running Dryad. It supports a data mining workload for a large web search engine. Jobs on this cluster are a mix of repetitive production scripts (e.g., hourly summaries) and jobs submitted by users. The IndexSrv dataset is from a production cluster with O(10K) servers. The cluster stores the web search index and assembles search results for queries. This workload is

latency sensitive. Unlike the Cosmos cluster, links here rarely see high utilizations. In both clusters, we instrumented every server to log network send and read system calls and the amount of data involved. The next two datasets are from an HPC platform with O(100) servers spread across 5 racks, running car simulation software. In most of the datasets, the servers were in racks underneath a single core switch pair. However, servers in the IndexSrv dataset spanned multiple core switches. In all clusters, ToR switches have enough backplane bandwidth such that intra-rack communication is only limited by the server NICs. However, the links connecting the ToR switches to the core are oversubscribed.

4.2 Estimating demand matrices

We want to understand the demands of data center applications without being impacted by the topology and capacity of the observed networks. To do so, we aggregate the traffic exchanged at time scales that are pertinent to the application. For example, most Dryad tasks finish within a few minutes, so the total traffic exchanged between racks in the Cosmos cluster every few minutes is a good indicator of application requirements. Unless otherwise noted, the datasets in this paper average traffic over 300 s periods to compute demands.

Consider an example demand matrix from the Cosmos dataset; Figure 11 depicts a heat map of the demands between pairs of the ToR switches. The color palette is on a logarithmic scale, i.e., black corresponds to the largest demand entry D, deep red (0.5 on the scale) corresponds to $\sqrt{D}$ and white indicates zero demand.

A few trends are apparent. First, only a few ToR pairs are hot, i.e., send or receive a large volume of traffic (darker dots). The bulk of the ToR pairs are yellow, i.e., less than $D^{\frac{1}{10}}$. Second, hot ToRs exchange much of their data with a few, but not all, of the other ToRs (horizontal and vertical streaks). It follows that providing additional bandwidth at hotspots would dramatically reduce the maximum temperature of the matrix. But, does this hold across all demand matrices? What form should the additional bandwidth take? How do the hotspots change over time? We look at these questions next.

4.3 Prevalence of hotspots

Figure 12(a) plots the fraction of hot links—links that are at least half as loaded as the most loaded link—in each of our datasets. In every dataset, over 60% of the matrices have fewer than 10% of their links hot at any time. In fact, every matrix in the Neon dataset has less than 7% hot links. *This means that for measured traffic patterns in the DC, avoiding oversubscription over the entire network may not be needed.* Instead, performance may be improved by adding capacity to a small set of links. We see in the evaluation of our system (§6) that, indeed, a few flyways have a large effect.

4.4 Traffic contributors to hotspots

To be useful, additional capacity provided to a hotspot should be able to offload a substantial fraction of the load. Prior proposals [7, 30] establish one additional flyway, in the form of an optical circuit, per congested link. Figure 12(b) estimates the maximum potential value of doing so, and suggests there will be little benefit in real data centers. Across hot links the traffic share of the largest ToR neighbor is quite small; on the Cosmos dataset, it is less than 20% for 80% of the matrices. In fact, Figure 12(c) shows that in some cases, even the top five ToR pairs can cumulatively add up to a small fraction of load on the hotlink. In other words, we find that hot links are associated with a high fan-in (or fan-out). This observation was a surprise; it means that *at hotspots, the existing proposals that offload traffic going to just the best neighbor would*

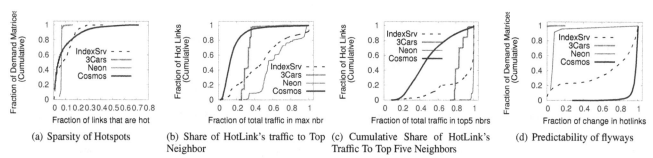

(a) Sparsity of Hotspots   (b) Share of HotLink's traffic to Top Neighbor   (c) Cumulative Share of HotLink's Traffic To Top Five Neighbors   (d) Predictability of flyways

Figure 12: Nature of hotspots in measured DC traffic

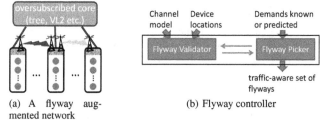

(a) A flyway aug-mented network   (b) Flyway controller

Figure 13: Proposed Architecture

be of limited value for real data center workloads. Even the optimistic wavelength multiplexing-based optical extensions proposed in Helios would not suffice in these cases. We propose and evaluate a one hop indirection technique (§5) that overcomes this weakness.

4.5 Predictability of hotspots

Figure 12(d) compares the change in the pairs of hot-links across consecutive matrices. We observe a dichotomy—some matrices are highly predictable, others are very unpredictable. In both HPC datasets, we see less than a 10% change in hot links whereas in the Cosmos dataset fewer than 10% of hot links repeat. We tried a few more complicated predictors, and find that the results are qualitatively similar. Likely, this is due to the nature of workload. While Cosmos churns work at the granularity of map and reduce tasks which typically last about a few minutes, work in HPC clusters manifests in more long lived groups. We also verify that flow sizes and arrival rates in the DC [6, 14] indicate that traffic in the DC lies in a fast-changing collection of medium-sized flows. This property of real DC workloads renders predictors that rely on identifying elephant flows [2] to be of less use.

Take-aways: In a broad study of many types of DC workload, we find that hotspots are sparse. The potential benefit of selectively providing additional bandwidth at these hotspots, as opposed to building for the worst case with non-oversubscribed networks, appears significant. We also see that real data center traffic matrices are more complex than synthetic workloads evaluated by prior proposals [7, 30], and flyway placement algorithms developed by these proposals are likely be of marginal value. The key issue is that hotspots are often correlated with a high fan-in (or fan-out) implying that to be useful traffic from (or to) many destinations needs to be offloaded. Our system design (§5) includes a novel one hop indirection method designed to resolve this problem.

5. FLYWAYS SYSTEM DESIGN

In this section, we propose a design for a DC network with flyways. The basic architecture is shown in Figure 13; we consider the set of racks in a cluster, each equipped with one or more wireless devices that can be used to construct flyways as needed. Our design is independent of the specific topology used in the oversubscribed core, which could be the typical tree structure, or recent proposals

for non-oversubscribed networks [1, 8, 9] with proportionally fewer switches and links.

Our goal is to configure the flyway links and the routing to improve the time to satisfy traffic demands. The metric of interest is the **completion time of the demands** (CTD), defined as the time it takes for the last flow to complete.

The system has three tasks: (*i*) measure and estimate traffic demands, (*ii*) decide which flyways to instantiate, and (*iii*) make appropriate routing changes to route traffic over flyways. Inputs to the system include the measured 60 GHz channel model, antenna characteristics, device locations and traffic demands if available. We focus on flyways instantiation, and discuss traffic estimation and routing only briefly (§5.3).

Computing an optimal choice of flyways is challenging since wireless constraints such as range and interference are hard to incorporate into a max-flow formulation. Hence, our design decomposes the problem into two sub-parts. A 'flyway picker' (§5.1) proposes flyways that will improve the completion time of demands. A measurement and channel-model driven 'flyway validator' (§5.2) confirms or rejects this proposal. The validator ensures that the system only adds feasible, non-interfering flyways. In addition, the validator also predicts how much capacity the flyways will have. This allows the picker to add the "approved" flyway and propose flyways for subsequent hotspots. The process repeats until no more flyways can be added. This decomposition is not optimal and there is room to improve. However, it finishes quickly, scales well and provides impressive gains, as we will show.

5.1 Choosing flyways

In this section, we will assume that traffic demands are known. We begin with an example. Consider the network in Figure 14(b). Six ToR switches A and C–G have traffic to send to ToR B. A has 100 units to send, whereas the rest each send 80 units. Each ToR has one wireless device connected to it. Wired link capacity in and out of the ToRs is 10 units/sec and for simplicity assume that these are the only potential bottlenecks. The downlink into B is the bottleneck here. It carries 500 units of traffic in total and takes 50 s to do so. Hence, completion time (CTD) is 50 s.

Suppose we add a flyway (capacity 3) from A to B to *improve performance of the straggler*, i.e., the ToR pair that sends the most amount of traffic on the bottleneck link and completes last, by bypassing the bottleneck. As Figure 14(c) shows, traffic on the bottleneck drops to 400 units, and time to complete drops to 40 s. However, as our traffic analysis shows, the straggler often contributes only a small proportion of the total demand on that link (in this case 100/500). Alleviating the straggler provides only 20% gains, reducing CTD to 40 s.

Note that there is room to spare on the flyway; the demand from A to B completes after 33.3 s, 6.7 s before traffic from C–G. Our datasets indicate that this is quite common; very few of the ToR pairs on hot links require substantial capacity. Hence, we also *allow*

Demand	A→B	100 units
	C,D,E,F,G→B	80 units
Capacity	wired links	10 units/s
	flyway: A→B	3 units/s
	flyway: C→B	6 units/s

(a) Setup   (b) Baseline: CTD=50s   (c) Direct flyway for the straggler: CTD=40s   (d) Allowing transit traffic: CTD=38.5s   (e) Greedy choice of flyways: CTD=31.2s

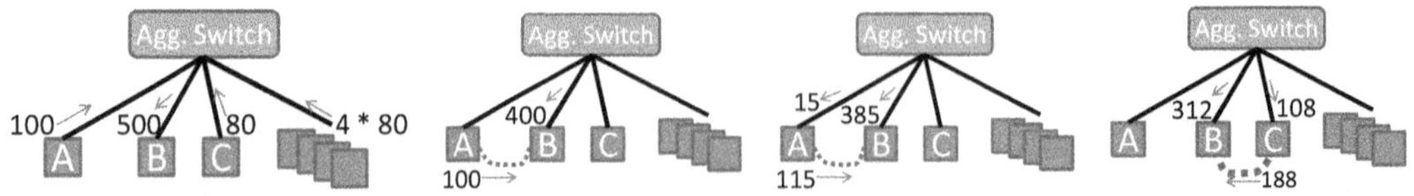

Figure 14: A motivating example: Greedy choice of flyways to add and allowing transit traffic through flyways are crucial.

indirect transit traffic to use the flyway, i.e., as Figure 14(d) shows, traffic from other sources to B bypasses the bottleneck by flowing via node A and the flyway. This improves CTD to $\frac{115}{3} = \frac{385}{10} = 38.5$ s.

Often the flyway to the straggler is infeasible or an inferior choice, the devices at either ends might be used up in earlier flyways or the link may interfere with an existing flyway or the ToR pairs might be too far apart. Allowing transit traffic ensures that *any flyway that can offload traffic on the bottleneck will be of use*, even if it is not between the straggler pair. In this case, it is more effective to enable the flyway from C to B, with twice the capacity of the flyway from A. This decision allows more traffic to be offloaded results in a CTD of $\frac{312}{10} = \frac{188}{6} = 31.2$ s.

Proposed algorithm: Our approach formalizes these two insights. By allowing transit traffic on a flyway, via indirection, we skirt the problem of high fan-in (or fan-out) that we saw to be correlated with congestion. Further, doing so opens up the space of potentially useful flyways, greedy choice among this set adds substantial value. In particular, at each step, we choose the flyway that diverts the most traffic away from the bottleneck link. For a congested downlink to ToR p, the best flyway will be from the ToR that has a high capacity flyway and sufficient available bandwidth on its downlink to allow transit traffic through, i.e.,

$$\arg\max_{\text{ToR } i} \min\left(C_{i \to p},\ D_{i \to p} + down_i\right).$$

The first term $C_{i \to p}$ denotes the capacity of the flyway. The amount of transit traffic is capped by $down_i$ the available bandwidth on the downlink to i and $D_{i \to p}$ is i's demand to p. Together, the second term indicates the maximum possible traffic that i can send to p. The corresponding expression of the best flyway for a congested uplink to ToR is similar,

$$\arg\max_{\text{ToR } i} \min\left(C_{p \to i},\ D_{p \to i} + up_i\right).$$

5.2 Validating flyway choice

The flyways validator determines whether a specified set of flyways can operate together — it computes the effects of interference and what capacity each link is likely to provide. It operates using the same principle as DIRC's conflict graph [17]: If we know how much signal is delivered between all pairs of nodes in all transmit and receive antenna orientations, we can combine these measurements with knowledge of which links are active, and how the antennas are oriented, to compute the SINR for all nodes. We can then use the simple SINR-based auto-rate algorithm (§B) to select rates.

Our SINR model (§B) is very conservative: we compute interference assuming *all nodes from all other flyways* send concurrently, and add an additional 3 dB. Hence, we disable carrier sense on our flyways links, managing contention between sender and receiver with other types of coordination (§C). Recall that both the SINR model and rate selection are appropriate for our data center environment because of the high directionality (§3 and [17]).

Obtaining the conflict graph: If there are N racks and K antenna orientations, the input to the validator is an $(NK)^2$-size table of re-

ceived signal strengths. How can we generate this very large table? In the simulator, we compute delivered signal power using the models of antennas and signal propagation developed in §3. In a real DC deployment, we can measure it—a data center provides a stable, line-of-sight environment (§3.3) and a fixed set of nodes with known geographic coordinates. Hence, unlike DIRC's dynamic, non-line-of-sight environment with unknown client locations, we can afford to measure this table only once when the data center is configured, and measurements will remain valid over time. We can refresh entries in the table opportunistically, without disrupting ongoing wireless traffic, by having idle nodes measure signal strength from active senders at various receive antenna orientations and sharing these measurements, along with transmitter antenna orientation, over the wired network.

The table can be used not just to compute interference, but also to determine the best antenna orientation for two ToRs to communicate with each other, and the complex antenna orientation mechanisms prescribed in 802.11ad are no longer needed. In this paper, we evaluate antennas that use purely directional radiation patterns and point directly at their intended receivers. Advanced, more powerful antenna methods such as null-steering to avoid interference [20] could increase flyway concurrency, but we defer these to future work. Our results (§6) will show that even this simple antenna model is effective at improving data center performance.

5.3 Traffic estimation and routing

Traffic estimation and routing are not the main focus of this paper, and our system design in these areas is largely similar to prior work [30, 7, 8]. We describe it briefly for the sake of completeness.

Estimating traffic demands: Traffic demand can be estimated in one of two ways. First, for clusters that are orchestrated by cluster-wide schedulers (e.g., map-reduce schedulers such as Quincy [11]), logically co-locating our system with such a scheduler makes traffic demands visible. In this mode, our system can pick flyways appropriate for these demands. C-Through [30] takes a somewhat similar approach: it assumes that applications hint at their traffic demands.

Second, in clusters that have predictable traffic patterns, such as the HPC datasets we analyzed, we can use instrumentation to estimate current traffic demands and pick flyways appropriate for demands predicted based on these estimates. Such distributed, end-host based, traffic measurement instrumentation is already used, for e.g., at EC2 and Windows Azure, for billing and accounting, and can provide up-to-date inputs for our system as well.

We have designed a simple traffic estimation scheme that uses a shim layer (an NDIS filter driver) on servers to collect traffic statistics, in a manner similar to prior work [6, 14]. We use a simple moving average of estimates from the recent past [13]. This estimator works as well with our traces as the more complex alternatives that we tried. Micro-benchmarks show this estimator to be feasible at line rate with negligible increase in server load.

In future work, we will address traffic that is neither predictable nor orchestrated. See (§7) for some ideas.

Routing: We present a simple mechanism that routes traffic across the potentially multiple paths that are made feasible with flyways.

Our approach is straightforward and similar to prior work [8, 7]. We treat flyways as point-to-point links. Note that every path on the flyway transits through exactly one flyway link, so all that the routing does is to encapsulate packets to the appropriate interface address. For example, to send traffic via $A \rightarrow Core \rightarrow C \rightarrow B$, the servers underneath A encapsulate packets with the address of C's flyway interface to B. The flyway picker computes the fraction of traffic to flow on each path and relays these decisions to the servers. We have built this functionality into the aforementioned NDIS filter driver. Our micro-benchmarks tests on standard DC servers equipped with 1 Gbps NICs indicate that these operations can be performed at line speed with negligible additional load.

When changing the flyway setup, we simply disable encapsulation, and remove the added routes. The default routes on the ToR and Agg switches are never changed, and direct traffic on the wired network. Thus, as soon as we remove the flyway route, the traffic flows over wired links. Thus, during flyway changes (and flyway failures, if any), packets are simply sent over wired network.

6. EVALUATING FLYWAYS

In this section we combine our measurement- and standard-driven wireless models with our traces from real data centers to evaluate the practical benefits to data center workloads in oversubscribed networks that come from our wireless flyways system.

6.1 Methodology

Demands: We replay the traffic described in §4, which is measured from four different clusters and includes workloads from latency- and throughput-sensitive applications and highly tuned HPC applications.

Wireless models: We use the wireless physical and MAC layers and channel models described in §B. Here, we recall a few salient specifics: We use the three channels defined in 802.11ad to increase the number of concurrent links. Devices use a uniform 10 mW transmit power. The system uses the interference model and rate selection algorithms described in §B and the flyways validator described in §5.2. We use the 802.11ad OFDM rates, which peak at 6.76 Gbps, only about 85% of which is usable for traffic (§C).

Geography: We mimic the geographical layout of racks as per measurements from an open floor-plan data center (see Figure 9). We assume that each ToR is equipped with K wireless devices, often 1, which are mounted atop the rack. ToR switches in the observed data centers have a few unused ports for occasional network management tasks.

We compare these variants of our system:

Straggler is the simplest alternative, in which the picker proposes a flyway between the pair of ToRs taking the longest time to complete. If the validator accepts this proposal as safe then the flyway is added, and if not then the process terminates — the CTD cannot be further improved.

Transit augments Straggler by allowing for transit traffic on the added flyways. As we saw in §5, doing so improves performance by offloading more traffic from the bottleneck link, and potentially changes which link will next be the bottleneck.

Greedy augments Transit by preferentially picking, in each iteration, the flyway that offloads the most traffic from the bottleneck link. In practice, this results in using flyways between close-by nodes that have high capacity. As a side-effect, this process tends to add shorter links and thus results in more feasible flyways than Straggler.

Metric: Our primary metric of goodness is the completion time of

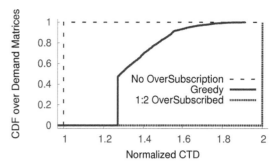

Figure 15: With just one device/ToR with NB antennas, the greedy traffic-aware choice of flyways provides significant improvements for demands observed in data centers.

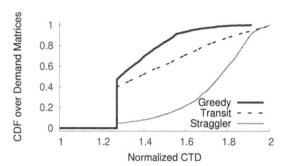

Figure 16: Improvements from the traffic-oblivious scheme as well as from each of the constituent ideas.

demands (CTD) as defined in §5 and shown in the example (Figure 14) of §5.1. To facilitate comparison, we report the *normalized CTD*: CTD/CTD$_{ideal}$, where CTD$_{ideal}$ is the CTD with an ideal, non-oversubscribed network. In a $1:N$ oversubscribed network, the baseline network has a CTD of N, and obtaining a CTD of 1 implies that with flyways, the network has performed as well as the ideal, non-oversubscribed network. We will also report statistics on the numbers of flyways used, the capacities of those flyways and their utilization.

6.2 Benefits from flyways

Figure 15 plots a CDF of the normalized CTD over all the demands in the dataset on a 1:2 oversubscribed network. For reference, the normalized CTD of the ideal non-oversubscribed network and the baseline are 2 and 1 as shown in the figure. With just one device per ToR (with NB antennas), Greedy provides significant improvements. About 50% of the demand matrices have a normalized CTD of 1.27, i.e., 27% off the optimal. More than 90% of the demand matrices experience a speed-up of at least 45% (normalized CTD < 1.55). This configuration trades roughly half the number of switches, links and ports (by running at 1:2 oversubscription) for one wireless device per ToR.

At first blush, it is surprising that a large number of demand matrices reach CTD=1.27, but none go lower. The reason is that CTD improvement is limited by the additional capacity in or out of each ToR. Given a baseline network oversubscribed N times and K flyways per ToR of capacity F, the best possible CTD is $N/\left(1 + \frac{KF}{C}\right)$, where C is the uplink capacity at each ToR. Then with the flyway capacity 85% of the ideal 6.756 Gbps wireless bitrate and a ToR uplink of 10 Gbps, it follows that for the default configuration of one device per ToR, the best possible normalized CTD value is about 1.27. Thus, half of the demand matrices obtain almost the best possible savings.

Figure 16 compares Greedy with other schemes. We see that Straggler performs quite poorly. Since high fan-in (and fan-out)

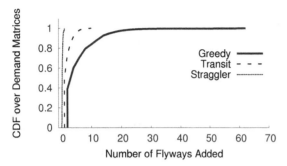

Figure 17: Average numbers of flyways used

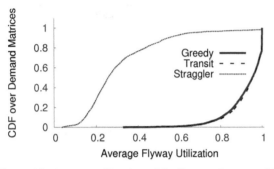

Figure 18: Average utilization of the flyways that are added

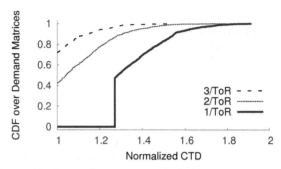

Figure 19: Increasing number of wireless devices/ToR: One more device per ToR provides significant additional benefit.

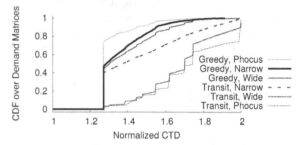

Figure 20: Different antenna configurations: The greedy approach is more robust with wide-beam antennas where flyways can have very different capacities.

correlate with congestion, Straggler runs out of flyways that it can add. As expected, the supporting result in Figure 17 shows that Straggler adds many fewer flyways than all of the other schemes. Offloading the demands to just the largest neighbor does not impact the hotlinks by much. Instead, by allowing indirect traffic across flyways, Transit improves the performance for every demand matrix. Greedy performs even better. Building on the ability to indirect, Greedy searches among many more flyway possibilities and adds those that allow the most traffic to be offloaded. Figure 18 shows that for both Transit and Greedy, almost all the flyways are fully utilized. In addition, Greedy primarily picks short flyways that achieve the full possible rate. This indicates that were more capacity achievable on the flyway link, Greedy's performance would improve. These results reaffirm the value of allowing transit traffic across flyways and greedily picking the best over the resulting many possibilities.

6.3 Evaluating alternate configurations

To understand the solution space better, we evaluate alternatives with more wireless devices available at each ToR, different antennas and different degrees of oversubscription on the core.

More wireless devices/ToR: Figure 19 plots the benefits due to flyways when more than one wireless device is available at each ToR. We see that with just one additional device ($K = 2$), the improvements in completion time are significant. In fact, over 40% of the matrices finish as fast as they would have in a non-oversubscribed network. There are two reasons for this. First, as we saw in Figure 15, with just one device available per ToR, some of the demand matrices are constrained by the maximum capacity that a flyway adds. Additional wireless devices provide immediate benefit to these matrices. Second, even matrices that are unconstrained by flyway capacity experience benefit because with more flyways many more indirect routes are now feasible. Ever more traffic gets diverted away from congested parts of the wired network via flyways to other wired links that have spare capacity.

Different antenna configurations: All the results so far were with a narrow beam, 23 dBi gain, antenna. Figure 20 compares the ben-

efits when different directional antennas are used. We compare Greedy with Transit, its next best alternative. We find that Greedy works best with the Phocus antennas, even though they are less directional than NB antennas, due to two reasons. First, Greedy biases the algorithm to use shorter higher capacity flyways and to then route traffic indirectly via these links. Most of these short links will continue to exist even with lower gain antennas. Second, the Phocus array has smaller back and side lobes, resulting in lower interference, and hence more simultaneously usable links. We find that unlike Greedy, Transit is sensitive to antenna directionality. With the wider beam antennas, Transit performs considerably worse and is on par with Straggler+NB. That is, the benefits from allowing transit traffic are lost with wider antennas. The reason is that with the wider antennas, there is a greater variation of capacities across flyways (as predicted by Figure 8) and quicker decay with distance. The inability to pick flyways other than those between the straggling ToR pair causes Transit to lose its gains. On the other hand, Greedy's selectivity allows it to retain most of its gains even with the wider antennas.

Different oversubscription factors: With a greater oversubscription factor, e.g., slower links between the ToR and the core or fewer core switches in a VL2-like architecture, the network core would be relatively less expensive. Figure 21 plots the median normalized CTD across demand matrices for different oversubscription factors. We see a reasonable trade-off: one can increase the oversubscription factor on the wired network and instead spend a small fraction of that amount to deploy additional wireless devices at each ToR. The marginal improvement from each additional device decreases, but the savings are considerable. On a 1:4 oversubscribed network, flyways with 3 devices per ToR provide a median CTD of 1.78, i.e., performance better than a 1:2 oversubscribed network.

7. DISCUSSION

Flyways limitations: For some workloads, such as all-pairs-shuffle, non-oversubscribed networks are indeed more appropriate. However, these workloads are not reflected in our many traces, and we

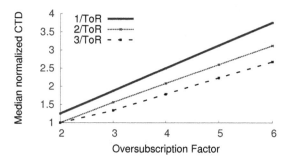

Figure 21: Flyway benefit vs. Oversubscription Ratio

believe that such workloads are rare in practice. Our current "flyway picker" algorithm requires knowledge of traffic patterns. In some cases (e.g., multi-tenant data centers) traffic patterns may not be predictable, and there may be no cluster-wide scheduler. In such cases, we believe that an online traffic engineering approach such as that described in [5], combined with the ability to rapidly steer antennas (every few seconds) may be the right solution. Design of flyway validator and flyway picker becomes more interesting when rapid beam steering is possible; since now a single flyway device can divide time across multiple neighbors. We are currently investigating the practical issues (e.g., routing) involved in this approach.

Scaling with faster wired networks: The maximum rate specified in 802.11ad is 6.76 Gbps. We have shown (§4) that flyway bandwidth needs to be only a fraction of the hot link's capacity. Still, as the speed of wired links in the data center continues to grow, we may need faster flyways. Our results in Figure 8 show that many links have ample SNR headroom and thus have plenty of room to grow with higher modulations. In addition, the flyway architecture is not specific to 60 GHz technology. Other frequencies in the 50–75 GHz band have similar properties and as 60 GHz devices become a mature technology, it may be possible to convince the FCC to open up more spectrum around the 60 GHz band for indoor data center use. Given the large lot sizes of data centers and the short propagation distance of 60 GHz links, it may be possible to use a wider band while ensuring that no detectable signal leaves the data center premises.

Scaling the data center size: Network architectures such as VL2 [8] and FatTree [1] allow the data center to scale easily in addition to providing full bisection bandwidth. In these designs it is easy to build a bigger network by simply adding additional switches, instead of investing in larger aggregation switches, or adding more layers to hierarchy. We can use the flyway architecture in conjunction with oversubscribed VL2-like networks. The VL2 architecture can be used for easy scaling, while the flyways are used to address congestion in a dynamic manner.

Containerized data center networks: While many of today's large data centers use a large, open floor plan (and new ones continue to be built), some of the new data centers are being built with containerized architecture. In a container environment, we can either deploy flyways inside a container, or between containers. Deploying flyways inside a container, instead of building a full bisection bandwidth network may allow for cheaper containers, as much less hardware will be required. On the other hand, inside a container, flyways may suffer from multipath effects, as radiation bounces off metal walls of the container. This issue can be addressed in numerous ways — by lining the inside of a container with adsorbent materials, or by employing very narrow beam antennas. For inter-container traffic, flyways are an ideal choice, since a number of devices can be mounted atop a container. At the same time, inter-

container links will need higher bandwidth. We plan to study this scenario further.

Comparison with Helios and c-Through: A direct comparison between Helios [7] and c-Through [30] is difficult to perform at this point. There are several reasons for this. First, the performance of any flyway scheme will depend on the speed at which flyways can be switched between nodes. We believe (Appendix A) that wireless flyways can be switched extremely fast compared to optical MEMs switches. However, to do a meaningful comparison, we would need access to electronically steerable antennas, which we do not have. Second, the Helios system is meant for inter-container traffic, while we focus on inter-rack traffic. Third, the workload used in Helios is artificial, while our evaluation is based on real traces. Finally, our modest attempt at comparison was not successful. We built a test-bed using MEMs optical switches from the same vendor as Helios. However, we found switching times to be above 100 ms and reducing it to the values in the Helios paper (10 ms) would have required significant resources and time (software switches and NIC modifications).

Signal leakage: A concern with using wireless in a data center environment is that the signal may leak outside the data center and be picked up by an attacker. Our measurements show that the concern is unfounded. We found that common construction materials such as wood, glass and metal significantly attenuate the signal by a large margin. Coupled with normal free-space attenuation, this margin makes it very unlikely that the signal can be decoded outside the data center, even with a highly directional antenna. We omit detailed results due to lack of space.

Power consumption: Our experimental 60 GHz HXI devices consume 25 Watts of power. Several startups report devices that consume at most a few Watts [24, 27]. As a typical server rack draws thousands of Watts of power, a few additional wireless devices per rack increase consumption by a negligible fraction.

8. RELATED WORK

60 GHz wireless: Millimeter wavelength wireless communication is a very active research area, especially at the hardware/PHY level, with several dedicated conferences and workshops. Much of this work focuses on characterizing signal propagation, proposing new modulation schemes and devising antenna hardware, and much has been synthesized into WiGig and WirelessHD standards. Our work benefits from advances in this area. However, our use of 60 GHz links for data center communications is significantly different from the other applications that the field has explored.

We are aware of only one other[1] paper [22] that has discussed using 60 GHz links in data centers. In it, the authors give a high-level vision for an all-wireless data center network. In contrast, we present a hybrid architecture, backed by an experimental study of 60 GHz wireless propagation in the data center environment and evaluate its merit upon several types of traffic measured in the data center.

Data center networks: A number of papers have addressed the problem of congestion in data center networks. We discuss a representative sample. Researchers have proposed [1, 8, 9] building full bisection bandwidth networks to eliminate hot-spots. Deploying such networks is expensive, and the cabling complexity of some of them is quite daunting [15].

Hedera [2] and MicroTE [5] advocate fine-grained traffic engineering over a fixed topology to alleviate congestion. However, this approach has limitations. For example, in a tree-structured net-

---

[1]Apart from the preliminary version [15] of this paper.

work, if the downlink from an aggregator switch to a ToR switch is congested, only extra bandwidth can relieve the congestion. At the other extreme, Proteus [28] explored the idea of a completely reconfigurable, all-optical network topology.

Instead, we explore the idea of adding additional bandwidth to data center networks on demand. The closest work to our own is Helios [7] and c-Through [30], both of which propose flyways using optical switches. Wireless flyways have the benefits of potentially lower costs and limited cabling complexity but also face challenges unique to wireless, such as interference, and we show how we address these.

There are other differences in the designs as well. C-Through delays TCP connections to ensure that optical links are used optimally; we do not require any such delay. Helios is targeted towards inter-container traffic; we target sub-agg-switch traffic. Most importantly, both Helios and c-Through use synthetic workloads, while we use extensive traffic traces from a variety of real data centers to motivate our system and assess the value of flyways.

9. CONCLUSION

We have presented the design and evaluation of a 60 GHz wireless flyway system. It adds wireless links to the wired data center network to relieve hotspots and thus improve performance. Working with prototype 60 GHz devices, we measured and simulated performance to show that wireless flyways can provide a dense deployment of stable, multi-Gbps paths in the DC environment. By analyzing traces of DC traffic for four real applications, we find that only a relatively small number of top-of-rack switches and links are congested at any time. This implies that a set of flyways with relatively small capacity can relieve hotspots and boost application performance. Informed by our exploration of 60 GHz and DC traffic, we designed a wireless flyway system that sets up the most beneficial flyways and routes over them both directly and indirectly to reduce congestion on hot links. Our trace-driven simulation shows this design speeds up network-limited DC applications with predictable traffic workloads by 45% in 95% of the cases at a fraction of the cost of avoiding oversubscription.

10. REFERENCES

[1] M. Al-Fares et al. A scalable, commodity data center network architecture. In *SIGCOMM*, 2008.
[2] M. Al-Fares et al. Hedera: Dynamic flow scheduling for data center networks. In *NSDI*, 2009.
[3] S. Alalusi. CMOS multi-antenna systems at 60 GHz. In *Communications Design Conference*, July 2004.
[4] M. Alizadeh et al. DCTCP: Efficient packet transport for the commoditized data center. In *SIGCOMM*, 2010.
[5] T. Benson et al. The case for fine-grained traffic engineering in data-centers. In *WREN*, 2010.
[6] T. Benson et al. Network traffic characteristics of data centers in the wild. In *IMC*, 2010.
[7] N. Farrington et al. Helios: A hybrid electrical/optical switch architecture for modular data centers. In *SIGCOMM*, 2010.
[8] A. Greenberg et al. VL2: A scalable and flexible data center network. In *SIGCOMM*, 2009.
[9] C. Guo et al. BCube: High performance, server-centric network architecture for data centers. In *SIGCOMM*, 2009.
[10] IEEE P802.11ad/D0.1: Enhancements for very high throughput in the 60 GHz band. Draft 0.1, June 2010.
[11] M. Isard et al. Quincy: fair scheduling for distributed ocmputing clusters. In *SOSP*, 2009.
[12] K. Jain et al. Impact of interference on multi-hop wireless network performance. In *MOBICOMM*, 2003.
[13] S. Kandula et al. Walking the tightrope: responsive yet stable traffic engineering. In *SIGCOMM*, 2005.
[14] S. Kandula et al. The nature of datacenter traffic: Measurements and analysis. In *IMC*, 2009.
[15] S. Kandula, J. Padhye, and P. Bahl. Flyways to de-congest data center networks. In *HotNets*, Nov. 2009.
[16] LightPointe. http://www.lightpointe.com/.
[17] X. Liu et al. DIRC: Increasing indoor wireless capacity using directional antennas. In *SIGCOMM*, 2009.
[18] T. Manabe et al. Effects of antenna directivity on indoor multipath propagation characteristics at 60 GHz. In *PIMRC*, 1995.
[19] V. Navda et al. MobiSteer: Using steerable beam directional antenna for vehicular network access. In *MobiSys*, 2007.
[20] G. Nikolaidis et al. (Poster) Cone of silence: Adaptively nulling interferers in wireless networks. In *SIGCOMM*, 2010.
[21] The ns-3 network simulator. http://www.nsnam.org/.
[22] K. Ramachandran et al. 60 GHz data-center networking: Wireless ⇒ worry less? Technical report, NEC, 2008.
[23] T. S. Rappaport. *Wireless Communications: Principles and Practice*. Prentice-Hall, 2002.
[24] Sayana Networks.
[25] A. Sheth et al. Geo-fencing: Confining Wi-Fi coverage to physical boundaries. In *Pervasive*, 2009.
[26] SiBeam. http://sibeam.com/whitepapers/.
[27] SiBeam. http://www.earthtimes.org/articles/press/generation-solutions-ces-2011,1604984.html.
[28] A. Singla et al. Proteus: A topology malleable data center network. In *HotNets*, 2010.
[29] Terabeam Wireless. http://www.terabeam.com/.
[30] G. Wang et al. c-Through: Part-time optics in data centers. In *SIGCOMM*, 2010.
[31] Wireless Gigabit Alliance. http://wirelessgigabitalliance.org/.
[32] WirelessHD. http://wirelesshd.org/.
[33] Y. Yu et al. A 60 GHz digitally controlled phase shifter in CMOS. In *ESSCIRC*, 2008.

APPENDIX

A. PHASED ARRAYS

Our assumptions about phased array design are based on three sources of information: (1) research literature on commercially available 2.4 GHz Phocus arrays from the wireless research communities, (2) existing 60 GHz silicon such as SiBeam's WirelessHD [26] products, and (3) research on 60 GHz phased arrays technology.

Phased array technology: A phased array comprises multiple antenna elements each transmitting (or receiving) an attenuated, phase-shifted copy of the same RF signal. By varying the amount of attenuation or phase shift, a device can control the radiation pattern of the antenna, including the direction of maximum gain or the size and location of lobes. The flexibility of a phased array increases rapidly with the number of antenna elements. The 2.4 GHz Phocus array is commercially available today and uses 8 elements; in contrast, 60 GHz phased array design is an area of ongoing research [3, 33], but SiBeam's initial WirelessHD products include 32 elements and fit into 1 in^2.

Antenna pattern: In this work, we simply replicate the radiation pattern used in the Geo-fencing project [25]. This pattern minimizes the size and extent of back and side lobes and can be produced by the 8-element Phocus arrays. Though 60 GHz and 2.4 GHz phased array technologies will likely differ, we expect that the increased number of elements at 60 GHz will enable patterns of similar or better flexibility. For simplicity, in this paper we assume that the antenna pattern can be steered to an arbitrary angle. Extrapolating from the Phocus array, a 30-element array might in practice have a 6° granularity.

Switching times: The phased array technology used in the Phocus arrays can be switched within 250 μs [19]. In personal communication, the authors of [33], informed us that their 60 GHz phase shifting technology can be switched in picoseconds. However since we cannot yet implement and evaluate phase-switched flyways, we ignore switching overhead in this paper and instead focus on individual traffic matrices in isolation.

Discovering the steering coefficients: Steering coefficients allow directional antennas of the sender and transmitter to point at each other. Optimizing the search process to discover steer coefficients is currently an active area of research. However, the flyways scenario greatly simplifies this problem. We use the wired network to coordinate the steering. Rather than needing to optimize the combination of multiple reflections off walls and in-home objects, in the DC, we can use physically meaningful steering patterns that point in a particular direction. A movement of a few mm does not dramatically reduce gains. The stable DC environment allows us to use history and retrain infrequently. Any nodes not involved in flyways (there will be many of these) can opportunistically measure their directional gains with respect to ongoing transmissions, as well as update measurements for patterns between idle nodes that will not interfere with ongoing traffic.

B. 60 GHz SIMULATOR

We implemented an 802.11ad simulator in `ns-3`. To have confidence that our simulations are a good reflection of reality, we base wireless effects directly on the physical layer measurements we took in §3 and the WiGig/802.11ad PHY and MAC design [31]. Here we describe wireless aspects of our `ns-3` model. We extended `ns-3` with other support too, such as automatic generation of DC layouts and routing, but these components are straightforward and we omit them due to lack of space.

Directional antennas: We built table-driven models from the measured radiation patterns of the antennas in our lab (Figure 3). We interpolate between measurements when needed. As well as using measured patterns, rather than the manufacturer antenna specifications, we take care to simulate the full 360° radiation pattern, not just the primary lobe. We also added a simple isotropic antenna model, and the radiation pattern used for Geo-fencing [25].

IEEE 802.11ad PHY and MAC: We implemented in `ns-3` the physical and MAC layers defined in the draft 802.11ad standard. We limit ourselves to the faster OFDM PHY. We fix transmit power to 10 mW to match commercial devices.

Signal propagation: We model signal propagation using Friis' law. Our measurements (§3.2) show that this is a good fit for line-of-sight environments. Still, we conservatively subtract an additional 3 dB from the signal power (but not from interference) to represent potential destructive multi-path interference received via side lobes.

Interference (SINR): To calculate the SINR needed for bit error rate estimation, `ns-3` uses the standard SINR modeling technique. It adds together the power from multiple interferers, combines it with noise, and compares it with signal strength. `ns-3` does not model symbol-level fading, i.e., it assumes that the received power (RSS) from each transmitter is consistent throughout its transmission. It does, however, compute different SINR levels for different parts of packets when interference stops or starts during reception.

Our measurements of the stability of real links (§3.3) show that we can use this SINR model and ignore fading at the sub-packet level. Prior work (DIRC [17]) has also found this simple SINR model to be appropriate with directional antennas, even when using the 802.11g OFDM rates in non-line-of-sight environments and omni-directional antennas at receivers. The model is much more fitting in our 60 GHz domain: both transmitter and receiver use directional antennas so that secondary rays (multi-path) have little impact (§3.2); and the channel is very stable due to little environ-

Ideal Rate	Wireless TCP	Offload ACKs to Wired	No DCF
693 Mbps	656 Mbps	672 Mbps	676 Mbps
6.76 Gbps	4.58 Gbps	5.36 Gbps	5.62 Gbps

Table 2: Impact of sending TCP ACKs over wire

mental mobility (§3.3).

Bit error rate (BER): Estimating the bit error rate, and hence whether a transmitted packet is received correctly, forms a key function of any wireless model. The input to this calculation is the SINR and the 802.11ad wireless rate. To estimate BER, we use the 802.11ad standard as our guide. It defines the sensitivity for each rate and coding as the (SINR) power level down to which a device much successfully receive more than 99% of 4096-byte packets sent using that rate. This reception rate corresponds to a BER less than 3.07×10^{-7}, and thus we calibrate our error model for each rate by assuming its BER is 3×10^{-7} when its SINR is the sensitivity threshold. The sensitivities defined in the standard implicitly include the (≈ -81 dBm) thermal noise for a 2.16 GHz channel, and a 15 dB combined implementation loss. We compute BERs at other SINR values using textbook formulas [23] for BER as a function of SNR in Gaussian noise. To receive a packet, all bits must be correct.

Auto-rate algorithm: The 802.11ad standard does not mandate use of a specific auto-rate algorithm. We select rates based on received SINR. This is reasonable for our stable data center environment.

C. IMPROVING WIRELESS PERF.

Data center performance will improve the most when the flyways deliver the largest possible throughputs. A unique aspect of our flyways scenario is the hybrid wired and wireless nature of the network, and in this section we describe and evaluate two wireless optimizations that leverage the wired backbone in the DC to increase flyway TCP throughput by 25%

Wired offload of MAC-inefficient packets: TCP ACKs are far smaller than data packets, and make inefficient use of wireless links because payload transmission time is dwarfed by overheads such as preamble and SIFS. The hybrid wired-wireless design of our network lets us improve efficiency by sending ACK packets over the wire instead. To measure the improvement, we simulated a single TCP flow on a 20 m link and configured `ns-3` to send the TCP ACKs over the wired network. Table 2 shows the resulting TCP throughput. For fast links enabled by the narrow-beam antenna, the performance improves 17%. Note that the TCP ACK traffic will use some wired bandwidth, but this will be trivial compared to the increase in throughput.

Removing DCF: For the common case of one-way TCP flows in the data center [4], if we divert TCP ACKs over the wire as above then all traffic over a given wireless link will flow in only one direction. Furthermore, our system design (§5) is based on independent flyways that do not interfere with one another. Thus, there are no collisions in our wireless network, and we can eliminate the DCF backoff mechanism. This change improves the TCP throughput by an additional 5%, as seen in the third column of Table 2.

Occasionally there may be bidirectional data flows over the flyway. Even in this case, we can remove the cost of DCF. Since only the two communicating endpoints can interfere with each other, we can easily schedule transmissions on the link by passing a token between the endpoints. This naturally fits into the 802.11 link layer protocol because after transmitting a packet batch, the sender waits for a link layer Block-ACK. We can exploit this scheduled hand-off to let the receiver take the token and send its own batch of traffic.

Better Never than Late: Meeting Deadlines in Datacenter Networks

Christo Wilson
christowilson@umail.ucsb.edu

Hitesh Ballani
hiballan@microsoft.com

Thomas Karagiannis
thomkar@microsoft.com

Ant Rowstron
antr@microsoft.com

Microsoft Research
Cambridge, UK

ABSTRACT

The soft real-time nature of large scale web applications in today's datacenters, combined with their distributed workflow, leads to deadlines being associated with the datacenter application traffic. A network flow is useful, and contributes to application throughput and operator revenue if, and only if, it completes within its deadline. Today's transport protocols (TCP included), given their Internet origins, are agnostic to such flow deadlines. Instead, they strive to share network resources fairly. We show that this can hurt application performance.

Motivated by these observations, and other (previously known) deficiencies of TCP in the datacenter environment, this paper presents the design and implementation of D^3, a deadline-aware control protocol that is customized for the datacenter environment. D^3 uses explicit rate control to apportion bandwidth according to flow deadlines. Evaluation from a 19-node, two-tier datacenter testbed shows that D^3, even without any deadline information, easily outperforms TCP in terms of short flow latency and burst tolerance. Further, by utilizing deadline information, D^3 effectively doubles the peak load that the datacenter network can support.

Categories and Subject Descriptors: C.2.2 [Computer-Communication Networks]: Network Protocols
General Terms: Algorithms, Design, Performance
Keywords: Online services, Datacenter, SLA, Deadline, rate control

1. INTRODUCTION

The proliferation of datacenters over the past few years has been primarily driven by the rapid emergence of user-facing online services. Web search, retail, advertisement, social networking and recommendation systems represent a few prominent examples of such services.

While very different in functionality, these services share a couple of common underlying themes. First is their *soft real* *time* nature resulting from the need to serve users in a timely fashion. Consequently, today's online services have service level agreements (SLAs) baked into their operation [10,16,24]. User requests are to be satisfied within a specified latency target; when the time expires, responses, irrespective of their completeness, are shipped out. However, the completeness of the responses directly governs their quality and in turn, operator revenue [17]. Second, the mantra of horizontal scalability entails that online services have a *partition-aggregate* workflow with user requests being partitioned amongst (multiple) layers of workers whose results are then aggregated to form the response [10].

The combination of latency targets for datacenter applications and their distributed workflow has implications for traffic inside the datacenter. Application latency targets cascade to targets for workers at each layer; targets in the region of 10 to 100ms are common [4], which in turn, yield targets for network communication between the workers. Specifically, for any network flow initiated by these workers, there is an associated *deadline*. The flow is useful and contributes to the *application throughput* if, and only if, it completes within the deadline.

Today's datacenter networks, given their Internet origins, are oblivious to any such implications of the application design. Specifically, the congestion control (TCP) and flow scheduling mechanisms (FIFO queuing) used in datacenters are unaware of flow deadlines and hence, strive to optimize network-level metrics: maximize network throughput while achieving fairness. This mismatch can severely impact application performance; this is best illustrated through a couple of simple examples:

– *Case for unfair sharing:* Consider two flows that share a bottleneck link; one flow has a tighter deadline than the other. As shown in figure 1, with today's setup, TCP strives for fairness and the flows finish at similar times.[1] However, only one flow makes its deadline and is included in the user response. Apart from hurting application performance, this wastes valuable network resources on a non-contributing flow. Alternatively, given explicit information about flow deadlines, the network can distribute bandwidth unequally to meet the deadlines.

– *Case for flow quenching:* Consider a common application setting involving multiple servers responding to an aggregator simultaneously. The resulting network flows share a bottleneck link and have the same deadline. Further, as-

---

[1]We use TCP as a running example since it is used in datacenters today. However, our arguments apply to other TCP variants and proposals like DCTCP [4], XCP [19], etc.

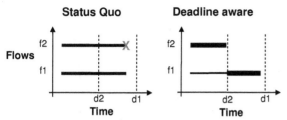

Figure 1: Two flows (f1, f2) with different deadlines (d1, d2). The thickness of a flow line represents the rate allocated to it. Awareness of deadlines can be used to ensure they are met.

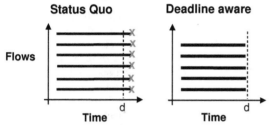

Figure 2: Multiple flows with the same deadline (d). The bottleneck capacity cannot satisfy the deadline if all six flows proceed. Quenching one flow ensures that the others finish before the deadline.

sume that congestion on the bottleneck link is such that the aggregate capacity available to these flows is not enough to finish all the flows before the deadline. Figure 2 shows that with today's setup, all flows will receive their fair share of the bandwidth, finish at similar times and hence, miss the deadline. This, in turn, results in an empty response to the end user. Given flow deadlines, it may be possible to determine that the network is congested and quench some flows to ensure that the remaining flows do meet the deadline.

Both these examples reflect a tension between the functionality offered by a deadline agnostic network and application goals. This tension is above and beyond the known deficiencies of TCP in the datacenter environment. These include the incast problem resulting from bursts of flows [8,23], and the queuing and buffer pressure induced by a traffic mix that includes long flows [4].

However, the goal of a deadline-aware datacenter network poses unique challenges:

1. Deadlines are associated with flows, not packets. All packets of a flow need to arrive before the deadline.

2. Deadlines for flows can vary significantly. For example, online services like Bing and Google include flows with a continuum of deadlines (including some that do not have a deadline). Further, datacenters host multiple services with diverse traffic patterns. This, combined with the previous challenge, *rules out traditional scheduling solutions, such as simple prioritization of flows based on their length and deadlines (EDF scheduling [21])*.

3. Most flows are very short (<50KB) and RTTs minimal ($\approx 300 \mu sec$). Consequently, reaction time-scales are short, and centralized, or heavy weight mechanisms to reserve bandwidth for flows are impractical.

In this paper, we present D^3, a Deadline-Driven Delivery control protocol, that addresses the aforementioned challenges. Inspired by proposals to manage network congestion through explicit rate control [11,19], D^3 explores the feasibility of exploiting deadline information to control the rate at which endhosts introduce traffic in the network. Specifically, applications expose the flow deadline and size information at flow initiation time. Endhosts use this information to request rates from routers along the data path to the destination. Routers thus allocate sending rates to flows to greedily satisfy as many deadlines as possible.

Despite the fact that flows get assigned different rates, instead of fair share, D^3 *does not* require routers to maintain per-flow state. By capitalizing on the nature of trust in the datacenter environment, both the state regarding flow sending rates and rate policing are delegated to endhosts. Routers only maintain simple aggregate counters. Further, our design ensures that rate assignments behave like "leases" instead of reservations, and are thus unaffected by host or router failures.

To this effect, this paper makes three main contributions:

- We present the case for utilizing flow deadline information to apportion bandwidth in datacenters.

- We present the design, implementation and evaluation of D^3, a congestion control protocol that makes datacenter networks deadline aware. Results from our testbed deployment show that D^3 can effectively double the peak load that a datacenter can support.

- We show that apart from being deadline-aware, D^3 performs well as a congestion control protocol for datacenter networks in its own right. Even without any deadline information, D^3 outperforms TCP in supporting the mix of short and long flows observed in datacenter networks.

While we are convinced of the benefits of tailoring datacenter network design to the soft real time nature of datacenter applications, we also realize that the design space for such a deadline-aware network is vast. There exists a large body of work for satisfying application demands in the Internet. While we discuss these proposals in Section 3, the D^3 design presented here is heavily shaped by the peculiarities of the datacenter environment — its challenges (lots of very short flows, tiny RTTs, etc.) and luxuries (trusted environment, limited legacy concerns, etc.). We believe that D^3 represents a good first step towards a datacenter network stack that is optimized for application requirements and not a retrofitted Internet design.

2. BACKGROUND: TODAY'S DATACENTERS

In this section, we provide a characterization of today's datacenters, highlighting specific features that influence D^3 design.

2.1 Datacenter applications

Partition-aggregate. Today's large-scale, user facing web applications achieve horizontal scalability by partitioning the task of responding to users amongst worker machines (possibly at multiple layers). This partition-aggregate structure is shown in Figure 3, and applies to many web applications like search [4], social networks [6], and recommendation systems [10]. Even data processing services like MapReduce [9] and Dryad [18] follow this model.

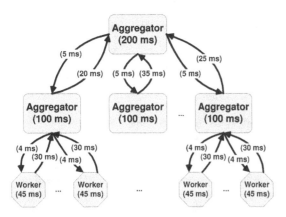

Figure 3: An example of the partition aggregate model with the associated component deadlines in the parentheses.

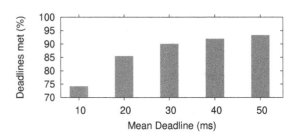

Figure 4: Deadlines met (%) based on datacenter flow completion times.

Application deadlines. The interactive nature of web applications means that latency is key. Customer studies guide the time in which users need to be responded to [20], and after accounting for wide-area network and rendering delays, applications typically have an SLA of 200-300ms to complete their operation and ship out the user reply [10]. These application SLAs lead to SLAs for workers at each layer of the partition aggregate hierarchy. The worker SLAs mean that network flows carrying queries and responses to and from the workers have deadlines (see Figure 3). Any network flow that does not complete by its deadline is not included in the response and typically hurts the response quality, not to mention wastes network bandwidth. Ultimately, this affects operator revenue; for example, an added latency of 100ms costs Amazon 1% of sales [17]. Hence, *network flows have deadlines and these deadlines are (implicitly) baked into all stages of the application operation.*

Deadline variability. Worker processing times can vary significantly. For instance, with search, workers operate on different parts of the index, execute different search algorithms, return varying number of response items, etc. This translates to varying flow deadlines. Datacenter traffic itself further contributes to deadline variability. We mentioned the short *query* and *response* flows between workers. Beyond this, much datacenter traffic comprises of time sensitive, *short messages* (50KB to 1MB) that update the control state at the workers and long *background* flows (5KB to 50MB) that move fresh data to the workers [4]. Of course, the precise traffic pattern varies across applications and datacenters. A Google datacenter running MapReduce jobs will have primarily long flows, some of which may carry deadlines. Hence, *today's datacenters have a diverse mix of flows with widely varying deadlines. Some flows, like background flows, may not have deadlines.*

Missed deadlines. To quantify the prevalence of missed deadlines in today's datacenters, we use measurements of flow completion times in datacenters [4]. We were unable to obtain flow deadline information, and resort to capturing their high variability by assuming that deadlines are exponentially distributed. Figure 4 shows the percentage of flows that meet their deadlines with varying mean for the deadline distribution. We find that even with lax deadlines (mean=40ms), more than 7% of flows miss their deadline. Our evaluation (section 6) shows that this results from network inefficiencies. Application designers struggle to cope

with the impact of such inefficiencies [4], and this might mean artificially limiting the peak load a datacenter can support so that application SLAs are met. Hence, *a significant fraction of flow deadlines are missed in today's datacenters.*

Flow sizes. Since deadlines are associated with flows, all packets of a flow need to arrive before its deadline. Thus, a-priori knowledge of the flow size is important. Indeed, for most interactive web applications today, the size of network flows initiated by workers and aggregators is known in advance. As a specific example, in web search, queries to workers are fixed in size while responses essentially include the top-k matching index records (where k is specified in the query). Thus, the size of the response flow is known to the application code at the worker even before it begins processing. The same holds for many other building block services like key-value stores [6,10], data processing [9,18], etc. Even for applications where this condition does not hold, the application designer can typically provide a good estimate of the expected flow sizes. Hence, *many web applications have knowledge of the flow size at flow initiation time.*

2.2 TCP in Datacenters

The problems resulting from the use of TCP in datacenters are well documented [8,23]. Bursts of concurrent flows that are all too common with the partition aggregate application structure can cause a severe drop in network throughput (incast). Beyond this, the presence of long flows, when combined with TCP's tendency to drive queues to losses, hurts the latency of query-response flows. These problems have placed artificial limitations on application design, with designers resorting to modifying application workflow to address the problems [4].[2]

Motivated by these issues, recent proposals have developed novel congestion control protocols or even moved to UDP to address the problems [4,22]. These protocols aim to ensure: (i) low latency for short flows, even in the face of bursts, and (ii) good utilization for long flows. We concur that this should be the baseline for any new datacenter transport protocol and aim to achieve these goals. *We further argue that these minimum requirements should ideally be combined with the ability to ensure that the largest possible fraction of flows meet their deadlines.* Finally, many application level solutions (like SEDA [25]) deal with variable application load. However, they are not well suited for network/transport problems since the datacenter network is shared amongst multiple applications. Further, applications do not have visibility into the network state (congestion, fail-

---

[2]Restrictions on the fan-out factor for aggregators and the size of the response flows from workers to aggregator are a couple of examples of the limitations imposed.

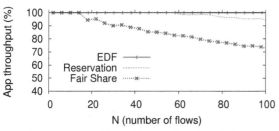

Figure 5: Application throughput with varying number of flows across a single bottleneck link and moderate deadlines. Confidence intervals are within 1% of the presented values.

ures, etc.). On the contrary, a deadline-aware network can complement load-aware applications by explicitly honoring their demands.

3. DESIGN SPACE AND MOTIVATION

The past work for satisfying application deadlines in the Internet can be categorized in two broad classes. The first class of solutions involve packet scheduling in the network based on deadlines. An example of such scheduling is Earliest Deadline First (EDF) [21] wherein routers prioritize packets based on their per-hop deadlines. EDF is an optimal scheduling discipline in that if a set of flow deadlines can be satisfied under any discipline, EDF can satisfy them too. The second solution category involves rate reservations. A deadline flow with size s and deadline d can be satisfied by reserving rate $r = \frac{s}{d}$. Rate reservation mechanisms have been extensively studied. For example, ATM supported Constant Bit Rate (CBR) traffic. In packet switched networks, efforts in both industry (IntServ, DiffServ) and academia [5,12] have explored mechanisms to reserve bandwidth or at least, guarantee performance.

Value of deadline awareness. Given this existing body of work, we attempt through simple Monte Carlo simulations, to build some intuition regarding the (possible) benefits of these approaches over fair sharing used in datacenters today.

Consider a 1Gbps link carrying several flows with varying deadlines. Flow parameters (such as the size and the fraction of short and long flows) are chosen to be consistent with typical datacenters [4]. For the flows with deadlines, the deadlines are chosen to be exponentially distributed around 20ms (tight), 30ms (moderate) and 40ms (lax). To capture the lack of application value of flows that miss their deadline, we use *application throughput* or the number of flows that meet their deadline as the performance metric of interest.

Using this simple simulation setup, we evaluate three "ideal" bandwidth allocation schemes: (i) *Fair-share*, where the link bandwidth is allocated evenly amongst all current flows and represents the best-case scenario for today's deadline agnostic protocols like TCP, DCTCP [4], XCP [19], etc. (ii) *EDF*, representing the first broad class of deadline aware solutions, where the flow with the earliest deadline receives all the bandwidth until it finishes, and (iii) *Rate reservation* (i.e., the second category), where flows, in the order of their arrival, reserve the rate needed to meet their deadline. In contrast to fair-share, the latter two approaches are deadline aware.

Figure 5 shows the application throughput for the three approaches with moderate deadlines (see [26] for similar results with tight and lax deadlines). *As the number of flows increases, deadline-aware approaches significantly outperform fair sharing.* Perhaps most important is the fact that they can support *three to five times* as many flows as fair share without missing any deadline (application throughput=100%). This, in effect, redefines the peak loads at which a datacenter can operate without impacting the user experience. Hence, deadline-aware approaches have a lot to offer towards datacenter performance. However, practical challenges remain for both types of solutions, scheduling as well as reservations.

For the former class, we use EDF as an example to explain its limitations, though our arguments are general. EDF is packet based. It works on per-hop packet deadlines while datacenter applications have end-to-end flow deadlines. As a result, even though EDF is optimal when the deadlines can be satisfied, when there is congestion, EDF can actually drive the network towards congestive collapse (see figure for tight deadlines in [26]). Second and perhaps more importantly, EDF still needs to be complemented by an endhost rate control design that will ensure that routers have the right packets to schedule. Designing such a distributed rate control scheme is far from trivial. Finally, EDF requires priority queuing at routers. Our testbed experiments in Section 6 illustrate some of these limitations for a simple priority scheme.

For the latter class, reservation schemes are too heavy weight for the datacenter environment where most flows are short. Further, unlike real-time traffic on the Internet, datacenter flows do not require a "constant" rate. Reservation schemes ignore this flexibility and reduce network efficiency, especially given the dynamics on datacenter networks, where network conditions change very fast (e.g., tiny RTTs, large bursts of short flows).

Overall, these limitations motivate the need for a practical datacenter congestion control protocol that, on the one hand, ensures flows meet their deadlines, but, on the other, avoids packet scheduling and explicit reservations.

4. D³ DESIGN

The discussion in the two previous sections leads to the following goals for datacenter congestion control:

1. *Maximize application throughput*: The protocol should strive to maximize the number of flows that satisfy their deadlines and hence, contribute to application throughput.

2. *Burst tolerance*: Application workflows often lead to flow bursts, and the network should be able to accommodate these.

3. *High utilization*: For flows without deadlines, the protocol should maximize network throughput.

D³ is designed to achieve these goals. Beyond these explicit goals, D³ accounts for the luxuries and challenges of the datacenter environment. For instance, an important luxury is the fact that the datacenter is a homogenous environment owned by a single entity. Consequently, incremental deployment, backwards compatibility, and being friendly to legacy protocols are *non-goals*.

The key insight guiding D³ design is the following: given a flow's size and deadline, one can determine the rate needed to satisfy the flow deadline. Endhosts can thus ask the network for the required rate. There already exist protocols for explicit rate control wherein routers assign sending rates to endhosts [11,19]. With D^3, we extend these schemes to assign flows with rates based on their deadlines, instead of the fair share.

Assumptions. Based on the previous discussion, our design assumes that the flow size and deadline information are available at flow initiation time. Further, we also assume that per-flow paths are static.

4.1 Rate control

With D^3, applications expose the size and deadline information when initiating a deadline flow. The source endhost uses this to request a *desired rate*, r. Given a flow of size s and deadline d, the initial desired rate is given by $r = \frac{s}{d}$. This rate request, carried in the packet header, traverses the routers along the path to the destination. Each router assigns an *allocated rate* that is fed back to the source through the acknowledgement packet on the reverse path. The source thus receives a vector of allocated rates, one for each router along the path. The sending rate is the minimum of the allocated rates. The source sends data at this rate for a RTT while piggybacking a rate request for the next RTT on one of the data packets.

Note however that neither does a flow need, nor does it obtain a reservation for a specific sending rate throughout its duration. The rate that the network can offer varies with traffic load and hence, each source must periodically (in our case, every RTT) ask the network for a new allocation. Since the actual rate allocated by the network can be more or less than the desired rate, endhosts update the desired rate as the flow progresses based on the deadline and the remaining flow size.

4.2 Rate allocation

For each of their outgoing interfaces, routers receive rate requests from flows with deadlines. Beyond this, there are flows without deadlines, where $r = 0$. Hence, the *rate allocation problem* is defined as: Given rate requests, a router needs to allocate rates to flows so as to maximize the number of deadlines satisfied (goal 1) and fully utilize the network capacity (goal 3). In a dynamic setting, this rate allocation problem is NP-complete [7].

We adopt a greedy approach to allocate rates. When a router receives a rate request packet with desired rate r, it strives to assign at least r. If the router has spare capacity after satisfying rate requests for all deadline flows, it distributes the spare capacity fairly amongst all current flows. Hence, when the router capacity is more than the capacity needed to satisfy all deadline flows, the allocated rate a given to a flow is:

- For a deadline flow with desired rate r, $a = (r + fs)$, where fs is the fair share of the spare capacity after satisfying deadline flow requests.

- For a non-deadline flow, $a = fs$.

We note that distributing the spare capacity between deadline and non-deadline flows allows us to balance the competing goals 1 and 3. Assigning deadline flows with a rate greater than their desired rate ensures that their subsequent rate requests will be lower and the network will be able to

satisfy future deadline flows. At the same time, assigning non-deadline flows with a share of the spare capacity ensures that they make progress and network utilization remains high.

However, in case the router does not have enough capacity to satisfy all deadline flows, it greedily tries to satisfy the rate requests for as many deadline flows as possible. The remaining flows, deadline and non-deadline, are assigned a **base rate** that allows them to send a header-only packet per RTT and hence, request rates in the future. For deadline flows, such low assignments will cause the desired rate to increase. The endhosts can thus decide whether to give up on flows based on an ever increasing desired rate. This is further discussed in Section 6.1.3.

4.3 Router operation

The rate allocation description above assumes the router has the rate requests for all flows at the same point in time. In reality, the router needs to make allocation decisions in an online, dynamic setting, i.e., rate requests are spread over time, and flows start and finish. To achieve this, the rate allocation operates in a slotted fashion (from the perspective of the endhosts). The rate allocated to a flow is valid for the next RTT, after which the flow must request again. A rate request at time t serves two purposes: (1). It requires the router to assign a_{t+1}, the allocated rate for the next RTT, and (2). It returns a_t, the allocation for the current RTT.

To achieve (1), the router needs to track its existing allocations. Consequently, routers maintain three simple, aggregate counters for each interface:

- N: number of flows traversing the interface. Routers use flow initiation and termination packets (TCP SYN/FIN) to increment and decrement N respectively.[3]

- Demand counter (D): sum of the desired rates for deadline flows. This represents the total demand imposed by flows with deadlines.

- Allocation counter (A): sum of allocated rates. This is the current total allocation.

To achieve (2), the router must know the current rate allocated to the flow. In a naive design, a router could maintain rate allocations for each active flow through it. However, since most deadline flows are very short, such an approach is too heavy-weight, not to mention router memory intensive. We avoid the need for per-flow state on routers by relying on endhosts to convey rate allocations for each flow. Specifically, each rate request packet, apart from the desired rate r_{t+1}, contains the rate requested in the previous interval (r_t) and a vector of the rates allocated in the previous interval ($[a_t]$). Each element in the vector corresponds to the rate allocated by a router along the path in the previous interval. The encoding of these in the rate request packet header is described in Section 5.

For topologies with multiple paths between endhosts [13] [1,2,15], D^3 relies on ECMP, VLB and other existing mechanisms used with TCP to ensure that a given flow follows a

---

[3]Note that past rate control schemes [11,19] approximate N as C/R, where C is the interface capacity and R is the current rate being assigned to flows. Yet, D^3 does not assign the same rate to each flow and this approximation is not applicable.

single path. Adapting D^3 to use multiple paths for a single flow requires additional mechanisms and is beyond the scope of this work.

Given this, we can now describe how packets are processed by routers. *Routers have no notion of flow RTTs.* Packets without rate request headers are forwarded just as today. Snippet 1 shows how a router processes a rate request packet. It applies to both deadline and non-deadline flows (for the latter, desired rate r_{t+1} is 0). The router first uses the packet header information to perform bookkeeping. This includes the flow returning its current allocation (line 3). Lines 7-13 implement the rate allocation scheme (Section 4.2) where the router calculates a_{t+1}, the rate to be allocated to the flow. The router adds this to the packet header and forwards the packet.

Snippet 1 Rate request processing at interval t

Packet contains: Desired rate r_{t+1}, and past information r_t and a_t. Link capacity is C.

Router calculates: Rate allocated to flow (a_{t+1}).
1: //For new flows only
2: **if** (new_flow_flag_set) $N = N + 1$
3: $A = A - a_t$ //Return current allocation
4: $D = D - r_t + r_{t+1}$ //Update demand counter
   //Calculate left capacity
5: $left\_capacity = C - A$
   //Calculate fair share
6: $fs = (C - D)/N$

7: **if** $left\_capacity > r_{t+1}$ **then**
8:    //Enough capacity to satisfy request
9:    $a_{t+1} = r_{t+1} + fs$
10: **else**
11:    //Not enough capacity to satisfy request
12:    $a_{t+1} = left\_capacity$
13: **end if**
   //Flows get at least base rate
14: $a_{t+1} = max(a_{t+1}, base\_rate)$
   //Update allocation counter
15: $A = A + a_{t+1}$

Of particular interest is the scenario where the router does not have enough capacity to satisfy a rate request (lines 11-12). This can occur in a couple of scenarios. First, the cumulative rate required by existing deadline flows, represented by the demand counter, may exceed the router capacity. In this case, the router simply satisfies as many requests as possible in the order of their arrival. In the second scenario, the demand does not exceed the capacity but fair share allocations to existing flows imply that when the rate request arrives, there is not enough spare capacity. However, the increased demand causes the fair share assigned to the subsequent rate requests to be reduced (line 6). Consequently, when the deadline flow in question requests for a rate in the next interval, the router should be able to satisfy the request.

4.4 Good utilization and low queuing

The rate given by a router to a flow is based on the assumption that the flow is bottlenecked at the router. In a multihop network, this may not be true. To account for bottlenecks that occur earlier along the path, a router ensures that its allocation is never more than that of the previous router. This information is available in the rate allocation vector being carried in the packet header. However, the flow may still be bottlenecked downstream from the router and may not be able to utilize its allocation.

Further, the veracity of the allocation counter maintained by a router depends on endhosts returning their allocations. When a flow ends, the final rate request packet carrying the FIN flag returns the flow's allocated rate. While endhosts are trusted to follow the protocol properly, failures and bugs do happen. This will cause the router to over-estimate the allocated rate, and, as a result, penalize the performance of active flows.

The aforementioned problems impact router utilization. On the other hand, a burst of new flows can cause the router to temporarily allocate more bandwidth than its capacity, which results in queuing. To account for all these cases, we borrow from [11,19] and periodically adjust the router capacity based on observed utilization and queuing as follows:

$$C(t + T) = C(t) + \alpha(C(t) - \frac{u(t)}{T}) - \beta(\frac{q}{T})$$

where, C is router capacity at time t, T is the update interval, u is bytes sent over the past interval, q is instantaneous queue size and α, β are chosen for stability and performance.[4]

Consequently, when there is under-utilization $(u/T < C)$, the router compensates by allocating more total capacity in the next interval, while when there is queuing $(q(t) > 0)$, the allocations reduce. Apart from addressing the downstream bottleneck problem, this ensures that the counters maintained by routers are soft state and divergence from reality does not impact correctness. The failure of endhosts and routers may cause flows to not return their allocation. However, the resulting drop in utilization drives up the capacity and hence, the allocation counters do not have to be consistent with reality. The router, during periods of low load, resets its counters to return to a consistent state. Even in an extreme worst case scenario, where bugs at endhosts lead to incorrect rate requests, this will only cause a degradation in the performance of the application in question, but will have no further effects in the operation of the router or the network.

4.5 Burst tolerance

Bursts of flows are common in datacenters. Such bursts are particularly challenging because of tiny RTTs in the datacenter. With a typical RTT of $300\mu s$, a new flow sending even just one 1500-byte packet per RTT equates to a send rate of 40Mbps! Most TCP implementations shipping today start with a send window of two packets and hence, a mere 12-13 new flows can cause queuing and packet loss on a 1Gbps link. This has been observed in past work [8,23] and is also present our experiments.

With D^3, a new flow starts with a rate request packet with the SYN flag set. Such a request causes N to be incremented and reduces the fair share for flows. However, pre-existing flows may already have been allocated a larger fair share rate

---

[4]The α, β values are chosen according to the discussion in [11] where the stability of this controller was shown, and are set to 0.1 and 1 in our implementation. The update interval T should be larger than the datacenter propagation RTT; in our implementation it is set to $800\mu s$. The equation assumes at least one flow is bottlenecked on the link.

(N was less when the earlier rate requests were processed). Hence, allocating each new flow with its proper fair share can cause the router to allocate an aggregate rate larger than its capacity, especially when a burst of new flows arrives.

We rely on D^3's ability to "pause" flows by assigning them the base rate to alleviate bursts. When a new flow starts, the fair share assigned to its rate request is set to base rate. For non-deadline flows, this effectively asks them to pause for a RTT and not send any data packets. The sender however does send a packet with only the rate request (i.e., a header-only packet) in the next RTT and the router assigns it with a fair share as normal. This implies that a new non-deadline flow does not make progress for an extra RTT at startup. However, such flows are typically long. Further, RTTs are minimal, and this approach trades-off a minor overhead in bandwidth and latency (one RTT $\sim 300\mu s$) for a lot of burst tolerance. Our evaluation shows that this vastly improves D^3's ability to cope with flow bursts over the state of the art. Additionally, this does not impact deadline flows much because the router still tries to honor their desired rate.

5. IMPLEMENTATION

We have created an endhost-based stack and a proof-of-concept router that support the D^3 protocol. This paper focuses on the congestion control aspects of D^3 but our implementation provides a complete transport protocol that provides reliable, in-order delivery of packets. As with TCP, reliability is achieved through sequence numbers for data packets, acknowledgements from receivers, timer-based retransmissions and flow control.

On endhosts, D^3 is exposed to applications through an extended Sockets-like API. The extensions allow applications to specify the flow length and deadline when a socket is created. The core logic for D^3, including the rate control scheme, runs in user space. We have a kernel driver that is bound to the Ethernet interface exposed by the NIC driver. The kernel driver efficiently marshals packets between NIC and the user-level stack.

The router is implemented on a server-grade PC and implements a shared buffer, store and forward architecture. To be consistent with shallow buffers in today's datacenters, the router has a buffer of 128KB per NIC. The router uses the same kernel driver as the endhosts, except the driver is bound to multiple Ethernet interfaces. All incoming packets pass to a user space process, which processes and forwards them on the appropriate interface. The design of the kernel driver and user-space application support zero-copy of packets.

Router overhead. To keep per-packet overhead low in the router, we use integer arithmetic for all rate calculations. Although each packet traverses the user-kernel space boundary, we are able to sustain four links at full duplex line rate. *Specifically, the average packet processing time was less than 1μs (0.208μs), and was indistinguishable from normal packet forwarding in user-space.* Thus, D^3 imposes minimal overhead on the forwarding path and the performance of our prototype leads us to believe that it is feasible to implement D^3 in a commodity router.

Packet header. The D^3 request and rate feedback packet header is shown in Figure 6. The congestion header includes the desired rate r_{t+1}, an index into the allocation vector and the current allocation vector ($[a_{t+1}]$). The header also includes the allocations for the previous RTT so that the

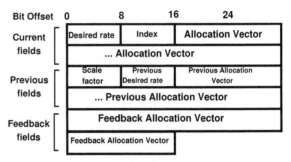

Figure 6: Congestion header for rate request and feedback packets.

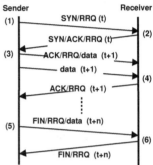

Figure 7: Packet exchange with D^3. RRQ is Rate Request. Text in parenthesis is the current RTT interval.

routers can update their relevant counters - the desired rate r_t and the vector of rates allocated by the routers ($[a_t]$). Finally, the header carries rate feedback to the destination - a vector of rates allocated by the routers for reverse traffic from the destination to the source.

All rates are in Bytes/μs and hence, can be encoded in one byte; 1Gbps equates to a value of 125. The scale factor byte can be used to scale this and would allow encoding of much higher rates. The allocation vectors are 6 bytes long, allowing for a maximum network diameter of 6 routers (or switches). We note that current datacenters have three-tiered, tree-like topologies [13] with a maximum diameter of 5 switches. The allocation vectors could be made variable length fields to achieve extensibility. Overall, our current implementation imposes an overhead of 22 bytes for every packet carrying rate requests.

Protocol description. The protocol operation is illustrated in Figure 7. (1). The sender initiates the flow by sending a SYN packet with a rate request. Routers along the path allocate rate and add it to the current allocation vector in the congestion header. (2). Receivers respond with a SYN/ACK and a rate request of their own. The congestion header of the response includes the allocated rate vector for the sender. (3). The sender uses this vector to determine its sending rate and sends data packets. One of these includes a rate request for the next RTT. (5). Once the sender is done, it sends a FIN packet and returns its existing allocation.

Calculating desired rate. The sender uses information about flow deadline and remaining flow length to determine the desired rate that would allow the flow to meet its deadline. At interval t, the desired rate for the next RTT is given by

$$rt + 1 = \frac{remaining\_flow\_length - s_t * rtt}{deadline - 2 * rtt}$$

where s_t is the current sending rate, and rtt is the sender's current estimate of the RTT for the flow, which is based on an exponential moving average of the instantaneous RTT values. The numerator accounts for the fact that by the next RTT, the sender would have sent $s_t * rtt$ bytes worth of more data. The denominator is the remaining time to achieve the deadline: one rtt is subtracted since the rate will be received in the next RTT, while the second rtt accounts for the FIN exchange to terminate the flow.

6. EVALUATION

We deployed D^3 across a small testbed structured like the multi-tier tree topologies used in today's datacenters. The testbed (Figure 8) includes twelve endhosts arranged across four racks. Each rack has a top-of-rack (ToR) switch, and the ToR switches are connected through a root switch. All endhosts and switches are Dell Precision T3500 servers with a quad core Intel Xeon 2.27GHz processor, 4GB RAM and 1 Gbps interfaces, running Windows Server 2008 R2. The root switch is further connected to two other servers that are used as traffic generators to model traffic from other parts of the datacenter. For two endhosts in the same rack communicating through the ToR switch, the propagation RTT, measured when there is no queuing, is roughly $500\mu s$. The endhosts are also connected to a dedicated 48-port 1Gbps NetGear GS748Tv3 switch (not shown in the figure). We use this for TCP experiments.

Our evaluation has two primary goals: (i). To determine the value of using flow deadline information to apportion network bandwidth. (ii). To evaluate the performance of D^3 just as congestion control protocol, without deadline information. This includes its queuing and utilization behavior, and performance in a multi-bottleneck, multi-hop setting.

6.1 Exploiting deadlines through D^3

To evaluate the benefit of exploiting deadline information, we compare D^3 against TCP. However, TCP is well known to not be amenable to datacenter traffic patterns. To capture the true value of deadline awareness, we also operate D^3 in fair share mode only, i.e., without any deadline information and all flows treated as non-deadline flows. We term this RCP_{dc} since it is effectively RCP optimized for the datacenter.[5] With RCP_{dc}, the fair share is explicitly communicated to the hosts (i.e., no probe-based exploration is required) and it has been shown to be optimal in terms minimizing flow completion times [11]. Hence, it represents the limit for any fair share protocol, such as DCTCP [4] and other recent proposals for datacenters like QCN [3] and E-TCP [14]. We further contrast D^3 against deadline-based priority queuing of TCP flows. Priority queuing was implemented by replacing the Netgear switch with a Cisco router that offers port-based priority capabilities. Flows with short deadlines are mapped to high priority ports. Our evaluation covers the following scenarios:

- *Flow burst microbenchmarks.* This scenario reflects the case where a number of workers start flows at the same

[5]While the core functionality of RCP_{dc} mimics RCP, we have introduced several optimizations to exploit the trusted nature of datacenters. The most important of these include: exact estimates of the number of flows at the router (RCP uses algorithms to approximate this), the introduction of base rate, the pause for one RTT to alleviate bursts, etc.

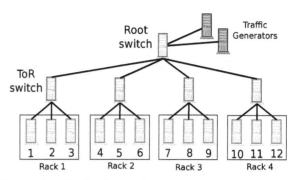

Figure 8: Testbed topology: red servers are end-hosts, blue are switches, grey are traffic generators.

time towards the same destination. It provides a lower-bound on the expected performance gain as all flows compete at the same bottleneck at the same time. Our results show that D^3 can *support almost twice the number of workers*, without compromising deadlines, compared to RCP_{dc}, TCP and TCP with priority queuing (henceforth referred to as TCP_{pr}).

- *Benchmark traffic.* This scenario represents typical datacenter traffic patterns (e.g., flow arrivals, flow sizes) and is indicative of the expected D^3 performance with current datacenter settings. The evaluation highlights that D^3 offers an order of magnitude improvement over out of the box TCP and a factor of two improvement over an optimized TCP version and RCP_{dc}.

- *Flow quenching.* We evaluate the value of terminating flows that do not contribute to application throughput. Our results show that flow quenching ensures the D^3 performance degrades gracefully under extreme load.

6.1.1 Flow burst microbenchmarks

In this scenario, a host in each rack serves as an aggregator (see Figure 3) while other hosts in the rack represent workers responding to an aggregator query. This is a common application scenario for online services. All workers respond at the same time and all response flows are bottlenecked at the link from the rack's ToR switch to the aggregator. Since there are only three hosts in each rack, we use multiple workers per host. We also repeated the experiment on a restructured testbed with more hosts per rack and the results remained qualitatively the same.

The response flow lengths are uniformly distributed across [2KB, 50KB] and the flow deadlines are distributed exponentially around 20ms (tight), 30ms (moderate) and 40ms (lax). As described earlier, the primary performance metric is *application throughput*, that is, the number of flows finishing before their deadline. *This metric was intentionally chosen as datacenter operators are primarily interested in the "operating regime" where the network can satisfy almost all flow deadlines.* Hence, we vary the number of workers sending flows and across 200 runs of this experiment, determine the maximum number of concurrent senders a given congestion control scheme supports while ensuring at least 99% application throughput. This is shown in Figure 9.

As compared to RCP_{dc}, D^3 *can support almost twice as many concurrent senders while satisfying flow deadlines* (3-4 times as compared to TCP and TCP_{pr}). This is because D^3 uses flow deadline information to guide bandwidth ap-

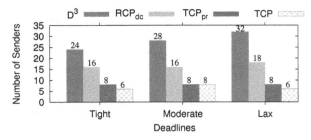

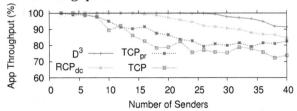

Figure 9: Number of concurrent senders that can be supported while ensuring more than 99% application throughput.

Figure 10: Application throughput for varying concurrent senders and moderate deadlines (the Y-axis starts at 60%).

portioning. This is further pronounced for relaxed deadlines where D^3 has more flexibility and hence, the increase in the number of senders supported compared to tight deadlines is greater than for other approaches. Note that since congestion occurs at the aggregator's downlink, richer topologies like VL2 [13] or FatTree [2] cannot solve the problem.

For completeness, Figure 10 shows the application throughput with moderate deadlines as we vary the number of concurrent senders to 40. Results look similar with tight and lax deadlines [26]. While the performance of these protocols beyond the regime of high application throughput may not be of primary operator importance, the figure does help us understand application throughput trends under severe (unplanned) load spikes. Apart from being able to support more senders while ensuring no deadlines are missed, when the number of senders does become too high for D^3 to satisfy all deadlines, it still improves application throughput by roughly 20% over TCP, and 10% or more, over RCP_{dc} and TCP_{pr}. Hence, even if we relax our "operating-regime" metric to be less demanding, for example, to 95% of application throughput, D^3 can support 36 senders with moderate deadlines compared to the 22, 10 and 8 senders of RCP_{dc}, TCP_{pr} and TCP respectively.

The figure also illustrates that RCP_{dc} outperforms TCP at high loads. This is because probe-based protocols like TCP attempt to discover their fair share by causing queues to build up and eventually, losses, ergo increasing latency for a number of flows. Instead, RCP_{dc} avoids queueing by equally dividing the available capacity. Figure 11 highlights this point by displaying the scatter plots of flow completion times versus flow deadlines for TCP, RCP_{dc} and D^3 for one of the experiments (moderate deadlines, 14-30 senders). For TCP, it is evident that packet losses result in TCP time-outs and very long completion times for some flows. Since the hardware switch has a buffer of 100KB, a mere eight simultaneous senders with a send-window of eight full sized packets can lead to a loss; this is why TCP performance starts degrading around eight senders in Figure 10.[6]

---

[6]The mean flow size in our experiments is 26KB. Hence, a

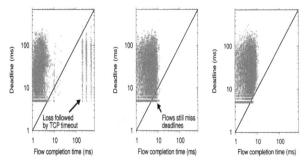

Figure 11: Scatter plot of flow completion times vs. deadlines for TCP (left), RCP_{dc} (middle), and D^3 (right). Points above the diagonal reflect flows that have met their deadlines.

Fair share protocols, like RCP_{dc} and DCTCP, address precisely this issue by ensuring no losses and short queues in the network; yet, as they are unaware of deadlines, a large number of flows still miss their associated deadlines (see middle Figure 11). For these particular experiments, RCP_{dc} misses 8.1% of flow deadlines as compared to 1% for D^3. Further, looking at flows that do miss deadlines, RCP_{dc} causes their completion time to exceed their deadline by 75% at the 95th percentile (30% on average). With D^3, completion times are extended by 27.7% at the 95th percentile (9% on average). This implies that *even if deadlines were "soft", fair share protocols still suffer, as a non-negligible fraction of flows exceed their deadline significantly.* This is not acceptable for datacenters where good performance has to be ensured for a very high percentile of flows.

For TCP_{pr}, we use two-level priorities. Flows with short deadlines are mapped to the higher priority class. Such "deadline awareness" improves its performance over TCP. However, it remains hampered by TCP's congestion control algorithm and suffers from losses. Increasing the priority classes to four (maximum supported by the switch) does not improve performance significantly. Simply using priorities with RCP_{dc} will not help either. This is because deadlines can vary a lot and require a high number of priority classes while today's switches only support O(10) classes. Further, as discussed in Section 3, switch prioritization is packet-based while deadlines are associated with flows. Finally, bursty datacenter traffic implies that instead of statically mapping flows to priority classes, what is needed is to dynamically prioritize flows based on deadlines and network conditions. D^3 tackles precisely all these issues.

With background flows. We repeat the above flow burst experiment by adding long, background flows. Such flows are used to update the workers with the latest data, and typically don't have deadlines associated with them. For each run, we start a long flow from a traffic generator to the receiver. This flow is bottlenecked at the link between the receiver and its ToR switch. After five seconds, all senders send their responses ([2KB, 50KB]).

Figure 12 shows the high application throughput operating regime for the three protocols. When compared to the response-flows-only scenario, the relative drop in the maximum number of senders supported is less for D^3 than for TCP, TCP_{pr} and RCP_{dc}. Performance significantly de-

---

majority of flows will require more than 3 RTTs to complete, at which point the TCP send window will exceed 8 packets.

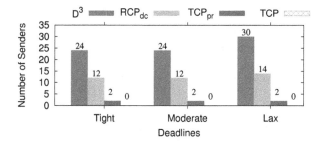

Figure 12: Number of concurrent senders supported while ensuring more than 99% application throughput in the presence of long background flows.

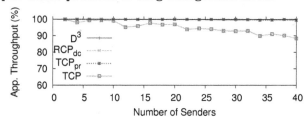

Figure 13: Application throughput with varying number of senders, 2.9KB response flows and one long background flow.

	TCP (reduced RTO)	RCP$_{dc}$	D^3
Flows/s	100 (1100)	1300	2000

Table 1: Flow arrival rate supported while maintaining >99% application throughput.

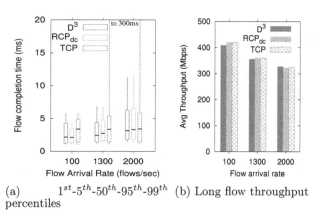

(a) 1st-5th-50th-95th-99th (b) Long flow throughput percentiles

Figure 14: Benchmark traffic including short response flows (poisson arrivals with varying arrival rate) and two long flows.

grades for TCP and TCP$_{pr}$ in the presence of queuing due to background flows, which has been well documented in the past [4]. It is noteworthy that even with only two senders, TCP cannot achieve 99% of application throughput. TCP$_{pr}$ implements a 3-level priority in this scenario, where background flows are assigned to the lowest priority class, and deadline flows are assigned according to their deadline value to the other two priority classes. However, the background flows still consume buffer space and hurt higher priority response flows. Hence, D^3 is even better at satisfying flow deadlines in the presence of background traffic.

With tiny response flows. TCP's travails with flow bursts seen in datacenters have forced application designers to use various "hacks" as workarounds. This includes restricting the response flow size [4]. Here, we repeat the flow burst experiment with a uniform response size of 2.9KB such that response flows are 2 packets long. Further, there exists one long background flow. Figure 13 shows the application throughput with moderate deadlines (mean=30ms). With TCP, the long flow fills up the queue, causing some of the response flows to suffer losses. Consequently, application throughput starts dropping at only 12 senders. As a contrast, the other three approaches satisfy all deadlines untill 40 senders. Since response flows are tiny, there is no room for D^3 to improve upon RCP$_{dc}$ and TCP$_{pr}$. However, our earlier results show that if designers were to be freed of the constraints imposed by TCP inefficiencies, D^3 can provide significant gains over fair sharing approaches and priorities.

Since RCP$_{dc}$ presents an upper limit for fair share protocols and performs better than priorities, in the following sections, we will compare D^3 against RCP$_{dc}$ only; TCP will also be presented as a reference for today's status quo.

6.1.2 Benchmark traffic

In this section, we evaluate the performance of D^3 under realistic datacenter traffic patterns and flow dynamics. As before, we choose one endhost in each rack as the aggrega-tor that receives response flows from the two other endhosts in the rack. The response flow size is uniformly distributed between [2KB, 50KB], and we focus on results with moderate deadlines (mean=30ms). Further, each sender also has one long flow to the aggregator. Both long flows are bottlenecked at the aggregator's link to its ToR switch. This represents the 75th percentile of long flow multiplexing observed in datacenter traffic [4]. We model the response flow arrival as a Poisson process and vary the mean arrival rate. As before, our primary focus is on the flow arrival rate that can be supported while maintaining more than 99% application throughput. This is shown in Table 1.

We find that under realistic traffic dynamics, both D^3 and RCP$_{dc}$ outperform TCP by more than an order of magnitude. These results are best understood by looking at the underlying network level metrics. Figure 14(a) plots the percentiles for flow completion times (1st-5th-50th-95th-99th) at different flow arrival rates. At very low load, the flow completion times for the three protocols are comparable (TCP's median flow completion time is 50% higher than D^3). However, as the flow arrival rate increases, the presence of long flows and the resulting queuing with TCP inevitably causes some response flows to drop packets. Even at 200 flows/s, more than 1% flows suffer drops and miss their deadlines. Given the retransmission timeout value (RTO=300ms), the 99th percentile flow completion time for TCP is more than 300ms. Reducing the RTO to a lower value like 10ms [23] does help TCP to improve its performance by being able to support roughly 1100 flows (Table 1). Yet, even with this optimization, TCP can support less than half the flows supported by D^3.

The flow completion times for D^3 and RCP$_{dc}$ are similar throughout. For instance, even at 2000 flows/s, the 99th percentile completion time is almost the same even though D^3 can satisfy 99% of flow deadlines while RCP$_{dc}$ can only satisfy 96.5% flow deadlines. We reiterate the fact that deadline awareness does not improve flow completion times over RCP$_{dc}$ (which minimizes them already). However, by being

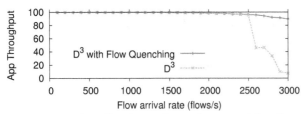

Figure 15: Application throughput with flow quenching

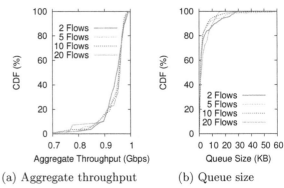

(a) Aggregate throughput   (b) Queue size

Figure 16: D^3 performance with long flows.

cognizant of the flow deadlines, it ensures a greater fraction of flows satisfy them.

We also look at the performance of the long flows to examine whether the gains offered by D^3 come at the expense of (non-deadline) long background flows. Figure 14(b) shows the average throughput achieved by each long flow during the experiment. The figure shows that long flows do not suffer with D^3. Instead, it achieves its gains by smarter allocation of resources amongst the deadline flows.

6.1.3 Flow quenching

The results above illustrate the benefits of unfair sharing. Beyond this, deadline awareness can also guide "flow quenching" to cope with severe congestion. As described in Section 1, under extreme duress, it may be better to shed some load and ensure that a good fraction of flows meet their deadlines, rather than to run all flows to completion even though most will miss their deadlines. D^3 design is particularly suited to such flow quenching. Since endhosts know the rate needed to satisfy their deadlines and the rate the network can offer, they can independently decide whether to continue with the flow or not.

We implemented a straightforward flow quenching mechanism wherein endhosts prematurely terminate flows (by sending a FIN) when: (i). desired rate exceeds their uplink capacity, or (ii). the deadline has already expired. Figure 15 shows the application throughput with such flow quenching for the benchmark traffic experiment.

Flow quenching leads to a smoother decline in performance at extreme loads. From the application perspective, fewer end users get empty responses. Beyond 2500 flows/s, D^3 cannot cope with the network load since the flow arrival rate exceeds the flow departure rate. Consequently, the application throughput drops drastically as the network suffers congestive collapse. However, with flow quenching, endhosts do not pursue intractable deadlines which, in turn, spares bandwidth for other flows whose deadlines can be met.

6.2 D^3 as a congestion control protocol

We also evaluated the performance of D^3 as a congestion control protocol in its own right, operating without any deadline information. Results in earlier sections already show that D^3 (and RCP_{dc}) outperforms TCP in terms of short flow latency and tolerance of flow bursts. Here we look at other aspects of D^3 performance.

Throughput and Queuing. We first evaluate the behavior of D^3 with long flows to determine the network throughput achieved. To this effect, we start a varying number of flows (2-20) to an endhost and record the flow throughput at 1ms intervals. Figure 16(a) shows that the aggregate throughput remains the same as we increase the number of long flows with a median and average network throughput of 0.95Gbps (95% of capacity). Overall, D^3 matches the performance offered by TCP for long flows.

We also measured the instantaneous queue length on the bottleneck link to determine D^3's queuing behavior. This is plotted in Figure 16(b). For all scenarios, the average queue size is 4-6KB, the median is 1.5KB while the 99th percentile is 16.5-48KB. As a contrast, TCP tends to drive long flows to fill switch buffers, resulting in much larger queues. This impacts any short (deadline) flows that share the same bottleneck. Even compared to DCTCP, D^3 achieves the same throughput with queues that are shorter by a factor of five. **Multi-hop, multi-bottleneck setting.** We have also evaluated the performance of D^3 in a multi-hop network. Due to space limitations, the results are discussed in [26]. Overall, our experiments show that D^3 performs well in scenarios with both multiple hops as well as multiple bottlenecks.

7. DISCUSSION

While we have evaluated many aspects of D^3 design and performance, a number of issues were not discussed in detail. We briefly comment on the most important of these here. *Deployability.* D^3 takes a radical tact to align the datacenter network to application requirements. It mandates changes to almost every participant: applications, endhosts, and network elements. While in all cases these changes might be considered easy to implement, the choice of modifying the main components is quite intentional. Discussions with both datacenter operators and application designers have revealed that they are quite willing to adopt new designs that would free them from the artificial restrictions posed by existing retrofitted protocols. This is especially true if the added benefit is significant, as in the case of D^3. The use of a UDP-based transport protocol by Facebook is a good example of the extra miles designers are willing to go to overcome current limitations [22].

The biggest hurdle to D^3 deployment may be the changes necessitated to network elements. From a technical perspective, we have strived to restrict the state maintained and the processing done by a D^3 router to a bare minimum. This allowed our user-space software implementation to easily achieve line-rates and bodes well for a hardware implementation. For instance, like RCP [11], D^3 can be implemented on NetFPGA boards.

As mentioned in Section 4, co-existence with existing protocols, such as TCP or other non-D^3 traffic, was a non-goal for D^3. However, we do admit that a flag day where an entire datacenter moves to D^3-only traffic may not be realistic, and incremental deployment is desirable. In this regard, we believe that D^3's performance should not be impacted by low-rate TCP or UDP traffic (e.g., control traffic), as rate allocations at routers do account for the observed utilization through the estimation of C. However, a detailed examination of D^3's performance in the presence of existing protocols, and incremental deployment with a mix of D^3-enabled and legacy switches is beyond the scope of this work.

Soft vs. hard deadlines. Throughout the paper, D^3 operates under the assumption that deadlines are hard, and once missed, flows are useless. This decision was intentional to stress a, perhaps, extreme design point: *Being deadline aware provides significant value to the network.* On the other hand, one can imagine applications and flows that operate on soft deadlines. Such flows may, for example, gracefully degrade their performance once the deadline is missed without needing to be quenched. The D^3 model can accommodate soft deadlines in a number of ways. For example, since the host controls the requested rate, flows with soft requirements could extend their deadlines if these are missed, or fall back to fair share mode; alternatively, a two-stage allocation process in the router could be implemented, where demands are met in the order of importance (e.g., where not all deadlines are of equal value) depending on the network congestion. Yet, even with the presence of soft deadlines, the evaluation in Section 6 stresses the benefits of deadline-aware protocols. Another extended use-case involves persistent flows with changing deadlines. D^3 can be modified to handle this as long as deadline changes are communicated to the protocol. Such modifications as well as the long-term stability of the protocol under various types of workloads or end-host failure need further investigation.

8. CONCLUDING REMARKS

D^3 is a control protocol that uses application deadline information to achieve informed allocation of network bandwidth. It explicitly deals with the challenges of the datacenter environment - small RTTs, and a bursty, diverse traffic mix with widely varying deadlines. Our evaluation shows that D^3 is practical and provides significant benefits over even optimized versions of existing solutions. This, we believe, is a good illustration of how datacenters that are tuned to application requirements and exploit inherent aspects of the underlying network can perform above and beyond the current state of the art. Emerging trends indicate that operators are willing to adopt new designs that address their problems and this bodes well for D^3 adoption.

Acknowledgements

We are grateful to Greg O'Shea, Austin Donnelly, and Paolo Costa for their valuable help. We would also like to thank David Oran for his help and comments during the shepherding process.

9. REFERENCES

[1] H. Abu-Libdeh, P. Costa, A. Rowstron, G. O'Shea, and A. Donnelly. Symbiotic routing in future data centers. In *ACM SIGCOMM*, 2010.

[2] M. Al-Fares, A. Loukissas, and A. Vahdat. A Scalable, Commodity Data Center Network Architecture. In *Proc. of ACM SIGCOMM*, 2008.

[3] M. Alizadeh, B. Atikoglu, A. Kabbani, A. Laksmikantha, R. Pan, B. Prabhakar, and M. Seaman. Data center transport mechanisms: congestion control theory and IEEE standardization. In *Proc. of Allerton Conference on Communications, Control and Computing*, Sept. 2008.

[4] M. Alizadeh, A. G. Greenberg, D. A. Maltz, J. Padhye, P. Patel, B. Prabhakar, S. Sengupta, and M. Sridharan. Data center TCP (DCTCP). In *ACM SIGCOMM*, 2010.

[5] C. Aras, J. Kurose, D. Reeves, and H. Schulzrinne. Real-time communication in packet-switched networks. *Proc. of the IEEE*, 82(1), 1994.

[6] D. Beaver, S. Kumar, H. C. Li, J. Sobel, and P. Vajgel. Finding a Needle in Haystack: Facebook's Photo Storage. In *Proc. of OSDI*, 2010.

[7] B. B. Chen and P.-B. Primet. Scheduling deadline-constrained bulk data transfers to minimize network congestion. In *CCGRID*, May 2007.

[8] Y. Chen, R. Griffith, J. Liu, R. H. Katz, and A. D. Joseph. Understanding TCP incast throughput collapse in datacenter networks. In *WREN*, 2009.

[9] J. Dean and S. Ghemawat. MapReduce: Simplified Data Processing on Large Clusters. In *USENIX OSDI*, 2004.

[10] G. DeCandia, D. Hastorun, M. Jampani, G. Kakulapati, A. Lakshman, A. Pilchin, S. Sivasubramanian, P. Vosshall, and W. Vogels. Dynamo: amazon's highly available key-value store. *ACM SIGOPS*, 41(6), 2007.

[11] N. Dukkipati. *Rate Control Protocol (RCP): Congestion control to make flows complete quickly.* PhD thesis, Stanford University, 2007.

[12] D. Ferrari, A. Banerjea, and H. Zhang. Network support for multimedia: A discussion of the tenet approach. In *Proc. of Computer Networks and ISDN Systems*, 1994.

[13] A. Greenberg, J. R. Hamilton, N. Jain, S. Kandula, C. Kim, P. Lahiri, D. A. Maltz, P. Patel, and S. Sengupta. VL2: a scalable and flexible data center network. In *Proc. of ACM SIGCOMM*, 2009.

[14] Y. Gu, C. V. Hollot, and H. Zhang. Congestion Control for Small Buffer High Speed Networks. In *Proc. of IEEE INFOCOM*, 2007.

[15] C. Guo, H. Wu, K. Tan, L. Shi, Y. Zhang, and S. Lu. Dcell: a scalable and fault-tolerant network structure for data centers. In *Proc. of ACM SIGCOMM*, 2008.

[16] T. Hoff. 10 eBay Secrets for Planet Wide Scaling, Nov. 2009. http://highscalability.com/blog/2009/11/17/10-ebay-secrets-for-planet-wide-scaling.html.

[17] T. Hoff. Latency is Everywhere and it Costs You Sales - How to Crush it, July 2009. http://highscalability.com/blog/2009/7/25/latency-is-everywhere-and-it-costs-you-sales-how-to-crush-it.html.

[18] M. Isard, M. Budiu, Y. Yu, A. Birrell, and D. Fetterly. Dryad: Distributed Data-Parallel Programs from Sequential Building Blocks. In *Proc. of EuroSys*, Mar. 2007.

[19] D. Katabi, M. Handley, and C. Rohrs. Congestion Control for High Bandwidth-Delay Product Networks. In *Proc. of ACM SIGCOMM*, Aug. 2002.

[20] R. Kohavi, R. Longbotham, D. Sommerfield, and R. M. Henne. Controlled experiments on the web: survey and practical guide. *Data Mining and Knowledge Discovery*, 18(1), 2009.

[21] C. L. Liu and J. W. Layland. Scheduling Algorithms for Multiprogramming in a Hard-Real-Time Environment. *Journal of the ACM*, 20(1), 1973.

[22] P. Saab. Scaling memcached at Facebook, Dec. 2008. http://www.facebook.com/note.php?note_id=39391378919.

[23] V. Vasudevan, A. Phanishayee, H. Shah, E. Krevat, D. G. Andersen, G. R. Ganger, G. A. Gibson, and B. Mueller. Safe and effective fine-grained TCP retransmissions for datacenter communication. In *ACM SIGCOMM*, 2009.

[24] W. Vogels. Performance and Scalability, Apr. 2009. http://www.allthingsdistributed.com/2006/04/performance_and_scalability.html.

[25] M. Welsh, D. Culler, and E. Brewer. Seda: an architecture for well-conditioned, scalable internet services. In *Proc. of ACM SOSP*, 2001.

[26] C. Wilson, H. Ballani, T. Karagiannis, and A. Rowstron. Better never than late: Meeting deadlines in datacenter networks. Technical Report MSR-TR-2011-66, Microsoft Research, May 2011.

NetLord: A Scalable Multi-Tenant Network Architecture for Virtualized Datacenters

Jayaram Mudigonda
Praveen Yalagandula
Jeff Mogul
HP Labs, Palo Alto, CA

Bryan Stiekes
Yanick Pouffary
HP

ABSTRACT

Providers of "Infrastructure-as-a-Service" need datacenter networks that support multi-tenancy, scale, and ease of operation, at low cost. Most existing network architectures cannot meet all of these needs simultaneously.

In this paper we present NetLord, a novel multi-tenant network architecture. NetLord provides tenants with simple and flexible network abstractions, by fully and efficiently virtualizing the address space at both L2 and L3. NetLord can exploit inexpensive commodity equipment to scale the network to several thousands of tenants and millions of virtual machines. NetLord requires only a small amount of offline, one-time configuration. We implemented NetLord on a testbed, and demonstrated its scalability, while achieving order-of-magnitude goodput improvements over previous approaches.

Categories and Subject Descriptors

C.2.1 [**Computer-Communication Networks**]: Network Architecture and Design

General Terms

Design, Experimentation, Management

Keywords

Datacenter Network, Network Virtualization, Multi-Tenant, Multi-Pathing, Scalable Ethernet

1. INTRODUCTION

Cloud datacenters such as Amazon EC2 [1] and Microsoft Azure [6] are becoming increasingly popular, as they offer computing resources at a very low cost, on an attractive *pay-as-you-go* model. Many small and medium businesses are turning to these cloud computing services, not only for occasional large computational tasks, but also for their IT jobs. This helps them eliminate the expensive, and often very complex, task of building and maintaining their own infrastructure.

Cloud datacenter operators, on the other hand, can provide cost-effective Infrastructure as a Service (IaaS), because they can time-multiplex the physical infrastructure among a large number of *tenants*. The advent of mature CPU virtualization techniques (e.g., VMWare [26] and Xen [28]) makes it possible to convert the dedicated, and often extremely underutilized, physical servers in an enterprise into *Virtual Machines* (VMs) that run in an IaaS datacenter.

To fully realize the benefits of resource sharing, these datacenters must scale to huge sizes. The larger the number of tenants, and the larger the number of VMs, the better the chances for multiplexing, which in turn achieves better resource efficiency and cost savings.

Increasing the scale alone, however, cannot fully minimize the total cost. Today, a great deal of expensive human effort is required to configure the equipment, to operate it optimally, and to provide ongoing management and maintenance. A good fraction of these human costs reflect the complexity of managing a multi-tenant network; IaaS datacenters cannot become cost-effective at scale unless we can reduce these costs.

Therefore, IaaS networks must support virtualization and multi-tenancy, at scales of tens of thousands of tenants and servers, and hundreds of thousands of VMs. They must keep costs down by exploiting commodity components and by facilitating automatic configuration and operation. Most existing datacenter network architectures, however, suffer one or more of the following drawbacks:

They are expensive to scale: Today, scaling the network to the sizes needed by IaaS datacenters remains very expensive. The straightforward scaling of existing datacenter networks requires huge core switches with thousands of ports [8]. Some approaches require complex new protocols to be implemented in hardware [5, 17], or may work only with specific features such as IP-in-IP decapsulation [13] and MAC-in-MAC encapsulation [5, 17]. Some approaches that do not require switch modifications (e.g., [18]) may require excessive switch resources – in particular, they require very large forwarding tables, because the MAC address of every VM is exposed to the switches. None of these architectures can easily leverage existing, inexpensive commodity switches.

They provide limited support for multi-tenancy: Ideally, a multi-tenant network should provide a network abstraction that allows a tenant to design its network as if it were the sole occupant of a datacenter. That is, a tenant should be able to define its own layer-2 (L2) and layer-3 (L3) addresses. Previous multi-tenancy architectures do not provide full address-space virtualization; they either focus on performance guarantees and performance isolation [14, 24, 25], or only provide IP address space sharing [11, 13].

They require complex configuration: Many existing architectures that might make use of cheaper switches often require careful manual configuration: for example, setting up IP subnets and configuring OSPF [8, 13].

In this paper, we present *NetLord*, a novel multi-tenant virtualized datacenter network architecture. NetLord encapsulates a tenant's L2 packets, to provide full address-space virtualization. NetLord employs a light-weight agent in the end-host hypervisors to transparently encapsulate and decapsulate packets from and to the local VMs. Encapsulated packets are transferred over an underlying, multi-path L2 network, using an unusual combination of IP and Ethernet packet headers. NetLord leverages SPAIN's approach to multi-pathing [18], using VLAN tags to identify paths through the network.

The encapsulating Ethernet header directs the packet to the destination server's edge switch, via L2 forwarding. By leveraging a novel configuration of the edge switch's IP forwarding table, the encapsulating IP header then allows the switch to deliver the packet to the correct server, and also allows the hypervisor on that server to deliver the packet to the correct tenant.

Because NetLord does not expose any tenant MAC addresses to the switches (and also hides most of the physical server addresses), the switches can use very small forwarding tables, thus reducing capital costs, while scaling to networks with hundreds of thousands of VMs. Because NetLord uses simple, static switch configurations, this reduces operational costs.

Our focus in this paper is only on *qualitative* isolation between tenants: tenants can design their L2 and L3 address spaces without any restrictions created by multi-tenancy. NetLord itself provides no guarantees on *performance* isolation between tenants [14, 24, 25]. However, because NetLord explicitly exposes tenant identifiers in the encapsulation header, it can efficiently support various slicing/QoS mechanisms using commodity switches.

In this paper, we present the NetLord design, and show through simple calculations how it can scale. We also describe an experimental evaluation, with up to 3000 tenants and 222K emulated VMs, showing that NetLord can achieve substantial goodput improvements over other approaches.

2. PROBLEM AND BACKGROUND

We start by describing the problems we are trying to solve, and then describe some prior work on similar problems.

2.1 Goals: scalable, cheap, and flexible

Our goal is to provide a network architecture for a multi-tenant virtualized cloud datacenter. We want to achieve large scale at low cost, with easy operation and configuration, and we want to provide tenants with as much flexibility as possible.

Scale at low cost: Cloud providers can offer services at low cost because they can leverage economies of scale. This implies that the network for a cloud datacenter must scale, at low cost, to large numbers of tenants, hosts, and VMs. The network must support lots of addresses, and provide ample bandwidth between the VMs of any tenant.

A provider's costs include both capital expenditures (CAPEX) and operational expenditures (OPEX). To reduce CAPEX, the network should use commodity, inexpensive components. However, commodity network switches often have only limited resources and limited features. For example, typical commercial switches can hold a few tens of thousands of MAC forwarding information base (FIB) table entries in their data-plane fast paths (e.g., 64K entries in the HP ProCurve 6600 series [20] and 55K in the Cisco Catalyst 4500 series [10]).

Small data-plane FIB tables in switches create a scaling problem

for MAC-address learning: if the working set of active MAC addresses is larger than the data-plane table, some entries will be lost, and a subsequent packet to those destinations will cause flooding. (Even when the table is large enough, a rapid arrival rate of new addresses can lead to flooding, if learning is done in software and the switch's local management CPU is too slow to keep up.) Therefore, we cannot afford to expose the switches to the MAC addresses of all tenant VMs, or even of all physical servers in a large network, because the resultant flooding will severely degrade performance. Section 5.3 demonstrates this effect experimentally.

We also want to be able to support high bisection bandwidth at low cost. In particular, we would like to allow the cloud provider to choose an efficient and cost-effective physical wiring topology without having to consider whether this choice interferes with multi-tenancy mechanisms or tenant-visible abstractions.

Easy to configure and operate: To reduce OPEX, cloud providers need networks that, as much as possible, can be configured and operated automatically. We would like to avoid any per-switch configuration that is hard to scale, or that is highly dynamic. We also want to avoid network-related restrictions on the placement of VMs, to allow the cloud provider to efficiently multiplex physical hosts, without worrying about resource fragmentation.

Cloud providers may wish to offer QoS features to tenants. We would also like to provide simple mechanisms that support per-tenant traffic engineering; we do not want to require the provider to individually manage QoS for each TCP flow for each tenant.

We also want the network to handle switch and link failures automatically. We would like the unfailed portions of the network to continue to work without being affected by failed components.

Flexible network abstraction: Different tenants will have different network needs. A tenant wishing to run a Map-Reduce job might simply need a set of VMs that can communicate via TCP. On the other hand, a tenant running a three-tier Web application might need three different IP subnets, to provide isolation between tiers. Or a tenant might want to move VMs or entire applications from its own datacenter to the cloud, without needing to change the network addresses of the VMs. This flexibility will also allow tenants to create networks that span VMs both in their own datacenters or on rented servers in the cloud datacenter [15].

These examples, and others, motivate our desire for a datacenter network that fully virtualizes the L2 and L3 address spaces for each tenant, without any restrictions on the tenant's choice of L2 or L3 addresses.

Also, in certain kinds of cloud environments, tenants might wish to use non-IP protocols, such as Fibre Channel over Ethernet (FCoE), ATA over Ethernet (AoE), or HyperSCSI. These protocols, while currently unsupported in public cloud networks, could be important for tenants trying to move existing applications into the cloud, and would be impossible to use in a network that did not support an L2 abstraction. Similarly, these tenants would benefit from a cloud network that supports tenant-level broadcasts or muliticasts.

2.2 State of the art

In this section, we first describe current practices and recent research proposals for multi-tenant datacenter networking. Also, since NetLord depends on an underlying large-scale L2 network, we discuss recent work on scalable network fabrics.

Multi-tenant datacenters: Traditionally, datacenters have employed VLANs [16] to isolate the machines of different tenants on a single L2 network. This could be extended to virtualized datacenters, by having the hypervisor encapsulate a VM's packets with a

VLAN tag corresponding to the VM's owner. This simple approach provides an L2 abstraction to the tenants, and can fully virtualize the L2 and L3 address spaces. However, to correctly support the Spanning Tree Protocol, each VLAN needs to be a loop-free subgraph of the underlying network, and that limits the bisection bandwidth for any given tenant. Also, unless VLANs are carefully laid out, this approach may expose all VM addresses to the switches, creating scalability problems. Finally, the VLAN tag is a 12-bit field in the VLAN header, limiting this to at most 4K tenants. (The IEEE 802.1ad standard on Provider Bridges [3] defines the "QinQ" protocol to allow stacking of VLAN tags, which would relieve the 4K limit, but QinQ is not yet widely supported.)

Amazon's Virtual Private Cloud (VPC) [2] provides an L3 abstraction and full IP address space virtualization. Tenants can specify up to 20 arbitrary IP subnets (at least /28 in size), and the provider will instantiate a VPC router to connect these IP subnets. We could not find any documentation of how the VPC router is implemented, and hence cannot comment on its routing efficiency. VPC does not support multicast and broadcast, which implies that the tenants do not get an L2 abstraction.

Greenberg et al. [13] propose VL2, a scalable and flexible datacenter network. VL2 provides each tenant (termed "service" in the paper) with a single IP subnet (L3) abstraction, but implements efficient routing between two different IP subnets without needing to divert the packets through an explicit router. Services running in VL2 are expected to use only IP-based protocols. VL2 works with a specific topology (Clos) to achieve a full bisection bandwidth network, and hence does not restrict VM placement. However, the approach assumes several features not common in commodity switches, such as IP-in-IP decapsulation support at line rates. VL2 handles a service's L2 broadcast packets by transmitting them on a IP multicast address assigned to that service. The VL2 paper does not explicitly address unicast non-IP packets, but we believe their approach can be extended, as it encapsulates all packets.

Diverter [11] presents an efficient fully-distributed virtualized routing system, which accommodates multiple tenants' logical IP subnets on a single physical topology. Similar to VL2, Diverter addresses the problem of efficient routing between subnets. Diverter's solution is to overwrite the MAC addresses of inter-subnet packets, allowing it to relay these packets via a single hop. Diverter provides an L3 network abstraction to tenants, but it assigns unique IP addresses to the VMs; that is, it does not provide L3 address virtualization.

Scalable network fabrics: Many research projects and industry standards address the limitations of Ethernet's Spanning Tree Protocol. Several, including TRILL (an IETF standard) [5], Shortest Path Bridging (an IEEE standard) [4], and Seattle [17], support multipathing using a single-shortest-path approach. These three need new control-plane protocol implementations and data-plane silicon. Hence, inexpensive commodity switches will not support them, for at least a few years.

One way to achieve scalable multipathing is through hierarchical addressing in specific topologies. Al-Fares et al.[7] proposed three-level FatTree topologies, combined with a specific IP address assignment scheme, to provide high bisection bandwidth without needing expensive, high-radix core switches. For scalability, their proposal depends on a two-level route lookup feature in the switches. Mysore et al. proposed PortLand [19], which replaces that IP address scheme with MAC-address rewriting, and requires switches with the ability to forward based on MAC-address prefixes. Both these approaches work only with multi-rooted tree topologies.

Scott et al. proposed MOOSE [22], which address Ethernet scaling issues by using hierarchical MAC addressing. MOOSE also uses shortest-path routing, and did not focus on multipathing for improved bisection bandwidth. MOOSE, like PortLand, needs switches that can forward packets based on MAC prefixes.

Mudigonda et al. [18] proposed SPAIN, which uses the VLAN support in existing commodity Ethernet switches to provide multipathing over arbitrary topologies. SPAIN uses VLAN tags to identify k edge-disjoint paths between pairs of endpoint hosts. The original SPAIN design may expose each end-point MAC address k times (once per VLAN), stressing data-plane tables even more than standard Ethernet, and hence it can not scale to large number of VMs.

To summarize, no current practices or prior research proposals meets all of the goals we described in section 2.1.

3. NETLORD'S DESIGN

The fundamental idea underlying NetLord is to encapsulate the tenant's L2 packets and transfer them over a scalable L2 fabric, using an L3+L2 (IP+Ethernet) encapsulation that exploits features of both layers. NetLord uses a light-weight agent in the hypervisors to encapsulate, route, decapsulate, and deliver tenant packets to virtual machines, addressed to the VMs' tenant-assigned Ethernet addresses. With two exceptions, described in sections 3.2 and 3.9, NetLord ignores any tenant-visible L3 (IP) issues.

The source NetLord Agent (NLA) creates the encapsulating L2 and L3 headers such that the Ethernet destination address directs the packet through the underlying L2 fabric to the correct edge switch, and such that the IP destination address both allows the egress edge switch to deliver the packet to the correct server, and allows the destination NLA to deliver the packet to the correct tenant. The details of this encapsulation are somewhat subtle; we discuss them in section 3.5.

One significant consequence of this encapsulation method is that tenant VM addresses are never exposed to the actual hardware switches. By using IP forwarding on (only) the last hop, we can effectively share a single edge-switch MAC address across a large number of physical and virtual machines. This resolves the problem of FIB-table pressure; in NetLord the switches, instead of needing to store millions of VM addresses in their FIBs, only need to store the addresses of the other switches. Even in a very large datacenter, we expect at most a few thousand switches. (Edge-switch FIBs must also store the addresses of their directly-connected server NICs – at most, one per switch port; they do *not* need to store the addresses of remote servers.)

Because of the specific encapsulation used in NetLord, edge switches require very limited configuration; in particular, this configuration requires only local information, plus some boilerplate configuration that is essentially identical on every switch. This aspect of NetLord dramatically simplifies the operation and configuration of the network hardware, obviates the need for complex routing protocols, and reduces the chances for software or human error to create failures. We describe the details of configuration in section 3.6.

Another consequence of NetLord's encapsulation method is that it exposes tenant IDs in the outer L3 header of packets moving through the fabric. This potentially allows a cloud provider to do per-tenant traffic management in the network fabric, without having to put per-flow ACLs in the switches, which would create significant scaling problems. We discuss tenant-level network management in section 6.

Since we intend NetLord for use in a large-scale datacenter, the underlying L2 fabric needs multi-path support, for high band-

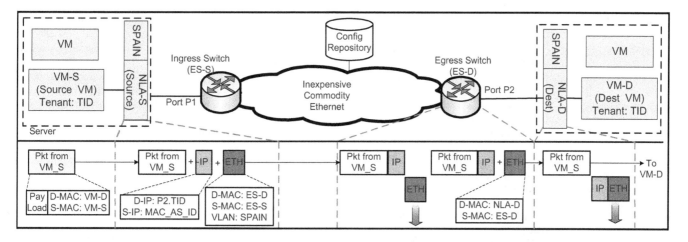

Figure 2: NetLord's high-level component architecture (top) and packet encapsulation/decapsulation flows (bottom)

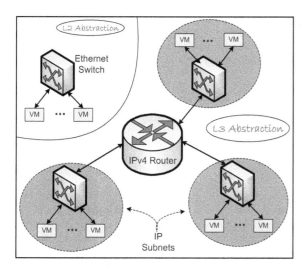

Figure 1: Network abstractions, as seen by the tenants

width and fault tolerance. NetLord leverages our previous work on SPAIN [18] to provide an underlying multi-path fabric using commodity switches. We provide a brief summary of SPAIN in section 3.4.

3.1 A tenant's view of NetLord

NetLord provides tenants with a very simple abstract view of the network: every tenant has one or more *private* MAC address spaces. In each of its MAC address spaces, the tenant can assign arbitrary MAC addresses. A tenant might wish to use multiple MAC address spaces to simplify address allocation, or to limit the scope of its broadcasts/multicasts. (NetLord does not currently implement tenant multicasting, but we believe this is feasible.)

Most tenants will also allocate and use L3 addresses (IPv4, IPv6, etc.). NetLord mostly ignores any tenant-visible L3 issues (except as discussed in sections 3.2 and 3.9). Therefore, by placing no restrictions on how tenants assign L2 or L3 addresses, NetLord provides full address-space virtualization: multiple tenants can use the same address without having their packets mis-routed.

3.2 Virtual routing

A tenant can divide its IP address space into networks and/or IP subnets, and connect these via software routers running on some of its VMs. This approach requires no support from NetLord.

However, for simple routing functions, the extra network hop and VM computation implied by that approach can add unnecessary overhead. Therefore, NetLord follows Diverter's model of supporting "virtual routing" within the hypervisor [11]. A tenant designates to NetLord certain sets of ⟨IP address, MAC address⟩ pairs (within their own address spaces) as virtual router interfaces. Whenever a tenant VM sends a packet to one of these MAC addresses, its local NetLord agent intercepts the packet, extracts the IP header, and does a route lookup to determine the destination tenant-assigned IP and MAC addresses (see section 3.9 for the latter). The NLA can then encapsulate the outgoing packet to send it directly to the final destination.

The virtual routing function could support simple firewall functions, although tenant-implemented SW routers might be needed for more complex router features. Tenants can also use virtual routing to exchange packets with hosts on the public Internet, or with other tenants, via a *public address space* that is exposed to all tenants and advertised externally. This public address space is associated with a reserved *Tenant_ID*=2, so the NLA allows any tenant to request that a VM's interface be given an address in that address space.

Figure 1 shows examples of several network abstractions available to NetLord tenants. The inset shows a pure L2 abstraction; the main figure shows a tenant with three IPv4 subnets connected by a virtual router.

3.3 NetLord's components

Figure 2 shows a high-level architectural view of NetLord. The top half of the figure depicts important components and their interconnections, while the lower half shows the header operations performed on a packet as it travels through these components.

As shown in the top half, NetLord consists of: (1) a fabric consisting of simple switches, (2) NetLord Agents (NLAs) in the hypervisor at each physical host, and (3) a configuration repository.

Fabric switches: NetLord relies on a traditional, switched Ethernet fabric, using unmodified commodity switches. We require only that these switches support VLANs (for multi-pathing; see section 3.4) and basic IP forwarding. We do not require full-fledged support for IP routing; in particular, the switches run no routing protocol. We do require that a switch can take an IP packet sent to its own MAC address, look up its destination using longest-prefix match (LPM) in a small forwarding table using statically-configured entries, and forward the packet appropriately. All of the datacenter switches we have examined, including the cheapest ones, can support NetLord.

These switches tend to be much cheaper than full routers, because they do not require support for complex routing protocols (e.g., IS-IS or OSPF), large routing tables, complex firewall functions, etc.

NetLord agents: A NetLord Agent (NLA) resides in the hypervisor (or the driver domain) of each physical server, and performs two major tasks. First, the NLA transparently encapsulates and decapsulates all packets from and to the local VMs.

Second, the NLA collaborates with other NLAs, and with the central configuration repository, to gather and maintain all the information needed for the encapsulation. For instance, the NLA builds and maintains a table that maps a VM's Virtual Interface (VIF) ID to the port number and MAC address of the edge switch to which the server hosting that VM is connected.

Configuration repository: The repository (which could be replicated for performance and availability) resides at an address known to the NLAs, and maintains several databases. Some are used for SPAIN-style multi-pathing; some are used for per-tenant configuration information. We envision this repository to be co-located with the datacenter-wide VM manager system (such as Eucalyptus[1]) that we expect all cloud datacenters to have. (Note that this repository differs from OpenFlow's central controller, since it is used to configure end-host parameters, not just switches).

3.4   SPAIN in a nutshell

NetLord relies on SPAIN to construct a high-bandwidth, resilient multi-path fabric using commodity Ethernet switches. We briefly sketch the pertinent features; for a full description, see [18].

SPAIN is based on three mechanisms: it pre-computes k edge-disjoint paths between pairs of edge switches; it pre-configures VLANs to identify these paths (not for isolation, as is the typical use of VLANs); and it uses an end-host agent to spread the traffic across paths (i.e., VLANs).

SPAIN's algorithms for computing edge-disjoint paths, merging these paths into trees, and optimally packing these into the 12-bit VLAN tag space are complex and somewhat computationally expensive, but are run only when the network topology is designed or significantly changed. These algorithms work with any topology, but are most useful when the topology provides a rich variety of paths (e.g., FatTree).

SPAIN uses an end-host agent, which can be incorporated into a hypervisor, and thus integrated with the NetLord Agent. On packet transmission, the agent looks up the destination Ethernet address D in a local table, yielding a set of k VLANs that reach that destination. It then chooses a VLAN (e.g., round-robin, but with flow affinity to prevent packet reordering), tags the packet with that VLAN, and transmits it normally. Because the k VLANs are constructed to take different paths to D, this provides high net bandwidth and load balancing among paths. The SPAIN agent also detects failed ⟨VLAN, destination⟩ pairs, and then re-routes around the failure by using a different VLAN.

SPAIN by itself (i.e., without NetLord) suffers from a major scalability problem: it not only exposes the fabric switches to end-host MAC addresses, but it exposes each VM MAC address k times: once per ⟨VLAN, VM-MAC⟩ pair. This means that SPAIN creates even more pressure on switch data-plane FIB tables than plain Ethernet does. (We demonstrate this problem in section 5.) However, NetLord encapsulates all tenant VM addresses, and also hides most physical NIC MAC addresses from most switches (as we will soon

---

1http://eucalyptus.cs.ucsb.edu/

describe). Thus, augmenting SPAIN with NetLord greatly reduces FIB pressure, because the switch FIBs need to hold only one entry for each ⟨VLAN, switch-MAC⟩ pair, and there are far fewer switches than VMs.

The SPAIN end-host agent relies on the repository to obtain the table that maps between destinations and sets of VLANs. When combined with the NetLord Agent, SPAIN requires one entry for each edge switch in the datacenter (not for each VM!); this table is loaded at boot time and updated only when the set of switches and wires changes. (Note that the NLAs on each edge switch will see a different table; the NLAs attached to one switch all see the same table.)

3.5   Encapsulation details

NetLord identifies a tenant VM's Virtual Interface (VIF) by the 3-tuple ⟨Tenant_ID, MACASID, MAC-Address⟩, where MACASID is a tenant-assigned MAC address space ID, to support the use of multiple L2 address spaces.

When a tenant VIF *SRC* sends a packet to a VIF *DST*, unless the two VMs are on the same server, the NetLord Agent must encapsulate the packet. The encapsulation is constructed as follows (and as depicted in the lower half of figure 2):

$$
\begin{aligned}
\text{VLAN.tag} &= \text{SPAIN\_VLAN\_for}(\text{edgeswitch}(DST),\text{flow}) \\
\text{MAC.src} &= \text{edgeswitch}(SRC).\text{MAC\_address} \\
\text{MAC.dst} &= \text{edgeswitch}(DST).\text{MAC\_address} \\
\text{IP.src} &= \text{MACASID} \\
\text{IP.dst} &= \text{encode}(\text{edgeswitch\_port}(DST), \text{Tenant\_ID}) \\
\text{IP.id} &= \text{same as VLAN.tag} \\
\text{IP.flags} &= \text{Don't Fragment}
\end{aligned}
$$

This encapsulation conveys all of the information that the receiving NLA needs to deliver the packet, since the Tenant_ID is encoded in the IP.dst field, the MACASID is carried in the IP.src field, and the original packet header contains the MAC-Address of the destination VIF. Because the sender NLA sets the "Don't Fragment" flag, it can use the IP.id field to transmit the SPAIN-assigned VLAN tag to the receiving NLA. The outer VLAN tag is stripped by the egress edge switch, but the receiving NLA needs to see this tag to support SPAIN's fault-tolerance mechanisms; see section 3.8.

Clearly, the NLA needs to know the remote edge switch MAC address, and the remote edge switch port number, for the destination VM; we will explain how this happens in section 3.9. (Section 3.7 explains how the NLA learns the local edge switch MAC address.) It also must use SPAIN to choose a VLAN for the egress edge switch; to avoid packet reordering, this function also takes a (tenant-level 5-tuple) flow ID.

The most subtle aspect of the encapsulation is the function $encode()$, which takes the egress edge switch port number p (for the destination server, represented as a 7-bit number) and the Tenant_ID tid to create an IP address. Our goal is to allow the egress edge switch to look up this address to generate the final forwarding hop. We construct this encoding by creating an IP address with p as the prefix, and tid as the suffix: $p.tid[16:23].tid[8:15].tid[0:7]$, which supports 24 bits of Tenant_ID. (Other similar encodings are possible, if, for example, the edge switches have more than 128 ports.) Note that since these addresses are never used outside the context of the egress edge switch, we can use any properly formed IP address.

This address encoding allows the egress edge switch to use longest-prefix matching, over a forwarding table with wildcard addresses of the form $p. * . * . * /8$ to do the final-hop lookup. This table needs only one entry per local switch port, and so will fit on the cheapest switches. Another key point is that this table is also the same on every edge switch.

In summary, the NetLord encapsulation uses the destination MAC address to cover all VMs attached to a single edge switch, and it uses the destination IP address both to direct the packet to the NLA on the correct server, and to allow that NLA to deliver the packet to the correct tenant.

3.6 Switch configuration

Switches require only static configuration to join a NetLord network. These configurations are set at boot time, and need never change unless the network topology changes.

The key idea behind edge-switch configuration is that there is a well-defined set of IP addresses that are reachable via a given switch port p: $encode(p, *)$, or more concretely, $p.*.*.*/8$. Therefore, when an edge switch boots, either a local process or a management station simply creates IP forwarding-table entries of the form $\langle prefix, port, next\_hop \rangle = \langle p.*.*.*/8, p, p.0.0.1 \rangle$ for each switch port p. The NLA on each server "owns" the next-hop IP address $p.0.0.1$, as described in section 3.7.

These forwarding-table entries can be set up by a switch-local script, or a management-station script via SNMP or the switch's remote console protocol. Since, as noted above, every edge switch has exactly the same IP forwarding table, this simplifies switch management, and greatly reduces the chances of misconfiguration.

All NetLord switches also need to be given their SPAIN VLAN configurations. This information comes from the configuration repository, and is pushed to the switches via SNMP or the remote console protocol. When there is a significant topology change, the SPAIN controller might need to update these VLAN configurations, but that should be a rare event.

3.7 NetLord Agent configuration

NetLord Agents need several kinds of configuration information. We defer discussion, until section 3.9, of how an NLA learns information about where remote tenants are in the network. We also assume that there already is a VM manager that places VMs on hosts, and so is already distributing VM configuration information (including tenant IDs) to the hypervisors. Finally, we assume that when a tenant VM creates a VIF, the VIF parameters become visible to the hypervisor.

The NLA must learn its own IP address and edge-switch MAC address. When a NetLord hypervisor boots, it listens to the Link Layer Discovery Protocol (LLDP - IEEE 802.1AB) messages sent by the edge switch to which it is connected. An LLDP message tells the server the switch's port number p and MAC address. The NLA then assumes the IP address $encode(p, 1) = p.0.0.1$ as its own, and responds to ARP queries for that address from the local edge switch.

If a server has multiple interfaces, the NLA repeats this process on all of them. Multiple interfaces of the same server could end up with the same IP address, because they could be connected to the same-numbered port on different switches. This is not a problem: the NetLord agent never actually uses these IP addresses, except to respond to ARP requests, which can be handled locally to a specific interface.

Since the $p.0.0.1$ address has no meaning beyond the local switch, an NLA needs a globally-usable address for communication with repositories, VM managers, and other hypervisors. NetLord reserves an address space for Tenant_ID=1, and each NLA must obtain an IP address in this address space. Therefore, when the hypervisor boots, it broadcasts a DHCP request directly over the L2 fabric, using its hardware MAC address, and the DHCP server

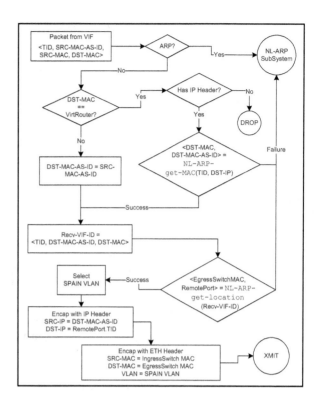

Figure 3: Flow Chart for Packet Send

responds with sufficient information for the NLA to continue with further operation in the Tenant_ID=1 space. (While this bootstrap mechanism does require L2 switches to learn the server's MAC address, this is needed only briefly, and so does not create much FIB pressure.)

3.8 The journey of a NetLord packet

We can now describe how a packet flows through the NetLord system.

VM operation: VMs send packets out exactly as they would have without NetLord, because NetLord is fully transparent to VMs. An outbound packet thus arrives at the local NLA.

Sending NLA operation: The flow chart in Figure 3 shows packet processing within the sending NLA. ARP messages are handled by NL-ARP subsystem (section 3.9). For all other packets, the first step is to determine the unique ID of the packet's destination Virtual Interface (VIF), $\langle$Tenant_ID, MACASID, MAC-Address$\rangle$.

The Tenant_ID of the receiving VIF is always the same as that of the sender VIF; NetLord does not allow direct communication between two tenants, except via the public address space with Tenant_ID=2. The NLA therefore needs to determine the other two fields of the VIF: MACASID and MAC-Address.

If the L2 packet is *not* addressed to the MAC of a designated virtual router within the VIF's MACASID (see section 3.2), then the destination VIF's MACASID must be the same as the source VIF's MACASID, and the destination VIF's MAC-Address can be found in the L2 packet header. A tenant that wants to move packets between two different MAC address spaces can do this by using a VM with VIFs in either address space as a software router.

If the packet *is* MAC-addressed to the virtual router, the NLA extracts the destination IP address from the packet, then obtains the destination VIF's $\langle$MACASID, MAC-Address$\rangle$ directly from the NL-ARP lookup table (which, because it also supports ARP-like functions, associates an IP address with a VIF, if that binding exists).

Once the NLA has the destination VIF ID, it must determine the destination edge-switch MAC address and server port number. This done by lookup in a table maintained by the NL-ARP protocol, which maps from a VIF ID to the correct ⟨MAC-Address, port⟩ tuple.

Once the egress edge switch MAC address is known, we invoke SPAIN's VLAN selection algorithm to select a path for the packet. If the outgoing packet is a TCP packet, NetLord also extracts the 5-tuple and provides it to SPAIN, so that all packets of a given TCP flow take the same path and avoid reordering.

At this point, the NLA has all the information it needs to create an encapsulated packet, using 802.1q and IP headers. The headers are created as described in section 3.5.

If the destination server is attached to the same switch, the NLA sets the source MAC address to its own hardware MAC address, rather than that of the switch. We do this because switches may drop packets if the source and destination MAC addresses are the same. Also, it is OK for the switch to learn the MAC addresses of its directly-connected servers in this case, because these addresses will not leak out to other switches, and the net increase in FIB pressure is limited. In this case, we also do not need to set a SPAIN VLAN tag, because there is only one possible path.

Network operation: The packet follows a path, defined by the SPAIN-provisioned VLAN, through the switched L2 network. All the switches *en route* learn the reverse path to the ingress edge switch, because its MAC address is carried in the packet as the source MAC.

On receiving the packet, the egress edge switch recognizes the destination MAC as its own, strips the Ethernet header, and then looks up the destination IP address in its IP forwarding table to determine the destination NLA next-hop information, which (by the construction in section 3.5) gives the switch-port number and local IP address of the server. The switch might occasionally need to do an ARP request to find the server's MAC address.

Receiving NLA operation: The receiving NLA decapsulates the MAC and IP headers, after extracting the Tenant_ID from the encapsulating IP destination address, the MACASID from the IP source, and the VLAN tag from the IP_ID field. It can then use its local information to look up the correct tenant's VIF, using the L2 destination address in the inner packet. (A tenant might have multiple VMs on a server, but each has a unique VIF.) Finally, it delivers the packet to the tenant VIF.

The NLA also notifies the local SPAIN agent that a packet was received from the ingress edge switch MAC address, via the copy VLAN tag carried in the IP.ID field. SPAIN needs this information to monitor the health of its paths. (The original SPAIN VLAN tag in the 802.1q header has already been stripped by the egress edge switch, so we need this copy to convey the tag to the receiving NLA.)

3.9 NL-ARP

An NLA needs to map a VIF to its location, as specified by an egress switch MAC address and port number. This mapping combines the functions of IP routing and ARP, and we use a simple protocol called NL-ARP to maintain an *NL-ARP table* in each hypervisor. The NLA also uses this table to proxy ARP requests made by the VMs, rather than letting these create broadcast load.

NL-ARP defaults to a push-based model, rather than the pull-based model of traditional ARP: a binding of a VIF to its location is pushed to all NLAs whenever the binding changes. In sec-

tion 4.2, we argue that the push model reduces overhead, and simplifies modelling and engineering the network.[2]

The NL-ARP protocol uses three message types: NLA-HERE, to report a location; NLA-NOTHERE, to correct misinformation; and NLA-WHERE, to request a location. Messages can either be broadcast on the L2 fabric, over a special VLAN that reaches all NLAs, or unicast to one NLA, through the NetLord mechanism via Tenant_ID=1. NL-ARP broadcasts are sent using the ingress switch MAC address as the source address, to avoid adding FIB pressure.

When a new VM is started, or when it migrates to a new server, the NLA on its current server broadcasts its location using an NLA-HERE message. Since NL-ARP table entries are never expired, in the normal case a broadcast is needed only once per VM boot or migration.

Broadcasts can be lost, leading to either missing or stale entries. If an entry is missing when a tenant sends a packet, the sending NLA broadcasts an NLA-WHERE request, and the target NLA responds with a unicast NLA-HERE. If a stale entry causes misdelivery of a packet, the receiving NLA responds with a unicast NLA-NOTHERE, causing deletion of the stale entry, and a subsequent NLA-WHERE broadcast. (Entries might also be missing after the unlikely event of a table overflow; see section 4.2.)

4. BENEFITS AND DESIGN RATIONALE

Having described NetLord's architecture and operation, we now explain its benefits, and the rationale behind some of the important design decisions. We first explain how NetLord meets the goals in Section 2.1. We then discuss some design alternatives we considered, and explain how we derived our architecture, subject to the restrictions imposed by our goals.

4.1 How NetLord meets the goals

Simple and flexible abstractions: NetLord gives each tenant a simple abstract view of its network: all of its VMs within a MAC address space (e.g., within an IP subnet) appear to be connected via a single L2 switch, and all IP subnets appear to be connected via a single virtual router. The switch and router scale to an arbitrary number of ports, and require no configuration aside from ACL and QoS support in the virtual router. The tenant can assign L2 and L3 addresses however it chooses, and for arbitrary reasons. NetLord's address space virtualization therefore facilitates development of novel network and transport protocols within a cloud datacenter.

Scale: Number of tenants: By using the $p.*.*.*/24$ encoding (see section 3.5), NetLord can support as many as 2^{24} simultaneous tenants. (We could increase this, if necessary, by using additional header fields for the encoding, at the cost of added complexity.)

Scale: Number of VMs: NetLord's encapsulation scheme insulates the L2 switches from all L2 addresses except those of the edge switches. Each edge switch also sees a small set of locally-connected server addresses. The switches are thus insulated from the much larger number of VM addresses, and even from most of the server addresses.

Because this limits FIB pressure, a NetLord network should scale to a huge number of VMs, but it is hard to exactly quantify this number. The actual number of FIB entries required depends upon a complex interaction of several factors that are either poorly understood, that vary widely over small time scales, or that are hard to quantify. These factors include the traffic matrix and its locality;

---

[2]An alternative to NL-ARP is to use a DHT, as in SEATTLE [17].

packet and flow sizes, application tolerance of lost packets; network topology; dynamics of load balancing schemes; etc.

Instead, we estimate the number of unique MAC addresses that NetLord can support, based on a set of wildly pessimistic assumptions. We assume a FatTree topology (these scale well and are amenable to analysis), and we assume a worst-case traffic matrix: simultaneous all-to-all flows between all VMs, with one packet per flow pending at every switch on the flow's path. We assume that the goal is to never generate a flooded packet due to a capacity miss in any FIB.

Table 1: NetLord worst-case limits on unique MAC addresses

Switch Radix	FIB Sizes			
	16K	32K	64K	128K
24	108,600	153,600	217,200	307,200
48	217,200	307,200	434,400	614,400
72	325,800	460,800	651,600	921,600
94	425,350	601,600	850,700	1,203,200
120	543,000	768,000	1,086,000	1,536,000
144	651,600	921,600	1,303,200	1,843,200

Based on these assumptions, NetLord can support $N = VR\sqrt{(F/2)}$ unique MAC addresses, where V is the number of VMs per physical server, R is the switch radix, and F is the FIB size (in entries). (SPAIN requires a FIB size proportional to the square of the number of edge switches.)

Table 1 shows the maximum number of MAC addresses (VM) that NetLord could support, for various switch port counts and FIB sizes. Following a rule of thumb used in industrial designs, we assume $V = 50$.

With existing single-chip switches that feature 72 ports and 64K FIB entries [12], a NetLord network could support 650K VMs. Using plausible future 144-port ASICs with the same FIB size, NetLord could support 1.3M VMs. The table suggests that ASIC designers might consider increasing port count at the expense of FIB size; the number of VMs scales linearly with ports, but only with the square root of the FIB size.

Note that the original SPAIN design can scale to large numbers of physical paths, but at the cost of large FIBs. NetLord removes this restriction, and so allows the network to support a number of VMs consistent with its physical scale.

Ease of operation: NetLord simplifies network operation in three different ways, thereby reducing operating costs. First, as explained in Section 3, NetLord automates all switch configuration. The configuration details are either computed offline (e.g., SPAIN's VLAN configuration), or are autonomously determined by individual entities (e.g., the IP forwarding tables in the switches). Also, most of the configuration is static; this not only eliminates the need for constant supervision by humans, but also makes debugging and trouble-shooting easier.

Second, NetLord makes it easy to exploit standard mechanisms on commodity switches to implement tenant-specific traffic engineering, ACL, and isolation policies. As a design principle, NetLord uses only standard header formats; this exposes all important tenant information in header fields supported by even the most basic ACL mechanisms. For instance, an ACL based on the low-order bits of the destination IP address (the tenant ID) can match all packets belonging to a single tenant. Similarly, a tenant's flow between two physical servers can be easily identified by matching on the source and destination MAC addresses, and on the port-number bits of the IP destination address. One could use these mechanisms, to-

gether with NLA support, to deploy sophisticated QoS via a central controller (analogous to OpenFlow).

Finally, by supporting high bisection bandwidth without concerns about FIB pressure, NetLord removes network-based restrictions on VM placement. The VM manager need not try to co-locate communicating VMs, and can instead place them based on resource availability (e.g., CPU or RAM) or power management.

Low-cost switches: NetLord can efficiently utilize inexpensive, feature- and resource-limited commodity switches. The datacenter operator need not pay for IP routing support, or to upgrade switches to support novel L3 features (e.g., IPv6).

4.2 Design rationale

Why encapsulate? VM addresses can be hidden from switch FIBs either via encapsulation or via header-rewriting. Encapsulation is often thought to suffer three major drawbacks: (1) Increased per-packet overhead – extra header bytes and CPU for processing them; (2) Heightened chances for fragmentation and thus dropped packets; and (3) Increased complexity for in-network QoS processing. Even so, we used encapsulation for two reasons. First, the header re-writing cannot simultaneously achieve both address-space virtualization and reduced FIB pressure. Second, in a datacenter, we can easily address the drawbacks of encapsulation.

Header rewriting clearly would not suffer from increased byte overheads or fragmentation. However, since we want to support an unconstrained L2 abstraction, and therefore cannot assume the presence of an IP header, the only two fields we could rewrite are the source and destination MAC addresses. But to avoid FIB pressure from exposed VM addresses, we would have to rewrite these header fields with the source and destination agent (server) MAC addresses; this would then make it impossible for the receiving agent to know which VM should receive the packet. Diverter [11] solves this problem by requiring tenant VMs to send IP packets (using a defined addressing scheme), which allows the agent to map the destination IP address to the correct VM. Also, this approach still exposes server MAC addresses to switch FIBs, which limits scalability. (Nor could we rewrite using edge-switch MAC addresses, because the egress edge switch would not know where to forward the packet.) Thus, we believe encapsulation is required to offer tenants an L2 abstraction.

What about per-packet overheads, both on throughput and on latency? Our measurements (section 5) show that these overheads are negligible. Modern multi-GHz CPUs need only a few tens of nanoseconds to add and delete the extra headers; the added wire delay at 10Gbps is even smaller. Throughput overheads should be negligible if tenants use 9000-byte "jumbo" packets, which all datacenter switches support.

Encapsulation in NetLord also adds one extra hop to Diverter's "one-hop" paths. However, NetLord suffers no performance loss, because unlike in Diverter, this extra hop is done in hardware of the egress edge switch.

We can also mitigate fragmentation by exploiting jumbo packets. Our NetLord virtual device (in the hypervisor) exports a slightly smaller MTU (34 bytes fewer) than the physical device. Because in a datacenter we can ensure a consistent, high MTU across all switches, and our encapsulation header always sets the "Do-not-fragment" bit, we completely eliminate the possibility of NetLord-generated fragments. (This also frees up the fragmentation-related IP header fields for us to use for other purposes; see section 3.5.)

Finally, as explained in section 4.1, we can exploit NetLord's encapsulation scheme to make it easier to identify tenants via simple ACLs.

Why not use MAC-in-MAC? We could have used a "MAC-in-MAC encapsulation", where the sending NLA encapsulates the packet with only a MAC header, setting the source and destination MAC addresses set to those of the ingress and egress switches. This would add less overhead than our chosen encapsulation, but would create some problems. First, this would require the egress edge-switch FIB to map a VM destination MAC address to one of its output ports. This implies that no two VMs connected to an edge switch could have the same MAC address, which would impose unwanted restrictions on VM placement. Further, since arbitrary tenant-assigned L2 addresses, unlike NetLord's encoded IP address, cannot be aggregated, this approach requires an order of magnitude more FIB entries. Perhaps worse, it also requires some mechanism to update the FIB when a VM starts, stops, or migrates. Finally, MAC-in-MAC is not yet widely supported in inexpensive datacenter switches.

NL-ARP overheads: NL-ARP imposes two kinds of overheads: bandwidth for its messages on the network, and space on the servers for its tables.

In steady-state operation, most NL-ARP messages would be the gratuitous NLA-HERE broadcasts. We show, through a simple analysis, that these impose negligible overheads.

All NLA messages fit into the 64-byte (512-bit) minimum-length Ethernet packet. With the worst-case 96-bit inter-frame gap, an NLA packet requires 608 bit-times.

Most new servers come with at least one 10Gbps NIC. If we limit NLA-HERE traffic to just 1% of that bandwidth, a network that supports full bisection bandwidth can sustain about 164,000 NLA-HERE messages per second. That is, the network could support that rate of VM migrations or boots. Assuming that most VMs persist for minutes or hours, that should be sufficient for millions of VMs. Further, we believe that NLA-WHERE broadcasts and NLA-NOTHERE unicasts should occur so rarely as to add only negligible load.

NL-ARP also requires negligible table space on servers. Each table entry is 32 bytes. A million such entries can be stored in a 64MB hash table, at 50% loading. Since even small datacenter servers have 8GB of RAM, this table consumes about 0.8% of that RAM.

5. EXPERIMENTAL ANALYSIS

We did an experimental analysis, both to measure the overhead of the NetLord Agent (NLA), and to evaluate the scalability of NetLord. We measured overheads using a micro-benchmark (section 5.1) and scalability by emulating thousands of tenants and hundreds of thousands of VMs. We have not yet measured the cost of the control plane, including NL-ARP.

We implemented the NetLord agent as a Linux kernel module. We started with our implementation of SPAIN [18], adding about 950 commented lines of code. This includes all components of NetLord, except the NL-ARP subsystem. We implemented NL-ARP lookup tables, but have not fully implemented the message handlers, so we ran our experiments using statically-configured lookup tables; thus, no NL-ARP messages are sent. We ran our tests using Ubuntu Linux 2.6.28.19.

5.1 NetLord Agent micro-benchmarks

Since the NLA intercepts all incoming and outgoing packets, we quantified its per-packet overheads using two micro-benchmarks, "ping" for latency and Netperf [3] for throughput. We compare our NetLord results against an unmodified Ubuntu ("PLAIN") and our

---

[3] www.netperf.org

---

original SPAIN implementation. We used two Linux hosts (quad-core 3GHz Xeon CPU, 8GB RAM, 1Gbps NIC) connected via a pair of switches that served as "edge switches."

Table 2: Microbenchmarks for NetLord overheads

Case	Metric	PLAIN	SPAIN	NetLord
Ping	avg	97	99	98
(in μs)	min/max	90/113	95/128	93/116
NetPerf	avg	987.57	987.46	984.75
1-way	min	987.45	987.38	984.67
(in Mbps)	max	987.67	987.55	984.81
NetPerf	avg	1835.26	1838.51	1813.52
2-way	min	1821.34	1826.49	1800.23
(in Mbps)	max	1858.86	1865.43	1835.21

Our ping (latency) experiments used 100 64-byte packets. The first row in Table 2 shows the results (average, minimum, and maximum). NetLord appears to add at most a few microseconds to the end-to-end latency.

We measured both one-way and bi-directional TCP throughput using Netperf. For each case, we ran 50 10-second trials. We used jumbo (9000-byte) packets, because we observed erratic results (even with PLAIN) when using 1500-byte packets in the two-way experiments. (We hypothesize, but have not confirmed, that this is due to the limited number of buffer descriptors in the specific NIC in our testbed hosts.) Note that, because of our 34-byte encapsulation headers, NetLord exposes an 8966-byte MTU to applications.

The second and third rows in Table 2 show throughput results (mean, min., and max.). NetLord causes a 0.3% decrease in mean one-way throughput, and a 1.2% drop in in mean two-way throughput. We attribute these nearly-negligible drops mostly to the smaller MTU.

5.2 Emulation methodology and testbed

We have asserted that NetLord can scale to large numbers of VMs using inexpensive switches. We were limited to testing on just 74 servers, so to demonstrate NetLord's scalability, we emulated a much larger number of VMs than could normally run on 74 servers.

We implemented a light-weight VM emulation by adding a shim layer to the NLA kernel module. Conceptually, each TCP flow endpoint becomes an emulated VM. The shim layer exposes a unique MAC address for each such endpoint, by mapping from a source or destination $\langle IP\_addr, TCP\_port \rangle$ tuple to synthesize a corresponding MAC address. The shim executes, for every outgoing packet, before the NLA code, and rewrites the packet's MAC source and destination addresses with these synthetic addresses. Thus, the NLA sees one such emulated VM for each flow from our workload-generator application.

Using this technique, we can emulate up to $V = 3000$ VMs per server. We emulated 74 VMs per tenant on our 74 servers (one VM per tenant per host), or $74N$ VMs in all for N tenants.

Multi-tenant parallel shuffle workload: Our workload generator emulates the *shuffle* phase of Map-Reduce. Each of the N tenants has 74 VMs, each emulating both a Map task and a Reduce task. Each Map task transfers 10MB to each of the tenant's 73 other Reduce tasks. A given Map tasks serializes these transfers, in a random order that differs for each tenant; the transfers originating from a single Map task do not run in parallel. To avoid overloading a Reduce task, we reject incoming connections beyond a limit of 3 simultaneous connections per Reduce task. A Map task

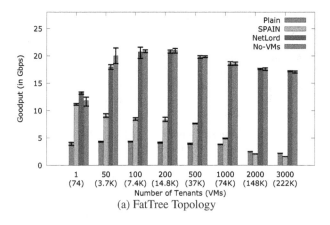

(a) FatTree Topology

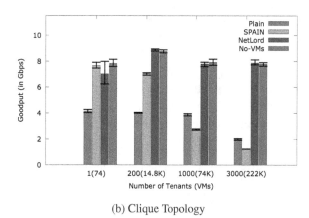

(b) Clique Topology

Figure 4: Goodput with varying number of tenants (number of VMs in parenthesis).

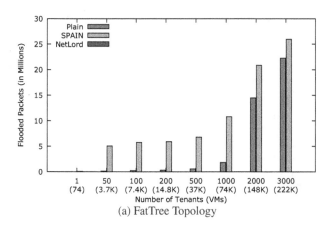

(a) FatTree Topology

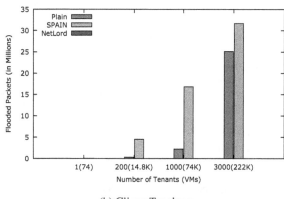

(b) Clique Topology

Figure 5: Number of flooded packets with varying number of tenants (number of VMs in parenthesis).

will postpone any such rejected transfer to a random position in its pending-transfer list; ultimately, all such tasks will complete.

Between each trial of the entire workload, we delay for 320 seconds, during which no packets are sent. Since our switches are set to expire learning table entries after 300 seconds, this ensures the FIBs are empty at the start of each trial.

Metrics: We run each shuffle trial either to completion or for 1800 seconds, and we compute the goodput as the total number of bytes transferred by all tasks, divided by the run-time. We also measure the number of unnecessarily-flooded packets during a trial, by counting, at each host, the total number of packets received that are not destined for any VM on that host.

Testbed: We ran the emulation experiments on 74 servers, part of a larger shared testbed. Each server has a quad-core 3GHz Xeon CPU and 8GB RAM. The 74 servers are distributed across 6 edge switches, with 10, 12, 12, 13, 13, and 15 servers/switch. All switch and NIC ports run at 1Gbps, and the switches can hold 64K FIB table entries.

We built two different topologies on this testbed: (i) **FatTree topology**: the entire testbed has 16 edge switches; using another 8 switches to emulate 16 core switches, we constructed a two-level FatTree, with full bisection bandwidth (i.e., no oversubscription). (ii) **Clique topology**: All 16 edge switches are connected to each other, thus creating a clique, which is oversubscribed by at most 2:1.

SPAIN and NetLord exploit these multi-path topologies by using VLANs to identify paths. For FatTree, we used 16 VLANs, each rooted at one core switch. For Clique, we used 6 VLANs, each rooted at one of the edge switches involved in our experiments.

5.3 Emulation results

As with the micro-benchmarks, we compared PLAIN, SPAIN, and NetLord. PLAIN does not support multi-pathing, and so its traffic follows a single spanning tree. We ran trials on both of the topologies with varying numbers of tenants (N), and for each N, we ran at least three trials and computed the means.

Figures 4(a) and 4(b) show the mean goodputs for the FatTree and Clique topologies, respectively. We include error bars showing the maximum and minimum results. The x-axis legend shows both the number of tenants, and the number of emulated VMs in parentheses.

Figure 4 shows that:

(1) As expected, PLAIN does not scale. Aside from failing to exploit the available bisection bandwidth, PLAIN's goodput drops after the number of VMs exceeds the switch FIB table size (64K entries) – by as much as 44% for 222K VMs. (At 74K VMs, the drop is only 3%, implying that the FIB table replacement policy might be LRU.)

(2) SPAIN outperforms PLAIN for <74K VMs, since it does exploit the multi-path fabrics.

(3) However, SPAIN performance degrades badly as the number of VMs increases. Above 74K VMs, SPAIN actually performs worse than PLAIN, because it maintains k distinct end-to-end paths between host pairs. Thus, instead of requiring $74N$ FIB table entries for N tenants, it requires $74kN$ entries (in the worst case), because a switch maintains a FIB entry for each $\langle$MAC-address,VLAN$\rangle$ tuple. SPAIN's goodput therefore drops even at relatively modest numbers of VMs.

(4) NetLord scales well, achieving far superior goodput, especially as the number of VMs increases.

We observe that NetLord's goodput declines slightly as the number of VMs exceeds 14.8K. We suspect this dip is caused by end-host overheads associated with maintaining lots of TCP connections. To validate this hypothesis, we re-ran the shuffle workload without VM emulation, using the PLAIN system. The goodput we achieved with this case (shown in Figure 4 s "No-VMs", with the number of connections matching the number of VMs) suffers from a similar dip – that is, NetLord's goodput closely matches the No-VMs goodput. The one exception, for Clique and $N = 1$, might be due to NetLord's slightly higher overheads.

Why does NetLord scale better? Our main hypothesis in this paper has been that PLAIN and SPAIN do not scale because of FIB-table misses. Our switches do not allow us to directly count these misses, so we use our counts of flooded packets as a proxy.

Figure 5 shows the mean number of packet floods received at each host during our experiments. (The error bars for this figure are too narrow to be worth showing, and we omit them to avoid clutter). Clearly, PLAIN and SPAIN suffer from lots of flooding, supporting our belief that their scaling problems result from FIB-table capacity misses. Since NetLord conceals all VM and most server MAC addresses from the switches, it experiences only a modest number of FIB misses, caused mostly by table timeouts.

We note that NetLord suffers from more misses than PLAIN when there is only one tenant, although the effect is too insignificant to see in Figure 5 – for FatTree, for example, PLAIN floods about 2,550 packets, SPAIN floods about 25,600, while NetLord floods about 10,500 packets. In the one-tenant case, we see more flooded packets than we expect during the first few connections. This could be because our switches implement their MAC learning process in control-plane software, and some FIB table updates might not complete within an RTT. However, the results are not fully consistent with this hypothesis, and they require further investigation.

In summary, through experimental evaluation on a real testbed with NetLord prototype, we have demonstrated that NetLord scales to several hundreds of thousands of VMs. We have also shown that it works with unmodified commodity switches.

6. DISCUSSION AND FUTURE WORK

In this section, we discuss how the NetLord architecture addresses several important considerations for operators of large datacenter networks. We also identify several limitations of NetLord, and areas for future work.

Fault-tolerance: An important aspect of scale is the increased likelihood of failures. NetLord directly inherits SPAIN's ability to handle transient network failures. SPAIN monitors the health of its VLAN-based paths by observing all incoming traffic, or by sending special *chirp* packets that serve (among other purposes) as heartbeats. This monitoring allows SPAIN (and therefore NetLord) to quickly detect failed paths, and to re-route load to alternate paths.

NetLord does not proactively monitor the health of the servers themselves. NetLord tolerates server failures, because there is no "hard state" associated with a specific NLA. We assume that a VM manager (such as Eucalyptus) is responsible for detecting failed servers and restarting affected VMs on other servers. When the VMs are restarted, their local NLAs broadcast NLA-HERE messages, which repopulate the NL-ARP tables at the NLAs for other VMs. It might be useful for the VM manager to provide this information directly to the surviving NLAs, thereby avoiding some lost packets during the restart phase.

Broadcasts and multicasts: ARP and DHCP account for a vast majority of broadcasts in today's typical datacenter. Because the NLAs proxy ARP requests, these are never broadcast. We expect the DHCP broadcast load to be similar to the NLA-HERE load, which (in section 4.2) we argued is just a small percentage of network capacity.

However, other tenant multicasts and broadcasts (particularly from malicious, buggy, or inefficient VMs) could become a problem. Scalable techniques for multi-tenant multicasting is a challenge for future work. Possible approaches include rate-limiting at the switches, or mapping broadcasts to a tenant-specific multicast group (as proposed in [11, 13]). But these techniques might not scale, because most switches either treat multicasts as broadcasts, or cannot scale the number of simultaneous multicast-tree pruning sessions to match the number of tenants [23].

Per-tenant management: A cloud provider might wish to manage traffic on a per-tenant basis: for example, to impose bandwidth limits or priorities. While this can often be done in the hypervisors [21], sometimes there might be reasons to exploit features of switch hardware. Doing so requires a way for switches to identify the packets of a specific tenant. If tenants can only be identified by the addresses of their individual VMs, this cannot scale. However, since NetLord exposes the tenant ID as part of the encapsulation's IP destination address, one can use a single ACL per tenant to control features such as rate limiting. This would probably still have to be limited to a small subset of the tenants, given the number of ACLs and rate-limiters supported by commodity switches. Or, the high-order bits of tenant IDs could encode service classes.

Inter-tenant and external communications: Currently, NetLord requires that the tenant implement some sort of routing within its own network, if a VM on its private address space needs to be able to contact the external world. We are currently working a few minor modifications to our basic design, so that we can provide a per-tenant "distributed virtual NAT" service.

Software overheads and SR-IOV: Although NetLord itself is frugal with server resources, the use of hypervisor-based (or driver domain-based) network virtualization imposes substantial overheads [27]. These overheads can be avoided by using Single Root I/O Virtualization (SR-IOV) NICs, which allow VMs direct access to NIC hardware. However, SR-IOV would appear to prevent the NLA from intercepting and encapsulating outgoing packets, and a standard SR-IOV NIC would not know how to decapsulate an incoming NetLord packet. We believe that techniques allowing hypervisors to inject code into the guest-domain drivers [9] could solve the outbound problem; the inbound problem would either involve the hypervisor on every received packet, or would require some modifications to SR-IOV.

Other L2 fabrics: Although NetLord as presented in this paper utilizes SPAIN as the underlying multipathing fabric, it is not closely tied to SPAIN. NetLord can use any fabric that provides an Ethernet abstraction such as TRILL [5], SPB [4], or SEATTLE [17]. NetLord might help with scaling these other solutions. For instance,

TRILL switches maintain a FIB entry for each destination MAC address (but mapping the destination MAC to a destination edge switch, rather than to a next-hop port), and so (without NetLord) suffer from the same FIB-pressure problems as traditional switches.

SEATTLE addresses scaling for the core switches. However, SEATTLE's edge switches probably still need relatively large FIB tables, to cache the working set of remote VM MAC addresses; otherwise, table misses incur the significant penalty of traversing the SEATTLE DHT. It would be useful to have a quantified analysis of how well SEATTLE scales in a virtualized environment.

7. CONCLUSIONS

In this paper we presented NetLord, a novel network architecture for multi-tenant cloud datacenters.

Through the encapsulation of a tenant's L2 (Ethernet) packets in its own IP packets, NetLord gains multiple advantages over prior solutions. It allows us to fully virtualize each tenant's L2 and L3 address spaces, which gives the tenants full flexibility in choosing their VM addresses — or not choosing these addresses, if they want to preserve their legacy addressing schemes. Encapsulation also allows NetLord to scale to larger numbers of VMs than could otherwise be efficiently supported using commodity Ethernet switches. NetLord's design can exploit commodity switches in a way that facilitates simple per-tenant traffic management in the network. Our new NL-ARP protocol simplifies the design, by proactively pushing the location information of VMs to all servers. NetLord improves ease of operation by only requiring static one-time configuration that is fully automated.

Our measurements show that the NetLord architecture scales to several thousands of tenants, and hundreds of thousands of VMs. Our experimental evaluation shows that NetLord can achieve at least 3.9X improvement in goodput over existing approaches, and imposes only negligible overheads.

Acknowledgements

We thank our shepherd, Jon Crowcroft, and the anonymous reviewers for their insightful comments. We thank Sujata Banerjee, Anna Fischer, Rick McGeer, and Jean Tourillhes for their help and feedback. Finally, we thank Ken Burden, Pete Haddad, and Eric Wu for their help in setting up the testbed network.

8. REFERENCES

[1] Amazon EC2. http://aws.amazon.com/ec2/.
[2] Amazon virtual private cloud. http://aws.amazon.com/vpc/.
[3] IEEE 802.1ad - Provider Bridging. http://www.ieee802.org/1/pages/802.1ad.html.
[4] IEEE 802.1aq - Shortest Path Bridging. http://www.ieee802.org/1/pages/802.1aq.html.
[5] IETF TRILL Working Group. http://www.ietf.org/html.charters/trill-charter.html.
[6] Windows Azure. https://www.microsoft.com/windowsazure/.
[7] M. Al-Fares, A. Loukissas, and A. Vahdat. A Scalable, Commodity Data Center Network Architecture. In *Proc. SIGCOMM*, 2008.
[8] M. Arregoces and M. Portolani. *Data Center Fundamentals*. Cisco Press, 2003.
[9] Broadcom Corp. Broadcom Ethernet Network Controller Enhanced Virtualization Functionality. http://tinyurl.com/4r8vxhh, Accessed on 1/31/11.
[10] Cisco Catalyst 4500 Series Model Comparison. http://tinyurl.com/yvzglk, Accessed on 1/31/11.
[11] A. Edwards, A. Fischer, and A. Lain. Diverter: A New Approach to Networking Within Virtualized Infrastructures. In *WREN 2009*.
[12] Fulcrum MicroSystems. FocalPoint FM6000 ProductBrief. http://tinyurl.com/4uqvale, Accessed on 1/31/11.
[13] A. Greenberg, J. Hamilton, and N. Jain. VL2: A Scalable and Flexible Data Center Network. In *Proc. SIGCOMM*, 2009.
[14] C. Guo, G. Lu, H. J. Wang, S. Yang, C. Kong, P. Sun, W. Wu, and Y. Zhang. SecondNet: A Data Center Network Virtualization Architecture with Bandwidth Guarantees. In *Co-NEXT*. ACM, 2010.
[15] M. Hajjat, X. Sun, Y.-W. E. Sung, D. Maltz, S. Rao, K. Sripanidkulchai, and M. Tawarmalani. Cloudward Bound: Planning for Beneficial Migration of Enterprise Applications to the Cloud. In *Proc. SIGCOMM*, 2010.
[16] IEEE 802.1q - Virtual Bridged Local Area Networks. http://tinyurl.com/5ok4f6, Accessed on 1/31/11.
[17] C. Kim, M. Caesar, and J. Rexford. Floodless in SEATTLE: A Scalable Ethernet Architecture for Large Enterprises. In *Proc. SIGCOMM*, pages 3–14, 2008.
[18] J. Mudigonda, P. Yalagandula, M. Al-Fares, and J. C. Mogul. SPAIN: COTS Data-Center Ethernet for Multipathing over Arbitrary Topologies. In *Proc. USENIX NSDI*, 2010.
[19] R. N. Mysore, A. Pamboris, N. Farrington, N. Huang, P. Miri, S. Radhakrishnan, V. Subramanya, and A. Vahdat. PortLand: A Scalable Fault-Tolerant Layer 2 Data Center Network Fabric. In *Proc. SIGCOMM*, 2009.
[20] HP ProCurve 6600 Series. http://tinyurl.com/4cg8qt9, Accessed on 1/31/11.
[21] H. Rodrigues, J. R. Santos, Y. Turner, P. Soares, and D. Guedes. Gatekeeper: Supporting Bandwidth Guarantees for Multi-tenant Datacenter Networks. In *Proc. 3rd Workshop on I/O Virtualization*, June 2011.
[22] M. Scott, A. Moore, and J. Crowcroft. Addressing the Scalability of Ethernet with MOOSE. In *Proc. DC CAVES Workshop*, Sept. 2009.
[23] R. Seifert and J. Edwards. *The All-New Switch Book: The Complete Guide to LAN Switching Technology*. Wiley, 2008.
[24] R. Sherwood, G. Gibb, K.-K. Yap, G. Appenzeller, M. Casado, N. McKeown, and G. Parulkar. Can the Production Network be the Testbed? In *Proc. of OSDI 2010*.
[25] A. Shieh, S. Kandula, A. Greenberg, and C. Kim. Seawall: Performance Isolation For Cloud Datacenter Networks. HotCloud'10.
[26] VMware. http://www.vmware.com.
[27] P. Willmann, J. Shafer, D. Carr, A. Menon, S. Rixner, A. L. Cox, and W. Zwaenepoel. Concurrent Direct Network Access for Virtual Machine Monitors. In *Proceedings of HPCA*, 2007.
[28] Xen. http://www.xen.org, Accessed on 1/31/11.

Inter-Datacenter Bulk Transfers with NetStitcher

Nikolaos Laoutaris, Michael Sirivianos, Xiaoyuan Yang, and Pablo Rodriguez
Telefonica Research
Barcelona, Spain
nikos@tid.es, msirivi@tid.es, yxiao@tid.s, pablorr@tid.es

ABSTRACT

Large datacenter operators with sites at multiple locations dimension their key resources according to the peak demand of the geographic area that each site covers. The demand of specific areas follows strong diurnal patterns with high peak to valley ratios that result in poor average utilization across a day. In this paper, we show how to rescue unutilized bandwidth across multiple datacenters and backbone networks and use it for non-real-time applications, such as backups, propagation of bulky updates, and migration of data. Achieving the above is non-trivial since leftover bandwidth appears at different times, for different durations, and at different places in the world.

To this end, we have designed, implemented, and validated *NetStitcher*, a system that employs a network of storage nodes to stitch together unutilized bandwidth, whenever and wherever it exists. It gathers information about leftover resources, uses a store-and-forward algorithm to schedule data transfers, and adapts to resource fluctuations.

We have compared *NetStitcher* with other bulk transfer mechanisms using both a testbed and a live deployment on a real CDN. Our testbed evaluation shows that *Net-Stitcher* outperforms all other mechanisms and can rescue up to five times additional datacenter bandwidth thus making it a valuable tool for datacenter providers. Our live CDN deployment demonstrates that our solution can perform large data transfers at a substantially lower cost than naive end-to-end or store-and-forward schemes.

Categories and Subject Descriptors

C.2.5 [**Computer-Communication Networks**]: Distributed Systems

General Terms

Algorithms, Design

Keywords

bulk transfers, inter-datacenter traffic, store-and-forward

1. INTRODUCTION

Online service companies such as Amazon, Facebook, Google, Microsoft, and Yahoo! have made huge investments in networks of datacenters that host their online services and cloud platforms. Similarly, hosting and co-location services such as Equinix and Savvis employ distributed networks of datacenters that include tens of locations across the globe. A quick look at any datacenter directory service [2]. reveals that datacenters are popping up in large numbers everywhere. The trend is driven primarily by the need to be co-located with customers for QoS (latency directly affects the revenues of web sites [26]), energy and personnel costs, and by the need to be tolerant to catastrophic failures [5].

1.1 The problem

The dimensioning of a site in terms of key resources, such as the number of servers and the amount of transit bandwidth to the Internet, depends highly on the peak demand from the geographic area covered by the site. In addition, the demand on a datacenter exhibits strong diurnal patterns that are highly correlated with the local time [21]. The combination of peak load dimensioning with strong diurnal patterns leads to poor utilization of a site's resources.

At the same time, Greenberg et al. [21] report that networking costs amount to around 15% of a site's total worth, and are more or less equal to the power costs [21]. They also report that wide-area transit bandwidth costs more than building and maintaining the internal network of a datacenter, a topic that has recently received much attention [22]. The transit bandwidth of a site is used for reaching end customers and for server-to-server communications with remote datacenters (Fig. 1). Datacenter operators purchase transit bandwidth from Telcos and pay based on flat or 95-percentile pricing schemes, or own dedicated lines.

Peak dimensioning and diurnal patterns hinder the amortization of the investment in bandwidth and equipment. In particular, with flat rate pricing, transit bandwidth sits idle when the local demand drops, *e.g.*, during early morning hours. Similarly, under 95-percentile billing, a datacenter operator pays a charged volume [30] according to its peak demand but does not use the already paid for bandwidth during the off-peak hours. Finally, in the case of owned dedicated lines, peak dimensioning pushes for constant upgrades even if the average utilization is low.

1.2 Our approach

The aim of our work is to rescue purchased but unutilized (leftover) bandwidth and put it to good use for the benefit

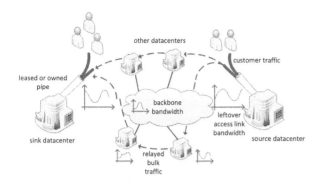

Figure 1: A source datacenter using its leftover transit bandwidth to perform a bulk backup to a remote sink datacenter. The two end points are in different time zones and thus their peak customer hours and their leftover bandwidth appear during non overlapping time intervals. Store-and-forward through intermediate nodes can solve the problem but needs to be aware of the constraints of these nodes and the backbone that connects them.

of backup, bulky updates propagation, and data migration applications running between different datacenters. Such applications can improve the fault tolerance and customer experience of a network of datacenters (Sect. 1.3). Their importance has been recently highlighted in a large scale survey of 106 large organizations that operate two or more datacenters conducted by Forrester, Inc. [10]. A key finding was that the vast majority (77%) of interviewed organizations run backup and replication applications among three or more sites. More than half of them reported having over a peta-byte of data in their primary datacenter and expect their inter-datacenter bandwidth requirements to double or triple over the next two to four years. As a general conclusion, IT managers agreed that the rate at which the price of inter-datacenter bandwidth is falling is outpaced by the growth rate of inter-datacenter traffic. Furthermore, Chen et al. [17] recently reported that background traffic is dominant in Yahoo!'s aggregate inter-datacenter traffic, and Google is deploying a large-scale inter-datecenter copy service [37].

By being elastic to delay, the aforementioned applications can postpone their transfers to non-peak hours when the interactive customer traffic is low. The challenge in efficiently rescuing such leftover bandwidth is that it can appear in multiple parts of the world at non-overlapping time windows of the day; such fluctuations in the availability of leftover bandwidth often relate to time zone differences but can also appear within the same time zone when mixing different types of traffic (*e.g.*, corporate and residential traffic). For example, a sending datacenter on the East Coast has free capacity during early morning hours (*e.g.*, from 3-6am) but cannot use it to backup data to another datacenter on the West Coast. The reason is that during that time the West Coast datacenter is still on night peak hours.

Our key insight is that we can rescue leftover bandwidth by using store-and-forward (SnF) algorithms that use relay storage points to temporarily store and re-route data. The intermediate datacenters are thus stitching together the leftover bandwidth across time and different locations. However to do so, we have to consider both the current and the future

constraints of the datacenters as well as the constraints on the backbone network that connects them (Fig. 1).

We have designed, implemented, and validated *NetStitcher*, a system that employs a network of commodity storage nodes that can be used by datacenter operators to stitch together their unutilized bandwidth, whenever and wherever it exists. Such storage nodes can be co-located with datacenters or expanded to other parts of the inter-datacenter network as needed. The premise of our design is that the cost of storage has been decreasing much faster than the cost of wide area bandwidth [20].

NetStitcher employs a store-and-forward algorithm that splits bulk data into pieces which are scheduled across space and long periods of time into the future, over multiple paths and multiple hops within a path. Scheduling is driven by predictions on the availability of leftover bandwidth at access and backbone links as well as storage constraints at storage relay nodes. With this information, the system maximizes the utilization of leftover resources by deriving an optimal store-and-forward schedule. It uses novel graph time expansions techniques in which some links represent bandwidth (carrying data across space), while others represent storage (carrying data across time). The system is also equipped with mechanisms for inferring the available future bandwidth and adapts to estimation errors and failures.

By performing intelligent store-and-forward, we circumvent the problems that plague other approaches, such as direct end-to-end (E2E) transfers or multipath overlay routing. Both of these approaches have no means to bridge the timing gap between non overlapping windows of leftover bandwidth at different sites. Its advanced scheduling, also gives *NetStitcher* an edge over simpler store-and-forward algorithms that do not schedule or use information regarding future availability of leftover resources. For instance, simpler random or greedy store-and-forward algorithms, such as BitTorrent's [18], have a partial view on the availability of leftover resources. Consequently, they may forward data towards nodes that are able to receive data very fast but are unable to relay them in fast paths towards the receiver.

1.3 NetStitcher applications

We now briefly discuss two applications that exchange inter-datacenter non-interactive bulk traffic and can therefore benefit from *NetStitcher*.

Fault tolerance. Improving the fault tolerance of datacenters by increasing the redundancy and security within a single site is too expensive. Quoting the VP of Amazon Web services, *"With incredible redundancy, comes incredible cost ... The only cost effective solution is to run redundantly across multiple data centers."* [5]. Instead of fortifying a single facility, a simpler solution is to periodically backup all the data to a remote location. The key challenge becomes the efficient use of WAN transit bandwidth. Hamilton points out that *"Bandwidth availability and costs is the prime reason why most customers don't run geo-diverse"* [5].

Customer experience. Since network latency impacts directly the usability and the revenues of a web site [26], firms with a global footprint replicate their information assets (such as collections of images and videos) at multiple locations around the world. For example, Facebook runs at least 3 datacenters [4] and holds more than 6 billion photographs [14]. To maintain a high quality customer experience, a new collection needs to be quickly replicated at

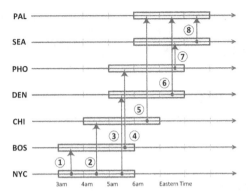

Figure 2: Timing diagram for backing up a datacenter in New York to another one in Palo Alto. The width of a rectangle indicates the window during which a datacenter can perform backups. The diagram shows the operation of a Store and Forward solution. To maximize the amount of data that can be moved between New York and Palo Alto, we need to introduce intermediate storage nodes across three time zones (Eastern, Central, Pacific): in Boston, Chicago, Phoenix, Denver and Seattle.

sites closer to the users. However, due to its "long-tail" profile, such user-generated content challenges traditional pull-based caching approaches: individual objects are accessed by a very small number of users [12]. This means that a large number (or all) of those objects needs to be proactively but cost-effectively replicated.

1.4 Our contributions and results

Our work makes the following contributions:
• The design and implementation of the first system that uses information about future bandwidth availability to provide optimally efficient bulk data transfers.
• The evaluation of *NetStitcher* on an emulation testbed showing that: a) for a large set of datacenter sender-receiver pairs in North America, *NetStitcher* doubles the median transferred volume over 24 hours. Especially when the sender is in the east and the receiver in the West Coast, *NetStitcher* can carry up five times more data than the second best policy; b) *NetStitcher* delivers tera-byte sized files in a few hours, whereas competing policies might take days; c) *NetStitcher* performs well even in international transfers in view of additional backbone network constraints.
• Our live deployment of *NetStitcher* on Telefonica's global CDN. The Points of Presence (PoP) of large CDNs are small datacenters that exchange large volumes of pushed or pulled content. We show that by using leftover CDN bandwidth when the video traffic subsides, our solution can perform bulk transfers at a very low cost per GB. Drawing from these results, *NetStitcher* is planned to augment our CDN service portfolio by allowing content owners to cheaply perform point-to-point high volume transfers. CDN services are more attractive "when viewed as as broader portfolio of services for content owners and providers" [11].

2. MOTIVATING EXAMPLE

We present a simple example to motivate the need for multipath and multi-hop store-and-forward (SnF) schedul-

ing, and to highlight the limitations of existing techniques. The example is based on the real topology of Equinix [3], a company offering hosting services over its global network of datacenter, which includes 22 locations in North America.

Specifically, we want to maximize the volume of data that a datacenter in New York can backup to another one in Palo Alto within 24 hours, assuming that datacenters have a 3 hour time window early in the morning (*e.g.*, 3-6am) for performing such backups. Windows are depicted as rectangles in Fig. 2. Two sites can exchange data directly only if their respective rectangles overlap in time. All sites are assumed to have the same bandwidth capacity.

End-to-end: The simplest mechanism to backup data across the two locations is to use a direct End-to-End transfer. As can be seen in Fig. 2, no data can be backed up using direct E2E transfers since the windows of New York and Palo Alto do not overlap in time. This is a consequence of the window width that we assume, and the 3 hour difference between Eastern and Pacific time. However, even with a wider window – assuming that the windows begin at the same local time – the two sites would be wasting at least 3 hours of valuable bandwidth due to their time difference.

Multipath overlay routing: Overlay routing [13] is used to bypass problematic links, or even entire network segments. In our case, however, the problem is caused by the first and the last hop of the transfer. Thus, overlay redirection does not help because it still requires New York and Palo Alto to have free bandwidth at the same time. In fact, no overlay spatial redirection suffices to address the misalignment of windows. We need a combination of spatial and temporal redirection through the use of storage nodes.

Figure 2 depicts how a scheduled SnF solution can use the bandwidth and storage of 5 intermediate sites to maximize the amount of data that can be transferred between two end points. During the first hour of its window, from 3am to 4am Eastern, New York transfers data to a site in Boston (arrow (1)), where it remains stored for up to 2 hours. Between 4am and 5am, New York uploads to Chicago (2), and between 5am and 6am to Denver (3).

If the above data can be delivered to their final destination before the closing of its window, then New York will have utilized optimally its bandwidth. Indeed this can be achieved as follows. Boston relays its data to Phoenix (4) where they remain for 2 hours. Subsequently Phoenix relays the data to Seattle (7), which finally delivers them to Palo Alto one hour later (8), utilizing the last hour of Palo Alto's window. Chicago delivers its data directly to Palo Alto (5) and so does Denver one hour later (6), thus filling up the first 2 hours of Palo Alto's window.

This simple example shows that multipath and multi-hop SnF succeeds where E2E and Overlay fail. However, real SnF scheduling is substantially more involved due to the existence of varying windows and capacities, as well as additional network and storage bottlenecks. *NetStitcher* copes with this complexity and hides it from the applications. Before discussing the details of its design we will consider whether simpler SnF solutions, such as BitTorrent suffice.

Simple store-and-forward: In a nutshell, simple greedy or random SnF algorithms fail as they do not have complete information on the duration, time and location of windows. This results in data being pushed to sites that cannot deliver it forward to the destination or any other intermediate relay node (or if they do, they do it in an inefficient manner).

For example a node in New York may start greedily feeding a faster node in London, but London's window may close before it can push the data towards any useful direction. All the capacity of New York, which is committed to feeding the London site, is wasted. This is only a motivating example. More intricate inefficiencies occur in complex networks due to the myopic view of simple SnF algorithms.

3. SYSTEM OVERVIEW

NetStitcher is an overlay system comprising of a sender, intermediate storage nodes, and a receiver node. Its goal is to minimize the transfer time of a given volume given the predicted availability of leftover bandwidth resources at the access links and the backbone.

It comprises the following modules: a) *overlay management*, which is responsible for maintaining the connectivity of the overlay; b) *volume prediction*, which is responsible for measuring and predicting the available network resources; c) *scheduling*, which computes the transfer schedule that minimizes the transfer time of the given volume; and d) *transmission management*, which executes the transfer schedule specified by the scheduling module.

The scheduling module is the core of our system and we describe it in detail in Sect. 4. It schedules data transfers across multiple hops and multiple paths over the overlay. The scheduling module only specifies the rate at which each node forwards data to the other nodes. The volume to be transferred is divided in pieces and nodes follow primarily a simple piece forwarding rule: a node can forward each piece only once and to a node that has not received it. (We violate this rule in exceptional cases as discussed in Sect. 4.4 and Sect. 4.4 of [29].) By decoupling the scheduling and forwarding we simplify the design.

3.1 Design Goals

We now discuss the goals of our design and summarize how we achieve them:

Use leftover bandwidth effectively: *NetStitcher*'s multi-hop and multipath transfer scheduler uses unutilized bandwidth resources whenever and wherever they become available. Multipath data transfers enable *NetStitcher* to deal with resource constraints at the intermediate storage nodes. Multi-hop data transfers allow *NetStitcher* to use leftover bandwidth even when the window of the intermediate storage nodes in a single intermediate time zone does not overlap with the window of the sender or the receiver.

Accommodate common pricing schemes: *NetStitcher* leverages unutilized but already paid-for bandwidth, irrespective of the pricing scheme details. Such bandwidth can be manifested in two ways: a) a backbone provider has unutilized transit bandwidth during off-peak hours, which he can offer for cheap to its customers; b) a customer may not be utilizing the capacity he has reserved on a dedicated line. Also, if the customer is billed under the 95th-percentile rule, *NetStitcher* can use the difference between the 95-percentile and the customer's actual utilization.

Easily deployable: *NetStitcher* works at the application layer of low or high-end servers and does not require modifications on network devices.

Adapt to churn and failures: Our design periodically revises the transfer schedule taking into consideration failures, resource prediction errors, and how much data have already been transferred to the intermediate storage nodes

and the receiver. By using optimal flow algorithms and resolving extreme estimation error through an end-game-mode (Sect. 4.4), we obviate the need for inefficient redundancy through re-transmissions or forward error correction codes. Due to prediction errors and unexpected events, the initially computed transfer schedule may be erroneous. Its revision may yield a longer transfer time than initially scheduled. Therefore, at the start of a transfer, *NetStitcher* can guarantee meeting a set deadline only in the absence of critical failures and unpredictable resource availability changes.

4. SCHEDULING

We now provide a detailed description of the scheduling component in three stages: a) perfect knowledge under network bottlenecks (backbone constraints) only; b) perfect knowledge under both network and edge bottlenecks; and c) imperfect knowledge under network and edge bottlenecks.

4.1 Scheduling problem statement

First, we formulate the problem that scheduling addresses. Consider a sender node v that wants to send a large file of size F to a receiver node u. The sender can utilize any leftover uplink bandwidth that cannot be saturated by its direct connection to the receiver to forward additional pieces of the file to storage nodes in the set W. Nodes in W can in turn store the pieces until they can forward them to the receiver or another storage node. We define the *Minimum Transfer Time* (MTT) problem as follows:

DEFINITION 1. *Let $MTT(F, v, u, W)$ denote the minimum transfer time to send a file of size F from v to u with the help of nodes $w \in W$ under given uplink, downlink, storage, and backbone network constraints (bottleneck) at all the nodes. The Minimum Transfer Time problem amounts to identifying a transmission schedule between nodes that yields the minimum transfer time $MTT(F, v, u, W)$.*

The task of *NetStitcher* is to achieve $MTT(F, v, u, W)$ in controlled environments where the available bandwidth is known a priori, or approximate it given some error in bandwidth prediction and occasional node churn. We also note that it is straightforward to adapt the algorithm that solves the MTT (Sect. 4.2.1) so that it maximizes the volume transferred in a given time period.

Figure 3 depicts a group of *NetStitcher* nodes and summarizes the notation for the rest of the section. $U_w(t)$ and $D_w(t)$ denote the volume of data from file F that can be sent on the *physical* uplink and downlink of node w during time slot t, which we refer to as *edge bottlenecks*. In the simplest case, edge bottlenecks are given by the nominal capacity of the access links and thus are independent of time. They become time dependent if a site's operator allocates bandwidth to the system only during specific time-of-day windows. $N_{ww'}(t)$ denotes the volume of data that can be sent on the *overlay* link from w to w' due to *network bottlenecks* (backbone constraints). Such bottlenecks capture the bandwidth allocation policies of backbone operators that might, for example, prohibit bulk transfers over links that are approaching their peak utilization. *NetStitcher* can use such information to derive backbone operator-friendly bulk transfer schedules (more in Sect. 7.3). $S_w(t)$ denotes the maximum volume of data from file F that can be stored at w during time slot t. It is dependent on the node's storage

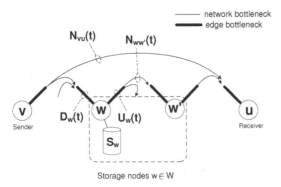

Figure 3: Model and definitions. $U_w(t)$, $D_w(t)$: uplink and downlink edge bottlenecks of w at time t. $N_{ww'}(t)$: network bottleneck of overlay connection $w \to w'$ at time slot t. $S_w(t)$: storage capacity of w at time slot t.

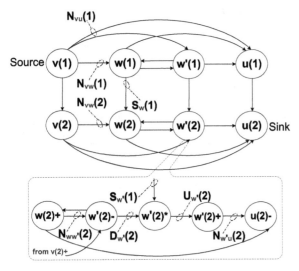

Figure 4: Reduction of the MTT problem to a variant of the maximum flow problem using time expansion. The upper portion of the figure shows the reduction when we consider only network bottlenecks. The bottom (zoomed-in) portion of the figure shows the reduction when we consider edge bottlenecks.

capacity and on the amount of storage required by other applications or *NetStitcher* sessions.

4.2 Perfect knowledge

Our approach is to reduce the MTT problem to the max-flow problem. We express the edge and network bottlenecks and the storage limits as the capacities of edges in a max-flow graph. We model the time dimension of the MTT problem through time expansion as we shortly describe.

First, we consider the case in which the bandwidth and storage resources, $U_w(t)$, $D_w(t)$, $N_{ww'}(t)$ and $S_w(t)$, are known a priori for all $w \in W$ and all time slots t that make up an entire day.

4.2.1 Network bottlenecks only

We initially consider the case when there are no edge bottlenecks. We reduce the MTT problem of minimizing the delivery time of volume F using nodes with time-varying

storage and bandwidth to a maximum flow problem with constant edge capacity. The reduction is performed through the time-expansion shown in Fig. 4. Let T_{max} be an upper bound on the minimum transfer time. We construct a max-flow problem over a flow network $G(V, E)$ as follows:
- *Node set V:* For each storage node $w \in W$ (Sect. 4.1), and for $1 \le t \le T_{max}$, we add T_{max} virtual nodes $w(t)$. Similarly for the sender v and the receiver u.
- *Edge set E:* To model storage constraints, for $1 \le t \le T_{max} - 1$, we connect $w(t)$ with $w(t+1)$ with a directed edge of capacity $S_w(t)$. We repeat the same for the sender v and the receiver u. To model network constraints, for $1 \le t \le T_{max}$, we connect $w(t)$ with $w'(t)$, $w, w' \in W$ with a directed edge of capacity $N_{ww'}(t)$ and similarly for the sender and the receiver.
- *Single source and sink:* The source is the sender virtual node $v(1)$. The sink is the receiver virtual node $u(T_{max})$.

The maximum flow from $v(1)$ to $u(T_{max})$ equals the maximum volume that *NetStitcher* can send over T_{max} time slots. We obtain an optimal transmission schedule for the volume F by performing a binary search to find the minimum T_{max} for which the maximum flow from $v(1)$ to $u(T_{max})$ equals the volume F. We can now map the max-flow solution to a transmission schedule as follows: if the max-flow solution involves flow f crossing the edge $(w(t), w'(t))$, an optimal schedule should transmit a volume of size f from w to w' during slot t.

In most cases, the network bottlenecks observed by *NetStitcher* flows are due to backbone operator rate-limiting policies with respect to bulk flows; namely whether they admit additional bulk traffic on a link during a certain time window. Although the rate-limiting policy may depend on bandwidth availability of the physical link, we assume that in most cases the *NetStitcher* flows comprise a small portion of the link's utilization and do not compete for capacity. Therefore, we model every link that connects two nodes as a distinct edge in E. In the rare cases of multiple *NetStitcher* flows competing on a link, one can detect the shared bottleneck [25] and model it as an additional edge.

4.2.2 Edge and network bottlenecks

We now incorporate the edge node uplink and downlink bottlenecks in the MTT problem. We split each virtual node $w(t)$ in three parts, as shown in the bottom of Fig. 4: the front part $w(t)-$ is used for modeling the downlink bottleneck $D_w(t)$, the middle part $w(t)\star$ models the storage capacity $S_w(t)$, whereas the back part $w(t)+$ models the uplink bottleneck $U_w(t)$. The sender node has only a "+" part and the receiver has only a "−" part. The complete reduction is:
- *Node set V:* For each storage node $w \in W$ (Sect. 4.1) and for $1 \le t \le T_{max}$ we add virtual nodes $w(t)-$, $w(t)\star$, $w(t)+$. Similarly for the sender v and the receiver u.
- *Edge set E:* For $1 \le t \le T_{max} - 1$, we connect $w(t)\star$ with $w(t+1)\star$ with a directed edge of capacity $S_w(t)$. We repeat the same for the sender v and the receiver u. For $1 \le t \le T_{max}$, we connect $w(t)-$ with $w(t)\star$ and $w(t)\star$ with $w(t)+$ with a directed edge of capacity $D_w(t)$ and $U_w(t)$, respectively. Also, we connect $v(t)\star$ with $v(t)+$ and $u(t)-$ with $u(t)\star$ with a directed edge of capacity $U_v(t)$ and $D_u(t)$, respectively. In addition, for $1 \le t \le T_{max}$, we connect $w(t)+$ with $w'(t)-$, $w, w' \in W$ with a directed edge of capacity $N_{ww'}(t)$ and similarly for the sender and the receiver.

- *Single source and sink:* The source is the sender virtual node $v(1)\star$. The sink is the receiver virtual node $u(T_{max})\star$.

As before, we obtain the optimal MTT transmission schedule by finding the max-flow for the smallest T_{max} that equals the volume to be transferred F.

4.3 Imperfect knowledge

We have so far assumed perfect prior knowledge of bandwidth bottlenecks which is exactly the case when the datacenter operator regulates explicitly the amount of bandwidth given to the system. The system is also capable of operating in environments with imperfect yet predictable periodic patterns and adapt gracefully to estimation error end node failure. We describe how next.

We periodically recompute the transmission schedule based on revised bottleneck predictions provided by the prediction module (Sect. 5). We also recompute the transmission schedule when we detect an unexpected component failure. The first computation of the transmission schedule is as described above. However, for the subsequent computations, apart from the updated bottlenecks, we need to take into account that the sender may have already delivered some part of the file to intermediate storage nodes and the final receiver. We capture this by augmenting our basic time-expansion: we assign a new demand at the source $F_v \le F$ and assign a new demand F_w at each intermediate storage node $w \in W$. F_w is equal to the volume of file data w currently stores. This casts the MTT problem into a multiple source maximum flow problem. The details are as follows:

- *Node and Edge sets:* The node and edge sets between the sender, the receiver and the intermediate storage nodes are obtained as described in Sect. 4.2.2.
- *Multiple sources and single sink:* We represent the volume that has yet to be transferred to the receiver as a flow from *multiple* sources to the sink node $u(T_{max})\star$. We then cast the multiple source max-flow problem to a single source max-flow as follows [19]. We create a virtual super-source node S. We connect S to the sender virtual node $v(1)$ with a directed edge of capacity equal to the demand F_v, which is equal to the volume of the file the sender has not yet transmitted to any storage node or the receiver. We also connect S to each storage virtual node $w(1)$ with a directed edge of capacity F_w equal to the volume of file data it currently stores.

An optimal transmission schedule is obtained by finding the minimum T_{max} for which the total flow from the super-source S to $u(T_{max})\star$ equals the remaining undelivered volume: $F_v + \sum_{w \in W} F_w$. The mapping from the resulting flow into a transmission schedule is as before.

We observe the following about our choice to address imperfect prediction with periodic recomputation:

Stateless. Each successive recomputation depends only implicitly on previous ones through the amount of data that has already been delivered to the storage nodes and the receiver. We do not need to consider past schedules.

Simplifies the admission of multiple jobs. The ability to revise the schedule of yet undelivered parts of a job can be used to handle multiple sender-receiver pairs. For example, a new job can run with the storage and bandwidth resources that are available given the already accepted jobs, or it can be allowed to "steal" resources from them. In that case, already accepted jobs will perceive this as estimation error and adjust. If the workload is known a priori, one can perform a joint optimization of all jobs in parallel instead of

the simpler online approach mentioned above by reducing it to a maximum concurrent flow problem [35].

Gracefully falls back to multipath overlay routing. Although it is not our intended deployment scenario, *NetStitcher* can be used for settings in which only short term predictions are available. In this case, we make the re-optimization intervals short. As a result, *NetStitcher* behaves similar to overlay routing – only the schedule for the first few time slots which is based on the available information executes. The schedule for later slots for which reliable information is not available will not execute, as it will be preceded by a re-optimization.

4.4 End-game mode

The above algorithm adapts to prediction errors by periodically revising the transmission schedule. In extreme situations however, even periodic revision does not suffice. For example, a node can go off-line, or its uplink can be substantially reduced, unexpectedly holding back the entire transfer due to pieces that get stuck at the node. Since we consider this to be an extreme case rather than the norm, we address it through a simple *end-game-mode* (EGM) [18] approach as follows. Due to the low cost of storage, we can keep at some storage nodes "inactive" replicas of already forwarded pieces. If the piece is deemed delayed by the time that the EGM kicks in, a replica can switch to "active" and be pulled directly by the receiver. Similar to BitTorrent, we further subdivide a piece in subpieces. The EGM starts after a large portion (*e.g.*, 95%) of the file has been delivered, and it pulls subpieces of the delayed piece simultaneously from the source and the storage nodes that store active replicas.

4.5 Computational cost

In both the perfect and imperfect knowledge case, if the demands and capacities are encoded as integer values, we can solve the MTT in $O(F|W|^2 T_{max} \log(T_{max}))$ using the Ford-Fulkerson (FF) algorithm. A typical scenario in our experiments (Sect. 8.1) involves $|W|=14$ intermediate storage nodes, $T_{max} = 100$ and $F = 100000$. Our Python FF implementation can solve this instance in less than 25 seconds on an Intel Duo 2.40GHz, 3MB CPU, with 4GB RAM. For further speedup we can use one of the many heuristic or approximation algorithms for max flow problems [31].

5. IMPLEMENTATION

NetStitcher is implemented as a library that exposes a simple API with the following calls: join(v), leave(v), and send(v,u,F). The first two are for joining and leaving the *NetStitcher* overlay and the third for initiating the transfer of a file F from v to u. It is implemented in *Python* and C++ and is approximately 10K lines. The system comprises of the following modules:

Overlay management: This module runs at the *broker process* and is responsible for adding a new node to the overlay and removing it.

Volume prediction: It runs at the broker process and the *peer processes* and its task is to maintain a time series with the maximum volume of data that can be forwarded to each neighbor during the slots that constitute an entire day. As it is usually the case, we assume that the bandwidth resources exhibit periodic behavior. Thus, the module uses the history of the time series to predict the future volumes. It obtains this history using the bandwidth monitoring tools of our backbone provider, Telefonica International WholeSale Services (TIWS). It uses the Sparse Periodic Auto-Regression (SPAR) estimator [16] to derive a prediction for the next 24 hours. It assumes a period of resource availability $T_p = 24\ hours$, and divides time in 1-hour-long time slots t. SPAR performs short-term forecasting of the volume at time t by considering the observed volumes at $t - kT_p$ and the differences between the volumes at $t - j$ and $t - j - kT_p$, where $t, j, k \in \mathbb{N}$. We derive a long-term forecasting by deriving a prediction for $t + 1$ considering the prediction for t, and continuing recursively until we predict the volume for $t + 24$.

Scheduling: This module is invoked at the *scheduler process* by peer v when it wishes to send a file to another receiver peer u. It is responsible for scheduling all data transfers between the sender v, the storage nodes W and the receiver node u. It uses volume predictions to calculate an initial transfer schedule and keeps updating it periodically as it receives updated predictions from the nodes (details in Sect. 4). The transfer schedules are computed by solving a maximum flow optimization problem using the GLPK simplex-based solver of the PuLP Python package [32].

Transmission management: This module runs at the peer processes, getting scheduling commands from the scheduler process. For each scheduling slot, the peers translate the scheduled amount volume to a set of pieces that are transferred during the slot. To avoid creating unnecessary spikes, transfers occur using CBR over the duration of the slot.

6. NORTH AMERICAN TRANSFERS

Since most datacenters are located in North America we begin our evaluation from there. In a subsequent section we look at international transfers. We build our case study around Equinix [3] which operates 62 datacenters in 22 locations across the four time zones that cover North America. The exact breakdown of locations and datacenters to time zones is: a) 16 datacenters in 3 locations in Pacific; b) 2 datacenters in 2 locations in Mountain; c) 12 datacenters in 4 locations in Central; and d) 32 datacenters in 13 locations in Eastern (see [3] for the exact list of locations).

6.1 Experimental setting

Sender-receiver pairs: We assume that only one datacenter in each location participates in the *NetStitcher* network. We consider all sender-receiver pairs of such datacenters that are located in different time zones.

Datacenter characteristics: We assume that each site has 1Gbps uplink and downlink transit bandwidth that is made available for inter-datacenter bulk transfer during early morning hours: 3am to 6am. This access link configuration is chosen based on [10] which reports that most firms had between 1 and 10 Gbps of transit bandwidth in each datacenter where they have a point of presence. The duration of the window was based on discussions with datacenter operators [6]. We vary it in Sect. 6.4 to show its effect. In this first set of results we do not consider backbone constraints.

Transfer policies: We consider the following policies: End-to-End (E2E), Overlay, Random store-and-forward, BitTorrent (BT), and *NetStitcher*. Since in this setting there are no bottlenecks in the backbone and the senders have the same capacity as the receivers, E2E and Overlay perform equally. Consequently, we refer to them as E2E/Overlay.

Overlay, Random SnF, BitTorrent, and *NetStitcher* are allowed to use any intermediate Equinix datacenter other than the sender and the receiver. Random SnF is the simplest store-and-forward policy in which the file is cut in pieces and forwarding decisions are completely random. It introduces no redundancy by relaying a single copy of each file part. An alternative approach is to use multiple copies of file parts to deal with the lack of informed scheduling. A simple way to do this with an existing technology is to set up a BT swarm with the initial seeder as the sender, a receiver, and a number of intermediate BT clients acting as relays.

Methodology: We run all the above policies on a dedicated server cluster using our *NetStitcher* implementation and the μTorrent client. Overlay is obtained from *NetStitcher* by setting the available storage of intermediate nodes to a very low value. Random SnF is obtained from *NetStitcher* by not imposing any rate limits specified by the scheduler. E2E is obtained from *NetStitcher* by removing intermediate storage nodes. We repeat each experiment 5 times and we report means and confidence intervals. In all experiments we attempt to sent a 1223GB file. 1223GB is actually the maximum that can be transferred due to access link capacities, independently of timing issues (1Gbps × 3 hours considering header overheads and TCP inefficiencies).

Metrics: For each pair of datacenters we attempt to send the above mentioned file and report the transferred volume to the receiver within 24 hours starting at the beginning of the window of the sender. We also look at the transfer completion time for a given file size.

6.2 Transferred volume

Figure 5(a) depicts the complimentary cumulative distribution function (CCDF) of transferred volume over 24 hours between all 286 pairs of locations in which Equinix operates at least one datacenter. We make the following observations:

• *NetStitcher* is always better than all other competing policies. E2E/Overlay is better than BT and Random SnF in most pairs. And BT is generally better than Random SnF.

• *NetStitcher* transfers up to 1223GB in one day whereas E2E/Overlay goes up to 833GB, BT up to 573GB and Random SnF up to 448GB.

• The median volume *NetStitcher* transfers (783GB) is almost double or more than that of all other policies .

To interpret the above results we start with the factor that has the most profound effect on performance – the amount of misalignment between windows of leftover bandwidth at the sender and the receiver. In this particular example, the misalignment is directly related to the local time. In Fig. 5(b) we plot the transferred volume of different policies against the time zone difference between the sender and the receiver, which ranges from -3 hours, in the direction from Eastern to Pacific time, and up to to +3 hours, in the opposite direction. To explain better the situation we also include the performance when both ends are on the same time zone (not included in the previous figure). We conclude:

• **When there is no time difference,** E2E/Overlay matches the optimal performance of *NetStitcher* which depends only on the capacity of the two end points. Random SnF suffers by permitting file parts to do random walks over intermediate datacenters. In some cases, they will be delivered through longer suboptimal paths, whereas in other cases they will get stuck in intermediate nodes and never be delivered. By creating multiple copies of the same file part

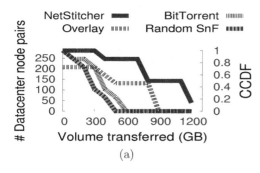

(a)

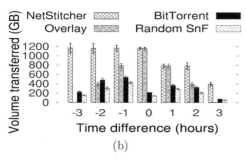

(b)

Figure 5: (a) CCDF of the volumes transferred between a *NetStitcher* sender and receiver among all possible sender/destination pairs in the North American Equinix topology. The y axis indicates the number of pairs that have transfered more than the specified volume during the first 24h of the transfer; (b) Mean volumes transferred in 24h and 95% confidence intervals. The x axis indicates the time difference between the receiver and the sender, e.g., -3 means that the receiver is 3h behind the sender.

and relaying them through all intermediate nodes BT pays a penalty in cases when Random SnF succeeds in delivering a file part to the final receiver without using redundant copies. When however Random SnF gets stuck, BT has a better chance to deliver due to the multiple copies it relays. The poor performance of the two extreme cases of simple store-and-forward, full (BT) and no (Random SnF) redundancy, highlights the value of *NetStitcher* scheduling.

• **When the time difference is negative,** *i.e.,* when transferring from east to west, *NetStitcher* remains optimal in terms of absolute transfer volume . In the same direction, E2E/Overlay, BT, and Random SnF decline progressively, suffering by the increasing misalignment of windows. E2E/Overlay however, is more severely penalized due to its lack of store-and-forward capabilities and eventually ends up carrying no data. BT is consistently better than Random SnF but is always at least 50% worse than *NetStitcher*.

• **With positive time difference,** even *NetStitcher* cannot avoid losing capacity. This is because when the window of a sender opens at 3am local time, the window of the receiver at a +1h time zone has already been open for one hour and has been effectively lost. The same applies to E2E/Overlay. With a +2h time zone difference between sender and receiver, E2E/Overlay loses two hours of available bandwidth but *NetStitcher* loses only one. This might seem odd but it is in fact expected. A +2h receiver will be opening its window for the second time 22 hours after the opening of the window of the sender. This hour can be used, not by

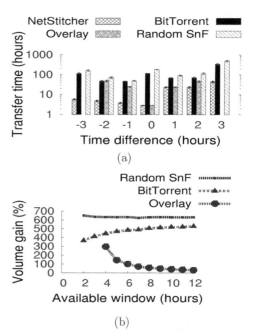

(a)

(b)

Figure 6: (a) Mean transfer times for 1150GB volume and 95% confidence intervals. The x axis indicates the time difference between the receiver and the sender. For -3h and +3h, difference overlay has infinite transfer time and is not depicted. (b) Normalized transfered volume gains of *NetStitcher* over another policy as a function of the available window.

the sender, but by a +1h intermediate storage node that received the data at a prior time and stored them until that point. This explains why the performance of *NetStitcher* deteriorates slower than E2E/Overlay when going from west to east.

6.3 Transfer time

Another way to observe the performance benefits of *Net-Stitcher* is to look at the transfer completion time of fixed size files. For this purpose, we set the volume equal to 1150GB, which is close to the maximum that can be shipped by *NetStitcher* in the 3 hours that the window of the sender opens. We measure the transfer time for all policies. The results are depicted in Fig. 6(a):

• For the -3h pairs (Eastern and Pacific), we see that *Net-Stitcher* delivers the volume on average in 5 hours 45 minutes whereas E2E/Overlay can never deliver it (infinite time), BT needs around 5 days, and Random SnF around 7 days.

• In the absence of time zone difference, *NetStitcher* and E2E/Overlay achieve the absolute minimum of 3 hours, as derived by the access link capacities.

• In the opposite direction, for the +3h pairs (Pacific, Eastern), we see that *NetStitcher* incurs its highest delay of approximately 1 day plus 21 hours approximately. This is approximately 7.5 times smaller than the second best BT.

6.4 Effect of the window

Next we look at the effect of variable available window on the volume transferred over 24. Specifically, we compute the normalized gain of *NetStitcher* against any of the competing policies (*i.e.,* (volume-of-*NetStitcher* − volume-of-policy)/volume-of-policy), for all sender and receiver pairs. As can be seen in Fig. 6(b), even with a 12 hour window, the gain of *NetStitcher* over E2E/Overlay is approximately 25%. BT and Random SnF are always substantially worse. We have experimented with several other parameters of the system such as the access bandwidth capacities, amount of storage, number of relay nodes, and the results are consistent and supportive of our above main observations.

6.5   North American transfers conclusions

The important lessons from our evaluation are:
- *NetStitcher* always outperforms store and forward policies that do not consider future resource availability, and instead redundantly and/or randomly forward data.
- The benefits of *NetStitcher* over end-to-end or multipath overlay policies, which do not utilize storage, increase with the decrease of the duration of the window and the increase of the time difference between the sender and the receiver.
- Store and forward policies are more effective when the time difference between the receiver and the sender is positive, *i.e.*, the receiver resides west of the sender.

7.   INTERNATIONAL TRANSFERS

In this section we turn our attention to international transfers between continents. We use this setting to study two issues: a) the effect of a larger time zone difference between the sender and receiver; and b) the effect of additional constraints appearing in the backbone network. Long haul links (*e.g.*, transatlantic) have more intricate peak and valley behavior than access links since they carry traffic from multiple time zones. Thus they can create additional constraints, e.g., by peaking at hours that do not coincide with the peak hours of their end points. *NetStitcher* can circumvent around such combined constraints due to its advanced network and edge constraint scheduling.

7.1   Experimental setting

Topology: We now present a case study in which Equinix uses the international backbone of TIWS to perform bulk transfers between its sites. TIWS is a transit provider [9] with PoPs in more than 30 countries and peering points with more than 200 other large networks. WS peers with Equinix datacenters in 7 locations in Europe, 1 in Asia, and 4 in US. We emulate a scenario in which *NetStitcher* nodes with 1Gbps uplink/downlink are collocated with Equinix datacenters in Frankfurt, Dusseldorf, Zurich, New York and Palo Alto as shown in Fig. 7. The figure shows the actual WS backbone links that connect the above cities Next to the name of each city we state the real number of Equinix datacenters in that city. For each setting we repeat the experiment 5 times and report mean values in Table 1.
Backbone constraints: We assume that the backbone operator permits bulk traffic to cross only links that are on a valley, *i.e.*, are close to their minimum utilization. Backbone operators naturally prefer to carry delay tolerant traffic during the off peak hours of their links thus improving their overall utilization. This can benefit both backbone operators who can postpone costly upgrades and datacenter operators who can be offered better pricing schemes/QoS if they stir their bulk traffic in an a backbone-friendly manner. *NetStitcher* achieves this objective through its ability to schedule around combined edge and network bottlenecks (described in Sect. 4.2.2). To showcase the above, we used

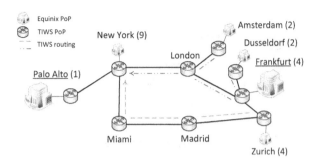

Figure 7: The joint Equinix/TIWS topology used in our transfer from Frankfurt to Palo Alto. In parenthesis we list the number of datacenters operated by Equinix in each city.

real 5-minute aggregate utilization data from TIWS and integrated these constraints to our emulation environment.

7.2   Crossing the Atlantic

We now zoom on the details of a transatlantic transfer between an Equinix datacenter in Frankfurt and one in Palo Alto. This example highlights the additional measures that need to be taken in terms of scheduling and provisioning of storage nodes when transfers are subjected to combined backbone and access link bottlenecks. The Atlantic presents one of the toughest barriers for inter datacenter bulk transfers since there are no major relay nodes in between to assist in the transfer. Therefore we study it to determine what can be achieved in this difficult but important case.

Starting with the sending and receiving windows of the datacenters we notice that these need to be at least 7 hours long. This is because the windows need to bridge the 6 hour gap between central Europe (GMT+1) and the East Coast of the US (GMT-5), and leave at least one hour of overlap for performing the transfer. We assume that the available window starts at 00:00 am local time and ends at 7:00 am local time at each datacenter. Assuming that there are no backbone constraints, the Frankfurt datacenter can upload for 2 hours to 2 datacenters in Amsterdam, another 2 hours to 2 datacenters in Dusseldorf, and another 2 hours to 2 datacenters in Zurich. Then during the last hour of its window (5am-6am GMT), which overlaps with the first hour of the window of New York, Frankfurt, and the other 6 datacenters in Amsterdam, Dusseldorf, and Zurich can push in parallel all their data to 7 datacenters in New York. The New York datacenters can eventually deliver them to Palo Alto, 16 hours after Frankfurt initiated the transfer. Effectively, Frankfurt can deliver to Palo Alto as much data as its window permits within a day (first row of Table 1).

7.3   Putting the backbone in the picture

The previous example shows that large enough windows at the end-points combined with sufficient intermediate storage nodes can bypass the Atlantic barrier. In reality, however, all the European datacenters of Equinix have to cross the Atlantic using one of TIWS's transatlantic links. In particular, due to the topology and routing of TIWS, Frankfurt, Amsterdam, and Dusseldorf cross the Atlantic through the London-New York link, whereas Zurich crosses through the Madrid-Miami link (Fig. 7). However, these links become available for bulk transfers at different times of the day and

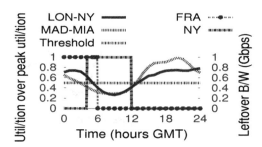

Figure 8: Diurnal utilizations of the London-New York (LON-NY) and Madrid-Miami (MIA-MAD) transatlantic TIWS backbone links. We also depict the cutoff threshold (0.5) and the available windows of the New York (GMT-5) and Central Europe, e.g., FRA, datacenters (GMT+1). Due to confidentiality reasons we report the utilization over peak utilization ratio, instead of the actual utilization.

for different durations. We assume that bulk traffic is allowed only as long as it does not exceed the cutoff threshold, which we set equal to 50% of the peak actual link utilization. Consequently based on our utilization traces, the London-New York link becomes available from 7am GMT to 2pm GMT, whereas the Madrid-Miami link becomes available from 3am GMT to 1pm GMT (see Fig. 8). Thus, the Madrid-Miami link is available for bulk transfers during a bigger part of the day than the London-New York link.

Backbone-constraint-unaware scheduler: A scheduler that is unaware of backbone constraints, such as the above, can push data to datacenters whose exit link over the Atlantic is unavailable when their available windows overlap with the available windows of their intended receiver datacenters in the East Coast. In particular, because of the unavailability of the London-New York link at 5am GMT, all the data at Frankfurt, Amsterdam, and Dusseldorf cannot cross the Atlantic. At the same time, however, the Madrid-Miami link is available, thus the 2 Zurich datacenters can push their data to New York. This way however, only 2 hours worth of data using Frankfurt's uplink capacity can be delivered to Palo Alto during a day.

Backbone-constraint-aware scheduler: The scheduler that is aware of both edge and backbone constraints (Sect. 4.2.2), can deliver up to 4 hours worth of data. This is done by sending 4 hours instead of 2 hours worth of data to Zurich, and having the 4 datacenters in Zurich forward their data to New York through the Madrid-Miami link. Note that the Madrid-Miami link is available between 5am and 6am GMT when the available window of the Central Europe datacenters overlaps with the window of New York. Approximately 4 hours worth of data is the best attainable performance given the number and locations of Equinix datacenters, and the topology and routing rules of TIWS.

To increase the performance to the maximum 7 hours worth of data, Zurich needs to have 7 datacenters. Alternatively, TIWS can install a dedicated *NetStitcher* node in its PoP in Madrid (last row of Table 1).

7.4 International transfers conclusions

The conclusions from this evaluation are:
• Backbone bottlenecks may appear on transatlantic links.

Conditions	Volume Transferred	Transfer Time
No backbone constraints	2720GB	16h
Backbone constraints and constraint-aware scheduler	1553GB	36.4h
Backbone constraints and constraint-unaware scheduler	799GB	∞
Backbone constraints, constraint-aware scheduler and *NetStitcher* node in Madrid	2720GB	16h

Table 1: Volumes transferred during 24h and the total time it takes to transfer 2720GB between the Frankfurt and Palo Alto Equinix datacenters. We repeat the experiment 5 times and report mean values. We consider as the start time of a transfer the moment the window of Frankfurt becomes available.

These bottlenecks render transfer schedules that do not consider them ineffective, and raise the need for a backbone-constraint-aware transfer scheduler.
• The introduction of *NetStitcher* storage nodes in strategically selected locations is needed to bypass network bottlenecks and maximize efficiency.

8. LIVE CDN DEPLOYMENT

In this section we present a real deployment of *NetStitcher* aiming to: a) assess the forecasting accuracy of the SPAR-based predictor; and b) quantify cost savings based on a simple, but realistic pricing scheme.

The system has been installed on a subset of nodes operated by a global CDN platform. The CDN serves video and other content and is deployed in 19 Points of Presence (PoP) in Europe, North and South America. For our experiments we had access to 49 CDN servers, each with direct Gbps access to the backbone and abundant storage. *NetStitcher* is planned to run on top of this infrastructure and take advantage of its resources when the critical operational traffic (video or file-sharing) to local customers subsides.

8.1 Experimental setting

We evaluate *NetStitcher* in the presence of emulated CDN operational traffic. Our purpose is to show that our scheduling algorithm can substantially reduce costs, even when the nodes have irregular but mostly predictable capacity.

Hardware and software: Each CDN server has a quad Intel Xeon 2GHz/4MB CPU, 4GB RAM, 2TB storage, and runs Red Hat 4.1.2-46 with a 2.6.18-164.el5 kernel. Each server has 1Gbps uplink/downlink capacity.

Sender-receiver pairs: We use 3 CDN servers in Spain (Madrid and Barcelona; GMT+1), 2 servers in the UK (London; GMT+0), 3 servers in Argentina (Buenos Aires; GMT-3), 3 servers in Chile (Valparaiso; GMT-4), 3 servers in the East Coast (Miami and New York; GMT-5), 1 server in the central US (Dallas; GMT-6), and 1 server in the West Coast (Palo Alto; GMT-8). We consider all the sender-receiver pairs between servers residing in distinct timezones.

Methodology: We use a 4-day trace of the CDN operational load of the node in Madrid. Unlike other nodes used in our experiment, Madrid's is currently part of our commercial deployment with a load largely induced by a TV broadcaster. Thus, as expected it exhibits a periodic diurnal behavior, allowing us to use it for a more faithful evaluation.

We depict the last 2 days of the trace in Fig. 9(a). For confidentiality reasons we report the ratio of the utilization over the 95th-percentile utilization. We normalize this ratio to correspond to the utilization of the server's 1Gbps capacity. We assign this diurnal load to all CDN servers for the time zone they reside in. We assign the remaining capacity as available resources for *NetStitcher*, E2E/Overlay and BT.

The transfers start on the 4th day of Madrid CDN trace at 0am GMT+1. *NetStitcher* knows the operational traffic load of the first 3 days. It uses it to predict the bandwidth availability during the 4th day with the autoregressive volume predictor. The predictor revises the prediction as described in Sect. 5. Considering the revisions, we recompute the transfer schedule (Sect. 4.3) every 1 hour.

According to this time series, the uplink capacity of the CDN servers suffices to upload at most 4260GB over a day. We therefore arrange for *NetStitcher* and BT to transfer a volume of this size. For each sender-receiver pair we repeat the experiment 5 times and we compute the cost savings of using *NetStitcher*, E2E/Overlay and BT.

Pricing scheme: The cost of leftover bandwidth used by *NetStitcher* and the other policies is zero. The transit bandwidth for our CDN costs $7/Mbps/month. In this deployment, the customer wants to transfer a 4260GB file in 24 hours. If the policy is unable to deliver all the file, the customer sends the remainder using a CBR end-to-end transfer over 24 hours, and pays for the excess transit bandwidth. This excess bandwidth is paid at both the sender and the receiver under the 95th-percentile billing scheme. *NetStitcher* and BT incur the additional cost of intermediate node storage. To compute this cost we consider the storage occupied on an hourly basis. We approximate the storage cost at the intermediate nodes by considering the per-hour normalized cost of Amazon S3 [1]: $0.000076 per GB per hour.

8.2 Live deployment results and conclusions

Performance of the autoregressive predictor: In Fig. 9(a) we depict the forecast of the autoregressive predictor as derived at the end of the 3rd day. As can be seen, the predictor approximates satisfactorily the actual CDN utilization, with a 0.18 maximum error.

Cost savings: Figure 9(b) shows the monthly cost for transferring 4260GB every day with *NetStitcher*, E2E/Overlay and BT against the time zone difference between the sender and the receiver. We observe that:

• *NetStitcher* yields up to 86% less cost compared to the E2E/Overlay when the sender is in GMT+1 and the receiver in GMT-6. It yields up to 90% less cost compared to BT when the sender is in GMT+0 and the receiver in GMT+3.

• *NetStitcher* yields the greatest cost savings when the time difference is negative, *i.e.*, when going from east to west. As the time difference between sender and receiver increases, the costs for all policies increase. BT however is more severely penalized due to its excessive replication, which forces the customer to send up to ~85% of its data using additional transit bandwidth, when the time difference is +9h. For +9h time difference, E2E/Overlay costs almost as much as *NetStitcher*. In this case, the extra paid bandwidth for *NetStitcher* is slightly lower than E2E/Overlay and do not compensate for *NetStitcher*'s storage requirements. We note that the reported monetary values would be proportionally higher if the deployment involved a larger file, and thereby more servers and more transit bandwidth.

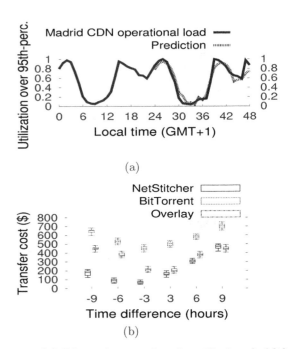

(a)

(b)

Figure 9: (a) Diurnal operational traffic bandwidth utilization of the Madrid CDN node; (b) Percentile plot of USD monthly cost for transferring 4260GB every day. The x axis indicates the time difference between the receiver and the sender. For each time difference, the boxes are shown in the horizontal order NetStitcher, BT and Overlay.

• The maximum storage required by *NetStitcher* is 619GB per 24 hours, when the sender resides in GMT-8 and the receiver in GMT+1. This entails a monthly cost of ~$33, which is substantially lower than the median bandwidth cost for this case: $438. On average, storage costs are only 14% of the total cost. This is because an intermediate storage node can delete a piece after forwarding it. On the other hand BT, which maintains copies of forwarded data, needs a maximum storage of 1872GB per 24 hours, yielding a $101 monthly cost.

9. RELATED WORK

Differentiated traffic classes: There have been proposals for bulk transfers at different layers of the protocol stack via differentiated treatment of traffic classes. For instance, the Scavenger service of Qbone [36] tags delay tolerant bulk traffic so that routers can service it with lower priority. However, such approaches use end-to-end flows, and thus suffer from the shortcomings of the E2E policy discussed before. That is, they allow a single bottleneck to block the utilization of bandwidth that gets freed up elsewhere in the path.

Delay tolerant networks: Store-and-forward has been used in proposals for wireless intermittently connected Delay Tolerant Networks (DTN) [24]. Mobile devices forward and store messages with the aim of eventually delivering them to the intended final recipient whose location is unknown and changing. Such systems have to operate in highly unpredictable environments and suffer from disconnections at both the control (routing) and the data plane (transmission). *NetStitcher* is designed to tap on periodic phenomena appearing in wireline networks while having at its disposal an always connected control plane that allows it to schedule and route efficiently. On a tangential but still related area, [23] shows that mobility combined with storage increases the capacity of wireless DTNs. *NetStitcher* does the same by using storage to stitch together leftover capacity that would otherwise be wasted due to time misalignments.

Breitgand et al. [15] used store and forward to deliver individual low priority messages of a network monitoring system over a single path. They proposed an online algorithm to deal with unpredictable changes in resource availability. We target multipath bulk transfers in mostly predictable environments, which dictates the reduction of our problem to an efficiently computable maximum flow formulation. We address unpredictability by recomputing the schedule sufficiently often and when component failure is detected.

Point-to-point multipath bulk transfers: Pucha et al.'s dsync [34] is a file transfer system that adapts to network conditions by determining which of its available resources (e.g. network, disk, network peers) is the best to use at any given time and by exploiting file similarity [33]. *NetStitcher* does not rely on network peers that store content of interest in advance, and it has different design goals. Signiant [8] and Riverbed [7] offer point-to-point intra-business content transfer and application acceleration platforms, which utilize WAN optimization technologies. One could view *NetStitcher* as an additional WAN optimization technology. To the best of our knowledge, Signiant and RiverBed do not employ store and forward techniques.

Kokku et al. [27] focus on the TCP implications of multipath background transfers. They do not consider store and forward, but instead aim at making bulk background transfers more TCP-friendly, while maintaining efficiency.

Single-hop and single-path SnF bulk transfers: The closest work to *NetStitcher* is [30, 28], which developed analytical models for transferring bulk data through single-hop and single-path transfers while minimizing 95th-percentile transit costs for Telcos. It quantified the cost for transferring bulk scientific data across time zones and compared it to the use of postal service. That work did not address design and implementation issues, whereas *NetStitcher* is a system deployed in a production setting for SnF bulk transfers. In this work, we extend SnF scheduling beyond the simple case of single-path and single-hop over a single unconstrained storage node presented in [30].

10. CONCLUSIONS AND FUTURE WORK

We have presented the design, implementation, and validation of *NetStitcher*. It is a system for stitching together unutilized bandwidth across different datacenters, and using it to carry inter-datacenter bulk traffic for backup, replication, or data migration applications. *NetStitcher* bypasses the problem of misaligned leftover bandwidth by using scheduled multipath and multi-hop store-and-forward through intermediate storage nodes. As future work, we consider results on bootstrapping deployments and on security. An additional interesting topic is to adapt our system for operations in a P2P setting (higher churn, free-riding, etc).

11. REFERENCES

[1] Amazon Simple Storage Service. aws.amazon.com/s3/.
[2] Datacenter map. www.datacentermap.com/datacenters.html.
[3] Equinix datacenter map. www.equinix.com/data-center-locations/map/.
[4] Facebook Statistics. www.facebook.com/press/info.php?statistics.
[5] James Hamilton's blog: Inter-datacenter replication & geo-redundancy. perspectives.mvdirona.com/2010/05/10/InterDatacenterReplicationGeoRedundancy.aspx.
[6] Personal communication.
[7] Riverbed Products&Services. http://www.riverbed.com/us/products/index.php.
[8] Signiant Products. www.signiant.com/Products-content-distribution-management/.
[9] Telefonica International Wholesale Services Network Map. http://www.e-mergia.com/en/mapaRed.html.
[10] Forrester Research. The Future of Data Center Wide-Area Networking. info.infineta.com/l/5622/2011-01-27/Y26, 2010.
[11] Ovum. CDNs The Carrier Opportunity. reports.innovaro.com/reports/cdns-the-carrier-opportunity, 2010.
[12] B. Ager, F. Schneider, J. Kim, and A. Feldmann. Revisiting Cacheability in Times of User Generated Content. In *IEEE Global Internet'10*.
[13] D. Andersen, H. Balakrishnan, F. Kaashoek, and R. Morris. Resilient Overlay Networks. In *ACM SOSP'01*.
[14] D. Beaver, S. Kumar, H. C. Li, J. Sobel, and P. Vajgel. Finding a Needle in Haystack: Facebook's Photo Storage. In *USENIX OSDI'10*.
[15] D. Breitgand, D. Raz, and Y. Shavitt. The Traveling Miser Problem. In *IEEE/ACM Transactions on Networking'06*.
[16] G. Chen, W. He, J. Liu, S. Nath, L. Rigas, L. Xiao, and F. Zhao. Energy-Aware Server Provisioning and Load Dispatching for Connection-Intensive Internet Services. In *USENIX NSDI'08*.
[17] Y. Chen, S. Jain, V. K. Adhikari, Z.-L. Zhang, and K. Xu. A First Look at Inter-Data Center Traffic Characteristics via Yahoo! Datasets. In *IEEE INFOCOM'11*.
[18] B. Cohen. Incentives Build Robustness in BitTorrent. In *P2P Econ'03*.
[19] T. H. Cormen, C. E. Leiserson, R. L. Rivest, and C. Stein. Introduction to Algorithms. MIT Press'01.
[20] J. Gray. Long Term Storage Trends and You, 2006. http://research.microsoft.com/~Gray/talks/IO_talk_2006.ppt.
[21] A. Greenberg, J. Hamilton, D. A. Maltz, and P. Patel. The Cost of a Aloud: Research Problems in Data Center Networks. *ACM SIGCOMM Comput. Commun. Rev.*, 39(1), '09.
[22] A. Greenberg, J. R. Hamilton, N. Jain, S. Kandula, C. Kim, P. Lahiri, D. A. Maltz, P. Patel, and S. Sengupta. VL2: a Scalable and Flexible Data Center Network. In *ACM SIGCOMM'09*.
[23] M. Grossglauser and D. Tse. Mobility Increases the Capacity of Ad-hoc Wireless Networks. In *IEEE/ACM Transactions on Networking'01*.
[24] S. Jain, K. Fall, and R. Patra. Routing in a Delay Tolerant Network. In *ACM SIGCOMM'04*.
[25] D. Katabi, I. Bazzi, and X. Yang. A Passive Approach for Detecting Shared Bottlenecks. In *IEEE ICCN'02*.
[26] R. Kohavi, R. M. Henne, and D. Sommerfield. Practical Guide to Controlled Experiments on the Web: Listen to Your Customers not to the HiPPO. In *ACM KDD'07*.
[27] R. Kokku, A. Bohra, S. Ganguly, and A. Venkataramani. A Multipath Background Network Architecture. In *IEEE INFOCOM'07*.
[28] N. Laoutaris and P. Rodriguez. Good Things Come to Those Who (Can) Wait or How to Handle Delay Tolerant Traffic and Make Peace on the Internet. In *ACM HotNets-VII'08*.
[29] N. Laoutaris, M. Sirivianos, X. Yang, and P. Rodriguez. Inter-Datacenter Bulk Transfers with NetSticher. Technical report, 2011. Available at the authors' website.
[30] N. Laoutaris, G. Smaragdakis, P. Rodriguez, and R. Sundaram. Delay Tolerant Bulk Data Transfers on the Internet. In *ACM SIGMETRICS'09*.
[31] T. Leighton, C. Stein, F. Makedon, E. Tardos, S. Plotkin, and S. Tragoudas. Fast Approximation Algorithms for Multicommodity Flow Problems. In *ACM STOC'91*.
[32] S. Mitchell and J. Roy. Pulp Python LP Modeler. code.google.com/p/pulp-or/.
[33] H. Pucha, D. G. Andersen, and M. Kaminsky. Exploiting Similarity for Multi-Source Downloads using File Handprints. In *USENIX NSDI'07*.
[34] H. Pucha, M. Kaminsky, D. Andersen, and M. Kozuch. Adaptive file transfers for diverse environments. In *USENIX ATC'08*.
[35] F. Shahrokhi and D. Matula. The Maximum Concurrent Flow Problem. In *Journal of the ACM'90*.
[36] S. Shalunov and B. Teitelbaum. Qbone Scavenger Service (QBSS) Definition. Internet2 Technical Report'01.
[37] D. Ziegler. Distributed Peta-Scale Data Transfer. www.cs.huji.ac.il/~dhay/IND2011.html.

The Power of Prediction:
Cloud Bandwidth and Cost Reduction

Eyal Zohar[*]
Technion - Israel Institute of
Technology
eyalzo@tx.technion.ac.il

Israel Cidon
Technion - Israel Institute of
Technology
cidon@ee.technion.ac.il

Osnat (Ossi) Mokryn[†]
Tel Aviv Academic College
ossi@mta.ac.il

ABSTRACT

In this paper we present PACK (Predictive ACKs), a novel end-to-end Traffic Redundancy Elimination (TRE) system, designed for cloud computing customers.

Cloud-based TRE needs to apply a judicious use of cloud resources so that the bandwidth cost reduction combined with the additional cost of TRE computation and storage would be optimized. PACK's main advantage is its capability of offloading the cloud-server TRE effort to end-clients, thus minimizing the processing costs induced by the TRE algorithm.

Unlike previous solutions, PACK does not require the server to continuously maintain clients' status. This makes PACK very suitable for pervasive computation environments that combine client mobility and server migration to maintain cloud elasticity.

PACK is based on a novel TRE technique, which allows the client to use newly received chunks to identify previously received chunk chains, which in turn can be used as reliable predictors to future transmitted chunks.

We present a fully functional PACK implementation, transparent to all TCP-based applications and network devices. Finally, we analyze PACK benefits for cloud users, using traffic traces from various sources.

Categories and Subject Descriptors

C.2.m [**Computer-Communication Networks**]: Miscellaneous

General Terms

Algorithms, Design, Measurement

Keywords

Caching, Cloud computing, Network optimization, Traffic redundancy elimination

---

[*]Also with HPI Research School.

[†]Also with Technion - Israel Institute of Technology.

1. INTRODUCTION

Cloud computing offers its customers an economical and convenient *pay as you go* service model, known also as *usage-based pricing* [6]. Cloud customers[1] pay only for the actual use of computing resources, storage and bandwidth, according to their changing needs, utilizing the cloud's scalable and elastic computational capabilities. Consequently, cloud customers, applying a judicious use of the cloud's resources, are motivated to use various traffic reduction techniques, in particular Traffic Redundancy Elimination (TRE), for reducing bandwidth costs.

Traffic redundancy stems from common end-users' activities, such as repeatedly accessing, downloading, distributing and modifying the same or similar information items (documents, data, web and video). TRE is used to eliminate the transmission of redundant content and, therefore, to significantly reduce the network cost. In most common TRE solutions, both the sender and the receiver examine and compare signatures of data chunks, parsed according to the data content prior to their transmission. When redundant chunks are detected, the sender replaces the transmission of each redundant chunk with its strong signature [16, 23, 20]. Commercial TRE solutions are popular at enterprise networks, and involve the deployment of two or more proprietary protocol, state synchronized middle-boxes at both the intranet entry points of data centers and branch offices, eliminating repetitive traffic between them (e.g., Cisco [15], Riverbed [18], Quantum [24], Juniper [14], Bluecoat [7], Expand Networks [9] and F5 [10]).

While proprietary middle-boxes are popular point solutions within enterprises, they are not as attractive in a cloud environment. First, cloud providers cannot benefit from a technology whose goal is to reduce customer bandwidth bills, and thus are not likely to invest in one. Moreover, a fixed client-side and server-side middle-box pair solution is inefficient for a combination of a mobile environment, which detaches the client from a fixed location, and cloud-side elasticity which motivates work distribution and migration among data centers. Therefore, it is commonly agreed that a universal, software-based, end-to-end TRE is crucial in today's pervasive environment [4, 1]. This enables the use of a standard protocol stack and makes a TRE within end-to-end secured traffic (e.g., SSL) possible.

In this paper, we show that cloud elasticity calls for a new TRE solution that does not require the server to continuously maintain clients' status. First, cloud load balancing and power optimizations may lead to a server-side process and data migration environment, in which TRE solutions that require full synchronization between the server and the client are hard to accomplish or may lose ef-

---

[1]We refer as *cloud customers* to organizations that export services to the cloud, and as *users* to the end-users and devices that consume the service

ficiency due to lost synchronization. Moreover, the popularity of rich media that consume high bandwidth motivates CDN solutions, in which the service point for fixed and mobile users may change dynamically according to the relative service point locations and loads.

Finally, if an end-to-end solution is employed, its additional computational and storage costs at the cloud-side should be weighed against its bandwidth saving gains. Clearly, a TRE solution that puts most of its computational effort on the cloud-side[2] may turn to be less cost-effective than the one that leverages the combined client-side capabilities. Given an end-to-end solution, we have found through our experiments that sender-based end-to-end TRE solutions [23, 1] add a considerable load to the servers, which may eradicate the cloud cost saving addressed by the TRE in the first place. Moreover, our experiments further show that current end-to-end solutions also suffer from the requirement to maintain end-to-end synchronization that may result in degraded TRE efficiency.

In this paper, we present a novel receiver-based end-to-end TRE solution that relies on the power of predictions to eliminate redundant traffic between the cloud and its end-users. In this solution, each receiver observes the incoming stream and tries to match its chunks with a previously received chunk chain or a chunk chain of a local file. Using the long-term chunks meta-data information kept locally, the receiver sends to the server predictions that include chunks' signatures and easy to verify hints of the sender's future data. Upon a hint match the sender triggers the TRE operation, saving the cloud's TRE computational effort in the absence of traffic redundancy.

Offloading the computational effort from the cloud to a large group of clients forms a load distribution action, as each client processes only its TRE part. The receiver-based TRE solution addresses mobility problems common to quasi-mobile desktop/laptops computational environments. One of them is cloud elasticity due to which the servers are dynamically relocated around the federated cloud, thus causing clients to interact with multiple changing servers. Another property is IP dynamics, which compel roaming users to frequently change IP addresses. In addition to the receiver-based operation, we also suggest a hybrid approach, which allows a battery powered mobile device to shift the TRE computation overhead back to the cloud by triggering a sender-based end-to-end TRE similar to [1].

To validate the receiver-based TRE concept, we implemented, tested and performed realistic experiments with PACK within a cloud environment. Our experiments demonstrate a cloud cost reduction achieved at a reasonable client effort while gaining additional bandwidth savings at the client side. The implementation code, over 25,000 lines of C and Java, can be obtained from [22]. Our implementation utilizes the TCP Options field, supporting all TCP-based applications such as web, video streaming, P2P, email, etc.

We propose a new computationally light-weight chunking (fingerprinting) scheme termed *PACK chunking*. PACK chunking is a new alternative for Rabin fingerprinting traditionally used by RE applications. Experiments show that our approach can reach data processing speeds over 3 Gbps, at least 20% faster than Rabin fingerprinting.

In addition, we evaluate our solution and compare it to previous end-to-end solutions using tera-bytes of real video traffic consumed by 40,000 distinct clients, captured within an ISP, and traffic obtained in a social network service for over a month. We demonstrate that our solution achieves 30% redundancy elimination without sig-

nificantly affecting the computational effort of the sender, resulting in a 20% reduction of the overall cost to the cloud customer.

The paper is organized as follows: Section 2 reviews existing TRE solutions. In Section 3 we present our receiver-based TRE solution and explain the prediction process and the prediction-based TRE mechanism. In Section 4 we present optimizations to the receiver-side algorithms. Section 5 evaluates data redundancy in a cloud and compares PACK to sender-based TRE. Section 6 details our implementation and discusses our experiments and results.

2. RELATED WORK

Several TRE techniques have been explored in recent years. A protocol-independent TRE was proposed in [23]. The paper describes a packet-level TRE, utilizing the algorithms presented in [16].

Several commercial TRE solutions described in [15] and [18], have combined the sender-based TRE ideas of [23] with the algorithmic and implementation approach of [20] along with protocol specific optimizations for middle-boxes solutions. In particular, [15] describes how to get away with three-way handshake between the sender and the receiver if a full state synchronization is maintained.

[3] and [5] present redundancy-aware routing algorithm. These papers assume that the routers are equipped with data caches, and that they search those routes that make a better use of the cached data.

A large-scale study of real-life traffic redundancy is presented in [11], [25] and [4]. Our paper builds on the latter's finding that "an end to end redundancy elimination solution, could obtain most of the middle-box's bandwidth savings", motivating the benefit of low cost software end-to-end solutions.

Wanax [12] is a TRE system for the developing world where storage and WAN bandwidth are scarce. It is a software-based middle-box replacement for the expensive commercial hardware. In this scheme, the sender middle-box holds back the TCP stream and sends data signatures to the receiver middle-box. The receiver checks whether the data is found in its local cache. Data chunks that are not found in the cache are fetched from the sender middle-box or a nearby receiver middle-box. Naturally, such a scheme incurs a three-way-handshake latency for non-cached data.

EndRE [1] is a sender-based end-to-end TRE for enterprise networks. It uses a new chunking scheme that is faster than the commonly-used Rabin fingerprint, but is restricted to chunks as small as 32-64 bytes. Unlike PACK, EndRE requires the server to maintain a fully and reliably synchronized cache for each client. To adhere with the server's memory requirements these caches are kept small (around 10 MB per client), making the system inadequate for medium-to-large content or long-term redundancy. EndRE is server specific, hence not suitable for a CDN or cloud environment.

To the best of our knowledge none of the previous works have addressed the requirements for a cloud computing friendly, end-to-end TRE which forms PACK's focus.

3. THE PACK ALGORITHM

For the sake of clarity, we first describe the basic receiver-driven operation of the PACK protocol. Several enhancements and optimizations are introduced in Section 4.

The stream of data received at the PACK receiver is parsed to a sequence of variable size, content-based signed chunks similar to [16][20]. The chunks are then compared to the receiver local storage, termed *chunk store*. If a matching chunk is found in the local chunk store, the receiver retrieves the sequence of subsequent chunks, referred to as a *chain*, by traversing the sequence of LRU

---

[2]We assume throughout the paper that the cloud-side, following the current Web service model, is dominated by a sender operation.

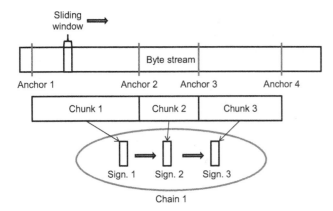

Figure 1: From stream to chain

chunk pointers that are included in the chunks' metadata. Using the constructed chain, the receiver sends a prediction to the sender for the subsequent data. Part of each chunk's prediction, termed a *hint*, is an easy to compute function with a small enough false-positive value, such as the value of the last byte in the predicted data or a byte-wide XOR checksum of all or selected bytes. The prediction sent to the receiver includes the range of the predicted data, the hint and the signature of the chunk. The sender identifies the predicted range in its buffered data, and verifies the hint for that range. If the result matches the received hint, it continues to perform the more computationally intensive SHA-1 signature operation. Upon a signature match, the sender sends a confirmation message to the receiver, enabling it to copy the matched data from its local storage.

3.1 Receiver Chunk Store

PACK uses a new *chains* scheme, described in Figure 1, in which chunks are linked to other chunks according to their last received order. The PACK receiver maintains a *chunk store*, which is a large size cache of chunks and their associated meta-data. Chunk's meta-data includes the chunk's signature and a (single) pointer to the successive chunk in the last received stream containing this chunk. Caching and indexing techniques are employed to efficiently maintain and retrieve the stored chunks, their signatures and the chains formed by traversing the chunk pointers.

When the new data is received and parsed to chunks, the receiver computes each chunk's signature using SHA-1. At this point, the chunk and its signature are added to the chunk store. In addition, the meta-data of the previously received chunk in the same stream is updated to point to the current chunk.

The unsynchronized nature of PACK allows the receiver to map each existing file in the local file system to a chain of chunks, saving in the chunk store only the meta-data associated with the chunks.[3] Using the latter observation, the receiver can also share chunks with peer clients within the same local network utilizing a simple map of network drives.

3.1.1 Chunk Size

The utilization of a small chunk size presents better redundancy elimination when data modifications are fine-grained, such as sporadic changes in a HTML page. On the other hand, the use of smaller chunks increases the storage index size, memory usage and magnetic disk seeks. It also increases the transmission overhead of the virtual data exchanged between the client and the server.

---

[3]De-duplicated storage systems provide similar functionality and can be used for this purpose.

Unlike IP level TRE solutions that are limited by the IP packet size (~1,500 bytes), PACK operates on TCP streams, and can, therefore, handle large chunks and entire chains. Although our design permits each PACK client to use any chunk size, we recommend an average chunk size of 8KB (see Section 6).

3.2 The Receiver Algorithm

Upon the arrival of new data, the receiver computes the respective signature for each chunk, and looks for a match in its local chunk store. If the chunk's signature is found, the receiver determines whether it is a part of a formerly received chain, using the chunks' meta-data. If affirmative, the receiver sends a prediction to the sender for several next expected chain chunks. The prediction carries a starting point in the byte stream (i.e., offset) and the identity of several subsequent chunks (PRED command).

Upon a successful prediction, the sender responds with a PRED-ACK confirmation message. Once the PRED-ACK message is received and processed, the receiver copies the corresponding data from the chunk store to its TCP input buffers, placing it according to the corresponding sequence numbers. At this point, the receiver sends a normal TCP ACK with the next expected TCP sequence number. In case the prediction is false, or one or more predicted chunks are already sent, the sender continues with normal operation, e.g., sending the raw data, without sending a PRED-ACK message.

Proc. 1 Receiver Segment Processing

1. **if** segment carries payload *data* **then**
2.   calculate chunk
3.   **if** reached chunk boundary **then**
4.   activate predAttempt()
5.   **end if**
6. **else if** PRED-ACK segment **then**
7.   processPredAck()
8.   activate predAttempt()
9. **end if**

Proc. 2 predAttempt()

1. **if** received *chunk* matches one in chunk store **then**
2.   **if** foundChain(*chunk*) **then**
3.   prepare PREDs
4.   send single TCP ACK with PREDs according to Options free space
5.   exit
6.   **end if**
7. **else**
8.   store *chunk*
9.   link *chunk* to current chain
10. **end if**
11. send TCP ACK only

Proc. 3 processPredAck()

1. **for all** offset ∈ PRED-ACK **do**
2.   read data from chunk store
3.   put data in TCP input buffer
4. **end for**

3.3 The Sender Algorithm

When a sender receives a PRED message from the receiver, it tries to match the received predictions to its buffered (yet to be sent) data. For each prediction, the sender determines the corresponding TCP sequence range and verifies the hint. Upon a hint match, the sender calculates the more computationally intensive SHA-1 signature for the predicted data range, and compares the result to the signature received in the PRED message. Note that in case the hint does not match, a computationally expansive operation is saved. If the two SHA-1 signatures match, the sender can safely assume that the receiver's prediction is correct. In this case, it replaces the corresponding outgoing buffered data with a PRED-ACK message.

Figure 2 illustrates the sender operation using state machines. Figure 2a describes the parsing of a received PRED command. Figure 2b describes how the sender attempts to match a predicted range to its outgoing data. First, it finds out if this range has been already sent or not. In case the range has already been acknowledged, the corresponding prediction is discarded. Otherwise, it tries to match the prediction to the data in its outgoing TCP buffers.

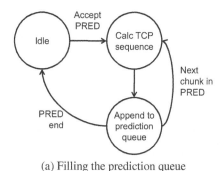

(a) Filling the prediction queue

(b) Processing the prediction queue and sending PRED-ACK or raw data

Figure 2: Sender algorithms

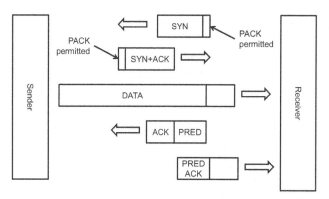

Figure 3: PACK wired protocol in a nutshell

3.4 The Wired Protocol

In order to conform with existing firewalls and minimize overheads, we use the TCP Options field to carry the PACK wired protocol. It is clear that PACK can also be implemented above the TCP level while using similar message types and control fields.

Figure 3 illustrates the way the PACK wired protocol operates under the assumption that the data is redundant. First, both sides enable the PACK option during the initial TCP handshake by adding a *PACK permitted* flag (denoted by a bold line) to the TCP Options field. Then, the sender sends the (redundant) data in one or more TCP segments, and the receiver identifies that a currently received chunk is identical to a chunk in its chunk store. The receiver, in turn, triggers a TCP ACK message and includes the prediction in the packet's Options field. Last, the sender sends a confirmation message (PRED-ACK) replacing the actual data.

4. OPTIMIZATIONS

For the sake of clarity, the previous section presents the most basic version of the PACK protocol. In the following one, we describe additional options and optimizations.

4.1 Adaptive Receiver Virtual Window

PACK enables the receiver to locally obtain the sender's data when a local copy is available, thus eliminating the need to send this data through the network. We term the receiver's fetching of such local data as the reception of *virtual data*.

When the sender transmits a high volume of virtual data, the connection rate may be, to a certain extent, limited by the number of predictions sent by the receiver. This, in turn, means that the receiver predictions and the sender confirmations should be expedited in order to reach high virtual data rate. For example, in case of a repetitive success in predictions, the receiver's side algorithm may become optimistic and gradually increase the ranges of its predictions, similarly to the TCP rate adjustment procedures.

PACK enables a large prediction size by either sending several successive PRED commands or by enlarging PRED command range to cover several chunks.

PACK enables the receiver to combine several chunks into a single range, as the sender is not bounded to the anchors originally used by the receiver's data chunking algorithm. The combined range has a new hint and a new signature that is a SHA-1 of the concatenated content of the chunks.

The variable prediction size introduces the notion of a *virtual window*, which is the current receiver's window for virtual data. The virtual window is the receiver's upper bound for the aggregated number of bytes in all the pending predictions. The virtual

Proc. 4 predAttemptAdaptive() - obsoletes Proc. 2

1. {new code for Adaptive}
2. **if** received *chunk* overlaps recently sent prediction **then**
3.   **if** received *chunk* matches the prediction **then**
4.   *predSizeExponent()*
5.   **else**
6.   *predSizeReset()*
7.   **end if**
8. **end if**
9. **if** received *chunk* matches one in signature cache **then**
10.   **if** foundChain(*chunk*) **then**
11.   {new code for Adaptive}
12.   prepare PREDs according to *predSize*
13.   send TCP ACKs with all PREDs
14.   exit
15.   **end if**
16. **else**
17.   store *chunk*
18.   append *chunk* to current chain
19. **end if**
20. send TCP ACK only

Proc. 5 processPredAckAdaptive() - obsoletes Proc. 3

1. **for all** offset $\in$ PRED-ACK **do**
2.   read data from disk
3.   put data in TCP input buffer
4. **end for**
5. {new code for Adaptive}
6. *predSizeExponent()*

Proc. 6 Receiver Segment Processing Hybrid - obsoletes Proc. 1

1. **if** segment carries payload *data* **then**
2.   calculate chunk
3.   **if** reached chunk boundary **then**
4.   activate predAttempt()
5.   {new code for Hybrid}
6.   **if** detected broken chain **then**
7.   calcDispersion(255)
8.   **else**
9.   calcDispersion(0)
10.   **end if**
11.   **end if**
12. **else if** PRED-ACK segment **then**
13.   processPredAck()
14.   activate predAttempt()
15. **end if**

Proc. 7 processPredAckHybrid() - obsoletes Proc. 3

1. **for all** offset $\in$ PRED-ACK **do**
2.   read data from disk
3.   put data in TCP input buffer
4.   {new code for Hybrid}
5.   **for all** chunk $\in$ offset **do**
6.   calcDispersion(0)
7.   **end for**
8. **end for**

---

window is first set to a minimal value, which is identical to the receiver's flow control window. The receiver increases the virtual window with each prediction success, according to the following description.

Upon the first chunk match, the receiver sends predictions limited to its initial virtual window. It is likely that, before the predictions arrive at the sender, some of the corresponding real data is already transmitted from it. When the real data arrives, the receiver can partially confirm its prediction and increase the virtual window. Upon getting PRED-ACK confirmations from the sender, the receiver also increases the virtual window. This logic resembles the slow-start part of the TCP rate control algorithm. When a mismatch occurs, the receiver switches back to the initial virtual window.

Proc. 4 describes the advanced algorithm performed at the receiver's side. The code at lines 2-8 describes PACK behavior when a data segment arrives after its prediction was sent and the virtual window is doubled. Proc. 5 describes the reception of a successful acknowledgement message (PRED-ACK) from the sender. The receiver reads the data from the local chunk store. It then modifies the next byte sequence number to the last byte of the redundant data that has just been read plus one, and sends the next TCP ACK, piggybacked with the new prediction. Finally, the virtual window is doubled.

The size increase of the virtual window introduces a trade-off in case the prediction fails from some point on. The code in Proc. 4 line 6 describes the receiver's behavior when the arriving data does not match the recently sent predictions. The new received chunk may, of course, start a new chain match. Following the reception of the data, the receiver reverts to the initial virtual window (conforming to the normal TCP receiver window size) until a new match

is found in the chunk store. Note that even a slight change in the sender's data, compared with the saved chain, causes the entire prediction range to be sent to the receiver as raw data. Hence, using large virtual windows introduces a tradeoff between the potential rate gain and the recovery effort in the case of a missed prediction.

4.2 The Hybrid Approach

PACK's receiver-based mode is less efficient if changes in the data are scattered. In this case, the prediction sequences are frequently interrupted, which, in turn, forces the sender to revert to raw data transmission until a new match is found at the receiver and reported back to the sender. To that end, we present the PACK hybrid mode of operation. When PACK recognizes a pattern of dispersed changes, it may select to trigger a sender-driven approach in the spirit of [23][15][18][5].

However, as was explained earlier, we would like to revert to the sender-driven mode with a minimal computational and buffering overhead at the server in the steady state. Therefore, our approach is to first evaluate at the receiver the need for a sender-driven operation and then to report it back to the sender. At this point, the sender can decide if it has enough resources to process a sender-driven TRE for some of its clients. To support this enhancement, an additional command (DISPER) is introduced. Using this command, the receiver periodically sends its estimated level of dispersion, ranging from 0 for long smooth chains, up to 255.

PACK computes the data dispersion value using an exponential smoothing function:

$$D \leftarrow \alpha D + (1 - \alpha)M \qquad (1)$$

Where α is a smoothing factor. The value M is set to 0 when a chain break is detected and 255 otherwise.

5. EVALUATION

The objective of this section is twofold: evaluating the potential data redundancy for several applications that are likely to reside in a cloud, and to estimate the PACK performance and cloud costs of the redundancy elimination process.

Our evaluations are conducted using (i) video traces captured at a major ISP, (ii) traffic obtained from a popular social network service, and (iii) genuine data sets of real-life workloads. In this section, we relate to an average chunk size of 8 KB, although our algorithm allows each client to use a different chunk size.

5.1 Traffic Redundancy

5.1.1 Traffic Traces

We obtained a 24 hours recording of traffic at an ISP's 10 Gbps PoP router, using a 2.4 GHz CPU recording machine with 2 TB storage (4 x 500 GB 7,200 RPM disks) and 1 Gbps NIC. We filtered YouTube traffic using deep packet inspection, and mirrored traffic associated with YouTube servers IP addresses to our recording device. Our measurements show that YouTube traffic accounts for 13% of the total daily web traffic volume of this ISP. The recording of the full YouTube stream would require 3 times our network and disk write speeds. Therefore, we isolated 1/6 of the obtained YouTube traffic, grouped by the video identifier (keeping the redundancy level intact) using a programmed load balancer that examined the upstream HTTP requests and redirected downstream sessions according to the video identifier that was found in the YouTube's URLs, to a total of 1.55 TB. We further filtered out the client IP addresses that were used too intensively to represent a single user, and were assumed to represent a NAT address.

Note that YouTube's video content is not cacheable by standard Web proxies since its URL contains private single-use tokens changed with each HTTP request. Moreover, most Web browsers cannot cache and reuse partial movie downloads that occur when end-users skip within a movie, or switch to another movie before the previous one ends.

Table 1 summarizes our findings. We recorded more than 146K distinct sessions, in which 37K users request over 39K distinct movies. Average movie size is 15 MB while the average session size is 12 MB, with the difference stemming from end-user skips and interrupts. When the data is sliced into 8 KB chunks, PACK brings a traffic savings of up to 30%, assuming the end-users start with an empty cache, which is a worst case scenario.

Figure 4 presents the YouTube traffic and the redundancy obtained by PACK over the entire period, with the redundancy sampled every 10 minutes and averaged. This end-to-end redundancy arises solely from self similarity in the traffic created by end-users. We further analyzed these cases and found that end-users very often download the same movie or parts of it repeatedly. The latter is mainly an inter-session redundancy produced by end-users that skip forward and backward in a movie and producing several (partially) overlapping downloads. Such skips occurred at 15% of the sessions and mostly in long movies (over 50 MB).

Since we assume the cache is empty at the beginning, it takes a while for the chunk cache to fill up and enter a steady state. In the steady state, around 30% of the traffic is identified as redundant and removed. We explain the length of the warm-up time by the fact that YouTube allows browsers to cache movies for 4 hours, which results in some replays that do not produce downloads at all.

Table 1: Data and PACK's results of 24 hours YouTube traffic trace

	Recorded
Traffic volume	1.55TB
Max speed	473Mbps
Est. PACK TRE	29.55%
Sessions	146,434
Unique videos	39,478
Client IPs	37,081

Figure 4: ISP's YouTube traffic over 24 hours, and PACK redundancy elimination ratio with this data

5.1.2 Static Data-set

We acquired the following static data-sets:

Linux source Different Linux kernel versions: all the forty 2.0.x tar files of the kernel source code that sum up to 1 GB.

Email A single-user Gmail account with 1,140 email messages over a year, that sum up to 1.09 GB.

The 40 Linux source versions were released over a period of two years. All tar files in the original release order, from 2.0.1 to 2.0.40, were downloaded to a download directory, mapped by PACK, to measure the amount of redundancy in the resulted traffic. Figure 5a shows the redundancy in each of the downloaded versions. Altogether the Linux source files show 83.1% redundancy, which accounts to 830 MB.

To obtain an estimate of the redundancy in email traffic we operated an IMAP client that fully synchronized the remote Gmail account with a new local folder. Figure 5b shows the redundancy in each month, according to the email message's issue date. The total measured traffic redundancy was 31.6%, which is roughly 350 MB. We found this redundancy to arise from large attachments that are sent by multiple sources, email correspondence with similar documents in development process and replies with large quoted text.

This result is a conservative estimate of the amount of redundancy in cloud email traffic, because in practice some messages are read and downloaded multiple times. For example, a Gmail user that reads the same attachment for 10 times, directly from the web browser, generates 90% redundant traffic.

Our experiments show that in order to derive an efficient PACK redundancy elimination, the chunk level redundancy needs to be applied along long chains. To quantify this phenomenon, we ex-

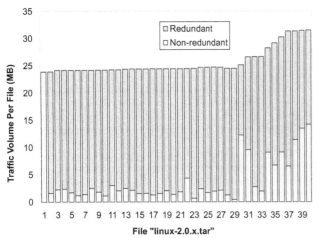

(a) Linux source: 40 different Linux kernel versions

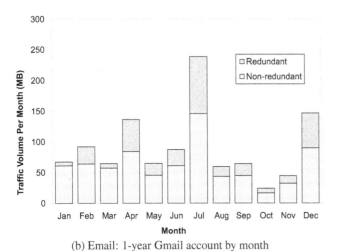

(b) Email: 1-year Gmail account by month

Figure 5: Traffic volume and detected redundancy

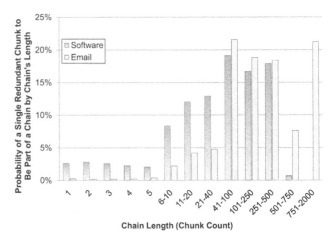

Figure 6: Chain length histogram Linux Software and Email data collections

plored the distribution of redundant chains in the Linux and Email data-sets. Figure 6 presents the resulted redundant data chain length distribution. In Linux 54% of the chunks are found in chains, and in Email about 88%. Moreover, redundant chunks are more probable to reside in long chains. These findings sustain our conclusion that once redundancy is discovered in a single chunk, it is likely to continue in subsequent chunks.

Furthermore, our evaluations show that in videos and large files with a small amount of changes, redundant chunks are likely to reside in very long chains that are efficiently handled by a receiver-based TRE.

5.2 Receiver-Based vs. Sender-Based TRE

In this subsection, we evaluate the sender performance of PACK as well as of a sender-based end-to-end TRE.

5.2.1 The Server Computational Effort

First, we evaluate the computational effort of the server in both cases. In PACK, the server is required to perform a SHA-1 operation over a defined range of bytes (the prediction determines a starting point, i.e., offset, and the size of the prediction) only after it verifies that the hint, sent as a part of the prediction, matches the data. In the sender-based TRE, the server is required to first com-

pute Rabin fingerprints in order to slice the stream into chunks, and then to compute a SHA-1 signature for each chunk, prior to sending it. Table 2 presents a summary of the server computational effort of each sender-based TRE described in the literature, as well as of PACK.

To further evaluate the server computational effort for the different sender-based and PACK TRE schemes, we measured the server effort as a function of time and traffic redundancy. For the sender-based scheme we simulated the approach of [12] using their published performance benchmarks[4]. We then measured the server performance as a function of the download time and redundant traffic for the Email data-set, that contains 31.6% redundancy. The sender effort is expressed by the number of SHA-1 operations per second.

Figure 7a demonstrates the high effort placed on a server in a sender-based scheme, compared to the much lower effort of a PACK sender, which performs SHA-1 operations only for data that matches the hint. Moreover, Figure 7b shows that the PACK server computational effort grows linearly with the amount of redundant data. As a result, the server works only when a redundancy is observed and the client reads the data from its local storage instead of receiving it from the server. This scenario demonstrates how the server's and the client's incentives meet: while the server invests the effort into saving traffic volume, the client cooperates to save volume and get faster downloads.

5.2.2 Synchronization

Several sender-based end-to-end TRE mechanisms require full synchronization between the sender and the receiver caches. When such synchronization exists, the redundancy is detected and eliminated upfront by the sender. While this synchronization saves an otherwise required three-way handshake, it ignores redundant chunks that arrive at the receiver from different senders. This problem is avoided in PACK, but we did not account this extra efficiency in our current study.

To further understand how TRE would work for a cloud-based web service with returning end-users, we obtained a traffic log from a *social network* site for a period of 33 days at the end of 2010. The data log enables a reliable long term detection of returning users, as users identify themselves using a login to enter the site. We

---

[4]The taken benchmarks: For 8 KB chunks the SHA-1 calculation throughput is about 250 Mbps with a Pentium III 850MHz and 500 Mbps with a Pentium D 2.8 GHz. Rabin fingerprint chunking is reported to be 2-3 times slower.

Table 2: Sender computational effort comparison between different TRE mechanisms

System	Avg. Chunk Size	Sender Chunking	Sender Signing	Receiver Chunking	Receiver Signing
PACK	Unlimited, receiver's choice	None	SHA-1: true predictions and 0.4% of false predictions	PACK chunking: all real data	SHA-1: all real data
Wanax [12]	Multiple	Multi-Resolution Chunking (MRC): all data	SHA-1: all data	Multi-Resolution Chunking (MRC): all data	SHA-1: all real data
LBFS [20]	Flexible, 8KB	Rabin: all modified data (not relying on database integrity)	SHA-1: all modified data (not relying on database integrity)	Rabin: all modified data (not relying on database integrity)	SHA-1: all modified data (not relying on database integrity)
[3]	None (representative fingerprints)	Rabin: all data (for lookup)	(see Sender Chunking)	None	None
EndRE [1] Chunk-Match	Limited, 32-64 bytes	SampleByte: all data (optionally less, at the cost of reduced compression)	SHA-1: all data (for chunk lookup)	None	None

identified the sessions of 7,000 registered users over this period. We then measured the amount of TRE that can be obtained with different cache sizes at the receiver (a synchronized sender-based TRE keeps a mirror of the last period cache size).

Figure 8 shows the redundancy that can be obtained for different caching periods. Clearly, a short-term cache cannot identify returning long-term sessions.

5.2.3 Users Mobility

Using the social network data-set presented above, we explored the effect of users' mobility on TRE. We focused on users that connected through 3G cellular networks with many device types (PCs, smartphones, etc.). Users are required to complete a registration progress, in which they enter their unique cellular phone number and get a password through SMS message.

We found that 62.1% of the cellular sessions were conducted by users that also got connected to the site through a non-cellular ISP with the same device. Clearly, TRE solutions that are attached to a specific location or rely on static client IP address cannot exploit this redundancy.

Another related finding was that 67.1% of the cellular sessions used IP addresses that were previously used by others in the same data-set. On non-cellular sessions we found only 2.2% of IP reuse. This one is also a major obstacle for synchronized solutions that require a reliable protocol-independent detection of returning clients.

5.3 Estimated Cloud Cost for YouTube Traffic Traces

As noted before, although TRE reduces cloud traffic costs, the increased server efforts for TRE computation result in increased server-hours cost.

We evaluate here the cloud cost of serving the YouTube videos described in Section 5.1 and compare three setups: without TRE, with PACK and with a sender-based TRE. The cost comparison takes into account server-hours and overall outgoing traffic throughput, while omitting storage costs that we found to be very similar in all the examined setups.

The baseline for this comparison is our measurement of a single video server that outputs up to 350 Mbps to 600 concurrent clients. Given a cloud with an array of such servers, we set the cloud policy to add a server when there is less than 0.25 CPU computation power unemployed in the array. A server is removed from this array if, after its removal, there is at least 0.5 CPU power left unused.

Table 3: Cloud operational cost comparison

	No TRE	PACK	Server-based
Traffic volume	9.1 TB	6.4 TB	6.2 TB
Traffic cost reduction (Figure 4)		30%	32%
Server-hours cost increase (Figure 9)		6.1%	19.0%
Total operational cost	100%	80.6%	83.0%

The sender-based TRE was evaluated only using a server's cost for a SHA-1 operation per every outgoing byte, which is performed in all previously published works that can detect YouTube's long-term redundancy.

Figure 9 shows, in the shaded part, the number of server-hours used to serve the YouTube traffic from the cloud, with no TRE mechanism. This is our base figure for costs, which is taken as the 100% cost figure for comparison. Figure 9 also shows the number of server-hours needed for this task with either PACK TRE or the sender-based TRE. While PACK puts an extra load of almost one server for only 30% of the time, which accounts for the amount of redundancy eliminated, the sender-based TRE scheme requires between one to two additional servers for almost 90% of the time, resulting in a higher operational cost for 32% redundancy elimination.

Table 3 summarizes the costs and the benefits of the TRE operations and compares them to a baseline with no TRE. The total operational cost is based on current Amazon EC2 [2] pricing for the given traffic-intensive scenario (traffic:server-hours cost ratio of 7:3). Both TRE schemes identify and eliminate the traffic redundancy. However, while PACK employs the server only when redundancy exists, the sender-based TRE employs it for the entire period of time, consuming more servers than PACK and no-TRE schemes when no or little redundancy is detected.

6. IMPLEMENTATION

In this section, we present PACK implementation, its performance analysis and the projected server costs derived from the implementation experiments.

Our implementation contains over 25,000 lines of C and Java

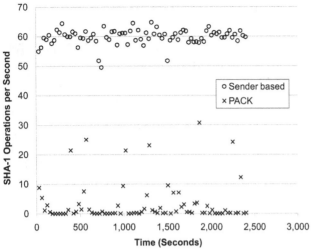

(a) Server effort as a function of time

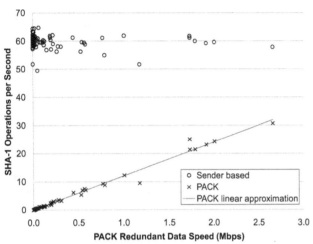

(b) Sender effort relative to redundant chunks signatures download time (virtual speed)

Figure 7: Difference in computation efforts between receiver and sender-driven modes for the transmission of Email data collection

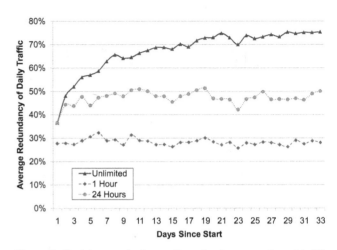

Figure 8: Social network site: traffic redundancy per day with different time-lengths of cache

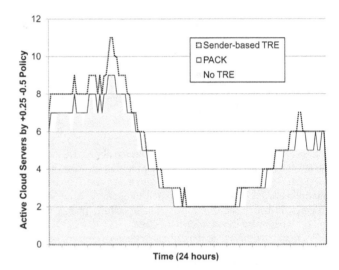

Figure 9: Number of cloud servers needed for serving YouTube traffic without TRE, with sender-based TRE or PACK

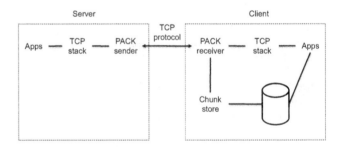

Figure 10: Overview of the PACK implementation

code. It runs on Linux with Netfilter Queue [21]. Figure 10 shows the PACK implementation architecture. At the server side, we use an Intel Core 2 Duo 3 GHz, 2 GB of RAM and a WD1600AAJS SATA drive desktop. The clients laptop machines are based on an Intel Core 2 Duo 2.8 GHz, 3.5 GB of RAM and a WD2500BJKT SATA drive.

Our implementation enables the transparent use of the TRE at both the server and the client. PACK receiver-sender protocol is embedded in the TCP Options field for low overhead and compatibility with legacy systems along the path. We keep the genuine operating systems' TCP stacks intact, allowing a seamless integration with all applications and protocols above TCP.

Chunking and indexing are performed only at the client's side, enabling the clients to decide independently on their preferred chunk size. In our implementation, the client uses an average chunk size of 8 KB. We found this size to achieve high TRE hit-ratio in the evaluated data-sets, while adding only negligible overheads of 0.1% in meta-data storage and 0.15% in predictions bandwidth.

For the experiments held in this section, we generated a workload consisting of Section 5 data-sets: IMAP emails, HTTP videos and files downloaded over FTP. The workload was then loaded to the server, and consumed by the clients. We sampled the machines' status every second to measure real and virtual traffic volumes and CPU utilization.

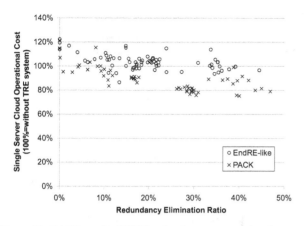

Figure 11: PACK vs. EndRE-like cloud server operational cost as a function of redundancy ratio

6.1 Server Operational Cost

We measured the server performance and cost as a function of the data redundancy level in order to capture the effect of the TRE mechanisms in real environment. To isolate the TRE operational cost, we measured the server's traffic volume and CPU utilization at maximal throughput without operating a TRE. We then used these numbers as a reference cost, based on present Amazon EC2 [2] pricing. The server operational cost is composed of both the network traffic volume and the CPU utilization, as derived from the EC2 pricing.

We constructed a system consisting of one server and seven clients over a 1 Gbps network. The server was configured to provide a maximal throughput of 50 Mbps per client. We then measured three different scenarios, a baseline no-TRE operation, PACK and a sender-based TRE similar to EndRE's Chunk-Match [1], referred to as *EndRE-like*. For the EndRE-like case, we accounted for the SHA-1 calculated over the entire outgoing traffic, but did not account for the chunking effort. In the case of EndRE-like, we made the assumption of unlimited buffers at both the server and client sides to enable the same long-term redundancy level and TRE ratio of PACK.

Figure 11 presents the overall processing and networking cost for traffic redundancy, relative to no-TRE operation. As the redundancy grows, the PACK server cost decreases due to the bandwidth saved by unsent data. However, the EndRE-like server does not gain a significant cost reduction since the SHA-1 operations are performed over non-redundant data too. Note that at above 25% redundancy, which is common to all reviewed data-sets, the PACK operational cost is at least 20% lower than that of EndRE-like.

6.2 PACK Impact on the Client CPU

To evaluate the CPU effort imposed by PACK on a client, we measured a random client under a scenario similar to the one used for measuring the server's cost, only this time the cloud server streamed videos at a rate of 9 Mbps to each client. Such a speed throttling is very common in real-time video servers that aim to provide all clients with stable bandwidth for smooth view.

Table 4 summarizes the results. The average PACK-related CPU consumption of a client is less than 4% for 9 Mbps video with 36.4% redundancy.

Figure 12a presents the client CPU utilization as a function of the real incoming traffic bandwidth. Since the client chunks the arriving data, the CPU utilization grows as more real traffic enters the client's machine. Figure 12b shows the client CPU utilization

Table 4: Client CPU utilization when streaming 9 Mbps video with and without PACK

No-TRE avg. CPU	7.85%
PACK avg. CPU	11.22%
PACK avg. TRE ratio	36.4%
PACK min CPU	7.25%
PACK max CPU	23.83%

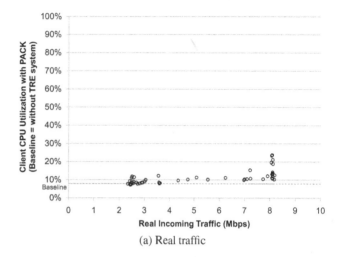

(a) Real traffic

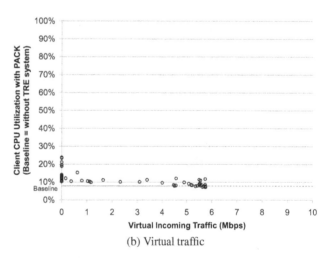

(b) Virtual traffic

Figure 12: Client CPU utilization as a function of the received traffic, when the client's CPU utilization without TRE is used as a baseline

as a function of the virtual traffic bandwidth. Virtual traffic arrives in the form of prediction approvals from the sender, and is limited to a rate of 9 Mbps by the server's throttling. The approvals save the client the need to chunk data or sign the chunks, and enable him to send more predictions based on the same chain that was just used successfully. Hence, the more redundancy is found, the less CPU utilization incurred by PACK.

6.3 Chunking Scheme

Our implementation employs a novel computationally light-weight chunking (fingerprinting) scheme, termed *PACK chunking*. The scheme, presented in Proc. 8 and illustrated in Figure 13, is a XOR-

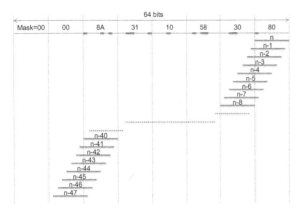

Figure 13: PACK chunking: a snapshot after at least 48 bytes were processed

Table 5: Chunking schemes processing speed tested with 10 MB random file over a client's laptop, without neither minimal nor maximal limit on the chunk size.

Scheme	Window	Chunks	Speed
SampleByte 8 markers	1 byte	32 bytes	1,913 Mbps
Rabin fingerprint	48 bytes	8 KB	2,686 Mbps
PACK chunking	48 bytes	8 KB	3,259 Mbps
SampleByte 1 marker	1 byte	256 bytes	5,176 Mbps

based rolling hash function, tailored for fast TRE chunking. Anchors are detected by the mask in line 1 that provides on average 8 KB chunks while considering all the 48 bytes in the sliding window.

Our measurements show that *PACK chunking* is faster than the fastest known Rabin fingerprint software implementation [8], due to a one less XOR operation per byte.

Proc. 8 PACK chunking algorithm
---
1. $mask \Leftarrow 0x00008A3110583080$ {48 bytes window; 8 KB chunks}
2. $longval \Leftarrow 0$ {has to be 64 bits}
3. **for all** byte $\in$ stream **do**
4.   shift left $longval$ by 1 bit {lsb $\leftarrow$ 0; drop msb}
5. $longval \Leftarrow longval$ bitwise-xor $byte$
6.   **if** processed at least 48 bytes **and** ($longval$ bitwise-and $mask$) == $mask$ **then**
7.   found an anchor
8.   **end if**
9. **end for**

We further measured *PACK chunking* speed and compared it to other schemes. The measurements were performed on an unloaded CPU whose only operation was to chunk a 10 MB random binary file. Table 5 summaries the processing speed of the different chunking schemes. As a baseline figure we measured the speed of SHA-1 signing, and found that it reached 946 Mbps.

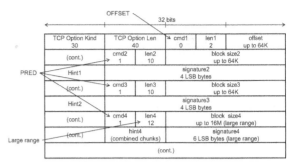

Figure 14: Receiver message example of a large range prediction

6.4 PACK Messages Format

In our implementation, we use two currently unused TCP option codes, similar to the ones defined in SACK [17]. The first one is an enabling option *PACK permitted* sent in a SYN segment to indicate that the PACK option can be used after the connection is established. The other one is a *PACK message* that may be sent over an established connection once permission has been granted by both parties. A single PACK message, piggybacked on a single TCP packet, is designed to wrap and carry multiple PACK commands, as illustrated in Figure 14. This not only saves message overhead, but also copes with security network devices (e.g. firewall) that tend to change TCP options order [19]. Note, that most TCP options are only used at the TCP initialization period, with several exceptions such as SACK [17] and timestamps [13][19]. Due to the lack of space, additional implementation details are left out and are available in [22].

7. CONCLUSIONS

Cloud computing is expected to trigger high demand for TRE solutions as the amount of data exchanged between the cloud and its users is expected to dramatically increase. The cloud environment redefines the TRE system requirements, making proprietary middle-box solutions inadequate. Consequently, there is a rising need for a TRE solution that reduces the cloud's operational cost, while accounting for application latencies, user mobility and cloud elasticity.

In this work, we have presented PACK, a receiver-based, cloud friendly end-to-end TRE which is based on novel speculative principles that reduce latency and cloud operational cost. PACK does not require the server to continuously maintain clients' status, thus enabling cloud elasticity and user mobility while preserving long-term redundancy. Besides, PACK is capable of eliminating redundancy based on content arriving to the client from multiple servers without applying a three-way handshake.

Our evaluation using a wide collection of content types shows that PACK meets the expected design goals and has clear advantages over sender-based TRE, especially when the cloud computation cost and buffering requirements are important. Moreover, PACK imposes additional effort on the sender only when redundancy is exploited, thus reducing the cloud overall cost.

Two interesting future extensions can provide additional benefits to the PACK concept. First, our implementation maintains chains by keeping for any chunk only the last observed subsequent chunk in a LRU fashion. An interesting extension to this work is the statistical study of chains of chunks that would enable multiple possibilities in both the chunk order and the corresponding predictions. The system may also allow making more than one prediction at a time and it is enough that one of them will be correct for successful traffic elimination. A second promising direction is the mode of operation optimization of the hybrid sender-receiver approach based on shared decisions derived from receiver's power or server's cost changes.

8. ACKNOWLEDGEMENTS

This work is partially supported by the VENUS-C project, co-funded within the 7th Framework Programme by the GÉANT & e-Infrastructure Unit, Information Society & Media Directorate General of the European Commission, Contract 261565. It is also partially supported by NET-HD MAGNET program of the office of the Chief Scientist of the Israeli Ministry of Industry, Trade, and Labor. We would like to thank our partners in Venus-C and NET-HD projects for their invaluable feedback and insight.

The authors would like to thank the anonymous SIGCOMM 2011 reviewers and our shepherd, Aditya Akella, for their comments and suggestions that considerably helped us to improve the final version.

9. REFERENCES

[1] B. Aggarwal, A. Akella, A. Anand, A. Balachandran, P. Chitnis, C. Muthukrishnan, R. Ramjee, and G. Varghese. EndRE: An End-System Redundancy Elimination Service for Enterprises. In *Proc. of NSDI*, 2010.

[2] Amazon Elastic Compute Cloud (EC2). http://aws.amazon.com/ec2/.

[3] A. Anand, A. Gupta, A. Akella, S. Seshan, and S. Shenker. Packet caches on routers: The implications of universal redundant traffic elimination. In *Proc. of SIGCOMM*, pages 219–230, New York, NY, USA, 2008. ACM.

[4] A. Anand, C. Muthukrishnan, A. Akella, and R. Ramjee. Redundancy in Network Traffic: Findings and Implications. In *Proc. of SIGMETRICS*, pages 37–48. ACM New York, NY, USA, 2009.

[5] A. Anand, V. Sekar, and A. Akella. SmartRE: an Architecture for Coordinated Network-Wide Redundancy Elimination. In *Proc. of SIGCOMM*, volume 39, pages 87–98, New York, NY, USA, 2009. ACM.

[6] M. Armbrust, A. Fox, R. Griffith, A. Joseph, R. Katz, A. Konwinski, G. Lee, D. Patterson, A. Rabkin, I. Stoica, et al. A view of cloud computing. *Communications of the ACM*, 53(4):50–58, 2010.

[7] BlueCoat Systems. http://www.bluecoat.com/, 1996.

[8] A. Z. Broder. Some Applications of Rabin's Fingerprinting Method. In *Sequences II: Methods in Communications, Security, and Computer Science*, pages 143–152. Springer-Verlag, 1993.

[9] Expand Networks: Application Acceleration and WAN Optimization. http://www.expand.com/technology/application-acceleration.aspx, 1998.

[10] F5: WAN Optimization. http://www.f5.com/solutions/acceleration/wan-optimization/, 1996.

[11] A. Gupta, A. Akella, S. Seshan, S. Shenker, and J. Wang. Understanding and Exploiting Network Traffic Redundancy. Technical Report 1592, UW-Madison, April 2007.

[12] S. Ihm, K. Park, and V. Pai. Wide-area Network Acceleration for the Developing World. In *Proc. of USENIX ATC*, pages 18–18, Berkeley, CA, USA, 2010. USENIX Association.

[13] V. Jacobson, R. Braden, and D. Borman. TCP Extensions for High Performance. *RFC 1323*, 1992.

[14] Juniper Networks: Application Acceleration. http://www.juniper.net/us/en/products-services/application-acceleration/, 1996.

[15] E. Lev-Ran, I. Cidon, and I. Z. Ben-Shaul. Method and Apparatus for Reducing Network Traffic over Low Bandwidth Links. *US Patent 7636767*, November 2009. Filed: November 2005.

[16] U. Manber. Finding similar files in a large file system. In *Proc. of the USENIX winter technical conference*, pages 1–10, Berkeley, CA, USA, 1994. USENIX Association.

[17] M. Mathis, J. Mahdavi, S. Floyd, and A. Romanow. TCP Selective Acknowledgment Options. *RFC 2018*, 1996.

[18] S. Mccanne and M. Demmer. Content-Based Segmentation Scheme for Data Compression in Storage and Transmission Including Hierarchical Segment Representation. *US Patent 6828925*, December 2004. Filed: December 2003.

[19] A. Medina, M. Allman, and S. Floyd. Measuring the evolution of transport protocols in the Internet. *ACM Computer Communication Review*, 35(2):37–52, 2005.

[20] A. Muthitacharoen, B. Chen, and D. Mazi'eres. A Low-Bandwidth Network File System. In *Proc. of SOSP*, pages 174–187, New York, NY, USA, 2001. ACM.

[21] netfilter/iptables project: libnetfilter_queue. http://www.netfilter.org/projects/libnetfilter_queue, Oct 2005.

[22] PACK source code. http://www.venus-c.eu/pages/partner.aspx?id=10.

[23] N. T. Spring and D. Wetherall. A Protocol-Independent Technique for Eliminating Redundant Network Traffic. In *Proc. of SIGCOMM*, volume 30, pages 87–95, New York, NY, USA, 2000. ACM.

[24] R. Williams. Method for Partitioning a Block of Data Into Subblocks and for Storing and Communcating Such Subblocks. *US Patent 5990810*, November 1999. Filed: August 1996.

[25] M. Zink, K. Suh, Y. Gu, and J. Kurose. Watch Global, Cache Local: YouTube Network Traffic at a Campus Network - Measurements and Implications. In *Proc. of MMCN*, San Jose, CA, USA, 2008.

Managing Data Transfers in Computer Clusters with Orchestra

Mosharaf Chowdhury, Matei Zaharia, Justin Ma, Michael I. Jordan, Ion Stoica
University of California, Berkeley
{mosharaf, matei, jtma, jordan, istoica}@cs.berkeley.edu

ABSTRACT

Cluster computing applications like MapReduce and Dryad transfer massive amounts of data between their computation stages. These transfers can have a significant impact on job performance, accounting for more than 50% of job completion times. Despite this impact, there has been relatively little work on optimizing the performance of these data transfers, with networking researchers traditionally focusing on per-flow traffic management. We address this limitation by proposing a global management architecture and a set of algorithms that (1) improve the transfer times of common communication patterns, such as broadcast and shuffle, and (2) allow scheduling policies at the transfer level, such as prioritizing a transfer over other transfers. Using a prototype implementation, we show that our solution improves broadcast completion times by up to $4.5\times$ compared to the status quo in Hadoop. We also show that transfer-level scheduling can reduce the completion time of high-priority transfers by $1.7\times$.

Categories and Subject Descriptors

C.2 [**Computer-communication networks**]: Distributed systems—*Cloud computing*

General Terms

Algorithms, design, performance

Keywords

Data-intensive applications, data transfer, datacenter networks

1 Introduction

The last decade has seen a rapid growth of cluster computing frameworks to analyze the increasing amounts of data collected and generated by web services like Google, Facebook and Yahoo!. These frameworks (*e.g.*, MapReduce [15], Dryad [28], CIEL [34], and Spark [44]) typically implement a data flow computation model, where datasets pass through a sequence of processing stages.

Many of the jobs deployed in these frameworks manipulate massive amounts of data and run on clusters consisting of as many as tens of thousands of machines. Due to the very high cost of

these clusters, operators aim to maximize the cluster utilization, while accommodating a variety of applications, workloads, and user requirements. To achieve these goals, several solutions have recently been proposed to reduce job completion times [11,29,43], accommodate interactive workloads [29,43], and increase utilization [26,29]. While in large part successful, these solutions have so far been focusing on scheduling and managing computation and storage resources, while mostly ignoring network resources.

However, managing and optimizing network activity is critical for improving job performance. Indeed, Hadoop traces from Facebook show that, on average, transferring data between successive stages accounts for 33% of the running times of jobs with reduce phases. Existing proposals for full bisection bandwidth networks [21, 23, 24, 35] along with flow-level scheduling [10, 21] can improve network performance, but they do not account for collective behaviors of flows due to the lack of job-level semantics.

In this paper, we argue that to maximize job performance, we need to optimize at the level of transfers, instead of individual flows. We define a *transfer* as the set of all flows transporting data between two stages of a job. In frameworks like MapReduce and Dryad, a stage cannot complete (or sometimes even start) before it receives all the data from the previous stage. Thus, the job running time depends on the time it takes to complete the *entire* transfer, rather than the duration of individual flows comprising it. To this end, we focus on two transfer patterns that occur in virtually all cluster computing frameworks and are responsible for most of the network traffic in these clusters: *shuffle* and *broadcast*. Shuffle captures the many-to-many communication pattern between the map and reduce stages in MapReduce, and between Dryad's stages. Broadcast captures the one-to-many communication pattern employed by iterative optimization algorithms [45] as well as fragment-replicate joins in Hadoop [6].

We propose Orchestra, a global control architecture to manage intra- and inter-transfer activities. In Orchestra, data movement within each transfer is coordinated by a Transfer Controller (TC), which continuously monitors the transfer and updates the set of sources associated with each destination. For broadcast transfers, we propose a TC that implements an optimized BitTorrent-like protocol called Cornet, augmented by an adaptive clustering algorithm to take advantage of the hierarchical network topology in many datacenters. For shuffle transfers, we propose an optimal algorithm called Weighted Shuffle Scheduling (WSS), and we provide key insights into the performance of Hadoop's shuffle implementation.

In addition to coordinating the data movements within each transfer, we also advocate managing *concurrent* transfers belonging to the same or different jobs using an Inter-Transfer Controller (ITC). We show that an ITC implementing a scheduling discipline as simple as FIFO can significantly reduce the average transfer times in

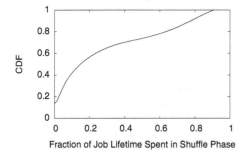

Figure 1: CDF of the fraction of time spent in shuffle transfers in Facebook Hadoop jobs with reduce phases.

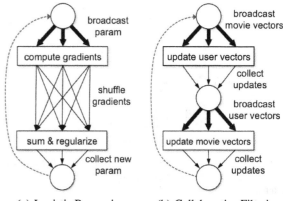

(a) Logistic Regression   (b) Collaborative Filtering

Figure 2: Per-iteration work flow diagrams for our motivating machine learning applications. The circle represents the master node and the boxes represent the set of worker nodes.

a multi-transfer workload, compared to allowing flows from the transfers to arbitrarily share the network. Orchestra can also readily support other scheduling policies, such as fair sharing and priority.

Orchestra can be implemented at the application level and overlaid on top of diverse routing topologies [10,21,24,35], access control schemes [12,22], and virtualization layers [37,38]. We believe that this implementation approach is both appropriate and attractive for several reasons. First, because large-scale analytics applications are usually written using high-level programming frameworks (*e.g.,* MapReduce), it is sufficient to control the implementation of the transfer patterns in these frameworks (*e.g.,* shuffle and broadcast) to manage a large fraction of cluster traffic. We have focused on shuffles and broadcasts due to their popularity, but other transfer patterns can also be incorporated into Orchestra. Second, this approach allows Orchestra to be used in existing clusters without modifying routers and switches, and even in the public cloud.

To evaluate Orchestra, we built a prototype implementation in Spark [44], a MapReduce-like framework developed and used at our institution, and conducted experiments on DETERlab and Amazon EC2. Our experiments show that our broadcast scheme is up to $4.5\times$ faster than the default Hadoop implementation, while our shuffle scheme can speed up transfers by 29%. To evaluate the impact of Orchestra on job performance, we run two applications developed by machine learning researchers at our institution—a spam classification algorithm and a collaborative filtering job—and show that our broadcast and shuffle schemes reduce transfer times by up to $3.6\times$ and job completion times by up to $1.9\times$. Finally, we show that inter-transfer scheduling policies can lower average transfer times by 31% and speed up high-priority transfers by $1.7\times$.

The rest of this paper is organized as follows. Section 2 discusses several examples that motivate importance of data transfers in cluster workloads. Section 3 presents the Orchestra architecture. Section 4 discusses Orchestra's inter-transfer scheduling. Section 5 presents our broadcast scheme, Cornet. Section 6 studies how to optimize shuffle transfers. We then evaluate Orchestra in Section 7, survey related work in Section 8, and conclude in Section 9.

2 Motivating Examples

To motivate our focus on transfers, we study their impact in two cluster computing systems: Hadoop (using trace from a 3000-node cluster at Facebook) and Spark (a MapReduce-like framework that supports iterative machine learning and graph algorithms [44]).

Hadoop at Facebook: We analyzed a week-long trace from Facebook's Hadoop cluster, containing 188,000 MapReduce jobs, to find the amount of time spent in shuffle transfers. We defined a "shuffle phase" for each job as starting when either the last map task finishes or the last reduce task starts (whichever comes later) and ending when the last reduce task finishes receiving map out-

puts. We then measured what fraction of the job's lifetime was spent in this shuffle phase. This is a conservative estimate of the impact of shuffles, because reduce tasks can also start fetching map outputs before all the map tasks have finished.

We found that 32% of jobs had no reduce phase (*i.e.,* only map tasks). This is common in data loading jobs. For the remaining jobs, we plot a CDF of the fraction of time spent in the shuffle phase (as defined above) in Figure 1. On average, the shuffle phase accounts for 33% of the running time in these jobs. In addition, in 26% of the jobs with reduce tasks, shuffles account for more than 50% of the running time, and in 16% of jobs, they account for more than 70% of the running time. This confirms widely reported results that the network is a bottleneck in MapReduce [10,21,24].

Logistic Regression Application: As an example of an iterative MapReduce application in Spark, we consider Monarch [40], a system for identifying spam links on Twitter. The application processed 55 GB of data collected about 345,000 tweets containing links. For each tweet, the group collected 1000-2000 features relating to the page linked to (*e.g.,* domain name, IP address, and frequencies of words on the page). The dataset contained 20 million distinct features in total. The applications identifies which features correlate with links to spam using logistic regression [25].

We depict the per-iteration work flow of this application in Figure 2(a). Each iteration includes a large broadcast (300 MB) and a shuffle (190 MB per reducer) operation, and it typically takes the application at least 100 iterations to converge. Each transfer acts as a barrier: the job is held up by the slowest node to complete the transfer. In our initial implementation of Spark, which used the the same broadcast and shuffle strategies as Hadoop, we found that communication accounted for 42% of the iteration time, with 30% spent in broadcast and 12% spent in shuffle on a 30-node cluster. With such a large fraction of the running time spent on communication, optimizing the completion times of these transfers is critical.

Collaborative Filtering Application: As a second example of an iterative algorithm, we discuss a collaborative filtering job used by a researcher at our institution on the Netflix Challenge data. The goal is to predict users' ratings for movies they have not seen based on their ratings for other movies. The job uses an algorithm called alternating least squares (ALS) [45]. ALS models each user and each movie as having K features, such that a user's rating for a movie is the dot product of the user's feature vector and the movie's. It seeks to find these vectors through an iterative process.

Figure 2(b) shows the workflow of ALS. The algorithm alter-

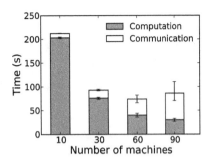

Figure 3: Communication and computation times per iteration when scaling the collaborative filtering job using HDFS-based broadcast.

nately broadcasts the current user or movie feature vectors, to allow the nodes to optimize the other set of vectors in parallel. Each transfer is roughly 385 MB. These transfers limited the scalability of the job in our initial implementation of broadcast, which was through shared files in the Hadoop Distributed File System (HDFS)—the same strategy used in Hadoop. For example, Figure 3 plots the iteration times for the same problem size on various numbers of nodes. Computation time goes down linearly with the number of nodes, but communication time grows linearly. At 60 nodes, the broadcasts cost 45% of the iteration time. Furthermore, the job stopped scaling past 60 nodes, because the extra communication cost from adding nodes outweighed the reduction in computation time (as can be seen at 90 nodes).

3 Orchestra Architecture

To manage and optimize data transfers, we propose an architecture called Orchestra. The key idea in Orchestra is global coordination, both within a transfer and across transfers. This is accomplished through a hierarchical control structure, illustrated in Figure 4.

At the highest level, Orchestra has an Inter-Transfer Controller (ITC) that implements cross-transfer scheduling policies, such as prioritizing transfers from ad-hoc queries over batch jobs. The ITC manages multiple Transfer Controllers (TCs), one for each transfer in the cluster. TCs select a mechanism to use for their transfers (*e.g.,* BitTorrent versus a distribution tree for broadcast) based on the data size, the number of nodes in the transfer, their locations, and other factors. They also actively monitor and control the nodes participating in the transfer. TCs manage the transfer at the granularity of flows, by choosing how many concurrent flows to open from each node, which destinations to open them to, and when to move each chunk of data. Table 1 summarizes coordination activities at different components in the Orchestra hierarchy.

Orchestra is designed for a cooperative environment in which a single administrative entity controls the application software on the cluster and ensures that it uses TCs for transfers. For example, we envision Orchestra being used in a Hadoop data warehouse such as Facebook's by modifying the Hadoop framework to invoke it for its transfers. However, this application stack can still run on top of a network that is shared with other tenants—for example, an organization can use Orchestra to schedule transfers inside a virtual Hadoop cluster on Amazon EC2. Also note that in both cases, because Orchestra is implemented in the framework, users' applications (*i.e.,* MapReduce jobs) need not change.

Since Orchestra can be implemented at the application level, it can be used in existing clusters without changing network hardware or management mechanisms. While controlling transfers at the application level does not offer perfect control of the network or protection against misbehaving hosts, it still gives considerable

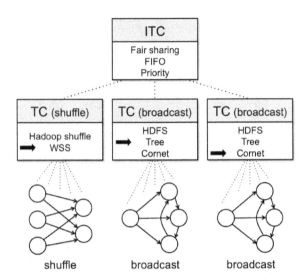

Figure 4: Orchestra architecture. An Inter-Transfer Controller (ITC) manages Transfer Controllers (TCs) for the active transfers. Each TC can choose among multiple transfer mechanisms depending on data size, number of nodes, and other factors. The ITC performs inter-transfer scheduling.

Table 1: Coordination throughout the Orchestra hierarchy.

Component	Coordination Activity
Inter-Transfer Controller (ITC)	- Implement cross-transfer scheduling policies (*e.g.,* priority, FIFO etc.) - Periodically update and notify active transfers of their shares of the network
Transfer Controller (TC)	- Select the best algorithm for a transfer given its share and operating regime
Cornet Broadcast TC	- Use network topology information to minimize cross-rack communication - Control neighbors for each participant
Weighted Shuffle Scheduling TC	- Assign flow rates to optimize shuffle completion time

flexibility to improve job performance. We therefore took this approach as a sweet-spot between utility and deployability.

In the next few sections, we present the components of Orchestra in more detail. First, we discuss inter-transfer scheduling and the interaction between TCs and the ITC in Section 4. Sections 5 and 6 then discuss two efficient transfer mechanisms that take advantage of the global control provided by Orchestra. For broadcast, we present Cornet, a BitTorrent-like scheme that can take into account the cluster topology. For shuffle, we present Weighted Shuffle Scheduling (WSS), an optimal shuffle scheduling algorithm.

4 Inter-Transfer Scheduling

Typically, large computer clusters are multi-user environments where hundreds of jobs run simultaneously [29, 43]. As a result, there are usually multiple concurrent data transfers. In existing clusters, without any transfer-aware supervising mechanism in place, flows from each transfer get some share of the network as allocated by TCP's proportional sharing. However, this approach can lead to extended transfer completion times and inflexibility in enforcing scheduling policies. Consider two simple examples:

- *Scheduling policies:* Suppose that a high-priority job, such as a report for a key customer, is submitted to a MapReduce cluster. A cluster scheduler like Quincy [29] may quickly assign CPUs and memory to the new job, but the job's flows will still experience fair sharing with other jobs' flows at the network level.

- *Completion times:* Suppose that three jobs start shuffling *equal amounts* of data at the same time. With fair sharing among the flows, the transfers will all complete in time $3t$, where t is the time it takes one shuffle to finish uncontested. In contrast, with FIFO scheduling across transfers, it is well-known that the transfers will finish faster on average, at times t, $2t$ and $3t$.

Orchestra can implement scheduling policies at the transfer level through the Inter-Transfer Controller (ITC). The main design question is what mechanism to use for controlling scheduling across the transfers. We have chosen to use weighted fair sharing at the cluster level: *each transfer is assigned a weight, and each congested link in the network is shared proportionally to the weights of the transfers using that link.* As a mechanism, weighted fair sharing is flexible enough to emulate several policies, including priority and FIFO. In addition, it is attractive because it can be implemented at the hosts, without changes to routers and switches.

When an application wishes to perform a transfer in Orchestra, it invokes an API that launches a TC for that transfer. The TC registers with the ITC to obtain its share of the network. The ITC periodically consults a scheduling policy (*e.g.,* FIFO, priority) to assign shares to the active transfers, and sends these to the TCs. Each TC can divide its share among its source-destination pairs as it wishes (*e.g.,* to choose a distribution graph for a broadcast). The ITC also updates the transfers' shares periodically as the set of active transfers changes. Finally, each TC unregisters itself when its transfer ends. Note that we assume a cooperative environment, where all the jobs use TCs and obey the ITC.

We have implemented fair sharing, FIFO, and priority policies to demonstrate the flexibility of Orchestra. In the long term, however, operators would likely integrate Orchestra's transfer scheduling into a job scheduler such as Quincy [29].

In the rest of this section, we discuss our prototype implementation of weighted sharing using TCP flow counts (§4.1) and the scalability and fault tolerance of the ITC (§4.2).

4.1 Weighted Flow Assignment (WFA)

To illustrate the benefits of transfer-level scheduling, we implemented a prototype that approximates weighted fair sharing by allowing different transfers to use different numbers of TCP connections per host and relies on TCP's AIMD fair sharing behavior. We refer to this strategy as Weighted Flow Assignment (WFA). Note that WFA is not a bulletproof solution for inter-transfer scheduling, but rather a proof of concept for the Orchestra architecture. Our main contribution is the architecture itself. In a full implementation, we believe that a cross-flow congestion control scheme such as Seawall [38] would improve flexibility and robustness. Seawall performs weighted max-min fair sharing between applications that use an arbitrary number of TCP and UDP flows using a shim layer on the end hosts and no changes to routers and switches.[1]

In WFA, there is a fixed number, F, of permissible TCP flows per host (*e.g.,* 100) that can be allocated among the transfers. Each transfer i has a weight w_i allocated by the scheduling policy in the ITC. On each host, transfer i is allowed to use $F \lceil \frac{w_i}{\sum w_j} \rceil$ TCP connections, where the sum is over all the transfers using that host.

Suppose that two MapReduce jobs (A and B) sharing the nodes of a cluster are both performing shuffles. If we allow each job to use 50 TCP connections per host, then they will get roughly equal shares of the bandwidth of each link due to TCP's AIMD behavior. On the other hand, if we allowed job A to use 75 TCP flows per host and job B to use 25 TCP flows per host, then job A would receive a larger share of the available bandwidth.[2]

Our implementation also divides all data to be transferred into chunks, so that a TC can shut down or launch new flows rapidly when its share in a host changes. In addition, for simplicity, we give transfers a $1.5\times$ higher cap for sending flows than for receiving on each host, so that a TC does not need to micromanage its flows to have sender and receiver counts match up exactly.

We found that our flow count approach works naturally for both broadcast and shuffle. In a BitTorrent-like broadcast scheme, nodes already have multiple peers, so we simply control the number of concurrent senders that each node can receive from. In shuffle transfers, existing systems already open multiple connections per receiver to balance the load across the senders, and we show in Section 6 that having more connections only improves performance.

WFA has some limitations—for example, it does not share a link used by different numbers of sender/receiver pairs from different transfers in the correct ratio. However, it works well enough to illustrate the benefits of inter-transfer scheduling. In particular, WFA will work well on a full bisection bandwidth network, where the outgoing links from the nodes are the only congestion points.

4.2 Fault Tolerance and Scalability

Because the ITC has fairly minimal responsibilities (notifying each TC its share), it can be made both fault tolerant and scalable. The ITC stores only soft state (the list of active transfers), so a hot standby can quickly recover this state if it crashes (by having TCs reconnect). Furthermore, existing transfers can continue while the ITC is down. The number of active transfers is no more than several hundred in our 3000-node Facebook trace, indicating that scalability should not be a problem. In addition, a periodic update interval of one second is sufficient for setting shares, because most transfers last seconds to minutes.

5 Broadcast Transfers

Cluster applications often need to send large pieces of data to multiple machines. For example, in the collaborative filtering algorithm in Section 2, broadcasting an $O(100 \text{ MB})$ parameter vector quickly became a scaling bottleneck. In addition, distributing files to perform a fragment-replicate join[3] in Hadoop [6], rolling out software updates [8], and deploying VM images [7] are some other use cases where the same data must be sent to a large number of machines. In this section, we discuss current mechanisms for implementing broadcast in datacenters and identify several of their limitations (§5.1). We then present Cornet, a BitTorrent-like protocol designed specifically for datacenters that can outperform the default Hadoop implementation by $4.5\times$ (§5.2). Lastly, we present a topology-aware variant of Cornet that leverages global control to further improve performance by up to $2\times$ (§5.3).

5.1 Existing Solutions

One of the most common broadcast solutions in existing cluster computing frameworks involves writing the data to a shared file system (*e.g.,* HDFS [2], NFS) and reading it later from that centralized storage. In Hadoop, both Pig's fragment-replicate join im-

---

[1] In Orchestra, we can actually implement Seawall's congestion control scheme directly in the application instead of using a shim, because we control the shuffle and broadcast implementations.

[2] Modulo the dependence of TCP fairness on round-trip times.

[3] This is a join between a small table and a large table where the small table is broadcast to all the map tasks.

plementation [6] and the DistributedCache API for deploying code and data files with a job use this solution. This is likely done out of a lack of other readily available options. Unfortunately, as the number of receivers grows, the centralized storage system can quickly become a bottleneck, as we observed in Section 2.

To eliminate the centralized bottleneck, some systems use d-ary distribution trees rooted at the source node. Data is divided into blocks that are passed along the tree. As soon as a node finishes receiving the complete data, it can become the root of a separate tree. d is sometimes set to 1 to form a chain instead of a tree (*e.g.,* in LANTorrent [7] and in the protocol for writing blocks in HDFS [2]). Unfortunately, tree and chain schemes suffer from two limitations. First, in a tree with $d > 1$, the sending capacity of the leaf nodes (which are at least half the nodes) is not utilized. Second, a slow node or link will slow down its entire subtree, which is problematic at large scales due to the prevalence of stragglers [15]. This effect is especially apparent in chains.

Unstructured data distribution mechanisms like BitTorrent [4], traditionally used in the Internet, address these drawbacks by providing scalability, fault-tolerance, and high throughput in heterogeneous and dynamic networks. Recognizing these qualities, Twitter has built Murder [8], a wrapper over the BitTornado [3] implementation of BitTorrent, to deploy software to its servers.

5.2 Cornet

Cornet is a BitTorrent-like protocol optimized for datacenters. In particular, Cornet takes advantage of the high-speed and low-latency connections in datacenter networks, the absence of selfish peers, and the fact that there is no malicious data corruption. By leveraging these properties, Cornet can outperform BitTorrent implementations for the Internet by up to $4.5\times$.

Cornet differs from BitTorrent in three main aspects:

- Unlike BitTorrent, which splits files into blocks and subdivides blocks into small chunks with sizes of up to 256 KB, Cornet only splits data into large blocks (4 MB by default).

- While in BitTorrent some peers (leechers) do not contribute to the transfer and leave as soon as they finish the download, in Cornet, each node contributes its full capacity over the full duration of the transfer. Thus, Cornet does not include a tit-for-tat scheme to incentivize nodes.

- Cornet does not employ expensive SHA1 operations on each data block to ensure data integrity; instead, it performs a single integrity check over the whole data.

Cornet also employs a cap on the number of simultaneous connections to improve performance.[4] When a peer is sending to the maximum number of recipients, it puts further requests into a queue until one of the sending slots becomes available. This ensures faster service times for the small number of connected peers and allows them to finish quickly to join the session as the latest sources for the blocks they just received.

During broadcast, receivers explicitly request for specific blocks from their counterparts. However, during the initial stage, the source of a Cornet broadcast sends out at least one copy of each block in a round-robin fashion before duplicating any block.

The TC for Cornet is similar to a BitTorrent tracker in that it assigns a set of peers to each node. However, unlike BitTorrent, each node requests new peers every second. This allows the TC to adapt to the topology and optimize the transfer, as we discuss next.

---

[4]The default limits for the number of receive and send slots per node are 8 and 12, respectively.

5.3 Topology-Aware Cornet

Many datacenters employ hierarchical network topologies with oversubscription ratios as high as 5 [21, 27], where transfer times between two nodes on the same rack are significantly lower than between nodes on different racks. To take network topology into account, we have developed two extensions to Cornet.

CornetTopology In this case, we assume that the network topology is known in advance, which is appropriate, for example, in private datacenters. In CornetTopology, the TC has a configuration database that specifies locality groups, *e.g.,* which rack each node is in. When a receiver requests for a new set of peers from the TC, instead of choosing among all possible recipients (as in vanilla Cornet), the TC gives priority to nodes on the same rack as the receiver. Essentially, each rack forms its individual swarm with minimal cross-rack communication. The results in Section 7.2 show that CornetTopology can reduce broadcast time by 50%.

CornetClustering In cloud environments, users have no control over machine placements, and cloud providers do not disclose any information regarding network topology. Even if the initial placements were given out, VM migrations in the background could invalidate this information. For these cases, we have developed CornetClustering, whose goal is to infer and exploit the underlying network topology. It starts off without any topology information like the vanilla Cornet. Throughout the course of an application's lifetime, as more and more broadcasts happen, the TC records block transfer times between different pairs of receivers and uses a learning algorithm to infer the rack-level topology. Once we infer the topology, we use the same mechanism as in CornetTopology. The TC keeps recalculating the inference periodically to keep an updated view of the network.

The inference procedure consists of four steps. In the first step, we record node-to-node block transfer times. We use this data to construct an $n \times n$ distance matrix $\mathbf{D}$, where n is the number of receiver nodes, and the entries are the median block transfer times between a pair of nodes. In the second step, we infer the missing entries in the distance matrix using a version of the nonnegative matrix factorization procedure of Mao and Saul [33]. After completing the matrix $\mathbf{D}$, we project the nodes onto a two-dimensional space using non-metric multidimensional scaling [31]. Finally, we cluster using a mixture of spherical Gaussians with fixed variance σ^2, and automatically select the number of partitions based on the Bayesian information criterion score [18]. In operational use, one can set σ to the typical intra-rack block transfer time (in our experiments, we use $\sigma = 200$ ms). With enough training data, the procedure usually infers the exact topology and provides a similar speedup to CornetTopology, as we show in Section 7.2.

5.4 Size-Aware Broadcast Algorithm Selection

While Cornet achieves good performance for a variety of workloads and topologies, it does not always provide the best performance. For example, in our experiments we found that for a small number of receivers, a chain distribution topology usually performs better. In such a case, the TC can decide whether to employ one algorithm or another based on the number of receivers. In general, as new broadcast algorithms are developed, the TC can pick the best one to match a particular data size and topology. This ability illustrates the advantage of our architecture, which enables the TC to make decisions based on global information.

6 Shuffle Transfers

During the shuffle phase of a MapReduce job, each reducer is assigned a range of the key space produced by the mappers and must

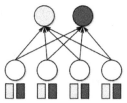

Figure 5: A shuffle transfer. The two receivers (at the top) need to fetch separate pieces of data, depicted as boxes of different colors, from each sender.

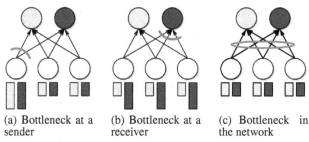

(a) Bottleneck at a sender

(b) Bottleneck at a receiver

(c) Bottleneck in the network

Figure 6: Different bottlenecks dictating shuffle performance.

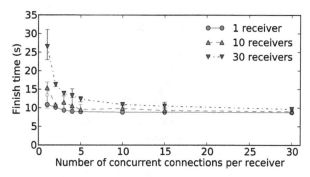

Figure 7: Transfer times for a shuffle with 30 senders and 1 to 30 receivers, as a function of the number of concurrent flows (to random senders) per receiver.

fetch some elements from every mapper. Consequently, shuffle transfers are some of the most common transfer patterns in datacenters. Similar constructs exist in other cluster computing frameworks, like Dryad [28], Pregel [32], and Spark [44]. In general, a shuffle consists of n receivers, $r_1, \ldots, r_n$, and m senders, $s_1, \ldots, s_m$, where each receiver i needs to fetch a distinct dataset d_{ij} from sender j. Figure 5 depicts a typical shuffle.

Because each piece of data goes from only one sender to one receiver, unlike in broadcasts, receivers cannot improve performance by sharing data. The main concern during a shuffle is, therefore, to keep bottleneck links fully utilized (§6.1). We find that the strategy used by systems like Hadoop, where each receiver opens connections to multiple random senders and rely on TCP fair sharing among these flows, is close to optimal when data sizes are balanced (§6.2). There are cases with unbalanced data sizes in which this strategy can perform 1.5× worse than optimal. We propose an optimal algorithm called Weighted Shuffle Scheduling (WSS) to address these scenarios (§6.3). However, situations where WSS helps seem to appear rarely in typical jobs; our main contribution is thus to provide a thorough analysis of this common transfer pattern.

6.1 Bottlenecks and Optimality in Shuffle Transfers

Figure 6 shows three situations where a bottleneck limits shuffle performance and scheduling can have little impact on the overall completion time. In Figure 6(a), one of the senders has more data to send than others (*e.g.*, a map produced more output in a MapReduce job), so this node's link to the network is the bottleneck. Even with the random scheduling scheme in current systems, this link is likely to stay fully utilized throughout the transfer, and because a fixed amount of data *must* flow along this link to finish the shuffle, the completion time of the shuffle will be the same regardless of the scheduling of other flows. Figure 6(b) shows an analogous situation where a receiver is the bottleneck. Finally, in Figure 6(c), there is a bottleneck in the network—for example, the cluster uses a tree topology with less than full bisection bandwidth—and again the order of data fetches will not affect the overall completion time as long as the contended links are kept fully utilized.

These examples suggest a simple optimality criterion for shuffle scheduling: *an optimal shuffle schedule keeps at least one link fully utilized throughout the transfer.* This condition is clearly necessary,

because if there was a time period during which a shuffle schedule kept all links less than 100% utilized, the completion time could be lowered by slightly increasing the rate of all flows during that period. The condition is also sufficient as long as unipath routing is used—that is, the data from each sender to each receiver can only flow along one path. In this case, there is a fixed amount of data, D_L, that must flow along each link L, so a lower bound on the transfer time is $\max_L \{D_L/B_L\}$, where B_L is the bandwidth of link L. If any link is fully utilized throughout the transfer, then this lower bound has been reached, and the schedule is optimal. Note that under multipath routing, multiple links may need to be fully utilized for an optimal schedule.

6.2 Load Balancing in Current Implementations

The optimality observation indicates that the links of both senders and receivers should be kept as highly utilized as possible. Indeed, if the amount of data per node is balanced, which is often the case in large MapReduce jobs simply because many tasks have run on every node, then all of the nodes' outgoing links can potentially become bottlenecks. The biggest risk with the randomized data fetching scheme in current systems is that some senders get too few connections to them, underutilizing their links.[5] Our main finding is that having multiple connections per receiver drastically reduces this risk and yields near-optimal shuffle times. In particular, Hadoop's setting of 5 connections per receiver seems to work well, although more connections can improve performance slightly.

We conducted an experiment with 30 senders and 1 to 30 receivers on Amazon EC2, using extra large nodes. Each receiver fetched 1 GB of data in total, balanced across the senders. We varied the number of parallel connections opened by each receiver from 1 to 30. We plot the average transfer times for five runs in Figure 7, with max/min error bars.

We note two trends in the data. First, using a single fetch connection per receiver leads to poor performance, but transfer times improve quickly with even two connections. Second, with enough concurrent connections, transfer times approach 8 seconds asymptotically, which is a lower bound on the time we can expect for nodes with 1 Gbps links. Indeed, with 30 connections per receiver, the overall transfer rate per receiver was 790 Mbps for 30 receivers, 844 Mbps for 10 receivers, and 866 Mbps for 1 receiver, while the best transfer rate we got between any two nodes in our cluster was 929 Mbps. This indicates that randomized selection of senders is within 15% of optimal, and may be even closer because there may

---

[5] Systems like Hadoop cap the number of receiving connections per reduce task for pragmatic reasons, such as limiting the number of threads in the application. Having fewer connections per receiver can also mitigate incast [41].

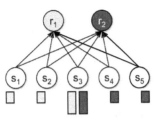

Figure 8: A shuffle configuration where Weighted Shuffle Scheduling outperforms fair sharing among the flows.

be other traffic on EC2 interfering with our job, or a topology with less than full bisection bandwidth.

The improvement in transfer times with more connections happens for two reasons. First, with only one connection per receiver, collisions (when two receivers pick the same sender) can only lower performance, because some senders will be idle. In contrast, with even 2 threads, a collision that slows down some flows may speed up others (because some senders are now sending to only one receiver). Second, with more connections per receiver, the standard deviation of the number of flows to each sender decreases relative to its mean, reducing the effect of imbalances.

6.3 Weighted Shuffle Scheduling (WSS)

We now consider how to optimally schedule a shuffle on a given network topology, where receiver r_i needs to fetch d_{ij} units of data from sender s_j. We aim to minimize the completion time of the shuffle, *i.e.*, the time when the last receiver finishes. For simplicity, we initially assume that the data from a sender/receiver pair can only flow along one path. Under this unipath assumption, the "fully utilized link" condition in Section 6.1 is sufficient for optimality.

We propose a simple algorithm called Weighted Shuffle Scheduling (WSS) that achieves this condition: *allocate rates to each flow using weighted fair sharing, such that the weight of the flow between receiver r_i and sender s_j is proportional to d_{ij}.* To see why this works, consider first a simpler scheduling scheme using progressive filling, where the flow from r_i to s_j is given a rate $t_{ij} = \lambda d_{ij}$ for the largest feasible value of λ. Under this scheme, all the pairwise transfers finish at the same time (because transfer rates are proportional to data sizes for each transfer), and furthermore, at least one link is fully utilized (because we use the largest feasible λ). Therefore, the schedule is optimal. Now, the WSS schedule based on max-min fair sharing with these same weights must finish at least as fast as this progressive filling schedule (because each flow's rate is at least as high as under progressive filling, but may also be higher), so it must also be optimal.

We found that WSS can outperform current shuffle implementations by up to 1.5×. In current systems, the flows between senders and receivers experience unweighted fair sharing due to TCP. This can be suboptimal when the flows must transfer different amounts of data. For example, consider the shuffle in Figure 8, where four senders have one unit of data for only one receiver and s_3 has two units for both. Suppose that there is a full bisection bandwidth network where each link carries one data unit per second. Under fair sharing, each receiver starts fetching data at $1/3$ units/second from the three senders it needs data from. After 3 seconds, the receivers exhaust the data on s_1, s_2, s_4 and s_5, and there is one unit of data left for each receiver on s_3. At this point, s_3 becomes a bottleneck, and the receivers take 2 more seconds to transfer the data off. The transfer thus finishes in 5s. In contrast, with WSS, the receivers would fetch data at a rate of $1/4$ units/second from s_1, s_2, s_4 and s_5 and $1/2$ units/second from s_3, finishing in 4s (25% faster).

This discrepancy can be increased in variants of this topology.

For example, with 100 senders for only r_1, 100 senders for only r_2, and 100 data units for each receiver on a shared sender, WSS finishes 1.495× faster than fair sharing. Nevertheless, we found that configurations where WSS outperforms fair sharing are rare in practice. If the amounts of data to be transferred between each sender and each reducer are roughly balanced, then WSS reduces to fair sharing. In addition, if there is a single bottleneck sender or bottleneck receiver, then fair sharing will generally keep this node's link fully utilized, resulting in an optimal schedule.

WSS can also be extended to settings where multipath transmissions are allowed. In this case, we must choose transfer rates t_{ij} between receiver i and sender j such that $\min_{i,j}\{t_{ij}/d_{ij}\}$ is maximized. This is equivalent to the Maximum Concurrent Multi-Commodity Flow problem [39].

Implementing WSS Note that WSS requires global knowledge of the amounts of data to transfer in order to set the weight of each flow. WSS can be implemented naturally within Orchestra by having the TC pass these weights to the nodes. In our prototype, the receivers open different numbers of TCP flows to each sender to match the assigned weights. We also tried a variant of where the TC adjusts the weights of each sender/receiver pair periodically based on the amount of data left (in case there is variability in network performance), but found that it provided little gain.

7 Evaluation

We have evaluated Cornet, WSS, and inter-transfer scheduling in the context of Spark and ran experiments in two environments: Amazon's Elastic Compute Cloud (EC2) [1] and DETERlab [5]. On EC2, we used extra-large high-memory instances, which appear to occupy whole physical nodes and had enough memory to perform the experiments without involving disk behavior (except for HDFS-based mechanisms). Although topology information is not provided by EC2, our tests revealed that nodes were able to achieve 929 Mbps in each direction and 790 Mbps during 30 nodes all-to-all communication (Figure 7), suggesting a near-full bisection bandwidth network. The DETERlab cluster spanned 3 racks and was used as ground-truth to verify the correctness of Cornet's clustering algorithm. Our experiments show the following:

- Cornet performs 4.5× better than the default Hadoop implementation of broadcast and BitTornado (§7.1), and with topology awareness in its TC, Cornet can provide further 2× improvement (§7.2).

- WSS can improve shuffle speeds by 29% (§7.3).

- Inter-transfer scheduling can speed up high priority jobs by 1.7×, and a simple FIFO policy can improve average transfer response times by 31% for equal sized transfers (§7.4).

- Orchestra reduced communication costs in the logistic regression and collaborative filtering applications in Section 2 by up to 3.6× and sped up jobs by up to 1.9× (§7.5).

Since data transfers act as synchronization steps in most iterative and data-intensive frameworks, capturing the behavior of the slowest receiver is the most important metric for comparing alternatives. We therefore use the *completion time* of the entire transfer as our main performance metric.

7.1 Comparison of Broadcast Mechanisms

Figure 9 shows the average completion times of different broadcast mechanisms (Table 2) to transfer 100 MB and 1 GB of data to multiple receivers from a single source. Error bars represent the minimum and the maximum observed values across five runs.

We see that the overheads of choking/unchoking, aggressive hashing, and allowing receivers to leave as soon as they are done, fail

Table 2: Broadcast mechanisms compared.

Algorithm	Description
HDFS (R=3)	Sender creates 3 replicas of the data in HDFS and receivers read from them
HDFS (R=10)	Same as before but there are 10 replicas
Chain	A chain of receivers rooted at the sender
Tree (D=2)	Binary tree with sender as the root
BitTornado	BitTorrent implementation for the Internet
Cornet	Approach proposed in Section 5
Theoretical Lower Bound	Minimum broadcast time in the EC2 network (measured to have 1.5 Gbps pairwise bidirectional bandwidth) using pipelined binomial tree distribution mechanism [19]

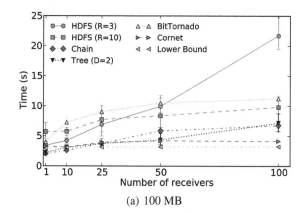

(a) 100 MB

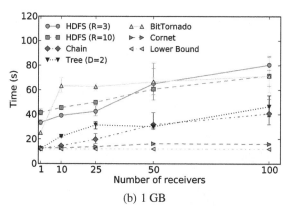

(b) 1 GB

Figure 9: Completion times of different broadcast mechanisms for varying data sizes.

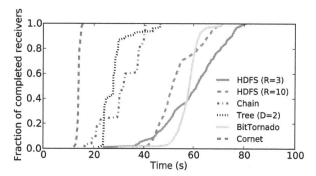

Figure 10: CDF of completion times of individual receivers while transferring 1 GB to 100 receivers using different broadcast mechanisms.

or a chain propagated and got magnified throughout the structure. Indeed, upon inspection, we found that the non-monotonicity of chain and tree completion times were due to this very reason in some experimental runs (*e.g.,* completion time for 25 receivers using a tree structure is larger than that for 50 receivers in 9(b)).

As expected, HDFS-based mechanisms performed well only for small amounts of data. While increasing the number of replicas helps, there is a trade-off between time spent in creating replicas vs. time all the receivers would spend in reading from those replicas. In our experiments, HDFS with 3 replicas performed better than HDFS with 10 replicas when the total number of receivers was less than 50. Overall, HDFS with 3 and 10 replicas were up to $5\times$ and $4.5\times$ slower than Cornet, respectively.

A Closer Look at Per-node Completion Times. We present the CDFs of completion times of individual receivers for each of the compared broadcast mechanisms in Figure 10.

Notice that almost all the receivers in Cornet finished simultaneously. The slight bends at the two endpoints illustrate the receivers ($< 10\%$) that finished earlier or slower than the average receiver. The CDF representing BitTornado reception times is similar to that of Cornet except that the variation in individual completion times is significantly higher and the average receiver is almost $4\times$ slower.

Next, the steps in the CDFs of chain and tree highlight how stragglers slow down all their children in the distribution structure. Each horizontal segment indicates a node that was slow in finishing reception and the subsequent vertical segment indicates the receivers that experienced head-of-line blocking due to a slow ancestor.

Finally, receivers in HDFS-based transfer mechanism with 10 replicas start finishing slower than those with 3 replicas due to higher replication overhead. However, in the long run, receivers using 10 replicas finish faster because of less reading contention.

The Case for a TC. As evident from Figure 9, the transfer mechanisms have specific operating regimes. In particular, chain and tree based approaches are faster than Cornet for small numbers of nodes and small data sizes, likely because the block sizes and polling intervals in Cornet prevent it from utilizing all the nodes' bandwidth right away. We confirmed this by running another set of experiments with 10 MB (not shown due to lack of space), where tree and chain outperformed the other approaches. In an Orchestra implementation, a TC can pick the best transfer mechanism for a given data size and number of nodes using its global knowledge.

7.2 Topology-aware Cornet

Next, we explore an extension of Cornet that exploits network topology information. We hypothesized that if there is a significant difference between block transfer times within a rack vs. between

to take full advantage of the faster network in a datacenter environment and made BitTornado[6] as much as $4.5\times$ slower than the streamlined Cornet implementation.

Cornet scaled well up to 100 receivers for a wide range of data sizes in our experiments. For example, Cornet took as low as 15.4 seconds to complete broadcasting 1 GB data to 100 receivers and remained within 33% of the theoretical lower bound. If there were too few participants or the amount of data was small, Cornet could not fully utilize the available bandwidth. However, as the number of receivers increased, Cornet completion times increased in a much slower manner than its alternatives, which convinces us that Cornet can scale well beyond 100 receivers.

We found structured mechanisms to work well only for smaller scale. Any delay introduced by a straggling internal node of a tree

---

[6]We used Murder [8] with a modification that forced every peer to stay in the swarm until all of them had finished.

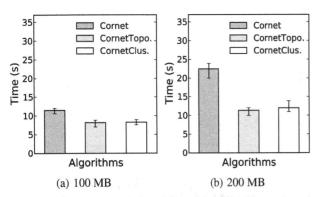

(a) 100 MB (b) 200 MB

Figure 11: Cornet completion times when the rack topology is unknown, given, and inferred using clustering.

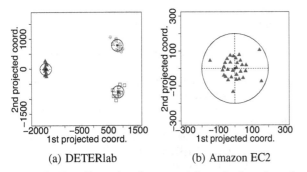

(a) DETERlab (b) Amazon EC2

Figure 12: Two-dimensional, non-metric projection of receiver nodes based on a distance matrix of node-to-node block transfer times. The ellipses represent the inferred clusters. The triangles, squares and circles in (a) represent Rack A, B and C respectively in the DETERlab testbed.

racks, then a topology-aware version of Cornet, which reduces cross-rack communication, will experience improved transfer times. To answer this question, we conducted an experiment on a 31 node DETERlab testbed (1 TC and 30 receivers). The testbed topology was as follows: Rack A was connected to Rack B and Rack B to Rack C. Each rack had 10 receiver nodes. The TC was in Rack B.

We ran the experiment with three TC configurations. The first was the default topology-oblivious Cornet that allowed any receiver to randomly contact any other receiver. The second was Cornet-Topology, where the TC partitioned the receivers according to Racks A, B, and C, and disallowed communication across partitions. The last one was CornetClustering, where the TC dynamically inferred the partitioning of the nodes based on the node-to-node block transfer times from 10 previous training runs.

The results in Figure 11 show the average completion times to transfer 100 MB and 200 MB of data to all 30 receivers over 10 runs with min-max error bars. Given the topology information (CornetTopology), the broadcasts' completion time decreased by 50% compared to vanilla Cornet for the 200 MB transfer. In 9 out of 10 runs for the 200 MB transfer, the TC inferred the exact topology (see Figure 12(a) for a typical partitioning). Only in one run did the TC infer 5 partitions (splitting two of the racks in half), though this only resulted in a 2.5 second slowdown compared to inferring the exact topology. With the ten runs averaged together, CornetClustering's reduction in completion time was 47%.

We also evaluated Cornet and CornetClustering on a 30 node EC2 cluster. Evaluating CornetTopology was not possible because

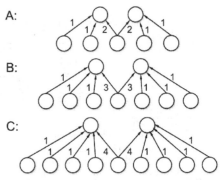

Figure 13: Transfer topologies used in the weighted shuffle experiment. The arrows show the number of units of data sent from each mapper to each reducer.

Table 3: Completion times in seconds for WSS compared to a standard shuffle implementation on the three topologies in Fig. 13. Standard deviations are in parentheses.

Topology	Standard Shuffle	WSS	Speedup	Theoretical Speedup
A	83.3 (1.1)	70.6 (1.8)	18%	25%
B	131 (1.8)	105 (0.5)	24%	33%
C	183 (2.6)	142 (0.7)	29%	38%

we could not obtain the ground-truth topology for EC2. The performance of Cornet using inferred topology did not improve over Cornet on EC2 — the algorithm found one cluster, likely due to EC2's high bisection bandwidth (Section 6.2). The projection in Figure 12(b) showed that with the exception of a few outliers (due to congestion), all the nodes appeared to be relatively close to one another and could not be partitioned into well-separated groups.

Overall, the results on the DETERlab demonstrate that when there is a sizable gap between intra-rack and inter-rack transfer times, knowing the actual node topology or inferring it can significantly improve broadcast times.

7.3 Weighted Shuffle Scheduling (WSS)

In this experiment, we evaluated the optimal Weighted Shuffle Scheduling (WSS) algorithm discussed in Section 6.3 using three topologies on Amazon EC2. Figure 13 illustrates these topologies, with arrows showing the number of units of data sent between each pair of nodes (one unit corresponded to 2 GB in our tests). Topology A is the example discussed in Section 6.3, where two receivers fetch differing amounts of data from five senders. Topologies B and C are extensions of topology A to seven and nine map tasks.

We ran each scenario under both a standard implementation of shuffle (where each reducer opens one TCP connection to each mapper) and under WSS. We implemented WSS by having each receiver open a different number of TCP connections to each sender, proportional to the amount of data it had to fetch. This allowed us to leverage the natural fair sharing between TCP flows to achieve the desired weights without modifying routers and switches.

We present average results from five runs, as well as standard deviations, in Table 3. In all cases, weighted shuffle scheduling performs better than a standard implementation of shuffle, by 18%, 24% and 29% for topologies A, B and C respectively. In addition, we present the theoretical speedup predicted for each topology, which would be achieved in a full bisection bandwidth network with a perfect implementation of fair sharing between flows. The measured results are similar to those predicted but somewhat

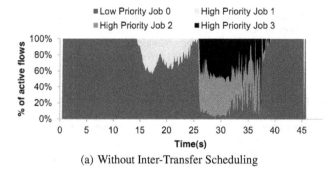

(a) Without Inter-Transfer Scheduling

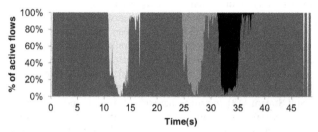

(b) Priority Scheduling with an Orchestra ITC

Figure 14: Percentage of active flows in the cluster for four different shuffle transfers in two priority classes with and without inter-transfer scheduling.

lower because fair sharing between TCP flows is not perfect (*e.g.,* if a node starts 2 GB transfers to several nodes at the same time, these transfers can finish 10-15 seconds apart).

7.4 Scheduling Across Transfers

Cross-Transfer Priority Scheduling In this experiment, we evaluated the average transfer completion times of three different smaller high priority jobs while a low priority larger job was running in the background in a 30-node cluster. The ITC was configured to put an upper limit on the number of flows created by the low priority transfer when at least one high priority job was running. Within the same priority class, the ITC used FIFO to schedule jobs. The larger transfer was shuffling 2 GB data per mapper, while the smaller ones were transferring 256 MB from each mapper. Both the experiments (with or without ITC) in Figure 14 follow similar timelines: the low priority transfer was active during the whole experiment. The first high priority transfer started after at least 10 seconds. After it finished, two more high priority transfers started one after another.

In the absence of any inter-transfer scheduler, the smaller high priority transfers had to compete with the larger low priority one throughout their durations. Eventually, each of the high priority transfers took 14.1 seconds to complete on average, and the larger low priority transfer took 45.6 seconds to finish. When using Orchestra for inter-transfer priority scheduling, the low priority transfer could create only a limited number of flows; consequently, the average completion time for the high priority transfers decreased 43% to 8.1 seconds. The completion time for the background transfer increased slightly to 48.7 seconds.

Cross-Transfer FIFO Scheduling In this experiment, we evaluated the average transfer completion times of four concurrent shuffle transfers that started at the same time in a 30 node cluster. We implemented a strict FIFO policy in the ITC as well as FIFO+, which enforces a FIFO order but gives a small share of the network (3% each) to other transfers as well. The intuition behind FIFO+ is to keep mappers busy as much as possible – if some reducers of the first transfer finish receiving from a particular mapper, it can send

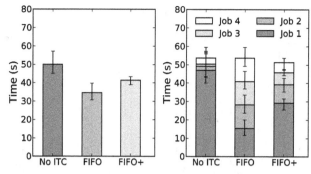

(a) Average completion times   (b) Individual completion times

Figure 15: Average completion times of four shuffles with no transfer-level scheduling, FIFO, and FIFO+ (which gives small shares of the network to the transfers later in the FIFO queue).

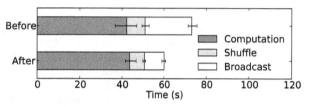

Figure 16: Per-iteration completion times for the logistic regression application before and after using Orchestra.

data to reducers from other transfers. In absence of the ITC, all the flows get their shares of the network as enforced by TCP fair sharing. During each shuffle transfer, each of the 30 reducers received a total of 1 GB data from 30 mappers.

We present the average results from five runs in Figure 15 with max-min error bars. Figure 15(a) shows the average transfer completion times for four transfers. FIFO achieved the best average completion time of 34.6s and was $1.45\times$ faster than TCP fair sharing. The theoretical maximum[7] speedup in this case is $1.6\times$.

The stacked bars in Figure 15(b) show how much longer Job i took to finish its transfer once Job $(i-1)$'s had finished. We observe that the finishing time of the slowest transfer remained the same in both FIFO ordering and TCP fair sharing. However, with FIFO, each transfer actively used the full network for equal amounts of time to complete its transfer and improved the average.

By allowing the latter transfers to have some share of the network, FIFO+ increased the completion time of the first transfer. Meanwhile, it decreased the completion times of all the other transfers in comparison to FIFO. The final outcome is a higher average completion time but lower total completion time than strict FIFO.

7.5 End-to-End Results on Full Applications

We revisit the motivating applications from Section 2 to examine the improvements in end-to-end run times after adopting the new broadcast and shuffling algorithms. In these experiments, we compare the applications before and after adopting Orchestra. In particular, "before" entails running with a HDFS-based broadcast implementation (with the default $3\times$ replication) and a shuffle with 5 threads per receiver (the default in Hadoop). Meanwhile, "after" entails Cornet and shuffle with 30 threads per receiver.

Figure 16 illustrates the breakdown of time spent in different activities in each iteration of Monarch in a 30 node EC2 cluster. We

---

[7]For n concurrent transfers, theoretical maximum speedup of the average completion time using FIFO over fair sharing is $\frac{2n}{n+1}\times$.

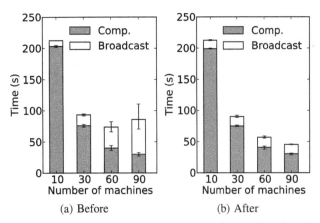

(a) Before   (b) After

Figure 17: Per-iteration completion times when scaling the collaborative filtering application using Orchestra.

see that its communication overhead in each iteration decreased from 42% of the run time to 28%, and iterations finished 22% faster overall. There is a 2.3× speedup in broadcast and a 1.23× speedup in shuffle. The improvements for both broadcast and shuffle are in line with the findings in Sections 7.1 and 6.2.

Figure 17(b) presents the per-iteration completion times for the collaborative filtering job while scaling it up to 90 nodes using Cornet. Unlike the HDFS-based solution (Figure 17(a)), broadcast time increased from 13.4 to only 15.3 seconds using Cornet. As a result, the job could be scaled up to 90 nodes with 1.9× improvement in iteration times. The average time spent in broadcast decreased by 3.6×, from 55.8s to 15.3s, for 90 nodes. These results are in line with Section 7.1 given 385 MB broadcast per iteration.

8 Related Work

Full Bisection Bandwidth Datacenter Networks. A large number of new datacenter network architectures have been proposed in recent years [9, 21, 23, 24, 35] to achieve full bisection bandwidth and improved network performance. However, full bisection bandwidth does not mean infinite bisection bandwidth. Orchestra is still valuable in full bisection bandwidth networks to enable inter-transfer prioritization and scheduling, to balance shuffle transfer rates using WSS, and to speed up broadcasts using Cornet. For example, the experiments in Section 7 show that Orchestra improves job performance even on EC2's network, which appears to have near-full bisection bandwidth.

Centralized Network Controllers. Centralized controllers for routing, access control, and load balancing in the network had been proposed by the 4D architecture [22] and projects like Tesseract [42], Ethane [12], PLayer [30], and Hedera [10]. While PLayer and Ethane focus on access control, our primary objective is application-level performance improvement. The scope of our work is limited to shared clusters and datacenters, whereas 4D, Tesseract, and Ethane are designed for wide-area and enterprise networks. However, unlike Hedera or any of the existing proposals for centralized control planes, we work at the granularity of *transfers* to optimize overall application performance, and not at the packet or flow level.

Performance Isolation in Datacenter Networks. Seawall [38] performs weighted fair sharing among cloud tenants running arbitrary numbers of TCP and UDP flows through a shim layer at the hypervisor using a cross-flow AIMD scheme. It can be leveraged by Orchestra to enforce inter-transfer scheduling policies. However, Seawall itself is not aware of transfer-level semantics.

Scheduling and Management in Data-intensive Applications. A plethora of schemes exist to schedule and manage tasks of data-intensive applications. Examples include fair schedulers for Hadoop [43] and Dryad [29], and Mantri [11] for outlier detection. The core tenet of existing work in this area is achieving data locality to avoid network transfers as much as possible. Mesos [26] provides a thin management layer to allow diverse cluster computing frameworks to efficiently share computation and storage resources, but leaves sharing of network resources to underlying transport mechanisms. Orchestra complements these systems by enabling the implementation of network sharing policies across applications.

One-to-many Data Transfer Mechanisms. Broadcast, multicast, and diverse group communication mechanisms in application and lower layers of the network stack have been studied extensively in the literature. Diot *et al.* provide a comprehensive survey and taxonomy of relevant protocols and mechanisms of distributed multipoint communication in [16]. Cornet is designed for transferring large amounts of data in high-speed datacenter networks.

SplitStream [13] improves network utilization and tackles the bottleneck problem observed in *d*-ary trees by creating multiple distribution trees with disjoint leave sets. However, it is designed primarily for multimedia streaming over the Internet, where frames can be dropped. Maintaining its structural constraints in presence of failure is complicated as well.

BitTorrent [4] is wildly popular for file-sharing. BitTorrent and similar peer-to-peer mechanisms are in use to distribute planet-scale software updates [20]. However, Murder [8] is the only known BitTorrent deployment inside a datacenter. Antfarm [36] uses a central coordinator across multiple swarms to optimize content distribution over the Internet. Cornet is a BitTorrent-like system that is optimized for datacenters and uses adaptive clustering algorithm in the TC to infer and take advantage of network topologies.

Incast or Many-to-one Transfers. TCP incast collapse is typically observed in barrier-synchronized request workloads where a receiver synchronously receives small amounts of data from a large number of senders [41]. However, incast collapse has been reported in MapReduce-like data-intensive workloads as well [14]. The latter case boils down to a special case of shuffle with only one reducer. With Orchestra, the TC can effectively limit how many senders are simultaneously sending and at what rate to alleviate this problem for data-intensive workloads.

Inferring Topology from Node-to-Node Latencies. Inferring node topology in CornetClustering (Section 5.3) is similar in spirit to inferring network coordinates [17]. These methods could act as a substitute for the non-metric multidimensional scaling step in the CornetClustering procedure.

9 Conclusion

We have argued that multi-node transfer operations have a significant impact on the performance of data-intensive cluster applications and presented an architecture called Orchestra that enables global control both across and within transfers to optimize performance. We focused on two common transfer patterns: broadcasts and shuffles. For broadcasts, we proposed a topology-aware BitTorrent-like scheme called Cornet that outperforms the status quo in Hadoop by 4.5×. For shuffles, we proposed an optimal algorithm called Weighted Shuffle Scheduling (WSS). Overall, our schemes can increase application performance by up to 1.9×. In addition, we demonstrated that inter-transfer scheduling can improve the performance of high-priority transfers by 1.7× and reduce average transfer times by 31%. Orchestra can be implemented at the application level and does not require hardware changes to run in current datacenters and in the cloud.

Acknowledgments

We thank the AMPLab members, the anonymous reviewers, and our shepherd, Yinglian Xie for useful comments on the paper, and Michael Armbrust, Jon Kuroda, Keith Sklower, and the Spark team for infrastructure support. This research was supported in part by gifts from AMPLab founding sponsors Google and SAP, AMPLab sponsors Amazon Web Services, Cloudera, Huawei, IBM, Intel, Microsoft, NEC, NetApp, and VMWare, and by matching funds from the State of California's MICRO program (grants 06-152, 07-010), the National Science Foundation (grants CNS-0509559 and CNS-1038695), the University of California Industry/University Cooperative Research Program (UC Discovery) grant COM07-10240, and the Natural Sciences and Engineering Research Council of Canada.

10 References

[1] Amazon EC2. http://aws.amazon.com/ec2.

[2] Apache Hadoop. http://hadoop.apache.org.

[3] BitTornado. http://www.bittornado.com.

[4] BitTorrent. http://www.bittorrent.com.

[5] DETERlab. http://www.isi.deterlab.net.

[6] Fragment replicate join – Pig wiki. http://wiki.apache.org/pig/PigFRJoin.

[7] LANTorrent. http://www.nimbusproject.org.

[8] Murder. http://github.com/lg/murder.

[9] H. Abu-Libdeh, P. Costa, A. Rowstron, G. O'Shea, and A. Donnelly. Symbiotic routing in future data centers. In *SIGCOMM*, pages 51–62, 2010.

[10] M. Al-Fares, S. Radhakrishnan, B. Raghavan, N. Huang, and A. Vahdat. Hedera: Dynamic flow scheduling for data center networks. In *NSDI*, 2010.

[11] G. Ananthanarayanan, S. Kandula, A. Greenberg, I. Stoica, Y. Lu, B. Saha, and E. Harris. Reining in the outliers in mapreduce clusters using Mantri. In *OSDI*, 2010.

[12] M. Casado, M. J. Freedman, J. Pettit, J. Luo, N. McKeown, and S. Shenker. Ethane: Taking control of the enterprise. In *SIGCOMM*, pages 1–12, 2007.

[13] M. Castro, P. Druschel, A.-M. Kermarrec, A. Nandi, A. Rowstron, and A. Singh. Splitstream: high-bandwidth multicast in cooperative environments. In *SOSP*, 2003.

[14] Y. Chen, R. Griffith, J. Liu, R. H. Katz, and A. D. Joseph. Understanding TCP incast throughput collapse in datacenter networks. In *WREN*, pages 73–82, 2009.

[15] J. Dean and S. Ghemawat. MapReduce: Simplified data processing on large clusters. In *OSDI*, pages 137–150, 2004.

[16] C. Diot, W. Dabbous, and J. Crowcroft. Multipoint communication: A survey of protocols, functions, and mechanisms. *IEEE JSAC*, 15(3):277 –290, 1997.

[17] B. Donnet, B. Gueye, and M. A. Kaafar. A Survey on Network Coordinates Systems, Design, and Security. *IEEE Communication Surveys and Tutorials*, 12(4), Oct. 2010.

[18] C. Fraley and A. Raftery. MCLUST Version 3 for R: Normal mixture modeling and model-based clustering. Technical Report 504, Department of Statistics, University of Washington, Sept. 2006.

[19] P. Ganesan and M. Seshadri. On cooperative content distribution and the price of barter. In *ICDCS*, 2005.

[20] C. Gkantsidis, T. Karagiannis, and M. VojnoviC. Planet scale software updates. In *SIGCOMM*, pages 423–434, 2006.

[21] A. Greenberg, J. R. Hamilton, N. Jain, S. Kandula, C. Kim, P. Lahiri, D. A. Maltz, P. Patel, and S. Sengupta. VL2: A scalable and flexible data center network. In *SIGCOMM*, 2009.

[22] A. Greenberg, G. Hjalmtysson, D. A. Maltz, A. Myers, J. Rexford, G. Xie, H. Yan, J. Zhan, and H. Zhang. A clean slate 4D approach to network control and management. *SIGCOMM CCR*, 35:41–54, 2005.

[23] C. Guo, G. Lu, D. Li, H. Wu, X. Zhang, Y. Shi, C. Tian, Y. Zhang, and S. Lu. BCube: A high performance, server-centric network architecture for modular data centers. In *SIGCOMM*, pages 63–74, 2009.

[24] C. Guo, H. Wu, K. Tan, L. Shi, Y. Zhang, and S. Lu. DCell: A scalable and fault-tolerant network structure for data centers. In *SIGCOMM*, pages 75–86, 2008.

[25] T. Hastie, R. Tibshirani, and J. Friedman. *The Elements of Statistical Learning: Data Mining, Inference, and Prediction*. Springer, New York, NY, 2009.

[26] B. Hindman, A. Konwinski, M. Zaharia, A. Ghodsi, A. Joseph, R. Katz, S. Shenker, and I. Stoica. Mesos: A Platform for Fine-Grained Resource Sharing in the Data Center. In *NSDI*, 2011.

[27] U. Hoelzle and L. A. Barroso. *The Datacenter as a Computer: An Introduction to the Design of Warehouse-Scale Machines*. Morgan and Claypool Publishers, 1st edition, 2009.

[28] M. Isard, M. Budiu, Y. Yu, A. Birrell, and D. Fetterly. Dryad: Distributed data-parallel programs from sequential building blocks. In *EuroSys*, pages 59–72, 2007.

[29] M. Isard, V. Prabhakaran, J. Currey, U. Wieder, K. Talwar, and A. Goldberg. Quincy: Fair scheduling for distributed computing clusters. In *SOSP*, 2009.

[30] D. A. Joseph, A. Tavakoli, and I. Stoica. A policy-aware switching layer for data centers. In *SIGCOMM*, 2008.

[31] J. B. Kruskal and M. Wish. Multidimensional Scaling. *Sage University Paper series on Quantitative Applications in the Social Sciences*, 07-001, 1978.

[32] G. Malewicz, M. H. Austern, A. J. Bik, J. C. Dehnert, I. Horn, N. Leiser, and G. Czajkowski. Pregel: A system for large-scale graph processing. In *SIGMOD*, 2010.

[33] Y. Mao and L. K. Saul. Modeling Distances in Large-Scale Networks by Matrix Factorization. In *IMC*, 2004.

[34] D. G. Murray, M. Schwarzkopf, C. Smowton, S. Smith, A. Madhavapeddy, and S. Hand. Ciel: A Universal Execution Engine for Distributed Data-Flow Computing. In *NSDI*, 2011.

[35] R. N. Mysore, A. Pamboris, N. Farrington, N. Huang, P. Miri, S. Radhakrishnan, V. Subramanya, and A. Vahdat. PortLand: A scalable fault-tolerant layer 2 data center network fabric. In *SIGCOMM*, pages 39–50, 2009.

[36] R. Peterson and E. G. Sirer. Antfarm: Efficient content distribution with managed swarms. In *NSDI*, 2009.

[37] B. Pfaff, J. Pettit, K. Amidon, M. Casado, T. Koponen, and S. Shenker. Extending networking into the virtualization layer. In *HotNets 2009*.

[38] A. Shieh, S. Kandula, A. Greenberg, and C. Kim. Sharing the data center network. In *NSDI*, 2011.

[39] D. B. Shmoys. *Cut problems and their application to divide-and-conquer*, chapter 5, pages 192–235. PWS Publishing Co., Boston, MA, USA, 1997.

[40] K. Thomas, C. Grier, J. Ma, V. Paxson, and D. Song. Design and evaluation of a real-time URL spam filtering service. In *IEEE Symposium on Security and Privacy*, 2011.

[41] V. Vasudevan, A. Phanishayee, H. Shah, E. Krevat, D. G. Andersen, G. R. Ganger, G. A. Gibson, and B. Mueller. Safe and effective fine-grained TCP retransmissions for datacenter communication. In *SIGCOMM*, pages 303–314, 2009.

[42] H. Yan, D. A. Maltz, T. S. E. Ng, H. Gogineni, H. Zhang, and Z. Cai. Tesseract: A 4D network control plane. In *NSDI '07*.

[43] M. Zaharia, D. Borthakur, J. Sen Sarma, K. Elmeleegy, S. Shenker, and I. Stoica. Delay scheduling: A simple technique for achieving locality and fairness in cluster scheduling. In *EuroSys*, 2010.

[44] M. Zaharia, M. Chowdhury, M. J. Franklin, S. Shenker, and I. Stoica. Spark: Cluster Computing with Working Sets. In *HotCloud*, 2010.

[45] Y. Zhou, D. Wilkinson, R. Schreiber, and R. Pan. Large-scale parallel collaborative filtering for the Netflix prize. In *AAIM*, pages 337–348. Springer-Verlag, 2008.

On Blind Mice and the Elephant[*]

Understanding the Network Impact of a Large Distributed System

John S. Otto[†]   Mario A. Sánchez[†]   David R. Choffnes[†]

Fabián E. Bustamante[†]   Georgos Siganos[‡]

† Northwestern University   ‡ Telefónica Research

ABSTRACT

A thorough understanding of the network impact of emerging large-scale distributed systems – where traffic flows and what it costs – must encompass users' behavior, the traffic they generate and the topology over which that traffic flows. In the case of BitTorrent, however, previous studies have been limited by narrow perspectives that restrict such analysis.

This paper presents a comprehensive view of BitTorrent, using data from a representative set of 500,000 users sampled over a two year period, located in 169 countries and 3,150 networks. This unique perspective captures unseen trends and reveals several unexpected features of the largest peer-to-peer system. For instance, over the past year total BitTorrent traffic has *increased by 12%*, driven by 25% increases in per-peer hourly download volume despite a 10% decrease in the average number of online peers. We also observe stronger diurnal usage patterns and, surprisingly, given the bandwidth-intensive nature of the application, a close alignment between these patterns and overall traffic. Considering the aggregated traffic across access links, this has potential implications on BitTorrent-associated costs for Internet Service Providers (ISPs). Using data from a transit ISP, we find a disproportionately large impact under a commonly used burstable (95th-percentile) billing model. Last, when examining BitTorrent traffic's paths, we find that for over half its users, most network traffic never reaches large transit networks, but is instead carried by small transit ISPs. This raises questions on the effectiveness of most in-network monitoring systems to capture trends on peer-to-peer traffic and further motivates our approach.

Categories and Subject Descriptors

C.2.4 [**Communication Networks**]: Distributed Systems—*Distributed applications*; C.2.5 [**Communication Networks**]: Local and Wide-Area Networks—*Internet*; C.4 [**Performance of Systems**]: Measurement techniques

---

[*]A variation on the Indian fable of the seven blind men and the elephant.

General Terms

Experimentation, Performance, Measurement

Keywords

Internet-scale Systems, Peer-to-Peer, Evaluation

1. INTRODUCTION

The network impact of popular, widely distributed services has implications for capacity planning, traffic engineering, and interdomain business relationships. Accurately characterizing and understanding this impact requires a view of the service in question that includes not only the traffic it generates and the networks it traverses, but also the underlying user behaviors that drive it. Such a comprehensive view is typically impossible to capture from any single network or in-network monitoring system.

It comes as no surprise, then, that the overall impact of BitTorrent, arguably the most widely distributed peer-to-peer system, remains unknown.

In this paper, we present the first comprehensive study of BitTorrent based on a longitudinal, representative view from the network edge, including two years of application traces from over 500,000 user IPs located in 3,150 ASes and 169 countries.

Our study reveals BitTorrent usage trends and traffic patterns that have been previously hidden or obscured by limited perspectives. After demonstrating the representativeness of our dataset as a sample of the overall BitTorrent system (Sec. 3), we discuss trends regarding how users interact with the system. We find that while the number of concurrent active users has decreased since 2008, the overall volume of traffic that BitTorrent generates has grown by 12%, likely due in part to increased bandwidth capacities. While session times have also decreased over this period (by 21%), the temporal patterns behind these sessions are increasingly aligned with those of rest of Internet traffic, despite BitTorrent's known high-bandwidth demands. This shift in usage patterns suggests an increasing role for BitTorrent on ISPs' infrastructure and costs.

After describing key trends regarding *how* BitTorrent is being used, we then focus on *where* the corresponding traffic is flowing. We leverage hundreds of millions of traceroute measurements between peers to map the vast majority (89%) of BitTorrent traffic to the networks it traverses. Our analysis reveals that the traffic surprisingly exhibits significant locality across geography (32% of BitTorrent traffic stays in the country of origin) and networks (49% of traffic is intradomain or crosses a single peering or sibling AS link). Using a recent network classification scheme, we unexpectedly find that most traffic does not reach the core of the network. Among other points, this raises questions on the effectiveness of in-network monitoring approaches to capture trends on BitTorrent traffic and further motivates our approach.

Using information about where BitTorrent traffic is flowing and when it is generated, we model its contribution to ISPs' costs. We observe that, under the 95th-percentile billing model typically used between transit ISPs and their customers, the *time* at which traffic occurs can be as important as the volume of traffic. Incorporating traffic volumes from a large, global ISP, using this cost model, we find that current time-of-day patterns of BitTorrent often result in significantly higher cost, byte-for-byte, when compared to other traffic on the network.

In sum, our results highlight how limited perspectives for analyzing Internet-wide systems do not generalize, demonstrating the need for comprehensive views when analyzing global features of such widely distributed systems. One application of our analyses is enabling ISPs to better understand the impact of such systems and reason about the effects of alternative traffic management policies.

2. BACKGROUND AND RELATED WORK

P2P systems have received much attention from operators and the research community due in part to their widespread popularity and their potential network impact. Among P2P systems, BitTorrent is the most popular one, potentially accounting for between 20% and 57% of P2P file-sharing traffic [17, 22]. A number of studies provide detailed summaries of the BitTorrent protocol, conventions and dynamics [11, 12, 19, 20]. In this paper, we focus on data connections between peers, the flows they generate, the network paths they traverse and their temporal characteristics.

Numerous studies have analyzed P2P usage trends and attempted to characterize the overall network impact from various perspectives based on either simulations or limited perspectives [14, 15, 17, 21, 22, 25]. Conclusions vary considerably among studies, due in part to variations in P2P usage in each ISP and the challenges with identifying P2P traffic from network flow summaries (e.g., due to randomized ports or use of connection encryption). Our study is the first to examine the network impact of the BitTorrent P2P system, based on the perspective of a set of users distributed over several thousand networks worldwide. Since these traces are gathered from within the application, they are not subject to classification errors.

Given the potential impact of P2P-associated cross-ISP traffic on network operational costs, several studies have investigated approaches to evaluate and improve P2P traffic's locality [5, 6, 13, 16, 18, 30]. Xie et al. [30] base their results on testbed evaluations in a small number of ISPs, Piatek et al. [18] use a single vantage point outside of classical research platforms, and Cuevas et al. [6] simulate peer interactions based on information derived from tracker scrape results. As in some of our previous work [5], we rely instead on a global view and actual BitTorrent connections to evaluate locality aspects of this system. Here we move beyond coarse-grained locality analysis in an attempt to understand the cost associated with BitTorrent traffic using a detailed Internet map that combines public BGP feeds with peer-based traceroute data [3]. As we demonstrate in Section 5.1, network paths collected from end-users are indispensable to determine the path that BitTorrent traffic takes through the network.

Understanding how P2P-associated traffic affects an ISP's transit charges is important for determining subscriber charges and informing traffic engineering policies. Following the approach used by Stanojevic et al. [23] (which examined the cost impact of individual ISP subscribers' traffic), we are the first to apply the game-theoretic Shapley analysis to examine the relative cost of interdomain BitTorrent traffic under the common 95th-percentile charging model.

3. DATASETS

We now describe the traces we use in the rest of this study. We posit that this dataset comprises the first comprehensive and representative view of BitTorrent. The following paragraphs demonstrate each of these properties in turn.

3.1 A Comprehensive View of BitTorrent

Our study is based on the largest collection of detailed end-user traces from a P2P system. Specifically, we use data gathered through users of the AquaLab's ongoing Ono [5] and NEWS [4] projects, our *vantage points (VP)*, collectively representing more than 1,260,000 installations. Our data collection software, implemented as extensions to the Vuze BitTorrent client [28], periodically report application and network statistics, excluding any information that can identify the downloaded content.[1] This dataset is comprehensive in that it is longitudinal across time and covers a broad range of networks and geographic regions.

To inform BitTorrent usage trends during the past year (Sec. 4), we use data from the second week of November 2008 and every two months from November 2009 through November 2010 (about 1 TB of trace data). For our detailed study of BitTorrent traffic, we use continuous data from March through May 2010 (Secs. 5-6). Altogether, our dataset includes traces from more than 500,000 IPs located in 3,150 ASes and 169 countries.

This dataset includes per-connection transfer data, such as source and destination (our vantage points and the peers they connect to), current transfer rates at 30-second intervals, and the cumulative volume of data transferred in each direction for each connection. It also allows us to compute user session time, i.e. the length of time that a user runs BitTorrent.

In addition to passively gathered data, the dataset contains traceroutes to a subset of peers connected to each vantage point. Targets for the probes are selected at random from connected peers, and at most one traceroute is performed at a time (to limit probing overhead). Each measurement is performed using the host's built-in traceroute command. From March through May 2010, our dataset comprises 202 million traceroute measurements. In Sec. 5.1, we discuss how we use these measurements to map per-connection flows to the AS paths they traverse.

3.2 Representativeness

We now analyze the representativeness of our dataset as a sample of activity in the Internet-wide BitTorrent system. While the vantage points are limited by the set of users who voluntarily install our extensions, we do not expect to find any strong platform or language-specific bias that could impact our results. The Vuze BitTorrent client, as well as our two instrumented plugins, run on all major platforms and are translated into nearly every language. There are several other potential sources of bias such as extension-specific behavior and the distribution of vantage points in terms of geography and networks, the peers they connect to, and the BitTorrent clients those peers use. We address these in the following paragraphs.

We first account for bias introduced by the extensions that our VPs run. While NEWS uses BitTorrent traffic to detect service-level network events without affecting the application, Ono biases peer selection using CDN redirections to reduce cross-ISP traffic. We avoid this bias by filtering out all data for connections that Ono selected for preferred peering.

---

[1]Anonymized traces are available to researchers through the EdgeScope project. [10]

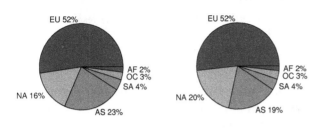

| | (a) Vantage points | (b) Connected peers |

Figure 1: Distribution of BitTorrent users by continent for our vantage points (left) and the set of all peers connected to our vantage points (right) in November 2010. Both distributions match closely but for small differences in North America and Asia.

Network type	Vantage points	Remote peers
Large transit	4.07 %	5.18 %
Small transit	53.7 %	51.6 %
Access providers	42.3 %	43.2 %

Table 1: Portion of VPs and remote peers located in each type of network, suggesting that the VP population is representative of the general BitTorrent population.

Given the default random peer selection strategy in BitTorrent, we expect that the remaining peers that the VPs connect to are representative of the system as a whole. We evaluate this by testing for similarities in geography, network topology, and BitTorrent client use.

We compare the VPs' geographic distribution to that of the peers they connect to, using geolocation information obtained from a popular IP-to-ASN mapping service [24]. Figure 1 shows, side by side, the distribution of VPs and their connected peers per continent. These distributions match closely, having equal portions in Europe (52%), with small differences of 16/20% in North America, and 23/19% in Asia.

For reference, we also compare the observed distributions with those reported in previous studies and find strong similarities. Zhang et al. [31] crawl tracker sites from 2008 to 2009 and report the number of BitTorrent users for the top-20 countries sorted by peer population. These data show that 49% of users are in Europe, 28% in North America and 18% in Asia. Note that these statistics under-represent the fractions of European and Asian peers since many countries in these regions did not appear in the top-20 list. This explains why North American peers are a larger portion of the peers (28%) relative to our distributions (16/20%). The reported fractions of European and Asian peers match closely those found in our dataset.

We also compare the distribution of VPs and remote peers in terms of network topology, by contrasting the number of IP addresses per network class, following the scheme recently proposed by Dhamdhere and Dovrolis [7]. Table 1 shows that these distributions align – the portion of peers in each network class differs by at most 2%.

Last, we determine whether there is any significant bias based on the types of BitTorrent clients that our VPs connect to. This could result, for example, from Vuze peers preferentially connecting to other Vuze peers. We evaluate this by comparing the distribution of BitTorrent clients connected to our VPs with that of an independent

Client	Our Data (Nov 2009)	Aug 2009 [27]
μTorrent	50.59 %	56.81 %
Azureus/Vuze	22.48 %	18.13 %
Mainline	9.28 %	11.79 %
BitComet	5.29 %	4.71 %
Transmission	2.68 %	2.95 %

Table 2: Comparison between connected client distribution in our dataset in November 2009 and results from a swarm crawl conducted in August 2009.

source (Table 2). We use VP data from November 2009 and a client distribution collected in August 2009 that is derived from crawls of 400 swarms [27]. As the table shows, there is a strong correspondence in both client rank and market share between the two sets.

Overall, we find no strong evidence of significant bias in our dataset using any of these metrics. In the following sections, we use this dataset to analyze the network impact of BitTorrent, starting with a description of observed usage patterns and trends.

4. BITTORRENT USAGE TRENDS

In this section, we use our BitTorrent traces to analyze several key usage trends that affect the system's network impact. In particular, we find that despite reports of declining usage [17] the absolute volume of BitTorrent traffic continues to rise. Further, we find that BitTorrent's temporal usage patterns are increasingly aligned with diurnal traffic patterns, which has implications for its contribution to ISPs' costs.

4.1 Sampling Methodology

Obtaining representative, longitudinal snapshots of BitTorrent traffic and user behavior is challenging, given the high degree of churn in the system. To enable comparisons across multiple time scales, we aggregate user statistics at one-hour granularity, then use random sampling of our dataset to obtain a constant number of users (1000) during each hour for inclusion in our analysis. We repeat this random sampling 5 times to derive a statistically significant average for each hour. In general, the standard deviations of our samples are relatively small, and we include corresponding error bars in our figures.

The following analysis focuses on comparisons using the second week of every 2 months over the year of study. In some cases, we use data collected in November 2008 to analyze trends over two years.

4.2 Key Trends

In the following paragraphs, we examine trends in overall BitTorrent traffic in terms of number of connected peers and per-peer download volumes.

We begin by examining the volume of traffic generated by individual peers. Figure 2 depicts average per-peer hourly download volumes over one year, between November 2009 and 2010. As the figure shows, BitTorrent's network impact in terms of hourly download volumes per-peer have grown consistently over this period, increasing by 25% on average.

Beyond the download volumes generated by users, we find two important and related trends that refer to (1) the number of BitTorrent users and (2) the temporal patterns behind their activities. Variations in the number of connected peers may hint at changes in the size of the overall BitTorrent population. An understanding of temporal patterns behind user activities, on the

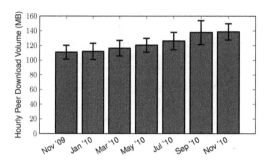

Figure 2: Average per-user hourly download volume between November 2009 and 2010, showing that download volumes have increased by 25%.

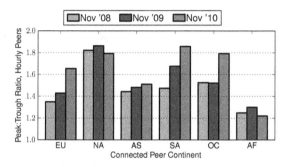

Figure 4: Average daily peak-to-trough ratio of hourly peers seen by continent, from 2008 to 2010. Peers in Europe, Oceania and South America appear to have increasingly strong diurnal patterns. The diurnal patterns of North American peers remain consistently strong.

	Metric	2009	2010	Δ
A	Peer download rate	110.9	138.7	+25.0%
B	Unique peers per hour	276.6	248.0	-10.3%
C	Concurrent flows	32.7	28.9	-11.6%
D (A/C)	Per-flow download rate	3.39	4.80	+41.5%
E (B*C)	Total flows	9040	7170	-20.7%
F (D*E)	Total download rate	30700	34400	**+12.1%**

Table 3: Summary of calculations to determine overall BitTorrent traffic, based on product of number of flows and per-flow download rate. All download rates are in MB/hr. We find that total BitTorrent traffic has increased 12.1% from 2009 to 2010.

other hand, is necessary to understand the potential contributions of BitTorrent to congestion and near-peak transit charging rates.

We begin by plotting weekly timelines of the number of peers connected to each vantage point in 2008 and 2010 (Fig. 3). We group peers by location to highlight variations in usage over time and across regions. Focusing first on Europe, the largest contributor to connected peers, we see increasingly defined diurnal patterns with peak usage in the late evening, and relatively larger peaks and troughs in 2010 compared to 2008. This is surprising given the logical, common belief that BitTorrent is used out-of-phase with other applications because of the high load it imposes on users connections [17].

To better illustrate changes in diurnal patterns for the number of connected peers over time, we plot the average peak-to-trough ratio of the hourly connected peers by continent (Fig. 4). Larger ratio values indicate that greater portions of peers in each region use BitTorrent at the same time. The figure shows that the ratio of connected peers in North America has remained consistently high over the last two years, with 80% more peers online during peak usage. Meanwhile, diurnal patterns in Europe have grown more pronounced during the same period. While the exact causes for this behavior are beyond the scope of this paper, we speculate that variations in copyright law and enforcement (which can affect how long users leave BitTorrent running) across time and regions may contribute to this effect.

Figure 3 also indicates that the average number of connections to each vantage point per hour has decreased during the observation period by 10% (compare the "All" curves in Figs. 3a and 3b). This could be explained in part by a drop in the system popularity and/or

shorter session times. While it is difficult to quantify the former, we can use our dataset to directly evaluate the latter. Figure 5 shows a typical distribution of session times, and also plots median session time for vantage points in each continent from November 2008 to 2010. We find that, from 2009 to 2010, median session times have decreased for each of the three main continents. Since 2008, session times in Europe, North America and Asia decreased by 13%, 23%, and 20%, respectively.

Finally, we note that changes in the average number of connected peers are dominated by a 30% drop in the number of European peers. This is aligned with previous reports that European users are increasingly using direct download sites in lieu of P2P [17]. In contrast, usage in Africa and Asia *increased* by 75% and 45% from 2008 levels, indicating a growing presence in developing regions.

These results reveal conflicting trends that make it difficult to estimate changes in aggregate BitTorrent traffic. With this in mind, we compute a measure of the total BitTorrent traffic as the product between the number of BitTorrent flows in the network and the average per-flow hourly traffic volume. For this, we determine the average number of concurrent connections (i.e. flows) maintained by each peer and use it to compute the average per-flow download rate and an estimate of the total flows in the system. Table 3 provides a summary of these metrics and calculations. We use the *Peer download rate (A)* and the number of *Concurrent flows (C)* to estimate the *Per-flow download rate (D)* and compute an estimate of the number of *Total flows (E)* as the product of the number of *Unique peers per hour (B)* and the number of *Concurrent flows (C)*. The *Total download rate (F)* is then computed as the product of the *Per-flow download rate (D)* and the number of *Total flows (E)*. The reduction in the number of flows per peer results in an increase in the per-flow download rate of 41.5%. Thus, while the total number of flows in the system has shrunk by 20.7%, the BitTorrent traffic has had a net increase of 12.1% between 2009 and 2010.

To summarize, we find that BitTorrent traffic volume is growing, and its traffic is increasingly generated from shorter sessions that tend to occur during peak hours. As we show in Sec. 6, these temporal trends have a significant impact on transit charges. The next sections build on the identified trends to determine which parts of the Internet are most affected by the corresponding traffic and the impact of this traffic in terms of costs and revenue.

5. WHERE BITTORRENT FLOWS

We now discuss *where* BitTorrent traffic flows through the network. We begin with a discussion of how to map traffic flows to the network paths they traverse. We use these mappings to study the geographic and topological characteristics of the traffic exchanged between users from March through the end of May 2010.

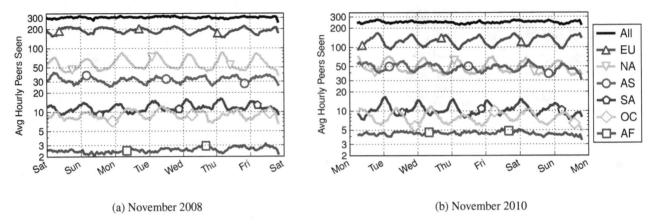

(a) November 2008

(b) November 2010

Figure 3: Distribution of connected peers per hour, grouped by continent, in 2008 and 2010 (semi-log scale). Vertical grid lines correspond with midnight, UTC. Note the increasingly defined diurnal patterns.

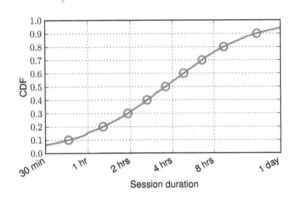

(a) All Session Times, Nov 2010

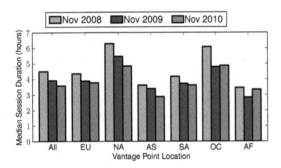

(b) Changes in Median Session Time

Figure 5: CDF of average session time per vantage point for all peers in Nov 2010 (top). Overall, session times have decreased from Nov 2008 to Nov 2010. For peers in Asia, Europe, and North America, median session times dropped by 13% to 23% over this time interval (bottom).

5.1 Mapping BitTorrent Flows

In the following paragraphs, we address the problem of mapping BitTorrent flows to the paths they traverse. In particular, we show that publicly available path information such as BGP feeds are insufficient for mapping the vast majority of BitTorrent traffic, and

address this by supplementing the public view with traceroutes collected between our vantage points and their connected peers. While the limitations of the public view of Internet topology are well known [3], we focus on what this implies for estimating P2P traffic locality and costs.

To infer traceroute-based AS path information, we combine over 202 M traceroutes between peers in our dataset with data gathered from public BGP feeds [26] using heuristics from Chen et al. [3]. Altogether, our dataset consists of 13.1 M distinct AS paths.

We then determine the portion of BitTorrent flows that, for the same time period, can be mapped to an AS path. First we map each flow's endpoint IP addresses to a source/destination AS pair [24]. For each of the resulting 2.1 million AS pairs, we determine whether an AS-level path exists, using either the paths in the BGP public view alone or using a combination of the public view with traceroute-derived AS paths. We say that such a path exists for a pair if both the source and destination of the pair appear in any path.

Figure 6 plots the cumulative distribution function of the portion of BitTorrent traffic per vantage point that can be mapped to an AS path using either BGP only paths (curve labeled "BGP") or the combined set of BGP and traceroute-derived paths ("BGP + Traceroute"). The figure shows that paths available in the BGP public view are not sufficient to account for the majority of flows in our traces – over 80% of vantage points cannot even map half of their traffic, while the median vantage point is able to map less than 14% of its traffic.

After adding traceroute-derived AS paths to this analysis, we can map nearly all BitTorrent traffic to AS paths. In particular, despite not having complete all-to-all traceroutes, for 90% of VPs we can map at least half of their traffic and are able to map over 96% of traffic for the majority (>50%) of peers.

These results show that when evaluating the Internet-wide impact of a globally distributed system, it is necessary and sufficient to supplement public views of Internet topology with topological information gathered from the edge of the network. The remainder of this paper uses this information to understand where BitTorrent flows and its impact on ISP costs and revenue.

5.2 Geographic Locality

While it is well known that BitTorrent is used in nearly every region and country worldwide, it is unclear how much of its traffic

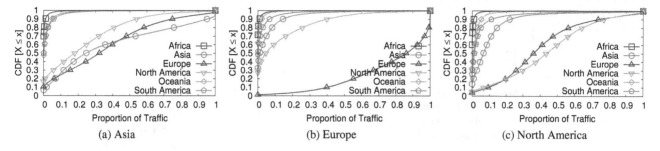

(a) Asia   (b) Europe   (c) North America

Figure 7: For each vantage point in a given continent, the proportion of its traffic according to the continent of destination. The curves show strong locality at the continent-level; this is particularly the case for Europe where most users are located.

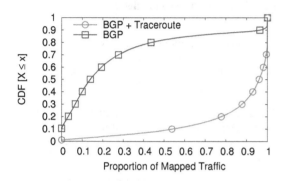

Figure 6: CDF of the portion of each vantage point's traffic that can be mapped to a path, using only BGP paths, or BGP and traceroute-derived paths. Paths in the public view cannot map most BitTorrent traffic, but adding traceroute paths results in nearly complete coverage.

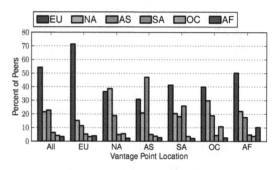

Figure 8: Distribution of the location of connected peers, according to the location of the vantage point, for November 2010. The VP's locale is always more strongly represented than in the "All" distribution.

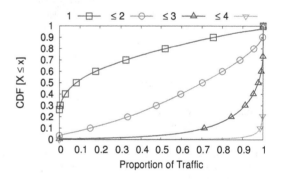

Figure 9: For each peer, the proportion of traffic that passes through up to C different countries. 73% of all traffic at most travels one country from its origin.

stays local. In this section, we show that traffic typically crosses few country boundaries, and the average distance it travels for a VP is strongly dependent on the VP location.

We first discuss the issue of locality of traffic. To represent this graphically, at the continent granularity, we determine the portion of each vantage point's traffic that flows to or from each continent. Figure 7 plots this as CDFs, where a point (x, y) for a given continent indicates that for a fraction y of the peers, the portion of their traffic flowing to endpoints in that continent is less than or equal to x. Curves closer to the lower right indicate continents receiving the largest share of peer traffic.

The figure includes these data for vantage points in each of the top three continents (by number of BitTorrent users). We observe that on average a VP exchanges more traffic with peers in the same continent than in any other. The effect is strongest in Europe (75% of traffic from European VPs stays within Europe), which contains the largest portion of BitTorrent users. Both North America and Asia exchange much larger portions of intracontinental traffic than their user populations would indicate.

Some of the reasons for the observed locality include content interest (e.g. based on language) as well as temporal trends – peers in a continent tend to use the system at the same time (as shown in Sec. 4). To test whether we find locality trends in traffic patterns, we plot the geographic distribution of connected peers, grouped by the continent for each VP (Fig. 8). The graph indeed shows that the distributions of connections per VP continent is similar to those for traffic.

To obtain a finer-grained view of how far aggregate BitTorrent traffic travels, we plot a CDF of each vantage point's traffic that passes through up to C countries (Figure 9). For 80% of vantage points, the majority of their traffic travels at most to one other country. Of the total traffic, we find that 32% stays within the same country, and an additional 41% travels to only one other country.

These results show that while BitTorrent's flows are geographically diverse, the location of a user (and the popularity of BitTorrent in that region) has a strong influence on the location of connected endpoints. In aggregate, BitTorrent traffic exhibits surprisingly high geographic locality – often traveling to at most one additional country. In the next section, we evaluate whether this locality holds when viewed in terms of the network topology.

Tier	Category [7]	AS Count
1	–	10
2	Large Transit Providers	20
3	Small Transit Providers	2012
4	Content/Access/Hosting Providers Enterprise Customers	40993

Table 4: Description of each network tier, as well as the number of networks in each tier. We define Tier 1 to consist of ten well-known transit-free networks, a subset of ASes that are classified as "Large Transit Providers" by Dhamdhere and Dovrolis [7].

	Tier-2	Tier-3	Tier-4
Vantage Points	13,838	181,981	143,368
VP ASes	17	611	2,524
Remote Peers	6,226,321	61,999,202	51,976,554
Remote ASes	18	1,363	14,562
Total ASes	18	1,364	14,573

Table 5: Distribution of vantage point and remote peer IPs and ASes, by tier. As expected, most of our VPs and remote peers are located in tier-3 and tier-4 networks.

5.3 Topological Locality

We now examine the topological properties of BitTorrent traffic to determine which types of networks it traverses. We note that while these results may be affected by ISP-imposed throttles on interdomain traffic, our goal is to understand the impact of the system in its current environment. For this analysis, we map traffic to Internet tiers based on the classifications by Dhamdhere and Dovrolis [7], last updated in January 2010. This work classifies ASes into the tiers shown in Table 4, based on inferred business relationships. We apply this to categorize peers and routers in our dataset and find that, as one would expect, most BitTorrent users are located in lower network tiers (Table 5).

An interesting question related to the network impact of BitTorrent traffic is how deep into the "core" of the network it flows. We want to understand whether the traffic more frequently enters large transit providers or stays at lower tiers of the topology. To evaluate this, we determine the portion of each vantage point's traffic that reaches tier T. For example, if a flow traverses from tier 4 to tier 2 and back to tier 4, the flow is counted as reaching tier 2. Figure 10 plots the result as a CDF for each originating tier. Curves near the bottom right indicate tiers receiving the largest portion of traffic.

We find that tier-3 networks handle more BitTorrent traffic than any other tier. While over 50% of the median peer's traffic stays in tier 3, less than 10% (20%) goes up to tier 2 (tier 1).

To understand the role of the endpoint locations on the spread of BitTorrent traffic, we separate individual traffic flows by their starting and ending Internet tiers, and determine the portion of that traffic flowing to each of the other tiers. Figure 11 plots, for traffic between Tier T and Tier U, the proportion of that traffic reaching Tier V (such that $V \leq T$) as CDFs. As an example, Figs. 11a–11c show that, for traffic with at least one endpoint in tier 2, the majority of traffic stays in a tier-2 AS without passing through a tier-1 network.

Overall, the figures show that BitTorrent traffic most often stays in the same tier from which it originated. For instance, the trends for tiers 3 and 4 – where the vast majority of BitTorrent users are located – show that most traffic *does not go above tier-3* (Figs. 11d–11f). Further, for traffic between two tier-4 ASes, we see that the

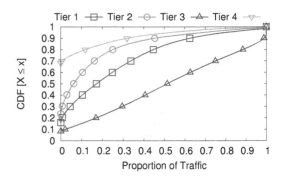

Figure 10: For each peer, the proportion of its traffic reaching Tier T. The vast majority of traffic only reaches tier 3, with significantly less traffic going to tier 1 or tier 2.

largest component of traffic unexpectedly *stays in tier 4*. When combined with results from geographic locality, this indicates that much of BitTorrent traffic remains in the same region and can be handed off among regional ISPs instead of using large transit providers.

This section showed that BitTorrent traffic exhibits strong locality, both geographically and in terms of network topology. In the next section, we evaluate the economic impact on ISPs as a result of these patterns.

6. ECONOMIC ASPECTS OF NETWORK IMPACT

In this section, we address one of the key question driving P2P research and ISP policies: how does the network impact of P2P translate to costs and revenue for ISPs? The following paragraphs present a detailed analysis of the potential impact of BitTorrent traffic on the variable costs/revenues of ISPs. For our analysis, we use detailed traces of BitTorrent traffic, comprehensive AS topologies annotated with business relationships, and additional information on interdomain traffic volumes from a large ISP.

6.1 Overview

Interdomain traffic is an important component of ISPs' operational costs. A number of research efforts have focused on reducing interdomain traffic generated by P2P systems [1, 2, 5, 30]. Earlier studies have assumed that *all* interdomain traffic incurs charges. In practice, however, charges are a function of both the total traffic flowing over each interdomain link and the business relationships between ISPs.

Thus, in the first step of our analysis, we map BitTorrent flows to inter-AS links annotated with actual business relationships – customer-provider, provider-customer, peer or sibling. To this end, we use the algorithm proposed by Xia et al. [29], which leverages the valley-free and selective export policies of BGP routing to infer the relationship between connected ASes. This allows us to infer relationships for 98.3% of the 222,675 AS links in our dataset. We assume that transit charges occur only between customers and providers, resulting in costs for the customer and revenue for the provider. We further assume peering and sibling relationships to be settlement free, with no side paying the other to carry traffic [8].

In the next step of our analysis (Sec. 6.2), we model the net impact of those flows on ISP costs. A significant challenge is the diverse and commonly confidential charging models for transit agreements between ISPs. Absent this information, we first use a basic cost model that focuses on variable costs, assigning transit

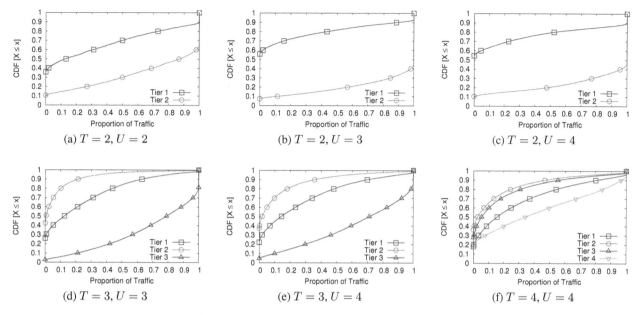

Figure 11: For each peer with data flowing between Tier T and U, the portion of that traffic that reaches up to Tier V.

charges in proportion to the volume of traffic traversing a link. This allows us to understand trends in the balance between revenue- and cost-generating flows for the ASes in our dataset (Sec. 6.3).

Finally, we conduct case studies of the economic impact of BitTorrent on several ISPs using the 95th-percentile charging model (Sec. 6.4), in which the *temporal pattern* of traffic – not just the overall volume – plays a significant role in determining cost [23]. This burstable billing model is generally considered the most popular model used between small, access networks and their providers [9]. We have shown (Sec. 5) that a significant fraction of BitTorrent traffic is handled by small transit providers near the edge of the network and that this traffic is increasingly exhibiting strong diurnal usage patterns (Sec. 4). While we cannot assign dollar values to 95th-percentile traffic, we can determine *whether BitTorrent is relatively more expensive* than the rest of the traffic traversing each link.

6.2 Portion of Charging Traffic

In this section, we analyze BitTorrent traffic in terms of the types of links that it traverses. To begin, we find that 8% of all traffic in our dataset stayed in the same AS. Though this may seem to be a small number, one should consider that peers in our dataset are distributed across nearly 16,000 ASes. For these flows, we assume that there are no transit charges and we exclude them from the remainder of our analysis.

We focus then on interdomain traffic and compute the portion of each AS's total BitTorrent traffic that crosses links to its customers, to its providers, and to its peers. This allows us to understand the portion of BitTorrent traffic that traverses charging links and thus contributes to ISPs' costs.

We begin by describing summary results for tier-1 traffic (not shown). Not surprisingly, none of this traffic flows to a provider (by definition), but interestingly the tier-1 ASes experience significantly more peering traffic relative to customer traffic. The implication is that even when traversing tier-1 networks, BitTorrent flows are relatively unlikely to incur variable charges.

For traffic in tiers 2, 3 and 4, Fig. 12 plots a CDF of the proportion of per-AS interdomain traffic grouped by business relationship. In tier-2 networks (Fig. 12a), the vast majority of traffic crosses no-cost peering links, while a small portion of the traffic crosses charging links. In the median case, over 95% of tier-2 traffic crosses no-cost links. We also note that, on average, more of their non-peering traffic traverses customer links than provider links.

For tier-3 ASes (Fig. 12b), we again find that significantly more traffic crosses peering links than provider or customer links; 25% of these ASes send the majority of BitTorrent traffic to provider links. Unlike with tier 2, provider traffic is much larger than customer traffic for tier 3, indicating that these ISPs on average are paying for rather than profiting from transit charges due to BitTorrent traffic.

Last, we analyze traffic distributions for tier-4 networks (see Fig. 12c). As expected, only a small fraction of these ASes have any customer traffic, so BitTorrent does not generate substantial revenue here. We also see that most tier-4 networks are connected either over peering or provider links. For half of tier-4 networks, the majority of BitTorrent traffic is handled by provider links, suggesting that BitTorrent is incurring significant transit charges for these networks.

6.3 Traffic Ratios

While the previous graphs indicate the portion of traffic along links for different business relationships, they do not allow straightforward calculations of the relative amounts of customer and provider traffic for each AS (and thus which direction of charging traffic dominates). Figure 13 plots CDFs of these ratios for each tier, except for tier 1 where the denominator would be zero. Values greater than one indicate cases where an AS receives more customer traffic than it sends to providers (presumably generating a net revenue). Overall, this is always the case for tier-2 ASes. For lower tiers we find that a significant fraction of them do not have any customer traffic, resulting in a ratio of 0. The ratio is less than one most of the time, indicating that BitTorrent traffic is costing these networks – only 17% of tier-3 and 15% of tier-4 ASes

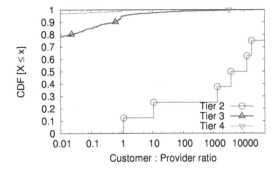

Figure 13: For each AS in Tier T, the ratio between traffic on customer and provider AS links. More customer traffic than provider traffic (a ratio > 1) indicates a net revenue (if provider and customer traffic have the same cost). This shows the proportion of ASes in each tier that have a net revenue.

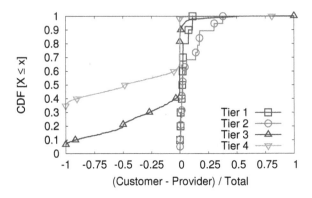

Figure 14: Average revenue per byte of BitTorrent traffic (i.e., the difference between customer traffic and provider traffic, divided by total traffic) for each AS, grouped by tier.

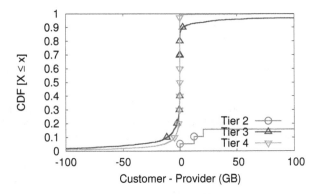

Figure 15: For each AS in Tier T, the difference between customer traffic and provider traffic. In contrast to the data in Figures 13 and 14, this perspective allows us to compare the scale of the revenue or expenses of ASes by tier.

with customer traffic have a ratio > 1. While this may seem to indicate that BitTorrent is harmful to lower-tier ASes, it is difficult to determine the relative cost of BitTorrent without understanding the volumes of non-BitTorrent traffic over the same links (an issue we address in Sec. 6.4).

The ratios above indicate when there is a net imbalance in charged traffic volumes but do not show their relative size compared to all BitTorrent traffic, including those flowing over no-cost links. We now address this by computing the average revenue (or cost) per byte for each AS (Fig. 14). This is defined as the balance of charging traffic (customer bytes minus provider bytes) divided by the total number of bytes flowing through the AS. When peering traffic accounts for a large proportion of AS traffic, the revenue of each byte of P2P traffic will be close to zero. However, when most AS traffic is from providers (or customers), it will have a more significant cost (or revenue) per byte for flows that travel through its network.

In Figure 14, all tier-1 ASes have a net revenue (values > 0) because, by definition, they do not have any provider links. In addition, all tier-2 ASes have a net revenue as well, reflecting the fact that the majority of their traffic is on peering, customer, or sibling links. The ASes in tiers 3 and 4 have incrementally larger average costs per byte overall, corresponding to the larger proportions of traffic traversing their provider links.

While most tier-4 ASes do not generate revenue from BitTorrent traffic, there are a few exceptions. This is explained by the fact that the tier classification algorithm is not strictly hierarchical, so a tier-4 AS can be a provider for another AS. In this case, large portions of traffic can traverse this revenue-generating link, resulting in a net profit per byte in the graph.

Finally, we attempt to quantify the relative scales of these costs and/or revenues by calculating a basic "balance sheet" for each AS in our study. In Fig. 15, we report customer minus provider traffic for each AS in tiers 2–4. Since tier-1 ASes do not have any providers, they have large net balances, several orders of magnitude larger than the net balances shown here. The balances of tier-2 networks range from 12 GB to 13 TB. By comparison, we see that the net differences from tier-3 and tier-4 ISPs are relatively small. Although tier-4 ASes had the largest average cost per byte of P2P traffic, we see that they have relatively small net balances of traffic compared to ASes in all other tiers.

6.4 Impact on 95th-Percentile Transit Costs

We now examine the cost of BitTorrent traffic under a 95th-percentile charging model, with a goal of understanding the impact of temporal trends in BitTorrent traffic on ISPs' costs. This is important because BitTorrent and network traffic are not uniform across time (e.g. due to diurnal trends), and costs computed under a 95th-percentile charging model are essentially set by usage in the busiest hours for network usage, typically in the evening. Intuitively, if BitTorrent traffic is more prevalent during these peak hours than off-peak hours, then we say it is *relatively more expensive* for the ISP, in comparison to the rest of the traffic. Appendix A provides a detailed description of the 95th-percentile charging model and the Shapley analysis that we use to determine the relative cost of BitTorrent traffic.

For this analysis, we obtain traces of total link volume between a major transit ISP "T" and several of its providers (A, B) and customers (C-G).[2] In addition, we compute for each pair of ASes the time series of BitTorrent traffic seen in our dataset. For both data sets, we use 5-minute intervals, a resolution commonly used in determining 95th-percentile charges. Both sets of traces are from the same 1-week period, January 6-14, 2011, and thereby

---

[2] The identities of these ISPs are protected by nondisclosure agreements.

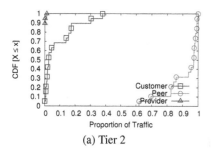
(a) Tier 2

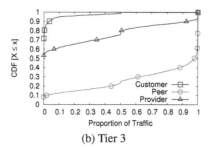
(b) Tier 3

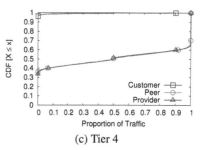
(c) Tier 4

Figure 12: For each AS located in Tier T, the CDF of the proportion of its traffic traversing provider, customer, or peering/sibling links.

are comparable and capture both weekday and weekend traffic patterns.

Following the typical use of 95th-percentile billing, we focus on the link direction with the greater 95th-percentile traffic volume. For ISP T's providers, this is the inbound direction (toward ISP T); for its customers, the dominant direction is outbound (from ISP T).

6.4.1 "Relative Cost" Metric and Scaling

For each type of traffic that we study – BitTorrent and "all the rest" – we compute that traffic's "relative cost". This is defined as the ratio between its Shapley value (how much it costs) and its overall fraction of traffic on the link. For example, if our BitTorrent trace accounts for 10% of all traffic seen over a link, but the Shapley value is 20% (e.g. if traffic occurs during peak hours), then BitTorrent traffic's "relative cost" is 2. Therefore, BitTorrent is contributing *more* to defining the 95th-percentile transit costs than the rest of the traffic. Using this metric, we can evaluate the *relative* contribution of any subset of network traffic over a link.

Though we have detailed BitTorrent traces for the networks we study in this section, it is important to note that there is no ground truth information to determine the relative volume of BitTorrent traffic compared to "all the rest" of traffic for the links that we study. To address this issue, we assume that our BitTorrent sample is representative of the larger population of all BitTorrent traffic on the network (following from our analysis in Sec. 3.2). This allows us to assess the relative cost of any BitTorrent traffic ratio by scaling our time-series of BitTorrent traffic to the corresponding fraction of overall link traffic.

Using the BitTorrent traffic ratio as a free variable, we scale each value in our time-series of BitTorrent traffic by a factor such that the sum of BitTorrent bandwidth matches a given percentage of the total aggregate link volume over the week. Then, we examine the impact of different fractions of BitTorrent traffic over a link on BitTorrent's role in setting the 95th-percentile costs.

6.4.2 Relative Impact of BitTorrent on 95th-Percentile Costs

We evaluate now the relative cost of BitTorrent traffic over several links between a large transit provider and several of its customers and providers.

First, we examine the trends in the relative cost of BitTorrent traffic as we vary the percentage of BitTorrent traffic ($X\%$) out of the total traffic on the link. To compute the relative cost for each X, we subtract the BitTorrent trace from the total trace to obtain the time-series of "all the rest" of the traffic and run the analysis described in Appendix A. A relative cost of 1 means that the Shapley value is the same as the fraction of traffic – BitTorrent traffic costs the same as other traffic, in terms of setting the ISP's

ISP	Cost	X-Corr	C.V.
Customer D	1.03	-0.4	109%
Provider A	1.15	-7.1	130%
Customer C	1.21	0.8	160%
Customer G	1.43	-0.2	186%
Provider B	1.50	3.2	188%
Customer E	1.52	1.6	158%
Customer F	1.83	7.4	325%

Table 6: For each link we study, we compute the cross-correlation offset ("X-Corr") that resulted in the best overlap between BitTorrent and total traffic, and the coefficient of variation ("C.V.") of the time series of BitTorrent traffic. We sort the links by increasing relative cost ("Cost", when BitTorrent is scaled to 10% of total traffic). Increased variation in the BitTorrent traffic curve is strongly correlated with increased relative cost of that traffic.

95th-percentile costs. Relative costs greater than 1 mean that BitTorrent is contributing *more* to setting the 95th-percentile costs than all the rest of the traffic crossing the link.

Figure 16 shows the results of this analysis for two providers and two customers of ISP T. Among these results, we find significant diversity in terms of the relative cost of BitTorrent, ranging from 0.95 (relatively less expensive) to over 1.5 (relatively more expensive). In general, BitTorrent tends to be relatively more expensive than the rest of traffic on the link. Note that as we increase the percent of BitTorrent traffic, the relative cost metric by definition approaches 1, which explains the downward trends in the figures.

To explain the diversity of the relative cost of BitTorrent traffic over different links, we characterize each of our BitTorrent traces by its variations over time, as well as how it aligns with the overall traffic on the link. To represent how much BitTorrent traffic varies over time for each link, we use the coefficient of variation (i.e., the normalized dispersion of values in a distribution). To capture the temporal alignment between BitTorrent traffic and total traffic, we conduct a cross-correlation analysis between normalized time-series of traffic data and report the time offset at which we found the peak overlap between BitTorrent and total traffic. Negative offsets occur if the peak in BitTorrent traffic appears *later* than the total traffic.

Table 6 shows the results of these analyses for all of ISP T's links that we study, sorted by increasing relative cost (when BitTorrent is scaled to 10% of total traffic). The relatively small values (e.g., ≤ 2) in the third column indicate that the peak traffic for BitTorrent indeed coincides with peak volumes for the rest of traffic for most

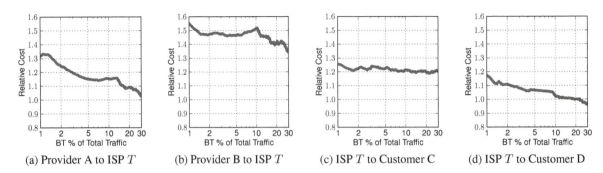

| (a) Provider A to ISP T | (b) Provider B to ISP T | (c) ISP T to Customer C | (d) ISP T to Customer D |

Figure 16: Trends in the relative cost of BitTorrent traffic for links between ISP T and several of its providers and customers, as we scale BitTorrent traffic to various percentages of the total link traffic.

of these links. Moreover, we find that larger variations in BitTorrent traffic (i.e., burstiness captured by the coefficient of variation metric) correlate strongly with higher relative cost. Customer E is the only exception to this trend, which can be explained by the fact that Customer E's BitTorrent traffic is more closely aligned with total traffic (according to the cross correlation metric) than either Provider B or Customer F.

6.5 Summary

In summary, this section showed that capturing the impact of BitTorrent on network costs requires a global view of where traffic flows as well as an understanding of the business relationships and charging billing models used. We found that large portions of BitTorrent traffic flow over settlement-free links, and the portion of interdomain traffic generating charges varies significantly among ISPs. This analysis also shows that the recent trend toward more diurnal usage patterns leads to traffic that is closely aligned with peak usage for other Internet traffic, which has a significant impact on the common 95th-percentile charging model. While the relative cost of BitTorrent traffic is variable, we found it to be generally more expensive than other traffic for links we evaluated.

These results can inform ISPs' decisions about the impact and efficacy of specific traffic management policies. Our BitTorrent-focused analysis is an example of how applications can have varied impacts on ISP costs, based on when the traffic occurs.

7. CONCLUSION

In this paper, we demonstrated the importance of a comprehensive view when evaluating the network impact of a globally distributed system like BitTorrent. By incorporating application traces gathered from hundreds of thousands of IPs, we answered key questions regarding trends in BitTorrent's traffic volumes and user behavior, where BitTorrent traffic flows, and whether such traffic incurs net costs or produces revenue for ISPs.

This unique view allowed us to reveal several properties of the system previously hidden from studies based on limited perspectives. First, we used a longitudinal view of user behavior to show that the BitTorrent system continues to evolve, both in terms of when and where the application is being used. We then evaluated the impact of this behavior on where BitTorrent traffic flows geographically and topologically, an analysis that requires extensive traceroutes between P2P users. We found that despite its global reach, BitTorrent is able to remain local for large portions of its traffic. Further, our results show that most traffic generated by BitTorrent users stays at or below tier 3. Some of our results call

into question the ability of in-network monitoring approaches to capture salient features of widely distributed systems, particularly when deployed in higher Internet tiers.

Last, we evaluated the economic impact of BitTorrent traffic on ISPs' variable costs. Using inferred business relationships between ISPs, we showed that most BitTorrent traffic flows over cost-free paths and that it generates substantial revenue potential for many higher tier ISPs. We also highlighted the importance of the temporal pattern behind the generated traffic under the common 95th-percentile charging model. By combining traces from operational interdomain links with our corresponding BitTorrent traces, we determined that the relative cost of BitTorrent is variable and tended to be higher than other traffic for several ISPs.

In summary, we emphasize that no single aspect of this study alone – application traces, topology information and in-network traces – were sufficient to develop a complete picture of a widely distributed system such as BitTorrent. Only in combination did these perspectives allow us to view the system as a whole and its impact on the network.

8. ACKNOWLEDGEMENTS

We would like to thank our shepherd, Augustin Chaintreau, and the anonymous reviewers for their detailed and helpful feedback. We are always grateful to Paul Gardner for his assistance with Vuze and the users of our software for their invaluable data. This work was supported in part by NSF Awards CNS 0644062, CNS 0917233 and CNS 0855253.

9. REFERENCES

[1] V. Aggarwal, A. Feldmann, and C. Scheideler. Can ISPs and P2P users cooperate for improved performance? *SIGCOMM Comput. Commun. Rev.*, 37(3):29–40, 2007.

[2] R. Bindal, P. Cao, W. Chan, J. Medved, G. Suwala, T. Bates, and A. Zhang. Improving traffic locality in BitTorrent via biased neighbor selection. In *Proc. of ICDCS*, 2006.

[3] K. Chen, D. Choffnes, R. Potharaju, Y. Chen, F. Bustamante, and Y. Zhao. Where the sidewalk ends: Extending the Internet AS graph using traceroutes from P2P users. In *Proc. of ACM CoNEXT*, 2009.

[4] D. Choffnes, F. Bustamante, and Z. Ge. Using the crowd to monitor the cloud: Network event detection from edge systems. In *Proc. of ACM SIGCOMM*, 2010.

[5] D. R. Choffnes and F. E. Bustamante. Taming the torrent: A practical approach to reducing cross-ISP traffic in peer-to-peer systems. In *Proc. of ACM SIGCOMM*, 2008.

[6] R. Cuevas, N. Laoutaris, X. Yang, G. Siganos, and P. Rodriguez. Deep diving into BitTorrent locality. In *Proc. of IEEE INFOCOM*, 2011.

[7] A. Dhamdhere and C. Dovrolis. Ten years in the evolution of the Internet ecosystem. In *Proc. of IMC*, 2008.

[8] A. Dhamdhere and C. Dovrolis. The Internet is Flat: Modeling the transition from a transit hierarchy to a peering mesh. In *Proc. of ACM CoNEXT*, 2010.

[9] X. Dimitropoulos, P. Hurley, A. Kind, and M. P. Stoecklin. On the 95-percentile billing method. In *Proc. of PAM*, 2009.

[10] EdgeScope – sharing the view from a distributed Internet telescope. http://www.aqualab.cs.northwestern.edu/projects/EdgeScope.html.

[11] L. Guo, S. Chen, Z. Xiao, E. Tan, X. Ding, and X. Zhang. Measurements, analysis, and modeling of BitTorrent-like systems. In *Proc. of IMC*, 2005.

[12] M. Izal, G. Urvoy-Keller, E. Biersack, P. Felber, A. Hamra, and L. Garces-Erice. Dissecting BitTorrent: Five months in a torrent's lifetime. In *Proc. of PAM*, 2004.

[13] T. Karagiannis, P. Rodriguez, and K. Papagiannaki. Should Internet service providers fear peer-assisted content distribution? In *Proc. of IMC*, 2005.

[14] H. Kim, k. Claffy, M. Fomenkov, D. Barman, M. Faloutsos, and K. Lee. Internet traffic classification demystified: myths, caveats, and the best practices. In *Proc. of ACM CoNEXT*, 2008.

[15] C. Labovitz, S. Iekel-Johnson, J. Oberheide, and F. Jahanian. Internet inter-domain traffic. In *Proc. of ACM SIGCOMM*, New Delhi, India, August 2010.

[16] S. Le Blond, A. Legout, and W. Dabbous. Pushing BitTorrent Locality to the Limit. http://hal.inria.fr/inria-00343822/PDF/bt_locality.pdf.

[17] G. Maier, A. Feldmann, V. Paxson, and M. Allman. On dominant characteristics of residential broadband Internet traffic. In *Proc. of IMC*, 2009.

[18] M. Piatek, H. V. Madhyastha, J. P. John, A. Krishnamurthy, and T. Anderson. Pitfalls for ISP-friendly P2P design. In *Proc. of HotNets*, 2009.

[19] J. A. Pouwelse, P. Garbacki, D. H. J. Epema, and H. J. Sips. The BitTorrent P2P file-sharing system: Measurements and analysis. In *Proc. of IPTPS*, 2005.

[20] D. Qiu and R. Srikant. Modeling and performance analysis of BitTorrent-like peer-to-peer networks. In *Proc. of ACM SIGCOMM*, 2004.

[21] H. Schulze and K. Mochalski. ipoque: Internet study 2007, Nov. 2007. http://www.ipoque.com/media/internet_studies.

[22] H. Schulze and K. Mochalski. ipoque: Internet study 2008/2009, Nov. 2009. http://www.ipoque.com/media/internet_studies.

[23] R. Stanojevic, N. Laoutaris, and P. Rodriguez. On economic heavy hitters: Shapley value analysis of 95th-percentile pricing. In *Proc. of IMC*, 2010.

[24] Team Cymru. The Team Cymru IP to ASN lookup page. http://www.cymru.com/BGP/asnlookup.html.

[25] R. D. Torres, M. Y. Hajjat, S. G. Rao, M. Mellia, and M. M. Munafo. Inferring undesirable behavior from P2P traffic analysis. In *Proc. of ACM SIGMETRICS*, 2009.

[26] University of Oregon Route Views project. http://www.routeviews.org/.

[27] uTorrent still on top, BitComet's market share plummets. http://torrentfreak.com/utorrent-still-on-top-bitcomets-market-share-plummets-090814/.

[28] Vuze, Inc. Vuze. http://www.vuze.com.

[29] J. Xia and L. Gao. On the evaluation of AS relationship inferences. In *In Proc. of IEEE GLOBECOM*, 2004.

[30] H. Xie, R. Yang, A. Krishnamurthy, Y. Liu, and A. Silberschatz. P4P: Provider portal for P2P applications. In *Proc. of ACM SIGCOMM*, 2008.

[31] C. Zhang, P. Dhungel, D. Wu, and K. W. Ross. Unraveling the BitTorrent ecosystem. *IEEE Transaction on Parallel and Distributed Systems*, July 2011. To appear.

APPENDIX

A. 95TH-PERCENTILE AND SHAPLEY

95th-percentile billing is one of the most common models used by providers to charge for traffic over interdomain links [9]. Under this billing model, costs are determined by near-peak usage, calculated by the 95th-percentile value at fixed intervals (e.g. 5 minute bins) over each billing cycle (usually 1 month). As a result, the effective cost of each byte of traffic varies depending on the particular time of day – bytes sent during times of high usage are more expensive than off-peak bytes.

Following the approach in [23], we use the game-theoretic concept of Shapley value to compute the *average marginal cost contribution* of individual classes of traffic under the 95th-percentile billing model.[3] This is obtained by averaging the marginal increase in 95th-percentile cost over all possible "arrival orders" for the classes of traffic being examined.

In our study of "BT" and "Other" traffic, we have two arrival orders: [BT, Other] and [Other, BT]. Given a function v_{95th} that returns the 95th-percentile value of a series of bandwidth measurements, we compute the Shapley value of BitTorrent traffic by averaging the marginal contributions:

$$m_1 = v_{95th}(BT)$$
$$m_2 = v_{95th}(Other + BT) - v_{95th}(Other)$$
$$SV_{BT} = (m_1 + m_2)/2$$

Since the Shapley value is *efficient* (i.e. the sum of the average marginal costs equals the total cost), we can compute the proportion of the total cost attributable to BitTorrent traffic:

$$p_{BT} = SV_{BT}/(SV_{BT} + SV_{Other})$$

Finally, we compare the proportion of total cost attributable to BitTorrent traffic relative to the overall fraction of BitTorrent traffic f_{BT} carried over the network:

$$\text{Relative Cost}_{BT} = p_{BT}/f_{BT}$$

When the relative cost of BitTorrent is > 1, that means that increases in BitTorrent traffic are temporally aligned with increases in the total traffic (typically during waking hours) and BitTorrent traffic is *comparatively more expensive* than other traffic. Likewise, a relative cost < 1 means that BitTorrent traffic is *comparatively less expensive* than other traffic, and tends to occur during off-peak (e.g,. overnight) periods.

---

[3]This analysis is general to any such cost model.

Predicting and Tracking Internet Path Changes

Ítalo Cunha[††‡]   Renata Teixeira[*‡]   Darryl Veitch[♮]   Christophe Diot[†]
[†]Technicolor   [‡]UPMC Sorbonne Universités   [*]CNRS
[♮]Dept. of Electrical and Electronic Eng., University of Melbourne
{italo.cunha, christophe.diot}@technicolor.com   renata.teixeira@lip6.fr   dveitch@unimelb.edu.au

ABSTRACT

This paper investigates to what extent it is possible to use trace-route-style probing for accurately tracking Internet path changes. When the number of paths is large, the usual traceroute based approach misses many path changes because it probes all paths equally. Based on empirical observations, we argue that monitors can optimize probing according to the likelihood of path changes. We design a simple predictor of path changes using a nearest-neighbor model. Although predicting path changes is not very accurate, we show that it can be used to improve probe targeting. Our path tracking method, called DTRACK, detects up to two times more path changes than traditional probing, with lower detection delay, as well as providing complete load-balancer information.

Categories and Subject Descriptors

C.2.3 [**Computer Systems Organization**]: Computer Communication Networks—*Network Operations—Network Monitoring*; C.4 [**Computer Systems Organization**]: Performance of Systems—*Measurement Techniques*

General Terms

Design, Experimentation, Measurement

Keywords

Topology Mapping, Tracking, Prediction, Path Changes

1. INTRODUCTION

Systems that detect Internet faults [9, 15] or prefix hijacks [34] require frequent measurements of Internet paths, often taken with traceroute. Topology mapping techniques periodically issue traceroutes and then combine observed links into a topology [14, 17, 25]. Content distribution networks continuously monitor paths and their properties to select the "best" content server for user requests [10]. Similarly, overlay networks monitor IP paths to select the best overlay routing [1]. In all these examples, a source host issues traceroutes to a large number of destinations with the hope of tracking paths as they change.

[♮]The work was done while Darryl Veitch was visiting Technicolor.

The classical approach of probing all paths equally, however, has practical limits. First, sources have a limited probing capacity (constrained by source link capacity and CPU utilization), which prevents them from issuing traceroutes frequently enough to observe changes on all paths. Second, Internet paths are often stable [8, 12, 24], so probing all paths at the same frequency wastes probes on paths that are not changing while missing changes in other paths. Finally, many paths today traverse routers that perform load balancing [2]. Load balancing creates multiple simultaneous paths from a source to a given destination. Ignoring load balancing leads to traceroute errors and misinterpretation of path changes [8]. Accurately discovering all paths under load balancing, however, requires even more probes [31].

This paper shows that a monitor can optimize probing to track path changes more efficiently than classical probing given the same probing capacity. We develop DTRACK, a system that separates the tracking of path changes into two tasks: *path change detection* and *path remapping*. DTRACK only remaps (measures again the hops of) a path once a change is detected. Path remapping uses Paris traceroute's multipath detection algorithm (MDA) [31], because it accurately discovers all paths under load balancing. The key novelty of this paper is to design a probing strategy that predicts the paths that are more likely to change and adapts the probing frequency accordingly. We make two main contributions:

Investigate the predictability of path changes. We use traceroute measurements from 70 PlanetLab nodes to train models of path changes. We use RuleFit [13], a supervised machine learning technique, to identify the features that help predict path changes and to act as a benchmark (Sec. 3). RuleFit is too complex to be used online. Hence, we develop a model to predict path changes, called NN4, based on the K nearest-neighbor scheme, which can be implemented efficiently and is as accurate as RuleFit (Sec. 4). We find that prediction is difficult. Even though NN4 is not highly accurate, it is effective for tracking path changes, as it can predict paths that are more likely to change in the short term.

A probing strategy to track path changes. (Sec. 5) DTRACK adapts path sampling rates to minimize the number of missed changes based on NN4's predictions. For each path, it sends a single probe per sample in a temporally striped form of traceroute. We evaluate DTRACK with trace-driven simulations and show that, for the probing budget used by DIMES [25], DTRACK misses 73% fewer path changes than the state-of-the-art approach and detects 93% of the path changes in the traces.

DTRACK tracks path changes more accurately than previous techniques. A closer look at path changes should enable research on the fine-grained dynamics of Internet topology as well as ensure that failure detection systems, content distribution, and overlay networks have up-to-date information on network paths.

2. DEFINITIONS, DATA, AND METRICS

In this section we define key underlying concepts and present the dataset we use. We establish the low-level path prediction goals which underlie our approach to path tracking, and then present a spectrum of candidate path features to be exploited to that end.

2.1 Virtual paths and routes

Following Paxson [24], we use *virtual path* to refer to the connectivity between a fixed source (here a monitor) and a destination d. At any given time, a virtual path is realized by a route which we call the *current route*. Since routing changes occur, a virtual path can be thought of as a continuous time process $P(t)$ which jumps between different routes over time.

A *route* can be *simple*, consisting of a sequence of IP interfaces from the monitor toward d, or *branched*, when one or more *load balancing* routers are present, giving rise to multiple overlapping sequences (branched routes are called "multi-paths" in [31]). A route can be a sequence that terminates before reaching d. This can occur due to routing changes (e.g., transient loops), or the absence of a complete route to the destination. By *route length* we mean the length of its longest sequence, and we define the *edit distance* between two routes as the minimum number of interface insertions, deletions, and substitutions needed to make the IP interface sequences of each route identical. In the same way we can define *AS length* and *AS edit distance* for a general route.

Let a virtual path P be realized by route r at time t, i.e., $P(t) = r$. Suppose that the path will next jump to a new route at time t_d, and last jumped to the current route r at time t_b. Then the *age* of this instance of route r is $A(r) = t - t_b$, its *residual life* is $L(r) = t_d - t$, and its *duration* is $D(r) = A(r) + L(r) = t_d - t_b$. Typically, as we have just done, we will write $A(r)$ instead of $A(P(t))$, and so on, when the context makes the virtual path, time instant, and hence route instance, clear.

In practice we measure virtual paths only at discrete times, resulting effectively in a sampling of the process $P(t)$. A change can be detected whenever two consecutive path measurements differ, however the full details of the evolution of the virtual path between these samples is unknown, and many changes may be missed. Unless stated otherwise, by *(virtual) path change* we mean a change observed in this way. The change is deemed to have occurred at the time of the second measurement. Hence, the measured age of a route instance is always zero when it is first observed. This conservative approach underestimates route age with an error smaller than the inter-measurement period.

2.2 Dataset

For our purposes, an ideal dataset would be a complete record of the evolution of virtual paths, together with all sequences of IP interfaces for each constituent route. Real world traces are limited both in the frequency at which each virtual path can be sampled, and the accuracy and completeness of the routing information obtained at each sample. In particular, the identification of the multiple IP interface sequences for branched routes requires a lot of probes [31] and takes time, reducing the frequency at which we can measure virtual paths. For this identification we use Paris traceroute's Multipath Detection Algorithm (MDA) [31]. MDA provides strong statistical guarantees for complete route discovery in the presence of an unknown number of load balancers. It is therefore ideal for reliable change detection, but is conservative and can be expensive in probe use (see Sec. 5.4).

We address the above limitations by using traces collected with *FastMapping* [8]. FastMapping measures virtual paths with a modified version of Paris traceroute [2] that sends a single probe per hop. Whenever a new IP interface is seen, FastMapping remeasures the route using MDA. In this way, the frequency at which it searches for path changes is high, but when a change is detected, the new route is mapped out thoroughly.

We use a publicly-available dataset collected from 70 PlanetLab hosts during 5 weeks starting September 1st, 2010 [8]. Each monitor selects 1,000 destinations at random from a list of 34,820 randomly chosen reachable destinations. Each virtual path is measured every 4.4 minutes on average. We complement the dataset with IP-to-AS maps built from Team Cymru[1] and UCLA's IRL [23]. Although almost all monitors are connected to academic networks, the destinations are not. As such, this dataset traverses 7,842 ASes and covers 97% of large ASes [23].

We lack ground truth about path changes and the FastMapping dataset may miss changes; however, all changes the dataset captures are real. Fig. 1 shows the distribution of all route durations in the dataset. It is similar to Paxson's findings that most routes are short-lived: 60% of routes have durations under one hour.

2.3 Prediction goals and error metrics

We study three kinds of prediction: (i) prediction $\hat{L}(r)$ of the residual lifetime $L(r)$ of a route $r = P(t)$ of some path observed at time t, (ii) prediction $\hat{N}_\delta(P)$ of the number of changes in the path occurring in the time interval $[t, t + \delta]$, and (iii) prediction, via an indicator function $\hat{I}_\delta(r)$, of whether the current route will change in the interval $[t, t + \delta]$ ($I_\delta(r) = 1$), or not ($I_\delta(r) = 0$).

In the case of residual lifetime, we measure the relative prediction error $E_L(r) = (\hat{L}(r) - L(r))/L(r)$. This takes values in $[-1, \infty)$, with $E_L(r) = 0$ corresponding to a perfect prediction. For $\hat{N}_\delta$, we measure the absolute error $E_{N_\delta}(P) = \hat{N}_\delta(P) - N_\delta(P)$ because the relative prediction error is undefined whenever $N_\delta(P) = 0$. For $\hat{I}_\delta$, we measure the error E_{I_δ}, the fraction of time $\hat{I}_\delta(r) \neq I_\delta(r)$. This takes values in $[0, 1]$, with $E_{I_\delta} = 0.5$ corresponding to a random predictor.

2.4 Virtual path features

A virtual path predictor needs to determine and exploit those features of the path and its history that carry the most information about change patterns.

Paxson characterized virtual path stability using the notions of route *persistence*, which is essentially route duration $D(r)$, and route *prevalence* [24], the proportion of time a given route is active. In the context of prediction, where only metrics derivable from past data are available, these two measures translate to the following two features of the route r which is current at time t: (i) the route age $A(r)$, and (ii) the (past) prevalence, the fraction of time r was active over the window $[t - \tau, t]$. We set the *timescale* τ to $\tau = \infty$ to indicate a window starting at the beginning of the dataset.

Route age and prevalence are important prediction features. A first idea of their utility is given in Figs. 2(a) and 2(b) respectively, where the median, 25th, and 75th percentiles of route residual lifetimes are given as a function of the respective features (these were computed based on periodic sampling of all virtual paths in the dataset with period five minutes). In Fig. 2(a) for example we observe that younger routes have shorter residual lifetimes than older routes, a possible basis for prediction. Similarly, Fig. 2(b) shows that when prevalence is measured over a timescale of $\tau = 1$ day, routes with lower prevalence are more likely to die young.

Although route age and prevalence are each useful for prediction, they are not sufficient, as shown by the high variability in the

---

[1] http://www.team-cymru.org/Services/ip-to-asn.html

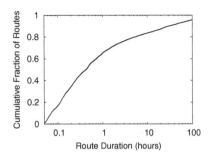

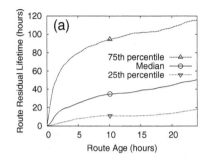

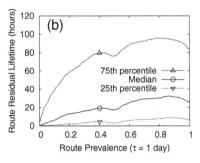

Figure 1: Distribution of all route durations in the dataset.

Figure 2: Relationship between virtual path features and residual lifetime: residual lifetime as a function of (a) route age and (b) route prevalence.

data (wide spread of the percentiles in Figs. 2(a) and 2(b)). To do better, additional features are needed. Our aim here is to define a spectrum of features broad enough to capture essentially all information computable from the dataset which may have predictive value. We do not know at this point which features are the important ones, nor how to combine them to make accurate predictions. This is a task we address in Sec. 3.

We do not attempt to exploit spatial dependencies in this paper for prediction, although they clearly exist. For example, changes in routing tables impact multiple paths at roughly the same time. The reason is that including spatial network information in Rule-Fit requires one predictive feature per link in the network, which is computationally prohibitive. However, we *can* exploit spatial dependencies to improve path tracking efficiency through the probing scheme, as we detail in Sec. 5.3.

Table 1 partitions all possible features into four categories: (i) Current route – characterize the current route and its state; (ii) Last change – capture any nearest neighbor interactions; (iii) Timescale-based – metrics measured over a given timescale; (iv) Event-based – metrics defined in 'event-time'. We use this scheme only as a framework to guide the selection of individual features. We aim to capture inherently different kinds of information and measures both of average behavior and variability. Only features that are computable based on the information in the dataset, together with available side-information (we use IP-to-AS maps), are allowed.

The last four features in the Timescale-based category allow us to identify virtual paths that are highly unstable and change repeatedly, as observed by previous work [22, 24, 30]. The features in the Event-based category may involve time but are not defined based on a preselected timescale. Instead, they try to capture patterns of changes in the past, like oscillation between two routes. For computational reasons we limit ourselves to looking up to the 5 most recent virtual path changes. In most of the cases this is already sufficient to reach the beginning of the dataset.

Feature properties. Paths in the FastMapping dataset are stable 96% of the time, but experience short-lived instability periods. Similar to Zhang et al. [32], we find that path changes are local and usually close to destinations: 86% of changes are inside an AS and 31% of path changes impact the destination's AS. We also find that 38% of path changes impact the path length, and 14% change the AS-level path. Our previous work [8] presents a more detailed characterization of path changes.

Tab. 1 shows the correlation between path features and residual lifetime, computed by sampling the dataset with a Poisson process with an average sampling period of 4 hours. For timescale-based

	CORRELATION WITH $L(r)$
CURRENT ROUTE	
Route Age	0.17
Length	-0.10
AS length	-0.10
Number of load balancers (i.e., hops with multiple next-hops)	-0.04
Indicator of whether the route reaches the destination	-0.03
LAST CHANGE	
Duration of the previous route	0.03
Length difference	-0.07
AS length difference	-0.02
Edit distance	0.05
AS edit distance	0.07
TIMESCALE-BASED (COMPUTED OVER $[t - \tau, t]$)	
Prevalence of the current route	0.20
Average route duration	-0.11
Standard deviation of route durations	-0.13
Number of previous occurrences of the current route	-0.11
Number of virtual path changes	-0.14
EVENT-BASED	
Times since the most recent occurrences of the current route	-0.08
Number of changes since the most recent occ. of the cur. route	-0.09

Table 1: Set of candidate features underlying prediction.

features we show correlation values for $\tau = 1$ day, and for event-based features we show the highest correlation. These low correlation values indicate that no single feature can predict changes; in the next section we study how to combine features for prediction.

3. PREDICTION FOUNDATIONS

Our path tracking approach is built on the ability to predict (albeit imperfectly) virtual path changes. We seek a predictor based on an intuitive and parsimonious model rather than a black box. However, virtual path changes are characterized by extreme variability and are influenced by many different factors, making model building, and even feature selection, problematic. We employ Rule-Fit [13], a state-of-the-art supervised machine learning technique, to bootstrap our modeling efforts. We use RuleFit for two main purposes. First, to comprehensively examine the spectrum of features of Tab. 1 to determine the most predictive. Second, to act as a benchmark representing in an approximate sense the best possible prediction when large (off-line) resources are available for training.

3.1 RuleFit Overview

RuleFit [13] trains predictors based on rule ensembles. We choose it over other alternatives (against which it compares favorably) for two reasons: (i) it ranks features by their importance for prediction, (ii) it outputs easy-to-interpret rules that allow an understanding of how features are combined. We give a brief overview of RuleFit, referring the reader to the original paper for details [13].

Rules combine one or more features into simple 'and' tests. Let $\boldsymbol{x}$ be the feature vector in Tab. 1 and s_f a specified subset of the possible values of feature f. Then, a rule takes the form

$$r(\boldsymbol{x}) = \prod_f I(x_f \in s_f), \qquad (1)$$

where $I(\cdot)$ is an indicator function. Rules take value one when all features have values inside their corresponding ranges, else zero.

RuleFit first generates a large number of rules using decision trees. It then trains a predictor of the form

$$\hat{\phi}(\boldsymbol{x}) = a_0 + \sum_k a_k r_k(\boldsymbol{x}), \qquad (2)$$

where the vector $\boldsymbol{a}$ is computed by solving an optimization problem that minimizes the *Huber loss* (a modified squared prediction error robust to outliers) with an L1 penalty term. RuleFit also employs other robustness mechanisms, for example it trains and tests on subsets of the training data internally to avoid overfitting.

Rule ensembles can exploit feature interdependence and capture complex relationships between features and prediction goals. Crucially, RuleFit allows rules and features to be ordered by their importance. *Rule importance* is the product of the rule's coefficient and a measure of how well it splits the training set:

$$I_k = |a_k| \sqrt{s_k(1 - s_k)}, $$

where s_k is the fraction of points in the training set where $r_k(\boldsymbol{x}) = 1$. *Feature importance* is computed as the sum of the normalized importance of the rules where the feature appears:

$$I_f = \sum_{k : f \in r_k} I_k / m_k, \qquad (3)$$

where m_k is the number of active features in r_k.

3.2 RuleFit training sets

RuleFit, like any supervised learning algorithm, requires a training set consisting of training points that associate features with the true values of metrics to be predicted. In our case, a training point, say for residual lifetime, associates a virtual path at some time t, represented by the features in Tab. 1, with the true residual lifetime $L(r)$ of the current route $r = P(t)$. Separate but similar training is performed for $N_\delta(P)$ and $I_\delta(r)$.

To limit the computational load of training, which is high for RuleFit, we control the total number of training points. For training point selection, first note that a given virtual path has a change history that is crucial to capture for good prediction of its future. We therefore build the required number of training points by extracting rich path change information from a subset of paths, rather than extracting (potentially very) partial information from each path. We retain path diversity through random path selection, and the use of multiple training sets (at least five for each parameter configuration we evaluate), obtained through using different random seeds.

For a given virtual path, we first include all explicit path change information by creating a training point for each entry in the dataset where a change was detected. However, such points all have (measured) current route age equal to zero (Sec. 2.1), whereas when running live predictions in general are needed at any arbitrary time point, with arbitrary route age. To capture the interdependence of features and prediction targets on route age we include additional synthetic points which do not appear in the dataset but which are functions of it. To achieve this we discretize route age into bins

and create a training point whenever the age of a route reaches a bin boundary. We choose bin boundaries as equally-spaced percentiles of the distribution of route durations in the training set, as this adapts naturally to distribution shape. Using five bins as example, we create training points whenever a route's age reaches zero seconds, 3.5 min., 12 min., 48 min., and 4 hours.

3.3 Test sets

Like training sets, test sets consist of test points which associate virtual path features with correct predictions. Unlike training sets, where the primary goal is to collect information important for prediction and where details may depend on the method to be trained, for test sets the imperative is to emulate the information available in the operational environment so that the predictor can be fairly tested, and should be independent of the prediction method.

The raw dataset has too many points for use as a test set. To reduce computational complexity, we build test sets by sampling each virtual path at time points chosen according to a Poisson process, using the same sampling rate for each path. This corresponds to examining the set of paths in a neutral way over time, which will naturally include a diversity of behavior. For example, our test sets include samples inside bursts of path changes, many samples from a very long-lived route, and rare events such as of an old route just before it changes.

We use an average per-path sampling period of four hours, resulting in at least two orders of magnitude more test points than training points. We test each predictor against eight test sets (from different seeds), for a total of 40 different training–test set combinations.

We ignore routes active at the beginning or the end of the dataset when creating training and test sets, as their duration, age, and residual lifetime are unknown. Similarly, we ignore all virtual path changes in the first τ hours of the dataset (if $\tau \neq \infty$) to avoid biasing timescale-dependent features.

3.4 RuleFit configuration

In this section we study the impact of key parameters on prediction accuracy, pick practical default values, and justify our use of RuleFit as a benchmark for predicting virtual path changes.

We study the impact of four parameters on prediction error: the number of rules generated during training, the number of age thresholds, the timescale τ, and the training set size. Each plot in Fig. 3.1 varies the value of one parameter while keeping the others fixed. We show results for E_{I_δ} with $\delta = 4$ hours because this is the prediction goal where the studied parameters have the greatest impact. Results for other values and other prediction goals are qualitatively similar. We compute the prediction error rate only for test points with route age less than 12 hours to focus on the differences between configurations. As we discuss later, prediction accuracy is identical for routes older than 12 hours regardless of configuration. We plot the minimum, median, and maximum error rate over 40 combinations of training and test sets for each configuration.

Fig. 3.1(a) shows that the benefit of increasing the number of generated rules is marginal beyond 200 for this data. Our interpretation is that at 200 or so rules, RuleFit has already been able to exploit all information relevant for prediction. Therefore, we train predictors with 200 rules unless stated otherwise.

Fig. 3.1(b) shows that prediction error decreases when we add additional points with age diversity into training sets as described in Sec. 3.2. However, as few as three age bins are enough to achieve accurate predictions, and improvement after six is minimal. Therefore, we train predictors with six age bins unless stated otherwise.

Fig. 3.1(c) shows that the timescale τ used to compute timescale-dependent features has little impact on prediction accuracy. A pos-

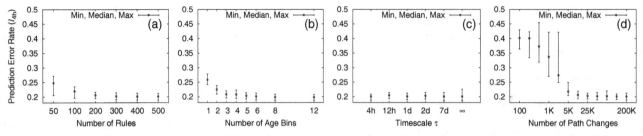

Figure 3: Impact of the (a) number of rules, (b) number of age bins, (c) timescale τ, and (d) training set size on RuleFit accuracy (test points with route age less than 12 hours).

PATH FEATURE	IMPORTANCE
Prevalence of the current route ($\tau = 1$ day)	1.0
Num. of virtual path changes ($\tau = 1$ day)	.624
Num. of previous occ. of the current route ($\tau = 1$ day)	.216
Route age	.116
Times since most recent occs. of the current route	$\leq .072$
Edit distance (last change)	.015
Duration of the previous route	.014
Standard deviation of route durations ($\tau = 1$ day)	.014
Length difference (last change)	.012
All other features	$\leq .010$

Table 2: Feature importance according to RuleFit.

sible explanation is that only the long term mean value of timescale-dependent features is predictive, and that RuleFit discovers this and only builds the means of these features into the predictor (or ignores them). Therefore, we train predictors with timescale-dependent features computed with $\tau = 1$ day.

Finally, Fig. 3.1(d) shows the impact of the number of virtual path changes in a training set. Training sets with too few changes fail to capture the virtual path change diversity present in test sets, resulting in predictors that do not generalize. Prediction accuracy increases quickly with training set size before flattening out. We use training sets with 200,000 virtual path changes (around 2.4% of those in the dataset) unless stated otherwise.

We justify our use of RuleFit as a benchmark for predicting changes, based on a given (incomplete) dataset, on: (i) we provide RuleFit with a rich feature set, (ii) RuleFit performs an extensive search of feature combinations to predict residual lifetimes, and (iii) our evaluation shows that changing RuleFit's parameters is unlikely to improve prediction accuracy significantly. This is an empirical approach to approximately measure the limits to prediction using a given dataset. Determining actual limits would only be possible given information-theoretic or statistical assumptions on the data, which is beyond the scope of this paper.

3.5 Feature selection

We compute feature importance with Eq. (3) and normalize using the most important feature. Tab. 2 shows the resulting ordered features, with normalized importance averaged over 50 predictors for each of residual lifetime, number of changes, and I_δ.

Route prevalence is the most important feature, helped by its correlation with route age. It is clear why route prevalence alone is insufficient. It cannot differentiate a young current route that also occurred repeatedly in the time window of width τ, from a middle-aged current route, as both have intermediate prevalence values.

The second, third, and fourth most important features are the number of virtual path changes, the number of occurrences of the current route, and route age. Predicted residual lifetimes increase as route age and prevalence increase, but decrease as the number of

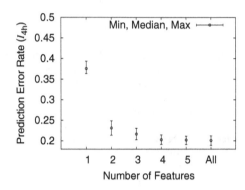

Figure 4: $E_{I_{4h}}$ for predictors trained with the most important features (test points with route age < 12 hours).

virtual path changes and occurrences of the current route increase. Results for the number of changes and I_δ are similar.

The fifth most important feature is the times (1st up to 5th) of the most recent occurrences of the current route. The low importance of this and the other event-based feature suggests that, contrary to our initial hopes, patterns of changes are too variable, or too rare, to be useful for prediction.

To evaluate more objectively the utility of RuleFit's feature importance measure, Fig. 4 shows $E_{I_{\delta=4h}}$ for predictors trained with training sets containing only the top p features, for $p = 1$ to 5. The improvements in performance with the addition of each new feature are consistent with the importance rankings from Tab. 2. Importantly, we see that the top four features generate predictors which are almost as accurate as those trained on all features.

4. NEAREST–NEIGHBOR PREDICTOR

We design and evaluate a simple predictor which is almost as accurate as RuleFit while overcoming its slow and computationally expensive training, its difficult integration into other systems, and the lack of insight and control arising from its black box nature.

4.1 NN4: Definition

We start from the observation that the top four features from Tab. 2 carry almost all of the usable information. Since virtual paths are so variable and the RuleFit models we obtained are so complex, simple analytic models are not serious candidates as a basis for prediction. We select a nearest-neighbor approach as it captures empirical dependences effectively and flexibly. Using only four features avoids the dimensionality problems inherent to such predictors [5] and allows for a very simple method, which we name NN4.

4.1.1 Method overview

Like all nearest-neighbor predictors, we compute predictions for a virtual path with feature vector x based on training points with feature vectors that are 'close' to x. The first challenge is to define a meaningful distance metric. This is difficult as feature domains differ (prevalence is a fraction, the number of changes and previous occurrences are integers, and route age is a real), have different semantics, and impact virtual path changes differently.

To avoid the pitfalls of some more or less arbitrary choice of distance metric, we instead partition the feature space into 4 dimensional 'cubes', or partitions, based on discretising each feature. Discretisation creates artifacts related to bin boundaries and resolution loss; however, the advantages are simplicity and the retention of a meaningful notion of distance for each feature individually. To avoid rigid fixed bin boundaries, for each feature we choose them as equally-spaced percentiles of their corresponding distribution, computed over all virtual path changes in the training set (as we did for route age in Sec. 3.2).

We denote the partition containing the feature vector of path P at time t as $\mathcal{P}(P, t)$ or simply $\mathcal{P}(P)$. We predict the residual lifetime of $r = P(t)$ and the number of changes in the next δ interval as the averages of the true values of these quantities over all training points in the partition $\mathcal{P}(P)$:

$$\hat{L}(r) = E[\{L(P_s(t_s)) \mid s \in \mathcal{P}(P)\}],$$
$$\hat{N}_\delta(P) = E[\{N_\delta(P_s) \mid s \in \mathcal{P}(P)\}],$$

where training point s corresponds to the path P_s at time t_s. Similarly, we predict $\hat{I}_\delta(r) = 1$ if more than half the training points in $\mathcal{P}(P)$ change within a time interval δ:

$$\hat{I}_\delta(r) = \lfloor E[\{I_\delta(P_s(t_s)) \mid s \in \mathcal{P}(P)\}] + 0.5 \rfloor.$$

The cost of a prediction in NN4 is $O(1)$, while in RuleFit it is $O(r)$, where r is the number of rules in the model. NN4 can be easily implemented, while RuleFit is available as a binary module that cannot be accessed directly and requires external libraries.

4.1.2 Training

To allow a meaningful comparison in our evaluation, each training for NN4 reuses the virtual paths of some RuleFit training set.

Consider a virtual path $P(t_s)$ chosen for training. As t_s progresses, the associated feature vector $x(t_s)$ moves between the different partitions. For example, for long-lived routes, $x(t_s)$ evolves toward the partition with 100% prevalence, zero changes, no previous occurrences, and the oldest age bin (before resetting to zero age etc. when/if the path changes). We need to sample this trajectory in a way that preserves all important information about the changes in the three prediction goals (L, N_δ, I_δ). Just as in RuleFit, we need to supplement the changes that occur explicitly in the dataset with additional training points occurring inbetween change points. Here we need to add additional samples to capture the diversity not only of age, but also the other three dimensions. In fact we can do much better than a discrete sampling leading to a set of training time points. From the dataset we can actually calculate when the path enters and exits the partitions it visits, its sojourn time in each, and the proportions of the sojourn time when a prediction goal takes a given value. For each partition (and prediction goal) we are then able to calculate the exact time-weighted average of the value over the partition. The result is a precomputed prediction for each partition traversed by the path that emulates a continuous-time sampling. Final per-partition predictions are formed by averaging over all paths traversing a partition.

4.1.3 Configuration

Apart from δ, the only parameter of our predictor is the number of bins b we use to partition each feature. We choose a shared

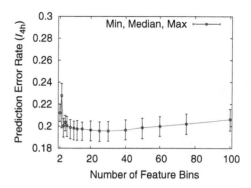

Figure 5: Impact of the number of feature bins on prediction accuracy (test points with age < 12 hours).

number of bins for parsimony, since when studying each feature separately (not shown) the optimal point was similar for each. The tradeoff here is clear. Too few bins and distinct change behaviors important for prediction are averaged away. Too many bins and partitions contain insufficient training information resulting in erratic predictions. We found in Sec. 3.4 that six bins were sufficient for route age. We now examine the three remaining features.

Fig. 5 shows E_{I_δ} with $\delta = 4$ hours as a function of b, restricting to test points with route age below 12 hours where the b dependence is strongest. We see that values in $[6, 20]$ achieve a good compromise. We use $b = 10$ in what follows.

4.2 NN4: Evaluation

We evaluate the prediction accuracy of NN4 and compare it to our operational benchmark, RuleFit, discovering in the process the limitations of this kind of prediction in general. We will find that only very rough prediction is feasible, but in the next section we show that it is nonetheless of great benefit to path tracking. For each method we generate new training and test sets in order to test the robustness of the configuration settings determined above.

4.2.1 Predicting residual lifetime

Fig. 6(Top) shows the distribution of $E_L(r)$, the relative error of $\hat{L}(r)$. An accurate predictor would have a sharp increase close to $E_L = 0$ (dotted line), but this is not what we see. Specifically, only 33.5% of the RuleFit and 31.1% of the nearest-neighbor predictions have $-0.5 \leq E_L \leq 1$ (see symbols on the curves). Predictions miss the true residual lifetimes by a significant amount around 70% of the time. As this is true not only of NN4 but also for RuleFit, we conjecture that accurate prediction of route residual lifetimes is too precise an objective with traceroute-based datasets. It does not follow, however, that $\hat{L}(r)$ is not a useful quantity to estimate. We can still estimate its order of magnitude well in most cases, and this is enough to bring important benefits to path tracking, as we show later. The error of NN4 is considerable larger than that of the benchmark but it is of the same order of magnitude.

4.2.2 Predicting number of changes

Fig. 6(Bottom) shows the distribution of E_{N_δ}, the error of $\hat{N}_\delta$, for NN4 for all test points with route age less than 12 hours. The errors for RuleFit are similar. Errors for test points in routes older than 12 hours are significantly smaller (not shown) because a predictor can perform well simply by outputting "no change" ($\hat{N}_\delta = 0$). We focus here on the difficult case of $A < 12$h.

Unlike residual lifetimes, the sharp increase near zero means most predictions are accurate. For example, 90.2% of test points have $-2 < E_{N_{4h}} < 2$, and accuracy increases for smaller val-

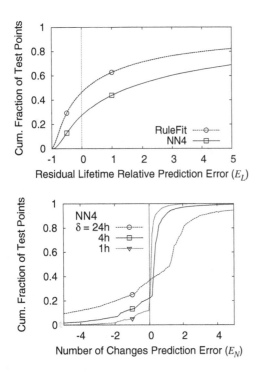

Figure 6: Distribution of prediction error. Top: L; Bottom: N_δ based on NN4 (for age $< 12h$).

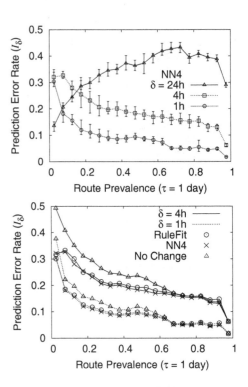

Figure 7: E_{I_δ} as a function of route prevalence for various values of δ. Top: NN4; Bottom: RuleFit comparison.

ues of δ. However, predicting the number of changes over long intervals such as 24 hours cannot be done accurately. Note that simply guessing that $N_\delta = 0$ also works well for very small δ. Although N_δ is a less ambitious target than L, it remains difficult to estimate from traceroute-type data. Again, however, prediction is sufficiently good to bring important tracking benefits.

4.2.3 Predicting a change in next δ interval

We now study whether the current route of a given path will change within the next time interval of width δ. We expect I_δ to be easier to predict than L or N_δ.

Fig. 7(Top) shows NN4's prediction error as a function of route prevalence for δ between 1 hour and 1 day (results for RuleFit are very similar and are omitted for clarity). We group route prevalence into fixed-width bins and compute the error from all test points falling within each bin (these bins are distinct from the constant-probability bins underlying NN4's partitions). For each bin, we show the minimum, median, and maximum error among the 40 training and test set combinations. Such a breakdown is very useful as it allows us to resolve where prediction is more successful, or more challenging. For example, since routes with prevalence 1 are very common, a simple global average over all prevalence values would drown out the results from routes with prevalence below 1.

First consider the results for $\delta = 1h$ and 4h. The main observation is that error drops as prevalence increases. This is because routes with high prevalence are unlikely to change, and a prediction of "no change" ($\hat{I}_\delta(r) = 0$), which the predictors output increasingly often, becomes increasingly valid as prevalence increases. We also see that, for all prevalence values, error is lower for smaller δ. This makes intuitive sense since prediction further into the future is in general more difficult. More precisely, the probability that a route will change in a time interval δ decreases as δ decreases, and predictors exploit this by predicting "no change" more often.

The situation is more complex when $\delta = 24h$, with errors beginning low and increasing substantially before finally peaking and then decreasing at very high prevalence. This happens because for larger values of δ, routes with low prevalence have a high probability of changing. Predictors exploit this and output $I_{24h}(r) = 1$ more often (in fact more than 80% of the time for paths with prevalence under 0.2). Prediction error is highest at intermediate prevalence values, as these routes have a probability close to 50% of changing in the next 24 hours. Finally, prediction error decreases for routes with high prevalence: as routes become stable the same mechanism noted above for smaller δ kicks in.

We now provide a comparison against RuleFit, focusing on small to medium δ. Fig. 7(Bottom) shows that NN4 and RuleFit have equivalent prediction accuracy across all values of prevalence. In fact NN4 is marginally (up to 2%) better here, where we used the default RuleFit configuration. Their performance is close to identical when using the more generous RuleFit configuration (see Sec. 3) with 500 rules and 12 age bins.

The plot also shows results for a simple baseline predictor that always predicts $\hat{I}_\delta(r) = 0$ (no change). Our predictor is better for routes with prevalence smaller than 0.7 which are more likely to change than not, but for high-prevalence routes all predictors predict "no change" and are equivalent. For routes with prevalence below 0.7, NN4 reduces the baseline predictor's $E_{I_{4h}}$ from 0.296 to 0.231 (22%), and $E_{I_{1h}}$ from 0.163 to 0.131 (20%).

Summary. Prediction is easiest when δ is small and prevalence is high. This is a promising result as most Internet routes are long-lived and have high prevalence; moreover, applications like topology mapping need to predict changes within short time intervals. NN4 predicts I_δ reasonably well, and errors ultimately fall to just a few percent as route prevalence increases and as δ decreases. We have tested the sensitivity to training and test sets, monitor choice, and overall probing rate, and found it to be very low.

5. TRACKING VIRTUAL PATH CHANGES

We now apply our findings to the problem of the efficient and accurate tracking of a set of virtual paths over time. We describe and evaluate our tracking technique, DTRACK.

5.1 DTRACK overview

Path tracking faces two core tasks: path change detection (how best to schedule probes to hunt for changes), and path remapping (what to do when they are found). For the latter, inspired by Fast-Mapping [8], DTRACK uses Paris traceroute's MDA to accurately measure the current route of monitored paths both at start up and after any detection of change. This is vital, since confusing path changes with load balancing effects makes 'tracking' meaningless.

For change detection, DTRACK is novel at two levels.

Across paths: paths are given dedicated sampling rates guided by NN4 to focus effort where changes are more likely to occur. Without this, probes are wasted on paths where nothing is happening.

Within paths: a path 'sample' is a single probe rather than a full traceroute, whose target interface is carefully chosen to combine the benefits of Paris Traceroute over time with efficiencies arising from exploiting links shared between paths. This allows changes to be spotted more quickly.

DTRACK monitors operate independently and use only locally available information. Each monitor takes three inputs: a predictor of virtual path changes, a set $\mathcal{D}$ of virtual paths to monitor, and a probing budget; and consists of three main routines: sampling rate allocation, change tracking, and change remapping. When a change is detected in a path through sampling, that path is remapped, and sampling rates for all paths are recomputed. A probing budget is commonly used to control the average resource use [14, 25].

5.2 Path sampling rate allocation

For each path p in $\mathcal{D}$, DTRACK uses NN4 to determine the rate λ_p at which to sample it. Sampling rates are updated whenever there is a change in the predictions, i.e., whenever any virtual path's feature vector changes its NN4 partition. This can happen as a result of a change detection or simply route aging.

We constrain sampling rates to the range $\lambda_{\min} \le \lambda_p \le \lambda_{\max}$. Setting $\lambda_{\min} > 0$ guarantees that all paths are sampled regularly, which safeguards against poor predictions on very long lived paths. An upper rate limit is needed to avoid probes appearing as an attack ($\lambda_{\max}$ implements the "politeness" of the tracking method [18]).

Based on the monitor's probe budget of B probes per second, a sampling budget of B_s samples per second for change detection alone can be derived (Sec. 5.4). To be feasible, the rate limits must obey $\lambda_{\min} \le B_s/|\mathcal{D}| \le \lambda_{\max}$, where $|\mathcal{D}|$ is the number of paths.

We now describe three allocation methods for the sampling rates λ_p. The first two are based on residual life and the third minimizes the number of missed changes.

Residual lifetime allocation. Since $1/L$ is precisely the rate that would place a sample right at the next change, allocating sampling rates proportional to $1/\hat{L}$ is a natural choice. We will see that despite the poor accuracy of $\hat{L}$ found before, this is far better than the traditional uniform allocation. To approximate this we define rates to take values in

$$\lambda_p \in \{\lambda_{\max}, a/\hat{L}(p), \lambda_{\min}\} \tag{4}$$

and require that $\lambda_p \ge \lambda_q$ if $L(p) < L(q)$ and $\lambda_{\min} \le \lambda_p \le \lambda_{\max}$ for all p, where a is a renormalisation constant which respects $\sum_p \lambda_p = B_s$ while minimizing the number of paths with rates clipped at $\lambda_{\min}$ or $\lambda_{\max}$.

We define two variants depending on the definition of $\hat{L}(p)$:

RL: $\hat{L}(p)$ is estimated by NN4,

RL-AGE: $\hat{L}(p)$ is predicted as the average residual lifetime of all route instances in the dataset with duration larger than $A(r)$, i.e.,

$$\hat{L}'(r) = \mathrm{E}[\{D(s) \mid s \in \mathcal{R} \text{ and } D(s) > A(r)\}] - A(r),$$

where $\mathcal{R}$ is the set of all route instances in the dataset.

Finally, for comparison we add an oracular method which knows the true $L(p)$ and is not subject to rate limits:

RL-ORACLE: $\lambda_p = a'/L(p)$ where $a' = B_s \sum_q 1/L(q)$.

Minimizing missed changes (MINMISS, used in DTRACK). We use a Poisson process as a simple model for when changes occur. With this assumption we are able to select rates that minimize the expected number of missed changes over the prediction horizon δ. This combines prediction of N_δ with a notion of sampling more where the pay off is higher. The rate $\mu_c(p)$ of the Poisson change process is estimated as $\mu_c(p) = \hat{N}_\delta(p)/\delta$.

We idealize samples as occurring periodically with separation $1/\lambda_p$. By the properties of a Poisson process, the changes falling within successive gaps between samples are i.i.d. Poisson random variables with parameter $\mu = \mu_c(p)/\lambda_p = \hat{N}_\delta/(\delta\lambda_p)$. Let C be the number of changes in a gap and M the number of these missed by the sample at the gap's end. It is easy to see that $M = \max(0, C-1)$, since a sample can see at most one change (here we assume that there is at most one instance of any route in the gap). The expected number of missed changes in a gap is then

$$
\begin{aligned}
\mathrm{E}[M(\mu)] &= \sum_{m=0}^{\infty} m \Pr(M=m) = \sum_{m=1}^{\infty} m \Pr(C = m+1) \\
&= e^{-\mu} \sum_{m=1}^{\infty} \frac{m\mu^{m+1}}{(m+1)!} = \mu - 1 + e^{-\mu} .
\end{aligned}
\tag{5}
$$

Summing over the $\delta\lambda_p$ gaps, we compute the sampling rates as the solution of the following optimization problem:

$$\min_{\{\lambda_p\}} : \sum_p \delta\lambda_p(\mu - 1 + e^{-\mu}) = \sum_p \hat{N}_\delta + \delta\lambda_p(e^{-\hat{N}_\delta/(\delta\lambda_p)} - 1)$$

$$\text{such that } \sum_p \lambda_p = B_s, \ \lambda_{\min} \le \lambda_p \le \lambda_{\max}, \forall p.$$

We also evaluated I_δ as the basis of rate allocation, but as it is inferior to MINMISS, we omit it for space reasons.

Implementation. Path sampling in DTRACK is controlled to be 'noisily periodic'. As pointed out in [4], strictly periodic sampling carries the danger of phase locking with periodic network events. Aided by the natural randomness of round-trip-times, our implementation ensures that sampling has the noise in inter-sample times recommended to avoid such problems [3].

DTRACK maintains a FIFO event queue which emits a sample every $1/B_s$ seconds on average. Path p maintains a timer $T(p)$. When $T(p) = 0$ the next sample request is appended to the queue and the timer reset to $T(p) = 1/\lambda_p$. Whenever DTRACK updates sampling rates, the timers are rescaled as $T_{\text{new}}(p) = T_{\text{old}}(p)\lambda_{\text{old},p}/\lambda_{\text{new},p}$. Path timers are staggered at initialization by setting $T(p_i) = i/B_s$, where i indexes virtual paths.

5.3 In-path sampling strategies

By a *sample* of a path we mean a measurement, using one or more probes, of its current route. At one extreme a sample could correspond to a detailed route mapping using MDA; however, when checking for route changes rather than mapping from scratch, this is too expensive. We now investigate a number of alternatives that are less rigorous (a change may be missed) but cheaper, for example sending just a single probe. In each case however the sample is load-balancing aware, that is we make use of the flow-id to interface mapping, established by the last full MDA, to target interfaces to test in an informed and strategic way. Thus, although a single sample takes only a partial look at a path and may miss a change, it will not flag a change where none exists, and can still cover the entire route through multiple samples over time.

In what follows we describe a single sample of each technique applied to a single path.

Per-sequence A single interface sequence from the route is selected, and its interfaces are probed in order from the monitor to the destination using a single probe each. Subsequent samples select other sequences in some order until all are sampled and the route is covered, before repeating. This strategy gives detailed information but uses many probes in a short space of time. FastMapping has a similar strategy only it probes a single sequence repeatedly rather than looping over all sequences.

Per-probe The interface testing schedule is exactly as for per-sequence, however only a single probe is sent, so the probing of each sequence (and ultimately each interface in the route) is spread out over multiple samples.

The above methods treat each path in isolation, but paths originated at a single monitor often have shared links. Doubletree [11] and Tracetree [17] assume that the topology from a monitor to a set of destinations is a tree. They reduce redundant probes close to the monitor by doing backwards probing (from the destinations back to the monitor). Inspired by this approach, we describe methods that exploit spatial information, namely knowledge of shared links, to reduce wasteful probing while remaining load-balancing-aware. We define a *link* as a pair of consecutive interfaces found on some path, which can be thought of as a set of links. Many paths may share a given link.

Per-link A single probe is sent, targeting the far interface of the least recently sampled link. The per-link sample sharing scheme means that the timestamp recording the last sampling of a given link is updated by *any* path that contains it. The result is that a given path does not have to sample shared links as often, instead focussing more on links near the destination. Globally over all links, the allocation of probes to links becomes closer to uniform.

Per-safelink As for per-link, except that a shared link only triggers sample sharing when in addition an entire subsequence, from the monitor down to the interface just past the link, is shared.

Any method that tries to increase probe efficiency through knowledge of how paths share interfaces can fail. This happens when a change occurs at a link (say ℓ) in some path p, but the monitor probes ℓ using a path other than p, for which ℓ has not changed. To help reduce the frequency of such events, per-link strengthens the definition of sharing from an interface to a link, and per-safelink expands it further to a subsequence.

Finally, for comparison we add an oracular method:

Per-oracle A single probe is sent, whose perfect interface targeting will always find a change if one exists.

5.4 Evaluation methodology

We describe how we evaluate DTRACK and compare it to other tracking techniques.

Trace-driven simulation. We build a simulator that takes a dataset with raw traceroutes as input, and for each change in each path extracts a timestamp and the associated route description. It then simulates how each change tracking technique would probe these

paths, complete with their missed changes and estimated (hence inaccurate) feature vectors.

We use the traces described in Sec. 2.2 as input for our evaluation. Different monitors in this dataset probe paths at different frequencies. Let $r_{\min}$ be the minimum interval between two consecutive path measurements from a monitor. We set $\lambda_{\max} = 1/r_{\min}$ per-sequence samples per second (the average value over all monitors is $1/190$), and this is scaled appropriately for other sampling strategies. This setting is natural in our trace-driven approach: probing faster than $1/r_{\min}$ is meaningless because the dataset contains no path data more frequent than every $r_{\min}$, and lower $\lambda_{\max}$ would guarantee that some changes would be missed. We set $\lambda_{\min} = 0$ for all monitors.

Setting probe budgets. The total probe budget B is the sum of a *detection budget* B_d used in sampling for change **d**etection, and a *remapping budget* or cost B_r for route **r**emapping. Let the number of probes per sample be denoted by $n(sam)$, where $sam \in \{s, p, l, sl, o\}$ is one of sampling methods above. The total budget (in probes per second) can be written as

$$B = B_d + B_r = n(sam)B_s + N_r \cdot \overline{\text{MDA}}, \qquad (6)$$

where $\overline{\text{MDA}}$ is the average number of probes in a remapping, and N_r is the average number of remappings per second.

When running live in an operational environment, typical estimates of N_r and $\overline{\text{MDA}}$ can be used to determine B_s based on the monitor parameter B. Our needs here are quite different. For the purposes of a fair comparison we control B_d to be the same for all methods, so that the sampling rates will be determined by $B_s = B_d/n(sam)$ where sam is the sampling method in use. This makes it much easier to give each method the same resources, since we cannot predict how many changes different methods may find. More importantly, it does not make sense in this context to give each method the same total budget B, since the principal measure of success is the detection of as many changes as possible. More detections inevitably means increased remapping cost, but it would be contradictory to focus on B_r and to view this as a failing. The remapping cost is essentially just proportional to the number of changes found and, although important for the end system, is not of central interest for assessing detection performance. We provide some system examples below based on equal B.

The default MDA parameters are very conservative, leading to high probe use. However, it is stated [31] that much less conservative parameters can be used with little ill effect. In this paper we use default parameters for simplicity, since the change detection performance is our main focus.

Performance metrics. We evaluate two performance metrics for tracking techniques: the fraction of missed virtual path changes, and the change detection delay.

A change can be missed through a sample failing to detect a change, or because of undersampling. We give two examples of the latter. If a path changes from r_1 to r_2 and back to r_1 before a sample, then the tracking technique will miss two changes and think that the path is stable between the two probes. If instead the path changes from r_1 to r_2 to r_3, then tracking will detect a change from r_1 to r_3. For each detected change (and only for detected changes), we compute the detection delay as the time of the detection minus the time of the last true change.

Alternative tracking techniques. We compare DTRACK against two other techniques: FastMapping [8] (Sec. 2.2) and Tracetree [17] (Sec. 5.3).

Comparing Tracetree against FastMapping and DTRACK is difficult because Tracetree assumes a tree topology, and is also obliv-

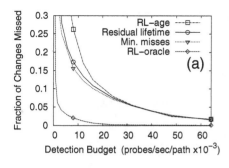 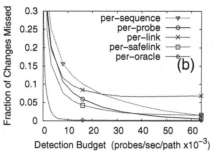 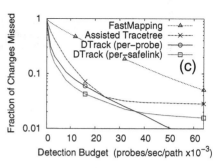

Figure 8: Fraction of missed changes versus detection budget per path $(B_d/|\mathcal{D}|)$**: (a) comparing path sampling rate allocation (using per-sequence) (b) comparing sampling methods (using** MINMISS**), (c) comparing** DTRACK **to alternatives.**

ious to load balancing. As such, Tracetree detects many changes that do not correspond to any real change in any path. To help quantify these false positives and to make comparison more meaningful, in addition to the total number of Tracetree 'changes' detected we compute a cleaned version by assisting Tracetree in three ways. We filter out all changes induced by load balancing; ignore all changes due to violation of the tree hypothesis; and whenever a probe detects a change, we consider that it detects changes in all virtual paths that traverse the changed link (even though they were not directly probed). The result is "Assisted Tracetree".

5.5 Evaluation of path rate allocation

This section evaluates RL, RL-AGE, and MINMISS, using per-sequence, the simplest sampling scheme. Fig. 8(a) shows the fraction of changes missed as a function of $B_d/|\mathcal{D}|$, the detection budget per path. Normalizing per-path facilitates comparison for other datasets. For example, CAIDA's Ark project [14] and DIMES [25] use approximately 0.17×10^{-3} and 8.88×10^{-3} probes per second per virtual path, respectively.

When the budget is too small, not even the oracle can track all changes; whereas in the high budget limit all techniques converge to zero misses. We see that Ark's probing budget is the range where even the oracle misses 72% of changes. To track changes more efficiently Ark would need more monitors, each tracking a smaller number of paths.

Comparing RL-AGE and RL shows that NN4 reduces the number of missed changes over the simple age-based predictor by up to 47% when the sampling budget is small. For sampling budgets higher than 30×10^{-3} both RL-AGE and RL perform similarly as most missed changes happen in old, high-prevalence paths where predictors behave similarly. MINMISS reduces the number of missed changes by less than 11% compared to RL. We adopt MINMISS in DTRACK. It is unlikely that we can improve its performance, even if we could it would require a significantly more complex model.

5.6 Evaluation of in-path sampling

We now use MINMISS as the path rate allocation method, and compare the performance of the in-path sampling strategies using Fig. 8(b) ("minimize misses" in Fig. 8(a) and "per-sequence" in Fig. 8(b) are the same).

The per-probe strategy improves on per-sequence by up to 54%. Per-sequence sampling often wastes probes as once a single changed interface is detected, there is no need to sample the rest of the sequence or route, the route can be remapped immediately, and so the search for the next change begins earlier. Per-probe also has a large advantage in spotting short-lived routes, as its sampling

rate is $n(s)$ times higher (around 16 times in our data) than per-sequence, greatly decreasing the risk of skipping over them.

Each of per-link and per-probe use a single probe per sample, but from Fig. 8(b) the latter is clearly superior. This is because the efficiency gains of the sample-sharing strategy of per-link are outweighed by the inherent risks of missed changes (as explained at the end of Sec. 5.3). This tradeoff becomes steadily worse as probing budget increases, in fact for this strategy the error saturates rather than tending to zero in the limit.

Per-safelink sampling addresses the worst risks of per-link, and over low detection budgets is the best strategy, with up to 28% fewer misses than per-probe. However, at high sampling rates a milder form of the issue affecting per-link still arises, and again the error saturates rather than tending to zero. These results show that exploiting spatial information (like shared links) must be done with great care in the context of tracking, as the very assumptions one is relying on for efficiencies are, by definition, changing (see Tracetree results below).

By default we use per-safelink sampling in DTRACK, as we expect most deployments to operate at low sampling budgets (e.g., DIMES and CAIDA's Ark). At very high sampling budgets we recommend per-probe sampling.

5.7 Comparing DTRACK to alternatives

Fig. 8(c) replots the per-probe and per-safelink curves from Fig. 8(b) on a logarithmic scale, and compares against FastMapping and the assisted form of Tracetree. Each variant of DTRACK outperforms FastMapping by a large margin, up to 89% at intermediate detection budgets. DTRACK also outperforms Assisted Tracetree for all detection budgets, despite the significant degree of assistance provided. We attribute this mainly to the failure of the underlying tree assumption because of load balancing, traffic engineering, and typical AS peering practices. Real (unassisted) Tracetree also suffers from false positives, which in fact grow linearly in probing budget. Already for a detection budget of 8×10^{-3} probes per second per path, Tracetree infers 17 times more false positives than there are real changes in the dataset!

As an example of the benefits that DTRACK can bring, DIMES, which uses $B_d/|\mathcal{D}| = 8.88 \times 10^{-3}$ probes per second per path, would miss 86% fewer changes (detect 220% more) by using DTRACK instead of periodic traceroutes.

Fig. 9 shows the average remapping cost as a function of sampling budget for DTRACK and FastMapping. Real deployments can reduce remapping costs compared to the results we show by configuring MDA to use less probes [31]. We omit Tracetree as it does not perform remapping.

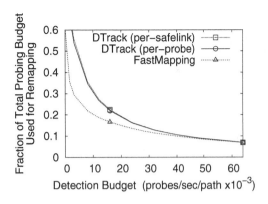

Figure 9: Remapping cost for a given detection budget.

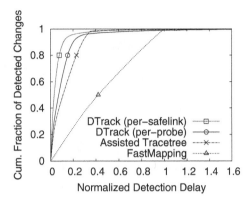

Figure 10: Distribution of detection delay normalized by Fast-Mapping's virtual path sampling period.

Fig. 9 gives $B_r/B = (B - B_d)/B$, the fraction of the probing budget that is used for remapping. At low detection budgets, sampling frequency is lower and each sample has a higher probability to detect a change (as well as to miss others). In such scenarios the remapping cost is comparable to the total budget. As the sampling budget increases, the number of changes detected stabilizes and the remapping cost becomes less significant relative to the total.

Taking again the example of DIMES, even including DTRACK's remapping cost, DIMES would miss 73% less (or detect twice as many) changes using DTRACK instead of periodic traceroutes, while providing complete load balancing information.

Fig. 9 allows an operator to compute an initial sampling budget so that DTRACK respects a desired total probing budget B in a real deployment. After DTRACK is running, the operator can readjust the sampling budget as a function of the actual remapping cost.

Fig. 10 shows the distribution of the detection delay of detected changes for the different tracking techniques, given a detection budget of $B_d/|\mathcal{D}| = 16 \times 10^{-3}$ probes per second per path. Results for other detection budgets are qualitatively similar. We normalize the detection delay by FastMapping's virtual path sampling period (which is common to all paths).

We see that FastMapping detection delay is in a sense the worst possible, being almost uniform over the path sampling period. Tracetree samples paths more frequently and achieves lower detection delay. However, both FastMapping and Tracetree are limited by sampling all paths at the same rate. DTRACK (per-safelink) reduces average detection delay by 57% over FastMapping and has lower delay 99.8% of the time, the exceptions being, not surprisingly, on paths with low sampling budgets.

Low detection delay is important to increase the fidelity of fault detection and tomographic techniques. To see the benefits, say that a monitor uses a total budget B of 64 kbits/sec to track 8,000 paths. It would detect 52% more changes by replacing periodic traceroutes with DTRACK (using safelink) and it would detect 90% of path changes with a delay below 125 seconds. Replacing classic traceroute by MDA also has the benefit of getting complete and accurate routes.

Summary. Our results indicate that DTRACK not only detects more changes, but also has lower detection delay, which should directly benefit applications that need up-to-date information on path stability and network topology.

6. RELATED WORK

Forwarding vs. routing dynamics. Internet path dynamics and routing behavior have captured the interest of the research community since the mid-90s with Paxson's study of end-to-end rout-

ing behavior [24] and Labovitz et al.'s findings on BGP instabilities [16]. In this paper, we follow Paxson's approach of using traceroute-style probing to infer end-to-end routes and track virtual path changes. Traceroute is appealing for tracking virtual paths from monitors located at the edge of the Internet for two main reasons. First, traceroute directly measures the forwarding path, whereas AS paths inferred from BGP messages may not match the AS-level forwarding path [21]. Second, traceroute runs from any host connected to the Internet with no privileged access to routers, whereas the collection of BGP messages requires direct access to routers. Although RouteViews and RIPE collect BGP data from some routers for the community, public BGP data lacks visibility to track all path changes from a given vantage point [7, 29]. When BGP messages from a router close to the traceroute monitor are available, they could help tracking virtual path changes. For instance, Feamster et al. [12] showed that BGP messages could be used to predict about 20% of the path failures in their study. We will study how to incorporate BGP messages in our prediction and tracking methods in future work.

Characterization and prediction of path behavior. Some of the virtual path features that we study are inspired by previous characterizations of Internet paths [2, 12, 24] as discussed in Sec. 2.4. None of these characterization studies, however, use these features to predict future path changes. Although to our knowledge there is no prior work on predicting path changes, Zhang et al. [33] studied the degree of constancy of path performance properties (loss, delay, and throughput); constancy is closely related to predictability. Later studies have used past path performance (for instance, end-to-end losses [28] or round-trip delays [6]) to predict future performance. iNano [20] also "predicts" a number of path properties including PoP-level routes, but their meaning for route prediction is different than ours. Their goal is to predict the PoP-level route of an arbitrary end-to-end path, even though the system only directly measures the route of a small sub-set of paths. iNano only refreshes measurements once per day and as such cannot track path changes.

Topology mapping techniques. Topology mapping systems [14, 17, 19, 25] often track routes to a large number of destinations. Many of the topology discovery techniques focus on getting more complete or accurate topology maps by resolving different interfaces to a single router [26, 27], selecting traceroute's sources and destinations to better cover the topology [27], or using the record-route IP option to complement traceroutes [26]. DTRACK is a good complement to all these techniques. We argue that to get more accurate maps, we should focus the probing capacity on the paths that are changing, and also explore spatio-temporal alternatives to simple traditional traceroute sampling. One approach to tracking the evolution of IP topologies is to exploit knowledge of shared links to reduce probing overhead and consequently probe the topology faster as Tracetree [17] and Doubletree [11] do. As we show in Sec. 5, Tracetree leads to a very large number of false detections. Thus, we choose to guarantee the accuracy and completeness of measured routes by using Paris traceroute's MDA [31]. Most comparable to DTRACK is FastMapping [8]. Sec. 5 shows that DTRACK, because of its adaptive probing allocation (instead of a constant rate for all paths) and single-probe sampling strategy (compared to an entire branch of the route at a time), misses up to 89% fewer changes than FastMapping.

7. CONCLUSION

This paper presented DTRACK, a path tracking strategy that proceeds in two steps: path change detection and path remapping. We designed NN4, a simple predictor of path changes that uses as input: route prevalence, route age, number of past route changes, and number of times a route appeared in the past. Although we found that the limits to prediction in general are strong and in particular that NN4 is not highly accurate, it is still useful for allocating probes to paths. DTRACK optimizes path sampling rates based on NN4 predictions. Within each path, DTRACK employs a kind of temporal striping of Paris traceroute. When a change is detected, path remapping uses Paris traceroute's MDA to ensure complete and accurate route measurements. DTRACK detects up to two times more path changes when compared to the state-of-the-art tracking technique, with lower detection delays, and whilst providing complete load balancer information. DTRACK finds considerably more true changes than Tracetree, and none of the very large number of false positives. More generally, we point out that any approach that exploits shared links runs the risk of errors being greatly magnified in the tracking application, and should be used with great care.

To accelerate the adoption of DTRACK, our immediate next step is to implement DTRACK into an easy-to-use system and deploy it on PlanetLab as a path tracking service. For future work, we will investigate the benefits of incorporating additional information, such as BGP messages, to increase prediction accuracy, as well as the benefits of coordinating the probing effort across monitors to further optimize probing.

Acknowledgements. We thank Ethan Katz-Bassett, Fabian Schneider, and our shepherd Sharon Goldberg for their helpful comments. This work was supported by the European Community's Seventh Framework Programme (FP7/2007-2013) no. 223850 (Nano Data Centers) and the ANR project C'MON.

8. REFERENCES

[1] D. Andersen, H. Balakrishnan, F. Kaashoek, and R. Morris. Resilient Overlay Networks. *SIGOPS Oper. Syst. Rev.*, 35(5):131–145, 2001.

[2] B. Augustin, T. Friedman, and R. Teixeira. Measuring Load-balanced Paths in the Internet. In *Proc. IMC*, 2007.

[3] F. Baccelli, S. Machiraju, D. Veitch, and J. Bolot. On Optimal Probing for Delay and Loss Measurement. In *Proc. IMC*, 2007.

[4] F. Baccelli, S. Machiraju, D. Veitch, and J. Bolot. The Role of PASTA in Network Measurement. *IEEE/ACM Trans. Netw.*, 17(4):1340–1353, 2009.

[5] K. Beyer, J. Goldstein, R. Ramakrishnan, and U. Shaft. When Is "Nearest Neighbor" Meaningful? In *Proc. Intl. Conf. on Database Theory*, 1999.

[6] A. Bremler-Barr, E. Cohen, H. Kaplan, and Y. Mansour. Predicting and Bypassing End-to-end Internet Service Degradations. *IEEE J. Selected Areas in Communications*, 21(6):961–978, 2003.

[7] R. Bush, O. Maennel, M. Roughan, and S. Uhlig. Internet Optometry: Assessing the Broken Glasses in Internet Reachability. In *Proc. IMC*, 2009.

[8] I. Cunha, R. Teixeira, and C. Diot. Measuring and Characterizing End-to-End Route Dynamics in the Presence of Load Balancing. In *Proc. PAM*, 2011.

[9] I. Cunha, R. Teixeira, N. Feamster, and C. Diot. Measurement Methods for Fast and Accurate Blackhole Identification with Binary Tomography. In *Proc. IMC*, 2009.

[10] J. Dilley, B. Maggs, J. Parikh, H. Prokop, R. Sitaraman, and B. Weihl. Globally Distributed Content Delivery. *IEEE Internet Computing*, 6(5):50–58, 2002.

[11] B. Donnet, P. Raoult, T. Friedman, and M. Crovella. Efficient Algorithms for Large-scale Topology Discovery. In *Proc. ACM SIGMETRICS*, 2005.

[12] N. Feamster, D. Andersen, H. Balakrishnan, and F. Kaashoek. Measuring the Effects of Internet Path Faults on Reactive Routing. In *Proc. ACM SIGMETRICS*, 2003.

[13] J. Friedman and B. Popescu. Predictive Learning via Rule Ensembles. *Annals of Applied Statistics*, 2(3):916–954, 2008.

[14] k. claffy, Y. Hyun, K. Keys, M. Fomenkov, and D. Krioukov. Internet Mapping: from Art to Science. In *Proc. IEEE CATCH*, 2009.

[15] E. Katz-Bassett, H. Madhyastha, J. P. John, A. Krishnamurthy, D. Wetherall, and T. Anderson. Studying Black Holes in the Internet with Hubble. In *Proc. USENIX NSDI*, 2008.

[16] C. Labovitz, R. Malan, and F. Jahanian. Internet Routing Instability. In *Proc. ACM SIGCOMM*, 1997.

[17] M. Latapy, C. Magnien, and F. Ouédraogo. A Radar for the Internet. In *Proc. Intl. Workshop on Analysis of Dynamic Networks*, 2008.

[18] D. Leonard and D. Loguinov. Demystifying Service Discovery: Implementing an Internet-Wode Scanner. In *Proc. IMC*, 2010.

[19] H. Madhyastha, T. Isdal, M. Piatek, C. Dixon, T. Anderson, A. Krishnamurthy, and A. Venkataramani. iPlane: an Information Plane for Distributed Services. In *Proc. USENIX OSDI*, 2006.

[20] H. Madhyastha, E. Katz-Bassett, T. Anderson, A. Krishnamurthy, and A. Venkataramani. iPlane Nano: Path Prediction for Peer-to-peer Applications. In *Proc. USENIX NSDI*, 2009.

[21] Z. M. Mao, J. Rexford, J. Wang, and R. H. Katz. Towards an Accurate AS-level Traceroute Tool. In *Proc. ACM SIGCOMM*, 2003.

[22] A. Markopoulou, G. Iannaccone, S. Bhattacharyya, C. N. Chuah, Y. Ganjali, and C. Diot. Characterization of Failures in an Operational IP Backbone Network. *IEEE/ACM Trans. Netw.*, 16(4):749–762, 2008.

[23] R. Oliveira, D. Pei, W. Willinger, B. Zhang, and L. Zhang. Quantifying the Completeness of the Observed Internet AS-level Structure. *IEEE/ACM Trans. Netw.*, 18(1):109–122, 2010.

[24] V. Paxson. End-to-end Routing Behavior in the Internet. *IEEE/ACM Trans. Netw.*, 5(5):601–615, 1997.

[25] Y. Shavitt and U. Weinsberg. Quantifying the Importance of Vantage Points Distribution in Internet Topology Measurements. In *Proc. IEEE INFOCOM*, 2009.

[26] R. Sherwood, A. Bender, and N. Spring. DisCarte: a Disjunctive Internet Cartographer. In *Proc. ACM SIGCOMM*, 2008.

[27] N. Spring, R. Mahajan, and D. Wetherall. Measuring ISP Topologies with Rocketfuel. In *Proc. ACM SIGCOMM*, 2002.

[28] S. Tao, K. Xu, Y. Xu, T. Fei, L. Gao, R. Guerin, J. Kurose, D. Towsley, and Z.-L. Zhang. Exploring the Performance Benefits of End-to-End Path Switching. In *Proc. ICNP*, 2004.

[29] R. Teixeira and J. Rexford. A Measurement Framework for Pin-pointing Routing Changes. In *Proc. SIGCOMM Workshop on Network Troubleshooting*, 2004.

[30] D. Turner, K. Levchenko, A. Snoeren, and S. Savage. California Fault Lines: Understanding the Causes and Impact of Network Failures. In *Proc. ACM SIGCOMM*, 2010.

[31] D. Veitch, B. Augustin, T. Friedman, and R. Teixeira. Failure Control in Multipath Route Tracing. In *Proc. IEEE INFOCOM*, 2009.

[32] M. Zhang, C. Zhang, V. Pai, L. Peterson, and R. Wang. PlanetSeer: Internet Path Failure Monitoring and Characterization in Wide-area Services. In *Proc. USENIX OSDI*, San Francisco, CA, 2004.

[33] Y. Zhang, N. Duffield, V. Paxson, and S. Shenker. On the Constancy of Internet Path Properties. In *Proc. IMW*, 2001.

[34] Z. Zhang, Y. Zhang, Y. C. Hu, Z. M. Mao, and R. Bush. iSPY: Detecting IP Prefix Hijacking on My Own. In *Proc. ACM SIGCOMM*, 2008.

Broadband Internet Performance: A View From the Gateway

Srikanth Sundaresan
Georgia Tech
Atlanta, USA
srikanth@gatech.edu

Walter de Donato
University of Napoli Federico II
Napoli, Italy
walter.dedonato@unina.it

Nick Feamster
Georgia Tech
Atlanta, USA
feamster@cc.gatech.edu

Renata Teixeira
CNRS/UPMC Sorbonne Univ.
Paris, France
renata.teixeira@lip6.fr

Sam Crawford
SamKnows
London, UK
sam@samknows.com

Antonio Pescapè
University of Napoli Federico II
Napoli, Italy
pescape@unina.it

ABSTRACT

We present the first study of network access link performance measured directly from home gateway devices. Policymakers, ISPs, and users are increasingly interested in studying the performance of Internet access links. Because of many confounding factors in a home network or on end hosts, however, thoroughly understanding access network performance requires deploying measurement infrastructure in users' homes as gateway devices. In conjunction with the Federal Communication Commission's study of broadband Internet access in the United States, we study the throughput and latency of network access links using longitudinal measurements from nearly 4,000 gateway devices across 8 ISPs from a deployment of over 4,200 devices. We study the performance users achieve and how various factors ranging from the user's choice of modem to the ISP's traffic shaping policies can affect performance. Our study yields many important findings about the characteristics of existing access networks. Our findings also provide insights into the ways that access network performance should be measured and presented to users, which can help inform ongoing broader efforts to benchmark the performance of access networks.

Categories and Subject Descriptors

C.2.3 [**Computer-Communication Networks**]: Network Operations—*Network Management*; C.2.3 [**Computer-Communication Networks**]: Network Operations—*Network Operations*

General Terms

Management, Measurement, Performance

Keywords

Access Networks, Broadband Networks, BISMark, Benchmarking

1. INTRODUCTION

Of nearly two billion Internet users worldwide, about 500 million are residential broadband subscribers [19]. Broadband penetration is likely to increase further, with people relying on home connectivity for day-to-day and even critical activities. Accordingly, the Federal Communication Commission (FCC) is actively

developing performance-testing metrics for access providers [5,15, 35]. Policymakers, home users, and Internet Service Providers (ISPs) are in search for better ways to benchmark home broadband Internet performance.

Benchmarking home Internet performance, however, is not as simple as running one-time "speed tests". There exist countless tools to measure Internet performance [7,14,29,32]. Previous work has studied the typical download and upload rates of home access networks [12,24]; others have found that modems often have large buffers [24], and that DSL links often have high latency [26]. These studies have shed some light on access-link performance, but they have typically run one-time measurements either from an end-host inside the home (from the "inside out") or from a server on the wide-area Internet (from the "outside in"). Because these tools run from end-hosts, they cannot analyze the effects of confounding factors such as home network cross-traffic, the wireless network, or end-host configuration. Also, many of these tools run as one-time measurements. Without continual measurements of the same access link, these tools cannot establish a baseline performance level or observe how performance varies over time.

This paper measures and characterizes broadband Internet performance from home gateways. The home gateway connects the home network to the user's modem; taking measurements from this vantage point allows us to control the effects of many confounding factors, such as the home wireless network and load on the measurement host (Section 4). The home gateway is always on; it can conduct unobstructed measurements of the ISP's network and account for confounding factors in the home network. The drawback to measuring access performance from the gateway, of course, is that deploying gateways in many homes is incredibly difficult and expensive. Fortunately, we were able to take advantage of the ongoing FCC broadband study to have such a unique deployment.

We perform our measurements using two complementary deployments; the first is a large FCC-sponsored study, operated by SamKnows, that has installed gateways in over 4,200 homes across the United States, across many different ISPs. The second, BISMark, is deployed in 16 homes across three ISPs in Atlanta. The SamKnows deployment provides a large user base, as well as diversity in ISPs, service plans, and geographical locations. We designed BISMark to allow us to access the gateway remotely and run repeated experiments to investigate the effect of factors that we could not study in a larger "production" deployment. For example, to study the effect of modem choice on performance, we were able to install different modems in the same home and conduct experiments in a controlled setting. Both deployments run a comprehensive suite of measurement tools that periodically measure throughput, latency, packet loss, and jitter.

We characterize access network throughput (Section 5) and latency (Section 6) from the SamKnows and BISMark deployments. We explain how our throughput measurements differ from common "speed tests" and also propose several different latency metrics. When our measurements cannot fully explain the observed behavior, we model the access link and verify our hypotheses using controlled experiments. We find that the most significant sources of throughput variability are the access technology, ISPs' traffic shaping policies, and congestion during peak hours. On the other hand, latency is mostly affected by the quality of the access link, modem buffering, and cross-traffic within the home.

This study offers many insights into both access network performance and the appropriate measurement methods for benchmarking home broadband performance. Our study has three high-level lessons, which we expand on in Section 7:

- ISPs use different policies and traffic shaping behavior that can make it difficult to compare measurements across ISPs.

- There is no "best" ISP for all users. Different users may prefer different ISPs depending on their usage profiles and how those ISPs perform along performance dimensions that matter to them.

- A user's home network equipment and infrastructure can significantly affect performance.

As the first in-depth analysis of home access network performance, our study offers insights for users, ISPs, and policymakers. Users and ISPs can better understand the performance of the access link, as measured directly from the gateway; ultimately, such a deployment could help an ISP differentiate performance problems within the home from those on the access link. Our study also informs policy by illustrating that a diverse set of network metrics ultimately affect the performance that a user experiences. The need for a benchmark is clear, and the results from this study can serve as a principled foundation for such an effort.

2. RELATED WORK

This section presents related work; where appropriate, we compare our results to these previous studies in Sections 5 and 6.

From access ISPs. Previous work characterizes access networks using passive traffic measurements from DSL provider networks in Japan [8], France [33], and Europe [26]. These studies mostly focus on traffic patterns and application usage, but they also infer the round-trip time and throughput of residential users. Without active measurements or a vantage point within the home network, however, it is not possible to measure the actual performance that users receive from their ISPs, because user traffic does not always saturate the user's access network connection. For example, Siekkinen *et al.* [33] show that applications (*e.g.*, peer-to-peer file sharing applications) often rate limit themselves, so performance observed through passive traffic analysis may reflect application rate limiting, as opposed to the performance of the access link.

From servers in the wide area. Other studies have characterized access network performance by probing access links from servers in the wide area [11, 12]. Active probing from a fixed set of servers can characterize many access links because each link can be measured from the same server. Unfortunately, because the server is often located far from the access network, the measurements may be inaccurate or inconsistent. Isolating the performance of the access network from the performance of the end-to-end path can be challenging, and dynamic IP addressing can make it difficult to determine whether repeated measurements of the same IP address are in fact measuring the same access link over time. A remote server

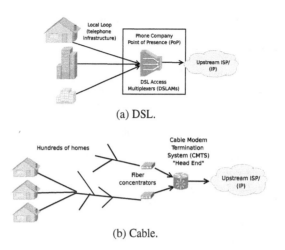

(a) DSL.

(b) Cable.

Figure 1: Access network architectures.

also cannot isolate confounding factors, such as whether the user's own traffic is affecting the access-link performance.

From inside home networks. The Grenouille project in France [1] measures the performance of access links using a monitoring agent that runs from a user's machine inside the home network. Neti@Home [23] and BSense [4] also use this approach, although these projects have fewer users than Grenouille. PeerMetric [25] measured P2P performance from about 25 end hosts. Installing software at the end-host measures the access network from the user's perspective and can also gather continuous measurements of the same access link. Han *et al.* [18] measured access network performance from a laptop that searched for open wireless networks. This approach is convenient because it does not require user intervention, but it does not scale to a large number of access networks, cannot collect continuous measurements, and offers no insights into the specifics of the home network configuration.

Other studies have performed "one-time" measurements of access-link performance. These studies typically help users troubleshoot performance problems by asking the users to run tests from a Web site and running analysis based on these tests. Netalyzr [29] measures the performance of commonly used protocols using a Java applet that is launched from the client's browser. Network Diagnostic Tool (NDT) [7] and Network Path and Application Diagnostics (NPAD) [14] send active probes to detect issues with client performance. Glasnost performs active measurements to determine whether the user's ISP is actively blocking BitTorrent traffic [17]. Users typically run these tools only once (or, at most, a few times), so the resulting datasets cannot capture a longitudinal view of the performance of any single access link. In addition, any technique that measures performance from a device inside the home can be affected by factors such as load on the host or features of the home network (*e.g.*, cross-traffic, wireless signal strength). Finally, none of these studies measure the access link directly from the home network gateway.

3. ACCESS NETWORKS: BACKGROUND

We describe the two most common access technologies from our deployments: Digital Subscriber Line (DSL) and cable. Then, we explain how a user's choice of service plan and local configuration can affect performance. Although a few users in our deployments have fiber-to-the-node (FTTN), fiber-to-the-premises (FTTP), and WiMax, we do not have enough users to analyze these technologies.

DSL networks use telephone lines; subscribers have dedicated lines between their own DSL modems and the closest DSL Access Multiplexer (DSLAM). The DSLAM multiplexes data between the access modems and upstream networks, as shown in Figure 1a. The most common type of DSL access is asymmetric (ADSL), which provides different upload and download rates. In cable access networks, groups of users send data over a shared medium (typically coaxial cable); at a regional *headend*, a Cable Modem Termination System (CMTS) receives these signals and converts them to Ethernet, as shown in Figure 1b. The physical connection between a customer's home and the DSLAM or the CMTS is often referred to as the *local loop* or *last mile*. Users buy a service plan from a provider that typically offers some *maximum* capacity in both the upload and download directions.

ADSL capacity. The ITU-T standardization body establishes that the achievable rate for ADSL 1 [20] is 12 Mbps downstream and 1.8 Mbps upstream. The ADSL2+ specification [21] extends the capacity of ADSL links to at most 24 Mbps download and 3.5 Mbps upload. Although the ADSL technology is theoretically able to reach these speeds, there are many factors that limit the capacity in practice. An ADSL modem negotiates the operational rate with the DSLAM (often called the *sync rate*); this rate depends on the quality of the local loop, which is mainly determined by the distance to the DSLAM from the user's home and noise on the line. The maximum IP link capacity is lower than the sync rate because of the overhead of underlying protocols. The best service plan that an ADSL provider advertises usually represents the rate that customers can achieve if they have a good connection to the DSLAM. Providers also offer service plans with lower rates and can rate-limit a customer's traffic at the DSLAM.

Modem configuration can also affect performance. ADSL users or providers configure their modems to operate in either *fastpath* or *interleaved* mode. In *fastpath* mode, data is exchanged between the DSL modem and the DSLAM in the same order that they are received, which minimizes latency but prevents error correction from being applied across frames. Thus, ISPs typically configure fastpath only if the line has a low bit error rate. *Interleaving* increases robustness to line noise at the cost of increased latency by splitting data from each frame into multiple segments and interleaving those segments with one another before transmitting them.

Cable capacity. In cable networks, the most widely deployed version of the standard is Data Over Cable Service Interface Specification version 2 (DOCSIS 2.0) [22], which specifies download rates up to 42.88 Mbps and upload rates up to 30.72 Mbps in the United States. The latest standard, DOCSIS 3.0, allows for hundreds of megabits per second by bundling multiple channels. Cable providers often offer service plans with lower rates. The service plan rate limit is configured at the cable modem and is typically implemented using a token bucket rate shaper. Many cable providers offer *PowerBoost*, which allows users to download (and, in some cases, upload) at rates that are higher than the contracted ones, for an initial part of a transfer. The actual rate that a cable user receives will vary with the network utilization of other users connecting to the same headend. The CMTS controls the rate at which cable modems transmit. For instance, Comcast describes that when a CMTS's port becomes congested, it ensures fairness by scheduling heavy users on a lower priority queue [3].

4. MEASUREMENT INFRASTRUCTURE

We describe the measurement infrastructure that we deployed and the datasets that we collected. We first motivate the need for

Factor	How we address it
Wireless Effects	Use a wired connection to modem.
Cross Traffic	Measure cross traffic and avoid it/account for it.
Load on gateway	Use a well-provisioned gateway.
Location of server	Choose a nearby server.
End-to-end path	Focus on characterizing the last mile.
Gateway configuration	Test configuration in practice and controlled settings.

Table 1: Confounding factors and how we address them.

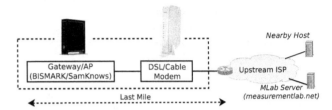

Figure 2: Our gateway device sits directly behind the modem in the home network. They take measurements both to the *last mile router* (first non-NAT IP hop on the path) and to wide area hosts.

deploying measurement infrastructure directly at the gateway; then, we describe the *SamKnows* and *BISMark* (Broadband Internet Service benchMark) gateway deployments.

4.1 Why a Gateway?

Deploying measurements at gateway devices offers the following advantages over the other techniques discussed in Section 2:

- *Direct measurement* of the ISP's access link: the gateway sits behind the modem; between the access link and all other devices at the home network as shown in Figure2. This allows us to isolate the effect of confounding factors such as wireless effects and cross traffic.

- *Continual/longitudinal measurements*, which allow us to meaningfully characterize performance of ISPs for individual users.

- *The ability to instrument a single home with different hardware and configurations*, which allows us to explore the effects of multiple factors on performance. In some deployments, we were even able to swap modems to study their effect on performance, holding all other conditions about the network setup equal.

Table 1 summarizes the challenges involved in conducting such a study, and how deploying gateways solves them. We now describe the two gateway deployments in our study.

4.2 Gateway Deployments

Our study uses two independent gateway deployments. The first, the FCC/SamKnows gateway deployment, collected data from over 4,200 users across different ISPs in the United States, as of January 2011. This deployment currently has over 10,000 users. Our goal in using the measurements from this deployment is to achieve *breadth*: we aim to classify a large set of users across a diverse set of ISPs and geographical locations. The second, the BISMark deployment, collects measurements from a smaller, focused group of users from different ISPs and service plans in Atlanta. Our goal with the measurements from this deployment is to achieve *depth*: this platform allows us to take measurements with detailed knowledge of how every gateway is deployed; we can also take repeated measurements and conduct specific experiments from the same deployment with different settings and configurations.

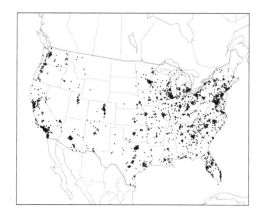

Figure 3: SamKnows deployment: 4,200 devices, 16 ISPs.

ISP	Technology	SamKnows Total	SamKnows Active	BISMark Total
Comcast	Cable	864	560	4
AT&T	DSL/FTTN	787	335	10
TimeWarner	Cable	690	381	-
Verizon	DSL/FTTP	551	256	-
Cox	Cable	381	161	-
Qwest	DSL/FTTN	265	117	-
Charter	Cable	187	51	-
Cablevision	Cable	104	53	-

Table 2: The SamKnows and BISMark deployments. *Active* deployments are those that report more than 100 download throughput measurements over the course of our study.

Gateway deployments entail significant challenges concerning the resource constraints of the gateway platform and the need to remotely maintain and manage the devices (especially because these devices are deployed in homes of "real users"); we omit discussion of these logistical challenges due to lack of space and instead focus on the details of the platforms and the measurements we collect.

4.2.1 SamKnows

SamKnows specializes in performance evaluation of access networks; it has studied access ISP performance in the United Kingdom and has now contracted with the FCC for a similar study in the United States. SamKnows deployed gateways in each participant's home either directly behind the home user's router or behind the home wireless router; the devices can be updated and managed remotely. The gateway is a Netgear WNR3500L RangeMax Wireless-N Gigabit router with a 480 MHz MIPS processor, 8 MB of flash storage, and 64 MB of RAM. We use active measurement data from the SamKnows study from December 14, 2010 to January 14, 2011. This dataset comprises measurements from 4,200 devices that are deployed across sixteen different ISPs and hundreds of cities in the United States. The volunteers for the study were recruited through http://www.testmyisp.com. Figure 3 shows a map of the deployment.

Table 2 lists the ISPs that we study, the number of gateways deployed in them, and the number of gateways that report more than 100 throughput measurements. Gateways are rolled out in phases. These devices perform measurements less aggressively when users are sending a lot of traffic. Therefore, not all gateways report data for the entire duration of the study. When we report averages and 95th percentile values for some metric, we only consider gateways that have reported more than 100 measurements for that metric. We also only consider the eight ISPs with the most gateways.

Table 3 shows the active measurements that we use from the SamKnows deployment; some of these (*e.g.*, *last mile latency*) were inspired from our experience running them on BISMark. The gateways conduct upstream and downstream measurements to servers hosted at Measurement Lab [27] about once every two hours.

There are many ways to measure throughput, though there is no standard method. Bauer *et al.* list several notions of "broadband speed": *capacity* is the total carrying capacity of the link; and the *bulk transfer capacity* is the amount of data that can be transferred along a path with a congestion-aware protocol like TCP. In Section 5.1, we evaluate several methods for measuring these metrics.

The SamKnows gateways measure bulk transfer capacity using an HTTP client that spawns three parallel threads; this approach increases the likelihood of saturating the access link. The software first executes a "warmup" transfer until throughput is steady to ensure that the throughput measurements are not affected by TCP slow start. The download tests that follows use the same TCP connection to exploit the "warmed up" session. The tests last for about 30 seconds; the software reports snapshots of how many bytes were transferred for every five-second interval.

The gateways also measure different aspects of latency: (1) end-to-end latency; (2) latency to the first IP hop inside the ISP (*last mile latency*); and (3) latency coinciding with an upload or download (*latency under load*). They measure end-to-end latency in two ways: (1) Using a UDP client that sends about six hundred packets an hour to the servers and measures latency and packet loss, and (2) using ICMP ping to the same set of servers at the rate of five packets per hour. To measure latency under load, the gateway measures end-to-end latency during both the upload and the download measurements. They also measure jitter based on RFC 5481 [28] and the time to download the home page of ten popular websites. Before any test begins, the measurement software checks whether cross traffic on the outgoing interface exceeds 64 Kbits/s down or 32 Kbits/s up; if traffic exceeds this threshold, it aborts the test.

4.2.2 BISMark

BISMark comprises gateways in the home, a centralized management and data collection server, and several measurement servers. The gateway performs passive and active measurements and anonymizes the results before sending them back to the central repository for further analysis. This gateway also periodically "phones home" to allow the central repository to communicate back through network address translators, to update network configurations and to install software updates. The gateway is based on the NOX Box [31], a small-form-factor computer resembling an off-the-shelf home router/gateway. The NOX Box hardware is an ALIX 2D13 6-inch by 6-inch single board computer with a 500MHz AMD Geode processor, 256 MB of RAM and at least 2 GB of flash memory. The Nox Box runs Debian Linux.

Table 3 lists the measurements that BISMark collects.[1] We collect throughput, latency, packet loss, and jitter measurements.

BISMark measures *bulk transfer capacity* by performing an HTTP download and upload for 15 seconds using a single-threaded TCP connection once every 30 minutes, regardless of cross traffic. We do this to have more readings, and to account for cross-traffic, we count bytes transferred by reading directly from /proc/net/dev, and compute the "passive throughput" as the

---

[1] The data is available at http://projectbismark.net/.

Parameter	Type	Prot.	Freq.	Comments
SamKnows: 4,200 devices, 16 ISPs				
Latency	End-to-end	UDP	600 pkts/hr	MLab
	End-to-end	ICMP	5 pkts/hr	MLab
	Last-mile	ICMP	5 pkts/hr	First IP hop
	Upstream load	ICMP	2 hours	During upload
	Downstream load	ICMP	2 hours	During download
Loss	End-to-end	UDP	600 pkts/hr	MLab
Downstream Throughput	Multi-threaded HTTP	TCP	2 hours	MLab, idle link
Upstream Throughput	Multi-threaded HTTP	TCP	2 hours	MLab, idle link
Jitter	Bi-directional	UDP	1 hour	500pkts/30sec
Web GET	HTTP	TCP	1 hour	Alexa sites
BISMark: 17 devices, 3 ISPs				
Latency	End-to-end	ICMP	5 min	Host
	Last-mile	ICMP	5 min	First IP hop
	Upstream load	ICMP	30 min	During upload
	Downstream load	ICMP	30 min	During download
Packet loss	End-to-end	UDP	15 min	D-ITG
Jitter	End-to-end	UDP	15 min	D-ITG
Downstream Throughput	Single-thread HTTP	TCP	30 min	curlget to Host
	Passive throughput	N/A	30 min	/proc/net/dev
	Capacity	UDP	12 hrs	ShaperProbe
Upstream Throughput	Single-thread HTTP	TCP	30 min	curlput to Host
	Passive throughput	N/A	30 min	/proc/net/dev
	Capacity	UDP	12 hrs	ShaperProbe

Table 3: Active measurements periodically collected by the SamKnows and BISMark deployments.

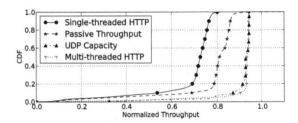

Figure 4: Comparison of various methods of measuring throughput. (SamKnows and BISMark)

byte count after the HTTP transfer minus the byte count before the transfer, divided by the transfer time. This yields the combined throughput of the HTTP transfer and the cross traffic. To measure *capacity*, we run ShaperProbe [32] once every twelve hours to measure UDP capacity. The gateways measure end-to-end latency to a nearby wide-area host, last-mile latency, and latency-under load to the last-mile router. They also measure packet loss and jitter using the D-ITG tool [6]. The gateways perform each measurement at the frequency presented in Table 3 regardless of cross traffic. All measurements are synchronized to avoid overlapping towards the same measurement server.

In January 2011, the BISMark deployment had 14 gateways across AT&T (DSL) and Comcast (Cable), and two more on Clear (WiMax). We recruited users from our research lab and other graduate students in the computer science department; some users were recruited using a recruiting firm.[2] We only study AT&T and Comcast using BISMark. The AT&T users form the most diverse set of users in the current deployment, with five distinct service plans. We use data from the same period as the SamKnows study.

5. UNDERSTANDING THROUGHPUT

We study throughput measurements from both the SamKnows and BISMark deployments. We first explore how different mechanisms for measuring throughput can generate different results and offer guidelines on how to interpret them. We then investigate the throughput users achieve on different access links, the consistency of throughput obtained by users, and the factors that affect it. Finally, we explore the effects of ISP traffic shaping and the implications it holds for throughput measurement.

5.1 Interpreting Throughput Measurements

Users of access networks are often interested in the throughput that they receive on uploads or downloads, yet the notion of "throughput" can vary depending on how, when, and who is mea-

---

[2] All of our methods have been approved by Georgia Tech's institutional review board.

suring it. For example, a sample run of www.speedtest.net in an author's home, where the service plan was 6Mbits/s down and 512Kbits/s up, reported a downlink speed of 4.4 Mbits/s and an uplink speed of 140 Kbits/s. Netalyzr reported 4.8 Mbits/s and 430 Kbits/s. Long-term measurements (from the SamKnows gateway deployed in that author's home) paint a different picture: the user achieves 5.6 Mbits/s down and 452 Kbits/s up. Both www.speedtest.net and Netalyzr measurements reflect transient network conditions, as well as other confounding factors. Users cannot complain to their ISPs based solely on these measurements. Although measuring throughput may seem straightforward, our results in this section demonstrate the extent to which different measurement methods can produce different results and, hence, may result in different conclusions about the ISP's performance.

We compare several methods for measuring upstream and downstream throughput from Table 3. We normalize the values of throughput by the service plan rates advertised by the ISP so that we can compare throughput across access links where users have different service plans.

Throughput measurement techniques—even commonly accepted ones—can yield variable results. We perform comparisons of throughput measurement techniques in two locations that have deployed both the SamKnows and BISMark gateways (we are restricted to two due to the logistical difficulty in deploying both gateways in the same location). In both cases, the ISP is AT&T, but the service plans are different (6 Mbits/s down and 512 Kbits/s up; and 3 Mbit/s down and 384 Kbits/s up). Figure 4 shows a CDF of the normalized throughput reported by the four methods we presented in Table 3. Each data point in the distribution represents a single throughput measurement by a client. A value of 1.0 on the x-axis indicates that the throughput matches the ISP's advertised rate. None of the four methods achieve that value. This could be due to many factors: the sync rate of the modem to the DSLAM; layer-2 framing overhead on the line; or overhead from the measurement techniques themselves. The throughput achieved by multiple parallel TCP sessions comes closer to achieving the advertised throughput. UDP measurements (obtained from ShaperProbe) also produce consistent measurements of throughput that are closer to the multi-threaded TCP measurement. A single-threaded TCP session may not be able to achieve the same throughput, but accounting for cross traffic with passive measurements can provide a better estimate of the actual achieved throughput.

The behavior of single-threaded TCP measurements varies for different access links. We compare the passive throughput for two BISMark users with the *same ISP and service plan* (AT&T; 3 Mbits/s down, 384 Kbits/s up) who live only a few blocks apart. Figure 5 shows that User 2 consistently sees nearly 20% more throughput—much closer to the advertised rate—than User 1. One possible explanation for this difference is the loss rates experienced by these two users; User 1 suffers more loss than User 2

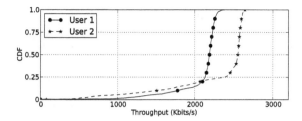

Figure 5: Users with the same service plan but different loss profiles see different performance. User 1 has higher loss and sees lower performance. (BISMark)

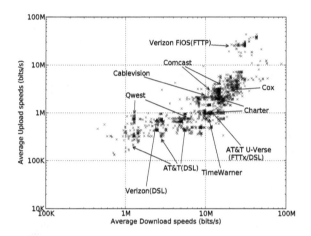

Figure 6: Average download rate versus the average upload rate obtained by individual users in the dataset. (SamKnows)

(0.78% vs. 0.20% on the downlink and 0.24% vs. 0.06% on the uplink). Their baseline latencies differ by about 16 milliseconds (8 ms vs. 24 ms). We confirmed from the respective modem portals that User 1 has interleaving disabled and that User 2 has interleaving enabled. Therefore, User 2 is able to recover from noisy access links that cause packet corruption or losses. Single-threaded downloads are more adversely affected by the loss rate on the access link than multi-threaded downloads (even when accounting for cross traffic); reducing the loss rate (e.g., by interleaving) can improve the performance of a single-threaded download. For the rest of the paper, we consider only multi-threaded TCP throughput.

Takeaway: Different throughput measurement techniques capture different aspects of throughput. A single-threaded TCP session is sensitive to packet loss. Augmenting this measurement with passive usage measurements improves its accuracy. Multi-threaded TCP and the UDP capacity measurements measure the access link capacity more accurately and are more robust to loss.

5.2 Throughput Performance

We investigate the throughput obtained by users in the Sam-Knows deployment. We then study the consistency of their performance.

What performance do users achieve? Figure 6 shows the average download and upload speeds obtained by each user in the Sam-Knows dataset. Each point in the scatter plot shows the average performance obtained by a single user in the deployment. Clusters of points in the plot reveal common service plans of different ISPs,

identified in the plot by labels. In general, these results agree with the findings from both Netalyzr [24] and Dischinger et al. [12], although our dataset also contains Verizon FiOS (FTTP) users that clearly stand out, as well as other more recent service offerings (e.g., AT&T U-Verse). Although the statistics do show some noticeable clusters around various service plans, there appears to be considerable variation even within a single service plan. We seek to understand and characterize both the performance variations and their causes. We do not yet have access to the service plan information of each user, so we focus on how and why throughput performance varies, rather than whether the measured values actually match the rate corresponding to the service plan.

Do users achieve consistent performance? We analyze how consistently users in the SamKnows achieve their peak performance deployment using the $Avg/P95$ metric, which we define as the ratio of the average upload or download throughput obtained by a user to the 95th percentile of the upload or download throughput value obtained by the same user. Higher values for these ratios reflect that users' upload and download rates that are more consistently close to the highest rates that they achieve; lower values indicate that user performance fluctuates.

Figure 7a shows the CDF of the Avg/$P95$ metric for each user; Figure 7b shows the same metric for uploads. Most users obtain throughput that is close to their 95th percentile value. Users of certain ISPs (e.g., Cox, Cablevision) experience average download throughput that is significantly less than their 95th percentile. (Both ISPs have more than 50 active users in our data set; see Table 2). Upload throughput performance is more consistent across ISPs. The big difference between download rates and upload rates for popular service plans could account for the fact that upstream rates are more consistent than downstream rates. We also studied the Median/$P95$ performance; which is similar to Avg/$P95$, and so we do not show them. Our results suggest that upload and download throughput are more consistent than they were when Dischinger et al. performed a similar study few years ago [12], especially for some cable providers.

Why is performance sometimes inconsistent? One possible explanation for inconsistent download performance is that the access link may exhibit different performance characteristics depending on time of day. Figure 8a shows the Avg/$P95$ metric across the time of day. We obtain the average measurement reported by each user at that particular time of day and normalize it with the 95th percentile value of that user over all reports. Cablevision users see, on average, a 40% drop in performance from early morning and evening time (when users are likely to be home). For Cox, this number is about 20%. As the figure shows, this effect exists for other ISPs to a lesser extent, confirming prior findings [12]. Because we do not know the service plan for each user, we cannot say whether the decrease in performance for Cox and Cablevision represents a drop below the service plans for those users (e.g., these users might see rates higher than their plan during off-peak hours). Figure 8b shows how the standard deviation of normalized throughput varies depending on the time of day. Performance variability increases for *all* ISPs during peak hours. Figure 8c shows the loss behavior for different times of day; although most ISPs do not see an increase in loss rates during peak hours, Cox does. This behavior suggests that some access ISPs may be under-provisioned; those ISPs for which users experience poor performance during peak hours may be experiencing congestion, or they may be explicitly throttling user traffic during peak hours.

Takeaway: Although there is no significant decrease in performance during peak hours, there is significant variation. A one-time

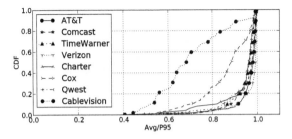

(a) Download throughput is mostly consistent, with some exceptions.

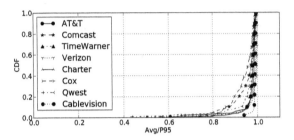

(b) Upload throughput is consistent across ISPs.

Figure 7: Consistency of throughput performance: The average throughput of each user is normalized by the 95th percentile value obtained by that user. (SamKnows)

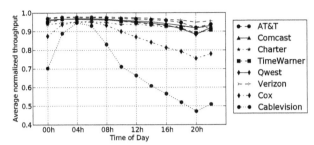

(a) The biggest difference between peak and worst performance is about 40%.

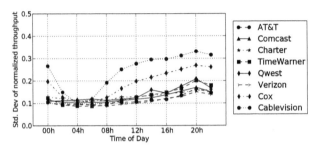

(b) The standard deviation of throughput measurements increases during peak hours, most significantly for ISPs that see lower throughputs at peak hours.

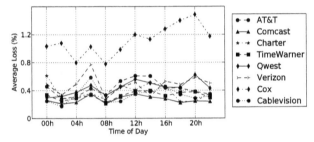

(c) Loss increases during peak hours for Cox. Other ISPs do not see this effect as much.

Figure 8: Time of day is significant: The average download throughput for Cablevision and Cox users drops significantly during the evening peak time. Throughput is also significantly more variable during peak time. (SamKnows)

"speed test" measurement taken at the wrong time could likely report misleading numbers that do not have much bearing on the long-term performance.

5.3 Effect of Traffic Shaping on Throughput

ISPs shape traffic in different ways, which makes it difficult to compare measurements across ISPs, and sometimes even across users within the same ISP. We study the effect of PowerBoost 3 across different ISPs, time, and users. We also explore how Comcast implements PowerBoost.

Which ISPs use PowerBoost, and how does it vary across ISPs? The SamKnows deployment performs throughput measurements once every two hours; each measurement lasts 30 seconds, and each report is divided into six snapshots at roughly 5-second intervals for the duration of the 30-second test (Section 4). This measurement approach allows us to see the progress of each throughput measurement over time; if PowerBoost is applied, then the throughput during the last snapshot will be less than the throughput during the first. For each report, we normalize the throughput in each period by the throughput reported for the first period. Without Power-Boost, we would expect that the normalized ratio would be close to one for all intervals. On the other hand, with PowerBoost, we expect the throughput in the last five seconds to be less than the throughput in the first five seconds (assuming that PowerBoost lasts less than 30 seconds, the duration of the test). Figure 9 shows the average progression of throughput over all users in an ISP: the average normalized throughput decreases steadily. We conclude that most cable ISPs provide some level of PowerBoost for less than 30 seconds, at a rate of about 50% more than the normal rate. Cablevision's line is flat; this suggests that either it does not provide PowerBoost, or it lasts well over 30 seconds consistently, in which case the throughput test would see only the PowerBoost effect. The

gradual decrease, rather than an abrupt decrease, could be because PowerBoost durations vary across users or that the ISP changes PowerBoost parameters based on network state. From a similar analysis for uploads (not shown), we saw that only Comcast and Cox seem to provide PowerBoost for uploads; we observed a decrease in throughput of about 20%. Dischinger *et al.* [12] also reported PowerBoost effects, and we also see that it is widespread among cable ISPs. For the DSL ISPs (not shown), the lines are flat.

Takeaway: Many cable ISPs implement PowerBoost, which could distort speedtest-like measurements. While some people may be only interested in short-term burst rates, others may be more interested in long-term rates. Any throughput benchmark should aim to characterize both burst rates and steady-state throughput rates.

Do different users see different PowerBoost effects? Using BIS-Mark, we study Comcast's use of PowerBoost in depth. According to Comcast [9], their implementation of PowerBoost provides

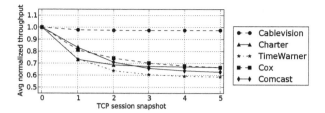

Figure 9: The average throughput obtained during the course of the measurement goes down significantly for the ISPs that enable PowerBoost. (SamKnows)

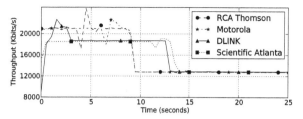

(a) PowerBoost download behavior for 4 users.

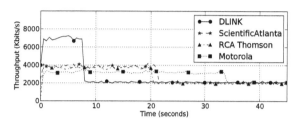

(b) PowerBoost upload behavior for 4 users.

Figure 10: The level and duration of the burstiness is different for users with different modems, suggesting different shaping mechanisms or parameters. (BISMark)

higher throughput for the first 10 MBytes of a download and the first 5 MBytes of an upload. We measure the shaped throughput for download and upload at the receiver using `tcpdump`. Because our tests are intrusive, we conducted them only a few times; however the results do not vary with choice of traffic generators or ports.

Figure 10 shows the observed throughput for four users for both download and uploads. All four users see PowerBoost effects, but, surprisingly, we see many different profiles even in such a small subset of users. Figure 10a shows download profiles for each user (identified by the modem they use; while the modem doesn't have an effect on burst rates, it does have an effect on buffering latencies as we show in Section 6). The user with a D-LINK modem sees a peak rate of about 21 Mbits/s for 3 seconds, 18.5 Mbits/s for a further ten seconds, and a steady-state rate of 12.5 Mbits/s. The Motorola user sees a peak rate of 21 Mbits/s for about 8 seconds. The PowerBoost technology [10] provides token buckets working on both packet and data rates; it also allows for dynamic bucket sizes. The D-LINK profile can be modeled as a cascaded filter with rates of 18.5 Mbits/s and 12.5 Mbits/s, and buffer sizes of 10MBytes and 1Mbyte respectively, with the line capacity being 21Mbits/s. We see varying profiles for uploads as well, although we only see evidence of single token buckets (Figure 10b). The D-LINK user sees about 7 Mbits/s for 8 seconds, Scientific Atlanta and Thomson users see about 4 Mbits/s for 20 seconds, and the Motorola user sees about 3.5Mbits/s for nearly 35 seconds. Because our results do not vary with respect to the packet size, we conclude that Comcast does not currently apply buckets based on packet rates.

Takeaway: Depending on how throughput measurements are conducted and how long they last, the measurements across users may vary considerably. Specifically, any speedtest measurement that lasts less than 35 seconds will *only* capture the effects of PowerBoost in some cases, and any short-term throughput measurement may be biased by PowerBoost rates.

6. UNDERSTANDING LATENCY

We show how latency can drastically affect performance, even on ISP service plans with high throughput. We then study how various factors ranging from the user's modem to ISP traffic shaping policies can affect latency.

6.1 How (and Why) to Measure Latency

Latency affects the performance that users experience. It not only affects the throughput that users achieve, it also affects *perceived* performance: on a connection with high latency, various operations ranging from resolving DNS queries to rendering content may simply take longer.

Although latency appears to be a straightforward characteristic to measure, arriving at the appropriate metric is a subtle challenge because our goal is to isolate the performance of the access link

from the performance of the end-to-end path. End-to-end latency between endpoints is a common metric in network measurement, but it reflects the delay that a user experiences along a wide-area path. We use two metrics that are more appropriate for access networks.

The first metric is the *last-mile latency*, which is the latency to the first hop inside the ISP's network. This metric captures the latency of the access link, which could affect gaming or short downloads. We measure last-mile latency in both of our deployments. As we show in this section, the last-mile latency is often a dominant factor in determining the end-user performance. The second metric we define is *latency under load*, which is the latency that a user experiences during an upload or download (*i.e.*, when the link is saturated in either direction). For BISMark, we measure the last-mile latency under load; on the SamKnows platform, we measure latency under load on the end-to-end path.

To investigate the effect of latency on performance, we measured how the time to download popular Web pages varies for users with different throughput and latency. Figure 11 shows the download time for `www.facebook.com` and how it varies by both the user's throughput and baseline last-mile latency. Figure 11a plots the 95th percentile of each user's downstream throughput versus the average time it takes to download all objects from `www.facebook.com`. The average size of the download is 125 KByte. As expected, the download times decrease as throughput increases; interestingly, there is negligible improvement beyond a rate of 6 Mbits/s. Figure 11b plots download time against the baseline latency for all users whose downstream throughput (95th percentile) exceeds 6 Mbits/s. Minimum download times increase by about 50% when baseline latencies increase from 10 ms to 40 ms. The fact that this effect is so pronounced, even for small downloads, underscores importance of baseline latency.

We investigate the effects of cable and DSL access-link technologies on last-mile latency, packet loss, and jitter. We also explore how different DSL modem configurations, such as whether the modem has interleaving enabled, affects last-mile latency and loss. Finally, we study the effect of modem hardware on perfor-

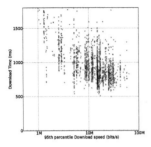
(a) Fetch time stabilizes above 6Mbits/s.

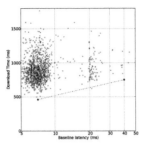
(b) Latency affects fetch times.

Figure 11: Effect of downstream throughput and baseline latency on fetch time from `facebook.com`. (SamKnows)

mance. Specifically, we investigate how oversized modem buffers that has recently received much attention from both operators and users [16]—affects interactivity and throughput.

ISP	Last mile latency		Loss	
	Average	Std. dev	Avg(%)	Std. dev
AT&T	25.23	33.47	0.48%	3.59
Comcast	10.36	14.49	0.27%	2.79
TimeWarner	11.87	25.18	0.33%	3.09
Verizon	12.41	20.60	0.51%	4.07
Charter	11.87	11.80	0.43%	3.29
Cox	13.88	28.02	1.11%	8.35
Qwest	39.42	32.27	0.33%	3.38
Cablevision	10.21	7.52	0.33%	3.14

Table 4: Last-mile latency and variation is significant; Variation in loss is high, suggesting bursty losses. (SamKnows)

ISP	Downstream		Upstream	
	Average	Std. dev	Average	Std. dev
AT&T	1.85	7.63	3.02	12.92
Comcast	1.15	6.37	3.24	6.60
TimeWarner	1.68	3.35	3.67	12.52
Verizon	1.71	5.01	1.97	4.82
Charter	1.17	1.66	2.66	7.48
Cox	1.18	1.89	4.27	7.10
Qwest	3.04	12.59	2.16	10.95
Cablevision	1.69	3.52	2.25	1.18

Table 5: Downstream jitter is quite low, however upstream jitter is significant. (SamKnows)

6.2 Last-Mile Latency

We obtain the last-mile latency by running `traceroute` to a wide-area destination and extracting the first IP address along the path that is not a NAT address. Note that we are measuring the latency to the first network-layer hop, which may not in fact be the DSLAM or the CMTS, since some ISPs have layer-two DSLAMs that are not visible in traceroute. This should not be problematic, since the latency between hops inside an ISP is typically much smaller than the last-mile latency.

How does access technology affect last-mile latency? Table 4 shows the average last-mile latency experienced by users in the ISPs included in our study. Last-mile latency is generally quite high, varying from about 10 ms to nearly 40 ms (ranging from $40 - -80\%$ of the end-to-end path latency). Variance is also high. One might expect that variance would be lower for DSL, since it is not a shared medium like cable. Surprisingly, the opposite is true: AT&T and Verizon have high variance compared to the mean. Qwest also has high variance, though it is a smaller fraction of the mean. To understand this variance, we divide different users in each ISP according to their baseline latency, as shown in Figure 12 Most users of cable ISPs are in the 0–10 ms interval. On the other hand, a significant proportion of DSL users have baseline last-mile latencies more than 20 ms, with some users seeing last-mile latencies as high as 50 to 60 ms. Based on discussions with network operators, we believe DSL companies may be enabling an interleaved local loop for these users.

Table 4 shows loss rates for users across ISPs. The average loss is small, but variance is high for all ISPs, suggesting bursty loss. Jitter has similar characteristics, as shown in Table 5; while the average jitter is low, the variation is high, especially on the upstream, also suggesting burstiness.

How does interleaving affect last-mile latency? ISPs enable interleaving for three main reasons: (1) the user is far from the DSLAM; (2) the user has a poor quality link to the DSLAM; or (3) the user subscribes to "triple play" services. An interleaved last-mile data path increases robustness to line noise at the cost of higher latency. The cost varies between two to four times the baseline latency.

Takeaway: Cable providers in general have lower last-mile latency and jitter. Baseline latencies for DSL users may vary significantly based on physical factors such as distance to the DSLAM or line quality.

6.3 Latency Under Load

We turn our attention to a problem that has gathered much interest recently because of its performance implications: modem buffering under load conditions [16]. We confirm that excessive buffering is a widespread problem afflicting most ISPs (and the equipment they provide). We profile different modems to study how the problem affects each of them. We also see the possible effect of ISP policies such as active queue and buffer management on latency and loss. Finally we explore exploiting shaping mechanisms such as PowerBoost might help mitigate the problem.

Problem: Oversized buffers. Buffers on DSL and cable modems are too large. Buffers do perform an important role: they absorb bursty traffic and enable smooth outflow at the configured rate [24]. Buffering only affects latency during periods when the access link is loaded, but during such periods, packets can see substantial delays as they queue up in the buffer. The capacity of the uplink also affects the latency introduced by buffering. Given a fixed buffer size, queuing delay will be lower for access links with higher capacities because the draining rate for such buffers is higher. We study the effect of buffering on access links by measuring latency when the access link is saturated, under the assumption that the last-mile is the bottleneck. We also present a simple model for modem buffering and use emulation to verify its accuracy.

How widespread are oversized buffers? Figure 13 shows the average ratios of latency under load to baseline latency for each user across different ISPs for the SamKnows data. The histogram shows the latencies when the uplink and the downlink are saturated separately. This figure confirms that oversized buffers affect users across all ISPs, though in differing intensity. The factor of increase when the uplink is saturated is much higher than when the downlink

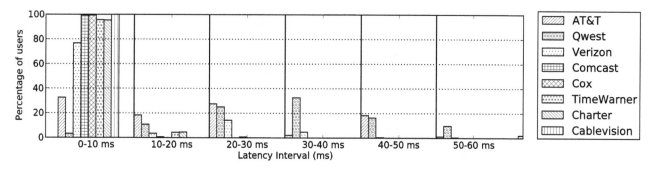

Figure 12: The baseline last mile latency for each user is computed as the 10th percentile of the last mile latency. Most users see latencies less than 10 ms, but there are a significant number of users with the last mile latency greater than 10 ms. (SamKnows)

is saturated. One plausible explanation is that the downlink usually has more capacity than the uplink, so buffering on the ISP side is lower. The home network (at least 10 Mbits/s) is also probably better provisioned than the downlink, so there is minimal buffering in the modem for downstream traffic. The high variability in the latency under load can be partly explained by the variety in service plans; for instance, AT&T offers plans ranging from 768 Kbits/s to 6 Mbits/s for DSL and up to 18 Mbits/s for UVerse and from 128 Kbits/s to more than 1 Mbit/s for upstream. In contrast, Comcast offers fewer service plans, which makes it easier to design a device that works well for all service plans.

How does modem buffering affect latency under load? To study the effects of modem buffers on latency under load, we conduct tests on AT&T and Comcast modems using BISMark. We ran tests on the best AT&T DSL (6 Mbits/s down; 512 Kbits/s up) and Comcast (12.5 Mbits/s down; 2 Mbits/s up) plans. We perform the fol-

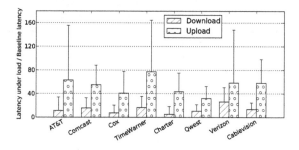

Figure 13: Latency under load: the factor by which baseline latency goes up when the upstream or the downstream is busy. The high ratios translate to significant real latencies, often in the order of seconds. (SamKnows)

lowing experiment: we start ICMP `ping` (at the rate of 10 pkts/s for Comcast and 2 pkts/s for AT&T as some modems were blocking higher rates) to the last mile hop. After 30 seconds, we flood the uplink (at 1 Mbits/s for AT&T and at 10 Mbits/s for Comcast using `iperf` UDP). After 60 seconds, we stop `iperf`, but let `ping` continue for another 30 seconds. The `ping` measurements 30 seconds on either side of the `iperf` test establishes baseline latency. The Motorola and the 2Wire modems were brand new, while the Westell modem is about 5 years old, and was in place at the home where we conducted the experiment. We also saw the same Westell modem in two other homes in the BISMark deployment.

Figure 14a shows the latency under load for the three modems. In all cases, the latency increases dramatically at the start of the

flooding and plateaus when the buffer is saturated. The delay experienced by packets at this stage indicates the size of the buffer, since we know the uplink draining rate. Surprisingly, we see more than an order of magnitude of difference between modems. The 2Wire modem has the lowest worst case latency, of 800 ms. Motorola's is about 1600 ms, while the Westell has a worst case latency of more than 10 seconds. Because modems are usually the same across service plans, we expect that this problem may be even worse for users with slower plans.

To model the effects of modem buffering, we emulated this setup in Emulab [13] with a 2 end-host, 1-router graph. We configured a token bucket filter using `tc`. We compute the buffer size to be: 512 Kbits/s × max(latency of modem), which yields a size of 640 Kbytes for Westell, 100 Kbytes for Motorola, and 55 Kbytes for 2Wire. This simple setup almost perfectly captures the latency profile that the actual modems exhibit. Figure 14b shows the emulated latencies. Interestingly, we observed little difference in throughput for the three buffer sizes. We also emulated other buffer sizes. For a 512 Kbits/s uplink, we observed that the modem buffers exceeding 20 KBytes do little for throughput, but cause a linear increase in latency under load. Thus, the buffer sizes in all three modems are too large for the uplink.

How does PowerBoost traffic shaping affect latency under load? To understand latency under load for cable users, we study the Comcast users from BISMark. All of the modems we study have buffers that induce less than one second of delay, but these users see surprising latency under load profiles due to traffic shaping. Figures 15a and 15b show the latency under load for two Comcast users. The other two Comcast users (with the Scientific Atlanta and the Motorola modems) had latency profiles similar to the user with the Thomson modem, so we do not show them. The difference in the two latency profiles is interesting; the D-LINK user sees a jump in latency when the flooding begins and about 8 seconds later, *another increase* in latency. The Thomson user sees an initial increase in latency when flooding starts but then a *decrease* in latency after about 20 seconds. The first effect is consistent with buffering and PowerBoost. Packets see lower latencies during PowerBoost because, for a fixed buffer, the latency is inversely proportional to the draining rate. The increase in latency due to PowerBoost (from 200 ms to 700 ms) is proportional to the decrease in the draining rate (from 7 Mbits/s to 2 Mbits/s, as shown in Figure 10b). The decrease in latency for the Thomson user cannot be explained in the same way. Figure 15 shows the average loss rates alongside the latencies for the two users; interestingly for the user with the Thomson modem, the loss rate is low for about 20 seconds after the link is saturated, but there is a sharp hike in loss corresponding

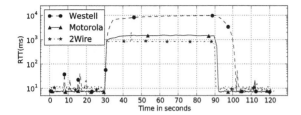

(a) *Empirical measurements* of modem buffering. Different modems have different buffer sizes, leading to wide disparities in observed latencies when the upstream link is busy. (BISMark)

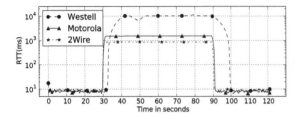

(b) *Emulated modems* with token bucket filters. We see similar latency progression. Emulated buffer sizes have minimal effect on throughput.

Figure 14: Buffering in AT&T modems. There is little benefit to the buffering seen in most modems.

to the drop in latency. This behavior may correspond to dynamic buffer sizing, as discussed in Section 5.3.

Can data transfer be modified to improve latency under load? We explore whether a user can modify their data transfer behavior so that large "bulk" flows and delay-sensitive flows can co-exist without interfering with one another. We compare the impact of a 50 MByte download on a G.711 VoIP call in three different conditions: (1) not applying any traffic control, (2) intermittent traffic at capacity on 10.8 seconds ON and 5.3 seconds OFF cycle, and (3) shaping using the WonderShaper [36] approach. Figure 16 shows the result of this experiment. In (1), the transfer takes 25.3 seconds; however, just after the PowerBoost period, the VoIP call starts suffering high latency and loss until the end of the transfer. In (2), traffic is sent in pulses, and the download takes 26.9 seconds. In (3), traffic is sent at just under the long term rate and the download takes 32.2 seconds. Both (2) and (3) do not increase latency significantly, this is because they do not deplete the tokens at any time, and therefore cause no queuing. In approach (2), the ON/OFF periods can be configured depending on the token bucket parameters,[3] and the size of the file to be transferred. Both approaches achieve similar long-term rates but yield significant latency benefit. The drawback is that any approach that exploits this behavior would need to know the shaping parameters.

Takeaway: Modem buffers are too large. Even the smallest buffers we see induce nearly one-second latency under load for AT&T and 300 ms for Comcast. Buffering is detrimental to both interactivity and throughput. Modifying data transfer behavior using short bursts or tools like WonderShaper might help mitigate the problem in the short term.

---

[3]If ρ_r is the rate we want to reserve for real-time applications, and ρ_t the token rate, the condition to be satisfied is: $(\rho_b + \rho_r - \rho_t) \times \tau_{on} \leq \tau_{off} \times (\rho_t - \rho_r)$, where ρ_b is the sending rate during the pulse, and τ_{on} and τ_{off} are the ON and the OFF times, respectively.

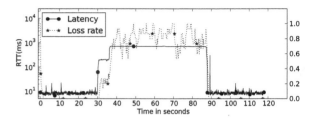

(a) Comcast user with D-LINK modem.

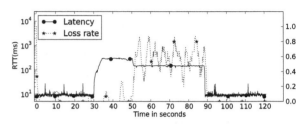

(b) Comcast user with RCA Thomson modem.

Figure 15: Possible effect of active buffer management: Loss rates increase when the latency drops. (BISMark)

7. LESSONS LEARNED

We conclude with some high-level lessons and suggestions for future research directions. One significant takeaway for users, policymakers, ISPs, and researchers is that *continual measurements, directly from home network gateways are crucial for understanding the details of home access network performance.* Existing "speed test" downloads and end-to-end latency measurements do not often reflect access network performance over an extended period of time, and they neglect various confounding factors on the host and within the home. Our ability to execute measurements directly, both from a small set of gateways where we can control the network conditions and measurements (BISMark) and a larger, more representative set of gateways across the United States (SamKnows), yields several lessons:

Lesson 1 (One Measurement Does Not Fit All) *Different ISPs use different policies and traffic shaping behaviors that make it difficult to compare measurements across ISPs.*

There is no single number that characterizes performance, or even throughput. Certain ISP practices such as PowerBoost can distort benchmarking measurements; ISPs might even design their networks so that widely used performance tests yield good performance. Developing a benchmarking suite for ISP performance that users can understand (*e.g.,* in terms of the applications they use) is critical; the measurements we develop in this paper may be a good starting point for that. Along these lines, more work is needed to understand the performance of specific applications, such as how video streaming performance compares across ISPs. The NetFlix study on ISP streaming performance [30] is a good start, but more such performance benchmarks are needed.

Lesson 2 (One ISP Does Not Fit All) *There is no "best" ISP for all users. Different users may prefer different ISPs depending on their usage profiles and how those ISPs perform along performance dimensions that matter to them.*

Different ISPs may be "better" along different performance dimen-

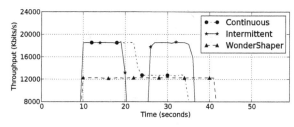

(a) Throughput.

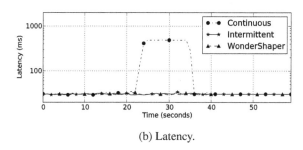

(b) Latency.

Figure 16: It is possible to maintain low latency by modifying data transfer behavior. (BISMark)

sions, and the service plan that a user buys is only part of the picture. For example, we saw that, above a certain throughput, latency is the dominant factor in determining Web page loading time. Similarly, a gamer might be interested in low latency or jitter, while an avid file swapper may be more interested in high throughput. An imminent technical and usability challenge is to summarize access network performance data so that users can make informed choices about the service plans that are most appropriate for them (akin to a "performance nutrition label" [2]). Our recent work proposes some first steps in this direction [34].

Lesson 3 (Home Network Equipment Matters) *A user's home network infrastructure can significantly affect performance.*

Modems can introduce latency variations that are orders of magnitude more than the variations introduced by the ISP. Other effects inside the home that we have not yet studied, such as the wireless network, may also ultimately affect the user's experience. More research is needed to understand the characteristics of traffic inside the home and how it affects performance.

Acknowledgments

We thank the participants in the SamKnows and BISMark studies, and to Walter Johnston at the FCC for help and access to the data from the SamKnows study. We are grateful to Dave Täht for his continuing support of the BISMark platform. We also thank Sam Burnett and Hyojoon Kim for constructive comments on paper drafts. This project is supported by the the National Science Foundation through awards CNS-1059350, CNS-0643974, a generous Google Focus Grant, the European Community's Seventh Framework Programme (FP7/2007-2013) no. 258378 (FIGARO), and the ANR project C'MON.

REFERENCES

[1] Grenouille. http://www.grenouille.com/.
[2] Does broadband need its own government nutrition label? http://arstechnica.com/tech-policy/news/2009/10/ does-broadband-needs-its-own-government-nutrition-label.ars, Oct. 2010. Ars Technica.
[3] C. Bastian, T. Klieber, J. Livingood, J. Mills, and R. Woundy. *Comcast's protocol-agnostisc congestion management system*. Internet Engineering Task Force, Dec. 2010. RFC 6057.
[4] G. Bernardi and M. K. Marina. Bsense: a system for enabling automated broadband census: short paper. In *Proc. of the 4th ACM Workshop on Networked Systems for Developing Regions (NSDR '10), June 2010.*, 2010.
[5] K. Bode. FCC: One Million Speedtests and Counting. http://www.dslreports.com/shownews/ FCC-One-Million-Speedtests-And-Counting-109440, July 2010.
[6] A. Botta, A. Dainotti and A. Pescapé. Multi-protocol and multi-platform traffic generation and measurement. IEEE INFOCOM, Demo session, May 2007.
[7] R. Carlson. Network Diagnostic Tool. http://e2epi.internet2.edu/ndt/.
[8] K. Cho, K. Fukuda, H. Esaki, and A. Kato. The impact and implications of the growth in residential user-to-user traffic. In *ACM SIGCOMM 2006*, 2006.
[9] Comcast FAQ. http://customer.comcast.com/Pages/FAQViewer.aspx? Guid=024f23d4-c316-4a58-89f6-f5f3f5dbdcf6, Oct. 2007.
[10] R. Compton, C.L. Woundy and J. Leddy. Method and packet-level device for traffic regulation in a data network. U.S. Patent 7,289,447 B2, Oct. 2007.
[11] D. Croce, T. En-Najjary, G. Urvoy-Keller, and E. Biersack. Capacity Estimation of ADSL links. In *CoNEXT*, 2008.
[12] M. Dischinger, A. Haeberlen, K. P. Gummadi, and S. Saroiu. Characterizing residential broadband networks. In *Proc. ACM SIGCOMM Internet Measurement Conference*, San Diego, CA, USA, Oct. 2007.
[13] Emulab. http://www.emulab.net/, 2006.
[14] M. M. et al. Network Path and Application Diagnosis. http://www.psc.edu/networking/projects/pathdiag/.
[15] National Broadband Plan. http://www.broadband.gov/.
[16] J. Gettys. Bufferbloat. http://www.bufferbloat.net/.
[17] Glasnost: Bringing Transparency to the Internet. http://broadband.mpi-sws.mpg.de/transparency.
[18] D. Han, A. Agarwala, D. G. Andersen, M. Kaminsky, K. Papagiannaki, and S. Seshan. Mark-and-sweep: Getting the inside scoop on neighborhood networks. In *Proc. Internet Measurement Conference*, Vouliagmeni, Greece, Oct. 2008.
[19] Internet World Stats. http://www.internetworldstats.com/dsl.htm.
[20] Asymmetric Digital Subscriber Line Transceivers. ITU-T G.992.1, 1999.
[21] Asymmetric Digital Subscriber Line (ADSL) Transceivers - Extended Bandwidth ADSL2 (ADSL2Plus). ITU-T G.992.5, 2003.
[22] Data-over-cable service interface specifications: Radio-frequency interface specification. ITU-T J.112, 2004.
[23] C. R. S. Jr. and G. F. Riley. Neti@home: A distributed approach to collecting end-to-end network performance measurements. In *the Passive and Active Measurement Conference (PAM)*, 2004.
[24] C. Kreibich, N. Weaver, B. Nechaev, and V. Paxson. Netalyzr: Illuminating the edge network. In *Proc. Internet Measurement Conference*, Melbourne, Australia, Nov. 2010.
[25] K. Lakshminarayanan and V. N. Padmanabhan. Some findings on the network performance of broadband hosts. In *Proceedings of the 3rd ACM SIGCOMM conference on Internet measurement*, IMC '03, pages 45–50, New York, NY, USA, 2003. ACM.
[26] G. Maier, A. Feldmann, V. Paxson, and M. Allman. On dominant characteristics of residential broadband internet traffic. In *ACM Internet Measurement Conference*, 2009.
[27] Measurement Lab. http://measurementlab.net.
[28] A. Morton and B. Claise. *Packet Delay Variation Applicability Statement*. Internet Engineering Task Force, Mar. 2009. RFC 5481.
[29] Netalyzr. http://netalyzr.icsi.berkeley.edu/.
[30] NetFlix Performance on Top ISP Networks. http://techblog.netflix.com/2011/01/ netflix-performance-on-top-isp-networks.html, Jan. 2011.
[31] NOX Box. http://noxrepo.org/manual/noxbox.html.
[32] ShaperProbe. http://www.cc.gatech.edu/~partha/diffprobe/shaperprobe.html.
[33] M. Siekkinen, D. Collange, G. Urvoy-Keller, and E. Biersack. Performance limitations of ADSL users: A case study. In *the Passive and Active Measurement Conference (PAM)*, 2007.
[34] S. Sundaresan, N. Feamster, R. Teixeira, A. Tang, K. Edwards, R. Grinter, M. Chetty, and W. de Donato. Helping users shop for isps with internet nutrition labels. In *ACM SIGCOMM Workshop on Home Networks*, 2011.
[35] D. Vorhaus. A New Way to Measure Broadband in America. http://blog.broadband.gov/?entryId=359987, Apr. 2010.
[36] WonderShaper. http://lartc.org/wondershaper/, 2002.

Random Access Heterogeneous MIMO Networks

Kate Ching-Ju Lin
Academia Sinica
katelin@citi.sinica.edu.tw

Shyamnath Gollakota
MIT
gshyam@csail.mit.edu

Dina Katabi
MIT
dk@mit.edu

ABSTRACT

This paper presents the design and implementation of 802.11n$^+$, a fully distributed random access protocol for MIMO networks. 802.11n$^+$ allows nodes that differ in the number of antennas to contend not just for time, but also for the degrees of freedom provided by multiple antennas. We show that even when the medium is already occupied by some nodes, nodes with more antennas can transmit concurrently without harming the ongoing transmissions. Furthermore, such nodes can contend for the medium in a fully distributed way. Our testbed evaluation shows that even for a small network with three competing node pairs, the resulting system about doubles the average network throughput. It also maintains the random access nature of today's 802.11n networks.

Categories and Subject Descriptors C.2.2 [**Computer Systems Organization**]: Computer-Communications Networks

General Terms Algorithms, Design, Performance, Theory

Keywords MIMO, Interference Alignment, Interference Nulling

1. INTRODUCTION

Multi-Input Multi-Output (MIMO) technology [6] is emerging as the default choice for wireless networks. The wireless industry is continuously pushing toward increasing the number of antennas per device. While 3×3 MIMO nodes represented the state of the art in 2009, 4×4 MIMO nodes were introduced on the market in 2010 [1]. Simultaneously, there is a proliferation of wireless devices with diverse form factors. These range from large devices, like desktops and laptops, to small devices, like temperature or light sensors, and a whole range of devices in between like smartphones and tablets. The physical size of these devices intrinsically limits the maximum number of antennas that they can support, and their differing capabilities and costs mean that they will naturally have different MIMO processing power. The combination of these two trends - a growth in the maximum number of antennas per device, and an increase in device diversity - means that future wireless networks will be populated by heterogeneous APs and clients supporting different numbers of antennas. For example, today a home

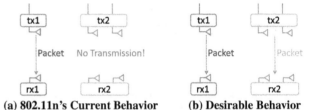

(a) **802.11n's Current Behavior**   (b) **Desirable Behavior**

Figure 1—Currently a 2×2 MIMO abstains from transmission in the presence of a single-antenna transmission as shown in (a), while it should be able to concurrently exchange a packet as shown in (b).

user may have a 2- or 3-antenna AP but one of her neighbors may have a single-antenna AP on the same channel. Even inside a single house, users can connect their HD TV to their video server using high-end 4×4 MIMO 802.11n devices [1], while continuing to use their 2- or 3- antenna wireless AP for the remaining devices in the home, while the home sensor network uses a single-antenna home controller that communicates with the sensors and actuators.

The existing design of 802.11n however uses the blueprint of traditional single-antenna networks, and as a result cannot efficiently support such heterogeneous MIMO networks. Consider for example the scenario in Fig. 1(a) where a single-antenna pair is exchanging a packet. A nearby 2×2 802.11n system will abstain from concurrently transmitting because it senses the medium as occupied. However, this is wasteful because a 2×2 MIMO pair can support two concurrent transmissions, and hence should be able to transmit a packet concurrently with the ongoing single-antenna transmission.

The objective of this paper is to develop a medium access protocol that enables as many concurrent transmissions as permitted by the MIMO transmitter with the maximum number of antennas. We would like for our design however to maintain the fully distributed random access nature of today's 802.11n. A distributed protocol will enable MIMO LANs to continue to support bursty traffic and have independent different networks share the same medium without explicit coordination.

We refer to our design as 802.11n$^+$ or simply n$^+$. It allows nodes to contend not just for time, but also for the degrees of freedom (i.e., concurrent transmissions) enabled by multiple antennas. Specifically, like 802.11, in n$^+$, nodes who have traffic contend for the medium using carrier sense. Unlike 802.11, however, which stops contending after a node wins the contention, in n$^+$, nodes with more antennas than the contention winner continue to carrier sense and contend for the medium. Once a node wins this secondary contention, it can transmit concurrently with the ongoing transmission. The process continues until the number of used degrees of freedom equals the maximum number of antennas on any MIMO transmitter with traffic demands.

To realize the above design, n$^+$ has to address two main challenges:

(a) How do nodes carrier sense in the presence of ongoing transmissions? n$^+$ extends carrier sense to work in the presence of ongoing transmissions. Specifically, since nodes with multiple antennas receive the signal in a multi-dimensional space, they can project on a space orthogonal to the ongoing transmission(s). This orthogonal space does not contain any interference from the ongoing signal(s). Nodes can hence contend for concurrent transmissions in this orthogonal space as if they were contending for an idle medium. We name this technique *multi-dimensional carrier sense*.

(b) How can a node transmit without interfering with ongoing transmissions? We use interference nulling [32] to zero out the signal at the receivers of the ongoing transmissions. For example, in the scenario in Fig. 1(b), the two-antenna transmitter, tx2, nulls its signal at rx1 and hence does not interfere with the ongoing transmission. Interference nulling on its own, however, does not allow nodes to achieve all the degrees of freedom available in the system. Specifically, consider a scenario where two transmitter-receiver pairs are already occupying the medium. tx1-rx1 is a single-antenna pair, while tx2-rx2 is a two-antenna MIMO system. Say that a 3-antenna transmitter-receiver pair, tx3-rx3, wants to transmit concurrently. Then tx3 will need to zero out its signal on three antennas, the antenna on rx1 and the two antennas on rx2. Since nulling requires a node to give up one of its antennas for every receive antenna where it wants to null its signal [7], it consumes the three antennas at tx3, leaving it no antenna to transmit to its own receiver. We will show in §2 that by using a combination of interference nulling and interference alignment, tx3 can indeed transmit concurrently with tx1 and tx2 and use all the available degrees of freedom, without interfering with the ongoing transmissions.

Our work is mostly related to recent empirical work on MIMO systems including [7, 31, 13]. n$^+$ is motivated by this work and builds on it. Past systems however require concurrent transmissions to be coordinated by a single node. Concurrent transmissions have to be pre-coded together at a single transmitter (as in beamforming [7]) or decoded together at a single receiver (as in SAM [31]), or the transmitters or the receivers have to be controlled over the Ethernet by a single master node (as in IAC [13]). In contrast, n$^+$ is a fully distributed medium access protocol where nodes with any number of antennas can transmit and receive concurrent packets without a centralized coordinator.

We have built a prototype of n$^+$ using the USRP2 radio platform and evaluated it over a 10 MHz channel. Our implementation uses an OFDM PHY-layer and supports the various modulations (BPSK, 4-64 QAM) and coding options used in 802.11. It also addresses practical issues like multipath and frequency and time synchronization.

Our evaluation considers three contending pairs of nodes that differ in the number of antennas, and have a maximum of three antennas at any node. We compare the throughput that these pairs obtain in today's 802.11n network with the throughput they obtain with n$^+$. Our findings are as follows:

- Though the maximum number of antennas in our testbed is relatively small – 3 antennas – n$^+$ nearly doubles the network throughput.
- Nodes that have more antennas experience a higher throughput gain with n$^+$. In our experiments, the average throughput gain of a 2×2 MIMO system is 1.5x and of a 3×3 MIMO system is 3.5x.

- In practice, interference nulling and alignment do not completely eliminate interference. They leave a residual error of 0.8 dB for nulling and 1.3 dB for alignment. This leads to a small average throughput reduction of 3% for single-antenna nodes. We believe this reduction is reasonable in comparison to the overall throughput gain.

Contributions: The paper presents a primitive that enables MIMO nodes to join ongoing transmissions without interfering with them. It then builds on this primitive to deliver a random access protocol where MIMO nodes contend for both time and degrees of freedom using multi-dimensional carrier sense, without any form of centralized coordination. Finally, it implements its design and evaluates it in a wireless testbed.

2. ILLUSTRATIVE EXAMPLES

Consider the network shown in Fig. 2, where tx1 wants to communicate with rx1, and tx2 wants to communicate with rx2. How do we design a MAC protocol that allows this network to use all available degrees of freedom?

Exploiting Interference Nulling: A key challenge we need to address is: how does tx2 transmit without interfering with the ongoing reception at rx1? To do this, we leverage a MIMO technique called interference nulling, i.e., the signal transmitted by tx2 creates a null at the antenna of rx1, as shown in Fig. 2. Say h_{ij} is the channel coefficients from the ith antenna at the transmitters to the jth antenna at the receivers. To create a null at rx1, for every symbol q transmitted, tx2 transmits q on the first antenna and αq on the second antenna. The signals from tx2's antennas combine on the medium, and rx1 receives $(h_{21} + \alpha h_{31})q$. By picking α to be $-\frac{h_{21}}{h_{31}}$, tx2 can ensure that the signals from its two antennas cancel each other at rx1, and hence do not create any interference at rx1.

Note that this nulling at rx1 does not prevent tx2 from delivering its packet to its own receiver rx2. In particular, say tx1 is transmitting the symbol p and tx2 is transmitting the symbol q. Intuitively, since rx2 has two antennas, the received signal lives in a 2-dimensional space. In this space, the two symbols p and q lie along two different directions, as shown in the bottom graph in Fig. 2. Thus, to decode its desired symbol, q, rx2 projects on a direction orthogonal to p, which is interference-free from the symbol, p.

The above intuition can be formalized as follows: rx2 receives the following signals on its two antennas:

$$y_2 = h_{12}p + (h_{22} + h_{32}\alpha)q \tag{1a}$$
$$y_3 = h_{13}p + (h_{23} + h_{33}\alpha)q \tag{1b}$$

Say rx2 knows the channel terms from tx1 and tx2 (which it can compute from the preamble in their packets), it can solve the above two equations for the two unknowns p and q, and obtain its desired symbol, q.[1]

The above discussion assumes that tx2 knows the channel from itself to rx1 so that it can compute the value of α. The naive way to do this would have tx2 and rx1 coordinate and exchange channel information before tx1 starts transmitting. Such a solution, however, requires tx1-rx1 to worry about which node pair may later join their transmission and coordinate with that pair to prevent interference. Fortunately, this is not necessary. To enable channel estimation in a distributed way, n$^+$ makes a communicating pair precede its data exchange with a light-weight handshake, operationally similar to

---

[1] Note that rx2 does not need to know α because tx2 sends its preamble while nulling at rx1, which means that rx2 computes the effective channels $(h_{22} + h_{32}\alpha)$ and $(h_{23} + h_{33}\alpha)$ directly from tx2's preamble.

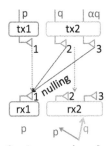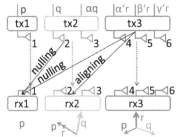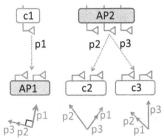

Figure 2—A scenario where a 2-antenna pair, tx2-rx2, can utilize the second degree of freedom to transmit concurrently with tx1-rx1. The bottom vector graph shows the decoding space at rx2.

Figure 3—A scenario where the tx2-rx2 and tx3-rx3 links can utilize the second and third degrees of freedom to transmit concurrently with tx1-rx1. The bottom vector graphs show the decoding space at multi-antenna receivers, rx2 and rx3.

Figure 4—A scenario where senders and receivers have a different number of antennas: The bottom vector graphs show the decoding space at each of the three receivers AP1, clients c2 and c3. For each 2-antenna receiver, the two unwanted packets have to be aligned.

RTS-CTS but significantly more efficient (as described in §3.5). A transmitter that wants to join the ongoing transmissions exploits the handshake messages of prior contention winners to compute the reverse channels from itself to receivers of ongoing transmissions, using channel reciprocity. Reciprocity states that electromagnetic waves travel forward and backward the same way, and hence the channel observed between any two antennas should be the same regardless of the direction [15]. Reciprocity has also been confirmed empirically in [4, 13, 14].[2]

Exploiting Interference Alignment: The above MAC protocol allows the network to achieve two degrees of freedom at any point in time, which is the maximum degrees of freedom available in this network. The design we described so far, however, does not trivially extend to more than two transmission pairs. To understand why, let us add a third communicating pair, tx3-rx3, to the above network as shown in Fig. 3. The new pair is a 3-antenna system and hence can support three degrees of freedom. This means that tx3 should be able to transmit an additional packet to rx3, concurrent to the two transmissions of tx1-rx1 and tx2-rx2. The transmitter tx3, however, is in a more challenging position, because it should interfere with neither rx1 nor rx2. So how does tx3 achieve this goal?

Say that tx3 uses only interference nulling as in the previous case. To ensure that it does not create any interference at rx1 and rx2, tx3 needs to null its signal at three antennas, the antenna at rx1 and the two antennas at rx2. Unfortunately, nulling at three antennas will prevent tx3 from sending any data. To see why this is the case, let tx3 transmit its packet r on its three antennas, after multiplying it with α', β' and γ', respectively. Let h_{ij} be the channel coefficients between antennas $i = 4, 5, 6$ on tx3 and antennas $j = 1, 2, 3$ on rx1 and rx2 where tx3 needs to perform nulling. The signals from tx3's antennas combine on the medium, creating a different equation at each receive antenna. Nulling the signal at rx1's antenna and rx2's two antennas can be expressed as follows:

$$r(h_{41}\alpha' + h_{51}\beta' + h_{61}\gamma') = 0 \quad (2a)$$
$$r(h_{42}\alpha' + h_{52}\beta' + h_{62}\gamma') = 0 \quad (2b)$$
$$r(h_{43}\alpha' + h_{53}\beta' + h_{63}\gamma') = 0, \quad (2c)$$

where r is tx3's symbol and h_{ij} are the channel coefficients.

The above three equations are satisfied for any value of the transmitted symbol, r, if and only if $(\alpha', \beta', \gamma') = (0, 0, 0)$. This solution, however, is clearly unacceptable because it will prevent tx3

from transmitting any signal from any of its antennas to its receiver. Therefore, interference nulling alone is not sufficient to prevent tx3 from interfering with concurrent transmissions while delivering a packet to its receiver.

We will show that a combination of interference nulling and interference alignment achieves the goal. To eliminate interference at the single antenna at rx1, tx3 is still going to use interference nulling. This constraint requires tx3 to satisfy only one additional equation, Eq. 2a. To eliminate interference at the 2-antenna receiver rx2, tx3 is however going to use interference alignment. This constraint requires satisfying only one additional equation, as opposed to the two equations required for nulling at the two antennas at rx2. Specifically, tx3 can align its signal at rx2 with the interference that rx2 already sees from the first transmitter, tx1, as shown in the bottom graph (below rx2) in Fig. 3. Then, rx2 only sees two signals, the symbol q transmitted by tx2 and the combined interference from tx1 and tx3, because the two signals from tx1 and tx3 are now aligned and look like coming from a single interferer. Specifically, the two equations received by rx2 are:

$$y_2 = h_{12}p + (h_{22} + \alpha h_{32})q + (\alpha' h_{42} + \beta' h_{52} + \gamma' h_{62})r \quad (3a)$$
$$y_3 = h_{13}p + (h_{23} + \alpha h_{33})q + (\alpha' h_{43} + \beta' h_{53} + \gamma' h_{63})r, \quad (3b)$$

and hence aligning the interference from tx1 and tx3 requires tx3 to satisfy the following equation:

$$\frac{(\alpha' h_{42} + \beta' h_{52} + \gamma' h_{62})}{h_{12}} = \frac{(\alpha' h_{43} + \beta' h_{53} + \gamma' h_{63})}{h_{13}} = L, \quad (4)$$

where L is any constant. If tx3 chooses the parameters α', β', and γ' to satisfy Eq. 4, Eqs. 3a and 3b can be rewritten as:

$$y_2 = h_{12}(p + Lr) + (h_{22} + \alpha h_{32})q$$
$$y_3 = h_{13}(p + Lr) + (h_{23} + \alpha h_{33})q.$$

The receiver, rx2, now has two independent equations in two unknowns, $(p + Lr)$ and q, and hence can decode its desired symbol q. (Note that rx2 cannot decode p and r separately but this is fine because it does not want these symbols.)

Thus, in total, tx3 has to satisfy two equations to ensure that it does not interfere with the ongoing transmissions: the nulling equation (Eq. 2a) at rx1 and the alignment equation (Eq. 4) at rx2. Then, tx3 can use the third degree of freedom to transmit to its own receiver.

We can continue adding additional transmitter-receiver pairs as long as they have additional antennas. By nulling at the first receiver and aligning at all the remaining receivers, each additional transmitter can transmit to its own receiver while ensuring no interference to ongoing transmissions.

---

[2] Applying reciprocity in a practical system requires taking into account the additional channel imposed by the hardware, which however is constant and hence can be computed offline [4, 14, 13]. Our implementation uses the method used in [4] to calibrate the hardware.

Generalizing to Different Numbers of Antennas at the Transmitter and Receiver: Finally, n^+ generalizes to scenarios where a transmitter and its receivers have different numbers of antennas. Consider, for example, the scenario in Fig. 4 where a 2-antenna access point, AP1, has a single-antenna client, c1, and a 3-antenna AP, AP2, has two 2-antenna clients, c2 and c3. Say that the single-antenna client is transmitting to its AP. In today's networks, this will prevent any other node from transmitting concurrently. However, with n^+, the 3-antenna AP can transmit concurrently two packets, one to each of its clients, i.e., p_2 to client c2 and p_3 to client c3 as shown in Fig. 4.

So how does the 3-antenna AP transmit these concurrent packets while protecting the ongoing reception at the 2-antenna AP? To protect the ongoing reception, the 3-antenna AP must ensure that both of its transmitted packets (p_2 and p_3) are received at the 2-antenna AP along a direction orthogonal to the signal of interest to that AP, i.e., the signal from c1 (called p_1 in Fig. 4). This allows the 2-antenna AP to continue to receive its client's signal without interference, as shown in the bottom graphs (below AP1) in Fig. 4. The 3-antenna AP also needs to ensure that its transmission to one client does not create interference at the other client. Since each of its clients has two antennas and hence receives signals in a 2-dimensional space, this goal can be achieved if the 3-antenna AP ensures that each client receives the unwanted signal aligned along the interference it already sees from the ongoing transmission of the single-antenna client, (i.e., along p_1), as shown in the bottom graphs in Fig. 4.

3. n^+'S DESIGN

n^+ is a random access protocol that enables nodes with any number of antennas to contend for both time and degrees of freedom. It also has bitrate selection built-in.

3.1 Overview

Similar to 802.11, in n^+, nodes listen on the wireless medium using carrier sense. If the channel is unoccupied, the nodes contend for the medium using 802.11's contention window and random backoff [5]. The node pair that wins the contention exchanges a light-weight RTS-CTS. The RTS-CTS allows nodes interested in contending for the remaining degrees of freedom to compute the channels to the receivers who won earlier contentions, in order to perform the required alignment or nulling. The RTS-CTS also includes the number of antennas that will be used in the transmission. After the RTS-CTS, the node pair proceeds to exchange the data packet followed by the ACK.

Unlike 802.11, n^+ allows nodes who have more antennas than the current number of used degrees of freedom to contend for concurrent transmissions. The number of used degrees of freedom is equal to the number of ongoing transmissions, which a node can learn from prior RTS-CTS messages. As nodes contend for the unused degrees of freedom, they again use a contention window and random backoff similar to 802.11. However, while carrier sensing, nodes need to ignore the signals from past contention winners. To do so, n^+ leverages that multi-antenna nodes receive the signal in a multi-dimensional space and, thus, can project on a space orthogonal to ongoing transmissions from past contention winners. Due to orthogonality, this space does not contain any interference from the ongoing transmissions, and thus, allows the nodes to perform carrier sense as if there were no ongoing transmissions. The process continues until all the degrees of freedom in the network have been used.

To illustrate how this design works, let us consider again the network in Fig. 3 which has three transmitter-receiver pairs. Each of the three transmitters carrier senses the medium and contends for the channel. Depending on who wins the contention, four different scenarios are possible. Fig. 5(a) shows the scenario where the 3-antenna pair, tx3-rx3, wins the contention and ends up using all three degrees of freedom. In this case, tx3 and rx3 exchange RTS-CTS, informing other nodes that they will use three degrees of freedom in their transmission. Since the other two transmitters have fewer than three antennas, they cannot support any additional degrees of freedom, and hence stop contending until the end of this transmission.

In the second scenario shown in Fig. 5(b), the two-antenna pair, tx2-rx2, wins the contention and uses two degrees of freedom. The first transmitter, tx1, notices that the channel is occupied and drops out of contention since it has only a single antenna. The third transmitter, tx3, on the other hand, has three antennas and therefore can deliver an additional packet. So it contends for the medium and wins the third degree of freedom. Since tx3 must not interfere with the ongoing transmission of tx2-rx2, it nulls its signal on the two antennas at rx2. This consumes two antennas at tx3, leaving it one antenna to transmit one stream to its own receiver, rx3.

The third scenario in Fig. 5(c) occurs when tx1-rx1 wins the contention. Since only a single degree of freedom is used, both tx2 and tx3 contend for the remaining two degrees of freedom. If tx3 wins, it needs to use one of its antennas to null its signal at rx1, which leaves it two antennas to send two concurrent streams to its own receiver, rx3, as in Fig. 5(c).

The last scenario shown in Fig. 5(d) occurs when the nodes win contention in the following order: tx1-rx1, tx2-rx2, tx3-rx3. It is similar to the example described in §2, where each of the pairs ends up transmitting a single packet.

Finally, a few additional points are worth noting:

- n^+ makes a node that joins ongoing transmissions end its transmission at about the same time as prior transmissions, which it learns from their light-weight RTS-CTS exchange. This design choice forces the medium to become idle at the end of each joint transmission, and hence prevents starving nodes that have only one antenna. Requiring all nodes to end their concurrent transmissions with the first contention winner means that nodes may need to fragment or aggregate packets. Various link layer protocols require packet fragmentation or aggregation. For example, 802.11n requires the driver to be able to aggregate multiple packets to create an aggregate frame [6], whereas old ATM networks require packet fragmentation [17]. n^+ leverages these methods.
- Instead of sending the ACKs one after the other, the receivers transmit their ACKs concurrently. These concurrent transmissions are analogous to the concurrent transmissions of the data packets, and can be achieved using a combination of nulling and alignment (see §3.3).

The above provides an overview of n^+. The next few sections explain how we realize this design. We first develop the details of the algorithms and the system architecture, and leave addressing the practical issues until §4.

3.2 Carrier Sense Despite Ongoing Transmissions

In n^+, nodes use 802.11's carrier sense to contend for additional concurrent transmissions, even after some nodes have already won earlier contention rounds and started their transmissions. For this approach to work effectively, carrier sense should be oblivious to the ongoing transmissions. n^+ satisfies this constraint as follows: In n^+, a node that is interested in sensing the medium first computes the channel for the ongoing transmissions (which it does using the

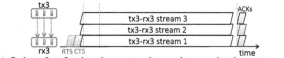

(a) Only tx3-rx3 wins the contention and transmits three streams.

(b) Both tx2-rx2 and tx3-rx3 win. tx2-rx2 transmits two streams, and tx3-rx3 transmits one stream using the third degree of freedom.

(c) tx1-rx1 and tx3-rx3 win. tx1-rx1 transmits one stream, and tx3-rx3 transmits two streams using the remaining degrees of freedom.

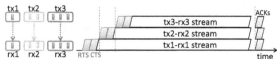

(d) All links win the contention, each of them transmits one stream using one degree of freedom.

Figure 5—Medium access for the three link scenario

preamble in their RTS messages). These channels define a subspace where the ongoing transmissions live. If the node projects on a space orthogonal to this subspace (using standard algebra [23]), the node will see no signal from ongoing transmissions, and hence can perform standard 802.11 carrier sense.

We name this approach multi-dimensional carrier sense. To illustrate how it works, consider again the example in Fig. 3, where we have three pairs of nodes: a single-antenna pair tx1-rx1, a 2-antenna pair tx2-rx2, and a 3-antenna pair tx3-rx3. Let us focus on the 3-antenna transmitter, tx3, as it senses the medium.

Say the single-antenna transmitter, tx1, wins the first round of contention and is already transmitting some signal p, hence using the first degree of freedom. Say tx3 wants to contend for the second degree of freedom. tx3 should sense the medium, but ignore the signal p from tx1. To do so, tx3 first computes the channel from tx1 to its three antennas using the preamble in tx1's RTS. We refer to these channels as h_1, h_2, and h_3. Since tx3 has three antennas, the received signal lies in a 3-dimensional space and can be written as:

$$\vec{y} = \begin{pmatrix} y_1 \\ y_2 \\ y_3 \end{pmatrix} = \begin{pmatrix} h_1 \\ h_2 \\ h_3 \end{pmatrix} p = \vec{h}_{tx1}p,$$

where $\vec{h}_{tx1}$ is the channel vector $[h_1, h_2, h_3]^T$. Thus, for different symbols p transmitted by tx1, the received signal at tx3 changes over time, but merely moves along the one-dimensional vector $\vec{h}_{tx1}$, shown in Fig. 6(a). Therefore, by projecting on the 2-dimensional subspace orthogonal to this vector, (the red plane in Fig. 6(a)), tx3 eliminates interference from tx1 and can carrier sense for the remaining degrees of freedom. Since a 2-dimensional subspace is defined by any two distinct vectors in it, tx3 can project on the subspace orthogonal to p by simply picking any two vectors in the subspace, e.g., $\vec{w}_1$ and $\vec{w}_2$, and projecting on them to get:

$$\vec{y}' = \begin{pmatrix} \vec{w}_1 \cdot \vec{y} \\ \vec{w}_2 \cdot \vec{y} \end{pmatrix},$$

where $\cdot$ denotes the dot product operation. If tx1's signal, p, is the only ongoing transmission, then $\vec{y} = \vec{h}_{tx1}p$, and by definition of orthogonality, $\vec{y}' = \vec{0}$. Thus, if tx3 performs carrier sense by sensing the signal after projection, $\vec{y}'$, it sees that the second degree of freedom is still unoccupied.

Now, say transmitter tx2 wins the second degree of freedom and starts transmitting its signal, q. Let h'_1, h'_2, and h'_3 be the channels from tx2 to tx3.[3] The three antennas at tx3 now receive the follow-

---

[3]For ease of expression we lump the channels from tx2's two antennas into one term, i.e., $h'_1 = (h_{22} + h_{32}\alpha)$ in Eqs. 1a and 1b.

(a) One transmission on the medium

(b) Two transmissions on the medium

Figure 6—The received signal space as perceived by a 3-antenna node.

ing combined signal from tx1 and tx2.

$$\vec{y} = \begin{pmatrix} y_1 \\ y_2 \\ y_3 \end{pmatrix} = \begin{pmatrix} h_1 \\ h_2 \\ h_3 \end{pmatrix} p + \begin{pmatrix} h'_1 \\ h'_2 \\ h'_3 \end{pmatrix} q = \vec{h}_{tx1}p + \vec{h}_{tx2}q,$$

where $\vec{h}_{tx2}$ is the channel vector for the second transmission. However, since tx3 is carrier sensing in the 2-dimensional space orthogonal to tx1's transmission, it computes:

$$\vec{y}' = \begin{pmatrix} \vec{w}_1 \cdot \vec{y} \\ \vec{w}_2 \cdot \vec{y} \end{pmatrix} = \begin{pmatrix} \vec{w}_1 \cdot \vec{h}_{tx1}p + \vec{w}_1 \cdot \vec{h}_{tx2}q \\ \vec{w}_2 \cdot \vec{h}_{tx1}p + \vec{w}_2 \cdot \vec{h}_{tx2}q \end{pmatrix} = \begin{pmatrix} \vec{w}_1 \cdot \vec{h}_{tx2} \\ \vec{w}_2 \cdot \vec{h}_{tx2} \end{pmatrix} q.$$

Thus, as opposed to the scenario in which only tx1 was transmitting and tx3 saw that the second degree of freedom is unused, tx3 sees that now $\vec{y}' \neq \vec{0}$, and hence the second degree of freedom is occupied.

Further, since the signal $\vec{y}'$ has no interference from tx1, and is equal to tx2's transmission, q, with a channel multiplier, tx3 can decode q using standard decoders. This allows tx3 to carrier sense not only by checking the power on the medium but also by cross correlating the preamble as in today's 802.11.

tx3 can use the same process to carrier sense and contend for the third degree of freedom. The only difference is that now it has to project on a space orthogonal to both tx1's and tx2's signals, as shown in Fig. 6(b). Thus, to summarize, for any number of concurrent transmissions the signal lives in a hyper-plane of the same dimension as the number of used degrees of freedom. To sense the medium, the node projects on the space orthogonal to the ongoing signals' hyper-plane, and performs carrier sense in this space.

3.3 Transmitting with Concurrent Transmissions

In n+, nodes that want to transmit in the presence of ongoing transmissions have to ensure that they do not interfere with those who already occupy the medium. This applies to the transmission of RTS, CTS, data, and ACK packets. In all of these cases, the approach is the same and relies on a combination of interference

Term	Definition
K	number of ongoing streams/transmissions
M	number of antennas on a transmitter tx
N	number of antennas on a receiver rx
m	the maximum number of streams tx can transmit without interfering with the ongoing streams
n	the number of streams destined to rx, i.e., its **wanted streams**
$U, U^\perp$	the matrices defining the space of unwanted streams at rx and its orthogonal space
$\mathcal{R}, \mathcal{R}'$	receivers of ongoing streams and receivers of tx respectively
$\vec{v}_i$	the pre-coding vector of stream i

Table 1—Terms used in the description of the protocol.

nulling and alignment. For ease of exposition, we will describe it for the case of data packets.

(a) Definitions: Consider a scenario where there are K concurrent streams (i.e., K transmissions) on the medium. Let tx be an M-antenna transmitter that wants to transmit in the presence of the ongoing streams. Let m be the maximum number of concurrent streams that tx can transmit without interfering with the ongoing streams. For each stream that tx transmits, s_i, tx sends $\vec{v}_i s_i$, where $\vec{v}_i$ is an M-element *pre-coding* vector and each element v_{ij} describes the scaling factor for stream s_i transmitted from antenna j. Thus, the signal that tx transmits can be expressed as $\sum_1^m s_i \vec{v}_i$.

Let $\mathcal{R}$ be the set of receivers of the ongoing streams, and $\mathcal{R}'$ be the set of receivers of tx. Each receiver, rx, is interested in decoding the streams destined to itself, which we call the *wanted streams*. An N-antenna receiver, rx, that wants $n \leq N$ streams receives signals in an N-dimensional space, a subset of which is wanted and the rest is *the unwanted space*. We will use the matrix U to represent the unwanted space and $U^\perp$ to represent the space orthogonal to U. Table 1 summarizes our definitions.

(b) Protocol: The goal of our protocol is to compute the pre-coding vectors such that tx delivers its streams to its receivers without interfering with any of the ongoing streams. Our protocol proceeds in three steps as follows:

Step 1: Deciding whether to align or null. How does the transmitter, tx, decide whether to perform interference alignment or nulling at a particular receiver? The answer is simple. If the receiver has an unwanted space (i.e., $N > n$), it does not hurt to align the new interference in the unwanted space. However, if the wanted streams occupy the whole N-dimensional space in which rx receives signals, the transmitter has to null its interference at the receiver. Thus:

CLAIM 3.1 (WHERE TO NULL AND WHERE TO ALIGN).
To avoid interfering with the n wanted streams at an N-antenna receiver, rx, the transmitter nulls all of its streams at rx if $n = N$, and aligns its streams in rx's unwanted space, otherwise.

Step 2: Computing the maximum number of concurrent streams that tx can transmit. The number of concurrent streams that tx can transmit is given by the following claim:

CLAIM 3.2 (NUMBER OF TRANSMITTED STREAMS). *A transmitter with M antennas can transmit as many as $m = M - K$ different streams concurrently without interfering with the ongoing K streams.*

The proof to this claim leverages the following two results:

CLAIM 3.3 (SATISFYING THE NULLING CONSTRAINT). *A transmitter can null its signal at an N-antenna receiver with n wanted streams (where $n = N$) by satisfying:*

$$\forall i = 1, \ldots, m, \qquad H_{N \times M} \vec{v}_i = \vec{0}_{n \times 1}, \qquad (5)$$

where $H_{N \times M}$ is the channel matrix from tx to rx.

CLAIM 3.4 (SATISFYING THE ALIGNMENT CONSTRAINT).
A transmitter can align its signal in the unwanted space, U, of an N-antenna receiver with n wanted streams by satisfying:

$$\forall i = 1, \ldots, m, \qquad U_{n \times N}^\perp H_{N \times M} \vec{v}_i = \vec{0}_{n \times 1}, \qquad (6)$$

where $H_{N \times M}$ is the channel matrix from tx to rx.

The proofs of Claims 3.3 and 3.4 follow directly from the definitions of nulling and alignment. These two claims articulate the linear equations that tx's pre-coding vectors must satisfy. Eqs. 5 and 6 show that, independent of nulling or alignment, a receiver $rx_j \in \mathcal{R}$ that wants n_j streams results in a matrix equation of n_j rows. Hence, tx's pre-coding vectors have to satisfy a total number of linear equations equal to $\sum n_j$, where the sum is taken over the receivers in $\mathcal{R}$. This sum is simply the total number of ongoing streams K. Further, these equations are independent because of the independence of the channel matrices, the H's. Given that tx has M antennas and its pre-coding vectors have to satisfy K independent linear equations, there are exactly $M - K$ linearly independent such vectors. Thus, the number of different streams that tx can send is $m = M - K$.

Step 3: Computing the pre-coding vectors. Next, tx has to compute the pre-coding vectors. If tx has a single receiver, this task is fairly simple. tx combines the various nulling and alignment equations into one matrix equation as follows:

$$[H_1^T H_2^T \ldots (U_j^\perp H_j)^T \ldots]^T \vec{v} = \vec{0},$$

where $[.]^T$ is the matrix transpose. The solutions to this equation are the basis vectors of the null space of the matrix. Since the matrix dimensions are $K \times M$, there are $M - K$ such vectors.

If tx however has multiple receivers, as in Fig. 4, it needs to ensure that a stream that it sends to one receiver does not interfere with a stream that it sends to another receiver. For example, in Fig. 4, AP2 had to align the stream sent to each client in the unwanted space of the other client. This process however is similar to aligning at the receivers of ongoing streams expressed in claim 3.4. Specifically, say stream i is destined to receiver $rx \in \mathcal{R}'$. For every receiver $rx_j \in \mathcal{R}'$, different from rx, and whose unwanted space is U_j', tx needs to ensure that $U_j'^\perp H_j' \vec{v}_i = \vec{0}$. Note that constraints for nulling or aligning at the receivers of ongoing streams are shared among all of tx's streams, whereas the constraints for nulling/aligning at tx's other receivers differ across tx's streams depending on the receiver of each stream. Combining all these constraints, tx can compute its pre-coding vectors as follows:

CLAIM 3.5 (COMPUTING THE CODING VECTORS). *Let $U_{n \times N}^\perp$ be the space orthogonal to the unwanted space at an N-antenna receiver, rx. For a receiver where the unwanted space is null, i.e., $n = N$, $U^\perp$ becomes the identity matrix, I. An M-antenna transmitter that wants to transmit m streams to receivers in $\mathcal{R}'$, while avoiding interference with receivers in $\mathcal{R}$, has to pick its coding vectors to satisfy:*

$$\begin{pmatrix} U_1^\perp H_1 \\ \vdots \\ U_{|\mathcal{R}|}^\perp H_{|\mathcal{R}|} \\ -- -- -- \\ U_1'^\perp H_1' \\ \vdots \\ U_{|\mathcal{R}'|}'^\perp H_{|\mathcal{R}'|}' \end{pmatrix}_{M \times M} [\vec{v}_1 \ldots \vec{v}_m]_{M \times m} = \begin{pmatrix} 0 \ldots 0 \\ \ddots \\ 0 \ldots 0 \\ -- -- \\ \\ I \end{pmatrix}_{M \times m}, \qquad (7)$$

where $|.|$ is the cardinality of the set.

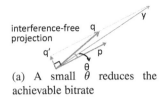
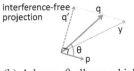

(a) A small θ reduces the achievable bitrate

(b) A larger θ allows a higher bitrate

Figure 7—The bitrate depends on the projection direction used to decode, and changes with the set of concurrent transmitters.

The proof follows directly from the discussion above. Thus, tx uses Eq. 7 to compute the pre-coding vectors. To do so, tx needs the channel matrices, H, which it obtains using reciprocity (as described in §2), and the alignment matrices, $U^\perp$, which are in the receivers' CTS messages. Once tx has the pre-coding vectors, it transmits its signal $\sum_1^m s_i \vec{v}_i$, which does not interfere with the wanted streams of any receiver.

3.4 Bitrate Selection

We discuss how a transmitter picks the best bitrate in the presence of ongoing transmissions. The challenge in this case is that bitrate selection has to be done on a per-packet basis because different packets share the channel with different sets of transmitters and hence require different bitrates. This constraint is very different from the standard assumptions made by today's bitrate selection algorithms, which use historical performance to predict the best bitrate.

We use a simple example to illustrate why the optimal bitrate of a MIMO node depends on concurrent transmitters. Consider a 2-antenna receiver that is interested in decoding a signal q in the presence of a concurrent transmission p. The 2-antenna receiver receives the combined signal y in a 2-dimensional space as shown in Fig. 7. To decode q, it uses the standard MIMO decoding algorithm called zero-forcing [32] to project the received signal y on a direction orthogonal to p. This projection removes all interference from p and yields a signal $q' = q \sin \theta$, where θ is the angle between the two signals p and q. The signal after projection is a scaled version of the original signal of interest and hence can be decoded using any standard decoder. The problem however is that, depending on the value of θ, the projected signal q' might have a large or small amplitude. A larger amplitude yields a higher SNR (signal-to-noise ratio) and hence a higher bitrate. A smaller amplitude yields a lower SNR and hence a lower bitrate.

In traditional MIMO systems where all concurrent streams/transmissions are from the same transmitter, p and q come from the same node and hence the angle between them does not change as long as the channels themselves do not change. However, when concurrent streams/transmissions are from different nodes, the angle changes from one packet to the next, as the set of concurrent transmitters changes, even if the channels themselves did not change. Thus, such a system requires a per-packet bitrate selection mechanism.

In n^+, each receiver uses the light-weight RTS of a packet to estimate the effective SNR (ESNR) after projection on the space orthogonal to ongoing transmissions. ESNR is a novel SNR-related metric that was recently proposed by Halperin et al [16]. Intuitively, the ESNR is similar to the SNR in that it captures the link quality; however, it is more useful for computing the best bitrate since it takes into account the impact of frequency selectivity. Given the ESNR, the receiver then chooses a valid bitrate using a table that maps ESNR to the optimal bitrate as shown by [16], and sends this decision back to the transmitter in the light-weight CTS message.

Note that a key characteristic of the above approach to bitrate se-

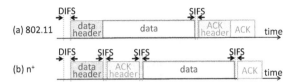

Figure 8—The Light-Weight RTS-CTS used in n^+: (a) a DATA-ACK exchange in 802.11n; (b) a DATA-ACK exchange in n^+, showing that n^+ does not send RTS-CTS, it rather separates the headers from the packets and sends all headers early on.

lection is that a node can pick the optimal bitrate at the time it wins the contention without worrying about future contention winners. This is because transmitters that join ongoing transmissions avoid creating interference to existing receivers. This means that a single-antenna transmitter that wins the first degree of freedom observes a link quality that is unaffected by concurrent transmissions, and hence can use any standard bitrate selection algorithm to decide its best bitrate. A transmitter that wins contention in the presence of ongoing transmissions needs to pick the best bitrate given the current transmissions, but needs not worry about additional concurrent transmissions.

3.5 Light-Weight RTS-CTS

Before data exchange, n^+ needs the receiver to inform its sender of the best bitrate, and broadcast the alignment space to nodes that are interested in concurrent transmissions. This objective can be achieved by preceding each packet with an RTS-CTS handshake. RTS-CTS frames, however, would introduce a relatively high overhead. n^+ adopts a different design that achieves the goal but without sending any control frames. To do so, n^+ uses a recent design called the light-weight handshake, described in [20]. A light-weight handshake is based on the observation that 802.11 channel coefficients do not change for periods shorter than multiple milliseconds [32]. Hence, one can split a packet header from the packet body, and make the sender and receiver first exchange the data and ACK headers and then exchange the data and ACK bodies without additional headers. Fig. 8 compares this process with a standard data-ack exchange in 802.11.

The empirical study in [20] shows that the impact of separating a packet's header from its body is insignificant on decodability, namely the packet loss rate increases on average by 0.0005, which is negligible for a wireless network.

The overhead of a light-weight handshake is minimal. Specifically, the overhead is two SIFS intervals, as shown in Fig. 8, and a per header checksum. In addition, each protocol may augment the standard data or ACK header with protocol-specific fields. In the case of n^+, the standard data and ACK headers already contain most of the needed information. Specifically, they contain a preamble for computing the channels, the packet length which implies its duration given a bitrate, the number of antennas, and the sender and receiver MAC addresses. In addition, n^+ augments the ACK header with the bitrate and the alignment space. Since n^+ performs nulling and alignment on each OFDM subcarrier independently, a receiver needs to send the alignment space for each of the 802.11's 64 OFDM subcarriers. n^+ leverages that the channel coefficients change slowly with OFDM subcarriers [9], and hence the alignment space in consecutive subcarriers is fairly similar. Thus, n^+ sends the alignment space U of the first OFDM subcarrier, and the alignment difference $(U_i - U_{i-1})$ for all subsequent subcarriers. Our results from a testbed of USRP2 radios in both line-of-sight and non-line-of-sight locations (see Fig. 10) show that differential encoding can on average compress the alignment space into three OFDM symbols. Since the CRC and bitrate values fit within one

OFDM symbol, the header size in n$^+$ increases by four OFDM symbols in the case of an ACK, and one OFDM symbol in the case of a data packet.

Thus, the total overhead from the light-weight handshake is 2 SIFS plus 4 OFDM symbols, which is about 4% overhead for a 1500-byte packet transmitted at 18 Mb/s. We note that these results are for USRP2 channels which have a 10 MHz width. 802.11 channels span 20 MHz and hence are likely to show more variability in the alignment space of different OFDM subcarrier. Hence, the number above should be taken as a rough estimate that indicates that the overhead is significantly smaller than the gain.

Finally, to support scenarios like the one in Fig. 4 where a single node transmits concurrently to multiple receivers, we allow a single light-weight RTS (i.e., the data header) to contain multiple receiver addresses along with the number of antennas used for each receiver. The receivers send their light-weight CTS's (i.e., their ACK headers), one after the other, in the same order they appear in the light-weight RTS.

4. PRACTICAL SYSTEM ISSUES

This section addresses a few practical issues.

Hidden Terminals and Decoding Errors: The light-weight handshake mechanism used by n$^+$ has the side-effect of providing the functionality of RTS-CTS which alleviates the hidden terminal problem. Further, in n$^+$, if a node misses or incorrectly decodes one of the RTS or CTS messages from prior contention winners or its own exchange, it does not transmit concurrently. Operationally this is similar to missing a traditional RTS or CTS.

Retransmissions: When an n$^+$ node transmits a packet, it keeps the packet in its queue until the packet is acked. If the packet is not acked, the next time the node wins the contention, it considers the packet for transmission. However, since the node always needs to finish with other concurrent transmissions, the packet may be fragmented differently or aggregated with other packets for the same receiver.

Multipath: Our discussion has been focused on narrowband channels. However, the same description can be extended to work with wideband channels which exhibit multipath effects. Specifically, such channels use OFDM, which divides the bandwidth into orthogonal subcarriers and treats each of the subcarriers as if it was an independent narrowband channel. Our model naturally fits in this context. Specifically, like today's 802.11, n$^+$ treats each OFDM subcarrier as a narrowband channel and performs nulling and alignment for each OFDM subcarrier separately.

Frequency Offset: To avoid inter-carrier interference, concurrent transmitters should have the same carrier frequency offset (CFO) with respect to every receiver. Thus, n$^+$'s senders compensate for their frequency offset in a manner similar to that used in [28, 30]. Specifically, as they decode the RTS from the transmitter that won the first degree of freedom, all concurrent transmitters naturally estimate their frequency offset with respect to the first transmitter. They compensate for that frequency offset by multiplying their digital signal samples by $e^{j2\pi \Delta ft}$ where Δf is the frequency offset and t is time since the beginning of the transmission. This process synchronizes all transmitters in the frequency domain without requiring any explicit coordination.

Time Synchronization: To prevent inter-symbol interference (ISI), concurrent transmitters have to be synchronized within a cyclic prefix of an OFDM symbol [30]. To do this without any explicit coordination, n$^+$ uses the technique in [30]. In particular, any transmitter that wants to join ongoing transmissions estimates the OFDM

symbol boundaries of ongoing transmissions and synchronizes its transmission with them. To deal with additional delays due to channel propagation and hardware turn-around time, both the cyclic prefix and the OFDM FFT size are scaled by the same factor. A longer cyclic prefix provides additional leeway for synchronization at the transmitters, as shown in [30]. Further, this scaling does not increase the overhead because the percentage of cyclic prefix to data samples stays constant.

Imperfections in Nulling and Alignment: In practice, it is impossible to get perfect nulling or alignment due to hardware non-linearities. This means that there is always some residual noise. The practical question however is: what level of residual noise is acceptable in these systems? The answer is: as long as the interference is reduced below the noise level of the hardware, the interference becomes negligible. For example, say that, in the absence of nulling or alignment, the interferer achieves a 25 dB SNR at a particular receiver. Then if nulling or alignment reduces the interference power by over 25 dB, the interference will be below the noise, and its impact is relatively negligible.

Thus, in n$^+$ we make a transmitter join an ongoing transmission only if it can reduce its interference power below the noise power. Specifically, say that interference nulling and alignment in practice can reduce the transmitter power by L dB (our empirical results show that L is about 25–27 dB). A transmitter that wants to contend for the unused degrees of freedom estimates the power of its signal at each receiver of the ongoing transmissions. The transmitter can do so because it knows the channel to these receivers and hence it knows the attenuation its signal would experience. If the resulting signal power after channel attenuation is below L dB, the transmitter contends for transmitting concurrently. On the other hand, if the signal power after channel attenuation is still higher than L, the transmitter reduces its own transmission power so that after attenuation it is less than L dB. The transmitter contends (and if it wins the contention transmits) at this lower power, which can be canceled using practical interference nulling and/or alignment.

Complexity: Components used in n$^+$ such as projections and estimation of the MIMO channel values are already used in current 802.11n for decoding point-to-point MIMO packets. Further, the computational requirement of computing the alignment and nulling spaces is similar to that of computing beamforming matrices in current 802.11n. Given the similarity between the components of n$^+$ and those used in today's hardware, we believe that n$^+$ can be built in hardware without significant additional complexity.

5. IMPLEMENTATION

We implement the design of n$^+$ using software radios. Each node in the testbed is equipped with USRP2 boards [3] and RFX2400 daughterboards, and communicates on a 10 MHz channel. Since USRP2 boards cannot support multiple daughterboards, we build a MIMO node by combining multiple USRP2's using an external clock [2]. In our evaluation, we use MIMO nodes which have up to three antennas. Further, we build on the GNURadio OFDM code base, using different 802.11 modulations (BPSK, 4QAM, 16QAM, and 64QAM) and coding rates, to implement the effective-SNR based bitrate selection algorithm.

We implement the following components of our design: carrier sense, light-weight RTS-CTS, alignment and nulling, bitrate selection, and frequency offset correction. However, due to the timing constraints imposed by GNURadio, we evaluate carrier sense independently from light-weight RTS-CTS and data transmission. Also, we do not implement ACKs. To perform nulling and alignment efficiently, concurrent transmitters have to be synchronized within a

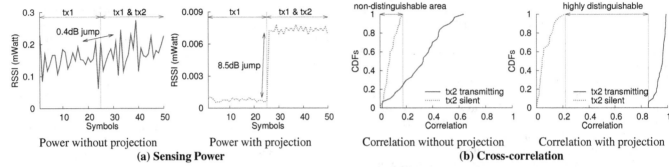

(a) Sensing Power   (b) Cross-correlation

Figure 9—Performance of Carrier Sense in the Presence of Ongoing Transmissions. The figures show that projecting on a space orthogonal to the ongoing transmissions provides a high distinguishability between a particular degree of freedom being occupied or free.

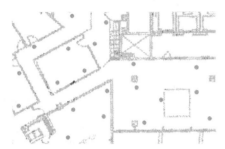

Figure 10—The testbed. Dots refer to node locations.

cyclic prefix. To achieve this goal, we exploit USRP2 timestamps to synchronize the transmitters despite the delays introduced by operating in software. We send a trigger signal and make the transmitters log the time of detecting the trigger, t_{start}. The transmitters then add a large delay, t_Δ, and set the timestamps of their concurrent transmissions to $t_{start} + t_\Delta$. The value of t_Δ depends on the maximum delay due to software processing, which in our testbed is 5 ms.

6. RESULTS

We evaluate n$^+$ in the testbed environment shown in Fig. 10, and compare it against the existing 802.11n design.

6.1 Performance of n$^+$'s Carrier Sense

We start by examining the effect of projection on the performance of carrier sense in the presence of ongoing transmissions. 802.11's carrier sense has two components which together allow it to detect if the medium is occupied [18]. The first component checks whether the power on the medium is above a threshold. The second component cross-correlates 10 short OFDM symbols in the preamble to detect the presence of other 802.11 transmissions. We investigate how projecting on a space orthogonal to the ongoing transmissions affects these components.

Experiment: We focus on the example in Fig. 3, where there are three pairs of nodes, tx1-rx1, tx2-rx2, and tx3-rx3, which have 1, 2, and 3 antennas, respectively. We make tx3 sense the medium using the projection technique described in §3.2. tx1 starts transmitting followed by tx2. The timing between tx1 and tx2 is ensured by sending a trigger, logging the USRP timestamps when the node detected the trigger, and scheduling their transmissions with respect to the timestamp of the common trigger as detailed in §5. We log the signal at tx3 and process the logs offline to measure the channels and then project tx3's received signals on the space orthogonal to tx1. We repeat the experiment for different transmission powers of tx1 and tx2 to check that carrier sense works at low powers.

Results: First, we show in Fig. 9(a) an illustrated power profile at

tx3, without and with projection. The graph on the left shows that if tx3 simply looks at the power on the medium without projecting, it might miss tx2's transmission because tx2's power is low in comparison with tx1's power. However, if tx3 projects on the space orthogonal to tx1, as in the graph on the right, it sees a relatively big jump in power when tx2 starts, and hence can more easily detect tx2's transmission.

Next, we show the result of cross correlating the preamble, without and with projection. We use the same size cross-correlation preamble as 802.11. We evaluate the system's ability to sense tx2's transmission in the presence of tx1's transmission. In this experiment, we focus on low SNR scenarios (SNR < 3 dB) because sensing becomes harder when the sensed signal from tx2 has a low SNR.

Fig. 9(b) plots the CDFs of the cross correlation values, without and with projection, both for the case of when tx2 is silent and transmitting. The figure shows that projecting on an orthogonal space (the graph on the right) provides a high distinguishability between the medium being unoccupied and occupied. This is because, with projection, the range of cross-correlation values measured when tx2 is silent is quite different from the cross-correlation values measured when tx2 is transmitting. In contrast, without projection (the graph on the left), about 18% of the cross-correlation values measured while tx2 is transmitting are not distinguishable from the case when tx2 is silent.

6.2 Performance of Nulling and Alignment

While in theory nulling and alignment can eliminate interference of unwanted transmissions, in practice, system noise and hardware nonlinearities lead to residual errors. Thus, we examine the accuracy of nulling and alignment in practice.

Experiment: To evaluate nulling, we use the scenario in Fig. 2, where a single-antenna pair tx1-rx1 and a 2-antenna pair tx2-rx2 transmit concurrently. The 2-antenna pair, tx2-rx2, nulls its signal at rx1 to avoid interfering with tx1's transmission. We randomly assign the four nodes, tx1, rx1, tx2, and rx2, to the marked locations in Fig. 10, and run the experiment in three phases: First, we make the link tx1-rx1 transmit alone to measure the SNR of the wanted traffic in the absence of the unwanted traffic. Second, we make the link tx2-rx1 transmit alone to measure the SNR of the unwanted traffic at rx1 in the absence of nulling. Third, we make tx1 and tx2 transmit concurrently and have tx2 null its signal at rx1. We measure the SNR of the wanted stream at rx1 after nulling, and compare it with its SNR in the absence of the unwanted stream. We repeat the experiment with different random locations in the testbed.

To evaluate alignment, we use the scenario in Fig. 3, i.e., we add a 3-antenna pair, tx3-rx3, to the two pairs, tx1-rx1 and tx2-rx2, used in the nulling experiment. As described in §2, the 3-antenna

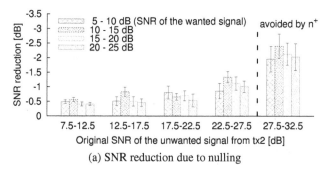

(a) SNR reduction due to nulling

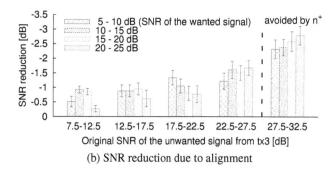

(b) SNR reduction due to alignment

Figure 11—Performance of Nulling and Alignment. The SNR loss of the wanted stream as a function of the original SNR of the unwanted streams in the absence of nulling or alignment. The figure shows that if the unwanted stream had a high SNR before nulling/alignment, it causes in a higher SNR loss for the wanted stream after nulling/alignment. Thus, n^+ allows unwanted streams to transmit concurrently only if their original SNR is below 27 dB, which results in an average SNR loss of 0.8 dB for nulling and 1.3 dB for alignment.

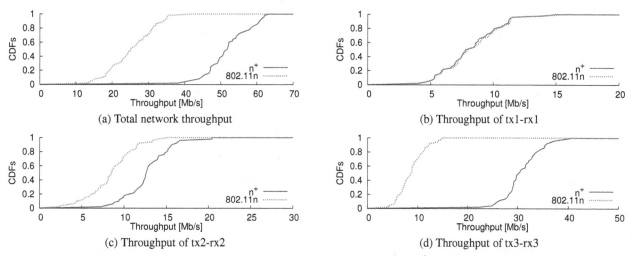

(a) Total network throughput

(b) Throughput of tx1-rx1

(c) Throughput of tx2-rx2

(d) Throughput of tx3-rx3

Figure 12—Throughput Comparison. The figure plots the throughput obtained under n^+ and the existing 802.11n design for the scenario in Fig. 3, where tx1-rx1 is a single-antenna node pair, tx2-rx2 is a 2-antenna node pair, and tx3-rx3 is a 3-antenna node pair.

pair, tx3-rx3, aligns its signal at rx2 along with the interference from tx1's transmission. Unlike the nulling experiment, the alignment experiment focuses on rx2, where the alignment is happening. Like the nulling experiment, however, it has three phases: First, tx1 and tx2 transmit concurrently, while tx3 stays silent to allow us to measure the SNR of the wanted stream at rx2, in the absence of interference from tx3. Second, tx3 transmits to rx2 alone to measure the SNR of the unwanted traffic in the absence of alignment. Last, all three transmitters transmit concurrently, and tx3 aligns its signal with that of tx1, as described in §2. We measure the difference in the SNR of rx2's wanted stream without interference and with interference alignment. We repeat the experiment with different random assignment of nodes to locations in Fig. 10.

Results: Fig. 11 plots the difference in the SNR of the wanted stream due to the presence of the unwanted stream, after nulling and alignment. The SNR difference is plotted as a function of the SNR of the unwanted (i.e., interfering) stream. Different bars refer to different SNRs of the wanted stream. The figure reveals four main points.

- When the power of the unwanted stream without nulling or alignment is in the range $[7.5, 32.5]$ dB, nulling and alignment reduce the impact of interference on the wanted signal to $[0.5, 3]$ dB.
- The residual interference after nulling or alignment depends on the original SNR of the unwanted signal before nulling or alignment. Thus, n^+ takes this issue into account, and forces a node

that wants to join ongoing transmissions to lower its interference power below a threshold $L = 27$ dB, as marked in the figure.

- Given n^+'s threshold, the average interference power after nulling is 0.8 dB, and after alignment is 1.3 dB.
- Nulling has a lower residual error than alignment. This is because nulling requires estimating only the channel from the interfering transmitter to the receiver. Alignment, on the other hand, also requires estimating the unwanted subspace at the receiver. Since the latter estimation adds additional noise, alignment is less accurate than nulling.

6.3 Throughput Comparison

Next, we investigate the impact of nulling and alignment on throughput. We also compare the throughput obtained with n^+ to that obtained with the existing 802.11n.

Experiment: Again, we consider the scenario in Fig. 3, which has three node pairs: tx1-rx1, tx2-rx2, and tx3-rx3, which have 1, 2, and 3 antennas respectively. Each run consists of a different assignment of nodes to locations in Fig. 10. The choice of which nodes win the contention is done by randomly picking winners. For 802.11n, an M-antenna node that wins the contention transmits an 1500 byte packet to its receiver using M concurrent streams. Similarly, for n^+, an M-antenna node that wins the first contention transmits an 1500 byte packet using M streams. Latter contention winners in n^+ end their transmissions at the same time as the first contention winner.

For both 802.11n and n^+, the bitrate is chosen according to the

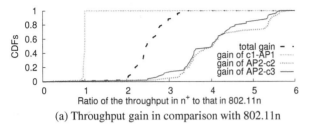 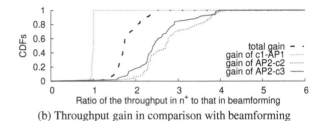

(a) Throughput gain in comparison with 802.11n (b) Throughput gain in comparison with beamforming

Figure 13—Throughput gain. For the scenario in Fig. 4 where the transmitter and receiver have a different number of antennas, n^+ provides an average network throughput improvement of 2.4x over 802.11n and 1.8x over beamforming.

algorithm in [16], which maps the effective SNR to the optimal bitrate. In n^+ each node picks its bitrate at the time of joining the concurrent transmission, independently of later contention outcomes. To achieve this behavior with GNURadios, the RTS-CTS messages are sent in a staggered fashion. For example, if the three pairs are each transmitting one stream, then tx1 first transmits its RTS message alone which is used by rx1 to compute its bitrate. Next, tx2 sends its RTS message in the presence of tx1's transmission, which rx2 uses to compute the bitrate for tx2. To compute the bitrate to be used by tx3, tx3 sends its RTS message in the presence of transmissions from both tx1 and tx2. Finally, tx1, tx2 and tx3 use the bitrates picked above to transmit their data packets concurrently.

Results: Fig. 12 plots the CDFs of the throughputs of each pair and the total throughput, both under n^+ and 802.11n. The CDFs are taken over different locations. They show:

- On average, the total network throughput doubles when the nodes use n^+, as opposed to current 802.11n.
- Nodes with multiple antennas achieve significant throughput gains, and the gains increase with increased number of antennas. Specifically, the 2-antenna pair experiences an average throughput gain of 1.5x, and the 3-antenna pair experiences an average throughput gain of 3.5x.
- There are three reasons for these throughput gains. First, n^+ allows the nodes to transmit three streams at any point in time, providing a multiplexing gain. Second, in 802.11n, each transmitter is given an equal chance to transmit a packet. Thus, nodes that have low throughput occupy more time on the medium than nodes with high throughput. Since single-antenna nodes typically have lower throughput as compared to multi-antenna nodes, which can transmit concurrent streams, the network throughput of existing 802.11n is bottlenecked by single-antenna nodes. In contrast, in n^+, since multi-antenna transmitters can join the ongoing transmission of single-antenna nodes, it does not matter that the single-antenna nodes take too much time on the medium. Third, allowing multiple nodes to transmit simultaneously provides a power gain [32]. In particular, the FCC limits the maximum transmission power of a single transmitter. Hence, 802.11n is limited by the amount of power on any single transmitter. In contrast, having multiple nodes transmit simultaneously (as in n^+) increases the total power on the medium, which increases the capacity of the system.
- The reduction in throughput at the single-antenna node is less than 3%. This number is fairly small because the residual interference after nulling is 0.8 dB (as shown above), which has a negligible impact on throughput.
- While the residual interference after alignment is slightly higher than nulling (1.3 dB), it does not translate to a throughput loss. This is because the 2-antenna receiver, where alignment occurs, gains more from concurrent transmissions than the small loss due to alignment errors.

6.4 Performance with a Different Number of Transmit and Receive Antennas

We check that n^+ increases the throughput even when the transmitter and receiver have a different number of antennas.

Experiment: We repeat the throughput evaluation experiment described in the last section but consider the scenario shown in Fig. 4 where a 2-antenna access point, AP1, is receiving from a single-antenna client, c1, and a 3-antenna AP, AP2, is transmitting to two 2-antenna clients. The rest of the setup mirrors that of the previous experiment. In addition to comparing the throughput of n^+ with 802.11n, we also compare it with prior work on beamforming [7] which can be applied to this scenario (but does not apply to the previous one). In particular, when the 3-antenna AP wins contention, beamforming allows it to transmit three streams concurrently, two to one client and one to the other.

Result: For space limitation we plot the CDFs of n^+'s throughput gains in comparison with 802.11n in Fig. 13(a) and beamforming [7] in Fig. 13(b), i.e., the ratio of the throughput in n^+ to that in 802.11n and beamforming, respectively. The figures show that the total network throughput increases by 2.4x and 1.8x over 802.11n and beamforming. Further, on average, the single-antenna client experiences a negligible reduction in throughput of 3.2%, whereas the other two clients experience a throughput gain of 3.5-3.6x over 802.11n and 2.5-2.6x over beamforming. As before, the large gains over 802.11n and beamforming are due to both having more concurrent transmissions and providing multi-antenna nodes more opportunities to transmit concurrently with the single-antenna transmitter. These results show that n^+ extends to scenarios where the transmitter and the receiver have a different number of antennas.

7. RELATED WORK

In the last few years, MIMO networks have attracted much attention from both the theoretical and empirical research communities. This resulted in new powerful theories including virtual MIMO and interference alignment [8, 22, 19] and led to pioneering systems that expanded and validated the theory [13, 31, 7]. Our work builds on this foundation to provide the first random access MIMO protocol where nodes contend for both degrees of freedom and medium time and pick the best bitrate for their transmissions in a fully distributed manner without a centralized coordinator.

Our work is mostly related to recent empirical work on MIMO systems [7, 31, 13]. Past systems however require concurrent transmissions to be pre-coded together at a single transmitter (as in beamforming [7]), decoded together at a single receiver (as in SAM [31]), or the transmitters or the receivers have to be controlled over the Ethernet by a single master node (as in IAC [13]). In contrast, n^+ does not require a centralized coordinator.

Our work on carrier sense in the presence of ongoing transmissions is related to packet detection in ZigZag [12] and carrier counting in SAM [31]. These schemes detect the number of concurrent transmissions using preamble correlation. In contrast, n$^+$ projects on a space orthogonal to ongoing transmissions, which cancels out the interference.

n$^+$ also builds on prior theoretical work on MIMO [29, 27]. The most relevant theoretical work to this paper is past work on multi-user MIMO, interference alignment and cognitive MIMO. Multi-user MIMO allows multiple clients to be served simultaneously by a single base station that has more antennas than any of the clients. A number of techniques, such as beamforming, dirty paper coding, linear decorrelators, and successive interference cancellation, have been proposed to achieve the capacity of both the uplink and the downlink [11, 21, 24]. More recently, work on interference alignment [8, 19, 22] has shown new capacity results for multi-user MIMO channels. Finally, theoretical work on cognitive MIMO [10, 26, 25] has advocated the use of MIMO to ensure that secondary users can coexist with the primary users, without creating interference to the primary users. These papers provide only theoretical solutions and typically target specific topologies. n$^+$ builds on this foundational work but differs from it in that it focuses on a random access protocol where nodes do not have to coordinate explicitly before they access the medium. Furthermore, n$^+$ is implemented and shown to work in actual wireless networks.

8. CONCLUSION

This paper presents n$^+$, a random access protocol for heterogeneous MIMO networks. We analytically show that n$^+$ can always use as many degrees of freedom as the transmitter with the maximum number of antennas while maintaining the random access property of 802.11. We show via a prototype implementation that n$^+$ can significantly improve the network throughput. We believe that as the diversity in the size and processing power of devices increases, n$^+$ is well positioned to exploit these differences and provide a better utilization of network resources.

Acknowledgments: We thank Nabeel Ahmed, Arthur Berger, Haitham Hassanieh, Nate Kushman, Hariharan Rahul, Lenin Ravindranath, Mythili Vutukuru, and Richard Yang for their insightful comments. This research is supported by DARPA IT-MANET, NSC and NSF.

9. REFERENCES

[1] 4x4 MIMO Technology. http://www.quantenna.com/4x4-mimo.html.

[2] ACQUITEK Inc., Fury GPS Disciplined Frequency Standard. http://www.acquitek.com/fury/.

[3] Ettus Inc., Universal Software Radio Peripheral. http://ettus.com.

[4] System Description and Operating Principles for High Throughput Enhancements to 802.11. IEEE 802.11-04/0870r, 2004.

[5] *IEEE Std 802.11-1997*, pages i –445, 1997.

[6] *IEEE Std 802.11n-2009*, pages c1 –502, 2009.

[7] E. Aryafar, N. Anand, T. Salonidis, and E. W. Knightly. Design and Experimental Evaluation of Multi-User Beamforming in Wireless LANs. In *ACM MobiCom*, 2010.

[8] V. Cadambe and S. Jafar. Interference Alignment and Degrees of Freedom of the K-User Interference Channel. *IEEE Trans. Inf. Theory*, 54(8):3425 –3441, 2008.

[9] O. Edfors, M. Sandell, J. Van de Beek, S. Wilson, and P. Borjesson. OFDM Channel Estimation by Singular Value Decomposition. *IEEE Trans. Comm.*, 46(7):931–939, 2002.

[10] S. Ganesan, M. Sellathurai, and T. Ratnarajah. Opportunistic Interference Projection in Cognitive MIMO Radio with Multiuser Diversity. In *IEEE DySPAN*, 2010.

[11] G.J.Foschini. Layered Space-Time Architecture for Wireless Communication in a Fading Environment When Using Multi-Element Antennas. In *Bell LAbs Technical Journal*, 1996.

[12] S. Gollakota and D. Katabi. Zigzag Decoding: Combating Hidden Terminals in Wireless Networks. In *ACM SIGCOMM*, 2008.

[13] S. Gollakota, S. D. Perli, and D. Katabi. Interference Alignment and Cancellation. In *ACM SIGCOMM*, 2009.

[14] M. Guillaud, D. Slock, and R. Knoop. A Practical Method For Wireless Channel Reciprocity Exploitation Through Relative Calibration. In *ISSPA*, 2005.

[15] M. Guillaud, D. Slock, and R. Knopp. A Practical Method for Wireless Channel Reciprocity Exploitation through Relative Calibration. In *Signal Processing and Its Applications*, 2005.

[16] D. Halperin, W. Hu, A. Sheth, and D. Wetherall. Predictable 802.11 Packet Delivery from Wireless Channel Measurements. In *ACM SIGCOMM*, 2010.

[17] R. Handel and M. Huber. *Integrated Broadband Networks; An Introduction to ATM-Based Networks*. Addison-Wesley Longman Publishing Co., Inc., 1991.

[18] J. Heiskala and J. Terry. *OFDM Wireless LANs: A Theoretical and Practical Guide*. Sams Indianapolis, IN, USA, 2001.

[19] S. Jafar and S. Shamai. Degrees of Freedom Region of the MIMO X Channel. *IEEE Trans. Inf. Theory*, 54(1):151–170, 2008.

[20] K. C.-J. Lin, Y. Chuang, and D. Katabi. A Light-Weight Wireless Handshake. In *MIT Tech Report, 2011*.

[21] R. Lupas and S. Verdu. Linear Multiuser Detectors for Synchronous Code-Division Multiple-Access Channels. *IEEE Trans. Inf. Theory*, 35(1):123–136, Jan. 1989.

[22] M. Maddah-Ali, A. Motahari, and A. Khandani. Communication over MIMO X Channels: Interference Alignment, Decomposition, and Performance Analysis. *IEEE Trans. Inf. Theory*, 54(8):3457–3470, 2008.

[23] C. D. Meyer. *Matrix Analysis and Applied Linear Algebra*. SIAM, 2001.

[24] M.K.Varanasi and T.Guess. Optimum Decision Feedback Multiuser Equalization and Successive Decoding Achieves the Total Capacity of the Gaussian Multiple-Access Channel. In *Proceedings of the Asilomar Conference on Signals, Systems and Computers*, 1997.

[25] B. Nosrat-Makoouei, J. Andrews, and R. Heath. User Admission in MIMO interference Alignment Networks. In *IEEE ICASSP, Prague, May 2011*.

[26] S. Perlaza, N. Fawaz, S. Lasaulce, and M. Debbah. From Spectrum Pooling to Space Pooling: Opportunistic Interference Alignment in MIMO Cognitive Networks. *IEEE Trans. Signal Process.*, 58(7):3728–3741, 2010.

[27] A. Poon, R. Brodersen, and D. Tse. Degrees of Freedom in Multiple Antenna Channels: a Signal Space Approach. *IEEE Trans. Inf. Theory*, 51(2):523–536, 2005.

[28] H. Rahul, H. Hassanieh, and D. Katabi. SourceSync: a Distributed Wireless Architecture for Exploiting Sender Diversity. In *ACM SIGCOMM*, 2010.

[29] A. Sayeed. Deconstructing Multiantenna Fading Channels. *IEEE Trans. Signal Process.*, 50(10):2563–2579, Oct. 2002.

[30] K. Tan, J. Fang, Y. Zhang, S. Chen, L. Shi, J. Zhang, and Y. Zhang. Fine-Grained Channel Access in Wireless LAN. In *ACM SIGCOMM*, 2010.

[31] K. Tan, H. Liu, J. Fang, W. Wang, J. Zhang, M. Chen, and G. M. Voelker. SAM: Enabling Practical Spatial Multiple Access in Wireless LAN. In *ACM MobiCom*, 2009.

[32] D. Tse and P. Vishwanath. *Fundamentals of Wireless Communications*. Cambridge University Press, 2005.

Strider: Automatic Rate Adaptation and Collision Handling

Aditya Gudipati, Sachin Katti
Stanford University
{adityag1,skatti}@stanford.edu

Abstract

This paper presents the design, implementation and evaluation of
Strider, a system that automatically achieves almost the optimal rate
adaptation without incurring any overhead. The key component in
Strider is a novel code that has two important properties: it is *rateless and collision-resilient*. First, in time-varying wireless channels,
Strider's rateless code allows a sender to effectively achieve almost
the optimal bitrate, without knowing how the channel state varies.
Second, Strider's collision-resilient code allows a receiver to decode
both packets from collisions, and achieves the same throughput as the
collision-free scheduler. We show via theoretical analysis that Strider
achieves Shannon capacity for Gaussian channels, and our empirical
evaluation shows that Strider outperforms SoftRate, a state of the art
rate adaptation technique by 70% in mobile scenarios and by upto
$2.8\times$ in contention scenarios.

Categories and Subject Descriptors

C.2 [**Computer Systems Organization**]: Computer-Communication
Networks

General Terms

Algorithms, Performance, Design

1. INTRODUCTION

Rate adaptation techniques face two challenging scenarios in wireless networks: time varying wireless channels and contention. To
pick the right bitrate in time-varying wireless channels, nodes have
to continuously estimate channel quality either via probing [2, 13, 21,
15] or by requiring channel state feedback from the receiver [4, 33].
However, probing is inaccurate since packet loss is a coarse measure
of channel strength. Channel state feedback from the receiver is more
accurate but incurs larger overhead, and can still be inaccurate in mobile scenarios when the channel varies every packet. The bitrate adaptation decision in contention is the opposite of time-varying wireless
channels, i.e. do not adapt the bitrate due to contention related losses.
Hence in such scenarios, nodes have to use probe packets such as RT-
S/CTS [1, 35] or require explicit notification from the receiver [33,
26] to discern the cause of packet loss and avoid making an incorrect bitrate change. Both techniques again incur overhead and reduce
throughput.

Prior work has made considerable progress in reducing the overhead and improving accuracy of bitrate adaptation, but the conventional wisdom is that there is a fundamental undesirable tradeoff between accuracy and overhead that cannot be avoided. Higher overhead lowers network goodput, but inaccurate bitrate adaptation also
significantly affects network performance. The performance impact
is especially bad in mobile or high contention scenarios.

In this paper we present **Strider** (for **Stri**pping Deco**der**, our decoding algorithm), a system that eliminates the undesirable tradeoff
between overhead and accuracy for rate adaptation. Strider designs a
novel coding technique that allows a node to achieve almost the optimal bitrate adaptation possible in any scenario without incurring any
overhead. Strider's code design has two important characteristics:

- Strider's code is *rateless*. Hence, senders do not have to perform any probing or require any channel state feedback or adjust their bitrates, they simply create a continuous stream of
encoded packets using Strider's algorithm until the receiver decodes and ACKs. We show that Strider's technique achieves
the same effective throughput as the omniscient conventional
scheme which knows the channel state exactly in advance and
always picks the right bitrate to transmit at.

- Strider's code is *collision-resilient*, i.e. it can take collided
packets and decode the individual packets from them. Hence
there is no need for the senders to discern the cause of packet
losses and take measures to avoid collisions. We show that
Strider's collision-resilient code achieves at least the same effective throughput as the omniscient collision-free scheduler,
i.e. a scheme which knows exactly what nodes are contending
in advance and schedules them in a collision-free manner.

The key intuition behind Strider is the concept of a *minimum distance transformer* (MDT). The MDT technique works by transmitting linear combinations of a batch of conventionally encoded symbols (e.g. QPSK symbols encoding bits that have been passed through
a 1/5 rate convolutional code). The intuition is that when we take
a batch of L conventional symbols, and transmit M linear combinations of them, in essence we are mapping points from a L dimensional space (the conventional symbols) to points in a M dimensional
space. Depending on the relative values of M and L, the minimum
distance in this new space can be controlled. Since every channel
code has a threshold minimum distance above which it can be decoded correctly, in Strider a sender can transmit linear combinations
until the minimum distance in the new space goes above the required
threshold and the packets are decoded correctly. Moreover, the minimum distance adjustment happens without any feedback from the
receiver or probing by the sender. Hence the technique automatically

achieves the best bitrate, since in effect it is finding the densest constellation possible that still allows correct decoding, which is what conventional rate adaptation protocols are attempting to accomplish.

The other important component of Strider is collision resilience. Currently, collided packets are thrown away and receivers wait for retransmissions, hoping they wont collide again. Instead, Strider decodes both (or more) packets from a collision. The key reason for our collision resilience is Strider's rateless code: it allows the receiver to treat the packets from the sender with the weaker channel as noise, and due to its rateless property, after the receiver has accumulated sufficient transmissions it can decode the packet from the sender with the stronger channel. After decoding the first packet, we can subtract its contribution from the received signal and decode the packets from the other sender. Hence, Strider's code has the nice benefit of completely eliminating hidden terminals.

We show theoretically that Strider's code asymptotically achieves Shannon capacity for AWGN channels. Further, Strider's algorithm has linear-time computational complexity and is efficient to implement. We have prototyped Strider in the GNURadio [6] SDR platform and evaluated it in an indoor testbed via experiments using USRP2s, as well as trace drive simulations. We compare Strider to the omniscient scheme and SoftRate [33], a state of the art conventional rate adaptation scheme. The omniscient scheme has perfect channel knowledge, and always picks the optimal bitrate and schedules nodes in a collision-free manner. Our evaluation shows that:

- Strider achieves a performance that is within 5% of the performance of the omniscient scheme across a wide range of SNRs (5-25dB).
- When collisions happen, our results show that Strider does at least as well as the omniscient collision free scheduler, and surprisingly in many cases Strider does better! The reason as we discuss later is that collision free scheduling is actually sub-optimal and in many cases concurrently transmitting and applying our technique can deliver even higher throughput. Strider thus completely eliminates hidden terminals in our testbed.
- In comparison with SoftRate [33], we show that Strider achieves nearly 70% throughput improvement in mobile scenarios. Further in networks with contention/hidden terminals, Strider provides a $2.8\times$ increase over SoftRate.

Strider is related in spirit to prior work on rateless codes such as fountain codes [19]. However, these rateless codes work only when the packets are correctly decoded, and cannot handle wireless distortions such as noise and interference. Similarly, prior work on incremental redundancy and hybrid ARQ [29, 18, 7] provides a limited form of rate adaptation by adaptively providing the right amount of redundancy needed to enable decoding of partially correct packets. However, these techniques still have to pick the right modulation, and further do not work in the presence of collisions or interference. Strider provides complete rate adaptation, and handles collisions and interference in a single framework.

2. RELATED WORK

There is a large body of prior work on rate adaptation. Most techniques use one of two approaches: estimate channel strength via direct channel state feedback (in the form of SNR or BER measurements) from the receiver, or infer channel strength based on packet delivery success/failures [4, 33, 2, 13, 21, 15, 27]. Channel state feedback in fast changing mobile channels can be expensive, and worse yet, inaccurate since by the time the transmitter uses the feedback, the channel might have changed. Inference based on packet delivery success can be highly inaccurate, since packet delivery is a very coarse

measure of channel strength. Further, none of these techniques work when there are collisions, and therefore often need to augment the rate adaptation protocol with extra overhead in the form of probing or feedback from the receiver to discern whether the packet loss was caused by a collision.

Strider is related to prior work in rateless codes and hybrid ARQ. Rateless codes such as LT [19] and Raptor codes [28] allow one to automatically achieve the capacity of an erasure channel without knowing the packet loss probability in advance. However these techniques require whatever packets are received to be correctly decoded, and do not work in wireless channels where packets are corrupted [28]. Second, hybrid ARQ schemes used in 4G wireless systems based on punctured turbo codes [18, 29] can be used to selectively provide extra redundancy in the form of coded bits, to help the receiver decode an erroneous frame. However, these techniques still need to pick the correct modulation and further do not work when there are collisions or external interference.

Strider's collision resilience component is related to prior work on interference cancellation [10, 9, 16, 17]. However, all prior techniques require that the colliding packets be encoded at the correct bitrate to enable them to decode collisions. For example in SIC, if the colliding packets have been encoded at a bitrate corresponding to the idle channel (which will happen because the colliding hidden terminal senders cannot know in advance that they will collide), SIC will fail to work [9]. Zigzag has a similar but less acute problem, since it also needs correct decoding of its interference free chunks, which requires the packets to be encoded at the correct bitrate. Further Zigzag needs the same set of packets to collide across successive collisions. Strider does not have any of these problems, since its rateless property automatically adjusts the effective bitrate to enable its stripping decoder to decode collisions, and it can decode even if collisions are between different sets of packets.

Strider's design is inspired by recent work on uplink power control in cellular CDMA systems, as well as theoretical work on rateless code design [3, 34, 23, 5, 24]. As we describe later, Strider treats each packet transmission as a set of virtual collisions among independent blocks, very similar to how multiple packet transmissions in a CDMA uplink wireless system collide. Hence decoding algorithms that are used in CDMA basestations have a similar structure to Strider's algorithm. Specifically, they need to control how power is allocated to each uplink transmitter to enable successful decoding, and we borrow from such algorithms to design Strider's encoding algorithm. The key contribution of Strider is the application of these techniques to design a rateless code for wireless channels, as well as an implementation and detailed evaluation of the technique using practical software radio experiments. Further, we also design a novel technique that extends the code design to handle packet collisions.

3. INTUITION

Senders have to adapt bitrates because of the threshold behavior of conventional techniques, i.e. they decode only at or above a particular SNR threshold depending on the coding rate and modulation choice. Even though it is fairly introductory material, we first discuss the reasons for this thresholding behavior since it provides insight into our eventual design.

In current schemes, data bits are first channel coded to add protection against noise. The level of protection is parameterized by the coding rate (e.g a $1/2$ rate code implies that every data bit is protected with one extra bit of redundancy). Coded bits are then modulated, i.e. they are mapped to points in a complex constellation and transmitted on the wireless channel. For example in BPSK, bits are mapped to two points on the real line $(\sqrt{P}, -\sqrt{P})$ (P is the transmission power) and transmitted. Due to attenuation and additive noise the receiver gets $y = x + n$, where n is Gaussian noise with variance σ^2. When decoding, the receiver first demodulates the received symbol, i.e. maps it to the nearest constellation point and infers what coded bit was transmitted. Hence if the Gaussian noise value is greater/less than $(\sqrt{P}/ - \sqrt{P})$ the receiver makes a bit error. However, the channel code decoder can correct a certain number of errors (depending on the amount of redundancy added) and decode the final data. Thus as long as the number of bit flips at the demodulation (BPSK) stage are less than the correcting power of the channel code, the data eventually gets decoded correctly.

Assuming the channel code rate is fixed, the key to ensuring decoding success is to make sure that the demodulation stage does not make more bit errors than the channel code can handle. This error rate is dictated by the *minimum distance* between any two constellation points (e.g. for BPSK it is $2\sqrt{P}$) and how it compares with the noise power (σ^2). To get good performance, the minimum distance has to be sufficiently large so that no more than the tolerable number of bit errors occur. If its too small, the channel code cannot correct, if its too large, the extra redundancy in the channel code is wasteful. Modulation schemes have different minimum distances (e.g. BPSK, QPSK, 16-QAM, 64-QAM have successively decreasing minimum distances), and depending on the channel SNR, the rate adaptation module's job is to pick the combination of modulation and channel coding that correctly decodes and maximizes throughput. Hence, different modulation and channel coding schemes have different SNR thresholds above which they begin to decode.

3.1 Our Approach

Strider takes a conventional fixed channel code and constellation which works only above a particular threshold SNR, and makes it **rateless**. In other words, it enables the fixed channel code and constellation to decode at any SNR. We refer to this fixed channel code and constellation as the *static code* in the rest of the paper. For exposition simplicity, we assume in this section that the static code is using BPSK, but the actual implementation uses QPSK.

The key idea behind Strider's rateless transformation is the concept of minimum distance transformation (MDT). Intuitively, MDT takes a batch of symbols from the static code and maps them to a different space where the minimum distance between the two closest points can be tuned to meet the static code's requirements. To understand how MDT works, we begin with a simple (but suboptimal) approach that demonstrates the basic idea. Assume we have a BPSK symbol x from the static code. A simple approach to amplify the minimum distance is to take the symbol x, and transmit it multiple (M) times, but multiply each transmission by a complex number of unit magnitude but random phase $r_i = e^{j\theta_i}$ (so transmission power does not change). The receiver therefore gets the following symbols after noise gets added

$$\vec{y} = \vec{r}x + \vec{n} \qquad (1)$$

where $\vec{r}$ is the M length vector of random complex numbers formed by the coefficients of each transmission, and $\vec{n}$ is the noise vector for the M transmissions.

The transmitter in essence has mapped a simple BPSK symbol x to a random point $\vec{y}$ in a M-dimensional space. To see why this amplifies minimum distance, lets compute the Euclidean distance in this new space between the original two BPSK constellation points $\sqrt{P}, -\sqrt{P}$. The new distance is $||2\sqrt{P}\vec{r}|| = 2\sqrt{MP}$, which is $\sqrt{M}$ times the original minimum distance, providing much higher resilience to noise. At some value of M (i.e. after a certain M number of transmissions), the static code will meet its minimum distance threshold and be able to decode.

As the reader can tell, the above naive approach is quite inefficient. It increases the minimum distance in large increments, whereas the

static code itself might need a much smaller increment to decode. Our key observation is that instead of operating over single symbols as above, we can spread the transmission power over a batch of K symbols belonging to K parallel blocks (each block is generated by passing data through the static code). Specifically, instead of transmitting the K symbols separately one by one, Strider transmits random linear combinations of the K symbols

$$\sqrt{(1/K)} \left(\sum_{i=1}^{i=K} r_i x_i \right) \qquad (2)$$

where the $\sqrt{1/K}$ factor is needed to ensure that every transmitted symbol has a power of P.

The transmitter picks separate random coefficients for each linear combination. Assuming the transmitter has to send M such linear combinations, the receiver receives the following system of linear equations distorted by noise.

$$\vec{y} = \sqrt{(1/K)}\mathbf{R}\vec{x} + \vec{n} \qquad (3)$$

where $\vec{x}$ is the K length vector corresponding to the batch of K static code symbols, $\mathbf{R}$ is the $M \times K$ matrix consisting of the random phase coefficients r_i defined above, and all the other definitions are the same.

To understand how this technique achieves minimum distance transformation, we can use the following visualization. Intuitively, this operation is taking K dimensional vectors $\vec{x}$ and mapping it to random points in a M dimensional space. As M increases, the minimum distance between the two closest points in this new space increases. When $M = 1$ the minimum distance is $2\sqrt{P/K}$. For any value M, the minimum distance between points in the M-dimensional space corresponding to the closest constellation points for the static code symbols x_i (assuming BPSK) is $||2\mathbf{R(i)}\sqrt{P/K}|| = 2\sqrt{MP/K}$, where $\mathbf{R(i)}$ is the i'th column of matrix $\mathbf{R}$. Thus the minimum distance increases monotonically with M. Hence, by controlling the value of M (i.e. by controlling the number of transmissions), we can control the minimum distance until the static code's requirements for each of the K blocks are met and they can decode. Thus, we can keep on transmitting linear combinations until all the K blocks can be decoded.

Stepping back, Strider's technique has taken a static code that used to operate at or above a fixed SNR threshold, and converted it using MDT to work at any SNR by adjusting the minimum distance. In other words, we have converted the static code to be *rateless*. To decode, the receiver estimates what are the likely symbols $\vec{x}$ given $\vec{y}$ and the matrix $\mathbf{R}$, and then passes the K symbols through the decoder for the static code. In the following section, we describe the design of an efficient algorithm that realizes this insight, as well as extend it to decode collided packets.

4. DESIGN

First, we describe the two main design goals for Strider, and discuss them in the context of how these goals fit into the larger picture of code design:

- **Complexity of the decoding algorithm**: The efficiency of a code (defined as how close it's achieved throughput is to the Shannon capacity at any SNR) is typically proportional to the computational complexity of the decoding algorithm. For example, Shannon himself used a random codebook construction that achieves channel capacity, but incurs exponential decoding computational complexity. Algorithms such as sphere decoding and maximum likelihood (ML) [14] decoders try to mimic the random decoding structure of Shannon's design and hence perform quite well, but still require at least cubic complexity, if not more. Recent code designs such as LDPC codes are the one exception to the rule, since they come close to achieving capacity yet only have linear decoding computational complexity. For practical implementations, low complexity algorithms are of course highly desirable. Our goal is to design an efficient code with ***linear decoding computational complexity***.

- **Feedback from the receiver**: In conventional code design, feedback from the receiver is often quite helpful in improving performance. For example, HARQ systems [29] use feedback from the receiver to determine how many extra parity bits to transmit and minimize wasteful transmission. Note that this is not channel-state feedback, but rather feedback about what data the receiver has already decoded. However, even such feedback can be expensive in wireless since spectrum is scarce, and can complicate protocol design since these feedback packets need to be scheduled and reliably delivered by the MAC protocol. More importantly, such feedback goes against the grain of rateless code designs [28, 19] which strive to operate so that the receiver has to only send a single ACK packet when *all* packets have been successfully decoded. Our goal is to design a code that requires the minimum possible feedback, i.e. it requires only ***one bit* of feedback from the receiver** when it has successfully decoded everything that was transmitted. The negligible feedback requirement simplifies protocol design.

Strider's encoding and decoding algorithms meet the above two design goals. Before describing the algorithm however, we summarize the operational algorithm in Strider to give the reader an overview of the end-to-end protocol, and also to harmonize notation. When a node has data to transmit, it uses the following four simple steps:

1. Data is divided into chunks of size 6KB. In each chunk we have $K = 33$ data blocks of length $L = 1500$bits each.

2. Each of the K data blocks is passed through the *static code* (currently we use a $1/5$ rate channel code and a QPSK constellation as the static code), to produce K blocks with $5L/2$ complex symbols each.

3. The K blocks are passed through Strider to create a packet for transmission.

4. Use the standard carrier sense mechanism to check if the medium is idle, and if it is transmit the packet. After transmission, wait for an ACK, which the receiver sends if it has successfully decoded the entire chunk consisting of K blocks. If no ACK is received, go to step 3 and repeat. Move to step 1 when an ACK is received.

We expand on Step 3 which is the core encoding step in Strider. To produce a packet for transmission, Strider linearly combines the K coded blocks from the static code to create one packet. For example to create the first symbol in the transmitted packet we would do the following computation

$$s_1 = r_1 x_{11} + r_2 x_{21} + \ldots + r_K x_{K1} \qquad (4)$$

where x_{i1} is the first complex symbol in the i'th block, and r_i is the i'th complex coefficient used to create the linear combination. The computation is repeated with the same coefficients for all L symbols in each block. We assume that the random coefficients have been normalized so that the energy of the symbols is P, the transmission power budget. The above technique produces one packet for transmission. The header of each packet includes the coefficients used to create the linear combination of the blocks (i.e. the symbols $r_1 \ldots r_K$).

The sender creates packets using different linear combinations for each packet, and transmits them until the receiver can decode all K

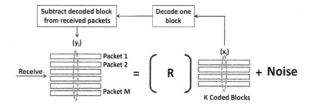

Figure 1: Strider's decoding algorithm

blocks and ACKs. Lets assume the receiver requires M packets before it can decode all K blocks. We can express the i'th symbol in each of the M packets received as:

$$\vec{y_i} = \mathbf{R}\vec{x_i} + \vec{n} \qquad (5)$$

where $\vec{y_i}$ is the M length vector consisting of the received symbols at the i'th position from the M received packets, and $\vec{x_i}$ is the K length input vector consisting of the i'th input symbols from the K coded blocks. $\mathbf{R}$ is the $M \times K$ matrix consisting of the coefficients used in creating the linear combinations for the M transmitted packets, with each row corresponding to one received packet. Finally $\vec{n}$ is the noise vector. Note that we did not include the channel attenuation in the above equation, we assume that the noise power has been scaled appropriately to account for channel attenuation.

4.1 Decoding Algorithm

As discussed before, we can visualize Strider as mapping K dimensional vectors ($\vec{x_i}$) to M dimensional vectors that are distorted by noise after they pass through the wireless channel to produce $\vec{y_i}$. Since the components of $\vec{x_i}$ can only take four discrete values (the four points of a QPSK constellation), the vector $\vec{x_i}$ can take at most 4^K different values. Since $\mathbf{R}$ is known to the receiver, the receiver can exactly estimate what 4^K possible points could have been transmitted. Hence one method to decode would be to calculate the closest constellation point among the 4^K possible points and then lookup the corresponding input. From that point, we can apply the traditional decoder for the static code to the K coded blocks and recover the original data.

However, this naive technique quickly gets complicated. For example, if $K = 10$ then the number of possible constellation points is $4^{10} = 1048576$! To compute the closest point, the decoder would require exponential memory and compute resources, which rules out this naive method.

4.1.1 Stripping Decoder

Strider's key insight is that *instead of trying to decode the entire vector $\vec{x_i}$ at once which incurs exponential complexity, we can try to decode it one component at a time*. Since each component in $\vec{x_i}$ can at most take 4 discrete values (QPSK), the computational complexity is significantly lower. Hence, Strider first decodes the first coded block's components, and passes them through the decoder for the static code to recover the original symbols. If decoding is successful, we can re-encode the first block and subtract it from the received vectors ($\vec{y_i}$) to remove the effect of the first coded block. Next, we can proceed to the second block and repeat the above process.

One way to visualize Strider's decoder is as follows: remember the received packets are each a linear combination of blocks belonging to one chunk. Strider's decoder is in effect trying to decode one block at a time, *strip* it from the received signals, and then decode the next block and strip it, and so on. Hence, we christen the scheme Strider for *stripping decoder*.

Operationally, the above intuition implies that Strider attempts to decode the first block while treating the other $K - 1$ blocks as interference. The algorithm would work as follows for the first block:

1. Take $\vec{R_1}$ (the first column of matrix $\mathbf{R}$) and form its complex transposed conjugate $\vec{R_1^*}$.

2. Take the dot product of $\vec{y_j}$ with $\vec{R_1^*}$ to obtain one symbol. Repeat for all $j = 1 \ldots L$ to obtain L complex symbols.

3. Attempt to decode the L symbols obtained in the previous step using the decoder for the static code.

4. If decoding is successful [1], block 1 is obtained. Subtract the symbols corresponding to block 1 from the received symbols, i.e. subtract $(x_{1j}\vec{R_1})$ from $\vec{y_j}$ to obtain a new vector $\vec{y_j'}$, and remove the first column from $\mathbf{R}$ to obtain a new matrix $\mathbf{R'}$. Go to step 1 and attempt to decode the second coded block using the same steps but with the new $\vec{y_j'}$ and $\mathbf{R'}$. Repeat until all blocks are decoded.

To see whats going on, consider what we have after carrying out the second step in the above algorithm:

$$\vec{R_1^*}\vec{y_i} = \vec{R_1^*}\vec{R_1}x_{1i} + \vec{R_1^*}\vec{R_2}x_{2i} + \ldots + \vec{R_1^*}\vec{R_K}x_{Ki} + \vec{R_1^*}\vec{n}$$
$$= |R_1|^2 x_{1i} + I \quad (6)$$

where $\vec{R_i}$ is the i'th column vector in matrix $\mathbf{R}$ and I is collapsing all the other terms except the contribution from the i'th symbol of the first block. This computation is performed for all $i = 1, \ldots L$ symbols.

In Step 3, we collect these L symbols from the computation above and attempt to decode the first block. We can show that [31] the decoding will be successful only if the minimum distance for block 1 $(MD(1))$, is above a threshold $C * (I + N)$, where C is a constant dependent on the static code, while I and N are the interference and noise powers respectively. The minimum distance for block 1 after M transmissions and the decoding condition while treating all other blocks as interference can therefore be expressed as:

$$MD(1, M) = \sqrt{2}\sum_{i=1}^{M}|R_{i1}|^2 \geq C*(\sum_{j=2}^{K}\Big|\sum_{i=1}^{M}R_{i1}^*R_{ij}\Big|^2 + \sum_{i=1}^{M}|R_{i1}|^2n_i^2) \quad (7)$$

The right half of the inequality thus consists of terms from the other blocks which are treated as interference and the noise.

There are two key takeaways from the equation above. First, as the receiver gets more packets (i.e. with increasing M), the minimum distance improves. Intuitively this makes sense, we expect our ability to decode to improve with every successive reception. Second, since the entries of $\mathbf{R}$ are picked randomly, any two columns in the matrix will be uncorrelated. The magnitude of the dot product of two uncorrelated complex vectors of equal magnitude will be less than the squared magnitude of either vector [31]. Hence, the right half of the inequality above grows relatively slower than the first block's minimum distance with M. Hence, with increasing M, the minimum distance for block 1 monotonically increases, until it exceeds the above threshold at which the static code can decode.

If block 1 is successfully decoded, we can subtract it and repeat the process for block 2. However, for this block, the interference will be only from blocks 3 to K, lesser than for the first block. Thus by stripping block 1 after decoding it, we reduce the minimum distance required for block 2 to decode, and as long as it is greater than the required threshold, the block will be decoded and the algorithm proceeds. All blocks will be decoded when the minimum distance for each is greater than the corresponding required threshold.

4.2 Encoding Algorithm

Our key deduction from the above analysis is that the *optimal design will have the property that all K blocks get decoded at once.* To

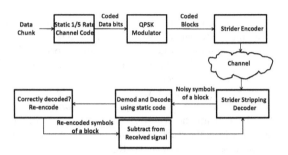

Figure 2: Strider's end-to-end design

see why, note that the receiver ACKs only when all K blocks are decoded, and that senders keep transmitting until an ACK is received. If at any point only a subset of the K blocks are decoded, then the next transmission will be wasted since it will contain components from the already decoded blocks. However this is a contradiction, since an optimal design by definition would not waste any transmission. Hence, the optimal design would guarantee that all K blocks get decoded at once.

The above insight has the following important consequence: *the minimum distance of all the K blocks should be greater than the required threshold for each block (defined in Eq. 8 below), when even any one of the blocks can be decoded.* This ensures, that if any block gets decoded, then all blocks get decoded. However the required minimum distance depends on the actual noise power in the channel, which the sender of course does not know. Hence the encoder just ensures the following condition: after every transmission it estimates the maximum possible noise power it can tolerate that still ensures that the minimum distance of each block is higher than the required threshold for each block. If the actual noise power is higher, then the sender will have to transmit more encoded packets. If the noise power is lesser than the maximum tolerable, then the receiver will decode and ACK.

To determine the entries of $\mathbf{R}$, we thus need to solve the following set of equations where the left hand side of the first equation represents the minimum distance $MD(b, m)$ that block b would need after m transmissions to decode,

$$\sqrt{2}\sum_{i=1}^{m}|R_{ib}|^2 \geq C * \Big(\sum_{j=b+1}^{K}\Big|\sum_{i=1}^{m}R_{ib}^*R_{ij}\Big|^2 + \sum_{i=1}^{m}|R_{ib}|^2n'^2 \Big)$$
$$\sum_{i=1}^{K}|R_{c,i}|^2 \leq P \quad \forall c = 1, \ldots, m \quad (8)$$

and n' is an unknown noise variable representing the maximum tolerable noise at the m'th transmission. The second equation ensures that the total power of any transmission cannot exceed P. We have to solve the above for every value of $b = 1, \ldots, K$ and $m = 1, \ldots, M$.

The above set of equations constitute a non-linear optimization problem that can be solved numerically [3], we omit the specifics of the solution. However, we make two comments:

- First, the solver only provides the magnitudes of the entries in the matrix $\mathbf{R}$, while the phases of the complex entries are completely free. Strider picks these phases at random for each entry.

- Second, note that we have to compute $\mathbf{R}$ *only once*, and the computation is performed *offline*. After that $\mathbf{R}$ is essentially a codebook which all nodes know in advance. Hence the computation above is not on the critical path.

To summarize, each row in $\mathbf{R}$ provides the coefficients for creating a separate packet. So the above computation is run to create a sufficiently large matrix of size $P \times K$, such that we can create

---
[1] each block has a CRC at the end to check decoding success

upto P packets. In practice we will likely require much less than P transmissions and hence the receiver will only see a submatrix of $\mathbf{R}$. The sender picks the rows of $\mathbf{R}$ one after the other and uses them to linearly combine the K blocks to produce packets for transmission. The receiver decodes using the stripping decoder method described before.

4.2.1 Why is the above design rateless?

Strider started out with the premise that it converts a conventional static code that operates at a fixed SNR into a rateless one that operates at any SNR. Remember that to decode the static code, the minimum distance of each block needs to be above a threshold. As discussed earlier, the minimum distance depends on two factors. First, with increasing number of transmissions it monotonically increases. Second, with increasing noise strength (i.e. with a weaker channel) the required minimum distance increases. After the right number of transmissions, the minimum distance for each block exceeds the corresponding required threshold, ensuring that the block decodes. Thus the above design converts a fixed static code into a rateless one. Further, we show theoretically in Section 6 that the rateless conversion is efficient, i.e. if the static code achieves Shannon capacity at its decoding threshold SNR, Strider's rateless conversion asymptotically achieves Shannon capacity for Gaussian wireless channels across a wide SNR range.

5. DECODING COLLISIONS

Strider also transforms the static code to be collision-resilient, i.e. it enables us to decode all the component packets from collided signals. To see why, consider how the Strider decoding algorithm works even when there are no collisions. The stripping decoder initially attempts to decode the first block, while treating all other blocks which have been added to it as interference. If decoding is successful, it subtracts the first block and attempts to decode the second block while treating all other blocks as interference and so on. As we can see, Strider's stripping decoder is intrinsically treating every received packet as a set of collisions, where the collisions are between the blocks in a chunk. And the decoding works by decoding one block at a time, or in effect one component of the collision at a time. Hence intuitively, we can model a collision from two senders as a collision between blocks of both senders, and apply the same stripping decoder algorithm as above. We expand on this insight below.

Lets assume we have a scenario where two nodes Alice and Bob are hidden terminals and their transmissions collide at the AP. Since they do not receive ACKs after their first transmission, they re-encode using Strider's algorithm and transmit a new packet again, which will likely collide. Lets assume the AP gets M collisions, we can represent the i'th received symbols in the M collisions as:

$$\vec{y_i} = h_{Al}\mathbf{R}x_i^{\vec{Al}} + h_{Bob}\mathbf{R}x_i^{\vec{Bob}} + \vec{n} \qquad (9)$$

where h_{Al} and h_{Bob} represent the channels, and x_i^{Al} and x_i^{Bob} represent the blocks for Alice and Bob respectively. For exposition simplicity we assume that the channel does not change through the M transmissions, but the results hold even if it does. We can rearrange the above equation into the following:

$$\vec{y_i} = \begin{bmatrix} h_{Al}\mathbf{R} & h_{Bob}\mathbf{R} \end{bmatrix} \begin{bmatrix} x_i^{\vec{Al}} \\ x_i^{\vec{Bob}} \end{bmatrix} + \vec{n} \qquad (10)$$

In effect, the new set of equations is quite similar to Equation 5 for the single sender case discussed in the previous section, except for the fact that the size of the encoding matrix $\mathbf{R}$ as well as the data symbol vector has doubled. Hence, we can use the same stripping decoder method as above. Specifically, Strider uses the following algorithm:

1. Estimate h_{Al} and h_{Bob} from the packet preambles. We discuss how to estimate these quantities in detail in Sec. 5.0.2.
2. Calculate which node has the stronger channel, i.e. calculate $max(|h_{Al}|^2, |h_{Bob}|^2)$. Next use Strider's stripping decoder algorithm on Eq. 10 to try and decode the blocks of the node with the stronger channel.
3. If the previous step is successful, the signal after the contribution from the decoded blocks have been stripped will only consist of blocks from the weaker node's blocks. The resulting equation will be exactly like a single sender case with no collisions, hence we can use the standard stripping decoder algorithm to decode.

Intuitively, assuming Alice has the stronger channel, the stripping decoder is treating the packets from Bob as noise, and attempting to decode Alice's blocks. If successful, it subtracts the contributions of all of Alice's blocks and moves on to decode Bob's blocks. The steps above are reminiscent of successive interference cancellation (SIC) [10]. However, there is one critical difference. Unlike SIC, Strider does not need the colliding packets to be encoded at the right bitrate. Traditional SIC requires that the bitrates of the colliding packets be picked correctly so that the packet with higher power can be decoded while treating the other as interference [9]. However, if the nodes do not know that their packets are going to collide, they will not pick the correct bitrates required for SIC to work. Consequently SIC will fail to decode. Strider does not have this issue, since due to its rateless property it ensures that after an appropriate number of transmissions, the bitrate is sufficient to kickstart the decoding of the first block, which then starts a chain reaction for all the other blocks.

5.0.2 Practical Challenges in Decoding Collisions

1) Asynchrony: The above description assumed that nodes were synchronized across collisions i.e. transmitted packets collide exactly at the same offset across collisions. However, in practice due to random backoffs nodes will not be synchronized, and different collisions will begin at different offsets.
2) Collisions between different senders, or different chunks from the same senders: In practice, successive collisions could be between packets from different senders. Second, in Strider the packets from the node with the stronger channel will get decoded first, and the node will move on to transmit the next chunk of blocks. Hence successive collisions can be between different chunks from the same senders.

Strider is actually invariant to both of these problems because of its stripping decoder structure. Specifically, Strider attempts to decode each block separately, while treating everything else as interference. So lets say we are trying to decode the first block of Alice from the collisions. We collect all of the collisions, and can express the decoding problem for Alice's first block as follows:

$$\vec{y_i'} = \vec{R_1}x_{1i}^{Al} + \vec{R_2}x_{2i}^{Al} + \ldots + \vec{R_K}x_{Ki}^{Al} + \vec{I} \qquad (11)$$

where the term $\vec{R_i}$ is the M length i'th column vector of $\mathbf{R}$, and $\vec{I}$ subsumes all the contributions from Bob's packets or from some other senders.

The above equation is collecting all the terms that have collided with the i'th symbol of Alice's first block across the M transmissions, and is just rearranging the terms in Eq. 10. To decode this block, we use the same stripping decoder technique. If successful, we re-encode it and subtract its contributions from all other symbols where it had a contribution. Thus, it does not matter what the identity of the terms in $\vec{I}$ is, since we do not use that knowledge in decoding Alice's blocks.

However, Strider does need to estimate the offsets where the collisions begin, so it knows where which symbol is. To do so we leverage the preamble and postamble trick used in prior work [33, 16, 9]. We include a pseudorandom sequence in the preamble/postamble of each packet, and the receiver correlates the received samples against this known sequence. Since the pseudorandom sequence is uncorrelated with any other sequence except itself, the correlation will spike exactly when a packet starts, even if there is a collision. The location of the spike gives us the offset where the collision begins.

3) Compensating for Frequency Offsets: Different senders will have different carrier frequency offsets (CFO) w.r.t the receiver. When we decode a block and subtract, we have to compute and compensate for this frequency offset. Strider's current implementation is on top of a WiFi style OFDM PHY implemented with USRP2s and GNURadio. Hence, we use the standard Schmidl-Cox algorithm [25] for OFDM carrier synchronization and offset estimation. The algorithm is based on exploiting a repeating preamble by computing the cross correlation of a signal with a delayed version of itself, and computing the phase offset across the correlation values at different delays to compute the CFO. However, the algorithm needs to be modified for collisions, since we wont have a clean copy of the repeating preamble for the packet that starts second. Like prior work [33], we use the postamble to get a clean copy of the repeating preamble. The Schmidl-Cox algorithm is run on the postamble for the second packet. The algorithm also estimates the symbol timing and subcarrier spacing offsets apart from the CFO, which are then used in OFDM demod. We refer the reader to [25] for a detailed description of the standard Schmidl-Cox implementation.

4) Channel Estimation: The receiver needs to estimate the channels at the receiver for decoding the collisions. We use the pilot tones in the OFDM subcarriers (e.g. WiFi uses 4 pilot tones) to estimate the channel using the Least Squares algorithm [32]. Strider uses 4 pilot tones that are inserted in the packet header. Suppose $p_1, \ldots, p_4$ and $\vec{y} = y_1, \ldots, y_4$ are the 4 pilot symbols sent and received respectively. The LS channel estimate is given by:

$$\vec{h} = \mathbf{P}^{-1}\vec{y} \qquad (12)$$

where $\mathbf{P}$ is diag$(p_1, \ldots, p_4)$, i.e. the 4×4 diagonal matrix of the 8 known pilot symbols. To estimate the channel at the other 48 data subcarriers we use linear interpolation at every subcarrier between two pilot subcarriers.

5) Collisions between more than two transmissions: Strider in principle can handle collisions between more than two packets. Specifically, Strider depends on the header of the packet being correctly decoded to handle collisions. Hence, similar to prior work [12], Strider appends the header to the end of the packet so that it can be recovered even under a collision. However if more than 2 packets collide, a receiver may not initially be able to decode all packet headers. But as decoding proceeds, one of the batches will get decoded after sufficient transmissions, and the decoded symbols are then subtracted from all collisions. After subtraction, a hidden header will be revealed at which point Strider can recover it and incorporate the new batch into the decoding process. We note however that in our experiments collisions between more than two nodes were quite rare, carrier sense works well enough that collisions happen only between hidden terminals, and configurations that involved three hidden terminals were very uncommon.

6. THEORETICAL ANALYSIS

Strider asymptotically achieves Shannon capacity for Gaussian channels. However, Strider's practical performance depends on how efficient the static code is at its decoding threshold. For example, a 1/2 rate convolutional code with QPSK (used in the 12Mbps WiFi bitrate) has a decoding threshold of around 6dB [11] and achieves a rate of 1b/s/Hz at that threshold. But the Shannon capacity at that SNR is

actually 2.3b/s/Hz. Hence convolutional codes are off from capacity, but we use them because they can be efficiently implemented.

Strider is orthogonal to the choice of the static code, and provides a technique for converting any static code into a rateless code that works at any SNR. Hence, what we wish to prove is that Strider's rateless conversion happens *without any loss in coding efficiency*, i.e., we would not achieve a higher rate than Strider by using a correctly picked conventional channel code and constellation at any SNR from the same class of static codes (e.g. convolutional codes in WiFi). Hence, we will assume that the rate $R(T)$ our static code achieves at its decoding threshold T is equal to the Shannon capacity at T, and intuitively show that after going through Strider's conversion it can achieve Shannon capacity across a larger SNR range.

When the sender uses Strider's algorithm, he is in effect dividing up the power among multiple blocks. Specifically, when he computes the entries of matrix $\mathbf{R}$, the magnitude of the column vectors corresponds to the powers that are allocated to the blocks. Lets assume we have K blocks and require M transmissions to decode. Hence, when the receiver manages to decode, the following condition is asymptotically true due to the way the matrix $\mathbf{R}$ is computed

$$\frac{P_1}{\sum_{i=2}^{K} P_i + N} = \ldots = \frac{P_j}{\sum_{i=j+1}^{K} P_i + N} = T \qquad (13)$$

Here P_i is total power allocated to i'th block across the M transmissions, and N is the unknown noise power. Thus the total power used by the sender is $P = \sum_{i=1}^{K} P_i$ and the actual SNR of the channel is $10 \log(P/N)$dB and is unknown to the sender. This equation is just restating the condition we developed in Eq. 8 that ensured that the minimum distance for each block is guaranteed to be greater than the required threshold for each block to decode.

The Strider decoder is a stripping decoder, i.e. it decodes the first block treating the second as noise, strips it after decoding and then decodes the second block. When the receiver decodes the K blocks, So the effective rate achieved by Strider at this point is:

$$R_{Strider} = \sum_{i=1}^{K} R(T) = \sum_{i=1}^{K} \log(1 + T) \qquad (14)$$

$$= \sum_{j=1}^{K} \log(1 + \frac{P_j}{\sum_{i=j+1}^{K} P_i + N}) \qquad (15)$$

$$= \log\left(\prod_{j=1}^{K} \frac{\sum_{i=j}^{K} P_j + N}{\sum_{i=j+1}^{K} P_i + N}\right) \qquad (16)$$

$$= \log(1 + \frac{\sum_{i=1}^{K} P_i}{N}) = \log(1 + \frac{P}{N}) \qquad (17)$$

Thus the effective rate is the same as the Shannon capacity at power P and noise N. In other words, Strider achieves the same throughput as if the user had used the full power P to transmit with a capacity achieving code at the unknown SNR.

For our practical implemented algorithm, we use a convolutional code at a fixed rate as the static code. Hence the practical performance of our scheme will be dictated by how good the fixed static code is at its decoding threshold. However, we stress that *Strider is orthogonal to the choice of the static code*. Hence, if in the future efficient codes (e.g. LDPC codes [8]) that achieve capacity at their decoding SNR threshold become practically available in hardware, we can immediately use Strider to convert them into a rateless capacity achieving code that works at every SNR.

7. IMPLEMENTATION

Strider is designed to work on top of a WiFi-style OFDM PHY, with a 64 length FFT out of which 48 subcarriers are used for data, 4 for pilot tones and the rest are padding. In Strider the data stream is first divided into chunks of $K = 33$ parallel blocks of size 1500 bits each. Each block is passed through the static code encoder, which in our current implementation is a $1/5$ rate channel code based on convolutional codes and a QPSK constellation. Next, these K coded blocks are linearly combined to create a single packet. The symbols in this packet are striped across the 48 data OFDM bins, which are then passed through an IFFT to obtain the time-domain signal. At the receiver, the process is reversed.

Strider's current implementation builds on top of a 802.11 style OFDM PHY implementation in GNURadio from MIT [33]. However, our frontends are USRP2/RFX2400s whose interconnects cannot support the full 20MHz width required in Wifi, and are currently configured to use 6.25MHz (interpolation and decimation rates of 16) due to PC processing constraints. Hence the subcarrier width in our current implementation is 97.6KHz.

Static Code: Strider's current implementation uses a static code that consists of a fixed $1/5$ rate channel code. However, implementing a convolutional code with such a large constraint length is infeasible in practice. Strider adopts a standard communication theory trick, concatenate a $1/2$ and $1/3$ rate code to together create a $1/2*1/3 = 1/6$ rate code, and then puncture it to make a rate $1/5$ code. Both $1/2$ and $1/3$ rate codes are widely available and implemented in hardware. We refer the reader to [20] for a description of this technique.

Packet Header: Similar to traditional WiFi, the Strider header has a known preamble. After the preamble, the packet header includes the following packet parameters: Sender MAC address, destination MAC address, frame no, chunk no, the index of the row in $\mathbf{R}$ that is used to create the linear combination and packet length. The header is repeated at the end of the packet to protect it from collisions.

Complexity: The computational complexity of Strider is linear in the number of input data symbols. Compared to traditional WiFi, Strider employs a stripping decoder in addition to the decoder for the static code. Since we use convolutional style coding for the static code (the same as WiFi), the only extra complexity in Strider is from the initial stripping decoder component. The stripping decoder algorithm requires $K \times L$ complex multiplications for every packet received. If a block is decoded, it is subtracted from the received signal, which requires another L complex subtractions. Thus the two extra operations are both linear in the length of the data block. Strider's current implementation is bottlenecked by the decoding complexity of the static code, the extra overhead of Strider's stripping decoder is only around 20% in terms of wallclock time. However, the static codes we use are widely implemented in conventional wireless hardware for very high data rates, hence we believe Strider can be easily ported to a realtime hardware implementation.

8. EVALUATION

We evaluate Strider on an indoor testbed of 15 USRP2s and trace driven simulations. We compare Strider with the following:

- **Omniscient Scheme**: This scheme has perfect advance knowledge of the channel strength, and picks the maximum possible bitrate that can be decoded error free. The bitrate choices are from the 9 different bitrates available in the 802.11 standard, listed in Table 1. We augment the above rates with a 16-QAM, 2/3 code rate that achieves a rate of 2.66b/s/Hz to give the omniscient scheme more fidelity in picking the right bitrate. The omniscient scheme also guarantees that concurrent transmissions are scheduled in a collision-free manner.

- **SoftRate**: This is a state of the art rate rate adaptation protocol that uses soft information at the receiver to estimate the BER of a packet. The BER information is sent back to the sender

Figure 3: Strider Indoor Testbed Layout

Table 1: WiFi Bitrates

BitRate	Channel Code/Modulation	b/s/Hz
6	1/2, BPSK	0.5
9	3/4, BPSK	0.75
12	1/2, QPSK	1.0
18	3/4, QPSK	1.5
24	1/2, 16-QAM	2.0
32*	2/3, 16-QAM	2.66
36	3/4, 16-QAM	3.0
48	2/3, 64-QAM	4.0
54	3/4, 64-QAM	4.5

via control packets, which uses it to make rate adaptation decisions. SoftRate's evaluation [33] shows that it outperforms almost all conventional rate adaptation techniques, so we compare against it as a representative of the best possible practical rate adaptation technique.

Before describing the experiments in detail, we briefly summarize our findings:

- In our testbed experiments, Strider achieves a throughput that is within 5% of the omniscient scheme across a wide range of SNRs (5-25dB). Note that Strider has no knowledge of the channel SNR, while the omniscient scheme has perfect advance knowledge.
- Strider eliminates hidden terminals in our testbed. Further, Strider achieves at least as good a throughput as the omniscient scheme which uses a collision free scheduler in most scenarios, and in the majority of the cases outperforms it.
- In comparison with SoftRate [33], a state of the art rate adaptation technique, we show that Strider outperforms by nearly 70% in mobile scenarios.
- In networks with contention and hidden terminals, Strider provides a throughput gain of $2.8\times$ over SoftRate and 60% over the omniscient scheme.

9. INDOOR TESTBED EXPERIMENTS

In this set of experiments, we evaluate Strider using experiments in our indoor testbed of USRP2s. We compare with the omniscient scheme, since current USRP2s do not meet the timing requirements needed to implement dynamic rate adaptation techniques such as SoftRate. However note that the omniscient scheme is an upper bound on the performance of any conventional rate adaptation technique.

9.1 Strider's Rateless Conversion

Method: In this experiment, we randomly place two USRP2 nodes in our testbed and measure the SNR of the link. We then transmit 1000 packets between the two nodes. For omniscient scheme, we transmit using all the different bitrates, and pick the one which achieves the maximum throughput. For Strider, we use Strider's encoding and decoding algorithm. We repeat this experiment 10 times

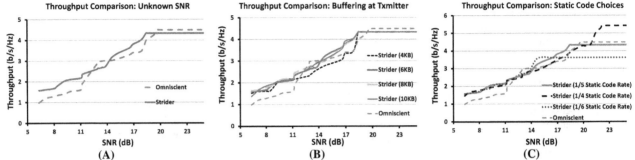

Figure 4: A) Strider performs almost as well as the omniscient scheme at all SNRs. B) Strider works fairly well even when the transmitter has a small amount of data to transmit. C) Strider's performance at high SNRs can be improved by selecting higher rate static codes.

for the same location of the nodes and take the average throughput for either scheme, expressed in terms of bits/second/Hz. We then change the locations of the two nodes to get a different SNR and repeat the above procedure. We plot the average throughput achieved by the two schemes vs SNR in Fig. 4.

Analysis: As Fig. 4 shows, Strider achieves a throughput that is atleast within 5% of the omniscient scheme at all SNRs between $4 - 24$dB. We comment on two regions of the graph. First, at medium to low SNRs ($4 - 16$dB), Strider often outperforms the omniscient scheme. The reason is that Strider has more granular steps, in fact it can achieve $K = 33$ different effective bitrates. The omniscient scheme is choosing within a relatively smaller set, the 10 different channel coding and modulation choices listed in Table 1. Hence at certain SNRs, the omniscient scheme is limited by the choices it has. However, note that Strider is close to the omniscient scheme at every SNR, implying that even if the omniscient scheme had more choices, it could not have done better than Strider.

On the other hand, Strider is around 5% worse at high SNRs greater than 18dB. The same granularity that helped Strider at the medium and lower SNRs slightly hurts Strider in the high SNR region. Remember that Strider's effective throughput drops as $2*33/5M$ where M is the number of transmissions needed. Hence, when M is small (around $2 - 5$), then the effective bitrate exhibits jumps. In high SNR regions, Strider decodes using $2 - 5$ transmissions, and does not have the high fidelity to achieve close to the omniscient in this region. However, Strider is still only 5% off omniscient.

How sensitive is Strider to buffering?: Strider buffers data so that it has enough to form a batch of blocks that it can code over. However, in practice some applications might not generate enough traffic to fill the buffer, and hence Strider might need to work with smaller buffers. Strider can handle these by changing two parameters: the size of a block, as well as the number of blocks in a batch. We conduct an experiment where the sender has different amounts of buffered data available, and picks the best block and batch size for that buffer size. We plot the average throughput vs SNR for buffer size in Fig. 4(b).

Analysis: Fig. 4(b) shows that Strider works fairly well even when the buffer size is as small as 4KB. There is a slight underperformance at medium SNRs (12-16dB). The reason is that at small buffer sizes, Strider has to use a smaller batch size than the normal value of 33. The smaller batch size impacts the granularity of the effective bitrates Strider can achieve, and leads to slightly lower effective throughputs. But overall, Strider works fairly well even when there is only a small amount of data (4KB) to transmit. In the extreme case where the amount of data queued up at the transmitter is smaller than 4KB, Strider might be overkill. In such cases, the sender can simply use a fixed low rate code to transmit the packet, and switch to Strider only when the outstanding buffer is greater than 4KB.

On the other hand larger buffers (i.e. larger batch sizes) slightly improve performance, especially at high SNRs. However, larger batch sizes come with the obvious tradeoff of needing more buffering at the transmitter. We chose $K = 33$ as the default since it gives good performance across our target SNR range, however the designer is free to choose a higher batch size if he wishes to target higher SNRs.

Impact of Static Code Choice: Strider's parameters, the 1/5 static code rate and the QPSK modulation, were picked to obtain the best performance in our target SNR range of $3 - 25$dB that is commonly found in deployed wireless networks. In the following experiment we vary the static code rate to check if Strider is sensitive to that choice. We note that varying the modulation is not necessary, since as we discussed in Sec. 6 what really matters for Strider's performance is the rate at which information is encoded in a block, because that parameter dictates the minimum distance required to decode a block. Changing the static code while keeping the QPSK modulation is sufficient to control the encoding rate of a block. We plot the average throughput vs SNR for different static code choices in Fig. 4(c).

Analysis: Fig. 4(c) plots the relative performance of different static code choices in Strider. As we can see, at most SNRs the different static code rates among the convolutional family do not make a big difference. The differences again are at high SNRs, and is mostly due to the granularity of the effective bitrates achieved for different static code rates. Higher static code rates (e.g. 1/4 code rate) in fact perform better at higher SNRs, achieving nearly 5.5b/s/Hz at SNRs$> 22dB$. Thus changing the static code rate provides the designer another lever if he wishes to optimize Strider for higher SNRs, outside our current target range of $3 - 25$dB.

9.2 Strider's Collision Decoding

To evaluate Strider with collisions, we set up hidden terminal scenarios in our testbed using USRP2 nodes. To evaluate if a particular node configuration is a hidden terminal scenario, we implement a simple threshold based carrier sense on the USRP2 nodes and check if they can carrier sense each other. The two hidden terminal nodes transmit to a fixed third USRP2 node, which acts as the receiver.

Method: We compare against the omniscient collision-free scheme where the two senders take turns transmitting 1000 packets to the receiver, and use the maximum error free bitrate for their channels during their transmissions. For Strider, the two senders transmit concurrently and the collided packets are decoded at the receiver using the Strider collision decoding algorithm. We compute the average throughput achieved by the omniscient scheme and Strider over 10 consecutive runs. We plot the CDF in Fig. 5(A).

Analysis: Fig. 5(A) shows that Strider surprisingly outperforms the omniscient collision free scheduler in most of the scenarios! The median throughput gain over the collision-free scheduler is nearly 30%. The reason is that in a hidden terminal scenario, if one node has a stronger channel than the other, then collision-free scheduling is actually suboptimal. The collision-free scheduler allows both nodes to transmit an equal number of packets, however the node with the weaker channel will take longer to transmit the same number of packets. Consequently, even though the node with the stronger channel can achieve higher rates when he is given the chance to transmit, he is limited due to the weaker channel node. Hence overall network throughput drops.

Strider on the other hand lets both nodes transmit concurrently and decodes from collisions. When the two senders have equal channels, it achieves the same throughput as the omniscient scheme. When the channels are unequal, the node with the stronger channel gets his packets decoded first, and moves on to the next chunk. Hence, unlike the collision-free omniscient scheme it does not have to wait for the weaker node to finish. Consequently, the medium is better utilized and leads to higher overall network throughput.

Impact of Relative SNRs: To better understand the above phenomenon, we conduct the following controlled experiment. We focus on a specific hidden terminal scenario where the SNRs of either sender to the receiver (when they are transmitting separately) is the same at around 10dB. We then keep one sender (lets say Bob) fixed and move the other sender (lets say Alice) closer to the receiver. For each location, we measure the average throughput achieved by Strider and the omniscient collision-free scheme as described in the previous experiment. We plot the relative throughput (i.e Strider throughput normalized by omniscient throughput) vs relative SNR (SNR of Alice - SNR of Bob) for both schemes in Fig. 5(B).

As Fig. 5(B) shows, the throughput of the collision free scheduler is slightly better ($\approx 5\%$) than Strider when the relative SNR is close to zero. The reason is that for Strider's decoding algorithm to get kickstarted, it needs to be able to decode the first block. But when the relative SNR is close to zero, Strider can take a long time before the first block can get decoded since collisions from the second node are treated as noise. However, as Alice moves closer to the receiver and her channel improves, Strider's throughput increases relative to the collision-free scheduler. The reason is that Alice's packets are decoded faster, while Bob achieves a throughput that is commensurate with his channel. In the collision-free omniscient scheme, even though Alice's channel has improved, she cannot take full advantage of it because Bob monopolizes the channel time to transmit his packets. When the SNR gap is nearly 10dB, the overall throughput is nearly 50% better than the collision-free scheduler.

10. TRACE DRIVEN EMULATION

Although Strider can run in real time on a USRP2 connected node, similar to prior work [33, 11] we turn to trace driven emulation to compare Strider with SoftRate, a state of the art conventional rate adaptation technique. This is for two reasons. First, SoftRate requires estimated BER control feedback immediately after every transmission from the receiver to the sender, but the USRP2s are not equipped to quickly transmit ACKs after a packet is received. Second, we want to compare the schemes over varied channel conditions, from static to rapidly changing, from no contention to heavy contention, to assess how consistently they perform across all scenarios. However, it is hard to generate controllable high-mobility and high-contention in experimental settings.

Trace: We collect real channel information for the simulations via two traces: one for mobility and the other for contention. We use the Stanford RUSK channel sounder [22] to collect channel state information for a 20MHz 802.11 wireless channel. The channel sounder is an equipment designed for high precision channel measurement, and provides almost continuous channel state information over the entire

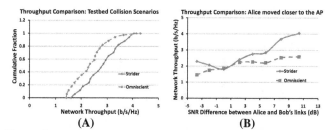

Figure 5: A) Strider eliminates hidden terminals. **B)** Strider's overall throughput improves as Alice is moved closer to the receiver.

measurement period, and can measure channel SNRs as low as -3dB. Our experiments are conducted at night on the band between 2.426 and 2.448GHz which corresponds to WiFi channel 6, and include some interference from the building's WiFi infrastructure which operates on the same channel.

- **Mobility Trace**: A mobile channel sounder node is moved at normal walking speed ($\approx$3mph) in the testbed and the channel sounder node at the center (the blue node at the center of the testbed figure 3) measures the channel from the mobile node. These nodes record and estimate detailed channel state information for all frequencies in the 20Mhz channel, and therefore include frequency selective fading which we would not have seen with USRP2s that operate on 6.25Mhz bands. We collect around 100000 measurements over a 100 second period, and get a CSI sample every $1ms$ for one trace. We use 10 different walking path to collect 10 different mobility traces.

- **Contention Trace**: The channel sounder is placed at ten different locations in our testbed, and their channel to the central blue node is measured over a period of 100 seconds similar to the mobility traces above. We therefore collect 10 such traces. We also place two USRP2 nodes at all pairs of these 10 locations and use our hidden terminal technique described in Sec. 9.2 to determine if the two nodes are hidden terminals. We record this information along with the trace.

Emulator: We feed this trace to a custom emulator written using the the MIT Gnuradio OFDM Code [33] and Strider's implementation. For Softrate, the emulator implements a 802.11 style PHY augmented with soft decoding since SoftRate uses it for BER estimation at the receiver. Further, for both Strider and Softrate, the emulator implements a 802.11 style MAC with ACKs, CSMA and exponential backoff with the default parameters.

Simulating Mobility: To vary mobility, we replay the trace at different speeds. For example, $4\times$ mobility implies the channel measurements that spanned T seconds now span $T/4$ seconds. When a packet is transmitted at time t in simulation, the symbols in the packet are distorted using the corresponding channel measurement from the trace at time t. If the trace has been sped up $4\times$ to simulate mobility, the channel measurement at time t in the new trace will be the channel measurement in the original trace at time $4t$.

Simulating Contention: To vary contention, we pick different subsets of the 10 nodes from the contention trace and let them send packets whenever the simulated 802.11 MAC lets them. If a node is allowed to transmit at time t, then we look up the channel measurements from its trace at time t and distort its transmitted symbols accordingly. If two nodes concurrently transmit and collide, their symbols are individually distorted according to their respective channel traces, and the distorted symbols are added up at the receiver.

10.0.1 Performance with Mobility

We compare the performance of Strider under varying mobility

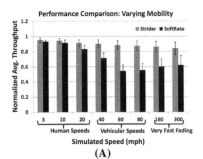 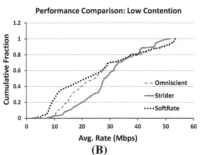 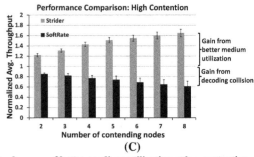

(A)   (B)   (C)

Figure 6: A) Strider outperforms SotfRate with increasing mobility. B) Strider provides gains because of better medium utilization at low contention. C) Strider outperforms both omniscient and SoftRate due to better medium utilization and ability to decode collisions in high contention scenarios.

by playing the trace at increasing speeds, from $1\times$ walking speed (3mph) to $20\times$ corresponding to vehicular speeds (60-80mph) to $100\times$ corresponding to 300mph. Note that the omniscient scheme has advance knowledge of all the channel states that affect each packet transmission, and picks the highest bitrate that can be correctly decoded at every instant. The other schemes are implemented as described before. The performance metric is the average throughput achieved by each scheme over a trace. We run the simulation for each trace and for each compared approach and for each speed. We compute the normalized throughput (i.e. throughput divided by throughput of omniscient scheme) achieved by each approach for all traces and for each speed, and then calculate the average normalized throughput at each speed. Fig. 6(A) plots the average normalized throughputs for the two schemes vs simulated speeds, along with error bars.

Analysis: Strider performs excellently, though it does exhibit some dropoff with increasing mobility compared to the omniscient scheme. At high mobility, Strider is around 15% off the omniscient scheme's rate. However, Strider still outperforms SoftRate by nearly 70% in vehicular mobility scenarios, and by 50% in very fast fading scenarios.

All schemes do fairly well at low mobility, which is expected. At human speeds, we do not see large fluctuations, the channel coherence time in our trace is around 100ms, a relatively long time given that a 802.11 sender would manage to transmit around 50 packets at the lowest bitrate, and probably more. Hence, once a rate adaptation algorithm locks on to the correct bitrate (which SoftRate achieves within one packet transmission time), bitrate adaptations are relatively infrequent. Therefore SoftRate performance is also close to the omniscient scheme.

SoftRate exhibits interesting behavior at higher mobilities. First, as mobility increases, channel coherence times drop, and bitrate adaptation decisions have to be made more frequently. Hence, the likelihood of a packet being transmitted at the incorrect bitrate increases, leading to the loss in performance. However, the surprising fact is that SoftRate performance drops and then recovers at very high mobility, corresponding to very fast fading scenarios. We *speculate* that the reason is the timescale at which Softrate adapts rate, which is every packet. Hence if a wireless channel has a coherence time which is on the order of $1-2$ packet transmission times, SoftRate is likely to make a mistake in the bitrate decision every second or third transmission. The coherence time in the vehicular mobility scenarios is on the order of a few milliseconds in our trace, just sufficient to transmit $1-4$ packets. Consequently SoftRate is constantly playing catchup, and often makes wrong bitrate decisions, leading to lower normalized average rate. However, as mobility increases further, the channel changes several times within a packet. Here SoftRate manages to average the channel over the packet transmission and accurately estimate BER. If the average around which the channel fluctuates stays the same across packets, then SoftRate finds the correct bitrate decision, and performance improves. This behavior is consistent with

the findings of the SoftRate paper [33]. The SoftRate authors present evaluations over slow and very fast fading scenarios, but mention that in intermediate mobility where the channel changes every $2-3$ packets, their scheme suffers. [2]

10.0.2 Low Contention

Method: We compare Strider's performance with the omniscient scheme and SoftRate under low contention scenarios. In these experiments, we randomly pick two nodes from the contention traces, and simulate a 802.11 network with both of them communicating to an AP. We let both nodes transmit, with the 802.11 MAC scheduling access for Strider and SoftRate and run the simulation for 100 seconds. If these two nodes are hidden terminals according to our testbed measurements, then they cannot carrier sense each other in the simulation. Among the C_2^{10} pairs in our traces, only 12 pairs are hidden terminals. The omniscient scheme however uses a collision-free scheduler, and concurrent transmissions will be scheduled one after the other to eliminate collisions. We compute the average total throughput for each two node scenario, and then repeat for a different two node scenario. Fig. 6(B) plots the CDF of the throughputs for the three compared schemes.

Analysis: Surprisingly, Strider outperforms even the omniscient scheme in the low contention scenario. The median rate gain over omniscient is around 25% and around 35% over SoftRate. With SoftRate approximately 15% of the simulations perform quite badly (shown in the first quartile of the CDF) because these topologies correspond to the hidden terminals in our set. However, given that hidden terminals are relatively rare and the omniscient scheme uses a collision free scheduler, where do Strider's gains come from?

The key reason for Strider's performance is *better medium utilization*. Consider what happens when the 802.11 MAC schedules contending nodes for transmission. If the nodes are within carrier sense range, the MAC ensures that all nodes get equal number of opportunities to transmit a packet. However, if the contending nodes have differing channel qualities to the AP, then the node with the weaker channel monopolizes the channel time because the same sized packet requires a larger transmission time (since it has to use a lower bitrate). Hence the stronger node is unfairly penalized, which hurts overall network performance. As prior work has observed [30], the right MAC policy in such scenarios is to ensure "time based fairness", i.e. give all nodes equal amount of channel time regardless of their respective channel strengths.

In Strider, due to its rateless nature, all transmissions occupy the same amount of channel time. Since the 802.11 MAC ensures equal number of transmission opportunities for all contending nodes, Strider ensures that every node gets equal time on the channel. Thus the stronger node is not unfairly penalized. This leads to better medium utilization and consequently higher overall throughputs. Thus, un-

---

[2]please see Sec. 3.4 of the SoftRate [33] paper for a discussion.

like prior work which used mechanisms such as regulating per node queues to ensure time-based fairness, Strider achieves it for free.

10.0.3 High Contention

Method: The experiment is conducted similar to the low contention scenario, except we pick increasing numbers of contending nodes from our contention traces. We normalize the throughput of each experiment by dividing it with the throughput achieved by the omniscient scheme. We calculate the average normalized throughput across all experiments that have the same number of contending nodes and plot it in Fig. 6(C) with increasing contention.

Analysis: Strider significantly outperforms both the omniscient scheme and SoftRate as contention increases. When 8 nodes are contending, Strider is nearly 60% better than the omniscient scheme, and $2.8\times$ better than SoftRate. There are three reasons for this outperformance:

- First, Strider does better because of efficient medium utilization, and the gain increases with higher contention. The reason is that with more nodes, the problem of weaker channel nodes dominating channel time becomes even more acute. Strider's rateless property ensures that every node gets an equal amount of channel time regardless of its channel quality, and hence performs better.
- Second, in high contention collisions are more frequent. SoftRate's performance suffers since it cannot decode from collisions and has to resort to expensive backoffs to ensure nodes don't collide. Strider decodes from collisions and also eliminates all hidden terminal problems. We note that the collisions we observed in our simulations were typically between two transmissions, it was quite rare to see collisions between higher number of transmissions because the required node geometry (three pairwise hidden terminals) as well as synchronization in channel access inspite of three independent random backoffs are quite unlikely.
- Finally, SoftRate relies on feedback from a previous packet's ACK to pick the bitrate for the next transmission. However, in high contention scenarios, a node may not get to transmit a packet for several milliseconds, and its bitrate estimate from the previous measurement gets stale. This leads to inaccurate bitrates and a loss in throughput.

11. CONCLUSION

Strider provides a rateless and collision-resilient design, that consistently achieves very good performance across a wide variety of scenarios, ranging from low mobility to high mobility, from low contention to high contention and unknown channels to hidden terminals. We believe Strider can greatly simply wireless PHY design by eliminating the need for complicated rate adaptation protocols. Strider suggests a number of avenues for future work, including redesigning the MAC to take advantage of Strider's collision resilient code and extending it to 802.11n MIMO scenarios.

12. REFERENCES

[1] V. Bharghavan, A. Demers, S. Shenker, and L. Zhang. MACAW: Media access protocol for wireless lans. In *Proceedings of the international conference on Applications, technologies, architectures, and protocols for computer communications (SIGCOMM)*, 1994.

[2] J. Bicket. Bit-rate selection in wireless networks. *MS Thesis, Massachusetts Institute of Technology*, 2005.

[3] G. Caire, S. Guemghar, A. Roumy, and S. VerdÃ². Maximizing the spectral efficiency of coded cdma under successive decoding. *IEEE Transactions on Information Theory*, Jan 2004.

[4] J. Camp and E. Knightly. Modulation rate adaptation in urban and vehicular environments:cross-layer implementation and experimental evaluation. In *ACM MOBICOM*, 2008.

[5] U. Erez, M. Trott, and G. Wornell. Rateless coding and perfect rate-compatible codes for gaussian channels. In *Information Theory, 2006 IEEE International Symposium on*, pages 528 –532, july 2006.

[6] Free Software Foundation. Gnuradio. `http://gnuradio.org`.

[7] P. Frenger, S. Parkvall, and E. Dahlman. Performance comparison of harq with chase combining and incremental redundancy for hsdpa. In *IEEE VTC*, 2001.

[8] R. Gallagher. Low density parity check codes. In *PhD thesis, MIT*, 1962.

[9] S. Gollakota and D. Katabi. ZigZag decoding: combating hidden terminals in wireless networks. In *SIGCOMM '08: Proceedings of the ACM SIGCOMM 2008 conference on Data communication*, pages 159–170, New York, NY, USA, 2008. ACM.

[10] D. Halperin, T. Anderson, and D. Wetherall. Taking the sting out of carrier sense: interference cancellation for wireless lans. In *MobiCom '08: Proceedings of the 14th ACM international conference on Mobile computing and networking*, pages 339–350, New York, NY, USA, 2008. ACM.

[11] D. Halperin, A. Sheth, W. Hu, and D. Wetherall. Predictable 802.11 packet delivery from wireless channel measurements. In *ACM SIGCOMM*, 2010.

[12] K. Jamieson and H. Balakrishnan. Ppr: Partial packet recovery for wireless networks. In *ACM SIGCOMM*, 2007.

[13] G. Judd, X. Wang, and P. Steenkiste. Efficient channel-aware rate adaptation in dynamic environments. In *ACM MOBISYS*, 2008.

[14] T. Kailath, H. Vikalo, and B. Hassibi. Mimo receive algorithms. *Space-Time Wireless Systems: From Array Processing to MIMO Communications*, 2005.

[15] A. Kamerman and L. Monteban. Wavelan r-ii: A high-performance wireless lan for the unlicensed band. *Bell Labs Technical Journal*, 2, 1997.

[16] S. Katti, S. Gollakota, and D. Katabi. Embracing wireless interference: analog network coding. In *SIGCOMM '07: Proceedings of the 2007 conference on Applications, technologies, architectures, and protocols for computer communications*, pages 397–408, New York, NY, USA, 2007. ACM.

[17] L. E. Li, K. Tan, Y. Xu, H. Viswanathan, and Y. R. Yang. Remap decoding: Simple retransmission permutation can resolve overlapping channel collisions. In *ACM MOBICOM*, Sep 2010.

[18] S. Lin and P. Yu. A hybrid arq scheme with parity retransmission for error control of satellite channels. *IEEE Trans. on Communications*, 1982.

[19] M. Luby. Lt codes. In *Proc. of FOCS 2002*, 2002.

[20] D. Mackay. *Information Theory, Inference and Learning Algorithms*. Cambridge University Press, 2003.

[21] MadWiFi. Onoe rate control. `http://madwifi.org/browser/trunk/ath_rate/onoe`.

[22] G. V. L. J. N. Czink, B. Bandemer and A. Paulraj. Stanford july 2008 radio channel measurement campaign. In *COST 2100*, October 2008.

[23] R. Palanki and J. Yedidia. Rateless codes on noisy channels. In *ISIT*, 2004.

[24] A. Sarwate and M. Gastpar. Rateless codes for avc models. *Information Theory, IEEE Transactions on*, 56(7):3105 –3114, july 2010.

[25] T. Schmidl and D. Cox. Robust frequency and timing synchronization for ofdm. *IEEE Transactions on Communications*, Dec. 1997.

[26] S. Sen, R. R. Choudhury, and S. Nelakuditi. Csma/cn: Carrier sense multiple access with collision notification. In *Mobicom*, 2010.

[27] S. Sen, N. Santhapuri, R. R. Choudhury, and S. Nelakuditi. Accurate: Constellation based rate estimation in wireless networks. In *NSDI*, 2010.

[28] A. Shokrollahi. Raptor codes. *IEEE/ACM Trans. Netw.*, 14(SI):2551–2567, 2006.

[29] E. Soljanin, R. Liu, and P. Spasojevic. Hybrid arq in wireless networks. In *DIMACS Workshop on Networking*, 2003.

[30] G. Tan and J. Guttag. Time-based fairness improves performance in multi-rate wlans. In *Usenix Annual Technical Conference*, 2004.

[31] D. Tse and P. Vishwanath. *Fundamentals of Wireless Communications*. Cambridge University Press, 2005.

[32] J. Van de Beek, O. Edfors, M. Sandell, S. Wilson, and P. Borjesson. On channel estimation in ofdm systems. 1995.

[33] M. Vutukuru, H. Balakrishnan, and K. Jamieson. Cross-layer wireless bit rate adaptation. In *ACM SIGCOMM, Barcelona, Spain*, August 2009.

[34] D. Warrier and U. Madhow. On the capacity of cellular cdma with successive decoding and controlled power disparities. In *Proc. 48th IEEE Vehicular Technology Conf.*, 1998.

[35] S. H. Y. Wong, H. Yang, S. Lu, and V. Bharghavan. Robust rate adaptation for 802.11 wireless networks. In *Proceedings of the 12th annual international conference on Mobile computing and networking*, New York, NY, USA, 2006.

Clearing the RF Smog: Making 802.11 Robust to Cross-Technology Interference

Shyamnath Gollakota [†]   Fadel Adib[†]   Dina Katabi[†]   Srinivasan Seshan[⋆]

[†]Massachusetts Institute of Technology   [⋆]Carnegie Mellon University
{gshyam, fadel, dina}@csail.mit.edu   srini@cs.cmu.edu

ABSTRACT

Recent studies show that high-power cross-technology interference is becoming a major problem in today's 802.11 networks. Devices like baby monitors and cordless phones can cause a wireless LAN to lose connectivity. The existing approach for dealing with such high-power interferers makes the 802.11 network switch to a different channel; yet the ISM band is becoming increasingly crowded with diverse technologies, and hence many 802.11 access points may not find an interference-free channel.

This paper presents TIMO, a MIMO design that enables 802.11n to communicate in the presence of high-power cross-technology interference. Unlike existing MIMO designs, however, which require all concurrent transmissions to belong to the same technology, TIMO can exploit MIMO capabilities to decode in the presence of a signal from a different technology, hence enabling diverse technologies to share the same frequency band. We implement a prototype of TIMO in GNURadio-USRP2 and show that it enables 802.11n to communicate in the presence of interference from baby monitors, cordless phones, and microwave ovens, transforming scenarios with a complete loss of connectivity to operational networks.

Categories and Subject Descriptors C.2.2 [**Computer Systems Organization**]: Computer-Communications Networks

General Terms Algorithms, Design, Performance, Experimentation

Keywords Cognitive MIMO, Cross-Technology Interference

1. INTRODUCTION

Cross-technology interference is emerging as a major problem for 802.11 networks. Independent studies in 2010 by the Farpoint Group [8], BandSpeed [17], and Miercom [10] all show that high-power interferers like baby monitors and cordless phones can cause 802.11n networks to experience a complete loss of connectivity. Other studies from Ofcom [7], Jupiter Research [1], and Cisco [14] report that such interferers are responsible for more than half of the problems reported in customer networks. Today's high-power non-WiFi sources in the ISM band include surveillance cameras, baby monitors, microwave ovens, digital and analog cordless phones, and outdoor microwave links. Some of these technologies transmit in a

frequency band as wide as 802.11, and all of them emit power that is comparable or higher than 802.11 devices [17]. Further, the number and diversity of such interferers is likely to increase over time due to the proliferation of new technologies in the ISM band.

Traditional solutions that increase resilience to interference by making 802.11 fall down to a lower bit rate are ineffective against high-power cross-technology interference. As a result, the most common solution today is to hop away to an 802.11 channel that does not suffer from interference [6, 38, 31, 32]. However, the ISM band is becoming increasingly crowded, making it difficult to find an interference-free channel. The lack of interference-free channels has led WiFi device manufacturers [6, 11, 3] and researchers [29] to develop signal classifiers that inform the 802.11 user about the root cause of the problem (e.g., Bluetooth, microwave, baby monitor). However, these classifiers put the burden of addressing the problem on the user and cannot solve the problem on their own.

In this paper, we ask whether it is possible to use the MIMO capability inherent to 802.11n to address high-power cross-technology interference. MIMO achieves most of its throughput gains by enabling multiple concurrent streams (e.g., packets). Current MIMO decoding, however, fails if any of these concurrent streams belongs to a different technology. Nonetheless, if MIMO can be made to work across technologies, a 3×3 802.11n transmitter can then treat the signal from a baby monitor or microwave as one stream and still deliver two concurrent streams to its receiver.

The challenge in harnessing MIMO across different technologies stems from the fact that MIMO decoding hinges on estimating the channel between all transmit and receive antennas. These estimates rely on understanding the signal structure and assume a known preamble. Hence, it has been infeasible to use MIMO across different and potentially unknown technologies.

We present TIMO,[1] an 802.11n receiver design robust to high-power cross-technology interference. TIMO introduces a MIMO technique that enables a receiver to decode a signal of interest, even when the channel from other concurrent transmissions is unknown. The intuition underlying TIMO is best explained via an example. Consider a pair of 2-antenna 802.11n nodes that want to communicate in the presence of a high-power unknown interferer. Let $s(t)$ be the signal of interest and $i(t)$ the interference signal. The 802.11n receiver node will receive the following signals on its two antennas:[2]

$$y_1(t) = h_i i(t) + h_s s(t) \qquad (1)$$
$$y_2(t) = h_i' i(t) + h_s' s(t), \qquad (2)$$

where h_i and h_i' are the channels from the interferer to the 802.11n

---

[1]Technology Independent Multi-Output (TIMO) receiver design.
[2]The equations here are for single-tap channels. Subsequent sections extend these equations to multi-tap channels.

receiver, and h_s and h'_s are the channels from the 802.11n sender to the 802.11n receiver. The 802.11n receiver has to solve these equations to obtain its signal of interest $s(t)$. It knows the received samples, $y_1(t)$ and $y_2(t)$, and the channels from its transmitter, h_s and h'_s, which can be computed in the presence of interference (see §6.4). The receiver, however, cannot compute the channels from the interferer, h_i and h'_i, because it does not know the interferer's signal structure or preamble. Hence, it is left with two equations in three unknowns $(s(t), h_i i(t),$ and $h'_i i(t)),$[3] which it cannot solve.

Note that the receiver can cancel the interference if it knows the interferer's channel ratio $\frac{h_i}{h'_i}$. In particular, the receiver can rewrite equations 1 and 2 to express the signal of interest as:

$$s(t) = \frac{y_1(t) - \beta y_2(t)}{h_s - \beta h'_s} \quad for \ \beta = \frac{h_i}{h'_i}. \tag{3}$$

The only unknown in the above equation is β. Thus, though the 802.11n receiver cannot compute the exact channels of the interferer, it can still cancel its interference using only its channel ratio.

Still, how do we obtain this ratio given no support from the interferer? The receiver can obtain this ratio as follows: Say that for some time instance $t = t_0$, our transmitter sends a known symbol $s(t_0)$. Our receiver can then substitute in equations 1 and 2 to obtain:

$$\frac{h_i}{h'_i} = \frac{y_1(t_0) - h_s s(t_0)}{y_2(t_0) - h'_s s(t_0)}, \tag{4}$$

where all terms are known except for the ratio $\frac{h_i}{h'_i}$. In §6, we develop this idea further and eliminate the need for having the transmitter send a known symbol, which makes the scheme applicable to existing 802.11n frames. We further generalize the solution to address scenarios in which different frequencies have different interferers, or the interferer hops across frequencies.

A MIMO transmitter can also encode its signal using interference nulling [36] so that it does not interfere with a concurrent transmission from a competing technology. However, using a similar computation, we show that it is necessary to obtain the ratio $\frac{h_{s1}}{h_{s2}}$, where h_{s1} and h_{s2} are the channels from the MIMO transmitter to the receiver of the competing technology. These channels can only be estimated if the receiving node transmits data at some point, i.e., if the competing technology uses bidirectional communication, e.g., a cordless phone. If this constraint is met, however, TIMO can be used not only to protect 802.11n networks from high-power interference, but also as a cognitive mechanism that enables MIMO-based nodes to peacefully coexist in the same frequency band with bidirectional non-MIMO nodes from a different technology. In this case, the simpler non-MIMO nodes just transmit bidirectionally, and the more complex MIMO nodes take on the burden of preventing interference. This approach can lead to a new form of spectrum sharing in which different technologies do not necessarily have to find unoccupied bands and, in crowded environments, could instead occupy the same band thereby increasing spectral efficiency.

We have built a prototype of TIMO using 2-antenna USRP2 radios [13]. We have evaluated our design in the presence of interference from three technologies: a microwave oven, an analog baby monitor, and a DSSS cordless phone. We first use commercial 802.11n cards and iperf [33] to transmit in the presence of these interferers. We find that, in our testbed, the cordless phone and the baby monitor prevent 802.11 from establishing any connection, reducing its throughput to zero. The microwave, on the other hand, results in a throughput reduction of 35–90%. We replace the commercial 802.11n cards with our USRP2 nodes and repeat the experiment with and without TIMO. We find that in the absence of

---

[3]We can lump $i(t)$ with the channel variable because we are not interested in decoding the symbols of the interferer.

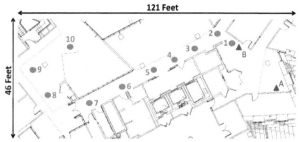

Figure 1—Testbed. An 802.11n transmitter located at A is communicating with an 802.11n receiver at B. The interferer is placed in one of the locations 1 to 10.

TIMO, when the USRP2 nodes are less than 31 feet away from the cordless phone or the baby monitors, they cannot deliver any packets. In contrast, in the presence of TIMO, and for the same locations, their throughput increases to 13-23 Mb/s. We also implement cross-technology interference nulling and show that it enables a MIMO node to significantly reduce the packet loss at the receiver of a competing technology, with the reduction in packet loss being as high as 14x in some locations.

2. IMPACT OF CROSS-TECHNOLOGY INTERFERENCE ON 802.11N

We study the interaction between high-power interferers and 802.11n and compare against the interaction between a low power interferer, Bluetooth, and 802.11n. We focus on three high-power technologies that are prevalent in today's environments [7]: DSSS cordless phones, baby monitors, and microwave ovens.

Experimental Setup: We use the Netgear N-300 USB-adapter and the Netgear N-300 router as the 802.11n client and AP respectively. Both devices support 2×2 MIMO. We place the AP and the client at positions A and B in Fig. 1. In each run, we place the interferer at one of the marked locations in Fig. 1. Our experiments include line-of-sight and non-line-of-sight situations, and show scenarios in which the interferer is within one foot of the 802.11n client as well as 90 feet away from it. We run iperf on the two 802.11n devices with the 802.11n client acting as the iperf server. The AP sends UDP packets for 2 minutes and logs the average throughput observed every 500 ms. In each location, we compute the observed 802.11n throughput first when the interferer is turned OFF and next when it is ON. Additionally, we use a USRP2 software radio to monitor a 25 MHz bandwidth. The USRP2 simply logs the time signal which we process offline to obtain the time and frequency characteristics of each interferer.

2.1 Digital Cordless Phone

We experiment with the Uniden TRU 4465-2 DSSS cordless handset system. The phone base and handset communicate using digital spread spectrum in the 2.4 GHz range. In each experiment, we fix the 802.11n AP and client at locations A and B and place both the cordless handset and the phone base at one of the locations in the testbed, 5 cm away from each other.

Fig. 2(a1) shows the 802.11n throughput with and without interference from the cordless phone. The figure shows that in the presence of the cordless phone, the 802.11n client and AP could not establish a connection and hence experienced zero throughput.

We next examine the time and frequency profile of the cordless phone to understand why 802.11 lost connectivity. Fig. 2(a2) plots the power profile of the phone as a function of time. The phone base and handset use Time-Division Duplexing (TDD) to communicate in the same frequency band. The handset transmits in the first time slot, followed immediately by a transmission from the phone base.

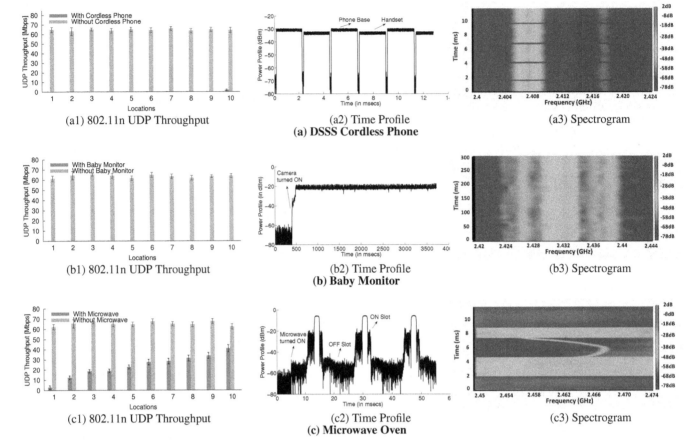

(a1) 802.11n UDP Throughput	(a2) Time Profile	(a3) Spectrogram
	(a) DSSS Cordless Phone	
(b1) 802.11n UDP Throughput	(b2) Time Profile	(b3) Spectrogram
	(b) Baby Monitor	
(c1) 802.11n UDP Throughput	(c2) Time Profile	(c3) Spectrogram
	(c) Microwave Oven	

Figure 2—Characteristics of High Power Interferers in the ISM Band.

Since these devices continuously transmit, the channel is never free. Thus, an 802.11n node that carrier senses the medium never gets the opportunity to transmit. Furthermore, since the phone transmits at about 25 mW [12], which is comparable to an 802.11 laptop, its interference continues even at distances as far as 90 feet.

The phone's spectrogram depicted in Fig. 2(a3) shows that the phone occupies about a 3-4 MHz wide band. Typically, the phone picks one channel out of 35 radio channels in the 2.407-2.478 GHz range. It stays on that channel as long as it does not experience persistent interference.

2.2 Baby Monitor

We experiment with the C-501 wireless monitoring toolkit, which has two units: a 2.4 GHz wireless camera that supports up to 4 different channels (i.e., 2.414 GHz, 2.432 GHz, 2.450 GHz and 2.468 GHz), and a wireless video receiver. For every interferer location, we measure the 802.11n throughput with the camera ON and OFF, and plot the results in Fig. 2(b1). The figure shows that the 802.11n client and AP could not establish a connection and, hence, could not exchange any packets for all tested locations.

We plot the time and frequency profile of the camera in Fig. 2(b2) and Fig. 2(b3). The frequency profile shows that the baby monitor occupies a relatively wide channel of 16 MHz. Further, the time profile shows that the camera transmits continuously, thus hogging the medium completely. These observations, compounded with the fact that the camera transmits at a fairly high power of 200 mW [2], explain the inability of 802.11n to obtain any throughput.

2.3 Microwave Ovens

We use the SHARP R-310CW microwave oven. Fig. 2(c1) shows the observed 802.11n average throughput for different placements

of the microwave. The figure shows that when the microwave is one foot away (in location 1), 802.11n suffers a throughput reduction of 90%. The 802.11n throughput improves as the microwave is moved away from the AP and its client, and the throughput loss decreases to 35% at the farthest location from the 802.11 client.

To understand this behavior, we plot the microwave's power profile over time in Fig. 2(b2). The figure shows that the microwave exhibits a periodic ON-OFF pattern, where an ON period lasts for about 10 ms and an OFF period lasts for 6 ms. In addition, the microwave also exhibits a continuous low interference, as evident from the 10 dB increase in the noise level after the microwave was turned on. The microwave time profile explains its impact on 802.11n. Specifically, at distant locations in our testbed, 802.11n transmits during the OFF periods but refrains from transmitting during the ON periods because it senses the medium as occupied. As a result, the throughput loss in such locations is about 35%. In contrast, at close distances, the 10 dB increase in the noise level generated by the microwave creates substantial interference for 802.11n causing most packets to be dropped even during the OFF periods.

2.4 Frequency Hopping Bluetooth

Finally, we evaluate the interference generated by Bluetooth devices. Bluetooth uses frequency hopping across a 79 MHz band in the 2.402-2.480 GHz range, occupying 1 MHz at any point in time. The most common devices use class 2 Bluetooth which transmits at a relatively low power of 2.5 mW [5].

For each interferer location, we transfer a 100 MB file between two Google Nexus One phones. We plot in Fig. 3 the throughput obtained by our 802.11n devices, in the presence and absence of the Bluetooth traffic. The figure shows that except in location 1, which

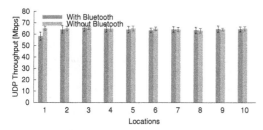

Figure 3—The impact of Bluetooth interference on 802.11n.

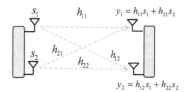

Figure 4—Decoding in a standard 2-by-2 MIMO system.

is one foot away from the 802.11n client, the Bluetooth exchange has no observable impact on the throughput of the 802.11n devices.

2.5 Summary

The above empirical study shows the following:

- High-power cross-technology interference can completely throttle 802.11n. Furthermore, loss of connectivity can occur even when the interferer is in a non-line-of-sight position and separated by 90 feet.
- While 802.11 and low-power interferers (e.g., Bluetooth) have managed a form of coexistence where both devices stay operational, coexistence with high-power devices (e.g., cordless phones, baby monitors, microwave, etc.) is lacking. Furthermore, the typical outcome of the interaction between 802.11n and a high-power interferer is that 802.11n either suffers a complete loss of connectivity or a significant throughput reduction. In §9 we show that even if carrier sense is deactivated, 802.11n continues to lose connectivity for many of the interferer's locations.
- Frequency isolation is increasingly difficult. Multiple of the studied interferers occupy relatively wideband channels of 16–25 MHz (e.g., camera and microwave). Moreover, these devices can occupy any band in the 802.11 spectrum. For example, both the cordless phone and the baby monitor have multiple channels that together cover almost the whole frequency range of 802.11.
- Finally, the characteristics of an interferer may change in time and frequency. The interferer may have ON-OFF periods, may move from one frequency to another, or change the width of the channel it occupies, like a microwave. This emphasizes the need for an agile solution that can quickly adapt to changes in the interference signal.

3. MIMO AND OFDM BACKGROUND

Consider the 2×2 MIMO system in Fig. 4. Say the sender transmits stream $s_1(t)$ on the first antenna, and $s_2(t)$ on the second antenna. The wireless channel linearly combines the signal samples corresponding to the two streams. Therefore, the receiver receives the following linear combinations on its two antennas:

$$y_1(t) = h_{11}s_1(t) + h_{21}s_2(t) \qquad (5)$$
$$y_2(t) = h_{12}s_1(t) + h_{22}s_2(t), \qquad (6)$$

where h_{ij} is a complex number whose magnitude and angle refer to the attenuation and delay along the path from the ith antenna on the sender to the jth antenna on the receiver, as shown in Fig. 4. If the receiver knows the channel coefficients, h_{ij}, it can solve the above two linear equations to obtain the two unknowns, $s_1(t)$ and $s_2(t)$, and decode the two transmitted streams.

To enable the receiver to estimate the channel coefficients, h_{ij}, a MIMO sender starts each frame by transmitting a known preamble from each of its antennas, one after the other. The receiver uses its knowledge of the transmitted preamble and the received signal samples to compute the channel coefficients, which it uses to decode the rest of the bits in the frame.

The above model assumes a narrowband channel, whose bandwidth is limited to a few MHz. In wideband channels, different frequencies may experience different channels. Thus, the channel function cannot be expressed as a single complex number; it has to be expressed as a complex filter, and the multiplication becomes a convolution:

$$y_1(t) = \mathbf{h}_{11} * s_1(t) + \mathbf{h}_{21} * s_2(t)$$
$$y_2(t) = \mathbf{h}_{12} * s_1(t) + \mathbf{h}_{22} * s_2(t),$$

Modern wireless technologies like 802.11a/g/n, WiMax, and LTE handle such wide channels by operating on the signal in the frequency domain using OFDM. OFDM divides the channel frequency spectrum into many narrow subbands called OFDM subcarriers. The receiver takes an FFT of the received signal and operates on individual OFDM subcarriers, as if they were narrowband channels, i.e., the receiver applies the model in Eqs. 5 and 6 to the frequency domain signal, and decodes the transmitted symbols.

In 802.11, there are 64 OFDM subcarriers, four of which are called pilots that have a known symbol pattern to allow the receiver track the channel [24]. Additionally, 48 subcarriers are used to transmit data and the rest are unused for distortion reasons.

4. PROBLEM DOMAIN

TIMO deals with high power cross-technology interference in 802.11n networks. We focus on typical situations that arise in the operation of 802.11 networks. In particular,

- TIMO tackles scenarios in which the interferer is a single antenna device. This is typically the case for current 802.11 interferers, like baby monitors, microwave ovens, cordless phones, surveillance cameras, etc.
- TIMO applies to scenarios in which the interfering signal lasts more than a few seconds. This constraint does not necessarily mean that the interferer transmits continuously for that duration. For example, a microwave signal that lasts for a few seconds satisfies our constraint despite having OFF periods.
- TIMO applies to scenarios where, in the absence of an interferer, the 802.11n receiver can use MIMO multiplexing, i.e., it can receive multiple concurrent streams at some bitrate. If the 802.11n receiver cannot multiplex streams from the same technology, it cannot be made to multiplex streams from different technologies.
- TIMO can address environments with multiple concurrent interferers, as long as the interferers are in different frequencies (i.e., different 802.11 OFDM subcarriers). We believe this to be the common case in today's networks because the presence of multiple high-power interferers in the same band will cause them to interfere with each other, and is likely to prevent the proper operation of the device.

5. TIMO

TIMO extends the MIMO design to operate across diverse wireless technologies that may differ in modulation, coding, packet format, etc. It develops two primitives: The first primitive enables a

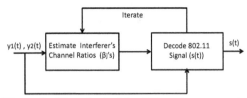

Figure 5—Flowchart of the different components.

MIMO 802.11n pair to exchange packets in the presence of an unknown interference signal, as if the unknown interference were a single-antenna 802.11 transmission. For example, an 802.11n AP-Client pair may use this primitive to correctly decode packets in the presence of the ON periods of a microwave oven. The second primitive enables a MIMO node to transmit in the presence of an unknown bi-directional technology without hampering reception at the receiver of the unknown technology. For example, an 802.11n node may use this primitive to transmit in the presence of a cordless phone without hampering the phone's operation. The next few sections describe these two primitives in detail.

6. DECODING IN THE PRESENCE OF CROSS-TECHNOLOGY INTERFERENCE

Consider a scenario in which two 802.11n nodes want to communicate in the presence of high-power cross-technology interference. For clarity, we will explain the design in the context of a 2-antenna 802.11n receiver decoding a single 802.11n transmission, in the presence of an interferer. The results extend to any number of antennas as we explain in the appendix.

In this case, the signal at the 2-antenna 802.11n receiver is the sum of the signal of interest, $s(t)$, and the interference signal, $i(t)$, after convolving them with their respective channels to the receiver:

$$y_1(t) = \mathbf{h}_i * i(t) + \mathbf{h}_s * s(t) \qquad (7)$$
$$y_2(t) = \mathbf{h}'_i * i(t) + \mathbf{h}'_s * s(t), \qquad (8)$$

where $\mathbf{h}_i$ and $\mathbf{h}'_i$ are the channel functions of the interference signal, and $\mathbf{h}_s$ and $\mathbf{h}'_s$ are channel functions of the signal of interest. We will explain TIMO's decoding algorithm assuming the receiver knows the channel of the signal of interest. In §6.4, we explain how the receiver obtains this channel in the presence of interference.

Since the signal of interest (i.e., that of 802.11n) is an OFDM signal, the receiver processes its input in the frequency domain by taking an FFT. Thus, for each OFDM subcarrier, j, the receiver obtains the following equations:

$$Y_{1j} = H_{ij}I_j + H_{sj}S_j \qquad (9)$$
$$Y_{2j} = H'_{ij}I_j + H'_{sj}S_j, \qquad (10)$$

where the terms in the above equations are the frequency version of the terms in Eqs. 7 and 8, for a particular OFDM subcarrier. Thus, the receiver can express the signal of interest as:

$$S_j = \frac{Y_{1j} - \beta_j Y_{2j}}{H_{sj} - \beta_j H'_{sj}} \quad for\ \beta_j = \frac{H_{ij}}{H'_{ij}}. \qquad (11)$$

All terms in Eq. 11 are known at the receiver, except for β_j. The objective of the receiver is to figure out β_j in each subcarrier, and use it to decode the signal of interest, S_j, in that subcarrier.

A TIMO receiver has three main components shown in Fig. 5. 1) An algorithm for computing the interferer's channel ratio in an OFDM subcarrier without knowing the interferer's preamble or signal structure. 2) A decoder that allows the receiver to decode the signal of interest given the interferer's channel ratio in every OFDM subcarrier. 3) An iteration mechanism that reduces the noise in the computation of channel ratios, hence increasing SNR. The following sections describe these components.

6.1 Computing the Interferer's Channel Ratio

A simplistic approach for computing the ratio $\beta_j = \frac{H_{ij}}{H'_{ij}}$ would rely on that the signal S_j in the OFDM pilots is known to the receiver. Thus, if one assumes β_j is the same for all OFDM subcarriers, one can simply substitute the signal S_j, where j is a pilot subcarrier, in Eq. 11, and use that equation to compute the ratio β. The receiver then uses this ratio to compute signal values in other OFDM subcarriers that contain data symbols. However, the assumption that the interferer channel ratio is the same in all OFDM subcarriers is typically invalid for several reasons. First, there might be multiple interferers each of them operating in a different frequency band. For example, the interfering signal may be a combination of two cordless phone signals each occupying upto 4 MHz and overlapping with a different set of 802.11n OFDM subcarriers. Second, there might be an interferer that hops across the OFDM subcarriers, but does not always occupy all subcarriers. This is the case for the narrowband signal during the microwave ON period. Finally, the interferer may have a relatively wideband channel, like the baby monitor which can span upto 16 MHz. In this case, the channel of the interferer may differ across the OFDM subcarriers due to multipath and hence the channel ratio also changes across the subcarriers.

Thus, the receiver should compute the interferer's channel ratio for each OFDM subcarrier independently. Since most OFDM subcarriers carry data and contain no known patterns, the receiver has to compute this ratio without any known symbols.

Below we use Eqs. 9 and 10 to obtain a closed form expression for the interferer's channel ratio in each OFDM subcarrier. To do so, we first eliminate the contribution from the signal of interest S_j, by multiplying Eq. 10 with $\frac{H_{sj}}{H'_{sj}}$ and subtracting it from Eq. 9:

$$Y_{1j} - \frac{H_{sj}}{H'_{sj}}Y_{2j} = (\frac{H_{ij}}{H'_{ij}} - \frac{H_{sj}}{H'_{sj}})H'_{ij}I_j$$

Next, we multiply the resulting equation with the conjugate of Y_{2j}, and take the expectation:

$$E[(Y_{1j} - \frac{H_{sj}}{H'_{sj}}Y_{2j})Y^*_{2j}] = (\frac{H_{ij}}{H'_{ij}} - \frac{H_{sj}}{H'_{sj}})E[H'_{ij}I_jY^*_{2j}]$$
$$= (\frac{H_{ij}}{H'_{ij}} - \frac{H_{sj}}{H'_{sj}})E[H'_{ij}I_j(H'^*_{ij}I^*_j + H'^*_{sj}S^*_j)]$$
$$= (\frac{H_{ij}}{H'_{ij}} - \frac{H_{sj}}{H'_{sj}})(E[|H'_{ij}I_j|^2] + H'^*_{sj}H'_{ij}E[I_jS^*_j])$$
$$= (\frac{H_{ij}}{H'_{ij}} - \frac{H_{sj}}{H'_{sj}})E[|H'_{ij}I_j|^2]$$
$$= (\beta_j - \frac{H_{sj}}{H'_{sj}})P'_{Ij}, \qquad (12)$$

where $|x|^2 = xx^*$ denotes the square of the amplitude of the complex number x, and $E[I_jS^*_j] = 0$ because the signal of interest is independent from the interference signal and hence their correlation is zero. Also $P'_{Ij} = E[|H'_{ij}I_j|^2]$ is the received interference power in OFDM subcarrier j on the second antenna of the 802.11n receiver.

Eq. 12 has two unknown β_j and P'_{Ij}. Thus, if the receiver knows the interferer's received power, P'_{Ij}, it can solve Eq. 12 to obtain the desired ratio. To compute P'_{Ij}, the receiver takes Eq. 10, multiplies it by its conjugate, and then computes the expectation, i.e.:

$$E[Y_{2j}Y^*_{2j}] = E[(H'_{ij}I_j + H'_sS_j)(H'_{ij}I_j + H'_sS_j)^*]$$
$$= E[|H'_{ij}I_j|^2] + E[|H'_sS_j|^2]$$
$$= P'_{Ij} + P'_{sj}, \qquad (13)$$

where P'_{sj} is the power of the signal of interest on the second antenna in the jth OFDM subcarrier. Again, to reach Eq. 13 we have exploited the fact that the interference signal and the signal of interest are independent of each other.

We can solve Eq. 12 and Eq. 13 together to obtain the ratio:

$$\beta_j = \frac{H_{ij}}{H'_{ij}} = \frac{E[(Y_{1j} - \frac{H_{sj}}{H'_{sj}} Y_{2j})Y^*_{2j}]}{E[|Y_{2j}|^2] - P'_{Sj}} + \frac{H_{sj}}{H'_{sj}}. \tag{14}$$

This equation enables the 802.11 receiver to compute the interferer's channel ratio without any known symbols, simply by substituting the power and the channel ratio for $s(t)$.

It is important to note that the above derivation exploits that expectations can be computed by taking averages. The accuracy of this estimate increases as one averages over more signal symbols. In §6.3 we will discuss how we can obtain a good accuracy without averaging over many symbols.

6.2 Decoding the Signal of Interest

Once the 802.11n receiver has an estimate of the interferer's channel ratio, β_j, in each OFDM subcarrier, it proceeds to decode its own signal of interest. One way to decode would be to substitute β_j in Eq. 11 to compute S_j in the frequency domain. This approach works well when the interferer is a narrowband signal, like a cordless phone. However, it has low accuracy in scenarios the interferer has a relatively wideband channel, like a baby monitor that spans 16 MHz. This is because wideband signals suffer from multipath effects; i.e., the signal travels from the sender to the receiver along multiple paths with different delays. A wideband receiver receives the combination of multiple copies of the same signal with different relative delays. This leads to inter-symbol interference (ISI), which mathematically is equivalent to convolving the time-domain signal with the channel on the traversed paths.

To deal with ISI, an OFDM transmitter inserts a cyclic prefix between consecutive symbols. The receiver discards the cyclic prefix and takes the remaining signal, thus eliminating any interference from adjacent symbols. This, however, does not work when we have a wideband interferer like the baby monitor. First, its signal may not have a cyclic prefix. Second, even if it does, as noted by past work on concurrent 802.11n transmissions [35], it is unlikely that the cyclic prefixes of the two devices are synchronized, in which case the receiver cannot discard a single cyclic prefix that eliminates ISI for both the devices.

The above discussion means that in the frequency domain, the interferer's signal, I_j, will experience ISI which would add noise. As a result, Eqs. 9 and 10 have additional noise terms due to ISI. While this is not a problem for the channel ratio estimation since one can average across more samples to obtain an accurate estimate of β_j; this additional noise would reduce the SNR for the signal of interest and, hence, affect its throughput.

The solution to the ISI problem is, however, simple. The 802.11n receiver needs to decode the signal of interest $s(t)$ by eliminating interference in the time domain. Here, ISI is simply a convolution with a filter, which can be removed by applying the inverse filter (i.e., an equalizer). Thus, we consider again the initial time domain Eqs. 7 and 8 which describe the signal at the 802.11n receiver:

$$y_1(t) = \mathbf{h}_i * i(t) + \mathbf{h}_s * s(t) \tag{15}$$
$$y_2(t) = \mathbf{h}'_i * i(t) + \mathbf{h}'_s * s(t), \tag{16}$$

We want to find a filter, $\mathbf{h}$, such that:

$$\mathbf{h} * \mathbf{h}'_i = \mathbf{h}_i$$

Given such a filter, the receiver can convolve $\mathbf{h}$ with Eq. 16 and subtract the resulting equation from Eq. 15 to eliminate $i(t)$ and

obtain an equation in $s(t)$, which it can decode using a standard 802.11 decoder.[4]

The above filter can be represented in the frequency domain as:

$$H_j H'_{ij} = H_{ij} \Rightarrow H_j = \frac{H_{ij}}{H'_{ij}} = \beta_j$$

Thus, we can compute the desired filter $\mathbf{h}$ by taking the IFFT of the interferer channel ratios, β_j's, computed in §6.1.

To summarize, the 802.11n receiver first moves the received signal to the frequency domain where it computes the interferer channel ratios using Eq. 14 while averaging over multiple samples to reduce the ISI and noise. Then, it transforms the interferer channel ratio into a time domain filter by taking an IFFT. Finally, it uses the filter to eliminate interference in the time domain. The receiver can now take this interference-free signal and decode its signal of interest using a standard 802.11 decoder.

6.3 Iterating to Increase Accuracy

The algorithm in §6.1 computes expectations by taking averages over multiple OFDM symbols. A packet, however, may not have enough OFDM symbols to obtain a highly accurate estimate. Also averaging over multiple packets will reduce TIMO's ability to deal with a dynamic interferer. Thus, in this section we are interested in obtaining an accurate estimate of the interferer's channel ratio, β_j, using only a few OFDM symbols.

To increase the accuracy of the estimate without much averaging, the receiver iterates over the following two steps:

Initialization: The receiver obtains a rough estimate of β_j by averaging over a limited number of OFDM symbols.

Step 1: The receiver uses its estimate of β_j to obtain the signal, $s(t)$, as in §6.2. The receiver then decodes $s(t)$ using the standard decoder to obtain the transmitted bits.

Step 2: The receiver re-modulates the decoded bits to obtain an estimate of $s(t)$, which we call $\hat{s}(t)$. The receiver convolves $\hat{s}(t)$ with the channel functions and subtracts the results from $y_1(t)$ and $y_2(t)$. Thus, we obtain the following:

$$\hat{y}_1(t) = \mathbf{h}_i * i(t) + \mathbf{h}_s * (s(t) - \hat{s}(t))$$
$$\hat{y}_2(t) = \mathbf{h}'_i * i(t) + \mathbf{h}'_s * (s(t) - \hat{s}(t)).$$

The receiver then obtains a new estimate for β_j while treating $(s(t) - \hat{s}(t))$ as the new signal of interest.

After iterating between Step 1 and 2 for two or three times, the receiver obtains an accurate estimate of the interferer's channel ratio β_j, which it uses to decode signal $s(t)$.

The reason why the above algorithm works is that in each iteration, the signal of interest used in Step 2, $(s(t) - \hat{s}(t))$, has a smaller magnitude. Since, in Step 2, the receiver is focused on estimating the interferer's ratio, the signal of interest plays the role of noise; reducing this signal's magnitude increases the accuracy of the ratio estimate. This higher accuracy in the ratio β_j percolates to the estimate of $s(t)$ in Step 1. Consequently, the decoded bits are more accurate and lead to even smaller difference between $\hat{s}(t)$ and $s(t)$, and hence an even more accurate β_j.

6.4 Estimating the 802.11n Channel Functions

So far, we have assumed that the 802.11n receiver knows the channel of the signal of interest, H_{sj} and H'_{sj}. To compute this channel we distinguish between two cases. First, the signal of interest

---

[4]As described in §3, such a decoder would apply FFT and decode in the frequency domain.

starts before the interference in which case the receiver can use the 802.11 preamble to compute the channel, as usual. Second, the interference signal starts before the signal of interest. In this case, the receiver can easily compute the interferer's channel ratio $\beta_j = \frac{H_{ij}}{H'_{ij}}$ by taking the ratio of the signals it receives on its two antennas $Y_{1j} = H_{ij}I_j$ and $Y_{2j} = H'_{ij}I_j$. Once the receiver knows the interferer's channel ratio, it computes the equalization filter described in §6.2 and uses it to eliminate the interference signal. The receiver can then use the 802.11n preamble to compute the channel as usual.

Two points are worth noting: First, while it is easy to compute the interferer's channel ratios when the interferer is alone on the medium, this does not eliminate the need to continue tracking the interferer's channel ratio using the algorithm in §6.1. In particular, the channel ratio may change as the interferer moves to a different frequency, as in the narrowband phase of a microwave signal, or it might change for a mobile interferer, as with the cordless phone.

Second, the above scheme will miss in scenarios in which the interference and the 802.11n signal starts during the same OFDM symbol. This event has a low probability, and the resulting packet loss is minor in comparison to the packet loss observed without TIMO. When such an event occurs the packet will be retransmitted by its sender as usual.

6.5 Finding the Interference Boundaries

Estimating the interferer's channel ratio, β_j, using Eq. 14 requires the 802.11n receiver to compute the expectations by taking averages over multiple OFDM symbols. This averaging, however, needs to be done only over symbols that are affected by interference. Thus, the 802.11n receiver needs to determine where, in a packet, interference starts and where it stops. The question of identifying the sequence of symbols affected by interference has been addressed in few recent systems, like PPR [25] and SoftRate [37]. Our approach follows the same principles. Specifically, when the interference signal starts, it causes a dramatic increase in decoding errors. As shown in Fig. 6(a), these errors appear at the PHY layer as large differences between the received symbol and the nearest constellation points in the I and Q diagram. We refer to these differences as soft errors. Thus, for each OFDM subcarrier, the 802.11n receiver computes the soft-error, and normalizes it by the minimum distance of the constellation. As shown in Fig. 6(b), when the interferer starts, the soft errors jumps; when it ends, they go back to their low values. In our implementation we consider a jump that is higher than doubling the errors as a potential interferer, i.e., interference above 3 dB. This means that we might miss low power interferers, but such interferers can be dealt with using traditional methods like reducing the bit rate.

6.6 Putting it together

A TIMO receiver first performs packet detection as usual by looking for jumps in received power (using standard window detection algorithms [24]). Then, the receiver computes the 802.11 preamble cross-correlation, in a manner similar to current 802.11. If the cross-correlation stays low, the receiver works under the assumption that the signal of interest may start later. Hence, it computes the channel ratios for the signal though it is not its signal of interest. On the other hand, if the cross-correlation spikes, the receiver identifies the packet as a signal of interest. It continues decoding the packet using a standard 802.11 decoder [15]. If the packet does not pass the checksum test, the receiver computes the soft-errors as described in §6.5. If the soft-errors jump by over 3 dB, the receiver initiates the channel ratio estimation algorithm. Specifically, for each OFDM bin, the TIMO decoder starts at the symbol where the soft errors jump and proceeds to compute the interference

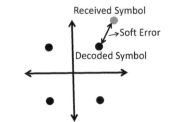

(a) Soft-errors in a 4QAM Constellation.

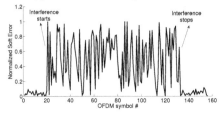

(b) Soft-errors with Interference.

Figure 6—Soft errors increase in the presence of interference.

channel ratios in an iterative manner as described in §6.3. Once the channel ratios are estimated for each OFDM subcarrier, the receiver uses the decoder in §6.2 to decode its signal of interest.

6.7 Complexity

While past work that deals with cross-technology interference [6, 34] typically employs different mechanisms for different technologies, TIMO is technology agnostic and hence its complexity stays constant as the number of technologies in the ISM band increases. Further, the components used in TIMO such as correlation, equalization and projection, are also used in MIMO receivers (though for a different purpose), and hence are amenable to hardware implementations.

7. ENSURING THE INTERFERER CAN DECODE

A MIMO transmitter can also encode its signal to prevent interference to a competing transmission from a different technology. Specifically, let $i(t)$ be the competing signal and $s_1(t)$ and $s_2(t)$ the two streams that a 2-antenna 802.11n node transmits. The receiver of the competing signal receives the following:

$$z(t) = h_i i(t) + h_{s1} s_1(t) + h_{s2} s_2(t), \quad (17)$$

where h_i refers to the channel from its transmitter and h_{s1} and h_{s2} are the channels from the 2-antenna 802.11n transmitter. The 802.11n transmitter can cancel its signal at the receiver of the competing technology by ensuring that the signals it transmits on its two antennas satisfy $s_2(t) = -\frac{h_{s1}}{h_{s2}} s_1(t)$. Such a technique is typically referred to as interference nulling [36].[5]

We note that nulling does not require the knowledge of the exact channels to the receiver. It is sufficient to know the channel ratios to null the signal at some receiver. This is crucial since for cross-technology scenarios, it is hard to estimate the exact channel.

But how does the 802.11n transmitter compute the channel ratio to the interferer's receiver? If the interfering technology is bidirectional in the frequency of interest, then our 802.11n nodes can use the interference caused by the receiver's response to compute the channel ratio from the receiver to itself. This can be done by leveraging the algorithm in §6.1. The required ratio for nulling, however, refers to the channels in the opposite direction, i.e., from our 802.11n transmitter to the interfering receiver. To deal with this

---

[5]Note that having the 802.11n transmitter perform interference nulling does not require any modification to decoding at the 802.11n receiver.

issue, TIMO exploits that wireless channels exhibit reciprocity, i.e., the channel function in the forward and backward direction is the same. Reciprocity is a known property that has been validated empirically by multiple studies [21, 39, 28].[6] Using reciprocity one can compute the required channel ratio. Once the ratio is computed, the transmitter can perform interference nulling. We note that since it is hard to synchronize wideband cross-technology interferers with 802.11, to avoid ISI we perform nulling by using a time-domain equalizer similar to §6.2.

Thus, interference nulling combined with our algorithm for estimating the interferer's channel ratio provide a new primitive that enables a MIMO node to transmit in the presence of a different technology without hampering reception of that technology. This primitive, however, requires the competing technology to be bidirectional, i.e., the competing receiver acks the signal or transmits its own messages, like a cordless phone.

If the technology is bidirectional, then the MIMO transmitter can learn the channel ratio to the communicating node pair, using the interference they create. The MIMO transmitter then alternates between nulling its signal at the two communicating nodes. For example, in the case of a cordless phone, the 802.11 transmitter has to switch between nulling its signal at the handset and nulling its signal at the base. In the case of the cordless phone, the switching time is constant, and for the tested phone it is 2.25 ms. Even if the switching time is not constant, as long as the pattern of the interference is persistent (e.g., one data packet, followed by one ack), the MIMO node can monitor the medium and immediately switch every time the medium goes idle.

On the other hand, if the receiver of the competing technology is not bidirectional, an 802.11n device has no way to compute its channel ratio, and hence cannot cancel its signal at the receiver of the competing technology. The impact of such interference will depend on the competing technology. For example, interference does not hamper a microwave oven function. Also, analog devices (e.g., an analog camera) have some level of resistance to interference which causes smooth degradation in their signal, and while they suffer from interference, they can still function if the interferer is not in close proximity (see §9).

In general, our objective is to create a form of coexistence between 802.11n and high-power interferers that approaches the coexistence it enjoys with low-power devices like Bluetooth, where the two technologies may interferer if they are in close proximity but the interference is limited and does not cause either device to become completely dysfunctional. Unidirectional devices which do not sense the medium or use any feedback from their receiver tend to show some level of resistance to interference. Hence, even if the 802.11n node did not cancel its interference at their receiver, they can still support some level of coexistence, as long as 802.11n can protect itself from their interference.

8. IMPLEMENTATION

We have built a prototype of TIMO using the USRP2 radio platform and the GNURadio software package. A 2×2 MIMO system is built using two USRP2 radio-boards connected via an external clock [9]. Each USRP2 is configured to span a 10 MHz channel by setting both the interpolation rate and decimation rate to 10. The resulting MIMO node runs a PHY layer similar to that

---

[6]To use it in our system, one needs to calibrate the effect of the hardware before applying reciprocity. This calibration, however, is done once for the hardware. Furthermore, an 802.11n transmitter can perform this task without the help of any other node because it merely involves taking the difference between the two transmit chains attached to its two antennas.

of 802.11n, i.e., it has 64 OFDM subcarriers, a modulation choice of BPSK, 4QAM, 16QAM, or 64QAM, and punctured convolution codes with standard 802.11 code rates [15]. Since we operate at half the 802.11 bandwidth, the possible bit rates span 3 to 27 Mbps.

We modify the receiver MIMO decoding algorithm to incorporate TIMO (summarized in §6.6). We also implemented interference nulling at the MIMO transmitters. To work with cross-technology interference, the transmitter first computes the channel ratios and then uses them for nulling (as described in §7).

9. PERFORMANCE EVALUATION

We evaluate TIMO with three high-power interferers: a DSSS cordless phone, a microwave oven, and a baby monitor.

9.1 Cordless Phone

Again, we use the Uniden TRU 4465-2 cordless phone as the interferer. We also use the same testbed in Fig. 1.

Addressing Cross-Technology Interference: We first evaluate TIMO's ability to help 802.11n nodes operate in the presence of high power cross-technology interference. We place two USRP-based 802.11n nodes in locations A and B in Fig. 1. In each run, we place the cordless phone system in one of the 10 interferer locations in Fig. 1. We transfer a 20 MB file between the 802.11n pair at the best bitrate for the channel in the presence of interference from the cordless phone. This rate is determined by initially trying all the possible bitrates and choosing the one which yields the highest throughput for the rest of the run. The 802.11 receiver logs the received samples and processes them both with and without TIMO.

Note that in contrast to the experiments done with commercial 802.11n nodes, the USRP implementation of 802.11n does not use carrier sense. Carrier sense is hard to implement in software due to its strict timing requirements. This constraint, however, can be beneficial. In particular, the lack of carrier sense provides insight into whether the throughput loss of commercial 802.11n is due to the nodes sensing the phone's signal and abstaining from transmitting, or due to their packets being corrupted by interference.

Fig. 7(a) plots the throughput of the 802.11 MIMO nodes in the presence of the phone signal, with and without TIMO. The figure reveals the following:

- Without TIMO, interference from the cordless phone causes the 802.11 nodes to completely lose connectivity in half of the testbed locations. This loss of connectivity occurs even though the nodes have deactivated carrier sense and are using the best bit rate for the channel. This means that the interference in these locations is too high even for the lowest bit rate supported by 802.11. This loss in connectivity can be attributed to the fact that the phone system transmits continuously at a high power. Hence, the 802.11 packets are always subject to strong interference. As the interferer moves away from the 802.11 USRP-based nodes, their throughput improves because of reduced interference.

- In contrast, with TIMO, the 802.11 nodes never experience disconnectivity. Also, their throughput becomes much higher and close to optimal (24.5Mbps) at most locations. The throughput decreases slightly as the phone moves closer to the 802.11 receiver in location B because of residual interference, but continues to be 78% of the optimal throughput even when the phone is one foot away from the 802.11 receiver. These results indicate that TIMO is successful at exploiting MIMO capability to address 802.11 cross-technology interference.

- Comparing the throughput of the USRP-based 802.11n implementation to that of commercial 802.11n in §2 shows that while carrier sense contributed to the loss of connectivity particularly

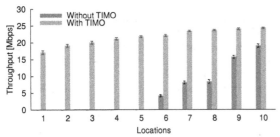
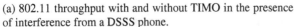
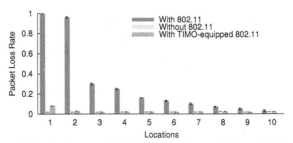

(a) 802.11 throughput with and without TIMO in the presence of interference from a DSSS phone.

(b) Packet loss at the DSSS phone with and without TIMO.

Figure 7—Interference from a DSSS Cordless Phone: Figure (a) shows that TIMO significantly improves the throughput of 802.11 USRP2-based nodes in the presence of interference from a DSSS phone. Figure (b) shows that if 802.11 nodes transmit concurrently with a DSSS cordless phone, they can cause the phone a dramatic packet loss at close distances. TIMO, however, enables such nodes to transmit concurrently with the phone without hampering its performance.

when the interferers are in locations 6–10, it is not the main reason since even though the USRP nodes do not implement carrier sense, they still lose connectivity in 50% of the locations.

Transmitting without Harming the Competing Technology:
Next, we evaluate TIMO's ability to allow 802.11n to transmit concurrently with a cordless phone in the same frequency band, but without harming the phone's transmission. The commercial phone does not give us access to packets, making it hard to evaluate the impact of TIMO's interference nulling. Instead, we implement the phone's physical layer in GNURadio and experiment with a USRP-based DSSS phone. We try to match the physical layer description of the Uniden phone. In particular, the transmitter feeds digital bits to a scrambler, differential encoder, and a spread spectrum module. The spread spectrum module sends bits at a data rate of 1.366 Mbps over FSK modulation. The receiver computes the correlation with the spreading code and outputs the data bits. For every packet we use the CRC to detect if it was correctly received.

We place the USRP nodes that perform the role of the phone base and handset at location A and B in the testbed. We then place a 802.11 USRP transmitter at each of locations 1 to 10 in the testbed, and let it transmit at the same time as the USRP phone. The 802.11 USRP transmitter uses TIMO to null its signal at the phone.

The 802.11 transmitter has to alternate between nulling its signal at the phone base and the handset. Since the Uniden phone packets have a fixed duration of 2.25 ms [12], this switching can easily happen on 802.11 hardware. However, due to the software nature of GNURadio, it is hard to alternate with the phone system at a granularity of about 2.25 ms. Thus, in our experiments, we increase the inter-packet time and the packet duration to 20 ms, which allows us to alternate with the phone system in software.

Each run of the experiment has three parts. First, the phone handset and base exchange packets without any interference from the 802.11n transmitter. Next, the handset and base exchange packets with interference from the 802.11 node but without TIMO. Finally, the handset and base exchange packets concurrently with the 802.11n node which uses TIMO.

Fig. 7(b) shows the packet loss rate at the handset for the above three cases. The figure shows three main trends.

- In comparison with 802.11n, the DSSS phone is more resilient to cross-technology interference. This is due to its use of FSK combined with a high redundancy DSSS code. Despite this resilience, without TIMO, the phone suffers a high loss rate at locations close to the 802.11 nodes.
- In contrast, TIMO significantly reduces the loss rate at the handset across all the locations. Further, in locations 2-10 the loss rate is almost as low as that without any interference. We note that this is true even for locations where the interferer is closer to the

handset than the base is to the handset (locations 2-4). Thus, we conclude that TIMO can help 802.11 and DSSS phones coexist.
- Finally, when the 802.11 interferer is less than a foot from the handset (location 1), the packet loss rate is higher than that without interference. This is because, in practice, it is difficult to completely eliminate interference using interference nulling. The residual interference may cause an increase in packet loss rate at such close distances. However, even at location 1, while TIMO did not completely eliminate interference, it still dramatically reduces the packet losses by more than 14x, from 100% to about 6-7%.

9.2 Baby Monitor

Next, we evaluate TIMO with a baby monitor.

Impact of baby monitors on 802.11n: To evaluate this, we repeat the previous experiment after replacing the microwave with the C-501 baby monitor. For every interferer location, we run the system with and without TIMO, and plot the results in Fig. 8(a). The figure shows that TIMO significantly increases the throughput in the presence of interference from the tested baby monitor. In particular, without TIMO the 802.11 nodes experience complete disconnectivity for 60% of locations of the baby monitor. In contrast, with TIMO no scenario causes disconnectivity and the overall throughput is significantly higher. We note that in comparison to the performance of commercial 802.11n nodes, the USRP-based 802.11n implementation does not use carrier sense, and hence was able to transmit and obtain some throughput in scenarios where the commercial 802.11n nodes refrained from transmitting due to carrier sense.

Impact of 802.11n transmissions on baby monitors: Communication in the baby monitor system is one-way. The camera continuously broadcasts the analog video. A monitor in range of the device receives the signal, decodes it and displays it on its screen. Given no signal from the video receiver, TIMO is limited in its ability to protect the transmitted video. Thus, we would like to check how the camera is affected by interference from our 802.11 implementation (which use the same power level as a laptop, i.e., about 30 mW).

To do so, we place the camera and its video receiver in locations A and B in the testbed. We move the 802.11-USRP node across the various interferer locations, and at each location, we ensure it interferes with the camera's transmission. We compare the received video quality with and without interference from 802.11. We measure video quality using PSNR, which is a standard video metric. A PSNR of less than 20 dB is hard to watch, whereas PSNRs in the range 25–30 dB are good. The PSNR can be computed only with respect to the original video. However, the camera does not provide us access to the original video before transmission over the wireless medium. To obtain a video baseline, we focus the camera on

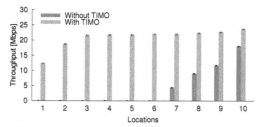

(a) 802.11 throughput with and without TIMO in the presence of interference from a baby monitor.

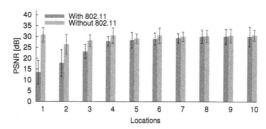

(b) Camera PSNR. (above 20 dB is watchable; above 25 is good [40]).

Figure 8—Interference from a Baby Monitor: Figure (a) shows that TIMO significantly improves the throughput of 802.11 nodes in the presence of interference from a baby monitor. Figure (b) shows that while TIMO cannot cancel its signal at the camera's receiver because it use a unidirectional communication, the impact of interference on the camera's signal is watchable in all locations but the two closest to the 802.11 nodes.

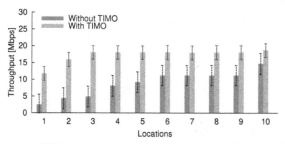

Figure 9—802.11 throughput with interference from a Microwave Oven: The figure shows that TIMO increases resilience to microwave interference.

a static image for all experiments, and make it transmit the same frame 1000 times. Then, we take the average pixel value in these 1000 versions of the same frame and consider this to be the ground truth. All experiments are run with the camera focused on the same picture so that they can be compared with this ground truth.

Fig. 8(b) shows the PSNR of the received video both with and without interference from our USRP-based 802.11 implementation. The figure shows that at the closest two locations, which are less than 6 feet away from the 802.11 interferer, the video is not watchable. However, for the rest of the locations, the video quality stays watchable. Further, for seven out of the ten testbed locations, the video PSNR hardly changes from its value without interference. This is expected because devices that blast the medium without checking for interference or without any feedback tend to be relatively resilient to some level of interference.

We note that since the monitoring system is uni-directional, TIMO cannot cancel its signal at potential video receivers; hence, we observe that interference degrades the monitoring system's performance at nearby locations. However, in contrast to the current mode of operation, where 802.11 loses connectivity in most locations due to interference, TIMO is an improvement over the status quo because it reduces the range of interference to close-by locations. This moves the system to a scenario where the two technologies enjoy some level of coexistence, which despite being far from optimal, is more acceptable than the current situation.

9.3 Microwave Oven

We evaluate TIMO's performance in the presence of interference from the microwave oven used in the experiments in §2. We repeat the experiment we conducted with the cordless phone, where we place the USRP-based 802.11 devices in locations A and B, and let them exchange traffic with the microwave on and off. We perform the experiment for each of the ten interferer locations in the testbed. In each run, the 802.11 transmitter uses the best bitrate as in §9.1.

Fig. 9 shows the average throughput and standard deviation, with and without TIMO. Without TIMO, the performance of the USRP2

nodes is relatively similar to that of the commercial 802.11n nodes. Specifically, at short distances, the throughput is very low due to increased interference. As the microwave is moved away, the nodes start getting packet through during the OFF periods of the microwave. In contrast, TIMO significantly increases resilience to interference from the microwave, allowing the 802.11 USRP node to deliver packets efficiently even during the ON periods of the microwave. Microwave ovens leak significantly high power during the ON periods, which could reach 1 Watt [17]. The results show that TIMO is effective even with such high-power interferers.

TIMO's approach is based on treating cross technology interference as if it were a stream from a single-antenna node of the same technology. Residential microwave ovens are equipped with a cavity magnetron which radiates energy in the 2.4 GHz range. Since they have only one magnetron radiating energy, theory concludes that they act as a single antenna device [34]. Our results confirm theoretical conclusions and show that TIMO can successfully treat a microwave as a single-antenna interferer.

9.4 Multiple Interferers

This experiment includes three node pairs with different transmission technologies: our 2×2 802.11n implementation, our DSSS phone implementation, and a GNURadio ZigBee implementation. The 802.11n devices occupy a 10 MHz channel, the DSSS phone occupies a 4 MHz channel, and the ZigBee devices occupy 5 MHz. The center frequencies of these devices are picked such that the phone interferes with the first half of the 802.11 channel, whereas the ZigBee device interferes with the second half. We place these six nodes randomly at the marked locations in Fig. 1. We make the three pairs transmit concurrently, and we repeat each run with and without TIMO. As before, we make the inter-packet arrival and the packet duration for the cordless phone and ZigBee nodes 20 ms, to allow for a software implementation.

Fig. 10(a) plots the CDF of 802.11 throughput with and without TIMO. The figure shows that without TIMO, about 67% of the locations cannot get any packets through and the average throughput is low. In contrast, with TIMO no locations suffer disconnectivity and the average throughput increases significantly.

Fig. 10(b) and 10(c) plot the packet loss rate of the competing technologies: the DSSS phone and ZigBee. The figure shows that if 802.11n transmits concurrently, without TIMO, these technologies can suffer significant packet loss. However, if 802.11n employs TIMO, then its interference increases loss rates by less than 0.5%, which is negligible. Thus, TIMO can help diverse technologies coexist in the same frequency band while placing the burden of interference prevention on high-end MIMO nodes instead of low-end single antenna systems.

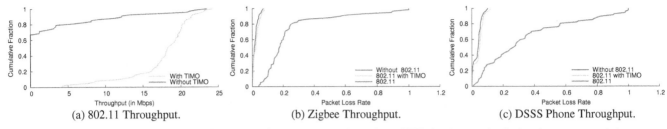

(a) 802.11 Throughput.   (b) Zigbee Throughput.   (c) DSSS Phone Throughput.

Figure 10—TIMO with Multiple Interferers. The figure shows the throughput CDFs for three technologies that are transmitting concurrently in overlapping frequencies: 802.11n, DSSS phone, and ZigBee.

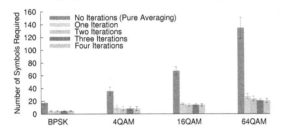

Figure 11—Tradeoff Between the Number of Averaged Symbols and the Number of Iterations: With three iterations, TIMO can achieve the same accuracy as a baseline that knows the structure and the preamble of the interferer, while maintaining the averaged symbols less than 22 for all modulations.

10. MICRO BENCHMARKS

Finally, we zoom in on the components of TIMO to examine the tradeoff between averaging over a larger number of symbols and applying the same algorithm iteratively over a smaller number of symbols.

We transfer a 20 MB file between two 2×2 802.11 USRP2 nodes. A third USRP2 node plays the role of an unknown interfering technology, and transmits a signal unknown to the 802.11 USRP2 nodes. We run the experiment for random placement of the three nodes in various locations in Fig. 1. We want to compute the amount of averaging and the number of iterations that TIMO needs to obtain an accurate estimate of the interferer's channel ratio. To obtain a ground truth of the channel ratios, we provide a baseline receiver with the full knowledge of the transmitted interference signal so that it can use the whole signal as if it were a preamble, and compute a very accurate estimate of the interferer's channel. We compute this estimate over periods of 1 ms each, which is significantly lower than the coherence time for indoor static channels at 2.4 GHz. For each run, we process the signal using the baseline receiver and TIMO.

Fig. 11 plots the number of symbols that TIMO needs to average over to obtain an estimate of the channel ratio that is within 3% of the value obtained with the baseline. The figure shows the results for the four modulations in 802.11 (BPSK, 4QAM, 16QAM and 64QAM). The plots reveal the following trends.

- The iterative algorithm yields a significant reduction in the number of symbols required to average over to obtain an accurate estimate of the interferer's channel ratio.
- Across all modulation schemes, two to three iterations are sufficient, and the return from more iterations is negligible. The reason why there is a ceiling for the iteration gain is that iterating does not provide more information; it only provides a better estimation using the collected information. After some point, the algorithm becomes limited by the intrinsic noise in the collected measurements.
- Given three iterations, TIMO needs to average over less than 22 symbols even at the highest modulation scheme.

11. RELATED WORK

Wireless interference has been the topic of much recent research. Work in this area falls under two broad categories:

(a) Interference Across Technologies: One can identify three main approaches within this category. The first approach attempts to eliminate interference by isolating the signals in time, frequency or space. The most common isolation approach is to employ frequency-based isolation, such as OFDM subcarrier suppression [30, 32, 23], variable channel width [19], or other fine grained frequency fragmentation techniques [38, 18, 31]. TIMO, on the other hand, enables independent technologies to share the same frequencies without interfering with each other. Directional antennas may also be used to provide spatial isolation and reduce interference. However, directional antennas are difficult to use in indoor scenarios where the signal tends to bounce off walls and furniture and scatter around [36]. In contrast, TIMO works in scattering environments and applies even when the two receivers are in the same direction.

The second approach uses mitigation schemes to modify transmissions to be more resilient to interference (e.g. by using coding or by lowering the bit rates). Mitigation proposals like PPR [25] and MIXIT [27], though designed and evaluated for the same technology, can work across technologies. These schemes however assume interference is fairly transient and limited to some bytes in each packet. In contrast, TIMO can deal with persistent interference.

Finally, some proposals identify the type of interference (is it ZigBee? Bluetooth?) and inform the user so he may switch off the interfering device [6, 29]. Others leverage the specific characteristic of a particular technology to design a suitable coexistence strategy [34]. Like this prior work, TIMO aims to provide coexistence of different wireless technologies. TIMO provides a single approach that works with different technologies, e.g., microwave ovens, cordless phones, etc, and applies even to unknown technologies.

(b) Interference from the Same Technology: Recent work in this category include interference cancellation [22], ZigZag [20] and analog network coding [26] which address the problem of interference from other 802.11 nodes. The closest to ours is prior work on MIMO systems which enables multiple transmitters to transmit concurrently without interference. This includes schemes like SAM [35], Interference Alignment and Cancellation [21], and beamforming systems [16]. Unlike these schemes, however, TIMO delivers a MIMO system that enables cooperation with multiple different wireless technologies.

Finally, TIMO is related to prior work on interference management in cellular networks, which uses multiple antennas to mitigate interference from nodes operating in adjacent cells [36, 4]. In contrast to this work, however, TIMO develops new algorithms that can address cross-technology interference.

12. CONCLUSION

This paper presents TIMO, a MIMO design that enables 802.11n to communicate in the presence of high-power cross-technology interference. TIMO exploits 802.11n's MIMO capability to treat a high-power signal from a different technology as if it were another stream from the same technology, hence enabling diverse technologies to share the same frequency band. We show via a proof-of-concept implementation that TIMO enables 802.11n to communicate effectively in the presence of typical interferers. Beyond 802.11n, we believe that TIMO provides the first step for a new form of coexistence, in which different technologies do not necessarily have to find unoccupied bands and could, in crowded environments, occupy the same band, thus increasing spectral efficiency.

Acknowledgments: We thank Nabeel Ahmed, Arthur Berger, Nate Kushman, Kate Lin, Hariharan Rahul, and Lili Qiu for their insightful comments. This research is supported by NSF Grants CNS-0831660 and CNS-0721857, and DARPA ITMANET.

13. REFERENCES

[1] 20 Myths of Wi-Fi Interference: Dispel Myths to Gain High-Performing and Reliable Wireless, White paper C11-44927.1-00, Cisco, 2007.

[2] 2.4GHz 4-Channel Wireless Receiver and 4 Wireless Infrared Color Cameras, Genica. www.genica.com.

[3] AirMaestro Spectrum Analysis Solution, Bandspeed. www.bandspeed.com.

[4] ArrayComm. www.arraycomm.com.

[5] Bluetooth Basics, Bluetooth SIG Inc., 2011. www.bluetooth.com.

[6] Cisco CleanAir Technology, Cisco. www.cisco.com/en/US/netsol/ns1070/index.html.

[7] Estimating the Utilisation of Key License-Exempt Spectrum Bands, Final Report REP003, Mass Consultants Ltd., Ofcom, April 2009.

[8] Evaluating Interference in Wireless LANs: Recommended Practice, White paper FPG 2010-135.1, Farpoint Group Technical Note, 2010.

[9] Fury GPS Disciplined Oscillator, Jackson Labs. www.jackson-labs.com.

[10] Miercom: Cisco CleanAir Competitive Testing, Lab Test Rerpot DR100409D, Miercom, 2010.

[11] Motorola Airdefense Solutions, Motorola. www.airdefense.net.

[12] Uniden TRU4465: Dual Handset Powermax 2.4GHz Cordless Systems, Uniden. www.uniden.com.

[13] Universal Software Radio Peripheral, Ettus Inc. www.ettus.com.

[14] Wireless RF Interference Customer Survey Result, White paper C11-609300-00, Cisco, 2010.

[15] Local and metropolitan area networks–specific requirements part 11: Wireless LAN medium access control (MAC) and physical layer (PHY) specifications. *IEEE Std 802.11*, 2009.

[16] E. Aryafar, N. Anand, T. Salonidis, and E. W. Knightly. Design and Experimental Evaluation of Multi-user Beamforming in Wireless LANs. In *Proc. ACM MobiCom*, 2010.

[17] Bandspeed. Understanding the Effects of Radio Frequency (RF) Interference on WLAN performance and Security, 2010.

[18] L. Cao, L. Yang, and H. Zheng. The Impact of Frequency-Agility on Dynamic Spectrum Sharing. In *Proc. IEEE DySPAN*, 2010.

[19] R. Chandra, R. Mahajan, T. Moscibroda, R. Raghavendra, and P. Bahl. A Case for Adapting Channel Width in Wireless Networks. In *Proc. ACM SIGCOMM*, 2008.

[20] S. Gollakota and D. Katabi. Zigzag Decoding: Combating Hidden Terminals in Wireless Networks. In *Proc. ACM SIGCOMM*, 2008.

[21] S. Gollakota, S. D. Perli, and D. Katabi. Interference Alignment and Cancellation. In *Proc. ACM SIGCOMM*, 2009.

[22] D. Halperin, J. Ammer, T. Anderson, and D. Wetherall. Interference Cancellation: Better Receivers for a New Wireless MAC. In *Proc. ACM HotNets*, 2007.

[23] Y. He, J. Fang, J. Zhang, H. Shen, K. Tan, and Y. Zhang. MPAP: Virtualization Architecture for Heterogenous Wireless APs. In *Proc. ACM SIGCOMM*, 2010.

[24] J. Heiskala and J. Terry. *OFDM Wireless LANs: A Theoretical and Practical Guide*. Sams Publishing, 2001.

[25] K. Jamieson and H. Balakrishnan. PPR: Partial Packet Recovery for Wireless Networks. In *Proc. ACM SIGCOMM*, 2007.

[26] S. Katti, S. Gollakota, and D. Katabi. Embracing Wireless Interference: Analog Network Coding. In *Proc. ACM SIGCOMM*, 2007.

[27] S. Katti, D. Katabi, H. Balakrishnan, and M. Medard. Symbol-Level Network Coding for Wireless Mesh Networks. In *Proc. ACM SIGCOMM*, 2008.

[28] J. Ketchum, S. Nanda, R. Walton, S. Howard, M. Wallace, B. Bjerke, I. Medvedev, S. Abraham, A. Meylan, and S. Surineni. System Description and Operating Principles for High Throughput Enhancements to 802.11, QUALCOMM Inc., 2005.

[29] K. Lakshminarayanan, S. Sapra, S. Seshan, and P. Steenkiste. RFDump: An Architecture for Monitoring the Wireless Ether. In *Proc. CoNEXT*, 2009.

[30] S. Mishra, R. Brodersen, S. Brink, and R. Mahadevappa. Detect and Avoid: An Ultra-Wideband/WiMAX Coexistence Mechanism. *IEEE Communications Magazine*, 2007.

[31] T. Moscibroda, R. Chandra, Y. Wu, S. Sengupta, P. Bahl, and Y. Yuan. Load-Aware Spectrum Distribution in Wireless LANs. In *Proc. IEEE ICNP*, 2008.

[32] H. Rahul, N. Kushman, D. Katabi, C. Sodini, and F. Edalat. Learning to Share: Narrowband-Friendly Wideband Networks. In *Proc. ACM SIGCOMM*, 2008.

[33] SourceForge. iperf.sourceforge.net.

[34] T. Taher, M. Misurac, J. LoCicero, and D. Ucci. Microwave Oven Signal Modelling. In *Proc. IEEE WCNC*, 2008.

[35] K. Tan, H. Liu, J. Fang, W. Wang, J. Zhang, M. Chen, and G. M. Voelker. SAM: Enabling Practical Spatial Multiple Access in Wireless LAN. In *Proc. ACM MobiCom*, 2009.

[36] D. Tse and P. Vishwanath. *Fundamentals of Wireless Communications*. Cambridge University Press, 2005.

[37] M. Vutukuru, H. Balakrishnan, and K. Jamieson. Cross-Layer Wireless Bit Rate Adaptation. In *Proc. ACM SIGCOMM*, 2009.

[38] L. Yang, W. Hou, L. Cao, B. Y. Zhao, and H. Zheng. Supporting Demanding Wireless Applications with Frequency-Agile Radios. In *Proc. USENIX NSDI*, 2010.

[39] P. Zetterberg. Experimental Investigation of TDD Reciprocity-Based Zero-Forcing Transmit Precoding. *EURASIP J. Adv. Signal Process*, 2010.

[40] H. Zhao, Y. Q. Shi, and N. Ansari. Hiding Data in Multimedia Streaming over Networks. In *Proc. CNSR*, 2010.

APPENDIX

Generalization to any number of antennas. Let M be the number of antennas at the 802.11 receiver. Say, there are K concurrent 802.11n transmissions, $s_1(t) \cdots s_K(t)$ whose channels are known at the receiver. We would like to estimate the interferer's channel in the presence of these K transmissions. Let, h_j^k be the channel coefficient of the kth transmission at the jth antenna on the receiver. Similarly, let h_j denote the channel of the interferer to the jth antenna on the receiver.

First, we note that one can always set h_1 to one. This can be done by considering the interferer to be the scaled value, $h_1 i(t)$, instead of $i(t)$. Thus, the received equation on the jth antenna is given by,

$$y_1(t) = i(t) + \sum h_1^k s_k(t)$$
$$y_j(t) = h_j i(t) + \sum h_j^k s_k(t), \forall j \neq 1$$

Now, since the channel of the interferer is given by $(1, h_1, \cdots, h_M)$, it is sufficient to find the h_is. To do this, the receiver correlates all the equations above with $y_1(t)^*$ and taking the expectation.

$$E[y_1(t) y_1(t)^*] = P_i + \sum h_1^k h_1^{k*} P_k$$
$$E[y_j(t) y_1(t)^*] = h_j P_i + \sum h_j^k h_1^{k*} P_k,$$

where P's are the corresponding powers. Since the only unknowns in the above equations are P_i and h_j's, they can be easily computed. Thus, even in the presence of K concurrent transmissions, a 802.11 receiver can estimate the channel of the interferer without knowing the preamble.

Design Space Analysis for Modeling Incentives in Distributed Systems

Rameez Rahman
Delft University of Technology
Delft, The Netherlands
rrameez@gmail.com

Tamás Vinkó
Delft University of Technology
Delft, The Netherlands
tamas.vinko@gmail.com

David Hales
The Open University
Milton Keynes, UK
david@davidhales.com

Johan Pouwelse
Delft University of Technology
Delft, The Netherlands
peer2peer@gmail.com

Henk Sips
Delft University of Technology
Delft, The Netherlands
h.j.sips@tudelft.nl

ABSTRACT

Distributed systems without a central authority, such as peer-to-peer (P2P) systems, employ incentives to encourage nodes to follow the prescribed protocol. Game-theoretic analysis is often used to evaluate incentives in such systems. However, most game-theoretic analyses of distributed systems do not adequately model the repeated interactions of nodes inherent in such systems. We present a game-theoretic analysis of a popular P2P protocol, Bit-Torrent, that models the repeated interactions in such protocols. We also note that an analytical approach for modeling incentives is often infeasible given the complicated nature of most deployed protocols. In order to comprehensively model incentives in complex protocols, we propose a simulation-based method, which we call *Design Space Analysis* (DSA). DSA provides a tractable analysis of competing protocol variants within a detailed design space. We apply DSA to P2P file swarming systems. With extensive simulations we analyze a wide-range of protocol variants and gain insights into their robustness and performance. To validate these results and to demonstrate the efficacy of DSA, we modify an instrumented BitTorrent client and evaluate protocols discovered using DSA. We show that they yield higher system performance and robustness relative to the reference implementation.

Categories and Subject Descriptors

C.2.4 [**Computer-Communication Networks**]: Distributed Systems – Distributed applications; H.1.0 [**Information Systems**]: Models and Principles – General; J.4 [**Computer Applications**]: Social and Behavioral Sciences – Economics

General Terms

Algorithms, Design, Economics, Theory

Keywords

Incentive systems, game theory, design space analysis, robustness

1. INTRODUCTION

Incentives play an important role in distributed systems with no centralized authority. Proper incentives ensure that the prescribed protocol is followed by all the nodes, i.e., the protocol is robust to strategic manipulation. A powerful tool for modeling incentives is game theory, the branch of economics that can model individual behavior in strategic situations [22]. The general applicability and predictive powers of game theory has allowed designers to employ it in a variety of contexts for the design of distributed systems [3, 29, 31].

In analyzing incentives in distributed systems, many papers model the node interaction as a one-shot game. However, many distributed settings involve repeated games in populations of interacting players where such approaches do not apply. In this paper, as our first contribution, we present a game-theoretic model of a distributed protocol that aims to capture some of the repeated aspects of such systems.

Furthermore, theoretical analyses often require high levels of abstraction to keep the models simple. This is required because involved models can become analytically intractable [19]. Thus, for modeling complex protocols, a theoretical analysis runs the risk of missing out on important variables that could have significant effects on protocol design. For instance, while designing a protocol, it is not uncommon for the designer to employ a variety of arbitrary design decisions and so-called "magic numbers". Modifying any of these can have negative effects on the robustness of the protocol's incentives. In other words, there are many elements in complex protocols that could be gamed by strategic nodes.

A simulation based approach has been used by Axelrod [1] to model strategic interactions in repeated games. As our second contribution, taking inspiration from Axelrod, we aim to devise a method which can be used to analyze protocols more comprehensively. To that end, we present a simulation-based approach that we call *Design Space Analysis* (DSA). DSA combines the specification of a design space with an analysis of varying protocols within that space.

The specification of a design space comprises two steps: *Parameterization* and *Actualization*. *Parameterization* involves identifying salient design dimensions for the space, while *Actualization* involves specifying multiple implementations for the identified dimensions.

For an analysis of the design space, we present a solution concept, which we term the *Performance, Robustness*, and *Aggressiveness* (PRA) quantification. For a protocol Π, *Performance* is the overall performance of the system when all nodes execute Π (where performance is defined by the application); *Robustness* is the ability of a majority of the population executing Π to outperform a minority executing a protocol other than Π; and *Aggressiveness* is the ability of a minority of the population executing Π to outperform a majority executing a protocol other than Π. PRA quantification takes the form of a tournament in which each protocol competes against every other protocol. By evaluating each protocol in the space, the PRA quantification simulates strategic variants and predicts their effects.

We choose the domain of peer-to-peer (P2P) systems for applying and exploring our ideas, because there are many such deployed systems, for which incentive-compatible design is of primary importance to counter strategic behavior. We undertake the following steps. We apply a game-theoretic analysis to the popular P2P protocol, BitTorrent, and devise a more robust variant by incorporating the repeated aspects of the protocol (Section 2). Then we perform a Design Space Analysis of P2P file swarming systems. We run experiments on a cluster and discover that there are several protocols that do better than this variant with respect to Performance, Robustness, and Aggressiveness (Section 3 & 4). Finally, we implement modifications to BitTorrent and with experiments on a cluster, analyze some protocols discovered using DSA. We show that they yield higher system performance and robustness as compared to the reference implementation, thus demonstrating the effectiveness of DSA (Section 5).

2. GAME-THEORETIC ANALYSIS OF BITTORRENT

We consider one of the most popular P2P protocols, BitTorrent (BT), for our analysis. Our reason for choosing BitTorrent is that this protocol has probably been the most widely studied P2P protocol in the literature. A game-theoretic approach has often been applied to BitTorrent [12, 16, 26].

First, we present a model of BitTorrent as a *strategy* in a *game*. In game theory, a game is a description of a strategic interaction that includes the constraints on the actions that the players can take and the players' interests [22]. Then we present an analysis of this model for multiple bandwidth classes. Under our assumptions, which are different from previous work [26], we show that BitTorrent is not a Nash equilibrium. Finally, we design a modification to BitTorrent, which is a Nash equilibrium.

We assume the reader is familiar with certain game-theoretic constructs such as the Prisoner's Dilemma (PD), a game between two players in which it is the dominant strategy of both players to defect.

2.1 BitTorrent as a strategy in a game

We explain the basics of the BitTorrent protocol from an iterated games setting perspective. Each peer plays a number of games with other peers in a given time period, following a Tit-for-Tat (TFT) like strategy. TFT is the strategy using which a player *cooperates* on the first move and then simply mimics what the other player did in the last round. In BitTorrent a peer cooperates with (i.e., uploads to) a certain number of preferred (fastest uploading) partners while it defects in the rest of the games. These are the 'regular unchokes' in BT terminology. Additionally, a peer also starts new games with other peers in search of better partners. These are 'optimistic unchokes' in BT terminology. In these games, a peer always cooperates unconditionally for some iterations. We do not model the seeders in BitTorrent as these do not affect our subsequent Nash equilibrium analysis. This is because we assume, like Chow *et al.* [4], that seeders interact uniformly with all peers.

We now present an analysis of our model in a system containing two classes of peers: fast and slow. The game interaction in Figure 1(a) captures the dynamics between a fast peer and a slow peer, where f is the upload speed of a fast peer and s is the upload speed of a slow peer. This game represents a single round in an iterated scenario, where the 'shadow of the future' is large (i.e., the payoff of subsequent moves is important relative to the previous move) and peers can form sustained relationships. It can be seen that given the payoffs, the dominant strategy for fast peers is to always defect on the slow peers. This is because when a fast peer cooperates with a slow peer, there is an *opportunity cost* associated with it. Opportunity cost is an important concept in economics. It is the cost of an alternative that must be given up in order to pursue a certain action [8].

We note here that by incorporating the 'shadow of the future' and opportunity costs in our 'game' we try to model two key aspects of the BitTorrent protocol usually ignored in traditional game-theoretical analysis. These aspects are: (a) the repeated interactions between peers; and (b) the wide choice of partners that peers can have.

A fast peer's opportunity cost in cooperating with a slow peer is a missed interaction with another fast peer. When a fast peer cooperates with a slow peer, it gets a negative utility of $s - f$. It gets s from the slow peer but on the other hand, loses out on a potential f from a fast peer. Conversely, for the slow peers, the dominant strategy is to always cooperate with the fast peers. A slow peer on defecting against a fast peer gets f from the fast peer and can form a relationship with a slow peer, where it gets $s - f$ (where $-f$ is the opportunity cost of cooperating with a slow peer), thus getting a final utility of $f + (s - f) = s$. Figure 1(b) depicts this scenario: a slow peer responds (with cooperation in the form of a 'regular unchoke' slot) upon being optimistically unchoked by a fast peer, while the converse does not hold. In light of this, we note here that the Prisoner's Dilemma is not an accurate model for BitTorrent under heterogeneous classes of peers. Instead, the way BitTorrent implements the interaction of a slow peer with a fast peer, resembles an interaction in the *Dictator game*, a game in which one player proposes to do something, while the other has no choice but to respond passively without any strategic input into the decision. It also resembles a game which has been called by some as the *One-Sided Prisoner's Dilemma* [28]. For simplicity, we refer to it here as the *BitTorrent Dilemma*.

Next we give an analytical model of BitTorrent for multiple bandwidth classes, using the BitTorrent Dilemma game as depicted in Figure 1(a).

2.2 Analytical model of BitTorrent Dilemma

In this section, we model the BitTorrent Dilemma game with multiple bandwidth classes of peers. We seek to calculate the expected number of games that a peer c from a particular class, with payoffs defined according to Figure 1(a), can win against other peers, where winning means getting cooperation from others.

In the remainder of this section we derive the formulae for the expected number of games that peer c wins against other players from different classes. We note that there are two types of games that a player c can win: 1) the games that it wins when others *reciprocate* to it; and 2) when other players start a new game with c and in line with TFT, cooperate unconditionally, thereby giving c a *free game win*.

We use the notation summarized in Table 1. Note that we assume, for notational simplicity, that the number of new partners that a peer cooperates with unconditionally (number of optimistic unchoke slots in BT terminology) is equal to 1. Moreover, it is also

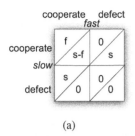
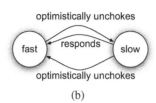
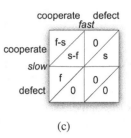

(a)   (b)   (c)

Figure 1: Analysis of the BitTorrent Dilemma: (a) The payoffs of the BT Dilemma for slow and fast peers; (b) An abstract illustration of interaction between slow and fast peers; (c) Modified BT payoffs in view of slow peers' opportunity costs.

assumed that there are always enough peers to exchange a particular piece of content.

Table 1: Model parameters. Classes are based on peers' bandwidth capacities.

Notation	Definition
N_A	number of TFT players in classes above c's class.
N_B	number of TFT players in classes below c's class.
N_C	number of TFT players in c's class.
U_r	number of players that c can reciprocate with simultaneously (number of regular unchoke slots in BT)
$E^r[X \to c]$	the expected number of games peer c wins against peers in the class $X \in \{A, B, C\}$, where A, B and C are the classes above, below and where peer c is from, respectively.
$E[X \to c]$	the expected number of 'free game wins' that peer c obtains from class $X \in \{A, B, C\}$.
N_r	$N_A + N_B + N_C - U_r - 1$

First, we calculate the expected number of games that can be won against higher classes. We assume that N_A is greater than U_r; thus, as per Figure 1(a), players employing TFT in higher classes will not reciprocate with peer c. Therefore,

$$E^r[A \to c] = 0.$$

However, as per the TFT policy, peers from higher classes, unknowingly, do offer first move cooperation to peers from lower classes in search for better partners. The probability that peers in class C are offered a 'free game win' by a peer from the higher classes is N_C/N_r, giving $E[A \to C] = N_A \times N_C/N_r$, which is the expected number of 'free game wins' that peers from higher classes offer to players in the considered class C. This leads to

$$E[A \to c] = N_A/N_r.$$

For the expected number of games won against the lower classes, using similar reasoning as above, we obtain

$$E[B \to c] = E^r[B \to c] = N_B/N_r.$$

The expected value for the number of games in which a peer c gets reciprocation from peers in the same class is U_r *minus* the number of 'free game wins' that peer c obtains from the higher classes (to which c always reciprocates as per its dominant strategy, thus breaking its relationship with a partner from the same class), *minus* the expected number of 'free game wins' that at least one of c's current partners gets from the higher classes (to which the partner reciprocates, thus breaking its relationship with c). This leads to

$$E^r[C \to c] = U_r - E[A \to c] - K, \qquad (1)$$

where $K = 1 - \left((1 - E[A \to c])(1 - \frac{1}{U_r})\right)^{U_r}$. Finally, the number of peers in contention for 'free game wins' by peer c in the same class is $N_C - 1 - E^r[C \to c]$, which gives

$$E[C \to c] = (N_C - 1 - E^r[C \to c])/N_r.$$

2.3 Is BitTorrent TFT a Nash equilibrium?

Under certain assumptions, it was shown in [26] that the TFT strategy as implemented in BitTorrent is a Nash equilibrium. However, by modifying the abstraction to incorporate more detail in our model, and taking a cue from formula (1), we find that BT is not a Nash equilibrium. In our model, the payoff structure in BitTorrent can be modified to devise a new protocol. This protocol can individually, in a population of all BitTorrent peers, do better than the BitTorrent peers, thereby showing that BitTorrent is not a Nash equilibrium.

Next, we discuss how we devise a protocol improvement called *Birds*[1] by modifying the payoffs in the BitTorrent Dilemma.

Birds: Modifying BitTorrent's payoffs. A fast peer upon being optimistically unchoked by a slow peer does not reciprocate, as given by Figure 1(a), because a fast peer realizes the opportunity cost of reciprocating to a slow peer, which is a missed interaction with another fast peer. A slow peer reciprocates to a fast peer because in its view there is an opportunity cost in defecting against a fast peer, which is a missed chance to form a long-term relationship with a fast peer. However, as stated, given the scenario described in Figure 1(a), this does not happen. This suggests that the payoff as calculated by a slow peer in the BitTorrent Dilemma could be modified. There is no opportunity cost in defecting against a fast peer. In fact there *is* an opportunity cost in cooperating with it: missing out on a sustained relationship with another slow peer. Therefore, in order to account for this fact, we modify the payoff structure of the BitTorrent Dilemma according to Figure 1(c) so that the dominant strategy of both slow and fast peers is to defect against each other. This new payoff structure leads to a new protocol that we call Birds and reflects the behavior of peers following this protocol.

Analytically, this leads to

$$E^r_B[A \to c] = E^r_B[B \to c] = 0,$$

and obviously

$$E^r_B[C \to c] = U_r.$$

For the 'free game wins', there is no change as compared to BitTorrent. For the interactions of peers in the same class, we find that we can use the same argument as used for BitTorrent, thus

$$E_B[C \to c] = (N_C - 1 - U_r)/N_r.$$

---

[1] Birds of a feather stick together. Using this protocol peers try to stick with others from their own bandwidth class.

For a proof of Birds being a Nash equilibrium and BitTorrent not being a Nash equilibrium, we refer the reader to the Appendix.

A practical approach to deploy Birds. We provide a simple, practical approach to incorporate Birds in current BitTorrent clients. We propose to change the peer selection policy of BitTorrent, so that it reciprocates not to the fastest peers but to those peers that are closest to its own upload bandwidth. Given Figure 1(c), a peer in Birds needs to sort others in increasing order of their *distance* to its own upload bandwidth.

We define a peer's distance to another peer to be equal to the absolute difference between its upload speed and the upload speed of the other peer. We note that a similar approach has been used for replica placement in P2P Storage Systems [30].

2.4 Discussion

We have applied a game-theoretic analysis to the popular P2P protocol, BitTorrent. Considering BT as a strategy in iterated games, and using the concept of 'opportunity costs', we were able to unearth new protocol aspects. Using a different abstraction as compared to previous work [26] under which BT is a Nash equilibrium, we demonstrated that in our abstraction, BitTorrent is not Nash equilibrium. We also devised a protocol variant that is a Nash equilibrium under our assumptions.

We now need to consider what we gain from our equilibrium analysis and what exactly is meant when a protocol is said to be robust. It was only subsequent to the proof that BitTorrent is a Nash equilibrium [26], that questions about BitTorrent's robustness were raised. Locher *et al.* [17] showed that BitTorrent's TFT policy is vulnerable to attack from an *Always Defect* strategy. Later on, yet another BT exploit was devised based on an adaptive policy for number of partners and variable rate of reciprocation [24]. Even in our case, simply by choosing an abstraction that incorporates the interactions between various classes of peers in more detail, we showed that BT is not a Nash equilibrium.

The literature of game-theoretic modeling of distributed systems often relies on the analytical analysis of simple models [30, 26]. The results of such analyses, as we have seen, can sometimes be misleading. In many other areas of networking, simulations are used when a faithful model of the real system is far too complicated, and it is not clear which details one can omit without changing the nature of the results. In the next section, we present Design Space Analysis, an approach inspired by the work of Axelrod [1], which uses a simulation based methodology for modeling incentives in complex protocols.

3. DESIGN SPACE ANALYSIS

We wish to design distributed protocols that maximize performance of the system under the assumption that protocol variants may enter the system. We present Design Space Analysis (DSA), a simulation based method, which emphasizes the specification and analysis of a design space, rather than proposing a single protocol. First, we list the key elements of DSA. Then we present the *Performance, Robustness, Aggressiveness* (PRA) quantification, a solution concept within DSA.

3.1 Key elements of DSA

We consider the elements that are integral to Design Space Analysis.

Flexible behavioral assumptions. In DSA, we relax behavioral assumptions. Specifically, we do not limit ourselves to the rational framework, where nodes are supposed to be self-interested. By foregoing the assumptions entailed in this framework, we consider a great variety of protocols, which may not necessarily be rational. Protocols may, in the words of Axelrod [1], "simply reflect standard operating procedures, rules of thumb, instincts, habits, or imitation".

Specification of design space. In DSA, keeping in view that complex protocols have many elements that can be gamed by strategic nodes, a design space should encompass relevant details that can affect the incentive structure. Design space specification occurs at two levels: i) *Parameterization*, which involves determining the salient dimensions of the design space, and ii) *Actualization*, which involves specifying a host of actual values for every individual dimension.

The specification of the design space can be inspired by consulting the relevant literature and analyzing existing systems. As an example, the Parameterization phase of the design space for *Gossip Protocols* [13] could result in the following salient dimensions: i) Selection function for choosing partners for exchanging data, ii) Periodicity of data exchange iii) Filtering function for determining data to exchange, iv) Record maintenance policy in local database.

The Actualization of this example design space for gossip protocols could be: For Selection Function, following policies could be used : 1) *Random:* Choose partners randomly; 2) *Best:* Choose partners who have given the best service; 3) *Loyal:* Choose most loyal partners; 4) *Similarity:* Choose partners based on similarity; etc. Similarly, different values could be chosen for each of the other dimensions.

An example of specifying a design space, with both the parameterization and actualization phases, will be described in detail in Sections 4.1 and 4.2 when we apply DSA to P2P file swarming systems.

Systematic analysis of the design space. In DSA, a desired feature of all solution concepts is a systematic exploration of the design space. This exploration could either follow an exhaustive approach, e.g., a parameter sweep, or a heuristic based approach. By a thorough scan of the space, DSA solution concepts can anticipate strategic variants and predict their effects. Heuristic based approaches can provide partial solutions relatively fast, however, without any guarantees on the level of goodness of the measures.

3.2 The PRA quantification

We now present the PRA quantification, a solution concept within DSA. We note that other solution concepts within DSA could also be devised. Using PRA, we can characterize any protocol, from a given design space, over three measures (or dimensions). For a given protocol Π, these three particular measures, are:

- Performance - the overall performance of the system when all peers execute Π (where performance is determined by the application);

- Robustness - the ability of a majority of the population executing Π to outperform a minority executing a protocol other than Π;

- Aggressiveness - the ability of a minority of the population executing Π to outperform a majority executing a protocol other than Π.

We formulate a way to assign values to each of the three measures normalized into the range $[0, 1]$. Hence the properties of any given Π can be characterized as a point within a three-dimensional Performance, Robustness, Aggressiveness (PRA) space. The importance of these three measures is evident from the literature. Performance and Robustness have been studied extensively [2, 12, 24].

Table 2: Existing protocols/designs mapped to our generic P2P protocol design space.

Protocol	P2P Replica Storage [30]	GTG [21]	Maze [32]	Pulse [23]	BarterCast [20]	Private BT Communities
Peer Discovery	Gossip based	orthogonal	Central server	Gossip based	Gossip based	Central server
Stranger Policy	Defect if set of partners full	Unconditional cooperation	Initialized with points	Give positive score	Unconditional cooperation	Initial credit
Selection Function	Closest to own profile	Sort on Forwarding Rank	Ranked on points	Missing list, Forwarding list	Rank/Ban according to reputation	Credits or sharing ratio above certain level
Resource Allocation	Equal	Equal	Differentiated according to rank	Equal	orthogonal	Equal / Differentiated according to credits

Aggressiveness has not been explicitly studied but the numerous papers that present protocol variants [11, 15, 16] suggest the need for an aggressiveness measure to determine the effectiveness of a new protocol variant in a population of peers following some other protocol(s).

It is desirable, in open systems in which strategic variants can enter, to design protocols which maximize all three measures. However, it can be conjectured that there will often be a trade-off between them. For example, one may design protocols with high performance but low robustness or conversely high robustness and low performance.

We now define more precisely how we can map a given protocol Π, which can be expressed as a point in the design space, to a point in the PRA space; formally, we define a function $S : D \rightarrow [0, 1]^3$, where D is the design space.

We assume that for each peer in a system of peers we can calculate a utility which quantifies individual performance. The measure of performance is application specific, such as download speed in P2P file swarming systems. Given this we define the performance P of protocol Π as the sum of all individual utilities in a population of peers executing Π normalized over the entire protocol design space. Hence, $P = 1$ indicates the best performance obtained from any protocol in the design space.

We define the Robustness R for protocol Π as the proportion of all other protocols from the design space that do not outperform Π in a *tournament*. A tournament consists of multiple *encounters* in which protocol Π plays against all other protocols in turn. An encounter is a mixed population of peers executing one of two protocols. The winning protocol is that which obtains the higher average utility for the peers executing it.

Aggressiveness A for protocol Π is defined in the same way as Robustness, but here Π is in the minority.

4. APPLYING DSA TO P2P FILE SWARMING SYSTEMS

In this section, we describe our methodology for applying DSA to P2P file swarming systems. First, we Parameterize a generic P2P design space. Next, based on this generic space, we Actualize a specific file swarming design space. Subsequently, we apply the PRA quantification on this space. Finally, we present the results of our analysis.

4.1 Parameterization of a Generic P2P Protocol Design Space

We have identified the following salient dimensions applicable to a large variety of P2P systems.

Peer Discovery: In order to perform productive peer interactions, it is necessary to find other partners. For example, when a peer is new in the system, looking for better matching partners or existing partners are unresponsive. The timing and nature of the peer discovery policy are the important aspects of this dimension.

Stranger Policy: When interacting with an unknown peer (stranger), past history cannot be used to inform actions. It is therefore necessary to apply a policy to deal with strangers. The way peers allocate resources to strangers is an important aspect of this dimension.

Selection Function: When a peer requires interaction with others this function determines which of the known peers should be selected. This could include, for example, past behavior (through direct experience or reputation system), service availability and liveness criteria.

Resource Allocation: During peer interactions resources must be allocated to the selected peers (given by the selection function). The way a peer divides its resources among the selected peers, defines the resource allocation policy.

Some existing implemented protocols and proposed designs are listed in Table 2. A protocol such as Give-to-Get (GTG) [21] employs unconditional cooperation with strangers as its *stranger policy*. A P2P replica storage design [30] presents a stranger policy which defects on strangers when its set of regular partners is full. For implementing the *selection function*, a deployed P2P reputation system like BarterCast [20] ranks peers in order of reputation score and also proposes to ban peers below a certain reputation score. P2P replica storage selects those peers which are closest to the selecting peer's own storage capacity. This selection policy is identical to the one proposed by us for implementing Birds in BitTorrent-like file-sharing systems. For *resource allocation*, Maze [32] allocates resources proportional to rank. These examples are a few implemented systems and proposed designs; a large variety of P2P systems that rely on eliciting cooperation from participating nodes rely on similar dimensions.

4.2 Actualization of a Specific P2P Protocol Design Space

We define some specific actualizations of a BitTorrent-like file swarming system, as described in Section 2, based on the general design space of Section 4.1. The ideas behind these actualizations have been taken directly from, or inspired by, various works on cooperation done in P2P and also some works done in biology and social sciences in general [1, 10, 25]. We were motivated to take inspiration from other fields, because eliciting cooperation in decentralized settings is a general problem that has been well-studied.

For the **Stranger Policy**, we define three different actualizations and a value h for the number of strangers to cooperate with:

B1) *Periodic:* Give resources to up to a certain number of strangers periodically.

B2) *When needed:* Only give resources to strangers when set of regular partners is not full. This particular implementation has been inspired by [11].

B3) *Defect:* Always defect on strangers, i.e., give nothing to strangers.

We set h, the number of strangers to cooperate with at any given time, to be in the range $[1, 3]$. This gives $3 \times 3 = 9$ different stranger policies. We further add one more stranger policy, where the number of strangers is zero. This gives a total of 10 different stranger policies.

We sub-divide the **Selection Function** into three parts: a candidate list, a ranking function over that candidate list, and finally a value k for the number of peers to select from the ranked candidate list.

For the 'Candidate List' we define two actualizations:

C1) *TFT*, used by default in BitTorrent, using which a peer only places those peers in the candidate list who reciprocated to it in the last round.

C2) *TF2T*, using which a peer places those peers in the candidate list who reciprocated to it in either of the last two rounds. TF2T has been taken from [1].

For the 'Ranking Function', we define six different actualizations:

I1) *Sort Fastest*, ranks peers in order of fastest first.

I2) *Sort Slowest*, ranks peers in order of slowest first.

I3) *Sort Based on Proximity*, ranks peers in order of proximity to one's own upload bandwidth, as in Birds.

I4) *Sort Adaptive*, ranks peers in order of proximity to an *aspiration level*, which is adaptive and changes based on a peer's evaluation of its performance. This has been inspired from [25].

I5) *Sort Loyal*, ranks peers in order of those who have cooperated with the peer for the longest durations. This has been inspired by [10].

I6) *Random*, does not rank peers and chooses them randomly. This has been inspired by [15].

After applying the ranking function, a peer chooses the k top peers, where k is the maximum number of partners that a peer can have. Currently, we set k to be in the range $[1, 9]$. This results in $2 \times 6 \times 9 = 108$ different possibilities for the selection function. We further add one more protocol, where the number of selected peers is zero. This gives a total of 109 different selection policies.

For **Resource Allocation**, we define three actualizations:

R1) *Equal Split*, gives all selected peers equal resources (upload bandwidth).

R2) *Prop Share*, gives others proportional to what they gave in the past. This has been inspired by [16].

R3) *Freeride*, gives nothing to partners.

Based on the above, the total number of unique protocols comes to $10 \times 109 \times 3 = 3270$. We note that this number can be larger or smaller based on what, and how many, specific implementations in the space, designers want to explore[2]. Our purpose here is to show the practicality of the DSA analysis by analyzing a considerable space of unique protocols.

---

[2]For instance, we do not consider variants for resource allocation to strangers. Also, we do not consider Peer Discovery.

4.3 Conducting the PRA quantification

First we describe our simulation model. Then we discuss our methodology for conducting the PRA quantification on the design space described in Section 4.2.

4.3.1 Simulation Model

We use a cycle-based simulation model, in which time consists of *rounds*. For *peer discovery* we assume that all peers can connect to each other. In each round, a peer decides to upload to a given number of peers based on some *selection* criterion. It uses its *resource allocation* policy to decide how much to give to each of the selected partners. Furthermore, it decides to cooperate with strangers based on its *stranger policy*. A peer also maintains a short history of actions by others. At the same time a peer also has some rate of requesting services from other peers that depends on specific actualizations. This is the basic model on top of which we explore the design space of Section 4.2. We run our simulation experiments with 50 peers, which is a good approximation of an average BitTorrent swarm-size [9]. These peers interact with each other for 500 rounds. We use a cluster for running our experiments. In order to lend realism to our experiments, we initialize the peers using the bandwidth distribution provided by Piatek *et al.* [24]. We assume that all peers always have data that others are interested in.

4.3.2 Methodology

Based on the PRA quantification, as described in Section 3.2, we first measure the Performance of each protocol in the space. For each protocol Π, we run simulations in which all peers execute Π and measure the average performance of the population. We perform 100 runs for each protocol. In these experiments we define average performance as throughput of the population.

Next we run Robustness experiments. We run simulations, where each protocol plays against every other protocol. We refer to a competition in which two protocols are pitted against each other as an *encounter*. For each encounter, the peer population is split up into two equal halves where half the peers execute Π and the other half executes another protocol. We chose 50% because this is the highest number that an invading protocol can have. Anything higher than 50% means that the invading protocol actually becomes the majority protocol. We hypothesize that if a protocol is robust when 50% of the population executes another protocol, then it will be robust against small invading populations. To verify this hypothesis, we also conduct simulations with the population split up into 90-10, where 90% of the peers follow protocol Π, while 10% execute other protocols in the space, and observe similar results (the Pearson's correlation coefficient of the two sets of results is 0.97). We do 10 runs for each particular encounter between two protocols. This means that a protocol Π plays against the same protocol ten times. For each run, we compare the average performance of Π with the average performance of the other protocol. If the performance of Π is greater than the performance of the other protocol, we mark it as a *Win* for Π, otherwise we mark it as a *Loss* for Π. The robustness value for Π is calculated by number of games that it wins against all opponents in all runs divided by the total number of games that it plays, which is constant for all protocols.

For Aggressiveness we use the same setup as for Robustness experiments, with the difference that the population is so divided that 10% of the peers execute Π while the rest execute another protocol.

Next, we present results of applying the PRA quantification over the design space[3] described in Section 4.2.

---

[3]We note here that the entire series of simulations for PRA took around 25 hours on a 50-node dual-core cluster.

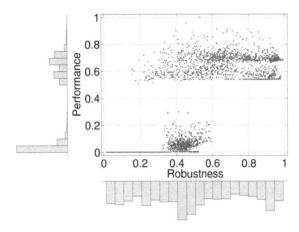

Figure 2: Scatter plot of all 3270 protocols in the design space with Robustness against Performance. The results presented here are a synthesis of over 107 million individual simulation runs. Histograms are also shown.

4.4 Results and Discussion

Figure 2 shows all the 3270 protocols actualized in Section 4.2, with their normalized Robustness and Performance values. Given the methodology of conducting the PRA quantification as described in Section 4.3.2, this figure represents a synthesis of 107 million individual runs. For performance, each point represents the average normalized performance of a protocol Π, over 100 runs. The robustness values are calculated as described in Section 4.3. The maximum variance in the runs for each protocol's performance and robustness was as low as 0.0014 and 0.0206, respectively.

Performance. We shall start by looking at different regions of Figure 2. It can be seen that numerous protocols have both very low performance and robustness in the range $[0, 0.2]$ (as can be seen from the large histogram bars in the bottom left hand corner). Upon inspection we discover that most of them are freeriders, although different kinds of freeriders. The freeriders with low robustness usually defect on strangers, while freeriders with low performance usually defect on their partners. The maximum performance that such freeriders get is 0.31. This can be seen in the form of two clusters in Figure 2, where the lower and upper clusters are below and above 0.4 performance, respectively.

The lower cluster for performance contains all freeriders that do not reciprocate with their partners. It also contains some freeriders that defect on strangers. The upper cluster for performance does not contain any freeriders that defect on their partners but interestingly does contain freeriders who defect on strangers. In fact, the protocol with the highest performance (of 1), is the one that always defects on strangers, has the *Sort Slowest* ranking function, and maintains one partner. We try to dissect why this particular protocol performs so highly. By defecting on a stranger, a protocol *in effect* uploads nothing to the stranger. Since, all peers follow the *Sort Slowest* ranking function, a peer p_1 on downloading nothing from another peer p_2, immediately discards its partner p_3 and chooses p_2 to be its partner. Peer p_3 now finds itself partner-less. However, it can also quickly find a partner for itself by uploading nothing to another peer. Thus by following this protocol, peers rarely find themselves without a fully occupied partner set and can always download at full speed.

Thus, counter-intuitively, by maintaining a single partner, by not uploading anything to strangers and by employing the *Sort Slowest*

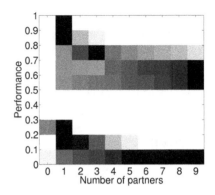

Figure 3: Normalized Performance histograms for different partner values. Darker squares represent high 'partner value' frequency for a particular Performance interval.

ranking function, a very high performing protocol can be designed. It is imperative of course in this case that the *resource allocation* method should *not* be *Prop Share*. This is because *Prop Share* will ensure that a peer on getting nothing from another peer, also uploads nothing in response. If that happens, the entire population that follows this protocol will fail to bootstrap.

In Figure 3 we observe that in fact many of the top performing protocols are those with one partner. In Figure 3, for each performance interval, darker squares represent higher relative frequency of the number of partners. The empty white spaces in Figure 3 reflect the empty spaces in the scatter plot and the histogram of the Performance values in Figure 2. All the top 15 performing protocols maintain one partner each and the overall trend in the top performing protocols shows a low number of partners. In the top hundred performing protocols only 11 maintain more than 2 partners. It can be seen from Figure 3, starting from the top, till the performance interval $[0.7, 0.8]$, the frequency of low number of partners is relatively higher than the frequency of high number of partners.

We analyze these high performing protocols with a low number of partners more closely now. We have already discussed the features of the highest performing protocol, which uses the *Sort Slowest* ranking function. However, not all high performing protocols with low number of partners have the same features. Many of them employ the *Sort Loyal* ranking function. With the *Sort Loyal* ranking function, it can be conjectured that peers which come to form cooperative relationships early on, stay committed in their relationships. This stability of relationships increases the performance of the system, because at no time do peers find themselves short of partners.

Apart from this, many such protocols often also use the *When needed* stranger policy. This policy also leads to more committed partnerships. With the *When needed* stranger policy, peers only cooperate with strangers when their set of partners is not full. Thus once its partner set is full, a peer will not cooperate with strangers. By not cooperating regularly with strangers, a peer protects itself from breaking relationships by avoiding temptation. This is because when a peer p defects against a stranger, it does not get back anything in response from the stranger. In this way peer p does not discover how much better or worse the stranger is than its current partners, and thus continues to stick with them.

It could be assumed that in the presence of churn, protocols with low number of partners will not perform so well. However, we ran Performance tests for the whole space under churn rates of 0.01 and 0.1 per round, and found that it was still the protocols that employed

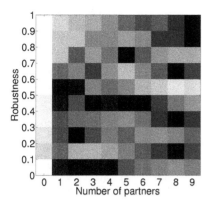

Figure 4: Normalized Robustness histograms for different partner values. Darker squares represent high 'partner value' frequency for a particular Robustness interval.

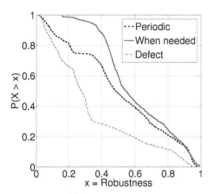

Figure 5: Complementary CDF plots of Robustness of different stranger policies.

a low number of partners that performed the best. Thus, it can be claimed that having low number of partners is a desirable feature of high performing protocols, given that everyone in the population runs the same protocol.

Robustness. It is interesting to compare Figure 3 with Figure 4. While a low number of partners seems to be a good choice for high performance, the situation is reversed when it comes to robustness. In Figure 4, we observe that most of the highly robust protocols have a high number of partners. This can be seen in the top right hand corner of the figure. This is intuitive, because protocols that employ a low number of partners would very likely perform worse in face of an invading protocol that employs high number of partners. This is because, in case of an invasion, peers employing a protocol that maintains a high number of partners are less likely to find themselves short of partners as compared to peers who follow a protocol that maintains a low number of partners. Hence, in the case that some partners defect, peers with a high number of partners can continue to download at high speeds while peers with a low number of partners are likely to suffer with poor speeds. To put it straightforwardly, a peer that maintains 9 partners will suffer less when one of its partners defects on it, as compared to a peer that only maintains one partner.

As we are considering the robustness of protocols, it can be seen from Figure 2 that there are some protocols that are highly robust with robustness values above 0.99. By analyzing these highly robust protocols, we discovered their interesting properties. Including

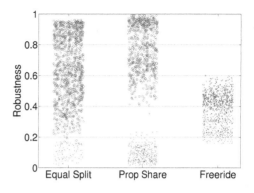

Figure 6: Robustness values using different resource allocation methods. Each circle is a unique protocol. Bigger circles represent better performance.

the most robust protocol in that cluster, these protocols use a combination of the *When needed* stranger policy, the *Sort Fastest* ranking function and the *Prop Share* reciprocation function. Figure 5 shows that only those protocols which use the *When needed* stranger policy reach robustness levels greater than 0.99. Similarly, it can be seen from Figure 7 that protocols which use the *Sort Fastest* ranking function, are the most robust protocols. Figure 6, shows that even though the *Equal Split* resource allocation policy does quite well, it is the *Prop Share* policy that manages to get robustness values greater than 0.99.

Since this is a vital point, as it tells us about the features of protocols that are almost completely robust, we consider these properties in detail. As discussed previously, the *When needed* stranger policy only cooperates with strangers when its set of partners is not full. The *Sort Fastest* ranking function, as the name implies, ranks peers in decreasing order of their speed, and finally the *Prop Share* resource allocation policy, allocates resources to peers in proportion to their contribution.

This combination, first of all, validates the claims about the robustness of the *Prop Share* mechanism [16]. However, it should be noted that, unlike their proposal, these protocols do not reciprocate with everyone. In fact, the most robust protocol maintains only 7 partners. Secondly, the combination of *When needed* with *Prop Share* is very important to note. In [16] a cryptographic bootstrapping technique was proposed to avoid exploitation by freeriding strangers. Our results suggest that the combination of the *When needed* stranger policy with the *Prop Share* resource allocation policy is a practical and lightweight alternative for designing robust protocols.

Trade-off between Performance and Robustness. Looking at the very robust protocols, we note that most of them are not among the high performing protocols. This suggests a trade-off between performance and robustness.

However, looking at the top right hand corner of Figure 2, we can see that there are at least some protocols that are robust and also have high performance (with robustness and performance values above 0.8). On inspection we find that there are 9 such protocols and *all* of these protocols follow the *Sort Loyal* ranking function. No other dimension (such as resource allocation, stranger policy, etc.) is uniform across all 9 protocols. *Sort Loyal* cooperates with those other peers who cooperate with it for the longest durations. It could have been assumed that a ranking policy like *Sort Loyal* would not fare very high in terms of robustness. This is because of the danger that a fast peer that employs the *Sort Loyal* ranking

Table 3: Multiple linear regression analysis applied for the PRA measures of the whole search space. The adjusted R^2 values are reported in the second row. The standard errors for all the variables are less than 0.012. Significance level is indicated as 'OK' if it was less than 0.001.

variable	Performance (adj.$R^2 = 0.68$)			Robustness (adj.$R^2 = 0.52$)			Aggressiveness (adj.$R^2 = 0.61$)		
	estimate	t value	sign.	estimate	t value	sign.	estimate	t value	sign.
(intercept)	0.661	64.372	OK	0.813	73.286	OK	0.801	96.300	OK
$\log(\bar{k})$	−0.008	−2.487	–	0.035	10.334	OK	0.037	14.591	OK
$\log(\bar{h})$	0.109	33.121	OK	0.115	32.287	OK	0.092	34.340	OK
B2	0.008	1.046	–	0.026	3.010	OK	0.026	4.012	OK
B3	−0.206	−26.257	OK	−0.241	−28.399	OK	−0.190	−29.778	OK
C2	−0.066	−10.567	OK	−0.045	−6.576	OK	−0.039	−7.716	OK
I2	0.023	2.151	–	−0.214	−18.186	OK	−0.212	−24.000	OK
I3	0.020	1.831	–	−0.199	−16.911	OK	−0.155	−17.503	OK
I4	0.022	1.975	–	−0.230	−19.517	OK	−0.193	−21.796	OK
I5	0.031	2.843	OK	−0.074	−6.262	OK	−0.097	−11.004	OK
I6	−0.009	−0.796	–	−0.082	−7.080	OK	−0.090	−10.259	OK
R2	−0.194	−25.260	OK	−0.093	−11.188	OK	−0.053	−8.511	OK
R3	−0.544	−70.848	OK	−0.220	−26.562	OK	−0.253	−40.697	OK

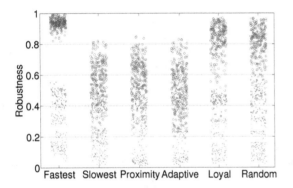

Figure 7: Robustness values using different ranking functions. Each circle is a unique protocol. Bigger circles represent better performance.

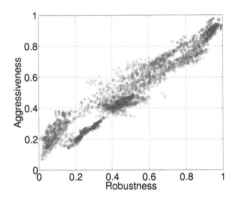

Figure 8: Scatter plot of robustness and aggressiveness values of the protocols. The Pearson's correlation coefficient is 0.96.

function, could get stuck with very slow peers (who follow another protocol) that keep cooperating with it. However, it is interesting to note that the highest robustness achieved by a protocol that sorts others based on loyalty, is actually a very high 0.97.

Aggressiveness. In Figure 8 we see that Robustness and Aggressiveness are linearly correlated with a Pearson's correlation coefficient of 0.96. This suggests that robust protocols are also very aggressive and there does not seem to be a major payoff between robustness and aggressiveness. We can conclude that the results for Robustness also hold for Aggressiveness.

4.4.1 Regression Analysis

We applied multiple linear regression analysis for the whole protocol design space, which is reported in Table 3. Values of h and k (i.e. number of strangers and partners) were treated as numerical values (in the table $\bar{h}$ and $\bar{k}$ are the standardized values of h and k, respectively), whereas the other variables are categorical, thus were substituted by dummy variables.

These results serve as a summary of our previous results and also examine some dimensions which were not covered in the previous section. From Table 3 we can conclude the following: i) Choosing *Freeride* as a resource allocation policy (R3) has the biggest negative impact on Performance and Aggressiveness and it is also has a big negative impact on Robustness. ii) Another bad choice is the *Defect* stranger policy (B3). This policy has the biggest neg-

ative effect on Robustness. On the other hand, the *When needed* policy (B2) increases Robustness and Aggressiveness, but is not statistically significant for Performance. iii) Increasing the number of strangers to cooperate with increases all three, Performance, Robustness, and Aggressiveness values and this variable has the biggest positive effect on all three measures. iv) Higher number of partners results in an increase in Robustness and Aggressiveness, but not for Performance. v) We can see that *TF2T* strategy (C2) plays a consistent negative role for all three measures. vi) The choice of the ranking function has a big effect on Robustness and Aggressiveness. This is in line with Figure 7. However, choice of ranking function does not have significant impact on Performance, except for the *Sort Loyal* ranking function (I5), which increases Performance.

4.4.2 Birds according to Design Space Analysis

We devised a robust variant of BitTorrent in Section 2.3 using a game-theoretic analysis. Subsequently, we augmented game-theoretic analysis for protocol design with Design Space Analysis. We would now like to inspect if the results that we obtained from our game-theoretic analysis have held. How does Birds fare in the larger design space, under a more comprehensive and more realistic analysis?

For the Performance measure, the best Birds variant, i.e., a protocol that at the very least ranks other by *Proximity* and employs

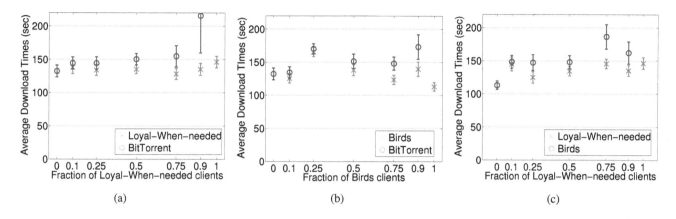

Figure 9: Encounters between three selected protocols.

Equal Split reciprocation, does well with a Performance value of 0.83 to rank at 30 among all 3270 protocols. In Robustness, Birds achieves a highest value of 0.76 and ranks at 714. For Aggressiveness, Birds achieves a highest value of 0.74 to rank at 630 among all protocols.

4.4.3 Discussion

Using DSA we were able to discover protocol variants that do well by employing interesting and counter-intuitive combinations of actualized dimensions. Some combinations lead to extremely high performance, while some lead to very high robustness. We also discovered a few protocols that are both highly robust and also have high performance.

The highly robust protocols are the best candidates for usage in open distributed systems, in which protocol variants may enter; whereas the protocols that achieve very high performance are perhaps more suited to closed systems, where incentives are not required. With the regression analysis on the whole design space we were able to measure the relative impacts of the different dimensions. This also gives new insights into practical protocol designs, and indicates the actualized dimensions that should be preferred and those that should be avoided.

Finally, we observed that Birds ranked very well in Performance and it is within the top quarter in Robustness. Given the fact that Birds was devised using a highly abstracted game-theoretic analysis, we claim to have: a) shown that a game-theoretic analysis is a useful tool which can be used to devise protocols through simple abstractions, that do reasonably well; and b) demonstrated the utility of DSA, by discovering *several* protocols that do better than Birds, in terms of Robustness and Performance.

5. VALIDATION OF DSA RESULTS

We discovered several interesting protocols using Design Space Analysis. In this section we want to explore how well DSA can be used to design deployable protocols. In order to prove the feasibility of using DSA to produce robust and high performing protocols that can be deployed, we modified an instrumented BitTorrent client provided by [14]. From the discovered protocols we choose one that uses the *Sort Loyal* ranking function and the *When needed* stranger policy because this variant resulted in both high Performance and Robustness according to DSA. We term this protocol as 'Loyal-When-needed'. Another variant was suggested by our Nash equilibrium analysis, which is the Birds protocol. Birds uses the *Proximity* ranking function. The third protocol type is the standard BitTorrent, which represents the baseline.

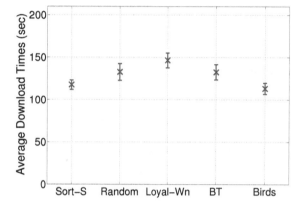

Figure 10: Performance of various protocols.

Experimental setup. In our experiments we pitted one protocol against another, with varying proportions of the two protocols. We adopted an experimental setup similar to [16] and [24]. The total number of leechers is 50. We setup one seeder with an upload bandwidth of 128 KBps. We setup a local tracker, with peers downloading 5MB files. We used the bandwidth distribution provided by [24]. Peers leave upon completing their download. The results of these runs can be seen in Figures 9 and 10, where each point in the figures represents the average over at least *10* runs and error bars mark 95% confidence intervals. Finally, we base our decision to use a cluster on the arguments and results in [27].

BitTorrent vs Loyal-When-needed. Figure 9(a) represents competitive encounters between BitTorrent and Loyal-When-needed clients. We can see the consistent trend of the Loyal-When-needed clients regarding the average download times: it is largely independent of the composition of the swarm. Moreover, Loyal-When-needed clients never do worse than BitTorrent, and they do significantly better if they are in a majority in the swarm.

Birds vs BitTorrent. Figure 9(b) represents a validation of our game-theoretic analysis from Section 2.3: Birds does as well or better than BitTorrent in all proportions. The difference is statistically significant if the proportion of Birds clients is more than or equal to three quarters. We can also conclude that the swarm with only Birds clients results in significantly better average download time than a swarm with only BitTorrent clients.

Birds vs Loyal-When-needed. Finally, in Figure 9(c) we compare the competitive encounters of Birds and Loyal-When-needed. We can immediately see that a swarm with only Birds clients results in better average download time. Together with the previous results, this validates our analysis using DSA, according to which Birds ranks high in performance (as discussed in Section 4.4.2). In line with our DSA results, the Loyal-When-needed protocol is more robust than Birds. The degradation in Birds performance becomes statistically significant when the two protocols compete; this is more evident when the Loyal-When-needed clients are in the majority.

Performance of various protocols. We now compare the performance of different protocols when all peers in the population execute the same protocol. For this, we consider two additional protocols that we discovered through DSA. Figure 10 shows that a protocol that we term Sort-S, together with Birds, fares the best when all peers in the swarm follow the same protocol. Sort-S is the interesting protocol that we discovered in our DSA analysis. It uses the *Sort Slowest* ranking function, defects on strangers and only has one partner. It is interesting to observe that a protocol that uses the *Sort Random* ranking function performs as well as BitTorrent. This recalls the results presented in [15]. We note that Figure 10 does not say anything about the Robustness of these protocols.

6. RELATED WORK

The study of incentive mechanisms for distributed systems has been a well-studied topic in the research community. Such works can be roughly categorized into the works, which came before the seminal papers by Feigenbaum and Shenker [6], and Dash *et al.* [5], and those that came subsequently. We concentrate on the latter works. Mahajan *et al.* [18] described their unsuccessful efforts at applying game theory for system design. They suggested that relaxing the notion of perfect selfishness could increase the applicability of game theory. We demonstrated that game theoretic analysis despite high level of abstraction, can result in a fruitful analysis, which, however, needs to be augmented with a detailed analysis.

Feldman *et al.* [7] applied an evolutionary game-theoretic analysis on a P2P design space. Their analysis differed from ours as it focussed on simple cooperation, defection and reciprocation, whereas we analyze a considerably vast space of protocols. Also, we apply the results of our analysis to BitTorrent to validate our approach.

Qiu *et al.* [26] under certain assumptions showed that BitTorrent is a Nash Equilibrium. We used a different abstraction and proved otherwise. Similarly Levin *et al.* [16] argued that BitTorrent is an auction, and with their model gained insights to develop a more robust variant. We showed that considering BitTorrent as a strategy in a game, also leads to insights, and we also developed a more robust variant.

Finally, many papers propose protocol variants not based on game-theoretic analysis [2, 15], but to our knowledge, ours is the first attempt to provide a comprehensive, simulation based approach.

7. CONCLUSION AND FUTURE WORK

We have presented Design Space Analysis (DSA), a simulation based approach that complements game-theoretic analysis of incentives in distributed protocols. DSA emphasizes the specification and analysis of a design space, rather than proposing a single protocol. We have shown that DSA can be used to gain an in-depth analysis of the properties of protocol variants, and it can be used for designing deployable protocols. For future work, we would like to explore if a solution concept similar to PRA quantification could be

developed which explores the design space using a heuristic based approach. This could be needed in situations where a thorough scan of the design space becomes infeasible due to its size. We would also like to test DSA on distributed domains other than P2P. In conclusion, we note that DSA is a general method, which is practical and easy to apply, and we have demonstrated its merits by applying it successfully to P2P file swarming systems.

Acknowledgement

This work was partially supported by the Higher Education Commission (HEC) of Pakistan; and by the European Community 7th Framework Program through the QLectives and P2P-Next projects (grant no. 231200, 216217). We thank Márk Jelasity and his group at Szeged, Hungary for their valuable feedback during the early phase of this work. We would also like to thank the anonymous reviewers who have helped to improve the paper. Finally, we thank our shepherd, Scott Shenker for guiding us in the final stages of this work.

8. REFERENCES

[1] R. Axelrod. *The Evolution of Cooperation*. Basic Books, New York, 1984.

[2] A. Bharambe, C. Herley, and V. Padmanabhan. Analyzing and improving a BitTorrent network's performance mechanisms. In *INFOCOM*, 2006.

[3] C. Buragohain, D. Agrawal, and S. Suri. A game theoretic framework for incentives in P2P systems. In *IEEE P2P*, 2003.

[4] A.L.H. Chow, L. Golubchik, V. Misra. BitTorrent: An extensible heterogeneous model. In *INFOCOM*, 2009.

[5] R. Dash, N. Jennings, and D. Parkes. Computational-mechanism design: A call to arms. *IEEE Intelligent Systems*, 18:40–47, 2003.

[6] J. Feigenbaum and S. Shenker. Distributed Algorithmic Mechanism Design: Recent Results and Future Directions. In *ACM DIALM*, 2002.

[7] M. Feldman, K. Lai, I. Stoica, and J. Chuang. Robust incentive techniques for peer-to-peer networks. In *ACM EC*, pp. 102–111, 2004.

[8] R. Hahnel and A. Library. *The ABCs of political economy: A modern approach*. Pluto Press, 2002.

[9] T. Hoßfeld, F. Lehrieder, D. Hock, S. Oechsner, Z. Despotovic, W. Kellerer, and M. Michel. Characterization of BitTorrent swarms and their distribution in the Internet. *Computer Networks*, 55:1197–1215, 2011.

[10] D. Hruschka and J. Henrich. Friendship, cliquishness, and the emergence of cooperation. *Journal of Theoretical Biology*, 239:1–15, 2006.

[11] R. Izhak-Ratzin. Collaboration in BitTorrent systems. In *IFIP-TC Networking*, pp. 338–351, 2009.

[12] S. Jun and M. Ahamad. Incentives in BitTorrent induce free riding. In *P2PECON*, 2005.

[13] A.-M. Kermarrec and M. van Steen, editors. *ACM SIGOPS Operating Systems Review 41, Special Issue on Gossip-Based Networking*. 2007.

[14] A. Legout, N. Liogkas, E. Kohler, and L. Zhang. Clustering and sharing incentives in bittorrent systems. In *ACM SIGMETRICS*, pp. 301–312, 2007.

[15] B. Leong, Y. Wang, S. Wen, C. Carbunaru, Y. Teo, C. Chang, and T. Ho. Improving peer-to-peer file distribution: winner doesn't have to take all. In *ACM APSys*, pp. 55–60, 2010.

[16] D. Levin, K. LaCurts, N. Spring, and B. Bhattacharjee. BitTorrent is an auction: analyzing and improving BitTorrent's incentives. In *ACM SIGCOMM*, 2008.

[17] T. Locher, P. Moor, S. Schmid, and R. Wattenhofer. Free riding in BitTorrent is cheap. In *HotNets-V*, 2006.

[18] R. Mahajan, M. Rodrig, D. Wetherall, and J. Zahorjan. Experiences applying game theory to system design. In *ACM PINS*, pp. 183–190, 2004.

[19] G. Mailath. Do people play Nash equilibrium? Lessons from evolutionary game theory. *Journal of Economic Literature*, 36:1347–1374, 1998.

[20] M. Meulpolder, J. Pouwelse, D. Epema, and H. Sips. BarterCast: A practical approach to prevent lazy freeriding in P2P networks. In *IEEE IPDPS*, 2009.

[21] J. Mol, J. Pouwelse, M. Meulpolder, D. Epema, and H. Sips. Give-to-get: Free-riding-resilient video-on-demand in p2p systems. In *SPIE/ACM MMCN*, 2008.

[22] M. Osborne and A. Rubinstein. *A course in game theory*. The MIT press, 1994.

[23] F. Pianese, J. Keller, and E. Biersack. PULSE, a flexible P2P live streaming system. In *INFOCOM*, 2006.

[24] M. Piatek, T. Isdal, T. Anderson, A. Krishnamurthy, and A. Venkataramani. Do incentives build robustness in BitTorrent. In *NSDI*, 2007.

[25] M. Posch. Win-Stay, Lose-Shift Strategies for Repeated Games–Memory Length, Aspiration Levels and Noise. *Journal of Theoretical Biology*, 198:183–195, 1999.

[26] D. Qiu and R. Srikant. Modeling and performance analysis of BitTorrent-like peer-to-peer networks. *ACM SIGCOMM Computer Communication Review*, 34:367–378, 2004.

[27] A. Rao, A. Legout, and W. Dabbous. Can Realistic BitTorrent Experiments Be Performed on Clusters? In *IEEE P2P*, 2010.

[28] E. Rasmusen. *Games and information: An introduction to game theory*. Wiley-Blackwell, 2007.

[29] T. Roughgarden and É. Tardos. How bad is selfish routing. *Journal of the ACM*, 49:236–259, 2002.

[30] K. Rzadca, A. Datta, and S. Buchegger. Replica placement in p2p storage: Complexity and game theoretic analyses. In *ICDCS*, pp. 599–609, 2010.

[31] S. Shenker. Making greed work in networks: A game-theoretic analysis of switch service disciplines. *IEEE/ACM Transactions on Networking*, 3:819–831, 2002.

[32] M. Yang, Z. Zhang, X. Li, and Y. Dai. An empirical study of free-riding behavior in the Maze P2P file-sharing system. *Peer-to-Peer Systems IV*, pp. 182–192, 2005.

Appendix: BitTorrent Nash Equilibrium

In the following we use the notation introduced in Table 1 and the results from Sections 2.2 and 2.3.

In order to show that *BitTorrent is not a Nash equilibrium* (NE), we consider a swarm with $N-1$ BitTorrent (BT) peers and assume that one peer using the Birds protocol enters this swarm.

In this setup the expected number of games won by the BT clients against higher and lower classes do not change. On the other hand, for the Birds client only the formula for the expected number of games won against the peers from the lower classes changes to $E_B^r[B \to c]' = N_B/N_r$, which is the same as for the BT clients.

Now, we consider the class C where the peer using the Birds protocol is located. The expected values of the number of games that the peers win due to reciprocation from other peers in this class

will be $E_B^r[C-c]' = U_r - K$ for Birds and

$$
\begin{aligned}
E^r[C \to c]' &= \frac{N_{C'} - U_r}{N_{C'}}(U_r - K - E[A \to c]) \\
&\quad + \frac{U_r}{N_{C'}}(U_r - E[A \to c] - K') \\
&= U_r - K - E[A \to c] - \frac{U_r}{N_{C'}}(K + K')
\end{aligned}
$$

for the BT clients, where $N_{C'} = N_C - 1$, and $K' = 1 - \left((1 - E[A \to c])(1 - \frac{1}{U_r})\right)^{U_r - 1}$, which leads us to the fact that

$$
E_B[C \to c]' > E[C \to c]'.
$$

Regarding the 'free game wins', the formulae change to

$$
E_B[C \to c]' = \frac{N_{C'}}{N_C}(N_C - E^r[C \to c]')/N_r,
$$

$$
E[C \to c]' = E_B[C \to c]' + \frac{N_C - E_B^r[C \to c]'}{N_C N_r},
$$

which says that $E[C \to c]' > E_B[C \to c]'$; however,

$$
E_B^r[C \to c]' + E_B[C \to c]' > E^r[C \to c]' + E[C \to c]'
$$

holds. Thus, the peer using the Birds protocol, on average, wins more games than any of the BT clients, proving that BT is not a NE.

Now we show that *it is a NE when all peers in the swarm follow the Birds protocol*.

We assume that there are $N-1$ peers following the Birds protocol and one peer using the BT protocol enters this swarm. We give a formal proof for the case when this new peer uses BT; the other three cases (regarding class-based reciprocation) can be proved in the similar way.

First, we consider the games where peers get reciprocation. Neither the Birds peers nor the BT peer get anything from the higher and lower classes. For that particular class C, where the BT peer is located we have

$$
\begin{aligned}
E_B^r[C \to c]'' &= \frac{N_{C'} - U_r}{N_{C'}}U_r + \frac{U_r}{N_{C'}}(U_r - E[A \to c]) \\
&= U_r - \frac{U_r}{N_{C'}}E[A \to c],
\end{aligned}
$$

where $N_{C'}$ is the number of Birds in class C, i.e. $N_{C'} = N_C - 1$. Moreover, we have $E^r[C \to c]'' = U_r - E[A \to c]$; from here it is easy to see that $E_B^r[C \to c]'' > E^r[C \to c]''$.

'Free game wins' remain the same. The expressions for the same class become

$$
E[C \to c]'' = \frac{N_{C'}}{N_C} \times \frac{N_{C'} - E_B^r[C \to c]}{N - U_r - 1},
$$

and

$$
E_B[C \to c]'' = E[C \to c]'' + \frac{N_{C'} - E^r[C \to c]}{N_{C'}(N - U_r - 1)},
$$

Thus we conclude that $E_B[C \to c]'' > E[C \to c]''$ which completes our proof that Birds is a NE.

How Many Tiers? Pricing in the Internet Transit Market

Vytautas Valancius*, Cristian Lumezanu*, Nick Feamster*,
Ramesh Johari† , and Vijay V. Vazirani*
* Georgia Tech † Stanford University

ABSTRACT

ISPs are increasingly selling "tiered" contracts, which offer Internet connectivity to wholesale customers in bundles, at rates based on the cost of the links that the traffic in the bundle is traversing. Although providers have already begun to implement and deploy tiered pricing contracts, little is known about how to structure them. Although contracts that sell connectivity on finer granularities improve market efficiency, they are also more costly for ISPs to implement and more difficult for customers to understand. Our goal is to analyze whether current tiered pricing practices in the wholesale transit market yield optimal profits for ISPs and whether better bundling strategies might exist. In the process, we offer two contributions: (1) we develop a novel way of mapping traffic and topology data to a demand and cost model; and (2) we fit this model on three large real-world networks: an European transit ISP, a content distribution network, and an academic research network, and run counterfactuals to evaluate the effects of different bundling strategies. Our results show that the common ISP practice of structuring tiered contracts according to the cost of carrying the traffic flows (*e.g.*, offering a discount for traffic that is local) can be suboptimal and that dividing contracts based on *both traffic demand and the cost of carrying it* into *only three or four tiers* yields near-optimal profit for the ISP.

Categories and Subject Descriptors

C.2.3 [**Network Operations**]: Network Management

General Terms

Algorithms, Design, Economics

1. INTRODUCTION

The increasing commoditization of Internet transit is changing the landscape of the Internet bandwidth market. Although residential Internet Service Providers (ISPs) and content providers are connecting directly to one another more often, they must still use major Internet transit providers to reach most destinations. These Internet transit customers can often select from among dozens of possible providers [28]. As major ISPs compete with one another, the price of Internet transit continues to plummet: on average, transit prices are falling by about 30% per year [24].

As a result of such competition, ISPs are evolving their business models and selling transit to their customers in many ways to try to retain profits. In particular, many transit ISPs implement pricing strategies where traffic is priced by volume or destination [9]. For example, most transit ISPs offer volume discounts for higher *commit levels* (*e.g.*, customer networks committing to a lower minimum bandwidth receive a higher per-bit price quote than customers committing to a higher minimum bandwidth [24]). Such a market is said to implement *tiered pricing* [13]. Through private communication with network operators, we identified many other instances of tiered pricing already being implemented by ISPs. These pricing instruments involve charging prices on traffic bundles based on various factors, such as how far the traffic is traveling, and whether the traffic is "on net" (*i.e.*, to that ISP's customers) or "off net". Still, we understand very little about the extent to which tiered pricing benefits both ISPs and their customers, or if there might be better ways to structure the tiers. In this paper, we study *destination-based tiered pricing*, with the goal of understanding how ISPs should bundle and price connectivity to maximize their profit.

In this study, we grapple with the balance between the prescriptions of economic theory and a variety of practical constraints and realities. On one hand, economic theory says that higher market granularity leads to increased efficiency [17]. Intuitively, an Internet transit market that prices individual flows is more efficient than one that sells transit in bulk, since customers pay only for the traffic they send, and since ISPs can price those flows according to their cost. On the other hand, various practical constraints prevent Internet transit from being sold in arbitrarily fine granularities. Technical hurdles and additional overhead can make it difficult to implement tiered pricing in current routing protocols and equipment. Additionally, tiered pricing can be more difficult for wholesale customers to understand if there are too many tiers. Transit ISPs would ideally like to come close to maximizing their profit with only a few pricing tiers, since implementing more pricing tiers introduces additional overhead and complexity. Our analysis shows that, indeed, in many cases, an ISP reaps most of the profit possible with infinitesimally fine-grained tiers using only two or three tiers, assuming that those two or three tiers are structured properly.

Although understanding the benefits of different pricing structures is important, modeling them is quite difficult. The model must take as an input existing customer demand and predict how traffic (and, hence, ISP profit) would change in response to pricing strategies. Such a model must capture how customers would respond to any pricing change—for any particular traffic flow—as well as the change in cost of forwarding traffic on various paths in an ISP's network. Of course, many of these input values are difficult to come by even for network operators, but they are especially elusive for researchers; additionally, even if certain values such as costs are known, they change quickly and differ widely across ISPs.

The model we develop allows us to estimate the relative effects of pricing and bundling scenarios, despite the lack of availability of precise values for many of these parameters. The general approach, which we describe in Section 3, is to start with a demand and cost model and assume both that ISPs are already profit-maximizing and that the current prices reflects both customer demand and the underlying network costs. These assumptions allow us to either fix or solve for many of the unknown parameters and run counterfactuals to evaluate the relative effects of dividing the customer demand into pricing tiers. To drive this model, we use traffic data from three real-world networks: a major international content distribution network with its own network infrastructure; an European transit ISP; and an academic research network. We map the demand and topology data from these networks to a model that reflects the service offerings that real-world ISPs use.

Using our model, we evaluate three scenarios:

- *What happens if an ISP increases the number of tiers for which it sells transit?* We find that profit increases, but the returns diminish as the number of tiers increases: with 3–4 tiers, it is possible to capture 90–95% of the profit that could be captured with an infinite number of granularities, assuming that these tiers are divided in the right way.

- *How do strategies for dividing capacity into distinct bundles and pricing those bundles affect an ISP's profit?* Our analysis shows that ISPs must judiciously choose how they divide traffic into pricing tiers. A naïve approach (*e.g.*, based only on traffic cost or on demand) might require dozens of pricing tiers to capture most of the possible profit. We find that dividing traffic into tiers in a way that accounts for *both traffic demand and the cost of carrying traffic* yields more profit than the current practice that is based only on cost, and is nearly as effective as an optimal division.

- *How do the benefits of various pricing strategies depend on the network topology and traffic demands?* We find that networks with high variability in *cost* of delivering traffic obtain greater benefit from bundling. We also observe that networks with high variability in *demand* require more bundles to capture maximum profit.

We evaluate these and other questions across two customer demand models, four network cost models, and a range of input parameters, such as price sensitivity. Although each of the models might not be perfectly accurate, they yield results that are consistent both across models and with our intuition about markets.

We make three contributions. First, we taxonomize the state of the art and trends in pricing instruments for Internet transit (Section 2). Second, to analyze the effects of tiered pricing, we develop a model that captures demands and costs in the transit market. One of the challenges in developing such a model is applying it to real traffic data, given many unknown parameters (*e.g.*, the cost of various resources, or how users respond to price). Hence, we develop methods for fitting empirical traffic demands to theoretical cost and demand models. We use this approach to evaluate ISP profit for pricing strategies under a range of possible cost models and network topologies (Section 3). Third, we apply our model to real-world traffic matrices and network topologies to characterize a range of simple bundling strategies that are close to optimal (Section 4); we also suggest how these strategies could be implemented in practice (Section 5).

2. BACKGROUND

In this section, we describe the current state of affairs in the Internet transit market. We first taxonomize *what* services (bundles) ISPs are selling. We then provide intuition on *why* ISPs are moving towards tiered wholesale Internet transit service.

2.1 Current Transit Market Offerings

Unfortunately, there is not much public information about the wholesale Internet transit market. ISPs are reluctant to reveal specifics about their business models and pricing strategies to their competitors. Therefore, to obtain most of the information in this section, we engaged in many discussions and email exchanges with network operators. Below, we classify the types of Internet transit service we identified during these conversations. Although much of the information in this section is widely known in the network operations community, it is difficult to find a concise taxonomy of product offerings in the wholesale transit market. The taxonomy below serves as a point of reference for our discussions of tiered pricing in this paper, but it may also be useful for anyone who wishes to better understand the state of the art in pricing strategies in the wholesale transit market.

Transit. Most ISPs offer conventional Internet transit service. Internet transit is sold at a *blended rate*—a single price (usually expressed in $/Mbps/month)—charged for traffic to all destinations. Historically, blended rates have been decreasing by 30% each year [24]. Blended rate is the simplest and yet the most crude way to charge for traffic. If network costs are highly variable, less costly flows in the blended-rate bundle subsidize other, more expensive flows. ISPs often innovate by offering more than one rate: We summarize three pricing models that require two or more rates: (1) *paid peering*, (2) *backplane peering*, and (3) *regional pricing*.

Paid peering is similar to settlement-free peering, except that one network pays to reach the other. A major ISP might separately sell *off-net* routes (wholesale transit) at one rate and *on-net* routes (to reach destinations inside its own network) at another (usually lower) rate. For example, national ISPs in Eastern Europe, Australia, and in other regions may sell local connectivity at a discount to increase demand for local traffic, which is is significantly cheaper than transit to outside global destinations [1]. The on-net routes are also offered at a discount by some major transit ISPs to large content providers, because such transit ISPs can recoup part of the costs from their customers, who congest paid upstream links to transit ISPs by downloading the content. Some instances of paid peering have spawned significant controversy: most recently, Comcast—primarily a network serving end-users—was accused of a network neutrality violation when it forced one tier-1 provider to pay to reach Comcast's customers [16].

Backplane peering occurs when an ISP, in addition to selling global transit through its own backbone, charges a discount rate for the traffic it can offload to its peers at the same Internet exchange. Smaller ISPs buy such a service because they might not meet all the settlement-free peering requirements to peer directly with the ISPs in the exchange. Although many large ISPs discourage this practice, some ISPs deviate by offering backplane peering to retain customers or to maintain traffic ratios with their peers. As with paid peering, the ISP selling backplane peering has to account and charge for at least two traffic flows: one to peers and another to its backbone.

Regional pricing occurs when transit service providers offer different rates to reach different geographic regions. The regions can be defined at different levels of granularity, such as PoP, metro area, regional area, nation, or continent. In some instances, the transit ISP offers access to all regions with different prices; in other instances, the downstream network purchases access only to a specific geographic region (*e.g.*, access only to South America or Australia). In practice, due to the overhead of provisioning and maintaining many sessions to the same customer, ISPs rarely use more than one or two extra price levels for different regions.

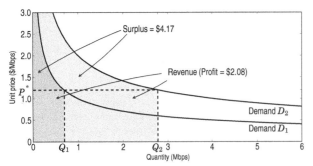

(a) **Blended-rate pricing.** ISP charges a single blended rate P_0.

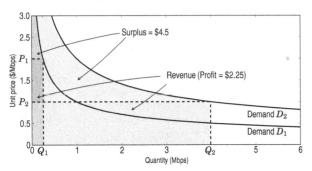

(b) **Tiered pricing.** ISP charges rates P_1 and P_2 for flows.

Figure 1: Market efficiency loss due to coarse bundling.

We speculate that the bundling strategies described above arose primarily from operational and cost considerations. For example, it is relatively easy for a transit ISP to tag which routes are coming from customers and which routes are coming from peers and then in turn sell them separately to its customers. Similarly, it is relatively easy to sell local (*i.e.*, less costly) routes separately. We show that these naïve bundling strategies might not be as effective as bundling strategies that account for both cost and demand.

2.2 The Trend Towards Tiered Pricing

Conventional blended rate pricing is simple to implement, but it may be inefficient. ISPs can lose profit as a result of blended-rate pricing, and customers can lose surplus. This is an example of *market failure*, where goods are not being efficiently allocated between participants of the market. Another outcome of blended-rate pricing is the *increase in direct peering* to circumvent "one-size-fits-all" transit. Both phenomena provide incentives for ISPs to improve their business models to retain revenue. We now explain each of these outcomes.

2.2.1 Profit and surplus loss

Selling transit at a blended rate could reduce profit for transit ISPs and surplus for customers. We define an ISP's *profit* as its revenue minus its costs, and *customer surplus* as customer utility minus the amount it pays to the ISP. Unrealized profit and surplus can occur when ISPs charge a single rate while incurring different costs when delivering traffic to destinations.

Figure 1 illustrates how tiered pricing can increase both the profit for an ISP and the surplus for a customer. The downward-sloping curves represent consumer demand[1] to two destinations. Since

---

[1]We model consumer demand as *residual demand*. Residual demand accounts for consumption change both due to inherent consumer demand and due to some consumers shifting consumption to substitutes, such as other ISPs (See Section 3.2.1.)

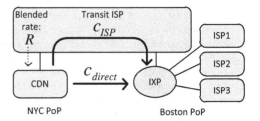

Figure 2: The customer procures a direct link if the cost for such a link is lower than the blended rate $c_{direct} < R$.

the demand slope D_2 is higher than demand slope D_1, the customer has higher demand for the second destination in the ISP's network. Assume that the ISP cost of serving demand D_1 is \$1, while the cost of serving demand D_2 is \$0.5. Modeling demand with constant elasticity (Section 3), the *profit maximizing price* can be shown to be $P_0 = \$1.2/Mbps$. If, however, the ISP is able to offer two bundles, then the profit maximizing prices for such bundles would be $P_1 = \$2.7$ and $P_2 = \$1$. Figure 1(b) shows that this price setup not only increases ISP profit but also increases consumer surplus and thus social welfare.

The market achieves higher efficiency because customers adjust their consumption levels of the ISP network according to their demand and to the prices that the ISP exposes, which directly depend on its costs. Without the ISP's indirect exposure of its costs, the customer consumes less of the cheaper capacity and more of the expensive capacity than it would otherwise. In Section 3, we formalize the market that we have used in this example and propose more complex demand and cost models.

2.2.2 Increase in direct peering

Charging for traffic at a blended rate also provides incentives for client networks to connect directly to geographically close Internet Exchange Points (IXPs). For instance, if a transit ISP charges only blended rate, client network might find geographically close IXPs cheaper to reach by leasing or purchasing private links. While direct peering is generally perceived as a positive phenomenon, for transit ISPs it means less revenue. Direct peering efforts can also diminish economies of scale: instead of using shared ISP infrastructure, customers provision their own connectivity to IXPs.

Figure 2 illustrates an interaction between an upstream ISP and a CDN client (*e.g.*, Google, Microsoft) with its own backbone, which extends to the NYC PoP. The CDN might, or might not, have a content cache at the Boston IXP, but since it does not have its own backbone presence at the IXP, the CDN must pay the upstream ISP to reach it. The ISP offers a blended rate R at the the NYC PoP for all the traffic, including the traffic to the Boston IXP. The blended rate R is set to compensate the upstream provider for the overall traffic mix and, therefore, is *higher* than the amortized cost of most of the cheaper (more localized) flows that ISP is serving (*i.e.*, the flows between the NYC and Boston PoPs). The CDN eventually will procure a direct link to the Boston IXP, if it finds that it can procure such a direct link at an amortized cost $c_{direct} < R$. Assuming the ISP's profit margin is M and flow accounting overhead is A (discussed in Section 5.2), such a direct link presents a *market failure* if $c_{direct} > (M + 1)c_{ISP} + A$, because the customer deploys additional capacity at a higher cost than the ISP could have charged in a tiered market.

Some operators we interviewed confirm that they periodically re-evaluate transit bills and expand their backbone coverage if they find that having own presence in an IXP pays off. In today's transit market, many customers increasingly opt for direct peering [14]; transit service providers are absorbing losses as a result of competitive pressure [24]. Naturally, this pressure increases the incentive for ISPs to adopt a tiered pricing model for local traffic. The central question, then, is how they should go about structuring these tiers. The rest of the paper focuses on this question.

3. MODELING PROFITS, COSTS, AND DEMANDS

We develop demand and cost models that capture ISP profit under various pricing strategies. Although we doubt there is a perfect model for demand in the Internet transit market, we perform our evaluation with two common demand models. Because cost is also difficult to model, we devise four network cost models. We first define ISP profit and then describe demand and cost models.

3.1 ISP Profit

We consider a transit market with multiple ISPs and customers. Each ISP is rational and maximizes its profit, which we express as the difference between its revenue and costs:

$$\Pi(\vec{P}) = \sum_{p_i \in \vec{P}} \left(p_i Q_i(\vec{P}) - c_i Q_i(\vec{P}) \right) \qquad (1)$$

where p_i is the price an ISP sets to deliver flow i, c_i is the unit cost for i, and $Q_i(\vec{P})$ is the demand for i given a vector of prices $\vec{P} = (p_1, p_2, \ldots, p_n)$. An ISP chooses the price vector $\vec{P}$ that maximizes its profit. Having a price for each flow allows us to explore different pricing strategies by bundling flows in different ways. For example, blended rate pricing requires p_i to be equal for all i; we can explore different tiered pricing approaches by requiring various subsets of all flows to have the same price.

Given knowledge of both the traffic demand of customers and the costs associated with delivering each flow, we can compute ISP profit. Unfortunately, it is difficult to validate any particular demand function or cost model; even if validation were possible, it is likely that cost structures and customer demand could change or evolve over time. Accordingly, we evaluate ISP profit for various tiered pricing approaches under a variety of demand functions and cost models. Section 3.2 describes the demand functions that we explore, and Section 3.3 describes the cost models that we consider.

3.2 Customer Demand

To compute ISP profit for each pricing scenario, we must understand how customers adjust their traffic demand in response to price changes. We consider two families of demand functions: *constant elasticity* and *logit*.

Constant elasticity demand. The constant elasticity demand (CED) is derived from the well-known *alpha-fair* utility model [21], which is often used to model user utility on the Internet. The alpha-fair utility takes the form of a concave increasing utility function, which emulates a decreasing marginal benefit to additional bandwidth for a user. In this model flow demands are *separable* (*i.e.*, changes in demand or prices for one flow have no effect on demand and prices of other flows). The CED model is most appropriate for scenarios when consumers have no alternatives (*e.g.*, when the content that a customer is trying to reach is not replicated, or the customer needs to communicate with a specific endpoint on the network).

Logit demand. To capture the fact that customers might sometimes have a choice between flows (*e.g.*, sending traffic to alternative destination if the current one becomes too expensive), we also perform our analysis using the *logit model*, where demands are not separable: the price and demand for any flow depend on prices and

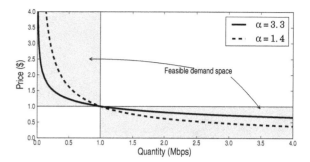

Figure 3: Feasible CED demand functions for $v = 1$.

demands for the other flows. The logit model is frequently used for this purpose in econometric demand estimation [19]. In the logit model, each consumer nominally prefers the flows that offers the highest utility. This matches well with scenarios when consumers have several alternatives (*e.g.*, when requested content is replicated in multiple places).

3.2.1 Constant elasticity demand

The CED demand function is as follows:

$$Q_i(p_i) = \left(\frac{v_i}{p_i} \right)^{\alpha} \qquad (2)$$

where p_i is the unit price (*e.g.*, \$/Mbit/s), $\alpha \in (1, \infty)$ is the price sensitivity, and $v_i > 0$ is the valuation coefficient of flow i. The demand function can be interpreted to represent either *inherent* consumer demand or *residual* consumer demand, which reflects not only the inherent demand but also the availability of substitutes.

Figure 3 presents example CED demand functions for $v = 1$ and two values of α, 3.3 and 1.4. Higher values of α indicate high elasticity (users reduce use even due to small changes in price). For example, the demand with elasticity $\alpha = 3.3$ might represent the traffic from residential ISPs, who are more sensitive to wholesale Internet prices and who respond to price changes in a more dramatic way. Similarly, the demand with elasticity $\alpha = 1.4$ might represent the traffic from enterprise customers, who are less sensitive to the Internet transit price changes. Although our model does not capture full dynamic interaction between competing ISPs (*e.g.*, price wars), modeling demand as residual allows us to account for the existing competitive environment and switching costs. As discussed above, high elasticity can also indicate that competitors are offering more affordable substitutes, and that switching costs for customers are low. In our evaluation, we use a range of price sensitivity values to measure how ISP profit changes for different values of the elasticity of user demand. The gray area in Figure 3 shows that we can cover all feasible demand functions simply by varying the sensitivity parameter.

CED profit. Using the expressions for ISP profit (Equation 1) and demand (Equation 2), and assuming separability of demand of different flows, the ISP profit is:

$$\Pi(\vec{P}) = \sum_{p_i \in \vec{P}} \left(\frac{v_i}{p_i} \right)^{\alpha} (p_i - c_i). \qquad (3)$$

CED profit-maximizing price. By differentiating the profit, we find the profit-maximizing price for each flow i:

$$p_i^* = \frac{\alpha c_i}{\alpha - 1}. \qquad (4)$$

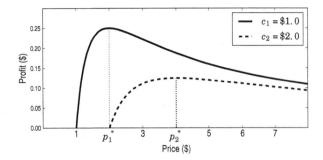

Figure 4: Profit for two flows with identical demand ($v_1 = v_2 = 1.0$, $\alpha = 2$) **but different cost.**

Figure 4 illustrates profit maximization for two flows that have identical demand functions but different costs. For example, the first flow costs $c_1 = \$1.0$ per unit to deliver and mandates optimal price $p^* = \$2.0$ which results in \$0.25 profit. The second flow is more costly thus the profit maximizing price is higher. In this case, the first plot might represent profit for local traffic, while the second plot represents national traffic: ISPs must price national traffic higher than local-area traffic to maximize profit.

CED price for bundled flows. In our evaluation, we test various pricing strategies that bundle multiple flows under the same profit-maximizing price. To find the price for each bundle, we first map real world demands to our model to obtain the valuation v_i and cost c_i for each flow. Then, we differentiate the profit (Equation 3) with respect to the price of each bundle. For example, when we have a single bundle for all flows, we obtain the following profit-maximizing price:

$$P^* = \frac{\alpha \sum_{i=1}^{n} c_i v_i^\alpha}{(\alpha - 1) \sum_{i=1}^{n} v_i^\alpha} \qquad (5)$$

where n is the number of flows. Section 4 details this approach.

3.2.2 Logit demand

The logit demand model assumes that each consumer faces a discrete choice among a set of available goods or services. In the context of data transit, the choice is between different destinations or flows. Following Besanko *et al.* [4], a consumer j using flow i will obtain the utility:

$$u_{ij} = \alpha(v_i - p_i) + \epsilon_{ij}$$

where $\alpha \in (0, \infty)$ is the elasticity parameter, v_i is the "average" consumer's *maximum willingness to pay* for flow i, p_i is a price of using i, and ϵ_{ij} represents consumer j's idiosyncratic preference for i (where ϵ_{ij} has a Gumbel distribution.) The logit model defines the probability that any given consumer will use flow i as a function of the price vector of all flows:

$$s_i(\vec{P}) = \frac{e^{\alpha(v_i - p_i)}}{\sum_j e^{\alpha(v_j - p_j)} + 1} \qquad (6)$$

where $\sum_i s_i(\vec{P}) = 1$. The demand for flow i equals the product of $s_i(\vec{P})$ and the total number of consumers (K):

$$Q_i(\vec{P}) = K s_i(\vec{P}). \qquad (7)$$

Here, s_i is also called the *market share* of flow i. The model also accounts for the possibility that some customers elect not to send traffic to any destination. The market share for traffic not sent is:

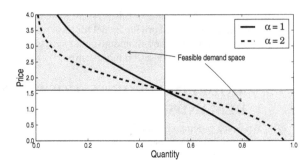

Figure 5: Logit demand function.

$$s_0(\vec{P}) = \frac{1}{\sum_j e^{\alpha(v_j - p_j)} + 1}.$$

Figure 5 shows examples of logit demand functions. We assume a setting with two flows, with two values for the valuation v_i, 1.6 and 1. We fix the price for the first flow to 1, and we vary the price for the second flow between 0 and 4. The figure shows demand curves for the second flow, for two values of α. Similar to the constant elasticity demand model, lower values of α indicate low elasticity of demand, where users need bigger price variations to modify their usage.

Logit profit. Using the expressions for ISP profit (Equation 1) and logit demand (Equation 7), the ISP profit is:

$$\Pi(\vec{P}) = K \sum_{p_i \in \vec{P}} s_i(\vec{P})(p_i - c_i). \qquad (8)$$

Logit profit-maximizing prices. To find the profit maximizing price for flow i, we find the first-order conditions for Equation 8:

$$p_i^* = c_i + \frac{1}{\alpha s_0}. \qquad (9)$$

Due to the presence of s_0, p_i^* recursively depends on itself and on profit-maximizing prices of other flows. To obtain maximum profit, we develop an iterative heuristic based on gradient descent that starts from a fixed set of prices ($p_i = P_0, \forall i$) and greedily updates them towards the optimum.

Valuation and cost of bundled flows. To test pricing strategies, we first map real traffic demands to the model to find the valuation v_i and cost c_i for each flow i. We then bundle the flows as described in Section 4.2.1. Knowing that $\sum_i s_i = 1$ and applying Equation 6 allows us to compute valuations for any bundle of flows as:

$$v_{bundle} = \frac{\ln\left(\sum_{i=1}^{n} e^{\alpha v_i}\right)}{\alpha} \qquad (10)$$

where v_i are valuations of the flows in the bundle. Similarly we can find the average unit cost of combined flows in each bundle:

$$c_{bundle} = \frac{\sum_{i=1}^{n} c_i e^{\alpha v_i}}{\sum_{i=1}^{n} e^{\alpha v_i}}. \qquad (11)$$

3.3 ISP Cost

Modeling cost is difficult: ISPs typically do not publish the details of operational costs; even if they did, many of these figures change rapidly and are specific to the ISP, the region, and other

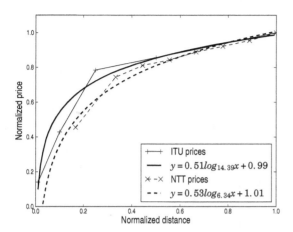

Figure 6: Using price data from ITU [11] and NTT [25] to fit concave distance to cost mapping curve.

factors. To account for these uncertainties, we evaluate our results in the context of several cost models. We also make the following assumptions. First, we assume the more traffic the ISP carries, the higher cost it incurs. Although on a small scale the bandwidth cost is a step function (the capacity is added at discrete increments), on a larger scale we model cost as a linear function of bandwidth. Second, we assume that ISP transit cost changes with distance. Both assumptions are motivated by practice: looking only at specific instances of connectivity, the cost is a step function of distance (*e.g.*, equipment manufacturers sell several classes of optical transceivers, where each more powerful transceiver able to reach longer distances costs progressively more than less powerful transceivers [7]). Over a large set of links, we can model cost as a smooth function of distance.

The cost models below offer only *relative* flow-cost valuations (*e.g.*, flow A is twice as costly as flow B); they do not operate on absolute costs. These relative costs must be reconciled with the blended prices used to derive customer valuations. We describe methods for reconciling these values in Section 4.1. Each cost model has a generic tuning parameter, denoted as θ, which we use in the evaluation.

Linear function of distance. The most straightforward way to model ISP's costs as a function of distance is to assume cost increases linearly with distance. Although, in some cases, this model does not hold (*e.g.*, crossing a mountain range is more expensive than crossing a region with flat terrain), we often observe that ISPs charge linearly in the distance of communication [5, 6]. As we model cost as linear function of distance, we set cost $c_i = \gamma d_i + \beta$, where γ is a scaling coefficient that translates from relative to real costs, β is a base cost (*i.e.*, the fixed cost that the ISP incurs for communicating over any distance), and d_i is the geographical distance between the source and destination served by an ISP. We describe how we determine γ in Section 4.1. We model the base cost β as a fraction of the maximum cost without the base component. More formally: $\beta = \theta \max_{j \in 1 \cdots n} \gamma d_j$, where θ in this cost model is a relative base cost fraction, and n is number of flows with different cost. For example, given distances 1, 10, and 100 miles, $\gamma = \$1/mile$, and $\theta = 0.1$, the resulting base cost β is $10, and thus flow costs are $11, $20, and $110. In the evaluation, we vary θ to observe the effects of different base costs. For example, low θ values (low base cost) here represent a case where link distance is the largest contributor to the total cost.

Concave function of distance. We are also aware of ISPs that price transit as a concave function of distance [11, 25]. For this scenario we model the ISP's cost as $c_i = \gamma(a \log_b d_i + c) + \beta$. Figure 6 shows a concave curve fitting to two price data sets, resulting in $a \approx 0.5$, $b \approx 6$, and $c \approx 1$ for normalized prices and distance. As in the case of linear cost, we set the base offset cost $\beta = \theta \max_{j \in 1 \cdots n} \gamma(a \log_b d_i + c)$. We use θ in the evaluation to change link distance contribution to the total cost.

Function of destination region. As described in Section 2.2, both private communication with network operators and publicly available data suggest that ISPs can also charge for traffic at rates depending on the region where traffic is destined [8,27,31]. For example, an ISP might have less expensive capacity in the metropolitan area than in the region, less expensive capacity in the region than in the nation, and less expensive capacity in the nation than across continental boundaries. We divide flows into three categories: *metropolitan*, *national*, and *international*. We map the flows into these categories by using data from the GeoIP [18] database: flows that originate and terminate in the same city are classified as metro, and flows that start and end in the same country are classified as national; all other flows are classified as international. For EU ISP we only have distances between traffic entry and exit points, thus we classify flows traveling less than 10 miles as metro, flows that travel less than 100 miles as national, and longer flows as international. We set the costs as follows: $c_{metro} = \gamma$, $c_{nation} = \gamma 2^\theta$, and $c_{int} = \gamma 3^\theta$. This form allows us to test scenarios when there is no cost difference between regions ($\theta = 0$), the cost differences are linear ($\theta = 1$), and costs are different by magnitudes ($\theta > 1$).

Function of destination type. As we described in Section 2.2, ISPs offer discounts for the traffic destined to their customers ("on net" traffic), while charging higher rates for traffic destined for their peers ("off net" traffic). These offerings are motivated by the fact that ISPs do recover some of their transport cost for the traffic sent to other customers. In our evaluation, we model this cost difference by setting the cost of the traffic to peers to be twice as costly than traffic to other customers. The logic behind such a model is that when an ISP sends the traffic between two customers, it gets paid twice by both customers, but when an ISP sends traffic between a customer and a peer it is only paid by the customer. The parameter θ indicates a fraction of traffic at each distance that is destined to clients, as opposed to traffic that is destined to peers and providers.

4. EVALUATING TIERED PRICING STRATEGIES

In this section, we evaluate the efficiency of destination-based tiered pricing using the model presented in Section 3 and real topology and demand data from large networks. Our goal is to understand how the profit that an ISP extracts from offering tiered-pricing depends on the number of tiers (or bundles), the bundling strategy used, and the network topology and traffic demand.

One of the major challenges we face is that we cannot know some aspects of the cost and demand models, or even which model to use. We use the ISP data to derive model parameters, such as valuation or cost, and evaluate the profit of each strategy across models and input parameters. Figure 7 presents an overview of our approach for computing ISP profits.

Our evaluation yields several important results. First, we show that an ISP needs only 3–4 bundles to capture 90–95% of the profit provided by an infinite number of bundles, if it bundles the traffic appropriately. Second, choosing a bundling strategy that considers both flow demand and cost is almost as effective as an exhaustive search for the best combination of bundles. Finally, we observe

```
┌─1. DEMAND──────────────────────────┐
│   Models: Constant elasticity, Logit (sec. 3.2)   │
│   ─────────────────────────────    │
│   Map to data to find valuations vᵢ (sec. 4.1.2)  │
└────────────────────────────────────┘
┌─2. COST────────────────────────────┐
│   Models: linear, concave, destination region (sec. 3.3) │
│   ─────────────────────────────    │
│   Map to data to find costs cᵢ (sec. 4.1.3)        │
└────────────────────────────────────┘
┌─3. BUNDLING────────────────────────┐
│   Models: optimal, profit-weighted, demand-weighted, │
│   cost-weightedcost division, index division (sec. 4.2.1) │
│   ─────────────────────────────    │
│   Compute profit maximizing prices (sec. 4.2.2)    │
└────────────────────────────────────┘
```

Figure 7: We evaluate the effect of tiered pricing on Internet transit by separately modeling the demand and cost of traffic and the way ISPs bundle flows under the same price. At each step we use real-world data to derive unknown parameters.

Data set	Date	Distance (miles)		Traffic (Gbps)	
		w-avg	CV	Aggregate	CV
EU ISP	11/12/09	54	0.70	37	1.71
CDN	12/02/09	1988	0.59	96	2.28
Internet 2	12/02/09	660	0.54	4	4.53

Table 1: Data sets used in our evaluation. The columns represent: the network, data capture date, demand-weighted average of flow distances, coefficient of variation (CV) of flow distances, aggregate traffic per second, and CV of demand of different flows.

that the topology and traffic of a network influences its bundling strategies: networks with higher coefficient of variation of demand need more bundles to extract maximum profit.

4.1 Mapping Data to Models

Because we do not know the parameters that we need to compute the profit-maximizing prices and the maximum profit for each bundling strategy, we must derive them. We first describe the data and how we extract the necessary information for computing model parameters. Then, we show how to apply the demand models to the real traffic demands to compute the valuation coefficients v_i for each flow i. Finally, we derive the ISP's cost for servicing the flow by applying flow distance information to each of the cost models.

4.1.1 Data Sources

We use demand and topology data from three networks: a European ISP serving thousands of business customers (EU ISP), one of the largest CDN providers in the world (CDN), and a major research network in United States (Internet 2). The data consists of sampled NetFlow records from core routers in each network for 24 hours. Table 1 presents more details about the data sets.

To drive our model, we must compute the traffic volume (which captures consumer demand) and the distance between the source and destination of each flow (which captures the relative cost of transit). To do so, we extract the source and destination IP and port information, as well as the traffic level, from each NetFlow record. We obtain the demand for each flow by aggregating all records of the flow, while ensuring that we do not double-count records that are duplicated on different routers.

To compute distances that reflect the ISP's cost of sending traffic, we use the following heuristics. For the EU ISP, the distance that each flow travels in the ISP's network is the geographical distance

between the flow's entry and exit points, whose identity and location is known. For the CDN, we use the GeoIP database [18] to estimate the distance to the destination. Although this may not reflect the real distance that a packet travels (because part of the path may be covered by another ISP), we assume that it is still reflective of the cost incurred by the CDN. Finally, for Internet2, because each flow may traverse multiple routers, we use the port information to identify the links the flow has traversed. The distance each flow traverses is the sum of the links in the path, where the link length is the geographical distance between the neighboring routers.

4.1.2 Discovering valuation coefficients

The valuation coefficient v_i indicates the valuation of flow i. We need the valuation coefficeint v_i to capture how the demand for flow i varies with price (Equations 2 and 7) and thus affect the ISP profit. To find v_i for each flow, we assume that ISPs charge the same blended price P_0 for each flow and map the observed traffic demand from the data to each demand model.

CED valuation coefficient. From Equation 2 we obtain:

$$v_i = \frac{q_i^{\left(\frac{1}{\alpha}\right)}}{P_0}$$

where q_i is observed demand on flow i and α is the sensitivity coefficient that we vary in the evaluation.

Logit demand valuation coefficient. Starting with Equation 7 and knowing that $s_0 + \sum s_i = 1$ and $s_0 = \frac{1}{\sum e^{\alpha(v_j - P_0)} + 1}$, we obtain:

$$v_i = \frac{\log s_i - \log s_0}{\alpha} + P_0$$

where s_i is the market share of flow i. We vary s_0 in the evaluation and compute the remaining market shares from observed traffic as $s_i = \frac{q_i(1-s_0)}{\sum q_i}$.

4.1.3 Discovering costs

To estimate the ISP profit, we must know the cost that an ISP incurs to service each flow. However, the data provides information only about the distance each flow traverses, which reflects only the relative cost (e.g., flow A is twice as costly as flow B), rather than an absolute cost value. To normalize the cost of carrying traffic to the same units as the price for the flow, we introduce a scaling parameter γ, where $c_i = \gamma f(d_i)$ and d_i is the distance covered by i (see Section 3.3). For each demand model, we compute the scaling parameter by assuming (as in computing valuation coefficients) that ISPs are rational and profit maximizing, and charge the same price P_0 for each flow.

CED. Using Equation 5 and substituting c_i for $\gamma f(d_i)$, we find:

$$\gamma = \frac{P_0(\alpha - 1)\sum_{i=1}^{n} v_i^{\alpha}}{\alpha \sum_{i=1}^{n} f(d_i)v_i^{\alpha}}$$

Logit demand. Differentiating profit Equation 8 and substituting c_i for $\gamma f(d_i)$, we can express γ:

$$\gamma = \frac{\sum \left(e^{\alpha(v_i - P_0)}\left(\alpha P_0 - 1 - \sum_{i=1}^{n} e^{\alpha(v_i - P_0)}\right)\right)}{\alpha \sum_{i=1}^{n} f(d_i)e^{\alpha(v_i - P_0)}}$$

4.2 How Should Tiers Be Structured?

ISPs must judiciously choose how they bundle traffic flows into tiers. As shown in Section 2.1, today's ISPs often offer at most two or three bundles with different prices. We define six bundling strategies that classify and group traffic flows according to their cost, demand, or potential profit to the ISP. We then evaluate them

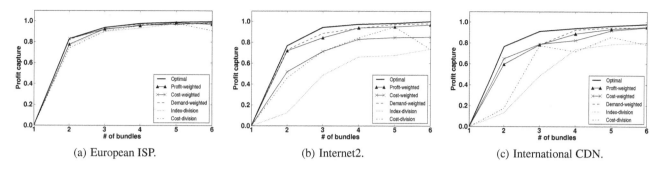

(a) European ISP. (b) Internet2. (c) International CDN.

Figure 8: Profit capture for different bundling strategies in constant elasticity demand.

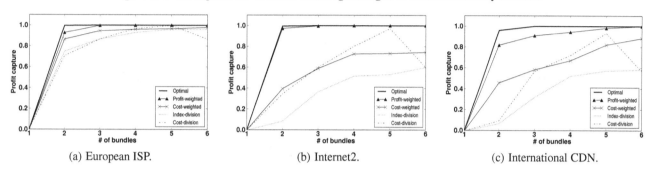

(a) European ISP. (b) Internet2. (c) International CDN.

Figure 9: Profit capture for different bundling strategies in logit demand.

and show that, assuming the right bundling strategy is used, ISPs typically need only a few bundles to collect near-optimal profit.

4.2.1 Bundling strategies

Optimal. We exhaustively search all possible combinations of bundles to find the one that yields the most profit. This approach gives optimal results and also serves as our *baseline* against which we compare other strategies. Computing the optimal bundling is computationally expensive: for example, there is more than a billion ways to divide one hundred traffic flows into six pricing bundles. Presented below, all of the other bundling strategies employ heuristics to make bundling computationally tractable.

Demand-weighted. In this strategy, we use an algorithm inspired by token buckets to group traffic flows to bundles. First, we set the overall token budget as the sum of the original demand of all flows: $T = \sum_i q_i$. Then, for each bundle j we assign the same token budget $t_j = T/B$, where B is the number of bundles we want to create. We sort the flows in decreasing order of their demand and traverse them one-by-one. When traversing flow i, we assign it to the first bundle j that either has no flows assigned to it or has a budget $t_j > 0$. We reduce the budget of that bundle by q_i. If the resulting budget $t_j < 0$, we set $t_{j+1} = t_{j+1} + t_j$. After traversing all the flows, the token budget of every bundle will be zero, and each flow will be assigned to a bundle. The algorithm leads to separate bundles for high demand flows and shared bundles for low demand flows. For example, if we need to divide four flows with demands 30, 10, 10, and 10 into two bundles, the algorithm will place the first flow in the first bundle, and the other three flows in the second bundle.

Cost-weighted. We use the same approach as in demand-weighted bundling, but we set the token budget to $T = \sum_i 1/c_i$. When placing a flow in a bundle we remove a number of tokens equal to the inverse of its cost. This approach creates separate bundles for local flows and shared bundles for flows traversing longer distances. The

current ISP practices of offering *regional pricing* and *backplane peering* maps closely to using just two or three bundles arranged using this cost-weighted strategy.

Profit-weighted. The bundling algorithms described above consider cost and demand separately. To account for cost and demand together, we estimate *potential profit* each flow could bring. We use the potential profit metric to apply the same weighting algorithm as in cost and demand-weighted bundling. In case of constant elasticity demand, we derive potential profit of each flow i:

$$\pi_i = \frac{v_i^\alpha}{\alpha} \left(\frac{\alpha c_i}{\alpha - 1} \right)^{1-\alpha} \tag{12}$$

For the logit demand, substituting p_i in Equation 9 yields:

$$\pi_i = K s_i (p_i - c_i) = \frac{K s_i}{\alpha s_0} \propto q_i \tag{13}$$

Cost division. We find the most expensive flow and divide the cost into ranges according to that value. For example, if we want to introduce two bundles and the most expensive flow costs \$10/Mbps/month to reach, we assign flows that cost \$0–\$4.99 to the first bundle and flows that cost \$5–\$10 to the second bundle.

Index division. Index-division bundling is similar to cost division bundling, except that we rank flows according to their cost and use the rank, rather than the cost, to perform the division into bundles.

4.2.2 The effects of different bundling strategies

To evaluate the bundling strategies described above, we compute the profit-maximizing prices and measure the resulting pricing outcome in terms of *profit capture*. Profit capture indicates what fraction of the maximum possible profit—the profit attained using an infinite number of bundles—the strategy captures. For example, if the maximum attainable profit is 30% higher than the original profit, while the profit from using two bundles is 15% higher than the original profit, the profit capture with two

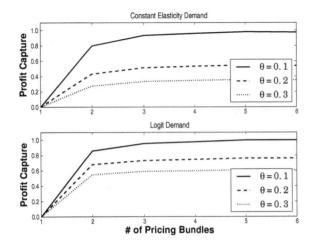

Figure 10: Profit increase in EU ISP network using linear cost model.

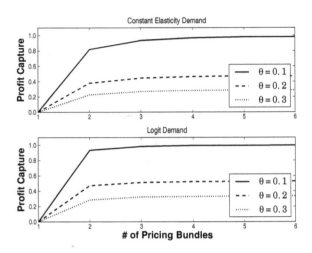

Figure 11: Profit increase in EU ISP network using concave cost model.

bundles attains 0.5 of profit capture. Formally, profit capture is $(\pi_{\text{new}} - \pi_{\text{original}})/(\pi_{\text{max}} - \pi_{\text{original}})$.

Figures 8 and 9 show the profit capture for different bundling strategies, across the three data sets, while varying the number of bundles. For the results shown here, we use both the constant elasticity and the logit demand models and the linear cost model. We set the price sensitivity α to 1.1, the original, blended rate P_0 to $20, the cost tuning parameter θ to 0.2, and the original market fraction that sends no traffic s_0 to 0.2. We explore the effect of varying these parameters in Section 4.3.

Optimal versus heuristics-based bundling. With an appropriate bundling strategy, the ISP attains maximum profit with just 3–4 bundles. As expected, the optimal flow bundling strategy captures the most profit for a given number of bundles. We observe that the EU ISP captures more profit with two bundles than other networks. We attribute this effect to the low coefficient of variation (CV) of demand to different destinations, which limits the benefits of having more pricing bundles. We also discover that, given fixed demand, a high CV of distance (cost) leads to higher absolute profits. With only minor exceptions, the profit-weighted bundling heuristic is almost as good as the the optimal bundling, followed by the cost-weighted bundling heuristic. Deeper analysis, beyond the scope of this work, could show what specific input data conditions cause the profit-weighted flow bundling heuristic to produce bundlings superior to the cost-weighted heuristic.

Logit profit capture. Maximum profit capture occurs more quickly in the logit model because (1) the total demand (including s_0 option) is constant, and (2) the model is sensitive to differences in valuation of different flows. When there is a flow with a significantly higher difference between valuation and cost ($v_i - c_i$), it absorbs most of the demand. In this model, with just two pricing tiers, local and non-local traffic are separated into distinct bundles that closely represent the *backplane peering* and *regional pricing* for local area service models.

4.3 Sensitivity Analysis

We explore the robustness of our results to cost models and input parameter settings. As we vary an input parameter under test, other parameters remain constant. Unless otherwise noted, we use profit-weighted bundling, the EU ISP dataset, sensitivity $\alpha = 1.1$, the linear cost model with base cost $\theta = 0.2$, blended rate $P_0 = \$20.0$,

and, in the logit model, $s_0 = 0.2$ (the original market fraction that sends no traffic).

4.3.1 Effects of cost models

We aim to see how cost models and settings within these models qualitatively affect our results from the previous section. We show how profit changes as we increase the number of bundles for different settings of the cost model parameters (θ), described in Section 3.3. We find that for different θ settings most of the attainable profit is still captured in 2-3 bundles. Unlike in other sections, in Figures 10–13, we normalize the profit of all the plots in the graphs to the highest observed profit. In other words, π_{max} in these figures is not the maximum profit of each plot, but the maximum profit of the plot with highest profit in the figure. Normalizing by the highest observed profit allows us to show how changing the parameter θ affects the amount of profit that the ISP can capture.

Linear cost. Figure 10 shows profit increase in the EU ISP network as we vary the number of bundles for different settings of θ. As expected, most of the profit is still attained with 2–3 pricing bundles. We also observe that the increase in the base cost (θ) causes a decline in the maximum attainable profit. The reduction in maximum attainable profit is expected, as increasing the base cost reduces the coefficient of variation (CV) of the cost of different flows and thus reduces the opportunities for variable pricing and profit capture. We can also see, as shown in previous section, that the logit demand model attains more profit than the constant elasticity demand model with the same number of pricing bundles.

Concave cost. Figure 11 shows the profit increase as we vary the number of bundles for different settings of θ for the concave cost model. The observations and results are similar to the linear cost model, with one notable exception. The amount of profit the ISP can capture decreases more quickly in the concave cost model than in the linear cost model for the same change in the base-cost parameter θ. This is due to the lower CV of cost in the concave model than in the linear cost model. In other words, applying the log function on distance (as described in Section 3.3) reduces the relative cost difference between flows traveling to local and remote destinations.

Regional cost. In the regional cost model, the parameter θ is an exponent which adjusts the price difference between three different regions: local, national, and international. Figure 12 shows the profit increase in the EU ISP network as we vary number of bundles for different settings of θ. Higher θ values result in a higher CV of

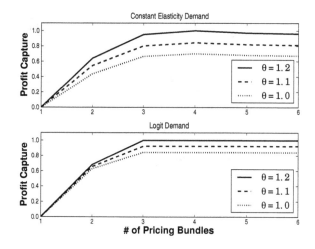

Figure 12: **Profit increase in the EU ISP network using regional cost model.**

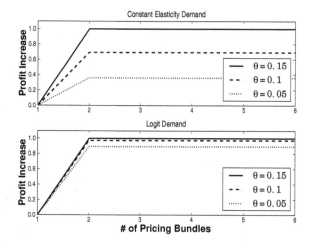

Figure 13: **Profit increase in the EU ISP network using destination type cost model.**

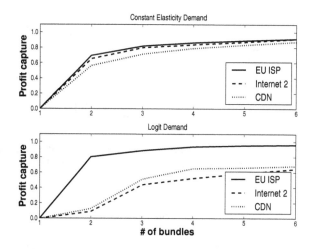

Figure 14: **Minimum profit capture for a fixed number of bundles over a range of α between 1 and 10.**

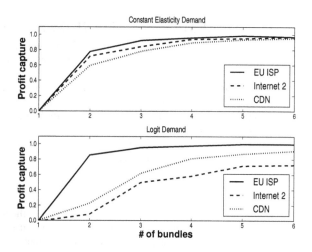

Figure 15: **Minimum profit capture for a fixed number of bundles over a range of starting prices $P_0 \in [5, 30]$.**

cost in different regions which, in turn, in both demand models produces higher profit. Using constant elasticity demand we observe a small dip in profit when using five and six bundles, which recovers later with more bundles. Such dips are expected when there are only a few traffic classes. For example, if traffic had just two distinct cost classes, two judiciously selected bundles could capture most of the profit. Adding a third bundle can reduce the profit if that third bundle contains flows from both of the classes (as may happen in a suboptimal bundling).

Destination type-based cost. Destination type-based cost model emulates "on-net" and "off-net" types of traffic in an ISP network. As described in Section 3.3, we assume that "on-net" traffic costs less than "off-net" traffic. We vary θ, which represents a fraction of "on-net" traffic in each flow. The standard profit-weighting algorithm does not work well with the destination type-based cost model. The effect observed in the regional cost model—where five bundles produce slightly lower profit then four bundles—is more pronounced when we have just two distinct flow classes. One heuristic that works reasonably well is as follows: we update the profit-weighting heuristic to never group traffic from two different classes into the same bundle. Figure 13 shows how profit increases

with an increasing number of bundles. Since there are two major classes of traffic ("on-" and "off-net"), most profit is attained with two bundles for both demand models. In this cost model, as in other cost models, the same change in CV of cost (induced by the parameter θ) causes a greater change in profit capture for constant elasticity demand than for logit demand.

4.3.2 Sensitivity to parameter settings

The models we use rely on a set of parameters, such as price sensitivity (α), price of the original bundle (P_0), and, in the logit model, the share of the market that corresponds to deciding not to purchase bandwidth (s_0). In this section, we analyze how sensitive the model is to the choice of these parameters.

Figures 14–16 show how profit capture is affected by varying price sensitivity α, blended rate P_0, and non-buying market share s_0, respectively. Each data point in the figures is obtained by varying each parameter over a range of values. We vary α between 1 and 10, P_0 between 5 and 30, and s_0 between 0 and 0.9. As we vary the parameters, we select and plot the *minimum* observed profit capture over the whole parameter range, for the profit-weighted strategy with different numbers of bundles. In other words, these plots

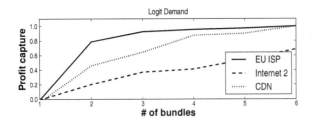

Figure 16: Maximum profit capture for a fixed number of bundles over a range of fractions of users who decide not to participate in the market $s_0 \in (0, 1)$.

show the worst case relative profit capture for the ISP over a range of parameter values. The trend of these minimum profit capture points is qualitatively similar to patterns in Figures 8 and 9. For example, using the CED model and grouping flows in two bundles in the EU ISP yields around 0.8 profit capture, regardless of price sensitivity, blending rate, and market share. These results indicate that our model is robust to a wide range of parameter values.

5. IMPLEMENTING TIERED PRICING

ISPs can implement the type of tiered pricing that we describe in Section 4 without any changes to their existing protocols or infrastructure, and ISPs may already be using the techniques we describe below. If that is the case, they could simply apply a profit-weighted bundling strategy to re-factor their pricing to improve their profit, possibly without even making many changes to the network configuration. We describe two tasks associated with tiered pricing: associating flows with tiers and accounting for the amount of traffic the customer sends in each tier.

5.1 Associating Flows with Tiers

Associating each flow (or destination) with a tier can be done within the context of today's routing protocols. When the upstream ISP sends routes to its customer, it can "tag" routes it announces with a label that indicates which tier the route should be associated with; ISPs can use BGP extended communities to perform this tagging. Because the communities propagate with the route, the customer can establish routing policies on every router within its own network based on these tags.

Suppose that a large transit service provider has routers in different geographic regions. Routers at an exchange point in, say, New York, might advertise routes that it learned in Europe with a special tag indicating that the path the route takes is trans-Atlantic and, hence, bears a higher price than other, regional routes. The customer can then use the tag to make routing decisions. For example, if a route is tagged as an expensive long-distance route, the customer might choose to use its own backbone to get closer to destination instead of performing the default "hot-potato" routing (i.e., offloading the traffic to a transit network as quickly as possible). A large customer might also use this pricing information to better plan its own network growth.

5.2 Accounting

Implementing tiered pricing requires accounting for traffic either on a *per-link* or *per-flow* basis.

Link-Based Accounting. As shown in Figure 17(a), an edge router can establish two or more physical or virtual links to the customer, with a Border Gateway Protocol (BGP) [29] session for each physical or virtual link. In this setup, each pricing tier would have a separate link. Each link carries the traffic only to the set of destinations

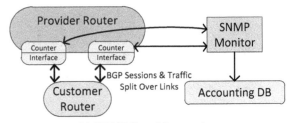

(a) SNMP-Based Accounting.

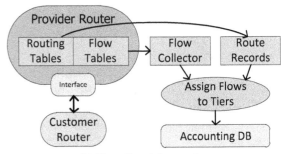

(b) Flow-Based Accounting.

Figure 17: Implementing accounting for tiered pricing.

advertised over that session (*e.g.*, on-net traffic, backplane peering traffic). Because each link has a separate routing session and only exchanges routes associated with that pricing tier, the customer and provider can ensure that traffic for each tier flows over the appropriate link: The customer knows exactly which traffic falls into which pricing tier based on the session onto which it sends traffic. Billing may also be simpler and easier to understand, since, in this mode, a provider can simply bill each link at a different rate. Unfortunately, the overhead of this accounting method grows significantly with the number of pricing levels ISP intends to support.

Flow-Based Accounting. In flow-based accounting, as in traditional peering and transit, an upstream ISP and a customer establish a link with a single routing session. As shown in Figure 17(b), the accounting system collects both flow statistics (*e.g.*, using Net-Flow [23]) and routing information to determine resource usage. For the purposes of accounting, bundling effectively occurs after the fact: flows can be mapped to distances using the routing table information and priced accordingly, exactly as we did in our evaluation in Section 4. Assuming flow and routing information collection infrastructure in place, flow-based accounting may be easier to manage, and it is easier to bundle flows into different bins according to various bundling strategies (*e.g.*, profit-weighted bundling) *post facto*.

6. RELATED WORK

Developing and analyzing pricing models for the Internet is well-researched in both networking and economics. Two aspects are most relevant for our work: the unbundling of connectivity and the dimensions along which to unbundle it. Although similar studies of pricing exist, none have been evaluated in the context of real network demand and topology data.

The unbundling of connectivity services refers to the setting of different prices for such services along various usage dimensions such as volume, time, destination, or application type. Seminal works by Arrow and Debreu [2] and McKenzie [20] show that markets where commodities are sold at infinitely small granularities are more efficient. More recent studies however, demonstrate that unbundling may be inefficient in certain settings, such as when selling information goods with zero or very low marginal cost (such as access to online information) [3, 15, 22]. This is not always the case with the connectivity market, where ISPs incur different costs to deliver traffic to different destinations. In addition, many service providers already use price discrimination [26].

Kesidis *et al.* [13] and Shakkottai *et al.* [30] study the benefits of pricing connectivity based on volume usage and argue that, with price differentiation, one can use resources more efficiently. In particular, Kesidis *et al.* show that usage-based unbundling may be even more beneficial to access networks rather than core networks. Time is another dimension along which providers can unbundle connectivity. Jiang *et al.* [12] study the role of time preference in network prices and show analytically that service providers can achieve maximum revenue and social welfare if they differentiate prices across users and time. Hande *et al.* [10] characterize the economic loss due to ISP inability or unwillingness to price broadband access based on time of day.

7. CONCLUSION

As the price of Internet transit drops, transit providers are selling connectivity using "tiered" contracts based on traffic cost, volume, or destination to maintain profits. We have studied two questions: How does tiered pricing benefit both ISPs and their customers? and How should ISPs structure the connectivity tiers they sell to maximize their profits? We developed a model for an Internet transit market that helps ISPs evaluate how they should arrange traffic into different tiers, and how they should set prices for each of those tiers. We have applied our model to traffic demand and topology data from three large ISPs to evaluate various bundling strategies.

We find that the common ISP practice of structuring tiered contracts according to the cost of carrying the traffic flows (*e.g.*, offering a discount for traffic that is local) is suboptimal. Dividing the contract into only three or four tiers based on *both traffic cost and demand* yields near-optimal profit for the ISP; other strategies such as cost division bundling also work well. We also find that networks with primarily lower cost traffic (either local or traveling short distances) require fewer tiers to extract maximum profit than other networks do.

Acknowledgments

We are grateful to the anonymous reviewers and our shepherd, David Clark, for feedback. We thank Guavus for early feedback and help with data. This research was primarily supported by grant N000140910755 from the Office of Naval Research. Vytautas Valancius and Nick Feamster were also supported by NSF CAREER Award CNS-06943974. Cristian Lumezanu was supported by NSF Grant 0937060 to the Computing Research Association for the CIFellows Project. Ramesh Johari was supported in part by NSF grants CMMI-0948434, CNS-0904609, CCF-0832820, and CNS-0644114. Vijay Vazirani was supported by NSF grants CCF-0728640 and CCF-0914732, and a Google Research Grant.

REFERENCES

[1] Adam Internet. Unmetered content. http://www.adam.com. au/unmetered/unmetered.php. Retrieved: June 2011.

[2] K. J. Arrow and G. Debreu. Existence of equilibrium for competitive economy. *Econometrica*, 22(3):265–290, 1954.

[3] Y. Bakos and E. Bronjolfsson. Bundling and competition on the Internet. *Marketing Science*, 19(1), Jan. 1998.

[4] D. Besanko, S. Gupta, and D. Jain. Logit demand estimation under competitive pricing behavior: An equilibrium framework. *Management Science*, 44:1533–1547, November 1998.

[5] BNSL. Tariff for leased lines. http://www.bsnl.co.in/ service/2mbps.pdf. Retrieved: June 2011.

[6] Chunghwa Telecom. Leased line pricelist. http://www.cht. com.tw/CHTFinalE/Web/Business.php?CatID=476. Retrieved: June 2011.

[7] Cisco. SFP optics for gigabit ethernet applications. http://www. cisco.com/en/US/prod/collateral/modules/ ps5455/ps6577/product_data_ sheet0900aecd8033f885.html. Retrieved: June 2011.

[8] Etisalat ISP. Leased circuit rental charges. http://tinyurl. com/66tfvj6. Retrieved: June 2011.

[9] Guavus. Profitable tiered pricing. http://www.guavus.com/ solutions/tiered-pricing. Retrieved: June 2011.

[10] P. Hande, M. Chiang, R. Calderbank, and J. Zhang. Pricing under constraints in access networks: Revenue maximization and congestion management. In *Proc. IEEE INFOCOM*, San Diego, CA, Mar. 2010.

[11] ITU Telecommunication Indicator Handbook. http://www.itu. int/ITU-D/ict/publications/world/material/ handbook.html. Retrieved: June 2011.

[12] L. Jiang, S. Parekh, and J. Walrand. Time-dependent network pricing and bandwidth trading. In *Proc. IEEE BoD*, 2008.

[13] G. Kesidis, A. Das, and G. D. Veciana. On flat-rate and usage-based pricing for tiered commodity Internet services. In *Proc. CISS*, 2008.

[14] C. Labovitz, S. Iekel-Johnson, D. McPherson, J. Oberheide, and F. Jahanian. Internet inter-domain traffic. In *Proc. ACM SIGCOMM*, New Delhi, India, Aug. 2010.

[15] J.-J. Laffont, S. Marcus, P. Rey, and J. Tirole. Internet interconnection and the off-net-cost principle. *The Rand Journal of Economics*, 34(2), 2003.

[16] Level 3 Communications. Level 3 statement concerning Comcast's actions. http://www.level3.com/index.cfm? pageID=491&PR=962. Retrieved: June 2011.

[17] A. Mas-Colell, M. Whinston, J. Green, and U. P. F. F. de Ciencies Econnmiques i Empresarials. *Microeconomic theory*, volume 981. Oxford university press New York, 1995.

[18] MaxMind GeoIP Country. http://www.maxmind.com/app/ geolitecountry. Retrieved: June 2011.

[19] D. McFadden. Conditional logit analysis of qualitative choice behavior. *Frontiers Of Econometrics*, 1974.

[20] L. W. McKenzie. On the existence of general equilibrium for a competitive economy. *Econometrica*, 1959.

[21] J. Mo and J. Walrand. Fair end-to-end window-based congestion control. *IEEE/ACM Trans. Netw.*, 8(5):556–567, 2000.

[22] P. Nabipay, A. M. Odlyzko, and Z.-L. Zhang. Flat versus metered rates, bundling, and "bandwidth hogs". In *6th Workshop on the Economics of Networks, Systems, and Computation*, San Jose, CA, June 2011.

[23] Cisco NetFlow. http://www.cisco.com/en/US/ products/ps6601/products_ios_protocol_group_ home.html. Retrieved: June 2011.

[24] W. Norton. DrPeering.net. http://drpeering.net.

[25] NTT East. Leased circuit price list. http://www.ntt-east. co.jp/senyo_e/charge/digital.html. URL retrieved January 2011.

[26] A. M. Odlyzko. Network neutrality, search neutrality, and the never-ending conflict between efficiency and fairness in markets. *Review of Network Economics*, 8(1):40–60, Mar. 2009.

[27] ORE. Wholesale leased lines price list. http://www. otewholesale.gr/Portals/0/LEASED%20LINES_ Pricelist_ENG_081110.pdf. Retrieved: June 2011.

[28] Peering Database. http://www.peeringdb.com.

[29] Y. Rekhter, T. Li, and S. Hares. *A Border Gateway Protocol 4 (BGP-4)*. Internet Engineering Task Force, Jan. 2006. RFC 4271.

[30] S. Shakkottai, R. Srikant, A. E. Ozdaglar, and D. Acemoglu. The price of simplicity. *IEEE Journal on Selected Areas in Communications*, 26(7):1269–1276, 2008.

[31] Telegeography. Bandwidth pricing report. http://www. telegeography.com/product-info/pricingdb/ download/bpr-2009-10.pdf. Retrieved: June 2011.

The Evolution of Layered Protocol Stacks Leads to an Hourglass-Shaped Architecture[*]

Saamer Akhshabi
College of Computing
Georgia Institute of Technology
sakhshab@cc.gatech.edu

Constantine Dovrolis
College of Computing
Georgia Institute of Technology
dovrolis@cc.gatech.edu

ABSTRACT

The Internet protocol stack has a layered architecture that resembles an hourglass. The lower and higher layers tend to see frequent innovations, while the protocols at the waist of the hourglass appear to be "ossified". We propose *EvoArch*, an abstract model for studying protocol stacks and their evolution. *EvoArch* is based on a few principles about layered network architectures and their evolution in a competitive environment where protocols acquire value based on their higher layer applications and compete with other protocols at the same layer. *EvoArch* produces an hourglass structure that is similar to the Internet architecture from general initial conditions and in a robust manner. It also suggests a plausible explanation why some protocols, such as TCP or IP, managed to survive much longer than most other protocols at the same layers. Furthermore, it suggests ways to design more competitive new protocols and more evolvable future Internet architectures.

Categories and Subject Descriptors: C.2.5 [Computer Communication Networks]: Internet

General Terms: Theory

Keywords: Internet Architecture, Future Internet, Layering, Network Science, Evolutionary Kernels, Evolution.

1. INTRODUCTION

Why does the Internet protocol stack resemble an hourglass? Is it a coincidence, intentional design, or the result of an evolutionary process in which new protocols compete with existing protocols that offer similar functionality and services? The protocol stack was not always shaped in this way. For instance, until the early nineties there were several other network-layer protocols competing with IPv4, including Novell's IPX, the X.25 network protocol used in Frame Relay, the ATM network layer signaling protocol, and several others. It was through a long process that IPv4 eventually prevailed as practically the only surviving protocol at layer-3, creating a very narrow waist at the Internet architecture hourglass (see Figure 1).

[*]This research was supported by the NSF award 0831848 ("Towards a Theory of Network Evolution").

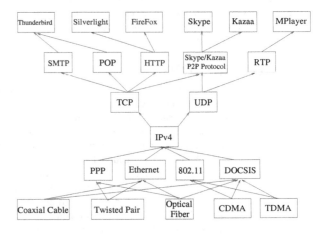

Figure 1: An (incomplete) illustration of the hourglass Internet architecture.

Another important question is: *why do we tend to see more frequent innovations at the lower or higher layers of the protocol hourglass, while the protocols at the waist of the hourglass appear to be "ossified" and difficult to replace?* During the last 30–40 years we have seen many new physical and data link layer protocols created and surviving. And of course the same can be said about applications and application-layer protocols. On the other hand, the protocols at the waist of the hourglass (mostly IPv4, TCP and UDP) have been extremely stable and they have managed to outcompete any protocols that offer the same or similar functionality. *How can a new protocol manage to survive the intense competition with those core protocols at the waist of the Internet hourglass?* In fact, *the ossification of the hourglass waist* has been a major motivation for "clean-slate" efforts to design a novel future Internet architecture [16]. There are two important questions in that context. First, *how can we make it more likely that a new (and potentially better) protocol replaces an existing and widely used incumbent protocol?* And second, how can we make sure that a new architecture we design today will not be ossified 10–20 years later? In other words, *what makes a protocol stack or network architecture evolvable?* The previous questions have generated an interesting debate [9, 10, 19].

In this paper, we attempt a first effort to study protocol stacks (and layered architectures, more generally) as well as their evolution in a rigorous and quantitative manner. Instead of only considering a specific protocol stack, we propose an abstract model in which protocols are represented by nodes, services are represented by directed links, and so a protocol stack becomes a layered directed acyclic graph (or network). Further, the topology of this graph changes with time as new nodes are created at different layers, and existing nodes are removed as a result of competition with other nodes at the same layer.

The proposed evolutionary model, referred to as *EvoArch*, is based on few principles about layered network architectures in which an "item" (or service) at layer-X is constructed (or composed) using items at layer-(X-1). These principles capture the following:

(a) the source of *evolutionary value* for an item,

(b) the *generality* of items as we move to higher layers,

(c) the condition under which two items compete,

(d) the condition under which one item causes the death or removal of a competing item.

Perhaps surprisingly, these few principles are sufficient to produce hourglass-shaped layered networks in relatively short evolutionary periods.

As with any other model, *EvoArch* is only an abstraction of reality focusing on specific observed phenomena, in this case the hourglass structure of the Internet protocol stack, and attempting to identify a parsimonious set of principles or mechanisms that are sufficient to reproduce the observed phenomena. As such, *EvoArch* is an *explanatory model* (as opposed to black-box models that aim to only describe statistically some observations). *EvoArch* deliberately ignores many aspects of protocol architectures, such as the functionality of each layer, technological constraints, debates in standardization committees, and others.[1] The fact that these practical aspects are not considered by *EvoArch* does *not* mean that they are insignificant; it means, however, that if the evolution of network architectures follows the principles that *EvoArch* is based on, then those aspects are neither necessary nor sufficient for the emergence of the hourglass structure.

EvoArch is certainly *not* going to be the only model, or "the correct model", for the emergence of hourglass-shaped network architectures. It is likely that there are other models that can produce the same hourglass structure, based on different principles and parameters. Additionally, *EvoArch* does not aim to capture every aspect of the Internet architecture; it only focuses on the emergence of the hourglass structure, and so it may be the wrong model to use for other purposes (e.g., to study the economics of new protocol deployment). G.Box wrote that *"all models are wrong but some models are useful"* [3]. We believe that *EvoArch* is a useful model for (at least) the following ten reasons:

1- It gives us a new way to think about protocol stacks and network architectures and to study their evolutionary properties based on few fundamental principles (§2).

2- *EvoArch* provides a plausible explanation (but certainly not the only explanation) for the emergence of hourglass-like architectures in a bottom-up manner (§3).

3- *EvoArch* shows how the location and width of the hourglass waist can follow from certain key parameters of the underlying evolutionary process (§5).

4- *EvoArch* can be parameterized to produce a structure that is similar to the TCP/IP protocol stack, and it suggests an intriguing explanation for the survival of these protocols in the early days of the Internet (§5.4).

5- *EvoArch* suggests how to make a new protocol more likely to survive in a competitive environment, when there is a strong incumbent (§5.5).

6- *EvoArch* provides recommendations to designers of future Internet architectures that aim to make the latter more evolvable (§5.5).

7- *EvoArch* predicts that few protocols at the waist (or close to it) become *ossified*, surviving much longer than most other protocols at the same layer, and it shows how such ossified protocols can be eventually replaced (§6).

8- When we extend *EvoArch* to capture the effect of different *protocol qualities*, we find that the lower part of the hourglass is significantly smaller than the upper part (§7.1).

9- The most stable protocols at the waist of the architecture are often *not* those with the highest quality (§7.2).

10- Finally, *EvoArch* offers a new way to think about the competition between IPv4 and IPv6 and to understand why the latter has not managed to replace the former (§7.3).

The rest of the paper is structured as follows. In Section 2, we describe *EvoArch* and explain how the model relates to protocol stacks and evolving network architectures. In Section 3, we present basic results to illustrate the behavior of the model and introduce some key metrics. Section 4 is a robustness study showing that the model produces hourglass structures for a wide range of parameter values. The effect of those parameters is studied in Section 5 focusing on the location and width of the waist. Section 6 examines the *evolutionary kernels* of the architecture, i.e., those few nodes at the waist that survive much longer than other nodes. Section 7 generalizes *EvoArch* in an important and realistic manner: what if different protocols at the same layer have different qualities (such as performance or extent of deployment)? We review related work in Section 8, present some criticism in Section 9, and conclude in Section 10.

2. MODEL DESCRIPTION

In *EvoArch*, a protocol stack is modeled as a directed and acyclic network with L layers (see Figure 2). Protocols are represented by nodes, and protocol dependencies are represented by directed edges. If a protocol u at layer l uses the service provided by a protocol w at layer $l-1$, the network includes an "upwards" edge from w to u.[2] The layer of a node u is denoted by $l(u)$. The incoming edges to a node u originate at the *substrates* of u, represented by the set of nodes $S(u)$. Every node has at least one substrate, except the nodes at the bottom layer. The outgoing edges of a node u terminate at the *products* of u, represented by the set of nodes $P(u)$. Every node has at least one product, except the nodes at the top layer.

The substrates of a node are determined probabilistically when that node is created.[3] Specifically, each layer l is associated with a probability $s(l)$: a node u at layer $l+1$ selects independently each node of layer l as substrate with probability $s(l)$. We refer to $s(l)$ as the *generality* of layer l. $s(l)$ *decreases* as we move to higher layers, i.e., $s(i) > s(j)$ for $i < j$. The decreasing generality probabilities capture that *protocols at lower layers are more general in terms of their function or provided service than protocols at higher layers*. For instance, in the case of the Internet protocol stack, a protocol at layer-1 offers a very general bit transfer service between two directly connected points; this is a service or function that almost any higher layer protocol would need. On the other extreme, an application-layer protocol, such as SMTP, offers a very specialized service and it is only used by applications that are related to

---

[1] The reader can see some of the criticism raised by anonymous reviewers in Section 9.

[2] In practice, the principle of strict layering is occasionally violated through tunnels or other forms of virtual networks. For the most part, however, layering is the norm in protocol architectures rather than the exception. Considering architectures without strict layering is outside the scope of this paper and an interesting subject for future research.

[3] Of course in practice substrates are never chosen randomly. The use of randomness in the model implies that a realistic mechanism of substrate selection is not necessary for the emergence of the hourglass structure.

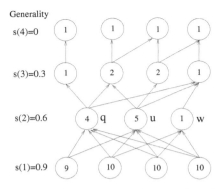

Generality

Figure 2: A toy network with four layers. The value of each node is shown inside the circle.

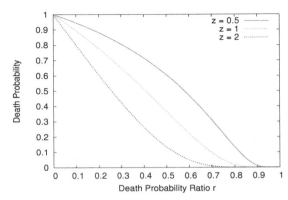

Figure 3: The death probability for three values of the mortality parameter z.

email exchanges. Note that if node u does not select any substrate from layer l we connect it to one randomly chosen substrate from that layer.

Each node u has an *evolutionary value*, or simply *value* $v(u)$ that is computed recursively based on the products of u,

$$v(u) = \begin{cases} \sum_{p \in P(u)} v(p) & l(u) < L \\ 1 & l(u) = L \end{cases} \quad (1)$$

The value of the top-layer nodes is assumed to be fixed; in the simplest version of *EvoArch* it is equal to one. So, the model captures that the value of a protocol u is driven by the values of the protocols that depend on u. For instance, TCP has a high evolutionary value because it is used by many higher layer protocols and applications, some of them being highly valuable themselves. A brand new protocol on the other hand, may be great in terms of performance or new features, but its value will be low if it is not used by important or popular higher layer protocols.

The value of a node largely determines whether it will survive the competition with other nodes at the same layer that offer similar services. Consider a node u at layer l. Let $C(u)$ be the set of *competitors* of u: this is the set of nodes at layer l that share at least a fraction c of node u's products, i.e.,

$$w \in C(u) \text{ if } l(w) = l(u) \text{ and } \frac{|P(u) \cap P(w)|}{|P(u)|} \geq c \quad (2)$$

The fraction c is referred to as the *competition threshold*. In other words, a node w competes with a node u if w shares a significant fraction (at least c) of u's products, meaning that the former offers similar services or functions with the latter. Note that the competition relation is not symmetric: w may provide a generic service, having many products, and thus competing with several protocols at the same layer; the latter may not be competitors of w if they provide more specialized functions and have only few products.

Given the set of competitors of a node u, we can examine whether u would survive the competition or die. The basic idea is that u dies if its value is significantly less than the value of its *strongest* (i.e., maximum value) competitor. Specifically, let $v_c(u)$ be the maximum value among the competitors of u

$$v_c(u) = \max_{w \in C(u)} v(w) \quad (3)$$

If u does not have competitors, $v_c(u)$ and the death probability for u are set to zero. Otherwise, we introduce the *death probability ratio* $r = \frac{v(u)}{v_c(u)}$. The death probability $p_d(r)$ is then computed as follows:

$$p_d(r) = \begin{cases} e^{\frac{-z\,r}{1-r}} & 0 < r < 1 \\ 0 & r \geq 1 \end{cases} \quad (4)$$

The death probability function $p_d(r)$ is shown in Figure 3 for three different values of the *mortality parameter z*. This parameter captures the intensity of the competition among protocols. As z decreases, the competition becomes more intense and it is more likely that a protocol will die if at least one of its competitors has higher value than itself.

When a node u dies, its products also die *if their only substrate is u*. This can lead to a *cascade effect* where the death of a node leads to the death of several nodes in higher layers.

To illustrate the previous concepts, Figure 2 shows a toy network with $L = 4$ layers. The generality probability for each layer is shown at the left of the corresponding layer. Note that, on average, the number of products per node decreases as we move to higher layers because the generality probability decreases in that direction. Assuming that $c = 3/5$, nodes u and q are competitors of node w in layer-2. It is likely (depending on the parameter z) that w would soon die because its value is much less than that of its maximum-value competitor, u. u is also a competitor of q but this competition is much less likely to be lethal for the latter because its value is comparable to that of u.

EvoArch captures the inherent competition between nodes at the same layer, and specifically, between nodes that offer about the same service. For instance, FTP and HTTP are two application-layer protocols that can both be used for the transfer of files. The large overlap of the services provided by HTTP with the services provided by FTP (i.e., HTTP is a competitor of FTP) and the fact that HTTP acquired over the years a larger evolutionary value from its own higher layer products (applications such as web browsers) leads to the extinction of FTP. On the other hand, TCP and UDP are two transport layer protocols that offer largely different services. Their competition, in terms of products (i.e., application layer protocols), is minimal and the two protocols have coexisted for more than 30 years.

In the simplest version of *EvoArch*, the creation of new nodes follows *the basic birth process*. Specifically, the number of new nodes at a given time is set to a small fraction (say 1% to 10%) of the total number of nodes in the network at that time, implying that the larger a protocol stack is, the faster it grows. Each new node is assigned randomly to a layer. In Section 6, we also examine a *death-regulated birth process*, in which the frequency of births at a layer depends on the death rate at that layer.

EvoArch is a discrete-time model. By t_k, we denote the *k'th round*. In each round, the model execution includes the following steps in the given order:
a) birth of new nodes and random assignment to layers,
b) examine each layer l, in top-down order, and perform three tasks:

b.1) connect any new nodes assigned to that layer, choosing substrates and products for them based on the generality probabilities $s(l-1)$ and $s(l)$, respectively,

b.2) update the value of each node at layer l (note that the value of a node in the k'th round can be affected by nodes added in that same round),

b.3) examine, in order of decreasing value in that layer, whether any node should die (considering the case of cascade deaths).

Initially, we start with a small number of nodes at each layer, and form the edges between layers as if all nodes were new births. Unless noted otherwise, the execution of the model stops when the network reaches a given number of nodes.[4] We refer to each execution as an *evolutionary path*.

We have mathematically analyzed a significantly simpler version of *EvoArch* [1]. Those simplifications are: static analysis (i.e., a non-evolving network), a node can compete only with the maximum-value node at that layer, each layer has the same number of nodes m, and $m\,s(L-1) \gg 1$. Under the previous assumptions, we derived a mathematical expression for the death probability ratio $r(l)$ for a node with the average number of products at layer l. Unfortunately the expression for $r(l)$ is not mathematically tractable and it does not allow us to examine whether it has a unique minimum. Numerically, however, that expression suggests that the ratio $r(l)$ has a unique minimum at a certain layer $\hat{l}$ that only depends on the generality probabilities and the competition threshold. Because the death probability decreases monotonically with $r(l)$ (see Figure 3), the previous observation means that the death probability has a unique maximum at layer $\hat{l}$, and it decreases monotonically at layers above and below $\hat{l}$. It is this death probability pattern that pushes, over several evolutionary rounds, the network to take the shape of a (generally asymmetric) hourglass with a waist at layer $\hat{l}$. The interested reader can find these derivations and further numerical results in our Technical Report [1].

In the rest of the paper, the results are generated from discrete-time simulations of the *EvoArch* model. The benefits of such computational analysis are threefold: first, we do not need to make further simplifying assumptions. Second, we can examine the dynamics of the model, focusing on how the shape of the network changes with time. And third, we can quantify the variability of the results across many different evolutionary paths, instead of only looking at expected values.

3. BASIC RESULTS

In this section, we illustrate the behavior of the *EvoArch* model focusing on the width of each layer across time. We also introduce the main metrics we consider, and the default values of the model parameters.

The default values of *EvoArch*'s parameters are: $L = 10$ layers, $s(l) = 1-l/L$ (i.e., the generality decreases as $0.9, 0.8, \ldots, 0.1, 0$, as we go up the stack), $c = 0.6$ (i.e., at least 3 out of 5 shared products), and $z = 1$ (see Figure 3). Each evolutionary path starts with 10 nodes at every layer, the average birth rate at each round is 5% of the current network size, and an evolutionary path ends when the network size reaches 500 nodes (but not sooner than 100 rounds). Unless noted otherwise, we repeat each experiment 1000 times, while the graphs show the median as well as the 10th, 25th, 75th and 90th percentiles across all evolutionary paths. We emphasize that the previous default values do *not* correspond, obviously, to

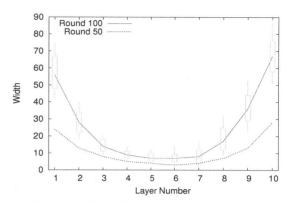

Figure 4: The median width of each layer at round-50 and round-100 (percentiles are only shown for the latter).

the characteristics of the Internet stack. A parameterization of the model for that specific architecture is given in Section 5.4. *EvoArch* is a general model for layered protocol stacks and it does not aim to *only* capture the existing Internet architecture.

Figure 4 shows the width of each layer at the 50th and 100th rounds of the evolutionary process (typically, the network reaches 500 nodes in about 100–150 rounds). Note that, at least in terms of the median, the width decreases as we move from the bottom layer to a middle layer, around layer 5, and then it increases again as we move towards the top layer. There is some variability across evolutionary paths however, and so we further examine if the network structure has the shape of an hourglass in every evolutionary path.

To do so, we introduce a metric that quantifies the resemblance of a layered network structure to an hourglass. Let $w(l)$ be the width of layer l, i.e., the number of nodes in that layer at a given round. Let w_b be the minimum width across all layers, and suppose that this minimum occurs at layer $l = b$; this is the *waist* of the network (ties are broken so that the waist is closer to $\lfloor L/2 \rfloor$). Consider the sequence $X = \{w(l)\}, l = 1, \ldots b\}$ and the sequence $Y = \{w(l)\}, l = b, \ldots L\}$. We calculate the normalized univariate *Mann-Kendall statistic for monotonic trend* on the sequences X and Y as coefficients τ_X and τ_Y respectively [12]. The coefficients vary between -1 (strictly decreasing) and 1 (strictly increasing), while they are approximately zero for random samples. We define $H = (\tau_Y - \tau_X)/2$; H is referred to as the *hourglass resemblance* metric. $H = 1$ if the network is structured as an hourglass, with a strictly decreasing sequence of b layers, followed by a strictly increasing sequence of $L - b$ layers. For example, the sequence of layer widths $\{10,6,8,2,4,7,10,12,9,16\}$ (from bottom to top) has $w_b = 4$, $\tau_X = -0.67$, $\tau_Y = 0.81$ and $H = 0.74$. Note that we do *not* require the hourglass to be symmetric, i.e., the waist may not always be at the middle layer.

Figure 5 shows H (median and the previous four percentiles) as function of time. Note that it only takes few rounds, less than 10, for the median H to exceed 80%. By the 100th round, the median H is almost 95% and even the 10th percentile is more than 80%. This illustrates that *EvoArch* generates networks that typically have the shape of an hourglass. Even though the accuracy of the hourglass structure improves with time, the basic hourglass shape (say $H > 0.8$) is formed within only few rounds. We have also examined the location of the waist as function of time, and the associated 10th and 90th percentiles across 1000 evolutionary paths (graph not shown due to space constraints). With the default parameter values, the median waist is almost always located at layer-6, while the 10th and 90th percentiles correspond to layers-5 and 7, respectively. So, even though there is some small variability in the exact location of

---

[4]We have also experimented with a termination condition based on the number of rounds, instead of the number of nodes. There is no significant difference as long as the network can evolve for at least few tens of rounds.

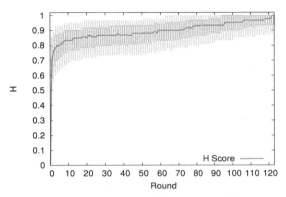

Figure 5: The hourglass resemblance metric H over time.

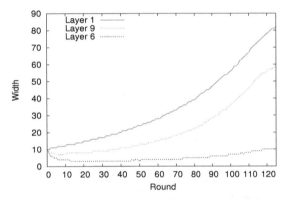

Figure 6: The median width of three layers over time.

the waist across time and across different evolutionary paths, the narrowest layer of the hourglass does not fluctuate significantly.

Figure 6 shows the median width of the typical waist (layer-6), as well as the median width of layers-1 and 9, as functions of time. Even though all three layers start from the same number of nodes, layers-1 and 9 become significantly wider with time, implying a low death probability. On the other hand, the width of the waist remains relatively low compared to other layers. It typically decreases significantly in the first few rounds, as several of the initial nodes are "unlucky" in terms of products and die soon. It then slowly increases because higher layers become much wider, the birth rate increases with the size of the network, and few additional nodes at the waist can acquire significant value compared to the maximum-value node in that layer.

Obviously, the major question is: *why does EvoArch generate hourglass-shaped networks?* Let us discuss separately what happens at layers close to the top, close to the bottom, and close to the waist.

Because the generality probability $s(l)$ is quite low at layers close to the top, those nodes typically have a small number of products. This means that they rarely compete with each other, and so the death probability is close to zero. For instance, in the application-layer a new protocol can compete and replace an incumbent only if the former provides a very similar service with the latter (e.g., recall the example with FTP and HTTP).

At layers close to the bottom, the generality probability is close to one, and so those nodes have many shared products and thus several competitors. Their value is often similar however, because those nodes typically share almost the same set of products. Thus, the death probability at layers close to the bottom is also quite low.

At layers close to waist, where the generality probability is close to 50%, the variability in the number of products is maximized—

recall that the variance of a Bernoulli random variable $X(p)$ is maximum when p=50%. So, few nodes in that layer may end up with a much larger number of products than most other nodes in the same layer, and so with a much higher value. Those nodes would compete with most others in their layer, often causing the death of their competitors. In other words, the death probability at bottom and top layers is quite low, while the death probability close to the waist is higher. The birth rate, on the other hand, is the same for all layers, and so the network's middle layers tend to become narrower than the bottom or top layers.

The reader should not draw the conclusion from the previous simplified discussion that the waist is always located at the layer with $s(l)$=0.5. As will be shown in Section 5, the competition threshold c also affects the location of the waist. Also, it is not true that the node with the maximum value at the waist never dies. Section 6 focuses on these "extraordinary" nodes, showing that, even though they live much longer than almost all other nodes in their layer, under certain conditions they can also die.

4. ROBUSTNESS

In this section, we focus on the robustness of the hourglass resemblance metric H with respect to the parameters of the *EvoArch* model. The robustness study has two parts. First, we show that wide deviations from the default value, for a single parameter at a time, do not cause significant changes in H. Second, we show that even if we simultaneously and randomly vary all *EvoArch* parameters, the model still produces hourglass-like structures with high probability.

Let us first focus on the three most important *EvoArch* parameters: the competition threshold c, the generality probability vector s, and the mortality parameter z. We have also examined the robustness of H with respect to the number of layers L, the birth rate, the number of initial nodes at each layer, or the stopping criterion, but those parameters have a much smaller impact on H.

Figure 7-a shows the median H score (together with the previous four percentiles) as we vary c between 0 and 1. The value $c = 0$ corresponds to "global" competition meaning that two nodes of the same layer compete with each other even if they do not share any products. When the competition threshold is so low, the death probability becomes significant even at higher layers, as those nodes start competing even without sharing many products. Thus, the upper part of the network deviates from the hourglass shape.

When $c = 1$, on the other hand, a node u competes with node w only if the former shares *all* products of w. This means that nodes rarely compete, and so most layers grow randomly, without a significant death probability. There is a wide range of c (between 0.1 and 0.9) in which we get reasonably good hourglass structures ($H > 0.8$) in most evolutionary paths. The best results, however, are produced in the range $0.5 < c < 0.8$. *In that range, almost all evolutionary paths produce $H > 0.9$.*

To study the robustness of the model with respect to the generality vector s, we consider a function $s(l)$ comprising of two linear segments that satisfy the constraints: $s(1)$=0.9, $s(\gamma)$=0.5 and $s(L)$=0, where γ is any layer between layer-2 and layer-(L-1). This function allows us to place the layer γ at which the generality probability is 50% at any (interior) layer of the architecture. Figure 7-b shows H as we vary the layer γ. The model is extremely robust with respect to variations in the generality vector s and layer γ.

Figure 7-c shows H as we vary the mortality parameter z. We limit the range of z to less than 2.0 so that the death probability is almost zero only if the value ratio r is close to one; this is not true for higher values of z (see Figure 3). Note that H is typically higher than 0.9 when $0.75 < z < 1.5$. For lower values of z, the death

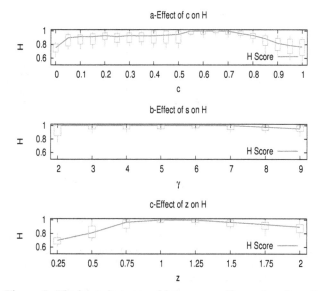

Figure 7: The hourglass resemblance score H as a function of the competition threshold c, the layer γ at which the generality is 50%, and the mortality parameter z.

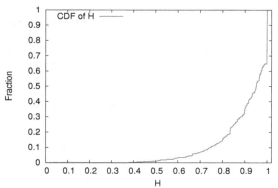

Figure 8: CDF of the hourglass resemblance score H when all parameters vary randomly in a certain range (see text).

probability becomes so high that only the most valuable node tends to survive in several layers. When z is higher than 1.5, the death probability becomes too low and several layers grow randomly.

In the previous experiments, we varied one parameter at a time. We now examine the robustness of the model when we randomly sample each parameter value simultaneously from a certain range (a Monte Carlo method). Together with the previous three parameters (c, s and z), we also consider here variations in the number of layers L, the random number of initial nodes n_0 separately at each layer, the birth rate μ, and the maximum network size N_{max} at the end of an evolutionary path. A subtle point here is that, as L increases, we need to make sure that N_{max} is also increased (with a larger number of layers the network should be allowed to grow larger). For this reason we set $N_{max} = \eta L$, and vary the factor η instead of N_{max}. We consider the following range for each parameter:
$0.25 \leq c \leq 0.75$, $3 \leq \gamma \leq L-2$, $0.75 \leq z \leq 1.5$, $5 \leq L \leq 15$, $1\% \leq \mu \leq 10\%$, $5 \leq n_0 \leq 20$, and $25 \leq \eta \leq 55$.

We generate 1000 evolutionary paths, each with a randomly chosen value for all previous parameters. The CDF of the hourglass resemblance scores is shown in Figure 8. Even when we vary all parameters randomly in the given ranges, the score H is still higher than 0.9 in 68% of the evolutionary paths, and higher than 0.75 in

90% of the evolutionary paths. We manually examined some evolutionary paths in which the score H is lower than 0.5. They typically result from "bad" combinations of parameter values. For instance, a large value of c in combination with a large value of z severely suppress deaths in all layers, allowing the network to grow randomly. Or, a small value of c pushes the waist towards higher layers, while a small γ pushes the waist towards lower layers, causing deviations from the basic hourglass shape (e.g., a double hourglass shape with two waists).

5. LOCATION AND WIDTH OF WAIST

In this section, we focus on the effect of the three major *EvoArch* parameters (competition threshold c, generality vector s, and mortality parameter z) on the location and width of the waist.[5] We also estimate the value of these three parameters in the case of the current Internet architecture (TCP/IP stack), and discuss several implications about the evolution of the latter and its early competition with the telephone network. We also discuss how to design a new architecture so that it has higher diversity (i.e., larger width) at its waist compared to the TCP/IP stack.

5.1 Effect of competition threshold

Figure 9-a shows the location and width of the waist as c increases. Recall from Section 4 that the model produces high values of H when c is between 0.1 to 0.9. As c increases in that range, the waist moves lower and its width increases. The competition threshold c quantifies how similar the services or products of two protocols must be before they start competing. As c increases, it becomes less likely that two nodes compete. Especially at higher layers, where the generality is low and nodes have few products, increasing c decreases the frequency of competition and thus the death probability. This means that those higher layers grow faster. Nodes at lower layers, where $s(l)$ is close to one, have many overlapping products and so they are less affected by c. Thus, *increasing c pushes the waist towards lower layers*. The same reasoning (increasing c decreases the death probability) explains why *the waist becomes wider as c increases*.

5.2 Effect of generality vector

As in Section 4, we focus on a two-segment piecewise linear generality vector: the first segment extends between $s(1) = 0.9$ and $s(\gamma) = 0.5$, and the second extends between $s(\gamma)$ and $s(L) = 0$. This function allows us to control the layer at which the generality is 50% (and the variance of the number of products is maximized) by modifying the parameter γ. Figure 9-b shows the location and width of the waist as γ increases from layer-2 to layer-(L-1). Recall that *EvoArch* produces high hourglass resemblance scores throughout that range. The general observation is that *as γ increases, the location of the waist increases*. It is important however that *the location of the waist is not exactly equal to γ*; in other words, the variance in the number of products is not sufficient to predict the layer at which the death probability is highest (and the width is lowest). The competition threshold c also influences the location of the waist, as previously discussed.

As γ increases, the width of the waist also increases. The reason is that the location of the waist moves to layers with larger generality. For instance, Figure 9-b shows that when $\gamma = 5$ the median waist is also at layer-5, while when $\gamma = 8$ the median waist is at layer-6. Thus, when $\gamma = 5$, the generality of the waist is 50%, while when $\gamma = 8$ the generality of the waist is approximately

---
[5] Any parameter we do not mention is set to the default value given in § 3.

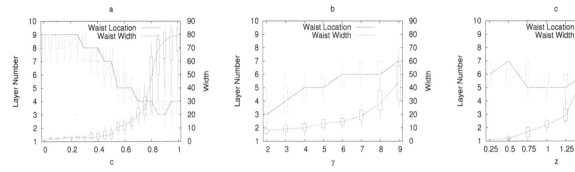

Figure 9: Location and width of the waist as a function of (a) competition threshold c, (b) layer γ with 50% generality, and (c) mortality parameter z.

61%. Higher generality, however, means a larger number of products for new nodes at the waist, a higher evolutionary value relative to the node with the maximum number of products in that layer, and thus a higher probability of survival.

5.3 Effect of mortality parameter

Recall that z controls the shape of the death probability (see Figure 3), with lower values of z causing more lethal competition. Figure 9-c shows the location and width of the waist when z varies between 0.25 and 2.0. As expected, *as z increases, the width of the waist increases*—the reason is that the death probability decreases, allowing more nodes to survive even though they compete with other nodes. On the other hand, *the parameter z does not have a significant effect on the location of the waist.*

5.4 Implications for the TCP/IP stack

In the current Internet architecture, the waist is located at the network layer and so it is practically at the mid-point of the protocol stack (see Figure 1). Further, the waist is very narrow: just one dominant networking protocol (IPv4) and two major transport protocols (TCP and UDP). We have estimated a good parameterization of the *EvoArch* model for the case of the TCP/IP stack (based on trial-and-error and also exploiting the trends shown in Figure 9). The values are: $L = 6$ (we distinguish between application-layer protocols such as HTTP at layer-5, and individual applications such as Firefox at layer-6), $c \approx 0.7$, $\gamma = 3$, and $z \approx 0.3$. With these parameter values the waist is almost always located at layer-3 and it consists of only few nodes (typically less than three). The median H score is 1 and the 10-90th percentiles are 0.66 and 1, respectively.[6]

What do these parameter values imply about the evolutionary characteristics of the current Internet architecture? In terms of the parameter c, a competition threshold around 70% implies that two protocols can co-exist in the TCP/IP stack as long as their relative product overlap (see Equation 2) is no more than about 70%; otherwise at least one of them will compete with the other. A good example of two protocols that co-exist at the same layer with little overlap in their services and functionality are TCP and UDP. The reason is that one of them is mostly used by applications that require reliability, while the other is chosen by a largely non-overlapping set of applications that prefer to avoid TCP's retransmissions, congestion control or byte-stream semantics. It is only few applications (e.g., DNS or Skype) that use both TCP and UDP.

The low value of z (approximately 0.3) implies that competition between protocols at the TCP/IP stack is very intense: *a protocol*

can survive only if its value is higher than about 90% of the value of its strongest component! A good survival strategy for a new protocol u would be to *avoid competition* with the highest-value protocol in that layer w. This can be achieved if u has largely non-overlapping products with w; in other words, *the new protocol should try to provide mostly different services or functionality than the incumbent.* The relatively high value of c (70%) means that a significant degree of service overlap would be tolerated, making it easier for the new protocol to also support some of the legacy applications.

The previous point also suggests an intriguing answer to a historical question. *How can we explain the survival of the TCP/IP stack in the early days of the Internet, when the telephone network was much more powerful?* During the 70s or 80s, the TCP/IP stack was not trying to compete with the services provided by the telephone network. It was mostly used for FTP, E-mail and Telnet, and those services were not provided by the incumbent (telephone) networks. So, TCP/IP managed to grow and increase its value without being threatened by the latter. In the last few years, on the other hand, the value of the TCP/IP protocols has exceeded the value of the traditional PSTN and Cable-TV networks, and it is now in the process of largely replacing them in the transfer of voice and video.

In terms of the parameter s, the fact that the waist of the TCP/IP stack is located at the network layer implies that the generality of that layer is close to 50%. This means that a new protocol at the network layer would see the highest variability (i.e., maximum uncertainty) in terms of whether it will be selected as substrate from protocols at the next higher layer. So, from an architect's perspective, the network layer of the TCP/IP stack is the layer at which a new protocol would experience the maximum uncertainty in terms of deployment and ultimate success.

5.5 Future Internet architectures

EvoArch also gives some interesting insights about the evolvability of future Internet clean-slate architectures. Suppose that a network architect would like to ensure that there is more diversity (i.e., larger width) in the waist of a new architecture compared to the TCP/IP stack—this goal has been suggested, for instance, by Peterson et al. [17]. *How can the network architect increase the likelihood that the evolution of a new architecture will lead to a wider waist, with several surviving protocols?* Based on the previous results, this will happen if we increase z—it is unlikely however that a network architect can control the intensity of competition; that is largely determined by economic and deployment considerations. A second and more pragmatic approach is to design protocols that are largely non-overlapping in terms of services and functionality, as previously discussed, so that they do not compete with each other. This approach was discussed in the previous section.

---

[6] A corresponding parameterization using the more realistic death-regulated birth process is given in Section 6.

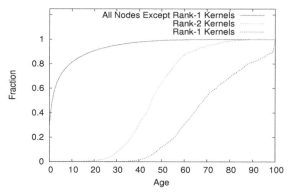

Figure 10: CDF of the age of various node subsets at layer-6.

A third approach is to design the architecture so that its waist is located at a layer with a high generality. As we saw in Figure 9-b, as we increase γ, increasing the generality of all layers, the waist moves higher, at a layer with higher generality. This also means that the waist is getting wider, allowing the co-existence of several protocols at that layer. How can this be done in practice? Suppose that we start from a 6-layer architecture X in which the waist is located at layer-3, and we want to redefine the functionality of each layer so that the waist of the new architecture Y is located at a higher layer. We should increase the generality of each layer (but still maintaining that $s(l)$ decreases as l increases) so that the corresponding protocols provide more general services in Y than in X. For instance, instead of defining HTTP as an application-specific protocol that is only used by web browsers, HTTP can be re-defined and used as a very general content-centric delivery protocol. This specific example, actually, has been recently proposed as a rather simple way to provide the benefits of clean-slate content-centric architectural proposals using an existing protocol [18].

6. EVOLUTIONARY KERNELS

It is often said that the core protocols of the Internet architecture (mostly IPv4, TCP and UDP) are "ossified", meaning that they are hard to modify or replace, creating an obstacle for network innovations [17]. At the same time however, they can be viewed more positively as the protocols that form the core of the architecture, creating a common interface between a large number of nodes at lower layers and a large number of nodes at higher layers. This is why we refer to them as *evolutionary kernels*, based on a similar concept about certain genes and gene regulatory networks in biology [10]. What can we learn from *EvoArch* about such ossification effects and evolutionary kernels? *Does the model predict the emergence of long-surviving nodes at the hourglass waist?* What is the reason that those nodes manage to survive much longer than their competitors? Do they ever get replaced by other nodes, and if so, under what conditions?

Let us focus on the waist—under the default parameters ($L = 10$) the waist is typically at layer-6. As previously discussed, the waist has the highest death probability, and so one may expect that it is unlikely to find any long-living nodes at that layer. We generate 1000 evolutionary paths, each lasting 100 rounds. At the end of the evolutionary path, we calculate the *maximum age* among all nodes that were ever born at layer-6. Figure 10 shows the CDF of the maximum age for various subsets of nodes: a) *the node with the maximum age* (we refer to such nodes as *rank-1 kernels* or simply *kernels*), b) the second older node (we refer to them as *rank-2 kernels*), c) all nodes, excluding only rank-1 kernels.

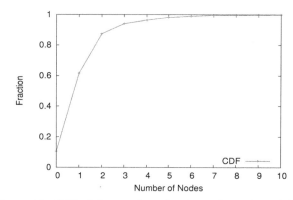

Figure 11: CDF of the number of nodes at layer-6 surviving more than half of the evolutionary path.

Note that almost all (rank-1) kernels survive for at least 50–60% of the entire evolutionary path. Actually, about 40% of the kernels are still alive at the end of the evolutionary path, meaning that their age is only determined by their birth time. On the other hand, the remaining nodes have much shorter life span. About 40% of them do not survive for more than a round or two and 90% of them survive for less than 20 rounds. The rank-2 kernels have much larger age than most nodes, but there is still a significant gap in the age of rank-1 and rank-2 kernels. So, our first observation is that *EvoArch predicts the emergence of very stable nodes at the waist that tend to survive for most of the evolutionary path.*

Figure 10 shows that only a small fraction of nodes survive for more than 50 rounds in an evolutionary path. So, let us identify in each evolutionary path those few nodes that survive for at least that long - we refer to them as "higher-rank kernels". Figure 11 shows the CDF of the number n of higher-rank kernels in each evolutionary path. In about half of the evolutionary paths only the rank-1 kernel exists. In almost all cases, $n \leq 4$. So, the number of nodes that can co-exist with the rank-1 kernel for more than 50 rounds is typically at most three. This confirms that it is difficult to survive for long at the waist in the presence of a rank-1 kernel. The nodes that manage to do so either have almost the same set of products with the rank-1 kernel (and thus almost the same value), or they have mostly different products than the rank-1 kernel, not competing with it. We have also examined the birth times of those nodes, and observed that in about 70% of the evolutionary paths rank-1 kernels are born earlier than higher rank kernels.

How large is the value of a kernel, and how can a kernel die? We define the *normalized value* $\hat{v}(u)$ of a node u at a given round as its value $v(u)$ divided by the value that u would have *if it was connected to all products at the next higher layer* in that round. So, $\hat{v}(u) \leq 1$. Note that because the death probability is almost zero when $r > 0.90$ (for the default value of z), if the normalized value of a node is higher than 90% that node cannot die even if it had a higher-value competitor.

Figure 12 shows the normalized value of all (rank-1) kernels, based on 1000 evolutionary paths. In the first 10–20 rounds, the normalized value increases as the upper layer grows larger and the kernels acquire new products. Then, during the next 30–40 rounds their normalized value varies around 80–90%, which means that those kernels are unlikely to die, even if they face competition. During the last 30–40 rounds, however, the normalized value of many kernels gradually drops. To understand this trend, and to explain how a kernel can be replaced, we have to examine the birth process. As time progresses, the upper layers of the network grow larger (recall that the death probability is low at higher layers due to low competition). In the basic birth model, however, the birth

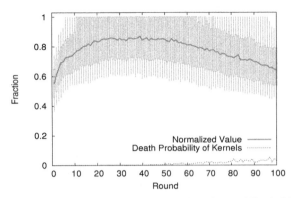

Figure 12: Normalized value for kernels at layer-6 (basic birth process).

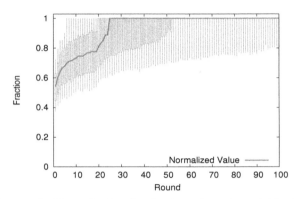

Figure 13: Normalized value for kernels at layer-6 (death-regulated birth process).

rate is proportional to the size of the network, and new nodes are distributed uniformly across all layers. Thus, the birth rate at the waist also increases with time.

The previous increase has two consequences. First, as the layer above the waist increases in size, new potential products appear for both the kernel and its competitors. Each of these new nodes will select the kernel as substrate with probability $s(l_b)$, where l_b is the waist. Second, as the birth rate at the waist increases, it becomes more likely that a new node at that layer will acquire enough new products so that its value becomes comparable, or even higher, than the value of the kernel. In other words, the death of kernels is largely due to the birth of several new nodes at the next higher layer: *if the kernel fails to quickly acquire most of those new potential products at the next higher layer it will experience a decrease in its normalized value, becoming more vulnerable to new or existing competitors at its own layer.*

The previous discussion raises the question: *what if the birth rate is not the same at all layers?* Specifically, what if the birth rate at a layer is negatively correlated with the death probability at that layer? This modification of the model, which we refer to as *death-regulated birth process*, captures situations in which the implementation or deployment of new protocols at a certain layer is discouraged by the intense competition that one or more incumbent protocols create at that layer. Arguably, this is a more realistic model than the basic birth model we considered earlier.

In the death-regulated birth process, we maintain an estimate of the death probability $\bar{d}(l)$ at layer l since the start of the evolutionary path. As in the basic birth process, the overall birth rate is proportional to the network size and the allocation of births to layers is random. However, a birth at layer l is successful with probability $1 - \bar{d}(l)$; otherwise the birth fails and it is counted as a death in that layer.

The death-regulated birth process creates a positive feedback loop through which the emergence of one or more kernels at the waist reinforces their position by decreasing the rate at which new nodes (and potential competitors) are created. Figure 13 shows the normalized value of the rank-1 kernel at layer-6, when we switch from the basic birth model to the death-regulated birth model after round-20. Note that the median normalized value (as well as the 25-th percentile) of the kernel becomes 100% within just few rounds. In other words, *with a death-regulated birth process it becomes practically impossible to replace a kernel at the waist of the hourglass.* Even when a new node u is somehow successfully born at the waist, the number of new nodes at the next higher layer is limited (because the birth process is also death-regulated at that layer) and so u's products will be most likely shared by the kernel.

This means that u will face the kernel's competition, and so u will most likely die.

We have also estimated a good parameterization of the *EvoArch* model for the case of the TCP/IP stack using the death-regulated birth process (again based on trial-and-error and exploiting the trends shown in Figure 9): $L = 6$, $c \approx 0.7$, $\gamma = 3$, and $z \approx 0.5$. With these values the waist is located at layer-3, its median width is one node, the median width of layer-4 is four nodes, while the width of the remaining layers increases with time. The median H score is 1 and the 10-90th percentiles are 0.66 and 1, respectively.

6.1 Kernels in the Internet architecture

There are several interesting connections between what *EvoArch* predicts about kernels and what happens in the Internet architecture. There is no doubt that IPv4, as well as TCP and UDP, are the kernels of the evolving Internet architecture. They provide a stable framework through which an always expanding set of physical and data-link layer protocols, as well as new applications and services at the higher layers, can interoperate and grow. At the same time, those three kernel protocols have been difficult to replace, or even modify significantly. Further, the fact that new network or transport layer protocols are rarely designed today implies that the birth process at those layers is closer to what we call "death-regulated", i.e., limited by the intense competition that the kernel protocols create.

EvoArch suggests an additional reason that IPv4 has been so stable over the last three decades. Recall that a large birth rate at the layer *above the waist* can cause a lethal drop in the normalized value of the kernel, if the latter is not chosen as substrate by the new nodes. In the current Internet architecture, the waist is the network layer but the next higher layer (transport) is also very narrow and stable. So, the transport layer acts as an *evolutionary shield* for IPv4 because any new protocols at the transport layer are unlikely to survive the competition with TCP and UDP. On the other hand, a large number of births at the layer above TCP or UDP (application protocols or specific applications) is unlikely to significantly affect the value of those two transport protocols because they already have many products. In summary, the stability of the two transport protocols adds to the stability of IPv4, by eliminating any potential new transport protocols that could select a new network layer protocol instead of IPv4.

In terms of future Internet architectures, *EvoArch* predicts that even if these architectures do not have the shape of an hourglass initially, they will probably do so as they evolve. When that happens, the emergence of new ossified protocols (kernels) will be a natural consequence. If the architects of such clean-slate designs want to proactively avoid the ossification effects that we now expe-

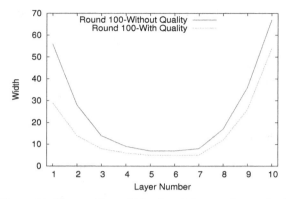

Figure 14: The median width of each layer when nodes have different quality factors (compared to the case that all nodes have the same quality).

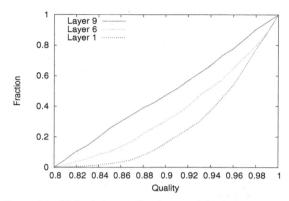

Figure 15: CDF of the quality factor $q(u)$ of the kernel node at the waist (layer-6). The corresponding CDFs for the oldest node at layer-1 and layer-9 are also shown.

rience with TCP/IP, they should try to design the functionality of each layer so that the waist is wider, consisting of several protocols that offer largely distinct but general services, as discussed in Section 5.5.

7. QUALITY DIFFERENTIATION

So far we have assumed that the value of a protocol is only determined by the value of its products. It would be more realistic however to consider that the evolutionary value of a protocol also depends on other factors, which we refer to as *quality*. The "quality factor" should be interpreted broadly; it can capture properties such as performance, extent of deployment, reliability or security, clarity of the corresponding specification or other features. The quality factor also allows *EvoArch* to capture the effect of incremental improvements in existing protocols: such improvements do not create a new node in the model, but they increase the quality parameter of an existing node. In the following, we assume that the quality factor of a node is constant—an interesting extension of the model will be to consider time-varying quality factors.

In this section, we conduct a simple extension to the *EvoArch* model so that each protocol u has a certain quality factor $q(u)$. We are mostly interested in two questions. First, *how does this quality differentiation affect the shape of the resulting architecture?* And second, *focusing on the kernel nodes at the waist, do they tend to be nodes with the highest quality factor?* The quality of a node u is represented by a multiplicative factor $q(u)$, uniformly distributed in $[q_{min}, 1]$ (with $0 < q_{min} < 1$). The value of node u is then the product of the quality factor $q(u)$ with the quality-independent value of u:

$$v(u) = \begin{cases} q(u) \sum_{p \in P(u)} v(p) & l(u) < L \\ q(u) & l(u) = L \end{cases} \quad (5)$$

7.1 Effect of quality differentiation

We have repeated the analysis of Section 3 with the previous model extension, with $q_{min} = 0.8$. Figure 14 shows the median width of each layer with the default parameter values, based on 1000 evolutionary paths. *The resulting network continues to have the hourglass shape* (decreasing width up to a certain layer and then increasing width), even when nodes have different quality factors; the median H score is 1.0 and the 10th and 90th percentiles are 0.9 and 1.0, respectively. The location of the waist does not change as a result of the quality factor heterogeneity.

There are two interesting differences however. First, *the network grows at a slower pace*. This is a result of the increased death

probability because of nodes with low quality factor. Second, *the lower part of the hourglass, below the waist, is now smaller in size than the upper part of the hourglass*. The reason is that nodes at lower layers have more competitors (due to higher generality at those layers) than nodes at higher layers. When all nodes have the same quality, nodes at lower layers compete widely but they usually survive the competition because their product sets are similar, and thus their values are similar. With heterogeneous qualities, on the other hand, the value of nodes at lower layers can be significantly different, increasing the death probability compared to the case of homogeneous qualities. This increased death probability makes the size of the lower part of the hourglass smaller than the upper part.

It is interesting that the TCP/IP stack has a similar asymmetry, with the bottom part of the hourglass being smaller in terms of size than the upper part. *EvoArch* offers a plausible explanation for this effect: the heterogeneity among different protocols at the same layer, in terms of performance, security, extent of deployment, etc, increases the death probability at lower layers more than at higher layers.

7.2 Quality of kernel nodes

Section 6 focused on the evolutionary kernels at the waist of the hourglass. In the case of heterogeneous qualities, *an important question is whether the kernels tend to also have the highest quality factor*. In other words, *can we expect that the "best" nodes (i.e., highest quality factor) are also the strongest nodes in terms of value?*

Figure 15 shows the CDF of the quality factor of the kernel node at the waist (layer-6), based on 1000 evolutionary paths. As a reference point, we also show the CDF of the quality factor of the oldest node at layer-1 and at layer-9.

If the quality of a node has no effect on its death probability, we would expect that the CDF of the quality factor of the oldest node would be a straight line between 0.8 and 1 (recall that the quality factor varies uniformly in that range). This is the case at layer-9. In that layer, which is almost at the top of the stack, nodes rarely compete with each other because of their low generality and small number of products. So, their quality does not influence their age, and the quality factor of the oldest node varies randomly between 0.8 and 1.

At the bottom layer (layer-1) on the other hand, we observe a strong bias towards higher quality values. As discussed earlier in this section, the nodes at the bottom layer have high generality, many competitors, and so their quality factor strongly affects their value and death probability. *It is mostly high-quality nodes that survive at the bottom layers.*

At the waist, where only few kernel nodes survive for most of the evolutionary path, the bias towards higher quality values is much weaker. In about 30% of the evolutionary paths the quality factor of the kernel is less than 0.9, which means that *those kernels are in the bottom half of all nodes in terms of quality.* Similarly, the probability that a node with high quality factor (say $q(u) > 0.95$) becomes the kernel of the waist is only 40%.

7.3 Implications for IPv4 and IPv6

In the Internet architecture, it would be hard to argue that IPv4 has dominated at the network layer because it was an excellent protocol in terms of design. During the last 30–40 years, several other network-layer protocols have been proposed, and probably some of them were better than IPv4 in several aspects. *EvoArch* gives us another way to understand the success of IPv4, and to also think about future protocols that could potentially replace it. It will help if such future protocols are better than IPv4; that is not a sufficient condition to replace IPv4 however. If the potential replacements attempt to directly compete with IPv4, having a large overlap with it in terms of applications and services but without offering a major advantage in terms of the previous "quality factor", it will remain difficult to replace IPv4.

What does EvoArch suggest about IPv6 and the difficulty that the latter faces in replacing the aging IPv4? We should first note that IPv6 does not offer new services compared to IPv4; it mostly offers many more addresses.[7] This means that IPv6 has, *at most,* the same products with IPv4, and so the latter is its competitor. Further, because IPv6 is not widely deployed, it is reasonable to assume that its quality factor is much lower than that of IPv4. So, even if the two protocols had the same set of products, IPv4 has much higher value and it wins the competition with IPv6. The situation would be better for IPv6 under two conditions. First, if IPv6 could offer some popular new services that IPv4 *cannot* offer—that would provide the former with additional products (and value) that the latter does not have. Second, IPv6 should avoid competition with IPv4, at least until it has been widely deployed. That would be the case if IPv6 was presented, not as a replacement to IPv4, but as "the second network layer protocol" that is required to support the previous new services.

8. RELATED WORK

To the extent of our knowledge, there is no prior work in modeling the evolution of protocol stacks or hourglass-like network architectures. At a high level however, our work is related to recent efforts that develop a rigorous theory of network layering and architecture, mostly using mathematical tools from optimization and control systems [4]. We agree with those authors that network architecture can become the subject of more quantitative and rigorous scientific methods. We have a different view however on how to get there: instead of thinking about each layer as the solution to an optimization problem, we focus on the evolutionary process that shapes a network architecture over time and we emphasize the role of robustness and evolvability instead of optimality. Also relevant is the work of Csete and Doyle [5], which has emphasized the role of hierarchical modularity and evolution in both technological and biological systems. Those authors have also identified the signif-

icance of the hourglass (or bowtie) structure in the corresponding network architectures.

Recent work has investigated the competition between incumbent and emerging network architectures [13, 14]. Their focus, however, is mostly on the deployment share of each architecture using economic models from the literature of technology diffusion. We think that the deployment effects represent just one of many instances of competition between protocols at the same layer. In the economics literature, several authors have focused on standards, compatibility, and on the diffusion of new technologies (see, for instance, the early work by Farrell and Saloner [11] or the review [7]). That line of work focuses on the positive externalities created by the requirement for compatibility, and how those externalities often lead to the dominance of a single standard or protocol. To the extent of our knowledge, however, there is no work in economics about multi-layer architectures or networks that involve multiple standards, and no studies of the hourglass or bowtie structure that can emerge in such architectures.

In a 2001 IETF talk, Steve Deering alarmed the community that the waist of the Internet architecture is getting bigger, as more functionality (such as QoS or native multicast) was then proposed for IPv4 [8]—*EvoArch* suggests that a wider waist, with different protocols offering largely non-overlapping but general services, is actually a good way to increase the evolvability of an architecture. Popa et al. argue that HTTP (a layer-5 protocol) can become the new narrow waist of the Internet architecture because almost all applications and services today can run over HTTP [18]. We argue that instead of pushing a single-protocol waist from layer-3 to layer-5, a more evolvable network architecture should have a wider waist that does not include only one protocol. Otherwise, HTTP will also be considered "ossified" and an obstacle to innovation in few years from now. Culler et al. argue that the narrow waist of a sensor network architecture should not be the network layer, as in the current Internet, but a single-hop broadcast with a rich enough interface to allow multiple network protocols [6]. *EvoArch* can help designers of such new and special-purpose architectures to think about the ideal location of the hourglass waist considering the generality of the services provided at each layer.

9. CRITICISM

EvoArch does not consider the semantics and various practical aspects of specific layers, protocols or architectures. There are certainly several objections to this abstract modeling approach. We include here some of the concerns expressed by the anonymous reviewers, including a brief response.

One reviewer summarized most of the criticism with the following quote: *"The strength of this work is the simplicity of the model as it makes fairly general assumptions that are not tied into, for instance, the semantics of what each layer does. However, the failure to take semantics into account is its biggest failing as well."* *EvoArch* shows that it is not necessary to consider the layer semantics for the emergence of the hourglass structure; the semantics are probably important for other architectural characteristics but not for the hourglass structure.

Another high-level concern relates to the confirmation-bias risk: *"The problem with a paper like this is that we know the answer the model must produce, so (like Jeopardy) we have to find a model that can be tweaked to give that answer, and then see if we learn anything beyond what we already knew about the answer."* It is true that our objective has been to identify a model that can produce the hourglass structure. Additionally, however, our objective was to identify a general, parsimonious and explanatory model based on a small set of principles about layered and evolving network archi-

---

[7]The original proposals for IPv6 included several novel services, such as mobility, improved auto-configuration and IP-layer security, but eventually IPv6 became mostly an IPv4-like protocol with many more addresses.

tectures. More importantly, *EvoArch* leads to several insights and explanations that were not expected from or "built-in" the model formulation.

Some reviewers offer different explanations for the narrow protocol waist at the network layer: *"The need for global addressing is a more important factor in having a single internetworking protocol than the evolutionary dynamics proposed here. IP does almost nothing else besides global addressing, and there is little reason to have two global addressing protocols."* This view is also reflected in the following quote: *"What if the reality is that the lower-most layer that provides end-to-end connectivity is the waist by default because that in effect represents the balance between generality and ease of use? It is hard to roll out an end-to-end connectivity service on top of lower-level primitives, and IP won because it got there (wide-area deployment) first."* Note that the previous plausible explanations for the presence of a narrow waist (with a single protocol at the network layer) do not explain, however, why we observe an hourglass structure. Another reviewer thinks that the hourglass structure is a result of a wide diversity of constraints at the lower layers and a wide diversity of services and applications at the upper layers: *"The more relevant dynamic at the bottom of the architecture is that there are different environmental niches (wireless, optical, etc.) that serve different needs in terms of deployability, bandwidth, and cost. So the model should have idiosyncratic applications at the top and idiosyncratic technologies at the bottom, tied together by layered protocols of varying generalities."* This is actually similar to *EvoArch*, even though it introduces more "semantics" about the function and constraints of lower layer protocols.

A more negative review questioned even whether the protocol stack has the shape of an hourglass: *"This model bears no intuitive relation to reality - in assumptions about the conditions under which protocols are invented, the process by which some are selected over others, or, indeed, that the protocol stack of the Internet is an hourglass (in practice, it is not: VPNs, tunnels, federation with other networks like the phone system, all complicate the picture)."* We believe that despite the former *architectural exceptions* (that are hard to place at a given layer), the Internet architecture is still shaped as an hourglass. Finally, we repeat what should be well-known to any scientist: the beauty and usefulness of a model is that it allows us to understand certain aspects of a system without having to describe or consider all the elements that constitute that system.

10. CONCLUSIONS

A main thesis behind this work is that we can study network architectures in a quantitative and scientific manner, in the same way that we study for instance the performance of transport protocols or the stability of routing protocols. In this spirit, we proposed a model for the evolution of layered protocol stacks. *EvoArch* is based on few principles about the generality of protocols at different layers, the competition between protocols at the same layer, and how new protocols are created. Even though *EvoArch* does not capture many practical aspects and protocol-specific or layer-specific details, it predicts the emergence of an hourglass architecture and the appearance of few stable nodes (not always of the highest quality) at the waist. Further, *EvoArch* offers some intriguing insights about the evolution of the TCP/IP stack, the competition between IPv4 and IPv6, and the evolvability of future Internet architectures. Possible extensions of *EvoArch* include a dynamic notion of quality (to capture, for instance, how the deployment of a protocol can change with time depending on the protocol's value), a growing number of layers as the complexity of the provided services increases with time, and architectures without strict layering.

Finally, we note that the presence of hourglass (or bowtie-like) architectures has been also observed in metabolic and gene regulatory networks [5, 20], in the organization of the innate immune system [2], as well as in gene expression during development [15]. Even though it sounds far-fetched, it is possible that there are similarities between the evolution of protocol stacks and the evolution of the previous biological systems. We explore these cross-disciplinary connections in on-going work.

Acknowledgements

We are grateful to Todd Streelman (School of Biology, Georgia Tech) for many long discussions about evolution that provided the inspiration for this work. We are also grateful to those anonymous reviewers that provided constructive comments and to our "shepherd" John Heidemann.

11. REFERENCES

[1] S. Akhshabi and C. Dovrolis. The Evolution of Layered Protocol Stacks Leads to an Hourglass-Shaped Architecture (extended version). Technical report, College of Computing, Georgia Tech, 2011. http://www.cc.gatech.edu/~dovrolis/Papers/evoarch-extended.pdf.

[2] B. Beutler. Inferences, Questions and Possibilities in Toll-like Receptor Signalling. *Nature*, 430(6996):257–263, 2004.

[3] G.E.P. Box. Robustness in the Strategy of Scientific Model Building. Technical report, DTIC Document, 1979.

[4] M. Chiang, S.H. Low, A.R. Calderbank, and J.C. Doyle. Layering as Optimization Decomposition: A Mathematical Theory of Network Architectures. *Proceedings of the IEEE*, 95(1):255–312, 2007.

[5] M. Csete and J. Doyle. Bow Ties, Metabolism and Disease. *TRENDS in Biotechnology*, 22(9):446–450, September 2004.

[6] D. Culler, P. Dutta, C. T. Ee, R. Fonseca, J. Hui, P. Levis, J. Polastre, S. Shenker, I. Stoica, G. Tolle, and J. Zhao. Towards a Sensor Network Architecture: Lowering the Waistline. In *USENIX HotOS*, 2005.

[7] P.A. David and S. Greenstein. The Economics of Compatibility Standards: An Introduction to Recent Research. *Economics of Innovation and New Technology*, 1(1):3–41, 1990.

[8] S. Deering. Watching the Waist of the Protocol Hourglass. 2001. www.iab.org/documents/docs/hourglass-london-ietf.pdf.

[9] C. Dovrolis. What would Darwin Think about Clean-Slate Architectures? *ACM SIGCOMM Computer Communications Review*, 38(1):29–34, 2008.

[10] C. Dovrolis and T Streelman. Evolvable Network Architectures: What can we Learn from Biology? *ACM SIGCOMM Computer Communications Review*, 40(2), 2010.

[11] J. Farrell and G. Saloner. Standardization, Compatibility, and Innovation. *The RAND Journal of Economics*, 16(1):70–83, 1985.

[12] M. Hollander and D. A. Wolfe. *Nonparametric Statistical Methods*. Willey Interscience, 1999.

[13] Y. Jin, S. Sen, R. Guérin, K. Hosanagar, and Z.L. Zhang. Dynamics of Competition between Incumbent and Emerging Network Technologies. In *NetEcon*, 2008.

[14] D. Joseph, N. Shetty, J. Chuang, and I. Stoica. Modeling the Adoption of New Network Architectures. In *Proceedings of ACM CoNEXT*, 2007.

[15] A.T. Kalinka, K.M. Varga, D.T. Gerrard, S. Preibisch, D.L. Corcoran, J. Jarrells, U. Ohler, C.M. Bergman, and P. Tomancak. Gene Expression Divergence Recapitulates the Developmental Hourglass Model. *Nature*, 468(7325):811–814, 2010.

[16] NSF-10528. Future Internet Architectures (FIA). *National Science Foundation*, 2010.

[17] L. Peterson, S. Shenker, and J. Turner. Overcoming the Internet Impasse through Virtualization. In *ACM SIGCOMM HotNets*, 2004.

[18] L. Popa, A. Ghodsi, and I. Stoica. HTTP as the Narrow Waist of the Future Internet. In *ACM SIGCOMM HotNets*, 2010.

[19] J. Rexford and C. Dovrolis. Future Internet Architecture: Clean-Slate versus Evolutionary Research. *Communications of the ACM*, 53:36–40, 2010.

[20] J. Zhao, H. Yu, J.H. Luo, Z.W. Cao, and Y.X. Li. Hierarchical Modularity of Nested Bow-Ties in Metabolic Networks. *BMC Bioinformatics*, 7(1):386, 2006.

What's the Difference?
Efficient Set Reconciliation without Prior Context

David Eppstein[1]   Michael T. Goodrich[1]   Frank Uyeda[2]   George Varghese[2,3]

[1]U.C. Irvine   [2]U.C. San Diego   [3]Yahoo! Research

ABSTRACT

We describe a synopsis structure, the Difference Digest, that allows two nodes to compute the elements belonging to the set difference in a single round with communication overhead proportional to the *size of the difference* times the logarithm of the keyspace. While set reconciliation can be done efficiently using logs, logs require overhead for every update and scale poorly when multiple users are to be reconciled. By contrast, our abstraction assumes no prior context and is useful in networking and distributed systems applications such as trading blocks in a peer-to-peer network, and synchronizing link-state databases after a partition.

Our basic set-reconciliation method has a similarity with the peeling algorithm used in Tornado codes [6], which is not surprising, as there is an intimate connection between set difference and coding. Beyond set reconciliation, an essential component in our Difference Digest is a new estimator for the size of the set difference that outperforms min-wise sketches [3] for small set differences.

Our experiments show that the Difference Digest is more efficient than prior approaches such as Approximate Reconciliation Trees [5] and Characteristic Polynomial Interpolation [17]. We use Difference Digests to implement a generic KeyDiff service in Linux that runs over TCP and returns the sets of keys that differ between machines.

Categories and Subject Descriptors

C.2.2 [**Computer-Communication Networks**]: Network Protocols; E.4 [**Coding and Information Theory**]:

General Terms

Algorithms, Design, Experimentation

1. INTRODUCTION

Two common tasks in networking and distributed systems are *reconciliation* and *deduplication*. In reconciliation, two hosts each have a set of keys and each seeks to obtain the union of the two sets. The sets could be file blocks in a Peer-to-Peer (P2P) system or link

state packet identifiers in a routing protocol. In deduplication, on the other hand, two hosts each have a set of keys, and the task is to identify the keys in the intersection so that duplicate data can be deleted and replaced by pointers [16]. Deduplication is a thriving industry: for example, Data Domain [1, 21] pioneered the use of deduplication to improve the efficiency of backups.

Both reconciliation and deduplication can be abstracted as the problem of efficiently computing the *set difference* between two sets stored at two nodes across a communication link. The set difference is the set of keys that are in one set but not the other. In reconciliation, the difference is used to compute the set union; in deduplication, it is used to compute the intersection. Efficiency is measured primarily by the bandwidth used (important when the two nodes are connected by a wide-area or mobile link), the latency in round-trip delays, and the computation used at the two hosts. We are particularly interested in optimizing the case when the set difference is small (e.g., the two nodes have almost the same set of routing updates to reconcile, or the two nodes have a large amount of duplicate data blocks) and when there is no prior communication or context between the two nodes.

For example, suppose two users, each with a large collection of songs on their phones, meet and wish to synchronize their libraries. They could do so by exchanging lists of all of their songs; however, the amount of data transferred would be proportional to the total number of songs they have rather than the size of the difference. An often-used alternative is to maintain a time-stamped log of updates together with a record of the time that the users last communicated. When they communicate again, A can send B all of the updates since their last communication, and vice versa. Fundamentally, the use of logs requires prior context, which we seek to avoid.

Logs have more specific disadvantages as well. First, the logging system must be integrated with any system that can change user data, potentially requiring system design changes. Second, if reconciliation events are rare, the added overhead to update a log each time user data changes may not be justified. This is particularly problematic for "hot" data items that are written often and may be in the log multiple times. While this redundancy can be avoided using a hash table, this requires further overhead. Third, a log has to be maintained for every other user this user may wish to synchronize with. Further, two users A and B may have received the same update from a third user C, leading to redundant communication. Multi-party synchronization is common in P2P systems and in cases where users have multiple data repositories, such as their phone, their desktop, and in the cloud. Finally, logs require stable storage and synchronized time which are often unavailable on networking devices such as routers.

To solve the set-difference problem efficiently without the use of logs or other prior context, we devise a data structure called a

Difference Digest, which computes the set difference with communication proportional to the size of the difference between the sets being compared. We implement and evaluate a simple key-synchronization service based on Difference Digests and suggest how it can improve the performance in several contexts. Settings in which Difference Digests may be applied include:

- *Peer-to-peer:* Peer A and B may receive blocks of a file from other peers and may wish to receive only missing blocks from each other.

- *Partition healing:* When a link-state network partitions, routers in each partition may each obtain some new link-state packets. When the partition heals by a link joining router A and B, both A and B only want to exchange new or changed link-state packets.

- *Deduplication:* If backups are done in the cloud, when a new file is written, the system should only transmit the chunks of the file that are not already in the cloud.

- *Synchronizing parallel activations:* A search engine may use two independent crawlers with different techniques to harvest URLs but they may have very few URLs that are different. In general, this situation arises when multiple actors in a distributed system are performing similar functions for efficiency or redundancy.

- *Opportunistic ad hoc networks:* These are often characterized by low bandwidth and intermittent connectivity to other peers. Examples include rescue situations and military vehicles that wish to synchronize data when they are in range.

The main contributions of the paper are as follows:

- *IBF Subtraction:* The first component of the Difference Digest is an Invertible Bloom Filter or IBF [9, 13]. IBF's were previously used [9] for straggler detection at a single node, to identify items that were inserted and not removed in a stream. We adapt Invertible Bloom Filters for set reconciliation by defining a new subtraction operator on whole IBF's, as opposed to individual item removal.

- *Strata Estimator:* Invertible Bloom Filters need to be sized appropriately to be efficiently used for set differences. Thus a second crucial component of the Difference Digest is a new Strata Estimator method for estimating the *size of the difference*. We show that this estimator is much more accurate for small set differences (as is common in the final stages of a file dissemination in a P2P network) than Min-Wise Sketches [3, 4] or random projections [14]. Besides being an integral part of the Difference Digest, our Strata Estimator can be used independently to find, for example, which of many peers is most likely to have a missing block.

- *KeyDiff Prototype:* We describe a Linux prototype of a generic KeyDiff service based on Difference Digests that applications can use to synchronize objects of any kind.

- *Performance Characterization:* The overall system performance of Difference Digests is sensitive to many parameters, such as the size of the difference, the bandwidth available compared to the computation, and the ability to do pre-computation. We characterize the parameter regimes in which Difference Digests outperform earlier approaches, such as MinWise hashes, Characteristic Polynomial Interpolation [17], and Approximate Reconciliation Trees [5].

Going forward, we discuss related work in Section 2. We present our algorithms and analysis for the Invertible Bloom Filter and Strata Estimator in Sections 3 & 4. We describe our KeyDiff prototype in Section 5, evaluate our structures in Section 6 and conclude in Section 7.

2. MODEL AND RELATED WORK

We start with a simple model of set reconciliation. For two sets S_A, S_B each containing elements from a universe, $\mathbb{U} = [0, u)$, we want to compute the set difference, D_{A-B} and D_{B-A}, where $D_{A-B} = S_A - S_B$ such that for all $s \in D_{A-B}$, $s \in S_A$ and $s \notin S_B$. Likewise, $D_{B-A} = S_B - S_A$. We say that $D = D_{A-B} \cup D_{B-A}$ and $d = |D|$. Note that since $D_{A-B} \cap D_{B-A} = \emptyset$, $d = |D_{A-B}| + |D_{B-A}|$. We assume that S_A and S_B are stored at two distinct hosts and attempt to compute the set difference with minimal communication, computation, storage, and latency.

Several prior algorithms for computing set differences have been proposed. The simplest consists of hosts exchanging lists, each containing the identifiers for all elements in their sets, then scanning the lists to remove common elements. This requires $O(|S_A| + |S_B|)$ communication and $O(|S_A| \times |S_B|)$ time. The run time can be improved to $O(|S_A| + |S_B|)$ by inserting one list into a hash table, then querying the table with the elements of the second list.

The communication overhead can be reduced by a constant factor by exchanging Bloom filters [2] containing the elements of each list. Once in possession of the remote Bloom Filter, each host can query the filter to identify which elements are common. Fundamentally, a Bloom Filter still requires communication proportional to the size of the sets (and not the difference) and incurs the risk of false positives. The time cost for this procedure is $O(|S_A| + |S_B|)$. The Bloom filter approach was extended using Approximate Reconciliation Trees [5], which requires $O(d \log(|S_B|))$ recovery time, and $O(|S_B|)$ space. However, given S_A and an Approximate Reconciliation Tree for S_B, a host can only compute D_{A-B}, i.e., the elements unique to S_A.

An exact approach to the set-difference problem was proposed by Minksy *et al.* [17]. In this approach, each set is encoded using a linear transformation similar to Reed-Solomon coding. This approach has the advantage of $O(d)$ communication overhead, but requires $O(d^3)$ time to decode the difference using Gaussian elimination; asymptotically faster decoding algorithms are known, but their practicality remains unclear. Additionally, whereas our Strata Estimator gives an accurate one-shot estimate of the size of the difference prior to encoding the difference itself, Minsky *et al.* use an iterative doubling protocol for estimating the size of the difference, with a non-constant number of rounds of communication. Both the decoding time and the number of communication rounds (latency) of their system are unfavorable compared to ours.

Estimating Set-Difference Size. A critical sub-problem is an initial estimation of the size of the set difference. This can be estimated with constant overhead by comparing a random sample [14] from each set, but accuracy quickly deteriorates when the d is small relative to the size of the sets.

Min-wise sketches [3, 4] can be used to estimate the set similarity ($r = \frac{|S_A \cap S_B|}{|S_A \cup S_B|}$). Min-wise sketches work by selecting k random hash functions $\pi_1, \ldots, \pi_k$ which permute elements within $\mathbb{U}$. Let $\min(\pi_i(S))$ be the smallest value produced by π_i when run on the elements of S. Then, a Min-wise sketch consists of the k values $\min(\pi_1(S)), \ldots, \min(\pi_k(S))$. For two Min-wise sketches, M_A and M_B, containing the elements of S_A and S_B, respectively, the set similarity is estimated by the of number of hash function returning the same minimum value. If S_A and S_B have a set-similarity r, then we expect that the number of matching cells in M_A and M_B

will be $m = rk$. Inversely, given that m cells of M_A and M_B do match, we can estimate that $r = \frac{m}{k}$. Given the set-similarity, we can estimate the difference as $d = \frac{1-r}{1+r}(|S_A| + |S_B|)$.

As with random sampling, the accuracy of the Min-wise estimator diminishes for smaller values of k and for relatively small set differences. Similarly, Cormode et al. [8] provide a method for dynamic sampling from a data stream to estimate set sizes using a hierarchy of samples, which include summations and counts. Likewise, Cormode and Muthukrishnan [7] and Schweller et al. [20] describe sketch-based methods for finding large differences in traffic flows. (See also [19].)

An alternative approach to estimating set-difference size is provided by [11], whose algorithm can more generally estimate the difference between two functions with communication complexity very similar to our Strata Estimator. As with our results, their method has a small multiplicative error even when the difference is small. However, it uses algebraic computations over finite fields, whereas ours involves only simple, and more practical, hashing-based data structures.

While efficiency of set difference *estimation* for small differences may seem like a minor theoretical detail, it can be important in many contexts. Consider, for instance, the endgame of a P2P file transfer. Imagine that a BitTorrent node has 100 peers, and is missing only the last block of a file. Min-wise or random samples from the 100 peers will not identify the right peer if all peers also have nearly finished downloading (small set difference). On the other hand, sending a Bloom Filter takes bandwidth proportional to the number of blocks in file, which can be large. We describe our new estimator in Section 3.2.

3. ALGORITHMS

In this section, we describe the two components of the Difference Digest: an Invertible Bloom Filter (IBF) and a Strata Estimator. Our first innovation is taking the existing IBF [9, 13] and introducing a subtraction operator in Section 3.1 to compute D_{A-B} and D_{B-A} using a single round of communication of size O(d). Encoding a set S into an IBF requires O($|S|$) time, but decoding to recover D_{A-B} and D_{B-A} requires only O(d) time. Our second key innovation is a way of composing several sampled IBF's of fixed size into a new Strata Estimator which can effectively estimate the size of the set difference using O($\log(|\mathbb{U}|)$) space.

3.1 Invertible Bloom Filter

We now describe the Invertible Bloom Filter (IBF), which can simultaneously calculate D_{A-B} and D_{B-A} using O(d) space. This data structure encodes sets in a fashion that is similar in spirit to Tornado codes' construction [6], in that it randomly combines elements using the XOR function. We will show later that this similarity is not surprising as there is a reduction between set difference and coding across certain channels. For now, note that whereas Tornado codes are for a fixed set, IBF's are dynamic and, as we show, even allow for fast set subtraction operations. Likewise, Tornado codes rely on Reed-Solomon codes to handle possible encoding errors, whereas IBF's succeed with high probability without relying on an inefficient fallback computation. Finally, our encoding is much simpler than Tornado codes because we use a simple uniform random graph for encoding while Tornado codes use more complex random graphs with non-uniform degree distributions.

We start with some intuition. An IBF is named because it is similar to a standard Bloom Filter—except that it can, with the right settings, be *inverted* to yield some of the elements that were inserted. Recall that in a counting Bloom Filter [10], when a key K is inserted, K is hashed into several locations of an array and a count, count, is incremented in each hashed location. Deletion of K is similar except that count is decremented. A check for whether K exists in the filter returns true if all locations that K hashes to have non-zero count values.

An IBF has another crucial field in each cell (array location) besides the count. This is the idSum: the XOR of all key IDs that hash into that cell. Now imagine that two peers, Peer 1 and Peer 2, doing set reconciliation on a large file of a million blocks independently compute IBF's, B_1 and B_2, each with 100 cells, by inserting an ID for each block they possess. Note that a standard Bloom filter would have a size of several million bits to effectively answer whether a particular key is contained in the structure. Observe also that if each ID is hashed to 3 cells, an average of 30,000 keys hash onto each cell. Thus, each count will be large and the idSum in each cell will be the XOR of a large number of IDs. What can we do with such a small number of cells and such a large number of collisions?

Assume that Peer 1 sends B_1 to Peer 2, an operation only requiring bandwidth to send around 200 fields (100 cells × 2 fields/cell). Peer 2 then proceeds to "subtract" its IBF B_2 from B_1. It does this cell by cell, by subtracting the count and XORing the idSum in the corresponding cells of the two IBF's.

Intuitively, if the two peers' blocks sets are almost the same (say, 25 different blocks out of a million blocks), all the common IDs that hash onto the same cell will be cancelled from idSum, leaving only the sum of the unique IDs (those that belong to one peer and not the other) in the idSum of each cell. This follows assuming that Peer 1 and Peer 2 use the same hash function so that any common element, c, is hashed to the same cells in both B_1 and B_2. When we XOR the idSum in these cells, c will disappear because it is XORed twice.

In essense, randomly hashing keys to, say three, cells, is identical to randomly throwing three balls into the same 100 bins for each of the 25 block ID's. Further, we will prove that if there are sufficient cells, there is a high probability that at least one cell is "pure" in that it contains only a single element by itself.

A "pure" cell signals its purity by having its count field equal to 1, and, in that case, the idSum field yields the ID of one element in the set difference. We delete this element from all cells it has hashed to in the difference IBF by the appropriate subtractions; this, in turn, may free up more pure elements that it can in turn be decoded, to ultimately yield all the elements in the set difference.

The reader will quickly see subtleties. First, a numerical count value of 1 is necessary but not sufficient for purity. For example, if we have a cell in one IBF with two keys X and Y and the corresponding cell in the second IBF has key Z, then when we subtract we will get a count of 1, but idSum will have the XOR of X, Y and Z. More devious errors can occur if four IDs W, X, Y, Z satisfy $W + X = Y + Z$. To reduce the likelihood of decoding errors to an arbitrarily small value, IBF's use a third field in each cell as a checksum: the XOR of the hashes of all IDs that hash into a cell, but using a different hash function H_c than that used to determine the cell indices. If an element is indeed pure, then the hash sum should be $H_c(\text{idSum})$.

A second subtlety occurs if Peer 2 has an element that Peer 1 does not. Could the subtraction $B_1 - B_2$ produce negative values for idSum and count? Indeed, it can and the algorithm deals with this: for example, in idSum by using XOR instead of addition and subtraction, and in recognizing purity by count values of 1 *or* -1. While IBF's were introduced earlier [9, 13], whole IBF subtraction is new to this paper; hence, negative counts did not arise in [9, 13].

Figure 1 summarizes the encoding of a set S and Figure 2 gives a small example of synchronizing the sets at Peer 1 (who has keys

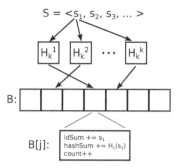

Figure 1: IBF Encode. Hash functions are used to map each element of the set to k cells of the IBF table.

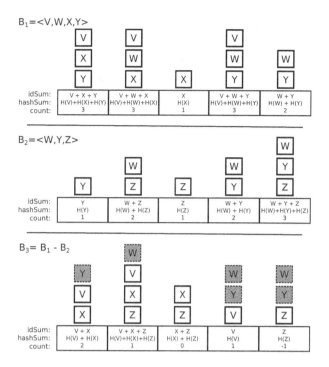

Figure 2: IBF Subtract. IBF B_3 results from subtracting IBF B_2 from IBF B_1 cell by cell. To subtract cells, the `idSum` and `hashSum` fields are XOR'ed, and `count` fields are subtracted. The elements common to B_1 and B_2 (shown shaded) are cancelled during the XOR operation.

V, W, X and Y) and Peer 2 (who has keys W, Y and Z). Each element is hashed into 3 locations: for example, X is hashed into buckets 1, 2 and 3. While X is by itself in bucket 3, after subtraction Z also enters, causing the `count` field to (incorrectly) be zero. Fortunately, after subtraction, bucket 4 becomes pure as V is by itself. Note that bucket 5 is also pure with Z by itself, and is signaled by a count of -1. Decoding proceeds by first deleting either V or Z, and then iterating until no pure cells remain.

Into how many cells should each element be hashed? We refer to this parameter as the `hash_count`. If the `hash_count` is too small, say 1, then there will be a high probability of finding pure cells initially, but once a pure element has been recorded and removed there are no other cells from which to remove it. Thus, two or more keys that have been hashed into the same cell cannot be decoded. On the other hand, if `hash_count` is too big, it is unlikely that there will be a pure element by itself to begin the process. We will show that `hash_count` values of 3 or 4 work well in practice.

Encode. First, assume that we have an oracle which, given S_A and S_B, returns the size of the set difference, d. We will describe the construction of such an oracle in Section 3.2. We allocate an IBF, which consists of a table B with $n = \alpha d$ cells, where $\alpha \geq 1$. Each cell of the table contains three fields (`idSum`, `hashSum` and `count`) all initialized to zero.

Additionally, hosts agree on two hash functions, H_c and H_k, that map elements in $\mathbb{U}$ uniformly into the space $[0, h)$, where $h \leq u$. Additionally, they agree on a value, k, called the `hash_count` which is the number of times each element is hashed. The algorithm for encoding a set S into an IBF is given in Algorithm 1 and illustrated in Figure 1. For each element in S, we generate k distinct random indices into B. To do this we recursively call $H_k()$ with an initial input of s_i and take the modulus by n until k distinct indices have been generated. More simply, an implementation could choose to use k independent hash functions. Regardless, for each index j returned, we XOR s_i into $B[j]$.idSum, XOR $H_c(s_i)$ into $B[j]$.hashSum, and increment $B[j]$.count.

Algorithm 1 IBF Encode

for $s_i \in S$ **do**
    for j in HashToDistinctIndices(s_i, k, n) **do**
        $B[j]$.idSum = $B[j]$.idSum $\oplus s_i$
        $B[j]$.hashSum = $B[j]$.hashSum $\oplus H_c(s_i)$
        $B[j]$.count = $B[j]$.count + 1

Subtract. For each index i in two IBF's, B_1 and B_2, we subtract $B_2[i]$ from $B_1[i]$. Subtraction can be done in place by writing the resulting values back to B_1, or non-destructively by writing values

to a new IBF of the same size. We present a non-destructive version in Algorithm 2. Intuitively, this operation eliminates common elements from the resulting IBF as they cancel from the `idSum` and `hashSum` fields as shown in Figure 2.

Algorithm 2 IBF Subtract ($B_3 = B_1 - B_2$)

for i in $0, \ldots, n-1$ **do**
    $B_3[i]$.idSum = $B_1[i]$.idSum $\oplus B_2[i]$.idSum
    $B_3[i]$.hashSum = $B_1[i]$.hashSum $\oplus B_2[i]$.hashSum
    $B_3[i]$.count = $B_1[i]$.count - $B_2[i]$.count

Decode. We have seen that to decode an IBF, we must recover "pure" cells from the IBF's table. Pure cells are those whose `idSum` matches the value of an element s in the set difference. In order to verify that a cell is pure, it must satisfy two conditions: the `count` field must be either 1 or -1, and the `hashSum` field must equal $H_c(\text{idSum})$. For example, if a cell is pure, then the sign of the `count` field is used to determine which set s is unique to. If the IBF is the result of subtracting the IBF for S_B from the IBF for S_A, then a positive `count` indicates $s \in D_{A-B}$, while a negative `count` indicates $s \in D_{B-A}$.

Decoding begins by scanning the table and creating a list of all pure cells. For each pure cell in the list, we add the value $s =$ idSum to the appropriate output set (D_{A-B} or D_{B-A}) and remove s from the table. The process of removal is similar to that of insertion. We compute the list of distinct indices where s is present, then decrement `count` and XOR the `idSum` and `hashSum` by s and $H_c(s)$, respectively. If any of these cells becomes pure after s is removed, we add its index to the list of pure cells.

Decoding continues until no indices remain in the list of pure cells. At this point, if all cells in the table have been cleared (i.e. all

Algorithm 3 IBF Decode $(B \rightarrow D_{A-B}, D_{B-A})$

> **for** $i = 0$ to $n - 1$ **do**
>> **if** $B[i]$ is pure **then**
>>> Add i to pureList
>> **while** pureList $\neq \emptyset$ **do**
>>> i=pureList.dequeue()
>>> **if** $B[i]$ is not pure **then**
>>>> continue
>>> $s=B[i]$.idSum
>>> $c=B[i]$.count
>>> **if** $c > 0$ **then**
>>>> add s to D_{A-B}
>>> **else**
>>>> add s to D_{B-A}
>>> **for** j in DistinctIndices(s, k, n) **do**
>>>> $B[j]$.idSum = $B[j]$.idSum $\oplus s$
>>>> $B[j]$.hashSum = $B[j]$.hashSum $\oplus H_c(s)$
>>>> $B[j]$.count = $B[j]$.count- c
>> **for** $i = 0$ to $n - 1$ **do**
>>> **if** $B[i]$.idSum $\neq 0$ OR $B[i]$.hashSum $\neq 0$ $B[i]$.count $\neq 0$
>>> **then**
>>>> **return** FAIL
>> **return** SUCCESS

fields have value equal to zero), then the decoding process has successfully recovered all elements in the set difference. Otherwise, some number of elements remain encoded in the table, but insufficient information is available to recover them. The pseudocode is given in Algorithm 3 and illustrated in Figure 3.

3.2 Strata Estimator

To use an IBF effectively, we must determine the approximate size of the set difference, d, since approximately $1.5d$ cells are required to successfully decode the IBF. We now show how to estimate d using $O(\log(u))$ data words, where u is the size of the universe of set values. If the set difference is large, estimators such as random samples [14] and Min-wise Hashing [3, 4] will work well. However, we desire an estimator that can accurately estimate very small differences (say 10) even when the set sizes are large (say million).

Flajolet and Martin (FM) [12] give an elegant way to estimate set sizes (not differences) using $\log(u)$ bits. Each bit i in the estimator is the result of sampling the set with probability $1/2^i$; bit i is set to 1, if at least 1 element is sampled when sampling with this probability. Intuitively, if there are $2^4 = 16$ distinct values in the set, then when sampling with probability $1/16$, it is likely that bit 4 will be set. Thus the estimator returns 2^I as the set size, where I is the highest strata (i.e., bit) such that bit I is set.

While FM data structures are useful in estimating the size of two sets, they do not help in estimating the size of the difference as they contain no information that can be used to approximate which elements are common. However, we can *sample the set difference* using the same technique as FM. Given that IBF's can compute set differences with small space, we use a hierarchy of IBF's as strata. Thus Peer A computes a logarithmic number of IBF's (strata), each of some small fixed size, say 80 cells.

Compared to the FM estimator for set sizes, this is very expensive. Using 32 strata of 80 cells is around 32 Kbytes but is the only estimator we know that is accurate at very small set differences and yet can handle set difference sizes up to 2^{32}. In practice, we build a lower overhead composite estimator that eliminates higher strata and replaces them with a MinWise estimator, which is more accu-

rate for large differences. Note that 32 Kbytes is still inexpensive when compared to the overhead of naively sending a million keys.

Proceeding formally, we stratify $\mathbb{U}$ into $L = \log(u)$ partitions, $P_0, \ldots, P_L$, such that the range of the ith partition covers $1/2^{i+1}$ of $\mathbb{U}$. For a set, S, we encode the elements of S that fall into partition P_i into the ith IBF of the Strata Estimator. Partitioning $\mathbb{U}$ can be easily accomplished by assigning each element to the partition corresponding to the number of trailing zeros in its binary representation.

A host then transmits the Strata Estimator for its set to its remote peer. For each IBF in the Strata Estimator, beginning at stratum L and progressing toward stratum 0, the receiving host subtracts the corresponding remote IBF from the local IBF, then attempts to decode. For each successful decoding, the host adds the number of recovered elements to a counter. If the pair of IBF's at index i fails to decode, then we estimate that the size of the set difference is the value of the counter (the total number of elements recovered) scaled by 2^{i+1}. We give the pseudocode in Algorithms 4 and 5.

We originally designed the strata estimator by starting with stratum 0 and finding the first value of $i \geq 0$ which decoded successfully, following the Flajolet-Martin strategy and scaling the amount recovered by 2^i. However, the estimator in the pseudocode is much better because it uses information in *all* strata that decode successfully and not just the lowest such strata.

In the description, we assumed that the elements in S_A and S_B were uniformly distributed throughout $\mathbb{U}$. If this condition does not hold, the partitions formed by counting the number of low-order zero bits may skew the size of our partitions such that strata i does not hold roughly $|S|/2^{i+1}$. This can be easily solved by choosing some hash function, H_z, and inserting each element, s, into the IBF corresponding to the number of trailing zeros in $H_z(s)$.

Algorithm 4 Strata Estimator Encode using hash function H_z

> **for** $s \in S$ **do**
>> i = Number of trailing zeros in $H_z(s)$.
>> Insert s into the i-th IBF

Algorithm 5 Strata Estimator Decode

> count $= 0$
> **for** $i = \log(u)$ down to -1 **do**
>> **if** $i < 0$ or $\text{IBF}_1[i] - \text{IBF}_2[i]$ does not decode **then**
>>> **return** $2^{i+1} \times$ count
>> count += number of elements in $\text{IBF}_1[i] - \text{IBF}_2[i]$

The obvious way to combine the Strata Estimator and IBF is to have node A request an estimator from node B, use it to estimate d, then request an IBF of size $O(d)$. This would take *two* rounds or at least two round trip delays. A simple trick is to instead have A initiate the process by sending its own estimator to B. After B receives the Strata Estimator from A, it estimates d and replies with an IBF, resulting in *one* round to compute the set difference.

4. ANALYSIS

In this section we review and prove theoretical results concerning the efficiency of IBF's and our stratified sampling scheme.

THEOREM 1. *Let S and T be disjoint sets with d total elements, and let B be an invertible Bloom filter with $C = (k + 1)d$ cells, where $k = \text{hash\_count}$ is the number of random hash functions in B, and with at least $\Omega(k \log d)$ bits in each hashSum field. Suppose that (starting from a Bloom filter representing the empty set) each*

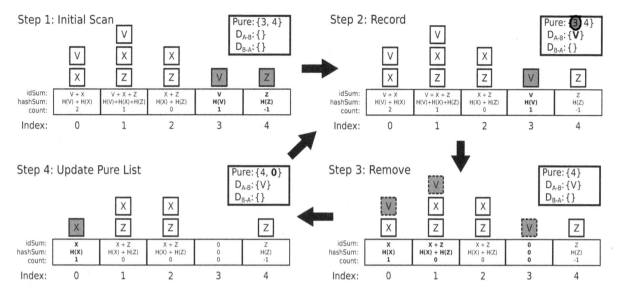

Figure 3: IBF Decode. We first scan the IBF for pure cells and add these indices (3&4) to the Pure list (Step 1). In Step 2, we dequeue the first index from the Pure list, then add the value of the `idSum` to the appropriate output set ($V \to D_{A-B}$). We then remove V from the IBF by using the k hash functions to find where it was inserted during encoding and subtracting it from these cells. Finally, if any of these cells have now become pure, we add them to the Pure list (Step 4). We repeat Steps 2 through 4 until no items remain in the Pure list.

item in S is inserted into B, and each item in T is deleted from B. Then with probability at most $O(d^{-k})$ the IBFDecode operation will fail to correctly recover S and T.

PROOF. The proof follows immediately from the previous analysis for invertible Bloom filters (e.g., see [13]). □

We also have the following.

COROLLARY 1. *Let S and T be two sets having at most d elements in their symmetric difference, and let B_S and B_T be invertible Bloom filters, both with the parameters as stated in Theorem 1, with B_S representing the set S and B_T representing the set T. Then with probability at most $O(d^{-k})$ we will fail to recover S and T by applying the IBFSubtract operation to B_S and B_T and then applying the IBFDecode operation to the resulting invertible Bloom filter.*

PROOF. Define $S' = S - T$ and $T' = T - S$. Then S' and T' are disjoint sets of total size at most d, as needed by Theorem 1. □

The corollary implies that in order to decode an IBF that uses 4 independent hash functions with high probability, then one needs an overhead of $k + 1 = 5$. In other words, one has to use $5d$ cells, where d is the set difference. Our experiments later, however, show that an overhead that is somewhat less than 2 suffices. This gap is narrowed in [13] leveraging results on finding a 2-core (analogous to a loop) in random hypergraphs.

Let us next consider the accuracy of our stratified size estimator. Suppose that a set S has cardinality m, and let i be any natural number. Then the ith stratum of our strata estimator for S has expected cardinality $m/2^i$. The following lemma shows that our estimators will be close to their expectations with high probability.

LEMMA 1. *For any $s > 1$, with probability $1 - 2^{-s}$, and for all $j < i$, the cardinality of the union of the strata numbered j or greater is within a multiplicative factor of $1 \pm O(\sqrt{s2^i/m})$ of its expectation.*

PROOF. Let Y_j be the size of the union of strata numbered j or greater for $j = 0, 1, \ldots, i$, and let μ_j be its expectation, that is, $\mu_j = E(Y_j) = m/2^j$. By standard Chernoff bounds (e.g., see [18]), for $\delta > 0$,

$$\Pr(Y_j > (1 + \delta)\mu_j) < e^{-\mu_j \delta^2/4}$$

and

$$\Pr(Y_j < (1 - \delta)\mu_j) < e^{-\mu_j \delta^2/4}.$$

By taking $\delta = \sqrt{4(s + 2)(2^i/m)\ln 2}$, which is $O(\sqrt{s2^i/m})$, we have that the probability that a particular Y_j is not within a multiplicative factor of $1 \pm \delta$ of its expectation is at most

$$2e^{-\mu_j \delta^2/4} \le 2^{-(s+1)2^{i-j}}.$$

Thus, by a union bound, the probability that any Y_j is not within a multiplicative factor of $1 \pm \delta$ of its expectation is at most

$$\sum_{j=0}^{i} 2^{-(s+1)2^{i-j}},$$

which is at most 2^{-s}. □

Putting these results together, we have the following:

THEOREM 2. *Let ϵ and δ be constants in the interval $(0, 1)$, and let S and T be two sets whose symmetric difference has cardinality d. If we encode the two sets with our strata estimator, in which each IBF in the estimator has C cells using k hash functions, where C and k are constants depending only on ϵ and δ, then, with probability at least $1 - \epsilon$, it is possible to estimate the size of the set difference within a factor of $1 \pm \delta$ of d.*

PROOF. By the same reasoning as in Corollary 1, each IBF at level i in the estimator is a valid IBF for a sample of the symmetric difference of S and T in which each element is sampled with probability $1/2^{i+1}$. By Theorem 1, having each IBF be of $C = (k+1)g$

cells, where $k = \lceil \log 1/\epsilon \rceil$ and $g \geq 2$, then we can decode a set of g elements with probability at least $1 - \epsilon/2$.

We first consider the case when $d \leq c_0^2 \delta^{-2} \log(1/\epsilon)$, where c_0 is the constant in the big-oh of Lemma 1. That is, the size of the symmetric difference between S and T is at most a constant depending only on ϵ and δ. In this case, if we take

$$g = \max \left\{ 2, \lceil c_0^2 \delta^{-2} \log(1/\epsilon) \rceil \right\}$$

and $k = \lceil \log 1/\epsilon \rceil$, then the level-0 IBF, with $C = (k+1)d$ cells, will decode its set with probability at least $1 - \epsilon/2$, and our estimator will learn the exact set-theoretic difference between S and T, without error, with high probability.

Otherwise, let i be such that $d/2^i \approx c_0^2 \delta^2 / \log(1/\epsilon)$ and let $g = \max \left\{ 2, \lceil c_0^2 \delta^{-2} \log(1/\epsilon) \rceil \right\}$ and $k = \lceil \log 1/\epsilon \rceil$, as above. So, with probability $1 - \epsilon/2$, using an IBF of $C = (k+1)d$ cells, we correctly decode the elements in the ith stratum, as noted above. By Lemma 1 (with $s = \lceil \log 1/\epsilon \rceil + 1$), with probability $1 - \epsilon/2$, the cardinality of the number of items included in the ith and higher strata are within a multiplicative factor of $1 \pm \delta$ of its expectation. Thus, with high probability, our estimate for d is within a $1 \pm \delta$ factor of d. $\square$

Comparison with Coding: Readers familiar with Tornado codes will see a remarkable similarity between the decoding procedure used for Tornado codes and IBF's. This follows because set reconciliation and coding are equivalent. Assume that we have a systematic code that takes a set of keys belonging to a set S_A and codes it using check words C_1 through C_n. Assume further that the code can correct for up to d erasures and/or insertions. Note that Tornado codes are specified to deal only with erasures not insertions.

Then, to compute set difference A could send the check words C_1 through C_n *without* sending the "data words" in set S_A. When B receives the check words, B can treat its set S_B as the data words. Then, together with the check words, B can compute S_A and hence the set difference. This will work as long as S_B has at most d erasures or insertions with respect to set S_A.

Thus any code that can deal with erasures and insertions can be used for set difference, and vice versa. A formal statement of this equivalence can be found in [15]. This equivalence explains why the existing deterministic set difference scheme, CPI, is analogous to Reed-Solomon coding. It also explains why IBF's are analogous to randomized Tornado codes. While more complicated Tornado-code like constructions could probably be used for set difference, the gain in space would be a small constant factor from say $2d$ to $d + \epsilon$, the increased complexity is not worthwhile because the real gain in set reconciliation is going down from $O(n)$ to $O(d)$, where n is the size of the original sets.

5. THE KEYDIFF SYSTEM

We now describe *KeyDiff*, a service that allows applications to compute set differences using Difference Digests. As shown in Figure 4, the KeyDiff service provides three operations, add, remove, and diff. Applications can add and remove keys from an instance of KeyDiff, then query the service to discover the set difference between any two instances of KeyDiff.

Suppose a developer wants to write a file synchronization application. In this case, the application running at each host would map files to unique keys and add these keys to a local instance of Key-Diff. To synchronize files, the application would first run KeyDiff's diff operation to discover the differences between the set stored locally and the set stored at a remote host. The application can then perform the reverse mapping to identify and transfer the files that differ between the hosts.

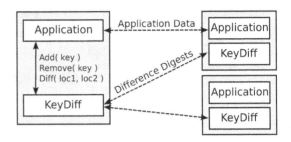

Figure 4: KeyDiff computes the set difference between any two instances and returns this information to the application.

The KeyDiff service is implemented using a client-server model and is accessed through an API written in C. When a client requests the difference between its local set and the set on a remote host, KeyDiff opens a TCP connection and sends a request containing an estimator. The remote KeyDiff instance runs the estimation algorithm to determine the approximate size of the difference, then replies with an IBF large enough for the client to decode with high-probability. All requests and responses between KeyDiff instances travel over a single TCP connection and the diff operation completes with only a single round of communication.

KeyDiff provides faster diff operations through the use of pre-computation. Internally, KeyDiff maintains an estimator structure that is statically sized and updated online as keys are added and removed. However, computing the IBF requires the approximate size of the difference, a value that is not know until after the estimation phase. In scenarios where computation is a bottleneck, Key-Diff can be configured to maintain several IBF's of pre-determined sizes online. After the estimation phase, KeyDiff returns the best pre-computed IBF. Thus, the computational cost of building the IBF can be amortized across all of the calls to add and remove.

This is reasonable because the cost of incrementally updating the Strata Estimator and a few IBF's on key update is small (a few microseconds) and should be much smaller than the time for the application to create or store the object corresponding to the key. For example, if the application is a P2P application and is synchronizing file blocks, the cost to store a new block on disk will be at least a few milliseconds. We will show in the evaluation that if the IBF's are precomputed, then the latency of diff operations can be 100's of microseconds for small set differences.

6. EVALUATION

Our evaluation seeks to provide guidance for configuring and predicting the performance of Difference Digests and the KeyDiff system. We address four questions. First, what are the optimal parameters for an IBF? (Section 6.1). Second, how should one tune the Strata Estimator to balance accuracy and overhead? (Section 6.2). Third, how do IBF's compare with the existing techniques? (Section 6.3). Finally, for what range of differences are Difference Digests most effective compared to the brute-force solution of sending all the keys? (Section 6.4).

Our evaluation uses a $\mathbb{U}$ of all 32-bit values. Hence, we allocate 12 bytes for each IBF cell, with 4 bytes given to each idSum, hashSum and count field. As input, we created pairs of sets containing *keys* from $\mathbb{U}$. The keys in the first set, S_A, were chosen randomly without replacement. We then chose a random subset of S_A and copied it to the second set, S_B. We exercised two degrees of freedom in creating our input sets: the number of keys in S_A, and the size of the difference between S_A and S_B, which we refer to as the experiment's *delta*. For each experiment we created 100

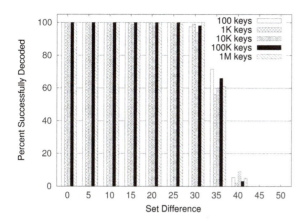

Figure 5: Rate of successful IBF decoding with 50 cells and 4 hash functions. The ability to decode an IBF scales with the size of the set difference, not the size of the sets.

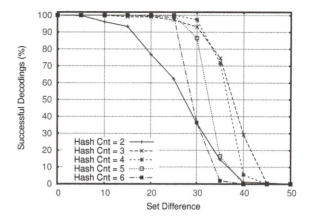

Figure 6: Probability of successful decoding for IBF's with 50 cells for different deltas. We vary the number of hashes used to assign elements to cells (`hash_count`) from 2 to 6.

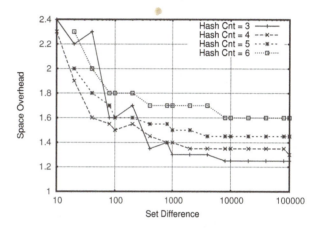

Figure 7: We evaluate sets containing 100K elements and plot the minimum space overhead (IBF cells/delta) required to completely recover the set difference with 99% certainty.

file pairs. As our objective is set reconciliation, we consider an experiment successful only if we are able to successfully determine all of the elements in the set difference.

6.1 Tuning the IBF

We start by verifying that IBF size scales with the size of the set difference and not the total set size. To do so, we generated sets with 100, 1K, 10K, 100K and 1M keys, and deltas between 0 and 50. We then compute the set difference using an IBF with 50 cells.

Figure 5 shows the success rate for recovering the entire set difference. We see that for deltas up to 25, the IBF decodes completely with extremely high probability, regardless of set size. At deltas of 45 and 50 the collision rate is so high that no IBF's are able to completely decode. The results in Figure 5 confirm that decoding success is independent of the original set sizes.

Determining IBF size and number of hash functions. Both the number of IBF cells and `hash_count` (the number of times an element is hashed) are critical in determining the rate of successful decoding. To evaluate the effect of `hash_count`, we attempted to decode sets with 100 keys and deltas between 0 and 50 using an IBF with 50 cells and `hash_count`'s between 2 and 6. Since the size of the sets does not influence decoding success, these results are representative for arbitrarily large sets. We ran this configuration for 1000 pairs of sets and display our results in Figure 6.

For deltas less than 30, `hash_count` = 4 decodes 100% of the time, while higher and lower values show degraded success rates. Intuitively, lower hash counts do not provide equivalent decode rates since processing each pure cell only removes a key from a small number of other cells, limiting the number of new pure cells that may be discovered. Higher values of `hash_count` avoid this problem but may also decrease the odds that there will initially be a pure cell in the IBF. For deltas greater than 30, `hash_count` = 3 provides the highest rate of successful decoding. However, at smaller deltas, 3 hash functions are less reliable than 4, with approximately 98% success for deltas from 15 to 25 and 92% at 30.

To avoid failed decodings, we must allocate IBF's with more than d cells. We determine appropriate memory overheads (ratio of IBF's cells to set-difference size) by using sets containing 100K elements and varying the number of cells in each IBF as a proportion of the delta. We then compute the memory overhead required for 99% of the IBF's to successfully decode and plot this in Figure 7.

Deltas below 200 all require at least 50% overhead to completely

decode. However, beyond deltas of 1000, the memory overhead reaches an asymptote. As before, we see a `hash_count` of 4 decodes consistently with less overhead than 5 or 6, but interestingly, `hash_count` = 3 has the lowest memory overhead at all deltas greater than 200.

6.2 Tuning the Strata Estimator

To efficiently size our IBF, the Strata Estimator provides an estimate for d. If the Strata Estimator over-estimates, the subsequent IBF will be unnecessarily large and waste bandwidth. However, if the Strata Estimator under-estimates, then the subsequent IBF may not decode and cost an expensive transmission of a larger IBF. To prevent this, the values returned by the estimator should be scaled up so that under-estimation rarely occurs.

In Figure 8, we report the scaling overhead required for various strata sizes such that 99% of the estimates will be greater than or equal to the true difference. Based on our findings from Section 6.1, we focus on Strata Estimators whose fixed-size IBF's use a `hash_count` of 4. We see that the scaling overhead drops sharply as the number of cells per IBF is increased from 10 to 40, and reaches a point of diminishing returns after 80 cells. With 80 cells per stratum, any estimate returned by a Strata Estimator

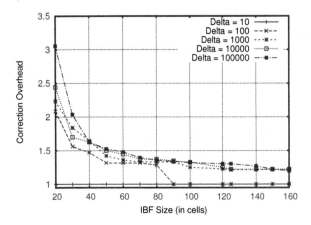

Figure 8: Correction overhead needed by the Strata Estimator to ensure that 99% of the estimates are greater than or equal to the true value of d when using strata IBF's of various sizes.

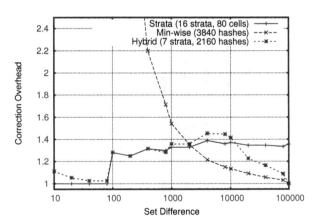

Figure 9: Comparison of estimators when constrained to 15.3 KB. We show the scaling overhead to ensure that 99% of estimates are greater than or equal to the true delta.

should be scaled by a factor of 1.39 to ensure that it will be greater than or equal to d 99% of the time.

Strata Estimator vs. Min-wise. We next compare our Strata Estimator to the Min-wise Estimator [3, 4] (see Section 2). For our comparison we used sets with 100K elements and deltas ranging from 10 to 100K. Given knowledge of the approximate total set sizes a priori, the number of strata in the Strata estimator can be adjusted to conserve communication costs by only including partitions that are likely to contain elements from the difference. Thus, we choose the number of strata to be $\lfloor \log_2(d_{max}) \rfloor$, where d_{max} is the largest possible difference. Since our largest delta is 100K, we configure our estimator with 16 strata, each containing 80 cells per IBF. At 12 bytes per IBF cell, this configuration requires approximately 15.3 KB of space. Alternatively, one could allocate a Min-wise estimator with 3840 4-byte hashes in the same space.

In Figure 9, we compare the scaling overhead required such that 99% of the estimates from Strata and Min-wise estimators of the same size are greater than or equal to the true delta. We see that the overhead required by Min-wise diminishes from 1.35 to 1.0 for deltas beyond 2000. Strata requires correction between 1.33 to 1.39 for the same range. However, the accuracy of the Min-wise estimator deteriorates rapidly for smaller delta values. In fact, for all deltas below 200, the 1st percentile of Min-wise estimates are 0, resulting in infinite overhead. Min-wise's inaccuracy for small deltas is expected as few elements from the difference will be included in the estimator as the size of the difference shrinks. This makes Min-wise very sensitive to any variance in the sampling process, leading to large estimation errors. In contrast, we see that the Strata Estimator provides reasonable estimates for all delta values and is particularly good at small deltas, where scaling overheads range between 1.0 and 1.33.

Hybrid Estimator. The Strata Estimator outperforms Min-wise for small differences, while the opposite occurs for large differences. This suggests the creation of a hybrid estimator that keeps the lower strata to accurately estimate small deltas, while augmenting more selective strata with a single Min-wise estimator. We partition our set as before, but if a strata does not exist for a partition, we insert its elements into the Min-wise estimator. Estimates are performed by summing strata as before, but also by including the number of differences that Min-wise estimates to be in its partition.

For our previous Strata configuration of 80 cells per IBF, each strata consumes 960 bytes. Therefore, we can trade a strata for 240

additional Min-wise hashes. From Figure 9 we see that the Strata Estimator performs better for deltas under 2000. Thus, we would like to keep at most $\lfloor \log_2(2000) \rfloor = 10$ strata. Since we expect the most selective strata to contain few elements for a difference of 2000, we are better served by eliminating them and giving more space to Min-wise. Hence, we retain 7 strata, and use the remaining 8640 bytes to allocate a Min-wise estimator with 2160 hashes.

Results from our Hybrid Estimator are plotted in Figure 9 with the results from the Strata and Min-wise estimators. We see that the Hybrid Estimator closely follows the results of the Strata Estimator for all deltas up to 2000, as desired. For deltas greater than 2000, the influence of errors from both Strata and Min-wise cause the scaling overhead of the Hybrid estimator to drift up to 1.45 (versus 1.39% for Strata), before it progressively improves in accuracy, with perfect precision at 100K. While the Hybrid Estimator slightly increase our scaling overhead from 1.39 to 1.45 (4.3%), it also provides improved accuracy at deltas larger than 10% where over-estimation errors can cause large increases in total data sent.

Difference Digest Configuration Guideline. By using the Hybrid Estimator in the first phase, we achieve an estimate greater than or equal to the true difference size 99% of the time by scaling the result by 1.45. In the second phase, we further scale by 1.25 to 2.3 and set `hash_count` to either 3 or 4 depending on the estimate from phase one. In practice, a simple rule of thumb is to construct an IBF in Phase 2 with twice the number of cells as the estimated difference to account for both under-estimation and IBF decoding overheads. For estimates greater than 200, 3 hashes should be used and 4 otherwise.

6.3 Difference Digest vs. Prior Work

We now compare Difference Digests to Approximate Reconciliation Trees (ART) [5], Characteristic Polynomial Interpolation (CPISync) [17], and simply trading a sorted list of keys (List). We note that ART's were originally designed to compute *most but not all* the keys in $S_A - S_B$. To address this, the system built in [5] used erasure coding techniques to ensure that hosts received pertinent data. While this approach is reasonable for some P2P applications it may not be applicable to or desirable for all applications described in Section 1. In contrast, CPISync and List are always able to recover the set difference.

Figure 10 shows the data overhead required by the four algorithms. Given that ART's were not designed for computing the

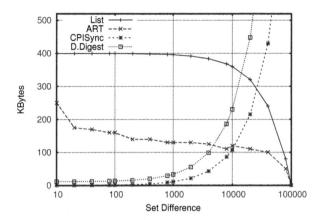

Figure 10: Data transmission required to reconcile sets with 100K elements. We show the space needed by `ART` **and Difference Digests to recover 95% and 100% of the set difference, respectively, with 99% reliability.**

complete set difference, we arbitrarily choose the standard of 95% of the difference 99% of the time and plot the amount of data required to achieve this level of performance with `ART`. For `CPISync`, we show the data overhead needed to recover the set difference. In practice, the basic algorithm must be run with knowledge of the difference size, or an interactive approach must be used at greater computation and latency costs. Hence, we show the best case overhead for `CPISync`. Finally, we plot the data used by Difference Digest for both estimation and reconciliation to compute the complete difference 99% of the time.

The results show that the bandwidth required by `List` and `ART` decreases as the size of the difference increases. This is intuitive since both `List` and the `ART` encode the contents of S_B, which is diminishing in size as the size of the difference grows ($|S_B| = |S_A| - |D|$). However, `ART` outperforms `List` since its compact representation requires fewer bits to capture the nodes in B.

While the size of the Hybrid Estimator stays constant, the IBF grows at an average rate of 24 Bytes (three 4-byte values and a factor of 2 inflation for accurate decoding) per key in the difference. We see that while Difference Digests and `CPISync` have the same asymptotic communication complexity, `CPISync` requires less memory in practice at approximately 10 bytes per element in the difference.

Algorithm Selection Guidelines. The results show that for small differences, Difference Digests and `CPISync` require an order of magnitude less bandwidth that `ART` and are better up to a difference of 4,000 (4%) and 10,000 (10%), respectively. However, the fact that `ART` uses less space for large deltas is misleading since we have allowed `ART` to decode only 95% of the difference. `CPISync` provides the lowest bandwidth overhead and decodes deterministically, making it a good choice when differences are small and bandwidth is precious. However, as we discuss next, its computational overhead is substantial.

6.4 KeyDiff Performance

We now examine the benefits of Difference Digest in system-level benchmarks using KeyDiff service described in Section 5. We quantify the performance of KeyDiff using Difference Digests versus `ART`, `CPISync`, and `List`. For these experiments, we deployed KeyDiff on two dual-processor quad-core Xeon servers

running Linux 2.6.32.8. Our test machines were connected via 10 Gbps Ethernet and report an average RTT of 93μs.

Computational Overhead. In the KeyDiff model, the applications at the client and server both add keys to KeyDiff. When `diff` is called the client requests the appropriate data from the server to compute the set difference. We begin by evaluating the computation time required to add new keys to KeyDiff and the time required by the server to generate its response when using each algorithm. For this experiment, we added 1 million keys to the KeyDiff server then requested a structure to decode a difference of 100. In Table 1, we show the average time required for these operations.

For adding new keys, we see that `List` and `ART` are slower than both `CPISync` and `IBF` since both perform $\log(|S|)$ operations — the `List` to do an ordered insertion, and `ART` to update hashes along a path in its tree. In contrast, `CPISync` and `IBF` simply store the new keys to an unordered list until they learn the size of the structure to build from the client's request.

For server compute time, we note that the latencies correspond closely with the number of memory locations each algorithm touches. `List` is quickest at 6.545 msec, as the server only needs to read and serialize the keys. In contrast, `IBF` and `CPISync` must allocate and populate appropriately-sized structures by scanning their stored lists of keys. For `IBF` this requires updating 4 cells per key, while `CPISync` must evaluate 100 linear equations, each involving all 1M keys. The time for `ART` is roughly twice that of `IBF` as it must traverse its tree containing $2|S|$ nodes, to build a Bloom Filter representation of its set.

At the bottom of Table 1, we show the add and server-compute times for the three estimation algorithms. Note that since the length of the IBF's in the Strata and Hybrid estimators are static, they can be updated online. We also note that although the Hybrid estimator maintains 2160 Min-wise hash values, its addition times are significantly lower that the original Min-wise estimator. This occurs because the Min-wise structure in the Hybrid estimator only samples the elements not assigned to one of the seven strata. Thus, while the basic Min-wise estimator must compute 3840 hashes for each key, the Hybrid Min-wise estimator only computes hashes for approximately $1/2^8$ of the elements in the set. Since each of the estimators is updated during its add operations, minimal server compute time is required to serialize each structure.

Costs and Benefits of Incremental Updates. As we have seen in Table 1, the server computation time for many of the reconciliation algorithms is significant and will negatively affect the speed of our `diff` operation. The main challenge for `IBF` and `CPISync` is that the size of the difference must be known before a space-efficient structure can be constructed. We can avoid this runtime computation by maintaining several IBF's of predetermined sizes within KeyDiff. Each key is added to all IBF's and, once the size of the difference is know, the smallest suitable IBF is returned. The number of IBF's to maintain in parallel will depend on the computing and bandwidth overheads encountered for each application.

In Table 1, we see that the time to add a new key when doing pre-computation on 8 IBF's takes 31μs, two orders of magnitude longer than IBF without precomputation. However, this reduces the server compute time to from 3.9 seconds to 22μs, a massive improvement for `diff` latency. For most applications, the small cost (10's of microseconds) for incremental updates during each add operation should not dramatically affect overall application performance, while the speedup during `diff` (seconds) is a clear advantage.

Diff Performance. We now look at time required to run the `diff` operation. As we are primarily concerned with the performance of computing set differences as seen by an application built on top of these algorithms, we use incremental updates and measure

Reconciliation Algorithm	Add (μs)	Serv. Compute
List (sorted)	1.309	6.545 msec
ART	1.995	6,937.831 msec
CPISync (d=100)	0.216	34,051.480 msec
IBF (no precompute)	0.217	3,957.847 msec
IBF (1x precompute)	3.858	0.023 msec
IBF (8x precompute)	31.320	0.022 msec

Estimation Algorithms (precompute)		
Min-wise (3840 hashes)	21.909	0.022 msec
Strata (16x80 cells)	4.224	0.021 msec
Hybrid (7x80 cells + 2160 hash)	4.319	0.023 msec

Table 1: Time required to add a key to KeyDiff and the time required to generate a KeyDiff response for sets of 1M keys with a delta of 100. The time per `add` call is averaged across the insertion of the 1M keys.

the wall clock time required to compute the set difference. Difference Digests are run with 15.3 KB dedicated to the Estimator, and 8 parallel, precomputed IBF's with sizes ranging from 256 to 400K cells in factors of 4. To present the best case scenario, CPISync was configured with foreknowledge of the difference size and the correctly sized CPISync structure was precomputed at the server side. We omit performance results for ART as it has the unfair advantage of only *approximating* the membership of D_{A-B}, unlike the other algorithms, which return all of D_{A-B} and D_{B-A}.

For our tests, we populated the first host, A with a set of 1 million, unique 32-bit keys, S_A, and copied a random subset of those keys, S_B, to the other host, B. From host A we then query KeyDiff to compute the set of unique keys. Our results can be seen in Figure 11a. We note that there are 3 components contributing to the latency for all of these methods, the time to generate the response at host B, the time to transmit the response, and the time to compare the response to the set stored at host A. Since we maintain each data structure online, the time for host B to generate a response is negligible and does not affect the overall latency.

We see from these results that the List shows predictable performance across difference sizes, but performs particularly well relative to other methods as the size of the difference increases beyond 20K. Since the size of the data sent *decreases* as the size of the difference increases, the transmission time and the time to sort and compare at A decrease accordingly. On the other hand, the Difference Digest performs best at small set differences. Since the estimator is maintained online, the estimation phase concludes very quickly, often taking less than 1 millisecond. We note that precomputing IBF's at various sizes is essential and significantly reduces the latency by the IBF's construction at host B at runtime. Finally, we see that even though its communication overhead is very low, the cubic decoding complexity for CPISync dramatically increases its latency at differences larger than 100.

In considering the resources required for each algorithm, List requires $4|S_B|$ bytes in transmission and touches $|S_A| + |S_B|$ values in memory. Difference Digest has a constant estimation phase of 15.3KB followed by an average of $24d$ bytes in transmission and $3d \times$ `hash_count` memory operations (3 fields in each IBF cell). Finally, CPISync requires only $10d$ bytes of transmission to send a vector of sums from it's linear equations, but d^3 memory operations to solve its matrix.

If our experimental setup were completely compute bound, we would expect List to have superior performance for large differences and Difference Digest to shine for small difference. If we assume a `hash_count` of 4, then Difference Digest's latency is

$12d$, while List's is $|S_A| + |S_B| = 2|S_A| - d$. Thus, they will have equivalent latency at $d = \frac{2}{12+1}|S_A|$, or a difference of 15%.

Guidance for Constrained Computation. We conclude that, for our high-speed test environment, precomputed Difference Digests are superior for small deltas (less than 2%), while sending a full list is preferable at larger difference sizes. We argue that in environments where computation is severely constrained relative to bandwidth, this crossover point can reach up to 15%. In such scenarios, precomputation is vital to optimize `diff` performance.

Varying Bandwidth. We now investigate how the latency of each algorithm changes as the speed of the network decreases. For this we consider bandwidths of 10 Mbps and 100Kbps, which are speeds typical in wide-area networks and mobile devices, respectively. By scaling the transmission times from our previous experiments, we are able to predict the performance at slower network speeds. We show these results in Figure 11b and Figure 11c.

As discussed previously, the data required by List, CPISync, and Difference Digests is $4|S_B|$, $10d$ and roughly $24d$, respectively. Thus, as the network slows and dominates the running time, we expect that the low bandwidth overhead of CPISync and Difference Digests will make them attractive for a wider range of deltas versus the sorted List. With only communication overhead, List will take $4|S_B| = 4(|S_A| - d)$, which will equal Difference Digest's running time at $d = \frac{4}{24+4}|S_A|$, or a difference of 14%. As the communication overhead for Difference Digest grows due to widely spaced precomputed IBF's the trade off point will move toward differences that are a smaller percentage of the total set size. However, for small to moderate set sizes and highly constrained bandwidths KeyDiff should create appropriately sized IBF's on demand to reduce memory overhead and minimize transmission time.

Guidance for Constrained Bandwidth. As bandwidth becomes a predominant factor in reconciling a set difference, the algorithm with the lowest data overhead should be employed. Thus, List will have superior performance for differences greater than 14%. For smaller difference sizes, IBF will achieve faster performance, but the crossover point will depend on the size increase between precomputed IBF's. For constrained networks and moderate set sizes, IBF's could be computed on-demand to optimize communication overhead and minimize overall latency.

7. CONCLUSIONS

We have shown how Difference Digests can efficiently compute the set difference of data objects on different hosts using computation and communication proportional to the size of the set difference. The constant factors are roughly 12 for computation (4 hash functions, resulting in 3 updates each) and 24 for communication (12 bytes/cell scaled by two for accurate estimation and decoding).

The two main new ideas are whole set differencing for IBF's, and a new estimator that accurately estimates small set differences via a hierarchy of sampled IBF's. One can think of IBF's as a particularly simple random code that can deal with both erasures and insertions and hence uses a simpler structure than Tornado codes but a similar decoding procedure.

We learned via experiments that 3 to 4 hash functions work best, and that a simple rule of thumb is to size the second phase IBF equal to twice the estimate found in the first phase. We implemented Difference Digests in a KeyDiff service run on top of TCP that can be utilized by different applications such as Peer-to-Peer file transfer. There are three calls in the API (Figure 4): calls to add and delete a key, and a call to find the difference between a set of keys at another host.

In addition, using 80 cells per strata in the estimator worked well and, after the first 7 strata, augmenting the estimator with Min-

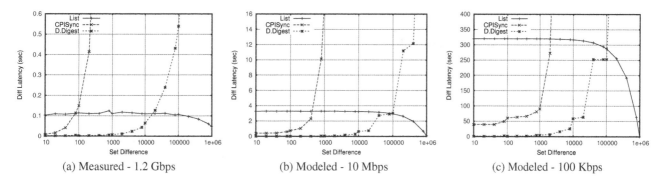

(a) Measured - 1.2 Gbps	(b) Modeled - 10 Mbps	(c) Modeled - 100 Kbps

Figure 11: Time to run KeyDiff `diff` for $|S_A| =$ 1M keys and varying difference sizes. We show our measured results in 11a, then extrapolate the latencies for more constrained network conditions in 11b and 11c.

wise hashing provides better accuracy. Combined as a Difference Digest, the IBF and Hybrid Estimator provide the best performance for differences less than 15% of the set size. This threshold changes with the ratio of bandwidth to computation, but could be estimated by observing the throughput during the estimation phase to choose the optimal algorithm.

Our system level benchmarks show that Difference Digests must be precomputed or the latency for computation at runtime can swamp the gain in transmission time compared to simple schemes that send the entire list of keys. This is not surprising as computing a Difference Digest touches around *twelve* 32-bit words for each key processed compared to *one* 32-bit word for a naive scheme that sends a list of keys. Thus, the naive scheme can be 10 times faster than Difference Digests *if we do no precomputation*. However, with precomputation, if the set difference is small, then Difference Digest is ten times or more faster. Precomputation adds only a few microseconds to updating a key.

While we have implemented a generic Key Difference service using Difference Digests, we believe that a KeyDiff service could be used by some application involving either reconciliation or deduplication to improve overall user-perceived performance. We hope the simplicity and elegance of Difference Digests and their application to the classical problem of set difference will also inspire readers to more imaginative uses.

8. ACKNOWLEDGEMENTS

This research was supported by grants from the NSF (CSE-2589 & 0830403), the ONR (N00014-08-1-1015) and Cisco. We also thank our shepherd, Haifeng Yu, and our anonymous reviewers.

9. REFERENCES

[1] Data domain. http://www.datadomain.com/.

[2] B. Bloom. Space/time trade-offs in hash coding with allowable errors. *Commun. ACM*, 13:422–426, 1970.

[3] A. Broder. On the resemblance and containment of documents. *Compression and Complexity of Sequences, '97*.

[4] A. Z. Broder, M. Charikar, A. M. Frieze, and M. Mitzenmacher. Min-wise independent permutations. *J. Comput. Syst. Sci.*, 60:630–659, 2000.

[5] J. Byers, J. Considine, M. Mitzenmacher, and S. Rost. Informed content delivery across adaptive overlay networks. In *SIGCOMM*, 2002.

[6] J. W. Byers, M. Luby, M. Mitzenmacher, and A. Rege. A digital fountain approach to reliable distribution of bulk data. In *SIGCOMM*, 1998.

[7] G. Cormode and S. Muthukrishnan. What's new: finding significant differences in network data streams. *IEEE/ACM Trans. Netw.*, 13:1219–1232, 2005.

[8] G. Cormode, S. Muthukrishnan, and I. Rozenbaum. Summarizing and mining inverse distributions on data streams via dynamic inverse sampling. *VLDB '05*.

[9] D. Eppstein and M. Goodrich. Straggler Identification in Round-Trip Data Streams via Newton's Identities and Invertible Bloom Filters. *IEEE Trans. on Knowledge and Data Engineering*, 23:297–306, 2011.

[10] L. Fan, P. Cao, J. Almeida, and A. Broder. Summary cache: a scalable wide-area web cache sharing protocol. *IEEE/ACM Transactions on Networking (TON)*, 8(3):281–293, 2000.

[11] J. Feigenbaum, S. Kannan, M. J. Strauss, and M. Viswanathan. An approximate L^1-difference algorithm for massive data streams. *SIAM Journal on Computing*, 32(1):131–151, 2002.

[12] P. Flajolet and G. N. Martin. Probabilistic counting algorithms for data base applications. *J. of Computer and System Sciences*, 31(2):182 – 209, 1985.

[13] M. T. Goodrich and M. Mitzenmacher. Invertible Bloom Lookup Tables. *ArXiv e-prints*, 2011. 1101.2245.

[14] P. Indyk and R. Motwani. Approximate nearest neighbors: towards removing the curse of dimensionality. *STOC*, 1998.

[15] M. Karpovsky, L. Levitin, and A. Trachtenberg. Data verification and reconciliation with generalized error-control codes. *IEEE Trans. Info. Theory*, 49(7), july 2003.

[16] P. Kulkarni, F. Douglis, J. Lavoie, and J. M. Tracey. Redundancy elimination within large collections of files. In *USENIX ATC*, 2004.

[17] Y. Minsky, A. Trachtenberg, and R. Zippel. Set reconciliation with nearly optimal communication complexity. *IEEE Trans. Info. Theory*, 49(9):2213 – 2218, 2003.

[18] R. Motwani and P. Raghavan. *Randomized Algorithms*. Cambridge Univ. Press, 1995.

[19] S. Muthukrishnan. Data streams: Algorithms and applications. *Found. Trends Theor. Comput. Sci.*, 2005.

[20] R. Schweller, Z. Li, Y. Chen, Y. Gao, A. Gupta, Y. Zhang, P. A. Dinda, M.-Y. Kao, and G. Memik. Reversible sketches: enabling monitoring and analysis over high-speed data streams. *IEEE/ACM Trans. Netw.*, 15:1059–1072, 2007.

[21] B. Zhu, K. Li, and H. Patterson. Avoiding the disk bottleneck in the data domain deduplication file system. In *FAST'08*.

DOF: A Local Wireless Information Plane

Steven Hong, Sachin Katti
Stanford University
{hsiying,skatti}@stanford.edu

Abstract

The ability to detect what unlicensed radios are operating in a neighborhood, their spectrum occupancies and the spatial directions their signals are traversing is a fundamental primitive needed by many applications, ranging from smart radios to coexistence to network management to security. In this paper we present DOF, a detector that in a single framework accurately estimates all three parameters. DOF builds on the insight that in most wireless protocols, there are hidden repeating patterns in the signals that can be used to construct unique signatures, and accurately estimate signal types and their spectral and spatial parameters. We show via experimental evaluation in an indoor testbed that DOF is *robust and accurate*, it achieves greater than 85% accuracy even when the SNRs of the detected signals are as low as 0 dB, and even when there are multiple interfering signals present. To demonstrate the benefits of DOF, we design and implement a preliminary prototype of a smart radio that operates on top of DOF, and show experimentally that it provides a 80% increase in throughput over Jello, the best known prior implementation, while causing less than 10% performance drop for co-existing WiFi and Zigbee radios.

Categories and Subject Descriptors

C.4 [**Computer Systems Organization**]: Performance of Systems

General Terms

Algorithms, Performance, Design

1. INTRODUCTION

The ability to detect what unlicensed radios are operating in a neighborhood, what parts of the spectrum they are occupying, and what spatial directions their signals are traversing is a fundamental primitive that is needed by many applications. For example, smart and agile radios such as [28, 22] could use it to detect what spectral resources are unused, and exploit them to provide high throughput. They could detect what spatial directions are unoccupied, and directionally steer their signals to further increase capacity. They could also use the primitive to be gentle when needed, if a low power medical wireless sensor is operating in the neighborhood, the smart ra-

dio could detect it and take extra measures to avoid causing interference to the sensor, lest some critical communication is impaired. Similarly, network administrators can use such a primitive to manage their "airspace", improve channel allocation and diagnose performance problems. Recent work [27] has explored using detectors that compute what spatial directions signals arrive at for wireless network security. Thus, a large and growing number of applications could benefit from such a primitive.

However, building such a detector that operates accurately across the large range of SNRs signals exhibit, in the presence of multiple interfering signals, or in the rich indoor multipath environment of the unlicensed ISM band is hard. Prior implemented systems have mostly focused on spectrum occupancy detection, and used threshold based methods that estimate changes in received signal energy [16] or the variations in the FFT [28] to estimate spectrum occupancy. However, optimal thresholds that work accurately across the rich variety of conditions (in SNR, multipath, interference etc) are hard to pick, and consequently these methods have low accuracy. Other work [22, 16] has used higher layer protocol behavior signatures to detect radio types. However, these techniques also rely on threshold based methods to detect the protocol behavior, and suffer from the same problems as above.

In this paper we present **D**egrees **O**f **F**reedom (DOF), *a single framework that accurately detects what radios exist in a neighborhood, what parts of the spectrum they occupy, and their angles of arrival (AoA) at the detector*. We believe this to be a first. DOF is *robust* and works accurately (around 90% accuracy) in a large SNR range (0 to 30dB) as well as in the presence of multiple interfering signals. DOF is *passive* and does not impose any measurement overhead, it can operate even when the detecting radio is being used for other communication. Finally, DOF is *efficient* to implement, it builds on top of commonly available FFT modules and requires modest extra resources (30% more computation compared to a standard FFT).

The key insight behind DOF is the observation that for most wireless protocols, *there are hidden repeating patterns that are unique and necessary for their operation*. For example, Wifi uses a repeating cyclic prefix to avoid intersymbol interference between consecutive OFDM symbols. A Zigbee radio has a repeating pulse which it uses for QPSK data transmission, Bluetooth has a Gaussian pulse on which it modulates data bits using FSK that is repeating with a different frequency and so on. DOF exploits the existence of these patterns to create unique signatures for each signal type. Further, DOF shows that the same signatures can also be exploited to determine the spectrum occupied and the AoA of that signal type.

Algorithmically, DOF extracts feature vectors using the following key idea: if a signal has a repeating hidden pattern, then a delayed version of the signal correlated with the original signal will show peaks at specific delay intervals. These intervals form a signature for each signal and can be used to extract feature vectors. We build on prior work [9, 19] in cyclostationary signal analysis to design an efficient feature extraction technique based on standard FFT operations. However, DOF's key contribution over prior work in cyclostationary analysis is to show that the extracted feature vector encodes information about the component signal types, what spectrum they occupy, as well as what AoAs they arrive at the detecting radio. DOF designs a novel SVM decision tree to classify component signal types, and new algorithms to estimate their spectrum occupancies as well as AoAs from the feature vector.

We implement DOF using the fftw [1] library and GnuRadio [3] software on a wideband radio that is capable of operating over the entire 100 MHz ISM band and has 4 MIMO antennas. We evaluate DOF using testbed experiments in an indoor office environment and compare it to three prior approaches, RFDump [16] for signal type, Jello [28] for spectrum occupancy, and SecureAngle [27] for AoA estimation (the best known implemented systems for each component respectively). We find that:

- DOF is accurate and robust at all SNRs, it classifies co-existing radio types with greater than 85% accuracy even at SNRs as low as 0dB. On the other hand, RFDump is at most 60% accurate at SNRs lower than 8dB.
- DOF is robust to interference, achieving more than 82% accuracy in detecting component signal types even when there are three overlapping and interfering signals. The compared approach RFDump cannot operate in this case.
- DOF's spectrum occupancy estimates are more than 85% accurate at low SNRs or in the presence of interference. The compared approach, Jello has an error of 35%, and cannot detect individual spectrum occupancies of interfering component signals.
- DOF's AoA estimation error is less than 6 degrees for SNRs as low as 0dB, and is the same as SecureAngle.

DOF is practical and can be applied to many problems. While we leave most of DOF's applications to future work, we demonstrate the potential benefits of DOF for building smart and agile radios by designing and implementing a preliminary prototype, DOF-SR. The key novel component in DOF-SR is that it's aggressiveness in scavenging for unused spectral resources can be tuned by a user specified policy so that interference to co-existing radios is controlled. To demonstrate this flexibility we implement three sample policies, from one which only uses unoccupied spectrum and minimizes interference to co-existing radios to ones which use microwave oven occupied spectrum and compete with co-existing WiFi radios. We deploy DOF-SR in our indoor testbed and compare it with Jello [28] (which uses edge detection for finding unused spectrum). Our evaluation shows that DOF-SR provides nearly a 80% throughput increase over Jello in crowded environments. Further, the co-existing WiFi/Zigbee radios suffer less than 10% throughput drop with DOF-SR, while Jello can cause nearly a 45% throughput drop. DOF-SR outperforms because it can accurately detect (un)occupied spectrum even at low SNRs as well as the occupying signal types, allowing it to more accurately scavenge unused spectrum, yet guarantee that it does not affect the co-existing radios.

2. RELATED WORK

DOF bridges and builds upon related work in signal detection and cyclostationary signal analysis. We discuss both of them below.

2.1 Signal Detection

Detecting Radio Type: Prior work such as RFDump and others [16, 22] has used unique protocol characteristics (e.g. $10\mu s$ delay between data and ACK WiFi packets) to infer radio type. The basic approach is to detect the start and end of packets using energy detection in the time domain, and use the delays between packets to estimate radio type. However, energy detection is not accurate at medium to low SNR, and fails if there are multiple interfering signals as we show in our evaluation in Sec. 6. Other work [20] has used preamble correlation to detect radio type by exploiting known preambles at the start of a packet. However this technique doesn't work for legacy analog signals such as microwaves, cordless phones etc which don't have preambles. Further, as prior work has shown [10], preamble correlation requires coarse synchronization to the carrier frequency of the detected signal, which becomes expensive given the large number of carrier frequencies for different radio types in the ISM band.

Detecting Spectrum Occupancy: Prior work such as Jello [28] has used edge detection on the power spectral density of the received signal to estimate spectrum occupancy. The basic idea is to compute the slope of the PSD at every point, and detect signal starts and ends based on thresholds on the slope. However, at low SNRs and for signals whose spectral masks are not of good quality, the accuracy of this approach is low because noise and spectral leakage can cause sharp spikes in the slope away from where the signal is located. Further, this approach fails when we have multiple interfering signals who also overlap in the frequency domain, since a edge will be detected as soon as the first signal ends, in spite of the second signal which occupies some more portion of the spectrum. Other approaches based on energy detection such as SpecNet [12] also suffer at low SNRs and are unable to distinguish between overlapping signals.

Detecting Angle of Arrival: Prior work such as SecureAngle [27] has used classic AoA estimation algorithms [14, 6, 23] to compute AoAs of the incoming signals. These approaches are highly accurate, and we show in our evaluation that DOF's accuracy is similar. Further, DOF can automatically associate a signal type with the AoA (e.g. a WiFi signal is impinging at $45°$), while prior approaches need separate detectors to associate signal type.

DOF thus provides a single framework that estimates all three parameters, and with accuracy better than the best known implemented techniques for each component.

2.2 Cyclostationary Signal Analysis

DOF builds on prior work in cyclostationary signal analysis, which was pioneered in the early 90's through the work of Gardner [9], and has been used widely in a variety of applications [11, 24, 17, 29]. Further, recent work [8, 7] has used neural network classifiers with cyclostationary features to detect the type of modulation used in a received signal. Finally, recent work has implemented cyclostationary techniques on the USRP platform [21, 19, 4] and evaluated its effectiveness for detection and rendezvous in cognitive networks.

As we will see in Sec. 3, DOF builds on this prior work to design an efficient feature extraction technique. However, DOF differentiates itself from all prior work in cyclostationary signal analysis in the following ways:

- DOF designs an efficient linear-time classification technique based on hierarchical SVMs to estimate the type of multiple overlapping signals. Prior approaches based on neural networks [8, 7] have cubic computational complexity and those based on SVMs [15] are limited to classifying a single signal. DOF's technique is robust to the presence of multiple interfering signals and can reuse the same SVM decision tree for classifying all component signal types. To the best of our knowledge, we are not aware of prior work in cyclostationary analysis that has handled detection of multiple interfering signals.
- DOF extends cyclostationary signal analysis to detect angle of arrivals, and designs a novel algorithm that computes AoAs as well as associates the signal type with the signal on each AoA.
- DOF is implemented on a wideband radio, and has been eval-

uated extensively in an indoor testbed with five different interfering signal types (WiFi, Bluetooth, Zigbee, Analog Cordless phones and microwave signals). We are not aware of any work that provides a similar extensive evaluation.

- We also design and build a preliminary prototype of a smart radio based on DOF, and show experimentally how it can be used to increase network capacity without harming other radios.

3. OVERVIEW & DESIGN

DOF operates on windows of raw samples from the ADC which do not undergo any demodulation, decoding or synchronization. These raw samples are processed to extract feature vectors, which are then used to detect signal types, the corresponding spectrum occupancies and the AoAs of the signals at the detector. Before discussing the detailed design, we provide the high level intuition behind DOF.

3.1 Intuition

The key insight behind DOF is that almost every radio protocol used for communication has hidden repeating patterns. For example, an OFDM PHY (used in WiFi) has a cyclic prefix (CP) where at the end of each OFDM symbol block, the symbols from the start are repeated. The CP serves two purposes, first it helps in avoiding intersymbol interference, and second it helps in preserving orthogonality of the OFDM subcarriers [26]. Thus a CP is an important attribute of the OFDM PHY itself, and necessary for its correct operation. Similarly, every other protocol operating in the ISM band has repeating patterns, that are unique and needed for their correct operation.

Note that these patterns are fundamental to the corresponding physical layers and are present in every packet (data, ACK and for every bitrate). These patterns are not some quirk of a specific hardware implementation or PHY layer parameter setting (e.g. different channel transmission times for a 1500B packet based on what bitrate is used in WiFi). Hence these patterns can potentially form a robust signature that is invariant to differences in hardware or PHY layer parameters.

How can we use the existence of these hidden patterns to detect the signal type, occupied spectrum and angle of arrival? We can use the following key trick from cyclostationary signal analysis [9]: *if a signal has a repeating pattern, then if we correlate the received signal against itself delayed by a fixed amount, the correlation will peak when the delay is equal to the period at which the pattern repeats.* Specifically, lets denote the raw signal samples we are receiving by $x[n]$. Consider the following function

$$R_x^\alpha(\tau) = \sum_{n=-\infty}^{\infty} x[n][x^*[n-\tau]]e^{-j2\pi\alpha n} \quad (1)$$

For an appropriate value of τ corresponding to the time period between the repeating patterns, the above value will be maximized, since the random patterns in $x[n]$ will be aligned. Further, these peak values occur only at periodic intervals in n. Hence the second exponential term $e^{-j2\pi\alpha n}$ is in effect computing the frequency α at which this hidden pattern repeats. We define such a frequency as a *pattern frequency*, and Eq. 1 is known as the Cyclic Autocorrelation Function (CAF) [9] at a particular pattern frequency α and delay τ. The CAF will exhibit a high value only for delays and pattern frequencies that correspond to repeating patterns in the signal.

Figure. 1 shows the 2-D CAF plots for a received signal that has WiFi and Zigbee signals interfering with each other. As explained above, WiFi uses OFDM, and has a repeating cyclic prefix, as well as other repeating patterns. In the CAF plot, we see spikes corresponding to these repeating patterns at different pattern frequencies and delays. Similarly, the Zigbee signal shows spikes at pattern frequencies corresponding to how its pulse repeats. Note the stark difference

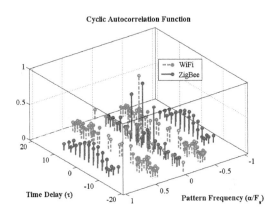

Figure 1: Cyclic Autocorrelation Function for WiFi and Zigbee - The spikes at different pattern frequencies are due to the repeating OFDM CP, and the repeating pulse on which QPSK symbols are modulated in Zigbee.

in the locations of the spikes for pattern frequencies for WiFi and Zigbee. The differentiability in spike locations enables DOF to distinguish both signals even when they are interfering with each other.

DOF uses the locations of these pattern frequencies as signatures for different signal types. In the following sections we expand on this insight and explain the design of the classifier, spectrum occupancy and AoA detection algorithms, which are DOF's main and novel contributions. However, to make these algorithms practical, we first need to efficiently evaluate the Cyclic Autocorrelation Function at the relevant pattern frequencies. Hence we first discuss DOF's feature extraction step, which borrows ideas from cyclostationary signal processing to design an efficient extraction algorithm.

4. DESIGN

DOF's design consists of 4 stages and an overview of the architecture is shown in Figure 2.

4.1 Feature Extraction

DOF's feature extraction component computes feature vectors from the digital samples delivered by the ADC. Our algorithm builds on a rich body of prior work in cyclostationary signal analysis [9], and is conceptually similar to recent work in whitespace radios that uses cyclostationary analysis to detect primary TV transmitters. Our main contribution here is the adaptation of the algorithm to work for the multitude of signals in the ISM band and an efficient implementation that works on a 100MHz wideband radio.

As described in 3.1 the feature extraction step is supposed to find the prominent pattern frequencies which represent the frequencies at which repeating patterns manifest in the different PHYs. However, instead of using the CAF defined in Eq. 1, we use an equivalent representation called the Spectral Correlation Function (SCF) [9]:

$$S_x^\alpha(f) = \sum_{\tau=-\infty}^{\infty} R_x^\alpha(\tau)e^{-j2\pi\tau} \quad (2)$$

The SCF is equal to the frequency transform of the CAF. Since frequency transforms are unitary, both representations are equivalent. If the CAF peaked for a certain value of τ, then the SCF will peak for a particular value of f that is inversely proportional to τ. Intuitively, the reason for this is that if a hidden pattern repeats at a lag of τ, then by definition it repeats for every integer multiple of τ.

The reason for moving to the SCF is that it can be computed efficiently [21] for discrete time windows as follows

$$S_x^\alpha(f) = \frac{1}{L}\sum_{l=0}^{L-1} X_{lN}(f)X_{lN}^*(f-\alpha) \quad (3)$$

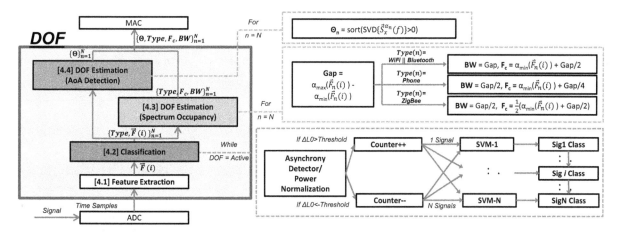

Figure 2: Overview of DOF showing the overall architecture and where it sits in the stack. Extracted features are first classified by signal type and then processed to determine which wireless degrees of freedom are in use. DOF then passes the distilled information up to the MAC layer which can utilize the information as it sees fit.

where $X_{lN}(f)$ is the FFT of the received signal for the l'th time window of length N samples, $*$ is the complex conjugate, and the summation is over L consecutive time windows of the received signal.

The key thing to note in Eq 3 is that the SCF can be expressed as a product of the FFTs of the received signal. Hence to compute the SCF at any pattern frequency α, one just has to take the product of the received signal's FFT with itself albeit shifted in the frequency domain by α. FFTs are very efficient to implement in hardware [13], and any wireless PHY that would use OFDM would already have an FFT hardware module. Hence we believe that the SCF can be easily computed using existing hardware. We compute and evaluate the computational complexity and verify the above claim in Sec. 5.

Feature Extraction: Finally, we summarize DOF's feature vector. Given the universe of signal types to detect (WiFi, Zigbee, cordless phones, microwaves and Bluetooth currently), we first determine the union of the unique sets of pattern frequency and frequency tuples contained in each type's signature. Let this union consist of the following M tuples, $(\alpha_1, f_1), ..., (\alpha_M, f_M)$, then the feature vector $\vec{F}$ is defined as:

$$F(i) = (S_x^{\alpha_i}(f_i)) \qquad \forall i = 1, ..., M \qquad (4)$$

The components of the feature vector are values of the SCF at different points, unique to the corresponding signal types.

4.2 Estimating Signal Type

DOF designs a novel decision tree based on SVMs [5] which allows it to classify multiple component signal types in an interfered signal using the extracted feature vectors. A SVM classifier takes an input feature vector, $\vec{F}$, and predicts the signal type T if any that exists in the received signal. These classifiers are trained using a small labeled dataset. It's common to regularize the feature vectors using a kernel function such as a Gaussian kernel [5] and project them to higher dimensions to make the feature vectors belonging to different types linearly separable, we use the same technique in DOF.

A naive method of using these classifiers is to train a SVM classifier using labeled data collected by transmitting from a particular radio and computing the corresponding feature vector from the received signal, and doing so for different radio types and locations. However, this generic off-the-shelf SVM design fails to work. The reason is that DOF expects to accurately detect signal types even when the received signal has multiple interfering signals in it. Interference significantly distorts feature vectors and throws off the SVM classifier. Specifically, the SCF for an interfered signal at a particular pattern

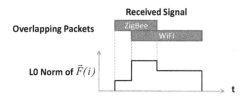

Figure 3: Detecting the Number of Signals - Asynchrony between packets causes differences in the L0 Norm of $\vec{F}$

frequency α can be shown to be equal to [9]:

$$S_X^\alpha(f) = a^2 S_{X_1}^\alpha(f) + b^2 S_{X_2}^\alpha(f) + R \qquad (5)$$

where X_1 and X_2 are the interfering signals with amplitudes a and b. R is a residual term representing cross-talk between the two signals. Thus the feature vector will be a sum of the feature vectors if the signals alone had been present without interference scaled according to their respective powers, plus a term that represents the crosstalk. The unique pattern frequencies for each component signal type are retained, but after kernel regularization, the test feature vector itself will not correspond to any of the training feature vectors the SVM classifier has been trained on.

One naive approach to this problem would be to train SVMs for all possible combinations of signals. However, this approach quickly gets out of hand, since the classifier has to account for the fact that the interfering signals will have different unknown powers, and consequently the feature vectors will be clustered differently for each combination of powers. Training classifiers for all possible signal combinations and powers is prohibitively expensive.

4.2.1 Robust & Efficient Classification

DOF builds a decision tree that can efficiently identify multiple component signal types in an interfering signal via two steps:

1) Exploiting Asynchrony: Transmissions from different nodes in the real world rarely overlap with each other perfectly since transmissions from two independent nodes will very likely be asynchronous as shown in Fig. 3. DOF exploits this idea to compute two quantities: the number of component signals in the received signal, and their average individual power.

To determine how many signals are present, DOF uses the following idea: if a new signal starts interfering, then the feature vector DOF extracts will start showing many new non-zero components due to the unique features belonging to the new signal. Hence, we can use the following algorithm to compute the number of interfering signals:

1. Keep track of the l_0 norm (i.e. the number of non-zero components) of the computed feature vector.

2. If the l_0 norm exhibits a sudden shift, then declare a change in the number of interfering signals. If the l_0 norm shift is positive, then a new signal has started interfering, if the change is negative, then one of the interfering signals has stopped.

The above algorithm begins by initializing the counter for the number of signals to zero. Hence, the algorithm continuously keeps track of the number of interfering signals at any point.

Second, DOF exploits the fact that the total power of the received signal is equal to the sum of the powers of the constituent signals and noise. Hence, as the received signal samples are received, DOF keeps a moving window average of the power at that point. If DOF detect a new signal, it estimates the power of the new signal, as the new received signal power minus the received signal power before the presence of a new signal was detected. Thus, DOF detects the number of component signals, as well as their powers in the received signal. It exploits this information in classifying the constituent signal types, as we explain next.

2) Constructing the SVMs: DOF exploits knowledge of the number of signal types and their powers computed above to design an efficient SVM decision tree for classification. The basic idea is to train a small number of classifiers equal to the number of signal types we wish to detect (currently five signal types in our implementation): one classifier for the case where the received signal has zero or one signal type, another classifier when the received signal has two signal types and so on. These classifiers are trained with labeled datasets that are generated by taking labeled data from experiments where there is a single signal type in the collected data, and adding them up after normalizing their powers. For example, if we have labeled data containing WiFi signals at power P_1 and another labeled dataset containing Zigbee signals at power P_2, to create one labeled data point for the classifier meant for two signals, we would add the two datasets above after normalizing their powers to be equal. By taking different numbers and combinations of signal types and repeating the above procedure, we create five training sets for the five SVM classifiers.

The above technique has two advantages. First, we only need to train five classifiers, significantly smaller than the naive approach which needs at least 31 different SVM classifiers (one for each combination of signal types and possibly more for different powers). Second, collecting training data is relatively easy, since we only have to collect data from controlled experiments where there is a single radio operating, and we can artificially add them up later to generate data for classifiers attempting to detect multiple interfering signal types.

To use these classifiers in practice however, we need to normalize the amplitudes of the computed feature vectors since the classifiers were trained on data where the component signals had equal power. To accomplish this, we exploit that we can compute the powers of the individual signals using asynchrony as we explained in the previous section. For example, lets say we are classifying a signal which we have estimated to have two different component signals with powers P_1 and P_2, and the signal X_1 starts before X_2. Due to asynchrony, we have an interference free part of X_1 and consequently an interference free estimate of the corresponding feature vector F_1. When we get to the part of the signal where these two signals interfere, we multiply the components of the new feature vector that were also non-zero in the original feature vector by P_2, and the remaining components by P_1. In effect, we have normalized the feature vectors corresponding to both components to have the same amplitude $P_1 P_2$. Now, the classifiers that were trained on normalized data can proceed to classify the component signal types.

The above technique recursively generalizes to any number of interfering signals, since we can use the above procedure whenever we detect that a new signal has started interfering. Similarly, we can reverse the technique when we detect that one of the signals has stopped. Specifically, if we detect via the l_0 norm technique that the number of signal types has reduced by 1, and the total observed power drops by P', then we just normalize the remaining feature vector components by $1/P'$.

4.3 Estimating Spectrum Occupancy

After identifying signal type, DOF computes the carrier frequency and bandwidth of each signal type. The key idea is that the feature vectors that were extracted for detecting type also encode information about the carrier frequency and the bandwidth of the signal. The reason is that almost every wireless communication signal modulates constellation symbols (e.g. QAM) on top of standard bandwidth-limited pulses such as raised cosine filters. The pulse rate is directly proportional to the bandwidth for that signal (e.g. 5MHz for Zigbee). This repeating pulse gives rise to specific pattern frequencies whose value is a function of the bandwidth and the carrier frequency of that signal. For OFDM signals like WiFi, instead of a pulse we have the CP that repeats at a frequency proportional to the bandwidth of the signal. DOF leverages these relationships in building its spectrum occupancy estimation algorithm.

To see why feature vectors encode information about the carrier frequency and bandwidth, consider the following BPSK signal that is representative of transmitted wireless signals

$$s(t) = b \cos(2\pi f_b t) e^{j 2\pi f_c t} \qquad (6)$$

where $b = \pm 1$ represents the bits and the $\cos(2\pi f_b t)$ represents the pulse on which the bits are modulated, and f_b is the bandwidth used for transmission, and f_c is the carrier frequency. Note that typically for spectrum masking purposes more specialized pulses than simple cosines are used, but for our explanation, this representation suffices.

Lets assume the center frequency of our detector is $f_{c'}$ and the gap with the transmitted signal's carrier frequency is $\delta f = |f_c - f_{c'}|$. This gap just shifts the FFT of the signal by the same amount δf. To see how the SCF for the received signal looks, lets first compute the CAF for this with $\tau = 0$

$$CAF(s(t)) = b^2 e^{-2\pi \delta f t} + b^2 \cos(4\pi f_b t) \qquad (7)$$

As discussed before, the SCF is just the FFT of the CAF. From the above equation it becomes clear that when we take its FFT, we will see two spikes, one at δf, and one at $2f_b$, giving us two prominent pattern frequencies at these locations. The location of the two pattern frequencies along with the knowledge of the detector's center frequency $f_{c'}$ is sufficient to compute the bandwidth and carrier frequency of the transmitted signal.

The above technique generalizes to every communication radio (including analog radios such as cordless phones), i.e. the Spectral Correlation Function of a signal will exhibit a prominent value at a pattern frequency corresponding to some function of f_c, f_b. Table 1 lists the pattern frequencies that are observed in the SCF which are direct functions of the carrier frequency and occupied bandwidth for different signal types. This table serves as the basis of DOF's algorithm for spectrum occupancy and carrier frequency estimation.

However, the above technique has two caveats. First, for Bluetooth signals which employ frequency hopping over 1 MHz intervals at a rate of 1600 hops/second, the per hop period is $1/1600 = 625 \mu s$. In our current implementation, our spectrum occupancy algorithm runs over a window of roughly $1ms$ intervals. Hence, DOF may estimate multiple spectrum occupancies for Bluetooth signals, since a Bluetooth signal could hop multiple times in 1ms. Second, the above

Table 1: Relationship between Pattern Frequencies and Bandwidth/Carrier Frequency

Signal Type	Pattern Frequency Locations
WiFi	all α's between $[f_c - \frac{BW}{2}, f_c + \frac{BW}{2}]$
Bluetooth	$f_c, f_c + \frac{BW}{2}, f_c - \frac{BW}{2}$
Analog Phone	$f_c, f_c + BW, f_c - BW$
ZigBee	$2f_c + BW, 2f_c - BW$

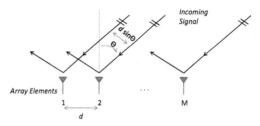

Figure 4: Uniform Linear Array - Sensing a plane wave impinging at an angle θ

intuition does not work for non communication signals such as microwave ovens because we are unable to exploit packet asynchrony to determine the number of signals present in the time window. However, as prior work has shown [25], microwave signals can be modeled as FM signals with a sweeping bandwidth that is equal to the AC power switching frequency. We can leverage this model to initialize our asynchrony detector counter based on the number of feature vectors when the counter is set to zero, and also compute the occupied spectrum for microwave signals due to these feature vectors.

Finally, note that one cannot determine bandwidth occupancy directly from signal type. While the detected signal type (e.g. WiFi) can tell us what is the expected signal bandwidth (e.g. 20MHz for Wifi), it cannot tell us what carrier frequency is used since WiFi has 11 different channels. The above technique determines both bandwidth and carrier frequency directly from the feature vectors.

4.4 Estimating Angles of Arrival

The final component of DOF is angle of arrival (AoA) estimation for each signal type detected. DOF designs a novel and efficient algorithm that extends cyclostationary analysis to also compute AoAs. The key insight is that we can leverage already known information about the unique pattern frequencies corresponding to a signal type to extract their AoAs. We demonstrate the basic idea using a simple uniform linear MIMO antenna array (ULA) [23] as our antenna geometry. Our algorithm generalizes to any antenna geometry, but ULA suffices for exposition.

Lets assume that we have M antennas and our radio receives $N < M$ signals that exhibit pattern features at unique $\alpha_n \; \forall n = 1, \ldots, N$ and arrive at AoAs $\theta_i \; \forall i = 1, \ldots, N$ respectively. A uniform linear array by definition has all its antennas on a line with equal spacing between them as shown in Fig. 4. Because the antennas are equally spaced, a signal at a particular angle of arrival θ has a difference in propagation distance that results in a time delay at the mth antenna with respect to the first antenna of

$$\tau_m(\theta) = (m-1)\frac{d \sin \theta}{c} \qquad (8)$$

where c is the rate of propagation (speed of light for free space) through the medium and d is the inter-antenna spacing. A delay in the time domain manifests itself as a phase shift as long as the narrowband assumption holds (the bandwidth of the signal does not exceed the channel's coherence bandwidth) and so the received signal at the M antennas modeled as a summation of all the interfering components is equal to

$$\boldsymbol{y}(t) = \sum_{n=1}^{N} \phi(\theta_n) x_n(t) + \boldsymbol{n}(t) \qquad (9)$$
$$= \boldsymbol{\Phi} \boldsymbol{x}(t) + \boldsymbol{n}(t)$$

where $\boldsymbol{x} = [x_1 \ldots x_N]^T$ with each x_n corresponding to the signal arriving at angle θ_n, $\boldsymbol{y} = [y_1 \ldots y_N]^T$ is the vector consisting of signals received at the M antennas, $\phi(\theta_n) = [1 \; e^{j2\pi f_c \tau_2(\theta_n)} \ldots e^{j2\pi f_c \tau_M(\theta_n)}]^T$ and $\boldsymbol{\Phi} = [\phi(\theta_1) \ldots \phi(\theta_n)]$ where f_c is the carrier frequency.

The objective of any AoA estimation algorithm is to compute the N column vectors in the AoA matrix ϕ, since they directly provide

the corresponding AoAs for each of the N signal types. The typical approach is to do a search over the space of possible matrices, and algorithms differ in how the search is conducted. The key contribution in our algorithm is a way to leverage the computed pattern frequencies to significantly reduce the search space and thus enable fast AoA computation, as well as automatically associate the computed AoAs with the corresponding signal type.

Lets assume we have detected a particular signal type and that it has a unique *pattern frequency* α_u and is arriving at a single AoA θ_u. DOF's algorithm first computes the Spectral Correlation Matrix $\mathbf{S}_{\mathbf{y}}^{\alpha_u}$ of the received signal at the M antennas [1] at the unique pattern frequency α_u. We omit the proof for brevity, but we can show that this matrix is related to the AoA vector $\phi(\theta_u)$ as follows:

$$\vec{S}_y^{\alpha_u}(f) = \Phi(\theta_u) \vec{S}_x^{\alpha_u}(f) \Phi(\theta_u)^H \qquad (10)$$

where $(\cdot)^H$ denotes the conjugate transpose operation. Since α_u is unique to this signal type, $\vec{S}_x^{\alpha_u}(f)$ will be a diagonal matrix, which implies that $\Phi(\theta_u)$ is the eigenvector of the computed matrix $\vec{S}_y^{\alpha_u}$. Hence, in order to compute the AoA for this signal type, we just have to compute the eigenvector of the matrix computed in Eq. 10. Because this computation is only performed at the *pattern frequencies corresponding to the received signal* and not all possible pattern frequencies, we are able to reduce the overall computation and associate signal type with each angle.

In practice due to multipath effects, each signal type will arrive at multiple AoAs. Due to this instead of a single eigenvector as above, we will have multiple eigenvectors, each corresponding to a different angle at which this signal arrives.

There are two important takeaways from this section:
- By detecting signal types we obtain a list of corresponding unique pattern frequencies. These are directly used in the AoA algorithm described above to efficiently calculate AoAs.
- By the very nature of the algorithm, i.e. our use of the unique pattern frequencies for the detected signal types, the computed AoAs are naturally and accurately associated with the corresponding signal types.

5. IMPLEMENTATION

DOF is implemented in C using a fast FFT implementation from FFTW [1] on a PC with an Intel Core i7 980x processor and 8GB of RAM. We use a wideband radio [18] (shown in Fig. 5) with a frontend bandwidth of 100MHz spanning the entire ISM band. The wideband radio is a modified channel sounder that was originally designed for taking channel measurements by sending user specified pilots. We modify the frontend to be able to send and receive arbitrary waveforms in the entire 100MHz ISM band. The frontend has a carrier

---

[1] a generalization for MIMO signals of the Spectral Correlation Function defined in earlier sections for single signals

20MHz	40MHz	60MHz	80MHz	100MHz
0.4	0.8	1.4	1.8	2.5

Table 2: Microbenchmarks - CPU time normalized wrt actual signal time of the trace

frequency of 2.45GHz and a max output power of 15dBm. However, similar to other SDR platforms such as USRP2s, the interconnect between the SDR frontend and the PC does not meet the latency requirements needed to implement timing sensitive MAC functions such as ACKs. DOF's algorithms operate on the raw digital samples collected by the wideband frontend. We provide a microbenchmark for our implementation in Sec. 5.1.

5.1 Complexity

In this section we discuss the computational complexity of DOF. We compare DOF's complexity against the simple and widely used PSD based edge/energy detector [28, 16, 22]. For AoA estimation, we compare it against the MUSIC algorithm [23] used in prior work such as SecureAngle [27].

Computational Complexity: The main computationally intensive task in DOF is the feature extraction step, which involves computing Eq. 3 for every component in the feature vector. The complexity is dictated by the choice of the FFT length N and the averaging window L. Higher values of N and L provide better resolution for the FFT and SCF respectively [9] and consequently higher accuracy for DOF, but also increase complexity. In our current implementation, we find that $N = 512$ and $L = 16$ suffices for DOF to work accurately over the 100MHz ISM band. Prior energy/edge based approaches [28] use a 256 point FFT, but were implemented over narrowband USRP2 radios with at most 10MHz bandwidth, while DOF works over a wideband radio with 100MHz bandwidth. We believe that prior work would have to use at least a 512 length FFT to operate over such widebands, otherwise the spectral resolution would be too low resulting in inaccuracy. (we verified the inaccuracy with 256 length FFTs experimentally for one prior approach [28]).

DOF and edge/energy detection share the same FFT complexity [2] of $5N \log N = 20384$ floating point operations per window. Next, DOF computes the $K = 80$ feature vector components by averaging over 16 windows, which costs another $4 * 16 * 80 = 5120$ floating point operations. Note that prior FFT based approaches [28, 22] also have to perform this averaging to smooth the FFT and avoid false positives. Our radio type classifier has an l_0 norm estimator and equalizer, that require $K + N \approx 600$ comparisons. The SVM classifiers require $K = 80$ real multiplications, while the spectrum occupancy estimation algorithm requires a small number of extra operations equal to the number of signal types detected. Thus in total, DOF requires 6000 extra floating point operations, in addition to the 20384 floating point operations that the FFT requires. Hence DOF's extra complexity is less than 30% over a standard FFT which we believe is reasonably modest.

Energy detection of course cannot compute AoAs, hence we compare DOF's complexity with the MUSIC algorithm [23] that is used in prior work [27]. The order computational complexity of MUSIC as well as DOF's AoA estimation algorithm is $O(PM^3)$, where M is the number of antennas and P is the number of distinct AoAs. However, we find empirically that the constant in the order notation is significantly smaller for DOF. This is because the MUSIC algorithm involves computing eigenvectors for a series of matrices as it converges to the correct AoAs. DOF on the other hand has to compute the eigenvectors only once as described in Section 4.4.

To summarize, DOF has modestly higher if not similar computational complexity compared to traditional energy/edge detectors, and actually lower complexity than other AoA methods. However,

Figure 5: Testbed layout and wideband software radio

as we will see in the next section, DOF significantly outperforms energy/edge based approaches and has additional features such as signal type detection that energy/edge based detectors do not provide. Hence, we believe that the additional complexity is a reasonable tradeoff given the significant gains in functionality and accuracy.

Micro-benchmark: Table 2 provides benchmark results for DOF's current software implementation. We calculate the normalized time by dividing the wall clock time used by our system divided by the actual signal time on the air. The goal is to see how close to "realtime" our system is. We provide benchmarks as we vary the bandwidth of the radio from 20MHz to 100MHz in increments of 20MHz. A larger bandwidth naturally means a faster stream of data to keep up with.

DOF performs in realtime for radios with bandwidths of up to 40MHz and starts falling behind with higher bandwidths. However, this is a software based implementation of the FFT (which requires the most computation), and we believe a hardware implementation would be significantly faster and be able to handle higher bandwidths. Further these benchmarks compare favorably with prior work [16].

6. EVALUATION

In this section we evaluate the accuracy of DOF and determine how different factors such as signal SNR, the number of interfering signals impact its performance using testbed experiments. Our current implementation is geared towards 5 common signal types in the ISM band - WiFi, Zigbee, Bluetooth, analog/digital cordless phones and microwave signals.

We first summarize our findings:

- DOF's performance is robust to the SNR of the detected signals. We find that DOF achieves greater than 85% accuracy even when the SNR of the detected signals is as low as 0dB. The best known prior approach have errors greater than 40% for SNRs below 8dB. [16]
- DOF's performance is robust to interference between detected signals. We find that DOF accurately classifies all component signals with greater than 82% accuracy even with 3 interfering signals. Prior approaches do not work with interfered signals.
- DOF's spectrum occupancy estimates are at least 85% accurate, at SNRs as low as 0dB and in the presence of multiple overlapping and interfering signals. The best known prior approach achieves an accuracy of 65% under similar conditions.
- DOF's AoA estimation is as accurate as the best known prior technique [23]. Further, unlike prior work it accurately associates the estimated AoAs with the correct type for the signal arriving at that angle.

Compared Approaches: We compare against the best known implemented systems for each component in DOF. First we compare against RFDump [16] which uses timing and phase analysis for detecting radio types. Second, we compare against Jello [28] which uses edge detection on the FFT to detect occupied spectrum. Finally, we compare against SecureAngle's [27] MUSIC technique [23] for computing AoA.

Testbed: The testbed for the experimental results consists of an indoor office environment with cubicle-style office rooms (see Fig.5). The total office size was 105ft × 48ft, the ceiling height was 10ft, and

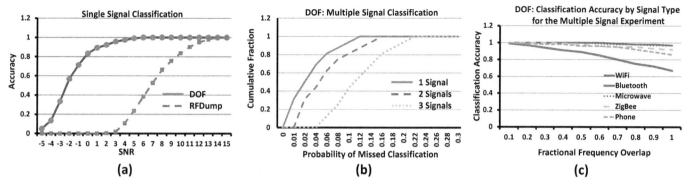

Figure 6: DOF has high classification accuracy over a large range of SNRs and for multiple interfered signals.

the height of the cubicle partitions was 5.5ft. Our wideband radio was placed at three different locations as shown by the shaded circles in Fig. 5, while the radios that we wish to detect (WiFi, Zigbee, cordless phones, bluetooth devices and microwaves) are placed randomly in the office and allowed to transmit. The measurements were taken when the office was empty, and ambient interference from sources outside our control (the departmental WiFi network, microwaves etc) was absent. While the design of DOF was tested using data from a 100 MHz channel sounder, note that conceptually DOF will work with any stream of raw data which can be obtained via commodity software radios such as USRPs. We used the channel sounder as opposed to USRPs because we wanted to demonstrate the full breadth of DOF's capabilities and did not want the range of our tests to be curbed by the limitations of the data acquisition device.

Training Data: The DOF SVM classifiers are first trained with labeled data generated via controlled experiments in the testbed. The training signals are generated by randomly turning on one of the five radios at a random location with randomly picked PHY parameters when applicable (bitrate, channel etc). Turning on means continuously transmitting packets for WiFi, Zigbee and Bluetooth radios, making a continuous call for the cordless phone and powering on for the microwave oven. We generate 30 labeled points for each radio type. The SVMs for detecting multiple signal types are trained by synthetically combining the single signal labeled data as described in Sec. 4.2. Hence the training complexity of DOF is relatively modest. Note that once DOF is trained, the training data allows DOF to operate in any physical environment so long as the training is representative of all possible parameters that a signal could have (bitrate, modulations, etc.). But for signals which aren't FCC-certified (e.g. microwaves), training has to be done specific to each instance since those protocols are not governed by a uniform specification.

Calculating SNR: In our plots, the reader will often see measurements at SNRs as low as −5dB. The reason we are able to calculate such low SNRs is our wideband radio, which is a modified channel sounder. Specifically, the sounder was initially designed to conduct wide area surveying for a WiMax network deployment. In such scenarios, such low SNRs need to be measured and the sounder comes equipped with a proprietary technique that allows two sounders to be placed at separate locations and yet accurately measure the SNR between them even when it is as low as −5dB. We leverage this capability to measure the SNRs in our experiments.

6.1 Estimating Signal Types

We evaluate DOF's accuracy in detecting component signal types in the received signal and compare it to the accuracy of RFDump [16], defining accuracy as the probability of correct classification.

Method: For each run, we pick a random subset of the five different radio types. We place the corresponding radios at a random location, randomly set their PHY parameters (bitrate, channel etc) in the

testbed and allow them to transmit. We also measure the SNR of the channel from each location. The same received samples are passed to the DOF detector and the RFDump detector - both algorithms are run at the same bandwidth. Because RFDump was not designed for such a large bandwidth, it does not work if there are multiple signals overlapping in time and for legacy radios such as cordless phones and microwave ovens. Hence for RFDump, we eliminate traces with multiple interfered signals, or if they have analog phone or microwave signals in them and compute its accuracy only for the remaining three signal types. Fig. 6 plots the accuracy of DOF and RFDump against SNR when there is a single signal. Because SNR doesn't work as a metric when there are multiple interfered signals, we plot the CDF of the error across all experimental runs in Fig. 6.

Analysis: Figs. 6(a) and 6(b) show that DOF has high classification accuracy over a large range of SNRs and for multiple interfered signals. DOF achieves an accuracy ranging from $85 - 100\%$, even for SNRs as low as 0dB when there is a single signal present. For multiple interfered signals, DOF achieves an accuracy greater than 85% at least 90% of the time even when there are three interfered signals in the trace. DOF is robust to SNR because our feature vector components are calculated by correlating and integrating repeated patterns over long intervals, hence even if individual samples have low power, the integration over the entire interval yields very prominent features. Also since the repeating patterns are unique to each signal and uncorrelated with other signal types, they are quite robust to the presence of interfering signals.

RFDump achieves an accuracy of at most 60% when the SNR of the detected signal is between between −5 to 8dB. RFDump uses two techniques, timing analysis and phase analysis to classify signal types. Timing analysis is based on detecting start and end of packets using energy detection, while the phase analysis component is dependent on computing statistics of the phases of received samples which use phase modulation such as Zigbee and Bluetooth. Both operations are error prone at medium to low SNRs, since noise significantly affects the accuracy of energy detection, and distorts the received phases affecting the phase statistics. Finally, RFDump fails to work in the presence of multiple interfering signals, since it cannot detect start or end of packets reliably when signals overlap in time, and phases are distorted when there is a strong additive interferer.

Why is accuracy slightly lower for interfering signals? DOF's accuracy is slightly lower when there are multiple interfering signals present in the received signal. Because DOF's ability to classify multiple interfering signals hinges on how well it is able to exploit asynchrony, at first glance it seems like this may be the root of the problem. Upon closer inspection, we found that while asynchrony detection errors are present, they account for a small fraction of the overall errors. Asynchrony detection errors occur when the offset between different transmissions is shorter than the cyclic feature pro-

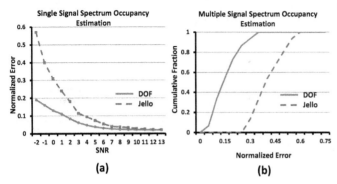

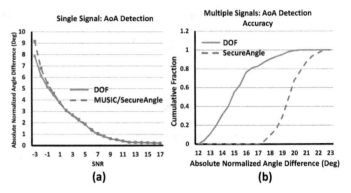

(a) (b) (a) (b)

Figure 7: DOF is more accurate than edge detection at low SNRs and with multiple interfering signals in estimating occupied spectrum

Figure 8: AoA Estimation Accuracy - Single Signal accuracy is accurate even at low SNRs but when multiple radios are operating, there are often more significant AoA's than our detectors are able to discern, a fundamental limit due to the number of antennas in our system.

cessing time. Because an FFT of length 512 using FFTW [1] can be performed in $4\mu s$ and the extra complexity of cyclic feature extraction is $< 30\%$ over that of a standard FFT (sec. 5), the probability of repeatedly missing the offset between asynchronous transmissions (WiFi, ZigBee, and Bluetooth all have packet lengths on the order of 100's of μs to a few ms) is small.

The main reason for the lower accuracy is that certain low-power and low-bandwidth signals are not detected in some corner cases when there is strong frequency overlap. Fig. 6 plots the accuracy of our classification for different signal types as a function of the frequency overlap from another signal. Frequency overlap between signals of the same type is rare because their identical MAC protocols act as a mechanism to prevent this. When signals do overlap, this is because they are of different types. Referring to Table 1, different types of signals centered at the same carrier frequency exhibit distinct patterns. Thus overall, DOF's classification accuracy does not deteriorate drastically when signals overlap, except for Bluetooth, which we can see drops with increasing overlap. The reason is that Bluetooth signals have a low bandwidth of 1 MHz. If the signal is overlapped in frequency by a stronger signal like WiFi, then DOF fails to even detect the Bluetooth signal. Bluetooth signals only have a few unique features because of their simple structure and small bandwidth, while a WiFi signal has a rich feature set some of which are close to the Bluetooth pattern frequencies. Consequently, DOF ends up not detecting the Bluetooth signal, resulting in lower accuracy.

6.2 Estimating Occupied Spectrum

In this section, we evaluate the accuracy of DOF's spectrum occupancy estimation, and compare it with the edge detection based approach in Jello [28]. To make a fair comparison, we allow Jello to use the same 512 length FFT as DOF.

Method: The experiment is conducted similar to the above classification experiments and the raw dump of the received signal at our wideband radio is sent to DOF's and Jello's spectrum occupancy estimators. We take the estimated occupied spectrum from both systems, and compute the absolute error for both. The error is computed as the sum of the estimated occupied spectrum components that are not actually occupied plus the estimated unoccupied spectrum which is actually occupied. We normalize the error by the ground truth spectrum occupancy. We plot two separate figures, Fig. 7(a) plots the error vs SNR of the detected signal when there is a single received signal in the trace and Fig. 7(b) plots the CDF of normalized errors when there are more than 1 potentially overlapping signals in the trace.

Analysis: Fig. 7(a) shows that DOF is reasonably accurate in estimating occupied spectrum. The normalized error in estimating occupied spectrum is around 15% at low SNR and reduces to 5% at higher SNR, but never approaches 0 because of the FFT size which inherently limits resolution.

Fig. 7(b) plots the CDF of errors when there is more than one signal in the received trace. DOF achieves a median error of 15% in these experiments, slightly higher than the single sender case. Apart from the FFT resolution, the other contributor to the error is overlapping signals in the frequency domain. As in the classification case, when a strong signal overlaps in frequency with a weak signal like Bluetooth, it becomes hard to even detect that the Bluetooth signal exists and consequently we miss its feature vector components. Hence, the spectrum occupancy error is slightly higher.

Jello performs less accurately, especially at low SNR and with multiple interfering signals. The reason is that edge detection (the technique used in Jello) is based on computing the slope of the PSD. However, at low SNRs noise introduces sufficient fluctuations that we encounter large slopes in the derivative of the signal at frequencies away from where the transmitted signal lies. Further, edge detection can get confused when there are two partially overlapping signals in frequency. The reason is that when the overlap ends, there will be a sharp drop in the PSD level (because we went from two signals to one signal at that frequency). This can be mistaken to be the end of the occupied spectrum since the PSD is relatively flat after that transition. Consequently, as we see in Fig. 7 Jello has a higher median error of 40% in our experiments.

6.3 Estimating Angle of Arrival

In this section, we evaluate the accuracy of DOF's AoA estimation component. However, unlike the prior experiments, we cannot compare against ground truth here. The indoor environment is a multipath environment, and a transmitted signal can arrive at multiple angles simultaneously. We have no way of knowing exactly what scattering takes place and consequently the ground truth AoAs. Hence we conduct the experiment as follows: We use two of our wideband radios, one equipped with 4 antennas and another with 8 antennas arranged in a ULA. As in the previous experiments, we randomly pick a subset of the radios among our five different types, place them at a random location and let them transmit. For the trace from the 8-antenna radio, we apply the standard MUSIC technique [23] to estimate all AoAs. The reason is that with such a large antenna array, MUSIC is almost guaranteed to accurately find all the significant AoAs. We consider these angles to be the ground truth.

Next, we give the trace collected at the 4-antenna radio to DOF as well as SecureAngle's [27] MUSIC method. Our logic for picking 4 antennas is to make it consistent with state of the art MIMO hardware, which comes with around 4 antennas. We then compute the absolute error of the estimates from DOF and SecureAngle, which is computed by summing the following values: absolute value of each estimated angle minus the closest ground truth angle. The absolute error is normalized by the number of estimated angles. Fig. 8(a) plots the normalized angle error vs the SNR when the trace contains a single signal type, while Fig. 8(b) plots the CDF of normalized errors when it contains more than one signal.

Analysis: Fig. 8(a) shows that DOF computes the AoAs with an accuracy of at least 5 degrees even at low SNRs when there is a single signal. SecureAngle's accuracy is similar. The reason for the relatively worse performance at very low SNR is that the estimation algorithm uses projections of the Spectral Correlation Function matrix to compute angles of arrival, and the projections have a slight contribution from noise. At very low SNRs, the contribution is relatively significant, and hence causes a higher estimation error.

As we see in Fig. 8(b) both DOF and SecureAngle perform slightly worse when there are multiple signals. DOF's median error is around 14 degrees, while SecureAngle's is 19 degrees. The reason is that the number of AoAs that can be accurately detected is a function of the number of antennas a radio has. With 4 antennas, we can detect at most 4 significant angles of arrival [23]. However with multiple signals in a rich multipath environment, there will be significant signal strength along a number of angles, sometimes larger than 4. Both DOF and SecureAngle get confused in this case. However, we note that this is a fundamental problem [23], regardless of the algorithm, the number of antennas a node has places a sharp upper bound on how many AoAs can be distinguished.

7. APPLICATION TO SMART RADIOS

The most direct uses of DOF are in designing smart radios, network management, indoor localization and performance diagnosis. While we leave most of these to future work, we design DOF-SR, a preliminary prototype of a wideband smart radio to demonstrate the benefits of DOF. Our design is inspired by recent work in smart radios, including Jello [28] and others [22]. We compare DOF-SR with Jello [28], the most recent state of the art system for such designs.

7.1 DOF-SR

DOF-SR is a wideband policy-aware smart radio design that operates over the entire 100MHz ISM band. The key technical contribution in DOF-SR is its ability to take advantage of the accurate detecting substrate DOF provides to let users specify a policy that tunes how aggressive the radio is going to be in scavenging for spectral resources. To demonstrate the policy flexibility, we design three sample policies and implement them in our current prototype of DOF-SR

1. **P0**: Only use unoccupied spectrum.
2. **P1**: Use all unoccupied spectrum. Further use spectrum occupied by microwave oven radiation.
3. **P2**: Use all unoccupied spectrum as well as parts occupied by microwave oven radiation. Further, compete for spectrum occupied by WiFi radios and get half the time share on that part of the spectrum.

The three policies are ordered in increasing amounts of aggressiveness. The first policy plays it safe and is similar to the one used by Jello. The second is more aggressive, but still avoids harming any co-existing radio that is used for communication. The third is the most aggressive, and encodes the notion that since WiFi is also another unlicensed radio, it is fair to compete and obtain half the time on spectrum used by WiFi too. However, our key point is that there is no "universal right policy", it will depend on the user's preferences and environmental constraints, but DOF-SR provides the flexibility needed to adapt the policy to those preferences and constraints.

7.1.1 Protocol

Measuring the RF Neighborhood: DOF-SR uses DOF as the substrate to accurately measure the RF environment and create a *RF-*

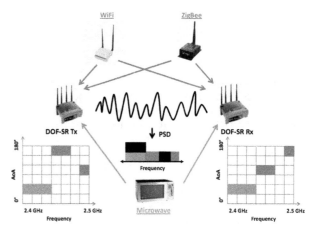

Figure 9: Evaluated scenario for DOF-SR

profile. In our design, both DOF-SR sender and receiver radios measure the environment using DOF, and the receiver sends its measurements to the sender. The measurement consists of the 2-D profile of the RF environment along the frequency and spatial (AoA) axes that DOF estimates, with each occupied point annotated by the occupying signal type. The sender combines the measurements from the receiver by taking the union of both spectrum occupancy measurements, but uses the AoA estimates from the receiver since AoA is specific to the detecting radio and only matters at the receiver for communication.

Estimating what spectral resources to use: Next, the sender uses the merged RF profile along with the user specified policy to estimate what spectral resources to use. For policy **P0**, this would be only the unoccupied spectrum, while for **P1** and **P2** this would also include spectrum occupied by microwave ovens and WiFi respectively.

Creating Packets: DOF uses an OFDM-MIMO PHY layer to create its packets for transmission. The key challenge here is to adaptively leverage the 4 antenna MIMO frontend to maximize throughput while minimizing interference from and to the co-existing radios. We first discuss how the system would work for the simplest policy **P0**, and then extend it to work for the other two policies.

Our current OFDM implementation uses a 1024 point FFT, and divides the 100MHz band into 1024 subcarriers of length 96KHz each. Among these subcarriers, it marks all subcarriers that intersect with the occupied parts from the RF profile as unusable. On the remaining subcarriers it uses MIMO spatial multiplexing to transmit 4 independent streams on each subcarrier. We omit the details here, but refer the reader to [26] for a description of this standard technique.

For policies **P1** and **P2**, we modify the above algorithm to take advantage of their aggressiveness. Specifically, for **P1** we include the subcarriers that were detected to be occupied by microwave ovens in the RF profile. However, we cannot use spatial multiplexing on these subcarriers, since the interference from the microwave signals would be too strong. Instead we leverage the 4 MIMO antennas to perform beamforming and null the interference from the microwave oven signals. Specifically, lets say the microwave oven signals are arriving at i significant AoAs $\theta_1, \ldots, \theta_i$ at the DOF-SR receiver. The sender calculates antenna weights $\vec{w}_p^S = (w_1^S, w_2^S, w_3^S, w_4^S)$ for the subcarrier centered at f_p, which is interfered by the microwave oven, such that the transmitted signal will not arrive at the same angles as the microwave. The receiver will then calculate antenna weights antenna weights $\vec{w}_p^R = (w_1^R, w_2^R, w_3^R, w_4^R)$ such that the microwave signal from the estimated AoAs at the receiver will be minimized:

$$\arg_{\vec{w}_p} \min |\vec{w}_p^* \phi(\vec{\theta}_1) + \ldots + \vec{w}_p^* \phi(\vec{\theta}_i)| \qquad (11)$$

where $\phi(\vec{\theta}_i)$ is the AoA vector corresponding to θ_i at the 4 antennas defined in Eq. 10, and $\vec{w}_p^*$ is the conjugate transpose. The estimated antenna weights are then applied to the streams on the corresponding OFDM subcarriers.

For policy **P3**, the DOF-SR radio will time share the medium with the co-existing WiFi radio, i.e. it will transmit on that spectrum half the time. The key parameter here is the time period over which the smart radio transmits and stays idle. If the time period is too short, then the WiFi radio won't have enough time to accurately estimate the bitrate and correctly utilize its channel time. In our current implementation we use a conservative period of 200ms, since that gives an 802.11 WiFi radio enough time to estimate the channel and get nearly 80 packets through even at the lowest bitrate. Hence, DOF-SR uses the WiFi spectrum for 200ms and then stays away for 200ms. During the time it uses that spectrum, DOF-SR uses spatial multiplexing on all 4 antennas.

Packet Transmission: Before transmitting the encoded packet, a DOF-SR sender transmits a short control packet over a predefined narrowband control channel to the receiver to synchronize state. This packet contains information on what subcarriers will be used, and the antenna weights on the used subcarriers. Then the sender transmits the packet and waits for an ACK, and repeats the above process.

Caveats: The goal of our current DOF-SR implementation is to show the potential benefits of a smart PHY that leverages the detection capabilities of DOF. Hence, it does not tackle MAC layer issues such as finding a usable control channel, rate adaptation on the used spectrum and contention among multiple DOF-SR nodes. The full design and implementation of a smart radio network stack based on DOF is beyond the scope of this paper and is part of our future work. However, the current prototype suffices to evaluate the relative benefits of DOF-SR over the compared state of the art approaches.

Compared Approach: We compare with Jello [28], which is a smart radio design that estimates unused spectrum using edge detection and allocates them among multiple radios for communication. We implement Jello also on our wideband radio. To make a fair comparison, since DOF-SR weaves non-contiguous spectrum together, we modify Jello to also weave non-contiguous spectrum using OFDM. Further, since we are using spatial multiplexing with 4 antennas, we let Jello also use the same spatial multiplexing capabilities with 4 MIMO antennas. Thus the only differences between DOF-SR and Jello in our current implementations are that DOF-SR uses DOF as its detector, while Jello uses edge detection. Second, DOF-SR with policies **P1** and **P2** uses microwave oven and WiFi occupied spectrum appropriately, while Jello does not since edge detection cannot detect that it is a microwave oven or WiFi occupied spectrum. Clearly, both these extra capabilities for DOF-SR come because of the DOF detector, and therefore help us quantify the benefits of using DOF.

Metric: We cannot use throughput as the metric to compare the two designs, since a naive scheme that uses no detection will always achieve the maximum throughput, but harmfully interfere with all co-existing radios. The right metric is therefore one that allows us to visualize the tradeoff between throughput and the harmful interference which the smart radio causes to co-existing radios. To evaluate this tradeoff, we compute two quantities and plot them against each other:

- **Normalized Throughput:** We compute the throughput achieved by DOF-SR and Jello, and normalize them by the throughput an optimal offline scheme implementing our policy would achieve. To compute the throughput of the optimal scheme, we take advantage of the fact that we know the ground truth of what radios are operating and what spectrum they are occupying. We also feed it the AoA measurements from DOF, since we cannot know the ground truth due to unknown multipath effects. We then use this information to compute the throughput of the optimal scheme which would use exactly the

unoccupied spectrum, and optimally beamforms its signals in the microwave occupied spectrum.

- **Normalized Harmful Interference:** We measure the throughput of the co-existing WiFi and Zigbee radios (which are supposed to be protected according to our policy) when neither DOF-SR or Jello are operating, and then when they are operating. We compute the difference in throughput, and normalize it by the throughput they achieve when the smart radios are not operating. This quantity represents the normalized performance drop due to the operation of DOF-SR or Jello.

The ideal scheme would have a normalized throughput of 1 and a normalized harmful interference of 0.

7.2 Evaluation

We evaluate DOF-SR and Jello on the same indoor testbed described in Sec. 6.

Method: We randomly place a WiFi sender-receiver pair, a Zigbee sender-receiver pair and a microwave oven in the testbed. The WiFi and Zigbee radios are operating on randomly picked non-intersecting channels, and the bitrate depends on their respective channel conditions. The WiFi and Zigbee links are continuously transmitting packets. We take a raw 10 second dump using our wideband radios at the sender and receiver, and provide the dumps to DOF and the edge detection algorithm of Jello. After their respective computations, we let the two smart radio systems compute what spectral resources they are going to use and how. They are then allowed to transmit one after the other for 50 seconds. For DOF-SR, we transmit three separate times corresponding to the three policies. We then take the traces at the receiver, decode the signals and compute the goodputs. Simultaneously, we measure the throughput of the WiFi and Zigbee links. We compute the normalized throughput and the normalized harmful interference as discussed before. We repeat this experiment for 50 such configurations and plot the points in Fig. 10.

Analysis: Fig. 10 plots normalized throughput on the y-axis and normalized harmful interference to the co-existing WiFi and Zigbee links on the x-axis for DOF-SR and Jello. We have three plots, corresponding to the three policies that DOF-SR currently implements. The blue circles are for DOF-SR, and the red crosses are for Jello. Note that the optimal scheme will achieve a normalized throughput of 1 and normalized harmful interference of 0.

We first summarize the results:

- With policy **P0**, DOF-SR achieves an average normalized throughput of 0.93 and the average harmful interference it causes is around 0.1, i.e. the throughput of the WiFi and Zigbee links drop only by around 10%. Jello on the other hand achieves a normalized throughput of 0.82 and causes a harmful interference of 0.44. Thus DOF-SR gets a gain of 15% over Jello purely from more accurate unoccupied spectrum estimation, and causes 35% less harm than Jello.
- With policy **P1**, DOF-SR achieves an average normalized throughput of 0.93 and causes an average harm of 0.1. Jello of course cannot use this policy and consequently its average normalized throughput drops to 0.61, while its average harm stays the same at 0.44. Thus with the ability to use microwave oven occupied spectrum, DOF-SR provides a 50% increase over Jello, while still causing minimal harm to co-existing radios.
- With policy **P2**, DOF-SR achieves an average normalized throughput of 0.87 and causes an average harm of 0.32. The reason for the higher harm is that DOF-SR is now competing with the WiFi device for half the time on the WiFi occupied spectrum. Hence WiFi throughput naturally drops compared to **P1**, and harm increases. However this is intended, policy **P2** was designed to be aggressive and steal throughput from the WiFi

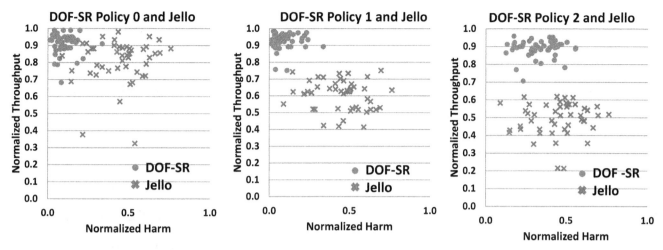

Figure 10: Throughputs and Harm with Smart Radios - More aggressive policies enable higher throughput but also cause greater harm to legacy systems. WiSpy-SR enables users to decide how aggressive their policy should be.

node. The normalized Jello throughput is around 0.5 with the harm the same at 0.44. Hence with policy **P2**, DOF-SR provides a performance gain of nearly 80% over Jello.

The relative gains over Jello help us understand the gains the increasingly aggressive policies provide to DOF-SR. The gain of 15% with policy **P0** is purely from DOF's more accurate spectrum detection. Further note that we achieve this gain while causing minimal harm to the co-existing radios, their average throughput loss is less than 10%. Next, with policy **P1**, DOF-SR's gains increase by another 35% to 50%. This gain comes from DOF-SR's extra capability of being able to detect microwave oven signals and their AoAs, and leverage that information to beamform and null the interference to increase throughput. Finally, with policy **P2**, DOF-SR gets a gain of 80% over Jello, i.e. an additional 30% over policy **P1**. However, the gains come with the price of increased interference to the co-existing WiFi radio since when competing DOF-SR is likely to cut the WiFi throughput, and hence the harm increases to 32%.

8. CONCLUSION

Historically, unlicensed band co-existence has been managed "socially". Different protocols would largely use non-overlapping bands, and given the low density of radios in a neighborhood, the likelihood of radios stepping on each other's toes was low. However, with the increasing number of protocols that operate in the ISM band and the increasing density of radios around us, this assumption is more and more on shaky ground. DOF provides the accurate substrate that future ISM band radios would need to operate and co-exist in this crowded space. DOF opens up a number of avenues of future work, including designing a generalized policy-aware smart radio, whose preliminary prototype design we briefly described in this paper. We also plan to apply DOF to other applications in network management, performance diagnosis and indoor localization.

9. REFERENCES

[1] Fftw. http://www.fftw.org.
[2] Fftw benchmark. http://www.fftw.org/benchfft.
[3] Gnu radio. http://gnuradio.org.
[4] Practical signal detection and classification in gnuradio. 2007.
[5] C. Bishop. Pattern recognition and machine learning, 2006.
[6] J. Capon. High-resolution frequency-wavenumber spectrum analysis. *Proceedings of the IEEE*, 57(8):1408 – 1418, aug. 1969.
[7] M. Davy, A. Gretton, A. Doucet, and P. Rayner. Optimized support vector machines for nonstationary signal classification. *Signal Processing Letters, IEEE*, 9(12):442 – 445, dec. 2002.
[8] A. Fehske, J. Gaeddert, and J. Reed. A new approach to signal classification using spectral correlation and neural networks. pages 144 –150, nov. 2005.
[9] W. Gardner. Exploitation of spectral redundancy in cyclostationary signals. *Signal Processing Magazine, IEEE*, 8(2):14 –36, apr. 1991.
[10] S. Gollakota and D. Katabi. ZigZag decoding: combating hidden terminals in wireless networks. In *SIGCOMM '08: Proceedings of the ACM SIGCOMM 2008 conference on Data communication*, pages 159–170, New York, NY, USA, 2008. ACM.
[11] S. Haykin, D. Thomson, and J. Reed. Spectrum sensing for cognitive radio. *Proceedings of the IEEE*, 97(5):849 –877, may. 2009.
[12] A. P. Iyer, K. Chintalapudi, V. Navda, R. Ramjee, V. N. Padmanabhan, and C. R. Murthy. Specnet: spectrum sensing sans frontières. In *Proceedings of the 8th USENIX conference on Networked systems design and implementation*, NSDI'11, pages 26–26, Berkeley, CA, USA, 2011. USENIX Association.
[13] L. Jia, Y. Gao, J. Isoaho, and H. Tenhunen. A new vlsi-oriented fft algorithm and implementation. In *IEEE International ASIC Conference*, 1998.
[14] D. H. Johnson and D. E. Dudgeon. *Array Signal Processing: Concepts and Techniques*. Simon & Schuster, 1992.
[15] M. O. C. R. L. Bixio, G. Oliveri. Ofdm recognition based on cyclostationary analysis in an open spectrum scenario. In *Vehicular Technology Conference*, 2009.
[16] K. Lakshminarayanan, S. Sapra, S. Seshan, and P. Steenkiste. Rfdump: an architecture for monitoring the wireless ether. In *Proceedings of the 5th international conference on Emerging networking experiments and technologies*, CoNEXT '09, 2009.
[17] E. Like, V. D. Chakravarthy, P. Ratazzi, and Z. Wu. Signal classification in fading channels using cyclic spectral analysis. *EURASIP J. Wirel. Commun. Netw.*, 2009:3–3, 2009.
[18] G. V. L. J. N. Czink, B. Bandemer and A. Paulraj. Stanford july 2008 radio channel measurement campaign. In *COST 2100*, October 2008.
[19] K. E. N. P D Sutton and L. E. Doyle. Cyclostationary signatures for rendezvous in ofdm-based dynamic spectrum access networks. In *IEEE DySPAN*, 2007.
[20] T. M. R. M. Paramvir Bahl, Ranveer Chandra and M. Welsh. White space networking with wi-fi like connectivity. In *ACM SIGCOMM*, 2009.
[21] K. N. Paul Sutton and L. Doyle. Cyclostationary signatures in practical cognitive radio applications. *IEEE Journal on Selected Areas of Communications*, 26, Jan 2008.
[22] H. Rahul, N. Kushman, D. Katabi, F. Edalat, and C. Sodini. Narrowband friendly wideband radios. In *ACM SIGCOMM 2008*.
[23] R. Schmidt. Multiple emitter location and signal parameter estimation. *Antennas and Propagation, IEEE Transactions on*, 34(3):276 – 280, mar. 1986.
[24] A. Swami and B. Sadler. Hierarchical digital modulation classification using cumulants. *Communications, IEEE Transactions on*, 48(3):416 –429, mar. 2000.
[25] T. Taher, M. Misurac, J. LoCicero, and D. R. Ucci. Microwave oven signal modeling. 2008.
[26] D. Tse and P. Vishwanath. *Fundamentals of Wireless Communications*. Cambridge University Press, 2005.
[27] J. Xiong and K. Jamieson. Secureangle: Improving wireless security using angle-of-arrival signatures. In *ACM HotNets 2010*.
[28] L. Yang, W. Hou, L. Cao, B. Y. Zhao, and H. Zheng. Supporting demanding wireless applications with frequency-agile radios. In *USENIX NSDI*, April 2010.
[29] O. Zakaria. Blind signal detection and identification over the 2.4ghz ism band for cognitive radio. In *Master's thesis, University of South Florida, Tampa, Florida, USA*, 2009.

Towards Predictable Datacenter Networks

Hitesh Ballani[†]
hiballan@microsoft.com

Paolo Costa[†‡]
costa@imperial.ac.uk

Thomas Karagiannis[†]
thomkar@microsoft.com

Ant Rowstron[†]
antr@microsoft.com

[†]Microsoft Research
Cambridge, UK

[‡]Imperial College
London, UK

ABSTRACT

The shared nature of the network in today's multi-tenant datacenters implies that network performance for tenants can vary significantly. This applies to both production datacenters and cloud environments. Network performance variability hurts application performance which makes tenant costs unpredictable and causes provider revenue loss. Motivated by these factors, this paper makes the case for extending the tenant-provider interface to explicitly account for the network. We argue this can be achieved by providing tenants with a virtual network connecting their compute instances. To this effect, the key contribution of this paper is the design of virtual network abstractions that capture the trade-off between the performance guarantees offered to tenants, their costs and the provider revenue.

To illustrate the feasibility of virtual networks, we develop Oktopus, a system that implements the proposed abstractions. Using realistic, large-scale simulations and an Oktopus deployment on a 25-node two-tier testbed, we demonstrate that the use of virtual networks yields significantly better and more predictable tenant performance. Further, using a simple pricing model, we find that the our abstractions can reduce tenant costs by up to 74% while maintaining provider revenue neutrality.

Categories and Subject Descriptors: C.2.3 [Computer-Communication Networks]: Network Operations

General Terms: Algorithms, Design, Performance

Keywords: Datacenter, Allocation, Virtual Network, Bandwidth

1. INTRODUCTION

The simplicity of the interface between cloud providers and tenants has significantly contributed to the increasing popularity of cloud datacenters offering on-demand use of computing resources. Tenants simply ask for the amount of compute and storage resources they require, and are charged on a pay-as-you-go basis.

While attractive and simple, this interface misses a critical

resource, namely, the (intra-cloud) network. Cloud providers do not offer guaranteed network resources to tenants. Instead, a tenant's compute instances (virtual machines or, in short, VMs) communicate over the network shared amongst all tenants. Consequently, the bandwidth achieved by traffic between a tenant's VMs depends on a variety of factors outside the tenant's control, such as the network load and placement of the tenant's VMs, and is further exacerbated by the oversubscribed nature of datacenter network topologies [14]. Unavoidably, this leads to high variability in the performance offered by the cloud network to a tenant [13,23,24,30] which, in turn, has several negative consequences for both tenants and providers.

–Unpredictable application performance and tenant cost. Variable network performance is one of the leading causes for unpredictable application performance in the cloud [30], which is a key hindrance to cloud adoption [10,26]. This applies to a wide range of applications: from user-facing web applications [18,30] to transaction processing web applications [21] and MapReduce-like data intensive applications [30,38]. Further, since tenants pay based on the time they occupy their VMs, and this time is influenced by the network, tenants implicitly end up paying for the network traffic; yet, such communication is supposedly free (hidden cost).

–Limited cloud applicability. The lack of guaranteed network performance severely impedes the ability of the cloud to support various classes of applications that rely on predictable performance. The poor and variable performance of HPC and scientific computing applications in the cloud is well documented [17,33]. The same applies to data-parallel applications like MapReduce that rely on the network to ship large amounts of data at high rates [38]. As a matter of fact, Amazon's ClusterCompute [2] addresses this very concern by giving tenants, at a high cost, a dedicated 10 Gbps network with no oversubscription.

–Inefficiencies in production datacenters and revenue loss. The arguments above apply to not just cloud datacenters, but to any datacenter with multiple tenants (product groups), applications (search, advertisements, MapReduce), and services (BigTable, HDFS, GFS). For instance, in production datacenters running MapReduce jobs, variable network performance leads to poorly performing job schedules and significantly impacts datacenter throughput [7,31]. Also, such network-induced application unpredictability makes scheduling jobs qualitatively harder and hampers programmer productivity, not to mention significant loss in revenue [7].

These limitations result from the mismatch between the desired and achieved network performance by tenants which hurts both tenants and providers. Motivated by these factors, this paper tackles the challenge of extending the interface between providers and tenants to explicitly account for network resources while maintaining its simplicity. Our overarching goal is to allow tenants to express their network requirements while ensuring providers can flexibly account for them. To this end, we propose "virtual networks" as a means of exposing tenant requirements to providers. Tenants, apart from getting compute instances, are also offered a virtual network connecting their instances. The virtual network isolates tenant performance from the underlying infrastructure. Such decoupling benefits providers too– they can modify their physical topology without impacting tenants.

The notion of a virtual network opens up an important question: *What should a virtual network topology look like?* On one hand, the abstractions offered to tenants must suit application requirements. On the other, the abstraction governs the amount of multiplexing on the underlying physical network infrastructure and hence, the number of concurrent tenants. Guided by this, we propose two novel abstractions that cater to application requirements while keeping tenant costs low and provider revenues attractive. The first, termed *virtual cluster*, provides the illusion of having all VMs connected to a single, non-oversubscribed (virtual) switch. This is geared to data-intensive applications like MapReduce that are characterized by all-to-all traffic patterns. The second, named *virtual oversubscribed cluster*, emulates an oversubscribed two-tier cluster that suits applications featuring local communication patterns.

The primary contribution of this paper is the design of virtual network abstractions and the exploration of the trade-off between the guarantees offered to tenants, the tenant cost and provider revenue. We further present Oktopus, a system that implements our abstractions. Oktopus maps tenant virtual networks to the physical network in an online setting, and enforces these mappings. Using extensive simulations and deployment on a 25-node testbed, we show that expressing requirements through virtual networks enables a symbiotic relationship between tenants and providers; tenants achieve better and predictable performance while the improved datacenter throughput (25-435%, depending on the abstraction and the workload) increases provider revenue.

A key takeaway from Oktopus is that our abstractions can be deployed today: they do not necessitate any changes to tenant applications, nor do they require changes to routers and switches. Further, offering guaranteed network bandwidth to tenants opens the door for explicit bandwidth charging. Using today's cloud pricing data, we find that virtual networks can reduce median tenant costs by up to 74% while ensuring revenue neutrality for the provider.

On a more general note, we argue that predictable network performance is a small yet important step towards the broader goal of offering an explicit cost-versus-performance trade-off to tenants in multi-tenant datacenters [36] and hence, removing an important hurdle to cloud adoption.

2. NETWORK PERFORMANCE VARIABILITY

Network performance for tenants in shared datacenters depends on many factors beyond the tenant's control: the volume and kind of competing traffic (TCP/UDP), placement of tenant VMs, etc. Here, we discuss the extent of net-

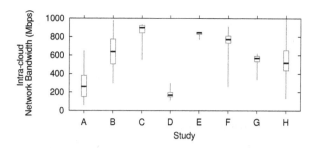

Figure 1: Percentiles ($1\text{-}25\text{-}50\text{-}75\text{-}99^{th}$) for intra-cloud network bandwidth observed by past studies.

work performance variability in cloud and production datacenters.

Cloud datacenters. A slew of recent measurement studies characterize the CPU, disk and network performance offered by cloud vendors, comment on the observed variability and its impact on application performance [13,23,24,30,35]. We contacted the authors of these studies and summarize their measurements of the intra-cloud network bandwidth, i.e., the TCP throughput achieved by transfers between VMs in the same cloud datacenter. Figure 1 plots the percentiles for the network bandwidth observed in these studies (A [13], B [30], C–E [23], F–G [35], H [24]). The figure shows that tenant bandwidth can vary significantly; *by a factor of five or more in some studies* (A, B, F and H).

While more work is needed to determine the root-cause for such bandwidth variations, anecdotal evidence suggests that the variability is correlated with system load (EU datacenters, being lightly loaded, offer better performance than US datacenters) [30,31], and VM placement (e.g., VMs in the same availability zone perform better than ones in different zones) [30]. Further, as mentioned in Section 1, such network performance variability leads to poor and unpredictable application performance [18,21,30,38].

Production datacenters. Production datacenters are often shared amongst multiple tenants, different (possibly competing) groups, services and applications, and these can suffer from performance variation. To characterize such variation, we analyze data from a production datacenter running data analytics jobs, each comprising multiple tasks. This data is presented in [7] while our results are discussed in [8]. Briefly, we find that runtimes of tasks belonging to the same job vary significantly, and this can adversely impact job completion times. While many factors contribute to such variability, our analysis shows that a fair fraction (>20%) of the variability can be directly attributed to variable network bandwidth. Further, we find that the bandwidth achieved by tasks that read data across cross-rack links can vary by an order of magnitude.

In summary, we observe significant variability in network performance in both cloud and production datacenters. This negatively impacts application performance. Evaluation in Section 5 also shows that in both settings, the mismatch between required and achieved network performance hurts datacenter throughput and hence, provider revenue. Since our proposed abstractions cover both cloud and production datacenters, we will henceforth use the term "multi-tenant" to refer to both.

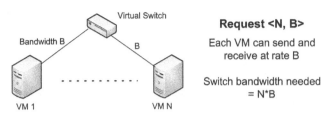

Figure 2: Virtual Cluster abstraction.

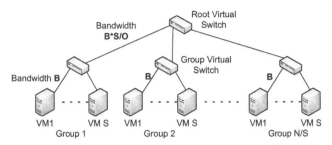

Request <N, S, B, O>
N VMs in groups of size S, Oversubscription factor O
Group switch bandwidth = S*B, Root switch bandwidth = N*B/O

Figure 3: Virtual Oversubscribed Cluster abstraction.

3. VIRTUAL NETWORK ABSTRACTIONS

In multi-tenant datacenters, tenants request virtual machines (VMs) with varying amounts of CPU, memory and storage resources. For ease of exposition, we abstract away details of the non-network resources and characterize each tenant request as $<N>$, the number of VMs requested. The fact that tenants do not expose their network requirements hurts both tenants and providers. This motivates the need to extend the tenant-provider interface to explicitly account for the network. Further, the interface should isolate tenants from the underlying network infrastructure and hence, prevent provider lock-in. Such decoupling benefits the provider too; it can completely alter its infrastructure or physical topology, with tenant requests being unaffected and unaware of such a change. To this end, we propose virtual networks as a means of exposing tenant network requirements to the provider. Apart from specifying the type and number of VMs, tenants also specify the virtual network connecting them.

The "virtual" nature of the network implies that the provider has a lot of freedom in terms of the topology of this network, and can offer different options to tenants for different costs. Beyond the overarching goal of maintaining the simplicity of the interface between tenants and providers, our topologies or *virtual network abstractions* are guided by two design goals:

1. *Tenant suitability.* The abstractions should allow tenants to reason in an intuitive way about the network performance of their applications when running atop the virtual network.

2. *Provider flexibility.* Providers should be able to multiplex many virtual networks on their physical network. The greater the amount of sharing possible, the lesser the tenant costs.

To this effect, we propose two novel abstractions for virtual networks in the following sections.

3.1 Virtual Cluster

The "Virtual Cluster" abstraction is motivated by the observation that in an enterprise (or any private setting), tenants typically run their applications on dedicated clusters with compute nodes connected through Ethernet switches. This abstraction, shown in figure 2, aims to offer tenants with a similar setup. With a *virtual cluster*, a tenant request $<N, B>$ provides the following topology: each tenant machine is connected to a virtual switch by a bidirectional link of capacity B, resulting in a one-level tree topology. The virtual switch has a bandwidth of $N * B$. This ensures that the virtual network has no oversubscription and the maximum rate at which the tenant VMs can exchange data is $N * B$. However, this data rate is only feasible if the communication matrix for the tenant application ensures that

each VM sends and receives at rate B. Alternatively, if all N tenant VMs were to send data to a single destination VM, the data rate achieved will be limited to B.

Since a *virtual cluster* offers tenants a network with no oversubscription, it is suitable for data-intensive applications like MapReduce and BLAST. For precisely such applications, Amazon's Cluster Compute provides tenants with compute instances connected through a dedicated 10 Gbps network with no oversubscription. This may be regarded as a specific realization of the *virtual cluster* abstraction with $<N, 10 \ Gbps>$.

3.2 Virtual Oversubscribed Cluster

While a network with no oversubscription is imperative for data-intensive applications, this does not hold for many other applications [19,34]. Instead, a lot of cloud bound applications are structured in the form of components with more intra-component communication than inter-component communication [16,25]. A "Virtual Oversubscribed Cluster" is better suited for such cases; it capitalizes on application structure to reduce the bandwidth needed from the underlying physical infrastructure compared to virtual clusters, thereby improving provider flexibility and reducing tenant costs.

With a *virtual oversubscribed cluster*, a tenant request $<N, B, S, O>$ entails the topology shown in Figure 3. Tenant machines are arranged in groups of size S, resulting in $\frac{N}{S}$ groups. VMs in a group are connected by bidirectional links of capacity B to a (virtual) group switch. The group switches are further connected using a link of capacity $B' = \frac{S*B}{O}$ to a (virtual) root switch. The resulting topology has no oversubscription for intra-group communication. However, intergroup communication has an oversubscription factor O, i.e., the aggregate bandwidth at the VMs is O times greater than the bandwidth at the root switch. Hence, this abstraction closely follows the structure of typical oversubscribed datacenter networks. Note, however, that O *neither depends upon nor requires physical topology oversubscription.*

Compared to *virtual cluster*, this abstraction does not offer as dense a connectivity. However, the maximum data rate with this topology is still $N * B$. The localized nature of the tenant's bandwidth demands resulting from this abstraction allows the provider to fit more tenants on the physical network. This, as our evaluation shows, has the potential to significantly limit tenant costs. By incentivizing tenants to expose the flexibility of their communication demands, the

Abstraction	Max Rate	Suitable for applications	Provider Flexibility	Tenant Cost
Virtual Cluster	$O(N)$	All	Medium	Medium
Oversub.	$O(N)$	Many	High	Low
Clique	$O(N^2)$	All	Very Low	Very High

Table 1: Virtual network abstractions present a trade-off between application suitability and provider flexibility.

abstraction achieves better multiplexing which benefits both tenants and providers. Amazon's EC2 Spot Instances [1] is a good example of how tenants are willing to be flexible, especially when it suits their application demands, if it means lowered costs.

For simplicity, in this paper we assume a single value of B for all VMs of a given request. For *virtual oversubscribed cluster*, we also assume that the group size is uniform. However, both the abstractions and the algorithms presented in Section 4 can be easily extended to support multiple values of B and variable-sized groups within the same request.

Other topologies. A number of network abstractions have been proposed in other contexts and could potentially be offered to tenants. However, they suffer from several drawbacks due to their dense connectivity, and hence significantly limit the true flexibility a multi-tenant datacenter can provide. For example, many topologies have been studied for HPC platforms, such as multi-dimensional cubes, hypercube and its variants, and even more complex topologies such as Butterfly networks, de Bruijn, etc [11]. These are of interest to a small niche set of applications (violating goal 1).

Similarly, SecondNet [15] provides tenants with bandwidth guarantees for pairs of VMs. While the resulting clique virtual topology can elegantly capture application demands, its dense connectivity also makes it difficult for the provider to multiplex multiple tenants on the underlying network infrastructure (violating goal 2). For instance, the analysis in [15] shows that with the oversubscribed physical networks prevalent in today's datacenters, only a few tenants demanding clique virtual networks are sufficient to saturate the physical network. This hurts the provider revenue and translates to high tenant costs.

Table 1 illustrates how the topologies discussed compare with respect to our design goals. The *virtual cluster* provides rich connectivity to tenant applications that is independent of their communication pattern but limits provider flexibility. The *virtual oversubscribed cluster* utilizes information about application communication patterns to improve provider flexibility. The clique abstraction, chosen as a representative of existing proposals, offers very rich connectivity but severely limits provider flexibility. Overall, our virtual networks closely resemble the physical topologies used in the majority of enterprise data centers. We expect that this will greatly simplify the migration of applications from a private cluster to a multi-tenant one.

4. Oktopus

To illustrate the feasibility of virtual networks, we present Oktopus, a system that implements our abstractions.[1] The provider maintains a datacenter containing physical machines

---

[1]Oktopus provides predictable performance, and is named

with slots where tenant VMs can be placed. With Oktopus, tenants requesting VMs can opt for a (virtual) cluster or a (virtual) oversubscribed cluster to connect their VMs. Further, to allow for incremental deployment, we also support tenants who do not want a virtual network, and are satisfied with the status quo where they simply get some share of the network resources. Two main components are used to achieve this:

- *Management plane.* A logically centralized network manager (*NM*), upon receiving a tenant request, performs admission control and maps the request to physical machines. This process is the same as today's setup except that the NM needs to further account for network resources and maintain bandwidth reservations across the physical network.

- *Data plane.* Oktopus uses rate-limiting at endhost hypervisors to enforce the bandwidth available at each VM. This ensures that no explicit bandwidth reservations at datacenter switches are required.

The network manager implements allocation algorithms to allocate slots on physical machines to tenant requests in an online fashion. For tenant requests involving a virtual network, the NM needs to ensure that the corresponding bandwidth demands can be met while maximizing the number of concurrent tenants. To achieve this, the NM maintains the following information- (i). The datacenter network topology, (ii). The residual bandwidth for each link in the network, (iii). The empty slots on each physical machine, and (iv). The allocation information for existing tenants, including the physical machines they are allocated to, the network routes between these machines and the bandwidth reserved for the tenant at links along these routes. In the following sections, we describe how the NM uses the above information to allocate tenant requests.

4.1 Cluster Allocation

A *virtual cluster* request $r :<N, B>$ requires a virtual topology comprising N machines connected by links of bandwidth B to a virtual switch. In designing the allocation algorithm for such requests, we focus on tree-like physical network topologies; for instance, the multi-rooted trees used in today's datacenters and richer topologies like VL2 [14] and FatTree [5]. Such topologies are hierarchical and are recursively made of *sub-trees* at each level. For instance, with a three-tier topology, the cluster is a collection of pods, pods comprise racks, and racks comprise hosts.

At a high level, the allocation problem involves allocating N empty VM slots to the tenant such that there is enough bandwidth to satisfy the corresponding virtual topology. We begin by characterizing the bandwidth requirements of an already allocated tenant on the underlying physical links. Further, we start with the assumption that the physical links connecting the tenant's N VMs form a simple tree T. This is shown in Figure 4. Section 4.4 relaxes the assumption. Note that the set of switches and links in T form a "distributed virtual switch" for the tenant. Given that the tenant's virtual switch has a bandwidth of $N * B$, a trivial yet inefficient solution is to reserve this bandwidth on each link in the tenant tree.

---

after "Paul the Oktopus" (German spelling), famous for his ability to *predict* the outcome of football World Cup games.

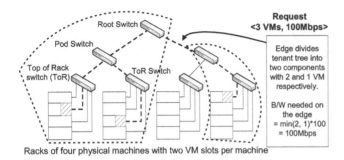

Racks of four physical machines with two VM slots per machine

Figure 4: An allocation for a cluster request r: **<3, 100 Mbps>. Three VMs are allocated for the tenant at the highlighted slots. The dashed edges show the tenant tree** T.

However, the actual bandwidth needed to be reserved is lower. Let's consider a link in T. As shown in Figure 4, removing this link from the tree leads to two components; if the first one contains m VMs, the other contains (N-m) VMs. The virtual topology dictates that a single VM cannot send or receive at rate more than B. Hence, traffic between these two components is limited to $\min(m, N - m) * B$. This is the *bandwidth required* for the tenant on this link.

For a *valid allocation*, the tenant's bandwidth requirement should be met on all links in the tenant tree. Hence, the *Virtual Cluster Allocation Problem* boils down to determining such valid allocations. An optimization version of this problem involves determining valid allocations that maximize Oktopus' future ability to accommodate tenant requests.

Allocation algorithm. Allocating *virtual cluster* requests on graphs with bandwidth-constrained edges is NP-hard [12]. We design a greedy allocation algorithm. The intuition is that the number of tenant VMs that can be allocated to a sub-tree (a machine, a rack, a pod) is constrained by two factors. The first is the number of empty VM slots in the sub-tree. The second is the residual bandwidth on the physical link connecting the sub-tree to the rest of the network. This link should be able to satisfy the bandwidth requirements of the VMs placed inside the sub-tree. Given the number of VMs that can be placed in any sub-tree, the algorithm finds the smallest sub-tree that can fit all tenant VMs.

Below we introduce a few terms and explain the algorithm in detail. Each physical machine in the datacenter has K slots where VMs can be placed, while each link has capacity C. Further, $k_v \in [0, K]$ is the number of empty slots on machine v, while R_l is the residual bandwidth for link l. We begin by deriving constraints on the number of VMs that can be allocated at each level of the datacenter hierarchy. Starting with a machine as the base case, the number of VMs for request r that can be allocated to a machine v with outbound link l is given by the set M_v:

$$M_v = \{m \in [0, \min(k_v, N)] \\ \text{s.t.} \min(m, N - m) * B \le R_l\}$$

To explain this constraint, we consider a scenario where m ($< N$) VMs are placed at the machine v. As described earlier, the bandwidth required on outbound link l, $B_{r,l}$ is $\min(m, N - m) * B$. For a valid allocation, this bandwidth should be less than the residual bandwidth of the link. Note that in a scenario where all requested VMs can fit in v (i.e., $m = N$), all communication between the VMs is internal to

---

Require: Topology tree T
Ensure: Allocation for request r :$< N, B >$
1: $l = 0$ //start at level 0, i.e., with machines
2: **while** true **do**
3:    **for** each sub-tree v at level l of T **do**
4:       Calculate M_v //v can hold M_v VMs
5:       **if** $N \le \max(M_v)$ **then**
6:          Alloc(r, v, N)
7:          **return true**
8:    $l = l + 1$ // move to higher level in T
9:    **if** $l ==$ height(T) **then**
10:       **return false**   //reject request

   //Allocate m VM slots in sub-tree v to request r
11: **function** Alloc(r, v, m)
12: **if** (level(v) ==0) **then**
13:    // Base case - v is a physical machine
14:    Mark m VM slots as occupied
15:    **return** m
16: **else**
17:    $count = 0$ //number of VMs assigned
18:    //Iterate over sub-trees of v
19:    **for** each sub-tree w in v **do**
20:       **if** $count < m$ **then**
21:          $count$ += Alloc(r, w, $\min(m - count, \max(M_w))$)
22:    **return** $count$

Figure 5: Virtual Cluster Allocation algorithm.

the machine. Hence, the bandwidth needed for the request on the link is zero.[2]

The same constraint is extended to determine the number of VMs that can be placed in sub-trees at each level, i.e., at racks at level 1, pods at level 2 and onwards. These constraints guide the allocation shown in Figure 5. Given the number of VMs that can be placed at each level of the datacenter hierarchy, the algorithm greedily tries to allocate the tenant VMs to the lowest level possible. To achieve this, we traverse the topology tree starting at the leaves (physical machines at level 0) and determine if all N VMs can fit (lines 2-10). Once the algorithm determines a sub-tree that can accommodate the VMs (line 5), it invokes the "Alloc" function to allocate empty slots on physical machines in the sub-tree to the tenant. While not shown in the algorithm, once the assignment is done, the bandwidth needed for the request is effectively "reserved" by updating the residual bandwidth for each link l as $R_l = R_l - B_{r,l}$.

The fact that datacenter network topologies are typically oversubscribed (less bandwidth at root than edges) guides the algorithm's optimization heuristic. To maximize the possibility of accepting future tenant requests, the algorithm allocates a request while minimizing the bandwidth reserved at higher levels of the topology. This is achieved by packing the tenant VMs in the smallest sub-tree. Further, when multiple sub-trees are available at the same level of hierarchy, our implementation chooses the sub-tree with the least amount of residual bandwidth on the edge connecting the sub-tree to the rest of the topology. This preserves empty VM slots in other sub-trees that have greater outbound bandwidth available and hence, are better positioned to accommodate future tenants.

---

[2]We assume that if the provider offers N slots per physical machine, the hypervisor can support N*B of internal bandwidth (within the physical machine).

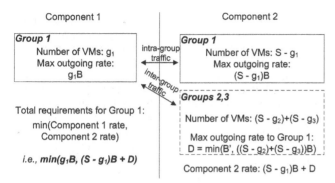

Figure 6: An oversubscribed cluster request with three groups. Figures illustrates bandwidth required by Group 1 VMs on a link dividing the tenant tree into two components.

4.2 Oversubscribed Cluster Allocation

An oversubscribed cluster request, $r : <N, S, B, O>$, requires N VMs arranged in groups of size S. VMs within the same group are connected by links of bandwidth B to a virtual switch. Inter-group bandwidth is given by $B' = \frac{S*B}{O}$ (see Section 3.2).

Consider a request with three groups. As with the *virtual cluster*, any physical link in the tenant tree divides the tree into two components. Let g_i denote the VMs of group i that are in the first component, implying that the rest are in the second component $(S - g_i)$. We observe that the bandwidth required by the request on the link is the sum of the bandwidth required by individual groups. Focusing on the Group 1 VMs in the first component, their traffic on the link in question comprises the intra-group traffic to Group 1 VMs in the second component and inter-group traffic to VMs of Groups 2 and 3 in the second component. This is shown in Figure 6.

In the first component, Group 1 VMs cannot send (or receive) traffic at a rate more than $g_i * B$. In the second component, Group 1 VMs cannot receive (or send) at a rate more than $(S - g_i) * B$ while the rate for VMs of other groups cannot exceed the inter-group bandwidth B'. The rate of these other VMs is further limited by the aggregate bandwidth of the Group 2 and 3 members in the second component, i.e., $((S - g_2) + (S - g_3)) * B)$. Hence, as shown in the figure, the total bandwidth needed by Group 1 of request r on link l, $B_{r,1,l} = \min(g_1 * B, (S - g_1) * B + D)$. Finally, the total bandwidth required on the link is the sum across all three groups, i.e., $\sum_{i=1,3} B_{r,i,l}$.

Generalizing the analysis above, the bandwidth required for Group i on link l is given by

$$B_{r,i,l} = \min(g_i * B, (S - g_i) * B + \\ + \min(B', \sum_{j \neq i} (S - g_j) * B)).$$

The bandwidth to be reserved on link l for request r is the sum across all the groups, i.e., $B_{r,l} = \sum_{i=1}^{P} B_{r,i,l}$. For the allocation to be valid, link l must have enough residual bandwidth to satisfy $B_{r,l}$. Hence, $B_{r,l} \leq R_l$ is the validity condition.

Allocation algorithm. The key insight guiding the algorithm is that allocating an oversubscribed cluster involves allocating a sequence of virtual clusters ($<S, B>$) for individual groups. This allows us to reuse the cluster allocation algorithm. Hence, the allocation for a request r proceeds

one group at a time. Let's assume that groups 1 to $(i-1)$ have already been allocated and we need to allocate VMs of group i. As with the cluster allocation algorithm, we derive constraints on the number of VMs for this group that can be assigned to each sub-tree. Consider a sub-tree with outbound link l already containing g_j members of group j, $j \in [1, i-1]$. Using the analysis above, the conditional bandwidth needed for the jth group of request r on link l is:

$$CB_{r,j,l}(i-1) = \min(g_j * B, (S - g_j) * B + \min(B', E))$$

where,

$$E = \sum_{k=1, k \neq j}^{i-1} (S - g_k) * B + \sum_{k=i}^{P} S * B.$$

This bandwidth is conditional since groups $i, \ldots, P$ remain to be allocated. We conservatively assume that all subsequent groups will be allocated outside the sub-tree and link l will have to accommodate the resulting inter-group traffic. Hence, if g_i members of group i were to be allocated inside the sub-tree, the bandwidth required by groups $[1,i]$ on l is at most $\sum_{j=1}^{i} CB_{r,j,l}(i)$. Consequently, the number of VMs for group i that can be allocated to sub-tree v, designated by the set $M_{v,i}$, is:

$$M_{v,i} = \{g_i \in [0, \min(k_v, S)] \\ \text{s.t. } \sum_{j=1}^{i} CB_{r,j,l}(i) \leq R_l\}.$$

Given the number of VMs that can be placed in sub-trees at each level of the datacenter hierarchy, the allocation algorithm proceeds to allocate VMs for individual groups using the algorithm in Figure 5. A request is accepted if all groups are successfully allocated.

4.3 Enforcing virtual networks

The NM ensures that the physical links connecting a tenant's VMs have sufficient bandwidth. Beyond this, Oktopus also includes mechanisms to *enforce* tenant virtual networks. **Rate limiting VMs.** Individual VMs should not be able to exceed the bandwidth specified in the virtual topology. While this could be achieved using explicit bandwidth reservations at switches, the limited number of reservation classes on commodity switches implies that such a solution certainly does not scale with the number of tenants [15].

Instead, Oktopus relies on endhost-based rate enforcement. For each VM on a physical machine, an *enforcement* module resides in the OS hypervisor. The key insight here is that given a tenant's virtual topology and the tenant traffic rate, it is feasible to calculate the rate at which pairs of VMs should be communicating. To achieve this, the enforcement module for a VM measures the traffic rate to other VMs. These traffic measurements from all VMs for a tenant are periodically sent to a tenant VM designated as the *controller VM*. The enforcement module at the controller then calculates the max-min fair share for traffic between the VMs. These rates are communicated back to other tenant VMs where the enforcement module uses per-destination-VM rate limiters to enforce them.

This simple design where rate computation for each tenant is done at a controller VM reduces control traffic. Alternatively, the enforcement modules for a tenant could use a gossip protocol to exchange their traffic rates, so that rate limits can be computed locally. We note that the enforcement modules are effectively achieving distributed rate limits; for instance, with a cluster request $<N, B>$, the aggregate rate at which the tenant's VMs can source traffic to a destination VM cannot exceed B. This is similar to other distributed rate control mechanisms like DRL [28] and Gatekeeper [32]. The authors discuss the trade-offs between accuracy and responsiveness versus the communication overhead in DRL; the same trade-offs apply here. Like Hedera [6], we perform centralized rate computation. However, our knowledge of the virtual topology makes it easier to determine the traffic bottlenecks. Further, our computation is tenant-specific which reduces the scale of the problem and allows us to compute rates for each virtual network independently. Section 5.4 shows that our implementation scales well imposing low communication overhead.

Tenants without virtual networks. The network traffic for tenants without guaranteed resources should get a (fair) share of the residual link bandwidth in the physical network. This is achieved using *two-level priorities*, and since commodity switches today offer priority forwarding, we rely on switch support for this. Traffic from tenants with a virtual network is marked as and treated as high priority, while other traffic is low priority. This, when combined with the mechanisms above, ensures that tenants with virtual networks get the virtual topology and the bandwidth they ask for, while other tenants get their fair share of the residual network capacity. The provider can ensure that the performance for fair share tenants is not too bad by limiting the fraction of network capacity used for virtual networks.

With the current implementation, if a VM belonging to a virtual network does not fully utilize its bandwidth share, the unused capacity can only be used by tenants without virtual networks. This may be sub-optimal since the spare capacity cannot be distributed to tenants with virtual networks. Oktopus can use weighted sharing mechanisms [22,31] to ensure that unused capacity is distributed amongst all tenants, not just fair share tenants and hence, provide minimum bandwidth guarantees instead of exact guarantees.

4.4 Design discussion

NM and Routing. Oktopus' allocation algorithms assume that the traffic between a tenant's VMs is routed along a tree. This assumption holds trivially for simple tree physical topologies with a single path between any pair of machines. However, datacenters often have richer networks. For instance, a commonly used topology involves multiple L2 domains inter-connected using a couple of layers of routers [27]. The spanning tree protocol ensures that traffic between machines within the same L2 domain is forwarded along a spanning tree. The IP routers are connected with a mesh of links that are load balanced using Equal Cost Multi-Path forwarding (ECMP). Given the amount of multiplexing over the mesh of links, these links can be considered as a single aggregate link for bandwidth reservations. Hence, *in such topologies with limited path diversity, the physical routing paths themselves form a tree and our assumption still holds.* The NM only needs to infer this tree to determine the routing tree for any given tenant. This can be achieved using SNMP queries of the 802.1D-Bridge MIB on switches (products like Netview and OpenView support this) or through active probing [9].

Data-intensive workloads in today's datacenters have motivated even richer, *fat-tree topologies* that offer multiple paths between physical machines [5,14]. Simple hash-based or randomized techniques like ECMP and Valiant Load Bal-

ancing (VLB) are used to spread traffic across paths. Hence, tenant traffic would not be routed along a tree, and additional mechanisms are needed to satisfy our assumption.

For the purpose of bandwidth reservations, multiple physical links can be treated as a single aggregate link if traffic is distributed evenly across them. Today's ECMP and VLB implementations realize hash-based, per-flow splitting of traffic across multiple links. Variations in flow length and hash collisions can result in a non uniform distribution of traffic across the links [6]. To achieve a uniform distribution, we could use a centralized controller to reassign flows in case of uneven load [6] or distribute traffic across links on a per-packet basis, e.g., in a round-robin fashion.

Alternatively, the NM can control datacenter routing to actively build routes between tenant VMs, and recent proposals present backwards compatible techniques to achieve this. With both SecondNet [15] and SPAIN [27], route computation is moved to a centralized component that directly sends routing paths to endhosts. The Oktopus NM can adopt such an approach to build tenant-specific routing trees on top of rich physical topologies. The fact that there are many VMs per physical machine and many machines per rack implies that multiple paths offered by the physical topology can still be utilized, though perhaps not as effectively as with per-flow or per-packet distribution.

We defer a detailed study of the relative merits of these approaches to future work.

Failures. Failures of physical links and switches in the datacenter will impact the virtual topology for tenants whose routing tree includes the failed element. With today's setup, providers are not held responsible for physical failures and tenants end up paying for them [36]. Irrespective, our allocation algorithms can be extended to determine the tenant VMs that need to be migrated, and reallocate them so as to satisfy the tenant's virtual topology. For instance, with the cluster request, the failed edge divides the tenant's routing tree into two components. If the NM cannot find alternate links with sufficient capacity to connect the two components, it will reallocate the VMs present in the smaller component.

5. EVALUATION

We evaluate two aspects of Oktopus. First, we use large-scale simulations to quantify the benefits of providing tenants with bounded network bandwidth. Second, we show that the Oktopus NM can deal with the scale and churn posed by datacenters, and benchmark our implementation on a small testbed.

5.1 Simulation setup

Since our testbed is restricted to 25 machines, we developed a simulator that coarsely models a multi-tenant datacenter. The simulator uses a three-level tree topology with no path diversity. Racks of 40 machines with 1Gbps links and a Top-of-Rack switch are connected to an aggregation switch. The aggregation switches, in turn, are connected to the datacenter core switch. By varying the connectivity and the bandwidth of the links between the switches, we vary the oversubscription of the physical network. The results in the following sections involve a datacenter with 16,000 physical machines and 4 VMs per machine, resulting in a total of 64,000 VMs.

Tenant workload. We adopt a broad yet realistic model for jobs/applications run by tenants. Tenant jobs comprise computation and network communication. To this effect, each tenant job is modeled as a set of independent tasks to be run on individual VMs, and a set of flows between the tasks. The minimum compute time for the job (T_c) captures the computation performed by the tasks. We start with a simple communication pattern wherein each tenant task is a source and a destination for one flow, and all flows are of uniform length (L). A job is complete when both the computation and the network flows finish. Hence, the completion time for a job, $T = \max(T_c, T_n)$, where T_n is the time for the last flow to finish. This reflects real-world workloads. For instance, with MapReduce, the job completion time is heavily influenced by the last shuffle flow and the slowest task [7].

This naive workload model was deliberately chosen; the job compute time T_c abstracts away the non-network resources required and allows us to determine the tenant's "network requirements". Since tenants pay based on the time they occupy VMs and hence, their job completion time, tenants can minimize their cost by ensuring that their network flows do not lag behind the computation, i.e., $T_n \leq T_c$. With the model above, the network bandwidth needed by tenant VMs to achieve this is $B = \frac{L}{T_c}$.

Baseline. We first describe the baseline setup against which we compare Oktopus abstractions. Tenants ask for VMs only, and their requests are represented as $<N>$. Tenants are allocated using a locality-aware allocation algorithm that greedily allocates tenant VMs as close to each other as possible. This baseline scenario is representative of the purely VM-based resource allocation today. Once a tenant is admitted and allocated, the simulator models flow level communication between tenant VMs. A flow's bandwidth is calculated according to max-min fairness; a flow's rate is its fair share across the most bottlenecked physical link it traverses.

Virtual network requests. To allow a direct comparison, we ensure that any baseline tenant request can also be expressed as a virtual network request. A baseline request $<N>$ is extended as $<N, B>$ and $<N, S, B, O>$ to represent a cluster and oversubscribed cluster request respectively. The requested bandwidth B is based on the tenant's network requirements, as detailed earlier. For oversubscribed clusters, the tenant's VMs are further arranged into groups, and to ensure that the underlying network traffic matches the requested topology, the number of inter-group flows is made proportional to the oversubscription factor O. For example, if O=10, on average $\frac{N}{10}$ inter-group flows are generated per request. These virtual network requests are allocated using the algorithms presented in Section 4.

Simulation breadth. Given the lack of datasets describing job bandwidth requirements to guide our workload, our evaluation explores the entire space for most parameters of interest in today's datacenters; these include tenant bandwidth requirements, datacenter load, and physical topology oversubscription. This is not only useful for completeness, but, further provides evidence of Oktopus' performance at the extreme points.

5.2 Production datacenter experiments

We first consider a scenario involving a large batch of tenant jobs to be allocated and run in the datacenter. The experiment is representative of the workload observed in production datacenters running data-analytics jobs from multiple groups/services. We compare the throughput achieved with virtual network abstractions against the status quo.

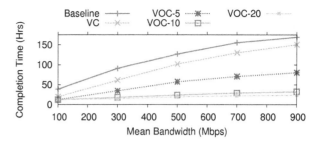

Figure 7: Completion time for a batch of 10,000 tenant jobs with Baseline and with various virtual network abstractions.

In our experiments, the number of VMs (N) requested by each tenant is exponentially distributed around a mean of 49. This is consistent with what is observed in production and cloud datacenters [31]. For oversubscribed cluster requests, the tenant VMs are arranged in $\sqrt{N}$ groups each containing $\sqrt{N}$ VMs. We begin with a physical network with 10:1 oversubscription, a conservative value given the high oversubscription of current data center networks [14], and 4 VMs per physical machine. We simulate the execution of a batch of 10,000 tenant jobs with varying mean bandwidth requirements for the jobs. To capture the variability in network intensiveness of jobs, their bandwidth requirements are taken from an exponential distribution around the mean. The job scheduling policy is the same throughout– jobs are placed in a FIFO queue, and once a job finishes, the topmost job(s) that can be allocated are allowed to run.

Job completion time. Figure 7 plots the time to complete all jobs with different abstractions for tenants– the Baseline setup, virtual cluster (VC), and virtual oversubscribed cluster with varying oversubscription ratio (VOC-10 refers to oversubscribed clusters with O=10). The figure shows that for any given approach, the completion time increases as the mean bandwidth requirement increases (i.e., jobs become network intensive).

In all cases, *virtual clusters provide significant improvement over the Baseline completion time*. For oversubscribed clusters, the completion time depends on the oversubscription ratio. The completion time for VOC-2, omitted for clarity, is similar to that of *virtual cluster*. With VOC-10, the completion time at 500 Mbps is 18% (*6 times less*) of Baseline (31% with 100 Mbps). Note that increasing O implies greater locality in the tenant's communication patterns. This allows for more concurrent tenants and reduces completion time which, in turn, improves datacenter throughput. However, the growth in benefits with increasing oversubscription diminishes, especially beyond a factor of 10.

Beyond improving datacenter throughput, providing tenants with virtual networks has other benefits. It ensures that network flows comprising a job do not lag behind computation. Hence, a tenant job, once allocated, takes the minimum compute time T_c to complete. However, with the Baseline setup, varying network performance can cause the completion time for a job to exceed T_c. Figure 8 plots the CDF for the ratio of today's job completion time to the compute time and shows that tenant jobs can be stretched much longer than expected. With BW=500 Mbps, the completion time for jobs is 1.42 times the compute time at the median (2.8 times at the 75th percentile). Such performance unpre-

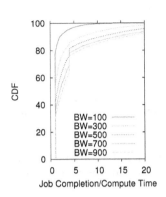
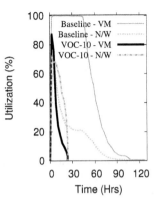

Figure 8: With Base-line, job duration is extended.

Figure 9: VM and network utilization with Baseline and VOC-10.

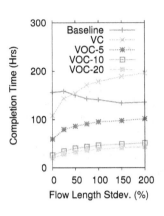
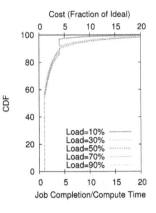

Figure 11: Completion time with varying flow lengths. Mean BW = 500 Mbps.

Figure 12: CDF for increase in completion time and cost (upper X-axis) with Baseline. Mean BW = 500Mbps.

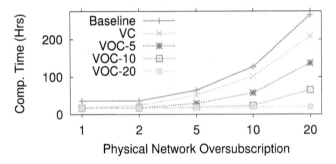

Figure 10: Completion time increases with physical oversub. Mean BW = 500 Mbps.

dictability is highly undesirable and given the iterative program/debug/modify development, hurts programmer productivity [7].

Utilization. To understand the poor Baseline performance, we look at the average VM and network utilization over the course of one experiment. This is shown in Figure 9. With Baseline, the network utilization remains low for a majority of the time. This is because the allocation of VMs, though locality aware, does not account for network demands causing contention. Thus, tenant VMs wait for the network flows to finish and hurt datacenter throughput. As a contrast, with oversubscribed cluster (VOC-10), the allocation is aware of the job's bandwidth demands and hence, results in higher network utilization.

We repeated the experiments above with varying parameters. Figure 10 shows how the completion time varies with the physical network oversubscription. We find that *even when the underlying physical network is not oversubscribed as in [5,14], virtual networks can reduce completion time (and increase throughput) by a factor of two.*[3] Further, increasing the virtual oversubscription provides greater benefits when the physical oversubscription is larger. Similarly, increasing the mean tenant size (N) improves the performance of our abstractions relative to today since tenant traffic is more likely to traverse core network links. We omit these results due to space constraints.

Diverse communication patterns. In the previous ex-

periments, all flows of a job have the same length. Consequently, all VMs for a tenant require the same bandwidth to complete their flows on time. We now diversify the job communication pattern by varying the length of flows between a tenant's VMs. The flow lengths are chosen from a normal distribution with a specified standard deviation. Consequently, each tenant VM requires a different bandwidth. While our abstractions can be extended to allow for a different bandwidth for individual VMs, here we restrict ourselves to the same bandwidth across a tenant's VMs.

Given the non-uniform communication pattern, each tenant needs to determine its desired bandwidth; we use the average length of a tenant's flows to calculate the requested bandwidth. This implies that some VMs will waste resources by not using their allocated bandwidth while for others, their flows will lag behind the computation.

Figure 11 shows the completion time with increasing standard deviation of the flow length. Since flow lengths are normally distributed, the average network load remains the same throughout, and there is not much impact on the Baseline completion time. For virtual networks, the completion time increases with increasing variation before tapering off. With oversubscribed clusters, the jobs complete faster than Baseline. For *virtual cluster*, completion time is greater than Baseline when flow lengths vary a lot. This is due to the diverse communication pattern and the resulting "imprecise" tenant demands that cause network bandwidth to be wasted. This can be rectified by modifying the semantics of Oktopus abstractions so that unused bandwidth can be utilized by other tenants.

5.3 Cloud datacenter experiments

The experiments in the previous section involved a static set of jobs. We now introduce tenant dynamics with tenant requests arriving over time. This is representative of cloud datacenters. By varying the tenant arrival rate, we vary the load imposed in terms of the number of VMs. Assuming Poisson tenant arrivals with a mean arrival rate of λ, the load on a datacenter with M total VMs is $\frac{\lambda N T_c}{M}$, where N is the mean request size and T_c is the mean compute time. Unlike the previous experiments in which requests could be delayed, in this scenario, we enforce an admission control

---

[3]Since there are 4 VMs per machine, flows for a VM can still be network bottlenecked at the outbound link.

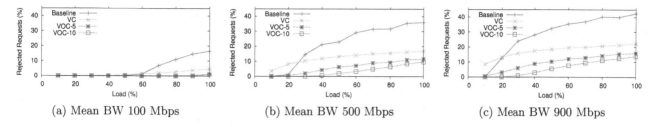

| (a) Mean BW 100 Mbps | (b) Mean BW 500 Mbps | (c) Mean BW 900 Mbps |

Figure 13: Percentage of rejected tenant requests with varying datacenter load and varying mean tenant bandwidth requirements. At load>20%, virtual networks allow more requests to be accepted.

scheme in which a request is rejected if it cannot be immediately allocated. For today's setup, requests are rejected if there are not enough available VMs when a request is submitted. For our virtual networks, instead, even if enough VMs are available, a request can still be rejected if the bandwidth constraints cannot be satisfied. We simulate the arrival and execution of 10,000 tenant requests with varying mean bandwidth requirements for the tenant jobs.

Rejected requests. Figure 13 shows that *only at very low loads, Baseline setup is comparable to virtual abstractions in terms of rejected requests, despite the fact that virtual abstractions explicitly reserve the bandwidth requested by tenants.* At low loads, requests arrive far apart in time and thus, they can always be allocated even though the Baseline setup prolongs job completion. As the load increases, Baseline rejects far more requests. For instance, at 70% load (Amazon EC2's operational load [3]) and bandwidth of 500 Mbps, 31% of Baseline requests are rejected as compared to 15% of VC requests and only 5% of VOC-10 requests.

Tenant costs and provider revenue. Today's cloud providers charge tenants based on the time they occupy their VMs. Assuming a price of k dollars per-VM per unit time, a tenant using N VMs for time T pays kNT dollars. This implies that *while intra-cloud network communication is not explicitly charged for, it is not free* since poor network performance can prolong tenant jobs and hence, increase their costs. Figure 12 shows the increase in tenant job completion times and the corresponding increase in tenant costs (upper X-axis) today. For all load values, many jobs finish later and cost more than expected– the cost for 25% tenants is more than 2.3 times their ideal cost had the network performance been sufficient (more than 9.2 times for 5% of the tenants).

The fraction of requests that are accepted and the costs for accepted requests govern the provider revenue. Figure 14 shows the provider revenue when tenants use virtual networks relative to Baseline revenue. At low load, the provider revenue is reduced since the use of virtual networks ensures that tenant jobs finish faster and they pay significantly less. However, as the load increases, the provider revenue increases since virtual network allow more requests to be accepted, even though individual tenants pay less than today. For efficiency, providers like Amazon operate their datacenters at an occupancy of 70-80% [3]. Hence, *for practical load values, virtual networks not only allow tenants to lower their costs, but also increase provider revenue!* Further, this estimation ignores the extra tenants that may be attracted by the guaranteed performance and reduced costs.

Charging for bandwidth. Providing tenants with virtual networks opens the door for explicitly charging for network bandwidth. This represents a more fair charging model

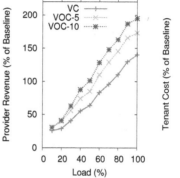

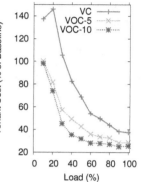

Figure 14: Provider revenue with virtual network abstractions. Mean BW = 500Mbps.

Figure 15: Relative tenant costs based on bandwidth charging model while maintaining provider revenue neutrality.

since a tenant should pay more for a *virtual cluster* with 500Mbps than one with 100Mbps. Given the lack of a reference charging model, we use a simple model to explore the economic benefits that the use of virtual networks would provide. Apart from paying for VM occupancy (k_v), tenants also pay a bandwidth charge of $k_b \frac{\$}{\text{bw*unit-time}}$. Hence, a tenant using a virtual cluster $<N, B>$ for time T pays $NT(k_v + k_b B)$.

Such a charging model presents an opportunity to redress the variability in provider revenue observed above. To this effect, we performed the following analysis. We used current Amazon EC2 prices to determine k_v and k_b for each virtual network abstraction so as to maintain provider revenue neutrality, i.e., the provider earns the same revenue as today.[4] We then determine the ratio of a tenant's cost with the new charging model to the status quo cost. The median tenant cost is shown in Figure 15. We find that except at low loads, *virtual networks can ensure that providers stay revenue neutral and tenants pay significantly less than Baseline while still getting guaranteed performance.* For instance, with a mean bandwidth demand of 500 Mbps, Figure 15 shows that tenants with virtual clusters at moderate load and 37% of Baseline at high load (31% and 25% respectively with VOC-10).

The charging model can be generalized from linear bandwidth costs to $NT(k_v + k_b f(B))$, where f is a bandwidth

---

[4]For Amazon EC2, small VMs cost 0.085\$/hr. Sample estimated prices in our experiments are at 0.04\$/hr for k_v, and 0.00016\$ /GB for k_b.

charging function. We repeated the analysis with other bandwidth functions ($B^{\frac{3}{2}}, B^2$), obtaining similar results.

5.4 Implementation and Deployment

Our Oktopus implementation follows the description in Section 4. The NM maintains reservations across the network and allocates tenant requests in an on-line fashion. The enforcement module on individual physical machines implements the rate computation and rate limiting functionality (Section 4.3). For each tenant, one of the tenant's VMs (and the corresponding enforcement module) acts as a controller and calculates the rate limits. Enforcement modules then use the Windows Traffic Control API [4] to enforce local rate limits on individual machines.

Scalability. To evaluate the scalability of the NM, we measured the time to allocate tenant requests on a datacenter with 10^5 endhosts. We used a Dell Precision T3500 with a quad-core Intel Xeon 5520 2.27 GHz processor and 4 GB RAM. Over 10^5 requests, the median allocation time is 0.35ms with a 99th percentile of 508ms. Note that this only needs to be run when a tenant is admitted, and hence, the NM can scale to large datacenters.

The rate computation overhead depends on the tenant's communication pattern. Even for a tenant with 1000 VMs (two orders of magnitude more than mean tenant size today [31]) and a *worst-case* scenario where all VMs communicate with all other VMs, the computation takes 395ms at the 99th percentile. With a typical communication pattern [20], 99th percentile computation time is 84ms. To balance the trade-off between accuracy and responsiveness of enforcement and the communication overhead, our implementation recomputes rates every 2 seconds. For a tenant with 1000 VMs and *worst-case* all-to-all communication between the VMs, the controller traffic is 12 Mbps (~1 Mbps with a typical communication pattern). Hence, the enforcement module imposes low overhead.

Deployment. We deployed Oktopus on a testbed with 25 endhosts arranged in five racks. Each rack has a Top-of-Rack (ToR) switch, which is connected to a root switch. Each interface is 1 Gbps. Hence, the testbed has a two-tier tree topology with a physical oversubscription of 5:1. All endhosts are Dell Precision T3500 servers with a quad core Intel Xeon 2.27GHz processor and 4GB RAM, running Windows Server 2008 R2. Given our focus on quantifying the benefits of Oktopus abstractions, instead of allocating VMs to tenants, we simply allow their jobs to run on the host OS. However, we retain the limit of 4 jobs per endhost, resulting in a total of 100 VM or job slots.

We repeat the experiments from Section 5.2 on the testbed and determine the completion time for a batch of 1000 tenant jobs (mean tenant size N is scaled down to 9). As before, each tenant job has a compute time (but no actual computation) and a set of TCP flows associated with it. Figure 16(a) shows that virtual clusters reduce completion time by 44% as compared to Baseline (57% for VOC-10). We repeated the experiment with all endhosts connected to one switch (hence, no physical oversubscription). The bars on the right in Figure 16(a) show that virtual clusters match the Baseline completion time while VOC-10 offers a 9% reduction. Since the scale of these experiments is smaller (smaller topology and tenants), virtual networks do not have much opportunity to improve performance and the reduction in completion time is less significant. However, tenant jobs still

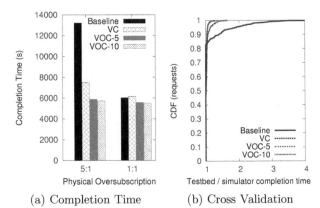

(a) Completion Time (b) Cross Validation

Figure 16: Testbed experiments show that virtual networks provide performance gains and validate our simulator.

get guaranteed network performance and hence, predictable completion times.

Cross-validation. We replayed the same job stream in our simulator and for each tenant request, we determined the ratio of the completion time on the testbed and the simulator. Figure 16(b) shows that for the vast majority of jobs, the completion time in the simulator matches that on the testbed. Some divergence results from the fact that network flows naturally last longer in the live testbed than in the simulator which optimally estimates the time flows take. We note that jobs that last longer in the testbed than the simulator occur more often with Baseline than with virtual networks. This is because the Baseline setup results in more network contention which, in turn, causes TCP to not fully utilize its fair share. Overall, the fact that the same workload yields similar performance in the testbed as in the simulator validates our simulation setup and strengthens our confidence in the results presented.

6. RELATED WORK

The increasing prominence of multi-tenant datacenters has prompted interest in network virtualization. Seawall [31] and NetShare [22] share the network bandwidth among tenants based on weights. The resulting proportional bandwidth distribution leads to efficient multiplexing of the underlying infrastructure; yet, in contrast to Oktopus, tenant performance still depends on other tenants. SecondNet [15] provides pairwise bandwidth guarantees where tenant requests can be characterized as $<N, [B_{ij}]_{N \times N}>$; $[B_{ij}]_{N \times N}$ reflects the complete pairwise bandwidth demand matrix between VMs. With Oktopus, we propose and evaluate more flexible virtual topologies that balance the trade-off between tenant demands and provider flexibility.

Duffield et al. [12] introduced the hose model for wide-area VPNs. The hose model is akin to the *virtual cluster* abstraction; however, the corresponding allocation problem is different since the physical machines are fixed in the VPN setting while we need to choose the machines. Other allocation techniques like simulated annealing and mixed integer programming have been explored as part of testbed mapping [29] and virtual network embedding [37]. These efforts focus on allocation of arbitrary (or, more general) virtual topologies on physical networks which hampers their scalability and restricts them to small physical networks ($O(10^2)$ machines).

7. CONCLUDING REMARKS

This paper presents virtual network abstractions that allow tenants to expose their network requirements. This enables a *symbiotic* relationship between tenants and providers; tenants get a predictable environment in shared settings while the provider can efficiently match tenant demands to the underlying infrastructure without muddling their interface. Our experience with Oktopus shows that the abstractions are practical, can be efficiently implemented and provide significant benefits.

Our abstractions, while emulating the physical networks used in today's enterprises, focus on a specific metric– inter-VM network bandwidth. Tenants may be interested in other performance metrics, or even non-performance metrics like reliability. Examples include bandwidth to the storage service, latency between VMs and failure resiliency of the paths between VMs. In this context, virtual network abstractions can provide a succinct means of information exchange between tenants and providers.

Another interesting aspect of virtual networks is cloud pricing. Our experiments show how tenants can implicitly be charged for their internal traffic. By offering bounded network resources to tenants, we allow for *explicit and fairer* bandwidth charging. More generally, charging tenants based on the characteristics of their virtual networks eliminates hidden costs and removes a key hindrance to cloud adoption. This, in effect, could pave the way for multi-tenant datacenters where tenants can pick the trade-off between the performance of their applications and their cost.

8. REFERENCES

[1] Amazon EC2 Spot Instances. http://aws.amazon.com/ec2/spot-instances/.

[2] Amazon Cluster Compute, Jan. 2011. http://aws.amazon.com/ec2/hpc-applications/.

[3] Amazon's EC2 Generating 220M, Jan. 2011. http://bit.ly/8rZdu.

[4] Traffic Control API, Jan. 2011. http://msdn.microsoft.com/en-us/library/aa374468%28v=VS.85%29.aspx.

[5] M. Al-Fares, A. Loukissas, and A. Vahdat. A scalable, commodity data center network architecture. In *Proc. of ACM SIGCOMM*, 2008.

[6] M. Al-Fares, S. Radhakrishnan, B. Raghavan, N. Huang, and A. Vahdat. Hedera: Dynamic Flow Scheduling for Data Center Networks. In *Proc. of USENIX NSDI*, 2010.

[7] G. Ananthanarayanan, S. Kandula, A. Greenberg, I. Stoica, Y. Lu, B. Saha, and E. Harris. Reining in the Outliers in Map-Reduce Clusters using Mantri. In *Proc. of USENIX OSDI*, 2010.

[8] H. Ballani, P. Costa, T. Karagiannis, and A. Rowstron. Towards Predictable Datacenter Networks. Technical Report MSR-TR-2011-72, Microsoft Research, May 2011.

[9] R. Black, A. Donnelly, and C. Fournet. Ethernet Topology Discovery without Network Assistance. In *Proc. of ICNP*, 2004.

[10] B. Craybrook. Comparing cloud risks and virtualization risks for data center apps, 2011. http://bit.ly/fKjwzW.

[11] J. Duato, S. Yalamanchili, and L. Ni. *Interconnection Networks: An Engineering Approach*. Elsevier, 2003.

[12] N. G. Duffield, P. Goyal, A. Greenberg, P. Mishra, K. K. Ramakrishnan, and J. E. van der Merive. A flexible model for resource management in virtual private networks. In *Proc. of ACM SIGCOMM*, 1999.

[13] A. Giurgiu. Network performance in virtual infrastrucures, Feb. 2010. http://staff.science.uva.nl/~delaat/sne-2009-2010/p29/presentation.pdf.

[14] A. Greenberg, J. R. Hamilton, N. Jain, S. Kandula, C. Kim, P. Lahiri, D. A. Maltz, P. Patel, and S. Sengupta. VL2: a scalable and flexible data center network. In *Proc. of ACM SIGCOMM*, 2009.

[15] C. Guo, G. Lu, H. J. Wang, S. Yang, C. Kong, P. Sun, W. Wu, and Y. Zhang. SecondNet: A Data Center Network Virtualization Architecture with Bandwidth Guarantees. In *Proc. of ACM CoNext*, 2010.

[16] M. Hajjat, X. Sun, Y.-W. E. Sung, D. Maltz, S. Rao, K. Sripanidkulchai, and M. Tawarmalani. Cloudward bound: Planning for beneficial migration of enterprise applications to the cloud. In *Proc. of SIGCOMM*, 2010.

[17] Q. He, S. Zhou, B. Kobler, D. Duffy, and T. McGlynn. Case study for running HPC applications in public clouds. In *Proc. of ACM Symposium on High Performance Distributed Computing*, 2010.

[18] A. Iosup, N. Yigitbasi, and D. Epema. On the Performance Variability of Production Cloud Services. Technical Report PDS-2010-002, Delft University of Technology, Jan. 2010.

[19] S. Kandula, J. Padhye, and P. Bahl. Flyways To Decongest Data Center Networks. In *Proc. of HotNets*, 2005.

[20] S. Kandula, S. Sengupta, A. Greenberg, P. Patel, and R. Chaiken. The Nature of Data Center Traffic: Measurements & Analysis. In *Proc. of ACM IMC*, 2009.

[21] D. Kossmann, T. Kraska, and S. Loesing. An Evaluation of Alternative Architectures for Transaction Processing in the Cloud. In *Proc. of international conference on Management of data (SIGMOD)*, 2010.

[22] T. Lam, S. Radhakrishnan, A. Vahdat, and G. Varghese. NetShare: Virtualizing Data Center Networks across Services. Technical Report CS2010-0957, University of California, San Deigo, May 2010.

[23] A. Li, X. Yang, S. Kandula, and M. Zhang. CloudCmp: comparing public cloud providers. In *Proc. of conference on Internet measurement (IMC)*, 2010.

[24] D. Mangot. Measuring EC2 system performance, May 2009. http://bit.ly/48Wui.

[25] X. Meng, V. Pappas, and L. Zhang. Improving the Scalability of Data Center Networks with Traffic-aware Virtual Machine Placement. In *Proc. of Infocom*, 2010.

[26] Michael Armburst et al. Above the Clouds: A Berkeley View of Cloud Computing. Technical report, University of California, Berkeley, 2009.

[27] J. Mudigonda, P. Yalagandula, M. Al-Fares, and J. Mogul. SPAIN: COTS Data-Center Ethernet for Multipathing over Arbitrary Topologies. In *Proc of NSDI*, 2010.

[28] B. Raghavan, K. Vishwanath, S. Ramabhadran, K. Yocum, and A. C. Snoeren. Cloud control with distributed rate limiting. In *Proc. of ACM SIGCOMM*, 2007.

[29] R. Ricci, C. Alfeld, and J. Lepreau. A Solver for the Network Testbed Mapping problem. *SIGCOMM CCR*, 33, 2003.

[30] J. Schad, J. Dittrich, and J.-A. Quiané-Ruiz. Runtime measurements in the cloud: observing, analyzing, and reducing variance. In *Proc. of VLDB*, 2010.

[31] A. Shieh, S. Kandula, A. Greenberg, and C. Kim. Sharing the Datacenter Network. In *Proc. of USENIX NSDI*, 2011.

[32] P. Soares, J. Santos, N. Tolia, and D. Guedes. Gatekeeper: Distributed Rate Control for Virtualized Datacenters. Technical Report HP-2010-151, HP Labs, 2010.

[33] E. Walker. Benchmarking Amazon EC2 for high-performance scientific computing. *Usenix Login*, 2008.

[34] G. Wang, D. G. Andersen, M. Kaminsky, K. Papagiannaki, T. S. E. Ng, M. Kozuch, and M. Ryan. c-Through: Part-time Optics in Data Centers. In *Proc. of ACM SIGCOMM*, 2010.

[35] G. Wang and T. S. E. Ng. The Impact of Virtualization on Network Performance of Amazon EC2 Data Center. In *Proc. of IEEE Infocom*, 2010.

[36] H. Wang, Q. Jing, S. Jiao, R. Chen, B. He, Z. Qian, and L. Zhou. Distributed Systems Meet Economics: Pricing in the Cloud. In *Proc. of USENIX HotCloud*, 2010.

[37] M. Yu, Y. Yi, J. Rexford, and M. Chiang. Rethinking Virtual Network Embedding: substrate support for path splitting and migration. *SIGCOMM CCR*, 38, 2008.

[38] M. Zaharia, A. Konwinski, A. D. Joseph, Y. Katz, and I. Stoica. Improving MapReduce Performance in Heterogeneous Environments. In *Proc. of OSDI*, 2008.

DevoFlow: Scaling Flow Management for High-Performance Networks*

Andrew R. Curtis
University of Waterloo

Jeffrey C. Mogul, Jean Tourrilhes, Praveen Yalagandula
Puneet Sharma, Sujata Banerjee
HP Labs — Palo Alto

ABSTRACT

OpenFlow is a great concept, but its original design imposes excessive overheads. It can simplify network and traffic management in enterprise and data center environments, because it enables flow-level control over Ethernet switching and provides global visibility of the flows in the network. However, such fine-grained control and visibility comes with costs: the switch-implementation costs of involving the switch's control-plane too often and the distributed-system costs of involving the OpenFlow controller too frequently, both on flow setups and especially for statistics-gathering.

In this paper, we analyze these overheads, and show that OpenFlow's current design cannot meet the needs of high-performance networks. We design and evaluate *DevoFlow*, a modification of the OpenFlow model which gently breaks the coupling between control and global visibility, in a way that maintains a useful amount of visibility without imposing unnecessary costs. We evaluate DevoFlow through simulations, and find that it can load-balance data center traffic as well as fine-grained solutions, without as much overhead: DevoFlow uses 10–53 times fewer flow table entries at an average switch, and uses 10–42 times fewer control messages.

Categories and Subject Descriptors.
C.2 [**Internetworking**]: Network Architecture and Design
General Terms. Design, Measurement, Performance
Keywords. Data center, Flow-based networking

1. INTRODUCTION

Flow-based switches, such as those enabled by the OpenFlow [35] framework, support fine-grained, flow-level control of Ethernet switching. Such control is desirable because it enables (1) correct enforcement of flexible policies without carefully crafting switch-by-switch configurations, (2) visibility over all flows, allowing for near optimal management of network traffic, and (3) simple and future-proof switch design. OpenFlow has been deployed at various academic institutions and research laboratories, and has been the basis for many recent research papers (e.g., [5,29,33,39,43]),

as well as for hardware implementations and research prototypes from vendors such as HP, NEC, Arista, and Toroki.

While OpenFlow was originally proposed for campus and wide-area networks, others have made quantified arguments that OpenFlow is a viable approach to high-performance networks, such as data center networks [45], and it has been used in proposals for traffic management in the data center [5,29]. The examples in this paper are taken from data center environments, but should be applicable to other cases where OpenFlow might be used.

OpenFlow is not perfect for all settings, however. In particular, we believe that it excessively couples central control and complete visibility. If one wants the controller to have visibility over all flows, it must also be on the critical path of setting up all flows, and experience suggests that such centralized bottlenecks are difficult to scale. Scaling the central controller has been the topic of recent proposals [11,33,47]. More than the controller, however, we find that the switches themselves can be a bottleneck in flow setup. Experiments with our prototype OpenFlow implementation indicate that its ratio of data-plane to control-plane bandwidth is four orders of magnitude less than its aggregate forwarding rate. We find this slow control-data path adds unacceptable latency to flow setup, and cannot provide flow statistics timely enough for traffic management tasks such as load balancing. Maintaining complete visibility in a large OpenFlow network can also require hundreds of thousands of flow table entries at each switch. Commodity switches are not built with such large flow tables, making them inadequate for many high-performance OpenFlow networks.

Perhaps, then, full control and visibility over all flows is not the right goal. Instead, we argue and demonstrate that effective flow management can be achieved by devolving control of most flows back to the switches, while the controller maintains control over only targeted *significant flows* and has visibility over only these flows and packet samples. (For example, load balancing needs to manage long-lived, high-throughput flows, known as "elephant" flows.) Our framework to achieve this, *DevoFlow*, is designed for simple and cost-effective hardware implementation.

In essence, DevoFlow is designed to allow aggressive use of wild-carded OpenFlow rules—thus reducing the number of switch-controller interactions and the number of TCAM entries—through new mechanisms to detect significant flows efficiently, by waiting until they actually become significant. DevoFlow also introduces new mechanisms to allow switches to make local routing decisions, which forward flows that do not require vetting by the controller.

The reader should note that we are not proposing any radical new designs. Rather, we are pointing out that a system like OpenFlow, when applied to high-performance networks, must account for *quantitative* real-world issues. Our arguments for DevoFlow are essentially an analysis of tradeoffs

---

*The version of this paper that originally appeared in the SIGCOMM proceedings contains an error in the description of Algorithm 1. This version has corrected that error.

between centralization and its costs, especially with respect to real-world hardware limitations. (We focus on OpenFlow in this work, but any centralized flow controller will likely face similar tradeoffs.)

Our goal in designing DevoFlow is to enable cost-effective, scalable flow management. Our design principles are:

- *Keep flows in the data-plane* as much as possible. Involving the control-plane in all flow setups creates too many overheads in the controller, network, and switches.
- *Maintain enough visibility over network flows* for effective centralized flow management, but otherwise provide only aggregated flow statistics.
- *Simplify the design and implementation of fast switches* while retaining network programmability.

DevoFlow attempts to resolve two dilemmas — a control dilemma:

- Invoking the OpenFlow controller on every flow setup provides good start-of-flow visibility, but puts too much load on the control plane and adds too much setup delay to latency-sensitive traffic, and
- Aggressive use of OpenFlow flow-match wildcards or hash-based routing (such as ECMP) reduces control-plane load, but prevents the controller from effectively managing traffic.

and a statistics-gathering dilemma:

- Collecting OpenFlow counters on lots of flows, via the pull-based Read-State mechanism, can create too much control-plane load, and
- Aggregating counters over multiple flows via the wild-card mechanism may undermine the controller's ability to manage specific elephant flows.

We resolve these two dilemmas by pushing responsibility over most flows to switches and adding efficient statistics collection mechanisms to identify significant flows, which are the only flows managed by the central controller. We discuss of the benefits of centralized control and visibility in §2, so as to understand how much devolution we can afford.

Our work here derives from a long line of related work that aims to allow operators to specify high-level policies at a logically centralized controller, which are then enforced across the network without the headache of manually crafting switch-by-switch configurations [10, 12, 25, 26]. This separation between forwarding rules and policy allows for innovative and promising network management solutions such as NOX [26, 45] and other proposals [29, 39, 49], but these solutions may not be realizable on many networks because the flow-based networking platform they are built on—OpenFlow—is not scalable. We are not the first to make this observation; however, others have focused on scaling the controller, e.g., Onix [33], Maestro [11], and a devolved controller design [44]. We find that the controller can present a scalability problem, but that switches may be a greater scalability bottleneck. Removing this bottleneck requires minimal changes: slightly more functionality in switch ASICs and more efficient statistics-collection mechanisms.

This paper builds on our earlier work [36], and makes the following major contributions: we measure the costs of OpenFlow on prototype hardware and provide a detailed analysis of its drawbacks in §3, we present the design and use of DevoFlow in §4, and we evaluate one use case of DevoFlow through simulations in §5.

2. BENEFITS OF CENTRAL CONTROL

In this section, we discuss which benefits of OpenFlow's central-control model are worth preserving, and which could be tossed overboard to lighten the load.

Avoids the need to construct global policies from switch-by-switch configurations: OpenFlow provides an advantage over traditional firewall-based security mechanisms, in that it avoids the complex and error prone process of creating a globally-consistent policy out of local accept/deny decisions [12, 39]. Similarly, OpenFlow can provide globally optimal admission control and flow-routing in support of QoS policies, in cases where a hop-by-hop QoS mechanism cannot always provide global optimality [31].

However, this does not mean that *all* flow setups should be mediated by a central controller. In particular, microflows (a *microflow* is equivalent to a specific end-to-end connection) can be divided into three broad categories: *security-sensitive flows*, which must be handled centrally to maintain security properties; *significant flows*, which should be handled centrally to maintain global QoS and congestion properties; and *normal flows*, whose setup can be devolved to individual switches.

Of course, all flows are potentially "security-sensitive," but some flows can be categorically, rather than individually, authorized by the controller. Using standard OpenFlow, one can create wild-card rules that pre-authorize certain sets of flows (e.g.: "all MapReduce nodes within this subnet can freely intercommunicate") and install these rules into all switches. Similarly, the controller can define flow categories that demand per-flow vetting (e.g., "all flows to or from the finance department subnet"). Thus, for the purposes of security, the controller need not be involved in every flow setup.

Central control of flow setup is also required for some kinds of QoS guarantees. However, in many settings, only those flows that require guarantees actually need to be approved individually at setup time. Other flows can be categorically treated as best-effort traffic. Kim *et al.* [31] describe an OpenFlow QoS framework that detects flows requiring QoS guarantees, by matching against certain header fields (such as TCP port numbers) while wild-carding others. Flows that do not match one of these "flow spec" categories are treated as best-effort.

In summary, we believe that the central-control benefits of OpenFlow can be maintained by individually approving certain flows, but categorically approving others.

Near-optimal traffic management: To effectively manage the performance of a network, the controller needs to know about the current loads on most network elements. Maximizing some performance objectives may also require timely statistics on some flows in the network. (This assumes that we want to exploit statistical multiplexing gain, rather than strictly controlling flow admission to prevent oversubscription.)

We give two examples where the controller is needed to manage traffic: load balancing and energy-aware routing.

Example 1: Load balancing via a controller involves collecting flow statistics, possibly down to the specific flow-on-link level. This allows the controller to re-route or throttle problematic flows, and to forecast future network loads. For example, NOX [45] "can utilize real-time information about network load ... to install flows on uncongested links."

However, load-balancing does not require the controller to be aware of the initial setup of every flow. First, some flows ("mice") may be brief enough that, individually, they are of no concern, and are only interesting in the aggregate. Second, some QoS-significant best-effort flows might not be distinguishable as such at flow-setup time – that is, the controller cannot tell from the flow setup request whether a flow will become sufficiently intense (an "elephant") to be worth handling individually.

Instead, the controller should be able to efficiently detect elephant flows as they become significant, rather than paying the overhead of treating every new flow as a potential elephant. The controller can then re-route problematic elephants in mid-connection, if necessary. For example, Al Fares *et al.* proposed Hedera, a centralized flow scheduler for data-center networks [5]. Hedera requires detection of "large" flows at the edge switches; they define "large" as 10% of the host-NIC bandwidth. The controller schedules these elephant flows, while the switches route mice flows using equal-cost multipath (ECMP) to randomize their routes.

Example 2: Energy-aware routing, where routing minimizes the amount of energy used by the network, can significantly reduce the cost of powering a network by making the network power-proportional [8]; that is, its power use is directly proportional to utilization. Proposed approaches including shutting off switch and router components when they are idle, or adapting link rates to be as minimal as possible [3,7,27,28,40]. For some networks, these techniques can give significant energy savings: up to 22% for one enterprise workload [7] and close to 50% on another [40].

However, these techniques do not save much energy on high-performance networks. Mahadevan *et al.* [34] found that, for their Web 2.0 workload on a small cluster, link-rate adaption reduced energy use by 16%, while energy-aware routing reduced it by 58%. We are not aware of a similar comparison for port sleeping vs. energy-aware routing; however, it is unlikely that putting network components to sleep could save significant amounts of energy in such networks. This is because these networks typically have many aggregation and core switches that aggregate traffic from hundreds or thousands of servers. It is unlikely that ports can be transitioned from sleep state to wake state quickly enough to save significant amounts of energy on these switches.

We conclude that some use of a central controller is necessary to build a power-proportional high-performance network. The controller requires utilization statistics for links and at least some visibility of flows in the network. Heller *et al.* [29] route all flows with the controller to achieve energy-aware routing; however, it may be possible to perform energy-aware routing without full flow visibility. Here, the mice flows should be aggregated along a set of least-energy paths using wildcard rules, while the elephant flows should be detected and re-routed as necessary, to keep the congestion on powered-on links below some safety threshold.

OpenFlow switches are relatively simple and future-proof because policy is imposed by controller software, rather than by switch hardware or firmware. Clearly, we would like to maintain this property. We believe that DevoFlow, while adding some complexity to the design, maintains a reasonable balance of switch simplicity vs. system performance, and may actually simplify the task of a switch designer who seeks a high-performance implementation.

3. OPENFLOW OVERHEADS

Flow-based networking involves the control-plane more frequently than traditional networking, and therefore has higher overheads. Its reliance on the control-plane has intrinsic overheads: the bandwidth and latency of communication between a switch and the central controller (§3.1). It also has implementation overheads, which can be broken down into implementation-imposed and implementation-specific overheads (§3.2). We also show that hardware changes alone cannot be a cost-effective way to reduce flow-based switching overheads in the near future (§3.3).

3.1 Intrinsic overheads

Flow-based networking intrinsically relies on a communication medium between switches and the central controller. This imposes both network load and latency.

To set up a bi-directional flow on an N-switch path, OpenFlow generates $2N$ flow-entry installation packets, and at least one initial packet in each direction is diverted first to and then from the controller. This adds up to $2N + 4$ extra packets.[1] These exchanges also add latency—up to twice the controller-switch RTT. The average length of a flow in the Internet is very short, around 20 packets per flow [46], and datacenter traffic has similarly short flows, with the median flow carrying only 1 KB [9,24,30]. Therefore, full flow-by-flow control using OpenFlow generates a lot of control traffic—on the order of one control packet for every two or three packets delivered if $N = 3$, which is a relatively short path, even within a highly connected network.

In terms of network load, OpenFlow's one-way flow-setup overhead (assuming a minimum-length initial packet, and ignoring overheads for sending these messages via TCP) is about $94 + 144N$ bytes to or from the controller—e.g., about 526 bytes for a 3-switch path. Use of the optional flow-removed message adds $88N$ bytes. The two-way cost is almost double these amounts, regardless of whether the controller sets up both directions at once.

3.2 Implementation overheads

In this section, we examine the overheads OpenFlow imposes on switch implementations. We ground our discussion in our experience implementing OpenFlow on the HP ProCurve 5406zl [1] switch, which uses an ASIC on each multi-port line card, and also has a CPU for management functions. This experimental implementation has been deployed in numerous research institutions.

While we use the 5406zl switch as an example throughout this section, the overheads we discuss are a consequence of both basic physics and of realistic constraints on the hardware that a switch vendor can throw at its implementation. The practical issues we describe are representative of those facing any OpenFlow implementation, and we believe that the 5406zl is representative of the current generation of Ethernet switches. OpenFlow also creates implementation-imposed overheads at the controller, which we describe after our discussion of the overheads incurred at switches.

3.2.1 Flow setup overheads

Switches have finite bandwidths between their data- and control-planes, and finite compute capacity. These issues can

---

[1]The controller could set up both directions at once, cutting the cost to $N + 2$ packets; NOX apparently has this optimization.

limit the rate of flow setups—the best implementations we know of can set up only a few hundred flows per second. To estimate the flow setup rate of the ProCurve 5406zl, we attached two servers to the switch and opened the next connection from one server to the other as soon as the previous connection was established. We found that the switch completes roughly 275 flow setups per second. This number is in line with what others have reported [43].

However, this rate is insufficient for flow setup in a high-performance network. The median inter-arrival time for flows at data center server is less than 30 ms [30], so we expect a rack of 40 servers to initiate approximately 1300 flows per second—far too many to send each flow to the controller.

The switch and controller are connected by a fast physical medium, so why is the switch capable of so few flow setups per second? First, on a flow-table miss, the data-plane must invoke the switch's control-plane, in order to encapsulate the packet for transmission to the controller.[2] Unfortunately, the management CPU on most switches is relatively wimpy, and was not intended to handle per-flow operations.

Second, even within a switch, control bandwidth may be limited, due to cost considerations. The data-plane within a linecard ASIC is very fast, so the switch can make forwarding decisions at line rate. On the other hand, the control data-path between the ASIC and the CPU is not frequently used in traditional switch operation, so this is typically a slow path. The line-card ASIC in the 5406zl switch has a raw bandwidth of 300 Gbit/sec, but we measured the loopback bandwidth between the ASIC and the management CPU at just 80 Mbit/sec. This four-order-of-magnitude difference is similar to observations made by others [13].

A switch's limited internal bandwidth and wimpy CPU limits the data rate between the switch and the central controller. Using the 5406zl, we measured the bandwidth available for flow-setup payloads between the switch and the OpenFlow controller at just 17 Mbit/sec.

We also measured the latency imposed. The ASIC can forward a packet within 5 μs, but we measured a round-trip time of 0.5 ms between the ASIC and the management CPU, and an RTT of 2 ms between that CPU and the OpenFlow controller. A new flow is delayed for at least 2 RTTs (forwarding the initial packet via the controller is delayed until the flow-setup RTT is over).

This flow-setup latency is far too high for high-performance networks, where most flows carry few bytes and latency is critical. Work from machines that miss their deadline in an interactive job is not included in the final results, lowering their quality and potentially reducing revenue. As a result, adding even 1ms delay to a latency-sensitive flow is "intolerable" [6]. Also, others have observed that the delay between arrival of a TCP flow's first packet and the controller's installation of new flow-table entries can create many out-of-order packets, leading to a collapse of the flow's initial throughput [50], especially if the switch-to-controller RTT is larger than that seen by the flow's packets.

Alternative approaches minimize these overheads but lose some of the benefits of OpenFlow. DIFANE [51] avoids these

overheads by splitting pre-installed OpenFlow wildcard rules among multiple switches, in a clever way that ensures all decisions can be made in the data-plane. However, DIFANE does not address the issue of global visibility of flow states and statistics. The types of management solutions we would like to enable (e.g., [5,29]) rely on global visibility and therefore it is unlikely they can be built on top of DIFANE. Another alternative, Mahout [17], performs elephant flow classifications at the end-hosts, by looking at the TCP buffer of outgoing flows, avoiding the need to invoke the controller for mice. Since this approach requires end-host modifications, it does not meet our goal of a drop-in replacement for Open-Flow.

3.2.2 Gathering flow statistics

Global flow schedulers need timely access to statistics. If a few, long-lived flows constitute the majority of bytes transferred, then a scheduler can get by collecting flow statistics every several seconds; however, this is not the case in high-performance networks, where most of the longest-lived flows last only a few seconds [30].

OpenFlow supports three per-flow counters (packets; bytes; flow duration) and provides two approaches for moving these statistics from switch to controller:

- **Push-based**: The controller learns of the start of a flow whenever it is involved in setting up a flow. Optionally, OpenFlow allows the controller to request an asynchronous notification when a switch removes a flow table entry, as the result of a controller-specified per-flow timeout. (OpenFlow supports both idle-entry timeouts and hard timeouts.) If flow-removed messages are used, this increases the per-flow message overhead from $2N+2$ to $3N+2$. The existing push-based mechanism does not inform the controller about the behavior of a flow before the entry times out, as a result, push-based statistics are not currently useful for flow scheduling.

- **Pull-based**: The controller can send a Read-State message to retrieve the counters for a set of flows matching a wild-card flow specification. This returns $88F$ bytes for F flows. Under ideal settings, reading the statistics for 16K exact-match rules and the 1500 wild-card rules supported on the 5406zl would return 1.3 MB; doing this twice per second would require slightly more than the 17 Mbit/sec bandwidth available between the switch CPU and the controller!

  Optionally, Read-State can request a report aggregated over all flows matching a wild-card specification; this can save switch-to-controller bandwidth but loses the ability to learn much about the behavior of specific flows.

Pull-based statistics can be used for flow scheduling if they can be collected frequently enough. The evaluation of one flow scheduler, Hedera [5], indicates that a 5 sec. control loop (the time to pull statistics from all access switches, compute a re-routing of elephant flows, and then update flow table entries where necessary) is fast enough for near-optimal load balancing on a fat-tree topology; however, their workload is based on flow lengths following a Pareto distribution. Recent measurement studies have shown data center flow sizes do not follow a Pareto distribution [9,24]. Using a workload with flow lengths following the distribution of flow sizes measured in [24], we find that a 5 sec. statistics-gathering interval can improve utilization only 1–5% over

---

[2]While it might be possible to do a simple encapsulation entirely within the data-plane, the OpenFlow specification requires the use of a secure channel, and it might not be feasible to implement the Transport Layer Security (TLS) processing, or even unencrypted TCP, without using the switch's CPU.

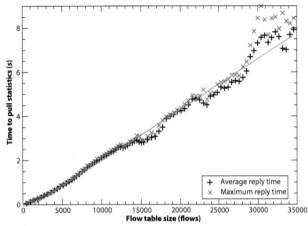

Figure 1: The latency of statistics gathering as the number of flow table entries is varied on the 5406zl Each point is the average of 10 runs, except for the maximum reply time points which are the maximum value seen out of those 10 runs. The switch was idle when the statistics were pulled.

randomized routing with ECMP (details are in §5). This is confirmed by Raiciu *et al.*, who found that the Hedera control loop needs to be less than 500ms to perform better than ECMP on their workload [41].

We measured how long it took to read statistics from the 5406zl as we varied the number of flow table entries. The results are shown in Figure 1. For this experiment (and all others in this section), we attached three servers to the switch: two servers were clients (A and B) and one was the Open-Flow controller. To get measurements with no other load on the switch, we configured the switch so that its flow table entries never expired. Then, both clients opened ten connections to each other. The controller waited 5 sec. to ensure that the switch was idle, and then pulled the statistics from the switch. This process was repeated until the flow table contained just over 32K entries.

From this experiment, we conclude that pull-based statistics cannot be collected frequently enough. We find that the statistic-gathering latency of the 5406zl is less than one second only when its flow table has fewer than 5600 entries and less than 500 ms when it has fewer than 3200 entries, and this is when there is no other load on the switch. Recall that a rack of 40 servers will initiate approximately 1300 flows per second. The default flow table entry timeout is 60 sec., so a rack's access switch can be expected to contain ~78K entries, which, extrapolating from our measurements, could take well over 15 sec. to collect! (The 5406zl does not support such a large table.) This can be improved to 13K table entries by reducing the table entry timeout to 10 sec.; however, it takes about 2.5 sec. to pull statistics for 13K entries with no other load at the switch, which is still too long for flow schedulers like Hedera.

In short, the existing statistics mechanisms impose high overheads, and in particular they do not allow the controller to request statistics visibility only for the small fraction of significant flows that actually matter for performance.

3.2.3 Impact on flow setup of statistics-gathering

Statistics-gathering and flow setup compete for the limited switch-controller bandwidth—the more frequently statistics are gathered, the fewer flows the switch can set up.

We performed an experiment to measure this interference.

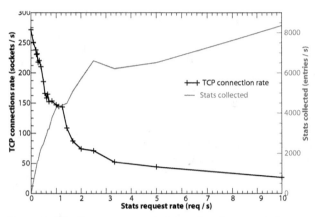

Figure 2: The flow setup rate between the clients and the number of statistics collected vs. the number of times statistics are requested per second. Each point is the average of 10 runs.

Here, each client has infinitely many flows to send to the other, and connections are established serially, that is, once one connection is established, another is opened. The client sends a single packet before closing each connection. We then vary the number of statistics-pulling requests between 0–10 requests per second.

The results are shown in Figure 2. We measured the number of connections achieved per second and the number of flow-entry statistics collected each second, as we varied the rate of requesting statistics for the entire flow table. It is clear that statistics-pulling interferes with flow setup. When statistics are never pulled, the clients can make 275 connections/sec.; when they are pulled once a second, collecting counters for just under 4500 entries, the clients can make fewer than 150 connections/sec.

3.2.4 Switch state size

A limited number of flow entries can be supported in hardware. The 5406zl switch hardware can support about 1500 OpenFlow rules, whereas the switch can support up to 64000 forwarding entries for standard Ethernet switching. One reason for this huge disparity is that OpenFlow rules are stored in a TCAM, necessary to support OpenFlow's wildcarding mechanism, and TCAM entries are an expensive resource, whereas Ethernet forwarding uses a simple hash lookup in a standard memory. It is possible to increase the number of TCAM entries, but TCAMs consume lots of ASIC space and power. Also, an OpenFlow rule is described by 10 header fields, which total 288 bits [35], whereas an Ethernet forwarding descriptor is 60 bits (48-bit MAC + 12-bit VLAN ID); so, even when fully optimized, OpenFlow entries will always use more state than Ethernet forwarding entries.

Finally, because OpenFlow rules are per-flow, rather than per-destination, each directly-connected host will typically require an order of magnitude more rules. (As we mentioned, an average ToR switch might have roughly 78,000 flow rules if the rule timeout is 60 sec.) Use of wildcards could reduce this ratio, but this is often undesirable as it reduces the ability to implement flow-level policies (such as multipathing) and flow-level visibility. Table 1 summarizes these limits.

Forwarding scheme	Descriptor size	Possible entries on 5406zl	Entries per active host
Ethernet learning	60 bits	~64000	1
OpenFlow	288 bits	~1500	10 (typical)

Table 1: State sizes: OpenFlow vs. Ethernet learning

3.2.5 Implementation-imposed controller overheads

Involving the controller in all flows creates a potential scalability problem: any given controller instance can support only a limited number of flow setups per second. For example, Tavakoli et al. [45] report that one NOX controller can handle "at least 30K new flow installs per second while maintaining a sub-10 ms flow install time ... The controller's CPU is the bottleneck." Kandula et al. [30] found that 100K flows arrive every second on a 1500-server cluster, implying a need for multiple OpenFlow controllers.

Recently researchers have proposed more scalable OpenFlow controllers. Maestro [11] is a multi-threaded controller that can install about twice as many flows per second as NOX, without additional latency. Others have worked on distributed implementations of the OpenFlow controller (also valuable for fault tolerance) These include Hyper-Flow (Tootoonchian and Ganjali [47]) and Onix (Koponen et al. [33]). These distributed controllers can only support global visibility of rare events such as link-state changes, and not of frequent events such as flow arrivals. As such, they are not yet suitable for applications, such as Hedera [5], which need a global view of flow statistics.

3.3 Hardware technology issues

A fair question to ask is whether our measurements are representative, especially since the 5406zl hardware was not designed to support OpenFlow. Hardware optimized for OpenFlow would clearly improve these numbers, but throwing hardware at the problem adds more cost and power consumption. Also, Moore's law for hardware won't provide much relief, as Ethernet speeds have been increasing at least as fast as Moore's law over the long term. Adding a faster CPU to the switch may improve control-plane bandwidth, but is unlikely to provide significant improvements without a bigger datapath and reorganized memory hierarchy. We believe such changes are likely to be complicated and expensive, especially because, for high-performance workloads, OpenFlow needs significantly more bandwidth between the data-plane and the control-plane than switches normally support (see §5.3). We expect this bandwidth gap will shrink as ASIC designers pay more attention to OpenFlow, but we do not think they will let OpenFlow performance drive their chip-area budgets for several generations, at least. And while Moore's Law might ameliorate the pressure somewhat, the need to reduce both ASIC cost and energy consumption suggests that hardware resources will always be precious.

An alternative implementation path is to use software-based OpenFlow switch implementations on commodity server hardware [18]. Such switches may have more control-plane bandwidth, but we do not believe these systems will be cost-effective for most enterprise applications in the foreseeable future. Casado et al. [13] have also argued that "network processors" are not ideal, either.

4. DEVOFLOW

We now present the design of DevoFlow, which avoids the overheads described above by introducing mechanisms for efficient devolved control (§4.1) and statistics collection (§4.2). Then, we discuss how to implement these mechanisms (§4.4), and end with an example of using DevoFlow to reduce use of the control-plane (§4.4).

4.1 Mechanisms for devolving control

We introduce two new mechanisms for devolving control to a switch, *rule cloning* and *local actions*.

Rule cloning: Under the standard OpenFlow mechanism for wildcard rules, all packets matching a given rule are treated as one flow. This means that if we use a wildcard to avoid invoking the controller on each microflow arrival, we also are stuck with routing all matching microflows over the same path, and aggregating all statistics for these microflows into a single set of counters.

In DevoFlow, we augment the "action" part of a wildcard rule with a boolean CLONE flag. If the flag is clear, the switch follows the standard wildcard behavior. Otherwise, the switch locally "clones" the wildcard rule to create a new rule in which all of the wildcarded fields are replaced by values matching this microflow, and all other aspects of the original rule are inherited. Subsequent packets for the microflow match the microflow-specific rule, and thus contribute to microflow-specific counters. Also, this rule goes into the exact-match lookup table, reducing the use of the TCAM, and so avoiding most of the TCAM power cost [37]. This resembles the proposal by Casado et al. [13], but their approach does per-flow lookups in control-plane software, which might not scale to high line rates.

Local actions: Certain flow-setup decisions might require decisions intermediate between the heavyweight "invoke the controller" and the lightweight "forward via this specific port" choices offered by standard OpenFlow. In DevoFlow, we envision rules augmented with a small set of possible "local routing actions" that a switch can take without paying the costs of invoking the controller. If a switch does not support an action, it defaults to invoking the controller, so as to preserve the desired semantics.

Examples of local actions include multipath support and rapid re-routing:

- **Multipath support** gives the switch a choice of several output ports for a clonable wildcard, not just one. The switch can then select, randomly from a probability distribution or round-robin, between these ports on each microflow arrival; the microflow-specific rule then inherits the chosen port rather than the set of ports. (This prevents intra-flow re-ordering due to path changes.)

  This functionality is similar to equal-cost multipath (ECMP) routing; however, multipath wildcard rules provide more flexibility. ECMP (1) uniformly selects an output port uniformly at random and (2) requires that the cost of the multiple forwarding paths to be equal, so it load balances traffic poorly on irregular topologies. As an example, consider a topology with two equal-cost links between s and t, but the first link forwards at 1 Gbps whereas the second has 10 Gbps capacity. ECMP splits flows evenly across these paths, which is clearly not ideal since one path has 10 times more bandwidth than the other.

  DevoFlow solves this problem by allowing a clonable wildcard rule to select an output port for a microflow according to some probability distribution. This allows implementation of *oblivious routing* (see, e.g., [20, 32]), where a microflow follows any of the available end-to-end paths according to a probability distribution. Oblivious routing would be optimal for our previous example, where it would route $10/11^{th}$ of the microflows for t on the 10Gbps link and $1/11^{th}$ of them on the 1Gbps link.

- **Rapid re-routing** gives a switch one or more fallback paths to use if the designated output port goes down. If the switch can execute this decision locally, it can recover from link failures almost immediately, rather than waiting several RTTs for the central controller to first discover the failure, and then to update the forwarding rules. OpenFlow *almost* supports this already, by allowing overlapping rules with different priorities, but it does not tell the switch *why* it would have multiple rules that could match a flow, and hence we need a small change to make indicate explicitly that one rule should replace another in the case of a specific port failure.

4.2 Efficient statistics collection

DevoFlow provides three different ways to improve the efficiency of OpenFlow statistics collection.

Sampling is an alternative to either push-based or pull-based collection (see §3.2.2). In particular, the sFlow protocol [42] allows a switch to report the headers of randomly chosen packets to a monitoring node—which could be the OpenFlow controller. Samples are uniformly chosen, typically at a rate of 1/1000 packets, although this is adjustable. Because sFlow reports do not include the entire packet, the incremental load on the network is less than 0.1%, and since it is possible to implement sFlow entirely in the data-plane, it does not add load to a switch's CPU. In fact, sFlow is already implemented in many switches, including the ProCurve 5406zl.

Triggers and reports: extends OpenFlow with a new push-based mechanism: threshold-based *triggers* on counters. When a trigger condition is met, for any kind of rule (wildcarded or not), the switch sends a *report*, similar to the Flow-Removal message, to the controller. (It can buffer these briefly, to pack several reports into one packet.)

The simplest trigger conditions are thresholds on the three per-flow counters (packets, bytes, and flow duration). These should be easy to implement within the data-plane. One could also set thresholds on packet or byte rates, but to do so would require more state (to define the right averaging interval) and more math, and might be harder to implement.

Approximate counters: can be maintained for all microflows that match a forwarding-table rule. Such counters maintain a view on the statistics for the top-k largest (as in, has transferred the most bytes) microflows in a space-efficient manner. Approximate counters can be implemented using streaming algorithms [21, 22, 23], which are generally simple, use very little memory, and identify the flows transferring the most bytes with high accuracy. For example, Golab *et al.*'s algorithm [23] correctly classifies 80–99% of the flows that transfer more than a threshold k of bytes. Implementing approximate counters in the ASIC is more difficult than DevoFlow's other mechanisms; however, they provide a more timely and accurate view of the network and can keep statistics on microflows without creating a table entry per microflow.

4.3 Implementation feasibility of DevoFlow

We have not implemented DevoFlow in hardware; however, our discussions with network hardware designers indicate that all of DevoFlow's mechanisms can be implemented cost-effectively in forthcoming production switches. (Sampling using sFlow, as we noted earlier, is already widely implemented in switch data-planes.)

Rule cloning: The data-plane needs to to directly insert entries into the exact-match table. This is similar to the existing MAC learning mechanism, the switch ASIC would need to be modified to take into account the formatting of entries in the flow table when learning new flows. If ASIC modification is not possible, rule cloning would require involving a CPU once per flow. Even so, this operation is considerably cheaper than invoking the centralized controller and should be orders of magnitude faster.

Multipath support: Can be implemented using specialized rule cloning or using a virtual port. Both methods require a small table to hold path-choice biasing weights for each multipath rule and a random number generator. The virtual port method is actually similar to link aggregation groups (LAG) and ECMP support, and could reuse the existing functional block with trivial modification.

Triggers: The mechanism needed to support triggers requires a counter and a comparator. It is similar to the one needed for rate limiters, and in some cases existing flexible rate limiters could be used to generate triggers. Most modern switches support a large number of flow counters, used for OpenFlow, NetFlow/IPFIX or ACLs. The ASIC would need to add a comparator to those counters to generate triggers; alternatively, the local CPU could poll periodically those counters and generate triggers itself.

Approximate counters: is the mechanism that would require the most extensive changes to current ASICs. It requires hashing on packet headers, which indirect to a set of counters, and then incrementing some of those counters. Switch ASICs have existing building blocks for most of these functions. It would also be non-trivial to support triggers on approximate counters; this might require using the local CPU.

4.4 Using DevoFlow

All OpenFlow solutions can be built on top of DevoFlow; however, DevoFlow enables scalable implementation of these solutions by reducing the number of flows that interact with the control-plane. Scalability relies on a finding a good definition of "significant flows" in a particular domain. These flows should represent a small fraction of the total flows, but should be sufficient to achieve the desired results.

As an example, we show how to load balance traffic with DevoFlow. First, we describe scalable flow scheduling with DevoFlow's mechanisms. Then, we describe how to use its multipath routing to statically load balance traffic without any use of the control-plane.

Flow scheduling: does not scale well if the scheduler relies on visibility over all flows, as is done in Hedera [5] because maintaining this visibility via the network is too costly, as our experiments in §3 showed.

Instead, we maintain visibility only over elephant flows, which is all that a system such as Hedera actually needs. While Hedera defines an elephant as a flow using at least

10% of a NIC's bandwidth, we define one as a flow that has transferred at least a threshold number of bytes X. A reasonable value for X is 1–10MB.

Our solution starts by initially routing incoming flows using DevoFlow's multipath wildcard rules; this avoids involving the control-plane in flow setup. We then detect elephant flows as they reach X bytes transferred. We can do this using using any combination of DevoFlow's statistics collection mechanisms. For example, we can place triggers on flow table entries, which generate a report for a flow after it has transferred X bytes; We could also use sampling or approximate counters; we evaluate each approach in §5.

Once a flow is classified as an elephant, the detecting switch or the sampling framework reports it to the DevoFlow controller. The controller finds the least congested path between the flow's endpoints, and re-routes the flow by inserting table entries for the flow at switches on this path.

The new route can be chosen, for example, by the decreasing best-fit bin packing algorithm of Correa and Goemans [16]. The algorithm's inputs are the network topology, link utilizations, and the rates and endpoints of the elephant flows. Its output is a routing of all elephant flows. Correa and Goemans proved that their algorithms finds routings with link utilizations at most 10% higher than the optimal routing, under a traffic model where all flows can be rearranged. We cannot guarantee this bound, because we only rearrange elephant flows; however, their theoretical results indicates their algorithm will perform as well as any other heuristic for flow scheduling.

Finally, we note that this architecture uses only edge switches to encapsulate new flows to send to the central controller. The controller programs core and aggregation switches reactively to flow setups from the edge switches. Therefore, the only overhead imposed is cost of installing flow table entries at the the core and aggregation switches—no overheads are imposed for statistics-gathering.

Static multipath routing: provides effective data-plane multipath load balancing with far greater flexibility than ECMP. By allowing clonable wildcard rules to select an output port for a microflow according to some probability distribution, we can implement *oblivious routing*, where an *s-t* microflow's path is randomly selected according to a precomputed probability distribution. This static routing scheme sets up these probability distributions so as to optimize routing any traffic matrix in a specified set; for example, in a data center one would generally like to optimize the routing of all "hose" traffic matrices [19], which is the set of all traffic matrices allowable as long as no end-host's ingress or egress rate exceeds a predefined rate.

Oblivious routing gives comparable throughput to the optimal dynamic routing scheme on many topologies. Kodialam *et al.* [32] found that packet-level oblivious routing achieves at least 94% of the throughput that dynamic routing does on the worst-case traffic matrix, for several wide-area network topologies.

However, these results assume that microflows can be split across multiple paths. While the flow-level multipath we implement with clonable wildcard rules does not conform to this assumption, we expect the theoretical results to be indicative of what to expect from flow-level oblivious routing on arbitrary topologies, just as it indicates the possible performance of oblivious routing on a Clos topology. Overall,

---

Algorithm 1 — Flow rate computation.

Input: set of flows F and a set of ports $\mathcal{P}$
Output: a rate $r(f)$ of each flow $f \in F$

begin
Initialize: $F_a = \emptyset$; $\forall f, r(f) = 0$
Define: $P.\text{used}() = \sum_{f \in F_a \cap P} r(f)$
Define: $P.\text{unassigned\_flows}() = P - (P \cap F_a)$
while $\mathcal{P} \neq \emptyset$ **do**
    Sort $\mathcal{P}$ in ascending order, where the sort key
        for P is $(P.\text{rate} - P.\text{used}())/|P.\text{unassigned\_flows}()|$
    $P = \mathcal{P}.\text{pop\_front}()$
    for each $f \in P.\text{unassigned\_flows}()$ **do**
        $r(f) = (P.\text{rate} - P.\text{used}())/|P.\text{unassigned\_flows}()|$
        $F_a = F_a \cup \{f\}$
end

---

the performance depends on the workload, as our results in §5 show. If oblivious routing does not achieve adequate performance on a particular topology and workload, it can be combined with DevoFlow's flow scheduler (described just above) to maximize utilization.

Finally, finding an oblivious routing is easy—one can be computed for any topology using linear programming [20]. Should the topology change, the forwarding probability distributions will need to be modified to retain optimality. Distributions for failure scenarios can be precomputed, and pushed to the switches once the central controller learns of a failure.

5. EVALUATION

In this section, we present our simulated evaluation of DevoFlow. We use load balancing as an example of how it can achieve the same performance as fine-grained, OpenFlow-based flow scheduling without the overhead.

5.1 Simulation methodology

To evaluate how DevoFlow would work on a large-scale network, we implemented a flow-level data center network simulator. This fluid model captures the overheads generated by each flow and the coarse-grained behavior of flows in the network. The simulator is event-based, and whenever a flow is started, ended, or re-routed, the rate of all flows is recomputed using the algorithm shown in Algorithm 1. This algorithm works by assigning a rate to flows traversing the most-congested port, and then iterating to the next most-congested port until all flows have been assigned a rate.

We represent the network topology with a capacitated, directed graph. For these simulations, we used two topologies: a three-level Clos topology [15] and a two-dimensional HyperX topology [4]. In both topologies, all links were 1Gbps, and 20 servers were attached to each access switch. The Clos topology has 80 access switches (each with 8 uplinks), 80 aggregation switches, and 8 core switches. The HyperX topology is two-dimensional and forms a 9×9 grid, and so has 81 access switches, each attached to 16 other switches. Since the Clos network has 8 core switches, it is 1:2.5 oversubscribed; that is, its bisection bandwidth is 640 Gbps. bandwidth. The HyperX topology is 1:4 oversubscribed and thus has 405 Gbps of bisection bandwidth.

The Clos network has 1600 servers and the HyperX network has 1620. We sized our networks this way for two reasons: first, so that the Clos and HyperX networks would have nearly the same number of servers. Second, our workload is based on the measurements of Kandula *et al.* [30], which are from a cluster of 1500 servers. We are not sure how to scale their measurements up to much larger data centers, so we kept the number of servers close to the number measured in their study.

We simulate the behavior of OpenFlow at switches by modeling (1) switch flow tables, and (2) the limited data-plane to control-plane bandwidth. Switch flow tables can contain both exact-match and wildcard table entries. For all simulations, table entries expire after 10 seconds. When a flow arrives that does not much a table entry, the header of its first packet is placed in the switch's data-plane to control-plane queue. The service rate for this queue follows our measurements described in Section 3.2.1, so it services packets at 17Mbps. This queue has finite length, and when it is full, any arriving flow that does not match a table entry is dropped. We experimented with different lengths for this queue, and we found that when it holds 1000 packets, no flow setups were dropped. When we set its limit to 100, we found that fewer than 0.01% of flow setups were dropped in the worst case. For all results shown in this paper, we set the length of this queue to 100; we restart rejected flows after a simulated TCP timeout of 300 ms.

Finally, because we are interested in modeling switch overheads, we do not simulate a bottleneck at the OpenFlow controller; the simulated OpenFlow controller processes all flows instantly. Also, whenever the OpenFlow controller re-routes a flow, it installs the flow-table entries without any latency.

5.1.1 Workloads

We consider two workloads in our simulations: (1) a MapReduce job that has just gone into its shuffle stage, and (2) a workload based on measurements, by Kandula *et al.* at Microsoft Research (MSR) [30], of a 1500-server cluster.

The MapReduce-style traffic is modeled by randomly selecting n servers to be part of the reduce-phase shuffle. Each of these servers transfers 128 MB to each other server, by maintaining connections to k other servers at once. Each server randomizes the order it connects to the other servers, keeping k connections open until it has sent its payload. All measurements we present for this shuffle workload are for a one-minute period that starts 10 sec. after the shuffle begins.

In our MSR workload, we generated flows based on the distributions of flow inter-arrival times and flow sizes in [30]. We attempted to reverse-engineer their actual workload from only two distributions in their paper. In particular, we did not model dependence between sets of servers. We pick the destination of a flow by first determining whether the flow is to be an inter- or intra-rack flow, and then selecting a destination uniformly at random between the possible servers. For these simulations, we generated flows for four minutes, and present measurements from the last minute.

Additionally, we simulated a workload that combines the MSR and shuffle workloads, by generating flows according to both workloads simultaneously. We generated three minutes of MSR flows before starting the shuffle. We present measurements for the first minute after the shuffle began.

5.1.2 Schedulers

We compare static routing with ECMP to flow scheduling with several schedulers.

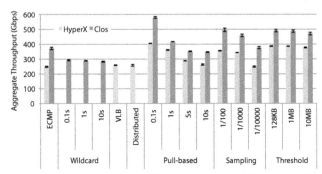

Figure 3: Throughput achieved by the schedulers for the shuffle workload with $n = 800$ and $k = 5$. OpenFlow-imposed overheads are not modeled in these simulations. All error bars in this paper show 95% confidence intervals for 10 runs.

The DevoFlow scheduler: behaves as described in Sec. 4, and collects statistics using either sampling or threshold triggers on multipath wildcard rules. The scheduler might re-reroute a flow after it has classified the flow as an elephant. New flows, before they become elephant flows, are routed using ECMP regardless of the mechanism to detect elephant flows. When the controller discovers an elephant flow, it installs flow-table entries at the switches on the least-congested path between the flow's endpoints. We model queueing of a flow between the data-plane and control-plane before it reaches the controller; however, we assume instantaneous computation at the controller and flow-table installations.

For elephant detection, we evaluate both sampling and triggers.

Our flow-level simulation does not simulate actual packets, which makes modeling of packet sampling non-trivial. In our approach:

1. We estimate the distribution of packets sent by a flow before it can be classified, with less than a 10% false-positive rate, as an elephant flow, using the approach described by Mori *et al.* [38].

2. Once a flow begins, we use that distribution to select how many packets it will transfer before being classified as an elephant; we assume that all packets are 1500 bytes. We then create an event to report the flow to the controller once it has transferred this number of packets.

Finally, we assume that the switch bundles 25 packet headers into a single report packet before sending the samples to the controller; this reduces the packet traffic without adding significant delay. Bundling packets this way adds latency to the arrival of samples at the controller. For our simulations, we did not impose a time-out this delay. We bundled samples from all ports on a switch, so when a 1 Gbps port is the only active port (and assuming it's fully loaded), this bundling could add up to 16 sec. of delay until a sample reaches the controller, when the sample rate is 1/1000 packets.

Fine-grained control using statistics pulling: simulates using OpenFlow in active mode. Every flow is set up at the central controller and the controller regularly pulls statistics, which it uses to schedule flows so as to maximize throughput. As with the DevoFlow scheduler, we route elephant flows using Correa and Goeman's bin-packing algorithm [16]. Here, we use Hedera's definition of an elephant flow: one with a demand is at least 10% of the NIC rate [5]. The rate of each flow is found using Algorithm 1 on an ideal network; that is, each access switch has an infinite-capacity uplink to a sin-

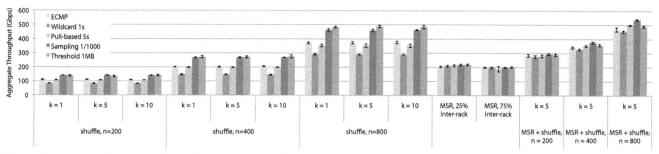

Figure 4: Aggregate throughput of the schedulers on the Clos network for different workloads. For the MSR plus shuffle workloads, 75% of the MSR workload-generated flows are inter-rack.

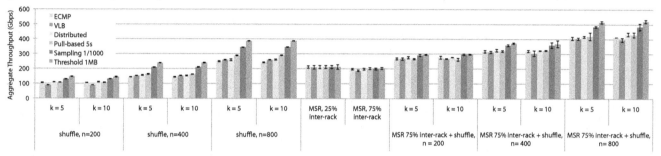

Figure 5: Aggregate throughput of the schedulers on the HyperX network for different workloads.

gle, non-blocking core switch. This allows us to estimate the demand of each flow when flow rates are constrained only by server NICs and not by the switching fabric.

Following the OpenFlow standard, each flow table entry provides 88 bytes of statistics [2]. We collect statistics only from the access switches. The ASIC transfers statistics to the controller at 17 Mbps, via 1500-byte packets. The controller applies the bin-packing algorithm immediately upon receiving a statistics report, and instantaneous installs a globally optimized routing for all flows.

Wildcard routing: performs multipath load balancing possible using only wildcard table entries. This controller reactively installs wildcard rules to create a unique spanning tree per destination: all flows destined to a server are routed along a spanning tree. When a flow is set up, the controller computes the least-congested path from the switch that registered the flow to the flow's destination's spanning tree, and installs the rules along this path. We simulated wildcard routing only on the Clos topology, because we are still developing the spanning tree algorithm for HyperX networks.

Valiant load balancing (VLB): balances traffic by routing each flow through an intermediate switch chosen uniformly at random; that switch then routes the flow on the shortest path to its destination [48]. On a Clos topology, ECMP implements VLB.

Distributed greedy routing: routes each flow by first greedily selecting the least-congested next-hop from the access switch, and then using shortest-path routing. We simulate this distributed routing scheme only on HyperX networks.

5.2 Performance

We begin by assessing the performance of the schedulers, using the aggregate throughput of all flows in the network as our metric. Figure 3 shows the performance of the schedulers under various settings, on a shuffle workload with $n = 800$ servers and $k = 5$ simultaneous connections/server. This simulation did *not* model the OpenFlow-imposed overheads;

for example, the 100ms pull-based scheduler obtains all flow statistics every 100ms, regardless of the switch load.

We see that DevoFlow can improve throughput compared to ECMP by up to 32% on the Clos network and up to 55% on the HyperX network. The scheduler with the best performance on both networks is the pull-based scheduler when it re-routes flows every 100 ms. This is not entirely surprising, since this scheduler also has the highest overhead. Interestingly, VLB did not perform any better than ECMP on the HyperX network.

To study the effect of the workload on these results, we tried several values for n and k in the shuffle workload and we varied the fraction of traffic that remained within a rack on the MSR workload. These results are shown in Figure 4 for the Clos topology and Figure 5 for the HyperX network. Overall, we found that flow scheduling improves throughput for the shuffle workloads, even when the network has far more bisection bandwidth than the job demands.

For instance, with $n = 200$ servers, the maximum demand is 200 Gbps. Even though the Clos network has 640 Gbps of bisection bandwidth, we find that DevoFlow can increase performance of this shuffle by 29% over ECMP. We also observe that there was little difference in performance when we varied k.

Flow scheduling did not improve the throughput of the MSR workload. For this workload, regardless of the mix of inter- and intra-rack traffic, we found that ECMP achieves 90% of the optimal throughput[3] for this workload, so there is little room for improvement by scheduling flows. We suspect that a better model than our reverse-engineered distributions of the MSR workload would yield different results.

Because of this limitation, we simulated a combination of the MSR workload with a shuffle job. Here, we see improvements in throughput due to flow scheduling; however, the gains are less than when the shuffle job is ran in isolation.

---

[3]We found the optimal throughput by attaching all servers to a single non-blocking switch.

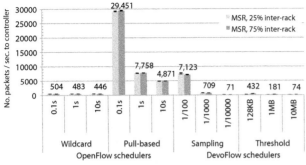

Figure 6: The number of packet arrivals per second at the controller using the different schedulers on the MSR workload.

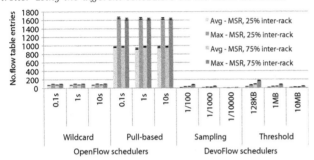

Figure 7: The average and maximum number of flow table entries at an access switch for the schedulers using the MSR workload.

5.3 Overheads

We used the MSR workload to evaluate the overhead of each approach because, even though we do not model the dependence between servers, we believe it gives a good indication of the rate of flow initiation. Figure 6 shows, for each scheduler, the rate of packets sent to the controller while simulating the MSR workload.

Load at the controller should scale proportionally to the number of servers in the data center. Therefore, when using an OpenFlow-style pull-based scheduler that collects stats every 100ms, in a large data center with 160K servers, we would expect a load of about 2.9M packets/sec., based on extrapolation from Figure 6. This would drop to 775K packets/sec. if stats are pulled once per second. We are not aware of any OpenFlow controller that can handle this message rate; for example, NOX can process 30K flow setups per second [45]. A distributed controller might be able to handle this load (which would require up to 98 NOX controllers, assuming they can be perfectly distributed and that statistics are pulled every 100 ms), but it might be difficult to coordinate so many controllers.

Figure 7 shows the number of flow table entries at any given access switch, for the MSR workload and various schedulers. For these simulations, we timed out the table entries after 10 sec. As expected, DevoFlow does not require many table entries, since it uses a single wildcard rule for all mice flows, and stores only exact-match entries for elephant flows. This does, however, assume support for the multipath routing wildcard rules of DevoFlow. If rule cloning were used instead, DevoFlow would use the same number of table entries as the pull-based OpenFlow scheduler because it would clone a rule for each flow. The pull-based scheduler uses an order of magnitude more table entries, on average, than DevoFlow.

We estimated the amount bandwidth required between a switch's data-plane and control-plane when statistics are

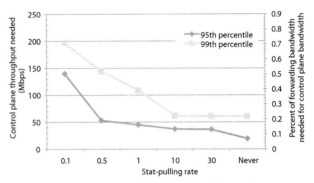

Figure 8: The control-plane bandwidth needed to pull statistics at various rates so that flow setup latency is less than 2ms in the 95th and 99th percentiles. Error bars are too small to be seen.

collected with a pull-based mechanism. Figure 8 shows the bandwidth needed so that the 95th and 99th percentile flow setup latencies on the MSR workload are less than 2ms. Here, we assume that the only latency incurred is in the queue between the switch's data-plane and control-plane; we ignore any latency added by communication with the controller. That is, the figure shows the service rate needed for this queue, in order to maintain a waiting time of less than 2 ms in the 95th and 99th percentiles. The data to control-plane bandwidth sufficient for flow setup is directly proportional to this deadline, so a tighter deadline of 1 ms needs twice as much bandwidth to meet.

The scale on the right of the chart normalizes the required data-to-control-plane bandwidth to a switch's total forwarding rate (which in our case is 28 Gbps, because each ToR switch has 28 gigabit ports). For fine-grained (100 ms) flow management using OpenFlow, this bandwidth requirement would be up to 0.7% of its total forwarding rate. Assuming that the amount of control-plane bandwidth needed scales with the forwarding rate, a 144-port 10 Gbps switch needs just over 10 Gbps of control-plane bandwidth to support fine-grained flow management. We do not believe it is cost-effective to provide so much bandwidth, so DevoFlow's statistics-collection mechanisms are the better option because they are handled entirely within the data-plane.

6. CONCLUSIONS

Flow-based networking frameworks such as OpenFlow hold great promise—they separate policy specification from its realization, and therefore enable innovative network management solutions. However, we have shown that OpenFlow's current design does not meet the demands of high-performance networks. In particular, OpenFlow involves the controller in the handling of too many microflows, which creates excessive load on the controller and switches.

Our DevoFlow proposal allows operators to target only the flows that matter for their management problem. DevoFlow reduces the switch-internal communication between control- and data-planes by (a) reducing the need to transfer statistics for boring flows, and (b) potentially reducing the need to invoke the control-plane for most flow setups. It therefore reduces both the intrinsic and implementation overheads of flow-based networking, by reducing load on the network, the switch control-plane, and the central controller. DevoFlow handles most microflows in the data-plane, and therefore allows us to make the most out of switch resources. Our evaluation shows that DevoFlow performs as well as fine-grained flow management when load balancing traffic in the data center. Beyond this use case, we believe that DevoFlow can simplify the design of high-performance OpenFlow switches and enable scalable management architectures to be built on OpenFlow for data center QoS, multicast, routing-as-a-service [14], network virtualization [43], and energy-aware routing [29].

Acknowledgments

We would like to thank Joe Curcio, Charles Clark, Paul Congdon, Mark Gooch, and many others from HP Networking for helping us to understand how real switches are designed. Our shepherd, Paul Barford, and the anonymous reviewers gave us helpful advice on comments for the final version of this paper. S. Keshav, Alex López-Ortiz, and Earl Oliver gave us beneficial feedback on earlier drafts. We thank Brent Stephens for pointing out an error in our description of Algorithm 1 in a previous version of this paper.

7. REFERENCES

[1] HP ProCurve 5400 zl switch series.
http://h17007.www1.hp.com/us/en/products/switches/HP_E5400_zl_Switch_Series/index.aspx.
[2] OpenFlow Switch Specification, Version 1.0.0. http://www.openflowswitch.org/documents/openflow-spec-v1.0.0.pdf.
[3] D. Abts, M. R. Marty, P. M. Wells, P. Klausler, and H. Liu. Energy proportional datacenter networks. In ISCA, 2010.
[4] J. H. Ahn, N. Binkert, A. Davis, M. McLaren, and R. S. Schreiber. HyperX: topology, routing, and packaging of efficient large-scale networks. In Proc. Supercomputing, 2009.
[5] M. Al-Fares, S. Radhakrishnan, B. Raghavan, N. Huang, and A. Vahdat. Hedera: Dynamic Flow Scheduling for Data Center Networks. In Proc. NSDI, Apr. 2010.
[6] M. Alizadeh, A. Greenberg, D. A. Maltz, J. Padhye, P. Patel, B. Prabhakar, S. Sengupta, and M. Sridharan. DCTCP: Efficient packet transport for the commoditized data center. In SIGCOMM, 2010.
[7] G. Ananthanarayanan and R. H. Katz. Greening the switch. In USENIX Workshop on Power Aware Computing and Systems, (HotPower 2008), 2008.
[8] L. A. Barroso and U. Hölzle. The case for energy-proportional computing. Computer, 40(12):33–37, 2007.
[9] T. Benson, A. Akella, and D. Maltz. Network traffic characteristics of data centers in the wild. In Proc. IMC, 2010.
[10] M. Caesar, D. Caldwell, N. Feamster, J. Rexford, A. Shaikh, and J. van der Merwe. Design and implementation of a routing control platform. In NSDI, 2005.
[11] Z. Cai, A. L. Cox, and T. S. E. Ng. Maestro: A System for Scalable OpenFlow Control. Tech. Rep. TR10-08, Rice University, 2010.
[12] M. Casado, M. J. Freedman, J. Pettit, J. Luo, N. McKeown, and S. Shenker. Ethane: taking control of the enterprise. In SIGCOMM, pages 1–12, Aug. 2007.
[13] M. Casado, T. Koponen, D. Moon, and S. Shenker. Rethinking Packet Forwarding Hardware. In Proc. HotNets, Oct. 2008.
[14] C.-C. Chen, L. Yuan, A. Greenberg, C.-N. Chuah, and P. Mohapatra. Routing-as-a-service (RaaS): A framework for tenant-directed route control in data center. In INFOCOM, 2011.
[15] C. Clos. A study of non-blocking switching networks. Bell System Technical Journal, 32(5):406–424, 1953.
[16] J. R. Correa and M. X. Goemans. Improved bounds on nonblocking 3-stage clos networks. SIAM J. Comput., 37(3):870–894, 2007.
[17] A. R. Curtis, W. Kim, and P. Yalagandula. Mahout: Low-overhead datacenter traffic management using end-host-based elephant detection. In INFOCOM, 2011.
[18] M. Dobrescu, N. Egi, K. Argyraki, B.-G. Chun, K. Fall, G. Iannaccone, A. Knies, M. Manesh, and S. Ratnasamy. RouteBricks: exploiting parallelism to scale software routers. In Proc. SOSP, pages 15–28, 2009.
[19] N. G. Duffield, P. Goyal, A. Greenberg, P. Mishra, K. K. Ramakrishnan, and J. E. van der Merive. A flexible model for resource management in virtual private networks. In SIGCOMM, 1999.
[20] T. Erlebach and M. Rüegg. Optimal bandwidth reservation in hose-model VPNs with multi-path routing. In IEEE INFOCOM, 2004.
[21] C. Estan and G. Varghese. New directions in traffic measurement and accounting. In SIGCOMM, 2002.
[22] P. B. Gibbons and Y. Matias. New sampling-based summary statistics for improving approximate query answers. In SIGMOD, 1998.
[23] L. Golab, D. DeHaan, E. D. Demaine, A. Lopez-Ortiz, and J. I. Munro. Identifying frequent items in sliding windows over on-line packet streams. In IMC, 2003.
[24] A. Greenberg, J. R. Hamilton, N. Jain, S. Kandula, C. K. P. Lahiri, D. Maltz, P. Patel, and S. Sengupta. VL2: a scalable and flexible data center network. In SIGCOMM, 2009.
[25] A. Greenberg et al.. A clean slate 4D approach to network control and management. SIGCOMM CCR, 35:41–54, 2005.
[26] N. Gude, T. Koponen, J. Pettit, B. Pfaff, M. Casado, N. McKeown, and S. Shenker. NOX: Towards an Operating System for Networks. In SIGCOMM CCR, July 2008.
[27] M. Gupta, S. Grover, and S. Singh. A feasibility study for power management in LAN switches. In ICNP, 2004.
[28] M. Gupta and S. Singh. Using low-power modes for energy conservation in ethernet LANs. In INFOCOM Mini-Conference, 2007.
[29] B. Heller, S. Seetharaman, P. Mahadevan, Y. Yiakoumis, P. Sharma, S. Banerjee, and N. McKeown. ElasticTree: saving energy in data center networks. In NSDI, 2010.
[30] S. Kandula, S. Sengupta, A. Greenberg, and P. Patel. The Nature of Datacenter Traffic: Measurements & Analysis. In Proc. IMC, 2009.
[31] W. Kim, P. Sharma, J. Lee, S. Banerjee, J. Tourrilhes, S.-J. Lee, and P. Yalagandula. Automated and Scalable QoS Control for Network Convergence. In Proc. INM/WREN, 2010.
[32] M. Kodialam, T. V. Lakshman, and S. Sengupta. Maximum throughput routing of traffic in the hose model. In Infocom, 2006.
[33] T. Koponen, M. Casado, N. Gude, J. Stribling, L. Poutievski, M. Zhu, R. Ramanathan, Y. Iwata, H. Inoue, T. Hama, and S. Shenker. Onix: a distributed control platform for large-scale production networks. In OSDI, 2010.
[34] P. Mahadevan, P. Sharma, S. Banerjee, and P. Ranganathan. Energy aware network operations. In Proc. 12th IEEE Global Internet Symp., 2009.
[35] N. McKeown, T. Anderson, H. Balakrishnan, G. Parulkar, L. Peterson, J. Rexford, S. Shenker, and J. Turner. OpenFlow: enabling innovation in campus networks. SIGCOMM CCR, 38(2):69–74, 2008.
[36] J. C. Mogul, J. Tourrilhes, P. Yalagandula, P. Sharma, A. R. Curtis, and S. Banerjee. Devoflow: Cost-effective flow management for high performance enterprise networks. In HotNets, 2010.
[37] N. Mohan and M. Sachdev. Low-Leakage Storage Cells for Ternary Content Addressable Memories. IEEE Trans. VLSI Sys., 17(5):604–612, may 2009.
[38] T. Mori, M. Uchida, R. Kawahara, J. Pan, and S. Goto. Identifying elephant flows through periodically sampled packets. In Proc. IMC, pages 115–120, Taormina, Oct. 2004.
[39] A. K. Nayak, A. Reimers, N. Feamster, and R. Clark. Resonance: Dynamic Access Control for Enterprise Networks. In Proc. WREN, pages 11–18, Aug. 2009.
[40] S. Nedevschi, L. Popa, G. Iannaccone, S. Ratnasamy, and D. Wetherall. Reducing network energy consumption via sleeping and rate-adaptation. In NSDI, 2008.
[41] C. Raiciu, C. Pluntke, S. Barre, A. Greenhalgh, D. Wischik, and M. Handley. Data center networking with multipath TCP. In HotNets, 2010.
[42] sFlow. http://sflow.org/about/index.php.
[43] R. Sherwood, G. Gibb, K.-K. Yap, G. Appenzeller, M. Casado, N. McKeown, and G. Parulkar. Can the production network be the testbed? In OSDI, 2010.
[44] A. S.-W. Tam, K. Xi, and H. J. Chao. Use of Devolved Controllers in Data Center Networks. In INFOCOM Workshop on Cloud Computing, 2011.
[45] A. Tavakoli, M. Casado, T. Koponen, and S. Shenker. Applying NOX to the Datacenter. In HotNets, 2009.
[46] K. Thompson, G. Miller, and R. Wilder. Wide-Area Internet Traffic Patterns and Characteristics. IEEE Network, 11(6):10–23, Nov. 1997.
[47] A. Tootoonchian and Y. Ganjali. HyperFlow: A Distributed Control Plane for OpenFlow. In Proc. INM/WREN, San Jose, CA, Apr. 2010.
[48] L. G. Valiant and G. J. Brebner. Universal schemes for parallel communication. In STOC, 1981.
[49] R. Wang, D. Butnariu, and J. Rexford. Openflow-based server load balancing gone wild. In Hot-ICE, 2011.
[50] C. Westphal. Personal communication, 2011.
[51] M. Yu, J. Rexford, M. J. Freedman, and J. Wang. Scalable Flow-Based Networking with DIFANE. In Proc. SIGCOMM, 2010.

Improving Datacenter Performance and Robustness with Multipath TCP

Costin Raiciu†*, Sebastien Barre‡, Christopher Pluntke†,
Adam Greenhalgh†, Damon Wischik†, Mark Handley†

†University College London, ‡Universite Catholique de Louvain, *Universitatea Politehnica Bucuresti
{c.raiciu, c.pluntke, a.greenhalgh, d.wischik, mjh}@cs.ucl.ac.uk, sebastien.barre@uclouvain.be

ABSTRACT

The latest large-scale data centers offer higher aggregate bandwidth and robustness by creating multiple paths in the core of the network. To utilize this bandwidth requires different flows take different paths, which poses a challenge. In short, a single-path transport seems ill-suited to such networks.

We propose using Multipath TCP as a replacement for TCP in such data centers, as it can effectively and seamlessly use available bandwidth, giving improved throughput and better fairness on many topologies. We investigate what causes these benefits, teasing apart the contribution of each of the mechanisms used by MPTCP.

Using MPTCP lets us rethink data center networks, with a different mindset as to the relationship between transport protocols, routing and topology. MPTCP enables topologies that single path TCP cannot utilize. As a proof-of-concept, we present a dual-homed variant of the FatTree topology. With MPTCP, this outperforms FatTree for a wide range of workloads, but costs the same.

In existing data centers, MPTCP is readily deployable leveraging widely deployed technologies such as ECMP. We have run MPTCP on Amazon EC2 and found that it outperforms TCP by a factor of three when there is path diversity. But the biggest benefits will come when data centers are designed for multipath transports.

Categories and Subject Descriptors

C.2.2[**Computer-Comms Nets**]: Network Protocols

General Terms: Algorithms, Design, Performance

1. INTRODUCTION

During the last decade, data centers have risen to dominate the computing landscape. Today's largest data centers have hundreds of thousands of servers, and run distributed applications that spread computation and storage across many thousands of machines. With so many hosts, it is impractical to manually manage the allocation of tasks to machines. While applications may be written to take advantage of locality within the data center, large distributed computations inevitably are spread across many racks of machines, with the result that the network can often be the bottleneck.

The research literature has proposed a number of data center topologies[1, 6, 7, 2] that attempt to remedy this bottleneck by providing a dense interconnect structure such as those shown in Fig. 1.

Topologies like these have started to be deployed; Amazon's latest EC2 data center has such a redundant structure - between certain pairs of hosts there are many alternative paths. Typically switches run a variant of ECMP routing, randomly hashing flows to equal cost paths to balance load across the topology. However, with most such topologies it takes many simultaneous TCP connections per host to generate sufficient flows to come close to balancing traffic. With more typical load levels, using ECMP on these multi-stage topologies causes flows to collide on at least one link with high probability. In traffic patterns that should be able to fill the network, we have observed flows that only manage 10% of the throughput they might expect and total network utilization below 50%.

In this paper we examine the use of Multipath TCP [4] within large data centers. Our intuition is that by exploring multiple paths simultaneously and by linking the congestion response of subflows on different paths to move traffic away from congestion, MPTCP will lead to both higher network utilization and fairer allocation of capacity to flows.

From a high-level perspective, there are four main components to a data center networking architecture:

- Physical topology
- Routing over the topology
- Selection between multiple paths supplied by routing
- Congestion control of traffic on the selected paths

These are not independent; the performance of one will depend on the choices made by those preceding it in the list, and in some cases by those after it in the list. The insight that we evaluate in this paper is that MPTCP's ability to balance load spans both path selection and congestion control, and fundamentally changes the dynamics of data center traffic management. Further, by exploring many paths and only utilizing the effective ones, it enables the use of network topologies that would be inefficient with single-path TCP. Thus we set out to answer two key questions:

- MPTCP can greatly improve performance in *today's* data centers. Under which circumstances does it do so, how big are the benefits, and on what do they depend?

- If MPTCP were deployed, how might we design data centers differently *in the future* to take advantage of its capabilities?

We have examined many topologies and traffic patterns, and in almost all of them MPTCP provided significant advantages over regular single-path TCP. Where there was no benefit, flows were limited at the sending or receiving host. We found no case where MPTCP performed significantly worse than single-path TCP.

We also looked at new network topologies designed to take advantage of MPTCP's end-host load-balancing mechanisms. For example, a dual-homed FatTree running MPTCP can, for the same cost, provide twice the throughput of a single-homed FatTree running MPTCP for a wide range of likely workloads. Without MPTCP, such a topology makes little sense, as the capacity is rarely usable.

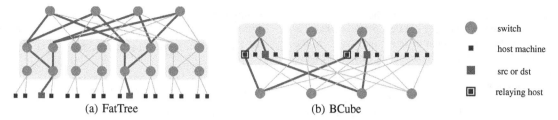

	switch
■	host machine
■	src or dst
▣	relaying host

(a) FatTree   (b) BCube

Fig. 1: Two proposed data center topologies. The bold lines show multiple paths between the source and destination.

Finally we have validated the results on Amazon's EC2 cloud using our Linux implementation. We observed that in the EC2 data center, the $^2/_3$ of flows that have access to multiple paths achieve approximately three times the throughput using MPTCP than with regular TCP. As MPTCP is no more aggressive than TCP, this indicates that MPTCP is very effective at finding unused capacity.

2. DATA CENTER NETWORKING

Before examining how MPTCP changes things, we will briefly discuss the components that comprise the data center architecture.

2.1 Topology

Traditionally data centers have been built using hierarchical topologies: racks of hosts connect to a top-of-rack switch; these switches connect to aggregation switches; in turn these are connected to a core switch. Such topologies make sense if most of the traffic flows into or out of the data center. However, if most of the traffic is intra-data center, as is increasingly the trend, then there is a very uneven distribution of bandwidth. Unless traffic is localized to racks, the higher levels of the topology become a serious bottleneck.

Recent proposals address these limitations. VL2[6] and FatTree (Fig. 1(a)) are Clos[3] topologies that use multiple core switches to provide full bandwidth between any pair of hosts in the network. They differ in that FatTree uses larger quantities of lower speed (1Gb/s) links between switches, whereas VL2 uses fewer faster (10Gb/s) links. In contrast, BCube[7] abandons the hierarchy in favor of a hypercube-like topology, using hosts themselves to relay traffic (Fig. 1(b)).

All three proposals solve the traffic concentration problem at the physical level — there is enough capacity for every host to be able to transmit flat-out to another randomly chosen host. However the denseness of interconnection they provide poses its own problems when it comes to determining how traffic should be routed.

2.2 Routing

Dense interconnection topologies provide many possible parallel paths between each pair of hosts. We cannot expect the host itself to know which of these paths is the least loaded, so the routing system must spread traffic across these paths. The simplest solution is to use randomized load balancing, where each flow is assigned a random path from the set of possible paths.

In practice there are multiple ways to implement randomized load balancing in today's switches. For example, if each switch uses a link-state routing protocol to provide ECMP forwarding then, based on a hash of the five-tuple in each packet, flows will be split roughly equally across equal length paths. VL2 provides just such a mechanism over a virtual layer 2 infrastructure.

However, in topologies such as BCube, paths vary in length, and simple ECMP cannot access many of these paths because it only hashes between the shortest paths. A simple alternative is to use multiple static VLANs to provide multiple paths that expose all the underlying network paths[9]. Either the host or the first hop switch can then hash the five-tuple to determine which path is used.

2.3 Path Selection

Solutions such as ECMP or multiple VLANs provide the basis for randomized load balancing as the default path selection mechanism. However, as others [2] have shown, randomized load balancing cannot achieve the full bisectional bandwidth in most topologies, nor is it especially fair. The problem, quite simply, is that often a random selection causes hot-spots to develop, where an unlucky combination of random path selections cause a few links to be overloaded and links elsewhere to have little or no load.

To address these issues, the use of a centralized flow scheduler has been proposed. Large flows are assigned to lightly loaded paths and existing flows may be reassigned to maximize overall throughput[2]. The scheduler does a good job if flows are network-limited, with exponentially distributed sizes and Poisson arrivals, as shown in Hedera [2]. The intuition is that if we only schedule the big flows we can fully utilize all the bandwidth, and yet have a small scheduling cost, as dictated by the small number of flows.

However, data center traffic analysis shows that flow distributions are not Pareto distributed [6]. In such cases, the scheduler has to run frequently (100ms or faster) to keep up with the flow arrivals. Yet, the scheduler is fundamentally limited in its reaction time as it has to retrieve statistics, compute placements and instantiate them, all in this scheduling period. We show later through simulation that a scheduler running every 500ms has similar performance to randomized load balancing when these assumptions do not hold.

2.4 Congestion Control

Most applications use single path TCP, and inherit TCP's congestion control mechanism which does a fair job of matching offered load to available capacity on whichever path was selected.

In proposing the use of MPTCP, we change how the problem is partitioned. MPTCP can establish multiple subflows on different paths between the same pair of endpoints *for a single TCP connection*. The key point is that by linking the congestion control dynamics on these multiple subflows, MPTCP can explicitly move traffic off more congested paths and place it on less congested ones.

Our hypothesis is that given sufficiently many randomly chosen paths, MPTCP will find at least one good unloaded path, and move most of its traffic that way. In so doing it will relieve congestion on links that got more than their fair share of ECMP balanced flows. This in turn will allow those competing flows to achieve their full potential, maximizing the bisectional bandwidth of the network and also improving fairness. Fairness is not an abstract concept for many distributed applications; for example, when a search application is distributed across many machines, the overall completion time is determined by the slowest machine. Hence worst-case performance matters significantly.

3. MULTIPATH TCP IN SUMMARY

Multipath TCP[4] extends TCP so that a single connection can be striped across multiple network paths. MPTCP support is negotiated in the initial SYN exchange and the client learns any additional IP addresses the server may have. Additional subflows can then be opened. An additional subflow can be between the same pair of IP addresses as the first subflow, but using different ports, or it can use any additional IP addresses the client or server may have. In the former case, MPTCP relies on ECMP routing to hash subflows to different paths; in the latter the paths are implicitly identified by the source and destination IP addresses. Both techniques may be used, depending on the routing scheme used in a particular data center.

Once multiple subflows have been established, the sending host's TCP stack stripes data across the subflows. Additional TCP options allow the receiver to reconstruct the received data in the original order. There is no requirement for an application to be aware that MPTCP is being used in place of TCP - in our experiments we have used unmodified applications running on our MPTCP-capable Linux kernel. However enhanced applications may themselves wish to use an extended sockets API to influence which subflows are set up and how data is striped between them (the full MPTCP protocol is described in [4]).

Each MPTCP subflow has its own sequence space and maintains its own congestion window so that it can adapt to conditions along the path. Although each subflow performs TCP-like additive-increase on acks and multiplicative decrease on losses, MPTCP links the behaviour of subflows by adapting the additive increase constant. The algorithm is:

- For each ACK on subflow r, increase the window w_r by $\min(a/w_{\text{total}}, 1/w_r)$.

- Each loss on subflow r, decrease the window w_r by $w_r/2$.

w_{total} is the sum of the windows on all subflows. a determines the aggressiveness of all the subflows; it is calculated as described in the IETF draft specification[12].

Broadly speaking, there are two key parts to this algorithm. First, by making the window increase depend on the total window size, subflows that have large windows increase faster than subflows with small windows. This actively moves traffic from more congested paths to less congested ones, load-balancing the network.

Second, by adapting a, MPTCP can compensate for different RTTs and can ensure that if all the subflows of a connection traverse the same bottleneck, they will compete fairly with a regular TCP flow. However, if the subflows encounter multiple unloaded paths, one connection can fill them all. The design of the algorithm has been detailed in [14].

4. MPTCP IN DATA CENTERS

It seems there might be three main benefits from deploying MPTCP in today's redundant data center networks:

- Better aggregate throughput, as exploring more paths and load-balancing them properly should reduce the number of underutilized and idle links.

- Better fairness; the throughputs of different MPTCP connections should be closer than if TCP were used, as congestion on network core links should be more evenly distributed.

- Better robustness. If a link or switch fails, routing will route around it, even without MPTCP, but this takes time. MPTCP uses many paths; if one fails the others can continue without pausing. Worse are failures that are not bad enough to trigger re-routing, but which cause link autonegotiation to fall back to a low link speed, or which cause very high packet loss rates. Single-path TCP has no choice but to trickle data through the slow path; MPTCP can simply avoid sending traffic on a very congested path.

In this section we examine the extent to which these potential benefits can be realized. As we will see, the benefits depend on:

- The congestion control scheme used.

- The physical topology.

- The traffic matrix generated by the applications.

- The level of load in the network.

Although we cannot predict what future data center applications will look like, we can at least map out broad areas where MPTCP gives considerable benefits and other areas where the bottleneck is elsewhere and MPTCP cannot help.

4.1 A Note on Simulation

In section 6, we give results from running our Linux MPTCP implementation on a small cluster in our lab, and on Amazon EC2. But most of the results in this paper come from simulation for two reasons. First, we do not have access to a large enough data center to examine issues of scale. But perhaps more importantly, simulation lets us tease apart the causes of complex behaviors.

For this paper, we wrote two simulators. The first, *htsim*, is a full packet level simulator that models TCP and MPTCP in similar detail to ns2, but which is optimized for large scale and high speeds. Even with this simulator, there are limits to what we can model. For example, simulating the 576-node Dual-homed FatTree in Section 5 with 100Mb/s links requires simulating 46,000 MPTCP subflows generating 115 Gb/s of traffic. Even a fairly small data center topology stresses the limits of simulation.

Today's larger data centers don't have hundreds of hosts. They have tens of thousands[1]. To examine these scales we must sacrifice some accuracy and the ability to model flow arrivals, and resort to flow-level simulation. Our second simulator models TCP and MPTCP throughput as a function of loss rate, and uses an iterative approach to find the equilibrium traffic pattern for a fixed set of arbitrary duration flows.

Comparing the two approaches on the same topology shows the flow-level simulator is a fairly good predictor of packet-level performance for long flows. Its main limitation is at high congestion levels, where it fails to model timeouts, and so predicts higher congestion levels than we see in reality. We mostly use packet-level simulation, but resort to flow-level to extrapolate to larger scales.

4.2 Examples of Benefits

Throughput Fig. 2 shows the aggregate throughput achieved by long-lived TCP and MPTCP in a FatTree network. The left histogram shows throughput in a FatTree with 128 hosts, 80 eight-port switches, and 100Mb/s links. The grey bars are from a detailed packet-level simulation, and the black bars are from the flow-level simulator. The right histogram scales up the topology to 8192 hosts, and shows only flow-level results. The traffic pattern is a permutation matrix; every host sends to one other host chosen at random, but with the constraint that no host receives more than one flow. This is a simple randomized traffic pattern that has the potential to saturate the FatTree. Of the multiple shortest paths, one is chosen at random for each subflow, simulating flow-based ECMP routing.

The bars show the number of MPTCP subflows used, or in the case of single subflow, shows the behavior with regular single-path TCP. The figure illustrates several points. Single-path TCP performs rather poorly, achieving less then half of the available capac-

---

[1]Microsoft's Chicago data center reputedly has the potential to hold as many as 300,000 hosts

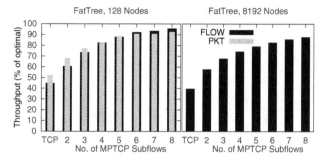

Fig. 2: Multipath needs eight paths to get good utilization in FatTree, independent of scale

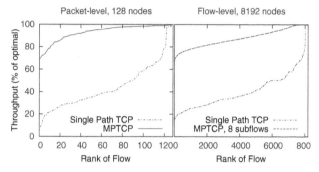

Fig. 3: Distribution of throughput in FatTree

ity. The reason is simple - the full capacity is only available if no two flows share the same link. If n flows share a link, each only achieves $1/n$ of the capacity it should achieve. ECMP's random hashing of a flow onto a path results in sufficiently many collisions that total throughput is less than 50% of the full bisectional bandwidth, while many links go idle.

MPTCP explores more paths. With the same ECMP hashing, fewer links go idle, and so total throughput increases. Interestingly, it takes around eight subflows per MPTCP connection to properly utilize the network.

Comparing the left and right histograms, we see the behavior is largely scale-invariant. In this and other experiments we find that increasing the network size by two orders of magnitude slightly reduces the overall performance for both TCP and MPTCP.

Comparing the grey and black histograms, we see that the packet and flow level simulations are in agreement about the performance benefits and the number of subflows required. The flow-level simulator slightly underestimates throughput in the single-path TCP and two-subflow cases.

Fairness Fig. 3 shows the throughput of individual connections from the 128 host packet level simulation and the 8,192 host flow-level simulation in Fig. 2, comparing the single-path TCP case with the eight subflow MPTCP case. Every host's throughput is shown ranked in order of increasing throughput. Is is clear that not only did the utilization improve with MPTCP, but also the fairness improved. With single-path TCP, some flows perform very well, but many perform poorly, and some get less than 10% of the potential throughput. With eight subflows, most MPTCP flows get at least 90% of the available capacity, and none get less than 50%. For applications that farm work out to many workers and finish when the last worker finishes, such fairness can greatly improve overall performance.

The subtle difference between packet-level and flow-level simulation is also visible in these curves. The flow-level simulator does not model timeouts, so flows that traverse multiple congested links

get a little more throughput than they should. These flows then degrade the performance of competing flows that do not traverse multiple congested links, so reducing overall performance a little.

4.3 Analysis

The permutation traffic matrix used above is rather artificial, but it serves to demonstrate that MPTCP can provide substantial gains over single-path TCP in today's data centers that are engineered to provide high bisectional bandwidth using commodity technology such as cheap gigabit switches. We will investigate where these gains come from, under which circumstances MPTCP provides large gains, and when it does not. In particular:

- How does the topology influence the performance of single-path vs MPTCP?

- How does the traffic matrix and load affect performance?

- How many subflows does MPTCP require? On what does this depend?

- Can these same benefits be provided using an application that simply opens multiple regular TCP flows?

4.3.1 Influence of Topology

We start by examining the effect that the network topology has on performance. The research literature proposes a number of different topologies for data centers, with the aim of providing high bisectional bandwidth. Two that are particularly enlightening are VL2[6] and BCube[7].

Like FatTree, VL2 is a Clos[3] topology - essentially a multi-routed tree using multiple core switches to provide full bandwidth between any pair of hosts in the network. Unlike FatTree where every link is cheap gigabit ethernet, VL2 uses ten times fewer links in the upper layers, but uses 10-gigabit ethernet for them. With current prices, a VL2 network costs more than a FatTree topology.

We also examined a future version of VL2 that might be built when 10 gigabit ethernet becomes cheap enough to be used by all hosts. The core links in this VL2-40 network are then upgraded to run at 40Gb/s.

The BCube topology shown in Fig. 1(b) is completely different; instead of using ethernet switches to perform all the switching, it uses a hybrid of host switching and hardware switching. To route between nodes on the same ethernet switch, a direct switched path is used, but to route between nodes that do not share an ethernet switch, an intermediate host relays the traffic. This provides a very large number of possible paths between any two hosts, but some of the host's resources are used for packet forwarding.

Fig. 4 shows the throughput of VL2, VL2-40 and BCube, using the permutation traffic matrix for single-path TCP and varying numbers of MPTCP flows. BCube shows similar performance gains to FatTree when using MPTCP, and also requires a large number of subflows to realize these gains. With VL2, the performance gains are smaller, and most of the gains are achieved with only two subflows.

Intuitively, BCube suffers from the same problem with collisions that FatTree does - when n flows share a link, each achieves approximately $1/n$ of the capacity (unless it is constrained elsewhere). With the permutation traffic matrix, the mean number of flows on a core VL2 link should be 10. However, when ECMP randomly puts n flows on such a VL2 core link, each of those flows either achieves 1 Gb/s if $n < 10$, or $10/n$ Gb/s if $n > 10$ (unless the flow is contained elsewhere). Thus the impact of uneven flow allocations to links is smoothed out across many more flows, and few links are severely underutilized. The result is that while FatTree needs eight

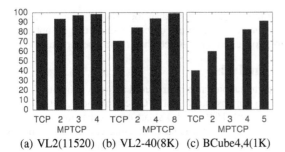

(a) VL2(11520) (b) VL2-40(8K) (c) BCube4,4(1K)

Fig. 4: VL2 and BCube throughput against number of flows, using a permutation traffic matrix.

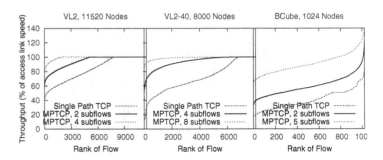

Fig. 5: Flow rates with VL2, VL2-40 and BCube. With BCube, multipath flows are not limited to a single interface.

MPTCP subflows to achieve 90% throughput, on VL2 only two subflows are needed per MPTCP connection. In VL2-40, the 4:1 ratio between core and host linkspeeds increases the effect of collisions compared to VL2; single path TCP throughput is around 70% of optimal, and we need 4 subflows to utilize 90% of the network.

The aggregate throughput does not tell the whole story. Fig. 5 shows the rates achieved by individual flows, comparing single-path TCP with MPTCP. Although the total VL2 throughput is fairly high using single-path TCP, the fairness is relatively low with approximately 25% of flows achieving less than 60% of what they should be able to achieve. While two MPTCP subflows bring most of the throughput gains, adding more subflows continues to improve fairness. VL2-40 gives less fairer throughputs compared to VL2; here too adding more subflows here significantly increases fairness. With BCube the distribution is similar to FatTree, except that as each BCube host has more than one interface, so hosts are not limited to the interface speed.

4.3.2 Number of Subflows

When we first started to examine MPTCP on FatTree, we were surprised that eight subflows were needed to achieve 90% throughput. Why eight, and on what does this depend? A simple analytical model casts some light on the issue.

In m-way multipath on a k-ary FatTree, let each path contribute weight $1/m$. Assume a permutation traffic matrix, with random (independent) routing. The total weight on an access link is always 1. To calculate the expected number of flows on intra-pod links and pod-core links, we need to factor in that some flows stay local to the rack and some stay local to the pod. The total weight on a within-pod link is random, with an expected value E_p and variance V_p. Similarly, E_c and V_c for the pod-core links:

$$E_p = 1 - \frac{n_2}{n_1}, \quad E_c = 1 - \frac{n_1}{n_0}$$

$$V_p = E_p \left(\left(\frac{m-1}{mn_2} + \frac{1}{m} \right) + \left(1 - \frac{1}{n_2} \right) \left(1 - \frac{n_2-1}{n_0-1} \right) - E_p \right)$$

$$V_c = E_c \left(\left(\frac{m-1}{mn_1} + \frac{1}{m} \right) + \left(1 - \frac{1}{n_1} \right) \left(1 - \frac{n_1-1}{n_0-1} \right) - E_c \right)$$

$$n_0 = \frac{k^3}{4}, \quad n_1 = \frac{k^2}{4}, \quad n_2 = \frac{k}{2}$$

Fig. 6 shows how variance V_p changes as we add subflows for varying sizes of network. V_c is very similar. Almost independent of the size of the network, the variance settles down above eight subflows. Although this model is too simplistic to predict throughput (it cannot factor in how congestion on one path can free capacity on another), it captures the dominant effect that determines how many subflows are required, at least for the permutation traffic matrix.

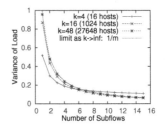

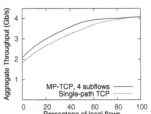

Fig. 6: Analytical model for variance of load on a link.

Fig. 7: Performance with locality, 4:1 oversubscribed 512-node FatTree.

4.3.3 Oversubscribed Topologies

All the topologies above all aim to provide full bisectional bandwidth; the goal is that every host should be able to transmit at the full interface speed, regardless of the location of the destination. This would allow applications to be deployed across any set of nodes without regard to the limitations of the network topology. We have seen that even with such topologies, it is hard to actually use all the network capacity with single-path transport protocols routed using flow-based ECMP routing. But in fact the goal itself may be misleading. Such topologies are expensive, and no data center application we know of sends at its full interface rate constantly.

In a large data center, running many simultaneous applications, it is extremely unlikely that all will burst simultaneously. Thus these topologies seem to be overkill for the task at hand - they are much more expensive than is necessary.

We must therefore consider topologies that oversubscribe the network core (at least in terms of potential load, not necessarily actual load). To do this, we created a Clos-style networks, but oversubscribed the capacity of the uplinks from the top-of-rack switches by 4:1 (for every four Gb/s from the hosts in the rack, one 1Gb/s uplink capacity is provided). Again we use a permutation matrix as a baseline, but now we also need to examine what happens when the oversubscribed network is overloaded (and underloaded).

Fig. 8(a) shows what happens as we increase the number of connections per host; the y-axis shows the total throughput achieved by MPTCP connections using four subflows, as a multiple of the total throughput achieved by single-path TCP using the same traffic pattern. At very low load, the few flows that exist almost never share a link with another flow, so they saturate the host NIC with both TCP and MPTCP. At very high load levels, the core is severely congested with high packet loss, and there are sufficient flows to saturate all the links in the core, irrespective of whether MPTCP is used. For a very wide range of load in between, MPTCP provides significant improvements in throughput, with the maximum improvement occurring at 0.25 connections per host, which is the

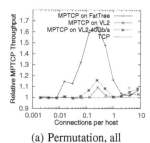
(a) Permutation, all

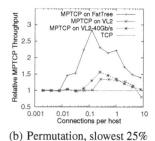
(b) Permutation, slowest 25%

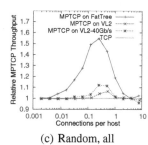
(c) Random, all

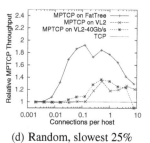
(d) Random, slowest 25%

Fig. 8: Relative MPTCP performance as a function of load when running Permutation or Random traffic matrices for differing topologies. Mean performance and the performance of the slowest quarter of flows are shown.

minimum load level to fill a 4:1 oversubscribed topology. The average throughput improvement depends on the topology used; the maximum for oversubscribed Fat-Tree is 65%, while VL2-40 and VL2 improve by 15% and 11% respectively.

It is also instructive to look at the speeds of the slower flows in these experiments, as these dictate when jobs finish. The average improvement again depends on topology and load, but the gains are bigger: MPTCP improves throughput for the slowest flows by 1.5x to 3x for medium to moderately high load levels.

There is one exception for a highly loaded VL2 where the slower flows have lower throughput with MPTCP. On closer inspection, in turns out that the slow flows have very small windows on each of their subflows, which leads to repeated timeouts and reduced throughput for those flows; this is despite total network throughput being higher for MPTCP compared to TCP. For VL2-40 and Fat Tree the same effect does not apply, as there is more heterogeneity in the speeds of the individual subflows; at least one or a few of these have a big enough window to avoid timeouts. A very simple heuristic can be applied to avoid VL2 throughput degradation for small flows: if the stack has many subflows with small windows, it will close some of them to reduce until the remaining windows are big enough to avoid timeouts.

Irrespective of whether MPTCP is used, we believe data center designers will be likely to attempt to engineer their networks so that the core is neither underloaded nor overloaded. An overloaded core is a performance bottleneck; an underloaded core costs money that would have been better spent elsewhere. So it appears likely that the sweet-spot for MPTCP is close to the load level for which the data center designer would provision.

4.3.4 Influence of the Traffic Matrix

The permutation traffic matrix is useful as a baseline for comparison because it is easy to reason about how much throughput should be available from the network. With a topology that provides full bisectional bandwidth, the load is just sufficient to fully load the network. It is however, not terribly realistic.

A random traffic matrix chooses randomly the sources and destinations, allowing traffic concentrations on access links. Because of this, traffic flowing through the core is much less than in a permutation TM for the same number of flows.

Fig. 8(c) shows average throughput improvement with MPTCP vs. TCP in the Fat Tree, VL2 and VL2-40 4:1 oversubscribed topologies. The results are very similar to the permutation TM, but the relative improvements are slightly smaller; this is the effect of access link collisions. Fig. 8(d) shows the throughput improvement for the slowest 25% of flows; MPTCP increases their throughput on average by 1.3 to 1.8 times, for a wide range of loads.

We ran the same experiments with full-bisection topologies. Fat-Tree improved by maximum of 30%, while BCube improved by 150% to 300%, depending on the load level. The BCube improve-

ments come from MPTCP's ability to simultaneously use multiple interfaces for the same flow.

Full-bisection VL2 and VL2-40 showed no improvement, which was puzzling. To understand this effect, say we randomly allocate n flows to n hosts. The probability that a host sends no flow is:

$$p[\text{no flow}] = \left(1 - \frac{1}{n}\right)^n \to \frac{1}{e}$$

The number of hosts that do not send are then $\frac{n}{e}$; this bounds the total throughput. In fact the throughput is lower. For example, of the hosts that send only one flow, many of these will be received by a host receiving more than one flow, so the sender will be unable to send at its full speed. Numerical analysis shows that when this is taken into account, the maximum achievable throughput by *any* load-balancing algorithm with random traffic is limited by colliding flows on the sending and receiving hosts to less than $\frac{1}{2}$ of the bisectional bandwidth.

With such a workload, none of VL2's 10Gb/s core links is ever saturated, so it makes no difference if TCP or MPTCP is used.

Locality of Traffic The random and permutation traffic matrices provide no locality of traffic. With a full bisection topology, it should in principle not be necessary for applications to localize traffic, although as we have seen, this is only really true under very light or heavy loads, or when multipath transport uses sufficiently many paths. However, with oversubscribed topologies, applications can always get better performance if they can localize traffic to the rack, because that part of the topology is not oversubscribed. MPTCP provides no performance improvement within the rack, because such flows are limited by their link to the top-of-rack switch. Just how good does application-based traffic localization have to be for the advantages of MPTCP to be nullified?

We simulated a 4:1 oversubscribed FatTree and generated a random traffic matrix, with the constraint that a fraction of the flows were destined for a random host with the sender's rack, while the rest were destined for an unconstrained random host. Every host sends one flow, so without locality this corresponds to the 1 flow-per-host data point from Fig. 8(a) - a rather heavily loaded network. Fig. 7 shows the aggregate throughput as locality is increased. Unsurprisingly, as traffic moves from the oversubscribed core to the non-oversubscribed local hosts, aggregate performance increases. However, MPTCP continues to provide approximately the same performance benefits until around 75% of the flows are rack-local. Above this point the network core is lightly loaded, and all flows are limited by the sending or receiving hosts, so MPTCP provides no improvement. We see similar benefit with a localized permutation traffic matrix, though the absolute throughput values are higher.

Finally, we examined many-to-one traffic patterns; there the access links are heavily congested, no alternative paths are available, and so MPTCP and TCP behave similarly.

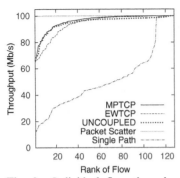

Fig. 9: Individual flow throughputs with different algorithms

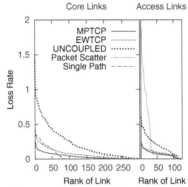

Fig. 10: Individual link loss rates from Figure 9

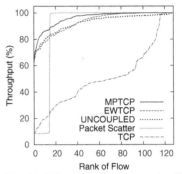

Fig. 11: Effects of a hot spot on the different algorithms

4.3.5 Influence of Congestion Control

Do we need all of MPTCP's mechanisms to get the performance and fairness benefits above? MPTCP establishes multiple subflows per connection, and links the congestion control behavior of these subflows to achieve two goals:

- It is fair to single-path TCP flows, even when multiple subflows of a connection traverse the same bottleneck.

- It explicitly moves traffic from the more congested subflows to the less congested subflows.

To understand what is going on, we must tease apart the mechanisms. We compare MPTCP with these algorithms:

Uncoupled TCP. Each subflow behaves independently, exactly as if an application had opened multiple TCP connections and striped data across them. An UNCOUPLED flow will be unfair to regular TCP; if it has n subflows through a bottleneck, it will achieve approximately n times the throughput of a competing TCP.

Equally-Weighted TCP (EWTCP). Each subflow runs TCP's additive increase, multiplicative decrease algorithm, but the increase constant is decreased depending on the number of active subflows. An EWTCP flow will be fair to regular TCP at a bottleneck, even if all the EWTCP subflows traverse that bottleneck. However, it will not actively move traffic away from congested paths.

A rather different multipath solution would be to deploy per-*packet* ECMP multipath routing, spreading the packets of a single flow across multiple paths, as opposed to per-*flow* ECMP which hashes the five-tuple to maintain a consistent path for each flow. For this to work, a single-path TCP endpoint must be modified to avoid unintentionally treating reordering as an indicator of packet loss. Thus we also tested:

PACKETSCATTER. The switches perform per-packet load balancing across all the available alternative paths. The TCP sender runs a more robust fast-retransmit algorithm, but retains a single congestion window as it is unaware of the multiple paths.

Fig. 9 shows the throughputs of individual connections for each algorithm. This is a packet-level simulation with 128 nodes in a FatTree topology, running a permutation traffic matrix of long flows. The result suegsts that it does not matter whether multipath transport is performed within TCP, or at the application level, and that the load balancing aspects of MPTCP's linked congestion control do not greatly affect throughput. In fact the best performance is

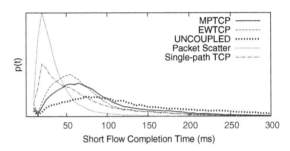

Fig. 12: The effect of short flows competing with different multipath congestion controllers

given by PACKETSCATTER, which spreads over all possible paths, but as we shall see, this result is fragile and only applies to over-provisioned networks with no hot spots.

It is clear that many of the performance benefits seen so far are the results of spreading load over many paths. Given this result, is there any reason to deploy MPTCP, as opposed to multipath-capable applications running over regular TCP?

To understand the differences between these algorithms, we have to look more closely. Fig. 10 shows the loss rates for all the links of the FatTree topology used in Fig. 9. We show core links separately from access links because congesting the core is qualitatively different from self-congestion at the host's own NIC.

UNCOUPLED TCP is clearly much more aggressive than single-path TCP, resulting in much higher packet loss rates, both in the core and access links. Although this does not directly impact performance for long-running UNCOUPLED flows, it does affect competing traffic.

MPTCP, EWTCP and Single-path TCP are equally aggressive overall, and so congest the access links equally. In the core, MPTCP performs as expected, and moves traffic from the more congested to the less congested paths, relieving congestion at hot spots. EWTCP lacks this active load redistribution, so although it does not increase loss at hot spots, it doesn't effectively relieve it either. EWTCP is also not as aggressive as MPTCP on the less loaded paths, so it misses sending opportunities and gets slightly lower throughput.

With per-packet round-robin ECMP, PACKETSCATTER cannot congest the core links; consequently the losses required to constrain its transmit rate are concentrated on access links.

Short Flows Fig. 12 examines how the algorithms affect competing short flows. The topology is the 4:1 oversubscribed Fat-Tree; each host sends to one other host; 33% send a continuous flow using either TCP or one of the multipath algorithms, providing enough traffic to congest the core. The remaining hosts send one 70 Kbyte file on average every 200ms (poisson arrivals) using single-path TCP (ECMP sends each via a new path), and we measure how long these flows take to complete. The averages in these experiments are:

Algorithm	Short Flow Finish Time (mean/stdev)	Network Core Utilization
SINGLE-PATH TCP	78 ±108 ms	25%
PACKETSCATTER	42 ± 63 ms	30%
EWTCP	80 ± 89 ms	57%
MPTCP	97 ± 106 ms	62%
UNCOUPLED	152 ± 158 ms	65%

It is clear that UNCOUPLED significantly hurts the short flows. Single-path TCP fails to spread load within the core, so while many short flows complete faster, some encounter more congestion and finish slower. MPTCP fills the core, but isn't overly aggressive, having much less impact than UNCOUPLED. Compared to TCP, MPTCP increases mean completion time by 25% but decreases the finish time of the slowest short flows by 10%. EWTCP has less impact on short flows than MPTCP, which should not be surprising - while it does use multiple paths, it does not load-balance as effectively as MPTCP, failing to use capacity quickly where it is available.

PACKETSCATTER lets short flows finish quickest, but gets very low network utilization, close to what TCP provides. This is because long flows back off on all paths as soon as one path looks congested, despite congestion being transient due to short flows. MPTCP achieves almost all of the performance that UNCOUPLED can manage, but its lower aggressiveness and better load balancing greatly reduce impact on competing traffic.

Robustness What happens when there is a hot spot in the network? We drop a single link in the core network from 1Gb/s to 100Mb/s. Such a failure is quite common: Gigabit ethernet requires two copper pairs in a Cat-5e cable; if one RJ45 conductor fails to seat properly, it can fall back to 100Mb/s which only requires a single pair. Similar results would be seen if a single unresponsive flow saturated one link (e.g. a FCoE or UDP flow).

Results, shown in Fig. 11, show that MPTCP does what it designed to do, moving traffic off the hot link onto alternative paths; other flows then move some of their traffic off these alternative paths, and so on, so the effect of the failure is negligible. EWTCP and UNCOUPLED do not shift traffic away from congestion, giving less throughput to the flows that pass through the bottleneck. PACKETSCATTER behaves worst: it has no way to separate the bad link from the good ones. It just observes a high loss rate, and backs off. Every single connection that has any available path through the bad link achieves about 10% of the throughput it should achieve.

Network Efficiency The example below shows another difference between EWTCP and MPTCP, and is taken from [14]. If there are multiple different length paths to a destination, pathological traffic matrices are possible where the network resources are wasted. MPTCP will explicitly move traffic off the paths that traverse multiple congested links, avoiding such pathologies. Such examples do not occur in FatTree-style topologies, but they can occur with BCube.

To illustrate the issue, consider a many-to-one traffic matrix, as in a distributed file system read from many servers. Typically the

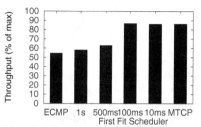

Fig. 13: First-fit scheduling compared to flow ECMP and MPTCP

distributed file systems store the data on hosts close in the network, to allow higher throughput writes. In our experiment each host reads from 12 other hosts, chosen to be the host's neighbors in the three levels in BCube(4,3). The per-host total read throughputs are:

SINGLE-PATH	297 Mb/s
EWTCP	229 Mb/s
MPTCP	272 Mb/s
PACKETSCATTER	115 Mb/s

Due to the locality, single-path TCP can saturate all three of the host's 100 Mb/s NICs, and achieves maximum throughput. EWTCP uses multiple paths and long paths congest short ones. MPTCP's linked congestion control mechanism moves almost all of the traffic onto the shortest path, avoiding paths that traverse multiple congested links, and so greatly reduces the self-congestion.

PACKETSCATTER suffers particularly badly in this case. It spreads traffic across both short and longer paths, and with this regular traffic matrix it actually succeeds in equalizing the loss rate across all paths. However, most of the traffic takes multi-hop paths using the network very inefficiently. If we wish to take advantage of multi-path in the cases where it benefits flows and also avoid this scenario and that of Fig. 11, it seems inevitable that each subflow must have its own sequence space and congestion window[11]. These choices dictate the core design of MPTCP.

4.4 Scheduling and Dynamic Flow Arrivals

With single-path TCP is it clear that ECMP's randomized load balancing does not perform sufficiently well unless the topology has been specifically tailored for it, as with VL2. Even with VL2, MPTCP can increase fairness and performance significantly.

ECMP however is not the only single path selection algorithm; Hedera proposes using a centralized scheduler to supplement random load balancing, with the goal of explicitly allocating large flows to paths. Specifically, Hedera flows start off using ECMP, but are measured by the centralized scheduler. If, during a scheduling period, a flow's average throughput is greater than 10% of the interface speed, it is explicitly scheduled. How well does MPTCP compare with centralized scheduling?

This evaluation is more difficult; the performance of a scheduler can depend on lag in flow measurement, path configuration, and TCP's response to path reconfiguration. Similarly the performance of MPTCP can depend on how quickly new subflows can slowstart.

We use a 128-host FatTree running a permutation traffic matrix with closed loop flow arrivals (one flow finishes, another one starts). Flow sizes come from the VL2 dataset. We measure throughputs for single-path TCP with ECMP, MPTCP (8 subflows), and a centralized scheduler using the First Fit heuristic Hedera [2].[2]

The total throughput is shown in Fig. 13. Again, MPTCP outperforms TCP over ECMP. Centralized scheduler performance depends on how frequently it is run. In [2] it is run every 5 sec-

---

[2]First Fit is much faster than Simulated Annealing; execution speed is essential to get benefits with centralized scheduling.

onds. Our results show it needs to run every 100ms to approach the performance of MPTCP; even if it runs every 500ms there is little benefit because in high bandwidth data center even large flows complete in around a second.

Host-limited Flows Hedera's flow scheduling algorithm is based on the assumption that it only needs to schedule long-lived flows because they contribute most of the bytes. Other flows are treated as background noise. It also assumes that a flow it schedules onto an unused link is capable of increasing to fill that link.

Both assumptions can be violated by flows which are end-host limited and so cannot increase their rate. For example, network bandwidth can exceed disk performance for many workloads. Host-limited flows can be long lived and transfer a great deal of data, but never exceed the scheduling threshold. These flows are ignored by the scheduler and can collide with scheduled flows. Perhaps worse, a host-limited flow might just exceed the threshold for scheduling, be assigned to an empty path, and be unable to fill it, wasting capacity. We ran simulations using a permutation matrix where each host sends two flows; one is host-limited and the other is not. When the host-limited flows have throughput just below the 10% scheduling threshold, Hedera's throughput drops 20%. When the same flows are just above the threshold for scheduling it costs Hedera 17%.

Scheduling	App Limited Flows	
Threshold	Over-Threshold	Under-Threshold
5%	-21%	-22%
10%	-17%	-21%
20%	-22%	-23%
50%	-51%	-45%

The table shows the 10% threshold is a sweet spot; changing it either caused too few flows to be scheduled, or wasted capacity when a scheduled flow cannot expand to fill the path. In contrast, MPTCP makes no such assumptions. It responds correctly to competing host-limited flows, consistently obtaining high throughput.

5. EVOLVING TOPOLOGIES WITH MPTCP

Our previous experiments showed that only a few workloads saturate the core of full-bisection topologies; these workloads are somewhat artificial. To justify full-bisection topologies requires:

- There is no locality to the traffic.

- There are times when all hosts wish to send flat-out.

- There is no concentration of traffic on any access link.

In practice, none of these assumptions seem valid, so building a topology that provides full bisectional bandwidth seems to be a waste of money.

In section 4.3.3, we examined an oversubscribed FatTree: one where for the same core network we connected four times as many hosts. This seems a more likely topology, and hits a better balance between being bottlenecked on the core and being bottlenecked on host access links. It also takes advantage of any locality provided by the application. For example, HDFS places two out of three replicas in the same rack, and map jobs in MapReduce are assigned to servers in the same rack as the data. For such topologies, MPTCP cannot help much with the local traffic, but it does ensure the core is used to maximal effect.

If we now take a leap and assume all hosts in the data center support MPTCP, then we should also ask whether different topologies enabled by MPTCP would perform even better. The obvious place to start is to consider cases where the workloads we have examined are bottlenecked on the access links between the hosts

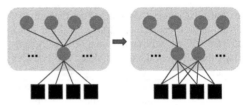

Fig. 14: Dual-homing in the Fat Tree Topology

and the top-of-rack (ToR) switches. These cases can only be improved by adding more capacity, but moving to 10Gb/s ethernet is expensive. With single-path TCP, there is limited benefit from additional 1Gb/s ethernet links to the ToR switches, because a single flow cannot utilize more than one path. MPTCP does not have this limitation. Almost all current servers ship with dual gigabit ethernet onboard, so an obvious solution is to dual-home hosts to ToR switches, as shown in Fig.14. Whether to overprovision the core is then an additional question a data center operator must consider, based on predicted workload.

For our experiments, we wish to keep the cost of the network constant, so we can directly compare new and existing topologies. To do so, we impose the artificial constraint that the number of switch ports remains constant, but that we can move ports from one place in the topology to another[3].

Consider the following two topologies:

Perfect Switch . FatTree and VL2 both try to emulate a single huge non-blocking switch. VL2 comes closer to succeeding than FatTree does, but a perfect switch serves as a good control experiment, giving an upper bound on what any network core might provide using single links to the hosts.

Dual-homed FatTree (DHFT) . A full FatTree requires five switch ports per host; one is to the host and four connect the links between the two layers of switches. If we remove one port per host from the core and use it to connect the second interface on each server, the network requires the same number of switch ports.

To produce a regular DHFT topology with this ratio of core-to-access capacity, we start with a k-port FatTree topology. We leave the upper-pod switches and aggregation switches the same, and replace each top-of-rack switch with two $11k/12$ port switches. With FatTree, each ToR switch had $k/2$ uplinks and connected $k/2$ hosts. With DHFT, each pair of DHFT ToR switches still has $k/2$ uplinks, but have $4k/3$ downlinks, supporting $2k/3$ hosts between them. In total, there are still five switch ports per host.

For sensible values of k, we cannot produce fully regular DHFT and FatTree networks with the same number of ports per host. For this reason we compare DHFT with the Perfect Switch, which should underestimate the benefits of DHFT.

5.1 Analysis

Effects of Locality It is not our aim to show that DHFT is in any sense optimal; we cannot define optimality without knowing the workload and which metrics are most important. Rather, we aim to show that MPTCP creates new options for data center topologies; DHFT is a simple example of such a topology.

DHFT presents opportunities single path TCP can't exploit. If the network is underutilized, any pair of communicating hosts should be able to utilize both their NICs, reaching a throughput of 2Gb/s.

---

[3]In a real network, the ports per switch would be fixed, and the number of hosts and switches varied, but this does not allow for a fair comparison, independent of the prices of hosts and switches

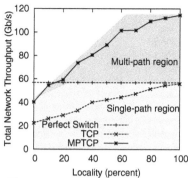

Fig. 15: Performance as a function of locality in the DHFT topology

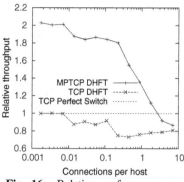

Fig. 16: Relative performance as a function of load in the DHFT

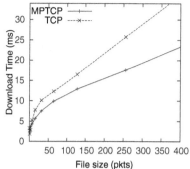

Fig. 17: Time to transfer short files.

We wish to tease apart the effects of the topology from the effects of running MPTCP over the topology. We compare:

- **TCP over the Perfect Switch.** This is the control experiment, and is an upper bound on what TCP can do in any single-homed topology. As there are no parallel paths, MPTCP cannot help on a Perfect Switch. Locality also has no effect on the results.

- **Single-path TCP over DHFT.** Although DHFT is not ideal for TCP, this provides a baseline for comparison.

- **MPTCP over DHFT.** We wish to understand when MPTCP over DHFT outperforms any single-homed topology, and see how much of this is due to MPTCP.

Our first experiment shown in Fig. 15 is a packet-level simulation of the permutation traffic matrix, using long-lived flows with varying degrees of intra-ToR traffic locality. The DHFT network has k=12, giving 576 hosts, and 100Mb/s links, giving a maximum throughput of 43 Gb/s if no traffic is local, and 115 Gb/s if all the traffic is local to the rack and both links from each host are used. The dark grey region shows throughputs that are feasible as locality changes. If only one of the two interfaces on each host is used, as is the case with single-path TCP, then the light grey region shows the possible throughputs.

Our baseline for comparison is a perfect switch directly connecting all 576 hosts via 100Mb/s links. This provides an upper bound on what a regular FatTree with the same number of switch ports as the DHFT could achieve with perfect traffic scheduling.

MPTCP using eight subflows achieves close to the theoretical maximum for all degrees of locality. In contrast, due to flow collisions on core links, single-path TCP does not even come close to the theoretical single-path limits until most of the traffic is not using the core. If the traffic resembles a permutation traffic matrix, building a DHFT topology without MPTCP makes little sense.

If no traffic is local, MPTCP on DHFT is outperformed by the Perfect Switch. But to achieve no locality requires effort - even with a random traffic, some flows stay local to the rack. In practice, applications often adaptively arrange for processing to take advantage of locality. MPTCP on DHFT outperforms the Perfect Switch when at least 12% of traffic is local, and costs the same in switch ports as a FatTree that is strictly worse than a Perfect Switch.

Effects of Load With a random traffic matrix, throughput can be limited by access links collisions. For single-path TCP, a DHFT can reduce this bottleneck, improving performance. Collisions in the DHFT core remain an issue though. The benefits are much greater for MPTCP, as it can utilize both access links even when there are no collisions. Fig. 16 shows how performance depends on load. At light-to-medium load, MPTCP achieves nearly twice the performance of the perfect switch. At high load, the DHFT core is the bottleneck, and the Perfect Switch core has higher bandwidth.

Interestingly, if we keep adding connections, we expect that around 20 connections per host MPTCP will again start to get more throughput than the perfect switch as more hosts gain at least one rack-local connection. In the extreme, an all-to-all traffic matrix will achieve twice the throughput of the perfect switch, with most traffic being rack-local flows. Such extreme workloads push the limits of our packet-level simulator, and have no practical relevance.

5.2 Discussion

DHFT costs the same as a Fat Tree (same port count), but has more links in the access. It provides benefits for traffic patterns with hotspots, and those where the network core is underutilized. Compared to an idealized Fat Tree (i.e. perfect switch), DHFT's worst case performance is 75% and best case is around 200%. If all traffic matrices we analyzed are equally likely to appear in practice, DHFT trades a bit of worst-case performance for substantial average-case gains.

Beyond performance, DHFT improves robustness: any lower-pod switch failure does not cut-off an entire rack of servers. As most racks have dual power supplies, switch redundancy eliminates the biggest single cause for correlated node failures. In turn, this will likely increase application locality; for instance HDFS could choose to store all three replicas of each block in the same rack.

DHFT is not optimal by any measure, but it shows that we can create topologies with better performance *if* we assume MPTCP is the transport protocol. DHFT makes little sense with TCP, as most of the benefits vanish either due to collisions in the core or TCP's inability to use multiple interfaces for a single connection.

With MPTCP as transport, a wider range of topologies are cost-effective. Multipath TCP allows us to linearly scale bisection bandwidth for the same increase in cost. For instance, to create a topology with 2Gb/s full bisection bandwidth, we could use a k-port Fat Tree with $k^3/8$ dual-homed hosts. Transport flows would need to be split across different host interfaces to reach 2Gb/s. Single path TCP can't effectively utilize such a topology.

For really large data centers with hundreds of thousands of hosts, Fat Tree may not be feasible to deploy. We expect there will be islands of Fat Trees, connected to a super core with 10Gb/s uplinks.

6. EXPERIMENTAL VALIDATION

Simulation is only as good as our ability to predict which properties of the environment we are modeling will turn out to be im-

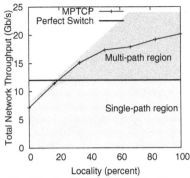

Fig. 18: Performance as a function of locality in the DHFT testbed

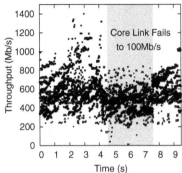

Fig. 19: Robustness to Link Failures in the DHFT testbed

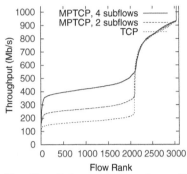

Fig. 20: 12 hours of throughput, all paths between forty EC2 nodes.

portant. Ideally we would cross-validate results against the full implementation. We had two opportunities to do this.

First, we built several small FatTree-like topologies in our lab, with 12 hosts and 7 switches. Although this is too small to see various statistical multiplexing effects, it does provide a controlled enviroment for experimentation. We primarily use this for microbenchmarks to validate aspects that cannot be accurately modeled in simulation.

Our second opportunity was to rent virtual machines on Amazon's Elastic Compute Cloud (EC2). This is a real large-scale production data center, but we can only infer topology and we cannot control or even measure competing traffic.

6.1 Microbenchmarks

Our Linux implementation is still research-grade code; it has not been optimized and mature code should perform better. All the same, it is important to verify that the implementation is capable of the performance indicated in the simulations. In particular, if eight subflows per connection are needed, can the implementation cope?

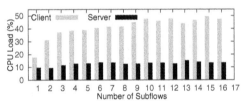

The histogram above shows host CPU load as the client sends to the server saturating a Gigabit link. Both machines are 2006-era, with 2.2GHz single-core Opteron CPUs. Even on old machines, growing beyond two subflows only increases CPU load by 10%.

Should MPTCP be enabled for all TCP connections in a data center? We connected two dual-interface machines to a gigabit switch, and measured the time to setup a connection and transfer a short file. TCP can only use one interface; MPTCP can also use the second, but only after the first subflow has negotiated the use of MPTCP and the second subflow has been established. Figure 17 shows that TCP is quicker for files of less than about 10 packets, but much slower thereafter. To avoid penalizing short flows, the code just needs to wait two RTTs after data transmission starts (or until the window of the first subflow is big enough) and only then start a second subflow.

6.2 DHFT Testbed Experiments

We built a small DHFT network with 12 hosts in two racks. Each host connects to the two ToR switches in its rack, which are dual homed to two aggregation switches, giving four static-routed paths

between hosts in different racks. The switches are soft switches running Linux on PCs. ToR-to-core links are oversubscribed 3:2.

Our aim is to validate some of the simulations, and to see how well our Linux MPTCP implementation behaves with multiple paths. To compare with Fig. 15 we ran the permutation locality traffic matrix, varying the fraction of rack-local connections. A traffic pattern quite similar to this is generated by HDFS writes, where ⅔ of the traffic is rack-local. The throughput curve, shown in Fig. 18, is close to the theoretical value; if 15% of traffic is local, DHFT equals the throughput of a perfect switch; with more local traffic, the improvements are bigger. Aggregate throughput levels off at 21Gb/s; although MPTCP could send more, the Linux soft-switches are saturated.

To validate MPTCP's robustness to link failures we ran the experiment from Fig. 11, downgrading a core link's speed from 1Gb/s to 100Mb/s. Single-path TCP cannot avoid this link as such a failure will not trigger re-routing. We ran a zero-locality permutation matrix to maximally load the core. Fig. 19 shows a time series of flow throughputs. Approximately 4 minutes into the experiment, we downgrade one of the core switches' links to 100Mb/s. MPTCP copes well: its congestion control fairly distributes the remaining core capacity between the flows. When the link returns to 1Gb/s, MPTCP flows increase to fill the capacity.

6.3 EC2

Amazon's EC2 compute cloud allows us to run real-world experiments on a production data center. Amazon has several data centers; their older ones do not appear to be have redundant topologies, but their latest data centers (us-east-1c and us-east-1d) use a topology that provides many parallel paths between many pairs of virtual machines.

We do not know the precise topology of the US East data center. Compared to our simulations, it is complicated slightly because each instance is a virtual machine, sharing the physical hardware with other users. Background traffic levels are also unknown to us, and may vary between experiments.

To understand the variability of the environment and the potential for MPTCP to improve performance, we ran our MPTCP-capable Linux kernel on forty EC2 instances, and for 12 hours sequentially measured throughput with iperf between each pair of hosts, using MPTCP with 2 and 4 subflows and TCP as transport protocols. The resultant dataset totals 3,000 measurements for each configuration, and samples across both time and topology.[4]

Fig. 20 shows the results ordered by throughput for each configuration. Traceroute shows that a third of paths have no diversity; of

---

[4]We also ran the same experiment for 24h with ten machines; results are qualitatively similar.

these paths 60% are local to the switch (2 IP hops), while the others have four IP hops. They roughly correspond to the right-hand 35% of the flows in the figure; they achieve high throughput, and their bottleneck is most likely the shared host NIC. MPTCP cannot help these flows; in fact some of these flows show a very slight reduction in throughput; this is likely due to additional system overheads of MPTCP.

The remaining paths are four IP hops, and the number of available paths varies between two (50% of paths), three (25%) up to nine. Traceroute shows all of them implement load balancing across a redundant topology. MPTCP with four subflows achieves three times the throughput of a single-path TCP for almost every path across the entire 12-hour period.

7. RELATED WORK

Multipath TCP spans routing, path selection and congestion control, offering a general solution to flow scheduling in data center networks. Our design of the MPTCP congestion controller was presented in [14]; there we also briefly analyzed the applicability of MPTCP to current data centers, and the effect of different congestion controllers. This paper provides a much more detailed analysis of MPTCP in existing data centers, as well as exploring new topologies enabled by MPTCP.

There has been much work on scheduling for Clos networks [10, 13, 8]. $m = n$ Clos networks are rearrangeably non-blocking: there is an assigment of flows to paths such that any source-destination traffic pattern can be satisfied at maximum speed. However, mapping flows to paths is difficult; random path selection can give less than 50% of the possible throughput. Many heuristic algorithms have been proposed to utilize Clos networks, but most have drawbacks either in convergence time or performance [8]. More recently, Hedera provided such a solution for data center networks using a centralized coordinator and programmable switches to place flows on paths in the Fat Tree topology [1].

VL2[6] sidesteps the scheduling issue by using 10Gb/s links in the core and per-flow Valiant Load Balancing (ECMP). The speed difference between core and access links reduces the effect of collisions. With BCube [7], sources probe congestion on all paths then use source routing. Unfortunately congestion varies rapidly, and the initial choice may quickly become suboptimal.

Spreading each connection over multiple paths makes the scheduling problem tractable. Geoffray [5] proposes striping packets across multiple paths, coupled with layer two back-pressure. The limitations of this solution stem from the limitations of back-pressure: it is unclear how well this scheme works over multi-hop paths with heterogeneous hardware, as found in todays data centers. In addition to changing the switches, the transport protocol must also be changed to cope with frequent reordering.

Multipath TCP takes the next logical step, making the end-host aware of the different paths, but not changing the network. MPTCP is topology agnostic, completely distributed, and can react on the timescale of a few round trip times to changes in load. MPTCP finds free capacity in the network, increases fairness and is robust to congested links or failures. Finally, it can cope with app-limited flows; network-based solutions struggle here because they have insufficient information. MPTCP gets these benefits because it combines path selection, scheduling and congestion control.

8. CONCLUSIONS

In this paper we examined how the use of MPTCP could improve data center performance by performing very short timescale distributed load balancing. This makes effective use of parallel paths

in modern data center topologies. Our experiments show that for any traffic pattern that is bottlenecked on the network core rather than on the hosts or their access links, MPTCP provides real performance benefits. Due to cost, we expect network cores to be oversubscribed in real data centers, so these benefits seem likely to be common; certainly we observed them in Amazon's EC2 network.

A surprising result is the need to use as many as eight subflows for FatTree and BCube to achieve both good throughput and fairness. Only then is the variance of load between core links reduced sufficiently. The MPTCP protocol and our implementation handle this without difficulty.

Multipath transport protocols such as MPTCP can change the way we think about data center design. With the right congestion control, they actively relieve hot spots, with no need for any form of network scheduling other than simple random ECMP routing. More importantly, network topologies that make no sense with TCP can be very effective with MPTCP. Even routing protocols might benefit. In recent years switch vendors have put a great deal of effort into reducing failure detection and routing reconvergence times. But as data centers scale to hundreds of thousands of hosts, this becomes increasingly difficult. In topologies with many redundant paths and hosts running MPTCP, perhaps fast routing reconvergence after failures is less critical.

Acknowledgements

We thank Olivier Bonaventure and Christoph Paasch for their help with improving MPTCP and the kernel implementation. We also want to thank the anonymous reviewers and our shepherd Jitendra Padhye for their suggestions that helped improve this paper. This work was partly funded by Trilogy, a research project funded by the European Comission in its Seventh Framework program.

9. REFERENCES

[1] M. Al-Fares, A. Loukissas, and A. Vahdat. A scalable, commodity data center network architecture. In *Proc. SIGCOMM 2010*.

[2] M. Al-Fares, S. Radhakrishnan, B. Raghavan, N. Huang, and A. Vahdat. Hedera: Dynamic flow scheduling for data center networks. In *Proc. Usenix NSDI 2010*.

[3] C. Clos. A study of non-blocking switching networks. *Bell System Technical Journal*, 32(5):406–424, 1952.

[4] A. Ford, C. Raiciu, M. Handley, and O. Bonaventure. TCP Extensions for Multipath Operation with Multiple Addresses. Internet-draft, IETF, 2011.

[5] P. Geoffray and T. Hoefler. Adaptive routing strategies for modern high performance networks. In *Proceedings of the 2008 16th IEEE Symposium on High Performance Interconnects*, pages 165–172, Washington, DC, USA, 2008. IEEE Computer Society.

[6] A. Greenberg el al. VL2: a scalable and flexible data center network. In *Proc. ACM Sigcomm 2009*.

[7] C. Guo, G. Lu, D. Li, H. Wu, X. Zhang, Y. Shi, C. Tian, Y. Zhang, and S. Lu. Bcube: a high performance, server-centric network architecture for modular data centers. In *Proc. SIGCOMM 2009*.

[8] K. Holmberg. Optimization models for routing in switching networks of clos type with many stages. *AMO - Advanced Modeling and Optimization*, 10(1), 2008.

[9] J. Mudigonda, P. Yalagandula, M. Al-Fares, and J. C. Mogul. Spain: Cots data-center ethernet for multipathing over arbitrary topologies. In *Proc. NSDI 2010*.

[10] E. Oki, Z. Jing, R. Rojas-Cessa, and H. J. Chao. Concurrent round-robin-based dispatching schemes for clos-network switches. *IEEE/ACM Trans. Netw.*, 10:830–844, December 2002.

[11] C. Raiciu, M. Handley, and A. Ford. Multipath TCP design decisions. Work in progress, www.cs.ucl.ac.uk/staff/C.Raiciu/files/mtcp-design.pdf, 2009.

[12] C. Raiciu, M. Handley, and D. Wischik. Coupled Congestion Control for Multipath Transport Protocols. Internet-draft, IETF, 2011.

[13] A. Smiljanic. Rate and delay guarantees provided by clos packet switches with load balancing. *IEEE/ACM Trans. Netw.*, 16:170–181, February 2008.

[14] D. Wischik, C. Raiciu, A. Greenhalgh, and M. Handley. Design, implementation and evaluation of congestion control for multipath TCP. In *Proc. Usenix NSDI 2011*.

NetQuery: A Knowledge Plane for Reasoning about Network Properties

Alan Shieh   Emin Gün Sirer   Fred B. Schneider

Department of Computer Science, Cornell University
Ithaca, NY, USA
{ashieh, egs, fbs}@cs.cornell.edu

ABSTRACT

This paper presents the design and implementation of NetQuery, a knowledge plane for federated networks such as the Internet. In such networks, not all administrative domains will generate information that an application can trust and many administrative domains may have restrictive policies on disclosing network information. Thus, both the trustworthiness and accessibility of network information pose obstacles to effective reasoning. NetQuery employs trustworthy computing techniques to facilitate reasoning about the trustworthiness of information contained in the knowledge plane while preserving confidentiality guarantees for operator data. By characterizing information disclosure between operators, NetQuery enables remote verification of advertised claims and contractual stipulations; this enables new applications because network guarantees can span administrative boundaries. We have implemented NetQuery, built several NetQuery-enabled devices, and deployed applications for cloud datacenters, enterprise networks, and the Internet. Simulations, testbed experiments, and a deployment on a departmental network indicate NetQuery can support hundreds of thousands of operations per second and can thus scale to large ISPs.

Categories and Subject Descriptors

C.2.3 [**Computer-Communication Networks**]: Network Operations—*network management, network monitoring*

General Terms

Design, Management

1. INTRODUCTION

Depending on their configuration, administration, and provisioning, networks provide drastically different features. For instance, some networks provide little failure resilience, while others provision failover capacity and deploy middleboxes to protect against denial of service attacks [13, 6]. Agreements between network operators often include requirements that are governed by such network features. Peering and service agreements, for example, can mandate topology, reliability, and forwarding policies, while terms-of-use agreements can mandate end host deployment of up-to-date security mechanisms. Yet the standard IP interface masks the differences between networks; each network appears to provide the same, undifferentiated "dial-tone" service. Consequently, clients and networks must resort to ad hoc techniques for advertising the quality of a network and for reasoning about meta-level properties of the network.

Knowledge planes [17] have been proposed to disseminate these underlying network features, thereby giving providers a channel for advertising network capabilities and enabling applications to use reasoning to find suitable networks for their requirements. This paper describes *NetQuery*, a knowledge plane for multi-operator networks, like the Internet. To our knowledge, NetQuery is the first instantiation of a knowledge plane for federated networks comprised of mutually untrusting administrative domains. NetQuery disseminates information (e.g., routing tables, neighbor lists, and configurations) about network entities (e.g., routers, switches, and end hosts) to support application-level reasoning. NetQuery enables reasoning while simultaneously respecting the information disclosure policies of participants, which may be hesitant to share information in a federated environment. Under NetQuery, reasoning can occur between mutually untrusting entities without leaking confidential information.

NetQuery applications act only on information from sources that they trust; NetQuery binds each property to a responsible principal. In environments where networked components are equipped with secure coprocessors, such as the Trusted Platform Module (TPM) [21], NetQuery can use this hardware as a root of trust for reasoning about information sources.

This paper outlines the design and implementation of NetQuery. First, it proposes mechanisms for disseminating and discovering facts about the state of network elements. These mechanisms also enable applications to track changes to such state. Second, it outlines a logic-based framework for using such facts, supported by attribution information, to assure that the network possesses an application-specific characteristic. NetQuery leverages trustworthy computing to achieve expressive reasoning while respecting the confidentiality requirements of each network operator. Finally, it describes our implementation of NetQuery devices and applications, as well as our experiences running NetQuery in simulated ISP networks and on an operational departmental network of 73 L2 and L3 Ethernet switches and over 700 end hosts. We show that NetQuery applications can derive guarantees about network performance that cannot be achieved with existing monitoring-based approaches. We also show that NetQuery imposes little overhead and supports topology sizes and event rates encountered in typical service provider networks. To wit, a single NetQuery server can handle 500,000 requests per second and store the full forwarding table state of an entire Internet POP.

The remainder of this paper describes the design and implementation of NetQuery. Section 2 describes the motivation for NetQuery and outlines the design. Section 3 discusses the NetQuery data model. Section 4 describes how the data model is coupled with a logical framework and with TPMs to support inference. Section 5 describes the security model, its architectural implications, and how analyses can determine that information sources are trustworthy. Section 6 describes the incremental deployment benefits of NetQuery. Section 7 describes and evaluates our implementation and applications. Section 8 presents related work and Section 9 concludes.

2. MOTIVATION AND OVERVIEW

Knowledge planes enable new applications that depend on reasoning about properties of the network. By providing mechanisms for determining the characteristics of a network, such as the expected level of performance, redundancy, or confidentiality, NetQuery enables network participants (e.g., peers, providers, or customers) to make better informed decisions when establishing sessions, entering into contracts with one another, or verifying compliance.

Sound network reasoning improves network transparency and accountability, facilitating many types of commercial transactions. On the Internet, the price that an operator can charge depends on the paths and performance that they advertise; since routing traffic on a different path may result in lower cost, operators are incentivized to deviate from their advertised behavior to maximize profit [26]. Existing reputation-based mechanisms have not proven sufficient to constrain selfish operators. Indeed, consumer advocates often accuse last mile ISPs of misrepresenting the quality and capacity of their networks [10]. Community forums often advise users to verify independently whether their datacenter provider is truly multi-homed [18]. Differences between networks are advertised through manual, ad hoc channels such as interstitial web pages. Absent automatic mechanisms for discovering and disseminating claims about network capacity and redundancy, agreements are difficult and costly to enact and competitors can engage in unscrupulous practices. With NetQuery, ISPs with good networks can advertise the quality of their networks in an automatic, remotely-verifiable fashion.

Transparency and accountability for claims improve market efficiency by reducing the economic transaction costs associated with establishing agreements. In particular, NetQuery allows applications to discover network properties that are otherwise difficult or impossible to determine by external data plane probing.

NetQuery reasoning is highly flexible and able to perform reasoning spanning multiple ASes. Since NetQuery's logic-based credential system supports many mechanisms for establishing trust besides a priori relationships, such reasoning can readily incorporate information from any principal. For instance, TPM-based credentials leverage trusted hardware to incorporate device-generated information and audit-based credentials incorporate network information added by trusted third parties.

2.1 Scenarios and applications

NetQuery enables a wide range of applications based on reasoning about the properties of a remote network.

Enforcing interconnection policies. Although the level of direct interconnection between ASes on the Internet has grown substantially [57], lack of trust limits the potential benefit of this dense graph. For instance, engaging in mutual backup, wherein each AS

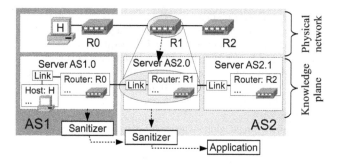

Figure 1: **NetQuery architecture.** A physical network and its knowledge plane representation, stored on knowledge plane servers operated by each AS.

allows the other to use its transit paths in emergencies, increases overall fault tolerance. Yet unscrupulous ASes might misuse these paths for non-emergency traffic. By checking a neighbor's BGP policies and forwarding table entries, a network can verify that backup paths are only used at appropriate times. This information is not currently available to external parties.

Verifying AS path length. Since performance typically degrades as packets traverse multiple ASes, ISPs are motivated to establish peering or transit relationships to shorten AS path lengths. A small content provider or access ISP that seeks to reduce AS path length but lacks the resources to establish many direct interconnections might instead purchase service from a provider that has low AS path length connections to the desired destinations [22]. The purchaser benefits from outsourcing the overhead of managing many peering relationships and can use NetQuery to verify that traffic will be forwarded with minimal stretch. By comparison, establishing this arrangement today by using BGP-reported path information and traceroute would necessitate a large trusted computing base as well as incur the cost of active probing.

Advertising network redundancy. Some networks are constructed with redundant devices and network links to increase availability. A provider with a highly redundant network can use NetQuery to advertise this fact by using a reasoning process that inspects the network topology. By comparison, it is difficult or impossible to detect redundancy with probing, since the extra resources are only visible during failure.

Avoiding rogue Wi-Fi hotspots. In urban areas, mobile users are typically within range of many wireless networks [44]. Users can employ NetQuery to differentiate between these, using analysis to select networks with better security and performance. By checking for a network built from trustworthy devices and link-level encryption, a user can avoid connecting to rogue Wi-Fi hotspots [37]; by checking the capacity of the backhaul path to the upstream provider, a user can choose the best performing network in an area.

Future opportunities. Many proposals for improving service discovery, such as those for bandwidth markets [56] and virtualized routing infrastructure [36], have the potential to greatly expand the set of service providers and peers available to a given ISP. NetQuery can maximize the benefits of such proposals by providing new ways to check whether a newly discovered service provider or peer is suitable.

2.2 System overview

Network information is disseminated in NetQuery using a *knowledge plane* that maintains a representation of the network topology and configuration (Figure 1). The knowledge plane makes this information available to applications for determining whether the network exhibits desired properties. The process of inferring some high-level *characteristic* of the network (such as the loss rate on a route between hosts) from low-level properties (such as routing tables) is called *analysis*. Status information about network entities is typically self-reported by these entities (e.g., routers export their forwarding tables), though a transition mode is supported for proxies to transfer management information from legacy entities to NetQuery.

Logically, a single, global knowledge plane incorporates all properties across multiple administrative domains on the Internet. Physically, this knowledge plane is federated — each administrative domain runs a cluster of servers that locally stores all information describing its network. Federation facilitates incremental deployment and protects confidentiality, since an operator can independently run NetQuery servers without making information accessible to operators of other administrative domains.

Applications can query the knowledge plane for information about any participating network. Networks will typically restrict direct access from external parties, but instead allow *sanitizers* to execute operator-authorized sets of analyses on behalf of external applications. These analyses export only the network characteristics that meet an operator's information disclosure policies. The exported sanitizer results are accompanied by credentials certifying that the correct analysis code was executed.

Each NetQuery application independently defines the set of principals it trusts. The knowledge plane can include conflicting information from different sources; applications can filter such information based on the principals that they trust. This trust can be predicated on any credential associated with a principal. Often, such credentials are issued by a TPM, which binds statements issued by a principal to a hardware/software platform. TPMs enable NetQuery to collect a broad pool of attributed properties at low cost since they are inexpensive and enable trust establishment costs to be amortized. In particular, rather than establish trust with every potential counterparty, analyses need only establish trust with platforms, with this cost amortized across all participants deploying those platforms. This enables TPM-bearing devices to automatically issue unforgeable, fine-grained certificates for information inserted into the knowledge plane.

Often, there are multiple ways to satisfied a desired network characteristic. For instance, the fault resilience of a network may be derived through an analysis of its topology or through independent vetting by an auditor. NetQuery employs a logic for sound, flexible derivation of characteristics. Logical reasoning yields a proof that is self-documenting in that it describes all the assumptions and inference steps used to conclude that a characteristic holds. Such proofs are useful in logging and auditing.

3. DATA MODEL

A key challenge in building a knowledge plane for the Internet is to contend with its many trust domains. A knowledge plane that spans multiple organizations must support access control policies to protect confidential properties. Because the knowledge plane might contain inaccurate information, applications should be able to express policies that specify what information is safe to use for analysis. Since the system includes a diverse range of devices and implementations, standardization of nomenclature is necessary for interoperability.

The knowledge plane in our NetQuery prototype is based on a *tuplespace* representation. Every *tuple* is named by a globally unique *tuple ID* (TID) and stores properties as typed attribute/value pairs; an attribute/value pair and its associated metadata is called

a *factoid*. NetQuery supports string, integer, references to tuples, dictionary, and vector values for factoids.[1]

NetQuery *principals* are the basis for policy decisions. Every producer and consumer of information from NetQuery is represented by a principal, which has a unique public/private key pair. The key pair is generated independently. NetQuery records two pieces of policy-associated metadata for every factoid it stores: *attribution*, the principal responsible for generating the factoid; and *export policy*, which defines what principals can read the factoid.

In a federated environment it is impractical to expect global consistency or uniform interpretation of properties contributed by diverse sources. But by retrieving attributions, applications have some basis to reason about whether a property is suitable for use based on whether the provider of that property is trustworthy.

To facilitate interoperability between devices and analyses, NetQuery information conforms to voluntary *schemas*. Each schema defines the set of properties that a given kind of network element must provide. NetQuery schemas prescribe a data format but do not prescribe associated code or operations. NetQuery provides standard schemas for representing devices (e.g., hosts, routers, and switches) and network abstractions (e.g., TCP connections, TCP/UDP endpoints, and IPsec security associations). NetQuery schemas are similar to those of network management systems (e.g., SNMP) that are supported by many devices. By adding to such devices a shim for outputting properties or by interfacing through an SNMP proxy, we enable them to participate in NetQuery.

Initializing factoids. Tuples and factoids for a network device can be initialized and maintained by different network participants, including the device itself, its administrator, or a third party. Since routers and switches have limited processing capacity, they offload their tuples to *tuplespace servers*, thereby insulating against application-induced query load.

On start up, a device discovers its local tuplespace server from a DHCP option and then transfers local configuration and initial state to that server by issuing **create**() operations to the tuplespace server to instantiate tuples and **update**() operations to write factoids. A newly activated router, for example, creates tuples for all of its interfaces and exports its initial forwarding table state. Hosts, routers, and switches also export local topology information to the tuplespace, using a neighbor-discovery protocol such as LLDP to generate ground facts. The device pushes any changes to its configuration and state to the tuplespace server.

Tuplespace servers and lookup protocol. Each AS or third-party information service operates tuplespace servers. The TID for a tuple embeds the IP of the tuplespace server storing that tuple, along with an opaque identifier. Device references are stored as TIDs, and therefore analysis can efficiently access the relevant tuplespace servers. To prevent changes to facts and metadata while in flight through man-in-the-middle attacks, tuplespace servers communicate over secure channels.

To prevent DoS attacks by applications that issue costly tuplespace server operations, all remote operations always terminate in bounded time. The tuplespace server only supports simple wildcard queries for attributes, which in the worst case loops over all attributes for a given tuple. NetQuery provides no mechanisms for invoking either

---

[1] A production version of NetQuery might well leverage the ongoing development of semantic web technologies such as RDF and OWL [43] for building the knowledge plane. Research into a semantic web has produced considerable infrastructure and theory for the federated knowledge stores, reasoning, and query processing that underpin any knowledge plane. NetQuery can also help ongoing efforts to extend the semantic web to cover network management information.

recursive queries or stored procedures. Clients, however, are free to aggregate data and locally perform expensive analyses.

Tuplespace servers make extensive use of soft-state to improve performance. Since the tuplespace contents derive from device state, a tuplespace server can always ask devices to re-export their state. This obviates the need for tuplespace servers to support a costly transactional recovery mechanism. The tuplespace uses lease-based storage management for factoids. Thus, once a device fails, the stale factoids will be garbage collected automatically.

3.1 Dynamics: changes and triggers

Changes in the network can invalidate properties in the knowledge plane. Time of check/time of use bugs can occur because network changes take place concurrently with analysis. Similar behavior can arise from probe-based measurements such as `traceroute`.

NetQuery provides a *trigger* interface to facilitate detection of changes to underlying properties during analysis. In addition to this, the interface allows applications that depend on long-running characteristics to be notified when some conclusion no longer holds. Once a trigger is installed, a callback packet is sent to an application-specified IP-port pair (*trigger port*) whenever a specified factoid has been modified. Triggers are stored by tuplespace servers as soft-state, so applications must periodically send keep-alives to refresh their triggers.

Our NetQuery applications check for relatively stable characteristics; here, triggers suffice to filter spurious analysis results that arise from observing transient states. Network tools built using probing interfaces typically would be fooled by such transients. To implement this filtering, applications install triggers for factoids being used. For instance, consider an application that enumerates all hosts in some given L2 Ethernet domain by issuing queries that traverse the network graph. Were the topology to change during these queries, the application might miss newly connected hosts. To guard against this, the application issues a **retrieve_and_ install_ trigger**() operation to atomically retrieve link information from a switch and thereafter to monitor it for changes. This atomic operation eliminates the window of vulnerability between the time a factoid is read to when monitoring for changes to that factoid starts.

Network delays in message delivery can cause updates from different devices to be received at a tuplespace server interleaved in unpredictable ways. A consistent cut guarantee would eliminate such inconsistent views, but the underlying network protocols and devices typically support neither consistency nor causality. We could augment devices with logical clocks, but that would be challenging to deploy incrementally, since means would be needed to approximate causal dependencies when exchanging messages with legacy devices. Fortunately, operator reasoning is typically focused on steady-state network characteristics, and causal consistency is less critical there. Future work will return to this problem.

4. ANALYSIS

NetQuery provides mechanisms that parse factoids acquired from tuplespace servers, determine whether a factoid is trustworthy, and check if a desired network characteristic is supported by trusted factoids.

Nexus Authorization Logic (NAL) provides the logical foundation for making inferences from factoids. A full discussion of NAL is beyond the scope of this paper (see [49]). Below, we simply outline the main features of NAL, describe how it is used in NetQuery, and discuss the implications of our choice. NAL admits reasoning about factoids and attribution information, enabling applications

to reconcile conflicting statements uttered by different principals. The `says` and `speaksfor` operators, along with a set of two dozen inference rules, permit inferences based on an application's trust assumptions.

NAL associates a *worldview* with each principal. This worldview contains beliefs the principal holds about the network. Reasoning in NAL is local to every worldview: by default, inference takes into account only local beliefs, rather than statements believed by other principals. This local reasoning restriction prevents reasoning by one principal from being corrupted by contradictory facts attributed to another principal. Using `speaksfor`, a principal can incorporate into its worldview beliefs from other principals that it trusts. An optional scoping parameter restricts `speaksfor` to import only a subset of statements that concern a specific matter of interest.[2]

Applications use NAL to derive theorems about the network from information provided by the NetQuery knowledge plane. Specifically, factoids are converted to logical statements, which are then used to prove some given *goal statement*. A goal statement is a NAL formula that characterizes what a client application wants to establish. An application initially populates its worldview with an *import policy*, specifying what factoids the client deems to be trustworthy. Import policies often include `speaksfor` statements that specify which hardware and software platforms are trusted sources for factoids.

Ground statements. Factoids from tuplespace servers translate into NAL *ground statements*. Tuplespace API operations, such as fetching factoids, translate their return values to NAL formulas. For instance, a **retrieve**() operation issued on router *R0*'s tuple returns factoids as NAL axioms of the form:

$$TuplespaceServer \text{ says}$$
$$R0 \text{ says } (R0\text{.Type} = \text{"Router"} \land$$
$$R0\text{.fwd\_table} = \{ip_A => nexthop, \ldots\})$$

where "$ip_A => nexthop$" denotes a forwarding table entry specifying the next hop for a given destination. The nesting of `says` formulas captures the full chain of custody during the factoid's traversal through the knowledge plane. Here, the factoid was exported from *R0* to a particular tuplespace server, *TuplespaceServer*.

The NAL *proof* for a goal statement is a derivation tree with the goal statement as the root, NAL inference rule applications as internal nodes, and ground statements and axioms as leaves. Analyses typically provide a proof generator that embodies a programmer's understanding of how to check whether a given characteristic holds into a proof generation strategy.

Proofs can be consumed entirely within a single application or exported to other parties as a self-documenting certificate. The certificate can be logged to create an audit trail for accounting, documentation, and debugging. Such audit trails are also useful in application domains governed by external compliance requirements, such as Sarbanes-Oxley and HIPAA.

4.1 Example: Checking network paths

This example shows how an application might use NAL to verify that a network complies with a performance requirement. Suppose site *A* wants to establish that the path to site *B* provides low loss rate (Figure 2).

---

[2]Since NAL does not encode a notion of degrees of trust, `speaksfor` is monolithic in that it incorporates all in-scope statements. NetQuery can switch to a logic that supports such reasoning [15, 41] should the need arise.

The goal statement for a path P to satisfy a bound r on the loss rate is

$$\exists P \in Routers^{2+} :$$
$$(P[1] = A) \wedge (P[|P|] = B) \wedge$$
$$(\forall i\ 1 \leq i < |P| : P[i] \rightarrow \texttt{fwd\_table}\langle B \rangle = P[i+1]) \wedge \qquad \text{(Goal)}$$
$$(\exists r' \in Reals : (r' < r) \wedge \text{TrustedLossRate}(P, r'))$$

We write "$Routers^{k+}$" for the set of all finite router-tuple sequences of length k or greater, "$\texttt{TID.name1} \rightarrow \texttt{name2} = v$" as shorthand for dereferencing a reference value factoid to access a second factoid, "$|P|$" for the length of a sequence, "$P[k]$" for the kth element in a sequence, and "$T\langle key \rangle$" for a lookup from a factoid of dictionary type. The first three lines constrain P to be a valid path given the source, destination, and forwarding table state. The last line asserts an upper bound on the expected one-way loss rate on P given information from trusted principals, and that predicate is defined as

$$\text{TrustedLossRate}(P, r) \triangleq$$
$$(\exists P', P'' \in Routers^{1+}\ \exists p \in Routers\ \exists r', r'' \in Reals :$$
$$(P = \text{Concat}(P', p, P'')) \wedge (r = r' + r'') \wedge \qquad \text{(Cjoin)}$$
$$\text{TrustedLossRate}(\text{Concat}(P', p), r') \wedge$$
$$\text{TrustedLossRate}(\text{Concat}(p, P''), r'')) \quad \vee$$

$$(\exists R, R_{next} \in Routers :$$
$$(P = \text{Concat}(R, R_{next})) \wedge$$
$$(R \text{ says } R.\texttt{curr\_loss\_rate\_to}\langle R_{next} \rangle = r) \wedge \qquad \text{(C0)}$$
$$\text{IsTrustedRouter}(R)) \quad \vee$$

$$(\exists I \in ISPs :$$
$$(\forall i\ 1 \leq i \leq |P| : P[i].\texttt{ISP} = I) \wedge$$
$$(I \text{ says } I.\texttt{sla\_loss\_rate}\langle P[1], P[|P|] \rangle = r) \wedge \qquad \text{(C1)}$$
$$\text{IsTrustedISP}(I)) \quad \vee$$

$$(\exists A \in Auditors :$$
$$(A \text{ says } A.\texttt{measured\_loss\_rate}\langle P[1], P[|P|] \rangle = r) \wedge \qquad \text{(C2)}$$
$$\text{IsTrustedAuditor}(A))$$

where "Concat()" denotes sequence concatenation. IsTrustedRouter(), IsTrustedISP(), and IsTrustedAuditor() are predicates derived from import policies, where the policy for IsTrustedRouter() checks the attestation and platform while the latter two check whether I and A are on a whitelist of trusted principals.

This analysis incorporates facts from multiple trustworthy sources, each having different ways to determine the loss rate of a path: (C0) expresses trust in certain routers to report their instantaneous link statistics, (C1) expresses trust in certain ISPs to claim SLAs, and (C2) expresses trust in certain auditors and measurement tools [40] to report measured performance. Each rule infers loss rate using different data schemas.

4.2 Using TPM attestations

Every TPM is uniquely identified by a set of keys that is certified by a PKI being operated by the device manufacturer. Attestations are remotely-verifiable, unforgeable, and tamper-proof certificates that use these device keys to bind a software-generated bit string (typically, a message) to the particular hardware and software platform that generated it [25]. By linking attestations to attribution metadata, NetQuery allows applications to unequivocally link each factoid back to some particular device.

Attestation is not a panacea against all misbehavior. Attestation merely establishes accountability; a NetQuery client using a factoid has to decide whether to trust the platform that is attesting to that factoid. For instance, suppose a routing platform is designed to honestly

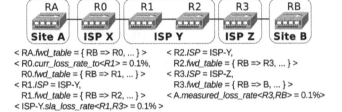

Figure 2: **Topology and tuplespace contents for network analyzer example.** Attribution metadata ("says" information) has been omitted for brevity.

reports its observations of the control- and data-plane as factoids. It is tempting to assume that attestation of this platform implies that the factoids agree with the real-world. But malicious operators can manipulate these observations and trick poorly-constructed devices into issuing factoids that disagree. Section 5.2.2 discusses such attacks.

TPM optimizations

NetQuery applications make their own determination about how factoids are interpreted based on attribution information. In the baseline system, every factoid and credential is signed, allowing clients to independently check that factoids are attributed to the right principals and that credentials are issued by the right parties. However, this checking is costly if clients use factoids and credentials from many different principals. Hence, NetQuery incorporates two optimizations.

Avoid TPM signatures. Whenever possible, NetQuery avoids obtaining signatures from the TPM, which is much slower than the CPU. Instead, NetQuery constructs software principal keys using a TPM-rooted certificate chain that the CPU uses for signing every factoid update. Thus, TPM attestations are used only once per boot, to bind the software principal to the platform.

Attest to tuplespace servers. Signatures provide end-to-end integrity and authentication for factoids. This helps when tuplespace servers might manipulate factoids, but it is unnecessary for tuplespace servers that are trusted to relay factoids correctly. By distinguishing such servers with attestation, NetQuery can replace per-factoid signatures with secure channels built from symmetric keys. Clients using this optimization specify an import policy that accepts tuples without signature-verification from attested tuplespace servers. These policies leverage the says information within ground statements, which encodes the tuplespace server's position as a repository of utterances from other principals.

4.3 Confidentiality and sanitizers

Agreements between network participants often stipulate the presence of certain network features. For instance, peering agreements mandate up-time and fault tolerance guarantees [3], SLAs mandate desired latency and loss rate characteristics, and service agreements for cloud datacenters reference the network bisection bandwidth and oversubscription levels. Verifying the accuracy of such advertised claims is at best difficult and often impossible. Trust establishment is typically performed manually, pairwise for each agreement, using ad hoc means.

In contrast, knowledge plane analysis can verify such claims in a principled fashion. However, most ASes have strict disclosure policies about internal network information. A naïve use of NetQuery, where external parties run analysis to verify properties of interest, can reveal detailed internal information. To be practical, a

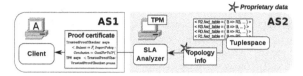

Figure 3: **Preserving confidentiality.** Sanitizers support external clients without leaking information, since the exported certificates serve as trusted proxies for the full proof.

knowledge plane needs some way to provide assurances to external parties without revealing confidential data.

NetQuery provides *sanitizers* for this purpose. A sanitizer is a service that converts secret factoids into unforgeable summary factoids suitable for release to other parties (Figure 3). Sanitizers execute analysis code on behalf of the remote party. To provide assurance that a remote analysis is done correctly, a sanitizer executes in a trusted execution environment and provides an attestation certificate that ties the output factoid to the sanitizer binary and the execution time. This approach does require both parties to agree on the sanitizer at the time of contract establishment, but once that agreement is in place, a sanitizer that checks the contract stipulations reveals no more information than what is revealed in the contract itself.

NetQuery provides confidentiality guarantees through its careful use of the trusted execution platform. A sanitizer executes on an AS's own computers, so factoids that it processes never leave the AS's custody. The trusted execution environment is used solely to provide an execution-integrity guarantee to a remote party. The data confidentiality guarantees then come from the sanitization embedded in the analysis itself—not from the underlying operating system. Using sanitizers means that NetQuery does *not* require an execution environment that can provide confidentiality guarantees against attackers with physical access to the execution hardware—such systems are difficult to build, even with TPMs. Further, since ASes have complete control over when, where and how often sanitizers execute and how much data they reveal to external parties, an AS can prevent outside applications from crafting query streams that consume excessive system resources or that induce a sanitizer to leak information.

4.4 Confidentiality-preserving applications

The following examples show how NetQuery supports different applications while preserving the confidentiality of factoids. These applications, along with the ones from Section 2.1, can all be implemented with sanitizers.

Verifying performance and reliability guarantees. Configuration generators that use global network optimization to achieve performance and reliability goals are increasingly prevalent [50, 4]. These tools automatically configure a network based on workload, topology, and performance constraints. Operators that rely on configuration generators can use NetQuery to advertise the achieved goals.

Configuration generators are typically complex and proprietary to an operator; so they are not disclosable to network clients as a means of certifying performance goals. But a sanitizer could run an industry standard configuration checker (such as [16]) to verify that the output configuration from a configuration generator meets the performance claim. Moreover, a network operator can upgrade to a new configuration generator without updating the contract or disclosing the new code.

As an example of this construction, suppose an operator offering MPLS-based VPNs advertises guaranteed bandwidth in the presence of a single node or link failure [34]. The operator could run a global optimizer to find an assignment of MPLS primary and backup paths that satisfies all reservations and link capacity constraints. A configuration checker can then validate this assignment by walking through the MPLS-related factoids: for each failure scenario, the checker would verify that backup paths do not overload any links.

Dynamic verification of contractual obligations. Some contractual obligations are easier to verify dynamically than statically. For instance, precomputed backup paths in MPLS VPNs provide bandwidth guarantees only for the first failure. To establish resilience against additional failures, the operator needs to compute a new set of primary and backup paths after each failure. A configuration checker can detect this by using triggers and updating its output factoids accordingly.

But updating the output factoid every time the provider-topology changes leaks information about outage and maintenance intervals. To prevent this disclosure, the operator can interpose another sanitizer certifying that the network successfully recovers from failures within a reasonable time. As long as this assertion is met, the sanitizer leaks no information beyond that found in the customer contract.

5. USING TRUSTWORTHY COMPUTING ABSTRACTIONS

Operators are not only well-positioned to launch attacks on NetQuery but they have incentives to do so. In this section, we outline the NetQuery security model and discuss the applicable results from trustworthy computing research in building routers that can provide assurances. We also discuss the vulnerabilities that can exist in analyses that improperly interpret knowledge plane information, along with defenses to protect against such concerns.

5.1 Security model assumptions

NetQuery depends on the following security assumptions:

- **Hardware and software security.** Attackers cannot tamper with the execution semantics of a device. The only way to affect running code is to use the explicit interfaces provided by the device (e.g., I/O ports, RPCs, configuration console) rather than side channels (e.g., installing hardware probes on its memory bus). Moreover, attackers cannot extract secrets stored in secure coprocessors.

- **Cryptographic algorithm security.** This assumption, shared by most work on security, implies that digital signatures used for attestation cannot be forged. It also implies the confidentiality and integrity of messages conveyed by secure channels.

Together, these assumptions imply that TPM attestations are unforgeable, since execution, encryption, and credentials cannot be compromised or spoofed. Consequently, messages used to implement the knowledge plane can be bound to the hardware/software platform responsible for generating them.

TPM-equipped commodity PC hardware approximates our hardware security assumptions. Network devices are substantially similar to PC hardware — the primary difference is an additional high-performance switching backplane not found on most PCs, but this backplane is logically equivalent to sophisticated I/O devices, which can be attested to [31].

Technology trends suggest that future trustworthy computing platforms will be even better approximations of our hardware resilience assumptions. This suggests that device manufacturers have incentives to further improve commodity platforms. It is already possible to build highly tamper-resistant platforms, ranging from high-performance encryption of buses to protect against probing attacks [53, 32] to highly secure processors for protecting major financial and PKI transactions [55]. Thus, even today, designers of trustworthy routers can choose a level of hardware security that can support the needs of NetQuery. Even without such improvements, TPMs are becoming more deeply integrated into platforms, raising the bar for physical attacks. Even if a TPM is compromised, the damage is localized, since the extracted keys can only be used to generate information attributed to that TPM.

5.2 Incomplete and inaccurate world views

The knowledge plane encodes an incomplete view of the data plane, control plane, and broader operating environment. Analyses must cope with the potential incompleteness to avoid deriving unsound analysis results. Inaccurate information may also arise due to poor device implementations.

Below, we present examples of incompleteness and inaccuracy, along with ways to ensure that analysis and devices are implemented correctly.

5.2.1 Exogenous information

Knowledge plane incompleteness can arise because relevant network information is outside the purview of NetQuery devices. For instance, consider a pair of routers connected with multiple links. Though they appear independent to the devices, these links could be physically separated or they could reside in the same undersea cable bundle and subject to correlated failures. Similarly, distinct devices might exhibit common mode failure due to physical breaches or financial insolvency of the operator.

A fault-tolerance analysis that equates multiple links, as reported by the device, with independence would derive unsound conclusions. Only by including more information in the knowledge plane, such as the physical location of fibers as compiled in databases [52], can one hope to avoid such errors. The NetQuery knowledge plane can incorporate such data.

5.2.2 Inaccurate information

Consider a network that has routers where the forwarding and control layers behave as today, but run NetQuery and satisfy its security assumptions. This strawman router design provides weak assurances; we will show how to improve on this.

Router implementations are complex; a malicious operator could well gain control of the control plane, data plane, or NetQuery processes, then induce them to export inaccurate facts. Trustworthy computing platforms provide isolated monitoring mechanisms [51] that operate independently of application code; using these to monitor the control plane and data plane and to export the inferred properties to the knowledge plane results in improved robustness.

A malicious operator could introduce non-NetQuery nodes into the real network such that the nodes are not reported to the knowledge plane, yet substantially change the behavior of the network. Any actions taken based on analysis of this knowledge plane could be misguided and violate the intended policy. This attack is inexpensive to launch, since the introduced nodes can be implemented with commodity devices.

To illustrate these attacks, suppose a dishonest ISP installs additional nodes to trick NetQuery analyses into inferring a high quality network even while the actual physical network supports only a fraction of the claimed capacity, provides no redundancy, and sends customer traffic over indirect routes.

In existing networks, operators have access to the keys used to secure control protocols such as OSPF and BGP. Malicious operators can use these keys to spoof routing advertisements, in a *forged control message attack*. Further, a malicious operator can also use network virtualization to hide a slower physical network or tunneling to redirect traffic along alternate paths. Such attacks embody forms of *data plane/control plane dissociation*.

In each of these cases, the knowledge plane reports that the routers are directly connected at the control or data link layer, yet they are in fact connected to an operator-controlled node. The solution is to add countermeasures to ensure that the knowledge plane and real network match. To protect against the forged control message attack, NetQuery encrypts all control messages between NetQuery-equipped devices with per-session keys known only to the devices. To protect against the dissociation attack, NetQuery devices can adopt standard solutions for monitoring the data plane for anomalies, such as trajectory sampling [20] to probabilistically detect packet redirection, link-layer encryption [33] to ensure that no control or data packets at all are redirected, and performance monitoring [7] to establish capacity bounds on every link.

5.3 Confidentiality-preserving analysis architectures

One of the design principles of NetQuery was to leverage existing trust relationships rather than requiring new ones to be forged. This principle comes into play if we consider the problem of protecting the confidentiality of operator information, which is a central concern of operators.

5.3.1 Sanitizers

NetQuery sanitizers execute in a machine controlled by the network operator, with the assurance that the right analysis was executed, as discharged by attesting to the code that ran on the machine. This leverages a pre-existing trust relation: in the absence of NetQuery, the external party has to trust the network operator to issue a properly-derived result. Hence, a NetQuery sanitizer does not change the extant trust relationship. Rather, it simply puts the original trust assumption on a mechanically-backed basis.

The alternative would be to execute the sanitizer in a TPM-equipped machine controlled by the external party. Here, the network operator would have to ship confidential information to external machines and would have to trust those machines to not reveal this information. The trust relation required here is substantially different from the original; operators might resist deploying this type of sanitizer. Their concern is well-founded: this architecture provides less defense-in-depth against the compromise of confidential information and there are indeed low-cost attacks that can extract confidential information from the memory of TPM-equipped machines [30].

5.3.2 Analyses spanning multiple domains

In preceding applications, we showed how to support multi-domain analyses that are decomposable into independent, per-domain sanitizers. We offer here a design for another approach that admits analyses that span multiple domains while preserving confidentiality. Such analyses are useful for implementing traffic engineering across multiple ASes while preserving confidentiality [39].

Our solution is to combine NetQuery with secure multiparty computation (MPC). In fact, NetQuery's strengths complement the weaknesses of MPC. Adding NetQuery helps to satisfy the trust assumptions of MPC. Since MPC protocols do not constrain participants to be honest about their inputs, each MPC application typically requires an application-specific security analysis of the implications of such cheating. Some MPC protocols leak information to participants that do not follow the protocol, which poses a deployment risk in realistic scenarios, but NetQuery obviates such concerns by protecting the MPC inputs and protocol implementation. This approach

Libraries	
Server & client	18,286
NAL	2,254

Data sources	
Nexus host	543
Software switch	1,853
Quagga router	+777
SNMP proxy	1,578

Applications	
Network access control	787
L2/L3 traceroute	483
Oversubscription	356
Maximum capacity	316
Redundancy	333

Figure 4: **Source line count for NetQuery libraries, devices, and analyses.** Router figure is the code size increase relative to Quagga. SNMP proxy supports HP and Cisco devices and exports a superset of the data for switch and router.

	Completion time (seconds)	Network cost (sent/recv'd)
L2/L3 traceroute	0.16 s	247 KB
Oversubscription	(pre-processing) 7.9 s	17 MB
	(per switch) 0.1 s	0 KB
Maximum capacity	0.16 s	247 KB
Redundancy	12.65 s	24 MB

Figure 5: **Performance of analyses on department network.** The execution time and network cost of each analysis suffices to support network management and data center SLA queries. Oversubscription analysis pre-processes the tuplespace to reduce query costs.

improves assurance by attesting to the execution of a trustworthy MPC implementation and restricting the MPC inputs to factoids from trusted devices.

5.4 TPM deployment

NetQuery's flexible import policies enables applications to benefit whether or not devices are equipped with TPMs.

Deployments without TPMs. For example, TPMs are not necessary in scenarios where pre-existing relationships are considered sufficient for trusting the claims of another party. Operators currently invest significant effort in establishing trust before entering peering agreements and may trust each other enough to exchange information through network diagnostic tools. This trust relationship can be represented by import policies that accept the remote ISP as a root of trust in lieu of a TPM key. In NetQuery, we have the remote ISP sign X.509 certificates with a self-generated key, and specify a corresponding import policy. Although this TPM-less configuration does not help with trust establishment, it still streamlines coordination and can be used to generate an audit log documenting why a claim was accepted.

Legacy network elements will lack a TPM with which to generate factoids. Here, an ISP can use its own self-signed key to issue statements on behalf of such legacy devices. Modern ISPs run extensive management software that collects information on the state of the network and devices within, and exporting the data from such systems into NetQuery enables even ISPs with pure legacy devices to support NetQuery applications. This approach supports a transparent transition as new TPM-equipped network devices are introduced, and ISP-signed statements are subsumed by device-issued factoids.

Finally, NetQuery sanitizers can enable external applications to participate in NetQuery even when they are not equipped with TPMs. Because sensitive factoids never leave an administrative domain, lack of a remote TPM can never lead to information leakage.

External checkers. Some trustworthy properties can be obtained by using TPM-equipped devices to infer or monitor legacy devices. Past work has examined how to obtain guarantees about the behavior of legacy BGP speakers by monitoring their inputs and outputs [47, 29]. Since monitors only need to inspect control traffic to infer details of BGP behavior, low cost monitoring hardware suffices to provide assurance about the behavior of expensive legacy equipment, such as high-performance routers.

6. INCREMENTAL DEPLOYMENT

NetQuery analyses can verify common advertised claims even when only some devices are upgraded to support NetQuery.

Bilateral benefits. Many claims in bilateral contracts can be computed almost entirely from factoids exported by one of the counterparties, and thus require minimal support for NetQuery outside of the participating networks. Since most Internet agreements are bilateral [22], this is a common case.

Some claims are completely self-contained within an ISP's network; these include those providing VPN service between multiple customer sites or guaranteeing an intra-domain latency or redundancy SLA. Other analyses, such as the Wi-Fi hotspot and AS hop count analyzers, require a modicum of support from ASes adjacent to the Wi-Fi or transit provider. These analyses verify that the provider routes traffic to a specific destination domain as promised: for the former, to the public Internet (e.g., outside the hotspot's domain), for the latter, to the destination AS. The adjacent networks need only install NetQuery devices at the edge and assert their ownership of these device, say by signing a factoid using a AS-number certificate issued by a regional Internet registry [11]. Adjacent networks need only ensure that they deliver packets into their network as claimed by the knowledge plane. To do so, they can simply deploy a low-cost TPM-equipped host, rather than upgrade edge routers.

NetQuery islands. In other scenarios, there may be islands of NetQuery-enabled devices separated by multiple legacy devices. Islands might arise within a single provider that deploys starting at the edge of each POP or in a few POPs at a time. Islands may also be isolated by legacy devices controlled by a third party. By establishing tunnels between one another, backed by encryption and performance monitoring [7], NetQuery devices can export properties describing the intervening legacy network. Such tunnels are similar to the defenses against the dissociation attack and the preceding deployment optimization for adjacent ASes.

7. PROTOTYPE AND FEASIBILITY STUDY

We have implemented a prototype of the NetQuery system described above. The core functionality is supported by an embeddable tuplespace server for building NetQuery devices and sanitizers; a C++ client library for writing NetQuery applications; NAL proof generators and checkers; and a stand-alone tuplespace server. Using these components, we have built a NetQuery switch for Linux, a NetQuery router adapted from the open source Quagga router [1], a NetQuery host that runs the Nexus trusted operating system, and an SNMP to NetQuery proxy (Figure 4). We also built a network access control (NAC) system and several network performance analyzers.

We describe, through our experience with building applications, the benefits of NetQuery-enabled analysis. We also demonstrate, through microbenchmarks of tuplespace operations and experiments and devices, that NetQuery achieves high throughput and low latency and that extending network devices to support NetQuery involves little code modification, low overhead, and low deployment cost.

All experiments used a testbed built from Linux 2.6.23 hosts equipped with 8-core 2.5GHz Intel Xeon processors and connected over a Gigabit Ethernet switch. Unless otherwise stated, all TPM and NAL optimizations from Section 4.2 were enabled.

7.1 Applications and production deployment

Here, we outline the implementation of each NetQuery application and describe the achieved performance and operational benefits.

7.1.1 Network access control

The NAC system restricts network access only to machines that are unlikely to harm the network, such as those running a firewall and virus checkers. Such policies are widely embraced today, yet often rely solely on user cooperation. This system installs triggers on local NetQuery switches to detect new hosts, which are initially allowed only limited network access. In response to a trigger notification, the application analyzes the new host. For each policy-compliant new hosts, the application sends a configuration command to the switch to grant network access. Such policy decisions are implemented in the switch enforcer process, consisting of 787 lines of code (LOC). The NetQuery switch consists of 1,853 LOC, including a full control plane and software data plane with link-level encryption to prevent dissociation attacks. The host runs the Nexus operating system, which exports its full process list to a locally running tuplespace server.

To prevent leakage of sensitive user information beyond the user's computer, NAC uses a sanitizer that releases the sanitized fact CompliantHost(H) if H's process list indicates that it is running the required software. NAC uses Nexus's process level attestation to verify execution of the sanitizer and tuplespace server, which run in separate processes. The proof tree consisted of eight ground statements: five tuplespace values, authenticated by tuplespace server MACs, and three attestations, authenticated by digital signatures.

Together, the proof generation and proof checking processes took less than 67 seconds of wall clock time, which is low compared to the long duration of typical Ethernet sessions. Digital signature verification at the enforcer dominated the cost.

7.1.2 Analysis of a production network

We deployed NetQuery on our department's production network consisting of 73 HP and Cisco L2 and L3 switches and over 700 end hosts. Using standard network management data exported by these switches, we built several analyses for detecting properties of interest to customers of cloud providers and ISPs; Figures 4 and 5 summarize the source code size and performance of each analysis. NetQuery enables these analyses to discover information that is otherwise difficult or impossible to obtain through the data plane. Our deployment relies on an SNMP-to-NetQuery proxy that periodically exports the neighbor, forwarding, routing, and ARP tables of every switch.

We implemented the following analyses, which can be used to generate remotely verifiable advertisements of datacenter network quality. These advertisements enable customer applications to pick the most appropriate network for a given workload.

L2/L3 traceroute analysis. Traceroute is widely used for diagnostics. Since standard IP traceroute returns only L3 information, it provides little information in a network composed primarily of L2 switches. We have built a NetQuery traceroute that iteratively traverses the topology graph contained in the knowledge plane, instead of using probe packets. At each switch, the analyzer performs forwarding table and ARP table lookups as appropriate to determine the next hop. To support traceroute on our network, the analysis understands many commonly used features of L2/L3 switched Ethernet networks, including link aggregation groups and VLANs. This analysis is often used as the basis for other analyses.

Over-subscription analysis computes internal network capacity and determines the ratio between the capacity of a given network link and the maximum amount of traffic that hosts downstream

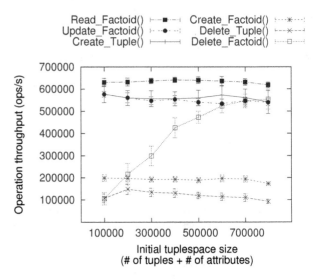

Figure 6: **Throughput of operations issued in bulk.** The throughput of all operations is independent of the tuplespace size.

from the link can generate or consume. To compute the aggregate capacity across all hosts, the analysis traces through the L3 core and L2 tree, down to the leaf switches, recording every host access link. Customers with network-intensive workloads such as MapReduce can benefit from choosing datacenters that are less oversubscribed.

Maximum capacity analysis determines the available bandwidth through the Internet gateway. This analysis determines the best-case throughput between a given host and network egress point by running NetQuery traceroute to find the host to egress path, then computing the minimum capacity across the links on that path. Customers deploying public services benefit from choosing datacenters with high available capacity through the gateway.

Redundancy analysis verifies that the network is robust against network failures. We implemented an analysis that decomposes the network graph into biconnected components, which are by definition robust against the failure of a single switch. Customers that require high availability should place their nodes in the same component as critical services and the Internet gateway.

In addition to using these analyses to support external customers, the datacenter operator can use them to debug network problems. For instance, we have used these tools to help us inventory and locate network equipment and to determine the network failure modes for our research group's externally-accessible servers.

7.2 Scalability

We evaluate the performance of a tuplespace server with throughput and latency microbenchmarks that correspond to different usages and scenarios. High throughput enables devices to initialize the knowledge plane quickly when they boot or are reconfigured. Reduced latency enables analysis to complete more quickly and limits exposure to concurrent changes to the network.

Throughput. In this experiment, a traffic generator issues a sequence of requests, without waiting for responses from a tuplespace server running on a separate machine. To fully utilize processor cores available on the server, the tuplespace is distributed across eight processes.

The results show that NetQuery can support large tuplestores and high tuplespace access and modification rates (Figure 6); a single tuplespace server can support more than 500,000 read and update operations per second. The throughput of all tuplespace operations

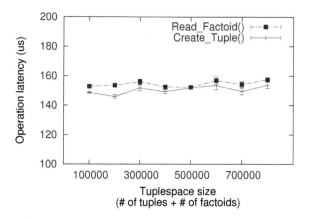

Figure 7: **Latency of operations issued sequentially.** The latency of all operations remains the same at all tuplespace sizes.

	NetQuery (Unoptimized)		NetQuery (Optimized)	
SNMPv3 Bulkwalk	Update	Read	Update	Read
46,572 ±300	29 ±0.06	2,723 ±30	97,422 ±2,000	94,844 ±8,000
Throughput in SNMP variables/s or				
NetQuery factoids/s (± 95% conf. interval)				

Figure 8: **Comparison of SNMP and NetQuery.** TPM- and NAL-based optimizations enable NetQuery to achieve better throughput than SNMP while providing stronger guarantees.

is decoupled from the size of the tuplespace, with the exception of **Delete_Factoid**(). For smaller tuplespace sizes, **Delete_Factoid**() experiments complete so quickly that initialization overheads dominate overall execution time. The tuplespace server achieves this high performance because it only holds soft-state, for which a simple in-memory implementation suffices.

Latency. The latency of accessing the tuplespace (Figure 7) affects the completion time of NetQuery applications. In this experiment, a single client issues sequential requests for the TID from **Create_Tuple**(); and for the factoid value from **Read_Factoid**(). Latency remains constant as tuplespace size increases.

Cryptographic optimizations and SNMP. To evaluate the overhead of accountability, we compared the performance of NetQuery to that of SNMPv3. To evaluate the benefits of the optimizations from Section 4.2, we measured the throughput of NetQuery with and without trusting the tuplespace server. Since the Linux SNMP server is not multithreaded, we ran both NetQuery and SNMP on a single core. We used multiple concurrent instances of snmpbulkwalk to retrieve SNMP server MIBs. The NetQuery experiments retrieved comparable amounts of data. SNMP and NetQuery were both configured to provide confidentiality and integrity.

When the tuplespace server is not trusted, devices sign all factoids on export and applications check signatures on all factoids on import, significantly increasing CPU overhead. When the tuplespace server is trusted, NetQuery provides better performance than SNMP (Figure 8). Thus, we expect that SNMP analyses that are ported to NetQuery will perform comparably well, yet provide accountability.

Since TPMs and trustworthy computing can be used to establish the trustworthiness of tuplespace servers, these results show that high performance knowledge planes that support accountability can be deployed at little additional cost.

7.3 Building NetQuery devices

We built several NetQuery devices to determine the implementation and runtime costs that NetQuery adds to devices. We also show that the knowledge plane and devices can efficiently support realistic workloads.

Quagga router. We modified a Quagga router to evaluate the cost of extending an existing device to support NetQuery. Only localized changes to the router's control plane were necessary to export all interface and routing table changes to the knowledge plane. NetQuery-Quagga interposes on Quagga's calls to rtnetlink, the low-level interface to the in-kernel dataplane, and translates all relevant requests, such as changes to the forwarding table and NIC state, into tuple updates. In total, only 777 lines of localized changes were needed, out of a total code base of 190,538 LOC.

Initialization. Quagga is a demanding macrobenchmark that exports significant amounts of state during operation. To demonstrate that routers can efficiently shed this data to a tuplespace server, we measured the initialization and steady state performance of the router. We used a workload derived from a RouteViews trace. The Quagga router, tuplespace server, and workload generator ran on separate machines. To demonstrate that NetQuery can efficiently import bulk data, we measured the completion time to load a full BGP routing table (268K prefixes) and the resulting tuplespace memory footprint.

Upon receiving routing updates, the BGP router downloads a full forwarding table to the IP forwarding layer. Added latency could affect network availability. Without NetQuery, an update of the full table took 5.70 s; with NetQuery, it took 13.5 s. Our prototype blocks all updates while waiting for NetQuery; a production implementation can eliminate this dependency by updating the knowledge plane in a background process.

Exporting the full forwarding table to the tuplespace server required 62.8 MB of network transfer and 10.7 MB of server memory to store the table. Though full updates are the most intense knowledge plane update workload, only a modest amount of hardware is needed to support them.

Steady state. To demonstrate that NetQuery routers perform well in steady state, we evaluated the router against a workload derived from RouteViews update traces. The workload generator batched updates into one second buckets, and submitted them as bursts. The experiment recorded the time needed to commit the resulting changes to the IP forwarding tables and to the knowledge plane. NetQuery increased the median completion time to 63.4 ms, from 62.2 ms in the baseline server. Thus, the NetQuery router reacts almost as quickly as a standard router, minimizing the disruption to forwarding table updates. NetQuery required only 3 KB, 92 KB, and 480 KB to transmit the median, mean, and maximum update sizes; thus, any server configuration provisioned to support initialization load can also support steady state load.

Convergence time. NetQuery does not impact eBGP convergence time: in eBGP, route propagation is governed by a thirty second Minimum Route Advertisement Interval, which exceeds the latency of exporting a full forwarding table update to NetQuery.

To measure the impact on IGP route convergence, we simulated the update traffic from large correlated link failures on the Sprint RocketFuel topology. This topology consists of 17,163 Sprint and customer edge routers. We converted the simulation trace into a POP-level NetQuery workload, which we fed to a single-core tuplespace server.

We measured for each run the convergence time after failure. For the five largest POPs, consisting of 51 to 66 routers, and link failure rates of up to 0.05, the mean and median increase in update completion times were less than 0.24 s and 0.14 s, respectively.

Thus, networks can deploy NetQuery while achieving sub-second IGP convergence time, which is the desired level of performance for operators [24].

8. RELATED WORK

Perhaps the work closest to NetQuery are network exception handlers (NEH) [35], ident++ [42], Maestro [12], NOX [27], and DECOR [14]. All are logically centralized systems for enterprise networks that disseminate network information to administrative applications. NetQuery supports such network management applications for enterprise networks, while also supporting applications that issue queries spanning multiple ASes. Moreover, the the NetQuery knowledge plane goes one step further and supports heterogeneous information sources by tracking the source of every statement and by leveraging trusted hardware.

Declarative programming [58] has been proposed as an alternative for building applications and for managing networks. In such systems, application logic is written as high-level rules that manipulate a database representation of the network. DECOR [14] uses declarative programming to autoconfigure network devices to meet high level operational goals. DECOR uses logical specifications for device semantics and state that can be helpful in writing NetQuery analyses and sanitizers. Both NetQuery and DECOR provide frameworks for extending existing devices to support policy analysis and management applications. NetQuery applications can span mutually distrusting administrative domains, for which we provide trust establishment and sanitization techniques not needed in the problem domain of DECOR.

Trusted Network Connect [54] and [48] are network access control systems with similar client authorization to NetQuery. Before an end host is allowed to join the network, these systems use attestation to verify that the end host's software and hardware configuration satisfies the access policy. Unlike NetQuery, these systems do not provide a channel that end hosts can use to discover properties of a network before deciding to connect.

The ubiquity of TPMs has inspired many systems that rely on trusted end host functionality to improve network security and performance. For instance, [19, 23] move middlebox, filtering, and monitoring functionality to end hosts, while [8, 46, 28] rely on end hosts to perform packet classification. NetQuery provides a standard interface for describing these local guarantees, enabling applications in other administrative domains to rely upon their presence.

Several extensions to IP have been proposed to provide guarantees about the sender of each packet. Accountable IP (AIP) [2], [9], and packet passports [38] provide accountability for network packets. These systems use optimizations whose safety rely on global network configuration invariants spanning multiple ASes. They can use NetQuery to verify these trust assumptions. Assayer attaches trustworthy sender information to packets as unforgeable annotations, obviating the need to reconstruct this information at middleboxes [45]. NetQuery and Assayer make similar use of the TPM.

NetReview [29] enforces fault detection for BGP behavior using a tamper-evident log. Since NetQuery supports analysis over router RIBs, it can check similar BGP policies as NetReview. NetReview relies on an AS's neighbors to achieve tamper-evidence and trustworthy detection on publicly-disclosable information. In contrast, NetQuery can bootstrap trust from TPMs where available, and it can also use sanitizers to perform trustworthy analysis on confidential network information.

Keller et al. [36] applies trustworthy computing techniques to a new operating model where service providers build wide area services using virtual router slices leased from infrastructure providers.

NetQuery uses similar techniques, but targets the existing operating model and uses a logical framework for analysis.

Network Confessional [5] provides verifiable performance measurements at the granularity of network paths and peering points. Such approaches are complementary to a knowledge plane; factoids extracted through Network Confessional can be extracted and disseminated through NetQuery.

9. CONCLUSIONS

This paper makes the case for leveraging trustworthy computing abstractions in building knowledge planes that are well-suited for heterogeneous, federated networks. We described NetQuery, a federated, lightweight, and scalable knowledge plane that uses these abstractions to assure the soundness of knowledge plane reasoning in such networks. Through granular access control, accountability, and sanitization, NetQuery supports the confidentiality policies and trust relationships found in real networks. It provides a logical analysis framework that enables applications to combine local information about network entities into global guarantees. Experiments show that NetQuery performs well on real routers and can support the volume of network events found in large enterprise and ISP networks. Overall, NetQuery's extensible data model and flexible logic supports a diverse range of applications and can help ISPs differentiate their services. We believe that NetQuery's design principles and abstractions address significant obstacles to building a practical federated knowledge plane and enable novel applications based on global network reasoning.

10. REFERENCES

[1] The Quagga routing suite. Available at http://www.quagga.net/.
[2] D. G. Andersen, H. Balakrishnan, N. Feamster, T. Koponen, D. Moon, and S. Shenker. Accountable Internet Protocol. In *ACM SIGCOMM*, Aug. 2008.
[3] AOL. AOL Transit Data Network: Settlement-Free Interconnection Policy, 2006. http://www.atdn.net/settlement\%5Ffree\%5Fint.shtml.
[4] D. Applegate, A. Archer, V. Gopalakrishnan, S. Lee, and K. K. Ramakrishnan. Optimal Content Placement for a Large-scale VoD System. In *ACM CoNEXT*, 2010.
[5] K. Argyraki, P. Maniatis, and A. Singla. Verifiable Network-Performance Measurements. In *ACM CoNEXT*, 2010.
[6] AT&T. AT&T Internet Protection Service, Aug. 2009. Available at http://www.corp.att.com/abs/serviceguide/docs/ip_sg.doc.
[7] I. Avramopoulos and J. Rexford. Stealth Probing: Efficient Data-Plane Security for IP Routing. In *USENIX Annual Technical Conference*, May 2006.
[8] K.-H. Baek and S. W. Smith. Preventing Theft of Quality of Service on Open Platforms. In *Securecomm*, Sept. 2005.
[9] A. Bender, N. Spring, D. Levin, and B. Bhattacharjee. Accountability as a Service. In *SRUTI*, June 2007.
[10] K. Bode. Why Are ISPs Still Advertising Limited Services As Unlimited?, Dec. 2008. http://www.dslreports.com/shownews/Why-Are-ISPs-Still-Advertising-Limited-Services-As-Unlimited-997
[11] R. Bush. An Operational ISP and RIR PKI, Apr. 2006. https://www.arin.net/participate/meetings/reports/ARIN_XVII/PDF/sunday/pki-bush.pdf.
[12] Z. Cai, F. Dinu, J. Zheng, A. L. Cox, and T. S. E. Ng. The Preliminary Design and Implementation of the Maestro Network Control Platform. Tech. Report TR08-13, Rice University, Oct. 2008.
[13] M. Casado, P. Cao, A. Akella, and N. Provos. Flow-Cookies: Using Bandwidth Amplification to Defend Against DDoS Flooding Attacks. In *IEEE IWQoS*, June 2006.
[14] X. Chen, Y. Mao, Z. M. Mao, and J. V. der Merwe. DECOR:

DEClarative network management and OpeRation. *ACM SIGCOMM CCR*, 40(1):61–66, 2010.

[15] P. Cheng, R. Pankaj, C. Keser, P. A. Karger, G. M. Wagner, and A. Reninger. Fuzzy Multi-Level Security: An Experiment on Quantified Risk-Adaptive Access Control. In *IEEE Symposium on Security and Privacy*, May 2007.

[16] Cisco Systems. IP SLAs–LSP Health Monitor, June 2006. http://www.cisco.com/en/US/docs/ios/12_4t/12_4t11/ht_hmon.html.

[17] D. D. Clark, C. Partridge, J. C. Ramming, and J. T. Wroclawski. A Knowledge Plane for the Internet. In *ACM SIGCOMM*, Aug. 2003.

[18] D. Collins. Is Your Provider Truly Multi-Homed? http://www.webmasterjoint.com/webmaster-articles/web-hosting/10-multi-homed-is-your-provider-truly-multi-homed.html.

[19] C. Dixon, A. Krishnamurthy, and T. Anderson. An End to the Middle. In *HotOS*, May 2009.

[20] N. Duffield and M. Grossglauser. Trajectory sampling for direct traffic observation. *IEEE/ACM Transactions on Networking*, 9(3):280–292, June 2001.

[21] P. England, B. Lampson, J. Manferdelli, M. Peinado, and B. Willman. A Trusted Open Platform. *Computer*, 36(7):55–62, 2003.

[22] P. Faratin, D. Clark, P. Gilmore, S. Bauer, A. Berger, and W. Lehr. Complexity of Internet Interconnections: Technology, Incentives and Implications for Policy. In *Annual Telecommunications Policy Research Conference*, Sept. 2007.

[23] W. Feng and T. Schluessler. The Case for Network Witnesses. In *NPSec*, Oct. 2008.

[24] P. Francois, C. Filsfils, J. Evans, and O. Bonaventure. Achieving sub-second IGP convergence in large IP networks. *ACM SIGCOMM CCR*, 35(3):35–44, July 2005.

[25] M. Gasser, A. Goldstein, C. Kaufman, and B. Lampson. The Digital Distributed System Security Architecture. In *NIST-NCSC*, pages 305–319, 1989.

[26] S. Goldberg, A. D. Jaggard, and R. N. Wright. Rationality and Traffic Attraction: Incentives for Honest Path Announcements in BGP. In *ACM SIGCOMM*, Aug. 2008.

[27] N. Gude, T. Koponen, J. Pettit, B. Pfaff, M. Casado, N. McKeown, and S. Shenker. NOX: Towards an Operating System for Networks. *ACM SIGCOMM CCR*, 38(3):105–110, 2008.

[28] R. Gummadi, H. Balakrishnan, P. Maniatis, and S. Ratnasamy. Not-a-Bot (NAB): Improving Service Availability in the Face of Botnet Attacks. In *ACM/USENIX NSDI*, Apr. 2009.

[29] A. Haeberlen, I. Avramopoulos, J. Rexford, and P. Druschel. NetReview: Detecting when interdomain routing goes wrong. In *USENIX NSDI*, Apr. 2009.

[30] J. Halderman, S. Schoen, N. Heninger, W. Clarkson, W. Paul, J. Calandrino, A. Feldman, J. Appelbaum, and E. Felten. Lest we remember: cold-boot attacks on encryption keys. In *USENIX Security Symposium*, 2008.

[31] J. Hendricks and L. van Doorn. Secure Bootstrap Is Not Enough: Shoring up the Trusted Computing Base. In *SIGOPS European Workshop*, Aug. 2004.

[32] IBM Corporation. IBM Extends Enhanced Data Security to Consumer Electronics Products. Press Release, Apr. 2006. http://www-03.ibm.com/press/us/en/pressrelease/19527.wss.

[33] IEEE Computer Society. IEEE Std 802.1AE-2006. Aug. 2006.

[34] G. F. Italiano, R. Rastogi, and B. Yener. Restoration Algorithms for Virtual Private Networks in the Hose Model. In *IEEE INFOCOM*, 2002.

[35] T. Karagiannis, R. Mortier, and A. Rowstron. Network Exception Handlers: Host-network Control in Enterprise Networks. In *ACM SIGCOMM*, Aug. 2008.

[36] E. Keller, R. Lee, and J. Rexford. Accountability in hosted virtual networks. In *ACM VISA*, pages 29–36, 2009.

[37] J. Kirk. 'Evil twin' hotspots proliferate, Apr. 2007. http://www.pcworld.com/businesscenter/article/131199/evil_twin_hotspots_proliferate.html.

[38] X. Liu, X. Yang, D. Wetherall, and T. Anderson. Efficient and Secure Source Authentication with Packet Passports. In *SRUTI*, July 2006.

[39] S. Machiraju and R. H. Katz. Reconciling Cooperation with Confidentiality in Multi-Provider Distributed Systems. Tech. Report UCB/CSD-4-1345, Computer Science Division (EECS), University of California, Berkeley, CA, 2004.

[40] H. V. Madhyastha, T. Isdal, M. Piatek, C. Dixon, T. Anderson, A. Krishnamurthy, and A. Venkataramani. iPlane: An Information Plane for Distributed Services. In *ACM/USENIX OSDI*, Nov. 2006.

[41] D. W. Manchala. E-Commerce Trust Metrics and Models. *IEEE Internet Computing*, (March-April):36–44, 2000.

[42] J. Naous, R. Stutsman, D. Mazieres, N. McKeown, and N. Zeldovich. Delegating Network Security Through More Information. In *WREN*, Aug. 2009.

[43] J. Z. Pan. Resource Description Framework. In *Handbook on Ontologies*, pages 71–90. Springer Berlin Heidelberg, Berlin, Heidelberg, 2009.

[44] J. Pang, B. Greenstein, M. Kaminsky, and D. Mccoy. Improving Wireless Network Selection with Collaboration. In *MobiSys*, June 2009.

[45] B. Parno, Z. Zhou, and A. Perrig. Help Me Help You: Using Trustworthy Host-Based Information in the Network. Tech. Report CMU-CyLab-09-016, Carnegie Mellon CyLab, 2009.

[46] A. Ramachandran, K. Bhandankar, M. B. Tariq, and N. Feamster. Packets with Provenance. Tech. Report GT-CS-08-02, Georgia Institute of Technology, 2008.

[47] P. Reynolds, O. Kennedy, E. Sirer, and F. Schneider. Securing BGP using external security monitors. Tech. Report TR2006-2065, Computer Science Department, Cornell University, Ithaca, NY, USA, 2006.

[48] R. Sailer, T. Jaeger, X. Zhang, and L. van Doorn. Attestation-based policy enforcement for remote access. In *ACM CCS*, pages 308–317, 2004.

[49] F. B. Schneider, K. Walsh, and E. G. Sirer. Nexus Authorization Logic (NAL): Design Rationale and Applications. In *TOSSEC*, Sept. 2010.

[50] V. Sekar, M. K. Reiter, W. Willinger, H. Zhang, R. R. Kompella, and D. G. Andersen. CSAMP: A System for Network-Wide Flow Monitoring. In *ACM/USENIX NSDI*, pages 233–246, 2008.

[51] A. Shieh, D. Williams, E. G. Sirer, and F. B. Schneider. Nexus: A New Operating System for Trustworthy Computing. In *ACM SOSP Work-in-Progress Session*, Oct. 2005.

[52] N. So and H.-H. Huang. Building a Highly Adaptive, Resilient, and Scalable MPLS Backbone. *MPLS World Congress*, 2007.

[53] G. Suh, D. Clarke, B. Gasend, M. van Dijk, and S. Devadas. Efficient memory integrity verification and encryption for secure processors. In *IEEE MICRO*, Dec. 2003.

[54] Trusted Computing Group. *TCG Trusted Network Connect: TNC Architecture for Interoperability, Specification Version 1.3*. Trusted Computing Group, Apr. 2008.

[55] T.W. Arnold and L. P. Van Doorn. The IBM PCIXCC: A new cryptographic coprocessor for the IBM eServer. *IBM Journal of Research and Development*, 48(3/4):491–503, 2004.

[56] V. Valancius, N. Feamster, R. Johari, and V. Vazirani. MINT: A Market for INternet Transit. In *ReArch*, Dec. 2008.

[57] B. Woodcock and V. Adhikari. Survey of Characteristics of Internet Carrier Interconnection Agreements. Tech. report, Packet Clearing House, May 2011.

[58] W. Zhou, Y. Mao, B. T. Loo, and M. Abadi. Unified Declarative Platform for Secure Networked Information Systems. In *IEEE ICDE*, Apr. 2009.

Debugging the Data Plane with Anteater

Haohui Mai
Matthew Caesar

Ahmed Khurshid
P. Brighten Godfrey

Rachit Agarwal
Samuel T. King

University of Illinois at Urbana-Champaign
{mai4, khurshi1, agarwa16, caesar, pbg, kingst}@illinois.edu

ABSTRACT

Diagnosing problems in networks is a time-consuming and error-prone process. Existing tools to assist operators primarily focus on analyzing control plane configuration. Configuration analysis is limited in that it cannot find bugs in router software, and is harder to generalize across protocols since it must model complex configuration languages and dynamic protocol behavior.

This paper studies an alternate approach: diagnosing problems through static analysis of the data plane. This approach can catch bugs that are invisible at the level of configuration files, and simplifies unified analysis of a network across many protocols and implementations. We present *Anteater*, a tool for checking invariants in the data plane. Anteater translates high-level network invariants into instances of boolean satisfiability problems (SAT), checks them against network state using a SAT solver, and reports counterexamples if violations have been found. Applied to a large university network, Anteater revealed 23 bugs, including forwarding loops and stale ACL rules, with only five false positives. Nine of these faults are being fixed by campus network operators.

Categories and Subject Descriptors

C.2.3 [**Computer-Communication Networks**]: Network Operation; D.2.5 [**Software Engineering**]: Testing and Debugging

General Terms

Algorithms, Reliability

Keywords

Data Plane Analysis, Network Troubleshooting, Boolean Satisfiability

1. INTRODUCTION

Modern enterprise networks are complex, incorporating hundreds or thousands of network devices from multiple vendors performing diverse codependent functions such as routing, switching, and access control across physical and virtual networks (VPNs and VLANs). As in any complex computer system, enterprise networks are prone to a wide range of errors [10, 11, 12, 14, 25, 32, 38, 41], such as misconfiguration, software bugs, or unexpected interactions across protocols. These errors can lead to oscillations, black holes, faulty advertisements, or route leaks that ultimately cause disconnectivity and security vulnerabilities.

However, diagnosing problems in networks remains a black art. Operators often rely on heuristics — sending probes, reviewing logs, even observing mailing lists and making phone calls — that slow response to failures.[1] To address this, automated tools for network diagnostics [14, 43] analyze configuration files constructed by operators. While useful, these tools have two limitations stemming from their analysis of high-level configuration files. First, configuration analysis *cannot find bugs in router software*, which interprets and acts on those configuration files. Both commercial and open source router software regularly exhibit bugs that affect network availability or security [41] and have led to multiple high-profile outages and vulnerabilities [11, 44]. Second, configuration analysis *must model complex configuration languages and dynamic protocol behavior* in order to determine the ultimate effect of a configuration. As a result, these tools generally focus on checking correctness of a single protocol such as BGP [14, 15] or firewalls [2, 43]. Such diagnosis will be unable to reason about interactions that span multiple protocols, and may have difficulty dealing with the diversity in configuration languages from different vendors making up typical networks.

We take a different and complementary approach. Instead of diagnosing problems in the control plane, our goal is to *diagnose problems as close as possible to the network's actual behavior* through formal analysis of data plane state. Data plane analysis has two benefits. First, by checking the results of routing software rather than its inputs, we can catch bugs that are invisible at the level of configuration

---

[1] As one example, a Cisco design technote advises that "Unfortunately, there is no systematic procedure to troubleshoot an STP issue. ... Administrators generally do not have time to look for the cause of the loop and prefer to restore connectivity as soon as possible. The easy way out in this case is to manually disable every port that provides redundancy in the network. ... Each time you disable a port, check to see if you have restored connectivity in the network." [10]

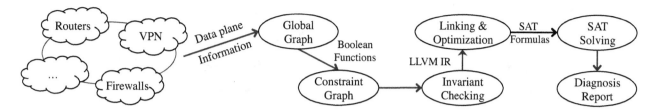

Figure 1: The work flow of Anteater. Clouds are network devices. Ovals are stages in the work flow. Text on the edges shows the type of data flowing between stages.

files. Second, it becomes easier to perform unified analysis of a network across many protocols and implementations, because data plane analysis avoids modeling dynamic routing protocols and operates on comparatively simple input formats that are common across many protocols and implementations.

This paper describes the design, implementation, and evaluation of Anteater, a tool that analyzes the data plane state of network devices. Anteater collects the network topology and devices' forwarding information bases (FIBs), and represents them as boolean functions. The network operator specifies an invariant to be checked against the network, such as reachability, loop-free forwarding, or consistency of forwarding rules between routers. Anteater combines the invariant and the data plane state into instances of boolean satisfiability problem (SAT), and uses a SAT solver to perform analysis. If the network state violates an invariant, Anteater provides a specific counterexample — such as a packet header, FIB entries, and path — that triggers the potential bug.

We applied Anteater to a large university campus network, analyzing the FIBs of 178 routers that support over 70,000 end-user machines and servers, with FIB entries inserted by a combination of BGP, OSPF, and static ACLs and routes. Anteater revealed 23 confirmed bugs in the campus network, including forwarding loops and stale ACL rules. Nine of these faults are being fixed by campus network operators. For example, Anteater detected a forwarding loop between a pair of routers that was unintentionally introduced after a network upgrade and had been present in the network for over a month. These results demonstrate the utility of the approach of data plane analysis.

Our contributions are as follows:

- Anteater is the first design and implementation of a data plane analysis system used to find real bugs in real networks. We used Anteater to find 23 bugs in our campus network.

- We show how to express three key invariants as SAT problems, and propose a novel algorithm for handling packet transformations.

- We develop optimizations to our algorithms and implementation to enable Anteater to check invariants efficiently using a SAT solver, and demonstrate experimentally that Anteater is sufficiently scalable to be a practical tool.

2. OVERVIEW OF ARCHITECTURE

Anteater's primary goal is to detect and diagnose a broad, general class of network problems. The system detects problems by analyzing the contents of forwarding tables contained in routers, switches, firewalls, and other networking equipment (Figure 1). Operators use Anteater to check whether the network conforms to a set of *invariants* (i.e., correctness conditions regarding the network's forwarding behavior). Violations of these invariants usually indicate a bug in the network. Here are a few examples of invariants:

- Loop-free forwarding. There should not exist any packet that could be injected into the network that would cause a forwarding loop.

- Connectivity. All computers in the campus network are able to access both the intranet and the Internet, while respecting network policies such as access control lists.

- Consistency. The policies of two replicated routers should have the same forwarding behavior. More concretely, the possible set of packets that can reach the external network through them are the same.

Anteater checks invariants through several steps. First, Anteater collects the contents of FIBs from networking equipment through vtys (terminals), SNMP, or control sessions maintained to routers [13, 22]. These FIBs may be simple IP longest prefix match rules, or more complex actions like access control lists or modifications of the packet header [1, 21, 28]. Second, the operator creates new invariants or selects from a menu of standard invariants to be checked against the network. This is done via bindings in Ruby or in a declarative language that we designed to streamline the expression of invariants. Third, Anteater translates both the FIBs and invariants into instances of SAT, which are resolved by an off-the-shelf SAT solver. Finally, if the results from the SAT solver indicate that the supplied invariants are violated, Anteater will derive a counterexample to help diagnosis.

The next section describes the design and implementation in more detail, including writing invariants, translating the invariants and the network into instances of SAT, and solving them efficiently.

3. ANTEATER DESIGN

A SAT problem evaluates a set of boolean formulas to determine if there exists at least one variable assignment such that all formulas evaluate to true. If such an assignment

Symbol	Description
G	Network graph $(V, E, \mathcal{P})$
V	Vertices (e.g., devices) in G
E	Directed edges in G
$\mathcal{P}$	Policy function for edges

Figure 2: Notation used in Section 3.

exists, then the set of formulas are *satisfiable*; otherwise they are *unsatisfiable*.

SAT is an NP-complete problem. Specialized tools called SAT solvers, however, use heuristics to solve SAT efficiently in some cases [8]. Engineers use SAT solvers in a number of different problem domains, including model checking, hardware verification, and program analysis. Please see §7 for more details.

Network reachability can, in the general case, also be NP-complete (see Appendix). We cast network reachability and other network invariants as SAT problems. In this section we discuss our model for network policies, and our algorithms for detecting bugs using sets of boolean formulas and a SAT solver.

Anteater uses an existing theoretical algorithm for checking reachability [39], and we use this reachability algorithm to design our own algorithms for detecting forwarding loops, detecting packet loss (i.e., "black holes"), and checking forwarding consistency between routers. Also, we present a novel algorithm for handling arbitrary packet transformations.

3.1 Modeling network behavior

Figure 2 shows our notation. A network G is a 3-tuple $G = (V, E, \mathcal{P})$, where V is the set of networking devices and possible destinations, E is the set of directed edges representing connections between vertices. $\mathcal{P}$ is a function defined on E to represent general policies.

Since many of the formulas we discuss deal with IP prefix matching, we introduce the notation $var =_{width} prefix$ to simplify our discussion. This notation is a convenient way of writing a boolean formula saying that the first $width$ bits of the variable var are the same as those of $prefix$. For example, $dst\_ip =_{24} 10.1.3.0$ is a boolean formula testing the equality between the first 24 bits of dst_ip and 10.1.3.0. The notion $var \neq_{width} prefix$ is the negation of $var =_{width} prefix$.

For each edge (u, v), we define $\mathcal{P}(u, v)$ as the policy for packets traveling from u to v, represented as a boolean formula over a symbolic packet. A *symbolic packet* is a set of variables representing the values of fields in packets, like the MAC address, IP address, and port number. A packet can flow over an edge if and only if it satisfies the corresponding boolean formulas. We use this function to represent general policies including forwarding, packet filtering, and transformations of the packet. $\mathcal{P}(u, v)$ is the conjunction (logical *and*) over all policies' constraints on symbolic packets from node u to node v.

$\mathcal{P}(u, v)$ can be used to represent a filter. For example, in Figure 3 the filtering rule on edge (B, C) blocks all packets destined to 10.1.3.128/25; thus, $\mathcal{P}(B, C)$ has $dst\_ip \neq_{25}$ 10.1.3.128 as a part of it. Forwarding is represented as a constraint as well: $\mathcal{P}(u, v)$ will be constrained to include only those symbolic packets that router u would forward to

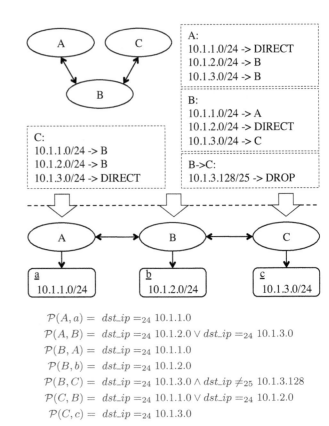

$$\mathcal{P}(A, a) = dst\_ip =_{24} 10.1.1.0$$
$$\mathcal{P}(A, B) = dst\_ip =_{24} 10.1.2.0 \lor dst\_ip =_{24} 10.1.3.0$$
$$\mathcal{P}(B, A) = dst\_ip =_{24} 10.1.1.0$$
$$\mathcal{P}(B, b) = dst\_ip =_{24} 10.1.2.0$$
$$\mathcal{P}(B, C) = dst\_ip =_{24} 10.1.3.0 \land dst\_ip \neq_{25} 10.1.3.128$$
$$\mathcal{P}(C, B) = dst\_ip =_{24} 10.1.1.0 \lor dst\_ip =_{24} 10.1.2.0$$
$$\mathcal{P}(C, c) = dst\_ip =_{24} 10.1.3.0$$

Figure 3: An example of a 3-node IP network. *Top:* Network topology, with FIBs in dashed boxes. *Bottom:* graph used to model network behavior. Ovals represent networking equipment; rounded rectangles represent special vertices such as destinations, labeled by lower case letters. The lower half of the bottom figure shows the value of $\mathcal{P}$ for each edge in the graph.

router v. The sub-formula $dst\_ip =_{24} 10.1.3.0$ in $\mathcal{P}(B, C)$ in Figure 3 is an example.

Packet transformations – for example, setting a quality of service bit, or tunneling the packet by adding a new header – might appear different since they intuitively modify the symbolic packet rather than just constraining it. Somewhat surprisingly, we can represent transformations as constraints too, through a technique that we present in §3.4.

3.2 Checking reachability

In this subsection, we describe how Anteater checks the most basic invariant: reachability. The next subsection, then, uses this algorithm to check higher-level invariants.

Recall that vertices V correspond to devices or destinations in the network. Given two vertices $s, t \in V$, we define the *s-t reachability* problem as deciding whether there exists a packet that can be forwarded from s to t. More formally, the problem is to decide if there exists a symbolic packet p and an $s \rightsquigarrow t$ path such that p satisfies all constraints $\mathcal{P}$ along the edges of the path. Figure 4 shows a dynamic programming algorithm to calculate a boolean formula f representing reachability from s to t. The boolean formula f has a satisfying assignment if and only if there exists a packet that can be routed from s to t in at most k hops.

```
function reach(s, t, k, G)
    r[t][0] ← true
    r[v][0] ← false for all v ∈ V(G) \ t
    for i = 1 to k do
        for all v ∈ V(G) \ t do
            r[v][i] ←    ⋁      (𝒫(v, u) ∧ r[u][i − 1])
                     (v,u)∈E(G)
        end for
    end for
    return   ⋁   r[s][i]
           1≤i≤k
```

Figure 4: **Algorithm to compute a boolean formula representing reachability from** s **to** t **in at most** k **hops in network graph** G.

```
function loop(v, G)
    v′ ← a new vertex in V(G)
    for all (u, v) ∈ E(G) do
        E(G) ← E(G) ∪ {(u, v′)}
        𝒫(u, v′) ← 𝒫(u, v)
    end for
    Test satisfiability of reach(v, v′, |V(G)|, G)
```

Figure 5: **Algorithm to detect forwarding loops involving vertex** v **in network** G.

This part of Anteater is similar to an algorithm proposed by Xie et al. [39], expressed as constraints rather than sets of packets.

To guarantee that all reachability is discovered, one would pick in the worst case $k = n − 1$ where n is the number of network devices modeled in G. A much smaller k may suffice in practice because path lengths are expected to be smaller than $n − 1$.

We give an example run of the algorithm for the network of Figure 3. Suppose we want to check reachability from A to C. Here $k = 2$ suffices since there are only 3 devices. Anteater initializes $\mathcal{P}$ as shown in Figure 3 and the algorithm initializes $s ← A$, $t ← C$, $k ← 3$, $r[C][0] ← $ true, $r[A][0] ← $ false, and $r[B][0] ← $ false. After the first iteration of the outer loop we have:

$$r[A][1] = \text{false}$$
$$r[B][1] = \mathcal{P}(B, C)$$
$$= (dst\_ip =_{24} 10.1.3.0 \land dst\_ip \neq_{25} 10.1.3.128)$$

After the second iteration we have:

$$r[A][2] = r[B][1] \land \mathcal{P}(A, B)$$
$$= dst\_ip =_{24} 10.1.3.0 \ \land dst\_ip \neq_{25} 10.1.3.128 \ \land$$
$$(dst\_ip =_{24} 10.1.2.0 \lor dst\_ip =_{24} 10.1.3.0)$$
$$r[B][2] = \text{false}$$

The algorithm then returns the formula $r[A][1] \lor r[A][2]$.

3.3 Checking forwarding loops, packet loss, and consistency

The reachability algorithm can be used as a building block to check other invariants.

```
function packet_loss(v, D, G)
    n ← the number of network devices in G
    d ← a new vertex in V(G)
    for all u ∈ D do
        (u, d) ← a new edge in E(G)
        𝒫(u, d) ← true
    end for
    c ← reach(v, d, n, G)
    Test satisfiability of ¬c
```

Figure 6: **Algorithm to check whether packets starting at** v **are dropped without reaching any of the destinations** D **in network** G.

Loops. Figure 5 shows Anteater's algorithm for detecting forwarding loops involving vertex v. The basic idea of the algorithm is to modify the network graph by creating a dummy vertex $v′$ that can receive the same set of packets as v (i.e., v and $v′$ have the same set of incoming edges and edge policies). Thus, v-$v′$ reachability corresponds to a forwarding loop. The algorithm can be run for each vertex v. Anteater thus either verifies that the network is loop-free, or returns an example of a loop.

Packet loss. Another property of interest is whether "black holes" exist: i.e., whether packets may be lost without reaching any destination. Figure 6 shows Anteater's algorithm for checking whether packets from a vertex v could be lost before reaching a given set of destinations D, which can be picked as (for example) the set of all local destination prefixes plus external routers. The idea is to add a "sink" vertex d which is reachable from all of D, and then (in the algorithm's last line) test the *absence* of v-d reachability. This will produce an example of a packet that is dropped or confirm that none exists.[2] Of course, in some cases packet loss is the correct behavior. For example, in the campus network we tested, some destinations are filtered due to security concerns. Our implementation allows operators to specify lists of IP addresses or other conditions that are intentionally not reachable; Anteater will then look for packets that are unintentionally black-holed. We omit this extension from Figure 6 for simplicity.

Consistency. Networks commonly have devices that are expected to have identical forwarding policy, so any differing behavior may indicate a bug. Suppose, for example, that the operator wishes to test if two vertices v_1 and v_2 will drop the same set of packets. This can be done by running packet_loss to construct two formulas $c_1 = $ packet_loss(v_1, D, G) and $c_2 = $ packet_loss(v_2, D, G), and testing satisfiability of $(c_1 \text{ xor } c_2)$. This offers the operator a convenient way to find potential bugs without specifically listing the set of packets that are intentionally dropped. Other notions of consistency (e.g., based on reachability to specific destinations) can be computed analogously.

3.4 Packet transformations

The discussion in earlier subsections assumed that packets

---

[2]This loss could be due either to black holes or loops. If black holes specifically are desired, then either the loops can be fixed first, or the algorithm can be rerun with instructions to filter the previous results. We omit the details.

traversing the network remain unchanged. Numerous protocols, however, employ mechanisms that *transform* packets while they are in flight. For example, MPLS swaps labels, border routers can mark packets to provide QoS services, and packets can be tunneled through virtual links which involves prepending a header. In this subsection, we present a technique that flexibly handles packet transformations.

Basic technique. Rather than working with a single symbolic packet, we use a *symbolic packet history*. Specifically, we replace each symbolic packet s with an array $(s_0, \ldots, s_k)$ where s_i represents the state of the packet at the ith hop. Now, rather than transforming a packet, we can express a transformation as a constraint on its history: a packet transformation $f(\cdot)$ at hop i induces the constraint $s_{i+1} = f(s_i)$. For example, an edge traversed by two MPLS label switched paths with incoming labels ℓ_1^{in}, ℓ_2^{in} and corresponding outgoing labels $\ell_1^{out}, \ell_2^{out}$ would have the transformation constraint

$$\bigvee_{j \in \{1,2\}} \left(s_i.label = \ell_j^{in} \wedge s_{i+1}.label = \ell_j^{out} \right).$$

Another transformation could represent a network address translation (NAT) rule, setting an internal source IP address to an external one:

$$s_{i+1}.source\_ip = 12.34.56.78$$

A NAT rule could be non-deterministic, if a snapshot of the NAT's internal state is not available and it may choose from multiple external IP addresses in a certain prefix. This can be represented by a looser constraint:

$$s_{i+1}.source\_ip =_{24} 12.34.56.0$$

And of course, a link with no transformation simply induces the identity constraint:

$$s_{i+1} = s_i.$$

We let $\mathcal{T}_i(v, w)$ refer to the transformation constraints for packets arriving at v after i hops and continuing to w.

Application to invariant algorithms. Implementing this technique in our earlier reachability algorithm involves two principal changes. First, we must include the transformation constraints $\mathcal{T}$ in addition to the policy constraints $\mathcal{P}$. Second, the edge policy function $\mathcal{P}(u, v)$, rather than referring to variables in a single symbolic packet s, will be applied to various entries of the symbolic packet array (s_i). So it is parameterized with the relevant entry index, which we write as $\mathcal{P}_i(u, v)$; and when computing reachability we must check the appropriate positions of the array. Incorporating those changes, Line 5 of our reachability algorithm (Fig. 4) becomes

$$r[v][i] \leftarrow \bigvee_{(v,u) \in E(G)} \left(\mathcal{T}_{i-1}(v, u) \wedge \mathcal{P}_{i-1}(v, u) \wedge r[u][i-1] \right).$$

The loop detection algorithm, as it simply calls reachability as a subroutine, requires no further changes.

The packet loss and consistency algorithms have a complication: as written, they test satisfiability of the *negation* of a reachability formula. The negation can be satisfied either with a symbolic packet that would be lost in the network, or a symbolic packet history that couldn't have existed because it violates the transformation constraints. We need to differentiate between these, and find only true packet loss.

To do this, we avoid negating the formula. Specifically, we modify the network by adding a node ℓ acting as a sink for lost packets. For each non-destination node u, we add an edge $u \rightarrow \ell$ annotated with the constraint that the packet is dropped by u (i.e., the packet violates the policy constraints on all of u's outgoing edges). We also add an edge $w \rightarrow \ell$ with no constraint, for each destination node $w \notin D$. We can now check for packet loss starting at v by testing satisfiability of the formula $\mathsf{reach}(v, \ell, n-1, G)$ where n is the number of nodes and G is the network modified as described here.

The consistency algorithm encounters a similar problem due to the xor operation, and has a similar solution.

Notes. We note two effects which are not true in the simpler transformation-free case. First, the above packet loss algorithm does not find packets which loop (since they never transit to ℓ); but of course, they can be found separately through our loop-detection algorithm.

Second, computing up to $k = n - 1$ hops does not guarantee that all reachability or loops will be discovered. In the transformation-free case, $k = n - 1$ was sufficient because after $n - 1$ hops the packet must either have been delivered or revisited a node, in which case it will loop indefinitely. But transformations allow the state of a packet to change, so revisiting a node doesn't imply that the packet will loop indefinitely. In theory, packets might travel an arbitrarily large number of hops before being delivered or dropped. However, we expect $k \leq n - 1$ to be sufficient in practice.

Application to other invariants. Packet transformations enable us to express certain other invariants succinctly. Figure 7 shows a simplified version of a real-world example from our campus network. Most servers are connected to the external network via a firewall, but the PlanetLab servers connect to the external network directly. For security purposes, all traffic between campus servers and PlanetLab nodes is routed through the external network, except for administrative links between the PlanetLab nodes and a few trusted servers. One interesting invariant is to check whether all traffic from the external network to protected servers indeed goes through the firewall as intended.

This invariant can be expressed conveniently as follows. We introduce a new field *inspected* in the symbolic packet, and for each edge (f, v) going from the firewall f towards the internal network of servers, we add a transformation constraint:

$$\mathcal{T}_i(f, v) = s_{i+1}.inspected \leftarrow 1.$$

Then for each internal server S, we check whether

$$(s_k.inspected = 0) \wedge R(ext, S)$$

where *ext* is the node representing the external network, and $R(S, ext)$ is the boolean formula representing reachability from *ext* to S computed by the reach algorithm. If this formula is true, Anteater will give an example of a packet which circumvents the firewall.

4. IMPLEMENTATION

We implemented Anteater on Linux with about 3,500 lines of C++ and Ruby code, along with roughly 300 lines of auxiliary scripts to canonicalize data plane information from

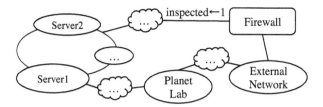

Figure 7: An example where packet transformations allow convenient checking of firewall policy. Solid lines are network links; text on the links represents a transformation constraint to express the invariant. Clouds represent omitted components in the network.

Foundry, Juniper and Cisco routers into a comma-separated value format.

Our Anteater implementation represents boolean functions and formulas in the intermediate representation format of LLVM [23]. LLVM is not essential to Anteater; our invariant algorithms could output SAT formulas directly. But LLVM provides a convenient way to represent SAT formulas as functions, inline these functions, and simplify the resulting formulas.

In particular, Anteater checks an invariant as follows. First, Anteater translates the policy constraints $\mathcal{P}$ and the transformation constraints $\mathcal{T}$ into LLVM functions, whose arguments are the symbolic packets they are constraining. Then Anteater runs the desired invariant algorithm (reachability, loop detection, etc.; §3), outputting the formula using calls to the $\mathcal{P}$ and $\mathcal{T}$ functions. The resulting formula is stored in the @main function. Next, LLVM links together the $\mathcal{P}$, $\mathcal{T}$, and @main functions and optimizes when necessary. The result is translated into SAT formulas, which are passed into a SAT solver. Finally, Anteater invokes the SAT solver and reports the results to the operator.

Recall the example presented in §3.2. We want to check reachability from A to C in Figure 3. Anteater translates the policy function $\mathcal{P}(B, C)$ into function @p_bc(), and puts the result of dynamic programming algorithm into @main():

```
define @p_bc(%si, %si+1) {        @pkt = external global
%0 = load %si.dst_ip
%1 = and %0, 0xffffff00          define void @main() {
%2 = icmp eq 0xa010300, %1        %0 = call @p_bc(@pkt, @pkt)
%3 = and %0, 0xffffff80          %1 = call @p_ab(@pkt, @pkt)
%4 = icmp eq 0xa010380, %3        %2 = and %0, %1
%5 = xor %4, true                call void @assert(%2)
%6 = and %2, %5                  ret void
ret %6 }                         }
```

The function @p_bc represents the function

$$\mathcal{P}(B, C) = dst\_ip =_{24} 10.1.3.0 \wedge dst\_ip \neq_{25} 10.1.3.128$$

The function takes two parameters %s_i and %s_{i+1} to support packet transformations as described in §3.4.

The @main function is shown at the right side of the snippet. @p_ab is the LLVM function representing $\mathcal{P}(A, B)$. @pkt is a global variable representing a symbolic packet. Since there is no transformation involved, the main function calls the policy functions @p_bc and @p_ab with the same symbolic packet. The call to @assert indicates the final boolean formula to be checked by the SAT solver. Next, LLVM performs standard compiler optimization, including inlining

and simplifying expressions, whose results are shown on the left:

```
define void @main() {
%0 = load @pkt.dst_ip     :formula
%1 = and %0, 0xffffff00   (let (?t1 (bvand p0 0xffffff00))
%2 = icmp eq %1, 0xa010300 (let (?t2 (= ?t1 0x0a010300))
%3 = and %0, 0xffffff80   (let (?t3 (bvand p0 0xffffff80))
%4 = icmp ne %3, 0xa010380 (let (?t4 (not (= ?t3 0x0a010380)))
%5 = and %2, %4           (let (?t5 (and ?t2 ?t4))
%6 = and %0, 0xffffffe00  (let (?t6 (bvand p0 0xfffffe00))
%7 = icmp eq %6, 0xa010200 (let (?t7 (= ?t6 0x0a010200))
%8 = and %5, %7           (let (?t8 (and ?t5 ?t7))
call void @assert(i1 %8)  (?t8)))))))))
ret void }
```

Then the result is directly translated into the input format of the SAT solver, which is shown in the right. In this example, it is a one-to-one translation except that @pkt.dst_ip is renamed to p0. After that, Anteater passes the formula into the SAT solver to determine its satisfiability. If the formula is satisfiable, the SAT solver will output an assignment to pkt.0/p0, which is a concrete example (the destination IP in this case) of the packet which satisfies the desired constraint.

The work flow of checking invariants is similar to that of compiling a large C/C++ project. Thus Anteater uses off-the-shelf solutions (i.e. make -j16) to parallelize the checking. Anteater can generate @main functions for each instance of the invariant, and check them independently (e.g., for each starting vertex when checking loop-freeness). Parallelism can therefore yield a dramatic speedup.

Anteater implements language bindings for both Ruby and SLang, a declarative, Prolog-like domain-specific language that we designed for writing customized invariants, and implemented on top of Ruby-Prolog [34]. Operators can express invariants via either Ruby scripts or SLang queries; we found that both of them are able to express the three invariants efficiently. The details of SLang are beyond the scope of this paper.

5. EVALUATION

Our evaluation of Anteater has three parts. First (§5.1), we applied Anteater to a large university campus network. Our tests uncovered multiple faults, including forwarding loops, traffic-blocking ACL rules that were no longer needed, and redundant statically-configured FIB entries.

Second (§5.2), we evaluate how applicable Anteater is to detecting router software bugs by classifying the reported effects of a random sample of bugs from the Quagga Bugzilla database. We find that the majority of these bugs have the potential to produce effects detectable by Anteater.

Third (§5.3), we conduct a performance and scalability evaluation of Anteater. While far from ideal, Anteater takes moderate time (about half an hour) to check for static properties in networks of up to 384 nodes.

We ran all experiments on a Dell Precision WorkStation T5500 machine running 64-bit CentOS 5. The machine had two 2.4 GHz quad-core Intel Xeon X5530 CPUs, and 48 GB of DDR3 RAM. It connected to the campus network via a Gigabit Ethernet channel. Anteater ran on a NFS volume mounted on the machine. The implementation used LLVM 2.9 and JRuby 1.6.2. All SAT queries were resolved by Boolector 1.4.1 with PicoSAT 936 and PrecoSAT 570 [8]. All experiments were conducted under 16-way parallelism.

Invariants	Loops	Packet loss	Consistency
Alerts	9	17	2
Being fixed	9	0	0
Stale config.	0	13	1
False pos.	0	4	1
No. of runs	7	6	6

Figure 8: Summary of evaluation results of Anteater on our campus network.

5.1 Bugs found in a deployed network

We applied Anteater to our campus network. We collected the IP forwarding tables and access control rules from 178 routers in the campus. The maximal length of loop-free paths in the network is 9. The mean FIB size was 1,627 entries per router, which were inserted by a combination of BGP, OSPF, and static routing. We also used a network-wide map of the campus topology as an additional input.

We implemented the invariants of §3, and report their evaluation results on our campus network. Figure 8 reports the number of invariant violations we found with Anteater. The row *Alert* shows the number of distinct violations detected by an invariant, as a bug might violate multiple invariants at the same time. For example, a forwarding loop creating a black hole would be detected by both the invariant for detecting forwarding loops and the invariant for detecting packet loss. We classified these alerts into three categories. First, the row *Being fixed* means the alerts are confirmed as bugs and currently being fixed by our campus network operators. Second, the row *Stale configuration* means that these alerts result from explicit and intentional configuration rules, but rules that are outdated and no longer needed. Our campus network operators decided to not fix these stale configurations immediately, but plan to revisit them during the next major network upgrade. Third, *False positive* means that these alerts flag a configuration that correctly reflected the operator's intent and these alerts are not bugs. Finally, *No. of runs* reports the total number of runs required to issue all alerts; the SAT solver reports only one example violation per run. For each run, we filtered the violations found by previous runs and rechecked the invariants until no violations were reported.

5.1.1 Forwarding loops

Anteater detected nine potential forwarding loops in the network. One of them is shown in Figure 9 highlighted by a dashed circle. The loop involved two routers: node and bypass-a. Router bypass-a had a static route for prefix 130.126.244.0/22 towards router node. At the same time, Router node had a default route towards router bypass-a.

As shown in the FIBs, according to longest prefix match rules, packets destined to 130.126.244.0/23 from router bypass-a could reach the destination. Packets destined to the prefix 130.126.244.0/22 but not in 130.126.244.0/23 would fall into the forwarding loop.

Incidentally, all nine loops happened between these two routers. According to the network operator, router bd 3 used to connect with router node directly, and node used to connect with the external network. It was a single choke point to aggregate traffic so that the operator could deploy Intrusion Detection and Prevention (IDP) devices at one

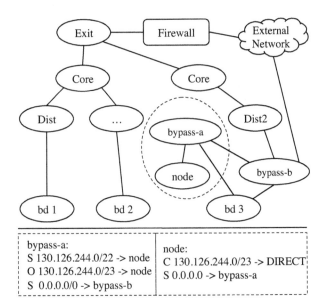

Figure 9: Top: Part of the topology of the campus network. Ovals and solid lines are routers and links respectively. The oval with dashed lines circles the location where a forwarding loop was detected. Bottom: Fragments of data plane information in the network. S stands for static, O stands for OSPF, and C stands for connected.

---

single point. The IDP device, however, was unable to keep up after the upgrade, so router bypass-a was introduced to offload the traffic. As a side effect, the forwarding loops were also introduced when the operator configured forwarding for that router incorrectly.

These loops are reachable from 64 of 178 routers in the network. All loops have been confirmed by the network operator and they are currently being fixed.

5.1.2 Packet loss

Anteater issued 17 packet loss alerts, scattered at routers at different levels of hierarchy. One is due to the lack of default routes in the router; three are due to blocking traffic towards unused IP spaces; and the other 13 alerts are because the network blocks traffic towards certain end-hosts.

We recognized that four alerts are legitimate operational practice and classified them as false positives. Further investigation of the other 13 alerts shows that they are stale configuration entries: seven out of 13 are internal IP addresses that were used in the previous generation of the network. The other six blocked IP addresses are external, and they are related to security issues. For example, an external IP was blocked in April 2009 because the host made phishing attempts to the campus e-mail system. The block was placed to defend against the attack without increasing the load on the campus firewalls.

The operator confirmed that these 13 instances can be dated back as early as September 2008 and they are unnecessary, and probably will be removed during next major network upgrade.

5.1.3 Consistency

Based on conversations with our campus network operators, we know that campus routers in the same level of hierarchy should have identical policies. Hence, we picked one representative router in the hierarchy and checked the consistency between this router and all others at the same level of hierarchy. Anteater issued two new alerts: (1) The two core routers had different policies on IP prefix 10.0.3.0/24; (2) Some building routers had different policies on the private IP address ranges 169.254.0.0/16 and 192.168.0.0/16.

Upon investigating the alert we found that one router exposed its web-based management interface through 10.0.3.0/24. The other alert was due to a legacy issue that could be dated back to the early 1990's: according to the design documents of the campus, 169.254.0.0/16 and 192.168.0.0/16 were intended to be only used within one building. Usually each department had only one building and these IP spaces were used in the whole department. As some departments spanned their offices across more than one building, network operators had to maintain compatibility by allowing this traffic to go one level higher in the hierarchy, and let the router at higher level connect them together by creating a virtual LAN for these buildings.

5.2 Applicability to router bugs

Like configuration errors, defects in router software might affect the network. These defects tend to be out of the scope of configuration analysis, but Anteater might be able to detect the subset of such defects which manifest themselves in the data plane.

To evaluate the effectiveness of Anteater's data plane analysis approach for catching router software bugs, we studied 78 bugs randomly sampled from the Bugzilla repository of Quagga [30]. Quagga is an open-source software router which is used in both research and production [31]. We studied the same set of bugs presented in [41]. For each bug, we studied whether it could affect the data plane, as well as what invariants are required to detect it. We found 86% (67 out of 78) of the bugs might have visible effects on data plane, and potentially can be detected by Anteater.

Detectable with `packet_loss` *and* `loop`. 60 bugs could be detected by the packet loss detection algorithm, and 46 bugs could be detected by the loop detection algorithm. For example, when under heavy load, Quagga 0.96.5 fails to update the Linux kernel's routing tables after receiving BGP updates (Bug 122). This can result in either black holes or forwarding loops in the data plane, which could be detected by either `packet_loss` or `loop`.

Detectable with other invariants. 7 bugs can be detected by other network invariants. For example, in Quagga 0.99.5, a BGP session could remain active after it has been shut down in the control plane (Bug 416). Therefore, packets would continue to follow the path in the data plane, violating the operator's intent. This bug cannot be detected by either `packet_loss` or `loop`, but it is possible to detect it via a customized query: checking that there is no data flow across the given link. We reproduced this bug on a local Quagga testbed and successfully detected it with Anteater.

No visible data plane effects. 11 bugs lack visible effects on the data plane. For example, the terminal hangs in Quagga 0.96.4 during the execution of `show ip bgp` when the data

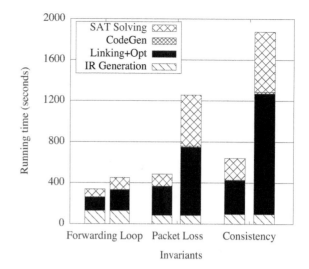

Figure 10: Performance of Anteater when checking three invariants. Time is measured by wall-clock seconds. The left and the right column represent the time of the first run and the total running time for each invariant.

plane has a large number of entries (Bug 87). Anteater is unable to detect this type of bug.

5.3 Performance and scalability

5.3.1 Performance on the campus network

Figure 10 shows the total running time of Anteater when checking invariants on the campus network. We present both the time spent on the first run and the total time to issue all alerts.

Anteater's running time can be broken into three parts: (a) compiling and executing the invariant checkers to generate IR; (b) optimizing the IR with LLVM and generating SAT formulas; (c) running the SAT solver to resolve the SAT queries.

The characteristics of the total running time differ for the three invariants. The reason is that a bug has different impact on each invariant; thus the number of routers needed to be checked during the next run varies greatly. For example, if there exists a forwarding loop in the network for some subnet S, the loop-free forwarding invariant only reports routers which are involved in the forward loop. Routers that remain unreported are proved to loop-free with respect to the snapshot of data plane, provided that the corresponding SAT queries are unsatisfiable. Therefore, in the next run, Anteater only needs to check those routers which are reported to have a loop. The connectivity and consistency invariants, however, could potentially report that packets destined for the loopy subnet S from all routers are lost, due to the loop. That means potentially all routers must be checked during the next run, resulting in longer run time.

5.3.2 Scalability

Scalability on the campus network. To evaluate Anteater's scalability, we scaled down the campus network while honoring its hierarchical structure by removing routers at the lowest layer of the hierarchy first, and continuing upwards

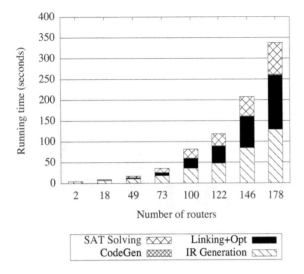

Figure 11: Scalability results of the loop-free forwarding invariant on different subsets of the campus network. The parameter k was set to $n-1$ for each instance.

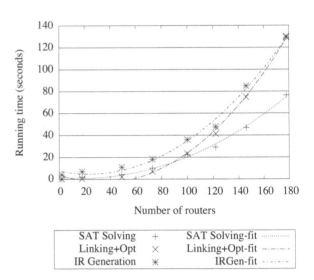

Figure 12: Scatter plots for individual components of the data of Figure 11. Solid lines are quadratic curves fitted for each category of data points.

until a desired number of nodes remain. Figure 11 presents the time spent on the first run when running the forwarding loop invariant on different subsets of the campus network.

Figure 12 breaks down the running time for IR generation, linking and optimization, and SAT solving. We omit the time of code generation since we found that it is negligible. Figure 12 shows that the running time of these three components are roughly proportional to the square of the number of routers. Interestingly, the running time for SAT solver also roughly fits a quadratic curve, implying that it is able to find heuristics to resolve our queries efficiently for this particular network.

Scalability on synthesized autonomous system (AS) networks. We synthesized FIBs for six AS networks (ASes 1221, 1755, 3257, 3967, 4755, 6461) based on topologies from the Rocketfuel project [36], and evaluated the performance of the forwarding loop invariant. We picked $k = 64$ in this experiment. To evaluate how sensitive the invariant is to the complexity of FIB entries, we defined L as a parameter to control the number of "levels" of prefixes in the FIBs. When $L = 1$, all prefixes are non-overlapping /16s. When $L = 2$, half of the prefixes (chosen uniform-randomly) are non-overlapping /16s, and each of the remaining prefixes is a sub-prefix of one random prefix from the first half — thus exercising the longest-prefix match functionality. For example, with $L = 2$ and two prefixes, we might have $p_1 = 10.1.0.0/16$ and $p_2 = 10.1.1.0/24$. Figure 13 shows Anteater's running time on these generated networks; the $L = 2$ case is only slightly slower than $L = 1$.

It takes about half an hour for Anteater to check the largest network (AS 1221 with 384 vertices). These results have a large degree of freedom: they depend on the complexity of network topology and FIB information, and the running time of SAT solvers depends on both heuristics and random number seeds. These results, though inconclusive, indicate that Anteater might be capable of handling larger production networks.

Scalability on networks with packet transformations. We evaluated the case of our campus network with network address translation (NAT) devices deployed. We manually injected NAT rules into the data in three steps. First, we picked a set of edge routers. For each router R in the set, we created a phantom router R' which only had a bidirectional link to R. Second, we attached a private subnet for each phantom router R', and updated the FIBs of both R and R' accordingly for the private subnet. Finally, we added NAT rules as described in §3.4 on the links between R' and R.

Figure 14 presents the running time of the first run of the loop-free forwarding invariant as a function of the number of routers involved in NAT. We picked the maximum hops k to be 20 since the maximum length of loop-free paths is 9 in our campus network.

The portion of time spent in IR generation and code generation is consistent among the different number of NAT-enabled routers. The time spent on linking, optimization and SAT solving, however, increases slowly with the number of NAT-enabled routers.

6. DISCUSSION

Collecting FIB snapshots in a dynamic network. If FIBs change while they are being collected, then Anteater could receive an inconsistent or incomplete view of the network. This could result in false negatives, false positives, or reports of problems that are only temporary (such as black holes and transient loops during network convergence).

There are several ways to deal with this problem. First, one could use a consistent snapshot algorithm [17, 24]. Second, if the network uses a software-defined networking approach [28], forwarding tables can be directly acquired from centralized controllers.

However, our experience shows that the problem of consistent snapshots may not be critical in many networks, as the time required to take a snapshot is small compared to

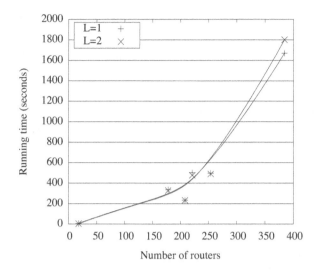

Figure 13: Scalability results of the loop-free forwarding invariant on six AS networks from [36]. L is the parameter to control the complexity of FIBs. Dots show the running time of the invariant for each network. Solid lines are fitted curves generated from the dots.

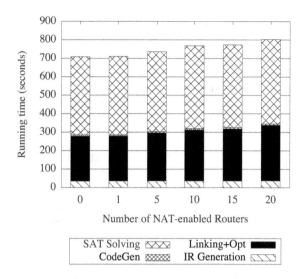

Figure 14: Running time of the loop-free forwarding invariant as a function of the number of routers that have NAT rules.

the average time between changes of the FIBs in our campus network. To study the severity of this problem over a longer timespan, we measured the frequency of FIB changes on the Abilene Internet2 IP backbone, by replaying Internet2's BGP and IS-IS update traces to reconstruct the contents of router FIBs over time. BGP was responsible for the majority (93%) of FIB changes. Internal network (IS-IS) changes occurred at an average frequency of just 1.2 events per hour across the network.

We also note that if changes do occur while downloading FIBs, we can avoid a silent failure. In particular, Cisco routers can be configured to send an SNMP trap on a FIB change; if such a trap is registered with the FIB collection device, and received during the FIB collection process, the process may be aborted and restarted.

Collecting FIB snapshots in the presence of network failures. Network reachability problems might make acquiring FIBs difficult. Fortunately, Anteater can make use of solutions available today, including maintaining separately tunneled networks at the forwarding plane [22, 13] or operating through out-of-band control circuits [3], in order to gather data plane state. (More philosophically, we note that if parts of the network are unreachable, then one problem has already been discovered.)

Would using control plane analysis reduce overhead? Anteater's runtime leaves room for improvement. However, using control plane analysis in place of Anteater does not address this problem, as the invariants of interest are computationally difficult (see Appendix) regardless of whether the information is represented at the control or data plane. It's unclear whether one approach can be fundamentally faster; differences may come down to the choice of which invariants to test, and implementation details. However, we note that the data plane analysis approach may be easier because un-

like control plane analysis, it need not predict future system inputs or dynamic protocol convergence.

Extending Anteater to handle more general properties. The generality of boolean satisfiability enables Anteater to handle other types of network properties beyond those presented in this paper. For example, Anteater could model network latency by introducing a new field in the symbolic packet to record the packet's total latency, and increasing it at each hop according to the link's latency using our packet transformation algorithms. (The SAT solver we used supports arithmetic operations such as $+, -, \leq$ that would be useful for representing network behavior and constraints involving latency.)

Of course, some bugs are beyond Anteater's reach, such as those that have no effect on the contents of forwarding state. That includes some hardware failures (e.g., corrupting the contents of the packet during forwarding), and configuration issues that do not affect the FIB.

7. RELATED WORK

Static analysis of the data plane. The research most closely related to Anteater performs static analysis of data plane protocols. Xie et al. [39] introduced algorithms to check reachability in IP networks with support for ACL policies. Their design was a theoretical proposal without an implementation or evaluation. Anteater uses this algorithm, but we show how to make it practical by designing and implementing our own algorithms to use reachability to check meaningful network invariants, developing a system to make these algorithmically complex operations (see the Appendix) tractable, and using Anteater on a real network to find 23 real bugs. Xie et al. also propose an algorithm for handling packet transformations. However, their proposal did not handle fully general transformations, requiring knowledge of an inverse transform function and only handling non-loopy paths. Our novel algorithm handles arbitrary packet transformations (without needing the inverse transform). This distinction becomes important for practical protocols that can cause packets to revisit the same node more than once (e.g., MPLS Fast Reroute).

Roscoe et al. [33] proposed predicate routing to unify the notions of both routing and firewalling into boolean expressions, Bush and Griffin [9] gave a formal model of integrity (including connectivity and isolation) of virtual private routed networks, and Hamed et al. [19] designed algorithms and a system to identify policy conflicts in IPSec, demonstrating bug-finding efficacy in a user study. In contrast, Anteater is a general framework that can be used to check many protocols, and we have demonstrated that it can find bugs in real deployed networks.

Static analysis of control plane configuration. Analyzing configurations of the control plane, including routers [6, 14] and firewalls [2, 5, 43], can serve as a sanity check prior to deployment. As discussed in the introduction, configuration analysis has two disadvantages. First, it must simulate the behavior of the control plane for the given configuration, making these tools protocol-specific; indeed, the task of parsing configurations is non-trivial and error-prone [26, 41]. Second, configuration analysis will miss non-configuration errors (e.g., errors in router software and inconsistencies between the control plane and data plane [18, 27, 41]; see our study of such errors in §5.2).

However, configuration analysis has the potential to detect bugs *before* a new configuration is deployed. Anteater can detect bugs only once they have affected the data plane — though, as we have shown, there are subtle bugs that fall into this category (e.g., router implementation bugs, copying wrong configurations to routers) that only a data plane analysis approach like Anteater can detect. Control plane analysis and Anteater are thus complementary.

Intercepting control plane dynamics. Monitoring the dynamics of the control plane can detect a broad class of failures [16, 20] with little overhead, but may miss bugs that only affect the data plane. As above, the approach is complementary to ours.

Traffic monitoring. Traffic monitoring is widely used to detect network anomalies as they occur [4, 29, 35, 37]. Anteater's approach is complementary: it can *provably* detect or rule out certain classes of bugs, and it can detect problems that are not being triggered by currently active flows or that do not cause a statistical anomaly in aggregate traffic flow.

SAT solving in other settings. Work on model checking, hardware verification and program analysis [7, 40, 42] often encounter problems that are NP-Complete. They are often reduced into SAT problems so that SAT solvers can solve them effectively in practice. This work inspired our approach of using SAT solving to model and analyze data-plane behavior.

8. CONCLUSION

We presented Anteater, a practical system for finding bugs in networks via data plane analysis. Anteater collects data plane information from network devices, models data plane behavior as instances of satisfiability problems, and uses formal analysis techniques to systematically analyze the network. To the best of our knowledge, Anteater is the first design and implementation of a data plane analysis system used to find real bugs in real networks.

We ran Anteater on our campus network and uncovered 23 bugs. Anteater helped our network operators improve the reliability of the campus network. Our study suggests that analyzing data plane information could be a feasible approach to assist debugging today's networks.

Acknowledgements

We would like to thank our shepherd, Emin Gün Sirer, and the anonymous reviewers for their valuable comments. We also thank our network operator Debbie Fligor for collecting data and sharing her operational experience. This research was funded by NSF grants CNS 0834738, CNS 0831212, CNS 1040396, and CNS 1053781, grant N0014-09-1-0743 from the Office of Naval Research, AFOSR MURI grant FA9550-09-01-0539, a grant from the Internet Services Research Center (ISRC) of Microsoft Research, and a Fulbright S&T Fellowship.

9. REFERENCES

[1] JUNOS: MPLS fast reroute solutions, network operations guide. 2007.

[2] E. S. Al-Shaer and H. H. Hamed. Discovery of policy anomalies in distributed firewalls. In *Proc. IEEE INFOCOM*, 2004.

[3] Apple. What is lights out management?, September 2010. http://support.apple.com/kb/TA24506.

[4] F. Baccelli, S. Machiraju, D. Veitch, and J. Bolot. The role of PASTA in network measurement. In *Proc. ACM SIGCOMM*, 2006.

[5] Y. Bartal, A. Mayer, K. Nissim, and A. Wool. Firmato: A novel firewall management toolkit. In *Proc. IEEE S&P*, 1999.

[6] T. Benson, A. Akella, and D. Maltz. Unraveling the complexity of network management. In *Proc. USENIX NSDI*, 2009.

[7] A. Biere, A. Cimatti, E. M. Clarke, and Y. Zhu. Symbolic model checking without BDDs. In *Proc. TACAS*, 1999.

[8] R. Brummayer and A. Biere. Boolector: An efficient smt solver for bit-vectors and arrays. In *Proc. TACAS*, 2009.

[9] R. Bush and T. G. Griffin. Integrity for virtual private routed networks. In *Proc. IEEE INFOCOM*, 2003.

[10] Cisco Systems Inc. Spanning tree protocol problems and related design considerations. http://www.cisco.com/en/US/tech/tk389/tk621/technologies_tech_note09186a00800951ac.shtml, August 2005. Document ID 10556.

[11] J. Duffy. BGP bug bites Juniper software. *Network World*, December 2007.

[12] J. Evers. Trio of Cisco flaws may threaten networks. *CNET News*, January 2007.

[13] D. Farinacci, T. Li, S. Hanks, D. Meyer, and P. Traina. Generic Routing Encapsulation (GRE). RFC 2784, March 2000.

[14] N. Feamster and H. Balakrishnan. Detecting BGP configuration faults with static analysis. In *Proc. USENIX NSDI*, 2005.

[15] N. Feamster and J. Rexford. Network-wide prediction of BGP routes. *IEEE/ACM Transactions on Networking*, 15:253–266, 2007.

[16] A. Feldmann, O. Maennel, Z. Mao, A. Berger, and B. Maggs. Locating Internet routing instabilities. In *Proc. ACM SIGCOMM*, 2004.

[17] D. Geels, G. Altekar, P. Maniatis, T. Roscoe, and I. Stoica. Friday: Global comprehension for distributed replay. In *Proc. USENIX NSDI*, 2007.

[18] G. Goodell, W. Aiello, T. Griffin, J. Ioannidis, P. McDaniel, and A. Rubin. Working around BGP: An

incremental approach to improving security and accuracy of interdomain routing. In *Proc. NDSS*, 2003.

[19] H. Hamed, E. Al-Shaer, and W. Marrero. Modeling and verification of IPSec and VPN security policies. In *Proc. ICNP*, 2005.

[20] X. Hu and Z. M. Mao. Accurate real-time identification of IP prefix hijacking. In *Proc. IEEE S&P*, 2007.

[21] Intel. The all new 2010 Intel Core vPro processor family: Intelligence that adapts to your needs, 2010. http://www.intel.com/Assets/PDF/whitepaper/311710.pdf.

[22] M. Lasserre and V. Kompella. Virtual private LAN service (VPLS) using label distribution protocol (LDP) signaling. RFC 4762, January 2007.

[23] C. Lattner and V. Adve. LLVM: A compilation framework for lifelong program analysis & transformation. In *Proc. CGO*, 2004.

[24] X. Liu, Z. Guo, X. Wang, F. Chen, X. Lian, J. Tang, M. Wu, M. F. Kaashoek, and Z. Zhang. D³S: Debugging deployed distributed systems. In *Proc. USENIX NSDI*, 2008.

[25] R. Mahajan, D. Wetherall, and T. Anderson. Understanding BGP misconfiguration. In *Proc. ACM SIGCOMM*, 2002.

[26] Y. Mandelbaum, S. Lee, and D. Caldwell. Adaptive parsing of router configuration languages. In *Workshop INM*, 2008.

[27] Z. M. Mao, D. Johnson, J. Rexford, J. Wang, and R. Katz. Scalable and accurate identification of AS-level forwarding paths. In *Proc. IEEE INFOCOM*, 2004.

[28] N. McKeown, T. Anderson, H. Balakrishnan, G. Parulkar, L. Peterson, J. Rexford, and S. Shenker. OpenFlow: Enabling innovation in campus networks. *ACM CCR*, April 2008.

[29] Nagios. http://www.nagios.org.

[30] Quagga Routing Suite. http://www.quagga.net.

[31] Quagga Routing Suite. Commercial Resources. http://www.quagga.net/commercial.php.

[32] Renesys. Longer is not always better. http://www.renesys.com/blog/2009/02/longer-is-not-better.shtml.

[33] T. Roscoe, S. Hand, R. Isaacs, R. Mortier, and P. Jardetzky. Predicate routing: Enabling controlled networking. *ACM CCR*, January 2003.

[34] Ruby-Prolog. https://rubyforge.org/projects/ruby-prolog.

[35] F. Silveira, C. Diot, N. Taft, and R. Govindan. ASTUTE: Detecting a different class of traffic anomalies. In *Proc. ACM SIGCOMM*, 2010.

[36] N. Spring, R. Mahajan, and D. Wetherall. Measuring ISP topologies with rocketfuel. In *Proc. ACM SIGCOMM*, 2002.

[37] P. Tune and D. Veitch. Towards optimal sampling for flow size estimation. In *Proc. IMC*, 2008.

[38] J. Wu, Z. M. Mao, J. Rexford, and J. Wang. Finding a needle in a haystack: Pinpointing significant BGP routing changes in an IP network. In *Proc. USENIX NSDI*, 2005.

[39] G. G. Xie, J. Zhan, D. A. Maltz, H. Zhang, A. Greenberg, G. Hjalmtysson, and J. Rexford. On static reachability analysis of IP networks. In *Proc. IEEE INFOCOM*, 2005.

[40] Y. Xie and A. Aiken. Saturn: A scalable framework for error detection using boolean satisfiability. *Proc. ACM TOPLAS*, 29(3), 2007.

[41] Z. Yin, M. Caesar, and Y. Zhou. Towards understanding bugs in open source router software. *ACM CCR*, June 2010.

[42] D. Yuan, H. Mai, W. Xiong, L. Tan, Y. Zhou, and S. Pasupathy. SherLog: Error diagnosis by connecting clues from run-time logs. In *ASPLOS*, 2010.

[43] L. Yuan, J. Mai, Z. Su, H. Chen, C.-N. Chuah, and P. Mohapatra. FIREMAN: A toolkit for FIREwall Modeling and ANalysis. In *Proc. IEEE S&P*, 2006.

[44] E. Zmijewski. Reckless driving on the Internet. http://www.renesys.com/blog/2009/02/the-flap-heard-around-the-worl.shtml, February 2009.

Appendix

In this appendix, we discuss the complexity of the basic problem of determining reachability in a network given its data plane state.

The difficulty of determining reachability depends strongly on what functions we allow the data plane to perform. If network devices implement only IP-style longest prefix match forwarding on a destination address, it is fairly easy to show that reachability can be decided in polynomial time. However, if we augment the data plane with richer functions, the problem quickly becomes difficult. As we show below, packet filters make reachability NP-Complete; and of course, reachability is undecidable in the case of allowing arbitrary programs in the data plane.

It is useful to mention how this complexity relates to the approach of Xie et al. [39], whose reachability algorithm is essentially the same as ours, but written in terms of set union/intersection operations rather than SAT. As pointed out in [39], even with packet filters, the reachability algorithm terminates within $O(V^3)$ operations. However, this algorithm only calculates a formula representing reachability, and does not evaluate whether that formula is satisfiable. In [39], it was assumed that evaluating the formula (via set operations in the formulation of [39]) would be fast. This may be true in many instances, but in the general case deciding whether one vertex can reach another in the presence of packet filters is *not* in $O(V^3)$, unless P = NP. Thus, to handle the general case, the use of SAT or similar techniques is required since the problem is NP-complete. We choose to use an existing SAT solver to leverage optimizations for determining satisfiability.

We now describe in more detail how packet filters make reachability NP-Complete. The input to the reachability problem consists of a directed graph $G = (V, E)$, the boolean policy function $\mathcal{Q}(e, p)$ which returns true when packet p can pass along edge e, and two vertices $s, t \in V$. The problem is to decide whether there exists a packet p and an $s \rightsquigarrow t$ path in G, such that $\mathcal{Q}(e, p) = true$ for all edges e along the path. (Note this problem definition does not allow packet transformations.) To complete the definition of the problem, we must specify what sort of packet filters the policy function $\mathcal{Q}$ can represent. We could allow the filter to be any boolean expression whose variables are the packet's fields. In this case, the problem can trivially encode arbitrary SAT instances by using a given SAT formula as the policy function along a single edge $s \rightarrow t$, with no other nodes or edges in the graph, with the SAT formula's variables being the packet's fields. Thus, that formulation of the reachability problem is NP-Complete.

One might wonder whether a simpler, more restricted definition of packet filters makes the problem easy. We now show that even when $\mathcal{Q}$ for each edge is a function of *a single bit* in the packet header, the problem is still NP-complete because the complexity can be encoded into the network topology.

PROPOSITION 1. *Deciding reachability in a network with single-bit packet filters is NP-Complete.*

PROOF. Given a packet and a path through the network, since the length of the path must be $< |V|$, we can easily verify in polynomial time whether the packet will be delivered. Therefore the problem is in NP.

To show NP-hardness, suppose we are given an instance of a 3-SAT problem with n binary variables $x_1, \ldots, x_n$ and k clauses $C_1, \ldots, C_k$. Construct an instance of the reachability problem as follows. The packet will have n one-bit fields corresponding to the n variables x_i. We create $k + 1$ nodes $v_0, v_1, \ldots, v_k$, and we let $s = v_0$ and $t = v_k$. For each clause C_i, we add three parallel edges e_{i1}, e_{i2}, e_{i3} all spanning $v_{i-1} \rightarrow v_i$. If the first literal in clause C_i is some variable x_i, then the policy function $\mathcal{Q}(e_{i1}, p) = true$ if and only if the ith bit of p is 1; otherwise the first literal in C_i is the negated variable $\overline{x}_i$, and we let $\mathcal{Q}(e_{i1}, p) = true$ if and only if the ith bit of p is 0. The policy functions for e_{i2} and e_{i3} are constructed similarly based on the second and third literals in C_i.

With the above construction a packet p can flow from v_{i-1} to v_i if and only if C_i evaluates to true under the assignment corresponding to p. Therefore, p can flow from s to t if and only if all 3-SAT clauses are satisfied. Thus, since 3-SAT is NP-complete, reachability with single-bit packet filters is NP-complete. □

Demystifying Configuration Challenges and Trade-Offs in Network-based ISP Services

Theophilus Benson, Aditya Akella
University of Wisconsin, Madison
Madison, WI, USA
{tbenson, akella}@cs.wisc.edu

Aman Shaikh
AT&T Labs – Research
Florham Park, NJ, USA
ashaikh@research.att.com

ABSTRACT

ISPs are increasingly offering a variety of network-based services such as VPN, VPLS, VoIP, Virtual-Wire and DDoS protection. Although both enterprise and residential networks are rapidly adopting these services, there is little systematic work on the design challenges and trade-offs ISPs face in providing them. The goal of our paper is to understand the complexity underlying the layer-3 design of services and to highlight potential factors that hinder their introduction, evolution and management. Using daily snapshots of configuration and device metadata collected from a tier-1 ISP, we examine the logical dependencies and special cases in device configurations for five different network-based services. We find: (1) the design of the core data-plane is usually service-agnostic and simple, but the control-planes for different services become more complex as services evolve; (2) more crucially, the configuration at the service edge inevitably becomes more complex over time, potentially hindering key management issues such as service upgrades and troubleshooting; and (3) there are key service-specific issues that also contribute significantly to the overall design complexity. Thus, the high prevalent complexity could impede the adoption and growth of network-based services. We show initial evidence that some of the complexity can be mitigated systematically.

Categories and Subject Descriptors

C.2.3 [**COMPUTER-COMMUNICATION NETWORKS**]: Network Operations - Network management

General Terms

Design, Management, Measurement

Keywords

Network services, network modeling, configuration analysis

1. INTRODUCTION

Conventional ISP operations have historically focused mainly on providing Internet access to customers and ensuring global connec-

tivity. In recent years, however, ISPs' focus has shifted toward providing large scale *network-based services*. These cater to groups of customers who need functions beyond best effort connectivity, such as virtual links or networks at layers 2 and 3, security, and quality-of-service. These services require the introduction of new layer-2/3 devices and/or significant modifications to the existing layer-2/3 setup. Customers of these services typically have fairly strict performance and availability requirements, which means ISPs have to enable the requisite support within their networks. Examples of network-based services include IPTV, Virtual-Wire (V-Wire), VPNs, VPLS, VoIP, DDoS protection, and teleconferencing.

The Internet is poised to experience rapid growth in the number of network-based services in the near future. There are several factors contributing to this. First, with growing traffic demands [1], merely providing IP connectivity is no longer a viable business model for ISPs; network-based services are seen as a crucial means to earn extra revenue. Second, router and switch vendors are responding to ISPs' desire to offer services by making their platforms virtualizable (e.g., through frameworks such as VRF [2, 3]) to ease creation of interesting new services. Finally, there is a growing demand for such services from both residential and enterprise customers. However, despite the growing importance and centrality of network-based services, few studies have examined the challenges ISPs face in offering them.

In this paper, we present a first-ever large-scale analysis of the *complexity* underlying the layer-3 design of a variety of network-based services in a tier-1 ISP. The central design issue in network-based services that motivates our work is how to make ISP networks *easier to evolve* to meet the growing demand for services and changing customer requirements. To a large extent, this hinges on the ease with which the infrastructure can be upgraded or reconfigured with new functionality.

Specifically, the focus of this paper is on the complexity arising from *device-level configurations*, which define the services and define how the devices are integrated into the network. We use configuration models to abstract away details of device configuration files and examine the difficulty in setting configuration *dependencies* (e.g., in setting up service-specific functionality on a router) and in creating the requisite *special cases* (e.g., to meet design constraints and differing customer requirements), which our prior work [7] shows to be indicative of the complexity in managing the underlying design and configuration. Based on our analysis, we then identify how to evaluate trade-offs in simplifying service designs to make them easier to evolve and manage.

There are several steps in creating and running a service over time, e.g., addition of layer-2/3 devices that have customer-, location- and service-specific configuration, integrating with the core, setting up the control-plane (e.g., routing between different sites of a VPN customer), and, occasionally, restructuring the network to achieve routing scalability as services expand. Using our configuration models, we analyze configuration snapshots collected from a large tier-1 ISP network over a period of several years. We study *five* services in all: VPN, VPLS, DDoS protection, Virtual Wire service and VoIP. We analyze the relative difficulty of all the above tasks, both within and across these services, and identifying what contributes most to complexity and why.

The key high-level findings from our analysis are as follows: (1) The design of the ISP core data-plane is usually service-agnostic and it appears simple to integrate new service infrastructures into it. Unfortunely, the good news ends here. In particular, we find that the design of service control-planes becomes more complex over time with growing service size. A key cause for this is the complexity underlying the establishment of BGP sessions. (2) More crucially, the configuration of a service at the network edge could rapidly become more complex over time, which could severely hinder key management issues such as service upgrades, adding customers, and troubleshooting. We find that a central factor in the growing complexity is the diversity of customer-provisioning requirements and the changes that occur to them over time. (3) There are several service-specific issues that also contribute significantly to the overall design complexity (e.g., introduction of a new vendor and implementation of new policies); thus, it appears that service-specific mechanisms may be fundamentally unavoidable in managing service design and configuration.

Thus, it appears that the high prevalent complexity may impede the growth and adoption of services. A natural question is whether it is possible to *control or mitigate* the complexity. This issue cannot be addressed in isolation as the complexity depends on other key considerations including the choice of available vendors, cost, performance and resource constraints. In this paper, we take initial steps in this direction and show how to systematically control or mitigate (where possible) the complexity in customer provisioning and service control-plane design by making an informed choice of vendors and by picking appropriate routing substrates.

The rest of the paper is structured as follows. Section 2 provides an overview of network-based services and their configuration in ISPs. Section 3 describes the ISP network analyzed and presents the configuration models used. Section 4 presents our findings regarding the complexity of service designs. Section 5 analyzes and explains some of the key causes of the complexity. Section 6 shows how it may be possible to reduce such complexity by using alternate designs. Section 7 presents implications of our results, and discusses limitations of our study. Finally, Section 8 presents related work, and Section 9 concludes.

2. BACKGROUND

Our work focuses on the network services that are implemented within, and require support from, the provider's router and switch infrastructure. We refer to such services as being *network-based*. Examples include VPN, VPLS, VoIP and DDoS protection. Our work does not extend to other key services such as CDNs, cloud services, data center and hosting services which ISPs offer by placing racks of servers in strategic locations within their network.

We focus specifically on the configuration of devices required to run network-based services. Device configurations define both the service semantics, i.e., how customers can use a service, and operational aspects, such as how a service integrates with the rest of the network. Thus, configuration is central to the correct and effective functioning of a service and the underlying network. Furthermore, device configuration is perhaps one of the most time-consuming and error-prone tasks in ISP operations [10], often requiring sig-

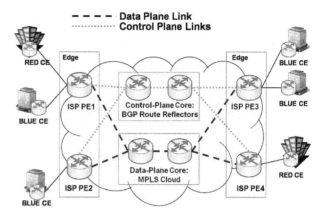

Figure 1: Architecture for a VPN service in an ISP.

nificant manual intervention [8]. We discuss other factors relevant to services such as configuration of customer-premise routers that connect to the ISP in Section 7.

Network-based services are realized through a combination of changes to layer-3 routing protocols and the deployment of new devices capable of supporting service-specific functionality. In this section, we present a brief overview of the roles played by various devices in supporting services, and then discuss how service introduction impacts the configuration of protocols within these devices. We also describe configuration steps required to provision a customer of a typical service.

2.1 ISP Network

In Figure 1, we show a typical tier-1 ISP network. The network devices are divided into the data-plane core, the control-plane core and the edge. The edge consists of a variety of specializable devices, known as *Provider Edge (PE)* devices. Each PE is configured to provide one or more services to the customers connected to it; customer devices that connect to PEs are called *Customer Edge (CE)* devices. For example, in Figure 1, we present an edge consisting of VPN PE devices which are used for creating virtual links and networks between the customer's CE devices. The data-plane core is a cloud of service-agnostic devices that provide transit for packets across the network in a highly efficient manner. The control-plane core consists of a set of BGP *route-reflectors (RRs)* [5] used for exachanging reachability information between Provider Edge devices (PEs).

2.2 Description of Services

As mentioned earlier, ISPs have traditionally provided Internet connectivity to business and residential customers. ISPs deploy networks consisting of routers, switches and links interconnecting them. These networks allow ISPs to provide other services to their customers. Two such services are VPN (Virtual Private Networks) and VPLS (Virtual Private LAN Service). These services are provided to enterprise customers, where an ISP uses its network to interconnect each customer's geographically distributed sites, thereby allowing the customer to form its own private intranet. With VPN, each customer gets a private IP (i.e., layer-3) network, allowing its sites to exchange IP packets amongst themselves. VPLS, on the other hand, provides a private ethernet (i.e., layer-2) network to the customer, thereby allowing its sites to exchange ethernet frames with one another. The implications of keeping these networks private are three-fold. First, the ISP needs to keep traffic of one customer separate from another customer. Second, the ISP needs to allow every customer to choose its own control-plane mechanisms to route packets across its sites. Finally, each customer needs to have freedom in the way addresses are assigned to its devices even if this means overlap of addresses across different customers. For example, the red and blue customers might end up assigning the same addresses to their hosts in the Figure 1.

To satisfy these requirements, ISPs essentially create a "virtual slice" of their network for each customer. For the example shown in Figure 1, the ISP creates two virtual slices, one for the red and another for the blue customers. Since the underlying network infrastructure is shared amongst these slices, an ISP needs several capabilities to keep the slices separate from one another. The first capability allows the ISP to form tunnels between PEs attached to the same customer. This in turn allows the ISP to maintain traffic separation even when addresses overlap between different customers. Although various tunneling mechanisms are available, most tier-1 ISPs have converged on the use of Multiprotocol Label Switching (MPLS) and Label Switched Path (LSP) as the tunneling technology.

The second capability allows ISPs to use (I-)BGP and an infrastructure of BGP route-reflectors for exchanging routes between sites attached to a virtual slice. This is similar to what ISPs do for providing Internet connectivity. Unlike with Internet connectivity though, the routes do not always carry IPv4 addresses (e.g., VPLS uses MAC addresses). Therefore, a Multi-protocol version of BGP, known as MP-BGP [4], is used. MP-BGP allows BGP to carry routes for various kinds of address families.

Finally, an ISP needs to keep routes of one slice separate from other slices especially when addresses can overlap. To achieve this, PEs need the capability to keep slice-specific routes in their own separate routing tables. This is achieved by creating virtual routing tables on PEs using *Virtual Routing and Forwarding (VRF)* technology, such that there is one VRF for every customer connected to a given PE. For example, PE1 in Figure 1 has VRFs for blue and red customers, whereas PE2 only carries a single VRF for the blue customer. MP-BGP stitches the VRFs together by allowing VRFs of a given customer which could be strewn across multiple PEs to exchange routes amongst themselves. MP-BGP also ensures that routes in the VRFs of a given customer do not leak into another customer's VRFs.

In addition to providing "basic connectivity", the VPN and VPLS services often allow customers to segregate traffic into multiple classes for different treatment across the core (e.g., VoIP calls between customer sites would be given higher priority over e-mail traffic). This capability is known as *Class of Service (CoS)* routing. Supporing CoS requires the ability to classify and mark packets at PEs, and providing appropriate treatment (via queuing mechanisms) to each traffic class within the core.

2.2.1 Configuration

Configuring VRF: At the edge of the network, VRFs are configured on the Provider Edge (PE) devices to interface with the customer site and create the virtual network. In Figure 2, we present the configuration commands used for such a PE device. The VRF is configured in lines 1-4. The virtual network for a customer is defined as a set of VRFs that import the same set of routes. In a simple setup, this is achieved by setting the same "route-target" on all VRFs as is done in lines 3-4. More complex setups, such as hub-and-spokes [22, 14], may be achieved by using an identical set of "route-targets" on the spokes and using multiple different "route-targets" or "route-maps" on the hub. While these setups are more complex to configure, they provide the ISP with the benefit of reducing the number of routes installed by a VRF into a PE's forwarding table. We discuss these trade-offs in section 6.2. Lines

```
     ! Configuration for the VRF for a customer's virtual network.
1    ip vrf blue
2    rd 23234:100223
3    route-target import 1000:1
4    route-target export 1000:1
     !
     ! Configuration for a customer facing interface.
5    interface ethernet1
6    ip address 128.105.82.66 255.255.255.252
7    ip vrf forwarding blue
8    service-policy output policy1
9    service-policy input policy2
     !
     ! Configuration for the CoS for a customer's virtual network.
10   policy-map policy1
11   class class1
12   police 10000 200 confirm-action transmit exceed-action drop
     !
13   class-map match-any class1
14   match mpls experimental 6
     !
     ! Configuration for BGP peering sessions with route-reflector.
15   router bgp 65000 !configuration for BGP
16   router-id 192.168.6.6
17   neighbor 192.168.2.1 remote-as 1
18   neighbor 192.168.2.1 update-source Loopback0
19   !
20   address-family vpnv4
21   neighbor 192.168.2.1 activate
22   neighbor 192.168.2.1 send-community extended
23   exit-address-family
```

Figure 2: Configuration for a VPN PE.

5-9 present the configuration for the customer-facing interface on the PE. Specifically, the customer's interface is attached to the VRF in line 7.

Configuring MPLS: As shown in Figure 1, the PE devices are interconnected by a cloud of core devices. In this architecture, the PEs act as MPLS edge devices which perform classification of packets and add/remove LSP labels from packets based on this classification. The PEs add two labels to every packet: an outer label to be used by the core devices to switch to the destination PE, and an inner label for the destination PE to select the appropriate VRF. The core devices, acting as label switch routers, switch packets based on the outer label contained in their headers.

Configuring BGP: Reachability information between different PEs is exchanged using MP-BGP [4] as mentioned earlier. Due to the size of the ISP networks, PEs are configured to exchange reachability information indirectly through the use of BGP route-reflectors. In lines 15-23 of Figure 2, we present the configurations for the PE to communicate with a BGP route-reflector. This involves setting up neighbor commands (for BGP peering sessions) with the appropriate route-reflectors (in lines 20-23).

In Figure 3, we present the configuration for the corresponding route-reflector. The route-reflector contains neighbor commands for peering sessions to each of the other route-reflectors (lines 5-6) and its clients (lines 3-4). Commands in lines 7-13 then activate use of MP-BGP for VPN addresses for these neighbors. Each route-reflector should have N such set of neighboring commands, where N is the number of route-reflectors and the PEs taken together.

Configuring CoS: The Class-of-Service primitives include policy maps (Figure 2, lines 10-12) and class maps (lines 13-14) which limit the amount of traffic that an interface of the virtual network allows to enter or leave the network (the interface itself is configured to use these in lines 8-9).

```
1   router bgp 65000
2   router-id 192.168.2.1
3   neighbor 192.168.6.6 remote-as 1
4   neighbor 192.168.6.6 update-source Loopback0
5   neighbor 192.168.2.2 remote-as 1
6   neighbor 192.168.2.2 update-source Loopback0
    !
7   address-family vpnv4
8   neighbor 192.168.6.6 activate
9   neighbor 192.168.6.6 send-community extended
10  neighbor 192.168.6.6 route-reflector-client
11  neighbor 192.168.2.2 activate
12  neighbor 192.168.2.2 send-community extended
13  exit-address-family
```

Figure 3: BGP configuration for a route-reflector.

2.3 Customer Provisioning

A customer of a network-based service is set up within this framework by (1) physically connecting the customer site to one or more PE devices and setting up customer-facing interfaces (Figure 2, lines 5-9); (2) configuring a VRF instance (Figure 2, lines 1-4) on each of the connected PE devices; and (3) setting up the appropriate CoS primitives (Figure 2, lines 10-14). Different customers have different CoS requirements and thus different types of configuration. For example, some customers may not have any CoS polices in which case lines 8 and 9 are not required, while others may have more complex policies requiring the policy map in lines 10-12 to be significantly larger and to use multiple different class maps (similar to those in lines 13-14).

3. APPROACH

In this section, we describe the data-set and configuration models we employ to study the complexity underlying the layer-3 design of network-based services.

3.1 Data

From a tier-1 ISP network, we gathered *daily snapshots* of device configurations as well as documentation about service deployment, installation and upgrades over a *30 month* period from June 2008 to December 2010. We also obtained metadata regarding device role (e.g., core or edge), associated services (e.g., VPLS or VPN), device vendor, and OS version.

We studied a total of **five** network-based services in this ISP: two of these – **VPN** and **VPLS** – were described in the previous section. Next, let us describe the remaining three.

The third service is **DDoS protection**, where the ISP offers mitigation to Denial of Service (DoS) attacks as a value-added service to enterprise customers that have subscribed to the Internet services. DDoS attacks are very prevalent in the Internet today. To mitigate such attacks, when the ISP detects an attack against a customer, it re-directs the customer's traffic to a "scrubbing farm". At the scrubbing farm the attack traffic is segregated from the normal traffic, and latter is sent back to the customer. Re-direction of the traffic to the scrubbing farm is achieved via a temporary BGP route announcement. The cleaned normal traffic is sent back over a dedicated VPN.

The fourth service, which we term **Virtual Wire**, is offered atop the VPLS infrastructure. It provides a customer with an "access link" to a PE offering layer-3 services like VPN and Internet access, and is realized by creating a point-to-point VPLS network – essentially a Virtual Wire – between the customer CE and the ISP's layer-3 PE.

The final service is a specific instantiation of VoIP targeted for the ISP's customers; we refer to this simply as **VoIP**. Traffic be-

Service	% of ISP Devices Used by the Service
VPN	48%
VPLS	27%
DDoS	31%
Virtual Wire (V-Wire)	25%
VoIP	5%

Table 1: Percentage of ISP devices used by the five services studied. The devices used by a service include both the PEs and the RRs, but not the MPLS core devices since the core devices are shared by all services.

longing to this service is routed between customer sites over a dedicated VPN.

We should mention that the DDoS protection, Virtual Wire, and VoIP services do not require the entire set of mechanisms and configuration steps outlined above, as these services are akin to customers of VPN and VPLS services. In particular, no special route-reflectors, MP-BGP setup or MPLS support is needed. However, they do require a group of VRFs with service specific configuration; the configuration of the VRFs may change over time to accommodate new customers of these services.

The services we study are quite diverse in terms of customer requirements, life-cycle, scale, and devices. The latter two aspects are captured in Table 1 where we show the percentage of overall devices used by each service. Note that the total of the first column exceeds 100% since a good fraction of devices are shared across services. Overall, we believe that this diversity offers a comprehensive view of network-based services.

3.2 Configuration Models

In order to understand the challenges of configuring services in ISP networks, we employ *configuration models*. These models allow us to abstract away the details of the underlying configuration files, while allowing us to systematically reason about the relative difficulty involved in various tasks such as configuring PE devices, core devices and control-plane mechanisms.

The models we use rely on first identifying *stanzas*, i.e., logical groupings of a set of configuration lines based on the functionality they directly define. For example, in Figure 2 lines 5-9, which specify properties for an interface are all grouped together into a single stanza. Various configuration languages provide different demarcators that can be used to identify stanzas.

Our models focus on two aspects of configuration: *creating and maintaining dependencies between stanzas*, and *creating special stanzas to cater to specific needs*.

Referential Graph. Since configuration files are modular in nature, when configuring a device, operators are often required to create references among different stanzas. For example, enabling a routing process on a router usually requires that the stanza defining the routing process refer to stanzas for the interfaces over which routing sessions are established. To model this dependency, we extract the referential graph for a device. Each node in the graph represents a configuration stanza. The edges between the nodes represent explicitly defined links between stanzas. To calculate the referential graph for a device, we developed a parser that reads through the configuration files, and determines stanzas and their names. Once all stanzas and their names are extracted, the parser re-processes the configuration file, creating links between stanzas everytime one stanza has a command explicitly referencing the name of another stanza.

The referential graph models the syntactic dependencies that operators must track in configuring services with various devices. We choose this model since, as prior work has shown, the higher the number of referential links that must be established within the subgraph of the referential graph corresponding to a functionality, the greater the difficulty of setting up the functionality [7]. Referential graphs help us understand both how difficult it is to introduce a service and to modify it over time.

Templates. Templates are often used in configuring similar functions across devices of an ISP network [8]. Our template model identifies groups of stanzas in various devices with similar configurations (meaning that the stanzas could be configured using a single configuration template). Thus, templates and the devices that constitute them help track *uniformity* in configuration; the greater the non-uniformity, the more special cases there are in the design and the more difficult it is to set up and maintain a service [7]. We use copy-paste analysis tools [13] to derive sets of configuration stanzas that are identical across devices, reflecting functionality that is replicated across devices. We set the grammar and parameters of the analysis tool such that a group of stanzas identical in size and consisting of the same commands form a template. Using templates, we are able to understand the ease of provisioning a new PE for an existing or a new service as well as modifying or updating the functions performed by existing PEs.

4. CONFIGURING SERVICES

In this section, we analyze the complexity of the layer-3 design and configuration for the five network-based services. The more involved the service configuration is, the greater the amount of manual intervention and time required to instantiate, modify or update it over time, and the more error-prone it gets. In particular, we study the relative amounts of complexity contributed by three aspects that make up a service: (1) PE configuration, (2) PE-Core configuration, and (3) control-plane configuration. For each aspect, we provide a longitudinal analysis of how configuration difficulty changes with time and what contributes to the observed complexity. Also, while prior works have examined services in isolation, we provide a comparative analysis and examine reasons for the differences observed across services. We apply the models described in the previous section to study various services.

4.1 PE Configuration

We start by analyzing the configuration employed for setting up PEs for each service.

4.1.1 Referential Dependence

We use the referential graph model to quantify the dependencies within PE configurations, with a greater number of dependencies as an indication of greater configuration complexity.

In Figure 4 we present various high-level properties of the referential graphs for the five services we studied. From Figure 4 (a), we observe that the ratio of the aggregate referential graphs - in terms of number of referential links computed over all PEs on which the service is configured at any point relative to the inital number at the beginning of the study - increases monotonically for each service. This indicates that, in general, configurations of the services require more dependencies to be tracked as they evolve. In Figure 4 (b), we examine the worst referential graph size for each service; we see that this too steadily increases over time. In the case of VPLS, it increases by a factor of 2 over a 12-month timespan.

In Figure 4 (c), we examine the referential graph size for the median PE device for each service. We find that the median referential graph size for VPN and VPLS is not strictly monotonic. Figure 4 (d) shows the corresponding timeline for the number of PEs in each service. From this, we note that the drops in the referential graph sizes in Figure 4 (c) correspond to time instances when new PEs

were added for the services: unlike existing devices, new devices do not have as many customers, and as such contain significantly simpler configurations. For other services, the median PE's referential graph increases in size over time.

We now examine the causes for the growing number of referential links in the services (Figures 4 (a) and (b)). To do this, in Figure 5, we present the relative numbers of various types of stanzas added within the overall referential graph of a service over time. Stanzas corresponding to the CoS include policers, filters, class maps and policy maps, while stanzas corresponding to the route control stanzas include route-maps, policy statements and community lists.

We make the following observations:
- For VPN (Figure 5 (a)) and VPLS (Figure 5 (b)), the changes in the referential graph sizes can be attributed to customer provisioning. With VPLS, this can be seen in the growing number of VRF stanzas – each VRF stanza indicates a different new customer site. In the case of VPN, the changes are due to a growing number of interfaces (whereas the proportion of VRF stays the same). This means existing customers are adding more sites to the same PEs.
- In the case of the DDoS protection service (Figure 5 (c)), the growing complexity was because the ISP started deploying PE routers from another vendor. The DDoS-related configuration on these PEs requires multiple stanzas since the configuration language of the vendor is more structured and modular. In contrast, the configuration language of the original vendor allows specification of multiple options and parameters within a single stanza, resulting in fewer stanzas and less complex configuration on its PEs to achieve the same purpose.
- For the Virtual Wire service (Figure 5 (d)), the somewhat fluctuating pattern for the number of interfaces and other stanzas is due to device provisioning over time and due to the semantics of the service. Recall that the Virtual Wire service provides the abstraction of a point-to-point access link to a layer-3 PE. When a new VPLS PE is provisioned for this service, it contains configuration for setting up the basic abstraction, i.e. VRF and route control stanzas, – this is reflected in the higher proportion of VRF and route control stanzas in the initial months. When a new customer is provisioned, the ISP configures an interface for physical connectivity to the customer and then configures the virtual network to include this interface– this is reflected in the higher proportion of interface stanzas at later times.
- For VoIP (Figure 5 (e)), we find that over time more policy maps and class maps are being used within the service to configure additional CoS constraints (in fact, the same policy maps and class maps are being uniformly applied across the PEs).

We also note that despite different services using the same basic router functionality (i.e., VRF and MP-BGP), Figure 5 shows that the relative composition of different stanzas in the devices of various services appear to be quite different. This, along with the observations above, indicates that mechanisms designed to manage the configuration for one service may not directly apply to other services. Service-specific optimizations and solutions may be necessary.

To summarize, we find that the aggregate and worst-case sizes for referential dependency graphs grow for PEs of all services. The implication of the growing complexity is that some configuration-related management tasks, such as updating functionality on PEs, or even adding new PEs may become tricky over time. There are a variety of different reasons for the growing complexity, several of which are service-specific. However, one common culprit across many of the services, is customer provisioning. Finally, the existence of key differences among service requirements means that

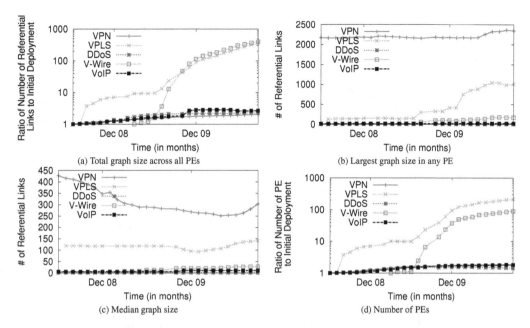

Figure 4: Longitudinal analysis of the referential graphs in service PE devices.

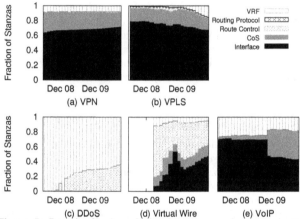

Figure 5: Longitudinal analysis of the types of stanzas in the referential graph (averaged over PEs).

one would require service-specific approaches for managing the complexity in designing and configuring services.

4.1.2 Templates

Next, we use templates to quantify the uniformity in the configuration between the devices being used for a particular service. Recall that greater uniformity (i.e., few templates and relatively even spread of templates across PEs) leads to simplicity in service configuration and ease in modifying or evolving it.

In Figure 6 (a), we show the number of templates across devices over time for various services. We observe that the number of templates in VPN-based services (i.e., VPN, DDoS and VoIP) grows more slowly over time compared to the VPLS-based services (i.e., VPLS and Virtual Wire). This can be explained by the fact that VPN and services based on it have been around longer than the VPLS-based services, and hence have had more time to "settle down".

Figure 6 (b) presents the median number of devices that a template is copied on as a fraction of the total number of PE devices for the service. For both sets of services, as the number of templates

rise, we observe a *decrease* in the median number of devices that share a given template, as one would expect.

Next we examine the cause for changes over time in the stanzas that make up templates and in the devices on which templates appear. We consider four types of changes: (1) *no change*: the template contains the same set of stanzas and devices, (2) *grow*: the stanzas within the template are replicated over more devices; (3) *new templates*: new stanzas are introduced to existing or new devices to form a new template, (4) *mutate*: exiting stanzas within the template are further specialized leading to a fragmentation of a template. For example, to add more customer sites to a customer's VPN, the VPN's VRF template is modified by adding configuration commands to specify the new interfaces. Note, while 'mutate' and 'new template' both result in essentially new templates, we differentiate between the two to highlight the number of new templates created by changing existing stanzas. Our observations are shown in Figure 7.

Across all the services, a significant fraction of templates remain unchanged over time. However, we note that significant template changes occur as well. Consider VPN whose relatively stable customer base explains the dominance of 'no change' templates. However, examining the other three categories shows that, over time, a large fraction (30-70%) of templates arise due to flux in the existing set of templates.

Upon closer examination, we find that tasks related to *provisioning of customers* (new or existing) contribute most to the flux in templates. Specifically, we find that 'new' templates are almost always for new customers' configurations which require specialization based on customers' locations; 'grow' corresponds to templates for shared functionality that gets replicated as new PE devices are provisioned (an example is configuration of management functions); finally, changes appear to be occurring in the requirements of existing customers over time, which contributes both to 'grow' and 'mutate' (most of these changes appear to be for customer CoS policies).

For the VPN service, the relative proportion of the four types of template changes remains mostly the same across time. However, the relative proportions change a lot over time for the VPLS and Virtual Wire services, and they reflect the service's evolution. Ini-

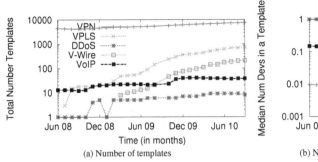
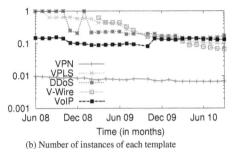

(a) Number of templates   (b) Number of instances of each template

Figure 6: Longitudinal analysis of configuration templates.

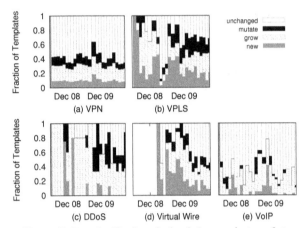

(a) VPN   (b) VPLS

(c) DDoS   (d) Virtual Wire   (e) VoIP

Figure 7: Longitudinal analysis of changes in templates.

tially, when new devices are being introduced, we find that 'new' templates dominate; when the service expands, 'grow' and 'mutate' dominate. Again, we find that customer provisioning contributes significantly to the overall flux in configuration templates.

On the whole, we note that the configuration templates in use constantly grow in number and become increasingly specialized as a service grows and as customer requirements evolve; we study this issue in greater depth in Section 5. The rate of flux in templates depends on how long a service has been offered – relatively new services tend to observe a far greater amount of flux.

Similar to our referential analysis, our analysis of templates indicates that a lot of the complexity arises from provisioning of customers, which includes adding new templates, and changing service definition for subsets of existing customers. The resulting high number of templates means that, for each candidate change to the service, a collection of templates across a small set of devices within the network would require consistent updates. As the service evolves, this would inevitably make key management tasks, especially those related to provisioning, more challenging.

4.2 PE-Core Configuration

Next, we examine configuration changes required to connect the PE devices to the MPLS core. This mainly involves configuring the interface on the core devices and thereby establishing the data plane for the services. We focus on VPLS and VPN. Since DDoS, Virtual Wire, and VoIP are built over VPLS and VPN, our results for VPN and VPLS include PEs used by these three services.

Figure 8 (a) shows the number of existing stanzas that must be changed to set up routing adjacencies over the PE-facing interface. Figure 8 (b) shows the number of interface-specific stanzas that must be set up to ensure that the appropriate data plane policies are applied to the interface, such as policing, queuing and access

control. From (a), we note that, across all three services, most interfaces require configuration of just two stanzas to set up routing (corresponding to IGP and BGP).

From (b), we see that setting up the interface-specific data plane policies appears complex at first glance, requiring the configuration of as many as 20 or so different stanzas for all three services – these stanzas include CoS specifications (class maps and policy maps), and NetFlow configuration. However, as we show in Figure 8 (c), few of these stanzas are "new" across interfaces corresponding to PEs of a particular service. Thus, most core router interfaces appear to be reusing exactly the same data plane policies across PEs for a service. Furthermore, we examined a time series of the stanzas on the core router and found few changes to them over time.

Thus, we conclude from our analysis of the PE-core configuration that: (i) the configuration on the core routers is fairly service-agnostic, and (ii) it is reasonably simple to integrate PEs of new services.

4.3 Control-Plane Configuration

As mentioned earlier, a common approach to designing the control-plane for network-based services is to use the MP-BGP protocol for redistributing routes between different service PEs. In what follows, we analyze the complexity in the configurations of the individual service-specific control-planes.

As shown in Section 2.2.1, BGP peering sessions among route-reflectors are set up by configuring different `neighbor` commands on the routers at both end-points of the peering session. We now examine the extent of referential dependencies underlying the configuration of the route-reflectors for various services.

We observe that the median number of links in the route-reflector referential graph remains stable over time across the services (Figure 9 (a)), but the worst case referential graph link count (Figure 9 (b)) increases over time. This increase is dramatic in the case of the VPLS service. For this service, the growing complexity is purely due to the service growth – growing number of PEs necessitate constant changes to the route-reflectors to maintain connectivity and reachability between the newly added PEs. Further examination reveals that a predominant number of referential links in Figure 9 is specifically due to BGP neighbor commands to set up BGP sessions across PEs.

In Figure 10, we show the relative proportions of stanzas of different types in the route-reflectors for the two services. We see that the relative proportions of the different stanza types vary across the two services. VPLS route-reflectors have about 50% of the stanzas attributed to CoS policies while the VPN route reflectors have only 15% attributed to CoS policies. The differences arise due to the fact that the VPLS service imposes more policies to protect the route-reflectors. For example, while both services restrict access to management services, only VPLS throttles the number of connec-

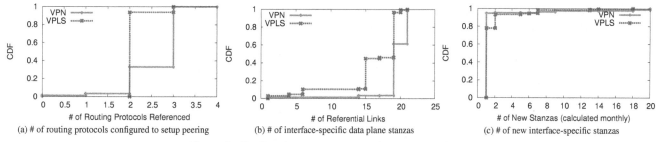

(a) # of routing protocols configured to setup peering (b) # of interface-specific data plane stanzas (c) # of new interface-specific stanzas

Figure 8: Configuring core routers to integrate services.

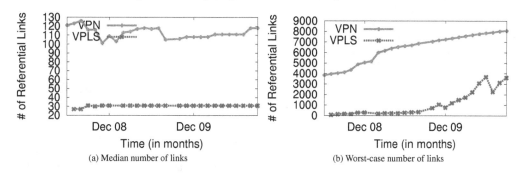

(a) Median number of links (b) Worst-case number of links

Figure 9: Properties of the per-service RR referential graph.

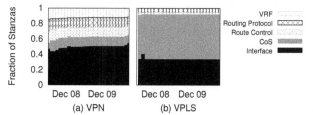

(a) VPN (b) VPLS

Figure 10: Longitudinal analysis of the types of stanzas in the referential graph (Averaged over RRs).

tions to the VPLS route-reflectors. The VPLS route reflectors are more safely guarded because the ratio of PEs to route-reflectors is much larger for the VPLS service than for the VPN service.

In conclusion, we find that the control-planes for the individual network services themselves are complex and distinct from each other, and the complexity grows as services themselves grow. The main reason is the establishment of BGP sessions required for route redistribution.

5. CUSTOMER PROVISIONING UNDER THE MICROSCOPE

In the previous section, we attributed the complexity in PE configurations mainly to customer-specific issues. In this section, we re-examine the referential graphs and templates for the PEs, focusing on the portions of the models created in response to the provisioning of the customers for a service. We compare these portions across different customers and over time. This comparison provides insights into why configuring the same services for different customers increases the complexity significantly rather than modestly. This section focuses on VPN and VPLS customers since customers for the other services are provisioned as part of the VPN/VPLS virtual networks.

Intuitively, we expect that provisioning the same services should entail only a slight change from one customer to the next. Due to the modularity of configuration languages, configuration across customers should differ mainly in a few parameters. Further, con-

figuration stanzas can, in theory, be reused across different customers provisioned on the same devices. However, as we show below, we find that complexity arises because customers often require significantly different configuration due to different ways in which a service is actually used. We find that reuse does exist between customers, but is rather limited.

5.1 Configuration Complexity

We evaluate the complexity of provisioning customers for a service by examining the referential graph on a per PE basis, and the number of templates used by a customer across all PEs.

In Figure 11 (a), we present the number of links in the PE referential graph that pertain to provisioning a customer site for all customers of VPLS and VPN services. In the figure, we observe two small jumps in the CDF for the VPLS service. These two jumps correspond to customers employing a point-to-point service, requiring only four stanzas as shown in Figure 12 (a), and a point-to-multipoint VPLS service, requiring six stanzas as shown in Figure 12 (b). As shown in the figure, VRF and interface stanzas are common to both types of VPLS services. In addition, the point-to-multipoint service requires filters and policers for incoming as well as outgoing traffic. Since point-to-point service only has two end-points, filters and policers for outgoing traffic are not required once they are applied to the incoming traffic.

Although some of the jumps in the number of referential links required for different customers of the VPN service (in Figure 11 (a)) arises for reasons similar to the VPLS services, remaining jumps are due to other reasons. The jumps at x equal to three and five are due to a VPN-equivalent of the VPLS point-to-point and point-to-multipoint services. However, the jumps at seven and fifteen are due to customers which require fine-grained control over CoS accorded to their traffic. The policies for these users divide traffic into different classes based on ToS/precedence fields, with each class getting a different treatment. For these customers, complexity increases because configuring the service requires references to a few policy maps which in turn reference class maps. The sharp jump at sixteen represents customers which require both fine-grained control over traffic as well as over how routes are redistributed in the

VPN. The customers use route-maps and community-list to filter out updates received from the route-reflectors. Finally, the tail is due to configuration of customer end-points on a PE from a different vendor. (We explore differences due to vendor configuration languages in greater detail in Section 6.1.)

Next, in Figure 11 (b), we examine the CDF of the number of templates used for provisioning the virtual networks of each customer. Most customers have a small number of templates: 90% of the customers have less than three templates. However, a small number of customers have a large number of templates. The differences between the tails for the two services arise because of the size of the customer's virtual networks. Customers with large virtual networks have sites with specialized configuration to overcome scale limitations; these require large number of templates resulting from the differences in the setup of VRFs across different sites.

To summarize, our findings are: (i) significant differences exist between customers of a service, (ii) these differences affect the difficulty of provisioning customers, and (iii) a small number of customers lead to high complexity in PE configuration.

5.2 Configuration Reuse

In this section, we aim to understand whether and how configuration reuse simplifies the action of customer provisioning. To do this, we examine the extent of such reuse both in provisioning individual customer sites as well as across the entire network. We start by analyzing reuse amongst the stanzas that exist within a PE. Next, we examine the amount of reuse amongst the stanzas in templates that are shared accross PEs.

In Figure 13 (a), we present the CDF of the fraction of the total number of stanzas in the referential graph that are reused for provisioning different customers of a service. Similar to the previous section, we limit out analysis to one customer -facing interface. We define a stanza in the referential graph to be reused, if at least two different stanzas explicitly refer to it, indicating that these two stanzas actively depend on it. We observe that although a significant amount of reuse exists (e.g., 40% of VPN customers reuse $\geq$ 75% of stanzas within a PE), there is never complete reuse in provisioning a customer. For VPLS, this occurs because at least two stanzas related to the configuration of the customer-facing interface and the VRF on it must be unique per interface. For VPN, limited reuse is due to the differences in policies that we described earlier in this section.

Using the templates, we extend the definition of reuse beyond a device to the entire network. We define a stanza in the referential graph as being reused if the stanza is in a template (indicating use across multiple devices). We observe, in Figure 13 (b), that using this definition of reuse brings downs the number of customers with no reuse (the jump at zero drops across all services). The CDFs shift down because while some policies are not shared by customers set up on a PE, these policies are shared by customers on different PEs. This indicates that certain customers have more in common with customers on other PEs than on their own PE. However, despite this sharing across customers, there is still a need for specialized stanzas as is evident from the fact that reuse is still limited.

Next in Figure 13 (c), we compare reuse over time for the VPN service. We observe that the fraction of unique stanzas grows over time indicating that customer provisioning does not become simpler, as the number of configuration stanzas being reused actually goes down. This observation also holds true for the VPLS service; however, we omit results due to space constraints.

Customers of the VPN service are in general more difficult to set up (i.e., referential graphs are larger) than customers of the VPLS

service, especially for VPN customers employing some of the complex usage patterns discussed earlier in this section. Further, the larger number of usage patterns mean that reuse is less prevalent across VPN customers. The consequences of this are twofold: first, given the same number of customers, the configuration on a VPLS PE should grow much more slowly than on a VPN PE; and second, much of the complexity on VPN PEs is unavoidable, and required to implement large number of distinct usage patterns.

To summarize, we find that: (i) overlap exists between the configuration required to provision a customer for a particular service; (ii) configuring a customer still requires unique elements that other customers on the same PE or even across the entire network do not require; (iii) this kind of specialization leads to increased complexity in customer provisioning; and (iv) the extent of specialization increases with time.

6. TRADE-OFFS IN CONFIGURATION COMPLEXITY

Our focus so far has been on evaluating the complexity of the configurations underlying network-based services. We found customer provisioning and the service control-planes contribute significantly to the complexity. Since configuration is a crucial aspect of a service's design, it is important to control the complexity arising from the above two causes. Despite this, whether it is actually possible to mitigate complexity depends on other important factors. In this section, we examine two such factors – choice of vendor for devices and performance/scalability constraints – and show how to make systematic choices that result in simpler configurations (where possible, given the constraints) for customer provisioning and control-plane design.

6.1 Choice of Vendor

Configuration languages of different vendors often vary a lot in language constructs, syntax and modularity. These differences affect the complexity of configuring the same functionality across devices from different vendors. Although configuration complexity has a huge bearing on service manageability, ISPs do not always choose their vendors solely based on ease or difficulty of configuring services on their devices. Other factors such as functionality and features, performance, price and management support play an equally important role.

To understand the impact of vendor on configuration complexity, we focus on the VPN service since it is a large service with PEs from different vendors. More specifically, we focus on customers whose sites are connected to PEs from different vendors. This allows us to perform a head-to-head comparison across vendors. The focus of this comparison is to examine the complexity of implementing the same policy across the two vendors and not to examine the complexity of the policy being implemented.

In Figure 14, we compare the configurations of the customers on the VPN service according to their referential dependencies. We use our model to compare the complexity of how configuration languages are used, and not the inherent complexity of the languages. Our results show that it is simpler to configure end-points on Vendor-1 than on Vendor-2: Vendor-2's configuration language requires more stanzas to express the exact same route control and CoS policies. For example, Vendor-1's language uses a combination of one route-map and several community lists to control the set of routes accepted into the VRF. Vendor-2, however, uses six different maps: two for input and four for output with each using on average two different community lists.

Since vendor configuration languages appear to play a role in

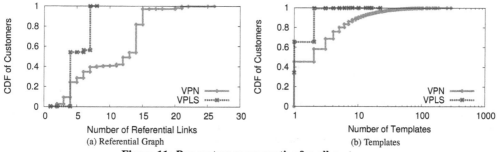

(a) Referential Graph   (b) Templates

Figure 11: Per customer properties for all customers.

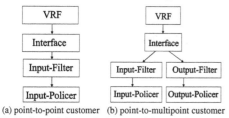

(a) point-to-point customer   (b) point-to-multipoint customer

Figure 12: Referential graph for provisioning VPLS customers.

	mesh	hub and spoke	multi-hub and spoke
# Routes (Spoke)	CE	$1 + C$	$1 + C$
# Routes (Hub)	n/a	CE	CE
# Routes (Total)	CE^2	$CE + (C+1)(E-1)$	$CEH + (C+1)(E-H)$
# Templates	1	2	$2H$
# Referential Links	0	0	0

Table 2: Number of routes and difficulty for maintaining each of the different VPN designs. Here, C is the number of customer routes, E is the number of customer sites, and H is the number of hubs.

determining the configuration complexity of customer end-points, an appropriate choice of vendors could lead to a significantly simpler configuration during provisioning, thereby improving service manageability.

6.2 Choices Based on Resource Limits

Due to resource limitations, operators are often forced to trade-off a simple design for an efficient but more complex design. In this section, we present the implications of such design choices on a service's configuration, and highlight how certain choices, while substantially reducing the resource usage, introduce little complexity, whereas other choices involving a slight reduction in resource usage can significantly increase the complexity of the service. We illustrate this by (i) examining connectivity between customer sites, a key issue tied to provisioning; and (ii) the performance/scalability trade-offs made in configuring the per-service control-plane.

6.2.1 Connectivity between Customer Sites

The connectivity between customer sites in a VPN, i.e., which sites can communicate directly with one another, has a significant bearing on the resource usage. Typical choices available to ISPs are: (i) full mesh, where every site is allowed to communicate directly with every other site; (ii) hub and spoke, where one customer site is chosen as a hub, while the rest are chosen as spokes; communication between spoke sites is only allowed through the hub site; and (iii) multi-hub and spoke, where a few customer sites are chosen as hubs, while the rest are chosen as spokes and assigned to specific hubs. The mesh configuration is usually employed by default, but depending on the traffic matrix among customer sites, one of the other choices could be employed [22]. The design changes over time in response to changes in the traffic matrix.

The hub and spoke design can offer significant savings in the number of routes stored by a VRF in the PE's forwarding table, which is often a critical resource for ISPs. This is because routes learned from a spoke site need to be propagated only to the hub site and not to other spoke sites. Thus, PEs with the spoke VRFs only need to store routes learned from the attached VRFs and a default route from all hubs in the VRF's virtual network. However, the savings in VRF space comes at the expense of additional latency the customer incurs for inter-spoke communication as well as extra bandwidth consumed by such traffic on the ISP's network.

In Table 2, we present the trade-offs between different choices in

terms of the amount of state and the number of templates required to realize different configurations. From the table, we observe that *given the choice between a mesh and hub and spoke design, the operator should choose hub and spoke* as it provides a large reduction in state with minimal configuration overhead. However, when *given the choice between mesh and multi-hub and spoke, the choice is not as clear, and depends on the properties of the virtual network.*

To illustrate, we present a simple example of a customer VPN with ten sites and 40 routes advertised by each customer's site. For this customer, full mesh ensures a single template but requires 400 routes in the VRF for each site. Transitioning to a hub and spoke reduces the VRF size to 41 at all but one PE, and increases the number of templates only to two. Finally, a transition from hub and spoke to a multi-hub and spoke with five hubs and one spoke per hub, increases the number of templates from two to ten and increases the VRF sizes to 400 at four sites. Thus, there is a significant increase in complexity but not a commensurate improvement in state. If the customer's traffic patterns allows a set up containing 3 hubs and 2-3 spokes per hub, then using multi-hub and spoke can result in significant state improvement relative to mesh (4000 vs 1487 routes per VRF) at low added complexity (1 vs 6 templates).

Conversations with the operators of the network indicate that the discussion above indeed crystallizes a trade-off they are facing in reality: for several VPN customers, the ISP is considering using multi-hub and spoke, but the design complexity is preventing operators from implementing it.

6.2.2 MP-BGP Route Distribution

The most common question for the MP-BGP control-plane is how to interconnect PEs for exchanging routes. Typical choices available to an ISP are: (i) full mesh, where every PE is connected to every other PE; (ii) route-reflectors, where every PE is connected to a set of route-reflectors (RRs), and routes between PEs are exchanged via RRs; and (iii) multi-plane route-reflectors [19], a recent proposal where RRs are divided into "planes", and those in a given plane only learn and distribute a subset of routes.

While making a choice, operators examine the number of peering sessions that PEs and RRs need to maintain, as well as the number of routes that RRs need to maintain. Depending on these parameters, operators choose a design that minimizes resource consump-

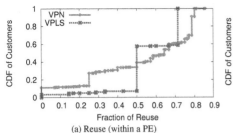

(a) Reuse (within a PE)

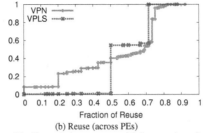

(b) Reuse (across PEs)

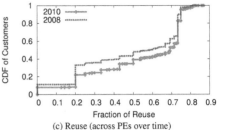

(c) Reuse (across PEs over time)

Figure 13: Examining reuse within a network.

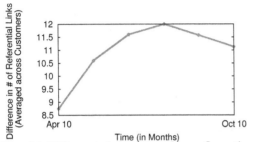

Figure 14: Differences between vendor configuration.

	mesh	Route-Reflectors	Multiplane Route-Reflectors
# Peering (PE)	N	2	2
# Peering (RR)	n/a	N	N
# Peering (Total)	$N(N-1)$	$R(R-1)+2N$	$M(R/M * (R/M - 1)) + 2N + M(M-1)$
# Routes (PE)	T	T	T/M
# Routes (RR)	T	T	T/M
# Templates	1	2	$2M$
# Referential Links	$N(N-1)$	$R(R-1)+2N$	$M(R/M * (R/M - 1)) + 2N + M(M-1)$

Table 3: Number of peering sessions, routes and difficulty for maintaining each of the different BGP control-plane designs. Here, N is the number of PEs, R is the number of route-reflectors, M is the number of different planes, and T the total number of routes contributed by all customers. We also assume that each PE is connected to two RRs for robustness purposes.

tion on PEs for maintaining peering sessions, including exchange of routing state.

In Table 3, we present the trade-offs between different designs. We examine the trade-off not only in the traditional terms of the number of peering sessions, the number of devices, and the size of the routing tables transferred, but also in terms of the configuration complexity (i.e., the number of templates and the size of the referential graphs).

From Table 3, we observe that a tremendous amount of reduction in the number of peering sessions arises by switching from the mesh to a single plane route-reflector setup, with only a modest change in the number of templates from one to two. Thus, *mesh is clearly inferior to using route-reflectors.*

However, with the multi-plane route reflector setup, the complexity may increase significantly. We illustrate this with a simple example. Consider an ISP service with 2,000 PEs, 50 RRs in a single plane, and 20,000 customer routes. For a single plane route-reflector design, the resulting number of peering sessions is 6,450 and each RR has to maintain 20,000 routes. However, if the ISP switches to a multi-plane solution with ten planes, the total number of peering sessions goes down to 4,290 while the number of routes in each RR is reduced to 2,000. This reduction in memory and peering sessions comes at a price though as the configuration complexity increases due to loss in uniformity – the number of templates used grows from 2 to 20 in this case. Thus, *the choice of multi-plane and its set up (i.e., number of planes) must be made carefully to ensure that the increase in the configuration complexity remains low.*

7. DISCUSSION

We describe key implications of our work on other proposals for network-based service design, as well as on tools for service configuration management. We then describe some limitations of our work.

Implications for other work on network-based services. Several prior works on network-based services have focused on issues related to the performance of the services (see for example, prior work which explores the reduction of VPN memory consumption [22, 14, 23, 6], diagnoses VPN problems [26], or models the usage patterns of IPTV networks [20, 21]). Our study is compli-

mentary as it shows that many of the proposed changes may require intricate (re)configuration which could make future changes to services hard. This aspect of service design should be considered as an equally important requirement to understand if the proposals are attractive in practice.

Configuration management. Our study also has implications for common configuration management tools. For example, our results show that template-based tools such as Presto [9], while effective for general management of an ISP's devices may prove inadequate for configuration management of certain services. For example, Presto may not really simplify PE configuration in VPNs, where the number of templates is very large (Section 4.1.2). In general, given the complexity underlying most services, a simpler alternative in the long term may be to configure and manage services through the use of new architectures, e.g, 4D [12], that eliminate the need for low-level configuration by allowing operators to specify high-level network policies and invariants.

Applicability to other ISPs. While we studied a single tier-1 ISP, we believe that our insights have a general applicability to the deployment of network-based services in other ISPs since most tier-1 ISPs utilize similar technologies to realize network-based services. For example, in deploying telepresence, a regional ISP on the west coast uses Cisco H323 gatekeepers as PEs to differentiate customers and employs similar trade-offs as discussed in Section 6.2 to configure the control-plane between these gatekeepers.

Limitations. End-to-end configuration of a service includes not only provider side mechanisms but also customer side configuration. Due to data limitations, our study focused mainly on the former. We leave a study of customer side (CE) configuration issues for future work. We also note that our work focuses on the configurations of devices used in network services, and related factors such as the vendors in use and resource limitations faced. A more comprehensive study of challenges and trade-offs in services, however, requires considering cost, ease of troubleshooting in alternate designs, and limitations imposed due to available functionality in various devices.

8. RELATED WORK

Our study is motivated by, and complimentary to, prior work that highlights the complexity in configuring Class-of-Service [24] and BGP policies [16, 10] in ISP networks. The latter also highlights the relatively high incidence of errors in BGP configuration, and blames the poorly designed router configuration languages for many of the errors. Note that our study examines complexity *given* commonly-used configuration languages, but it does not examine how much of this complexity arises from the basic design of these languages themselves. We leave this for future work.

While we focus on complexity within an ISP's network configuration, prior works [7, 15, 18, 11] have focused on the causes for complexity in enterprises. These studies found core enterprise network designs to be complex due to the usage of VLANs, route-redistribution commands, and network security and filtering policies. For ISP network services, we find that a significant amount of complexity can be attributed to the configuration of customer virtual networks at the edge, which involves the usage of CoS, VRFs, and route control stanzas, while the core network itself is simple.

The models we employed in this study are similar to those used in [7] to study enterprise networks, but with key extensions to focus on network-based services and the unique functionality found in ISP networks (e.g., the extensive use of route-reflectors, MPLS and router virtualization).

Finally, our study adds to a growing body of work that has found mining configurations to be a useful way to obtain insights about networks. E.g., recent works [17, 25] have used configuration files to perform root cause analysis, and troubleshooting of anomalies and performance problems in ISPs.

9. CONCLUSIONS

The usage and deployment of network-based services is growing as ISPs aim to provide advanced features to residential and enterprise customers. In this paper, we present the first large-scale analysis of these services, focusing on their design and configuration. We study several years' worth of configuration data corresponding to five services in a tier-1 ISP. We decompose the configurations into various tasks performed by operators and systematically highlight the complexity underlying each. We show that complexity grows over time. We find that while the exact causes of complexity may differ across different services, two factors – customer provisioning differences and control-plane (BGP) configuration – consistently make the overall designs complex. We conclude the study by exploring ways to reduce complexity, specifically, by considering the alternatives in, and the trade-offs imposed by, factors such as the choice of vendors and resource scaling.

We hope that our findings can lead to a broader discussion on understanding service configurations, on the design of both service-specific and service-agnostic support mechanisms, and potentially on alternate network architectures and router mechanisms with much better intrinsic support for network-based services.

10. ACKNOWLEDGMENTS

We would like to thank the operations team at the tier-1 ISP for providing the data and documentation about the services. We would also like to thank Katerina Argyraki (our shepherd), Aaron Gember, Seungjoon Lee, Kobus van der Merwe, Dan Pei, Kevin D'Souza, Adrian Cepleanu, Stephen Hutnik, Maria Napierala and the anonymous reviewers for their insightful feedback. This work is supported in part by NSF grants CNS-0746531, CNS-1017545 and CNS-1050170. Theophilus Benson is supported by an IBM PhD Fellowship.

11. REFERENCES

[1] Cisco visual networking index: Forecast and methodology, 2009-2014. http://www.cisco.com/en/US/solutions/collateral/ns341/ns525/ns537/ns705/ns827/white_paper_c11-481360_ns827_Networking_Solutions_White_Paper.html.

[2] Virtual routing and forwarding. http://www.cisco.com/en/US/docs/net_mgmt/active_network_abstraction/3.7/reference/guide/vrf.html.

[3] Virtual routing and forwarding. http://www.juniper.net/techpubs/software/junos/junos61/swconfig61-routing/html/instance-overview.html#1017937.

[4] T. Bates, R. Chandra, D. Katz, and Y. Rekhter. Multiprotocol Extensions for BGP-4. RFC 4760 (Draft Standard), Jan. 2007.

[5] T. Bates, E. Chen, and R. Chandra. BGP Route Reflection: An Alternative to Full Mesh Internal BGP (IBGP). RFC 4456 (Draft Standard), Apr. 2006.

[6] Z. ben Houidi and M. Meulle. A new VPN routing approach for large scale networks. In *Proc. IEEE ICNP*, 2010.

[7] T. Benson, A. Akella, and D. A. Maltz. Unraveling the complexity of network management. In *NSDI*, April 2009.

[8] D. Caldwell, A. Gilbert, J. Gottlieb, A. Greenberg, G. Hjalmtysson, and J. Rexford. The cutting edge of IP router configuration. In *In Proc. of Hotnets-II*, 2003.

[9] W. Enck, P. Mcdaniel, A. Greenberg, S. Sen, P. Sebos, S. Spoerel, and S. Rao. Configuration management at massive scale: System design and experience. In *In 2007 USENIX ATC*, pages 73–86, 2007.

[10] N. Feamster and H. Balakrishnan. Detecting BGP configuration faults with static analysis. In *Proceedings of USENIX NSDI*, pages 43–56, Berkeley, CA, USA, 2005.

[11] P. Garimella, Y.-W. E. Sung, N. Zhang, and S. Rao. Characterizing VLAN usage in an operational network. In *ACM INM '07*, pages 305–306, New York, NY, USA, 2007.

[12] A. Greenberg, G. Hjalmtysson, D. A. Maltz, A. Myers, J. Rexford, G. Xie, H. Yan, J. Zhan, and H. Zhang. A clean slate 4D approach to network control and management. *SIGCOMM Comput. Commun. Rev.*, 35(5):41–54, 2005.

[13] T. Kamiya, S. Kusumoto, and K. Inoue. Ccfinder: a multilinguistic token-based code clone detection system for large scale source code. *IEEE Trans. Softw. Eng.*, 28(7), 2002.

[14] C. Kim, A. Gerber, C. Lund, D. Pei, and S. Sen. Scalable VPN routing via relaying. In *Proceedings of SIGMETRICS*, pages 61–72, New York, NY, USA, 2008. ACM.

[15] F. Le, G. G. Xie, D. Pei, J. Wang, and H. Zhang. Shedding light on the glue logic of the Internet routing architecture. In *Proceedings of ACM SIGCOMM*, pages 39–50, New York, NY, USA, 2008.

[16] R. Mahajan, D. Wetherall, and T. Anderson. Understanding BGP misconfiguration. In *Proceedings of ACM SIGCOMM*, pages 3–16, New York, NY, USA, 2002.

[17] A. A. Mahimkar, H. H. Song, Z. Ge, A. Shaikh, J. Wang, J. Yates, Y. Zhang, and J. Emmons. Detecting the performance impact of upgrades in large operational networks. In *Proceedings of ACM SIGCOMM*, pages 303–314, New York, NY, USA, 2010.

[18] D. A. Maltz, G. Xie, J. Zhan, H. Zhang, G. Hjálmtýsson, and A. Greenberg. Routing design in operational networks: a look from the inside. In *Proceedings of ACM SIGCOMM*, pages 27–40, New York, NY, USA, 2004.

[19] M. Napierala. AT&T MPLS network and VPN services. PLNOG, 2008.

[20] T. Qiu, Z. Ge, S. Lee, J. Wang, J. Xu, and Q. Zhao. Modeling user activities in a large IPTV system. In *Proceedings of ACM IMC*, pages 430–441, New York, NY, USA, 2009.

[21] T. Qiu, Z. Ge, S. Lee, J. Wang, Q. Zhao, and J. Xu. Modeling channel popularity dynamics in a large IPTV system. In *Proceedings of ACM SIGMETRICS*, pages 275–286, New York, NY, USA, 2009.

[22] S. Raghunath and K. K. Ramakrishnan. Trade-offs in resource management for Virtual Private Networks. In *Proc. IEEE INFOCOM*, 2005.

[23] S. Raghunath, K. K. Ramakrishnan, and S. Kalyanaraman. Measurement-based characterization of IP VPNs. *IEEE/ACM Trans. Netw.*, 15:1428–1441, December 2007.

[24] Y.-W. E. Sung, C. Lund, M. Lyn, S. G. Rao, and S. Sen. Modeling and understanding end-to-end class of service policies in operational networks. In *Proceedings of SIGCOMM*, pages 219–230, New York, NY, USA, 2009. ACM.

[25] D. Turner, K. Levchenko, A. C. Snoeren, and S. Savage. California fault lines: understanding the causes and impact of network failures. In *Proceedings of ACM SIGCOMM*, pages 315–326, New York, NY, USA, 2010.

[26] Y. Zhao, Z. Zhu, Y. Chen, D. Pei, and J. Wang. Towards efficient large-scale VPN monitoring and diagnosis under operational constraints. In *Proc. IEEE INFOCOM*, pages 531–539, 2009.

Seamless Network-Wide IGP Migrations[*]

Laurent Vanbever[*], Stefano Vissicchio[†],
Cristel Pelsser[‡], Pierre Francois[*], Olivier Bonaventure[*]

[*] Université catholique de Louvain [†] Roma Tre University [‡] Internet Initiative Japan
[*]{laurent.vanbever, pierre.francois, olivier.bonaventure} @uclouvain.be
[†]vissicch@dia.uniroma3.it   [‡]cristel@iij.ad.jp

ABSTRACT

Network-wide migrations of a running network, such as the replacement of a routing protocol or the modification of its configuration, can improve the performance, scalability, manageability, and security of the entire network. However, such migrations are an important source of concerns for network operators as the reconfiguration campaign can lead to long and service-affecting outages.

In this paper, we propose a methodology which addresses the problem of seamlessly modifying the configuration of commonly used link-state Interior Gateway Protocols (IGP). We illustrate the benefits of our methodology by considering several migration scenarios, including the addition or the removal of routing hierarchy in an existing IGP and the replacement of one IGP with another. We prove that a strict operational ordering can guarantee that the migration will not create IP transit service outages. Although finding a safe ordering is NP-complete, we describe techniques which efficiently find such an ordering and evaluate them using both real-world and inferred ISP topologies. Finally, we describe the implementation of a provisioning system which automatically performs the migration by pushing the configurations on the routers in the appropriate order, while monitoring the entire migration process.

Categories and Subject Descriptors: C.2.3 [Computer-Communication Networks]: Network Operations

General Terms: Algorithms, Management, Reliability

Keywords: Interior Gateway Protocol (IGP), configuration, migration, summarization, design guidelines

1. INTRODUCTION

Among all network routing protocols, link-state Interior Gateway Protocols (IGPs), like IS-IS and OSPF, play a critical role. Indeed, an IGP enables end-to-end reachability

---

[*]Minor typo corrected in Section 2.1

between any pair of routers within the network of an Autonomous System (AS). Many other routing protocols, like BGP, LDP or PIM, also rely on an IGP to properly work. As the network grows or when new services have to be deployed, network operators often need to perform large-scale IGP reconfiguration [1]. Migrating an IGP is a complex process since all the routers have to be reconfigured in a proper manner. Simple solutions like restarting the network with the new configurations do not work since most of the networks carry traffic 24/7. Therefore, IGP migrations have to be performed gradually, while the network is running. Such operations can lead to significant traffic losses if they are not handled with care. Unfortunately, network operators typically lack appropriate tools and techniques to seamlessly perform large, highly distributed changes to the configuration of their networks. They also experience difficulties in understanding what is happening during a migration since complex interactions may arise between upgraded and non-upgraded routers. Consequently, as confirmed by many private communications with operators, large-scale IGP migrations are often avoided until they are absolutely necessary, thus hampering network evolvability and innovation.

Most of the time, network operators target three aspects of the IGP when they perform large-scale migrations. First, they may want to replace the current protocol with another. For instance, several operators have switched from OSPF to IS-IS because IS-IS is known to be more secure against control-plane attacks [2, 3]. Operators may also want to migrate to an IGP that is not dependent on the address family (e.g., OSPFv3, IS-IS) in order to run only one IGP to route both IPv4 and IPv6 traffic [4, 3], or to change IGP in order to integrate new equipments which are not compliant with the adopted one [5]. Second, when the number of routers exceeds a certain critical mass, operators often introduce a hierarchy within their IGP to limit the control-plane stress [6, 7]. Removing a hierarchy might also be needed, for instance, to better support some traffic engineering extensions [8]. Another reason operators introduce hierarchy is to have more control on route propagation by tuning the way routes are propagated from one portion of the hierarchy to another [1]. Third, network operators also modify the way the IGP learns or announces the prefixes by introducing or removing route summarization. Route summarization is an efficient way to reduce the number of entries in the routing tables of the routers as IGP networks can currently track as many as 10,000 prefixes [9]. Route summarization also helps improving the stability by limiting the visibility of local events. Actually, some IGP migrations combine several of these scenarios, such as the migration from a hierarchical OSPF to a flat IS-IS [2]. There have also been cases where, after having performed a migration, the network no longer met the original requirements, forcing the operators to fallback to the initial configuration [10]. Finally, given the recent trend of deploying virtual networks [11, 12], we believe that the need for reconfiguring the IGP will become more frequent.

In this paper, we aim at enabling *seamless IGP migrations*, that is, progressive modifications of the IGP configuration of a running network without loosing packets. Our main contribution is threefold. First, we analyze in detail the various scenarios of link-state IGP migrations and explain problems that can arise. In particular, we show that long-lasting forwarding loops can appear, both theoretically and practically, when modifications are made to the IGP hierarchy and when route summarization is introduced or removed. To deal with all the identified migration problems, we propose a generic IGP model. Second, we show that, in real-world networks, it is possible to find an ordering for the configuration changes that prevents forwarding loops. Although finding such an ordering is an NP-complete problem, we propose algorithms and heuristics and we show their practical effectiveness on several ISP networks. Furthermore, we describe how our techniques can be extended to prevent congestion and deal with network failures. Third, we describe the design and the evaluation of a complete system that automates the whole migration process. Our system generates router configurations, assesses the proper state of the network and updates all the routers in an appropriate sequence.

The rest of the paper is structured as follows. Section 2 provides a background on link-state IGPs and presents our abstract model. Section 3 formalizes the IGP migration problem and describes the migration scenarios we tackle. Section 4 presents our methodology. Section 5 proposes algorithms to compute a loop-free migration ordering. Section 6 presents our implementation. Section 7 evaluates our migration techniques on both inferred and real-world topologies. Section 8 defines design guidelines that make IGP migrations easier. Section 9 presents related work. Section 10 discusses the limitation of the approach and the impact on BGP. Finally, Section 11 contains the conclusions.

2. LINK-STATE INTERIOR GATEWAY PROTOCOLS

In this section, we summarize the most important features of link-state IGPs. Then, we present the model we use throughout the paper.

2.1 Background

An IGP is a protocol that routers use to decide how to forward packets within an AS. IGPs are divided in two main families: distance-vector and link-state protocols. Although some enterprise networks still use distance-vector protocols, most ISPs and large enterprises deploy link-state IGPs, namely OSPF [13] or IS-IS [14]. In this paper, we focus on network-wide migrations of link-state IGPs.

Link-state IGPs can be configured either in a flat or in a hierarchical *mode*. In flat IGPs, every router is aware of the entire network topology and forwards IP packets according to the shortest-paths towards their respective destinations.

In hierarchical IGPs, routers are not guaranteed to always prefer the shortest paths. Hierarchical IGP configurations break the whole topology into a set of *zones* (called areas in OSPF and levels in IS-IS), which we denote as $B, Z_1, \ldots, Z_k$. B is a special zone, called *backbone*, that connects all the other *peripheral zones* together, such that packets from a router in the network to a destination inside a different zone always traverse the backbone. IGP routers establish adjacencies, that could be represented as links in a logical graph. Each link in the logical graph belongs to only one zone. By extension, we say that a router is in a zone if it has at least one link in that zone. We call *internal routers* the routers that are in one zone only and *Zone Border Routers* (ZBRs) (e.g., ABRs in OSPF and L1L2 systems in IS-IS) the routers that are in more than one zone, among which there must be the backbone. Both internal routers and ZBRs *prefer intra-zone over inter-zone paths*. This means that, to choose the path on which to forward packets towards a certain destination, each router prefers a path in which all the links belong to the same zone over a path containing at least one link belonging to a different zone, no matter the weight of the two paths.

Moreover, in hierarchical IGPs, ZBRs can be configured to perform *route summarization*. In this configuration, ZBRs hide the internal topology of a zone Z to routers in different zones, advertising aggregated prefixes outside Z. In practice, they announce their ability to reach groups of destinations with paths of a certain weight. The weight announced by a ZBR is the same for all the destinations in an aggregated prefix and either it is customly configured or it is decided on the basis of the actual weights of the preferred paths towards that destinations (e.g., picking the highest one [13]).

2.2 An Abstract Model for IGPs

In this section, we aim at capturing IGP configurations and forwarding behavior of routers in a model that abstracts protocol-specific details. Transient IGP behaviors are not modeled since we ensure that both the initial and the final IGPs have converged before starting the migration process (see Section 4).

We formally define an *IGP configuration* as a tuple $< p, G, D, w, m >$. In such a tuple, p is the identifier of an IGP protocol, e.g., OSPF or IS-IS, and m is the mode in which the protocol is configured, namely flat or hierarchical. $G = (V, E)$ is the *logical graph*, i.e., a directed graph that represents the IGP adjacencies among routers participating in p. Each node in V represents an IGP router, and each edge in E represents an adjacency on which the two routers are allowed to exchange protocol-specific messages. Edges are labeled with additional information. In hierarchical configurations they are labeled with the name of zones they belong to. Moreover, $D \subseteq V$ is a set of IGP *destinations* for traffic that flows in the network. We associate each destination to a single node in G, assuming that each IP prefix is announced by one router only. This assumption is without loss of generality, as we can use virtual nodes to model peculiarities of the considered IGP (see [15]). To be as generic as possible, we consider as destinations a subset of the IGP routers. Finally, the function $w : E \to \mathbb{N}$ associates a positive integer, called *weight*, to each edge in G.

Packets destined to one router $d \in D$ follow paths on G. A forwarding path or simply *path* P on G is denoted as

$P = (s\ r_1\ \ldots\ r_k\ d)$, where s is the first router in G that is required to forward packets destined to d, and routers r_i, with $i = 1, \ldots, k$, are routers traversed by the traffic flow. The weight of a path is the sum of the weights of all the links in the path.

According to the IGP configuration, each router chooses its preferred path towards each destination and forwards packets to the next-hops in such preferred paths. To capture this behavior, we define the *next-hop* function nh, and the *actual path* function $\pi(u, d, t)$. We denote with $nh(u, d, t)$ the set of successors (next-hops) of u in the paths router u uses at time t to send traffic destined to destination d. Notice that $|nh(u, d, t)|$ is not guaranteed to be equal to 1, since our model encompasses the case in which routers uses multiple paths to reach the same destination, e.g., Equal Cost Multi-Path (ECMP). The paths actually followed by packets sent by u towards d at time t can be computed as a function π: $\pi(u, d, t)$ is the set of paths resulting from a recursive concatenation of next-hops. More formally, $\pi(u, d, t)$ is a function that associates to each router u the set of paths $\{(v_0\ v_1\ \ldots\ v_k)\}$, such that $v_0 = u$, $v_k = d$ and $v_{i+1} \in nh(v_i, d, t)$, $\forall i \in \{0, \ldots, k-1\}$. Notice that the actual path function does not always coincide with the preferred path of each router, since deflections can happen in the middle of a path [16]. A series of deflections can even build a forwarding loop, as shown in different examples described in Section 3.1. More formally, we say that there exists a *forwarding loop*, or simply a *loop*, for a certain destination d at a certain time t if $\exists r$ such that $\pi(r, d, t) = (r\ v_0\ \ldots\ v_j\ r)$, with $j \geq 0$.

By appropriately tuning the next-hop function, our model is able to represent specific details of IGP configurations such as the corresponding forwarding rules in hierarchical and flat mode, and route summarization. In Section 3.1, we provide some examples of next-hop functions, actual path functions, and migration loops in different migration scenarios.

3. THE IGP MIGRATION PROBLEM

In this section, we study the problem of seamlessly migrating a network from one IGP configuration to another. Both configurations are provided as an input (i.e., by network operators) and are loop-free.

PROBLEM 1. *Given a unicast IP network, how can we replace an initial IGP configuration with a final IGP configuration without causing any forwarding loop?*

Assuming no congestion and no network failures, solving this problem leads to seamless migrations. These assumptions are reasonable, since management operations are typically performed during convenient time slots, in which traffic is low. Moreover, our approach is time efficient, reducing the opportunities for failures during the migration process. Also, we discuss how to extend our techniques to remove these assumptions in Section 5.2.

In the rest of the paper, we call *router migration* the replacement of nh_{init} with nh_{final} on one router. Formally, we define the operation of *migrating a router* r at a certain time $\bar{t}$, the act of configuring the router such that $nh(r, d, t) = nh_{final}(r, d)$, $\forall d \in D$ and $\forall t > \bar{t}$. Since only one IGP can be configured to control the forwarding of each router (i.e., either the initial or the final), routers cannot be migrated on a per-destination basis. We call *router migration ordering* the ordering in which routers are migrated. A

scenario	IGP configuration changes
protocol	protocol replacement
flat2hier	zones introduction
hier2flat	zones removal
hier2hier	zones reshaping
summarization	summarization introduction/removal

Table 1: IGP Migration Scenarios.

network migration is completed when all routers have been migrated.

Throughout the paper, we consider only *migration loops*, that is, loops arising during an IGP migration because of a non-safe router migration ordering. Migration loops are not-protocol dependant, and can be longer and more harmful than loops that arise during protocol convergence, since migration loops last until specific routers are migrated (e.g., see Section 3.1). Observe that, if the nh function does not change, the π function does not change either, hence any migration order does not create loops during the migration.

3.1 IGP migration scenarios

Table 1 presents the IGP migration scenarios we address in this paper. We believe that those scenarios cover most of the network-wide IGP migrations that real-world ISPs can encounter. Each scenario concerns the modification of a specific feature of the IGP configuration. Moreover, different scenarios can be combined if more than one feature of the IGP configuration have to be changed. We do not consider the change of link weights as a network-wide migration. Since traffic matrices tend to be almost stable over time [17], ISPs can prefer to progressively change the weight of few links at a time. Effective techniques have been already proposed for the graceful change of few link weights [18, 19, 20, 21, 22]. Nevertheless, our generalized model and the techniques we present in Section 5 can also be used when link weights have to be changed. In the following, we describe the issues that must be addressed in each scenario using the notation introduced in Section 2.2.

Protocol replacement

This migration scenario consists of replacing the running IGP protocol, but keeping the same nh function in the initial and in the final configurations. A classical example of such a scenario is the replacement of an OSPF configuration with the corresponding IS-IS configuration [1]. Since the nh function is the same in both IGPs, routers could be migrated in any order without creating loops.

Hierarchy modification

Three migration scenarios are encompassed by the modification of the IGP hierarchy. First, a flat IGP can be replaced by a hierarchical IGP by introducing several zones. Second, a hierarchical IGP can be migrated into a flat IGP by removing peripheral zones and keeping only one zone. Third, the structure of the zone in a hierarchical IGP can be changed, e.g., making the backbone bigger or smaller. We refer to these scenarios as *flat2hier*, *hier2flat* and *hier2hier*, respectively.

Unlike to protocol replacement, changing the mode of the IGP configuration can require a specific router migration

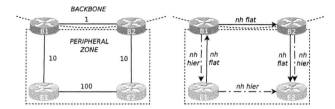

Figure 1: Bad Square Gadget. When the IGP hierarchy is modified, a given migration ordering is needed between $B1$ and $E1$ to avoid forwarding loops.

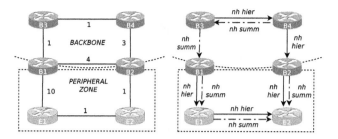

Figure 3: Route summarization gadget. When summarization is introduced or removed, a specific migration ordering is needed between $B3$ and $B4$ to avoid forwarding loops.

ordering. Indeed, the nh function can change in hierarchy modification scenarios because of the intra-zone over inter-zone path preference rule applied by routers in hierarchical IGPs (see Section 2). Hence, forwarding loops can arise due to inconsistencies between already migrated routers and routers that are not migrated yet. Consider for example the topology depicted on the left side of Fig. 1. In a *flat2hier* scenario, some routers change their next-hop towards destinations $E1$ and $E2$. In particular, the right side of Fig. 1 shows the next-hop function for all the routers when the destination is $E2$. During the migration process, a forwarding loop arises for traffic destined to $E2$ if $B1$ is migrated before $E1$. Indeed, $B1$ reaches $E2$ via $E1$ in hierarchical mode, and $E1$ reaches $E2$ via $B1$ in flat mode. Hence, for each time t where $B1$ is already migrated and $E1$ is not, the forwarding path used by $B1$ is $\pi(B1, E2, t) = \{(B1\ E1\ B1)\}$, since $nh_{final}(B1, E2) = \{E1\}$ and $nh_{init}(E1, E2) = \{B1\}$. Notice that such a loop lasts until $E1$ is migrated. A symmetric constraint holds between routers $B2$ and $E2$ for traffic destined to $E1$. A loop-free migration can be achieved by migrating $E1$ and $E2$ before $B1$ and $B2$.

Nevertheless, there are also cases in which it is not possible to avoid loops during the migration. Consider, for example, the topology represented in Fig. 2. In this topology, symmetric constraints between $B1$ and $B2$ for traffic destined to $E2$ and $E3$ imply the impossibility of finding a loop-free ordering. We refer the reader to the central and the right parts of Fig. 2 to visualize the next-hop functions in flat and hierarchical modes.

Similar examples can be found for *hier2flat* and *hier2hier* migrations. They are omitted for brevity. Observe that problems in hierarchy modification scenarios are mitigated in protocols such as IS-IS that natively support multiple adjacencies [14]. In fact, multiple adjacencies belonging to different zones decrease the number of cases in which the nh function changes during the migration. However, migration loops can still arise, depending on the initial and the final configurations.

Route summarization

Introducing or removing route summarization (i.e., *summ* scenarios) in a network can lead to forwarding loops. For example, consider the topology represented in the left part of Fig. 3. The right part of the figure visualizes the nh functions before and after the introduction of route summarization. It is evident that the introduction of route summarization on $B1$ and $B2$ can lead to a forwarding loop between $B3$ and $B4$ for traffic destined to $E2$. Indeed, before summarizing routes, $B3$ and $B4$ prefer to send traffic destined

---

Steps for a Seamless IGP Migration

1. *Compute a loop-free order* in which routers can be migrated without creating loops.

2. *Introduce the final IGP configuration* network-wide. In this step, routers still forward packets according to the initial IGP configuration only.

3. *Monitor the status* of the IGP configurations. Wait for the convergence of the final IGP configuration.

4. *Migrate routers* following the pre-computed loop-free order. Migrating a router means configuring it to forward packets according to the final IGP configuration.

5. *Remove the initial IGP configuration* from all the routers.

Figure 4: Proposed methodology for seamless IGP migrations.

to $E2$ via $B2$. On the other hand, when summarization is introduced, $B1$ and $B2$ propagate one aggregate for both $E1$ and $E2$ with the same weight. Hence, $B3$ and $B4$ change their next-hop since the path to $B1$ has a lower weight than the path to $B2$.

As for hierarchy modifications, no loop-free ordering exists in some cases. An example of such a situation can be built by simply replicating the topology in Fig. 3 so that symmetric constraints on the migration order hold between $B3$ and $B4$.

4. METHODOLOGY

Fig. 4 illustrates the main steps of our methodology. In the first step, we pre-compute an ordering in which to seamlessly migrate routers, with no packet loss (Section 5). When such an ordering does not exist, we use technical fallback solutions (see [15]). Fallback solutions are only exploited as a backup since they make the whole migration process slower and harder to pilot. As we always could find an ordering for all the ISP topologies we analyzed (Section 7), we believe that fallback solutions will be rarely needed in practice.

The actual migration process begins in the second step of our methodology. As a basic operation, we exploit a known migration technique called *ships-in-the-night* [1, 2, 4], in which both the initial and the final IGP configurations are

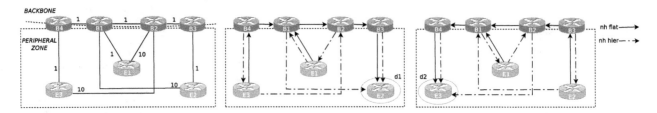

Figure 2: Loop Gadget. No migration ordering is loop-free for *flat2hier* **and** *hier2flat* **scenarios because of contradictory constraints between** $B1$ **and** $B2$.

running at the same time on each router in separate routing processes. Routing processes are ranked on the basis of their priority, the Administrative Distance (AD). When a route for a given prefix is available from several processes, the one with the lowest AD is installed in the FIB. In this step, we set the AD of the routing process running the final IGP configuration to 255, since this setting ensures that no route coming from that process is installed in the FIB [23]. All ISP routers typically support this feature.

In the third step of the migration, we wait for network-wide convergence of the final IGP configuration. After this step, both IGPs have reached a stable routing state. In the fourth step, we progressively migrate routers following the ordering pre-computed in the first Step of the methodology. For this purpose, we lower the AD of the routing process running the final IGP such that it is smaller than the AD of the process running the initial configuration. Doing so, the router installs the final routes in its FIB. Since a routing entry change takes about $100ms$ before being reflected in the FIB [24], we wait for a given amount time (typically few seconds) before migrating the next router in the ordering. This step ensures a loop-free migration of the network. Notice that switching the AD and updating the FIB are lossless operations on ISP routers [25]. Lowering the AD on all the routers at once is not a viable solution in practice as it can generate protocol-dependent loops and control-plane traffic storms concerning all the protocols (BGP, LDP, PIM, etc.) that rely on the IGP. Moreover, this approach prevents operators from controlling the migration process and from backtracking to a previously working state when a problem is detected, e.g., a router that does not receive an intended command. All the discussions that we had with network operators further confirm that they prefer to gradually migrate their network to have full-control of the process.

In the last step, we remove, in any order, the initial IGP configuration from the routers. This is safe since all of them are now using the final IGP to forward traffic.

5. LOOP-FREE MIGRATIONS

In this section, we study the problem of migrating a network from one link-state IGP configuration to another without creating any loop. Firstly, we present the algorithms we use to compute a loop-free router migration ordering. Then, we discuss how to adapt the algorithms to address congestion and network failures.

5.1 Migration Ordering Computation

We now study the following problem from an algorithmic perspective.

PROBLEM 2. *Given an initial and a final next-hop func-*

```
1:  loop_enumeration_run(G = (V, E),D,nh_init,nh_final)
2:    CS ← ∅
3:    for d ∈ D do
4:      Ḡ_d = (V, Ē), with Ē = {(u v)} such that v ∈ nh_init(u, d)
         or v ∈ nh_final(u, d)
5:      for each cycle L in Ḡ_d do
6:        V_init,L = {u ∈ L : ∃v, (u v) ∈ L, v ∈ nh_init(u, d) but
           v ∉ nh_final(u, d)}
7:        V_final,L = {u ∈ L : ∃v, (u v) ∈ L, v ∈ nh_final(u, d)
           but v ∉ nh_init(u, d)}
8:        CS ← CS ∪ {u_0 ∨ ··· ∨ u_k < v_0 ∨ ··· ∨ v_l}, where
           u_i ∈ V_init,L ∀i = 0, . . . , k, and v_j ∈ V_final,L ∀j = 0, . . . , l.
9:      end for
10:   end for
11:   LP ← new LP problem
12:   for u_0 ∨ ··· ∨ u_k < v_0 ∨ ··· ∨ v_l ∈ CS do
13:     add to LP the following constraints
14:     t_{u_0} − MAX_INT × Y_1 < t_{v_0}
15:     . . .
16:     t_{u_0} − MAX_INT × Y_l < t_{v_l}
17:     t_{u_1} − MAX_INT × Y_{l+1} < t_{v_0}
18:     . . .
19:     t_{u_k} − MAX_INT × Y_{l×k} < t_{v_l}
20:     t_{u_0}, . . . , t_{u_k}, t_{v_0}, . . . , t_{v_l} integer
21:     Y_1, . . . , Y_{l×k} binary
22:     ∑_{1<i<=l×k} Y_i < l × k
23:   end for
24:   return solve_lp_problem(LP)
```

Figure 5: Loop Enumeration Algorithm.

tions, a logical graph G*, and a set of destinations* D*, compute a router migration ordering, if any, such that no forwarding loop arises in* G *for any* $d \in D$.

Even the problem of deciding if a loop-free router migration ordering exists, that we call *RMOP*, is an $\mathcal{NP}$-complete problem. Indeed, a reduction from the well-known 3-SAT problem [26] can be built in polynomial time. The complete proof is described in [15].

In the following, we present an algorithm to find a loop-free ordering (when it exists). Because of the complexity of the problem, the algorithm is inefficient and can take several hours to run on very large ISP networks (see Section 7). We also propose an efficient heuristic that is correct but not complete.

Loop Enumeration Algorithm

The Loop Enumeration Algorithm (Fig. 5) enumerates all the possible migration loops that can arise during a migration, and outputs the sufficient and necessary constraints that ensure that no loop arises. To identify all possible migration loops, for each destination d, the algorithm builds the graph G_d (line 4) as the union of the actual paths in

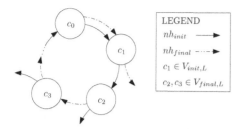

LEGEND
nh_{init} ——→
nh_{final} ----→
$c_1 \in V_{init,L}$
$c_2, c_3 \in V_{final,L}$

Figure 6: Abstract representation of a migration loop.

the initial and in the final configuration. G_d contains all the possible combinations of paths followed by traffic destined to d for any migration order. Then, all the cycles are enumerated and for each cycle, the algorithm outputs the constraint (line 8) of migrating at least one router that participates in the loop in the initial configuration before at least one router that is part of the loop in the final configuration (lines 5-8). In the example of Fig. 6, indeed, migrating c_1 before at least one among c_2 and c_3 avoids the loop. In the algorithm, $V_{init,L}$ represents the set of routers that participate in the loop when they are in the initial configuration (line 6), and $V_{final,L}$ contains only routers that participate in the loop when they are in the final configuration (line 7). The constraints identified by the algorithm are encoded in an Integer Linear Program (lines 12-22), where the variables t_{u_i} represent the migration steps at which routers can be safely migrated (lines 14-19). Finally, the algorithm tries to solve the linear program and returns a loop-free ordering, if one exists (line 24).

We now prove that the loop enumeration algorithm is correct and complete. This depends on the fact that the constraints it outputs encode the sufficient and necessary conditions to prevent loops during the migration.

LEMMA 1. *Let $u_0 \vee \cdots \vee u_k < v_0 \vee \cdots \vee v_l$ be the ordering constraint that the Loop Enumeration Algorithm identifies for a loop L concerning traffic destined to $d \in D$. Then, L does not arise during the migration if and only if the constraint is satisfied.*

PROOF. Let $L = (c_0 \; c_1 \; \ldots \; c_k \; c_0)$. We prove the statement in two steps.

If the loop does not arise then the constraint is satisfied. Suppose by contradiction that the constraint is not satisfied. Then, there exists a time $\bar{t}$ such that all the routers in $V_{final,L}$ are migrated while all the routers in $V_{init,L}$ are not migrated. Consider c_0. If $c_0 \in V_{final,L}$, then it is already migrated, i.e., $nh(c_0, d, \bar{t}) = nh_{final}(c_0, d)$, hence $c_1 \in nh(c_0, d, \bar{t})$, by definition of $V_{final,L}$. If $c_0 \in V_{init,L}$, then $nh(c_0, d, \bar{t}) = nh_{init}(c_0, d)$ and $c_1 \in nh(c_0, d, \bar{t})$. Finally, if $c_0 \notin V_{init,L}$ and $c_0 \notin V_{final,L}$, then $c_1 \in nh(c_0, d, t) \; \forall t$. In any case, $c_1 \in nh(c_0, d, \bar{t})$. Iterating the same argument for all the routers in L, we conclude that $c_{i+1} \in nh(c_i, d, \bar{t})$, with $i = 0, \ldots, k$ and $c_{k+1} = c_0$. Thus, L arises at time $\bar{t}$.

If the constraint is satisfied then the loop does not arise. Assume, without loss of generality, that $c_u \in V_{init,L}$ is migrated at time t', while at least one router $c_v \in V_{final,L}$ is migrated at $t'' > t'$. Then, L cannot arise $\forall t < t''$, since $nh(c_v, d, t) = nh_{init}(c_v, d)$ implies that $c_{v+1} \notin nh(c_v, d, t)$ by definition of $V_{final,L}$. Moreover, L cannot arise $\forall t > t'$, since $nh(c_u, d, t) = nh_{final}(c_u, d)$ implies that $c_{u+1} \notin nh(c_u, d, t)$

```
1:  routing_trees_run(G = (V, E), D, nh_init, nh_final)
2:  C ← ∅
3:  for d ∈ D do
4:      S_d ← greedy_run(V, d, nh_init, nh_final)
5:      V̄_d ← {v_i : nh_init(v_i, d) ≠ nh_final(v_i, d)}
6:      G_d = (V, E'), with E' = {(u, v) : v ∈ nh_final(u, d)}
7:      for P = (v_0 ... v_k), with v_k = d, (v_i, v_{i+1}) ∈ E', and
               predecessors(v_0) = ⊘ do
8:          last ← Null
9:          for u ∈ P ∩ V̄_d and u ∉ S_d do
10:             if last ≠ Null then
11:                 C ← C ∪ {(u, last)}
12:             end if
13:             last ← u
14:         end for
15:     end for
16: end for
17: G_c ← (V, C)
18: return topological_sort(G_c)
19:
20: greedy_run(V, d, nh_init, nh_final)
21: S_d ← ∅
22: N ← {d}
23: while N ≠ ∅ do
24:     S_d = S_d ∪ N
25:     N = ∅
26:     for u ∈ V, u ∉ S_d do
27:         if nh_init(u, d) ∪ nh_final(u, d) ⊆ S_d then
28:             N = N ∪ {u}
29:         end if
30:     end for
31: end while
32: return S_d
```

Figure 7: Routing Trees Heuristic.

by definition of $V_{init,L}$. Since $t'' > t'$, no time exists such that L arises during the migration. □

THEOREM 1. *The Loop Enumeration Algorithm is correct and complete.*

PROOF. The statement follows by Lemma 1, since the linear program encodes all the sufficient and necessary conditions for any migration loop to not arise. □

It is easy to verify that the algorithm requires exponential time. Indeed, the algorithm is based on the enumeration of all the cycles in a graph, and the number of cycles in a graph can be exponential with respect to the number of nodes.

Routing Trees Heuristic

The Routing Tree Heuristic is illustrated in Fig. 7. As the first step, for each destination $d \in D$, the heuristic exploits a greedy procedure to compute a set S_d of nodes that are guaranteed not to be part of any loop (line 4). The greedy procedure (lines 20-32) incrementally (and greedily) grows the set S_d, adding a node to S_d at each iteration if and only if all the next-hops of the node in the initial and in the final configurations are already in S_d (lines 27-28). After this step, the Routing Trees Heuristic builds the directed acyclic graph G_d [1] containing only the actual paths followed by packets to reach d in the final configuration (line 6). Then, it generates a constraint for each pair of routers (u, v) such that $(u \ldots v \ldots d) \in \pi_{final}(u, d)$, and both u and v do not belong

---

[1]G_d is an acyclic since the final configuration is loop-free

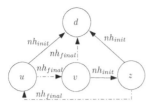

Figure 8: In some migration scenarios, the Routing Trees Heuristic generates unnecessary constraints.

to S_d and change at least one next-hop between the initial and the final configuration (lines 7-15). In particular, among the routers that change one or more next-hops during the migration (set $\bar{V}_d$ at line 5), each router is forced to migrate after all its successors in the actual path towards d (line 11). In the final step, the heuristic tries to compute an ordering compliant with the union of the constraints generated for all the destinations (lines 17-18).

It is easy to check that the algorithm is polynomial with respect to the size of the input. We now prove that the algorithm is correct. First, we show that the routers in S_d can be migrated in any order without creating loops towards d, hence it is possible not to consider them in the generation of the ordering constraints. Then, we prove that the constraints are sufficient to guarantee that the ordering is loop-free.

LEMMA 2. *If the greedy procedure adds a router u to S_d, then u cannot be part of any migration loop towards destination $d \in D$.*

PROOF. Suppose, by contradiction, that there exists a router u added to S_d by the greedy procedure at a given iteration i, such that $(u\ v_0\ \dots\ v_k\ u) \in \pi(u, d, t)$, with $k \geq 0$, at a given time t and for a given migration ordering. By definition of the algorithm, one router is added to S_d if and only if all its next-hops $w_0, \dots, w_n$ (in both the initial and final IGP configurations) are already in S_d, since each node in $\{w_0, \dots, w_n\}$ is added to S_d at a given iteration before i. Hence, $v_k \notin S_d$ at iteration i, because u is one of the next-hops of v_k and it is added to S_d at iteration i by hypothesis. Iterating the same argument, all routers $v_h \notin S_d$ at iteration i, $\forall h = 0, \dots, k$. As a consequence, GREEDY does not add u to S_d at iteration i, which is a contradiction. □

THEOREM 2. *Let $S = x_1, \dots, x_n$ be the sequence computed by the Routing Tree Heuristic. If the routers are migrated according to S, then no migration loop arises.*

PROOF. Suppose by contradiction that migration is performed according to S but migrating a router u creates a loop for at least one destination d. In that case, there exists a set of routers $\tilde{V} = \{v_1, \dots, v_k\}$, such that $C = (u\ v_0\ \dots\ v_k\ u) \in \pi(u, d, t)$, at a certain time t. By Lemma 2, all $v_i \notin S_d$. By definition of the heuristic, all routers v_i are such that $nh(v_i, d, t) = nh_{final}(v_i, d)$, with $i = 0, \dots, k$, because either they do not change their next-hop between the initial and the final configuration or they precede u in S. Hence, at time t, both u and all the routers $v_i \in \tilde{V}$ are in the final configuration. This is a contradiction, since we assumed that the final IGP configuration is loop-free. □

Note that the heuristic is not complete; while the constraints it generates are sufficient to guarantee no forwarding

loops, they are not necessary. Indeed, for each destination d, it imposes specific orderings between all the routers (not belonging to S_d) that change one of their next-hops towards d, even if it is not needed. For instance, in the scenario of Fig. 8, the heuristic mandates v to be migrated before u and u before z. However, no loop arises also if v is migrated before z and z before u. Generating unnecessary constraints prevents the heuristic from identifying a loop-free migration ordering every time it exists. Nonetheless, if state of the art best practices for PoP design are followed [27], such cases are rare. In Section 7, we show that the heuristic found an ordering in most of our experiments on realistic topologies.

5.2 Dealing with Congestion and Failures

Even if there is no congestion in both the initial and the final IGP configurations, congestion could transiently appear during the migration because of forwarding paths in temporary states in which only some routers are migrated. To deal with congestion, we can add constraints (e.g., routers u and v must not be migrated both before z) that the algorithms must take into account in looking for a proper router migration ordering. Assuming that the traffic matrix does not consistently change during the migration, such constraints can be statically computed, given the traffic matrix, the capacity of the links, and the nh function. Note that the assumption on the stability of the traffic matrix is reasonable since traffic shifts are rare for the most popular destinations [17] and our approach requires a short time to complete the migration process (see Section 7).

On the other hand, link or node failures modify the topology, hence they may modify the nh function and the loop-free migration ordering to be followed. Thanks to the high time efficiency of our heuristic (see Section 7), we can pre-compute loop-free router orderings and the corresponding ordering constraints that are needed for seamless migrations in the most important failure scenarios (e.g., all possible single link failures). When a failure happens, we can use such constraints to minimize the duration of the loops generated by the failure, and to dynamically adapt the order in which migration steps are performed. Because of the high efficiency of the heuristic on small and medium-sized topologies, we can even directly recompute the ordering just after the failure, taking into account the fact that some routers could have already been migrated.

6. THE PROVISIONING SYSTEM

We implemented a software system which is able to compute and automate all the required steps for a seamless migration. The main architectural components of our system are represented in Fig. 9. In the following, we describe how data flow through the system (dashed lines in the figure), by stressing the role of each component.

In order to assess the properties of the initial and the final IGPs, we rely on a monitoring system which collects the IGP Link-State Advertisements (LSAs) circulating in the network. The *IGP LSA Listener* component parses the LSAs, continuously filling a database (DB) with data on the IGP adjacencies, on the weight of the links, and on the announced IP prefixes. We implemented the IGP LSA Listener by using packet-cloning features available on routers [28]. The *IGP State Asserter* component is responsible for querying the DB and assessing properties of the monitored IGPs state. The current implementation of the IGP State Asserter is able to

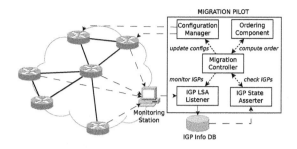

Figure 9: System architecture.

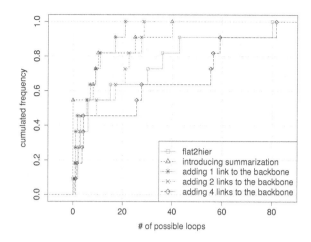

Figure 10: CDF of the number of loops that can arise on Rocketfuel topologies.

check an IGP for convergence completion by evaluating the stability over time of the IGP adjacencies and of the prefixes announced by each router. A custom time threshold can be set to assess the stability of the IGP. Moreover, the IGP State Asserter is able to verify the announcement of a given set of prefixes in an IGP, and the equivalence of two IGPs, i.e., the equivalence of the logical graph, and of the forwarding paths towards a given set of destinations.

The IGP State Asserter is triggered at specific moments in time by the *Migration Controller*, which is the central component of the system, responsible for tasks' coordination. Before the actual migration process starts, it delegates the computation of a loop-free router migration ordering to the *Ordering Component*. This component implements the ordering algorithms described in Section 5.1. Then, the Migration Controller runs the IGP LSA Listener. When needed (see Section 4), the Migration Controller asks the IGP State Asserter to assess whether it is possible to safely modify the configuration of the devices in the network without incurring transient states. This boils down to checking the stability of the current IGP. At each step of the migration process the controller also requires the *Configuration Manager* to properly update the configuration on the routers as described in Section 4. Based on a network-wide model, the Configuration Manager generates the necessary commands to be sent to routers for each migration step. The Configuration Manager is based on an extended version of NCGuard [29].

7. EVALUATION

In this section, we evaluate the ordering algorithms and the provisioning system. The system is evaluated on the basis of a case study in which a network is migrated from a flat to a hierarchical IGP.

7.1 Data Set and Methodology

Our data set contains both publicly available and confidential data relative to commercial ISP topologies. Concerning publicly available topologies, we used the inferred topologies provided by the Rocketfuel project [30]. Rocketfuel topologies represent ISPs of different sizes, the smallest one having 79 nodes and 294 edges while the biggest one contains 315 nodes and 1944 edges. In addition, some network operators provided us with real-world IGP topologies. In this section, we discuss the result of our analyses on all the Rocketfuel data and on the anonymized topologies of three ISPs, namely *tier1.A*, *tier1.B* and *tier2*. *tier1.A* is the largest Tier1, and its IGP logical graph has more than 1000 nodes and more than 4000 edges. *tier1.A* currently

uses a flat IGP configuration. The other two ISPs are one order of magnitude smaller but use a hierarchical IGP.

On this data set, we performed several experiments. We considered the introduction of summarization, as well as *flat2hier* and *hier2hier* scenarios. Since most of the topologies in our data set are flat, we artificially built a hierarchy (i.e., the separation in zones) in order to consider scenarios in which hierarchical configurations are needed. In particular, we grouped routers according to geographical information present in the name of the routers. Doing so, we built two hierarchical topologies out of each flat topology. In the first one, zones are defined per city. In the second one, zones are defined per-continent. In both topologies, we built the backbone by considering routers connected to more than one zone as $ZBRs$ and routers connected only to $ZBRs$ as pure backbone routers. To simulate a *hier2hier* scenario, we artificially enlarged the backbone by adding to it a fixed number (from 1 up to 32) of links. Such links were randomly chosen among the links between a ZBR and a router that does not participate in the backbone. For the summarization scenario, we aggregated all the destinations inside the same zone into a single prefix. This was done for all the zones but the backbone. Our hierarchy construction methodology and the way prefixes are summarized follow the guidelines proposed in [31]. All the tests were run on a Sun Fire X2250 (quad-core 3GHz CPUs with 32GB of RAM). We omit the results of some experiments due to space limitations.

7.2 Ordering Algorithms

We first evaluate usefulness and efficiency of the Loop Enumeration Algorithm and of the Routing Tree Heuristic. Fig. 10 shows the cumulative distribution function of the number of loops that can arise in Rocketfuel topologies. Different migration scenarios are considered. Each point in the plot corresponds to a specific topology and a specific scenario. In *flat2hier*, up to 80 different loops can arise in the worst case and at least 30 loops can arise for 4 topologies out of 11. Other scenarios follow similar trends. Observe that, in the *hier2hier* scenario (curves "adding x links to the backbone"), the number of possible loops significantly increases with the number of links which change zone. In all the scenarios, almost all the loops involve two routers, with a few exceptions of three routers loops. Also, the vast major-

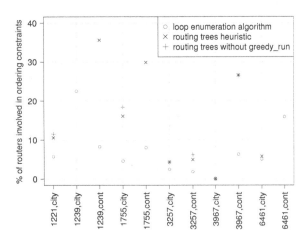

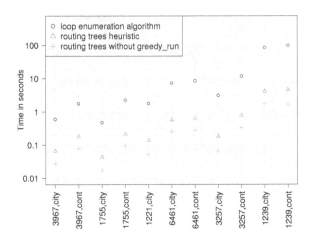

Figure 11: Percentage of routers involved in the ordering in *flat2hier* **(Rocketfuel topologies). Results for other scenarios are similar.**

Figure 12: Time taken to compute an ordering in *flat2hier* **(Rocketfuel topologies). Results for other scenarios are similar.**

ity of loops concerns traffic destined to routers that do not participate in the backbone. These routers are at the border of the network (e.g., BGP border routers or MPLS PEs) and normally attract most of the traffic in ISP networks. It is, thus, important to compute an ordering in which they are not involved in loops. The number of migration loops is topology dependent, hence it can be influenced by our design approach. However, these results clearly show that migrating routers in a random order is not a viable option in arbitrary networks. Additionally, it is desirable that migrations of world-wide networks be carried out on a per-zone basis, that is, migrating all the routers in the same zone (e.g., a continent) before routers in other zones. We observe that this is indeed possible since all the loops that occur, in both Rocketfuel and real-world topologies, arise between routers in the same zone or between backbone routers and routers in a peripheral zone. Thus, it is often possible to compute per-zone orderings. These considerations further motivate our effort to find a router migration ordering which is guaranteed to be loop-free. We found slightly different results on the real ISP topologies we analyzed. For the two hierarchical ISPs, none or few migration loops can arise in the considered scenarios. This is mainly due to a sensible design of the hierarchy. We discuss simple design guidelines that ease IGP migrations in Section 8. On the other hand, we found that huge number of problems could arise in a migration from a poor design to a neat one. In the *hier2flat* scenario, more than 2000 loops, involving up to 10 routers, might arise within the *tier1.A*. Such a large number of loops is mainly a consequence of the way we built the hierarchy.

As a second group of experiments, we ran the ordering algorithms on the Rocketfuel topologies. In the following, we present results for the *flat2hier* scenario but similar results and considerations hold for the other scenarios. Fig. 11 shows for each topology the percentage of routers that need to be migrated in a specific order according to each algorithm (implying that other routers can be migrated in any order). When a point is missing, it means that the corresponding algorithm was not able to find a loop-free ordering for the topology. The enumeration algorithm was always able to find a loop-free ordering in all situations. In the worst case, the computed ordering involves more than 20%

of the routers in the network. We believe that finding ordering constraints for such a number of routers is not practical at a glance. This stresses the importance of our algorithms. The Routing Trees Heuristic, instead, found a loop-free ordering on 9 topologies out of 11. Fig. 11 also highlights the gain of relying on the greedy subprocedure, as the heuristic could find a solution for only 6 topologies without it.

Fig. 12 plots the median of the computation time taken by each algorithm over 50 separated runs. Standard deviation is always under 40 for the loop enumeration algorithm, except for the two cases corresponding to topology 1239. In that cases, the standard deviation is around 450. Moreover, the standard deviation of the time taken by the Routing Trees Heuristic is always less than 25. Even if correct and complete, the Loop Enumeration Algorithm is inefficient, especially for large topologies. The heuristic is always one order of magnitude faster. In Fig. 12, the low absolute value of the time taken by the Loop Enumeration Algorithm can be explained by the relatively small size of the Rocketfuel topologies. Nevertheless, for the *tier1.A* topology, the Loop Enumeration Algorithm took more than 11 hours to complete. To further evaluate the performance degradation of the complete algorithm, we enlarged *tier1.B*'s and *tier2*'s topologies. The operation consisted in replicating multiple times the structure of one peripheral zone, and attaching these additional zones to the network in order to reach a size similar to *tier1.A*. In such experiments, we found that the Loop Enumeration Algorithm took several hours even if routers can be migrated in any order, while the heuristics always took less than 1.5 minutes. Typically, the time taken by the ordering algorithm is not a critical factor in our approach, since a loop-free router migration ordering can be computed before actually performing the migration. However, time efficiency is highly important to support advanced abilities like promptly reacting to failures that could happen during the migration (see Section 5.2).

7.3 Provisioning System

We evaluated the performance of the main components of our provisioning system by means of a case study. In the case study, we performed a *flat2hier* migration of Geant, the pan-european research network, that we emulated by

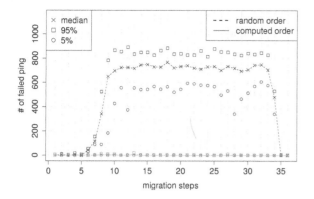

Figure 13: Our system guarantees that no packet is lost during migration while long-lasting connectivity disruptions can happen with a naive approach.

using a major router vendor routing operative system image. In particular, we simulated the migration from a flat IS-IS configuration to a hierarchical OSPF. Geant's topology is publicly available [32]. It is composed of 36 routers and 53 links. For the case study, we artificially built zones on the basis of the geographical location of the routers and their interconnections [33]. In addition to the backbone (12 routers), we defined three peripheral zones: the south west area (6 routers), the north east area (11 routers) and the south east area (17 routers). We defined the IGP link weights to be inversely proportional to the bandwidth of the links. By executing the Loop Enumeration Algorithm (see Section 5.1), we found that 8 different loops towards 5 different destinations could arise on that topology.

We ran two experiments. In the first experiment, we relied on the ordering computed by the Loop Enumeration Algorithm, while in the second we adopted a random order. In order to have statistically relevant data, we repeated each experiment 50 times. To measure traffic disruptions due to the migration, we injected data probes (i.e., ICMP echo request) from each router towards the 5 troublesome destinations. Fig 13 reports the median, the 5th and the 95th percentiles of ICMP packets lost that arose after each migration step.

The case study showed the ability of our provisioning system to perform seamless IGP migrations. Following the ordering computed by the Loop Enumeration Algorithm, we were able to achieve no packet loss during the migration (the few losses reported in Fig. 13 should be ascribed to the virtual environment). On the other hand, adopting the naive approach of migrating routers in the random order, forwarding loops arose at step 6 and are only solved at step 34. Thus, the network suffered traffic losses during more than 80% of the migration process. Finally, we observe that, even migrations on a per-zone basis require the use of an ordering algorithm because all the ordering constraints are among routers in the same zone.

Our system also enables faster migrations than known migration [2, 4]. The IGP LSA Listener is able to process IGP messages in a few milliseconds. The performance of the module is confirmed by a separate experiment we ran. We forced the Listener to process messages from a pcap file containing 204 LSAs (both OSPF and IS-IS). On 50 runs, the monitor was able to decode and collect each IGP message

in about 14 milliseconds on average and 24 milliseconds at most. We evaluated the performance of the IGP State Asserter on the IS-IS and the OSPF DBs generated during the case study. The DBs contained information about 106 directed links and 96 IP prefixes. The IGP State Asserter took about 40 milliseconds to assess equivalence of the logical graph, routing stability, and advertisement of the same set of prefixes in both IGPs. Even if the code could be optimized, current performance is good, also considering that the IGP Asserter does not need to be invoked more than once in absence of network failures (see Section 4). On average, the Configuration Manager took 8.84 seconds to push one intermediate configuration on a router. The average size of an intermediate configuration is around 38 lines. The entire migration process took less than 20 minutes. On the contrary, a similar real-world Geant migration took several days to be completed [4].

All the intermediate configurations that our system generated in the case study described above are available online [33].

8. DESIGN GUIDELINES

In this section, we state simple design guidelines that make the entire IGP migration process easier, since all the router migration orderings are loop-free. In the following, we consider the design of zones in hierarchical IGPs, since the most problematic migrations involve hierarchies.

GUIDELINE A. *For each zone Z, the shortest path from each ZBR to any destination in Z is an intra-zone path.*

Guideline A enables easier *flat2hier* and *hier2flat* migrations. In fact, the guideline enforces sufficient conditions to guarantee that the nh function does not change for any router and any destination in any zone Z, since an intra-zone path is preferred in both flat and hierarchical modes. Since no router in Z changes its path, then $nh_{init}(v, d) = nh_{final}(v, d)$ also for all routers $v \notin Z$ and $d \in Z$. This implies that no loop can arise during the migration. Notice that Guideline A refers only to ZBRs, since if they use intra-zone paths, then non-ZBR routers cannot use inter-zone paths. Establishing multiple adjacencies (e.g., $L1L2$ adjacencies in IS-IS) between ZBRs also guarantees the nh function does not change, but backbone links could be unnecessarily traversed in this case.

GUIDELINE B. *For each zone Z, an aggregation layer of routers connects the ZBRs to the destinations in Z (e.g., BGP border routers or MPLS PE). Link weights are set so that the weight of the path from any ZBR to any destination in Z is the same.*

Guideline B guarantees easy IGP migrations when route summarization is introduced or removed. We assume that aggregated prefixes are announced with a cost equal to the highest weight among the destinations in the aggregate (as in OSPF, by default [13]). In this case, both with and without summarization, each backbone router chooses the closest ZBR in Z as entry point for destinations in the aggregated prefix. It is easy to check that, as a consequence, the nh function does not change with or without summarization, hence no specific migration ordering is needed during the migration.

9. RELATED WORK

Seamless IGP operation and maintenance have been the focus of many previous studies. For example, several protocol extensions have been proposed [34, 35, 36] to gracefully restart a routing process. However, few research effort has been specifically devoted to network-wide IGP migrations.

In [18], Raza *et al.* propose the Graceful Network Operations (GNO) framework which formalizes the problem of minimizing a certain disruption function (e.g., link congestion) when the link weights change. They also describe an algorithm to find a congestion-free ordering when several IGP weights have to be modified. Although their work is close in spirit to ours, the migration scenarios we analyzed cannot always be mapped to a reweighting problem. For example, in hierarchical IGP configurations, both the weight of a link and the zone to which it belongs are considered in the computation of the next-hop from a router to a destination and a unique link weight assignment that generates the same next-hop for each router-to-destination pair could not exist. In [37], Keralapura *et al.* study the problem of finding the optimal way in which to add nodes and links to a network to minimize disruptions. Even if our techniques can be adapted to address topological changes, this problem is beyond the focus of this paper.

In [38], Chen *et al.* describe a tool that is able to automate status acquisition and configuration change on network devices according to rules specified by domain experts. The tool can be used to automate the ships-in-the-night approach, but not to compute a loop-free ordering. The authors also provide a rule of thumb to avoid problems during IGP migrations, i.e., update edge routers before the backbone ones. However, this rule does not hold in general. For example, migrating $E1$ before $B1$ in Fig. 1 creates a forwarding loop in a *hier2flat* scenario.

In [39], Alimi *et al.* extend the ship-in-the-night approach by allowing multiple configurations to run simultaneously on a router. They also describe a commitment protocol to support the switch between configurations without creating forwarding loops. While the technique looks promising, it cannot be exploited on current routers and a commitment ordering could still be needed.

Recently, some techniques [12, 40] have been proposed to enable virtual routers or parts of the configuration of routers (e.g., BGP session) to be moved from one physical device to another. Their work differ from ours as we aim at seamlessly changing network-wide configurations.

Regarding the problem of avoiding forwarding loops in IGPs during transient states, some previous work has also been done. Francois *et al.* propose protocol extensions that allow routers to update their FIB without creating a transient loop after a link addition or removal [41]. Fu *et al.* [21] and Shi *et al.* [22] generalize the results by defining a loop-free FIB update ordering for any change in the forwarding plane and considering traffic congestion, respectively. However, these approaches cannot be used in practice to carry out IGP migrations since they assume that the FIB can be updated on a per-destination basis which is not the case on current routers.

IGP migrations could also be performed by using route redistribution. Although new primitives have been recently proposed [42], we believe that relying on a ships-in-the-night approach (when possible) makes the entire migration process easier and more manageable.

10. DISCUSSION

In this section, we discuss the limitations of our methodology, especially in terms of its application to other types of migrations.

First of all, our methodology is adapted to link-state IGP migrations and it cannot be directly applied to other IGPs (e.g., distance-vector IGPs). Contrary to link-state protocols, where routers always have a global view of the topology and can take decisions autonomously, in distance-vector protocols a change of the next-hop of one router can affect the visibility other routers have of some destinations. This poses different problems with respect to those tackled by our techniques.

Moreover, our methodology does not take into consideration the interactions between the changing IGP and the protocols relying on it. In particular, our approach is not suitable for all the scenarios in which BGP is deployed on the migrated network. BGP uses the IGP to both discriminate among several exit-points and to learn how to reach the preferred exit-point [43]. Migrating the underlying IGP can thus cause BGP routers to change their preferred exit-point which can lead to forwarding loops. Currently, our algorithms ensure that no loop occurs during the migration towards any internal destination of an AS. For all the networks whose forwarding is based on tunneling or encapsulation mechanisms like MPLS, this property is sufficient to guarantee loop-free forwarding towards inter-domain destinations as well. Indeed, no loop occurs in the IGP and the tunneling mechanism ensures that the BGP traffic will reach the proper exit-point. Though, in the migration of a pure IP network, the exclusive presence of BGP can induce forwarding loops due to conflicting BGP decisions between updated routers and non-updated routers. Theoretically, our ordering algorithms can be adapted to deal with BGP-induced loops. However, the ordering problem is much more complicated since it needs to consider: (i) the fact that BGP prefixes could be reached via any combination of exit-points, (ii) the iBGP topology and its relationship to the IGP [44], and (iii) BGP dynamism. For these reasons, we expect that a loop-free migration ordering for all the BGP prefixes does not exist in most of the cases. We believe that finding an effective technique to prevent BGP-induced loops during the migration of pure IP networks is an interesting open problem raised by this paper.

11. CONCLUSIONS

Network-wide IGP migrations are a source of concerns for network operators. Unless carried on with care, IGP migrations can cause long-lasting forwarding loops and thus significant packet losses. In this paper, we proposed a migration strategy that enables network operators to migrate an entire IGP configuration seamlessly, rapidly, and without compromising routing stability. Our strategy relies on effective techniques for the computation of a router migration ordering and on a provisioning system to automate most of the process. These techniques encompass a complete, time-consuming algorithm and a heuristic. The evaluation we performed on several ISP topologies confirms the practical effectiveness of both the heuristic and the provisioning system.

Although we focused on link-state IGP migrations, the applicability of our techniques is broader since it can encompass any migration issues involving changes of next-hops. We plan to make our approach suitable for seamless migrations involving distance-vector IGPs. Also, we plan to study seamless migrations of other routing protocols (e.g., MPLS or BGP). Our vision is that network-wide migrations could become a basic operation enabling the seamless replacement or reconfiguration of any protocol.

12. ACKNOWLEDGEMENTS

We thank Luca Cittadini, Randy Bush, Bruno Quoitin, Virginie van den Schriek and our shepherd, Walter Willinger, for their help in improving the paper. This work was partially supported by Alcatel-Lucent. Laurent Vanbever is supported by a FRIA scholarship. Stefano Vissicchio is partially supported by ESF project 10-EuroGIGA-OP-003 GraDR and MIUR PRIN Project ALGODEEP. Pierre Francois is supported by the "Fonds National de la Recherche Scientifique", Belgium.

13. REFERENCES

[1] G. G. Herrero and J. A. B. van der Ven, *Network Mergers and Migrations: Junos Design and Implementation*. Wiley Publishing, 2010.

[2] V. Gill and M. Jon, "AOL Backbone OSPF-ISIS Migration," NANOG29 Presentation, 2003.

[3] NANOG thread, "IPv6: IS-IS or OSPFv3," http://mailman.nanog.org/pipermail/nanog/2008-December/006194.html, 2008.

[4] "Results of the GEANT OSPF to ISIS Migration," GEANT IPv6 Task Force Meeting, 2003.

[5] NANOG thread, "OSPF -vs- ISIS," http://www.merit.edu/mail.archives/nanog/2005-06/msg00406.html, 2005.

[6] B. Decraene, J. L. Roux, and I. Minei, "LDP Extension for Inter-Area Label Switched Paths (LSPs)," RFC 5283 (Proposed Standard), Jul. 2008.

[7] T. M. Thomas, *OSPF Network Design Solutions, Second Edition*. Cisco Press, 2003.

[8] J.-L. L. Roux, J.-P. Vasseur, and J. Boyle, "Requirements for Inter-Area MPLS Traffic Engineering," RFC 4105, Jun. 2005.

[9] N. Leymann, B. Decraene, C. Filsfils, M. Konstantynowicz, and D. Steinberg, "Seamless MPLS Architecture," Internet draft, 2011.

[10] P. Templin, "Small Network Operator - Lessons Learned," NANOG45 Presentation, 2009.

[11] "Virtual Network Operator (VNO) hosting opportunities with orbit research." [Online]. Available: http://www.orbitresearch.co.uk/services/virtual-network-operator

[12] Y. Wang, E. Keller, B. Biskeborn, J. van der Merwe, and J. Rexford, "Virtual routers on the move: live router migration as a network-management primitive," in *Proc. SIGCOMM*, 2008.

[13] Moy, J., "OSPF Version 2," RFC 2328, 1998.

[14] Oran D., "OSI IS-IS Intra-domain Routing Protocol," RFC 1142, 1990.

[15] L. Vanbever, S. Vissicchio, C. Pelsser, P. Francois, and O. Bonaventure, "Seamless Network-Wide IGP Migrations," Université catholique de Louvain, Tech. Rep., June 2011, http://hdl.handle.net/2078.1/75312.

[16] S. Iasi, P. François, and S. Uhlig, "Forwarding deflection in multi-area OSPF," in *CoNEXT*, 2005.

[17] J. Rexford, J. Wang, Z. Xiao, and Y. Zhang, "BGP Routing Stability of Popular Destinations," in *Proc. IMW*, 2002.

[18] S. Raza, Y. Zhu, and C.-N. Chuah, "Graceful Network Operations," in *Proc. INFOCOM*, 2009.

[19] P. Francois and O. Bonaventure, "Avoiding transient loops during the convergence of link-state routing protocols," *Trans. on Netw.*, vol. 15, pp. 1280–1292, December 2007.

[20] P. Francois, M. Shand, and O. Bonaventure, "Disruption-free topology reconfiguration in OSPF Networks," in *Proc. INFOCOM*, 2007.

[21] J. Fu, P. Sjodin, and G. Karlsson, "Loop-free updates of forwarding tables," *Trans. on Netw. and Serv. Man.*, vol. 5, no. 1, pp. 22–35, 2008.

[22] L. Shi, J. Fu, and X. Fu, "Loop-free forwarding table updates with minimal link overflow," in *Proc. ICC*, 2009.

[23] H. Ballani, P. Francis, T. Cao, and J. Wang, "Making routers last longer with ViAggre," in *Proc. NSDI*, 2009.

[24] P. Francois, C. Filsfils, J. Evans, and O. Bonaventure, "Achieving sub-second IGP convergence in large IP networks," *Comput. Commun. Rev.*, vol. 35, no. 3, pp. 33–44, 2005.

[25] C. Filsfils, P. Mohapatra, J. Bettink, P. Dharwadkar, P. D. Vriendt, Y. Tsier, V. V. D. Schrieck, O. Bonaventure, and P. Francois, "BGP Prefix Independent Convergence (PIC) Technical Report," Cisco, Tech. Rep., 2011.

[26] M. R. Garey and D. S. Johnson, *Computers and Intractability; A Guide to the Theory of NP-Completeness*. Freeman, 1990.

[27] C. Filsfils, P. Francois, M. Shand, B. Decraene, J. Uttaro, N. Leymann, and M. Horneffer, "LFA applicability in SP networks," Internet Draft, May 2011.

[28] S. Vissicchio, L. Cittadini, M. Pizzonia, L. Vergantini, V. Mezzapesa, and M. L. Papagni, "Beyond the Best: Real-Time Non-Invasive Collection of BGP Messages," in *Proc. INM/WREN 2010*, 2010.

[29] L. Vanbever, G. Pardoen, and O. Bonaventure, "Towards validated network configurations with NCGuard," in *Proc. of Internet Network Management Workshop 2008*, Orlando, USA, October 2008, pp. 1–6.

[30] N. Spring, R. Mahajan, and D. Wetherall, "Measuring ISP topologies with rocketfuel," in *Proc. SIGCOMM*, 2002.

[31] J. Yu, "Scalable Routing Design Principles," RFC 2791, 2000.

[32] "GEANT Backbone Topology," 2010, http://www.geant.net/network/networktopology/pages/home.aspx.

[33] "Seamless Network-Wide IGP Migrations," 2011, http://inl.info.ucl.ac.be/softwares/seamless-network-migration.

[34] A. Shaikh, R. Dube, and A. Varma, "Avoiding instability during graceful shutdown of multiple OSPF routers," *Trans. on Netw.*, vol. 14, pp. 532–542, June 2006.

[35] J. Moy, P. Pillay-Esnault, and A. Lindem, "Graceful OSPF Restart," RFC 3623, 2003.

[36] M. Shand and L. Ginsberg, "Restart Signaling for IS-IS," RFC 5306, 2008.

[37] R. Keralapura, C.-N. Chuah, and Y. Fan, "Optimal Strategy for Graceful Network Upgrade," in *Proc. INM*, 2006.

[38] X. Chen, Z. M. Mao, and J. Van der Merwe, "PACMAN: a platform for automated and controlled network operations and configuration management," in *Proc. CONEXT*, 2009.

[39] R. Alimi, Y. Wang, and Y. R. Yang, "Shadow configuration as a network management primitive," in *Proc. SIGCOMM*, 2008.

[40] E. Keller, J. Rexford, and J. Van Der Merwe, "Seamless BGP migration with router grafting," in *Proc. NSDI*, 2010.

[41] P. Francois and O. Bonaventure, "Avoiding transient loops during IGP Convergence in IP Networks," in *Proc. INFOCOM*, 2005.

[42] F. Le, G. G. Xie, and H. Zhang, "Theory and new primitives for safely connecting routing protocol instances," in *Proc. SIGCOMM*, 2010.

[43] Y. Rekhter, T. Li, and S. Hares, "A Border Gateway Protocol 4 (BGP-4)," RFC 4271, 2006.

[44] T. Griffin and G. Wilfong, "On the Correctness of IBGP Configuration," *SIGCOMM Comput. Commun. Rev.*, vol. 32, no. 4, pp. 17–29, 2002.

A Content Propagation Metric for Efficient Content Distribution

Ryan S. Peterson
Cornell University &
United Networks, L.L.C.
Dept. of Computer Science
Ithaca, NY
ryanp@cs.cornell.edu

Bernard Wong
Cornell University &
United Networks, L.L.C.
Dept. of Computer Science
Ithaca, NY
bwong@cs.cornell.edu

Emin Gün Sirer
Cornell University &
United Networks, L.L.C.
Dept. of Computer Science
Ithaca, NY
egs@cs.cornell.edu

ABSTRACT

Efficient content distribution in large networks comprising data-centers, end hosts, and distributed in-network caches is a difficult problem. Existing systems rely on mechanisms and metrics that fail to effectively utilize all available sources of bandwidth in the network. This paper presents a novel metric, called the Content Propagation Metric (CPM), for quantitatively evaluating the marginal benefit of available bandwidth to competing consumers, enabling efficient utilization of the bandwidth resource. The metric is simple to implement, imposes only a modest overhead, and can be retrofitted easily into existing content distribution systems. We have designed and implemented a high-performance content distribution system, called V-Formation, based on the CPM. The CPM guides V-Formation toward a global allocation of bandwidth that maximizes the aggregate download bandwidth of consumers. Results from a PlanetLab deployment and extensive simulations show that V-Formation achieves high aggregate bandwidth and that the CPM enables hosts to converge quickly on a stable allocation of resources in a wide range of deployment scenarios.

Categories and Subject Descriptors

C.2.4 [**Computer-Communication Networks**]: Distributed Systems

General Terms

Design, Performance

Keywords

Content distribution, Hybrid, Peer-to-peer

1. INTRODUCTION

Multimedia content distribution is a critical problem that accounts for a majority of all Internet traffic [3]. Delivering content at large scale with low cost requires taking advantage of all resources avail-able. Yet existing approaches to content distribution have architectural and protocol limitations that fail to utilize available resources effectively.

Content distribution systems have three sources of bandwidth: content distributors' origin servers, in-network cache servers, and clients. Content distribution systems based on a client-server architecture, such as YouTube, place the entire resource burden on the first two sources of bandwidth, and thus necessitate a large initial investment and incur high running costs [16]. In contrast, peer-to-peer protocols, such as BitTorrent [1] and others [7,31,35], rely primarily on bandwidth contributed by clients. While these protocols permit the utilization of bandwidth from origin servers and in-network caches [4,5], they lack mechanisms for managing such bandwidth to achieve commercial objectives and service level guarantees a content distributor might seek. Finally, a new class of emerging content distribution systems based on a hybrid, peer-assisted architecture [32] manage the bandwidth from a single centralized server using a global optimization. Yet the optimization mechanism in such systems does not support in-network caches or distributed datacenters that house only a partial subset of the managed content. As a result, hybrid systems cannot provide performance guarantees for a deployment that comprises origin servers in datacenters, cache servers, and clients.

Achieving a performance objective of any kind requires a *metric* that can measure the performance of the system and thus help adjust its behavior to progress toward the performance goal. But the design of a suitable metric is non-trivial. For instance, BitTorrent hosts use a ranking derived from continuous block auctions [19] to determine which peers to unchoke in order to maximize their reciprocal bandwidth. This ranking is of limited use in other systems because it is intertwined with the BitTorrent block transfer mechanisms, is vulnerable to attack [21, 27], and can lead to undesirable global behaviors such as swarm starvation [32]. An ideal metric would be effective at achieving globally-desirable performance objectives, easy to implement, able to handle network churn, and backwards compatible with existing systems.

This paper presents a unifying metric, called the *Content Propagation Metric (CPM)*, that enables a content distribution system to efficiently manage the resources of origin servers, in-network cache servers, and clients. The key insight behind this metric is to capture how quickly a host's uploaded content propagates transitively throughout a set of peers downloading that content (a swarm). To this end, the CPM is calculated by computing the average size of recent block propagation trees rooted at a particular host for a given swarm. The CPM handles changing swarm dynamics, such as changes in swarm size, changes in link capacities, churn, block availability, and content uploads from other hosts, which can all affect the rate of content propagation. The CPM offers a consistent way for hosts to measure their marginal utility to a particular swarm, and to make informed decisions with their bandwidth among swarms competing for content.[1]

This paper makes three contributions. First, it introduces and defines the content propagation metric, discusses how it can be realized in practice, and examines its effectiveness in dynamic settings. Second, it outlines the design and implementation of a content distribution system, called V-Formation, that uses the CPM to guide hosts toward an efficient allocation of bandwidth that maximizes global aggregate bandwidth. The CPM enables V-Formation to converge on an efficient system-wide allocation of bandwidth in a broad range of deployment scenarios that include origin servers, cache servers, and clients in multiple swarms. Finally, it evaluates the performance impact of using the CPM to existing content distribution systems through a deployment and simulations. PlanetLab experiments show that V-Formation can improve aggregate bandwidth by approximately 60% and 30% over BitTorrent and Antfarm, respectively.

The rest of this paper is structured as follows. Section 2 gives background on allocating bandwidth in the presence of multiple swarms. Section 3 states the general content distribution problem that this paper addresses, incorporating in-network caches. Section 4 describes the CPM in detail and the core approach for allocating bandwidth based on measurements from individual hosts. Section 5 describes our implementation of V-Formation, which we use to evaluate the CPM in Section 6. Section 7 places our approach to content distribution in the context of related work, and Section 8 concludes.

2. BACKGROUND

Existing swarming protocols, such as BitTorrent (Figure 1), use mechanisms that allocate bandwidth efficiently within a single swarm, but their policies do not make efficient use of bandwidth from multiple origin servers and in-network cache servers.

To address content distribution in deployments where multiple swarms compete for bandwidth from a server, Antfarm [32] introduced a peer-assisted protocol that offers coordination among peers using a logically centralized coordinator. Antfarm uses active measurements to compute the optimal allocation of bandwidth from a single origin server, called the *seeder* (Figure 2). Every swarm exhibits a response to bandwidth that it receives from peers: everything else remaining constant, increasing the bandwidth that a peer contributes to a swarm increases the aggregate bandwidth within the swarm. Antfarm represents this relationship with a *response curve*, which captures a swarm's aggregate bandwidth as a function of the seeder's bandwidth allocated to that swarm. The seeder can use response curves collected for every swarm to determine which swarms benefit most from its bandwidth: the steeper the slope of a response curve, the more aggregate bandwidth the corresponding swarm achieves from additional seeder bandwidth.

Response curves are costly to obtain in practice, which renders them impractical for highly dynamic swarms. Measuring a single data point in a response curve requires a seeder to operate at a particular bandwidth for sufficiently long that the swarm's aggregate bandwidth stabilizes. While it is clearly unnecessary to measure a swarm's entire response curve in order to derive meaningful information, a response curve must contain sufficient data near the point of operation to obtain the curve's slope and calculate the expected benefit of an increase in seeder bandwidth. Furthermore, the opti-

[1]The word "metric" is used in the networking, not mathematical, context. http://en.wikipedia.org/wiki/Metrics_(networking).

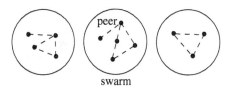

Figure 1: BitTorrent architecture. BitTorrent swarms are logically isolated; peers make bandwidth allocation decisions independently for each swarm.

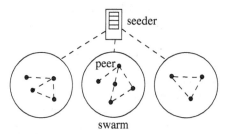

Figure 2: Antfarm architecture. Antfarm introduces a logically centralized coordinator to optimize bandwidth from a single origin server across multiple swarms, but neglects other inter-swarm bandwidth in its allocations.

mal point of operation can change rapidly as swarm memberships, network conditions, and block availability change.

Response curves provide an efficient allocation of bandwidth from a single seeder, but deployments where peers belong to multiple swarms add a level of complexity that response curves do not address. In a measurement study of over 6000 torrents and 960,000 users, we found that more than 20% of users simultaneously participated in more than one monitored torrent. Such peers are faced with choosing which swarms should receive their bandwidth, and their decisions can have dramatic effects on the performance of the system.

We discuss two approaches for adapting response curves to allocate bandwidth from multiple hosts, both of which result in suboptimal performance. In the first approach, the coordinator measures a set of response curves for each peer that belongs to multiple swarms, where each curve represents a swarm's response to bandwidth from a particular peer. Obtaining accurate measurements is difficult because peers' response curves are dependent on each other. The problem is exacerbated by the large time interval that a peer must wait for the swarm to stabilize at an aggregate bandwidth before taking a measurement; another peer's shift in point of operation during the time interval will perturb the measured value.

In an alternative approach, the coordinator instead maintains a single response curve per swarm, which captures the swarms' responses to bandwidth, independent of which particular hosts supply the bandwidth. The coordinator performs Antfarm's optimization on the response curves to calculate the optimal amount of bandwidth that each swarm should receive. Then, the coordinator assigns hosts to upload to particular swarms in order to realize the optimal bandwidth allocation based on the computed target swarm bandwidths and swarm memberships and upload capacities of individual peers. There are two problems with this approach. First, the assignment problem of assigning peers to swarms is difficult to solve at large scales, and greedy algorithms for assigning peer bandwidth to swarms can result in poor use of peers' resources. Second, using a single response curve for each swarm neglects variations among peers, such as which blocks they possess and network conditions to members of each of their swarms.

Overall, response curves offer an intuitive model for swarms that enables a logically centralized seeder to allocate bandwidth optimally among competing swarms. However, real-world issues render them less useful for highly dynamic swarms, and infeasible when swarms compete for bandwidth from multiple hosts distributed throughout the network or peers that belong to multiple swarms.

3. PROBLEM STATEMENT

To formalize bandwidth allocation among multiple swarms, we introduce the *general multi-swarm content distribution problem*. This defines a global performance goal over a class of realistic content distribution scenarios comprising origin servers, in-network caches, and end hosts organized into swarms (Figure 3).

Formally, given a set of peers P, a set of swarms S, and a set of memberships $M \subseteq P \times S$, the general multi-swarm content distribution problem is to determine the upload bandwidth $U_{p,s}$ that peer p should allocate to swarm s for all $(p,s) \in M$ in order to maximize global aggregate bandwidth $\sum_{p \in P} D_p$, where D_p is the download bandwidth of peer p.

This general formalization removes restrictions on the location of content and membership of peers in swarms. The CPM addresses the general multi-swarm content distribution problem by guiding hosts to an efficient allocation of bandwidth in these deployment scenarios.

4. APPROACH

The Content Propagation Metric provides an accurate measure of hosts' contributions, offering a practical approach for addressing the general multi-swarm content distribution problem. This section describes the CPM in detail. It then explores how peers use measured CPM values to compute an efficient allocation of bandwidth. The section concludes with discussions of how the CPM remains effective in the presence of highly dynamic swarms. We leave implementation details, including how to obtain and process CPM measurements, to Section 5.

4.1 Block Propagation Bandwidth

Peers that simply aim to saturate their upstream bandwidth without regard to the selection of the download recipients are not necessarily acting in the best interest of the global ecosystem. A recipient that fails to forward blocks to other peers provides little benefit to the swarm. The propagation of a block is hindered if a peer that receives it is unwilling to contribute its upstream bandwidth, or if the receiving peer's neighbors already possess the block. It is more beneficial to upload blocks to peers that are willing to contribute their bandwidth but lack desirable blocks that enable them to saturate their own upload capacities. As a result, blocks of equal rarity can have vastly different values to a swarm depending on which particular peers have those blocks and what other blocks those peers possess.

Block propagation bandwidth is a metric that captures these complex multi-peer interactions by encompassing the global demand for blocks, block availability, network conditions and topologies, and peer behavior. Block propagation bandwidth is defined for a particular block transfer between two peers, called a *tracked transfer*. Informally, the metric is the system-wide bandwidth during a specified time interval resulting from block transfers that occurred as a direct consequence of the tracked transfer. This metric provides

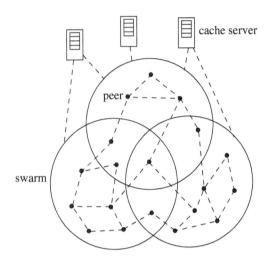

Figure 3: General multi-swarm content distribution. Peers, which includes all hosts that upload or download content, belong to arbitrary sets of potentially overlapping swarms.

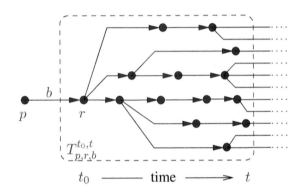

Figure 4: Propagation of a block. The dashed box indicates the propagation tree that results from peer p's tracked transfer of block b to peer r. The block propagates exponentially during the measurement time interval $\tau = t - t_0$, resulting in propagation bandwidth $v_{p,r,b}^{t_0,t} = 14 \cdot 256 \text{ KBytes}/30 \text{ s} \approx 120 \text{ KBytes/s}$, assuming 256-KByte blocks and $\tau = 30$ seconds.

an estimate of the benefit that results from a single block transfer from one peer to another.

Formally, for the upload of block b from peer p to peer r, where the transfer completes at time t_0, we define a *block propagation tree* $T_{p,r,b}^{t_0,t}$ rooted at r with a directed edge from p_1 to p_2 if r is an ancestor of p_1, and p_1 finishes uploading b to p_2 at time t' such that $t_0 < t' \le t$. Thus, $T_{p,r,b}^{t_0,t}$ is essentially an implicit multicast tree rooted at peer r for block b during the time interval $\tau = t - t_0$. The block propagation bandwidth, then, is

$$v_{p,r,b}^{t_0,t} = \left| T_{p,r,b}^{t_0,t} \right| \cdot \text{size}(b)/(t - t_0),$$

the download bandwidth enabled by p's tracked transfer to r over the time interval τ. Figure 4 shows an example propagation of a block and the resulting propagation tree. Assuming 256-KByte blocks and a τ of 30 seconds, the example block propagation bandwidth is approximately 120 KBytes/s.

Block propagation bandwidth enables peers to compare the relative benefits of their block uploads to competing swarms over a common time interval τ. To illustrate the metric and its relation to

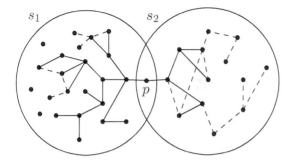

Figure 5: Block propagations in two competing swarms. Solid edges indicate the propagation of a particular block uploaded by peer p. Dashed edges indicate transfers of other blocks that compete with p's block for peers' upload bandwidth. p's block propagates more widely in swarm s_1 than in s_2.

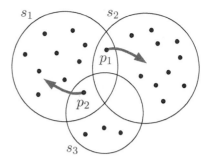

Figure 6: Three competing swarms. Peer p_1 in swarms s_1 and s_2 and peer p_2 in swarms s_1 and s_3 converge on the allocation of bandwidth indicated by the gray arrows. p_2's CPM value for s_3 is smaller than for s_1 due to the swarms' sizes; p_1 allocates its bandwidth to s_2, where its blocks do not compete with p_2's uploads.

the value of a block upload, consider the block propagations shown in Figure 5. Peer p is a member of swarms s_1 and s_2, to which p uploads tracked blocks. On average, peers in s_1 distribute their blocks more widely than peers in s_2, as indicated by solid edges. Dashed edges indicate peer-to-peer transfers of other blocks, which compete for peers' upload bandwidth. The higher average block propagation in s_1 can be due to several factors, including swarm size, competing uploads, peer behavior, and network conditions.

4.2 Content Propagation Metric

Block propagation bandwidth captures the utility of a given block upload, which may suffer from a high rate of fluctuation depending on that block's relative rarity and peer r, the peer that receives the block in the tracked transfer. To compensate for such fluctuations, the CPM is based on a statistical sample of blocks that are disseminated by each peer.

The CPM captures the utility of a peer to a given swarm based on its recent uploads. A peer's CPM value for a particular swarm is computed from block propagation bandwidths obtained within a recent time interval $\pi = t' - t$. Formally, let

$$V_{p,s}^{t,t'} = \left\{ v_{p,r_1,b_1}^{t_1,t'_1}, v_{p,r_2,b_2}^{t_2,t'_2}, \ldots \right\}$$

be the set of all block propagation measurements where blocks $b_1, b_2, \ldots$ are from swarm s and $t < t'_i \le t'$ for all i. Then,

$$\mathrm{CPM}_{p,s}^{t,t'} = \left(\sum_{v \in V_{p,s}^{t,t'}} v \right) / |V_{p,s}^{t,t'}|,$$

the average of the measurements. We define

$$\mathrm{CPM}_{p,s} = \mathrm{CPM}_{p,s}^{t^* - \pi, t^*},$$

with the times omitted, to be p's current value for swarm s during the most recent time interval π, where t^* is the current time. Each value $\mathrm{CPM}_{p,s}$ is implemented as a rolling average that is continually updated as new block propagation bandwidths become available and old measurements become stale.

The CPM distills the salient properties of response curves for deciding to which swarms peers should upload their blocks in order to yield high aggregate bandwidth. A peer's CPM value for a particular swarm approximates the instantaneous slope of the swarm's response curve at its point of operation. Whereas Antfarm measures a response curve and uses its slope to predict a swarm's bandwidth yield for any amount of seeder bandwidth, the CPM directly mea-

sures the slope of the response curve without the need to explicitly generate the curve.

To illustrate the CPM, consider the bandwidth allocation of two peers originating content for three new swarms with identical network conditions and no competition from other uploaders, as depicted in Figure 6. Swarms s_1 and s_2 distribute popular content, with new downloaders joining at a higher rate than swarm s_3. Peer p_1 possesses content for s_1 and s_2, and peer p_2 possesses content for s_1 and s_3. After uploading a few blocks and measuring CPM values, p_2 identifies s_1 as the swarm that benefits more from its bandwidth due to, in this example, its larger size. p_1 likewise measures a high CPM value for s_1, but blocks uploaded by p_2 interfere with p_1's uploads, causing both peers' CPM values for s_1 to diminish. Consequently, p_1 allocates its bandwidth to s_2, which lacks the competition of p_2's uploads.

As swarm dynamics change, CPM values shift to adjust peers' bandwidth allocations. Continuing the above example, after s_1 has received sufficiently many blocks, its peers may be able to sustain high aggregate bandwidth without support from p_2. In this case, p_2's block uploads to the swarm would compete with a large number of uploads from the peers themselves, causing p_2's blocks to propagate less. In turn, p_2's CPM value for s_3 may exceed its CPM value for s_1, causing p_2 to allocate its bandwidth to s_3 instead.

The CPM provides peers information to allocate bandwidth based on current swarm dynamics. It might be tempting to instead use a global rarest policy, where peers request rare blocks from neighbors regardless of swarm, and peers in multiple swarms preferentially satisfy requests for blocks that are rarest within their respective swarms. However, such a policy operates solely based on the number of replicas of each block, and disregards swarm dynamics and peer behavior.

A peer's CPM value provides an accurate estimate of the peer's value to a swarm relative to competing swarms. The CPM captures the average benefit that peers' recent block uploads had on their swarms, providing a useful prediction of the value of future block uploads.

4.3 Robustness of the CPM

The CPM handles changes in swarm membership and highly dynamic swarms, and achieves high performance in deployments with swarms of vastly different sizes. The CPM naturally dampens oscillations to converge on a stable allocation of bandwidth. We discuss these issues in turn.

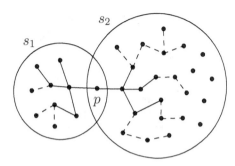

Figure 7: Measurement time interval. Edges indicate the propagation of blocks originating at peer p in swarms s_1 and s_2. Solid edges show the propagations within a time interval τ that is too small for p to differentiate its benefit to the competing swarms. Using a larger τ, indicated by dashed edges, makes it clear that s_2 receives more benefit from p's blocks.

4.3.1 Probing Swarms

Highly dynamic swarms pose two challenges for determining efficient bandwidth allocations. First, when peers join swarms for which they have no block propagation data, they are unable to compute the marginal benefit to the system from uploading blocks to the new swarm versus uploading blocks to a competing swarm. Second, swarms with high peer churn can respond very differently to a peer's contributions from one moment to the next. Consequently, such swarms can regularly invalidate many peers' CPM values, causing them to operate suboptimally.

Probing swarms enables calculation of CPM values for these problematic swarms with minimal overhead. To probe a swarm, a peer temporarily prioritizes requests for blocks in that swarm above other block requests until it has uploaded a small, constant number of blocks to the swarm. Data blocks are typically 128–256 KBytes, and we have found two block uploads to be sufficient for computing provisional CPM values to adapt to highly dynamic swarms.

4.3.2 Measurement Time Interval

The CPM measures the initial surge of block exchanges that occurs when a peer injects blocks into a swarm. The growth of a block's propagation tree reflects the swarm's demand for the block with respect to block availability, peer behavior, and network conditions within the vicinity of its tracked uploader. The wide range of swarm behavior means that using a globally constant time interval τ for measuring block propagations from all peers is insufficient.

Figure 7 gives an intuition of how the choice of measurement time interval affects a peer's ability to differentiate among competing swarms. Swarm s_1 is significantly smaller than s_2, but, assuming comparable network conditions and competition for blocks, using a small τ prevents p from recognizing that s_2 receives more benefit from each block. The propagation trees for small τ, represented by solid edges, are nearly identical in the two swarms, causing p to allocate its bandwidth equally between them. Increasing τ enables p to discover s_2's ability to achieve higher aggregate bandwidth than s_1 for each block.

Measuring block propagation with a τ that is unnecessarily large likewise decreases performance. A large measurement time interval increases the delay between the time p finishes uploading a block and the time p has an updated CPM value that incorporates the newly measured block propagations. Thus, choosing a suitable τ is a tradeoff between system performance, measured as aggregate bandwidth, and system adaptability, or the time required for

the system to converge on a new allocation of bandwidth in highly dynamic deployments.

Our implementation of V-Formation addresses the CPM's sensitivity to the measurement time interval by choosing an interval for each peer that teases apart the peer's highest-valued swarms. The system maintains a measurement time interval τ_p specific to each peer p. Based on recent block propagation data, the system adjusts τ_p in order to account for changes in size of p's swarms. To do this, the system periodically uses its record of p's recent block uploads to measure block propagation bandwidths for three different values of τ: τ_p, $\tau_p^{\text{low}} = 1/2 \cdot \tau_p$, and $\tau_p^{\text{high}} = 2 \cdot \tau_p$. It then updates τ_p with the smallest of the three time intervals for which p achieves different CPM values for its two swarms with the largest CPM values, corresponding to the swarms for which p has the greatest impact. Thus, the system continuously and iteratively computes τ_p, adjusting its value over time.

4.3.3 Stabilization

The CPM mitigates oscillations in bandwidth allocations despite complex interactions among peers that influence multiple swarms. First, changes in CPM values only affect the bandwidth allocations of peers that belong to multiple swarms. The remaining majority of peers propagate blocks within their respective swarms regardless of CPM values, dampening the effects of shifting bandwidth allocations on a swarm's aggregate bandwidth. Second, a peer's CPM values for competing swarms regulate the peer's bandwidth allocation among the swarms. A peer's CPM value for a swarm naturally decreases as the peer uploads to the swarm because the uploads increase competition for downloading peers' upload bandwidth. Once the CPM value drops below the CPM value of a competing swarm, the uploading peer allocates its bandwidth elsewhere, leaving the swarm with sufficient content to temporarily maintain a steady aggregate bandwidth. In Section 6, we show that system aggregate bandwidth converges stably when there are multiple swarms vying for bandwidth from cache servers with limited upload capacity.

5. IMPLEMENTATION

We have implemented our approach to content distribution based on the CPM in a system called V-Formation. V-Formation adopts a hybrid architecture that combines peer-to-peer exchanges with bandwidth from optional cache servers managed by a logically centralized coordinator. The coordinator tracks block exchanges in swarms based on the transfer of tokens and uses its measurements to compute CPM values. Tokens are unforgeable credits minted by the coordinator that function as a virtual currency; peers exchange tokens with each other for content blocks and reveal spent tokens to the coordinator as proof of contribution. Each token can only be spent once, and the coordinator verifies that each token is spent for a block within the swarm for which it was minted. V-Formation augments Antfarm's token protocol to include an identifier for the specific block for which a token was exchanged.

This section first discusses the operation of the coordinator, then the operation of peers based on the coordinator's guidance. For simplicity, the discussion assumes compliant peers that follow the protocol as proscribed; we address incentive compatibility in Section 5.4.

5.1 Coordinator

V-Formation's logically centralized coordinator consists of three components: web servers, processors, and a shared state layer (Figure 8). First, web servers process requests from peers to dispense

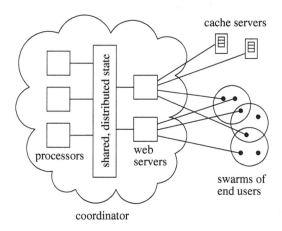

Figure 8: The V-Formation coordinator. Web servers communicate with peers (including cache servers) to gather information on swarm dynamics. Processors use swarm dynamics to compute peer bandwidth allocations. Web servers and processors communicate via a distributed state layer.

fresh tokens, collect spent tokens, and notify peers of computed bandwidth allocations. Second, *processors* use token exchanges aggregated by the web servers to calculate peer bandwidth allocations. Third, a distributed state layer grants web servers and processors read and write access for consolidating block exchange information and bandwidth allocations. The web servers, processors, and state can be distributed across multiple physical machines, or they can run on a single physical host for smaller deployments. We describe the operations of web servers and processors in turn, followed by a summary of all information stored in the distributed state layer.

5.1.1 Web Servers

V-Formation's peer-facing web servers function as an augmented tracker for facilitating swarms, similar a BitTorrent tracker. Web servers accept three types of requests asynchronously from peers: announce, get_tokens, and deposit_tokens. Peers issue periodic announce requests for each of their swarms to obtain addresses of other peers and to discover how to allocate bandwidth to swarms. An announce request contains the requesting peer's identifier and a swarm's identifier, represented as a 20-byte hash. A web server responds to an announce request with addresses of a random set of peers and the requesting peer's most recent CPM value for the swarm. Announce intervals are dynamically adjusted to achieve a constant CPU utilization of the web servers.

The get_tokens and deposit_tokens requests facilitate the exchange of fresh and spent tokens between peers and the coordinator, respectively. The coordinator maintains a credit balance for each peer that represents the total number of tokens that the peer can obtain across all swarms. A get_tokens request deducts from the issuer's credit balance in exchange for fresh tokens for a particular swarm, to be exchanged for blocks within a specific time interval. When a peer receives a token from another peer in exchange for a block, the peer sends it to the coordinator in a deposit_tokens request. The web server verifies the token's authenticity, increases the peer's balance accordingly, and, if the coordinator is tracking the block referenced in the token, records the block exchange in the state layer.

Web servers record block exchanges in *block exchange forests*

for use by processors. A block exchange forest contains a set of peer identifiers as vertices and recent block exchanges as timestamped, directed edges. Each forest is specific to a particular block in a particular swarm; web servers build a separate forest for each block that the coordinator is tracking. To add a block exchange to a forest, a web server simply adds an edge from the block's sender to its recipient, timestamped using the coordinator's clock upon receiving the token.

5.1.2 Processors

Processors continuously iterate over block exchange forests to extract block propagation bandwidths. A single forest contains a propagation bandwidth for each edge timestamped prior to the current time minus τ, the time interval over which block propagations are measured. A processor extracts a propagation bandwidth for each such edge, prunes those edges from the forest, and records the new propagation bandwidths in the state layer.

Before extracting propagation bandwidths, the processor adjusts the timestamps on the forest's edges such that no edge is timestamped later than any edge in its subtree. Such an inconsistency occurs if a peer deposits its spent tokens before an ancestor in a block propagation tree deposits its own tokens for the same block. To make the adjustment, the processor recurses on each of the forest's roots, setting each timestamp to the minimum of its own timestamp and the earliest timestamp in its subtree. This makes the forest reflect the constraint that a peer can only upload a block after it has received that block.

To extract block propagation bandwidths, the processor recurses on each vertex in a forest, summing up the number of edges in each subtree. The processor only calculates and reports propagation bandwidths for edges older than the measurement time interval τ. It removes the corresponding edges from the forest and appends each new propagation bandwidth to a list in the state layer of propagation bandwidths for the tracked uploader's contribution to the forest's swarm. Each new propagation bandwidth is timestamped with the time on the forest's tracked transfer edge, equal to the time that the tracked transfer completed.

Web servers compute CPM values for a peer's swarms by averaging the propagation bandwidths in the list that are timestamped within a recent time interval π, a global constant set to five minutes in our implementation. In an announce response, web servers report the most recent CPM value, or, if there are no recent propagation bandwidths, instruct the requester to upload blocks to the swarm to obtain fresh measurements.

Operating on block exchange forests is a highly parallel task. Each forest represents exchanges of a single block for a single swarm, enabling processors to operate on block exchange forests in isolation. Multiple processors coordinate their behavior through the state by atomically reading and incrementing the swarm and block identifiers for the next forest to process. Thus, increasing the number of processor machines linearly increases the supported processing workload of the coordinator.

If high load renders the coordinator unable to process all block propagation forests, the coordinator sheds load by decreasing the fraction of blocks that it tracks. The coordinator maintains a dynamically adjusted parameter that dictates the fraction of blocks to track, enabling web servers and processors to independently determine whether a particular block should be tracked. Web servers do not insert forest edges for untracked blocks, and processors do not iterate over forests of untracked blocks. The coordinator adjusts the parameter such that for each swarm, some block is processed with a target frequency.

5.1.3 Distributed State Layer

V-Formation uses memcached to implement a distributed, shared state layer for web servers and processors. The coordinator's state is linear in the number of swarms it supports and in the number of peers.

The coordinator maintains data structures for each of the swarms it supports as well as for each peer in the system. Since this state is stored in memcached, it is distributed across multiple servers. Atomic compare and swap operations supported by memcached enable nodes to update this state quickly and concurrently. Since all such state is soft and can be recreated through remeasurement, if necessary, it need not be stored on disk. All lookups are performed with a specific key, so the memcached key-value store suffices, and an expensive relational database insertion is unnecessary.

For each peer, the state layer maintains its address, port, identifier, credit balance, and the set of swarms to which it belongs. For each swarm, the state layer keeps a swarm identifier and the set of peers in the swarm. To make bandwidth allocations, for each peer the state layer records its current τ for computing block propagation bandwidths, its current CPM value for each swarm, and a history of block propagation bandwidths for each measured block over the past time interval π. Recent block transfers for measured blocks are stored as block propagation forests linear in size to the number of peers and edges that they contain. Forests are pruned as block propagation bandwidths are extracted, based on peers' values of τ. Lastly, the state layer maintains a single value representing the next block that a processor should analyze, which processors advance each time they read it.

5.2 Peers

Peers interact with the coordinator by issuing announce requests periodically for each swarm, get_token requests when their fresh tokens are nearly depleted, and deposit_token requests when they possess spent tokens from other peers. They interact with other peers through block requests for the rarest blocks among directly connected neighbors, and they satisfy block requests according to their CPM values for competing swarms. Upon receiving a block, a peer responds with a fresh token embedded with the block's identifier.

To allocate bandwidth among competing swarms, peers prioritize their swarms based on the CPM values contained in announce responses. Upon receiving a CPM value, a peer updates a local prioritized list of its swarms. When a peer has received multiple outstanding block requests from peers in different swarms, it satisfies the request from the swarm with the largest CPM value.

If the coordinator lacks current information on recent block exchanges for any swarm to which a peer belongs, the coordinator reports that the peer should probe the swarm. The special probe flag instructs a peer to upload a small, constant number of blocks to the swarm for the coordinator to track.

5.3 QoS Guarantees

In some cases, it may be desirable to guarantee a minimum bandwidth for particular swarms in order to meet service-level agreements or to provide a certain quality of service to designated swarms. V-Formation enables system administrators to specify lower bounds for swarms where necessary, sacrificing overall system performance in favor of control. V-Formation satisfies such requests by diverting upload bandwidth from members of the swarm whose CPM values suggest that they should upload to other competing swarms instead. In order to minimize impact on overall system performance, the co-ordinator iteratively reassigns bandwidth from peers with low CPM values for competing swarms until the target service level has been achieved.

5.4 Security

Securing a peer-assisted content distribution system from malicious users or free-loaders is significantly more tractable than securing pure peer-to-peer systems. The coordinator in a peer-assisted systems serves as a trusted entity in the system that can detect attacks and enforce access control when coupled with a secure wire protocol.

The V-Formation wire protocol is an extension of the Antfarm wire protocol [32] and shares the same security guarantees. It makes standard cryptographic assumptions on the infeasibility of reversing a one-way cryptographic hash function. It also assumes that packets cannot be read or modified by untrusted third parties at the IP level. Such an attack is difficult without collusion from ISPs, and a successful attack only influences peers whose packets can be snooped and spoofed. We support SSL on peer-to-peer and peer-to-coordinator exchanges, respectively. While a formal treatment of the security properties of the protocol is beyond the scope of this paper, prior work [35] has established the feasibility of a secure, cryptographic wire protocol using a trusted, logically centralized server.

V-Formation's token protocol incentivizes peers to report accurate and timely information about block exchanges to the coordinator. Fresh tokens contain unforgeable identifiers known only to the coordinator and the peers for which they are minted. When a peer receives a token in exchange for a block, the token's recipient embeds the identifier of its original owner and verifies the block identifier embedded in the token before depositing the token at the coordinator. The coordinator verifies that the token's spender and depositor are members of the swarm for which the token was minted, according to its records. In addition, the coordinator checks that the token was deposited before its expiration time, ensuring that it represents a recent block exchange. If a check fails, at least one of the two peers known to have touched the token are at fault, and the coordinator marks both peers possible culprits.

Peers are incentivized to deposit tokens soon after receiving them in exchange for blocks, resulting in accurate block propagation forests at the coordinator. All tokens must be deposited at the coordinator before they expire, placing an upper bound on the deviance of a block exchange's timestamp. Peers with small credit balances are incentivized to deposit tokens earlier than their expiration times in order to receive fresh tokens to spend. Consequently, when the coordinator adjusts timestamps on forest edges before extracting propagation bandwidths, promptly deposited tokens result in early timestamps that percolate up the forest trees, replacing timestamps of exchanges whose tokens were deposited significantly after the block exchanges actually occurred.

6. EVALUATION

We have implemented the full V-Formation protocol described in this paper, both in a deployed system that is actively running on FlixQ [2], and in a simulator for fine-grain analysis of its performance. Through a deployment on PlanetLab [6] and extensive simulations, we compare V-Formation's performance to Antfarm, BitTorrent, and a BitTorrent-like *global rarest* policy where peers request the rarest blocks for which they are interested across all swarms. We also evaluate secondary features of the CPM, such as convergence time to a stable allocation and sensitivity to changing swarm dynamics.

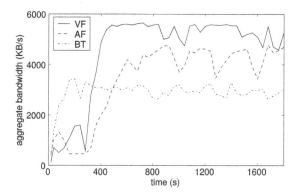

Figure 9: Performance on PlanetLab. 380 nodes in 200 swarms download movies from FlixQ using the V-Formation protocol and the same movies using the Antfarm and BitTorrent protocols.

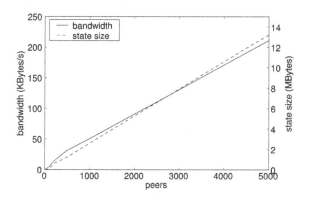

Figure 10: Scalability. Both memory consumption and bandwidth at the coordinator scale linearly with the size of the system.

6.1 Live Deployment

We evaluated our live deployment of V-Formation against Antfarm and version 5.0.9 of the official BitTorrent implementation. Our V-Formation deployment uses a distributed coordinator deployed in the Amazon EC2 cloud. In this experiment, 380 PlanetLab nodes each download one or more of 200 simulated movies, where a random 20% of the downloading nodes join two or more swarms to reflect the results of our BitTorrent trace. Two cache servers running on PlanetLab nodes seed the swarms. We scaled down the upload capacities of the cache servers to 50 KBytes/s each to reflect our relatively small deployment size. Peer upload capacities are drawn from the distribution of BitTorrent peer bandwidth collected by Pouwelse et al. [25]. This distribution specifies a median and 90th percentile peer upload capacity of 30 and 250 KBytes/s, respectively. The peers' download capacities are set 50% higher than their upload capacities to simulate asymmetric links.

The results of the experiment (Figure 9) show the three systems' aggregate bandwidths over time. V-Formation exhibits similar initial behavior as Antfarm, with lower aggregate bandwidth than BitTorrent in the first six minutes as peers probe swarms to determine an efficient allocation of bandwidth. V-Formation transitions to its steady state more quickly than Antfarm as a result of its lightweight probes, and it maintains a significantly higher steady state aggregate bandwidth than Antfarm and BitTorrent.

V-Formation's logically centralized coordinator is a potential performance bottleneck, and a poor implementation could limit the

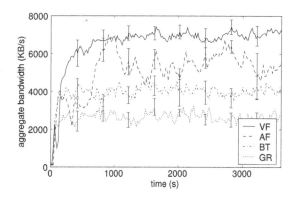

Figure 11: Comparison of protocols. Peers download movies with lengths and popularities randomly drawn from the Internet Movie Database. Peers have link capacities drawn from a distribution determined by a BitTorrent measurement study. Error bars indicate 95% confidence.

system's scalability. The next experiment examines how our implementation of the coordinator scales as a function of the size of the deployment; we found that the coordinator's bandwidth and memory requirements scale linearly with the total number of peers (Figure 10). In this experiment, peers are simulated across hosts in a computer cluster. Each peer is assigned a random bandwidth drawn from the same measured BitTorrent distribution as in the PlanetLab deployment. A peer's bandwidth is proportional to the rate at which the peer simulates receiving blocks from random participants in its swarm. Hosts in the cluster issue realistic deposit_token requests to the coordinator according to these simulated block transfers, as well as periodic announce requests. We made minor modifications to the coordinator to accept deposited tokens as if they were coming from legitimate peers with different IP addresses. In the experiment, three new peers enter the system every second and join a swarm for a 1-GByte file with 256-KByte blocks. The coordinator is distributed over two Amazon EC2 instances, each running a web server, a processor, and a slice of the memcached shared state layer. The reported memory usage includes all CPM, swarm, and peer metadata stored in the state layer, as discussed in Section 5.1.3. Coordinator bandwidth includes all outgoing tokens, CPM values, and responses to announce requests.

6.2 Simulations

Simulation experiments provide an in-depth examination of the CPM and how it affects hosts' bandwidth allocations in V-Formation. We first show the system-wide aggregate bandwidth of V-Formation, Antfarm, BitTorrent, and a global rarest policy for a realistic simulation based on movies in the Internet Movie Database (IMDb). The experiment is based on the number of votes and lengths of 425,000 movies, scaled down to 500 peers and 300 swarms to make simulations feasible. Each swarm facilitates the download of a single movie file, and each swarm's popularity is proportional to the number of votes that its movie has received on IMDb, resulting in a power-law distribution of swarm sizes. Each file's size is based on the movie's length and 1 Mbit/s video compression, common for 480p video. Swarm memberships are assigned iteratively, each of approximately 670 movie downloads randomly assigned either to a peer that has already been assigned one or more downloads, or to a fresh peer with no assigned downloads, the probability of each case calibrated so that 20% of peers belong to multiple swarms to reflect our BitTorrent trace. As in the PlanetLab deployment, nodes draw their bandwidth distribution from the measured BitTorrent band-

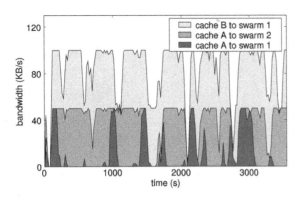

Figure 12: Cache bandwidth to a pair of swarms. Two swarms of similar size achieve comparable aggregate bandwidth even though cache B does not possess content for swarm s_2. Cache A gives more bandwidth to s_2 (medium gray area) than to s_1 (dark gray area) to compensate.

width distribution. Content originates from two cache servers, simulating a distributed cache of movie files. Cache server A contains a copy of every movie; cache server B has only a random 50% of the library's files to mitigate load on cache server A. Both servers upload content at 50 KBytes/s, scaled down from a realistic datacenter bandwidth due to the number of simulated downloaders. We show the system-wide aggregate bandwidth of each protocol over a one-hour run (Figure 11).

Both BitTorrent and the global rarest policy ignore swarm- and system-wide performance. The result is that singleton swarms and small swarms from the long tail receive a high proportion of the servers' bandwidth. Such peers are unable to forward blocks as rapidly as members of larger swarms, resulting in low aggregate bandwidth for pure peer-to-peer approaches. V-Formation achieves 66% higher aggregate bandwidth than BitTorrent.

V-Formation differs from Antfarm in both the time to converge on an allocation of bandwidth and the aggregate bandwidth itself after convergence. Since V-Formation uses lightweight probes to determine bandwidth allocations, it reaches a stable allocation of bandwidth four times faster than Antfarm. Antfarm instead relies on response curves to assess swarms, which requires the Antfarm coordinator to remain at a particular bandwidth allocation for a longer time before it becomes apparent which swarms benefit most from bandwidth.

Further, after the protocols converge, V-Formation and Antfarm achieve different aggregate bandwidths due to constraints imposed by individual peers' bandwidths and swarm memberships. From the experiment shown in Figure 11, consider two swarms s_1 and s_2 for which peers measure comparable CPM values, where s_1's movie is cached on both servers and s_2's movie is only cached on server B. In this scenario, the Antfarm coordinator measures a response curve for each of the two swarms and determines that both swarms should receive approximately equal bandwidth from the servers. However, Antfarm is unable to realize this allocation due to the constraints of peers' upload capacities and their swarm memberships. The coordinator's greedy solution to the assignment problem results in suboptimal performance.

In contrast, the V-Formation coordinator uses each individual peer's benefit to arrive at a more efficient allocation of bandwidth. A representative run of the experiment shows that both swarms receive comparable bandwidth from the cache servers despite the imbalance in the cache servers' content (Figure 12). Cache server B

can only upload to swarm s_1 because it only contains one of the movies, as depicted by the light gray area. Cache server A, on the other hand, possesses both movies, so it can upload blocks to either swarm. The dark gray and medium gray areas indicate that swarm s_2 receives more bandwidth from cache server A than s_1. Fluctuations in the caches' bandwidth is due to allocating bandwidth to other swarms in the system as measured CPM values vary over time. Averaged over eight runs of the experiment, cache server A uploads a majority of its bandwidth to the swarm with only one source (with an average of 124 peers) and only 12.6 KBytes/s to the swarm also sourced by cache server B (with an average of 120 peers) in order to offset cache server B's asymmetric contribution of 42.1 KBytes/s to the swarm sourced by both servers. Interactions among swarms similar to the two swarms we have examined account for V-Formation's 30% higher system-wide bandwidth over Antfarm.

To provide further insight into V-Formation's bandwidth allocation algorithm, we empirically show how V-Formation allocates bandwidth to competing swarms. We set up a scenario where peer p_1 possesses content for two swarms s_1 and s_2 with 25 downloaders each, and peer p_2 possesses content for s_1 and a small swarm s_3 with only three downloaders (Figure 6). All peers have upload and download capacities of 50 KBytes/s. The two peers p_1 and p_2 converge on an efficient, stable allocation (Figure 13). The left-hand graph shows p_1's CPM values for its swarms over time; the right-hand graph shows the same for p_2. When the simulation begins, p_1 and p_2 probe their respective swarms to obtain initial CPM values. They both measure comparable CPM values for s_1, which are similar to p_1's initial measurement of s_2. p_2 quickly discovers that s_3 receives little benefit from its block uploads, so it allocates its bandwidth to s_1. The competition that p_2's uploads create diminishes p_1's CPM value for s_1, causing it to dedicate its bandwidth to s_2. This sequence of events matches the expected behavior of the V-Formation protocol, with peer p_1 preferentially providing bandwidth to s_2 as s_1 can be sourced by both p_1 and p_2. The periodic fluctuations of measured CPM values are the result of probing; CPM values go stale after five minutes of no activity, at which time peers probe swarms for new block propagation bandwidths.

In order to differentiate peers' effects on competing swarms, the coordinator adjusts the block propagation measurement time interval τ for each peer. We measure a single peer p's block propagation bandwidths for three competing swarms s_1, s_2, and s_3, as well as the aggregate bandwidth that results from using each value. Swarm s_1 has 30 downloaders, and s_2 and s_3 each have 20 downloaders. Swarm s_3 has an additional source of content whose uploads compete with p's uploads. All peers have upload and download capacities of 50 KBytes/s. The coordinator chooses a value for τ that enables it to differentiate among swarms (Figure 14). The left-hand graph shows the resulting CPM values as a function of the coordinator's choice of τ. All three swarms exhibit comparable CPM values for small τ, but with sufficiently large τ, the swarms' different behaviors become prominent. The right-hand graph shows the system-wide aggregate bandwidth that results from each value of τ, with values 30 seconds and above providing approximately equal aggregate bandwidth. The vertical dashed line in the graph indicates the coordinator's dynamic choice of τ for determining p's bandwidth allocation. The coordinator chooses the smallest τ such that it is able to distinguish p's contribution to the swarms that receive the most benefit from p's blocks. The selected τ is safely above 30 seconds, enabling the system to operate at a high aggregate bandwidth.

The next two experiments evaluate how the CPM enables V-Formation to converge on a stable allocation of bandwidth in the

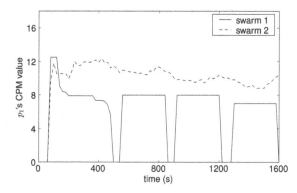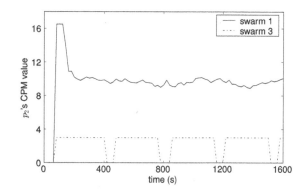

Figure 13: CPM values for competing swarms. Peer p_1 has cached content for two large swarms s_1 and s_2 (left), and peer p_2 has content for s_1 and a small swarm s_3 (right). p_2 creates competition for block uploads in s_1, causing p_1 to upload to s_2.

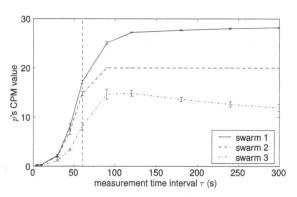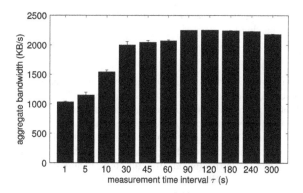

Figure 14: Sensitivity to the measurement time interval. Competing swarms are indistinguishable for small τ. Sufficiently large τ enables peer p to discover the swarm that receives the most benefit from its blocks. The vertical dashed line shows the coordinator's choice of τ based on the measurements. Error bars indicate 95% confidence.

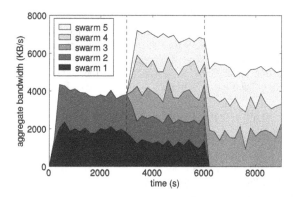

Figure 15: Convergence and stability. Three cache servers concurrently upload to two, five, and three identical swarms, indicated by shaded areas. The protocol adapts quickly to the changes introduced at the dotted lines, achieving equal aggregate bandwidth across swarms in each interval.

presence of churn. In both experiments, three cache servers initially provide content to two identical swarms s_1 and s_2, each with 50 peers. Again, peers have asymmetric upload and download links drawn from the same measured BitTorrent distribution. Due to symmetry, both swarms receive an even split of the servers' bandwidth and achieve equal aggregate bandwidth (Figure 15). At 3000 seconds, identical swarms s_3, s_4, and s_5 simultaneously join.

The cache servers adjust their allocations to maintain proportional swarm aggregate bandwidths by slightly sacrificing the aggregate bandwidths of s_1 and s_2 to bootstrap the new swarms. The caches' bandwidth is too small to saturate peers' upload capacities across the five swarms, but V-Formation manages to converge on equal aggregate bandwidths despite limited cache bandwidth. At 6000 seconds, all peers in s_1 and s_2 leave simultaneously; the remaining swarms each achieve an equal increase in aggregate bandwidth. V-Formation adapts within five minutes to dramatic changes in swarm memberships by choosing an appropriate block propagation time measurement interval τ that enables hosts to efficiently detect the swarms that benefit most from their bandwidth (Figure 16). Cache servers continuously shift their allocations based on changing CPM values, and swarms dampen the effect that the fluctuating allocations have on the swarms' aggregate bandwidths.

7. RELATED WORK

Past work on content distribution falls into two categories: content distribution networks in general and peer-to-peer swarming systems in particular.

Content distribution networks leverage distributed hosts to alleviate load at content origin servers and to improve latency and bandwidth performance for clients. Akamai [18] is an infrastructure-based CDN that many content providers use to distribute their content. ECHOS [20] proposes introducing infrastructure at the Internet's periphery to cache content near clients. Choffnes et al. [11] reduce cross-ISP traffic in peer-to-peer systems by harvesting data

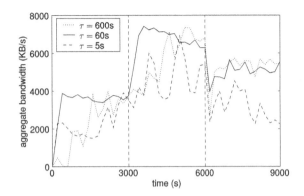

Figure 16: Time measurement interval and churn. Swarm memberships change drastically at the two vertical dashed lines. A measurement time interval τ that is too large or too small results in suboptimal performance. V-Formation chooses τ to maximize aggregate bandwidth.

from existing CDNs for locality information. Numerous CDNs rely on consistent hashing within distributed hash tables to replicate content for faster downloads and higher availability [14, 38]; in general, cooperative web caching dissipates load at servers [8, 15, 17, 37]. CoBlitz [26] uses proxies to disseminate content in pieces and assemble it near downloaders. V-Formation uses the CPM to make efficient use of bandwidth from all hosts, including server-class machines that cache content in the network.

Swarming systems leverage bandwidth contributed by peers in a mesh network for increased scalability and resiliency. BitTorrent [9], a swarming protocol that contributes to much of the Internet's traffic [25, 36], encourages peers to contribute their bandwidth using a bilateral tit-for-tat mechanism. Much prior work has measured and modeled BitTorrent's performance and tit-for-tat strategy, showing that it is susceptible to Sybil attacks [12] and is easily gamed [21, 27, 34]. New protocols have responded to BitTorrent's incentive mechanism that emphasize fairness using cryptographic- or auction-based mechanisms [24, 33, 35]. Such protocols encourage peers to contribute bandwidth in order to be rewarded with a proportional or equal number of content blocks. Fairness is not a primary concern of V-Formation; while some protocols rely on fairness for incentive compatibility, V-Formation enforces behavior with its coordinator, freeing it to maximizing system-wide performance instead.

Many swarming protocols rely on cryptographic virtual currencies to incentivize peers to contribute bandwidth. Dandelion [35] and BAR Gossip [22] employ tamper-resistant protocols that ensure that peers are honest. Similarly, microcurrencies [10, 23, 30, 39] rely on cryptographic tokens exchanged between parties to enforce correct behavior. V-Formation extends the lightweight token protocol introduced by Antfarm [32] to incentivize peers to follow the prescribed protocol and risk being discovered and blacklisted if they deviate.

One-Hop Reputations [28] and Contracts [29] use propagation trees of depth one to increase peer accountability in bulk download and live streaming systems, respectively. The protocols introduce peer incentivization strategies that outperform BitTorrent's bilateral tit-for-tat approach. The CPM is defined by content propagation trees that measure the benefit of a host to particular swarms.

Freedman et al. [13] propose a protocol that manages downloads in a multi-file system. Peers use a distributed algorithm to determine the relative values of content files and the market-based supply and demand for content blocks at each peer according to available network resources. The protocol enables ISPs to set a cost on transferring data over specific network links. It enables peers to adjust block prices based on local content demand; V-Formation, on the other hand, takes a holistic view of the relative contributions that peers bring to their swarms.

The work most similar to V-Formation is Antfarm [32], a content distribution system that measures swarms' responses to seeder bandwidth in order to optimize its uploads among competing swarms. Antfarm does not efficiently allocate bandwidth from multiple origin servers or from in-networking cache servers, which belong to multiple, overlapping swarms. In contrast, V-Formation accounts for bandwidth from all hosts based on real-time measurements using the CPM.

8. CONCLUSIONS

This paper introduced the Content Propagation Metric, which enables content distribution systems to make efficient use of bandwidth from all sources, including content distributors' origin servers, in-network caches, and clients. The CPM captures how quickly content propagates throughout swarms, providing hosts a basis of comparison that they can use to preferentially upload content to swarms that exhibit high marginal utility. A new content distribution system called V-Formation, based on a hybrid, peer-assisted architecture, uses the CPM to allocate hosts' bandwidth among competing swarms. V-Formation achieves a global performance goal of maximizing system-wide aggregate bandwidth by using the CPM to guide hosts toward an efficient use of resources. The CPM naturally handles dynamic swarm and peer behavior, and enables V-Formation to stabilize quickly on an efficient allocation of bandwidth. The flexibility of the CPM makes V-Formation efficient and scalable, rendering it well-suited to address the increasing demand for online media content.

9. ACKNOWLEDGMENTS

We would like to thank our shepherd Michael J. Freedman and the anonymous reviewers for their insights and comments. This material is based upon work supported by the National Science Foundation under Grant No. 0546568 and the 2009 Google Fellowship in Distributed Systems.

10. REFERENCES

[1] BitTorrent. http://bittorrent.com.

[2] FlixQ.com – Videosharing For The Masses. http://flixq.com.

[3] Ipoque – Internet Studies http://www.ipoque.com/resources/internet-studies.

[4] Velocix – New Generation Content Delivery Network http://www.velocix.com.

[5] Verivue – OneVantage Content Delivery Solution http://verivue.com.

[6] A. C. Bavier, M. Bowman, B. N. Chun, D. E. Culler, S. Karlin, S. Muir, L. L. Peterson, T. Roscoe, T. Spalink, and M. Wawrzoniak. Operating Systems Support For Planetary-scale Network Services. *Symposium on Networked System Design and Implementation*, San Francisco, CA, March 2004.

[7] J. W. Byers, M. Luby, M. Mitzenmacher, and A. Rege. A Digital Fountain Approach To Reliable Distribution Of Bulk Data. *SIGCOMM Conference*, Vancouver, Canada, August 1998.

[8] A. Chankhunthod, P. B. Danzig, C. Neerdaels, M. F. Schwartz, and K. J. Worrell. A Hierarchical Internet Object

Cache. *USENIX Annual Technical Conference*, San Diego, CA, January 1996.

[9] B. Cohen. Incentives Build Robustness In BitTorrent. *Workshop on the Economics of Peer-to-Peer Systems*, Berkeley, CA, May 2003.

[10] J. Camp, M. Sirbu, and J. D. Tygar. Token And Notational Money In Electronic Commerce. *USENIX Workshop on Electronic Commerce*, New York, NY, July 1995.

[11] D. R. Choffnes and F. E. Bustamante. Taming The Torrent: A Practical Approach To Reducing Cross-ISP Traffic In Peer-to-Peer Systems. *SIGCOMM Conference*, Seattle, WA, August 2008.

[12] J. R. Douceur. The Sybil Attack. *International Workshop on Peer-to-Peer Systems*, Springer Lecture Notes in Computer Science 2429, Cambridge, MA, March 2002.

[13] M. J. Freedman, C. Aperjis, and R. Johari. Prices Are Right: Managing Resources And Incentives In Peer-Assisted Content Distribution. *International Workshop on Peer-to-Peer Systems*, Tampa Bay, FL, February 2008.

[14] M. J. Freedman, E. Freudenthal, and D. Mazières. Democratizing Content Publication With Coral. *Symposium on Networked System Design and Implementation*, San Francisco, CA, March 2004.

[15] S. Gadde, J. S. Chase, and M. Rabinovich. Web Caching And Content Distribution: A View From The Interior. *Computer Communications*, 24(2), May 2001.

[16] C. Huang, J. Li, and K. W. Ross. Can Internet Video-on-Demand Be Profitable? *SIGCOMM Conference*, 2007.

[17] D. Karger, A. Sherman, A. Berkheimer, B. Bogstad, R. Dhanidina, K. Iwamoto, B. Kim, L. Matkins, and Y. Yerushalmi. Web Caching With Consistent Hashing. *International World Wide Web Conference*, Toronto, Canada, May 1999.

[18] D. R. Karger, E. Lehman, F. T. Leighton, R. Panigrahy, M. S. Levine, and D. Lewin. Consistent Hashing And Random Trees: Distributed Caching Protocols For Relieving Hot Spots On The World Wide Web. *ACM Symposium on Theory of Computing*, El Paso, TX, May 1997.

[19] D. Levin, K. LaCurts, N. Spring, and B. Bhattacharjee. BitTorrent Is An Auction: Analyzing And Improving BitTorrent's Incentives. *SIGCOMM Conference*, Seattle, WA, August 2008.

[20] N. Laoutaris, P. Rodriguez, and L. Massoulie. Echos: Edge Capacity Hosting Overlays Of Nano Data Centers. *ACM SIGCOMM: Computer Communication Review*, 38, January 2008.

[21] T. Locher, P. Moor, S. Schmid, and R. Wattenhofer. Free Riding In BitTorrent Is Cheap. *Workshop on Hot Topics in Networks*, Irvine, CA, November 2006.

[22] H. C. Li, A. Clement, E. L. Wong, J. Napper, I. Roy, L. Alvisi, and M. Dahlin. Bar Gossip. *Symposium on Operating System Design and Implementation*, Seattle, WA, November 2006.

[23] M. Manasse. The Millicent Protocol For Electronic Commerce. *USENIX Workshop on Electronic Commerce*, New York, NY, August 1995.

[24] T.-W. Ngan, D. S. Wallach, and a. P. Druschel. Enforcing Fair Sharing Of Peer-to-Peer Resources. *International Workshop on Peer-to-Peer Systems*, Springer Lecture Notes in Computer Science 2735, Berkeley, CA, February 2003.

[25] J. Pouwelse, P. Garbacki, D. Epema, and H. Sips. The BitTorrent P2P File-Sharing System: Measurements And Analysis. *International Workshop on Peer-to-Peer Systems*, Springer Lecture Notes in Computer Science 3640, Ithaca, NY, February 2005.

[26] K. Park and V. S. Pai. Scale And Performance In Coblitz Large-file Distribution Service. *Symposium on Networked System Design and Implementation*, San Jose, CA, May 2006.

[27] M. Piatek, T. Isdal, T. Anderson, A. Krishnamurthy, and A. Venkataramani. Do Incentives Build Robustness In BitTorrent? *Symposium on Networked System Design and Implementation*, Cambridge, MA, April 2007.

[28] M. Piatek, T. Isdal, A. Krishnamurthy, and T. Anderson. One Hop Reputations For Peer To Peer File Sharing Workloads. *Symposium on Networked System Design and Implementation*, San Francisco, CA, April 2008.

[29] M. Piatek, A. Krishnamurthy, A. Venkataramani, R. Yang, D. Zhang, and A. Jaffe. Contracts: Practical Contribution Incentives For P2P Live Streaming. *Symposium on Networked System Design and Implementation*, San Jose, CA, April 2010.

[30] T. Poutanen, H. Hinton, and M. Stumm. Netcents: A Lightweight Protocol For Secure Micropayments. *USENIX Workshop on Electronic Commerce*, Boston, MA, August 1998.

[31] J. A. Pouwelse, P. Garbacki, J. Wang, A. Bakker, J. Yang, A. Iosup, D.H.J. Epema, M. Reinders, M. van Steen, and H.J. Sips. *International Workshop on Peer-to-Peer Systems*, Santa Barbara, CA, February 2006.

[32] R. S. Peterson and E. G. Sirer. Antfarm: Efficient Content Distribution With Managed Swarms. *Symposium on Networked System Design and Implementation*, Boston, MA, April 2009.

[33] A. Sherman, J. Nieh, and C. Stein. Fairtorrent: Bringing Fairness To Peer-to-Peer Systems. *Conference on emerging Networking EXperiments and Technologies*, Rome, Italy, December 2009.

[34] M. Sirivianos, J. H. Park, R. Chen, and X. Yang. Free-riding In BitTorrent Networks With The Large View Exploit. *International Workshop on Peer-to-Peer Systems*, Bellevue, WA, February 2007.

[35] M. Sirivianos, X. Yang, and S. Jarecki. Dandelion: Cooperative Content Distribution With Robust Incentives. *USENIX Annual Technical Conference*, Santa Clara, CA, June 2007.

[36] S. Saroiu, P. K. Gummadi, R. J. Dunn, S. D. Gribble, and H. M. Levy. An Analysis Of Internet Content Delivery Systems. *Symposium on Operating System Design and Implementation*, Boston, MA, December 2002.

[37] A. Wolman, G. M. Voelker, N. Sharma, N. Cardwell, A. R. Karlin, and H. M. Levy. On The Scale And Performance Of Cooperative Web Proxy Caching. *Symposium on Operating Systems Principles*, Kiawah Island, SC, December 1999.

[38] L. Wang, K. Park, R. Pang, V. S. Pai, and L. L. Peterson. Reliability And Security In The Codeen Content Distribution Network. *USENIX Annual Technical Conference*, Boston, MA, June 2004.

[39] P. Wayner. *Digital Cash: Commerce On The Net*. Morgan Kaufmann, April 1996.

337

Insomnia in the Access

or How to Curb Access Network Related Energy Consumption

Eduard Goma†, Marco Canini*, Alberto Lopez Toledo†, Nikolaos Laoutaris†,
Dejan Kostić*, Pablo Rodriguez†, Rade Stanojević‡*, and Pablo Yagüe Valentín†
†Telefonica Research, *EPFL, ‡Institute IMDEA Networks
†{goma,alopezt,nikos,pablorr,payv}@tid.es, *{marco.canini,dejan.kostic}@epfl.ch,
‡rade.stanojevic@imdea.org

ABSTRACT

Access networks include modems, home gateways, and DSL Access Multiplexers (DSLAMs), and are responsible for 70-80% of total network-based energy consumption. In this paper, we take an in-depth look at the problem of greening access networks, identify root problems, and propose practical solutions for their user- and ISP-parts. On the user side, the combination of *continuous light traffic* and *lack of alternative paths* condemns gateways to being powered most of the time despite having Sleep-on-Idle (SoI) capabilities. To address this, we introduce Broadband Hitch-Hiking (BH²), that takes advantage of the overlap of wireless networks to aggregate user traffic in as few gateways as possible. In current urban settings BH² can power off 65-90% of gateways. Powering off gateways permits the remaining ones to synchronize at higher speeds due to reduced crosstalk from having fewer active lines. Our tests reveal speedup up to 25%. On the ISP side, we propose introducing simple inexpensive switches at the distribution frame for batching active lines to a subset of cards letting the remaining ones sleep. Overall, our results show an 80% energy savings margin in access networks. The combination of BH² and switching gets close to this margin, saving 66% on average.

Categories and Subject Descriptors

C.2.5 [**Computer-Communication Networks**]: Local and Wide-Area Networks—*Access schemes*; C.2.1 [**Computer-Communication Networks**]: Network Architecture and Design

General Terms

Design, Experimentation, Measurement

Keywords

Energy, Broadband access networks

---

*Work partly done when the author was with Telefonica Research.

1. INTRODUCTION

Recognizing the importance of improving the energy efficiency of the Information and Communication Technologies (ICT)[1], recent research efforts focused on reducing the energy consumption of datacenters [2, 3, 4], networks [5, 6, 7], and networked computers [8, 9, 10]. Out of the overall ICT energy expenditure, around 37% goes to powering telecommunication infrastructures [11]. The annual energy consumption figures reported by telecommunication companies are indeed staggering — Telecom Italia 2.1 TWh [12], France Telecom - Orange 3.7 TWh [13], Telefonica 4.5 TWh [14], Verizon 9.9 TWh [15]. In this paper, we seek energy saving opportunities in broadband access networks including: (i) on the user side, modem, wireless Access Point (AP), and router (hereafter collectively referred to as *gateway*), and (ii) on the ISP side DSLAM modems and line cards. Access networks consume 70-80% of the overall energy going into powering wired networks [16]. The above devices, despite being smaller than backbone/metro devices, are responsible for a major share of this fraction, due to their sheer number and high per bit consumption [17].

Insomnia at the user part. Like most ICT devices, access network devices are not energy proportional [18], *i.e.*, they consume close to maximum power even if only lightly loaded. Until the long term vision of energy proportional computing becomes reality, the most practical approach for cutting down on energy consumption is to implement Sleep-on-Idle (SoI) mechanisms which by now have become obligatory [19]. Herein, however, access networks have a problem that backbones and metro networks don't have – *they lack alternative paths*. This means that a household, or a small office connecting through a single Digital Subscriber Line (DSL) or cable connection can only power off its gateway when there is absolutely no traffic to be sent or received. This is possible when all terminal devices are powered off, but highly unlikely if some of them are online, and especially if the user is actively engaged.

Home gateways might take up to a minute to boot and synchronize their modem with the DSLAM, so traffic inactivity periods need to be sufficiently long. However, it is known [8, 10, 9], and we also demonstrate in Sec. 2, that most usages of the Internet (including leaving a machine idle

---

[1]While the energy consumption attributed to ICT might be smaller than in other areas like transportation, manufacturing, *etc.*, the ongoing exponential increase of Internet traffic on one side [1], and the successful efforts for reducing energy consumption in other societal systems on the other, will only increase the importance of greening ICT.

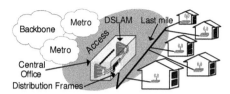

Figure 1: Illustration of a residential DSL broadband network. User gateways are connected to DSLAM ports via telephone lines in shared bundles up to few km long.

to maintain network presence) include at least some *continuous light traffic* that puts packets on the wire at time intervals that are much shorter than this. The problem is exacerbated by the fact that broadband connections typically serve multiple terminal devices like PCs, home entertainment systems and smart-phones, any of which can be injecting light, or not so light traffic.

Inflexibility at the ISP part. As shown in Fig. 1, the individual copper twisted pairs of nearby DSL subscribers are bundled in a common cable that travels all the way to the ISP central or regional office where individual pairs split again and terminate on the Main Distribution Frame (MDF) from where short local connections bring them to the Handover Distribution Frame (HDF) and ultimately to the ISP terminating modems. Each modem occupies a port in a line card and multiple line cards are controlled by a DSLAM. The insomniac state of the user part implies that ISP modems and line cards cannot sleep either. Later in the paper we will show that it is possible to put a large percentage of gateways to sleep yielding substantial energy savings for users. This implies that an equal percentage of ISP modems can also be powered off through SoI. The total energy gains however for an ISP are rather small. The reason is that a single ISP modem consumes around 1 W whereas the shared circuitry of the line card that hosts it consumes at least about 100 W. Line cards, however, are unlikely to sleep, even if they employ SoI. This is due to the inflexibility in terms of *lack of switching capability* at the HDF that permits a single active port to keep a card with 12-72 ports awake.

Our contributions and results. Our main contribution is a rigorous quantification of energy saving margins in access networks, and a breakdown of the gains between user and ISP parts. Overall, using a combination of trace-driven simulation and system prototype deployment (Sec. 5), we demonstrate that there exists an 80% energy saving margin at access networks. Straightforward techniques that do not require any expensive substitution of equipment can get close to this margin and save 66% of the current consumption. This will hopefully serve as a call to arms for ISPs and users to offer and use techniques in the spirit of those that we developed for demonstrating the claimed margins. Our specific technical contributions include the following:

• *Traffic aggregation:* We show that by aggregating user traffic to a minimum number of gateways it is possible to overcome the lack of alternative paths and the continuous light traffic problems and save up to 72% of the energy consumed by individual users without negatively impacting on their QoS. To demonstrate this, we introduce Broadband Hitch-Hiking (BH^2), a distributed algorithm implemented in the driver of wireless home devices (Sec. 3). In dense urban areas where most users are, BH^2 permits devices to direct their light traffic to neighboring gateways within range, thus letting the local gateway to power off through SoI.

• *Impact on crosstalk*[2]: Apart from energy savings, BH^2 yields an additional – surprising – "bonus" for QoS. Owing to the broadband lines being powered off by BH^2, the remaining copper twisted pairs on the common cable connecting users to an ISP office are able to achieve higher data rates due to reduced crosstalk [20] (Sec. 6). Our detailed experiments using an Alcatel DSLAM with 24 VDSL2 modems and cable lengths from 50 up to 600 m show substantial gains – having half of the lines powered off gives the remaining ones a speedup of around 15% whereas powering off 75% of the lines increases the speedup to 25%.

• *Line switching:* Going over to the ISP side, we show that the probability of a line card powering off using SoI decreases exponentially with the number of modems it carries (Sec. 4). We propose solving this problem using switches at the HDF for terminating lines at different DSLAM ports depending on their state (active/inactive). We develop a model for deciding how large a switch needs to be and obtain the very positive result that even tiny 8×8 switches (8 DSL lines being able to rearrange between a fixed set of 8 ports on different line cards) permit batching together the active lines to a minimum number of line cards, letting the remaining ones sleep. Our experiments show that these simple switches allow us to power off a percentage of line cards that tracks well the percentage of gateways that BH^2 can power off.

Putting it all together, simple aggregation at the user part and switching at the ISP part can save 66% of total energy consumed in access networks. Extrapolating to all DSL users world-wide, assuming comparable link utilizations and wireless gateway density that we observe, the savings collectively amount to about 33 TWh per year, comparable to the output of 3 nuclear power plants in the US or equivalent to half of the energy used by US datacenters in 2006[3].

2. CHALLENGES IN GREENING ACCESS NETWORKS

DSL is the most widely deployed broadband access network technology (58% of broadband subscriptions as of June 2010 in OECD countries [22]). DSL works on top of ordinary twisted copper pairs used originally for telephony. DSL enables digital transmission between a modem at the user's premises and a second modem at the ISP (Fig. 1). ISP modems reside inside a DSL Access Multiplexer (DSLAM) which contains one such device for each serviced phone line. Similar to IP routers, a DSLAM is often designed as a shelf supporting a number of slots for line cards. A DSL line card typically services 12 to 72 lines. Since DSL is by far the most widespread access technology connecting over 320 million subscribers world-wide [21], and the one for which we have extensive datasets, we will focus our study around it. Notice, however, that our proposed techniques operate one level above the component level so they are applicable to other technologies as well. Next, we look at the reasons behind the high energy consumption of access networks.

2.1 Huge number of devices

The access is the only part of the network where there exists a direct proportionality between the number of net-

---

[2]The electromagnetic interference produced by other DSL lines packed closely in the same cable bundle.
[3]Analysis based on public data available at http://www. eia.gov, http://www.energystar.gov and in [21].

work devices and the number of customers. Indeed each subscriber has its own gateway and modem whereas a second modem is terminating every customer line at the DSLAM. Individual DSLAMs, despite servicing up to few thousands customers, are still by far the most numerous shared device of a network. In [16], it is shown that the number of DSLAMs is at least one order of magnitude more than metro devices and two orders of magnitude more than core devices.

2.2 Very high energy consumption per bit

Due to their sheer number, access devices need to be as cheap as possible. This requirement has an impact on several aspects including their efficiency in terms of energy consumption. Due to lack of energy proportionality [18], the lowest energy consumption per bit transmitted is achieved when a device is fully utilized. Using data sheets for different devices, researchers have computed the ratio of maximum transmission capacity to maximum energy consumption and reported the per bit consumption of devices at the different levels of a network [6, 17, 23]. From these reports it is clear that access devices consume two to three orders of magnitude more energy per bit transmitted than core devices.

2.3 Poor statistical multiplexing

Access devices not only have higher per bit consumption than other network devices under full load but have even worse per bit consumption under typical load. This is due to the fact that dedicated access devices are typically much less utilized than shared core devices (while always consuming close to maximum power [18]). Take for example an ADSL line. Its utilization depends almost exclusively on the behavior of a single customer (whether an individual or a family). Therefore, the amount of statistical multiplexing achieved is much lower than in higher levels of the network, *e.g.*, in an access or a core router. To get an idea of the level of utilization of typical ADSL lines, we plot in Fig. 2 the median and the average utilization of a set of 10K ADSL subscribers of a large commercial ISP providing subscriptions with 1-20 Mbps downlink, and 256 Kbps to 1 Mbps uplink. We observe a very low average utilization throughout the day that does not exceed 9% even during the peak hour as also noted by others [24, 25, 26]. Such levels of utilization are smaller by a multiplicative factor than the level of utilization of backbone links (typically 30-50%). This makes the average per bit consumption of access devices yet another multiplicative factor worse than their corresponding per bit consumption under maximum load.

2.4 Failure of Sleep-on-Idle

The above mentioned low utilization should make access devices a prime target for applying simple "Sleep-on-Idle" (SoI) techniques that power off devices when there is no traffic. Unfortunately, SoI is inhibited on access devices by the following two problems. First, as noted earlier *in the access there exist no alternative wired paths*. If a DSL line is put to sleep, the customer is effectively disconnected from the network. Disconnection is ok as long as the customer has no traffic to send or receive. This, however, brings us to the second problem – "*continuous light traffic*". We are referring to low average rate traffic (see Fig. 2) that however is constantly present as long as one or more terminal devices are on. Gateways and modems might take up to a minute to boot and synchronize and thus cannot sleep using SoI

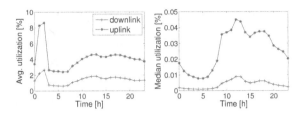

Figure 2: Daily average and median utilization of access links in a commercial ADSL provider (July 2009).

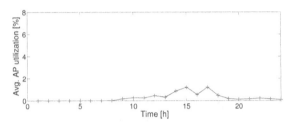

Figure 3: Average downlink utilization of access 6 Mbps links when using the UCSD CRAWDAD traces [27].

under such traffic. Web browsing, email, chat, or leaving a machine on to maintain online presence generate such light continuous traffic [8, 9, 10].

We want to illustrate this effect with data collected from real users. Given that packet-level traces of residential users are not publicly available, we use traces of wireless activity in the UCSD Computer Science building from [27] (see Sec. 5.1 for a detailed description). We assume for each AP in the building a backhaul bandwidth of 6 Mbps, which is the average downlink speed of the 10K residential ADSL subscribers presented in Fig. 2. We then compute the sum of inter-packet gaps in second-long bins (*i.e.*, 0-1 s, 1-2 s, *etc.*) for the peak hour (16-17 h), and show them in Fig. 4. We can see that for more than 80% of the time the inter-packet gaps are lower than 60 s, despite the utilization being as low as 1%. This continuous light traffic effectively condemns the SoI technique to a maximum saving of only 20%. Our results in Fig. 4 are strikingly consistent with the distribution of the inter-packet gaps of the non-publicly available dataset of residential traffic analyzed in Fig. 3 of [8]. In addition, the UCSD dataset matches very well with the aggregate utilization levels from 10K ADSL customers presented in Fig. 2. Therefore, we will use it later for our evaluation.

2.5 Summary

Access networks involve a huge number of devices that are particularly inefficient in terms of per bit energy consumption. Therefore it is not surprising that they end up consuming a very high percentage (70-80% [16]) of the total energy spent in networks costing ISPs millions per year. Powering off access networks is inhibited by the lack of alternative paths which implies that the single connecting path can only be put to sleep when there is no user traffic. This, however, is seldom possible due to continuous light traffic that does not permit SoI functionalities to be effective.

3. GREENING THE USER PART

In this section, we develop a simple technique for aggregating the traffic of multiple users to a sufficient subset of gateways letting the rest sleep. *Aggregation* is the key to solving the lack of alternative paths and continuous traffic

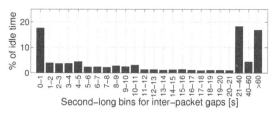

Figure 4: Histogram of the fraction of the idle time made up of inter-packet gaps of different size for the peak hour in Fig. 3.

problems discussed before. Currently, the simplest form of aggregation is via the wireless channel, taking advantage of the overlap of coverage area from multiple WiFi gateways in typical urban areas. In the future, femtocells or other wireless technologies can be used for the same purpose. Next, we formulate the problem and then present the design and implementation of a practical and efficient algorithm.

3.1 Formulation

Let U denote a set of users and let $d_i(t)$ denote the traffic demand of user $i \in U$ at time slot t. Let also G be a set of gateways and let c_j denote the capacity of gateway $j \in G$, *i.e.*, the speed of its broadband connection to the Internet. Additionally, with $w_{i,j}$ we denote the maximum available bandwidth between user i and gateway j due to the physical characteristics of the wireless channel. The parameters *backup* (a nonnegative integer) and $q \in (0, 1]$ denote the minimal number of backup gateways each user must connect to in order to do smooth hand-offs (more on this shortly) and the maximum allowed utilization of a gateway for protecting the QoS of the local user, respectively.

To formulate the problem of minimizing the number of online gateways we define o_j, a binary decision variable that becomes 1 iff gateway j is online. We also define the variables a_{ij} that becomes 1 iff i's traffic is "assigned" (routed) to gateway j. Our optimization problem at time slot t can now be stated as the following binary integer program:

$$\underset{o_j, a_{i,j}}{\text{minimize}} \quad \sum_{j \in G} o_j \quad (1)$$

$$\text{subject to} \quad \sum_{j \in G} a_{ij} \geq 1 + backup, \quad \forall i \in U$$

$$d_i \cdot a_{ij} \leq w_{ij}, \quad \forall i \in U, j \in G$$

$$\sum_{i \in U} d_i \cdot a_{ij} \leq q \cdot c_j \cdot o_j, \quad \forall j \in G$$

It is easy to see that the decision version of the above problem is NP-complete (reduction from SET-COVER to a version of our problem with no backups and infinite capacity at gateways). Next, we describe BH^2, a simple distributed heuristic algorithm that we developed for the above problem. BH^2 runs on user terminals permitting them to direct traffic to remote gateways in range under certain conditions. The operation of the algorithm can be summarized easily by looking at the following two cases:

User connected to its home gateway: If the load of the home gateway falls below a *low threshold*, the algorithm looks for available remote gateways in range that are both not heavily loaded (*i.e.*, their load is below a *high threshold*), and not candidates for going to sleep (their load is above the *low threshold*). If the number of gateways that meet

the above conditions is greater than the minimum number of *backup*, the algorithm selects one randomly among them with a probability proportional to their load, and redirects its traffic there. The randomness in the selection is introduced to prevent synchronization. The use of *backup* gateways is introduced to allow users to perform smooth hand-offs if they need to leave the remote gateway.

User connected to a remote gateway: Similar to when it is at its home, if the load of the remote gateway falls below the *low threshold*, the algorithm looks for available gateways in range whose load is below the *high threshold* and above the *low threshold*. If the number of candidate gateways is enough to meet the backup requirement, it selects among them randomly with probability proportional to their load. If the minimum number of *backup* gateways cannot be met, or if the load of the assigned remote gateway increases above the *high threshold*, the algorithm returns the user to its home gateway, waking it up if necessary.

3.2 BH^2: Implementation

BH^2 needs the following to be in place: (*i*) gateways need to implement some form of SoI that puts them to sleep after a period of traffic absence; (*ii*) gateways need to wake up when traffic reappears; and (*iii*) terminal devices running BH^2 need to be able to estimate the load of all gateways in range in order to compare with the above mentioned thresholds and also be able to route traffic through the assigned gateway — all irrespective of the channel in which the gateways operate.

For (*i*), there already exist several implementations in the literature (see *e.g.*, [8]). Regarding (*ii*) technologies such as Wake-on-WirelessLAN (WoWLAN) [28] or Remote Wake Technology (RWT) [29] are readily available in popular hardware and operating systems. Note that to wake up a system using WoWLAN or RWT, it is necessary to know the MAC address of the target device. In BH^2 users can only wake their own home gateway, so knowing the MAC address is not a problem.

Finally, for (*iii*) we use the methods described in [30] and [31], that allow a user to be simultaneously connected to all the gateways in range. Briefly, the user's wireless card is virtualized, *i.e.*, it appears as independent virtual cards associated to each available gateway. The solution then is to rely on the standard 802.11 Power Saving (PS) mode to implement a Time-Division Multiple Access (TDMA) by sequentially cycling through the gateways in a round-robin fashion devoting enough time to the selected gateway to collect the bandwidth from its backhaul, and a small amount of time to the other gateways in order to be able to estimate their load. The load estimation employs a trick that relies on the fact that every 802.11 frame sent by a gateway carries a MAC Sequence Number (SN) in the header [30]. The user can listen periodically to the traffic sent by the monitored gateways and store its SNs. By counting the SNs, the amount of packets traversing the gateway backhaul, and hence its load, can be estimated.

3.3 Discussion

We implemented BH^2 on Linux laptops by only modifying the open source wireless card drivers, without requiring any explicit communication with gateways, or other terminals (see Sec. 5.3). To realize, however, the benefits of BH^2 a gateway needs to allow remote terminals to connect to it.

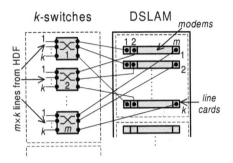 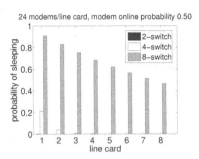 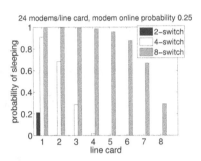

Figure 5: [left] k-switches and connection to DSLAM. [middle and right] Probability of line card $1,2,\ldots,k$ sleeping on a batch of k line cards connected through m k-switches. Each line card has $m = 24$ modems and each modem is active with probability $p = 0.5$ (middle) or $p = 0.25$ (right).

In our testbed this is not an issue, but on a real deployment it implies the cooperation of the owner of the gateway.

The wide adoption of such technologies is clearly a non trivial matter since it involves incentive, security, and privacy issues. Our implementation surely does not solve such issues since it was developed merely for demonstrating the technical feasibility of BH^2 and to permit computing energy gains in a real setting. However our hope is that due to the important energy gains that we report, users and ISPs will find ways to realize them in practice. We are confident that this is possible. Security and privacy concerns can be addressed with off-the-shelf solutions that already exist and have been deployed commercially[4]. Similar to the case of collaborative downloading [32], we believe that the right incentives can be found since (i) there is no penalty for users from participating — they all save energy, the gains are almost balanced, and QoS is preserved as we show later, and (ii) ISPs or regulators can provide additional incentives if there is need (*e.g.*, ISPs could temporarily increase a user's backhaul capacity to allow large uploads or downloads). Finally, notice that although we have solved the aggregation problem in a distributed way, more centralized/coordinated techniques, potentially involving changes to the gateway, can be developed for offering strict accountability and strengthened security (see *e.g.*, [33, 32]).

4. GREENING THE ISP PART

Aggregation is the key primitive in reducing the consumption at the user part of access networks. In this section, we will argue that *switching* is the key primitive for saving energy on the ISP part by putting line cards to sleep. By switching we mean the ability to terminate a customer's twisted pair in a modem/line card of choice at the DSLAM instead of having it always fixed to the same port.

4.1 Problem description

Consider a line card carrying m modems and assume that in a certain time slot individual gateways terminating in these modems have traffic with probability p (independently of each other) and with probability $1 - p$ they don't, and so can be powered off using SoI. Then, the probability that the entire line card can be put to sleep is $(1 - p)^m$, *i.e.*, it *drops exponentially with the line card size* m. This means that even if instead of continuous traffic we had well behaved burst traffic that utilizes a link fully and then leaves it idle

---

[4]For example, FON uses double ESSID (one private, one shared), combined with RADIUS-based WPA authentication (http://www.fon.com).

for a long period, the probability that a 48 port card can sleep under just 5% utilization would still be only 8% – *i.e.*, it is highly unlikely that line cards will sleep using just SoI.

What can be done to improve this? If we knew in advance the traffic profile of users, *i.e.*, had $p_i(t)$ for each user $i \in U$ and each time slot t of the day, we would assign users i and j to the same line card if their profiles were similar ($p_i \approx p_j$) and to different ones otherwise. The rationale is that if a user is active we would like also the remaining users to be active (to fully utilize the line card) and the reverse (to be able to put it to sleep).

The above strategy has several practical problems including that p_i's are not known in advance, are changing, and that traffic is not well behaved but rather continuous as shown in Sec. 2. For these reasons, our proposal is to introduce switching at the HDF for being able to select dynamically based on state (on/off) the line card/port to which a line terminates. A full switching capability that allows any line to terminate at any port can power off $\lfloor n \cdot (1-p)/m \rfloor$ line cards, where n is the total number of ports of the DSLAM. Percentage wise this is asymptotically equal to the percentage of powered off gateways.

4.2 Our proposal: small k-switches are enough

A full switching capability maximizes the number of line cards that can be put to sleep but incurs a cost that depends on n, the number of ports of a DSLAM (can be 1000 or more). In this section, we argue that much smaller constant size switches (as low as 8×8) suffice for getting close to optimal performance.

We propose to use a series of k-switches each of which gets k lines from the HDF and terminates them at k modems at the DSLAM, allowing any mapping between lines and modems. We connect arbitrary lines to the switch at the HDF but take care to connect modems that belong to k different line cards at the DSLAM. As a simple convention (but this is not necessary or constraining), we assume that line cards are batched in groups of k (as shown in Fig. 5) and that a given k-switch connects to one modem at each line card at the same position (*e.g.*, 1th, 2nd, ..., m^{th}). The operation of the switch is simple — it checks the state of each line and when a line is inactive, it maps that line to the next free modem starting from the first line card and going down until it finds an unallocated port. Effectively the k-switch packs the inactive lines on the top part of its k positions and the active lines on its bottom part. This way, m k-switches try to batch the active lines on a minimum number of line cards out of the k that they cover. Of course, unlike with a full switching capability, they might fail to do so, *e.g.*, if there is a switch whose k lines happen to be all active.

Next, we compute the impact of having these switches on the ability of line cards to power off through SoI. Assuming that individual lines are active with probability p independent of each other, it is easy to verify that the probability that the lth line card out of a set of k line cards can be put to sleep is:

$$
\begin{aligned}
&P\{l^{th} \text{ line card sleeps}\} \\
&= P\{\text{at least } l \text{ out of } k \text{ lines at every switch are inactive}\} \\
&= (P\{\text{at least } l \text{ out of } k \text{ lines of a switch are inactive}\})^m \\
&= \left(1 - \sum_{i=0}^{l-1}(1-p)^i p^{k-i}\right)^m
\end{aligned}
\tag{2}
$$

We can use Eq. (2) to select how big k needs to be in order to be able to put a good number of line cards to sleep given m (property of the line card) and p (performance of BH^2 under a given traffic load, topology, *etc.*). Fig. 5 shows that even very small switches of size $k = 4$ or 8 are in position to put to sleep a good number of line cards even in the case that BH^2 is able to turn off only half of the gateways ($p = 0.5$, something that is not at all uncommon according to the results shown later in Sect. 5.2.2). The above results are derived assuming independent traffic between users but as we will show experimentally later, such small switch sizes are indeed sufficient for reaping most of the benefits.

4.3 Discussion

Regarding the feasibility and the cost of installing 4- or 8-switches at the HDF, we note that switches of much greater size have already been constructed by large vendors, and used by several ISPs, albeit, for different applications than the one we envision here. For example, switches for Automated MDF (ADF) are available from companies like Network Automation[5] (ranging from $k = 20$ up to $k = 160000$) and Telepath Networks[6] ($k = 100$ up to $k = 100000$ with ms switching times). Given that the cost of switching depends on k, we believe that their cost will be more than covered by their contribution in achieving great reductions in energy consumption as we show next. Finally, we note that the power consumption of the switches themselves is negligible as these provide simple line switching, not datagram switching, and therefore do not need a packet processor or other complicated circuitry. They are simple micro-electromechanical relays that operate with near-zero power consumption [34] and have very low manufacturing costs [35].

5. EVALUATION

5.1 Evaluation methodology

Metrics: Our main quantitative evaluation metric is the total *energy savings* of the different schemes with respect to a *no-sleep* operation. Two indicators of performance are the number of gateways and the number of DSLAM line cards that each scheme can put to sleep. We also analyze how the schemes impact on the *completion time* of the network flows compared to the *no-sleep* scheme. As a measure of *fairness*,

we also look at the distribution of the sleeping time of the gateways compared to the basic *Sleep-on-Idle* scheme.

Traffic traces: We use the packet-level wireless traces from the CRAWDAD repository in [27]. The traces were obtained during the 24 hours of Thursday, January 11, 2007, by monitoring the activity of the wireless clients in the four-story UCSD Computer Science building. The traces contain packets of 272 clients accessing 40 APs. For simplicity we only consider downlink traffic. The dataset is detailed in [36].

Scenario: Since the traces do not contain topology information, we use the algorithm proposed in [37] to generate a wireless overlap topology. The resulting topology has node degrees that follow the distribution of per-household wireless networks in a residential area, as measured in [38]. The resulting average number of networks in range of a client is 5.6, consistent with previous studies (*e.g.*, [39]), and also with our own independent measurements. We uniformly distribute the 272 clients over the 40 gateways, and assign a wireless channel capacity of 12 Mbps between a client and its home gateway, and, based on the findings in [40], we assign half of that capacity (*i.e.*, 6 Mbps) between a client and gateways adjacent to the home gateway. As discussed in Sec. 2.4, we use ADSL speeds of 6 Mbps for consistency with our residential traces depicted in Fig. 2. On the ISP side, we consider a single DSLAM with 48 ports distributed in 4 line cards of 12 ports each. The gateways are connected to the ports randomly, as shown by our analysis of the distribution of the ADSL attenuations measured at two production DSLAMs covering more than 2K users in two major European cities (see Appendix). Since we only have 4 line cards, the k-switch schemes use 12 4-switches, where the ith 4-switch is connected to the ith port of each line card, following a configuration similar to the one in Fig. 5.

Power consumption: We performed detailed measurements of the power consumption of a Netgear WNR 3500L wireless router for different loads and distances from the clients. We obtained an average consumption of 5 W, with less than 10% of variation across the load range. We also measured the power consumption of a Telsey CPVA642WA ADSL gateway, and obtained a consumption of about 9 W mostly constant across all utilization levels. This implies that in terms of bits/Joule it is more efficient to operate the devices at higher utilization levels. We further measured the power consumption of the DSLAM we used in our experiments (reported later in Sec. 6). The ISAM 7302 datasheet reports for the shelf a typical consumption of 21 W and 53 W max. Each DSL line card is reported to consume typically 98 W, and a maximum of 112 W. We use the above figures as inputs for our evaluation.

Algorithms for comparison:

No-sleep: Users only connect to their home gateways. Gateways and line cards never go to sleep. This scheme represents today's regular residential network operation, and it is our baseline for comparison.

Sleep on Idle (SoI): Users only connect to their home gateways. Gateways go to sleep after an *idle timeout* (see below). When a gateway goes to sleep, the corresponding modem on the DSLAM also goes to sleep, and if all the modems in a line card are sleeping, the entire line card is put to sleep. When new traffic arrives there is a *wake-up time* (also see below), that includes the time that the gateway, the line

[5] http://www.networkautomation.se/
cdd9db52-3383-439a-b08e-fe20800e3937-9.html
[6] http://www.telepathnetworks.com/s.nl/sc.5/
category.22/.f

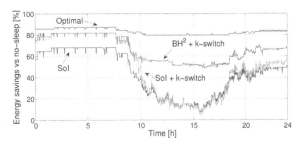

Figure 6: Energy saving vs. not sleeping.

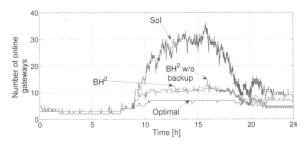

Figure 7: Number of online gateways for the aggregation schemes.

card (if necessary) and the DSLAM modem take to wake up, and the time needed for the modem synchronization.

SoI + k-switch: Same as *SoI*, but DSL lines are connected to 12 4-switches as described before in the scenario. To prevent the disruption of active flows, the switching operations happen only when the gateway is being woken-up.

BH² + k-switch: Users employ the BH² algorithm described in Sec. 3.1. We use a *low threshold* and *high threshold* of 10% and 50% respectively. BH² decides which gateways to use every 150 s, with a random offset to prevent synchronizations. When a user is assigned to a new gateway, it routes all its new traffic to the new gateway. However, its existing flows are not dropped, but remain at the current gateway until they finish. If BH² has to wake up the user's home gateway in order to return to it, the user's traffic remains routed over the current remote gateway until the home gateway becomes operative. Similar to the *SoI + k-switch scheme*, the DSL lines are connected to 12 4-switches. Unless explicitly stated, BH² refers to the scheme with one backup.

Optimal: Every minute, the optimal assignment of users to gateways is computed by solving the centralized ILP of Eq. (1) and assuming that the users' flows can then instantaneously "migrate" to the optimal assignment. Also, the DSL lines are connected to a full-switch in the DSLAM, covering all the available ports. Every minute, all the active ports are switched optimally to minimize the number of active line cards. The switching "migrates" all active flows with zero downtime and no disruption. Note that *optimal* is certainly infeasible in practice with current technology, but represents a useful upper bound of the potential savings from aggregating traffic at the user side and packing active ports on the DSLAM line cards.

Wake-up time and idle timeout: We measured the *wake-up time* using several gateways connected to both commercial ADSL lines and our DSLAMs in the testbed, and we obtained an average time of 60 s. Note that the ADSL resynchronization can be as high as 3 minutes in some cases. Following a similar analysis with [9], we computed the idle timeout that has a low probability of putting the device to sleep right before a new packet arrives (and hence paying the *wake-up time* penalty). This is justified by the results of Fig. 4 showing that even in peak hours, roughly 82% of the inter-packet gaps are lower than 60 s.

Sensitivity analysis: We performed extensive sensitivity analysis and selected the parameters that provide the best performance in a wider range of situations — we tested both the convergence and stability of the BH² algorithm under different loads, by scaling up to 3 times up and down the DSL capacities. We tested a large range of the *low threshold* and the *high threshold*, and selected the ones that provided a good trade-off between convergence and stability. In particular, we saw that 50% utilization in the gateways was an accurate estimator of a future saturation (given the low load this does not happen often). Also, a 10% of *low threshold* absorbed most of the high frequency changes in load. We paid special attention to oscillations, and selected the values that minimized the number of gateway changes, especially those that required powering on the sleeping gateways. For the employed traces, executing BH² every 2.5 minutes and estimating load over 1-minute intervals achieved this goal.

5.2 Results

We evaluate the performance of the different algorithms over the scenario discussed above using simulation. For each scheme, we run the experiments 10 times and average the results for every second of the day. The simulation starts with all the gateways sleeping.

5.2.1 Energy savings

Fig. 6 shows the energy savings of the different schemes compared to *no-sleep* for the duration of the day. Some important observations:

- During off-peak hours, most schemes can achieve energy savings greater than 60%. However, *optimal* can consistently achieve 80% savings compared to *no-sleep*.
- During peak hours, both *SoI* and *SoI + k-switch* schemes suffer considerably, dropping to less than 20%.
- *BH² + k-switch* tracks the *optimal* much better, and achieves consistently at least 50% savings, even during peak hours.
- Focusing on *SoI* and *SoI + k-switch*, we see that unlike *SoI*, the k-switches allow *SoI + k-switch* to match the performance of *BH² + k-switch* during off-peak hours, but become ineffective during peak hours.

5.2.2 The effect of aggregation on the user side

To understand and interpret the above results we look deeper at gateway aggregation. Fig. 7 shows the number of active gateways during the course of the day for *BH²*, *SoI* and the *optimal* aggregation. Also, for the sake of comparison, we show *BH²* when one backup is required, and also when no backup is enabled. The main observations are:

- During off-peak hours, there is almost no traffic in our dataset so all schemes can carry the traffic with 3-4 gateways online out of the total 40.
- *SoI* powers on many gateways (up to 95% of them at 15h) during the peak hours.
- On the contrary, *BH²* manages to track closely the *optimal* in terms of active gateways, even during peak.
- Using a backup does not penalize performance in terms of number of active gateways.

The above results verify our main proposition that the

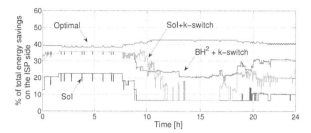

Figure 8: Contribution of the ISP part to the total energy savings.

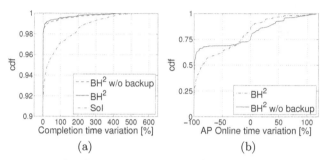

Figure 9: [left] Increase in flow completion time vs. *no-sleep*. [right] Increase in gateway online time vs. *SoI*.

lack of alternative paths combined with continuous traffic discussed in Fig. 4 do not permit *SoI* to be effective, despite operating under an average load of less than 2%. They also explain why *SoI + k-switch* can match the energy savings of $BH^2 + k\text{-}switch$ during off-peak hours – most user terminals are switched off so both of them use the same number of active gateways. Last, these results reveal why the *k*-switches do not make much difference when used with SoI (*SoI + k-switch*) during peak hours – *SoI* just fails to power off gateways therefore there is not much that the *k*-switches can do to power off line cards (the *p* of Sec. 4 is close to 1). Next, we show that the picture changes completely when *k*-switches are combined with BH^2 .

5.2.3 The effect of switching on the ISP side

Fig. 8 shows what percentages of the total savings of the various schemes correspond to the ISP side (DSLAM). We observe the following:

• Under *optimal* and $BH^2 + k\text{-}switch$, ISP-side savings due to switching are a substantial part of the overall savings, 40% and 30% (day average), respectively. This highlights that reaping the full energy savings requires actions at both the user and ISP sides.

• *SoI* saves very little for the ISP during peak hours as it only powers off terminating modems but no line cards. *SoI+k-switch* does only marginally better. The reason is that the *k*-switch does not have enough inactive lines at hand to be able to put entire cards to sleep.

Looking at the number of online cards, during off-peak hours we can see that all schemes can cope with just a single line card. During peak hours though, the average number of online cards varies significantly – *optimal*: 1, BH^2 +full-switch: 2, BH^2 +k-switch: 2.88, *SoI* +full-switch: 3, *SoI+k-switch*: 3.74, *SoI*: 3.99. Comparing BH^2 and *SoI* with full-switch and with 4-switch, we can verify also experimentally that even very small switches track closely the performance of full switching.

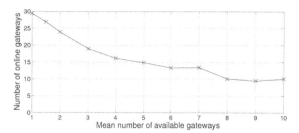

Figure 10: The impact of gateway density on the number of gateways that can sleep.

5.2.4 A look into QoS

An obvious question is whether powering off gateways and migrating to neighbors affects the QoS of the users. While the definition of QoS is ample, we focus as in [33] on whether the schemes increase the *completion time* of flows compared to *no-sleep*. Fig. 9a plots the CDF of the percentage of variation of flow completion time with respect to *no-sleep*. We can see the following:

• Even for *SoI*, only 8% of the flows see their completion time increased. Moreover, the increase can be as high as 7 times the original.

• BH^2 schemes perform much better, with as few as 2% of the flows being affected, and less heavily.

• Having a backup gateway slightly reduces the impact on completion time for BH^2 .

The few flows that see a large percentage-wise increase in their duration are short lived-flows (few seconds) that happen to coincide with waking up of a sleeping gateway, and thus get stretched by an additional 60 s. Finally, with low utilizations such as the one observed in our traces, having a backup gateway does not significantly change the behavior. We have observed, however, that as utilization increases, the positive effect of the backup is more noticeable.

5.2.5 The effect of gateway density

The results shown up to this point are all obtained using the same wireless overlapping topology and might raise the question of whether they are only valid for this gateway density. We assess the effect of the network density over the user aggregation capabilities of BH^2 running simulations where the mean number of networks that a user can connect to varies from 1 (*i.e.*, the user can only connect to the home gateway) to 10. We use a binomial distribution to generate the connectivity matrices with different mean number of gateways per user.

Fig. 10 shows the mean number of online gateways during the peak hours (from 11am to 7pm) versus the mean number of gateways users can connect to. As one might expect, the results show that the mean number of online gateways decreases with the increasing available gateway density. However, even in a low density deployment the number of online gateways is substantially reduced. For example, when users have just two neighboring gateways available on average, the number of online gateways is reduced to 19 (35% fewer powered-on gateways than when users can only connect to their home network).

5.2.6 Fairness

In this section, we examine whether the energy savings are shared in a fair manner among the different gateways. Fig. 9b shows the CDF of the variation in online time for

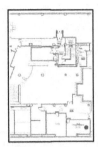

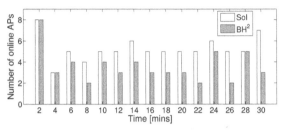

Figure 11: Testbed deployment. Gateways and terminals have been deployed over 3 floors, first floor [left], mezzanine [middle], and second floor [right]. Each circle represents a gateway, while terminals are placed nearby the gateways, one terminal per gateway. Obstacles, like walls and desks are present between all gateway links.

Figure 12: Number of online APs for a live experiment in the testbed in Fig. 11.

the gateways when using BH^2 compared to *SoI*. We want to see whether the traffic aggregation performed by BH^2 creates inequalities on the amount of online time a gateway experiences compared to running the simple *SoI* scheme (no change would be considered *fair*). We observe the following:

• As expected, BH^2 maintains a larger number of gateways always sleeping, hence the 25% of gateways with 100% decrease in online time.

• BH^2 increases the online time of 14% of the gateways compared to *SoI*.

• BH^2 without backup shows a more unfair situation, with several gateways completely eliminating their online time, and a larger number of them increasing it.

We see that using one backup gateway results in a more fair distribution of the sleeping times, while not harming performance (Fig. 7), therefore we opt for keeping it.

5.3 Realistic deployment

Testbed description: We deployed a testbed spanning three floors of a multi-story building. The testbed consists of 10 commercial 3 Mbps ADSL subscriptions with their corresponding gateways and 10 BH^2 terminals, *i.e.*, the "owners" of each line. The gateways are distributed approximately every 850 sq. ft. to emulate an average residential apartment size (see Fig. 11) and are randomly set to independent radio-frequencies in the 2.4 GHz ISM band. Similar to our evaluation scenario, each BH^2 terminal is in range of approximately 5.5 gateways and can communicate over the wireless channel at an average speed higher than 6 Mbps.

BH^2 implementation details: We implemented the BH^2 algorithm described in Sec. 3.1 on Linux laptops equipped with a single-radio Atheros-based wireless card. The BH^2 algorithm is implemented in the MadWiFi 0.9.4 driver [41] and the Click modular router 1.6.0 [42]. BH^2 terminals communicate with gateways at different radio-frequencies using the TDMA techniques described in Sec. 3.2. During the time BH^2 is connected to a gateway, it transmits and receives traffic according to the standard 802.11 DCF protocol. BH^2 uses a TDMA period of 100 ms, of which 60% is devoted to the gateway currently selected by BH^2, and the rest is distributed evenly among the rest of the gateways in range to collect their utilization statistics[7]. To be transparent to the applications, BH^2 implements a Reverse-NAT module that

ensures packets leave the terminals with the correct source IP address, while exposing a single *dummy* IP address to the upper layers [30].

Gateways: We use off-the-shelf Linksys DD-WRTv24, running unmodified firmware. All wireless routers and terminals have the wireless multimedia extensions and the RTS/CTS handshake disabled. Any non-standard 802.11 feature is also disabled, and H/W queues are set up with 802.11 best effort parameters. Each wireless router is connected to a Zyxel P-600 modem that provides the ADSL connectivity.

Methodology: We use the traces described in Sec. 5.1 as our source of data. For each flow, we record the timestamp t and the amount of bytes b reported in the traces and we *replay* it: at the specified time t the terminal makes a *HTTP request* to download b bytes of the DVD image of a very popular Linux distribution from the local national repository.

Since the testbed has just a few clients, each BH^2 terminal replays the flows of all clients that are *originally associated* with one of traced APs selected at random. When the BH^2 algorithms selects a new gateway, the terminal starts routing the new flows through it. However it does not modify the existing downloads, *i.e.*, they will continue through the same gateway until finished.

The BH^2 algorithm runs independently and in a totally distributed manner. Each BH^2 terminal wirelessly monitors the load in the gateways as described in Sec. 3.2 and takes independent decisions based on the *low* and *high thresholds*. However, since our gateways do not have any *SoI* capabilities, they do not actually go to sleep. Instead, we emulate the state of the gateway as follows: a script running in a central server monitors the load of the gateways and flags them as "sleeping" when the idle timeout expires. Each BH^2 terminal checks the status of the gateway in the server via an independent local area network. If a terminal decides to "wake-up" a gateway, it changes the status on the server as "waking-up". The server automatically updates the status to "active" after the appropriate *wake-up time*.

Results: We conducted numerous experiments to verify the correct operation of BH^2. Specifically, we used the BH^2 laptops in browsing, YouTube video streaming, BitTorrent and even P2P live video streaming sessions. We did not experience performance problems (*i.e.*, glitches, video rebuffering or choppy audio) even after several gateway changes.

To validate BH^2 performance, we made 10 independent experiments that *replay* the traces using 9 laptops, each of them having one of the 9 gateways of Fig. 11 as their "home" gateway. In each run we randomly assign one of the APs of the CRAWDAD traces to a gateway in our testbed. The corresponding laptop replays all the clients in the traces that were originally associated with the AP represented by that gateway. Our testbed allows a client to connect to a max-

---

[7]We verified that 60% of the wireless card's time is enough to collect all the bandwidth available at any gateway, since wireless capacities are higher than ADSL backhaul speeds.

imum of 3 gateways. Fig. 12 shows the number of active gateways from 15:00 to 15:30 h for BH^2 without a backup and SoI. We observe the following:

• Of the 9 gateways, on average BH^2 puts 5.46 to sleep (60%), while SoI only puts to sleep 3.72 (41%).

• BH^2 consistently outperforms SoI at all times, even for the small load of our traces and 3-gateway limitation we imposed in our implementation.

These experiments show that in our realistic experiments, BH^2 yield energy savings that *doubles* those of SoI, consistent with the results we reported earlier through simulation.

5.4 Summary

The results of this section have demonstrated that there is an 80% margin for energy savings in access networks. Simple aggregation and switching techniques like $BH^2 + k\text{-}switch$ can save 66% on average, of which 2/3 go to users and 1/3 to the ISP. Extrapolating to all DSL users world-wide, the savings collectively amount to about 33 TWh per year.

6. A CROSSTALK BONUS

Apart from the energy gains, the aggregation effect of BH^2 permits modems to lock at higher speeds due to lower crosstalk. In this section, we present a number of experiments with a real DSLAM and copper lines to demonstrate that the speedup can be as high as 25%.

6.1 Crosstalk

Crosstalk [20] refers to the electromagnetic coupling between lines in the same cable bundle. Crosstalk increases with attenuation (~cable length) and signal frequency. It also depends on the distance between lines inside the bundle and it is worst for adjacent lines (*e.g.*, 1 and 2 in Fig. 13a).

To deal with varying conditions of crosstalk, ADSL and VDSL adapt the frequency plan to the line length and crosstalk noise. To do so, there are two options while initializing the connection: (*i*) maximize the bit rate subject to the currently sensed line conditions and crosstalk while leaving a safe margin of at least 6 dB, or (*ii*) maximize the noise guard margin while having a bit rate fixed (usually set according to the subscribed plan). Once the connection is established it is being monitored and adjusted whereas re-synchronization occurs if the noise margin falls to 0 dB.

6.2 Experimental setup and methodology

Our testbed consists of an Alcatel 7302 ISAM DSLAM equipped with a 48-port, NVLT-C line card and 24 VDSL2 modems[8]. Each modem is connected through a cable bundle of 25 twisted pairs (Fig. 13a) to a switchboard that allows us to vary the length of the twisted pair connecting the modem to the DSLAM, as illustrated in Fig. 13b.

We measure the actual bit rate as we vary the number of active lines using the following methodology. First, we define 5 random orders in which to activate the 24 lines. The sequences activate 4 lines at a time up to 12 lines, and then 2 at a time up to 24 lines. At each step in a sequence, we activate certain lines and force each one to resynchronize, one at a time in random order.

We use two different line length setups and two different service profiles for a total of four set of experiments. Specifically, we experiment with a fixed line length of 600 m for

[8]21 modems are Huawei HG520v, other 3 are Zyxel P-870HW.

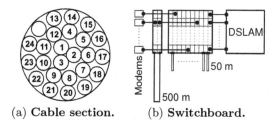

| (a) Cable section. | (b) Switchboard. |

Figure 13: Diagrams of the measurement testbed.

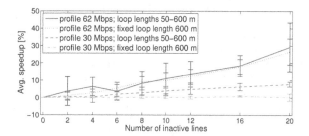

Figure 14: Average speedup as more lines become inactive. Standard deviations are plotted as error bars. Following the profile order of the legend, the baselines are at 41.3, 43.7, 27.8, and 29.7 Mbps.

all lines and with line lengths chosen to match a real distribution of lengths between 50 and 600 m as given to us by a large telco. We use two different service profiles: (*i*) the first with plan downstream bit rate of 30 Mbps, (*ii*) the second with plan downstream bit rate of 62 Mbps.

6.3 Results

Based on the average bit rate measured as we vary the number of active lines, we compute the average per-line speedup as the relative bit rate gain w.r.t. the baseline rate of having all lines active. Fig. 14 presents the average and standard deviation of the per-line performance increase, computed over all random sequences each of which is measured twice to account for the non-deterministic nature of the measured medium.

Considering the profile at 62 Mbps, it can be seen that there is an increase in bit rate of 1.1-1.2% for each modem that becomes inactive. When half of the modems are off, the remaining modems can obtain 13.6% more bandwidth, whereas when increasing the powered off modems to around 75% the speedup climbs to 25%.

7. RELATED WORK

Greening networks. Improving the energy efficiency of the Internet is currently a very active area of research (see [43] for a detailed survey). Most of the efforts have focused on backbone networks. For instance, Chabarek *et al.* [6] presented an energy-aware network design methodology. Vasić *et al.* [7] proposed a traffic engineering scheme that matches active network devices to the current traffic load. Heller *et al.* [44] discussed a similar approach for datacenter networks.

Arguing for hardware support of energy-aware capabilities, Nedevschi *et al.* [5] quantified the savings that can be achieved by shaping traffic into bursts to enable putting network components to sleep during idle times and by adapting the rate of network operation to the offered load. Applying such techniques to DSL is not straightforward due to two main issues: (*i*) putting a DSL modem to sleep would tear down the connection and restoring it with the current DSL specifications would require a new synchronization phase that can last tens of seconds, and (ii) rate adaption may lower the transmission power to the point where crosstalk from other active lines becomes a severe impairment.

Greening access networks. Approaches for saving energy in access networks include those that advocate network re-engineering and works that improve energy efficiency of broadband technologies. Bianco et al. [45] provided an analysis of the energy consumption trends in Telecom Italia and discussed the deployment of VDSL2 in FTTx architectures. Tsiaflakis et al. [46] and Guenach et al. [47] suggested a reformulation of dynamic spectrum management for minimizing power consumption of DSL. These works showed that adding objectives or constraints for limiting the transmit power in DSL modems ultimately reduces date rate performance and may render active lines less stable.

Looking at the enterprise environment, Jardosh et al. [33] proposed an approach for powering off APs in enterprise wireless networks. Although the underlying ideas and objectives are similar to BH^2, the two settings are substantially different. Jardosh et al. assumed a centralized controller that can map terminals to APs in a setting where APs communicate through a shared backbone. In our case, assuming a centralized controller would be challenging in terms of both scalability and amount of change to the existing architecture. However, we consider this work complementary and some of its techniques may be utilized to provide a centralized solution to the problem BH^2 solves.

Exploiting neighbor's wireless. Building on the observation of increasingly frequent high-density wireless deployments, several schemes have been proposed to aggregate bandwidth from neighboring wireless networks. Systems like FatVAP [31] and THEMIS [30] demonstrated the feasibility of aggregating the backhaul capacity of multiple APs using a single virtualized wireless card. PERM [38] discussed how to schedule flows across accessible APs based on predicting of flow round-trip time or traffic volume. CUBS [26] and Link-alike [39] focused on sharing the idle upload bandwidth of neighbors to improve P2P applications and file uploads. COMBINE [32] presented a system for collaborative downloading and specified a framework of incentives that could also help address several practical issues in our proposal. While different in their specifics all of them are in essence trying to maximize the transmission capacity. Our work is dual to that objective as it attempts to minimize the committed energy for carrying a given amount of traffic. At the same time, BH^2 takes advantage of some of these techniques to carry traffic on different gateways.

Network connectivity proxies. Tackling the problem of reducing power consumption from a different angle, several works (e.g., Nedevschi et al. [8], Reich et al. [9], Agarwal et al. [10]) argued that putting end hosts to sleep yields substantial energy savings that, however, are difficult to obtain because users keep unused end hosts fully powered-on only to maintain their network presence. They suggested using network connectivity proxies that allow idle hosts to sleep and still maintain full network presence. Unlike our proposal, such proxies cannot be used when the user is actively using its terminal. By maintaining the connections, they also eliminate energy saving opportunities at the ISP.

8. CONCLUSION

The biggest fraction of wired network energy is consumed by the access network, even though the individual access devices themselves have small power requirements. Unfortunately, straightforward techniques for sleeping during idle periods are inefficient in this environment because of the continuous lightweight traffic, and the absence of alternative paths that could carry the traffic.

In this paper, we formalize the problem of saving energy in the predominantly DSL-based access networks, and describe two simple techniques: (i) wireless user traffic aggregation that enables access devices to firmly sleep, and (ii) switching at the ISP side that significantly increases the number of power-hungry line cards that can sleep. Our thorough evaluation using trace-based simulation and a live prototype shows that for typical urban settings it is possible to save 66% of access network energy on average, while being within 7-35% of the computationally-hard optimal aggregation and impractical optimal switching. Moreover, our results show that both of our proposed techniques significantly contribute to the overall savings, which argue for their individual importance. Finally, we demonstrate using live experiments that energy-saving in the access network brings a surprising speedup in achievable access link bit rates due to reduced crosstalk.

Acknowledgments We thank our shepherd Vijay Sivaraman and the anonymous reviewers who provided excellent feedback. A. Lopez Toledo is supported by the Institució Catalana de Recerca i Estudis Avançats (ICREA). Part of this work was carried out with assistance of financial support from the European Community under grants FP7-ICT-258378 (FIGARO Project) and FP7-ICT-257263 (FLAVIA Project). This research was also supported in part by the Swiss NSF (grant FNS 200021-130265).

9. REFERENCES

[1] Cisco Visual Networking Index: Forecast and Methodology, 2008-2013., 2009.

[2] K. Church, A. Greenberg, and J. Hamilton. On Delivering Embarrassingly Distributed Cloud Services. In *Proc. of HotNets-VII*, 2008.

[3] V. Valancius, N. Laoutaris, L. Massoulié, C. Diot, and P. Rodriguez. Greening the Internet with Nano Data Centers. In *Proc. of CoNEXT'09*, 2009.

[4] S. Nedevschi, S. Ratnasamy, and J. Padhye. Hot Data Centers vs. Cool Peers. In *Proc. of HotPower'08*, 2008.

[5] S. Nedevschi, L. Popa, G. Iannaccone, S. Ratnasamy, and D. Wetherall. Reducing Network Energy Consumption via Sleeping and Rate-Adaptation. In *Proc. of NSDI'08*, 2008.

[6] J. Chabarek, J. Sommers, P. Barford, C. Estan, D. Tsiang, and S. Wright. Power awareness in network design and routing. In *Proc. of INFOCOM'08*, 2008.

[7] N. Vasić and D. Kostić. Energy-Aware Traffic Engineering. In *Proc. of e-Energy'10*, 2010.

[8] S. Nedevschi, J. Chandrashekar, J. Liu, B. Nordman, S. Ratnasamy, and N. Taft. Skilled in the Art of Being Idle: Reducing Energy Waste in Networked Systems. In *Proc. of NSDI'09*, 2009.

[9] J. Reich, A. Kansal, M. Gorackzo, and J. Padhye. Sleepless in Seattle No Longer. In *Proc. of USENIX ATC'10*, 2010.

[10] Y. Agarwal, S. Savage, and R. Gupta. SleepServer: A Software-Only Approach for Reducing the Energy Consumption of PCs within Enterprise Environments. In *Proc. of USENIX ATC'10*, 2010.

[11] The Climate Group. SMART 2020: Enabling the low carbon economy in the information age, 2008.

[12] Telecom Italia 2009 Sustainability Report.

[13] France Telecom 2009 Corporate Responsibility Report.

[14] Telefonica 2009 Corporate Responsibility Report.

[15] Verizon 2009-2010 Corporate Responsibility Report.

[16] R. Bolla, R. Bruschi, K. Christensen, F. Cucchietti, F. Davoli, and S. Singh. The Potential Impact of Green Technologies in Next-Generation Wireline Networks – Is There Room for Energy Saving Optimization? *IEEE Communications Magazine*, 2011.

[17] R. S. Tucker. Modelling Energy Consumption in IP Networks. In *Cisco Green Research Symposium*, 2008.

[18] L. A. Barroso and U. Hölzle. The Case for Energy-Proportional Computing. *Computer*, 40(12):33–37, 2007.

[19] European Commission. Code of Conduct on Energy Consumption of Broadband Equipment ver. 3, Nov 2008.

[20] P. Golden, H. Dedieu, and K. Jacobsen. *Fundamentals of DSL Technology.* Auerbach Publications, 2005.

[21] Point topic. World Broadband Statistics: Short report Q3 2010. http://point-topic.com/content/dslanalysis/.

[22] OECD Broadband Portal. http://www.oecd.org/sti/ict/broadband.

[23] U. Lee, I. Rimac, and V. Hilt. Greening the Internet with Content-Centric Networking. In *Proc. of e-Energy'10*, 2010.

[24] M. Dischinger, A. Haeberlen, K. P. Gummadi, and S. Saroiu. Characterizing Residential Broadband Networks. In *Proc. of IMC'07*, 2007.

[25] G. Maier, A. Feldmann, V. Paxson, and M. Allman. On Dominant Characteristics of Residential Broadband Internet Traffic. In *Proc. of IMC'09*, 2009.

[26] E. Tan, L. Guo, S. Chen, and X. Zhang. CUBS: Coordinated Upload Bandwidth Sharing in Residential Networks. In *Proc. of ICNP'09*, 2009.

[27] Y.-C. Cheng. CRAWDAD trace ucsd/cse/tcpdump/wired (v. 2008-08-25), 2008.

[28] Microsoft Technet. Configure Wake on Wireless LAN. http://technet.microsoft.com/en-us/library/ee851581(WS.10).aspx.

[29] Intel. Remote Wake Technology. http://www.intel.com/support/chipsets/rwt/.

[30] D. Giustiniano, E. Goma, A. Lopez Toledo, I. Dangerfield, J. Morillo, and P. Rodriguez. Fair WLAN Backhaul Aggregation. In *Proc. of MobiCom'10*, 2010.

[31] S. Kandula, K. C.-J. Lin, T. Badirkhanli, and D. Katabi. FatVAP: Aggregating AP Backhaul Capacity to Maximize Throughput. In *Proc. of NSDI'08*, 2008.

[32] G. Ananthanarayanan, V. N. Padmanabhan, L. Ravindranath, and C. A. Thekkath. COMBINE: Leveraging the Power of Wireless Peers through Collaborative Downloading. In *Proc. of MobiSys'07*, 2007.

[33] A. P. Jardosh, K. Papagiannaki, E. M. Belding, K. C. Almeroth, G. Iannaccone, and B. Vinnakota. Green WLANs: On-demand WLAN Infrastructures. *Mobile Networks and Applications (MONET)*, pages 1–26, 2009.

[34] G. M. Rebeiz. RF MEMS switches: status of the technology. In *Proc. of TRANSDUCERS'03*, 2003.

[35] J. Bouchaud, B. Knoblich, H. Tilmans, F. Coccetti, and A. El Fatatry. RF MEMS roadmap. In *Proc. of EuMIC*, 2007.

[36] Y.-C. Cheng, M. Afanasyev, P. Verkaik, P. Benkö, J. Chiang, A. C. Snoeren, S. Savage, and G. M. Voelker. Automating Cross-Layer Diagnosis of Enterprise Wireless Networks. In *Proc. of SIGCOMM'07*, 2007.

[37] F. Viger and M. Latapy. Efficient and Simple Generation of Random Simple Connected Graphs with Prescribed Degree Sequence. In *Proc. of COCOON'05*, 2005.

[38] N. Thompson, G. He, and H. Luo. Flow Scheduling for End-host Multihoming. In *Proc. of INFOCOM'06*, 2006.

[39] S. Jakubczak, D. G. Andersen, M. Kaminsky, K. Papagiannaki, and S. Seshan. Link-alike: Using Wireless to Share Network Resources in a Neighborhood. *ACM SIGMOBILE Mobile Computing and Communications Review*, 12(4), 2008.

[40] D. Han, A. Agarwala, D. G. Andersen, M. Kaminsky, K. Papagiannaki, and S. Seshan. Mark-and-Sweep: Getting the "Inside" Scoop on Neighborhood Networks. In *Proc. of IMC'08*, 2008.

[41] Madwifi project. http://madwifi-project.org.

[42] E. Kohler, R. Morris, B. Chen, J. Jannotti, and F. M. Kaashoek. The Click Modular Router. *ACM Trans. Comput. Syst.*, 18(3):263–297, August 2000.

[43] R. Bolla, R. Bruschi, F. Davoli, and F. Cucchietti. Energy Efficiency in the Future Internet: A Survey of Existing Approaches and Trends in Energy-Aware Fixed Network Infrastructures. *IEEE Communications Surveys and Tutorials*, 13(4), 2011.

[44] B. Heller, S. Seetharaman, P. Mahadevan, Y. Yiakoumis, P. Sharma, S. Banerjee, and N. McKeown. ElasticTree: Saving Energy in Data Center Networks. In *Proc. of NSDI'10*, 2010.

[45] C. Bianco, F. Cucchietti, and G. Griffa. Energy consumption trends in the Next Generation Access Network – a Telco perspective. In *Proc. of INTELEC'07*, 2007.

[46] P. Tsiaflakis, Y. Yi, M. Chiang, and M. Moonen. Green DSL: Energy-Efficient DSM. In *Proc. of ICC'09*, 2009.

[47] M. Guenach, C. Nuzman, J. Maes, and M. Peeters. On Power Optimization in DSL Systems. In *GreenComm'09*, 2009.

APPENDIX

We investigate if there is any correlation between the geographical distance of two customers and the relative distances of their ports in the DSLAM. We collect information from two production ADSL2+ DSLAMs of a large ISP in two major cities. We discuss one of them, since both yield similar results. Fig. 15 shows the distribution of the port attenuations measured in each of the 14 active line cards of 72 ports each. We plot the attenuations from n to $n + 100$, where n is not disclosed to protect sensitive information.

It is important to know that the attenuation measured for a line indicates the reduction in signal strength on that line, and represents the natural deterioration of the signal over distance from the MDF. We assume that there are no other external sources of attenuation, such as poor/unequal quality of the copper wires or the MDF connections. The production DSLAMs we measure are being actively maintained, and the ISP routinely discards lines that show subpar quality. In ADSL2+, a difference of 1dB in attenuation corresponds to a cable length of roughly 230 feet (70 m). Fig. 15 shows that across all line cards the attenuation has a similar Gaussian distribution with a standard deviation of one mile with minimal variations in mean. Given this randomness in the attenuation distribution, we assume that the assignment of gateways to DSLAM ports is random, and does not depend on their geographical proximity.

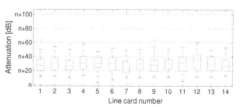

Figure 15: Distribution of the attenuations observed in a production DSLAM of a large ISP.

Understanding Network Failures in Data Centers: Measurement, Analysis, and Implications

Phillipa Gill
University of Toronto
phillipa@cs.toronto.edu

Navendu Jain
Microsoft Research
navendu@microsoft.com

Nachiappan Nagappan
Microsoft Research
nachin@microsoft.com

ABSTRACT

We present the first large-scale analysis of failures in a data center network. Through our analysis, we seek to answer several fundamental questions: which devices/links are most unreliable, what causes failures, how do failures impact network traffic and how effective is network redundancy? We answer these questions using multiple data sources commonly collected by network operators. The key findings of our study are that (1) data center networks show high reliability, (2) commodity switches such as ToRs and AggS are highly reliable, (3) load balancers dominate in terms of failure occurrences with many short-lived software related faults, (4) failures have potential to cause loss of many small packets such as keep alive messages and ACKs, and (5) network redundancy is only 40% effective in reducing the median impact of failure.

Categories and Subject Descriptors: C.2.3 [Computer-Communication Network]: Network Operations

General Terms: Network Management, Performance, Reliability

Keywords: Data Centers, Network Reliability

1. INTRODUCTION

Demand for dynamic scaling and benefits from economies of scale are driving the creation of mega data centers to host a broad range of services such as Web search, e-commerce, storage backup, video streaming, high-performance computing, and data analytics. To host these applications, data center networks need to be scalable, efficient, fault tolerant, and easy-to-manage. Recognizing this need, the research community has proposed several architectures to improve scalability and performance of data center networks [2, 3, 12–14, 17, 21]. However, the issue of reliability has remained unaddressed, mainly due to a dearth of available empirical data on failures in these networks.

In this paper, we study data center network reliability by analyzing network error logs collected for over a year from thousands of network devices across tens of geographically distributed data centers. Our goals for this analysis are two-fold. First, we seek to characterize network failure patterns in data centers and understand overall reliability of the network. Second, we want to leverage lessons learned from this study to guide the design of future data center networks.

Motivated by issues encountered by network operators, we study network reliability along three dimensions:

- **Characterizing the most failure prone network elements.** To achieve high availability amidst multiple failure sources such as hardware, software, and human errors, operators need to focus on fixing the most unreliable devices and links in the network. To this end, we characterize failures to identify network elements with high impact on network reliability e.g., those that fail with high frequency or that incur high downtime.

- **Estimating the impact of failures.** Given limited resources at hand, operators need to prioritize *severe* incidents for troubleshooting based on their impact to end-users and applications. In general, however, it is difficult to accurately quantify a failure's impact from error logs, and annotations provided by operators in trouble tickets tend to be ambiguous. Thus, as a first step, we estimate failure impact by correlating event logs with recent network traffic observed on links involved in the event. Note that logged events do not necessarily result in a service outage because of failure-mitigation techniques such as network redundancy [1] and replication of compute and data [11, 27], typically deployed in data centers.

- **Analyzing the effectiveness of network redundancy.** Ideally, operators want to mask all failures before applications experience any disruption. Current data center networks typically provide 1:1 redundancy to allow traffic to flow along an alternate route when a device or link becomes unavailable [1]. However, this redundancy comes at a high cost—both monetary expenses and management overheads—to maintain a large number of network devices and links in the multi-rooted tree topology. To analyze its effectiveness, we compare traffic on a per-link basis during failure events to traffic across all links in the network redundancy group where the failure occurred.

For our study, we leverage multiple monitoring tools put in place by our network operators. We utilize data sources that provide both a static view (e.g., router configuration files, device procurement data) and a dynamic view (e.g., SNMP polling, syslog, trouble tickets) of the network. Analyzing these data sources, however, poses several challenges. First, since these logs track low level network events, they do not necessarily imply application performance impact or service outage. Second, we need to separate failures that potentially impact network connectivity from high volume and often noisy network logs e.g., warnings and error messages even when the device is functional. Finally, analyzing the effectiveness of network redundancy requires correlating multiple data sources across redundant devices and links. Through our analysis, we aim to address these challenges to characterize network failures, estimate the failure impact, and analyze the effectiveness of network redundancy in data centers.

1.1 Key observations

We make several key observations from our study:

- **Data center networks are reliable.** We find that overall the data center network exhibits high reliability with more than four 9's of availability for about 80% of the links and for about 60% of the devices in the network (Section 4.5.3).

- **Low-cost, commodity switches are highly reliable.** We find that Top of Rack switches (ToRs) and aggregation switches exhibit the highest reliability in the network with failure rates of about 5% and 10%, respectively. This observation supports network design proposals that aim to build data center networks using low cost, commodity switches [3, 12, 21] (Section 4.3).

- **Load balancers experience a high number of software faults.** We observe 1 in 5 load balancers exhibit a failure (Section 4.3) and that they experience many transient software faults (Section 4.7).

- **Failures potentially cause loss of a large number of small packets.** By correlating network traffic with link failure events, we estimate the amount of packets and data lost during failures. We find that most failures lose a large number of packets relative to the number of lost bytes (Section 5), likely due to loss of protocol-specific keep alive messages or ACKs.

- **Network redundancy helps, but it is not entirely effective.** Ideally, network redundancy should completely mask all failures from applications. However, we observe that network redundancy is only able to reduce the median impact of failures (in terms of lost bytes or packets) by up to 40% (Section 5.1).

Limitations. As with any large-scale empirical study, our results are subject to several limitations. First, the best-effort nature of failure reporting may lead to missed events or multiply-logged events. While we perform data cleaning (Section 3) to filter the noise, some events may still be lost due to software faults (e.g., firmware errors) or disconnections (e.g., under correlated failures). Second, human bias may arise in failure annotations (e.g., root cause). This concern is alleviated to an extent by verification with operators, and scale and diversity of our network logs. Third, network errors do not always impact network traffic or service availability, due to several factors such as in-built redundancy at network, data, and application layers. Thus, our failure rates should not be interpreted as impacting applications. Overall, we hope that this study contributes to a deeper understanding of network reliability in data centers.

Paper organization. The rest of this paper is organized as follows. Section 2 presents our network architecture and workload characteristics. Data sources and methodology are described in Section 3. We characterize failures over a year within our data centers in Section 4. We estimate the impact of failures on applications and the effectiveness of network redundancy in masking them in Section 5. Finally we discuss implications of our study for future data center networks in Section 6. We present related work in Section 7 and conclude in Section 8.

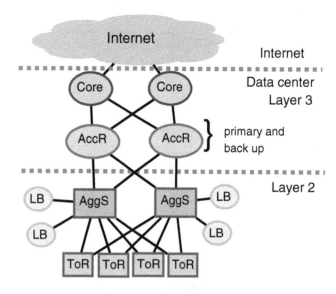

Figure 1: A conventional data center network architecture adapted from figure by Cisco [12]. The device naming convention is summarized in Table 1.

Table 1: Summary of device abbreviations

Type	Devices	Description
AggS	AggS-1, AggS-2	Aggregation switches
LB	LB-1, LB-2, LB-3	Load balancers
ToR	ToR-1, ToR-2, ToR-3	Top of Rack switches
AccR	-	Access routers
Core	-	Core routers

2. BACKGROUND

Our study focuses on characterizing failure events within our organization's set of data centers. We next give an overview of data center networks and workload characteristics.

2.1 Data center network architecture

Figure 1 illustrates an example of a partial data center network architecture [1]. In the network, rack-mounted servers are connected (or dual-homed) to a Top of Rack (ToR) switch usually via a 1 Gbps link. The ToR is in turn connected to a primary and back up aggregation switch (AggS) for redundancy. Each redundant pair of AggS aggregates traffic from tens of ToRs which is then forwarded to the access routers (AccR). The access routers aggregate traffic from up to several thousand servers and route it to core routers that connect to the rest of the data center network and Internet.

All links in our data centers use Ethernet as the link layer protocol and physical connections are a mix of copper and fiber cables. The servers are partitioned into virtual LANs (VLANs) to limit overheads (e.g., ARP broadcasts, packet flooding) and to isolate different applications hosted in the network. At each layer of the data center network topology, with the exception of a subset of ToRs, 1:1 redundancy is built into the network topology to mitigate failures. As part of our study, we evaluate the effectiveness of redundancy in masking failures when one (or more) components fail, and analyze how the tree topology affects failure characteristics e.g., correlated failures.

In addition to routers and switches, our network contains many middle boxes such as load balancers and firewalls. Redundant pairs of load balancers (LBs) connect to each aggregation switch and

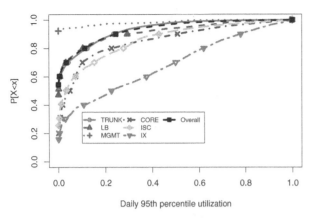

Figure 2: The daily 95th percentile utilization as computed using five-minute traffic averages (in bytes).

Table 2: Summary of link types

Type	Description
TRUNK	connect ToRs to AggS and AggS to AccR
LB	connect load balancers to AggS
MGMT	management interfaces
CORE	connect routers (AccR, Core) in the network core
ISC	connect primary and back up switches/routers
IX	connect data centers (wide area network)

perform mapping between static IP addresses (exposed to clients through DNS) and dynamic IP addresses of the servers that process user requests. Some applications require programming the load balancers and upgrading their software and configuration to support different functionalities.

Network composition. The device-level breakdown of our network is as follows. ToRs are the most prevalent device type in our network comprising approximately three quarters of devices. LBs are the next most prevalent at one in ten devices. The remaining 15% of devices are AggS, Core and AccR. We observe the effects of prevalent ToRs in Section 4.4, where despite being highly reliable, ToRs account for a large amount of downtime. LBs on the other hand account for few devices but are extremely failure prone, making them a leading contributor of failures (Section 4.4).

2.2 Data center workload characteristics

Our network is used in the delivery of many online applications. As a result, it is subject to many well known properties of data center traffic; in particular the prevalence of a large volume of short-lived latency-sensitive "mice" flows and a few long-lived throughput-sensitive "elephant" flows that make up the majority of bytes transferred in the network. These properties have also been observed by others [4, 5, 12].

Network utilization. Figure 2 shows the daily 95th percentile utilization as computed using five-minute traffic averages (in bytes). We divide links into six categories based on their role in the network (summarized in Table 2). TRUNK and LB links which reside lower in the network topology are least utilized with 90% of TRUNK links observing less than 24% utilization. Links higher in the topology such as CORE links observe higher utilization with 90% of CORE links observing less than 51% utilization. Finally, links that connect data centers (IX) are the most utilized with 35% observing utilization of more than 45%. Similar to prior studies of data center network traffic [5], we observe higher utilization at upper layers of the topology as a result of aggregation and high

bandwidth oversubscription [12]. Note that since the traffic measurement is at the granularity of five minute averages, it is likely to smooth the effect of short-lived traffic spikes on link utilization.

3. METHODOLOGY AND DATA SETS

The network operators collect data from multiple sources to track the performance and health of the network. We leverage these existing data sets in our analysis of network failures. In this section, we first describe the data sets and then the steps we took to extract failures of network elements.

3.1 Existing data sets

The data sets used in our analysis are a subset of what is collected by the network operators. We describe these data sets in turn:

- **Network event logs (SNMP/syslog).** We consider logs derived from syslog, SNMP traps and polling, collected by our network operators. The operators filter the logs to reduce the number of transient events and produce a smaller set of *actionable* events. One of the filtering rules excludes link failures reported by servers connected to ToRs as these links are extremely prone to spurious port flapping (e.g., more than 100,000 events per hour across the network). Of the filtered events, 90% are assigned to NOC tickets that must be investigated for troubleshooting. These event logs contain information about what type of network element experienced the event, what type of event it was, a small amount of descriptive text (machine generated) and an ID number for any NOC tickets relating to the event. For this study we analyzed a year's worth of events from October 2009 to September 2010.

- **NOC Tickets.** To track the resolution of issues, the operators employ a ticketing system. Tickets contain information about when and how events were discovered as well as when they were resolved. Additional descriptive tags are applied to tickets describing the cause of the problem, if any specific device was at fault, as well as a "diary" logging steps taken by the operators as they worked to resolve the issue.

- **Network traffic data.** Data transferred on network interfaces is logged using SNMP polling. This data includes five minute averages of bytes and packets into and out of each network interface.

- **Network topology data.** Given the sensitive nature of network topology and device procurement data, we used a static snapshot of our network encompassing thousands of devices and tens of thousands of interfaces spread across tens of data centers.

3.2 Defining and identifying failures

When studying failures, it is important to understand what types of logged events constitute a "failure". Previous studies have looked at failures as defined by pre-existing measurement frameworks such as syslog messages [26], OSPF [25, 28] or IS-IS listeners [19]. These approaches benefit from a consistent definition of failure, but tend to be ambiguous when trying to determine whether a failure had impact or not. Syslog messages in particular can be spurious with network devices sending multiple notifications even though a link *is* operational. For multiple devices, we observed this type of behavior after the device was initially deployed and the router software went into an erroneous state. For some devices, this effect was severe, with one device sending 250 syslog "link down" events *per hour* for 2.5 months (with no impact on applications) before it was noticed and mitigated.

We mine network event logs collected over a year to extract events relating to device and link failures. Initially, we extract all logged "down" events for network devices and links. This leads us to define two types of failures:

Link failures: A link failure occurs when the connection between two devices (on specific interfaces) is down. These events are detected by SNMP monitoring on interface state of devices.

Device failures: A device failure occurs when the device is not functioning for routing/forwarding traffic. These events can be caused by a variety of factors such as a device being powered down for maintenance or crashing due to hardware errors.

We refer to each logged event as a "failure" to understand the occurrence of low level failure events in our network. As a result, we may observe multiple component notifications related to a single high level failure or a correlated event e.g., a AggS failure resulting in down events for its incident ToR links. We also correlate failure events with network traffic logs to filter *failures with impact* that potentially result in loss of traffic (Section 3.4); we leave analyzing application performance and availability under network failures, to future work.

3.3 Cleaning the data

We observed two key inconsistencies in the network event logs stemming from redundant monitoring servers being deployed. First, a single element (link or device) may experience multiple "down" events simultaneously. Second, an element may experience another down event before the previous down event has been resolved. We perform two passes of cleaning over the data to resolve these inconsistencies. First, multiple down events on the same element that start at the same time are grouped together. If they do not end at the same time, the earlier of their end times is taken. In the case of down events that occur for an element that is already down, we group these events together, taking the earliest down time of the events in the group. For failures that are grouped in this way we take the earliest end time for the failure. We take the earliest failure end times because of occasional instances where events were not marked as resolved until long after their apparent resolution.

3.4 Identifying failures with impact

As previously stated, one of our goals is to identify failures that potentially impact end-users and applications. Since we did not have access to application monitoring logs, we cannot precisely quantify application impact such as throughput loss or increased response times. Therefore, we instead *estimate* the impact of failures on network traffic.

To estimate traffic impact, we correlate each link failure with traffic observed on the link in the recent past before the time of failure. We leverage five minute traffic averages for each link that failed and compare the median traffic on the link in the time window preceding the failure event and the median traffic during the failure event. We say a failure has impacted network traffic if the median traffic during the failure is less than the traffic before the failure. Since many of the failures we observe have short durations (less than ten minutes) and our polling interval is five minutes, we do not require that traffic on the link go down to zero during the failure. We analyze the failure impact in detail in Section 5.

Table 3 summarizes the impact of link failures we observe. We separate links that were transferring no data before the failure into two categories, "inactive" (no data before or during failure) and "provisioning" (no data before, some data transferred during failure). (Note that these categories are inferred based only on traffic observations.) The majority of failures we observe are on links that are inactive (e.g., a new device being deployed), followed by link failures with impact. We also observe a significant fraction of link

Table 3: Summary of logged link events

Category	Percent	Events
All	100.0	46,676
Inactive	41.2	19,253
Provisioning	1.0	477
No impact	17.9	8,339
Impact	28.6	13,330
No traffic data	11.3	5,277

failure notifications where no impact was observed (e.g., devices experiencing software errors at the end of the deployment process).

For link failures, verifying that the failure caused impact to network traffic enables us to eliminate many spurious notifications from our analysis and focus on events that had a measurable impact on network traffic. However, since we do not have application level monitoring, we are unable to determine if these events impacted applications or if there were faults that impacted applications that we did not observe.

For device failures, we perform additional steps to filter spurious failure messages (e.g., down messages caused by software bugs when the device is in fact up). If a device is down, neighboring devices connected to it will observe failures on inter-connecting links. For each device down notification, we verify that at least one link failure with impact has been noted for links incident on the device within a time window of five minutes. This simple sanity check significantly reduces the number of device failures we observe. Note that if the neighbors of a device fail simultaneously e.g., due to a correlated failure, we may not observe a link-down message for that device.

For the remainder of our analysis, unless stated otherwise, we consider only failure events that impacted network traffic.

4. FAILURE ANALYSIS

4.1 Failure event panorama

Figure 3 illustrates how failures are distributed across our measurement period and across data centers in our network. It shows plots for links that experience at least one failure, both for all failures and those with potential impact; the y-axis is sorted by data center and the x-axis is binned by day. Each point indicates that the link (y) experienced at least one failure on a given day (x).

All failures vs. failures with impact. We first compare the view of all failures (Figure 3 (a)) to failures having impact (Figure 3 (b)). Links that experience failures impacting network traffic are only about one third of the population of links that experience failures. We do not observe significant widespread failures in either plot, with failures tending to cluster within data centers, or even on interfaces of a single device.

Widespread failures: Vertical bands indicate failures that were spatially widespread. Upon further investigation, we find that these tend to be related to software upgrades. For example, the vertical band highlighted in Figure 3 (b) was due to an upgrade of load balancer software that spanned multiple data centers. In the case of planned upgrades, the network operators are able to take precautions so that the disruptions do not impact applications.

Long-lived failures: Horizontal bands indicate link failures on a common link or device over time. These tend to be caused by problems such as firmware bugs or device unreliability (wider bands indicate multiple interfaces failed on a single device). We observe horizontal bands with regular spacing between link failure events. In one case, these events occurred weekly and were investigated

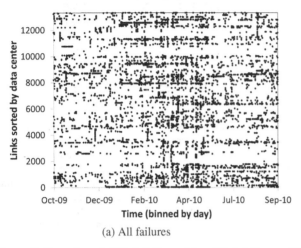
(a) All failures

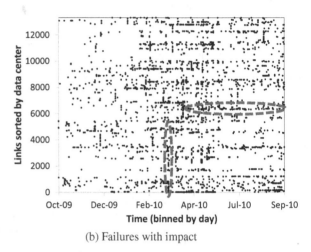
(b) Failures with impact

Figure 3: Overview of all link failures (a) and link failures with impact on network traffic (b) on links with at least one failure.

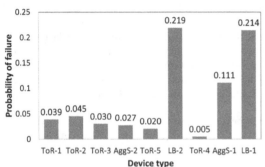

Figure 4: Probability of device failure in one year for device types with population size of at least 300.

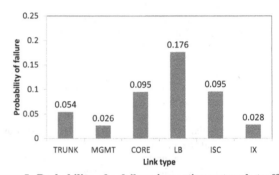

Figure 5: Probability of a failure impacting network traffic in one year for interface types with population size of at least 500.

in independent NOC tickets. As a result of the time lag, the operators did not correlate these events and dismissed each notification as spurious since they occurred in isolation and did not impact performance. This underscores the importance of network health monitoring tools that track failures over time and alert operators to spatio-temporal patterns which may not be easily recognized using local views alone.

Table 4: Failures per time unit

Failures per day:	Mean	Median	95%	COV
Devices	5.2	3.0	14.7	1.3
Links	40.8	18.5	136.0	1.9

4.2 Daily volume of failures

We now consider the daily frequency of failures of devices and links. Table 4 summarizes the occurrences of link and device failures per day during our measurement period. Links experience about an order of magnitude more failures than devices. On a daily basis, device and link failures occur with high variability, having COV of 1.3 and 1.9, respectively. (COV > 1 is considered high variability.)

Link failures are variable and bursty. Link failures exhibit high variability in their rate of occurrence. We observed bursts of link

failures caused by protocol issues (e.g., UDLD [9]) and device issues (e.g., power cycling load balancers).

Device failures are usually caused by maintenance. While device failures are less frequent than link failures, they also occur in bursts at the daily level. We discovered that periods with high frequency of device failures are caused by large scale maintenance (e.g., on all ToRs connected to a common AggS).

4.3 Probability of failure

We next consider the probability of failure for network elements. This value is computed by dividing the number of devices of a given type that observe failures by the total device population of the given type. This gives the probability of failure in our one year measurement period. We observe (Figure 4) that in terms of overall reliability, ToRs have the lowest failure rates whereas LBs have the highest failure rate. (Tables 1 and 2 summarize the abbreviated link and device names.)

Load balancers have the highest failure probability. Figure 4 shows the failure probability for device types with population size of at least 300. In terms of overall failure probability, load balancers (LB-1, LB-2) are the least reliable with a 1 in 5 chance of experiencing failure. Since our definition of failure can include incidents where devices are power cycled during *planned* maintenance, we emphasize here that not all of these failures are unexpected. Our analysis of load balancer logs revealed several causes of these

354

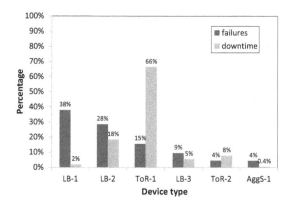

Figure 6: Percent of failures and downtime per device type.

Table 5: Summary of failures per device (for devices that experience at least one failure).

Device type	Mean	Median	99%	COV
LB-1	11.4	1.0	426.0	5.1
LB-2	4.0	1.0	189.0	5.1
ToR-1	1.2	1.0	4.0	0.7
LB-3	3.0	1.0	15.0	1.1
ToR-2	1.1	1.0	5.0	0.5
AggS-1	1.7	1.0	23.0	1.7
Overall	2.5	1.0	11.0	6.8

transient problems such as software bugs, configuration errors, and hardware faults related to ASIC and memory.

ToRs have low failure rates. ToRs have among the lowest failure rate across all devices. This observation suggests that low-cost, commodity switches are not necessarily less reliable than their expensive, higher capacity counterparts and bodes well for data center networking proposals that focus on using commodity switches to build flat data center networks [3, 12, 21].

We next turn our attention to the probability of link failures at different layers in our network topology.

Load balancer links have the highest rate of logged failures. Figure 5 shows the failure probability for interface types with a population size of at least 500. Similar to our observation with devices, links forwarding load balancer traffic are most likely to experience failures (e.g., as a result of failures on LB devices).

Links higher in the network topology (CORE) and links connecting primary and back up of the same device (ISC) are the second most likely to fail, each with an almost 1 in 10 chance of failure. However, these events are more likely to be masked by network redundancy (Section 5.2). In contrast, links lower in the topology (TRUNK) only have about a 5% failure rate.

Management and inter-data center links have lowest failure rate. Links connecting data centers (IX) and for managing devices have high reliability with fewer than 3% of each of these link types failing. This observation is important because these links are the most utilized and least utilized, respectively (cf. Figure 2). Links connecting data centers are critical to our network and hence back up links are maintained to ensure that failure of a subset of links does not impact the end-to-end performance.

4.4 Aggregate impact of failures

In the previous section, we considered the reliability of individual links and devices. We next turn our attention to the aggregate impact of each population in terms of total number of failure events

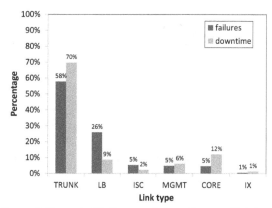

Figure 7: Percent of failures and downtime per link type.

and total downtime. Figure 6 presents the percentage of failures and downtime for the different device types.

Load balancers have the most failures but ToRs have the most downtime. LBs have the highest number of failures of any device type. Of our top six devices in terms of failures, half are load balancers. However, LBs do not experience the most downtime which is dominated instead by ToRs. This is counterintuitive since, as we have seen, ToRs have very low failure probabilities. There are three factors at play here: (1) LBs are subject to more frequent software faults and upgrades (Section 4.7) (2) ToRs are the most prevalent device type in the network (Section 2.1), increasing their aggregate effect on failure events and downtime (3) ToRs are not a high priority component for repair because of in-built failover techniques, such as replicating data and compute across multiple racks, that aim to maintain high service availability despite failures.

We next analyze the aggregate number of failures and downtime for network links. Figure 7 shows the normalized number of failures and downtime for the six most failure prone link types.

Load balancer links experience many failure events but relatively small downtime. Load balancer links experience the second highest number of failures, followed by ISC, MGMT and CORE links which all experience approximately 5% of failures. Note that despite LB links being second most frequent in terms of number of failures, they exhibit less downtime than CORE links (which, in contrast, experience about 5X fewer failures). This result suggests that failures for LBs are short-lived and intermittent caused by transient software bugs, rather than more severe hardware issues. We investigate these issues in detail in Section 4.7.

We observe that the total number of failures and downtime are dominated by LBs and ToRs, respectively. We next consider how many failures each element experiences. Table 5 shows the mean, median, 99th percentile and COV for the number of failures observed per device over a year (for devices that experience at least one failure).

Load balancer failures dominated by few failure prone devices. We observe that individual LBs experience a highly variable number of failures with a few outlier LB devices experiencing more than 400 failures. ToRs, on the other hand, experience little variability in terms of the number of failures with most ToRs experiencing between 1 and 4 failures. We make similar observations for links, where LB links experience very high variability relative to others (omitted due to limited space).

4.5 Properties of failures

We next consider the properties of failures for network element types that experienced the highest number of events.

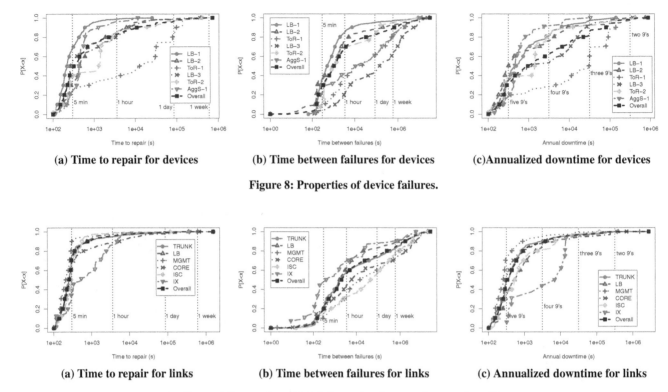

| (a) Time to repair for devices | (b) Time between failures for devices | (c)Annualized downtime for devices |

Figure 8: Properties of device failures.

| (a) Time to repair for links | (b) Time between failures for links | (c) Annualized downtime for links |

Figure 9: Properties of link failures that impacted network traffic.

4.5.1 Time to repair

This section considers the time to repair (or duration) for failures, computed as the time between a down notification for a network element and when it is reported as being back online. It is not always the case that an operator had to intervene to resolve the failure. In particular, for short duration failures, it is likely that the fault was resolved automatically (e.g., root guard in the spanning tree protocol can temporarily disable a port [10]). In the case of link failures, our SNMP polling interval of four minutes results in a grouping of durations around four minutes (Figure 9 (a)) indicating that many link failures are resolved automatically without operator intervention. Finally, for long-lived failures, the failure durations may be skewed by when the NOC tickets were closed by network operators. For example, some incident tickets may not be termed as 'resolved' even if normal operation has been restored, until a hardware replacement arrives in stock.

Load balancers experience short-lived failures. We first look at the duration of device failures. Figure 8 (a) shows the CDF of time to repair for device types with the most failures. We observe that LB-1 and LB-3 load balancers experience the shortest failures with median time to repair of 3.7 and 4.5 minutes, respectively, indicating that most of their faults are short-lived.

ToRs experience correlated failures. When considering time to repair for devices, we observe a correlated failure pattern for ToRs. Specifically, these devices tend to have several discrete "steps" in the CDF of their failure durations. These steps correspond to spikes in specific duration values. On analyzing the failure logs, we find that these spikes are due to groups of ToRs that connect to the same (or pair of) AggS going down at the same time (e.g., due to maintenance or AggS failure).

Inter-data center links take the longest to repair. Figure 9 (a) shows the distribution of time to repair for different link types. The majority of link failures are resolved within five minutes, with the exception of links between data centers which take longer to repair. This is because links between data centers require coordination between technicians in multiple locations to identify and resolve faults as well as additional time to repair cables that may be in remote locations.

4.5.2 Time between failures

We next consider the time between failure events. Since time between failure requires a network element to have observed more than a single failure event, this metric is most relevant to elements that are failure prone. Specifically, note that more than half of all elements have only a single failure (cf. Table 5), so the devices and links we consider here are in the minority.

Load balancer failures are bursty. Figure 8 (b) shows the distribution of time between failures for devices. LBs tend to have the shortest time between failures, with a median of 8.6 minutes and 16.4 minutes for LB-1 and LB-2, respectively. Recall that failure events for these two LBs are dominated by a small number of devices that experience numerous failures (cf. Table 5). This small number of failure prone devices has a high impact on time between failure, especially since more than half of the LB-1 and LB-2 devices experience only a single failure.

In contrast to LB-1 and LB-2, devices like ToR-1 and AggS-1 have median time between failure of multiple hours and LB-3 has median time between failure of more than a day. We note that the LB-3 device is a newer version of the LB-1 and LB-2 devices and it exhibits higher reliability in terms of time between failures.

Link flapping is absent from the _actionable_ network logs. Figure 9 (b) presents the distribution of time between failures for the different link types. On an average, link failures tend to be separated by a period of about one week. Recall that our methodology leverages actionable information, as determined by network operators. This significantly reduces our observations of spurious link down events and observations of link flapping that do not impact network connectivity.

MGMT, CORE and ISC links are the most reliable in terms of time between failures, with most link failures on CORE and ISC links occurring more than an hour apart. Links between data centers experience the shortest time between failures. However, note that links connecting data centers have a very low failure probability. Therefore, while most links do not fail, the few that do tend to fail within a short time period of prior failures. In reality, multiple inter-data center link failures in close succession are more likely to be investigated as part of the same troubleshooting window by the network operators.

4.5.3 Reliability of network elements

We conclude our analysis of failure properties by quantifying the aggregate downtime of network elements. We define annualized downtime as the sum of the duration of all failures observed by a network element over a year. For link failures, we consider failures that impacted network traffic, but highlight that a subset of these failures are due to planned maintenance. Additionally, redundancy in terms of network, application, and data in our system implies that this downtime _cannot_ be interpreted as a measure of application-level availability. Figure 8 (c) summarizes the annual downtime for devices that experienced failures during our study.

Data center networks experience high availability. With the exception of ToR-1 devices, all devices have a median annual downtime of less than 30 minutes. Despite experiencing the highest number of failures, LB-1 devices have the lowest annual downtime. This is due to many of their failures being short-lived. Overall, devices experience higher than four 9's of reliability with the exception of ToRs, where long lived correlated failures cause ToRs to have higher downtime; recall, however, that only 3.9% of ToR-1s experience any failures (cf. Figure 4).

Annual downtime for the different link types are shown in Figure 9 (c). The median yearly downtime for all link types, with the exception of links connecting data centers is less than 10 minutes. This duration is smaller than the annual downtime of 24-72 minutes reported by Turner _et al._ when considering an academic WAN [26]. Links between data centers are the exception because, as observed previously, failures on links connecting data centers take longer to resolve than failures for other link types. Overall, links have high availability with the majority of links (except those connecting data centers) having higher than four 9's of reliability.

4.6 Grouping link failures

We now consider correlations between link failures. We also analyzed correlated failures for devices, but except for a few instances of ToRs failing together, grouped device failures are extremely rare (not shown).

To group correlated failures, we need to define what it means for failures to be correlated. First, we require that link failures occur in the same data center to be considered related (since it can be the case that links in multiple data centers fail close together in time but are in fact unrelated). Second, we require failures to occur within a predefined time threshold of each other to be considered correlated. When combining failures into groups, it is important to pick an appropriate threshold for grouping failures. If the threshold is too

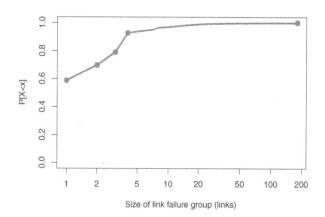

Figure 10: Number of links involved in link failure groups.

Table 6: Examples of problem types

Problem Type	Example causes or explanations
Change	Device deployment, UPS maintenance
Incident	OS reboot (watchdog timer expired)
Network Connection	OSPF convergence, UDLD errors, Cabling, Carrier signaling/timing issues
Software	IOS hotfixes, BIOS upgrade
Hardware	Power supply/fan, Replacement of line card/chassis/optical adapter
Configuration	VPN tunneling, Primary-backup failover, IP/MPLS routing

small, correlated failures may be split into many smaller events. If the threshold is too large, many unrelated failures will be combined into one larger group.

We considered the number of failures for different threshold values. Beyond grouping simultaneous events, which reduces the number of link failures by a factor of two, we did not see significant changes by increasing the threshold.

Link failures tend to be isolated. The size of failure groups produced by our grouping method is shown in Figure 10. We see that just over half of failure events are isolated with 41% of groups containing more than one failure. Large groups of correlated link failures are rare with only 10% of failure groups containing more than four failures. We observed two failure groups with the maximum failure group size of 180 links. These were caused by scheduled maintenance to multiple aggregation switches connected to a large number of ToRs.

4.7 Root causes of failures

Finally, we analyze the types of problems associated with device and link failures. We initially tried to determine the root cause of failure events by mining diaries associated with NOC tickets. However, the diaries often considered multiple potential causes for failure before arriving at the final root cause, which made mining the text impractical. Because of this complication, we chose to leverage the "problem type" field of the NOC tickets which allows operators to place tickets into categories based on the cause of the problem. Table 6 gives examples of the types of problems that are put into each of the categories.

Hardware problems take longer to mitigate. Figure 11 considers the top problem types in terms of number of failures and total downtime for devices. Software and hardware faults dominate in

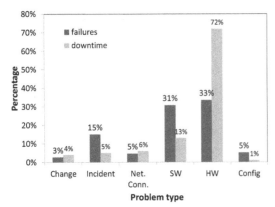

Figure 11: Device problem types.

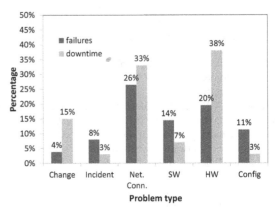

Figure 12: Link problem types.

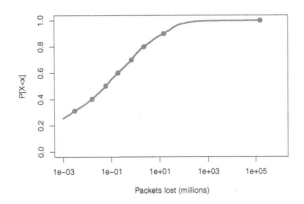

Figure 13: Estimated packet loss during failure events.

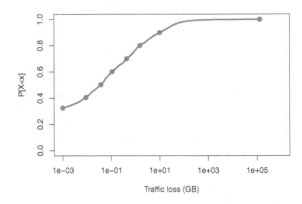

Figure 14: Estimated traffic loss during failure events.

terms of number of failures for devices. However, when considering downtime, the balance shifts and hardware problems have the most downtime. This shift between the number of failures and the total downtime may be attributed to software errors being alleviated by tasks that take less time to complete, such as power cycling, patching or upgrading software. In contrast, hardware errors may require a device to be replaced resulting in longer repair times.

Load balancers affected by software problems. We examined what types of errors dominated for the most failure prone device types (not shown). The LB-1 load balancer, which tends to have short, frequent failures and accounts for most failures (but relatively low downtime), mainly experiences software problems. Hardware problems dominate for the remaining device types. We observe that LB-3, despite also being a load balancer, sees much fewer software issues than LB-1 and LB-2 devices, suggesting higher stability in the newer model of the device.

Link failures are dominated by connection and hardware problems. Figure 12 shows the total number of failures and total downtime attributed to different causes for link failures. In contrast to device failures, link failures are dominated by network connection errors, followed by hardware and software issues. In terms of downtime, software errors incur much less downtime per failure than hardware and network connection problems. This suggests software problems lead to sporadic short-lived failures (e.g., a software bug causing a spurious link down notification) as opposed to severe network connectivity and hardware related problems.

5. ESTIMATING FAILURE IMPACT

In this section, we estimate the impact of link failures. In the absence of application performance data, we aim to quantify the impact of failures in terms of lost network traffic. In particular, we estimate the amount of traffic that would have been routed on a failed link had it been available for the duration of the failure.

In general, it is difficult to precisely quantify how much data was *actually* lost during a failure because of two complications. First, flows may successfully be re-routed to use alternate routes after a link failure and protocols (e.g., TCP) have in-built retransmission mechanisms. Second, for long-lived failures, traffic variations (e.g., traffic bursts, diurnal workloads) mean that the link may not have carried the same amount of data even if it was active. Therefore, we propose a simple metric to approximate the magnitude of traffic lost due to failures, based on the available data sources.

To estimate the impact of link failures on network traffic (both in terms of bytes and packets), we first compute the median number of packets (or bytes) on the link in the hours preceding the failure event, med_b, and the median packets (or bytes) during the failure med_d. We then compute the amount of data (in terms of packets or bytes) that was *potentially* lost during the failure event as:

$$loss = (med_b - med_d) \times duration$$

where $duration$ denotes how long the failure lasted. We use median traffic instead of average to avoid outlier effects.

As described in Section 2, the network traffic in a typical data center may be classified into short-lived, latency-sensitive "mice" flows and long-lived, throughput-sensitive "elephant" flows. Packet loss is much more likely to adversely affect "mice" flows where the loss of an ACK may cause TCP to perform a timed out retransmission. In contrast, loss in traffic throughput is more critical for "elephant" flows.

Link failures incur loss of many packets, but relatively few bytes. For link failures, few bytes are estimated to be lost relative to the number of packets. We observe that the estimated median number of packets lost during failures is 59K (Figure 13) but the estimated median number of bytes lost is only 25MB (Figure 14). Thus, the average size of lost packets is 423 bytes. Prior measurement study on data center network traffic observed that packet sizes tend to be bimodal with modes around 200B and 1,400B [5]. This suggests that packets lost during failures are mostly part of the lower mode, consisting of keep alive packets used by applications (e.g., MYSQL, HTTP) or ACKs [5].

5.1 Is redundancy effective in reducing impact?

In a well-designed network, we expect most failures to be masked by redundant groups of devices and links. We evaluate this expectation by considering median traffic during a link failure (in packets or bytes) normalized by median traffic before the failure: med_d/med_b; for brevity, we refer to this quantity as "normalized traffic". The effectiveness of redundancy is estimated by computing this ratio on a per-link basis, as well as across all links in the redundancy group where the failure occurred. An example of a redundancy group is shown in Figure 15. If a failure has been masked completely, this ratio will be close to one across a redundancy group i.e., traffic during failure was equal to traffic before the failure.

Network redundancy helps, but it is not entirely effective. Figure 16 shows the distribution of normalized byte volumes for individual links and redundancy groups. Redundancy groups are effective at moving the ratio of traffic carried during failures closer to one with 25% of events experiencing no impact on network traffic at the redundancy group level. Also, the median traffic carried at the redundancy group level is 93% as compared with 65% per link. This is an improvement of 43% in median traffic as a result of network redundancy. We make a similar observation when considering packet volumes (not shown) .

There are several reasons why redundancy may not be 100% effective in eliminating the impact of failures on network traffic. First, bugs in fail-over mechanisms can arise if there is uncertainty as to which link or component is the back up (e.g., traffic may be regularly traversing the back up link [7]). Second, if the redundant components are not configured correctly, they will not be able to re-route traffic away from the failed component. For example, we observed the same configuration error made on both the primary and back up of a network connection because of a typo in the configuration script. Further, protocol issues such as TCP backoff, timeouts, and spanning tree reconfigurations may result in loss of traffic.

5.2 Redundancy at different layers of the network topology

This section analyzes the effectiveness of network redundancy across different layers in the network topology. We logically divide links based on their location in the topology. Location is determined based on the types of devices connected by the link (e.g., a CoreCore link connects two core routers). Figure 17 plots quartiles of normalized traffic (in bytes) for links at different layers of the network topology.

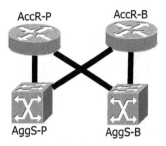

Figure 15: An example redundancy group between a primary (P) and backup (B) aggregation switch (AggS) and access router (AccR).

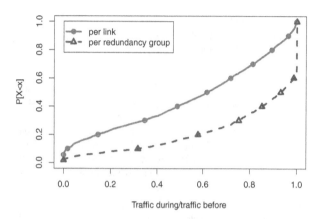

Figure 16: Normalized traffic (bytes) during failure events per link as well as within redundancy groups.

Links highest in the topology benefit most from redundancy. A reliable network core is critical to traffic flow in data centers. We observe that redundancy is effective at ensuring that failures between core devices have a minimal impact. In the core of the network, the median traffic carried during failure drops to 27% per link but remains at 100% when considered across a redundancy group. Links between aggregation switches and access routers (AggAccR) experience the next highest benefit from redundancy where the median traffic carried per link during failure drops to 42% per link but remains at 86% across redundancy groups.

Links from ToRs to aggregation switches benefit the least from redundancy, but have low failure impact. Links near the edge of the data center topology benefit the least from redundancy, where the median traffic carried during failure increases from 68% on links to 94% within redundancy groups for links connecting ToRs to AggS. However, we observe that on a per link basis, these links do not experience significant impact from failures so there is less room for redundancy to benefit them.

6. DISCUSSION

In this section, we discuss implications of our study for the design of data center networks and future directions on characterizing data center reliability.

Low-end switches exhibit high reliability. Low-cost, commodity switches in our data centers experience the lowest failure rate with a failure probability of less than 5% annually for all types of ToR switches and AggS-2. However, due to their much larger population, the ToRs still rank third in terms of number of failures and

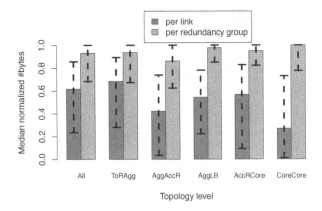

Figure 17: Normalized bytes (quartiles) during failure events per link and across redundancy group compared across different layers in the data center topology.

dominate in terms of total downtime. Since ToR failures are considered the norm rather than the exception (and are typically masked by redundancy in application, data, and network layers), ToRs have a low priority for repair relative to other outage types. This suggests that proposals to leverage commodity switches to build flat data center networks [3, 12, 21] will be able to provide good reliability. However, as populations of these devices rise, the absolute number of failures observed will inevitably increase.

Improve reliability of middleboxes. Our analysis of network failure events highlights the role that middle boxes such as load balancers play in the overall reliability of the network. While there have been many studies on improving performance and scalability of large-scale networks [2, 3, 12–14, 21], only few studies focus on management of middle boxes in data center networks [15]. Middle boxes such as load balancers are a critical part of data center networks that need to be taken into account when developing new routing frameworks. Further, the development of better management and debugging tools would help alleviate software and configuration faults frequently experienced by load balancers. Finally, software load balancers running on commodity servers can be explored to provide cost-effective, reliable alternatives to expensive and proprietary hardware solutions.

Improve the effectiveness of network redundancy. We observe that network redundancies in our system are 40% effective at masking the impact of network failures. One cause of this is due to configuration issues that lead to redundancy being ineffective at masking failure. For instance, we observed an instance where the same typo was made when configuring interfaces on both the primary and back up of a load balancer connection to an aggregation switch. As a result, the back up link was subject to the same flaw as the primary. This type of error occurs when operators configure large numbers of devices, and highlights the importance of automated configuration and validation tools (e.g., [8]).

Separate control plane from data plane. Our analysis of NOC tickets reveals that in several cases, the loss of keep alive messages resulted in disconnection of portchannels, which are virtual links that bundle multiple physical interfaces to increase aggregate link speed. For some of these cases, we manually correlated loss of control packets with application-level logs that showed significant traffic bursts in the hosted application on the egress path. This interference between application and control traffic is undesirable. Software Defined Networking (SDN) proposals such as Open-Flow [20] present a solution to this problem by maintaining state in

a logically centralized controller, thus eliminating keep alive messages in the data plane. In the context of proposals that leverage location independent addressing (e.g., [12, 21]), this separation between control plane (e.g., ARP and DHCP requests, directory service lookups [12]) and data plane becomes even more crucial to avoid impact to hosted applications.

7. RELATED WORK

Previous studies of network failures have considered application-level [16, 22] or network connectivity [18, 19, 25, 26, 28] failures. There also have been several studies on understanding hardware reliability in the context of cloud computing [11, 23, 24, 27].

Application failures. Padmanabhan *et al.* consider failures from the perspective of Web clients [22]. They observe that the majority of failures occur during the TCP handshake as a result of end-to-end connectivity issues. They also find that Web access failures are dominated by server-side issues. These findings highlight the importance of studying failures in data centers hosting Web services.

Netmedic aims to diagnose application failures in enterprise networks [16]. By taking into account state of components that fail together (as opposed to grouping all components that fail together), it is able to limit the number of incorrect correlations between failures and components.

Network failures. There have been many studies of network failures in wide area and enterprise networks [18, 19, 25, 26, 28] but none consider network element failures in large-scale data centers.

Shaikh *et al* study properties of OSPF Link State Advertisement (LSA) traffic in a data center connected to a corporate network via leased lines [25]. Watson *et al* also study stability of OSPF by analyzing LSA messages in a regional ISP network [28]. Both studies observe significant instability and flapping as a result of external routing protocols (e.g., BGP). Unlike these studies, we do not observe link flapping owing to our data sources being geared towards actionable events.

Markopolou *et al.* use IS-IS listeners to characterize failures in an ISP backbone [19]. The authors classify failures as either router related or optical related by correlating time and impacted network components. They find that 70% of their failures involve only a single link. We similarly observe that the majority of failures in our data centers are isolated.

More recently, Turner *et al.* consider failures in an academic WAN using syslog messages generated by IS-IS [26]. Unlike previous studies [19, 25, 28], the authors leverage existing syslog, e-mail notifications, and router configuration data to study network failures. Consistent with prior studies that focus on OSPF [25, 28], the authors observe link flapping. They also observe longer time to repair on wide area links, similar to our observations for wide area links connecting data centers.

Failures in cloud computing. The interest in cloud computing has increased focus on understanding component failures, as even a small failure rate can manifest itself in a high number of failures in large-scale systems. Previous work has looked at failures of DRAM [24], storage [11, 23] and server nodes [27], but there has not been a large-scale study on network component failures in data centers. Ford *et al.* consider the availability of distributed storage and observe that the majority of failures involving more than ten storage nodes are localized within a single rack [11]. We also observe spatial correlations but they occur higher in the network topology, where we see multiple ToRs associated with the same aggregation switch having correlated failures.

Complementary to our work, Benson *et al.* mine threads from customer service forums of an IaaS cloud provider [6]. They report on problems users face when using IaaS and observe that problems related to managing virtual resources and debugging performance of computing instances that require involvement of cloud administrators, increase over time.

8. CONCLUSIONS AND FUTURE WORK

In this paper, we have presented the first large-scale analysis of network failure events in data centers. We focused our analysis on characterizing failures of network links and devices, estimating their failure impact, and analyzing the effectiveness of network redundancy in masking failures. To undertake this analysis, we developed a methodology that correlates network traffic logs with logs of actionable events, to filter a large volume of non-impacting failures due to spurious notifications and errors in logging software.

Our study is part of a larger project, NetWiser, on understanding reliability in data centers to aid research efforts on improving network availability and designing new network architectures. Based on our study, we find that commodity switches exhibit high reliability which supports current proposals to design flat networks using commodity components [3, 12, 17, 21]. We also highlight the importance of studies to better manage middle boxes such as load balancers, as they exhibit high failure rates. Finally, more investigation is needed to analyze and improve the effectiveness of redundancy at both network and application layers.

Future work. In this study, we consider occurrence of interface level failures. This is only one aspect of reliability in data center networks. An important direction for future work is correlating logs from application-level monitors with the logs collected by network operators to determine what fraction of observed errors *do not* impact applications (false positives) and what fraction of application errors are not observed (e.g., because of a server or storage failure that we cannot observe). This would enable us to understand what fraction of application failures can be attributed to network failures. Another extension to our study would be to understand what these low level failures mean in terms of convergence for network protocols such as OSPF, and to analyze the impact on end-to-end network connectivity by incorporating logging data from external sources e.g., BGP neighbors.

Acknowledgements

We thank our shepherd Arvind Krishnamurthy and the anonymous reviewers for their feedback. We are grateful to David St. Pierre for helping us understand the network logging systems and data sets.

9. REFERENCES

[1] Cisco: Data center: Load balancing data center services, 2004. www.cisco.com/en/US/solutions/collateral/ns340/ns517/ns224/ns668/net_implementation_white_paper0900aecd8053495a.html.

[2] H. Abu-Libdeh, P. Costa, A. I. T. Rowstron, G. O'Shea, and A. Donnelly. Symbiotic routing in future data centers. In *SIGCOMM*, 2010.

[3] M. Al-Fares, A. Loukissas, and A. Vahdat. A scalable, commodity data center network architecture. In *SIGCOMM*, 2008.

[4] M. Alizadeh, A. Greenberg, D. Maltz, J. Padhye, P. Patel, B. Prabhakar, S. Sengupta, and M. Sridharan. Data Center TCP (DCTCP). In *SIGCOMM*, 2010.

[5] T. Benson, A. Akella, and D. Maltz. Network traffic characteristics of data centers in the wild. In *IMC*, 2010.

[6] T. Benson, S. Sahu, A. Akella, and A. Shaikh. A first look at problems in the cloud. In *HotCloud*, 2010.

[7] J. Brodkin. Amazon EC2 outage calls 'availability zones' into question, 2011. http://www.networkworld.com/news/2011/042111-amazon-ec2-zones.html.

[8] X. Chen, Y. Mao, Z. M. Mao, and K. van de Merwe. Declarative configuration management for complex and dynamic networks. In *CoNEXT*, 2010.

[9] Cisco. UniDirectional Link Detection (UDLD). http://www.cisco.com/en/US/tech/tk866/tsd_technology_support_sub-protocol_home.html.

[10] Cisco. Spanning tree protocol root guard enhancement, 2011. http://www.cisco.com/en/US/tech/tk389/tk621/technologies_tech_note09186a00800ae96b.shtml.

[11] D. Ford, F. Labelle, F. Popovici, M. Stokely, V.-A. Truong, L. Barroso, C. Grimes, and S. Quinlan. Availability in globally distributed storage systems. In *OSDI*, 2010.

[12] A. Greenberg, J. Hamilton, N. Jain, S. Kandula, C. Kim, P. Lahiri, D. Maltz, P. Patel, and S. Sengupta. VL2: A scalable and flexible data center network. In *SIGCOMM*, 2009.

[13] C. Guo, H. Wu, K. Tan, L. Shiy, Y. Zhang, and S. Lu. DCell: A scalable and fault-tolerant network structure for data centers. In *SIGCOMM*, 2008.

[14] C. Guo, H. Wu, K. Tan, L. Shiy, Y. Zhang, and S. Lu. BCube: A high performance, server-centric network architecture for modular data centers. In *SIGCOMM*, 2009.

[15] D. Joseph, A. Tavakoli, and I. Stoica. A policy-aware switching layer for data centers. In *SIGCOMM*, 2008.

[16] S. Kandula, R. Mahajan, P. Verkaik, S. Agarwal, J. Padhye, and P. Bahl. Detailed diagnosis in enterprise networks. In *SIGCOMM*, 2010.

[17] C. Kim, M. Caesar, and J. Rexford. Floodless in SEATTLE: a scalable ethernet architecture for large enterprises. In *SIGCOMM*, 2008.

[18] C. Labovitz and A. Ahuja. Experimental study of internet stability and wide-area backbone failures. In *The Twenty-Ninth Annual International Symposium on Fault-Tolerant Computing*, 1999.

[19] A. Markopoulou, G. Iannaccone, S. Bhattacharyya, C.-N. Chuah, Y. Ganjali, and C. Diot. Characterization of failures in an operational IP backbone network. *IEEE/ACM Transactions on Networking*, 2008.

[20] N. Mckeown, T. Anderson, H. Balakrishnan, G. Parulkar, L. Peterson, J. Rexford, S. Shenker, and J. Turner. Openflow: enabling innovation in campus networks. In *SIGCOMM CCR*, 2008.

[21] R. N. Mysore, A. Pamboris, N. Farrington, N. Huang, P. Miri, S. Radhakrishnan, V. Subramanya, and A. Vahdat. PortLand: A scalable fault-tolerant layer 2 data center network fabric. In *SIGCOMM*, 2009.

[22] V. Padmanabhan, S. Ramabhadran, S. Agarwal, and J. Padhye. A study of end-to-end web access failures. In *CoNEXT*, 2006.

[23] B. Schroeder and G. Gibson. Disk failures in the real world: What does an MTTF of 1,000,000 hours mean too you? In *FAST*, 2007.

[24] B. Schroeder, E. Pinheiro, and W.-D. Weber. DRAM errors in the wild: A large-scale field study. In *SIGMETRICS*, 2009.

[25] A. Shaikh, C. Isett, A. Greenberg, M. Roughan, and J. Gottlieb. A case study of OSPF behavior in a large enterprise network. In *ACM IMW*, 2002.

[26] D. Turner, K. Levchenko, A. C. Snoeren, and S. Savage. California fault lines: Understanding the causes and impact of network failures. In *SIGCOMM*, 2010.

[27] K. V. Vishwanath and N. Nagappan. Characterizing cloud computing hardware reliability. In *Symposium on Cloud Computing (SOCC)*, 2010.

[28] D. Watson, F. Jahanian, and C. Labovitz. Experiences with monitoring OSPF on a regional service provider network. In *ICDCS*, 2003.

Understanding the Impact of
Video Quality on User Engagement

Florin Dobrian,
Asad Awan, Dilip Joseph,
Aditya Ganjam, Jibin Zhan
Conviva

Vyas Sekar
Intel Labs

Ion Stoica
Conviva, UC Berkeley

Hui Zhang
Conviva, CMU

ABSTRACT

As the distribution of the video over the Internet becomes mainstream and its consumption moves from the computer to the TV screen, user expectation for high quality is constantly increasing. In this context, it is crucial for content providers to understand if and how video quality affects user engagement and how to best invest their resources to optimize video quality. This paper is a first step towards addressing these questions. We use a unique dataset that spans different content types, including short video on demand (VoD), long VoD, and live content from popular video content providers. Using client-side instrumentation, we measure quality metrics such as the join time, buffering ratio, average bitrate, rendering quality, and rate of buffering events.

We quantify user engagement both at a per-video (or view) level and a per-user (or viewer) level. In particular, we find that the percentage of time spent in buffering (buffering ratio) has the largest impact on the user engagement across all types of content. However, the magnitude of this impact depends on the content type, with live content being the most impacted. For example, a 1% increase in buffering ratio can reduce user engagement by more than three minutes for a 90-minute live video event. We also see that the average bitrate plays a significantly more important role in the case of live content than VoD content.

Categories and Subject Descriptors

C.4 [**Performance of Systems**]: [measurement techniques, performance attributes] ; C.2.4 [**Computer-Communication Networks**]: Distributed Systems—*Client/server*

General Terms

Human Factors, Measurement, Performance

Keywords

Video quality, Engagement, Measurement

1. INTRODUCTION

Video content constitutes a dominant fraction of Internet traffic today. Further, several analysts forecast that this contribution is set

to increase in the next few years [2, 29]. This trend is fueled by the ever decreasing cost of content delivery and the emergence of new subscription- and ad-based business models. Premier examples are Netflix which now has reached 20 million US subscribers, and Hulu which distributes over one billion videos per month. Furthermore, Netflix reports that video distribution over the Internet is significantly cheaper than mailing DVDs [7].

As video distribution over the Internet goes mainstream and it is increasingly consumed on bigger screens, users' expectations for quality have dramatically increased: when watching on the TV anything less than SD quality is not acceptable. To meet this challenge, content publishers and delivery providers have made tremendous strides in improving the server-side and network-level performance using measurement-driven insights of real systems (e.g., [12,25,33, 35]) and using these insights for better system design (e.g., for more efficient caching [18]). Similarly, there have been several user studies in controlled lab settings to evaluate how quality affects user experience for different types of media content (e.g., [13,23,28,38]). There has, however, been very little work on understanding how the quality of Internet video affects *user engagement* in the wild and at scale.

In the spirit of Herbert Simon's articulation of attention economics, the overabundance of video content increases the onus on content providers to maximize their ability to attract users' attention [36]. In this respect, it becomes critical to systematically understand the interplay between *video quality* and *user engagement* for different *types of content*. This knowledge can help providers to better invest their network and server resources toward optimizing the quality metrics that *really matter* [3]. Thus, we would like to answer fundamental questions such as:

1. How much does *quality matter*–Does poor video quality significantly reduce user engagement?
2. Do different metrics vary in the *degree* in which they impact the user engagement?
3. Do the critical quality metrics differ across content genres and across different granularities of user engagement?

This paper is a step toward answering these questions. We do so using a dataset which is unique in two respects:

1. *Client-side:* We measure a range of video quality metrics using lightweight client-side instrumentation. This provides critical insights into what is happening at the client that cannot be observed at the server node alone.
2. *Scale:* We present summary results from over 2 million unique views from over 1 million viewers. The videos span several popular mainstream content providers and thus representative of Internet video traffic today.

Using this dataset, we analyze the impact of quality on engagement along three dimensions:

- **Quality metrics:** We measure several quality metrics that we describe in more detail in the next section. At a high level, these capture characteristics of the start up latency, the rate at which the video was encoded, how much and how frequently the user experienced a buffering event, and what was the observed quality of the video rendered to the user.

- **Time-scales of user engagement:** We quantify the user engagement at the granularity of an individual *view* (i.e., a single video being watched) and *viewer*, the latter aggregated over all views associated with a distinct user. In this paper, we focus specifically on quantifying engagement in terms of the total play time and the number of videos viewed.

- **Types of video content** We partition our data based on video type and length into *short VoD*, *long VoD*, and *live*, to represent the three broad types of video content being served today.

To identify the critical quality metrics and to understand the dependencies among these metrics, we employ the well known concepts of *correlation* and *information gain* from the data mining literature [32]. Further, we augment this qualitative study with regression based analysis to measure the quantitative impact for the most important metric(s). Our main observations are:

- The percentage of time spent in buffering (buffering ratio) has the largest impact on the user engagement across all types of content. However, this impact is quantitatively different for different content types, with live content being the most impacted. For a highly popular 90 minute soccer game, for example, an increase of the buffering ratio of only 1% can lead to more than three minutes of reduction in the user engagement.

- The average bitrate at which the content is streamed has a significantly higher impact on live content than on VoD content.

- The quality metrics affect not only the per-view engagement but also the number of views watched by a viewer over a time period. Further, the join time which seems non-critical at the view-level, becomes more critical for determining viewer-level engagement.

These results have significant implications on how content providers can best use their resources to maximize user engagement. Reducing the buffering ratio can significantly increase the engagement for all content types, minimizing the rate of buffering events can improve the engagement for long VoD and live content, and increasing the average bitrate can increase the engagement for live content. Access to such knowledge implies the ability to optimize engagement. Ultimately, increasing engagement results in more revenue for ad supported businesses as the content providers can play more ads, as well as for subscription based services as better quality increases the user retention rate.

The rest of the paper is organized as follows. Section 2 provides an overview of our dataset and also scopes the problem space in terms of the quality metrics, types of video content, and granularities of engagement. Section 3 motivates the types of questions we are interested in and briefly describes the techniques we use to address these. Sections 4 and 5 apply these analysis techniques for different types of video content to understand the impact of different metrics for the view- and viewer-level notions of user engagement respectively. We summarize two important lessons that we learned in the course of our work and also point out a key direction of future work in Section 6. Section 7 describes our work in the context of other related work before we conclude in Section 8.

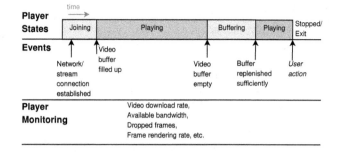

Figure 1: An illustration of a video session life time and associated video player events. Our client-side instrumentation collects statistics directly from the video player, providing high fidelity data about the playback session.

2. PRELIMINARIES AND DATASETS

We begin this section with an overview of how our dataset was collected. Then, we scope the three dimensions of the problem space: user engagement, video quality metrics, and types of video content.

2.1 Data Collection

We have implemented a highly scalable and available real-time data collection and processing system. The system consists of two parts: (a) a client-resident instrumentation library in the video player, and (b) a data aggregation and processing service that runs in data centers. Our client library gets loaded when Internet users watch video on our affiliates' sites. The library listens to events from the video player and additionally polls for statistics from the player. Because the instrumentation is on the client side we are able to collect very high fidelity raw data, process raw client data to generate higher level information on the client side, and transmit fine-grained reports back to our data center in real time with minimal overhead. Our data aggregation back-end receives real time information and archives all data redundantly in HDFS [4]. We utilize a proprietary system for real time stream processing and Hadoop [4] and Hive [5] for batch data processing. We collect and process 0.5TB of data on average per day from various affiliates over a diverse spectrum of end users, video content, Internet service providers, and content delivery networks.

Video player instrumentation: Figure 1 illustrates the life time of a video session as observed at the client. The video player goes through multiple states (connecting and joining, playing, paused, buffering, stopped). Player events or user actions change the state of a video player. For example, the player goes to paused state if the user presses the pause button on the screen, or if the video buffer becomes empty then the player goes in to buffering state. By instrumenting the client, we can observe all player states and events and also collect statistics about the play back.

We acknowledge that the players used by our affiliates differ in their choice of adaptation and optimization algorithms; e.g., selecting the bitrate or server in response to changes in network or host conditions. Note, however, that the focus of this paper is not to design optimal adaptation algorithms or evaluate the effectiveness of such algorithms. Rather, our goal is to understand the impact of quality on engagement in the wild. In other words, we take the player setup as a given and evaluate the impact of quality on user engagement. To this end, we present results from different affiliate providers that are diverse in their player setup and choice of optimizations and adaptation algorithms.

2.2 Engagement Metrics

Qualitatively, engagement is a reflection of user involvement and interaction. We focus on engagement at two levels:

1. **View level:** A user watching a single video continuously is a *view*. For example, this could be watching a movie trailer clip, an episode of a TV serial, or a football game. The view-level engagement metric of interest is simply *play time*, the duration of the viewing session.

2. **Viewer level:** To capture the aggregate experience of a single viewer (i.e., an end-user as identified by a unique system-generated clientid), we study the viewer-level engagement metrics for each unique viewer. The two metrics we use are *number of views* per viewer, and the *total play time* across all videos watched by the viewer.

We do acknowledge that there are other aspects of user engagement beyond play time and number of views. Our choice of these metrics is based on two reasons. First, these metrics can be measured directly and objectively. For example, things like how focused or distracted the user was while watching the video or whether the user is likely to give a positive recommendation are subjective and hard to quantify. Second, these metrics can be translated into providers' business objectives. Direct revenue objectives include number of advertisement impressions watched and recurring subscription to the service. The above engagement metrics fit well with these objectives. For example, play time is directly associated with the number (and thus revenue) of ad impressions. Additionally, user satisfaction with content quality is reflected in the play time. Similarly, viewer-level metrics can be projected to ad-driven and recurring subscription models.

2.3 Quality Metrics

In our study, we use five industry-standard video quality metrics [3]. We summarize these below.

1. **Join time** (*JoinTime*): Measured in seconds, this metric represents the duration from the player initiates a connection to a video server till the time sufficient player video buffer has filled up and the player starts rendering video frames (i.e., moves to playing state). In Figure 1, join time is the duration of the joining state.

2. **Buffering ratio** (*BufRatio*): Represented as a percentage, this metric is the fraction of the total session time (i.e., playing plus buffering time) spent in buffering. This is an aggregate metric that can capture periods of long video "freeze" observed by the user. As illustrated in Figure 1, the player goes into a buffering state when the video buffer becomes empty and moves out of buffering (back to playing state) when the buffer is replenished.

3. **Rate of buffering events** (*RateBuf*): *BufRatio* does not capture the frequency of induced interruptions observed by the user. For example, a video session that experiences "video stuttering" where each interruption is small but the total number of interruptions is high, might not have a high buffering ratio, but may be just as annoying to a user. Thus, we use the rate of buffering events $\frac{\#buffer\ events}{session\ duration}$.

4. **Average bitrate** (*AvgBitrate*): A single video session can have multiple bitrates played if the video player can switch between different bitrate streams. Average bitrate, measured in kilobits per second, is the average of the bitrates played weighted by the duration each bit rate is played.

5. **Rendering quality** (*RendQual*): Rendering rate (frames per second) is central to user's visual perception. Rendering rate may drop due to several reasons. For example, the video player

Dataset	# videos	# viewers (100K)
LiveA	107	4.5
LiveB	194	0.8
LvodA	115	8.2
LvodB	87	4.9
SvodA	43	4.3
SvodB	53	1.9
LiveH	3	29

Table 1: Summary of the datasets in our study. We select videos with at least 1000 views over a one week period.

may drop frames to keep up with the stream if the CPU is overloaded. Rendering rate may drop due to network congestion if the buffer becomes empty (causing rendering rate to become zero). Note that most Internet video streaming uses TCP (e.g., RTMP, HTTP chunk streaming). Thus, network packet loss does not directly cause a frame drop. Rather, it could deplete the client buffer due to reduced throughput. To normalize rendering performance across videos, which may have different encoded frame rates, we define rendering quality as the ratio of the rendered frames per second to the encoded frames per second of the stream played.

Why we do not report rate of bitrate switching? In this paper, we avoid reporting the impact of bitrate switching for two reasons. First, in our measurements we found that the majority of sessions have either 0, 1, or 2 bitrate switches. Now, such a small discrete range of values introduces a spurious relationship between engagement (play time) and the rate of switching.[1] That is, the rate of switches is $\approx \frac{1}{PlayTime}$ or $\approx \frac{2}{PlayTime}$. This introduces an artificial dependency between the variables! Second, only two of our datasets report the rates of bitrate switching; we want to avoid reaching general conclusions from the specific bitrate adaptation algorithms they use.

2.4 Dataset

We collect close to four terabytes of data each week. On average, one week of our data captures measurements over **300 million views** watched by about **100 million unique viewers** across all of our affiliate content providers. The analysis in this paper is based the data collected from five of our affiliates during the fall of 2010. These providers serve a large volume of video content and consistently appear in the Top-500 sites in overall popularity rankings [1]. Thus, these are representative of a significant volume of Internet video traffic. We organize the data into three content types. Within each content type we use a pair of datasets, each corresponding to a different provider. We choose diverse providers in order to eliminate any biases induced by the particular provider or the player-specific optimizations and algorithms they use. For live content, we use additional data from the largest live Internet video streaming sports event of 2010: the FIFA World Cup. Table 1 summarizes the total number of unique videos and views for each dataset, described below. To ensure that our analysis is statistically meaningful, we only select videos that have at least 1000 views over the week-long period.

- **Long VoD:** Long VoD clips have video length of at least 35 minutes and at most 60 minutes. They are often full episodes of TV shows. The two long VoD datasets are labeled as *LvodA* and *LvodB*.

- **Short VoD:** We categorize video clips as short VoD if the video length is at least 2 and at most 5 minutes. These are often

---

[1]This discretization effect does not occur with *RateBuf*.

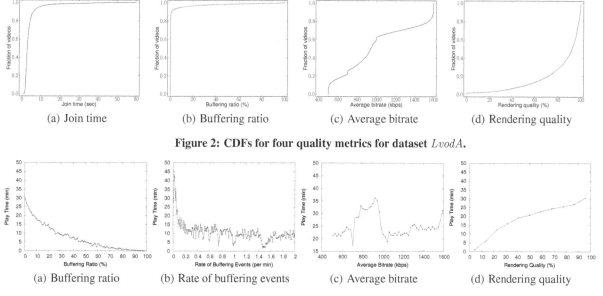

| (a) Join time | (b) Buffering ratio | (c) Average bitrate | (d) Rendering quality |

Figure 2: CDFs for four quality metrics for dataset *LvodA*.

| (a) Buffering ratio | (b) Rate of buffering events | (c) Average bitrate | (d) Rendering quality |

Figure 3: Qualitative relationships between four quality metrics and the play time for a video from *LvodA*.

trailers, short interviews, and short skits. The two short VoD datasets are labeled as *SvodA* and *SvodB*.

- **Live:** Sports events and news feeds are typically delivered as live video streams. There are two key differences between the VoD-type content and live streams. First, the client buffers in this case are sized such that the viewer does not lag more than a few seconds behind the video source. Second, all viewers are roughly synchronized in time. The two live datasets are labeled *LiveA* and *LiveB*. As a special case study, dataset *LiveH* corresponds to the three of the final World Cup games with almost a million viewers per game on average (1.2 million viewers for the last game from this dataset).

3. ANALYSIS TECHNIQUES

In this section, we begin with real-world measurements to motivate the types of questions we want to answer and explain our analysis methodology toward addressing these questions.

3.1 Overview

To put our work in perspective, Figure 2 shows the cumulative distribution functions (CDF) of four quality metrics for dataset *LvodA*. As expected, most viewing sessions experience very good quality, i.e., have very low *BufRatio*, low *JoinTime*, and relatively high *RendQual*. However, the number of views that suffer from quality issues is not trivial. In particular, 7% of views experience *BufRatio* larger than 10%, 5% of views have *JoinTime* larger than 10s, and 37% of views have *RendQual* lower than 90%. Finally, only a relatively small fraction of views receive the highest bit rate. Given that a non-negligible number of views experience quality issues, it is critical for content providers to understand if improving the quality of these sessions could have potentially increased the user engagement.

To understand how the quality could potentially impact the engagement, we consider one video object each from *LiveA* and *LvodA*. For this video, we bin the different sessions based on the value of the quality metrics and calculate the average play time for each bin. Figures 3 and 4 show how the four quality metrics interact with the play time. Looking at the trends visually confirms that

quality matters. At the same time, these initial visualizations spark several questions:

- How do we *identify* which metrics matter the most?
- Are these quality metrics *independent* or are they manifestations of the same underlying phenomenon? In other words, is the observed relationship between the engagement and the quality metric M really due to M or due to a hidden relationship between M and another more critical metric M'?
- How do we *quantify* how important a quality metric is?
- Can we explain the seemingly counter-intuitive behaviors? For example, *RendQual* is actually negatively correlated for the *LiveA* video (Figure 4(d)), while the *AvgBitrate* shows an unexpected non-monotone trend for *LvodA* (Figure 3(c)).

To address the first two questions, we use the well-known concepts of correlation and information gain from the data mining literature that we describe next. To measure the quantitative impact, we also use linear regression based models for the most important metric(s). Finally, we use domain-specific insights and experiments in controlled settings to explain the anomalous observations.

3.2 Correlation

The natural approach to quantify the interaction between a pair of variables is the correlation. Here, we are interested in quantifying the magnitude and direction of the relationship between the engagement metric and the quality metrics.

To avoid making assumptions about the nature of the relationships between the variables, we choose the Kendall correlation, instead of the Pearson correlation. The Kendall correlation is a *rank correlation* that does not make any assumption about the underlying distributions, noise, or the nature of the relationships. (Pearson correlation assumes that the noise in the data is Gaussian and that the relationship is roughly linear.)

Given the raw data–a vector of (x,y) values where each x is the measured quality metric and y the engagement metric (play time or number of views)–we *bin* it based on the value of the quality metric. We choose bin sizes that are appropriate for each quality metric of interest: for *JoinTime*, we use 0.5 second intervals, for *BufRatio* and *RendQual* we use 1% bins, for *RateBuf* we use 0.01/min

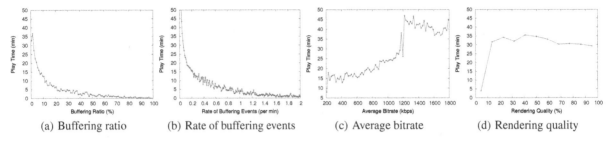

| (a) Buffering ratio | (b) Rate of buffering events | (c) Average bitrate | (d) Rendering quality |

Figure 4: Qualitative relationships between four quality metrics and the play time for a video from *LiveA*.

sized bins, and for *AvgBitrate* we use 20 kbps-sized bins. For each bin, we compute the empirical *mean* of the engagement metric across the sessions/viewers that fall in the bin.

We compute the Kendall correlation between the mean-per-bin vector and the values of the bin indices. We use this "binned" correlation metric for two reasons. First, we observed that the correlation coefficient[2] was biased by a large mass of users that had high quality but very low play time, possibly because of low user interest. Our primary goal, in this paper, is not to study user interest in the specific content. Rather, we want to understand if and how the quality impacts user engagement. To this end, we look at the average value for each bin and compute the correlation on the binned data. The second reason is scale. Computing the rank correlation is computationally expensive at the scale of analysis we target. The binned correlation retains the qualitative properties that we want to highlight with lower compute cost.

3.3 Information Gain

Correlations are useful for quantifying the interaction between variables when the relationship is roughly *monotone* (either increasing or decreasing). As Figure 3(c) shows, this may not always be the case. Further, we want to move beyond the single metric analysis. First, we want to understand if a pair (or a set) of quality metrics are complementary or if they capture the same effects. As an example, consider *RendQual* in Figure 3; *RendQual* could reflect either a network issue or a client-side CPU issue. Because *BufRatio* is also correlated with *PlayTime*, we suspect that *RendQual* is mirroring the same effect. Identifying and uncovering these hidden relationships, however, is tedious. Second, content providers may want to know the top k metrics that they should to optimize to improve user engagement. Correlation-based analysis cannot answer such questions.

To address the above challenges, we augment the correlation analysis using the notion of *information gain* [32], which is based on the concept of entropy. The entropy of random variable Y is $H(Y) = \sum_i P[Y = y_i] \log \frac{1}{P[Y=y_i]}$, where $P[Y = y_i]$ is the probability that $Y = y_i$. The conditional entropy of Y given another random variable X is defined as $H(Y|X) = \sum_j P[X = X_j]H(Y|X = x_j)$ and the information gain is then $H(Y) - H(Y|X)$, and the relative information gain is $\frac{H(Y)-H(Y|X)}{H(Y)}$. Intuitively, this metric quantifies how our knowledge of X reduces the uncertainty in Y.

Specifically, we want to quantify what a quality metric informs us about the engagement; e.g., what does knowing the *AvgBitrate* or *BufRatio* tell us about the play time distribution? As with the correlation, we bin the data into discrete bins with the same bin specifications. For the play time, we choose different bin sizes depending on the duration of the content. From this binned data, we compute $H(Y|X_1, \ldots, X_N)$, where Y is the discretized play time

and $X_1, \ldots, X_N$ are quality metrics. From this estimate, we calculate the relative information gain.

Note that these two classes of analysis techniques are *complementary*. Correlation provides a first-order summary of monotone relationships between engagement and quality. The information gain can corroborate the correlation or augment it when the relationship is not monotone. Further, it provides a more in-depth understanding of the interaction between the quality metrics by extending to the multivariate case.

3.4 Regression

Rank correlation and information gain are largely qualitative analyses. It is also useful to understand the *quantitative* impact of a quality metric on user engagement. Specifically, we want to answer questions of the form: *What is the expected improvement in the engagement if we optimize a specific quality metric by a given amount?*

For quantitative analysis, we rely on *regression*. However, as the visualizations show, the relationships between the quality metrics and the engagement are not always obvious and several of the metrics have intrinsic dependencies. Thus, directly applying regression techniques with complex non-linear parameters could lead to models that lack a physically meaningful interpretation. While our ultimate goal is to extract the relative quantitative impact of the different metrics, doing so rigorously is outside the scope of this paper.

As a simpler alternative, we use linear regression based curve fitting to quantify the impact of specific ranges of the most critical quality metric. However, we do so only after visually confirming that the relationship is approximately linear over the range of interest. This allows us to employ simple linear data fitting models that are also easy to interpret.

4. VIEW LEVEL ENGAGEMENT

The engagement metric of interest at the view level is *PlayTime*. We begin with long VoD content, then proceed to live and short VoD content. In each case, we start with the basic correlation based analysis and augment it with information gain based analysis. Note that we compute the binned correlation and information gain coefficients on a per-video-object basis. Then we look at the distribution of the coefficients across all video objects. Having identified the most critical metric(s), we quantify the impact of improving this quality using a linear regression model over a specific range of the quality metric.

In summary, we find that *BufRatio* consistently has the highest impact on user engagement among all quality metrics. For example, for a 90 minutes live event, an increase of *BufRatio* by 1% can decrease *PlayTime* by over 3 minutes. Interestingly, the relative impact of the other metrics depend on the content type. For live video, *RateBuf* is slightly more negatively correlated with *PlayTime* as compared to long VoD; because the player buffer

---

[2]This happens with Pearson and Spearman correlation metrics also.

is small there is little time to recover when the bandwidth fluctuates. Our analysis also shows that higher bitrates are more likely to improve user engagement for live content. In contrast to live and long VoD videos, for short videos *RendQual* exhibits correlation similar to *BufRatio*. We also find that various metrics are not independent. Finally, we explain some of the anomalous observations from Section 3 in more depth.

4.1 Long VoD Content

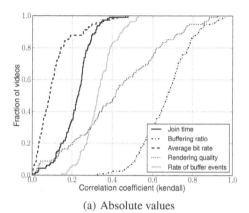

(a) Absolute values

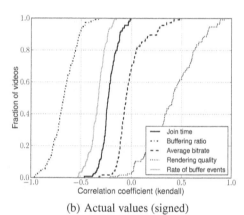

(b) Actual values (signed)

Figure 5: Distribution of the Kendall rank correlation coefficient between the quality metrics and play time for *LvodA*.

Figure 5 shows the distribution of the correlation coefficients for the quality metrics for dataset *LvodA*. We include both *absolute value* and *signed* values to measure the magnitude and the nature (i.e., increasing or decreasing) of the correlation. We summarize the median values for both datasets in Table 2. The results are consistent across both datasets for the common quality metrics *BufRatio*, *JoinTime*, and *RendQual*. Recall that the two datasets correspond to two different content providers; these results confirm that our observations are not unique to dataset *LvodA*.

The result shows that *BufRatio* has the strongest correlation with *PlayTime*. Intuitively, we expect a higher *BufRatio* to decrease *PlayTime* (i.e., a negative correlation) and a higher *RendQual* to increase *PlayTime* (i.e., a positive correlation). Figure 5(b) confirms this intuition regarding the nature of these relationships. We notice that *JoinTime* has little impact on the play duration. Surprisingly, *AvgBitrate* has very low correlation as well.

Next, we proceed to check if the univariate information gain analysis corroborates or complements the correlation results in Figure 6. Interestingly, the relative order between *RateBuf* and *BufRatio*

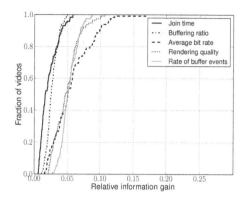

Figure 6: Distribution of the univariate gain between the quality metrics and play time, for dataset *LvodA*.

Quality metric	Correlation coefficient	
	LvodB	*LvodA*
JoinTime	-0.17	-0.23
BufRatio	-0.61	-0.67
RendQual	0.38	0.41

Table 2: Median values of the Kendall rank correlation coefficients for *LvodA* **and** *LvodB*. **We do not show** *AvgBitrate* **and** *RateBuf* **for** *LvodB* **because the player did not switch bitrates or gather buffering event data. For the remaining metrics the results are consistent with dataset** *LvodA*.

is reversed compared to Figure 5. The reason (see Figure 7) is that most of the probability mass is in the first bin (0-1% *BufRatio*) and the entropy here is the same as the overall distribution. Consequently, the information gain for *BufRatio* is low; *RateBuf* does not suffer this problem (not shown) and has higher information gain. We also see that *AvgBitrate* has high information gain even though its correlation was very low. We revisit this observation in Section 4.1.1.

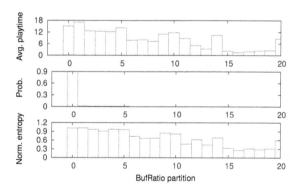

Figure 7: Visualizing why buffering ratio does not result in a high information gain even though it is correlated.

So far we have looked at each quality metric in isolation. A natural question is: Does combining two metrics provide more insights? For example, *BufRatio* and *RendQual* may be correlated with each other. In this case knowing that both correlate with *PlayTime* does not add new information. To evaluate this, we show the distribution of the bivariate relative information gain in Figure 8. For clarity, rather than showing all pairwise combinations, for each metric we include the bivariate combination with the highest relative information gain. For all metrics, the combination with the *AvgBitrate* provides the highest bivariate information gain. Also, even though *BufRatio*, *RateBuf*, and *RendQual* had strong correlations in Figure 5(a), their combinations do not add much new information because they are inherently correlated.

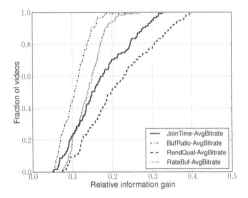

Figure 8: Distribution of the best bivariate relative information gains for *LvodA*

4.1.1 Strange behavior in *AvgBitrate*

Between Figures 5 and 6, we notice that *AvgBitrate* is the metric with the weakest correlation but the second highest information gain. This observation is related to Figure 3 from Section 3. The relationship between *PlayTime* and *AvgBitrate* is not monotone; it shows a peak between the 800-1000 Kbps, is low on either side of this region, and increases slightly at the highest rate. Because of this non-monotone relationship, the correlation is low. However, knowing the value of *AvgBitrate* allows us predict the *PlayTime*; there is a non-trivial information gain.

Now this explains why the information gain is high and the correlation is low, but does not tell us why the *PlayTime* is low for the 1000-1600 Kbps band. The reason is that the values of bitrates in this range correspond to clients having to switch bitrates because of buffering induced by poor network conditions. Thus, the *PlayTime* is low here mostly as a consequence of buffering, which we already observed to be the most critical factor. This also points out the need for robust bitrate selection and adaptation algorithms.

4.2 Live Content

Figure 9 shows the distribution of the correlation coefficients for dataset *LiveA*. The median values for the two datasets are summarized in Table 3. We notice one key difference with respect to the *LvodA* results: *AvgBitrate* is more strongly correlated for live content. Similar to dataset *LvodA*, *BufRatio* is strongly correlated, while *JoinTime* is weakly correlated.

Quality metric	Correlation coefficient	
	LiveB	*LiveA*
JoinTime	-0.49	-0.36
BufRatio	-0.81	-0.67
RendQual	-0.16	-0.09

Table 3: Median values of the Kendall rank correlation coefficients for *LiveA* **and** *LiveB***. We do not show** *AvgBitrate* **and** *RateBuf* **because they do not apply to** *LiveB***. For the remaining metrics the results are consistent with dataset** *LiveA***.**

For both long VoD and live content, *BufRatio* is a critical metric. Interestingly, for live, we see that *RateBuf* has a much stronger negative correlation with *PlayTime*. This suggests that the Live users are *more sensitive* to each buffering event compared to the

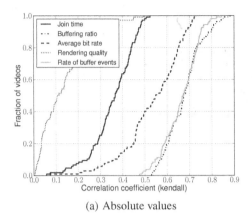

(a) Absolute values

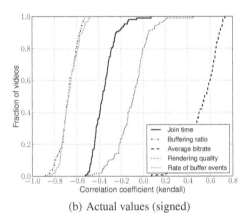

(b) Actual values (signed)

Figure 9: Distribution of the Kendall rank correlation coefficient between the quality metrics and play time for *LiveA***.**

Long VoD audience. Investigating this further, we find that the average buffering duration is much smaller for long VoD (3 seconds), compared to live (7s), i.e., each buffering event in the case of live content is more disruptive. Because the buffer sizes in long VoD are larger, the system fares better in face of fluctuations in link bandwidth. Furthermore, the system can be more proactive in predicting buffering and hence preventing it by switching to another server, or switching bitrates. Consequently, there are fewer and shorter buffering events for long VoD. For live, on the other hand, the buffer is shorter, to ensure that the stream is current. As a result, the system is less able to proactively predict throughput fluctuations, which increases both the number and the duration of buffering events. Figure 10 further confirms that *AvgBitrate* is a critical metric and that *JoinTime* is less critical for Live content. The bivariate results (not shown for brevity) mimic the same effects from Figure 8, where the combination with *AvgBitrate* provides the best information gains.

4.2.1 Why is *RendQual* negatively correlated?

We noticed an anomalous behavior for *PlayTime* vs. *RendQual* for live content in Figure 4(d). The previous results from both *LiveA* and *LiveB* datasets further confirm that this is not an anomaly specific to the video shown earlier, but a more pervasive phenomenon in live content.

To illustrate why this negative correlation arises, we focus on the relationship between the *RendQual* and *PlayTime* for a particular live video in Figure 11. We see a surprisingly large fraction of viewers with low rendering quality and high play time. Further, the

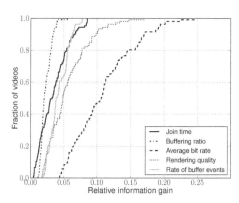

Figure 10: Distribution of the univariate gain between the quality metrics and play time for *LiveA*.

BufRatio values for these users is also very low. In other words, these users have no network issues, but see a drop in *RendQual*, but continue to watch the video for a long duration despite this poor frame rate.

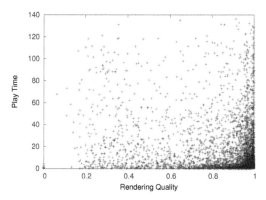

Figure 11: Scatter plot between the play time and rendering quality. Notice that there are a lot of points where the rendering quality is very low but the play time is very high.

We speculate that this counter-intuitive negative correlation between *RendQual* and *PlayTime* arises out of a combination of two effects. The first effect has to do with user behavior. Unlike long VoD viewers (e.g., TV episodes), live video viewers are also likely to run the video player in background (e.g., listening to the sports commentary). In such situations the browser is either minimized or the player is in a hidden browser tab. The second effect is an optimization by the player to reduce the CPU consumption when the video is being played in the background. In these cases, the player decreases the frame rendering rate to reduce CPU use. We replicated the above scenarios–minimizing the browser or playing a video in a background window–in a controlled setup and found that the player indeed drops the *RendQual* to 20% (e.g., rendering 6-7 out of 30 frames per second). Curiously, the *PlayTime* peak in Figure 4(d) also occurs at a 20% *RendQual*. These controlled experiments confirm our hypothesis that the anomalous relationship is in fact due to these player optimizations for users playing the video in the background.

4.2.2 Case study with high impact events

A particular concern for live content providers is whether the observations from typical events can be applied to *high impact* events [22]. To address this concern, we consider the *LiveH* dataset.

Because the data collected during the corresponding period of time does not provide the *RendQual* and *RateBuf*, we only focus on *BufRatio* and *AvgBitrate*, which we observed as the most critical metrics for live content in the previous discussion. Figures 12(a) and 12(b) show that the trends and correlation coefficients for *LiveH1* match closely with the results for datasets *LiveA* and *LiveB*. We also confirmed that the values for *LiveH2* and *LiveH3* are almost identical to *LiveH1*; we do not show these for brevity. These results, though preliminary, suggest that our observations apply to such singular events as well.

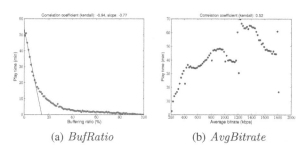

(a) *BufRatio*	(b) *AvgBitrate*

Figure 12: Impact of two quality metrics for *LiveH1*, **one of the three final games from the 2010 FIFA World Cup. A linear data fit is shown over the 0-10% subrange of** *BufRatio*. **The results for** *LiveH2* **and** *LiveH3* **are almost identical and not shown for brevity.**

With respect to the average bitrate, the play time peaks around a bitrate of 1.2 Mbps. Beyond that value, however, the engagement decreases. The reason for this behavior is similar to the previous observation in Section 4.1.1. Most end-users (e.g., DSL, cable broadband users) cannot sustain such a high bandwidth stream. As a consequence, the player encounters buffering and also switches to a lower bitrate midstream. As we already saw, buffering adversely impacts the user experience.

Quality metric	Correlation coefficient	
	SvodB	*SvodA*
JoinTime	0.06	0.12
BufRatio	-0.53	-0.38
RendQual	0.34	0.33

Table 4: Median values of the Kendall rank correlation coefficients for *SvodA* **and** *SvodB*. **We do not show** *AvgBitrate* **and** *RateBuf* **because the player did not switch bitrates and did not gather buffering event data. The results are consistent with** *SvodA*.

4.3 Short VoD Content

Finally, we consider the short VoD category. For both datasets *SvodA* and *SvodB* the player uses a discrete set of 2-3 bitrates (without switching) and was not instrumented to gather buffering event data. Thus, we do not show the *AvgBitrate* (it is meaningless to compute the correlation on 2 points) and *RateBuf*. Figure 13 shows the distribution of the correlation coefficients for *SvodA* and Table 4 summarizes the median values for both datasets.

We notice similarities between long and short VoD: *BufRatio* and *RendQual* are the most critical metrics that impact *PlayTime*. Further, *BufRatio* and *RendQual* are themselves strongly correlated (not shown). As before, *JoinTime* is weakly correlated. For brevity, we do not show the univariate/bivariate information gain results for short VoD because they mirror the results from the correlation analysis.

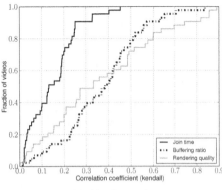

(a) Absolute values

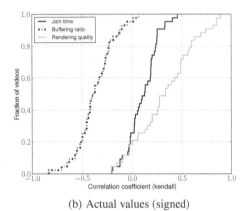

(b) Actual values (signed)

Figure 13: Distribution of the Kendall rank correlation coefficient between the quality metrics and play time for *SvodA*. **We do not show** *AvgBitrate* **and** *RateBuf* **because the player did not switch bitrates and did not gather buffering event data.**

4.4 Quantitative Impact

As we discussed earlier and as our measurements so far highlight, the interaction between the *PlayTime* and the quality metrics can be quite complex. Thus, we avoid blindly applying quantitative regression models on our dataset. Instead, we only apply regression when we can visually confirm that this has a meaningful real-world interpretation and when the relationship is roughly linear. Thus, we restrict this analysis to the most critical metric, *BufRatio*. Further, we only apply regression to the 0-10% range of *BufRatio*, where we confirmed a simple linear relationship.

We notice that the distribution of the linear-fit slopes are very similar within the same content type in Figure 14. The median magnitudes of the slopes are one for long VoD, two for live, and close to zero for short VoD. That is, *BufRatio* has the strongest quantitative impact on live, then on long VoD, then on short VoD.

Figure 12(a) also includes linear data fits on the 0-10% subrange for *BufRatio* for the *LiveH* data. These show that, within the selected subrange, a 1% increase in *BufRatio* can reduce the average play time by more than *three minutes* (assuming a game duration of 90 minutes). Conversely, providers can increase the average user engagement by more than three minutes by investing resources to reduce *BufRatio* by 1%.

4.5 Summary of view-level analysis

The key observations from the view-level analysis are:

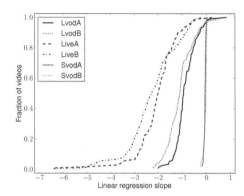

Figure 14: CDF of the linear-fit slopes between *PlayTime* **and the 0-10% subrange of** *BufRatio*.

- For long and short VoD content, *BufRatio* is the most important quality metric.
- For live content, *AvgBitrate* in addition to *BufRatio* is a key quality metric. Additionally, the requirement of small buffer for live videos exacerbates buffering events.
- A 1% increase in *BufRatio* can decrease 1 to 3 minutes of viewing time.
- *JoinTime* has significantly lower impact on view-level engagement than the other metrics.
- Finally, our analysis for the negative correlation of *RendQual* in live video highlights the need to put the statistics in the context of actual user and system behavior.

5. VIEWER LEVEL ENGAGEMENT

Content providers also want to understand if good video quality improves customer retention or if it encourages users to try more videos. To address these questions we analyze the user engagement at the viewer level in this section. For brevity, we highlight the key results and do not duplicate the full analysis as in the previous section.

For this analysis, we look at the *number of views* per viewer and the *total play time* aggregated over all videos watched by the viewer in a one week interval. Recall that at the view level we filtered the data to only look at videos with at least 1000 views. At the viewer level, however, we look at the aggregate number of views and play time per viewer across all objects irrespective of that video's popularity. For each viewer we correlate the average of each quality metric with the two engagement metrics.

Figure 15 visually confirms that the quality metrics also impact the number of views. One curious observation is that the number of views increases in the range 1–15 seconds before starting to decrease. We also see a similar effect for *BufRatio*, where the first few bins have fewer total views. This effect does not, however, occur for the total play time. We speculate that this is an effect of user interest. Many users have very good quality but little interest in the content; they "sample" the content and leave without returning. Users who are actually interested in the content are more tolerant of longer join times (and buffering). However, the tolerance drops beyond a certain point (around 15 seconds for *JoinTime*). Figure 16 summarizes the values of the correlation coefficients for the six datasets. The values are qualitatively consistent across the different datasets and also similar to the trends we observed at the view level. One significant difference is that while *JoinTime* is uninteresting at the view level, it has a more pronounced impact

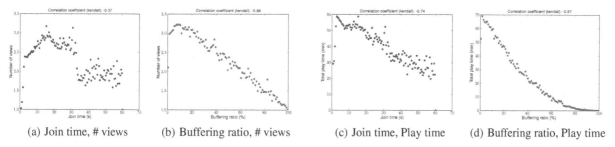

| (a) Join time, # views | (b) Buffering ratio, # views | (c) Join time, Play time | (d) Buffering ratio, Play time |

Figure 15: Visualizing the impact of *JoinTime* and *BufRatio* on the number of views and play time for *LvodA*

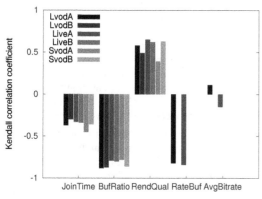

(a) Number of views

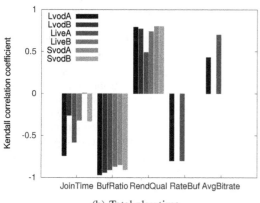

(b) Total play time

Figure 16: Viewer-level correlations w.r.t the number of views and play time. *AvgBitrate* and *RateBuf* values do not apply for *LvodB*, *LiveB*, *SvodA*, and *SvodB*.

on the total play time at the viewer level. This has interesting system design implications. For example, consider a scenario where a provider decides to increase the buffer size to alleviate the buffering issues. However, increasing buffer size can increase join time. The above result shows that doing so without evaluating the impact at the viewer level may be counterproductive, as increasing the buffer size may reduce the likelihood of a viewer visiting the site again.

As with the view-level analysis, we complement the qualitative correlations with quantitative results. Figure 17 shows linear data fitting for the total play time as a function of the buffering ratio for *LvodA* and *LiveA*. This shows that reducing *BufRatio* by 1% translates to an effective increase the total play time by 1.2 minutes for long VoD content and by 2.4 minutes for live content on average per user.

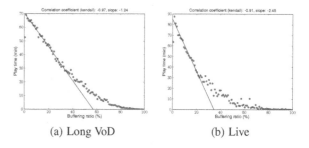

| (a) Long VoD | (b) Live |

Figure 17: Linear data fitting between the buffering ratio and the total play time, for datasets *LvodA* and *LiveA*.

Summary of viewer-level analysis:

- Both the number of views and the total play time are impacted by the quality metrics.
- The quality metrics that impact the view level engagement consistently impact the viewer level engagement. We confirm that these results are consistent across different datasets.
- The correlation between the engagement metrics and the quality metrics becomes visually and quantitatively even more striking at the viewer level.
- Additionally, the join time, which seemed less relevant at the view level, has non-trivial impact at the viewer level.

6. DISCUSSION

The findings presented in this paper are the result of an iterative process that included more false starts and misleading interpretations than we care to admit. We present two of the main lessons we learned in this process. Then, we discuss an important direction of future research for Internet video measurement.

6.1 The need for complementary analysis

All of you are right. The reason every one of you is telling it differently is because each one of you touched a different part of the elephant. So, actually the elephant has all the features you mentioned. [10]

For the Long VoD case, we observed that the correlation coefficient for the average bitrate was weak, but the univariate information gain was high. The process of trying to explain this discrepancy led us to visualize the behaviors similar to Figure 3(c). In this case, the correlation was weak because the relationship was non-monotone. The information gain, however, was high because the intermediate bins near the natural modes had significantly lower engagement and consequently low entropy in the play time distribution.

This observation guided us to a different phenomenon, sessions that were forced to switch rates because of poor network quality.

If we had restricted ourselves to a purely correlation-based analysis, we may have missed this effect and incorrectly inferred that *AvgBitrate* was not important. This highlights the value of using multiple *views* from complementary analysis techniques in dealing with large datasets.

6.2 The importance of context

Lies, damned lies, and statistics

Our second lesson is that while statistical data mining techniques are excellent tools, they need to be used with caution and with a judicious appreciation of the context in which they are applied. That is, we need to take the results of these analysis together with the context of the *human* and *operating* factors. For example, naively acting on the observation that the rendering quality is negatively correlated for live content can lead to an incorrect understanding of its impact on engagement. As we saw, this negative correlation is the outcome of both user behavior and player optimizations. Users who intend to watch a live event for a long time may run these in background windows; the player cognizant of this background window effect tries to reduce CPU consumption by reducing the rendering quality. This highlights the importance of backing the statistical analysis with a more in-depth domain knowledge and controlled experiments in replicating the observations.

6.3 Toward a video quality index

Our ultimate vision is to use measurement-driven insights to develop an *empirical Internet video quality index*, analogous to the notion of mean opinion scores and subjective quality indices [8, 9]. Given that there are multiple quality metrics, it is difficult for video providers and consumers to objectively compare different video services. At the same time, the lack of a concrete metric makes it difficult for delivery infrastructures and researchers to focus their efforts. If we can derive such a quality index, content providers and consumers can use it to choose delivery services while researchers and delivery providers can use it to guide their efforts for developing better algorithms for video delivery and adaptation.

However, as our measurements and lessons show the interactions between the quality metrics and engagement can be complex, interdependent, and counterintuitive even for a somewhat simplified view with just three content types and five quality metrics. Furthermore, there are other dimensions that we have not explored rigorously in this paper. For example, we considered three broad genres of content: Live, Long VoD, and Short VoD. It would also be interesting to analyze the impact of quality for other aspects of content segmentation. For example, is popular content more/less likely to be impacted by quality or is the impact likely to differ depending on the types of events/videos (e.g., news vs. sports vs. sitcoms)? Our preliminary results in these directions show that the magnitude of quality impact is marginally higher for popular videos but largely independent of content genres. Similarly, there are other fine-grained quality measures which we have not explored. For example, anecdotal evidence suggests that temporal effects can play a significant role; buffering during the early stages or a sequence of buffering events are more likely to lead to user frustration. Working toward such a unified quality index is an active direction of future research.

7. RELATED WORK

Content popularity: There is an extensive literature on modeling content popularity and its subsequent implications for caching (e.g., [15, 18, 22, 24, 26]). Most of these focus on the heavy-tailed nature of the access popularity distribution and its system-level impact. Our work on analyzing the interplay between quality and engagement is orthogonal to this extensive literature. One interesting question (that we address briefly) is to analyze if the impact of quality is different across different popularity segments. For example, providers may want to know if niche video content is more or less likely to be impacted by poor quality.

User behavior: Yu *et al.* present a measurement study of a VoD system deployed by China Telecom [24] focusing on modeling user arrival patterns and session lengths. They also observe that many users actually have small session times, possibly because many users just "sample" a video and leave if the video is of no interest. Removing the potential bias from this phenomenon was one of the motivations for our binned correlation analysis in Section 3. Other studies of user behaviors also have significant implications for VoD system design. For example, there are measurement studies of channel switching dynamics in IPTV systems (e.g., [19]), and understanding seek-pause-forward behaviors in streaming systems (e.g., [16]). As we mentioned in our browser minimization example for live video, understanding the impact of such behavior is critical for putting the measurement-driven insights in context.

P2P VoD: In parallel to the reduction of content delivery costs, there have also been improvements in building robust P2P VoD systems that can provide performance comparable to a server-side infrastructure at a fraction of the deployment cost (e.g., [14, 25, 26, 34]). Because these systems operate in more dynamic environments (e.g., peer churn, low upload bandwidth), it is critical for them to optimize judiciously and improve the quality metrics that really matter. While our measurements are based on a server-hosted infrastructure for video delivery, the insights in understanding the most critical quality metrics can also be used to guide the design of P2P VoD systems.

Measurements of deployed video delivery systems: The networking community has benefited immensely from measurement studies of *deployed* VoD and streaming systems using both "black-box" inference (e.g., [12, 25, 33, 35]) and "white-box" measurements (e.g., [22, 27, 30, 37]). Our work follows in this rich tradition of providing insights from real deployments to improve our understanding of Internet video delivery. At the same time, we believe that we have taken a significant step forward in qualitatively and quantitatively measuring the impact of the video quality on user engagement.

User perceived quality: There is prior work in the multimedia literature on metrics that can capture user perceived quality (e.g., [23, 38]) and how specific metrics affect the user experience (e.g., [20]). Our work differs on several key fronts. The first is simply an issue of timing and scale. Internet video has only recently attained widespread adoption and revisiting user engagement is ever more relevant now than before. Prior work depend on small-scale experiments with a few users, while our study is based on real-world measurements with millions of viewers. Second, these fall short of linking the perceived quality to the actual user engagement. Finally, a key difference is with respect to methodology; user studies and opinions are no doubt useful, but difficult to objectively evaluate. Our work is an empirical study of engagement in the wild.

Engagement in other media: The goal of understanding user engagement appears in other content delivery mechanisms as well. The impact of page load times on user satisfaction is well known (e.g., [13, 21, 28]). Several commercial providers measure the impact of page load times on user satisfaction (e.g., [6]). Chen *et al.* study the impact of quality metrics such as bitrate, jitter, and delay on call duration in Skype [11] and propose a composite metric to quantify the combination of these factors. Given that Internet video has become mainstream only recently, our study provides similar insights for the impact of video quality on engagement.

Diagnosis: In this paper, we focused on measuring the quality metrics and how they impact user engagement. A natural follow up question is whether there are mechanisms to pro-actively diagnose quality issues to minimize the impact on users (e.g., [17, 31]). We leave this as a direction for future work.

8. CONCLUSIONS

As the costs of video content creation and dissemination continue to decrease, there is an abundance of video content on the Internet. Given this setting, it becomes critical for content providers to understand if and how video quality is likely to impact user engagement. Our study is a first step towards addressing this goal.

We present a systematic analysis of the interplay between three dimensions of the problem space: quality metrics, content types, and quantitative measures of engagement. We study industry-standard quality metrics for Live, Long VoD, and Short VoD content to analyze engagement at per view and viewer-level.

Our key takeaways are that at the view-level, buffering ratio is the most important metric across all content genres and the bitrate is especially critical for Live (sports) content. Additionally, we find that the join time becomes critical in terms of the viewer-level engagement and thus likely to impact customer retention.

These results have key implications both from commercial and technical perspectives. In a commercial context, they inform the policy decisions for content providers to invest their resources to maximize user engagement. At the same time, from a technical perspective, they also guide the design of the technical solutions (e.g., tradeoffs in the choice of a suitable buffer size) and motivate the need for new solutions (e.g., better pro-active bitrate selection, rate switching, and buffering techniques).

In the course of our analysis, we also learned two cautionary lessons that more broadly apply to measurement studies of this nature: the importance of using multiple complementary analysis techniques when dealing with large datasets and the importance of backing these statistical techniques with system-level and user context. We believe our study is a significant step toward an ultimate vision of developing a unified quality index for Internet video.

Acknowledgments

We thank our shepherd Ratul Mahajan and the anonymous reviewers for their feedback that helped improve this paper. We also thank other members of the Conviva staff for supporting the data collection infrastructure and for patiently answering our questions regarding the player instrumentation and datasets.

9. REFERENCES

[1] Alexa Top Sites. http://www.alexa.com/topsites/countries/US.
[2] Cisco forecast. http://blogs.cisco.com/sp/comments/cisco_visual_networking_index_forecast_annual_update/.
[3] Driving Engagement for Online Video. http://events.digitallyspeaking.com/akamai/mddec10/post.html?hash=ZD1BSGhsMXBidnJ3RXNWSW5mSE1HZz09.
[4] Hadoop. http://hadoop.apache.org/.
[5] Hive. http://hive.apache.org/.
[6] Keynote systems. http://www.keynote.com.
[7] Mail service costs Netflix 20 times more than streaming. http://www.techspot.com/news/42036-mail-service-costs-netflix-20-times-more-than-streaming.html.
[8] Mean opinion score for voice quality. http://www.itu.int/rec/T-REC-P.800-199608-I/en.
[9] Subjective video quality assessment. http://www.itu.int/rec/T-REC-P.910-200804-I/en.
[10] The tale of three blind men and an elephant. http://en.wikipedia.org/wiki/Blind_men_and_an_elephant.
[11] K. Chen, C. Huang, P. Huang, C. Lei. Quantifying Skype User Satisfaction. In *Proc. SIGCOMM*, 2006.
[12] Phillipa Gill, Martin Arlitt, Zongpeng Li, Anirban Mahanti. YouTube Traffic Characterization: A View From the Edge. In *Proc. IMC*, 2007.
[13] A. Bouch, A. Kuchinsky, and N. Bhatti. Quality is in the Eye of the Beholder: Meeting Users' Requirements for Internet Quality of Service. In *Proc. CHI*, 2000.
[14] B. Cheng, L. Stein, H. Jin, and Z. Zheng. Towards Cinematic Internet Video-On-Demand. In *Proc. Eurosys*, 2008.
[15] B. Cheng, X. Liu, Z. Zhang, and H. Jin. A measurement study of a peer-to-peer video-on-demand system. In *Proc. IPTPS*, 2007.
[16] C. Costa, I. Cunha, A. Borges, C. Ramos, M. Rocha, J. Almeida, and B. Ribeiro-Neto. Analyzing Client Interactivity in Streaming Media. In *Proc. WWW*, 2004.
[17] C. Wu, B. Li, and S. Zhao. Diagnosing Network-wide P2P Live Streaming Inefficiencies. In *Proc. INFOCOM*, 2009.
[18] M. Cha, H. Kwak, P. Rodriguez, Y.-Y. Ahn, and S. Moon. I Tube, You Tube, Everybody Tubes: Analyzing the World's Largest User Generated Content Video System. In *Proc. IMC*, 2007.
[19] M. Cha, P. Rodriguez, J. Crowcroft, S. Moon, and X. Amatriain. Watching Television Over an IP Network. In *Proc. IMC*, 2008.
[20] M. Claypool and J. Tanner. The effects of jitter on the peceptual quality of video. In *Proc. ACM Multimedia*, 1999.
[21] D. Galletta, R. Henry, S. McCoy, and P. Polak. Web Site Delays: How Tolerant are Users? *Journal of the Association for Information Systems*, (1), 2004.
[22] H. Y. et al. Inside the Bird's Nest: Measurements of Large-Scale Live VoD from the 2008 Olympics. In *Proc. IMC*, 2009.
[23] S. R. Gulliver and G. Ghinea. Defining user perception of distributed multimedia quality. *ACM Transactions on Multimedia Computing, Communications, and Applications (TOMCCAP)*, 2(4), Nov. 2006.
[24] H. Yu, D. Zheng, B. Y. Zhao, and W. Zheng. Understanding User Behavior in Large-Scale Video-on-Demand Systems. In *Proc. Eurosys*, 2006.
[25] X. Hei, C. Liang, J. Liang, Y. Liu, and K. W. Ross. A measurement study of a large-scale P2P IPTV system. *IEEE Transactions on Multimedia*, 2007.
[26] Y. Huang, D.-M. C. Tom Z. J. Fu, J. C. S. Lui, and C. Huang. Challenges, Design and Analysis of a Large-scale P2P-VoD System. In *Proc. SIGCOMM*, 2008.
[27] W. W. Hyunseok Chang, Sugih Jamin. Live Streaming Performance of the Zattoo Network. In *Proc. IMC*, 2009.
[28] I. Ceaparu, J. Lazar, K. Bessiere, J. Robinson, and B. Shneiderman. Determining Causes and Severity of End-User Frustration. In *International Journal of Human-Computer Interaction*, 2004.
[29] K. Cho, K. Fukuda, H. Esaki. The Impact and Implications of the Growth in Residential User-to-User Traffic. In *Proc. SIGCOMM*, 2006.
[30] K. Sripanidkulchai, B. Maggs, and H. Zhang. An Analysis of Live Streaming Workloads on the Internet. In *Proc. IMC*, 2004.
[31] A. Mahimkar, Z. Ge, A. Shaikh, J. Wang, J. Yates, Y. Zhang, and Q. Zhao. Towards Automated Performance Diagnosis in a Large IPTV Network. In *Proc. SIGCOMM*, 2009.
[32] T. Mitchell. *Machine Learning*. McGraw-Hill.
[33] S. Ali, A. Mathur, and H. Zhang. Measurement of Commercial Peer-to-Peer Live Video Streaming. In *Proc. Workshop on Recent Advances in Peer-to-Peer Streaming*, 2006.
[34] S. Guha, S. Annapureddy, C. Gkantsidis, D. Gunawardena, and P. Rodriguez. Is High-Quality VoD Feasible using P2P Swarming? In *Proc. WWW*, 2007.
[35] S. Saroiu, K. P. Gummadi, R. J. Dunn, S. D. Gribble, and H. M. Levy. An Analysis of Internet Content Delivery Systems. In *Proc. OSDI*, 2002.
[36] H. A. Simon. Designing Organizations for an Information-Rich World. Martin Greenberger, Computers, Communication, and the Public Interest, The Johns Hopkins Press.
[37] K. Sripanidkulchai, A. Ganjam, B. Maggs, and H. Zhang. The Feasibility of Supporting Large-Scale Live Streaming Applications with Dynamic Application End-Points. In *Proc. SIGCOMM*, 2004.
[38] K.-C. Yang, C. C. Guest, K. El-Maleh, and P. K. Das. Perceptual Temporal Quality Metric for Compressed Video. *IEEE Transactions on Multimedia*, Nov. 2007.

An Untold Story of Middleboxes in Cellular Networks

Zhaoguang Wang[1], Zhiyun Qian[1], Qiang Xu[1], Z. Morley Mao[1], Ming Zhang[2]

[1]University of Michigan   [2]Microsoft Research

[1]{zgw, zhiyunq, qiangxu, zmao}@umich.edu   [2]mzh@microsoft.com

ABSTRACT

The use of cellular data networks is increasingly popular as network coverage becomes more ubiquitous and many diverse user-contributed mobile applications become available. The growing cellular traffic demand means that cellular network carriers are facing greater challenges to provide users with good network performance and energy efficiency, while protecting networks from potential attacks. To better utilize their limited network resources while securing the network and protecting client devices the carriers have already deployed various network policies that influence traffic behavior. Today, these policies are mostly opaque, though they directly impact application designs and may even introduce network vulnerabilities.

We present *NetPiculet*, the first tool that unveils carriers' NAT and firewall policies by conducting intelligent measurement. By running *NetPiculet* on the major U.S. cellular providers as well as deploying it as a smartphone application in the wild covering more than 100 cellular ISPs, we identified the key NAT and firewall policies which have direct implications on performance, energy, and security. For example, NAT boxes and firewalls set timeouts for idle TCP connections, which sometimes cause significant energy waste on mobile devices. Although most carriers today deploy sophisticated firewalls, they are still vulnerable to various attacks such as battery draining and denial of service. These findings can inform developers in optimizing the interaction between mobile applications and cellular networks and also guide carriers in improving their network configurations.

Categories and Subject Descriptors

C.2.3 [**Computer-Communication Networks**]: Network Operations

General Terms

Measurement, performance, security

Keywords

NAT, firewall, middlebox, TCP performance, cellular data network

1. INTRODUCTION

Data cellular networks have undergone tremendous growth in recent years due to the increasing popularity of mobile devices such as smartphones, tablets, and eBook readers. Their ever-growing coverage and capacity have enabled a wave of flashy mobile applications ranging from gaming and video to social networking. In contrast to their Internet counterparts, cellular networks bear more constraints due to the scarcity of physical resources in network infrastructure and mobile devices as well as the complexity in managing these resources. Cellular carriers usually deploy various types of middleboxes to make efficient use of these precious resources and protect them from potential attacks. For instance, many carriers use NAT (Network Address Translation) to provide data service to millions of users over a limited public IP address space. They also deploy firewalls to isolate mobile users from rampant malicious activities (*e.g.,* worms and DoS attacks) on the Internet.

Today, cellular network middleboxes and mobile applications are independently managed by two groups of entities: cellular operators (*e.g.,* AT&T, T-Mobile) and application developers. The latter group is often unaware of the middlebox policies enforced by operators while the former has limited knowledge about the application behavior and requirements. Such knowledge mismatch could potentially impair application performance, aggravate energy consumption, or even introduce security vulnerabilities. One illustrative example is that a carrier sets an aggressive timeout value to quickly recycle the resources held by inactive TCP connections in the firewall, unexpectedly causing frequent disruptions to long-lived and occasionally idle connections maintained by applications such as push-based email and instant messaging.

Prior work has studied middleboxes on the Internet by characterizing NAT properties such as mapping type and filtering rule [22, 15, 20, 18, 21], and proposed various schemes to perform NAT traversal. It is unclear whether the NAT box behavior remains the same or the NAT traversal schemes are still applicable in cellular networks. Other work quantified the end-to-end performance degradation (*e.g.,* lower throughput or larger transaction delay) induced by middleboxes [13]. In addition to performance, energy consumption is another critical perspective in the cellular network context. However, no previous studies have investigated how middleboxes affect energy consumption on mobile devices. Several research efforts revealed that cellular infrastructure and mobile handsets are vulnerable to various types of DoS attacks [34, 36, 25]. However, they did not investigate the feasibility of launching these attacks when the targets are behind middleboxes.

In this study, we design and implement *NetPiculet*, a measurement tool for accurately and efficiently identifying middlebox policies in cellular networks. We focus on firewalls and NAT boxes, which are widely deployed by many cellular carriers. Although a carrier may employ many policies, we focus on those that directly impact mobile users and their applications in terms of important properties including connectivity, performance, energy consumption, and security. Informed by our findings, we propose new techniques and modifications to applications to better cope with existing policies. We also offer concrete suggestions on policy changes for carriers to improve the experience and protection of their mobile users as well as robustness of their network infrastructure in response to attacks.

We released *NetPiculet* on Android Market in January 2011 and attracted 393 unique mobile users within merely two weeks. Leveraging the data from these users, we report our findings from 107 cellular carriers around the world. In particular, we studied the policies of two large nation-wide U.S. carriers in more depth and corroborated our findings carefully with controlled experiments. Due to security and privacy concerns, we anonymize their names and label them as Carrier A and Carrier B. We summarize our key findings as follows:

- In some cellular networks, a single mobile device can encounter more than one type of NAT, likely due to load balancing. We also discovered some NAT mappings increment external port number with time which was not documented in any prior NAT study. Accordingly, we develop new NAT traversal techniques to handle both cases.

- Four cellular networks are found to allow IP spoofing, which provides attack opportunities by punching holes on NATs and firewalls "on behalf of" a victim from inside the networks, and thus directly exposing the victim to further attacks from the Internet.

- Eleven carriers are found to impose a quite aggressive timeout value of less than 10 minutes for idle TCP connections, potentially frequently disrupting long-lived connections maintained by applications such as push-based email. The resulting extra radio activities on a mobile device could use more than 10% of battery per day compared to those under a more conservative timeout value (*e.g.,* 30 minutes).

- One of the largest U.S. carriers is found to configure firewalls to buffer out-of-order TCP packets for a long time, likely for the purpose of deep packet inspection. This unexpectedly interferes with TCP Fast Retransmit and Forward RTO-Recovery, severely degrading TCP performance triggered merely by a single packet loss.

- At least one firewall of a major cellular ISP liberally accepts TCP packets within a very large window of sequence numbers, greatly facilitating the traditional blind data injection attacks, endangering connections that transfer relatively large amount of data (*e.g.,* streaming applications).

- Some cellular network firewalls do not immediately remove the TCP connection state after a connection is closed, allowing attackers to extend his attack on a victim even after the victim has closed the connection to a malicious server. This also dramatically lengthens the NAT traversal time to a few minutes, given that the same TCP five tuple cannot be reused quickly.

2. OVERVIEW

Today's cellular data networks are susceptible to DoS attacks [34, 36, 25] and face the problem of IPv4 address depletion, which prompts carriers to deploy NATs and firewalls at network boundaries to protect cellular infrastructure and mobile users from unsolicited traffic from the Internet and to effectively share public IP

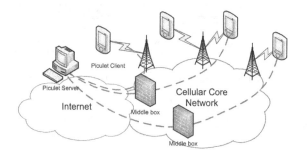

Figure 1: Physical view of the NetPiculet system

Count by # of	Technology		Continent						IP address		
	UMTS	EVDO	EU	AS	NA	SA	AU	AF	Public	Private	Both[1]
Carriers	97	10	46	26	20	11	2	2	25	72	10
Users	246	148	113	35	231	11	2	2	73	316	5[2]

[1] Some carriers assign both public and private IP addresses
[2] A single user is observed to have public IP or private IP at different times

Table 2: Properties of the studied carriers

addresses. However, they also directly impact end-to-end performance, connectivity, energy consumption, and security. Popular mobile P2P applications, *e.g.,* Fring [5] and Tango [6] for video chatting, use NAT traversal to establish direct connections between peers behind NAT. Correctly determining the NAT mapping type and filtering policy is crucial for the success of NAT traversal. Firewalls attempt to block unwanted traffic by detecting anomalous traffic patterns. Such behavior, however, may tamper with TCP's control and feedback mechanism, resulting in longer transaction delay and higher energy consumption. Furthermore, firewalls in cellular networks must accommodate a diverse and large set of mobile devices and applications. Such flexibility may come at the expense of security, leaving opportunities for mindful attackers.

Our goal is to develop a tool that can help application designers gain insight into NAT and firewall policies in cellular networks and make targeted improvements to applications. It can also help carriers fine-tune their middlebox policies to attain better user experience and security. A few technical challenges remain. First, the middlebox policies in a cellular network can be quite complex and are usually proprietary. We need to design a suite of end-to-end probes to accurately infer the policies and quantify their impact. Second, the middleboxes usually block unsolicited traffic from the Internet, making purely server-based probing infeasible. We need to carefully coordinate probing between a mobile client and an Internet server to infer these policies, while ensuring the policies inferred are not due to middleboxes on the Internet. Third, cellular carriers are diverse, often spanning a large geographic area and offering multiple types of subscription plan. We need to make our tool both efficient and user-friendly to attract different types of users from many carriers and locations.

We have built the *NetPiculet* tool that comprises of client software running on mobile devices inside cellular networks and a dedicated server on the Internet as shown in Figure 1. The server's upstream provider and border router are verified to not impose any restrictive policies. The client software is an Android application that is publicly available on the Android Market. In order to save both user time and device battery, except for the TCP connection timeout measurement running as a background service, the other tests are parallelized and finish within 10 seconds. By informing users about their network polices, *e.g.,* the feasibility of running P2P applications in their networks, the client software is able to attract users around the world. Both the server and client are implemented in C and Java with approximately 3000 LoC in total.

Category	Policy	Main findings and implications
NAT	NAT Mapping type (§3.1.1) Endpoint filtering (§3.1.2) TCP state tracking (§3.1.2) Filtering response (§3.1.2) Packet mangling (§3.1.2)	- A new NAT mapping was identified that increases external port number with time (§3.2.1) - One device may experience more than one NAT mapping in the same cellular network (§3.2.1) - New NAT traversal techniques are proposed to handle the challenges imposed by the above two findings (§3.3)
Firewall	IP spoofing (§4.1.1) Stateful firewall (§4.1.2) TCP connection timeout (§4.1.3) Out-of-order packet buffering (§4.1.4)	- 4 large carriers allow IP spoofing, which weakens the network security (§4.2.1) - 11 carriers timeout idle connections aggressively, which wastes device energy (§4.3.1) - One large U.S. carrier buffers out-of-order packets, which negatively affects TCP performance (§4.3.2) - One large U.S. carrier sets a large TCP sequence window, which facilitates TCP RST attack (§4.3.3) - Some carriers do not clear TCP state immediately after connection close, which invites battery draining attack (§4.3.4)

Table 1: *NetPiculet*'s key functionality, findings, and implications.

Table 1 summarizes the policies inferred by *NetPiculet* and where they are described. Because the TCP state diagram inference is time-consuming, we measure the full TCP state diagram only in local experiments and replace it with a simpler TCP connection timeout measurement in the released tool. Our results are based on two weeks of data collected in January 2011 from about 400 users in 107 carriers. Table 2 breaks down the carriers and users by technology, continent, and IP type. Note that for certain type of tests we may observe smaller number of data points as some tests such as IP spoofing require root privilege which is not available on every phone. Also, NAT tests only consider the carriers that assign private IP addresses. Moreover, we conducted extensive local experiments to validate the findings and quantify their impact for two major U.S. carriers: Carrier A and Carrier B.

Although the policies in Table 1 are associated with either NAT or firewall, we emphasize that this is simply a classification and may have little to do with the actual implementation. A carrier usually has a variety of options in implementing these policies. For instance, a single network device could have both the NAT and firewall functionalities. Our end-to-end probes treat NAT and firewall as black boxes, thus only inferring the *existence* of the policies but not their *inner workings*.

3. NAT POLICIES

In this section, we study the feasibility of NAT traversal in cellular networks. We focus on TCP NAT traversal because it is much more challenging than UDP NAT traversal. Our findings, however, can be easily applied to UDP NAT traversal as well. We first provide some background knowledge on several key NAT properties related to NAT traversal and describe the methodology for measuring these properties. We then present the results from *NetPiculet* clients executed by 316 mobile users in 72 carriers with NAT boxes deployed. We identify a new NAT mapping that increments external port number with time. We also find that a single mobile device may encounter more than one NAT mapping. Since techniques for traversing NAT with such previously unknown behavior were not studied, we design and implement a light-weight scheme to traverse the new NAT mapping with high success rate.

3.1 Methodology

At the high level, existing TCP NAT traversal approaches (*e.g.,* STUNT#1 [22], STUNT#2 [18], NATBlaster [15], and P2PNAT [20]) follow a similar idea. Two clients behind NAT first learn each other's external IP address through an out-of-band channel, *e.g.,* a third party server. Then both clients initiate a TCP connection to each other by sending a SYN packet, which creates a mapping on their own NATs. The destination port, which the SYN packet was sent to, is determined from *port prediction* based on the NAT mapping. The two connections are finally reconciled into one if the traversal succeeds. The key difference among various approaches is the distinct sequence of packets exchanged between two clients during the reconciliation process. Besides the NAT mapping, these approaches also heavily depend on several other NAT properties, which will be described below.

3.1.1 Identifying NAT Mapping

A NAT box maps a TCP connection to an external endpoint (IP address and port) based on the TCP five tuple. Based on previous work [21], the NAT box can map connections from *the same local endpoint* in the following ways:

- *Independent:* external endpoint remains the same for all connections.
- *Address and Port$_\delta$:* external endpoint changes when destination endpoint changes.
- *Connection$_\delta$:* external endpoint changes for each new connection.

The subscript δ indicates how the external port number changes relative to its previous value. It can be either a fixed value n (usually $n = 1$) or a random value R.

It is important for both clients to know each other's mapping type so that they can predict the external endpoint a new connection will use based on that of a previous connection. This allows each client to send a SYN packet to the appropriate external endpoint of the other client and create necessary connection mapping state on its own NAT.

To discover the mapping type of a NAT box, we follow the approach in previous work [21] to create 12 back-to-back connections to 4 destinations (3 connections to each destination) while using the same local port. Different from prior approaches, we add another 12 connections to the same destination but with different local ports. As explained in §3.2.1, this helps us discover a new time-dependent NAT mapping type.

3.1.2 Identifying Other NAT Properties

Endpoint filtering: A NAT box forwards an incoming packet to a destination based on its existing connection mapping state. A packet will be filtered if its destination address and port are not found in the maintained mapping state. Even if they do exist on the NAT, the packet can still be filtered based on its source address and/or port. This is referred to as the endpoint filtering policy.

To measure endpoint filtering policy, a *NetPiculet* client behind NAT first establishes a TCP connection to the *NetPiculet* server and thus creates the corresponding mapping state on the NAT. Outside the NAT, the *NetPiculet* server varies the source IP address and port and sends back SYN packets to the external endpoint of the connection established earlier. The client checks if it can receive the SYN packets from the server to determine the endpoint filtering policy.

TCP state tracking: A NAT may also track TCP state and filter certain sequence of TCP packets that are considered invalid. We test the following two types of packet sequence that are critical for existing TCP NAT traversal schemes (*e.g.,* STUNT#2, NATBlaster, and P2PNAT):

NAT Mapping	# carriers
Independent	30
Address and Port$_1$	15
Connection$_R$	19
Connection$_T$	5
Address and Port$_T$ & Connection$_T$	3
Total	72

Table 3: NAT mapping results for 72 cellular networks that deploy NAT boxes.

- *SYN-out SYN-in* tests if a NAT allows an incoming SYN packet after an outgoing SYN.
- *SYN-out SYN-ACK-out* tests if a NAT allows a client to send out a SYN-ACK packet after sending a SYN packet.

Filtering response: Recall that at the beginning of NAT traversal, each client sends out a SYN packet to create a connection mapping on its own NAT. However, when the SYN packet reaches the other NAT, it could be dropped or trigger a TCP RST or ICMP packet. The returning RST or ICMP packet may cause the newly-created mapping to be removed from the NAT and thus disrupt the NAT traversal process.

To test the filtering response, the *NetPiculet* server sends SYN packets to some random ports on the external IP address of a pre-established TCP connection. If no response packet is received, it means the NAT box drops the packet.

Packet mangling: A NAT may mangle TCP packets by modifying sequence number, which is vital to STUN#1 and NATBlaster. To test if a NAT box implements this, the *NetPiculet* client sends several SYN packets to the *NetPiculet* server with a predefined sequence number. The server can check if the sequence numbers in the received packets match the predefined value.

3.2 NAT Characteristics

3.2.1 NAT Mapping Results

Table 3 shows the NAT mapping results of 72 cellular carriers deploying NAT. A majority of them exhibit either *Independent* or *Address and Port$_1$* mappings, which are quite easy to traverse. Surprisingly, 19 of them (26.4%) fall into *Connection$_R$*, which cannot be handled by most existing NAT traversal schemes. This percentage number is significantly higher than the 0.5% number for home NAT boxes [21]. NATBlaster [15] proposes to use the birthday paradox to deal with *Connection$_R$*. However, NATBlaster requires root access to the mobile device, which is usually not easily obtained on mobile devices. The results suggest that NAT traversal is much more challenging in cellular networks.

Time-dependent NAT mapping: There are 8 carriers that were initially classified as *Connection$_R$* or *Address and Port$_1$*. However, a closer examination revealed that the external ports of the 24 connections created during the test are well correlated with time. To further validate this observation, we conducted controlled experiments in Carrier B's network. We have a mobile client create new connections to the *NetPiculet* server with a random interval between 0 and 60 seconds. Each new connection uses the same destination port but a different local port so that it will be assigned a new external port by NAT. The experiment lasts half an hour. Figure 2 plots the start time and external port number of each connection. It is clear that the external port number increases linearly with time, and it restarts from a small number after reaching the maximum value.

In Table 3, we use *Connection$_T$* and *Address and Port$_T$* to denote this new type of mapping. The former means the external port increments with time for each new connection. The latter means

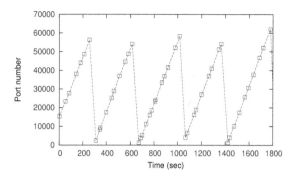

Figure 2: External port number linearly increases over time for new connections in Carrier B's network. (Each square denotes a new connection.)

the external port increments with time if a new connection has a different destination endpoint from the previous connection. Unaware of this new mapping type, existing NAT traversal schemes can easily misclassify it as *Connection$_R$*. To traverse *Connection$_R$*, NATBlaster [15] proposes to use the birthday paradox by initiating 439 connections. Besides the heavy-weight design, it also requires root access to the mobile devices, which normal users do not have. In contrast, as shown in §3.3, by leveraging the time-dependent information we propose a light-weight traversal scheme for time-dependent mapping, which only requires initiating a few connections without any root privilege.

Multiple NAT boxes for a single client: Interestingly, Table 3 shows that the *NetPiculet* clients in 3 carriers encounter two different mapping types. Sometimes, the connections from the same client are even assigned two distinct external IP addresses although the client's private IP address remains the same. To validate this observation, we conducted controlled experiments in Carrier B whose clients experience both *Connection$_T$* and *Address and Port$_T$* mappings. By establishing many connections with different five tuples between a mobile client and the *NetPiculet* server, we found that the mapping type encountered by a connection is determined by its source and destination ports. If the two port numbers add up to an even number, the connection experiences *Address and Port$_T$* mapping. Otherwise, the mapping type is *Connection$_T$*. Similarly, a connection is mapped to one of two external IP addresses depending on the sum of the source and destination port numbers.

NAT boxes are usually deployed at the top of the network infrastructure hierarchy of a cellular network, *e.g.*, near GGSN (Gateway GPRS Support Nodes) [4]. They serve the aggregate traffic from a large number of mobile users. It is likely that a carrier deploys multiple NAT boxes to balance their load based on the hash of the five tuple (source and destination ports in Carrier B). This again may interfere with NAT traversal and will be further discussed in §3.3.

3.2.2 Other NAT Results

Because the *NetPiculet* client requires raw socket to measure the remaining four NAT properties, we are only able to report the results from users who run *NetPiculet* client with root privilege in 20 cellular networks shown in Table 4.

Endpoint filtering: All the 20 carriers (100%) employ *Address and Port* filtering, which requires the source IP address and port of an incoming packet to exactly match the destination IP address and port of an existing connection in NAT. This is the most restrictive filtering policy. Given that only 82% of home NATs use *Address and Port* filtering [21], NAT traversal in cellular networks appears to be more challenging.

TCP state tracking: 18 carriers allow an incoming SYN packet

NAT property	# carriers
Endpoint filtering	20 use Address and Port
SYN-out SYN-in	18 allow, 2 disallow
SYN-out SYN-ACK-out	18 allow, 2 disallow
Filtering response	19 silently drop, 1 sends RST
Packet mangling	0 modifies sequence number

Table 4: NAT properties for 20 cellular networks.

after an outgoing SYN packet. 18 carriers allow an outgoing SYN-ACK packet following an outgoing SYN packet. One carrier in Hungary does not allow either sequence of packets. This suggests that the two underlying mechanisms (TCP simultaneous open and packet forging) of the existing NAT traversal schemes [21] are still viable in most cellular networks that we studied.

Filtering response: 19 carriers drop unsolicited incoming SYN packets silently while only one carrier in France responds with RST packets. This means the NAT traversal process is unlikely to be disrupted by the removal of an existing connection mapping triggered by a RST packet.

Packet mangling: None of the 20 carriers modifies TCP sequence number. Hence, packet mangling does not appear to be an issue for NAT traversal in cellular networks.

3.3 Implications on NAT Traversal

As we have explained, the connections from a single mobile client may be handled by more than one NAT. Even worse, these NATs may have different mapping types and external IP addresses. Because the existing NAT traversal approaches assume a client is behind only one NAT box [21], they will have trouble in determining the correct NAT mapping type and external IP address. For instance, suppose a client obtains two different external IP addresses (IP_s and IP_c) when connecting to the third-party server S and the other client C respectively. Then C will attempt to establish a connection to IP_s learned from S. This attempt will fail because the NAT we studied applies *Address and Port* filtering and only permits connection to IP_s from S.

Handling NAT load balancing: network load balancing is typically performed at the flow level, *e.g.,* based on the five tuple hash, to avoid packet reordering within a flow [16]. If the five tuple hash is configured statically, we need to discover the hash rule and only establish connections through the same NAT during NAT traversal. For instance, in Carrier B, we can ensure that the connections traverse only one NAT by making the sum of source and destination port numbers an even (or odd) number. We consider it as 2-way balancing solely based on our measurement observation. This problem becomes much more challenging if the hash function is more complicated, *e.g.,* based on the real-time load or n-way balancing where (n>2). We leave it for our future study.

Traversing time-dependent NAT: Since the external port number linearly increments over time on this type of NAT, we can predict the port number according to the port increment rate r and elapsed time t between a new and an old connection. We now describe how to establish a connection between $client_a$ and $client_b$ behind an independent and a time-dependent NATs. Suppose $client_b$ learns the external endpoint (1.2.3.4:5678) of $client_a$ through a third-party server S. $Client_b$ first creates two connections to S and 1.2.3.4:5678 respectively. It also records the time interval t between the two connections and sends the predicted port number increase ($\delta = r \times t$) to S. Upon receiving this information, S relays the external port number of $client_b$'s first connection (*e.g.,* 9000) and δ to $client_a$. $Client_a$ then attempts to connect to $client_b$ from the same external endpoint (1.2.3.4:5678) to multiple destination ports in the range of $[9000 + \delta - n, 9000 + \delta + n]$ (starting from the middle), until

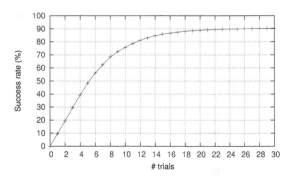

Figure 3: Success rate for traversing independent and time-dependent NATs.

it successfully hits the true external port value of $client_b$'s second connection. Here n is introduced to deal with imprecision in port prediction and is set to 15 by default.

Note that $client_a$ must be behind an independent NAT for the traversal to succeed. Because it is difficult to precisely predict the external port of $client_b$'s second connection, $client_a$ has to try multiple destination ports when connecting to $client_b$. If $client_a$ is behind other types of NAT, *e.g., Address and Port$_8$* or *Connection$_8$*, the external port of $client_a$'s trial connections will keep changing. Thus, a trial connection will be rejected by $client_b$'s NAT (because of *Address and Port* filtering) even if it does hit the right destination port.

We implemented this traversal scheme on Android and studied the success rate for establishing a connection between a smartphone in Carrier A and one in Carrier B. We learned from our previous measurements that the two carriers use independent and time-dependent NAT mappings respectively. Figure 3 shows the success rate of NAT traversal through 1,000 runs. The x-axis is the number of trials $client_a$ makes before successfully establishing a connection with $client_b$. It also roughly corresponds to the number of seconds the NAT traversal takes to succeed since we use a one-second timeout between two consecutive trials. The figure shows an 80% success rate within 12 seconds. It is noteworthy that we also tried out two popular P2P video chatting applications on Android, Fring [5] and Tango [6], none of which can successfully establish direct TCP connection in the same experimental environment.

3.4 Summary
To summarize our study on NAT in cellular networks.

- We discovered a previously-unknown NAT mapping that linearly increments port numbers with time. We designed and implemented a corresponding traversal scheme, which can succeed with high probability.

- A single mobile client may encounter more than one NAT mapping in cellular networks, likely due to load balancing, which requires extra care to ensure the same mapping during the traversal process.

- 19 out of the 72 carriers we studied assign random ports for connections on their NATs, which is the worst scenario for NAT traversal. To better support P2P applications, we suggest operators and vendors implement or configure consistent mapping on their NATs.

4. FIREWALL POLICIES
Firewalls are essential for carriers to protect their networks. As mentioned earlier, without such protection, attackers can more eas-

ily launch various attacks targeting either the network infrastructure [26] or mobile devices [32]. Even though some carriers deploy NATs, which naturally protect internal networks by dropping unsolicited incoming packets that do not have existing NAT mappings, they often still configure firewalls to further enhance network security (*e.g.,* by performing deep packet inspection and tracking TCP connection state). In this section, we study the key properties of firewalls in cellular networks from the perspective of their effectiveness to guard against potentially malicious traffic as well as policies that can negatively impact performance and energy. Indeed, we uncovered policies and configuration settings that unexpectedly impact both performance and energy.

4.1 Methodology

NetPiculet consists of several firewall tests targeting different aspects of the firewall. We describe the motivation and methodology of those tests in this section. We study the properties of firewall policies in two aspects: IP spoofing and stateful firewall. IP spoofing policy is one that can be potentially overlooked but in fact can undermine the purpose of NAT and firewall to protect mobile phones from probing and scanning. Stateful firewall can impact reachability, affecting both security and performance.

4.1.1 Testing IP Spoofing

Previous study on Internet IP spoofing [14] has shown that IP spoofing is still widely allowed. However, it unclear how prevalent it is in cellular networks. The unique implication of IP spoofing can be summarized in the following story [30]: There has been a well-known attack on jailbroken iPhones' sshd program where a default password is used. A worm scanned the public IP ranges and propagated via this weakness and eventually infected more than 21,000 phones.

Obviously, networks with NATs or firewalls that block unsolicited incoming traffic are not vulnerable to this worm, as external hosts cannot scan phones inside the cellular network. The ability to perform IP spoofing completely changes this by allowing a single phone to punch many holes on the NATs and firewalls, thus allowing external servers to scan the phones in the internal networks. More specifically, as long as the attacker controls a phone in the network, she can send spoofed SYN packets to an attacker-controlled server which can then send SYN back to the spoofed IP (victim). Besides scanning, attackers can also launch battery draining attacks [32] by continuously sending packets to the target phones.

To determine whether a given phone's network allows IP spoofing, *NetPiculet* client modifies the source IP field in the IP header for outgoing TCP SYN packets. We randomly choose 10 source IP addresses in its own /24 and /16 IP prefixes and send a SYN packet using the chosen IP. The SYN packet is to mimic a legitimate TCP connection establishment request initiated by a device inside the cellular network which will be allowed by the firewall and NAT. We also studied UDP packets. Note that other packets are not of interest as they can be easily blocked by NAT. If the *NetPiculet* server sees the corresponding public IP address translated by NAT, it records the spoofed private IP address, obtained from the payload, and the mapped public IP address pair and consider the carrier as permitting IP spoofing.

4.1.2 Testing Stateful Firewall

Stateful firewalls can determine legitimate packets under different connection states (*e.g.,* states associated with a TCP connection). In each state, only packets matching certain criteria are allowed to traverse through the firewall (for either incoming or outgoing traffic). For mobile carriers deploying NAT boxes (Carrier A and Carrier B), external traffic cannot reach devices directly without

out devices initiating an outbound connection first. Hence, the *NetPiculet* client and server have to coordinate to reveal the firewall policies for those carriers. We first perform this test in a local environment setting to help us understand properties of interest, *i.e.,* those impact performance and security. We subsequently deployed only tests associated with such properties on *NetPiculet* client to ensure they finish quickly on end-users' phones.

Note that we verified using local experiments, the packet blocking behavior imposed by the firewall is applicable to both incoming and outgoing traffic. However, the net effect of which incoming and outgoing packets are allowed may not be symmetric because of the presence of NAT. Also, the buffering behavior described later in §4.1.2 applies to both directions as well.

Due to the popularity of TCP, we conduct controlled experiments between *NetPiculet* client and server to infer the firewall policies in various TCP states such as SYN-SENT, SYN-REVD, ESTABLISHED *etc.* Specifically, in each state, we perform the following tests:

1. Single packet filter test: Probing using SYN, SYN-ACK, ACK, DATA, FIN, RST packets from the *NetPiculet* server to check if they are allowed.

2. Timeout test for each state: If any such probing packet is allowed, we infer the timeout value in each state by incrementally increasing the interval between consecutive probes.

3. Sequence (SEQ) window test for state transition: for packets that trigger state transitions, we probe with a range of SEQ number and ACK number to verify if they can still enable the correct transitions.

4. SEQ window test for ESTABLISHED state: we vary the SEQ number of DATA packets via binary search to infer the SEQ window size adopted by the firewall.

Given that some of these tests are quite time-consuming, we selected a subset, expected to significantly impact application security and performance, as shown in §4.1.3 and §4.1.4, to be integrated into the *NetPiculet* client.

4.1.3 Testing TCP Connection Timeout

Through local experiments, we found that firewalls deployed by Carrier B have a very short timeout for idle TCP connections. Thus TCP connections of chat applications are frequently timed out. Such applications require long-lived connections, *e.g.,* MSN Talk on Android. To understand the timer values of firewalls, we integrate the timeout inference test into *NetPiculet*.

To infer the timer value on the firewall that times out idle TCP connections, *NetPiculet* client creates multiple connections in parallel to *NetPiculet* server without enabling keep-alive option. Each connection sends a message to the server after a specific amount of idle time. The server responds to the client upon receiving the message. If the connection is still alive when the message is sent, the client should receive the response message from the server. Otherwise, the connection is timed out by the firewall. *NetPiculet* client tries four idle time intervals: 5, 10, 20, and 30 minutes, to bound the inferred timeout timer value within these ranges.

4.1.4 Testing Out-of-Order Packet Buffering

During our controlled experiments to test the SEQ window size, we accidentally discovered that some firewalls buffer out-of-order TCP packets. We inject packets with large sequence numbers to check if the firewall has a SEQ window such that packets with sequence number out of the window would be dropped. Initially we thought packets were dropped whenever the other end did not receive them, after accounting for network loss. We then discovered that after those missing packets arrive, the injected packets with large sequence numbers are released, indicating the buffering behavior. This ensures packets are delivered in order, most likely motivated by the need to perform deep packet inspection (DPI) to detect security attacks, a feature we found to be available in some commercial routers [10]. As we discuss later in §4.3.2, this buffering behavior has significant impact on TCP performance in the presence of packet loss. We implement this test in *NetPiculet*.

To realize this test for detecting buffering in both directions, we intentionally drop one packet from the many packets on the sender side, and observe whether there will be any ACK packet received for beyond the lost packet. If there is no response after certain time window (*e.g.*, 5 seconds), we conclude the firewall does buffer out-of-order packets. 5 seconds is chosen as it is sufficiently large to account for some of the performance impact on TCP, as described in §4.3.2.

4.2 Firewall Characteristics

We next describe the firewall testing results, including results from both local controlled experiments and tests implemented in the *NetPiculet* client deployed in the wild.

4.2.1 IP Spoofing

For local experiments, we studied one of the carriers found to allow IP spoofing to quantify how fast one can scan inside a cellular network. We scanned a randomly chosen /24 IP range as fast as possible by sending spoofed SYN packets back to back. We repeat the experiment for 10 times, and the result shows that it takes on average 2 – 3 seconds for all IP spoofing packets to be received by the external server, and then 3 – 4 seconds are spent for the servers to scan and wait for the response. Note that to receive packets, mobile devices have to obtain radio resource first, which normally takes 1 – 2 seconds [31]. The probing packets will likely experience such delay before reaching the scanned devices. In practice, if the attacker is continuously scanning a large range of IPs, the throughput of spoofing is usually the bottleneck, which we found to be around 90 packets/second. Compared to data packets, we do not find any signs of rate limiting on the spoofed SYN packets, as their throughput numbers are very close. In our scanning of the /24 prefix, we found 54 hosts on average responding to the probing.

NetPiculet was able to perform the IP spoofing test in 60 cellular networks, among which 4 allow IP spoofing. Despite the low absolute number, the percentage is still significant: 6.7%. Further, all four carriers are large cellular ISPs, covering U.S. and Europe respectively. Thus they can be profitable targets for attackers. Given that specifications and commercial products are already available [11, 9] that can prevent IP spoofing at finest granularity (using subscriber information IMSI/MSISDN available in each packet header), it is surprising to see that these four large carriers allow IP spoofing.

We further investigate the range of spoofable IP addresses (/24 and /16). Surprisingly, each of the four carriers allows /24 and /16 to be spoofed. This is likely due to the fact the NAT box is shared at the very high level of the network infrastructure inside the cellular network, usually co-located with GGSN [4]. We expect IP spoofing prevention to be enforced at GGSNs, as confirmed by commercial products available [9] that advertise such features.

4.2.2 Stateful Firewall

We observe that the stateful firewall policies usually do not strictly follow the TCP specifications (*e.g.*, packets with an invalid ACK number can still traverse the firewall). There are two key reasons for this: (1) It is expensive to check all the low-level details to the degree that a host networking stack does. (2) There are many TCP variants; thus, firewall policies should be flexible enough to accom-

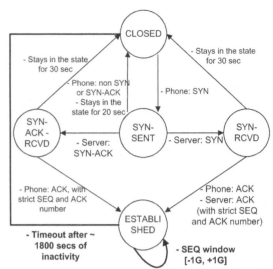

Figure 4: TCP State diagram of Carrier A's firewall.

modate most if not all of them. The latter is an inherent problem of network-based firewalls and intrusion detection systems [35]. In our study, we found significant variations among the stateful firewall policies adopted by various carriers. Next we explain in detail the key properties of the inferred TCP state machine on the firewalls, which serves as the necessary prelude for discussing their implication.

Figures 4 shows the TCP state diagram we inferred for the firewalls in Carrier A. Carrier B has a similar diagram except for some minor differences, which can still have significant implications for applications as explained below.

Carrier A's firewall: In Figure 4, we infer that there are 5 states, slightly different from the TCP states defined on end-host. The figure is fairly self-explanatory. We only highlight the key interesting state transitions identified, as indicated with bold lines.

There are several observations associated with the ESTABLISHED state. We found that even after a legitimate close sequence (FIN, FIN-ACK, ACK), one can still send packets into the cellular networks from external networks, indicating that the firewall did not go back to the CLOSED state. We discuss implications of this unexpected behavior in §4.3.4.

The ESTABLISHED state has an inactivity timer associated with each TCP connection. If the timer expires, the connection state is removed from the firewall and no additional packets are allowed until a new connection is established (starting over from TCP's three-way handshake). This timer value is 1800 seconds which we compare with another carrier and discuss its impact in §4.3.1.

In the ESTABLISHED state, the firewall checks the TCP SEQ of all packets from either direction to ensure that they fall into a window of SEQ from previously seen packets. The problem is that this window size δ seems to be statically configured to liberally accommodate packet reordering. As an example, if the server's first packet has SEQ of n, the second packet must have a SEQ from $[n - \delta, n + \delta]$. The range $[n - \delta, n)$ is to allow retransmission of lost packets. The range $(n, n + \delta)$ is to allow out-of-order packets. Dropping them would cause unnecessary retransmission from the sender. Surprisingly, we found that δ can be as large as 1G (and sometimes 128K), depending on the types of firewall encountered. We also found that different IP ranges go through different firewalls likely due to different network paths. 128K is normally good enough in today's 3G networks as the *delay* × *bandwidth* is typically capped at 0.2s × 4Mbps = 100KB, which is smaller than 128KB. However, for future networks such as 4G with higher net-

Timeout (min)	(0,5]	(5, 10]	(10, 20]	(20, 30]	(30, ∞)	Total
# carriers	4	7	6	8	48	73

Table 5: Measured TCP timeout timers in cellular network firewalls.

work capacity, a loss of one packet may cause its following packets overflow the 128KB window and be unnecessarily dropped.

Also, another important finding is that for packets that fall within $(n, n + \delta]$, they are not delivered immediately. Instead, they are buffered until in-order packets arrive. This behavior actually leads to security issues as well as performance impact due to unexpected interaction with TCP stack as discussed later in §4.3.3 and §4.3.2.

Carrier B's firewall: Its state diagram closely resembles that of Carrier A's. One major difference is that its firewall is much less restrictive in determining if a TCP connection is established (from SYN-ACK-RCVD and SYN-RCVD to ESTABLISHED). As long as the SEQ of the ACK packet falls into a (-128K, +128K) window from the previous SEQ, the firewall advances the state to ESTABLISHED. This may allow fake connections to be established on the firewall. Also, unlike Carrier A's firewall, Carrier B's firewall does not buffer out-of-order packets.

In the ESTABLISHED state, the inactivity timeout value is much smaller (255 seconds) compared to that of Carrier A's, more seriously affecting long-lived connections such as push-based services as elaborated in §4.3.1. In addition, the SEQ window of 128K for the ESTABLISHED state is much smaller compared to Carrier A's.

4.3 Implications and Recommendations

Given our previous discussions on several interesting observations from the firewall policy inference results, we elaborate on their impact on application performance and security. To quantify such impact we conduct further controlled experiments. We also describe the important implications and recommendations for the firewall.

4.3.1 Energy Impact of TCP Connection Timeout

Long-lived connections (*e.g.*, push-based services such as email) assume persistent TCP connections. Given the inactivity timer on the firewall, periodic keep-alive messages must be sent to maintain the connection. Otherwise, applications' ability to receive timely notifications can be impaired. The default TCP keep-alive timer of 2 hours [7] is clearly too large to help maintain the connection. In fact, we tested MSN Talk, one of the MSN messenger applications on Android, and discovered that Carrier B's firewall terminates idle connections (using spoofed RST packet) after 255 seconds, forcing the application to re-establish the connection immediately to restore the service. This may appear to be equivalent to sending keep-alive messages but transmitting more data and incurring additional delays.

Table 5 summarizes the measured TCP timeout timers of various carriers tested by *NetPiculet*. Among the 73 carriers measured, 11 have a timer shorter than 10 minutes, four of them with a timer of only at most 5 minutes. Since radio resource is allocated every time a keep-alive packet is sent for an idle connection, over time such packets can consume significant amount of energy for end devices and also incur high signaling overhead for cellular networks. To quantify the energy impact, we assume a long-lived connection which regularly sends keep-alive to reset the firewall timer right before it is about to expire. We use existing cellular interface power models [31] to estimate the ratio of energy spent on keep-alive per day for a common smartphone battery capacity (1350 mhA). While the actual energy consumption may vary across different networks and devices, the overall conclusion that significant energy waste due to small timers shown in Figure 5 is generally applicable. For example, more than 17% of the battery capacity is spent on keep-

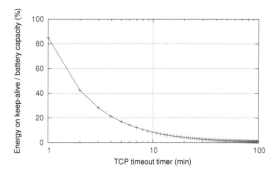

Figure 5: The ratio of energy of sending keep-alive messages per day to the battery capacity (1350 mAh).

alive everyday when the timer is less than 5 minutes, while it drops sharply as the timer becomes longer. The waste is reduced to less than 2% for 30 minute timers.

Network operators must consider an inherent tradeoff when setting the timer for terminating idle TCP connections. On one hand, larger timer values reduce the energy cost and signaling overhead caused by keep-alive packets to maintain the connection. On the other hand, they use up more memory at the firewalls for keeping track of existing connections. Firewalls generally have limited capacity to process concurrent connections; thus, carriers have incentives to set smaller timers to terminate idle connections in order to support more concurrent active users.

It is of interest to investigate the best way for developers to implement push-based services which are becoming more popular. One approach is to use the push service framework in the SDK. Both Apple and Google provide such framework API, which developers can use to implement push based services [2, 3]. The way it works is that when the third-party application server α has data to push to the mobile device, it informs the push notification server β, which belongs to Apple or Google, β then sends a notification message to the targeted mobile device through a long-lived TCP connection maintained by the framework. The framework provides two benefits. First, since the framework takes care of maintaining the long-lived connection, developers do not need to deal with diverse timer values in different networks. Second, since notifications of different applications share the single long-lived connection, energy cost on the mobile device is lower compared with the case where each application has its own long-lived connection.

It is interesting to note that in Carrier B's network, port 5228 stands out from others with a larger timeout value of 1600 seconds compared to the default of 255 seconds. Port 5228 is actually used by Google's push service framework [3] to send notifications. We suspect that Carrier B intentionally makes this optimization for Google, which reduces the overhead of re-establishing the connection repeatedly. However, verified by our experiments, Carrier B only uses the port number to make the distinction. Therefore, developers can take advantage of this port number to obtain a longer connection timeout value.

4.3.2 Performance and Energy Impact of Buffering

As described before, some firewalls buffer out-of-order packets within a configured range of sequence numbers and deliver them when in-order packets arrive. Two legitimate cases trigger such buffering behavior: 1) packet loss; 2) packets re-ordered along the path. Normally the first scenario happens much more frequently than the second one. It is worth mentioning that Carrier A, a U.S. nation-wide cellular service provider, shows the buffering behavior, and it buffers out-of-order packets for more than an hour.

Disabling "TCP fast retransmit". A major problem with such buffering behavior is that it disables TCP fast retransmission, which

381

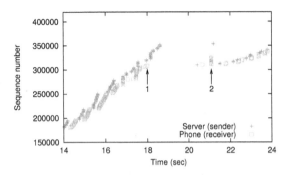

Figure 6: Sender's TCP sequence numbers monitored on server and client in Carrier A's network.

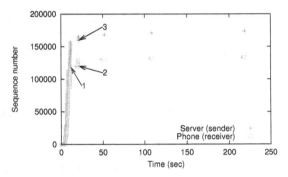

Figure 7: The impact of firewall buffering on TCP flow when FRTO is implemented on the sender side.

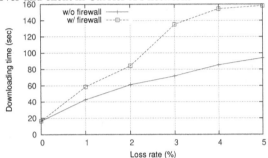

Figure 8: The average downloading time for 1MB file under different loss rates.

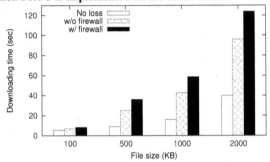

Figure 9: The firewall impact on downloading time for different file size under 1% loss rate.

is used to reduce the time a sender waits before retransmitting a lost segment and without which a sender has to use a timer to detect any lost segment. It works as follows: if a TCP sender receives three duplicate acknowledgements with the same acknowledge (ACK) number, *i.e.,* a total of four ACKs with the same ACK number, the sender can be reasonably confident that the segment with the next higher sequence number was dropped. The sender then retransmits the packet before waiting for its timeout.

Buffering disables fast retransmission because the sender is unable to observe any duplicate ACKs. For instance, if packet 1 is dropped and packets 2, 3, 4 and 5 arrive. The firewall buffers packets 2 – 5 since it never sees 1. This way, the receiver does not see any packets and cannot send any response. As a result, the sender has to resort to timeout-based retransmission.

Figure 6 illustrates the problem using a packet trace from our local experiment in Carrier A's network. A packet loss occurs at arrow 1, and the sender keeps sending more packets to fill the congestion window. Since the firewall does not see the lost packet, it buffers all the later packets, which are considered out-of-order. The sender thus is unable to get any response from the receiver and has to fall back to time-out based retransmission noted as the gap in the figure.

Bad interaction with TCP "Protect Against Wrapped Sequence number (PAWS)". At arrow 2 in Figure 6, the firewall released all the buffered packets upon seeing the retransmitted lost packet. However, those packets were retransmitted later by the sender through slow start, even though they have successfully reached the receiver. We investigated this behavior and found the explanation in RFC [24] where PAWS is defined. PAWS uses TCP timestamp to reject potentially old packets that might corrupt an ongoing TCP connection. With TCP timestamp option enabled, the timestamp on the buffered packets was strictly smaller than the timestamp on the retransmitted packet. Consequently the receiver rejected the buffered packets by sending back duplicate ACKs which then triggered the

following retransmission. The pile of packets at arrow 2 also indicates that the firewall has a limited buffer size. We measured the buffer size to be 10 packets per TCP flow and confirmed the setup with the documentation of commercial routers [10].

To quantify the impact of disabling fast retransmit on application performance and energy, we perform controlled experiments to measure the time and energy consumption for downloading files of different size from our server. We use WiFi to emulate the delay of 3G network (400ms RTT derived from a recent study [23]) to have full control over the loss rate and firewall configuration. On the hosting server, a small Perl script is used to control the loss rate by randomly dropping packets with certain probabilities. To emulate the firewall buffering behavior for the same TCP flow, the script buffers the first 10 packets (as we observed in Carrier A's network) with sequence number larger than the packet previously dropped intentionally and drops the remaining ones. Upon receiving a retransmitted packet with the same sequence number as the intentionally dropped packet, it releases all the buffered packets. We vary the loss rate from 0 to 5% and download each file 10 times under each setting.

Figure 8 shows that even with a loss rate of 1%, the downloading time for a 1MB file is increased by 50% due the firewall buffering behavior. And the degradation is worse with higher loss rate. Under the same loss rate, the buffering has less impact on smaller files. As shown in Figure 9 compared with normal loss without firewall, the firewall incurs 21% extra delay for a 100KB file while 44% increased delay for 500KB files for a loss rate of 1%. However, a recent study [1] points out that TCP-based streaming applications that typically send large amount of data contribute to majority of smartphone traffic. So the overall network performance could be significantly affected by firewall with such buffering behavior. Note that the cellular radio interface always stays in high power state during the entire download process. Even when there is no traffic during RTO, the interface still remains in high power state due to the tail time [31]. The energy consumption for downloading the same amount of data increases almost linearly with the downloading time.

Bad interaction with "TCP Forward RTO-Recovery (F-RTO)"
Since PAWS makes the buffered packets useless to the receiver, we were wondering whether letting the receiver accept the buffered packet would reduce the negative impact of buffering on TCP performance. Therefore, we disabled the TCP timestamp option on the sender side and repeated the experiments to measure the downloading time. Surprisingly, we found the TCP connection almost hung up after a single packet loss. As we figured out later, it is due to the bad interaction between buffering and F-RTO, a TCP extension defined in RFC [33].

F-RTO is designed to detect spurious TCP retransmission timeouts which cause unnecessary retransmissions when no segments are lost. After a spurious retransmission timeout, the late acknowledgments of the original segments arrive at the sender, usually triggering unnecessary retransmissions of the entire window of segments. This can happen when, for instance, some mobile networking technologies introduce sudden delay spikes on transmission due to actions taken during a hand-off.

When a retransmission timeout (RTO) occurs, the F-RTO sender retransmits the first unacknowledged segment as usual. Deviating from the normal operation after a timeout, it then tries to transmit new, previously unsent data, for the first ACK that arrives after the timeout given that the ACK advances the window. If the second ACK that arrives after the timeout also advances the window, *i.e.,* acknowledges data that was not retransmitted, the F-RTO sender declares the RTO as spurious and exits the RTO recovery. However, if either of the next two ACKs is a duplicate ACK, no sufficient evidence is found for a spurious RTO. The F-RTO sender retransmits the unacknowledged segments in slow start similar to the traditional algorithm.

This behavior is illustrated in Figure 7. A packet loss occurred at arrow 1, marked on the figure. The sender keeps sending about 30 more packets to fill the congestion window, 10 of which are buffered at the firewall, the rest dropped due to buffer space constraints. At arrow 2, the sender retransmits the lost packet after retransmission timeout which triggers the buffered packets to be released (since it is now in-order). The receiver then receives 11 packets including the retransmitted one. At this point, the sender behaves according to F-RTO. At arrow 3, instead of retransmitting unacknowledged packets in the congestion window, it now tries to transmit new, previously unsent data. If no duplicate ACKs are received, the sender can save the unnecessary effort of retransmitting the unacknowledged packets. However, this optimization fails to consider the case where the newly transmitted packets are buffered at the firewall causing no ACKs to be received. Later, the sender has to repeat the entire process of F-RTO again and further transmit new, previously unsent data. As we can see in the figure, in each round, the retransmission timeout is doubled with only one packet successfully delivered, effectively rendering the connection useless. And this is triggered by only a single packet loss shown by arrow 1.

The fundamental problem here is that this F-RTO algorithm does not expect packets to be buffered by the firewall for so long. Intuitively, one way to address this issue is to limit the buffering time to a small value (*e.g.,* $< 1s$). However, we found that firewalls with Intrusion Prevention Systems (IPS) capability must examine or perform deep packet inspection (DPI) on in-order packets before they can be delivered to provide strong security guarantees. Indeed, many such IPS boxes are sold today by major vendors such as Cisco [10]. At the moment, we did not observe other carriers im-

plementing similar buffering policy yet, but we did observe consistent buffering behavior from 14 users in 8 U.S. states. Further, this behavior can become more prevalent in the future due to increasing security concerns for mobile cellular networks. Since F-RTO was implemented in Linux kernel 2.6.22 in 2007, the majority of Linux servers are likely impacted.

In summary, regardless of the TCP timestamp option, the buffering behavior always disables the TCP fast retransmission which can degrade TCP performance significantly. If the TCP timestamp option is enabled, it can have bad interaction with PAWS. Without the TCP timestamp option, it can have adverse interaction with F-RTO, seriously rendering the TCP connection completely useless.

4.3.3 Exploiting Large Sequence Number Window

We have discussed the property of a SEQ window $[-\delta, +\delta]$ on the firewall to allow legitimate TCP packets through while blocking potentially malicious packets. In general, this window size should not be much bigger than the receiver window size, which is mostly 64K or 128K in most smartphone operating systems today (with the TCP window scaling option). For Carrier A, the window of [-1G, +1G] is too large. This allows arbitrary data packets to be injected assuming the knowledge of the 5 tuple, since the data packets are being buffered instead of being dropped immediately.

As the firewall can buffer 10 packets at most, an attacker can equally spread 40 data packets across the 4G SEQ space where at most 10 of them are buffered at (0, +1G]. Some of the buffer space can be occupied by legitimate packets that arrive out of order. To simplify the discussion, we assume for now that attackers can occupy all the 10 buffer slots. In this case, a TCP connection will always be injected with a packet with any payload within at most 100MB of data transfer. On average, about 50MB of data transfer is needed. The likelihood of success is much higher if this attack is attempted concurrently on many users and at different times of the day. Given that it takes only 40 packets for one trial, it is fairly cheap to blindly launch such attacks. For example, every 500 trials, an attacker can with high probability succeed at least one connection within 500KB of data transfer. Therefore, the large sequence number window property of such firewalls effectively amplifies the severity of blind data injection attacks [12] against TCP. TCP connections which transfer more data are especially vulnerable. The effect of this attack varies depending on different types of applications. For file downloading, it can corrupt the file content and render it unusable or even dangerous (imagine an executable file with altered instructions). For video streaming, however, a single corrupted packet can be tolerated by the video codec without much problem.

4.3.4 Flaws with Closing TCP Connections

For Carrier A, when the state transitions to the CLOSED state, the server can still send SYN packets continuously to drain the phones' battery even though the phone has invoked socket `close()` on its side. This is because some state is not properly de-allocated by the firewall and NAT, which operate independently. More specifically, the NAT still keeps an entry for the previous connection which gets cleaned up only after 20 seconds of timeout if it sees FIN packets. It is easy to keep resetting the timer by sending a packet every 20 seconds. The firewall always allows an incoming SYN packet as it treats it as a new connection. By maintaining the state at the NAT and the firewall, a malicious server can keep sending packets to the phone that it previously communicated with to drain its battery, even though the phone has already closed the connection. Such battery-draining attack can cause up to 22.3 times energy consumption and deplete the battery within several hours [32].

Due to the same problem, the back-to-back connections using the same five tuple could be delayed up to 25 seconds. As a consequence, the whole process of NAT mapping discovery (described in §3.1.1) could take more than three minutes. Comparing the packet traces dumped from both the server and client, we noticed that the SYN packets sent by the client to create new connections are dropped in the network during the delayed time duration.

4.4 Summary

Next we summarize the key findings for the firewall study.

- We discovered that 4 of 60 cellular networks allow IP spoofing, which can make hosts vulnerable to scanning and battery draining attacks even though they are behind the firewall and NAT.

- We discovered 11 of 73 carriers set the TCP inactivity timeout to be less than 10 minutes, which can cost significant amount of energy in maintaining long-lived connections used by push-based services. For carriers, we recommend a 30-minute timeout value. For application developers, we suggest they follow the push service framework in SDK where multiple services share a single persistent connection.

- We discovered the TCP out-of-order buffering behavior in some firewalls causing several unexpected interaction with common TCP behavior defined in the TCP specifications, leading to degraded performance and energy waste. Reducing the buffering time or increasing the buffer size both have negative impact on security. Thus, there is an inherent trade-off between performance and security.

5. DISCUSSION

As we demonstrate throughout the paper, inappropriate middlebox policies have severe impact on application performance, mobile device energy consumption, and network security. With all the potential impact in mind, carriers should take the responsibility to carefully avoid bad middlebox policies in their networks. Due to some constraints (*e.g.,* cost and security), sometimes they have to configure policies which may not be friendly to applications. However, working towards a neutral network environment, instead of concealing those policies they should inform network users and application developers on the middlebox policies and their associated impact. Despite our focus on cellular network policies, our methodologies for inferring NAT and firewall policies and the identified implications of such policies are also applicable to wired networks. For example, time-dependent NAT mapping may also exist on the Internet, and the new traversal scheme we proposed can be used to traverse such NATs. Firewalls on the Internet may also buffer out-of-order TCP packets, and the resulting bad interaction with TCP extensions would still hold. We leave it as future work to monitor those policies on the wired networks. We notice that some of the bad policies are identified only in a few carriers, but our findings are still valuable in preventing operators from falling into the same pitfalls in the future. The measurement results could also change over time as carriers modify the policies or upgrade their network devices. In this case, our tool can still monitor such policy changes in the long run.

6. RELATED WORK

We heavily draw on prior work on NAT characterization and traversal. MacDonald *et al.* [27] defined in an IETF draft a few key attributes of NAT box, *e.g.,* mapping, filtering, and binding time, as well as their corresponding tests. NUTSS [22] demonstrated the feasibility of TCP NAT traversal through a combination

of tricks including port prediction, IP address spoofing, and TCP packet forgery. Ford *et al.* [20] identified a few important properties relevant to NAT traversal and measured them in the wild. In parallel, Guha and Francis [21] tested nearly 100 commercial NAT boxes and compared the effectiveness of several NAT traversal solutions. Majority of the NAT boxes they studied exhibit predictability in port allocation. Makinen and Nurminen [28] measured the NAT properties from one vantage point in each of the six cellular networks. They suggested that the existing NAT traversal techniques would work in cellular networks without modifications. In contrast, we discovered some previously unknown NAT properties not handled by existing techniques and proposed new solutions accordingly. Our focus is on cellular ISPs, and by releasing *NetPiculet* to mobile users, we covered significantly more carriers and users.

While providing security and flexibility in IP address allocation, middleboxes have been shown to have undesirable performance impact on Internet users and content providers. They can inflate transaction time, disrupt long-lived connections, and reduce TCP throughput [13]. A follow-up study revealed that middleboxes may also interfere with ECN negotiation, MTU discovery, and IP and TCP options [29]. More recently, Casado and Freedman [17] investigated web clients behind middleboxes by injecting active content. They find most NATs cover a small number of hosts and their IP addresses are stable over at least several days. They also devised a suite of classifiers for detecting hosts behind middleboxes. In contrast, our work focuses on the middlebox behavior in cellular networks and reveals the implications on radio energy consumption, a unique perspective in cellular network context.

Besides the characterization work focusing on the usage of middleboxes, several studies investigated various security issues in cellular networks. Compared to their wired counterparts, cellular networks have relatively scarce network resource, making them vulnerable to various DoS attacks. Some attacks can be carried out by exploiting the complex and heavy-weight procedure of establishing a communication channel between a handset and the cellular infrastructure. Serror *et al.* found the paging channel can be easily overloaded in CDMA networks [34], Traynor *et al.* proposed attacks abusing the setup and teardown processes between mobile devices and base stations in GPRS/EDGE networks *et al.* [36], and Lee *et al.* showed well-timed traffic can trigger excessive radio resource control messages [25]. Compared with these studies that identified and exploited resource bottlenecks, our work sheds light on the feasibility of such attacks in real cellular networks that are protected by middleboxes. Moreover, we discovered some unexpected behavior of middleboxes, which can make cellular networks and devices vulnerable.

The popularity of cellular data network has inspired a growing number of measurement studies in this area as well. WindRider [8] proposed to capture network neutrality violations by monitoring application and system information on mobile devices. A previous study [23] leveraging dataset from a deployed mobile application compared the network and application performance of four major U.S. cellular carriers with the inputs from over 30,000 mobile users. Falaki [19] collected traces from 255 users and observed dramatic diversity in their usage behaviors. Our work differs in its emphasis on middlebox characteristics and implications on mobile users.

7. CONCLUSION

We have presented *NetPiculet*, the first system that effectively discovers cellular network policies focusing on NAT and firewall policies. Beyond the known properties of such middleboxes, we also focus on unique aspects of cellular networks as they impact mobile devices, mobile application developers, and cellular ISPs from perspectives of energy, performance, and security. Based on the data collected in January 2011, we studied more than 100 cellular networks around the world, illustrating how a diverse set of policies can lead to several important implications for network carriers as well as mobile application developers. Results from *NetPiculet* demonstrate the importance of understanding such policies especially due to potential complex and unexpected interaction among various policy components. In the long run, *NetPiculet* is highly valuable to help make cellular network policies less opaque and expose their impact as networks and applications continue to evolve.

8. REFERENCES

[1] Allot: Video streaming dominated mobile data traffic in first half 2010. http://www.indiatelecomtracker.com/archives/2669.

[2] Apple Push Notification Service. http://en.wikipedia.org/wiki/Apple_Push_Notification_Service.

[3] Building Push Applications for Android. http://dl.google.com/googleio/2010/android-push-applications-android.pdf.

[4] Cisco Mobile Exchange. http://docstore.mik.ua/univercd/cc/td/doc/product/wireless/moblwrls/cmx/mmg_sg/cmxdesc.htm.

[5] Fring. http://www.fring.com.

[6] Tango. http://tango.me.

[7] tcp(7) - Linux man page. http://linux.die.net/man/7/tcp.

[8] WindRider: A Mobile Network Neutrality Monitoring System. http://www.cs.northwestern.edu/~ict992/mobile.htm.

[9] Cisco GGSN Release. http://www.cisco.com/en/US/prod/collateral/iosswrel/ps8802/ps6947/ps5413/prod_bulletin0900aecd802e0859.html, 2005.

[10] TCP Out-of-Order Packet Support for Cisco IOS Firewall and Cisco IOS IPS. http://www.cisco.com/en/US/docs/ios/12_4t/12_4t11/ht_ooop.html, 2006.

[11] Interworking between the Public Land Mobile Network (PLMN) supporting packet based services and Packet Data Networks (PDN). 3GPP TS 29.061 V6.15.0, 2008.

[12] Improving TCP's Robustness to Blind In-Window Attacks. http://tools.ietf.org/html/rfc5961, 2010.

[13] M. Allman. On the Performance of Middleboxes. In *Proc. ACM SIGCOMM IMC*, 2003.

[14] R. Beverly, A. Berger, Y. Hyun, and k claffy. Understanding the Efficacy of Deployed Internet Source Address Validation Filtering. In *Proc. ACM SIGCOMM IMC*, 2009.

[15] A. Biggadike, D. Ferullo, G. Wilson, and A. Perrig. NATBLASTER: Establishing TCP Connections Between Hosts Behind NATs. In *Proc. of ACM SIGCOMM ASIA Workshop*, 2005.

[16] Z. Cao, Z. Wang, and E. Zegura. Performance of HashingnBased Schemes for Internet Load Balancing. In *INFOCOM*, 2000.

[17] M. Casado and M. J. Freedman. Peering through the shroud: The effect of edge opacity on IP-based client identification. In *Proc. Symposium on Networked Systems Design and Implementation*, 2007.

[18] J. L. Eppinger. TCP Connections for P2P Apps: A Software Approach to Solving the NAT Problem. http://reports-archive.adm.cs.cmu.edu/anon/isri2005/CMU-ISRI-05-104.pdf.

[19] H. Falaki, R. Mahajan, S. Kandula, D. Lymberopoulos, R. Govindan, and D. Estrin. Diversity in Smartphone Usage. In *Proc. ACM MOBISYS*, 2010.

[20] B. Ford, P. Srisuresh, and D. Kegel. Peer-to-Peer Communication Across Network Address Translators. In *Proc. of the USENIX Annual Technical Conference*, 2005.

[21] S. Guha and P. Francis. Characterization and Measurement of TCP Traversal through NATs and Firewalls. In *Proc. ACM SIGCOMM IMC*, 2005.

[22] S. Guha, Y. Takeda, and P. Francis. NUTSS: A SIP-based Approach to UDP and TCP Network Connectivity. In *Proc. of SIGCOMM'04 Workshop*, 2004.

[23] J. Huang, Q. Xu, B. Tiwana, Z. M. Mao, M. Zhang, and P. Bahl. Anatomizing Application Performance Differences on Smartphones. In *Proc. ACM MOBISYS*, 2010.

[24] V. Jacobson, R. Braden, and D. Borman. TCP Extensions for High Performance. http://tools.ietf.org/html/rfc1323, 1992.

[25] P. P. Lee, T. Bu, and T. Woo. On the Detection of Signaling DoS Attacks on 3G Wireless Networks. In *Proc. IEEE INFOCOM*, 2007.

[26] P. P. C. Lee, T. Bu, and T. Woo. On the Detection of Signaling DoS Attacks on 3G Wireless Networks. In *Proc. IEEE INFOCOM*, 2007.

[27] D. MacDonald and B. Lowekamp. NAT Behavior Discovery Using STUN. http://tools.ietf.org/html/draft-ietf-behave-nat-behavior-discovery-08.

[28] L. Makinen and J. K. Nurminen. Measurements on the Feasibility of TCP NAT Traversal in Cellular Networks. In *Proc. of the 4th EURO-NGI Conference on Next Generation Internet Networks*, 2008.

[29] A. Medina, M. Allman, and S. Floyd. Measuring Interactions Between Transport Protocols and Middleboxes. In *Proc. ACM SIGCOMM IMC*, 2004.

[30] P. Porras, H. Saidi, and V. Yegneswaran. An Analysis of the iKee.B iPhone Botnet. In *Proc. of International ICST Conference on Security and Privacy in Mobile Information and Communication Systems*, 2010.

[31] F. Qian, Z. Wang, A. Gerber, Z. M. Mao, S. Sen, and O. Spatscheck. Characterizing Radio Resource Allocation for 3G Networks. In *Proc. ACM SIGCOMM IMC*, 2010.

[32] R. Racic, D. Ma, and H. Chen. Exploiting mms vulnerabilities to stealthily exhaust mobile phone's battery. In *Proc. of SecureComm*, 2006.

[33] P. Sarolahti and M. Kojo. Forward RTO-Recovery (F-RTO): An Algorithm for Detecting Spurious Retransmission Timeouts with TCP and the Stream Control Transmission Protocol (SCTP). http://tools.ietf.org/html/rfc4138, 2005.

[34] J. Serror. Impact of paging channel overloads or attacks on a cellular network. In *Proceedings of the 5th ACM workshop on Wireless security*, WiSe, 2006.

[35] U. Shankar and V. Paxson. Active Mapping: Resisting NIDS Evasion Without Altering Traffic. In *Proc. IEEE Symposium on Security and Privacy*, 2003.

[36] P. Traynor, P. McDaniel, and T. La Porta. On Attack Causality in Internet-connected Cellular Networks. In *Proc. of 16th USENIX Security Symposium*, 2007.

Automatic Inference of Movements from Contact Histories

Pengcheng Wang   Zhaoyu Gao   Xinhui Xu   Yujiao Zhou
Haojin Zhu*   and   Kenny Q. Zhu*
Shanghai Jiao Tong University
Shanghai, China
{wpc009, gaozy1987, xuxinhui08, yujiao.zhou}@gmail.com
*{zhu-hj, kzhu}@cs.sjtu.edu.cn

ABSTRACT

This paper introduces a new security problem in which individuals movement traces (in terms of accurate routes) can be inferred from just a series of mutual contact records and the map of the area in which they roam around. Such contact records may be obtained through the bluetooth communication on mobile phones. We present an approach that solve the trace inference problem in reasonable time, and analyze some properties of the inference algorithm.

Categories and Subject Descriptors

C.2.m [**Computer-Communication Networks**]: Miscellaneous

General Terms

Algorithm, Experimentation, Security

Keywords

Traces, Inference, Contacts, Location privacy

1. INTRODUCTION

Location privacy and, in particular, privacy of individuals' timestamped movements is receiving increasing interest. Recent research indicates that the widespread use of WiFi and Bluetooth enabled smartphones opens new doors for malicious attacks, including geolocating individuals by illegitimate means (e.g. spreading worm based malware) and even legitimate means (e.g. location based advertisement networks and theft locators) [4, 3, 1]. However, most existing geo-localization techniques require GPS information or additional control of hardware infrastructures such as WiFi access points or GSM base stations. This paper presents a new technique to infer individuals' complete movement traces using only their mutual contact histories and a map. This technique can be deployed both indoors and outdoors, so long as the area map is available. To the best of our knowledge, the only other work that attempts to infer traces from bluetooth contact histories is by Whitbeck et al. [5]. However, they did not make use of a map and therefore only produces rough moving trajectories. It also relies on the existence of various imaginary forces that are supposed to bias

the person's movement, though it is not clear how to determine the parameters involved in the forces calculation. The technique in this paper, on the contrary, produces detailed movement traces according to a map.

Next we describe the *Trace Inference Problem*. We define a map M as a graph (V, E), where V is a set of road junctions each with geographic coordinates (x, y), and E is a set of straight road segment. Note that a curved road can be approximated by a sequence of straight road segments. Let a set of nodes N move on the edges of the map at various but constant speeds. We assume that a node never backtracks unless it's at a dead end. Let the trace of node i be a location function on time $l_i(t)$, and a *contact* between node i and j be a 4-tuple: (i, j, t_{in}, t_{out}) where t_{in} is when the encounter of i and j begins, and t_{out} is when their encounter ends. Further, a *contact history* is a set of contacts. Given the set of traces of N, we can *induce* all the contacts by solving inequality $\|l_i(t) - l_j(t)\| \leq r$ for all pairs of traces by node i and j, where r is the range in which two nodes are considered in contact. For simplicity, we assume $r = 0$ in the rest of this paper, and the contact induction can be computed in $O(|N|^2|V|^2)$ time.

Trace Inference Problem(TIP): Given a map M, a set of moving nodes N, their speeds $\{v_i\}$, their initial locations $\{l_i(0)\}$, and a contact history H, find the traces of N whose induced contacts $H_{ind} = H$.

Suppose the last contact in H is at t_{max}, the maximum speed is v_{max}, the length of the shortest edge in M is e_{min}, and largest degree of any vertex on M is d_{max}, then a naive search across all possible paths costs

$$O\left(|N|^2|V|^2(d_{max}-1)^{\frac{|N|v_{max}t_{max}}{e_{min}}}\right).$$

2. OUR APPROACH

Our main idea is to decompose **TIP** into $|H|$ subproblems, each resolving a single contact in H. To solve a contact of i and j at time t, we consider the locations of their last contacts. The key observation is that even though there can be many possible traces spanning from the previous locations of i and j, only a small number of them can produce the contact, due to the distance constraints of the map.

Fig.1 illustrates this approach. Suppose nodes A, B and C starts their movements at t_0 from point A, B and C in the diagram. A and B contact at t_1. Given A's speed, we know by t_1, there are 5 possible traces for A ending at $A1$-$A5$ respectively. Similarly, B has 6 possible traces and 5 locations up to time t_1. Of all 15 pairs of traces between A

and B, only 4 pairs of traces satisfy the contact constraint, which may occur at locations marked by $(A1, B1)$, $(A4, B3)$ and $(A2/A3, B2)$. The rest of the traces are pruned and not considered further. In the next round, B and C contact at time t_2. We repeat the above process, using $B1$, $B2$ and $B3$ as the B's initial locations for this round. As the figure shows, the only possible trace for B left is $B1 \rightarrow B6$ given the short time interval between t_1 and t_2.

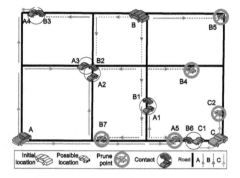

Figure 1: Inference of a Short Contact History

If we model the movements and contacts as a stochastic process, the time interval t between two successive contacts of i and j follows the exponential distribution [2]:

$$P\{t \leq x\} = 1 - e^{-\lambda_{ij}x}, x \in [0, \infty)$$

where λ_{ij} is the contact rate between i and j, the expected contact interval between i and j is $E[t] = \frac{1}{\lambda_{ij}}$. Let λ_{ij} be its mean value $\bar{\lambda}$, the number of contacts $|H|$ is

$$|H| = \frac{1}{2} \sum_i \sum_{j \neq i} t_{max} / \frac{1}{\lambda_{ij}} \approx \frac{1}{2} \bar{\lambda} t_{max} |N|^2$$

Let t_c be the expected time to infer each contact. If the contact interval of all nodes is bounded, then t_c is also bounded. Therefore, the time cost of our approach is linear to $|H|$, which is also linear to t_{max} and $|N|^2$.

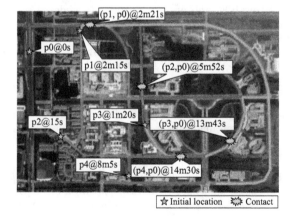

Figure 2: Five Inferred Traces on SJTU Campus

3. PRELIMINARY RESULTS

We implement the approach, run it on numbers of synthetic data sets and get the following results. Each trace

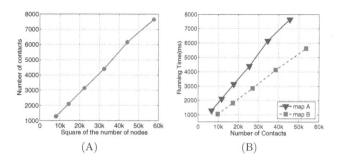

Figure 3: Induced Contacts vs. Nodes (A) Scale-up on Contacts (B)

is generated by randomly selecting an origin and a destination on a map of Shanghai Jiao Tong University campus and has a duration of 1 hour. Starting from the origin, we randomly select the next location among all adjacent junctions. A junction is more likely to be selected if it is closer to the destination. From the traces, we can induce a list of contacts and their locations like the following:

p0	p2	339.7877	154.0384	17.5236
p0	p2	41.2401	276.1339	87.4113
p0	p179	41.3582	284.7934	92.3681
...	...	...	...	...

Each row contains information for one contact. The columns represent the ids of two nodes in contact, the X and Y coordinates of the contact location, and contact time. The coordinates are not used in inference but in validation. We run 11 experiments in which the sizes of contact histories range from hundreds to 60,000. All traces are correctly inferred. Fig.2 shows 5 inferred trace fragments of nodes p_0 through p_4, along with their initial locations and contacts. Fig.3(A) shows the number of contacts induced in the data set is roughly proportional to the square of the number of nodes. Fig.3(B) shows the running times of the algorithm on various data sets. The solid line represents results for data on map A with 48 junctions which corresponds to the area in Fig.2. The dotted line represents the results for data on a smaller map B with 25 junctions. The running time is almost linear to size of contact histories. These preliminary results are in line with the discussion in Section 2.

4. ACKNOWLEDGEMENT

This work was partially supported by NSFC (Grant Nos. 61033002 and 61003218).

5. REFERENCES

[1] I. Constandache, X. Bao, M. Azizyan, and R. R. Choudhury. Did you see Bob?: human localization using mobile phones. In *MOBICOM*, 2010.

[2] W. Gao and G. Cao. User-centric data dissemination in disruption tolerant networks. In *IEEE Infocom*, 2011.

[3] N. Husted and S. Myers. Mobile location tracking in metro areas: malnets and others. In *ACM CCS*, 2010.

[4] C. Y. T. Ma, D. K. Y. Yau, N. K. Yip, and N. S. V. Rao. Privacy vulnerability of published anonymous mobility traces. In *MOBICOM*, 2010.

[5] J. Whitbeck, M. D. de Amorim, and V. Conan. Plausible mobility: Inferring movement from contacts. In *ACM MobiOpp*, 2010.

Poster: Towards A Fully Distributed N-Tuple Store

Yan Shvartzshnaider
NICTA and The University of Sydney
Sydney, Australia
yan.shvartzshnaider@sydney.edu.au

Maximilian Ott
NICTA
Sydney, Australia
max.ott@nicta.com.au

ABSTRACT

We present our work towards building a novel distributed n-tuple store by extending the Kademlia DHT [1] algorithm to support n dimensional keys as well as an $multi\_get$ operator, where some of the dimensions of the "query" key can be left unspecified.

Categories and Subject Descriptors

C.2 [**Computer-Communications Networks**]: Distributed Systems

General Terms

Algorithm, Design, Theory

Keywords

Distributed Pattern Matching, Kademlia

1. MOTIVATION

The growing volumes and rapidly changing heterogeneous nature of the data behind popular online services such as Amazon, Google, and Facebook pose new challenges to traditional data storage solutions. A possible alternative comes in the emerging NoSQL (Not Just SQL) systems. This class of systems can be roughly sorted into two categories: some that offer different "schema-less" storage abstractions to capture and describe data, and other that loosen the ACID properties to offer a more horizontally scalable storage. The choice of a particular solution comes down to a trade-off between expressiveness and scalability. This is mainly due to the fact that, many of the highly scalable NoSQL systems use key/value stores such as Distributed Hash Table (DHT) as a building block.

Despite providing features such as self-organisation, high availability, fault and network partition tolerance, DHT-based systems by design operate with single dimensional data, which significantly restricts the expressiveness of queries running on top. In particular, multi-attribute queries are not trivial to implement.

Much of prior work, such as [2], has focused on facilitating a rendezvous between the query and the published data, either through adding a supplementary indices layer or replacing the key elements of the DHT (e.g., hash function)

to ensure a non-uniform distribution. The rendezvous approach suffers from load balancing issues and requires extra effort to mitigate the overall impact on the system.

Motivated by these challenges, we present our work towards a novel n-tuple store. We extended the Kademlia DHT [1] algorithm to support n dimensional keys as well as an $multi\_get$ operator, where some of the dimensions of the "query" key can be left unspecified.

For many of the use cases we are considering, the keys within each dimension would not be uniformly distributed, but there is usually little correlation between dimensions. Concatenation of the n keys from each dimension, followed by a sequence of bit swapping operations leads to fairly well behaved one-dimensional flat keys. In such a scheme, query keys with unspecified dimensions map into bit patterns with wildcards.

In this paper we describe our extensions to the Kademlia algorithm and protocol to support queries with unconstraint wildcard patterns and present preliminary results on its performance.

2. PROBLEM DEFINITION

We first formalise the concepts on which we base our problem.

We define a **key** as a bit vector of length K and a **pattern** as a pair of bit vectors key_p and $mask_p$, where $mask_p$ is also of length K and any "0" denoting a wildcard at that vector index. We further denote a **P-distance** (pd) as the distance of a key to a pattern $\mathbb{P}$ that is calculated as $pd = (key \oplus key_p) \wedge mask_p$. The **matching set** for a pattern $\mathbb{P}$ is defined as the set of all keys for which $pd(key, P) = 0$.

We also define a network $\mathbb{W}$ consisting of N nodes, where each node selects a random key as its ID and "knows" at least one node from any of the $log_2(K)$ regions as long as that region contains a node. Finally, we define a "lookup" as a RPC call for nodes to discover additional nodes from nodes they already know.

Problem Statement: *Define an algorithm which allows a node to obtain the complete matching set for a given pattern $\mathbb{P}$ and network $\mathbb{W}$ with the minimum number of lookups.*

3. APPROACH

We introduce a new $multi\_get$ operator and a QUERY_PATTERN RPC to the Kademlia DHT protocol.

The $multi\_get$ takes a pattern as a parameter and returns the matching set over all known keys in the systems with their respective values. The QUERY_PATTERN(pattern)

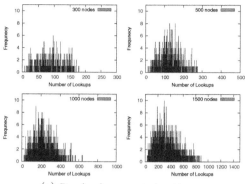
(a) Randomly generated patterns.

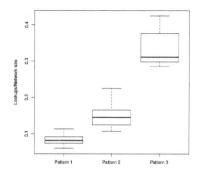
(b) The ratio of number of lookups to network size for Pattern 1, 2 and 3

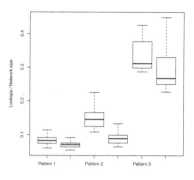
(c) Heuristic vs. Non-heuristic approach.

Figure 1: The experimental results

call returns the k nearest nodes to the specified pattern from the set of nodes known to the call's receiver.

Our algorithm is comprised of the following steps: *1)* Initialise a "target" set with the k nearest nodes from the local routing table. *2)* Select an "unused" node from the "target" set, call QUERY_PATTERN on it, and add all the returned nodes to the set. *3)* Repeat (2) until all nodes in the "target" set have been called.

4. PRELIMINARY RESULTS

We have run several experiments to evaluate our algorithm using the Oversim [3] P2P network simulator with the following Kademlia DHT parameters: $k - bucket$ size 16, id length $160bit$. We create random patterns using the *generate_pattern(msb_window, w)* function, which returns a pattern with w wildcards randomly distributed within the most significant msb_window bits. By selecting $msb\_window < log_2(N)$ the probability of any wildcard bit affecting the matching set is high. Throughout the experiments we set $msb\ window = 10$ and $w = 5$. All experiments run without network churn.

We performed three different experiments. In the first experiment, each node generated a random pattern and executed a local *multi_get* operation. We ran this for four different networks comprised of 300, 5000, 1000, 1500 nodes, respectively and after the completion of OverSim's *init* phase. Figure 1(a) depicts the lookup count distribution for the four network configurations. We do observe a fairly high number of lookups in a considerable number of cases which is the result of our overly conservative search strategy. We have begun work on incorporating network size estimations, which will allow us to terminate searches much earlier.

For the second set of experiments, we selected three different patterns 1, 2, and 3, which consistently incurred a minimum, average and maximum number of lookups, respectively. We then constructed ten differently sized networks ranging from 500 to 5000 nodes. For each combination of pattern and network, we randomly picked 20 nodes, which executed a local *multi_get* using the same pattern and reported the number of lookup. Figure 1(b) depicts the box plot of all the measurements for each pattern normalised by the respective network size. This demonstrates that the positioning of wildcard bits has a consistent impact on the number of lookups irrespective of network size.

For the third experiment we are using the same setup as in the previous experiment, but compare the baseline algorithm described above with one using a 'greedy'-type heuristic to determine which nodes to query next. Due to lack of space, we omit details of this approach because we believe there is further room for improvements. Instead, we focus on showing that such improvements are indeed statistically significant. Figure 1(c) shows the same type of box plot as before, but two box plots per pattern, one for the baseline, and one for the heuristic approach. To further validate our claims we performed a statistical analysis of variance (two way ANOVA test) to measure the impact of the two factors: the pattern composition with three levels of treatment (pattern 1, 2, and 3) and the algorithm with two levels (base and heuristics). The ANOVA test results confirm that both factors have statistically significant impact.

5. CONCLUSION

The above preliminary results show that is possible to get all the matching keys in a reasonable number of queries, particularly, while using a specially constructed pattern. We look to build on these results to optimise further the algorithm to develop a distributed n-tuple store.

6. REFERENCES

[1] P. Maymounkov and D. Mazieres, "Kademlia: A peer-to-peer information system based on the xor metric," *Proc. of IPTPS02, Cambridge, USA*, vol. 1, pp. 2–2, 2002.

[2] M. Cai and M. Frank, "RDFPeers: a scalable distributed RDF repository based on a structured peer-to-peer network," in *Proc. of the 13th Int. Conf. on World Wide Web*, 2004, p. 657.

[3] I. Baumgart, B. Heep, and S. Krause, "OverSim: A flexible overlay network simulation framework," in *IEEE Global Internet Symposium*. IEEE, 2007, pp. 79–84.

ASAP: A Low-Latency Transport Layer

Qingxi Li, Wenxuan Zhou, Matthew Caesar, Brighten Godfrey

Dept. of Computer Science, University of Illinois at Urbana-Champaign

Urbana, Illinois, USA

qli10@illinois.edu, wzhou10@illinois.edu, caesar@cs.illinois.edu, pbg@illinois.edu

Categories and Subject Descriptors

C.2.2 [**Computer-Communication Networks**]: Network Protocols

General Terms

Design, Security, Performance

Keywords

Latency, TCP, DNS

1. MOTIVATION

Achieving low latency is a key challenge for interactive web applications and other online services, as even relatively small delays cause user frustration, loss of usability of web services, and loss of customers and revenue. A recent study by Google [2] found that delays as small as 100 milliseconds measurably reduced users' frequency of conducting searches; the effect increased over time and persisted for weeks after the artificial delay was eliminated. As most web requests are small, and downloading one web page usually involves connecting to several web servers, application latency is fundamentally limited by the connection establishment delay in the underlying network protocols.

This poster studies how transport protocols can be designed to perform transactions with delay as close as possible to a single round-trip time between the endpoints and proposes a new transport protocol, Accelerated Secure Association Protocol (ASAP), to achieve that goal. ASAP merges functionality of DNS and TCP's connection establishment functions by piggybacking the connection establishment procedure atop the DNS lookup process and when the server receives the request, instead of doing three-way handshaking (3WH), the server directly sends data back to the client. From our evaluation, ASAP can reduce the response time of small web request by up to two thirds.

However, doing this in a naive fashion suffers from potential problems. First, eliminating TCP's 3WH creates the possibility of denial of service (DoS) attacks. Most significantly, the attacker can perform *reflection and amplification attacks* [6]: it sends requests with the source address set to a *victim*'s address. The attacker thus instructs servers to conduct DoS attacks on the attacker's behalf.[1] To solve

[1]Even with a 3WH, an attacker can reflect packets off a

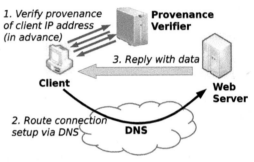

Figure 1: *Overview of ASAP.*

this, we design a *Provenance Verifier* (PV) which verifies a client's location, providing a certificate that the client can give to a server when opening a transport connection. In addition, embedding connection establishment information into a DNS request requires care to interact well with DNS caching.

2. DESIGN OF ASAP

ASAP comprises a new protocol that combines the functions of DNS and TCP. We next describe ASAP's transport-layer design (§2.1) and name resolution (§2.2).

2.1 Fast transport connection establishment

In this subsection, we present ASAP's core transport connection establishment protocol.

Verifying provenance without a handshake: Typically, the 3WH lets the server test the provenance of an incoming request from some source IP S by sending a pseudorandom initial sequence number (ISN) back to S. If the client is able to reply acknowledging this ISN, then it is *effectively* located at S. Without the 3WH, some DoS vulnerabilities would be exposed (§1). However, we demonstrate a practical means for a server to verify source provenance similar to the 3WH's guarantee, yet without introducing an RTT delay.

First, the client handshakes with a **provenance verifier (PV)** to obtain a **provenance certificate (PC)**. Before this process, the client and PV have each generated a public/private key pair (K_{pub}^c/K_{priv}^c and $K_{pub}^{pv}/K_{priv}^{pv}$ respectively) using a cryptosystem such as RSA. The client

server; but only a single packet will be reflected for every packet the attacker sends, limiting the damage per unit work by the attacker.

then sends a request to the PV of the form

$$\{K^c_{pub}, d_c\}$$

where d_c is the duration for which the client requests that the PC be valid. The PV replies with the PC:

$$PC = \{K^c_{pub}, a_c, t, d\}_{K^{pv}_{priv}}.$$

Here a_c is the address of the client, t is the time when the PC becomes valid (current time), and d is the duration for which the PC is valid. The PV sets d to the minimum of d_c and the PV's internal maximum time, for example, 1 day (that is, the client only needs to contact the PV once per day). Once the client has a current PC for its present location, it can contact a server using the ASAP protocol and include the PC in its request to bypass the 3WH. To do this, the client begins by constructing a **request certificate (RC)** encrypted with its private key:

$$RC = \{hash(m_{net}, m_{trans}, data), t_{req}\}_{K^c_{priv}}.$$

Here $hash$ is a secure hash function, m_{net} is the network-layer metadata (source and destination IP address, protocol number), m_{trans} is the transport-layer metadata for the connection (source and destination port, initial sequence number), t_{req} is the time the client sent the request, and $data$ is the application-level data (such as an HTTP request). The RC makes it more difficult for adversaries (such as malicious web servers) to replay a connection request or use the PC for requests not initiated by the client.

The client then opens a transport connection to the server with a message of the form:

$$m_{net}, m_{trans}, PC, RC, data.$$

Upon receipt, the server verifies validity of the request. The server must already know the public key of each PV that it trusts. It determines whether the PC is valid by checking that it decrypts correctly, the current time lies within $[t, t+d]$, and a_c matches the source address. If so, it uses the client's public key K^c_{pub} from PC to check that RC decrypts correctly, the hash value in RC matches $hash(m_{net}, m_{trans}, data)$, and the time t_{req} is recent, e.g., within the last 5 minutes. (This timeout only needs to be long enough to cover most clock inaccuracy, and packet transit time.) If all these tests pass, then the request is accepted and the connection proceeds as in TCP after the 3WH: $data$ is passed to the application, and an application-level response (e.g., a web page) may be sent immediately to the client. Thus, the client can receive results within a single RTT.

Security properties: (i) Even if the attacker is able to eavesdrop on the RC and PC, it can only replay existing client requests for an amount of time limited by the timeout. (ii) If the attacker is able to take over the IP address owned by a client (e.g., by hijacking a prefix or compromising a router along the path), it can contact the PV and generate the RC itself. To mitigate this, we can run multiple PVs, and require clients to authenticate with all of them.

2.2 Fast name resolution

To reduce delay, we encode the connection information (e.g., initial sequence number, the source IP address and port, the PC and RC and data request) into the hostname field of the DNS request. For example, if the client is looking up `www.xyz.com`, it would generate a DNS request for

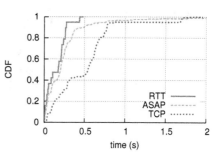

Figure 2: *CDF of total delay to download a 1K-byte file.*

`CI.www.xyz.com` where CI is the connection information. Since CI is unique, the local DNS will route the DNS request to the authoritative nameserver which supports ASAP. The ADNS will then strip off the CI and forward it to the server. It will also return an A record mapping `CI.www.xyz.com` to the web server's IP address. However, since CI is unique, even though the local nameserver caches this A record, it will never be used by the other ASAP queries even if they are looking up the same host. To address this, thereby reducing the workload of the ADNS, in addition to the ASAP query, we let the client send a normal DNS query (Fig. 1) which will cause the name to be cached at the local nameserver. Using the IP address result, the client then sends a transport connection request directly to the server.

3. EVALUATION

We evaluate our implementation of ASAP through a deployment on PlanetLab (Fig. 2). Overall, ASAP reduces transmission time by between one and two round trip times (depending on DNS caching and location), significantly reducing latency of short web traffic.

4. RELATED WORK

T/TCP [1], an extension of TCP, bypasses the 3WHS and truncates TIME-WAIT State to reduce latency, but is vulnerable to malicious attacks [4]. Recently, Google proposed the TCP Fast Open (TCPFO) [3] extension that allows hosts to exchange data during the 3WHS. However, TCPFO only accelerates connections to a single server after the client has connected to that server once, while ASAP clients only need to contact PV once to get a valid certificate to accelarate connections to all the servers that trust the PV. DEW [5] explores ways by which a variety of Web requests and responses could be piggybacked on DNS messages, but requires modifications on both LDNSs and ADNSs.

5. REFERENCES

[1] R. Braden. T/TCP - TCP extensions for transactions, functional specification. 1994.
[2] J. Brutlag. Speed matters for Google web search, June 2009. http://code.google.com/speed/files/delayexp.pdf.
[3] Y. Cheng. TCP Fast Open. Unpublished work in progress (IETF Informational), March 2011.
[4] C. Hannum. Security problems associated with T/TCP. Unpublished work in progress (IETF Informational), September 1996.
[5] B. Krishnamurthy, R. Liston, and M. Rabinovich. DEW: DNS-enhanced web for faster content delivery. May 2003.
[6] V. Paxson. An analysis of using reflectors for distributed denial-of-service attacks. *ACM SIGCOMM Computer Communications Review*, July 2001.

What Can Free Money Tell Us on the Virtual Black Market?

Kyungmoon Woo
Seoul National University
kwoo@popeye.snu.ac.kr

Hyukmin Kwon
Korea University
hack@korea.ac.kr

Hyun-chul Kim
Seoul National University
hyunchulk@gmail.com

Chong-kwon Kim
Seoul National University
ckim@snu.ac.kr

Huy Kang Kim
Korea University
cenda@korea.ac.kr

ABSTRACT

"Real money trading" or "Gold farming" refers to a set of illicit practices for gathering and distributing virtual goods in online games for real money. Unlike previous work, we use *network-wide economic interactions* among in-game characters as a lens to monitor, detect and identify gold farming networks. Our work is based on a set of real in-game trade activity logs collected for one month in year 2010 from the world's second largest MMORPG called AION (with 3.4 million subscribers). This is the first work that empirically (i) shows that "free money network" is a promising measure/approximation for detecting and characterizing gold farming networks, and (ii) measures the size of the free money net and in-game virtual economy in a large-scale MMORPG in terms of the cash flow.

Categories and Subject Descriptors

J.4 [**Computer Applications**]: Social and Behavioral Sciences

General Terms

Economics, Human Factors, Measurement, Security

Keywords

Online game security, Gold farming, Real money trading

1. INTRODUCTION

"Real money trading" or "Gold farming" refers to a set of illicit practices for gathering and distributing virtual goods in online games for real money [1]. During the last decade gold farming has become a vast enterprise (a best estimate suggests that in Asia, where most of the gold farmers dwell, more than 400,000 players spend their days stocking up on gold [2]). Gold farming industries have been grown up on the periphery of the virtual world of online games known as MMORPGs (Massively Multiplayer Online Role Playing Games) such as World of Warcraft, EverQuest, and AION.

One of the core components of the virtual world that helps to attract millions of gamers along with its fantastic settings of landscape, characters and creatures is a virtual economy. Originally, virtual goods (e.g., armor and weapons) and in-game currency are designed to be acquired only through the substantial time investments, typically

from several months to even years, thus their acquisition is definitely a main goal of gamers. Yet, these goods and currencies can also be sold to or obtained from other players via trade or exchange. Trade often leads gamers with limited time for play to rather purchase virtual capital (with real money) to enjoy more exciting challenges [1,3]. That is where the business model (i.e., black market) of Gold farmers has been established.

Gold farming has been considered malicious by both the game companies and the player communities [1,2] due to the following reasons: (i) While in-game economies are carefully designed in a way that virtual products serve as sinks to remove money from circulation, gold farmers and buyers inject currency into the economy which creates hyper-inflationary pressure, unintended arbitrage opportunities, and other perverse incentives for market agents [1]. (ii) Farmers affect other players' experiences in a disturbing, distracting, malicious, and even illegal way, by employing anti-social computer scripts (i.e., bots) to automate the farming process, as well as often engaging in the theft of account, ID, and financial information from their customers [4]. (iii) Farming explicitly and unfairly violates the rules of play and upsets the meritocratic and fantasy-based nature of the games thus potentially driving legitimate players away [1]. For these reasons, game companies have tried to detect and ban farming accounts.

So far, the existing methods for combating gold farmers have mostly focused on distinguishing individual, automated game bots from human players using data mining techniques, Turing test based human interactive proofs (HIPs) (e.g., CAPTCHA), and human observational proofs (HOPs) [5]. These methods differentiate bots from human players by their in-game behavioral biometrics or responses to interactive (often intrusive to users) tests. The arms race between game vendors and bot developers has given birth to much more elusive and human-like bots [6] capable of avoiding and neutralizing even state-of-the art detection techniques.

Unlike previous defense methods mostly focused on individual bot behavior, we investigate *network-wide economic interactions* among in-game characters to detect and identify gold farming networks as a whole, not individual automated bots comprising (only) a part of those networks. In particular, as an initial step pursuing that direction we first show empirically that "free money network" is a light-weight, promising vehicle for detecting

(a) Goods trading network   (b) Free money net only

Figure 1: AION Trade Networks.

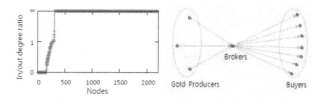

(a) In/out degree ratios   (b) A typical 3-tier shape

Figure 2: In/out degree ratios and a typical 3-tier shape.

and characterizing gold farmers. We also measure the size of the free money network as well as in-game virtual economy in terms of the cash flow based on a vast amount of real data. We use a set of (anonymized) in-game trade activity logs of AION, collected for one month from one of 41 independent yet identical game worlds (servers) in 2010.

2. PRELIMINARY RESULTS

"Trade" in MMORPGs means bartering or buying goods with in-game money. Our conjecture is that *free money* trade activities which only give in-game money without getting any goods/items in return are likely to be either free gifts among friends or somehow related with real money trading of gold farmers. Fig. 1(a) visualizes all the trade activities logged in our dataset where nodes and edges represent characters and trade activities among them, respectively. Fig. 1(b) is a subgraph of 1(a) consists of free gift edges and related nodes only. Note that in the AION community there are two character tribes (heavenly vs. diabolic) who cannot communicate with each other, thus each tribe forms its own trade clusters.

To our surprise, while the free money network involves with only 9.7% (2,884/29,612) and 1.9% (4,719/252,859) of the nodes and edges (i.e., transactions) in the whole trade network, it takes account of 62.2% of the total transaction money during the observed period ($62,526 out of total $100,593 when converted to USD). We also observe that Fig. 1(b), in particular the two central clusters, clearly unveils nodes whose interaction graphs look very similar to the typical cone-shaped N-to-1 and/or 1-to-N interaction patterns of gold farmers [1] (see Fig. 2(b)). Gold farming networks mainly consists of (i) gold producers who repeatedly send free money to only a small number of designated players (i.e., brokers), (ii) brokers who collect lots of free money from many gold producers and then transfer them to buyers at no charge back, and (iii) a lot of buyers receiving free money from the brokers. This 3-tier structure shown in Fig. 2(b) naturally comes from the survival strategy of gold farmers. Brokers intervene between gold producers and buyers to maximize farming efficiency and to establish the secrecy of their network. Indirect transactions also hide the identities of high-level gold producers/bots that are, raised with substantial investments of time, the most valuable assets for gold farmers.

Fig. 2(a) plots the distribution of the ratio of the number of incoming edges to that of outgoing edges for the 2,205 nodes forming the two larger central clusters in Fig. 1(b). Interestingly, we observe that 97.1% of all the nodes have either incoming or outgoing edges only. 10.8% and 86.3% of the nodes have either outgoing or incoming edges only, respectively. These uni-directional edges are the typical network-wide interaction patterns of gold producers and buyers shown in Fig. 2(b). The remaining 2.9% of the nodes mostly have a lot more number of outgoing edges (to buyers) than incoming edges (from producers), which is also the typical interaction pattern of gold brokers.

To summarize, we have found that (i) 62.2% of the total in-game cash flow was of free money, and (ii) 93.4% of the free money is highly likely to be related/connected with real money trading, i.e., virtual black market. Our current on-going work includes: (1) quantifying accuracy of the proposed approach based on the ground truth information (e.g., banned accounts), (2) finding out how many new gold farmers our approach can detect hitherto impossible, (3) further in-depth characterization of gold farmer networks, expanding our focus onto more diverse in-game social relationships as well, and (4) comparison of the revealed characteristics with those of other in-game normal users as well as real-world crime networks like drug trafficking [1] or money laundering ones.

3. ACKNOWLEDGMENTS

This work was supported by NAP of Korea Research Council of Fundamental Science and Technology and the ITRC support program (NIPA-2011-C1090-1111-0004) of MKE/NIPA.

4. REFERENCES

[1] B. Keegan *et al.*, "Dark Gold: Statistical Properties of Clandestine Networks in Massively Multiplayer Online Games," IEEE SocialCom, 2010.

[2] R. Heeks, "Real Money from Virtual Worlds," Scientific American, 302(1), Jan. 2010.

[3] E. Castronova, Synthetic Worlds: The Business and Culture of Online Games, University of Chicago Press, 2005.

[4] G. Lastowka, "ID theft, RMT, & Lineage," TerraNova, 2006; http://terranova.blogs.com/terra_nova/2006/07/id_theft_rmt_nc.html\

[5] S. Gianvecchio *et al.*, "Battle of Botcraft: Fighting Bots in Online Games with Human Observational Proofs," ACM CCS, 2009.

[6] S. Hill, MMO Subscriber Populations, http://www.brighthub.com/video-games/mmo/articles/ 35992.aspx

LoKI: Location-based PKI for Social Networks

Randy Baden
University of Maryland
randofu@cs.umd.edu
http://www.cs.umd.edu/~randofu/loki

Categories and Subject Descriptors

C.2.0 [**Computer Communications Networks**]: General—*Data communications*; C.2.1 [**Computer Communications Networks**]: Network Architecture and Design—*Wireless communication*; C.2.4 [**Computer Communications Networks**]: Distributed Systems—*Client/server, Distributed applications*; C.5.3 [**Computer System Implementation**]: Microcomputers—*Portable devices (e.g., laptops, personal digital assistants)*; E.3 [**Data Encryption**]: [Public key cryptosystems]

General Terms

Security, Design, Performance

Keywords

Public Key Infrastructure, Online Social Networks, Location, Mobility

1. INTRODUCTION

The existence of a public key infrastructure (PKI) is a linchpin of many systems that provide security, privacy, or accountability [2, 3]. For many systems, there are adequate solutions to providing a PKI that, while never perfect, are resilient to attack. Certificate authorities (CA) are a common solution, but they have limitations. Obviously, the CA must be trusted, a reasonable assumption in many systems, especially centralized ones. Less obviously, the CA must be able to independently verify the identities of those principals that the CA certifies.

For this reason, a trusted CA is at best an insufficient solution to the PKI problem for a decentralized online social network (OSN). The problem is not one of trustworthiness; a CA such as Verisign could be just as scrupulous and well-intentioned whether they certify web sites or people. The problem is a practical one: it would require prohibitively many resources for a central authority to independently verify every social identity in the system.

This problem is not new, but the changing landscape of how users interact with social networks — and with each other — offers opportunities for new, complementary solutions. The PGP web-of-trust is a good starting point, effectively making each user her own certificate authority. This matches the notion of a user being in charge of her own privacy and security within her *domain* of the social network, a primary guiding principal in

decentralized OSNs. The out-of-band exchange of keys, however, has proven too onerous for typical users [7]. We therefore choose to design techniques that users are able to more readily employ based on how users interact with each other in modern settings.

Our main contribution is a system, LoKI, in which we use the ubiquity of mobile devices to provide users with a new method for verifying identities that does not require immediate user interaction. Concretely, we propose collecting shared secrets from nearby mobile devices over the course of typical mobile activity, then using these shared secrets post-hoc to perform identity verification based on user recollection of when real-world meetings occurred. We estimate the frequency of real-world meetings among social network users with a data set of interactions recorded by Foursquare, Facebook, and Twitter. We evaluate the technical constraints of collecting and storing shared secrets in terms of storage space and power consumption based on the frequency of mobile device encounters. Finally, we provide a solution to allow peer-to-peer bluetooth communication on mobile devices when neither device is able to enter discoverable mode, such as in a background service on an Android phone that has not been rooted. We believe that this problem of peer-to-peer rendezvous on typical mobile devices is an important consideration that has heretofore gone unrecognized in research on mobile peer-to-peer systems.

2. DESIGN OVERVIEW

We design LoKI with one goal in mind: to transform real-world social interactions into secure online public key exchanges. We realize this goal using shared secret data frequently exchanged between proximal devices, where an exchange of secret data represents a real-world meeting. This secret data can later be used to establish a secure channel based on the user's recollection of when real-world meetings occurred [1]. This basic design goal requires proximal devices to be able to communicate privately without user intervention; though this seems like a simple requirement, a number of practical constraints make this non-trivial in practice.

2.1 Assumptions and Constraints

We assume that two users who wish to be friends on an OSN meet in person while in possession of their mobile devices; though not every pair of OSN friends will fall under this assumption, we will show that many do. We also assume that these devices have wifi and bluetooth capabilities along with some means of accessing the Internet. We assume that every user runs our key exchange application at all times, so we restrict the key exchange application to only be able to access features available to non-

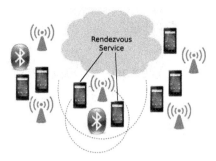

Figure 1: Non-rooted androids cannot observe each other, but they can observe similar nearby wifi access points and discoverable bluetooth devices to detect proximity with the help of a rendezvous service.

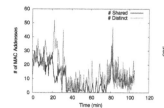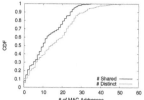

Figure 2: The number of common and distinct MAC addresses (wifi and bluetooth) visible from two colocated Motorola Droids while walking through the University of Maryland campus.

rooted devices. Otherwise, a user would have to void the warranty on the device.

Bluetooth's range of about 10 meters is a physical means of verifying locality, making bluetooth the intuitive communication channel for our purposes. If two devices are able to communicate via bluetooth, it most likely means that the device's users are near each other; this may indicate social interaction between the users that is reflected in the social graph in an OSN. Bluetooth is also an appealing choice because it requires less power than alternative communication technologies.

We focus on the case of "disengaged" users[1], i.e., users who do not actively establish OSN friendships during a real-world meeting, but later seek to establish the OSN friendship when they have left the presence of the other user. In particular, it is not possible to put an android device into bluetooth discoverable mode without periodically requesting permission from the user. However, bluetooth communication is still possible as long as once of the devices can learn the other device's bluetooth MAC address.

2.2 Rendezvous

We considered many strategies for advertising bluetooth MAC addresses using broadcast or multicast over either bluetooth or wifi. None of these solutions were viable because there is no way to access broadcast packets from non-rooted phones. Our ultimate solution relies on a third-party rendezvous service, analogous to the role of a STUN server in NAT hole-punching.

Given a request from a client containing spatiotemporal data and information about the client's bluetooth MAC address, the rendezvous service matches that data with other requests and return the data necessary to construct nearby users' bluetooth MAC addresses. Ideally, another user should only learn the user's MAC address if that user is sufficiently close, i.e., within bluetooth range.

Narayanan et al. [5] describe a set of possible location tags that can be used to confirm device location. Unlike most of their suggestions, the list of visible wifi access point MAC addresses and the list of discoverable bluetooth device MAC addresses are both available to non-rooted phones. Our setting is depicted in Figure 1. Visible MAC addresses provide a way to match based on location, though these values do not depend on time, so an attacker who visits a location once will be able to forever after check to see which devices are in that location. We believe it may be possible to extend the android API to report information

about the timestamps from beacon frames during a wifi scan to incorporate temporal dependence into the rendezvous service.

Complicating matters further, two colocated devices have remarkably different views of visible MAC addresses, as shown in Figure 2. We therefore consider two phones to be likely colocated during epoch t if they agree on some threshold k of visible MAC addresses.

We now describe what the clients communicate to the rendezvous service. First, if the client does not already know the current (publicly known) epoch t, it requests it from the rendezvous service. Let B be the client's bluetooth MAC address. Let $H(\cdot)$ be a one-way hash function, $Enc(\cdot, K)$ be a symmetric encryption function using key K, and let $S(\cdot)$ be a function that computes a secret share according to Shamir's secret sharing [6]. For each visible MAC address M, the client computes and transmits:

- The location tag: $H(M\|t)$
- The secret share: $Enc(S(B, M\|t, k), M\|t)$

The location tags can be used by the rendezvous service to match users who share at least k visible MAC addresses through set intersection. The secret shares can be decrypted and combined to reconstruct B by anyone who knows at least k matching visible MAC addresses, i.e., someone present at the location.

Once one of the pair of devices has B, it can establish an insecure channel and perform Diffie-Hellman key exchange to establish a secure channel over which a secret can be agreed upon. These agreed-upon secrets can thereafter be used to perform SPEKE [4] and exchange public keys with the certainty that the public key belongs to a user who was present at the times that the secrets were collected.

Since an attacker cannot selectively block bluetooth transmissions, the Diffie-Helman exchange is not vulnerable to a classical man-in-the-middle attack, though it can be vulnerable to impersonation; the attacker cannot hide the honest user, but she can create an indistinguishable duplicate. One defense against this attack is to require secrets from multiple meeting times, enough to ensure that no other user could be present at every meeting.

3. REFERENCES

[1] R. Baden, N. Spring, and B. Bhattacharjee. Identifying close friends on the internet. In *HotNets*, 2009.
[2] R. Baden, *et al*. Persona: An online social network with user-defined privacy. In *SIGCOMM*, 2009.
[3] A. Haeberlen, P. Kouznetsov, and P. Druschel. Peerreview: practical accountability for distributed systems. In *SOSP*, 2007.
[4] D. P. Jablon. Strong password-only authenticated key exchange. *SIGCOMM CCR*, 1996.
[5] A. Narayanan, *et al*. Location privacy via private proximity testing. In *NDSS*, 2011.
[6] A. Shamir. How to share a secret. *Commun. ACM*, 1979.
[7] A. Whitten, J. D. Tygar, A. Whitten, and J. D. Tygar. Usability of security: A case study. Tech. rep., CMU, 1998.

---

[1]The case of engaged users requires trivial technical solutions, though it remains part of the complete OSN PKI bootstrapping solution.

"Roto-Rooting" your Router:

Solution against New Potential DoS Attacks on Modern Routers

Danai Chasaki
Department of Electrical and Computer Engineering
University of Massachusetts, Amherst, MA, USA
{dchasaki}@ecs.umass.edu

ABSTRACT

Our work presents the first practical example of an entirely new class of network attacks – attacks that target the network infrastructure. Modern routers use general purpose programmable processors, and the software used for packet processing on these systems is potentially vulnerable to remote exploits. We describe a specific attack that can launch a devastating denial-of-service attack by sending just a single packet. We also show that there are effective defense techniques, based on processor monitoring, that can help in detecting and avoiding such attacks.

Categories and Subject Descriptors

C.2.6 [**Computer-Communication Networks**]: Internetworking—*Routers*; C.2.0 [**Computer-Communication Networks**]: General—*Security and protection*

General Terms

Design, Performance, Security

1. INTRODUCTION

Modern routers are becoming vulnerable to new attacks because of the technology shift towards programmable infrastructure [3]. Most service provider core routers contain programmable multi-core architectures, e.g. Cisco Carrier Routing Systems (CRS-1, CRS-3) and Juniper's T series. These routers are equipped with functionality beyond simple packet forwarding, ranging from load balancing to application security, access control, e.g. F5's BIG-IP products, where these services are available on a single device. While a lot of attention has been given to end system security, very little work has addressed security concerns in the network infrastructure itself. In our work, we consider the data plane of the network where modern routers are now exposed to vulnerabilities like any other software-based system.

We have shown that a single cleverly crafted malicious packet can change the protocol that runs on the processor of the router, and launches a denial-of-service attack [2]. All bandwidth of the outgoing link on the router is absorbed, and the attack propagates to all vulnerable downstream routers. An overview of such an attack example is illustrated in Figure 1. If we think of the impact of "clogging" a series of core routers with "attack" packets causing

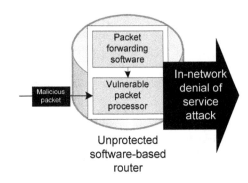

Figure 1: Example of in-network attack.

denial of service, we realize the importance of protecting them. One could think of tackling the problem using a virus scanner or an intrusion prevention mechanism. However, the multi-processor systems-on-chip that lie inside modern routers have relatively small amount of available resources. They cannot support an operating system and cannot afford the computationally heavy security solutions that are traditionally used to protect end systems. More importantly, any software based solution is not fast enough for our problem. A single packet's processing cycle lasts for only a few microseconds, which means that if the attack is launched by only one packet, its effects will be visible instantaneously. The whole system will "clog" before the intrusion detection scheme is able to detect the attack.

Our router "roto-rooting" technique is a hardware based solution adapted from embedded systems security literature. It monitors the router's processor in real time, and once deviation from normal behavior is detected, the processor is reset and the router is brought back to correct operation. This happens within 6 instruction cycles (∼100 ns), which is a quick enough response to detect and recover from the DoS attack. Our monitoring system is a light-weight method that does not slow down the system and consumes a small amount of resources.

2. ATTACK DEMONSTRATION

Routers perform a variety of protocol processing operations (IP forwarding, intrusion detection, tunneling etc.). While we don't have access to confidential network development source code, we can safely assume that some protocol operations will require adding a header to a packet. Thus, the kind of attack we describe can be realized in any network protocol that contains hidden vulnerabilities.

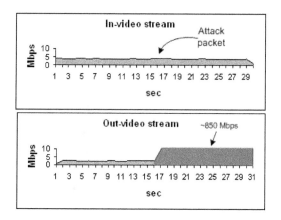

Figure 2: Traffic Rates at Input Port and Output Port of Vulnerable Router. Benign video traffic is shown in green, attack traffic is shown in red.

Here, we demonstrate that vulnerabilities in software-based routers are not only hypothetical, but can occur in common protocol processing code. For the discussion of our attack, we picked the congestion management (CM) protocol, which uses a custom protocol header that is inserted between the IP header and the UDP header. A security aware programmer would perform a check on the packet's total size, before shifting the UDP datagram and inserting the new header into the original packet. Since the total length field of the UDP header is a 16-bit field, the programmer could choose to assign the packet length to a 'unsigned short' integer type, so that the embedded processor's limited resources are not wasted. That is the part of the protocol that contains an integer overflow vulnerability.

The vulnerability does not exhibit problematic behavior for most "normal" packets that are short enough to accommodate the new CM header within the maximum IP packet length. However, if an attacker sends a packet with malformed UDP length field (e.g. 65532), the size check passes even though it should not. The, a large number of bytes is copied into the new packet buffer, which is designed to hold data up to the maximum datagram size. This last step has resulted in the notorious buffer overflow attack, which will overwrite the processor's stack, and finally overwrite the return address of the program. Thereby, the attacker can make the program jump to malicious code that is carried inside the packet payload. In our attack, we insert a few instructions of assembly code into the payload, which repeatedly broadcast the same attack packet in an infinite loop.

We have implemented our attack on the Click modular router and on a custom packet processor [1] based on the NetFPGA platform. We send video traffic into a router that implements the CM header insertion routine, which exhibits the integer overflow vulnerability. Figure 2 shows our results. Benign traffic is sent and the router forwards it as expected until a single attack packet is injected into the incoming traffic. Since the attack packet triggers an infinite loop of retransmitting itself, all output traffic consists of attack traffic. Only one packet of this type has caused a denial-of-service attack that jams the router's outgoing link at full data rate.

3. DEFENSE MECHANISM

To defend against this type of attack on the packet processing systems of routers, we proposed a secure packet processor design [1]. We briefly describe the operation here and demonstrate that it can defend against the attack we describe.

It uses a fine-grained hardware monitor to track the instruction-level operations of the packet processor. These operations are compared to a reference model of operation that has been obtained through offline analysis of the processor's binary file. Under normal conditions, the operations reported by the processor match the offline model. If an attack occurs, the behavior of the processor changes in an unexpected way (e.g., executes malicious code instead of executing the functions that it was programmed for) and the executed operations no longer match the reference model. The secure packet processor can detect this condition, drop the offending packet, and initiate a recovery process that resets the processor core and allows the normal operation to resume.

We have implemented this type of monitor on the same custom processor used for the experiments shown in Figure 2. The security monitor runs in parallel to the packet processor, and is designed to use four pipeline stages. Thanks to the tight hardware architecture, the prototype successfully detects the example attack, halts the processor, drops the packet, and restores the system within 6 instruction cycles. This small recovery time allows our router to operate at full data rate even when under attack. The overhead for adding a monitoring system to the packet processor is very small (0.8% increase on slice LUTs and 5.6% on memory elements).

Since the security monitoring performance results on a single core processor are encouraging, we are planning to extend this work to highly parallel routing systems. The ultimate goal is to have a 16-core version of the secure packet processor running on a development board, and evaluate its throughput performance and scalability. The challenges of a design where security monitors run in parallel to each core are a) how to share programs between the cores, and b) how to share the offline models of the programs between the monitors.

Acknowledgements

This material is based upon work supported by the National Science Foundation under Grant No. CCF-0952524.

4. REFERENCES

[1] CHASAKI, D., AND WOLF, T. Design of a secure packet processor. In *Proc. of ACM/IEEE Symposium on Architectures for Networking and Communication Systems (ANCS)* (La Jolla, CA, Oct. 2010).

[2] CHASAKI, DANAI, W. Q., AND WOLF, T. Attacks on network infrastructure. In *Proc. of IEEE International Conference on Computer Communications and Networks (ICCCN)* (Maui, HI, Aug. 2011).

[3] CUI, A., SONG, Y., PRABHU, P. V., AND STOLFO, S. J. Brave new world: Pervasive insecurity of embedded network devices. In *Proc. of 12th International Symposium on Recent Advances in Intrusion Detection (RAID)* (Saint-Malo, France, Sept. 2009).

Limiting Large-scale Crawls of Social Networking Sites

Mainack Mondal
MPI-SWS
mainack@mpi-sws.org

Bimal Viswanath
MPI-SWS
bviswana@mpi-sws.org

Allen Clement
MPI-SWS
aclement@mpi-sws.org

Peter Druschel
MPI-SWS
druschel@mpi-sws.org

Krishna P. Gummadi
MPI-SWS
gummadi@mpi-sws.org

Alan Mislove
Northeastern University
amislove@ccs.neu.edu

Ansley Post
MPI-SWS
abpost@mpi-sws.org

ABSTRACT

Online social networking sites (OSNs) like Facebook and Orkut contain personal data of millions of users. Many OSNs view this data as a valuable asset that is at the core of their business model. Both OSN users and OSNs have strong incentives to restrict large scale crawls of this data. OSN users want to protect their privacy and OSNs their business interest. Traditional defenses against crawlers involve rate-limiting browsing activity per user account. These defense schemes, however, are vulnerable to Sybil attacks, where a crawler creates a large number of fake user accounts. In this paper, we propose Genie, a system that can be deployed by OSN operators to defend against Sybil crawlers. Genie is based on a simple yet powerful insight: *the social network itself can be leveraged to defend against Sybil crawlers*. We first present Genie's design and then discuss how Genie can limit crawlers while allowing browsing of user profiles by normal users.

General Terms

Security, Design, Algorithms

Categories and Subject Descriptors

C.2.0 [**Computer-Communication Networks**]: General—*Security and protection*

Keywords

Sybil attacks, social networks, network-based Sybil defense

1. INTRODUCTION

Online social networking sites (OSNs), such as Facebook, Twitter, and Orkut, contain data about millions of users. These OSNs allow users to browse the profile of other users in the network, making it easy for users to connect, communicate and share content. This core functionality of OSNs, however, can be exploited by crawlers to aggregate data about large numbers of OSN users for re-publication [1] or other more nefarious purposes [2] that violate users' privacy.

Crawlers present a significant problem not only for OSN users but also for OSN site operators. First, many OSNs view the user data as a valuable asset that could be leveraged to generate revenue in the future, for example, via targeted advertisements. So OSNs have an incentive to prevent third party crawlers from accessing their data. Second, while OSN operators can ensure that data is used according to privacy policies specified on their sites, they cannot make any guarantees about how crawlers will use that data. A third party that crawls an OSN can do anything with that data (e.g. re-publish the data or infer private information [2]). Yet, if the third party crawler does something nefarious, the OSN operator is likely to be held responsible, at least in the court of public opinion. For example, Facebook was widely blamed in the popular press for allowing a crawler to gather public profiles of a large number of users [1].

Today OSN operators employ various rate-limiting techniques to restrict a crawler's ability to scrape the network. These techniques typically rely on limiting the number of user profiles a single user account or IP address can view in a given period of time [4]. Unfortunately, these schemes can be easily circumvented by a Sybil attack, in which the crawler creates a large number of fake user accounts and/or hires a botnet to gain access to multiple IP addresses.

In this work, we propose Genie, a system that OSN operators can deploy to limit Sybil crawlers. Genie relies on a key assumption about OSNs, namely, that *it would be hard for crawlers to establish an arbitrarily large number of links to users in an OSN*. Intuitively, this assumption is based on the observation that forming a new link between two users requires a certain amount of familiarity between the users involved. Genie leverages this insight to limit large scale crawls. It ties the ability of a user to crawl the OSN to the number of links she establishes with the rest of the network.

2. GENIE DESIGN

At its core, Genie models the trust between nodes in a social network as a credit network [3] and leverages this network to ensure crawlers cannot collect additional information by creating many identities. Specifically, Genie maps the nodes and links in the OSN to nodes and edges in a credit network. Each edge in the credit network is assigned some initial credit that is refreshed periodically. User A is allowed to view the profile of user B only if there exists a path in the credit network that connects the two users and has sufficient

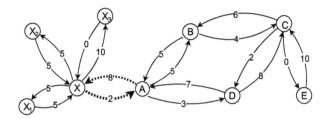

Figure 1: Genie represents the social network as a directed graph with available credit on the links as shown above. X is a crawler with Sybil identities (X_1, X_2, X_3). **The links between crawlers and the rest of the network are shown with bold dotted lines.**

credit on each link along the path. If no such path exists, then user A is blocked from browsing the data of user B.

Figure 1 illustrates how Genie represents the social network as a credit network consisting of directed links and leverages the credit network to determine which profile visits are allowed. For example, in the figure, Genie allows user A to visit the profile for user C because there exists a directed path from A to C with every edge on the path having a credit value of at least one. Once A visits C's profile, the credit on each directed edge in the selected path is decremented by one. User A, on the other hand, is not allowed to visit the profile for user E because there is no path from A to E in which all edges have sufficient credit to support the profile visit.

In the above example, we focussed on a pricing model that deducts one unit of credit from each edge along the path from A to C. We note, however, that there exist different pricing models that bound the ability of users to browse other users' profiles to different extents. While the pricing model that best suits an OSN depends on the OSN's workload (i.e., users' browsing behavior) and the OSN's social graph, Genie ensures that the following property holds for any valid pricing scheme: *Given any cut through the social network graph, the rate of profile view requests between nodes on different sides of the cut is proportional to the number of edges in the cut.* Thus with Genie, the ability of a user to crawl the OSN is tied to and limited by the number of social links she establishes with the rest of the network. Coupled with the observation that it is hard for crawlers to establish arbitrarily large number of links to other OSN users, this suggests that, even when a crawler creates a large number of Sybil identities, her ability to crawl the network would be limited.

We illustrate this situation in Figure 1 where crawler X creates three Sybil identities: X_1, X_2 and X_3. However, these Sybil identities do not give the crawler any extra benefit since the available credit on the cut between the crawler nodes and the rest of the network remains the same. Thus the crawlers, having a limited number of links to the rest of the network, would be allowed to perform only a limited number of crawls.

While the basic operation of Genie is straightforward, there are a few obvious points of concern:
Does Genie restrict access to popular content? A side effect of deploying Genie is that it limits the total number of profile views (exposures) that a OSN user may receive to the amount of credit on all the incoming links to the user. We argue that such a restriction is often in the interests

of ordinary users, many of whom make their personal data accessible to the public, under the implicit (though incorrect) assumption that their data would not be viewed by the whole world. There is a subtle but important difference between data being *accessible* to the public at large and data being *viewed* by the public at large. Thus, we argue that the limit Genie imposes on the number of views a user's data might receive, even as the data is accessible to the public at large, might be a desirable side-effect.

On the other hand, certain users, such as politicians, celebrities, and marketeers, might not want the profile views that they receive to be limited by Genie. We would argue that these users would in any case have many friend links, which would naturally allow more views. A side-effect of this approach is that a celebrity would be able to crawl a large number of users. But it is hard to imagine a celebrity behaving like a Sybil crawler. Some of these celebrities may further desire that their profile could be viewed by everyone without any limits. OSN sites can accommodate such users by explicitly allowing them to keep some or all of their profile contents outside the Genie framework. Access to the content would not be moderated by Genie and the content would not be protected from aggregation by crawlers.
Does Genie introduce new DDoS attacks? If Genie is deployed it may be feasible for a group of OSN users to launch a DDoS attack against a specific user A or against a small group of users. They can visit user A's profile repeatedly, exhaust credit on A's incoming links, and thus, block further access to A's profile for everybody, including A's friends. Genie solves this problem by allowing user A to create a whitelist of users (e.g., all direct friends of A), who would be granted access to A's profile regardless of the availability of credit. This ensures that the user A's profile data is always available to her direct friends.

3. DEPLOYMENT CHALLENGES

The primary challenge that OSN operators will face when deploying Genie lies in managing liquidity (i.e., credits) in the network. The OSN must decide upon the pricing model, the amount of credit value that is initially assigned to the directed edges of the OSN, and the rate at which credit is refreshed. The credits should be managed such that it would allow normal user browsing activities, while limiting the crawler or data aggregator activities. If an OSN assigns too much credit, it would allow too much of the undesired crawling activity. But, if it assigns too little then it could affect normal browsing activities of users.

We are currently investigating methods to determine suitable credit values by analyzing past user behavior. We are experimenting with different settings and have some promising preliminary results. We are still in the process of completing a thorough evaluation of the system. For more details, please refer to `www.mpi-sws.org/~mainack/genie/`

4. REFERENCES

[1] `http://tcrn.ch/9JvvmU`.
[2] `http://bit.ly/jlarLI`.
[3] D. DeFigueiredo and E. T. Barr. Trustdavis: A non-exploitable online reputation system. In *CEC'05*.
[4] T. Stein, E. Chen, and K. Mangla. Facebook Immune System. In *SNS'11*.

Designing a Testbed for Large-scale Distributed Systems

Christof Leng   Max Lehn[*]   Robert Rehner[†]   Alejandro Buchmann
Databases and Distributed Systems
TU Darmstadt, Germany
{cleng,mlehn,rehner,buchmann}@dvs.tu-darmstadt.de

ABSTRACT

Different evaluation methods for distributed systems like prototyping, simulation and emulation have different trade-offs. We present a testbed for Internet applications that supports real-network prototypes and multiple simulators with unchanged application code. To ensure maximum portability between runtimes, a compact but flexible system interface is defined.

Categories and Subject Descriptors

C.2.4 [**Distributed Systems**]: Distributed Applications; I.6.8 [**Simulation and Modeling**]: Discrete Event

General Terms

Design, Experimentation, Performance

1. MOTIVATION

Evaluation of prototypes for distributed systems is challenging. A few hundred nodes can be deployed on the Internet with PlanetLab [9], but it is not easy to get repeatable results when using a shared and public infrastructure like the Internet. Emulation testbeds like Emulab [4] are more controllable, but are expensive to acquire and maintain. Packet simulators like ns-3 [3] can run hundreds of nodes on commodity hardware and still give a good approximation of real networks, but become slow if scaled up to larger networks.

In research areas that deal with extremely large networks like peer-to-peer systems or massively multiplayer online games (MMOG) overlay simulators like PlanetSim [2] or ProtoPeer [1] have become very popular. By providing high-level APIs and a rather abstract network model they scale to many thousands of nodes. The downside is that the abstraction leads to reduced realism and the specialization makes it hard or impossible to implement anything beyond peer-to-peer systems. Additionally, most overlay simulators are implemented in Java, rendering them practically useless for applications written in native code (e.g. typical computer games).

---

[*]Supported by the DFG Research Group 733, Quality in Peer-to-Peer Systems (QuaP2P).

[†]Supported by the DFG Research Training Group 1343, Topology of Technology.

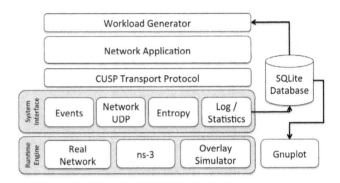

Figure 1: Testbed overview

It seems desirable to combine the advantages of several of the described approaches. On the other hand maintaining several independent implementations of a research prototype would be wasteful. ProtoPeer can be used to generate stand-alone applications for real networks, but only provides an overlay simulator. In our approach we define a system interface that can be used for real networks, low-level, and high-level simulators.

The identification of a common interface that works for all of these scenarios is a useful insight by itself, but our custom high-level simulator provides useful techniques for debugging complex large-scale systems. The system (Figure 1) consists of multiple runtimes which implement the system interface and applications which build on the system interface and (optionally) the CUSP transport protocol [11]. A workload module is used to generate application load. In a simulation the workload and scenario definitions are read from a central database and simulator output is written to the same database.

We have already used the testbed to implement CUSP demo applications [11], BubbleStorm [10], pSense [8], Kademlia [7], and the Planet PI4 online game [6]. The system is implemented in StandardML and provides language bindings to Java and C/C++.

In order to use the testbed environment an application developer must follow a few simple rules. Firstly, the system interface must be used exclusively for the offered functionality and most not be circumvented (e.g. by using the native network socket interface). This ensures that all relevant calls can be redirected to the current runtime engine. Secondly, the application must be written in an event-driven, asynchronous fashion. This enables the simulator engines to run many nodes in parallel without timing conflicts. Although such restrictions have to be considered when porting an existing application to the testbed, porting the non-trivial Planet PI4 game was surprisingly easy.

2. SYSTEM INTERFACE

The system interface consists of four modules: scheduling of events, networking, entropy, and output. An application using the interface must be written in an event-driven fashion in order to be executed by the simulator.

Event scheduling is responsible for scheduling new events and executing them on time. The interface also supports UNIX signals which can be used to trigger application handlers for workload or simulator events (e.g. node shutdown) without breaking the abstraction.

The networking interface is an asynchronous UDP networking interface. It also includes an opaque network address structure. This allows for a relatively smooth transition path from IPv4 to IPv6 addresses.

The entropy interface provides random numbers to the application for cryptographic or stochastic operations. In the real-network it is implemented using operation system means such as /dev/random. In a simulation it provides pseudo random numbers from the simulator's random number generator and thus ensures repeatability of the experiments.

The output interface is used for logging and statistics. The log interface can write short messages to a logging facility. The statistics interface can monitor performance metrics and system parameters measured by the application. In a simulation the output data is written to the scenario database whereas in the real network log files or standard output can be used.

Not strictly a part of the system interface, but being a module shared between many applications, is the CUSP transport protocol. It provides reliable in-order message streams for applications that require more than UDP. Moving the transport protocol implementation out of the runtime has made the system interface much easier to port, since it reduces not only the interface complexity but also the implementation complexity of the runtime (i.e. simulator) itself.

This collection of interfaces has proven to be sufficient for the networking applications we have worked with so far. Nonetheless we consider adding a data storage interface to improve the support for applications that store persistent data between sessions.

3. RUNTIME ENGINES

We currently support three runtime engines: real network, ns-3 [3], and our own overlay simulator. The real-network mode connects the application more or less directly with the operating system. With ns-3 we support a sophisticated and widespread packet-level simulator which can be used to validate results from our custom runtime engines. In day-to-day use we prefer our lightweight overlay simulator which is not as precise but more scalable and easier to configure.

4. OVERLAY SIMULATOR

Our custom simulator is completely event-based and builds on a lightweight end-to-end delay model [5]. It receives the node configuration, session times, and simulation workload from an SQLite database. The output of nodes is written to

the same database. This ensures that simulation results are always kept together with the scenario setup that produced the results. Gnuplot scripts can generate statistics plots directly from the database. The log table in the database can be used to track bugs not only between nodes but also forward and backward in time, a feature that step debuggers do not provide. This is especially useful if the conditions that lead to a bug have built up through time.

5. CONCLUSION

The testbed has proven to be a very useful tool for distributed system development and is in day-to-day use in our lab. Being constrained to an interface that also supports the real-network runtime helps to avoid unrealistic shortcuts in the application code that might have happened in a less strict simulation environment. The post-mortem debugging with the log database makes bug-hunting in distributed systems much easier.

6. REFERENCES

[1] W. Galuba, K. Aberer, Z. Despotovic, and W. Kellerer. ProtoPeer: a P2P toolkit bridging the gap between simulation and live deployement. In *Procs. of Simutools*, 2009.

[2] P. García, C. Pairot, R. Mondéjar, J. Pujol, H. Tejedor, and R. Rallo. Planetsim: A new overlay network simulation framework. In *Software Engineering and Middleware*, LNCS. Springer, 2005.

[3] T. R. Henderson, S. Roy, S. Floyd, and G. F. Riley. ns-3 project goals. In *Procs. of WNS2*, 2006.

[4] M. Hibler, R. Ricci, L. Stoller, J. Duerig, S. Guruprasad, T. Stack, K. Webb, and J. Lepreau. Large-scale virtualization in the Emulab network testbed. In *Procs. of USENIX*, 2008.

[5] S. Kaune, K. Pussep, A. Kovacevic, C. Leng, G. Tyson, and R. Steinmetz. Modelling the Internet Delay Space Based on Geographic Locations. In *Procs. of PDP*, 2009.

[6] M. Lehn, T. Triebel, C. Leng, A. Buchmann, and W. Effelsberg. Performance Evaluation of Peer-to-Peer Gaming Overlays. In *Procs. of P2P*, 2010.

[7] P. Maymounkov and D. Mazières. Kademlia: A Peer-to-Peer Information System Based on the XOR Metric. In *Procs. of IPTPS*, 2001.

[8] A. Schmieg, M. Stieler, S. Jeckel, P. Kabus, B. Kemme, and A. Buchmann. pSense - Maintaining a Dynamic Localized Peer-to-Peer Structure for Position Based Multicast in Games. In *Procs. of P2P*, 2008.

[9] N. Spring, L. Peterson, A. Bavier, and V. S. Pai. Using PlanetLab for network research: Myths, realities, and best practices. *Operating Systems Review*, 40(1), 2006.

[10] W. W. Terpstra, J. Kangasharju, C. Leng, and A. P. Buchmann. BubbleStorm: Resilient, Probabilistic, and Exhaustive Peer-to-Peer Search. In *Procs. of SIGCOMM*, 2007.

[11] W. W. Terpstra, C. Leng, M. Lehn, and A. P. Buchmann. Channel-based Unidirectional Stream Protocol (CUSP). In *Procs. of INFOCOM*, 2010.

Spider: Improving Mobile Networking with Concurrent Wi-Fi Connections

Hamed Soroush
University of Massachusetts
hamed@cs.umass.edu

Peter Gilbert
Duke University
gilbert@cs.duke.edu

Nilanjan Banerjee
University of Arkansas
nilanb@uark.edu

Brian Levine
University of Massachusetts
brian@cs.umass.edu

Mark Corner
University of Massachusetts
mcorner@cs.umass.edu

Landon Cox
Duke University
lpcox@cs.duke.edu

ABSTRACT

We investigate attempting concurrent connections to multiple Wi-Fi access points (APs) from highly mobile clients. Previous multi-AP solutions are limited to stationary wireless clients and do not take into account a myriad of mobile factors. We show that connection duration, AP response times, channel scheduling, available and offered bandwidth, node speed, and dhcp joins all affect performance. Building on these results, we present a system, Spider, that establishes and maintains concurrent connections to 802.11 APs in a mobile environment. While Spider can manage multiple channels, we demonstrate that it achieves maximum throughput when using multiple APs on a single channel.

Categories and Subject Descriptors

C.2.m [**Computer Systems Organization**]: Computer-Communication Networks—*Mobile and Wireless Systems*

General Terms

Concurrent Wi-Fi, Mobile Networks

1. INTRODUCTION

To realize their fullest extent of gains, Wi-Fi systems can aggregate a large number of access points (APs) *concurrently* to achieve improved network characteristics, unlike cellular, where devices are relegated to a single access point assignment. Recent *virtualized* Wi-Fi systems, such as VirtualWi-Fi [1], FatVAP [2], and Juggler [3], have shown that stationary users connected to multiple APs can achieve up to $3x$ greater bandwidth than users connected to a single AP [2]. These systems work by switching between APs on *multiple channels* rapidly, aggregating bandwidth at the client.

We show that multi-AP solutions designed for stationary users, like the ones mentioned above, are not useful at all in truly mobile scenarios. Our results show that at higher speeds, mobile users receive better performance by connecting to multiple APs only if they appear on the same channel. Only at lower speeds can mobile users recover from the throughput loss resulting from dhcp joins to APs on separate channels. In the extended technical report of this work [4], we present a general model of this problem that isolates the critical

factors that determine an optimal schedule using one or more channels. These factors include the user's speed, the AP's dhcp response time, the AP's offered bandwidth, and the attained bandwidth. Based on this model, we find the mentioned *dividing speed* to be about 10 m/s ($\sim$22 mph) in a typical environment; mobile users moving at this speed or faster would have to form concurrent Wi-Fi connections only within a single channel. Furthermore, we empirically show that link-layer association, dhcp and, TCP performance are affected negatively by multi-channel solutions.

We present a practical version of a mobile, virtualized Wi-Fi system called Spider that is designed for high-speed mobile users. Evaluation of Spider on a vehicular testbed crystalizes tradeoffs between throughput and connectivity. Spider can be used to manage and schedule joins to APs on multiple channels, and at a serious penalty to achieved bandwidth as our model predicts [1].

2. CHALLENGES

Joining to Multiple APs. Since APs can be instructed by the client to buffer packets, concurrent connections between a static client and multiple APs [1–3] are possible for Wi-Fi. The client falsely claims it is entering *power-save mode* (PSM), implicitly asking the AP to queue the incoming packets, and then communicates with another AP. Given that the backhaul bandwidth is typically smaller than the wireless bandwidth, such a scheme results in higher aggregate throughput if switching delays are kept very short. Static multi-AP solutions are not concerned with the delay incurred by the process of joining to the APs, and they do not need to be. In a static scenario joining process (association and dhcp) happens once, and its duration is negligible compared to the total connection time. In a mobile Wi-Fi environment, on the other hand, clients must continuously associate and obtain dhcp leases from APs as they become available. In addition, the packets associated with the join process cannot be buffered by the PSM request, and therefore, the client cannot switch away without reducing its chances of getting a dhcp lease.

To evaluate how the amount of time spent on the wireless channel affects the success rate of getting a dhcp lease, we performed several experiments, each lasting six hours on five vehicles moving around a small town, representing hundreds

---

[1]Detailed information about our analysis and design are available in our technical report [4] at http://www.cs.umass.edu/publication/docs/2011/UM-CS-2011-016.pdf.

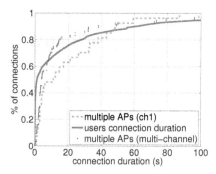

Figure 1: Comparison of connection lengths for wireless users and Spider.

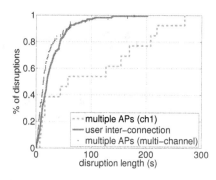

Figure 2: Comparison of disruption lengths for wireless users and Spider.

of trials. Since join delays are affected by link-layer timeouts, we reduced them from a standard of $1s$ to $100ms$ in these experiments. Detailed results of these experiments are presented in [4]. Our results show that reducing both `dhcp` and link-layer timeouts has a significant effect on performance, and that link-layer associations are robust to channel switching. However, while reconfigured `dhcp` timers are a boost to performance, we could not make `dhcp` robust to low fractions of scheduled time. This result suggests that the driver's time cannot be divided among more than two channels at 50% each in a mobile setting where the duration of time in range of an AP is limited.

Sustaining "Concurrent" TCP Connections. In a practical setting, if the channel schedule is skewed towards spending a large fraction of the time on a single channel, TCP connections on an orthogonal channel can timeout, potentially strangling performance. There is an inherent tension between the probability of successfully associating with APs on one channel and sustaining TCP connections on another channel. The results of our indoor experiments [4] show that when the total scheduling time is fixed, the TCP throughput increases monotonically with amount of time spent on AP's channel. However, when the total scheduling time is varied instead, the throughput increase is non-monotonic. This behavior is a result of increasing the total schedule which increases the amount of time *spent away* from the channel which can lead to TCP timeouts.

The Dividing Speed. In addition to these experiments, we have developed and validated a model in [4], that predicts the probability of obtaining a `dhcp` lease from an AP as a function of the amount of time spent in range in truly mobile scenarios. Based on the model, we have formulated an optimization framework to determine schedules that maximize aggregate throughput for a multi-AP solution. Our framework suggests that for highly mobile networks (where the average node speed is greater than $10m/s$), the best policy to maximize bandwidth is to stay on a *single* channel.

3. SOLUTION: SPIDER

Based on the results of our model and experimental analysis briefly presented in Section 2, we have designed and implemented Spider, a system that leverages concurrent 802.11 connections to improve performance in highly mobile networks. Our implementation is a freely available, open source Linux kernel module. Unlike previous workSpider designed for static scenarios that slice time across *individual* APs, Spi-

der schedules a physical Wi-Fi card among 802.11 channels as our analysis suggests is most appropriate to do. Use of per-channel queues in Spider's driver allows it to communicate with *all* the APs on the same channel simultaneously with no switching overhead. In [4], we show that selecting multiple APs while maximiz-ing a given system utility function is NP-hard and use a practically efficient heuristic for that purpose. We have evaluated Spider on a vehicular platform in two different cities [4].

But can open Wi-Fi solutions such as Spider cater to connectivity needs of mobile users? To answer this question, we performed a study using data from a permanent Wi-Fi mesh we deployed in our downtown. The mesh consists of 25 nodes and covers an area of about $0.50 \ km^2$. We collected performance data on all TCP flows from 161 wireless users for an entire day. Although, all users might not be mobile, the data provides us with a plausible baseline. We compare the traffic needs of wireless users with those provided by Spider based on two key metrics: (1) distribution of the duration of TCP connections, and (2) distribution of inter-connection time. Fig. 1 compares the TCP flow lengths gathered from actual users using our mesh network and Spider in its multi-channel and single-channel modes. The figure shows that Spider can support all the TCP flows that users need. Additionally, in Fig. 2 we compare the time between two connections for the mesh users and disruption time for Spider. When Spider uses multiple channels and multiple APs, it experiences disruptions comparable to what real users can sustain.

These results present Spider as a plausible complement to cellular data services. However, more data on mobile user's connectivity needs and network usage pattern is required in order to find out the degree to which Spider can *align* itself with the needs of each individual user. Conducting this study forms part of our future work with Spider.

4. REFERENCES
[1] R. Chandra, P. Bahl, and P. Bahl. MultiNet: Connecting to Multiple IEEE 802.11 Networks Using a Single Wireless Card. In *Proc. IEEE INFOCOM*, March 2004.

[2] S. Kandula, K. C.-J. Lin, T. Badirkhanli, and D. Katabi. FatVAP: aggregating AP backhaul capacity to maximize throughput. In *Proc NSDI*, pages 89–104, 2008.

[3] A. Nicholson, S. Wolchok, and B. Noble. Juggler: Virtual Networks for Fun and Profit. In *IEEE Trans. Mobile Computing*, 2009.

[4] H. Soroush, P. Gilbert, N. Banerjee, B. N. Levine, M. D. Corner, and L. Cox. Spider: Improving mobile networking with concurrent wi-fi connections. *UMass UM-CS-2011-016 Technical Report*, 2011.

Covert Channels in Multiple Access Protocols

Seyed Ali Ahmadzadeh
University of Waterloo, Canada
ahmadzdh@uwaterloo.ca

Gordon B. Agnew
University of Waterloo, Canada
gbagnew@uwaterloo.ca

ABSTRACT

In this paper, the use of structural behavior of communication protocols in designing new covert channels is investigated. In this way, a new covert transmitter is designed based on a modified CSMA protocol that enables the transmitter to embed a covert message in its overt traffic. The proposed scheme provides high covert rate without compromising the stealthiness of the channel.

Categories and Subject Descriptors

C.2.1 [**Computer-Communication Networks**]: Network Architecture and Design—*Wireless communication*

General Terms

Algorithms, Design, Security

1. INTRODUCTION

Covert communication often refers to the process of communicating through a channel that is neither designed, nor intended to transfer data [1]. Covert channels may be used to allow information to be leaked to an unauthorized recipient by exploiting weaknesses in conventional communication systems. Kemmer [1] identified three necessary conditions for existence of a covert channel. (i) a global resource that is shared between the transmitter and the receiver, (ii) ability to modify the shared resource, and (iii) a method to achieve synchronization between the transmitter and the receiver.

The wireless channel provides all three conditions making it a perfect medium for a covert channel. In [2] a covert channel based on jamming over slotted ALOHA was introduced. Later, a covert channel that exploits the properties of splitting tree collision resolution algorithm was proposed in [3]. Wang *et al.* extended the aforementioned approach into an anonymous covert channel [4] in which the receiver decodes the message using a voting approach that considers the probabilistic decisions of multiple covert transmitters.

Although the above schemes provide stealth covert channels, they trade the achievable covert rate in favor of the channel secrecy. Moreover, in order to avoid detection, these schemes are designed based on keeping the covert transmitter's long-term statistical characteristics as close as possible to an ordinary transmitter. However, to achieve this goal, the transmitter has to deviate from short-term behaviors of a regular source which may be used by a system observer to uncover the existence of the covert channel.

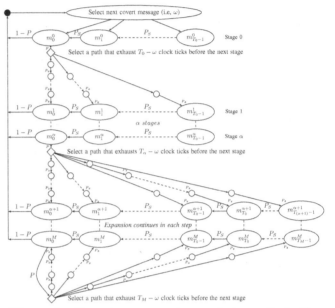

Figure 1: Covert message transmission. P_S is the probability of a successful transmission by members of the covert set.

In this paper, we present a new approach that systematically exploits the probabilistic nature of multiple access protocols in order to open a covert channel in the system. To this end, we turn our attention to the *carrier sense multiple access* (CSMA) protocol and design a covert transmitter that mimics the characteristics of a regular CSMA node while communicates covertly with the covert receiver.

2. COVERT CHANNEL DESIGN

In principle, the proposed covert channel benefits from the channel activities of a subset of users in the system (i.e., the covert set) as the mean of synchronization, and the covert transmitter's overt traffic is used in order to modify the shared medium. The design is based on a modified version of the CSMA protocol that gives the transmitter enough freedom to embed the covert message into its overt traffic, yet the transmitter reacts to the network events (e.g., collision) similar to an ordinary CSMA node.

Figure 1 depicts the modified CSMA protocol which is used by the covert transmitter. The transmitter and the receiver are equipped with a virtual clock called *covert clock*. The covert clock is incremented every time a packet from members of the covert set is detected. Due to the broadcast nature of the wireless channel, the transmitter and the receiver can observe the channel activities of the members of the covert set and increment their clock synchronously. This only requires that both sides track the same set of users and

Table 1: Details of Simulation Scenarios

Parameter	SC1	SC2	SC3	SC4
Number of users (N)	25	35	50	15
Size of the covert set ($\|S\|$)	16	21	33	10
Covert transmitter min window size (T_0)	4	7	8	4
Expansion postpone parameter (α)	1	1	1	1
Regular user min window size (W_{min})	16	32	32	16
Number of back off stages (M)	6	5	5	6

Table 2: Security Tests for Different Scenarios

Scenario	KS-test	Regularity Score (Covert Transmitter)	Regularity Score (Regular Transmitter)
SC 1	0.0432	0.2704	0.2757
SC 2	0.0398	0.2322	0.2509
SC 3	0.0367	0.3772	0.3794
SC 4	0.0353	0.2327	0.2534

are equipped with proper error correction methods in case a mismatch happens between the transmitter and the receiver.

Each covert message (i.e., ω) is associated to a *unique state* in the first stage of the transmitter's transmission window (i.e., stage 0). The covert communication begins as the transmitter moves to the corresponding state of the covert message. Then, the transmitter monitors the channel to catch packets from members of the covert set. For each packet, the transmitter's clock is incremented by one unit and it moves down one state in its transmission window (to the left in Figure 1). The transmitter sends its next packet when it reaches the last state of the transmission window.

The receiver also maintains its covert clock similar to the transmitter. Hence, upon receiving a packet from the transmitter, the receiver reads the value of its clock, decodes the covert message, and resets the clock for the next message.

However, if the transmitter fails to transmit the packet on the proper time slot (e.g., due to collision), it expands its contention window and selects a new time slot that corresponds to the covert message. Indeed, this window expansion plays a critical role to maximize the stealthiness of the covert transmitter as it mimics the behavior of an ordinary CSMA node to handle collisions in the network. Thus,

$$T_i = \begin{cases} T_0 & 0 \leq i \leq \alpha \\ 2 \times T_{i-1} & \alpha < i \leq M \\ T_M & i > M \end{cases} \quad (1)$$

Where, T_i is the size of the transmitter's contention window in the ith stage, and M is the number of backoff stages. The parameter α, is a design parameter that controls how far the transmitter deviates from behaviors of a regular user.

Finally, in order to keep synchronization between the transmitter and the receiver, following each unsuccessful packet transmission attempt, the transmitter waits for $T_i - \omega$ extra clock ticks (i.e., packets from members of the covert set) before moving to the next stage. Hence, at the beginning of the ith stage, the covert clocks at the receiver and the transmitter would be equal to $\sum_{j=0}^{i-1} T_j$, regardless of the covert message. The receiver removes this offset from its covert clock (i.e., C_r) and decodes the message as: $\omega = C_r \bmod T_0$.

3. PERFORMANCE ANALYSIS RESULTS

The performance analysis is performed on four scenarios (Table 1) using a CSMA testbed with Slot time = $20\mu s$, SIFS = $10\mu s$, DIFS = $50\mu s$, Payload = $1.5KB$, and Channel overt rate = $1Mbps$.

In order to evaluate the stealthiness of the channel, we use the *Kolmogorov-Smirnov test* (KS-test) [5] and the *reg-*

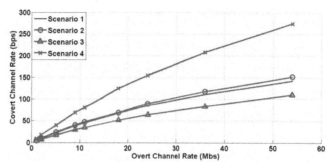

Figure 2: Covert rate of the proposed channel.

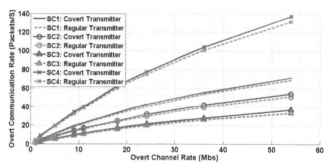

Figure 3: Overt rate of the covert transmitter

ularity test [6]. The KS-test shows the difference between the distributions of the inter-packet delays sampled from the covert transmitter's traffic and the traffic originated from a regular node. The regularity test is designed to detect the abnormal behavior of the covert transmitter in reacting to the network events (e.g., packet loss). The test results in Table 2 verifies that the transmitter has similar long-term characteristics (KS-test) and short-term behaviors (regularity test) as compared to a regular CSMA node.

Figure 2 shows the achievable rate of the proposed covert channel. It is noted that the covert channel rate increases linearly with the capacity of the overt channel. The overt communication rate of the covert transmitter and regular users in the system are depicted in Figure 3. From the graph, it can be observed that the transmitter conveys the same overt rate as compared to regular users of the system. Thus, it is extremely difficult for a system observer to track the transmitter based on overt communication rate.

4. REFERENCES

[1] R. Kemmerer. Shared resource matrix methodology: An approach to identifying storage and timing channels. *ACM Trans. on Computer Systems*, 1(3):277, 1983.

[2] S. Bhadra, S. Bodas, S. Shakkottai, and S. Vishwanath. Communication Through Jamming Over a Slotted ALOHA Channel. *IEEE Trans. on Information Theory*, pages 54(11):5257, 2008.

[3] S. Li and A. Ephremides. A covert channel in MAC protocols based on splitting algorithms. In *IEEE WCNC*, pages 1168-1173, 2005.

[4] Z. Wang, J. Deng, R. Lee, and P. Princeton. Mutual anonymous communications: a new covert channel based on splitting tree MAC. In *IEEE INFOCOM*, pages 2531-2535, 2007.

[5] Y. Liu, D. Ghosal, F. Armknecht, A. Sadeghi, S. Schulz, and S. Katzenbeisser. Hide and Seek in Time: Robust Covert Timing Channels. *In ESORICS*, pages 120-135, 2010.

[6] S. Cabuk, C. Brodley, and C. Shields. IP covert timing channels: design and detection. In *ACM CCS*, pages 178–187, 2004.

Pomelo: Accurate and Decentralized Shortest-path Distance Estimation in Social Graphs

Zhuo Chen[1], Yang Chen[2], Cong Ding[3], Beixing Deng[1] and Xing Li[1]
[1] Department of Electronic Engineering, Tsinghua University, Beijing, China
[2] Department of Computer Science, Duke University, Durham, USA
[3] Institute of Computer Science, University of Goettingen, Goettingen, Germany
E-mail: chenzhuo08@mails.tsinghua.edu.cn, ychen@cs.duke.edu,
cong@cs.uni-goettingen.de, dengbx@mail.tsinghua.edu.cn, xing@cernet.edu.cn

ABSTRACT

Computing the shortest-path distances between nodes is a key problem in analyzing social graphs. Traditional methods like breadth-first search (BFS) do not scale well with graph size. Recently, a Graph Coordinate System, called Orion, has been proposed to estimate shortest-path distances in a scalable way. Orion uses a landmark-based approach, which does not take account of the shortest-path distances between non-landmark nodes in coordinate calculation. Such biased input for the coordinate system cannot characterize the graph structure well. In this paper, we propose Pomelo, which calculates the graph coordinates in a decentralized manner. Every node in Pomelo computes its shortest-path distances to both nearby neighbors and some random distant neighbors. By introducing the novel *partial BFS*, the computational overhead of Pomelo is tunable. Our experimental results from different representative social graphs show that Pomelo greatly outperforms Orion in estimation accuracy while maintaining the same computational overhead.

Categories and Subject Descriptors

J.4 [**Computer Application**]: Social and behaviorial sciences

General Terms

Algorithms, Human Factors, Measurement

Keywords

Online social network, Graph Coordinate System

1. INTRODUCTION

Recently, online social networks (OSN), such as Facebook and Flickr, have gained significant popularity among users of the Internet. Computing the shortest-path distances between nodes in the social graph is one of the essential problems in analyzing the graph properties, such as computing centrality, detecting mutual friends and detecting community. Many widely used applications also benefit from the knowledge of node distances in the social graph. For instance, users of e-commerce sites may select more trustworthy sellers according to the shortest-path distances to the

sellers. One can also filter out query results using shortest-path distances in websites like LinkedIn [6].

However, traditional shortest-path computation algorithms like breadth-first search and Dijkstra do not scale with graph size. They calculate all pairs shortest-paths in $\Theta(N^3)$, where N is the number of nodes. This is not tolerable for nowadays real-world massive networks, especially when the shortest-path distance must be provided in the order of several milliseconds in online applications. In [6], Zhao et al. try to embed the nodes of a social graph into a Euclidean space by assigning each node a set of low-dimensional coordinates. They propose Orion, a Graph Coordinate System, which simply uses the Euclidean distance between two nodes to estimate the actual shortest-path distance. However, similar to landmark-based Network Coordinate (NC) systems for Internet latency estimation such as GNP [5], Orion does not take account of the shortest-path distances between non-landmark nodes when calculating coordinates. Such biased input cannot characterize the graph structure well and will lead to an inaccurate estimation.

In this paper, we propose Pomelo, an accurate and decentralized Graph Coordinate System. Our contributions are three-folds: (1) The coordinate calculation of every Pomelo node refers to both the nearby neighbors and some distant neighbors. This hybrid neighbor selection policy is in accordance with the intuition in [3], thus achieving the better overall estimation accuracy. (2) Instead of conducting a complete BFS for every node as the starting node, which is $\Theta(N^3)$ in computational overhead, we propose the novel *partial BFS* for every node bounded by a pre-defined budget. This tunable budget balances the tradeoff between computational cost and estimation accuracy. In Section 3, we adjust this budget to ensure fair comparison between Orion and Pomelo. (3) In evaluating Pomelo on representative social graphs, we show that with the same computational overhead, Pomelo estimates the shortest-path distances much more accurately than Orion does.

2. SYSTEM DESIGN OF POMELO

Since we want to choose a decentralized architecture for Pomelo, the representative distributed NC system, called Vivaldi [3], is a natural choice for coordinate calculation framework. Pomelo utilizes the spring model proposed in Vivaldi to characterize the social graph. In each updating round, every node adapts its coordinates by referring to one of its neighbors. Some rounds later, Pomelo converges to minimize the sum of squares of the absolute errors, i.e., the

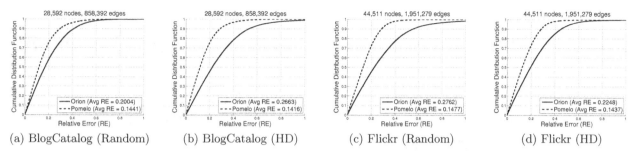

(a) BlogCatalog (Random)	(b) BlogCatalog (HD)	(c) Flickr (Random)	(d) Flickr (HD)

Figure 1: Compare Pomelo with Orion using Different Landmark Selection Strategies

differences between the estimated and computed shortest-path distances. In addition, since Vivaldi (with height) has been demonstrated as the most widely used implementation of Vivaldi [4], we also apply a *height* element to the coordinates of each node in Pomelo.

As argued in [6], there is a critical challenge to apply Vivaldi directly. When utilizing the original Vivaldi algorithm, the knowledge of all pairs shortest-path distances is required in order to randomly select neighbors for each node. That said, we have to perform a complete BFS for every node as the starting point. This $\Theta(N^3)$ method is cost prohibitive for processing large social graphs. In contrast, we conduct a partial BFS for each node in Pomelo, where a pre-defined budget T is set. Whenever the total number of nodes and edges visited exceeds this budget, we terminate the BFS procedure and the nodes that have been visited become the qualified nearby neighbors for the starting node. This method is scalable, since it tunes the computational overhead for N nodes to $\Theta(TN)$. Moreover, some extra computational budget is set for conducting complete BFS from a randomly selected set of nodes. In this way, an arbitrary node can also refer to this set of relatively distant nodes, which we refer to as distant neighbors, in the algorithm of Pomelo. That said, the neighbor set of every node in Pomelo is a combination of some nearby neighbors and some distant neighbors. It is shown in [3] that such hybrid neighbor selection policy can actually increase the estimation accuracy in the original Vivaldi system, which can be viewed as a positive indicator for Pomelo.

3. EVALUATION

Firstly, Orion is implemented with a couple of landmark selection strategies, including Random and High-degree (HD) [6]. And then, we calculate BFS_i, which is the total number of nodes and edges visited to complete a BFS procedure starting from node $i(1 \leqslant i \leqslant N)$. Suppose there are K landmarks in Orion, namely $l_1, l_2, ..., l_K$, the total overhead in computing BFS in Orion is then $\sum_{1 \leqslant j \leqslant K} BFS_{l_j}$, which is denoted as O_{sum}. In Pomelo, we let all N nodes share the same set of randomly selected distant neighbors, consisting of $K/2$ nodes, namely $r_1, r_2, ..., r_{K/2}$. Therefore, the total overhead of computing every node's shortest-path distances to these $K/2$ distant neighbors is $\sum_{1 \leqslant j \leqslant K/2} BFS_{r_j}$, which is denoted as $Rand_{sum}$. For the sake of fair comparison, we set the budget for every node when doing the partial BFS in Pomelo as $T = \frac{O_{sum} - Rand_{sum}}{N}$. Since a complete BFS procedure for one node is $\Theta(N^2)$, the above equation shows that T is actually $\Theta(KN)$, so that the partial BFS used in Pomelo is much more efficient than a complete BFS.

We use two representative datasets, named Flickr and BlogCatalog, from [1]. In practice, we randomly sample some nodes in each dataset and includes all the edges between these nodes. The sampled Flickr dataset has 44,511 nodes and 1,951,279 edges and the sampled BlogCatalog dataset has 28,592 nodes and 858,392 edges. The dimension in Orion is 8, and Pomelo uses 7 dimensions with a height element. The number of landmarks is set to be 100, the same as [6]. We use relative error (RE [3, 6]) to compare the accuracy of different systems:

$$RE = \frac{|EstimatedDist - ComputedDist|}{ComputedDist} \qquad (1)$$

Figure 1 depicts REs in the format of CDF using different datasets and landmark selection methods. As we see, estimation with Pomelo is much more accurate than that with Orion. Compared with Orion (Random), Pomelo reduces the average RE by between 28.08% (BlogCatalog) and 46.51% (Flickr). Moreover, compared with Orion (HD), Pomelo reduces the average RE by between 36.12% (Flickr) and 46.82% (BlogCatalog).

4. CONCLUSIONS AND FUTURE WORK

In this paper, we propose Pomelo, a decentralized Graph Coordinate System using a hybrid neighbor selection policy. According to our evaluation, Pomelo achieves much better estimation accuracy than Orion does while maintaining the same computational overhead. For future work, we would like to explore the matrix factorization model [2] for Graph Coordinate System.

5. ACKNOWLEDGMENTS

This work is supported by the National Basic Research Program of China (No.2007CB310806) and National Science Foundation of China (No.60850003) .

6. REFERENCES

[1] Social computing data repository at arizona state university. http://socialcomputing.asu.edu/.

[2] Y. Chen, X. Wang, X. Song, and et al. Phoenix: Towards an accurate, practical and decentralized network coordinate system. In *Proc. of IFIP/TC6 Networking*, 2009.

[3] F. Dabek, R. Cox, and et al. Vivaldi: A decentralized network coordinate system. In *Proc. of ACM SIGCOMM*, 2004.

[4] J. Ledlie, P. Gardner, and M. Seltzer. Network coordinates in the wild. In *Proc. of NSDI*, 2007.

[5] T. Ng and H. Zhang. Predicting internet network distance with coordinates-based approaches. In *Proc. of INFOCOM*, 2002.

[6] X. Zhao, A. Sala, C. Wilson, H. Zheng, and B. Y. Zhao. Orion: shortest path estimation for large social graphs. In *Proc. of The 3rd Workshop on Online Social Networks (WOSN)*, 2010.

Dummy Rate Analysis of Buffer Constrained Chaum Mix

Abhishek Mishra
Lehigh University
PA, USA 18015
abm210@lehigh.edu

Parv Venkitasubramaniam
Lehigh University
PA, USA 18015
parv.v@lehigh.edu

Categories and Subject Descriptors

C.2.0 [**Computer-Communication Networks**]: General—
Security and Protection; C.2.6 [**Computer-Communication
Networks**]: Internetworking—*Routers*

General Terms

Security

Keywords

Chaum Mix, Dummy rate, Buffer constraint

1. PROBLEM DESCRIPTION

Providing anonymity to network communication refers to
the prevention of "networking information" retrieval, not
only using the *content* of transmitted data packets but also
from their *timing information*. Access to such timing information can reveal the source-destination pairs or path of
data flow which is a violation of user privacy, and can further be used to jam a particular flow or create black holes.
Chaum Mixes [1] are often used to obfuscate this timing information from malicious eavesdroppers. A Chaum Mix is a
relay node or a proxy server that collects packets from different users, then uses layered encryption and packet padding
to make outgoing packets appear indistinguishable to eavesdroppers. Furthermore, it also alters the timing information
by reordering and batching together packets from different
users, so that the probability of any outgoing packet belonging to a particular user is identical for all users, thus
achieving perfect anonymity.

A drawback of the ideal Chaum Mix is that if long data
streams (eg. media streaming) are transmitted, then it may
require a very large buffer capacity to work well. In fact, it
has been proven that any batching strategy, under the constraint of a limited buffer size, would eventually reveal the
source identities [2]. It is, however, possible to mask the actual pattern of traffic flow through the insertion of **dummy
traffic**. For example, consider a network where all nodes
transmit packets according to scheduled departure times. If
an actual packet is unavailable for transmission at its time of
departure, a dummy packet can be transmitted in its place
and perfect anonymity is still maintained. But the extensive use of dummy packets can reduce network throughput,
which leads to some interesting questions:

1. For a fixed buffer size, what is the optimal mixing
   strategy to achieve perfect anonymity with minimum
   possible dummy rate (number of dummy packets per
   second)?

2. For a fixed buffer size, what is the minimum dummy
   rate required for a mix to achieve perfect anonymity?
   Further, how does this minimum dummy rate scale
   with buffer size?

In this work, the above questions are addressed using an
analytical approach.

2. APPROACH AND CONTRIBUTION

Optimal mixing strategy Ψ: For a fixed buffer size B,
the mix waits until at least one packet from each user arrives or until the buffer is full. If packets from all users arrive
before the buffer is full, then one packet of each user is selected and they are randomly ordered and sent in succession.
Otherwise, the mix generates one additional dummy packet
for each user missing in the buffer, and performs the above
operation treating the dummy packets as actual packets of
missing users.

THEOREM 1. *The strategy Ψ is optimal for achieving minimum dummy rate.*

Due to the constraint of page limit, we omit the proof here.
Using strategy Ψ, we can compute the exact rate of dummy
transmission for a two source mix.

THEOREM 2. *The minimum dummy rate required by a
mix serving two sources of rates λ_1, λ_2 respectively is given
by*

$$\mu = \frac{\lambda_1 \rho^{2B+1} - \lambda_1 \rho^{2B} + \lambda_2 \rho - \lambda_2}{\rho^{2B+1} - 1} \quad \text{where } \rho = \frac{\lambda_1}{\lambda_2}.$$

and hence when $\lambda_1 = \lambda_2 = \lambda$,

$$\mu = \frac{2\lambda}{2B+1}.$$

The proof is omitted for brevity. The same proof technique
can also be applied when more than two users are present,
but it involves the analysis of multidimensional Markov chains
which are analytically intractable. We can, however, provide
lower and upper bounds on the minimum achievable dummy
rate for the general k user case.

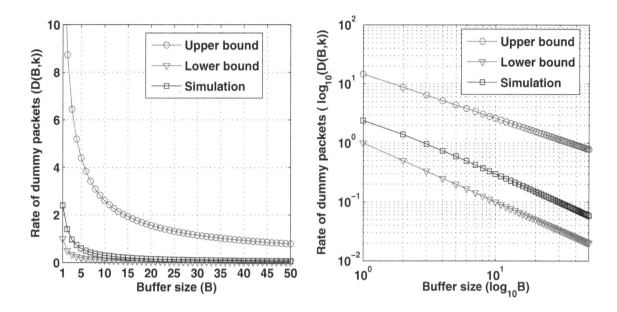

Figure 1: Bounds on dummy packets as a function of buffer size

THEOREM 3. *For a k−source mix with buffer size B, there exists constants K_1, K_2 independent of B such that the minimum required dummy rate $D(B, k)$ satisfies:*

$$\frac{K_1}{B} \leq D(B, k) \leq \frac{K_2}{B^{3/4}}.$$

The lower bound on the dummy rate holds true regardless of the mixing strategy employed, thus providing a useful performance benchmark.

To get the upper-bound, we consider a sub-optimal strategy $\overline{\Psi}$, under which the mix first divides the buffer into two equal halves, each of size $B/2$. The mix stores all incoming packets in the first half of the buffer until it is full. Amongst the $B/2$ packets now present in the buffer, the mix transmits the maximum number of packets in a batch, such that the number of packets from each source is equal. The remaining packets are shifted to the second half of the buffer. This process is repeated until the second half of the buffer is full. At this point, all the packets in the second half of the buffer are transmitted in a single batch with enough dummy transmissions such that the number of packets from each source is equal. Thus, by calculating the upper limit on the required dummy rate for strategy $\overline{\Psi}$, we obtain an upper bound on $D(B, k)$. The detailed proof is omitted due to paucity of space.

In Fig. 1, we plot the numerically computed dummy rate using the multidimensional Markov chain (optimal strategy), and compare it with the bounds. As is evident from the plots, the convergence rate of the optimal strategy matches that of the lower bound. This fact, in conjunction with the result on the convergence rate for the two-source system indicates that the optimal convergence rate is $O\left(\frac{1}{B}\right)$.

3. ANONYMITY IN A NETWORK

Thus far, we studied the dummy transmission rate required at a single mix to achieve perfect anonymity. The anonymity, as quantified using the Shannon entropy of packet sources would amount to $\log k$, if there are k sources transmitting to the mix. In a general multihop network, as the packet streams traverse through multiple mixes, the anonymity of packet sources at any given link would be the result of cumulative mixing at previous nodes in the path of the streams. This cumulative anonymity can be computed using the chain rule of entropy [3].

THEOREM 4. *If $A_1, A_2, \cdots, A_k$ denote the entropy of packet sources of k streams that are mixed at a given intermediate node, then the entropy of sources on the outgoing stream of packets is given by:*

$$A = \frac{\sum A_i}{k} + 1.$$

Using the fact that mixes that received packets directly from sources achieve anonymity of $\log k$, we can recursively compute the anonymity of packets on any link.

It is important to note that to achieve this anonymity, it is critical that the generated dummy packets are relayed by subsequent nodes as though they were data packets, and consequently, while anonymity builds up at successive mixes, the true rate of data packets drops, thus resulting in a trade-off between anonymity and throughput.

4. REFERENCES

[1] D. Chaum, "Untraceable electronic mail, return addresses and digital pseudonyms," *Communications of the ACM*, vol. 24, pp. 84–88, February 1981.

[2] X. Fu, B. Graham, R. Bettati, and W. Zhao, "On countermeasures to traffic analysis attacks," in *Information Assurance Workshop, 2003. IEEE Systems, Man and Cybernetics Society*, pp. 188–195, 18-23 June 2003.

[3] T. Cover and J. Thomas, *Elements of Information Theory*. John Wiley & Sons, Inc., 1991.

Minimising Cell Transmit Power: Towards Self-organized Resource Allocation in OFDMA Femtocells

David López-Pérez,
Xiaoli Chu
King's College London
London, UK
david.lopez@kcl.ac.uk

Athanasios V. Vasilakos
National Technical University
of Athens
Athens, Greece
vasilako@ath.forthnet.gr

Holger Claussen
Alcatel-Lucent Bell-Labs
Dublin, Ireland
holger.claussen@alcatel-lucent.com

ABSTRACT

With the introduction of femtocells, cellular networks are moving from the conventional centralised architecture to a distributed one, where each network cell should make its own radio resource management decisions, while providing inter-cell interference mitigation. However, realising this distributed cellular network architecture is not a trivial task. In this paper, we first introduce a simple self-organisation rule under which a distributed cellular network is able to converge into an efficient resource allocation pattern, then propose a novel resource allocation model taking realistic resource allocation constraints into account, and finally evaluate the performance of the proposed self-organisation rule and resource allocation model using system-level simulations.

Primary Classification: A. General Literature, A.m MISCELLANEOUS; General Terms: Algorithms; Keywords: Femtocell, Interference, Resource Allocation.

1. BACKGROUND AND MOTIVATION

Femtocells, which are low-cost, low-power cellular base stations (BSs) deployed by end-users in homes and offices, have been widely considered as a cost-effective solution to enhance indoor coverage and spectral efficiency in cellular networks. By reducing the distance between BSs and end-users and alleviating the traffic burden on macrocells, femtocells can potentially improve spatial reuse, allow higher user data-rates and provide energy savings. However, femtocell roll-outs are facing their own technical challenges. For instance, since the user-provided backhaul connection between an femto BS and the operator's core network usually has limited capacity, it is difficult to manage inter-cell interference using classic centralised network planning and optimisation tools. This has led to a new inter-cell interference management problem that must be solved in a decentralised and distributed manner. However, to achieve good performance across the network with each cell taking its own radio resource management decisions is an intricate problem [1].

2. RADIO RESOURCE MANAGEMENT

In orthogonal frequency division multiple access (OFDMA) -based networks, e.g., Long Term Evolution (LTE) and Wireless Interoperability for Microwave Access (WiMAX), the smallest resource unit that can be assigned is a resource block (RB). An RB is comprised of a set of adjacent subcarriers in the frequency domain and OFDM symbols in the time domain. The scheduling question to be addressed by each cell is how RBs are to be allocated to users and how much transmit power is to be applied to each RB, so that network capacity is enhanced. This radio resource allocation problem is complex because users may have different quality of service demands and may experience various channel and interference conditions in each RB. Moreover, both LTE and WiMAX standards have a scheduling constraints, e.g., when more than one RB are allocated to a user, all these RBs must utilise the same Modulation and Coding Scheme (MCS) [2].

3. OUR SELF-ORGANISATION RULE

For the independent and dynamic optimisation of radio resource assignments at each cell, it is necessary to have an objective that results in a good self-organising behaviour. Accordingly, our proposed cell optimisation rule is defined as: *each cell assigns MCSs, RBs and transmit power levels to users independently, while minimising the cell total transmit power and meeting its users' throughput demands.* The reasons for minimising the cell total transmit power are two:

1. A cell that aims at minimising its own transmit power mitigates inter-cell interference to neighbouring cells, because less power is allocated to those users with good channel conditions or lower throughput demands. This is straightforward from Shanon-Hartley theorem.
2. A cell that aims at minimising its own transmit power tends to allocate those RBs that are not being used by its neighbouring cells, because less transmit power is required for a less interfered and/or faded RB to get a targeted signal to interference plus noise ratio (SINR).

Following this rule, a cell will tend to allocate users that are closer to the BS or have lower data-rate requirements (hence requiring lower MSCs as well as transmit powers) to RBs that are used by cell-edge users in neighbouring cells.

4. RESOURCE ALLOCATION MODEL

The transmit power $p_{u,k,r}^f$ that femtocell F_f should assign to every subcarrier of RB k assign in the downlink to user u to achieve the SINR threshold γ_r of its assigned MCS r is

$$p_{u,k,r}^f = \gamma_r \cdot \frac{w_{u,k} + \sigma^2}{\Gamma_{f,u}} \quad (1)$$

$\Gamma_{f,u}$ is the channel gain between femto BS F_f and user u, $w_{u,k}$ is the inter-cell interference power suffered by user u in RB k, and σ^2 is the noise power. Femtocell F_f can 'know' $\Gamma_{m,u}$ and $w_{u,k}$ from its user measurement reports (MRs) [2].

Thus, the joint MCS, RB and power allocation problem in femtocell F_f, following our proposed self-organisation rule, can be formulated as the following integer linear problem:

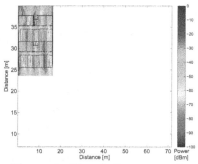

Figure 1: Simulation scenario.

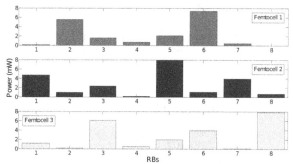

Figure 2: RB allocation.

Table 1: System-Level Simulation Results

Deployed users	Scheme	Rand.	MNL	IM	Our Method
4 users/cell 8 RB network	Outage	15.09 %	8.62 %	2.59 %	0.86 %
	Tx.-ing Users	31.13	33.11	35.20	35.75
	Mbps	7.65	8.24	8.77	8.83
8 users/cell 8 RB network	Outage	19.87 %	19.77 %	15.52 %	3.19 %
	Tx.-ing Users	58.36	58.59	60.47	69.63
	Mbps	14.40	14.48	14.98	16.78

$$\min_{\chi_{u,k,r}} \sum_{u=1}^{U} \sum_{k=1}^{K} \sum_{r=1}^{R} p_{u,k,r}^{f} \cdot \chi_{u,k,r} \qquad (2a)$$

subject to:

$$\sum_{u=1}^{U} \sum_{r=1}^{R} \chi_{u,k,r} \leq 1 \qquad \forall k \qquad (2b)$$

$$\sum_{r=1}^{R} \rho_{u,r} \leq 1 \qquad \forall u \qquad (2c)$$

$$\chi_{u,k,r} \leq \rho_{u,r} \qquad \forall u,k,r \qquad (2d)$$

$$\sum_{k=1}^{K} \sum_{r=1}^{R} \Theta \cdot eff_{r} \cdot \chi_{u,k,r} \geq TP_{u}^{req} \qquad \forall u \qquad (2e)$$

$$\rho_{u,r} \in \{0,1\} \qquad \forall u,r \qquad (2f)$$

$$\chi_{u,k,r} \in \{0,1\} \qquad \forall u,k,r \qquad (2g)$$

where $\chi_{u,k,r}$ (2g) is a binary decision variable that is equal to 1 if user u uses MCS r in RB k, or 0 otherwise, $\rho_{u,r}$ (2f) is a binary decision variable that is equal to 1 if user u makes use of MCS r, or 0 otherwise, constraint (2b) makes sure that RB k is only assigned to at most one user u, constraints (2c) and (2d) together guarantee that each user is allocated to at most one MCS, and constraint (2e) makes sure that each user u obtains a throughput no less than its demand TP_{u}^{req}.

Average channel quality in the form of instantaneous $w_{u,k}$ averaged over tens of user MRs is utilised to compute $p_{u,k,r}^{f}$, thus avoiding rapid fluctuations of $p_{u,k,r}^{f}$ due to fast-fading, which may result in fast variations of resource assignments.

One possible approach to solve (2) is to apply integer linear programming (ILP) techniques readily available in software packages. However, although ILP solvers are able to solve (2) up to optimality, their running times are unpredictable (exponential in the worst case), which renders them inappropriate for real-time use at femto BSs. Hence, to solve (2) in short time, we propose a two-level decomposition approach based on an heuristics search and a minimum cost network flow problem. Assuming that a MCS r_u has been assigned to user u $\forall u$, i.e., $\rho_{u,r} \forall u \forall r$ is known a priori as part of the input, (2) can be reduced to a simpler form, i.e., a user-to-RB assignment problem weighted by $p_{u,k,r}^{f} \forall u \forall k$. This assignment problem can be formulated as a minimum cost network flow problem, an optimally solved using a network simplex algorithm. Thereafter, a heuristic search can be performed over the MCS assignment solution space, where

for each MCS assignment to cell users, the optimal RB and power allocation can be found by using our network simplex algorithm. Since network simplex runs fast, RB and power allocations to users can be updated on a millisecond basis (dealing with fast channel variations), while the MCS assignment can be updated in a half-second basis (dealing with traffic load and mobility).

5. PERFORMANCE AND CONCLUSIONS

The performance of the proposed self-organisation rule has been investigated in an enterprise femtocell scenario (Fig. 1). Simulation results show that compared to existing radio resource management techniques in the literature, i.e., random [3], network listening mode (NLM) [4] and interference minimisation (IM) [5], our approach is able to significantly decrease the number of user outages, increase the average number of simultaneously transmitting users in the network (around 15%), and enhance the average network sum throughput (around 12%) (Tab. 1). This is because our approach (self-organization rule) achieves inter-cell interference coordination without the need of assigning orthogonal RBs among neighbouring cells. Instead, it allows all cells to allocate all RBs to their users in an intelligent manner: A cell that minimises its own transmit power assigns less power to those RBs allocated to users having good channel conditions or with lower data-rate demands. Thus, neighbouring cells will 'see' low interference in such RBs and will allocate them to users having bad channel conditions or with large data-rate demands, thereby improving spatial reuse. To illustrate this self-organising feature, Fig. 2 shows the transmit power allocated by 3 neighbouring femtocells at a given time in 8 available RBs. We can see that each femtocell tends to allocate higher power levels in RBs in which neighbouring femtocells assign lower power levels and vice versa. In this way, a same RB can be dynamically reused in neighbouring femtocells. Therefore, our proposed sefl-organisation rule and resource allocation model effectively introduce an implicit coordination among independently operating femtocells through distributed dynamic radio resource allocations.

6. REFERENCES

[1] V. Chandrasekhar et. al. Femtocell Networks: A Survey. *IEEE Comm. Mag.*, 46(9):59–67, Sep. 2008.

[2] E. Dahlman et. al. *3G Evolution. HSPA and LTE for Mobile Broadband.* Elsevier, 2 edition, Aug. 2008.

[3] V. Chandrasekhar et. al. Spectrum Allocation in Tiered Cellular Networks. *IEEE Transactions on Communications*, 57(10):3059–3068, Oct. 2009.

[4] J. Ling et. al. On Resource Allocation in Dense Femto-Deployments. In *IEEE COMCAS*, Nov. 2009.

[5] J. Zhang et. al. *Femtocells: Technologies and Deployment.* John Wiley and Sons, Jan. 2010.

Building Virtual Networks Across Multiple Domains

Christoph Werle and
Roland Bless
Karlsruhe Institute of
Technology, Germany
{werle, bless}@kit.edu

Panagiotis Papadimitriou
Leibniz University of
Hannover, Germany
panagiotis.papadimitriou
@ikt.uni-hannover.de

Ines Houidi, Wajdi Louati,
and Djamal Zeghlache
Institut Telecom, Telecom
SudParis, France
{ines.houidi, wajdi.louati,
djamal.zeghlache}
@it-sudparis.eu

Laurent Mathy
Lancaster University, UK
l.mathy@lancaster.ac.uk

ABSTRACT

This paper presents a platform for virtual network (VN) provisioning across multiple domains. The platform decomposes VN provisioning into multiple steps to address the implications of limited information disclosure on resource discovery and allocation. A new VN embedding algorithm with simultaneous node and link mapping allows to assign resources within each domain. For inter-domain virtual link setup, we design and realize a signaling protocol that also integrates resource reservations for providing virtual links with Quality-of-Service guarantees. Experimental results show that small VNs can be provisioned within a few seconds.

Categories and Subject Descriptors: C.2.1 [*Computer Communication Networks*]: Network Architecture and Design

General Terms: Design, Management, Performance

Keywords: Network virtualization, resource provisioning, Quality-of-Service, platform design

1. INTRODUCTION

Network virtualization has been seen as a promising solution for the concurrent deployment and operation of service-tailored network slices. The wide-area deployment of *virtual networks* (VNs) creates the need for separation between the network operations and the physical infrastructure. A newly envisioned level of indirection already exists in GENI [3], 4WARD [1], and Cabernet [8]. In this context, *VN Providers* (VNPs) that act as brokers for virtual resources between *VN Operators*[1] (VNOs) and *Infrastructure Providers* (InPs) will have to provision VNs without having control or even knowledge of any aspect of the physical infrastructure. This entails serious implications on resource discovery and allocation. Existing VN embedding approaches are limited to a single administrative domain, assuming complete knowledge

---

[1]VN Operators are responsible for the operation of VNs according to the needs of the Service Provider. In some cases VNOs and VNPs (as well as VNOs and Service Providers) may be realized by a single organization.

of physical resources and the underlying substrate topology. Hence, they cannot be used to provision VNs at large scale, i.e., across multiple domains. Recent work [2] presents an inter-domain VN embedding framework but lacks the required embedding algorithms and a prototype implementation.

In this paper, we present a platform for VN provisioning across multiple domains that particularly addresses the intricacies of inter-domain aspects. The platform allows VNOs to request VNs from VNPs, which subsequently coordinate their construction by assembling resources from multiple InPs, in line with the VN architecture exemplified in [7]. Since these actors access VN descriptions at different levels of abstraction, we decompose VN provisioning into a sequence of steps: (i) resource discovery, (ii) resource assignment, and (iii) VN instantiation. We propose and use a new VN embedding algorithm with simultaneous node and link mapping for resource assignment within InPs. To provide the required interoperability for virtual link setup across multiple domains, we design and implement a corresponding signaling protocol.

2. PLATFORM OVERVIEW

This section gives an overview of our platform. The platform provides (i) a control plane for VN provisioning and management, (ii) an XML-based resource and network topology description language, and (iii) on-the-fly VN embedding and instantiation by synthesizing existing technologies, such as Xen for node virtualization and Click Modular Router (running in Linux kernel) for packet encapsulation / decapsulation and packet forwarding. For virtual link setup, we employed *IETF's Next Steps in Signaling* (NSIS) Framework and extended the *QoS NSIS Signaling Layer Protocol* (QoS NSLP) to additionally carry required information within a *Virtual Link Setup Protocol* (VLSP) object [5, 6].

Inter-domain VN provisioning is coordinated by VNPs, which have limited resource and topology information of the underlying substrates. Hence, virtual resources should be initially discovered and matched at a rather high level of abstraction (i.e., VNP) to identify candidate resources from which the most appropriate resources will be selected based on detailed information only available to InPs. To this end, our platform provisions VNs as a sequence of the three following steps, which are illustrated in Fig. 1.

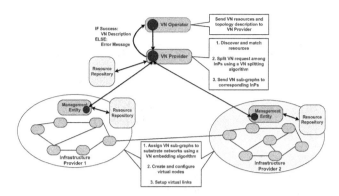

Figure 1: Platform overview with control interfaces and VN provisioning steps.

Resource Discovery: The VNP matches a requested set of virtual nodes and links (which represent a VN topology) to virtual resources offered by InPs. For each virtual node/link instance, the VNP identifies all candidate resources and estimates the cost. Subsequently, the VNP splits the VN topology among the InPs; the objective is to minimize the expenditure for Service Providers. VN partitioning algorithms are discussed in previous work [4].

Resource Assignment: Resource assignment takes place within each InP, since full knowledge of the physical resources and network topology is required. Each InP assigns its partial VN to its substrate network using a VN embedding algorithm. Previous approaches mainly rely on greedy algorithms where node and link mapping is achieved sequentially. Nodes are preselected and assigned, during the node mapping stage, without considering their relation to the link-mapping stage. We use a new heuristic embedding algorithm where node and link mapping phases are simultaneously executed in one stage. The main objective of this algorithm is to optimize load balancing over substrate nodes.

VN Instantiation: Upon resource assignment, the selected substrate resources are allocated by the InPs in order to instantiate the requested VN. VN instantiation is coordinated by a management node within each InP, which signals requests to substrate nodes for virtual node and link setup. We use NSIS to setup virtual links within and between InPs and correspondingly create tunnels with IP-in-IP encapsulation (other tunneling technologies can be used as well). We further discuss virtual link setup in the following section.

3. VIRTUAL LINK SETUP

We use the NSIS protocol suite and integrate the virtual link setup with the resource reservation signaling via the QoS NSLP. This integration reduces the setup time of a virtual link, as the resource reservation at the same time conveys the necessary address information of the virtual link. A QoS NSLP extension mechanism for carrying new objects is used to integrate the newly created *virtual link setup protocol* object (VLSP object). Only the substrate nodes hosting the virtual nodes at the edges of the virtual link need to support the VLSP object and act on it accordingly by, e.g., installing any state required for the setup of the virtual link. Intermediate substrate nodes might be involved in guaranteeing QoS properties of the virtual link or an aggregate of vir-

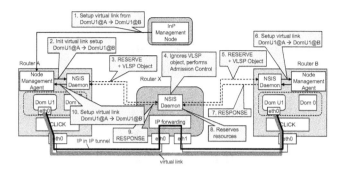

Figure 2: Virtual link setup.

tual links and therefore need to process the remaining QoS NSLP content. They can, however, simply ignore and forward the contained VLSP object, which is ensured by the NSLP object extensions flags in the VLSP object header. Moreover, the path-coupled signaling approach of NSIS assures that a viable substrate path with sufficient resources exists to accommodate the new virtual link.

Fig. 2 illustrates the sequence of events during the setup of a unidirectional virtual link. Experimental results with this setup using a prototypical implementation [6] show that the combined QoS/VLSP signalling does not incur a notable delay during virtual link setup (also if authenticated [5]). Even if the substrate path across two domains comprises several hops, we expect that resource reservation will not dominate the virtual link setup time.

4. CONCLUSIONS

We presented a VN platform that complies with the restrictions imposed by multiple domains, such as limited information disclosure. The platform also provides the required interoperability for inter-domain virtual link setup with QoS guarantees.

The platform design shows what technological ingredients are needed and how these can be combined efficiently to provision VNs at large scale. The main building blocks of the platform, such as node virtualization technologies, packet encapsulation/decapsulation and signaling protocols for virtual link setup, are readily available today. This shows that a shift towards full network virtualization is viable in the not too distant future.

5. REFERENCES

[1] 4WARD Project, http://www.4ward-project.eu.
[2] M. Chowdhury, F. Samuel, and R. Boutaba, PolyViNE: Policy-based Virtual Network Embedding Across Multiple Domains, Proc. ACM SIGCOMM VISA, New Delhi, India, September 2010.
[3] GENI: Global Environment for Network Innovations, http://www.geni.net.
[4] I. Houidi, W. Louati, W. Bean-Ameur, and D. Zeghlache, Virtual Network Provisioning Across Multiple Substrate Networks, Computer Networks, Vol. 55, No. 4, March 2011.
[5] R. Bless, M. Röhricht and C. Werle, Authenticated Setup of Virtual Links with Quality-of-Service Guarantees, Proc. IEEE ICCCN 2011, Hawaii, USA, July 2011.
[6] NSIS-ka, A free C++ implementation of NSIS protocols, KIT, https://svn.tm.kit.edu/trac/NSIS
[7] G. Schaffrath et al., Network Virtualization Architecture: Proposal and Initial Prototype, Proc. ACM SIGCOMM VISA, Barcelona, Spain, August 2009.
[8] Y. Zu, R. Zhang-Shen, S.Rangarajan, and J. Rexford, Cabernet: Connectivity Architecture for Better Network Services, Proc. ACM ReArch '08, Madrid, Spain, December 2008.

Multi-relational Social Networks in a Large-scale MMORPG

Seokshin Son
Seoul National University
ssson@mmlab.snu.ac.kr

Ah Reum Kang
Korea University
armk@korea.ac.kr

Hyun-chul Kim
Seoul National University
hyunchulk@gmail.com

Ted "Taekyoung" Kwon
Seoul National University
tkkwon@snu.ac.kr

Juyong Park
Kyunghee University
perturbation@gmail.com

Huy Kang Kim
Korea University
cenda@korea.ac.kr

ABSTRACT

We analyze multi-relational social interaction networks in a large-scale commercial Massively Multiplayer Online Role-Playing Game (MMORPG). Our work is based on data from AION, currently the world's second most-played MMORPG with 3.4 million subscribers as of mid 2010, created and serviced by NCSoft, Inc. We construct and characterize six distinct interactivity networks (Friend, Private Messaging, Party invitation, Trade, Mail, and Shop), each representing diverse player interaction types.

Categories and Subject Descriptors

J.4 [**Computer Applications**]: Social and Behavioral Sciences

General Terms

Human Factors, Measurement

Keywords

Social network analysis, Quantitative social science, Massively multiplayer online game

1. INTRODUCTION

It has been reported that more than 15 million people worldwide enjoy MMORPGs [1] that feature online social arenas in fantastical settings where gamers can engage in individual or group battles, exchange or trade items, or simply socialize with one another via in-game communication channels. Given that the complexity and variety of in-game interactions may now rival those of real-world interactions, the digital archive of online activities opens up an attractive avenue to researchers for a deep understanding of human social behaviors. Yet, such research is often hindered by the lack of access to the data. In this work we investigate multi-relational social and collective aspects of MMORPG players' interactions based on data collected from AION[1], the world's second largest MMORPG from NCSoft, Inc. Specifically, we construct and charactersize six distinct interactivity networks, each representing diverse player interaction types. To the best of our knowledge, this is the first work that analyzes

---

[1] AION Online, http://www.aiononline.com

multi-relational social networks in a large-scale commercial MMORPG.

Our study is based on the anonymized database dumps from one AION server/world out of 41 identically designed but independently running parallel game worlds/servers. The dataset includes all in-game interactions between player characters for 87 days, in mid 2010. Each interaction record contains anonymized IDs of the sender and receiver, and the type of the interaction record, most of which fall into one of the following six categories: (i) Friend **F**: A directed edge is created from user A to B when A adds B to A's buddy list. (ii) Whisper **W**: A directed edge is created from user A to B when A sends a private message to B. (iii) Party Invitation **P**: A directed edge is created from user A to user B when A invites B to join his party. A party is a group of up to six players that can carry out missions or engage in battles as a team. (iv) Trade **T**: A directed edge is formed from A to B when A requests a trade of items to B, then B accepts it. (v) Mail **M**: An edge is formed from user A to B when A sends a mail to B. (vi) Shop **S**: users can enter a private market mode, becoming a merchant (and unable to do any other actions while in the mode) who can announce publicly the list of items for sale. Other users can then buy items from the merchant using in-game currency, in which case a directed edge is drawn from the buyer to the merchant.

2. RESULTS

Table 1[2] shows how many gamers were engaged in each interaction type, and the number of interactions (for simplicity, we have not considered weights on the edges, which is the frequency of the interactions between user pairs). We see that the Party invitation, a truly social activity, is the most prevalent interaction while Shop is the least so. Note that the Giant Connected Components (GCCs) [2] take up approximately 50% of the nodes and the edges across the networks, while the second largest connected components (not shown) are very similar in size. While this phenomenon would be extremely unusual, it is expected in AION, since it features a Realm-vs-Realm design where a player belongs to either of two major tribes (Heavenly and Diabolical) that cannot communicate with each other. The clustering coefficients [2] in the networks are shown in Fig. 1(a), where Trade, Party, Whisper, and Friend networks exhibit clustering coefficients $C > 0.03$, higher than others. In Fig. 1(b), we show by how many factors they are larger than expected

---

[2] Due to space limitations, we refer readers to [2] for the definitions of all the graph measures used.

Table 1: Summary of the basic network characteristics.

	Party(P)	Friend(F)	Whisper(W)	Trade(T)	Mail(M)	Shop(S)
# of Nodes	45,590	29,995	20,107	45,567	56,040	9,423
# of Edges	910,171	103,437	176,245	179,277	170,774	18,882
% of Nodes in GCC [2]	47.44%	46.83%	50.24%	47.06%	49.34%	51.17%
% of Edges in GCC [2]	49.32%	49.47%	47.80%	49.12%	51.24%	58.38%
Network Diameter [2]	15	15	11	27	13	13
Avg. Path Length [2]	3.90	4.80	3.81	5.70	7.63	6.85
Avg. Degree [2]	43.8	13.5	26.2	9.6	6.8	4.0

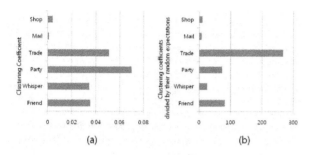

(a)   (b)

Figure 1: (a) The clustering coefficients C. (b) Clustering coefficients divided by their expected values in randomized networks of identical sizes.

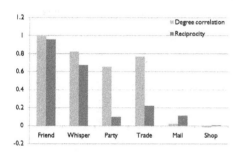

Figure 2: The Pearson correlation coefficients between the in- and the out-degrees of nodes, and the reciprocity of the interactions.

in randomized networks with the same number of nodes and edges. Again, we see that the four social-type networks (F, W, P, T) show factors of 20 or larger indicating the strong clustering tendency.

The Pearson correlation coefficients [3] between the in- and the out-degree of each node, and the reciprocity [2] of interactions are shown in Fig. 2. First, we see that in the four social-type networks (F, W, P, T) the in- and the out-degrees of nodes are high correlated (green, 0.6 or higher); if a user has a long buddy list, then they are likely to be in many buddy lists themselves, and people engaging in Party or Trade initiation are also likely to be actively invited to Parties and Trade. Again, Shop and Mail show very small in- and out-degree correlation. The case of Shop is due to the nature of the interaction and the preferred role that users take: Since a high in-degree represents the role of a merchant, the low correlation means that users who prefer to be one is seldom a buyer from a merchant, and vice versa. In Mail, on the other hand, we found that spammers who send many mails indiscriminately and receive few have a large effect on the statistics.

When we inspect the reciprocity, however, only two of the social-type networks (F and W) are highly reciprocated, while the other two (P and T) are generally not. This presents an interesting observation of the two interactions: when one invites others to a Party, becoming a "Party Leader", it is not necessarily the case that the invitee will at some point invite the original initiator to join their Party. Also, one who initiates a Trade will not necessarily be invited to a Trade by the same person. It indicates that a preferred partner of Party and Trade activities in a gamer's mind tends not to reciprocate the feeling; perhaps the level of strategic thinking necessary for starting a Party or Trade for items is higher – it is conceivable that one may be more interested in joining stronger players when one goes out on a mission – than for Friend or Whisper activities that do not require as much strategizing.

Our current on-going work includes further in-depth investigation of degree distributions [2], triangular motif statistics [5], and the network link and node overlap [4], etc. We believe they will shed light on the correlations and overlap between different types of networks, which in turn would help us understand the organization principles of the social system. In thie paper we reported on the very first results from the analysis of massive interaction data from AION. We believe that there are many promising avenues for more detailed research, for understanding not only human social behavior themselves in a virtual world, but also offline behavior otherwise difficult or impossible to study.

3. ACKNOWLEDGEMENT

This work was funded by KHU-20110088 from Kyung Hee University, KRF-20110005499 from the Korean Research Foundation, the Korea Broadcasting Service, the ITRC support program NIPA-2011-C1090-1001-0004 of MKE/NIPA, and the NAP of Korean Research Council of Fundamental Science and Technology.

4. REFERENCES

[1] S. Hill. MMO Subscriber Populations. http://www.brighthub.com/video-games/mmo/articles/35992.aspx, March 2011.

[2] M. Newman. The Structure and Function of Complex Networks. *SIAM Rev.*, 45(2), 2003.

[3] J. Rodgers and W. Nicewander. Thirteen Ways to Look at the Correlation Coefficient. *The American Statistician*, 42(1), 1988.

[4] J. Onnela, J. Samamaki, J. Hyvonen, G. Szabo, M. Menezes, K. Kaski, A. Barabasi, and J. Kertesz. Analysis of a Large-scale Weighted Network of One-to-one Human Communication. *New Journal of Physics*, 9(6), 2007.

[5] R. Milo, S. Shen-Orr, S. Itzkovitz, N. Kashtan, D. Chklovskii, and U. Alon. Network Motifs: Simple Building Blocks of Complex Network. *Science*, 298(5594), 2002.

Taming Power Peaks in MapReduce Clusters

Nan Zhu*
Dept. of Computer Science
Shanghai Jiaotong University
Shanghai, China
zhunan@sjtu.edu.cn

Lei Rao*
School of Computer Science
McGill University
Montreal, Canada
leirao@cs.mcgill.ca

Xue Liu
School of Computer Science
McGill University
Montreal, Canada
xueliu@cs.mcgill.ca

Jie Liu
Microsoft Research
Microsoft Corp.
Redmond, USA
jie.liu@microsoft.com

Haibin Guan
Dept. of Computer Science
Shanghai Jiaotong University
Shanghai, China
hbguan@sjtu.edu.cn

ABSTRACT

Along with the surging service demands on the cloud, the energy cost of Internet Data Centers (IDCs) is dramatically increasing. Energy management for IDCs is becoming ever more important. A large portion of applications running on data centers are data-intensive applications. MapReduce (and Hadoop) has been one of the mostly deployed frameworks for data-intensive applications. Both academia and industry have been greatly concerned with the problem of how to reduce the energy consumption of IDCs. However the critical power peak problem for MapReduce clusters has been overlooked, which is a new challenge brought by the usage of MapReduce. We elaborate the power peak problem and investigate the cause of the problem in details. Then we design an adaptive approach to regulate power peaks.

Categories and Subject Descriptors

H.m [**Information Systems**]: Miscellaneous; D.0 [**Software**]: General

General Terms

Algorithms, Design, Performance

1. MOTIVATION AND PROBLEM STATEMENT

The energy consumption of Internet Data Centers (IDCs) is an important aspect of data center efficiency. It is reported [4] that IDC operators pay extremely large bill for the energy consumption for their IDCs. As computational needs increase, this trend will continue or even be intensified. Recently both academia and industry are greatly concerned about the problem of energy management for IDCs. Among these research, regulating high power peaks have received considerable attentions. With high power peaks, Power Distribution Units (PDUs) and other power provisioning infrastructures should be subscribed with high level configura-

tions, which greatly increase the capital cost for building and operation of IDCs. Power capping technique is a regulated way to enable additional machines to be hosted and prevent overload situations in IDCs [3]. MapReduce [2] is one of the mostly deployed frameworks for large scale data-intensive applications. However the usage of MapReduce brings new challenges for IDC energy management problems. As we will show in this paper, the decision of when and where to schedule the map and reduce tasks significantly affects the peak power in IDCs.

We observed this problem from Microsoft Production Servers. The power consumption of computing servers running on MapReduce framework does not keep in a stable level and temporary peaks appear at certain moments. We use the Hadoop official software [1] to elaborate this problem and replicate the phenomenon similar to the production system. We elaborate the power peak problem on a 200-nodes Hadoop cluster. The power consumption of the cluster is shown in Figure 1 (More details are in Section 2). The power consumption curve starts at around 10 kilowatts, which is close to the idle power of the nodes in the cluster. It takes about 210 virtual minutes for the cluster to finish the calculation of the workload. During the simulation time, the curve surges at a few time intervals. According to the power consumption distribution, there are less than 8% time intervals where the cluster is operating close to its peak power. If we could remove these few intervals we might be able to further increase the number of machines hosted within a given power budget or decrease the power budget to a lower value, which can both greatly improve the energy efficiency of the IDCs. In this paper, we systematically study the cause of these temporary power peaks in MapReduce clusters and propose an adaptive approach to address the power peak problem.

2. ANALYSIS ON THE POWER CONSUMPTION AND SCHEDULING

In this section, we elaborate the power peak problem on a 200-nodes Hadoop cluster, in which each node has 8 processing cores with the frequency of 2.4 GHz. We use the workload trace file in Mumak provided by Yahoo!.

We first show that the scheduling of the map and reduce tasks affects the power peaks of the Hadoop cluster. We trace both the power consumption and the number of arrived

---

*The first two authors contribute equally for the work in this paper.

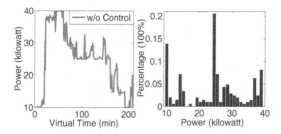

Figure 1: Power Consumption and its Distribution of the Hadoop Cluster

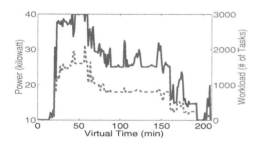

Figure 2: Power Consumption vs. Workload Scheduling Along with Virtual Time in Mumak

tasks with the sampling frequency of 1 minute and present the power consumption and workload scheduling trace in Figure 2. We can observe that the power consumption surges with the increase of the arrived task number for most cases. There are some interesting points in the figure. At the 44th virtual minute, the power consumption goes down when the workload surges. This is because the sizes of jobs at the 42nd and 43rd minutes are large and during these two minutes the system utilization is very high. At the 44th virtual minute, these large size jobs have left the system and only a number of jobs with small sizes have been invoked. The system utilization becomes lower. It is important to remind that the power consumption is linear in the processor utilization (for fixed processor frequency) and is not directly related to the workload arrival rate.

From the above observations and corresponding analysis, we can conclude that the default scheduling in the Hadoop system leads to poor system performances: at a few time intervals the cluster is operating at high power, and during most of the total time interval the cluster operates at low power. This indicates that the system utilization is very low. It is desirable that the system is utilized more evenly with the high power to be relative lower.

3. THE DESIGN OF ADAPTIVE APPROACH

The design of our adaptive approach mainly consists of two modules: The model building module and the controller module. The model building module dynamically estimates the input-output model of the Hadoop cluster. The input is the workload arrival rate and the output is the power of each node in the Hadoop cluster. Based on the dynamic model, the controller module adjusts the input in order to regulate power peaks.

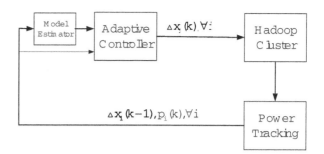

Figure 3: Architecture of the Adaptive Approach

The architecture of the adaptive approach is shown in Figure 3. We consider a general power consumption model of each node i in the Hadoop cluster as following

$$p_i(k) = A_i p_i(k-1) + B_i \Delta x_i(k), \qquad (1)$$

where A_i and B_i are the unknown system parameters and these parameters may vary due to the varying workload; Δx_i represents the change to the arrival rate threshold for node i. For $k = 1, 2 ...,$, the kth control point represents the time k. At each time point, the model estimator gets the change to the workload arrival rate threshold Δx_i form the adaptive controller and the real nodes' power from the power tracking. Based on them, the model estimator calculates the system parameters. We use the recursive least square (RLS) estimator with exponential forgetting to identify the system parameters A_i and B_i for all node i. Then the model estimator sends the updated system parameters to the adaptive controller. The adaptive controller decides the system input, i.e., the workload arrival rate for each node in the Hadoop cluster, according to the power budget.

To achieve the control objective with power capping, we define the following cost function for each server i:

$$J_i(k) = \left(p_i(k+1) - p_i^{cap}(k+1) \right)^2. \qquad (2)$$

This stands for the differences between the consumed power and the power cap value should be as small as possible. It can ensure the power consumed is limited around the expected level. We want to optimize the above cost function so as to regulate the power consumption of the Hadoop cluster.

4. REFERENCES

[1] Hadoop. *http://hadoop.apache.org/*.
[2] J. Dean and S. Ghemawat. Mapreduce: Simplified data processing on large clusters. *OSDI 04'*, pages 137–150, 2004.
[3] X. Fan, W.-D. Weber, and L. A. Barroso. Power provisioning for a warehouse-sized computer. In *ISCA*, 2007.
[4] J. Koomey. Worldwide electricity used in data centers. *Environmental Research Letters*, Sept. 2008.

Towards Scalable and Realistic Node Models for Network Simulators

Stein Kristiansen, Thomas Plagemann, Vera Goebel
Department of Informatics, University of Oslo, Gaustadalléen 23 D, N-0373, Oslo, Norway
{steikr, plageman, goebel}@ifi.uio.no

ABSTRACT

Network simulators typically do not include node models. Our studies show that in networks such as mobile networks, the impact of nodes on performance can be significant. Existing techniques to simulate nodes' are not scalable for network simulations, and require a too large modelling effort to be feasible for network research. In this paper, we propose to capture flexible per-protocol performance profiles from real, running systems using instrumentation and traffic benchmarking techniques. By using the obtained profiles as input into an extended scheduler simulator, the behaviour of the node can be accurately reproduced. Since the processing overhead is represented statistically, we preserve scalability and a low modelling overhead.

Categories and Subject Descriptors

I.6.5 [**Simulation and Modeling**]: Model Development—*Modeling methodologies*

General Terms

Experimentation, Measurement, Performance

1. MOTIVATION AND PROBLEM

Network protocols are most commonly evaluated with network simulators. These simulators rely on accurate models of protocols and communication media, which are assumed to primarily impact the performance. The impact of nodes on the performance is generally ignored. We claim that it is important, especially in mobile networks, that node models in network simulators properly reflect the impact of protocol execution in the nodes onto the protocol performance. Our general observation is that the weaker the node is and the more workload it has to handle, the larger is its impact on the performance. Furthermore, the more nodes involved in protocol execution, the less accurate the results will get, i.e, in an end-to-end protocol over several hops in a Mobile Ad-Hoc Network (MANET). The severity of this problem grows with the time sensitivity of the involved protocols and applications. In network technologies such as sensor networks, MANETs, or opportunistic networks, this problem is particularly prominent as nodes might have to work as end-user devices and routers. We recently studied the forwarding capacity of the Nokia N900 smart phone in real-world experiments [2]. Only with the simple task of IP forwarding, the device was not capable of forwarding more than 6 Mbps over a 54 Mbps network. By analysing traces from a run with 2 Mbps, we found that most packets spent 10-40 ms within the device, depending on the bus frequency. The equivalent experiment in ns-3 yields an average end-to-end delay of 6.85 ms.

Requirements: To overcome the discrepancy between results from real world experiments and simulation experiments it is necessary to enable the network simulator to calculate the impact of protocol execution in the nodes. This requires an accurate model of the protocol execution in a particular device, which we call *node model*. In addition to accuracy, we require the node model to be sufficiently lightweight to allow network simulations with many nodes. Furthermore, it is important that the effort to create node models is not too high, otherwise it would be unrealistic to assume that models for the multitude of possible combinations of protocols and devices will be developed. Therefore, it should be possible to (1) re-use the large base of existing models present in popular, general-purpose network simulators such as ns-2/3, and (2) combine models of individual protocols to models of entire protocol stacks.

2. APPROACH

Our overall approach is based on four elements. First, we take on a modular approach where protocol stacks can be composed from individual protocol execution profiles. Second, for these profiles to be realistic, they are obtained from analysis of traces from real, running systems. To preserve scalability, the profiles contain execution duration distributions rather than implementation details. Third, to capture the dynamics of multi- threaded systems, they are used as input to a scheduler simulator. Fourth, to facilitate the re-use of existing protocol models, we provide the framework to integrate the scheduler simulator with a network simulator. The goal is to make the timing behaviour of protocol models in the network simulator reflect that of a real-world implementation. We focus primarily on small, handheld devices operating in MANETs, but the usefulness of our model extends to other scenarios where nodes can have a significant performance impact. Although we use ns-3 and Linux in our implementation, our approach can be implemented with other OSes and simulators as well.

The overall contribution is a solution to improve accuracy of network simulations where nodes have a considerable impact on performance. This contribution is twofold. First, we provide a tracing and analysis technique to capture the timing behaviour of protocols running on existing multi-threaded devices. Then, we provide the framework to map this behaviour onto existing protocol models in network simulators. As opposed to existing techniques, our model realistically captures the dynamics of multi-threaded systems, while preserving scalability and a low modelling overhead.

3. KEY CHALLENGES

Due to the increasing heterogeneity of available hardware, OSes and protocol implementations, finding parameter values for models is an inherently difficult task. Establishing representative default values is in many cases impossible. Furthermore, a protocol's timing behaviour is determined by its implementation complexity rather than its specification. Since there are several ways to implement protocols, it is clear that it is not feasible to predict execution time from a protocol model alone. If we have the implementation available, along with an architectural description of a device, we can estimate its execution time with existing code analysis techniques. These techniques typically only estimate the number of CPU cycles consumed, and are therefore by themselves not sufficient to characterize overall timing behaviour of a node. Modern devices are usually equipped with several physical execution units in the form of CPUs, DMAs and processors on the NIC. How protocol processing is delegated among these, and the degree of parallelism achieved, has a large impact on performance. Different protocols can run concurrently within different time-shared Logical Execution Units (LEUs) on the same CPU. Their time of execution, and the length of their time-slice, depends on scheduling rules, timers and the amount of workload. This concurrency results in queuing delays between execution units and causes traffic burstiness and tail-dropping of packets. Since packets traverse several protocols, the processing for each packet can be spread across different LEUs. This results in an intermixing of processing stages of different packets, which we call *pre-emptive packet handling*. Our experience with the Nokia N900 demonstrates that the high number of LEUs involved in packet packet forwarding results in a significant amount of imposed traffic burstiness. The reason for the burstiness stems from the common approach to distribute the handling of individual packets among several LEUs. It is important that a node model is able to reproduce this effect.

4. STATE-OF-THE-ART

Although it is possible with existing techniques to model nodes, none of these fulfill all the above mentioned requirements. System simulators are generally too computationally expensive to be used for large scale, long-lasting network simulations. They impose an unreasonably large modelling effort onto a network researcher, because it is required to gain a deep insight into the OS and hardware, and because existing network simulators can not be re-used. To address the latter, a co-simulation framework has been proposed to combine OMNeT++ with SystemC [3]. Scalable models target either sensors or routers. Sensor simulators either do not provide any means to relate processing overhead to real implementations [4], or they generate their model directly from real implementations. The latter is unsuitable for general purpose network simulators. Works on modelling routers [1] do not consider pre-emptive packet handling, and focus on forwarding only.

5. DETAILED APPROACH

We extract per-protocol models from real-world traces. The traces are obtained from protocol-centric traffic benchmarking on a device running an instrumented Linux kernel. We instrument entry- and exit-points of protocol services to obtain service execution time distributions. To unveil the effect of concurrent workload, we perform the benchmark with varying CPU load and parallel memory usage. We also instrument the request queues between (logical) execution units to trace per-packet and -service workflows, and to account for queuing during resource contention. To quantify resource utilization and to unveil the distribution of services among execution units, we instrument the scheduler queues, context switches and subsystems for handling interrupts, timers and deferred work. To be as non-intrusive as possible, we use a combination of dynamic and static tracing techniques. Low-overhead, compiled-in static tracing is used for the scheduler, context switches and the different OS-specific subsystems. These events occur frequently and the location of the trace points do not change with the composition of the network stack. Dynamic tracing is used for services and request queues between protocols. This is to preserve the flexibility of tracing different protocols without the need to re-compile the kernel. To reduce the overhead of dynamic traces, we traverse a user-specified list of services and request queues, adjusting the configuration of dynamic probes to target individual services at a time. To quantify the overhead of processing on the NIC, we deduct intra-OS delay from the intra-node delay obtained by an external monitoring computer. By statistically analysing the resulting traces, we obtain Service Execution Profiles (SEPs) containing (1) per-packet and -service resource utilization distributions, (2) service-to-execution unit mappings and (3) blocking and non-blocking requests made between execution units. We are currently implementing the static tracing component using the *ftrace* tracing utility, and are analysing the traces to ensure that the approach yields acceptable accuracy. To aid our understanding, we have created tools to visualize these traces.

The only currently available alternative to accurately model pre-emptive packet handling is system simulation. We are convinced that our approach will yield a significantly lower modelling effort. Obtaining SEPs mainly involves providing the list of services and request queues of a given protocol, which protocol designers will have readily available. Once the SEP is obtained, it can be made publicly available for reuse by other researchers. Adjusting models in existing network simulators is significantly less work than re-modelling them in a system simulator. SEPs are composed of statistical representations of execution durations, and do not contain any details of the operations performed on packets. Determining simulation durations is simply a matter of distribution sampling rather than actually running or analysing code. Therefore, we are convinced our approach will be scalable.

6. FUTURE WORK

We will complete the dynamic part of the tracing framework, and plan to extend LinuxSched to meet our needs for a scheduler simulator. The next step is to implement the co-simulation framework to integrate the modified LinuxSched with ns-3. The design should allow primitives to be inserted in-line with existing network simulator code to synchronize the virtual time in both simulators.

7. REFERENCES

[1] R. Chertov, S. Fahmy, and N. B. Shroff. A device-independent router model. INFOCOM, Phoenix, USA, 2008.

[2] S. Kristiansen, M. Lindeberg, D. Rodriguez-Fernandez, and T. Plagemann. On the forwarding capability of mobile handhelds for video streaming over manets. MobiHeld '10, New Delhi, India, 2010.

[3] B. Muller-Rathgeber and H. Rauchfuss. A cosimulation framework for a distributed system of systems. In *Vehicular Technology Conference, 2008. VTC 2008-Fall. IEEE 68th*, Calgary, USA, 2008.

[4] P. Pagano, M. Chitnis, G. Lipari, C. Nastasi, and Y. Liang. Simulating real-time aspects of wireless sensor networks. *EURASIP J. Wirel. Commun. Netw.*, 2010:2:1–2:12, April 2010.

Revisiting Next-hop Selection in Multipath Networks

Simon van der Linden
simon.vanderlinden@uclouvain.be

Gregory Detal
gregory.detal@uclouvain.be

Olivier Bonaventure
olivier.bonaventure@uclouvain.be

ICTEAM Institute
Université catholique de Louvain
Louvain-la-Neuve, Belgium

ABSTRACT

Multipath routing strategies such as Equal-Cost MultiPath (ECMP) are widely used in IP and data-center networks. Most current methods to balance packets over the multiple next hops toward the destination base their decision on a hash computed over selected fields of the packet headers. Because of the non-invertible nature of hash functions, it is hard to determine the values of those fields so as to make the packet follow a specific path in the network. However, several applications might benefit from being able to choose such a path. Therefore, we propose a novel next-hop selection method based on an invertible function. By encoding the selection of successive routers into common fields of packet headers, the proposed method enables end hosts to force their packets to follow a specific path.

Categories and Subject Descriptors

C.2.1 [**Computer-Communication Networks**]: Network Architecture and Design—*Packet-switching networks*; C.2.6 [**Computer-Communication Networks**]: Internetworking—*Routers*

General Terms

Algorithms, Management, Performance

Keywords

multipath, load balancing, path selection

1. INTRODUCTION

Load balancing allows to improve the performance and the scalability of the Internet by distributing the load evenly across network links, servers, or other resources, in order to maximize the throughput, achieve redundant connectivity, obtain an optimal resource utilization, or avoid congestion. Different forms of load balancing are deployed at various layers of the protocol stack. At the network layer, multipath routing strategies such as ECMP are widely deployed.

Most multipath routers use a hash computed over selected fields of the packet headers to select a next hop. Because of the avalanche effect hash functions exhibit, a fair distribution of the packets over the next hops is ensured even though the values of their header fields fed to the hash function

might not vary widely[2]. By carefully selecting these fields, next-hop selection methods avoid distributing the packets of a transport-level flow over more than one next hop in order to prevent packet reordering at the destination.

Due to the design of hash functions, it is hard to find the values of these fields in order to force a next hop to be selected at a multipath router. It is even harder to find them to control the decisions of multiple routers in a row, i.e., to force a packet to follow a specific path.

Hash-based next-hop selection methods bring two challenges that could be relieved by letting end hosts possibly control the selection of next hops at multipath routers.

First, it is hard to monitor paths in multipath networks to test and verify the performance and quickly detect problems. The simplest monitoring tool, traceroute, gives erroneous measurements [1]. Paris traceroute fixes most of the problems traceroute experienced with multipath networks, and is able to discover various paths between the source and a destination. Unfortunately, its probabilistic approach causes it to send quite a large amount of probes and leaves undiscovered paths when path diversity increases.

Second, it is difficult for end hosts to use disjoint paths in the network to get better performance and resiliency. There has recently been a growing interest in being able to use multiple paths in transport protocols. While it was initially focused on multi-homed hosts, single-homed hosts could also benefit from multiple paths in the core network. To leverage on multipath with hash-based next-hop selection methods, end hosts can barely do better than creating enough flows in the hope that they will be bound to different paths [3].

For these applications, solutions like source routing or a shim header with routing information are impractical. Monitoring packets should not be handled differently than regular packets. Protocol changes should be avoided to keep compatibility with legacy routers on the path and allow for incremental deployment.

In this paper, we propose a novel next-hop selection method that allows to determine the ports to use for a TCP or UDP flow to choose the path the latter will follow. Compared to a modulo-N hash, the most deployed next-hop selection method, the proposed method mainly differs in two points. First, instead of using a hash function, we use an invertible function, e.g.., a block cipher. Second, we use a different part of the output of that function at each router. Notwithstanding, with ordinary traffic, modulo-N hashes and our method achieve equally-fair distributions.

2. DESIGN

We propose to apply a function over selected fields of the packet header – the source and destination IP address, the protocol identifier, and the source and destination TCP or UDP ports – to pick one next hop among the multiple available at each router along the path to the destination. More precisely, an invertible function F is applied over the source and destination ports, while the rest is fed to a injective function H. F and H should exhibit the avalanche effect to keep the distribution of their output as uniform as possible even if the input is not. We use block ciphers such as RC5 and KATAN for F, and CRC, as in many implementations of hash-based methods, for H. The output of both functions is xor-ed to form a 32-bit value that we call path selector. Albeit the computed path selector is the same at each router on the path, routers pick a different part of it according to the Time-to-Live (TTL) of the packet. This part can serve as a finger into a table of next hops to select one to relay the packet. We call it the next-hop selector.

Using this method, the end host can determine the ports to use to make its flow follow a specific path. The next-hop selectors of all routers on the path are concatenated into a 32-bit value and sorted according to the initial TTL to form a path selector. The latter is then xor-ed with the output of H applied over the source and destination IP addresses, and the protocol identifier. The inverse function F^{-1} is applied over the resulting value. The latter value provides the source and destination ports to use.

If the end hosts do not have enough knowledge of the network topology to construct a useful path selector, the construction could be relegated to a dedicated service. Such a service could be offered to end hosts by a server that gathers information about the topology, e.g., by listening to link-state advertisements.

This next-hop selection method can be used to implement a monitoring tool that deterministically probes any particular path or all paths between a source and a destination. Another example enables hosts using a multipath-aware transport protocol like Multipath TCP [3] to spread flows over disjoint paths. Indeed, while the destination port of the first TCP flow can hardly be chosen, the ports of the subflows are not actually used. They can be freely set in order to make the subflows take different paths than the first one.

Albeit only the ports are controlled and the lattitude of choice their 32 bits offer is limited, our analysis of ISP and data-center networks has shown it should be enough to implement the aforementioned applications in these networks. We are investigating ways to get more bits to control and to use them more efficiently. We are also looking at ways to control the path beyond the network of the packet sender.

3. PRELIMINARY EVALUATION

We implemented the proposed method in a module for the Click modular router. We implemented the Skip32, RC5, and KATAN block ciphers as invertible functions. We also implemented a monitoring tool to validate the ability to control the path the proposed method offers. Due to space limitation, we are not going to evaluate the tool here.

We then analyze how the proposed method preserves a fair distribution of packets at each router, compared to a modulo-2 hash. Therefore, we replay a CAIDA trace [4] of 10 million of packets. Fig. 1 shows the difference in packet dis-

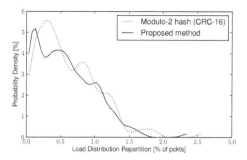

Figure 1: The difference in packet distribution over two next hops is comparable to the distribution offered by the modulo-2 hash.

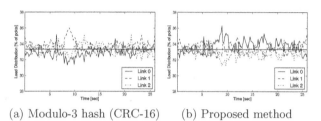

(a) Modulo-3 hash (CRC-16)   (b) Proposed method

Figure 2: The packet distribution over three next hops is similar over time too.

tribution over two next hops for the modulo-2 hash and the proposed method with RC5. We observe two things. First, as the maximum difference value never reaches 3%, the distribution is almost equal. Second, the variation around the optimum is in most cases smaller than 1%. Fig. 2 shows the packet distribuition over time over two next hops. Both the modulo-2 hash and the proposed method slightly fluctuate within the same tight interval [31%, 36%] and their median is close to 33,3%. We observe that there is no strong difference between the two methods.

Thus, the ability to control path offered by the proposed method does not significantly impact the fairness of the local packet distribution. Nevertheless, such a fair distribution might not be preserved if end hosts somehow control the next-hop selection.

4. ACKNOWLEDGMENT

Simon van der linden is supported by a FRIA grant. This work has been partially funded by the FP7 EU project CHANGE.

5. REFERENCES

[1] B. Augustin, X. Cuvellier, B. Orgogozo, F. Viger, T. Friedman, M. Latapy, C. Magnien, and R. Teixeira. Avoiding traceroute anomalies with Paris traceroute. In *Proc. ACM SIGCOMM IMC*, 2006.

[2] Z. Cao, Z. Wang, and E. Zegura. Performance of Hashing-Based Schemes for Internet Load Balancing. In *Proc. IEEE INFOCOM*, 2000.

[3] C. Raiciu, C. Pluntke, S. Barre, A. Greenhalgh, D. Wischik, and M. Handley. Data Center Networking with Multipath TCP. In *Proc. ACM SIGCOMM HotNets Workshop*, 2010.

[4] C. Shannon, E. Aben, K. Claffy, and D. Andersen. The CAIDA Anonymized 2008 Internet Traces – 2008-07-17 12:59:07 - 2008-07-17 14:01:00.

netmap: Memory Mapped Access To Network Devices*

Luigi Rizzo and Matteo Landi, Università di Pisa
http://info.iet.unipi.it/~luigi/netmap/

ABSTRACT

Recent papers have shown that wire-speed packet processing is feasible in software even at 10 Gbit/s, but the result has been achieved taking direct control of the network controllers to cut down OS and device driver overheads.

In this paper we show how to achieve similar performance in safer conditions on standard operating systems. As in some other proposals, our framework, called **netmap**, maps packet buffers into the process' memory space; but unlike other proposals, any operation that may affect the state of the hardware is filtered by the OS. This protects the system from crashes induced by misbehaving programs, and simplifies the use of the API.

Our tests show that **netmap** takes less than 90 clock cycles to move one packet between the wire and the application, almost one order of magnitude less than using the standard OS path. One core at 1.33 GHz can send or receive packets at wire speed on 10 Gbit/s links (14.88 Mpps), with very good scalability in the number of cores and clock speed.

At least three factors contribute to this performance: A i) no overhead for encapsulation and metadata management; ii) no per-packet system calls and data copying; iii) much simpler device driver operation, because buffers have a plain and simple format that requires no run-time decisions.

Categories and Subject Descriptors: C.2.1 [Network Architecture and Design]: Network communications

General Terms: Design, experimentation, performance

Keywords: Software packet processing, operating systems.

1. INTRODUCTION

Moving packets quickly between the wire and the application is a must for systems such as software routers, switches, firewalls, traffic generators and monitors.

The task involves three components: Network Interface Controllers (*NICs*), device drivers, and the Operating System (*OS*). NICs typically handle packets through circular arrays of buffers (*NIC rings*) managed directly by the hardware. Device drivers wrap the buffers in containers (`mbuf`, `skbuf`, `NdisPacket`) to exchange information with the OS about data fragmentation, buffer sharing, offloading of tasks

*Work supported by EC FP7-ICT Project CHANGE 257422. Thanks to Intel Research Berkeley for funding the hardware used to run the experiments.

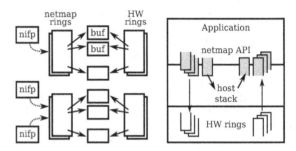

Figure 1: netmap disconnects the adapter's datapath from the host stack, and makes buffers and rings visible to applications through a shared memory area (right).

to the NIC, etc.. The OS in turn introduces further encapsulations and data copies in the path to/from the application. This layering imposes large per-packet overheads, impacting performance in many ways, including energy efficiency and the ability to work at very high packets-per-second rates.

Dedicated appliances address the problem by taking direct control of the hardware, and removing unnecessary software layers. Researchers have followed a similar approach, using modified Click drivers [1, 2], or exporting packet buffers to user space [3], to reach processing speeds of millions of packets per second per core. But giving applications direct access to the hardware (even if mediated by libraries), makes the system extremely vulnerable in case of a crash of the application itself, and often prevents the use of some convenient OS primitives (e.g. select/poll).

The **netmap** framework [4] presented in this paper supports wire-speed packet processing for user-space applications in a conventional OS, while at the same time preserving the safety and convenience of a rich and portable execution environment. **netmap** is mostly meant for trusted applications in charge of special tasks (software router/switches, firewalls, traffic generator and analyzers). Existing applications can benefit of the performance improvements even without using the native **netmap** API, thanks to wrapper libraries (e.g. mapping libpcap calls onto **netmap** calls).

2. ARCHITECTURE

To achieve its performance, our framework changes the way applications talk to the NIC. A program using the **netmap** API opens the special file `/dev/netmap` and issues an `ioctl()` to switch the NIC to "netmap" mode. This *partially* disconnects the NIC from the host stack: standard ioctl()s are still operational to let the operating system configure the interface, but packets are no more exchanged with the host. Instead, they are stored into statically allocated buffers accessible in the program's address space (Fig. 1), with an mmap() call. Structures called *netmap rings*, also residing in the mmap-ed memory, replicate, in a device-independent way, the essential content of the NIC rings: size, cur-rent read/write position, number of available slots (representing received packets on the RX side, empty slots on the TX side), and for each slot, the corresponding buffer index and payload size. This change, as we will see, greatly reduces the packet processing costs.

2.1 Receiving and sending packets

Packet reception is normally preceded by calls to either ioctl(fd, NIOCRXSYNC) (non blocking), or poll() (blocking). On return, these system calls update the netmap ring to reflect the status of the NIC ring. At this point the program can process some of the available packets, adjusting the cur and avail fields of the netmap ring accordingly. These values will be used in the subsequent system call to tell the kernel which buffers have been consumed. Packet data is available through the buffer indexed by the slot.

A similar mechanism is used on the transmit side, with the system calls used to wait for available buffers and/or push out newly queued packets.

Buffers and netmap rings reside in shared memory, so the system calls involve no memory copies; besides, their cost can be amortized over potentially large batches of packets.

2.2 Multiple rings, cores and NICs

Recent 1-10 Gbit cards implement multiple NIC rings to spread load to multiple CPU cores without lock contention. **netmap** supports this feature in a very natural way: NIC rings map to an equivalent number of netmap rings, which can be associated to independent file descriptors and possibly used by different processes/threads. The standard setaffinity() system call permits the mapping of threads to cores without any new or special mechanism.

netmap exports two more rings per NIC to communicate with the host stack. Packets from the host are made visible in an RX netmap ring; packets written to the extra TX netmap ring are encapsulated and passed to the host.

2.3 Efficient packet forwarding

All buffers and netmap rings for all adapters in netmap mode are in the same memory region, shared by the kernel and all **netmap** clients. Hence, handling multiple NICs within one process (e.g. for routing) is straightforward. Zero copy forwarding between interfaces requires no special tricks, either: swapping the buffer index between the source and destination slot enqueues the received buffer for transmission, and at the same time provides a fresh buffer on the receive ring. A similar approach can be followed to let the host stack use the NIC while in netmap mode.

2.4 Security considerations

netmap exposes the system to the same vulnerabilities as libpcap: programs can read all incoming packets, and inject arbitrary traffic into the network. However, they cannot possibly crash the system by writing invalid buffer indexes or packets sizes, because the content of the netmap rings is validated by the system calls before being used.

3. STATUS AND PERFORMANCE

netmap is available on FreeBSD. It consists of about 2000 lines of code for system calls and and general functions, plus individual driver modifications (mostly mechanical, about 500 lines each) currently supporting Intel 10 Gbit and 1 Gbit, and RealTek 1 Gbit adapters. The most tedious parts of the drivers (initialization, the PHY interface, ioctls etc.) do not need changes. Additionally, we have developed some native applications (packet sources and sinks, bridges) and a library to run unmodified libpcap clients on top of **netmap**, often with a 5..20x performance improvement.

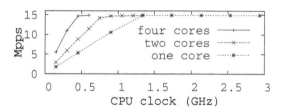

Figure 2: Send rate for a packet generator using netmap with different CPU clock speeds.

netmap dramatically reduces the per-packet overheads compared to the ordinary host stack. As an example, Fig.2 shows the send rate of a packet generator using an Intel 10G card, and an i7-870 CPU at different clock frequencies from 150 MHz to 2.93 GHz. One core achieves line rate (14.88Mpps) at just 1.3GHz, and even at 150 MHz can push out 1.76 Mpps. These numbers correspond to roughly 90 clock cycles/packet. The receive side gives similar numbers. Using 2 or 4 cores is marginally less efficient (going to 100-110 clocks/packet) probably due to memory and bus contention. As a comparison, a native traffic generator on the same system and OS delivers barely 790 Kpps per core at maximum clock speed. A more detailed performance analysis is presented in [4].

4. FUTURE WORK

In addition to porting existing applications, we are working on extending the API to support more features such as better insulation among clients (e.g. providing virtual rings in excess of those supported by the hardware) and a semi-transparent operation mode where the host stack remains connected to the NIC even in netmap mode. These and other extension are likely to expose different tradeoffs between performance and features.

5. REFERENCES

[1] E.Kohler, R.Morris, B.Chen, J.Jannotti, M.F.Kaashoek, The Click modular router, ACM TOCS, vol.18 n.3, pp.263-297, ACM, 2000

[2] M.Dobrescu, N.Egi, K.Argyraki, B.G.Chun, K.Fall, G. Iannaccone, A.Knies, M.Manesh, S.Ratnasamy, RouteBricks: Exploiting parallelism to scale software routers, ACM SOSP, 2009

[3] S. Han, K.Jang, K.Park, S.Moon, PacketShader: a GPU-accelerated software router, Proc. of ACM SIGCOMM 2010, New Delhi, India

[4] L. Rizzo, netmap: fast and safe access to network adapters for user programs, Tech. Report, Univ. di Pisa, June 2011, http://info.iet.unipi.it/~luigi/netmap/

Detecting and Assessing the Hybrid IPv4/IPv6 AS Relationships

Vasileios Giotsas
University College London
v.giotsas@cs.ucl.ac.uk

Shi Zhou
University College London
s.zhou@cs.ucl.ac.uk

ABSTRACT

The business relationships between the Autonomous Systems (ASes) play a central role in the BGP routing. The existing relationship inference algorithms are profoundly based on the valley-free rule and generalize their inference heuristics for both the IPv4 and IPv6 planes, introducing unavoidable inference artifacts. To discover and analyze the Type-of-Relationship (ToR) properties of the IPv6 topology we mine the BGP Communities attribute which provides an unexploited wealth of reliable relationship information. We obtain the actual relationships for 72% of the IPv6 AS links that are visible in the RouteViews and RIPE RIS repositories. Our results show that as many as 13% of AS links that serve both IPv4 and IPv6 traffic have different relationships depending on the IP version. Such relationships are characterized as hybrid. We observe that links with hybrid relationships are present in a large number of IPv6 AS paths. Furthermore, an unusually large portion of IPv6 AS paths violate the valley-free rule, indicating that the global reachability in the IPv6 Internet requires the relaxation of the valley-free rule. Our work highlights the importance of correctly inferring the AS relationships and the need to appreciate the distinct characteristics of IPv6 routing policies.

Categories and Subject Descriptors

C.2.1 [**Computer Communication Networks**]: Network Architecture and Design; C.2.3 [**Computer Communication Networks**]: Network Operations—*Network Management*

General Terms

Measurement, Algorithms

Keywords

Internet, Autonomous Systems, inter-domain routing, BGP, AS relationship, topology, IPv6, inference algorithms

1. INTRODUCTION

The business relationships between the Autonomous Systems (ASes) play a central role in the Internet BGP decision process. Knowledge on the AS relationships is essential for

measuring and analyzing the Internet inter-domain properties and operational trends. AS relationships are coarsely categorized as the transit relationship, i.e. provider-to-customer (p2c) or customer-to-provider (c2p); and the peering relationship, i.e. peer-to-peer (p2p). In a transit relationship the customer pays the provider to transit its traffic to the rest of the Internet. In a peering relationship the peers freely exchange traffic but only between themselves or their customers.

AS relationships are usually treated as confidential. A number of algorithms [1, 2, 4] have been proposed to infer the Type-of-Relationship (ToR) between ASes, utilizing a variety of heuristics. Their common ground is the valley-free property [1], according to which an AS path is valid only if it has one of the following formats: (1) $n \times c2p + m \times p2c$, or (2) $n \times c2p + p2p + m \times p2c$, where $n, m \geqslant 0$.

The existing ToR algorithms analyze the IPv4 and IPv6 AS links using exactly the same principles. However, the AS links carrying IPv6 traffic may follow unconventional BGP routing policies, including relaxed peering requirements and even free IPv6 transit. These distinct policies may result in AS links with different relationship type between the IPv4 and the IPv6 Internet. Such relationships are called *hybrid* IPv4/IPv6 relationships and cannot be captured by the existing ToR algorithms. Hence, measurement artifacts are unavoidable under the current ToR inference approaches.

To rigorously analyze the IPv6 AS relationships and detect the hybrid relationships we rely on the BGP Communities relationship information [3], and the Local Preference (LocPrf) attribute. We utilize the metric of "customer tree" [2] to assess the impact of hybrid links on the IPv6 routing structure.

2. DATA COLLECTION METHODOLOGY

The Communities attribute tags a BGP advertisement with additional information. Communities values are not standardized but the Internet Routing Registries (IRR) provide abundant information on their interpretation. Only Communities that describe relationship types and traffic-engineering requests are relevant to our analysis (the latter to facilitate the interpretation of LocPrf values).

LocPrf expresses the degree of preference that an AS has to a certain route. Usually LocPrf are ordered as follows: $LocPrf_{customer} > LocPrf_{peer} > LocPrf_{provider}$. However, LocPrf can be adjusted to any value for traffic engineering purposes.

The Communities relationships function as the Rosetta Stone for the LocPrf values. A LocPrf value is assigned to a

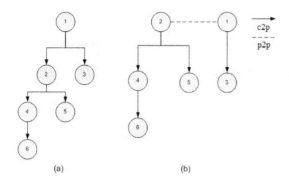

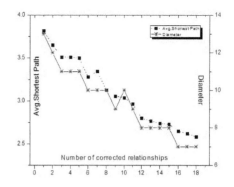

Figure 1: The change in the customer tree when the link 1–2 is (a) p2c or (b) p2p. In (a) AS1 can reach all the nodes through p2c links, while in (b) it can reach only AS3 through a p2c link.

Figure 2: The change of the average shortest path and the diameter of the IPv6 AS customer trees as we gradually correct the misinferred relationship of the 20 hybrid AS relationships with the highest visibility in the IPv6 AS paths.

relationship type only if we can validate it from the collected Communities. The traffic engineering Communities allow us to detect and filter-out LocPrf values used for non-standard preference tuning of specific paths.

3. ANALYSIS AND RESULTS

We collect daily BGP data from RouteViews and RIPE RIS repositories to extract the IPv6 AS paths and AS links. In August 2010, there are 346,649 IPv6 AS paths and 10,535 IPv6 AS links. 7,618 IPv6 AS links are also visible in the IPv4 topology. From the Community and the Local Preference attributes we are able to extract the actual AS relationship for 72% (7,651) of the all IPv6 links and for 81% (6,160) of the IPv4/IPv6 links. We have a number of interesting observations.

Firstly, 779 (or 13%) of the IPv4/IPv6 links have hybrid AS relationships. 67% of such hybrid links have a peering relationship for IPv4 and a transit relationship for IPv6; the rest are p2p for IPv6 and p2c for IPv4, except a single case where the two ASes have a p2c for IPv4 and a c2p for IPv6.

Secondly, the hybrid links usually happen among tier-1 or tier-2 ASes with large numbers of connections. As a result the hybrid links have a high visibility in IPv6 AS paths. More than 28% of the IPv6 paths contain at least one IPv4/IPv6 link with hybrid AS relationships.

Thirdly, 13% of the IPv6 paths do not follow the valley-free rule. We call them the *valley* paths. The large number of IPv6 valley paths is a major reason underlying the inference errors of the existing ToR algorithms. Our analysis indicates that 16% of the valley paths are due to the relaxation of the valley-free rule in order to expand the reachability of IPv6 prefixes. The IPv6 topology is partitioned in terms of valley-free routing [1] and the relaxation of the valley-free rule is necessary in some cases to maintain IPv6 reachability.

4. DISCUSSION

The substantial existence of hybrid IPv4/IPv6 links suggests that the IPv4 and IPv6 Internet topologies should be studied separately. This is consistent with our recent study on the evolution of IPv4 and IPv6 AS topologies [5].

[1] An example is the peering dispute between two transit-free ASes in the IPv6 plane, AS6939 and AS174, as described in http://mailman.nanog.org/pipermail/nanog/2009-October/014017.html

The ToR-annotated AS topology is very sensitive to misinference of AS relationship. An expressive metric to assess the impact of misinferred relationships is the "customer tree" of an AS (root), which contains all the ASes that the root can reach through p2c links. Figure 1 shows an example where the change of relationship between two ASes results in two different topologies. We find that when we replace the IPv6 AS relationships that were misinferred in [4] with the correct relationships inferred from the BGP Communities, the average length and the longest length (diameter) of the shortest valley-free AS paths of the union of the IPv6 customer trees are reduced from 3.8 to 2.23, and from 11 to 7 hops, respectively (Figure 2).

In summary, our results reveal substantial differences between the IPv4 and IPv6 relationships, including a significant number of IPv6 paths that are not valley-free, sometimes in exchange for better reachability. The IPv6 topology should be studied separately using new models that capture its distinct characteristics. Our future work will validate and expand our inference results, investigate the reasons for hybrid links and revisit the valley-free rule. Our dataset and more details are available at the project's website [6].

5. REFERENCES

[1] L. Gao. On inferring autonomous system relationships in the Internet. *IEEE/ACM Trans. Netw.*, 9(6):733–745, 2001.

[2] X. Dimitropoulos, D. Krioukov, M. Fomenkov, B. Huffaker, Y. Hyun, k. claffy, and G. Riley. AS relationships: inference and validation. *SIGCOMM Comput. Commun. Rev.*, 37(1):29–40, 2007.

[3] J. Xia and L. Gao. On the evaluation of as relationship inferences. In *Global Telecommunications Conference, 2004. GLOBECOM '04. IEEE*, 2004.

[4] R. Oliveira, D. Pei, W. Willinger, B. Zhang, and L. Zhang. The (in)completeness of the observed internet as-level structure. *IEEE/ACM Trans. Netw.*, 18:109–122, February 2011.

[5] G.Q. Zhang, B. Quoitin, and S. Zhou. Phase changes in the evolution of the IPv4 and IPv6 AS-Level Internet topologies. *COMPUT COMMUN*, 34(5):649–657, 2011.

[6] http://www.cs.ucl.ac.uk/BAB/

CloudProphet: Towards Application Performance Prediction in Cloud

Ang Li, Xuanran Zong, Srikanth Kandula[†], Xiaowei Yang, Ming Zhang[†]
Duke University
Durham, NC
{angl,xrz,xwy}@cs.duke.edu

[†]Microsoft Research
Redmond, WA
{srikanth,mzh}@microsoft.com

ABSTRACT

Choosing the best-performing cloud for one's application is a critical problem for potential cloud customers. We propose Cloud-Prophet, a trace-and-replay tool to predict a legacy application's performance if migrated to a cloud infrastructure. CloudProphet traces the workload of the application when running locally, and replays the same workload in the cloud for prediction. We discuss two key technical challenges in designing CloudProphet, and some preliminary results using a prototype implementation.

Categories and Subject Descriptors

C.4 [**Performance of Systems**]: General—*measurement techniques, performance attributes*; C.2.4 [**Computer-Communication Networks**]: Distributed Systems—*distributed applications*

General Terms

Design, Performance, Measurement.

Keywords

Cloud computing, performance, prediction.

1. INTRODUCTION

The public cloud computing market has grown dramatically in the recent years. Many companies, including Amazon, Microsoft, and Rackspace, have all released their own public cloud computing infrastructures, such as Amazon AWS, Microsoft Azure, and Rackspace CloudServers. These infrastructures, albeit offering similar services, can diverge significantly in terms of performance [3]. Hence, if a potential cloud customer is planning to migrate her legacy application into cloud, it is critical to know: *which cloud does my application perform best on?*

The most straightforward way is to actually migrate the application to different clouds, so that the customer can field test her application's performance inside the cloud infrastructures. However, migration is not cheap. For infrastructure providers, the whole software stack of the application needs to be deployed on the cloud VMs, incurring huge configuration effort. The application data also need to be migrated to ensure realistic benchmarking, raising the data security concern.

In this work, we focus on *predicting* an application's performance running on a target cloud infrastructure, prior to any migration effort. Depending on accuracy, the prediction result can di-

rectly point the customer to the best-performing provider, or at least limit the scope for actual migration and field testing. There are two common approaches for performance prediction. Standard benchmarks [1, 3] can provide a baseline to compare the performance of different providers. However, as the benchmarks are simple by design, it is challenging to map the complex and multi-tiered cloud applications to the limited set of benchmarks. Modeling is another widely used approach to predict the performance of simple computation and I/O-intensive applications [5]. Yet it remains a challenging task to describe the complex and often distributed cloud applications' workload using concise model characteristics.

In this paper, we propose CloudProphet, a performance prediction tool aiming to provide accurate and application-specific prediction results. CloudProphet takes a trace-and-replay approach [4]. During *tracing*, CloudProphet records the detailed workload information and the internal dependency of a representative application run. During *replaying*, CloudProphet runs an agent in the target cloud platform, which emulates the workload of the traced application run by replaying the recorded workload and dependency. The performance of the agent is then used to predict the application performance after migration.

We choose this approach for several reasons. First, it does not require any *a priori* knowledge of the performance characteristics of the target cloud infrastructure, because the agent uses real workload to test the infrastructure's efficiency. This is particularly suitable for the cloud environment, as the performance of a cloud can change frequently due to interferences and equipment upgrades. Second, the approach is less likely to be limited by the complexity of the application. As long as we can trace the correct dependency, the approach should work with applications with multiple components and rich inter-component communication, which is essential for the practicality of the tool.

In the following, we describe several key design challenges of CloudProphet.

2. CHALLENGES

2.1 Non-deterministic Application Workload

For many multi-threaded applications, such as databases and scientific computation tools [6], the workload on each thread depends on the order of the synchronization events (*e.g.*, locks), which in turn depends on how the threads interleave with each other. Due to the performance (e.g. CPU and I/O speed) difference in cloud, the application threads may interleave differently if migrated, which then leads to different workload. In this case, simply replaying the workload events collected locally can result in poor prediction accuracy.

We first illustrate the problem using a real example. Figure 1(a) shows part of the request handling code of a file hosting application UDDropBox, and (b) shows the lock and I/O events triggered by two application threads during tracing. Note that thread $T2$ fails to acquire the lock and has to sleep for a while before retrying.

A naive replay mechanism simply replays all events in each thread's trace one after another. This may cause the replayed events to diverge from the real events of the application if migrated. For instance, if the cloud VM has faster disk I/O, $T1$'s unlock event may happen earlier than the first trylock event of $T2$ (Figure 1(c)). In this case, the first trylock of $T2$ would succeed, and the application would directly trigger open instead of usleep. However, if we replay strictly according to the event trace, $T2$ still needs to replay usleep and another trylock before open. This adds unnecessary overhead to $T2$.

CloudProphet introduces a novel mechanism to address this. During replay, CloudProphet *detects* any synchronization event that occurs out-of-order compared to the order in the recorded trace. An out-of-order synchronization event may cause the future workload events to diverge from the events in the current trace. If such an event is detected, CloudProphet pauses the replay process, and starts a new application run on the local machine to update the workload events after the diverged point. Specifically, the new run is steered by enforcing the new synchronization events order occurred in cloud [2]. After the application run has reached the diverged point, CloudProphet then collects the updated workload events, resumes the replay process, and uses those events for future replaying. The process is repeated if new out-of-order events are detected.

Consider again the previous example. With the new mechanism the cloud replayer will detect that the first trylock of $T2$ occurs out-of-order, because the event happens before $T1$'s unlock in the trace, while during replay it occurs after. CloudProphet then pauses the replay right after the trylock, and tries to update the future events through a new run of the application. During the new run, CloudProphet enforces the order between the trylock and the unlock, so that the trylock always happens after the unlock. In this way, the trylock is guaranteed to succeed, and therefore the application will immediately trigger open and other I/O functions afterwards. Finally, CloudProphet updates the event trace using the new local events that do not contain the extra usleep and trylock, and resumes the replay.

The mechanism does not make any assumption on the application model, and therefore theoretically works for arbitrary application. On the other hand, one practical limitation is that it requires multiple runs of the application to obtain the right workload to replay. It is our ongoing work to adopt optimizations to reduce the overhead.

2.2 Replay Computation Workload

To faithfully replay the computation (CPU and memory) workload of the original application, we need to trace the exact CPU instructions executed and the memory footprint. However, this can incur significant tracing overhead and increase the replayer complexity. CloudProphet instead adopts a simple linear model to map the local computation workload to the one in cloud. The model scales the CPU time measured locally by a constant factor calibrated by standard CPU benchmarks. The cloud replayer then uses a busy-loop to emulate the scaled workload. The model works reasonably well for most applications we have tested (the error rate is smaller than 30% for most cases), including memory-intensive applications in the SPLASH-2 benchmark [6].

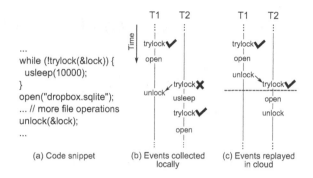

```
...
while (!trylock(&lock)) {
  usleep(10000);
}
open("dropbox.sqlite");
... // more file operations
unlock(&lock);
...

        (a) Code snippet
```

Figure 1: (a) The UDDropBox code snippet that accesses the lock-protected database file; (b) The events collected locally; (c) The events replayed in the cloud by CloudProphet.

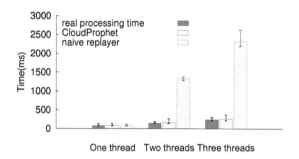

Figure 2: The prediction results of the UDDropBox application.

3. PRELIMINARY RESULTS

Figure 2 shows the prediction results of UDDropBox with 1, 2, and 3 concurrent clients. Each client uploads ten 1MB files back-to-back. We predict the total processing time on an Amazon AWS m1.large instance. In comparison, we also show the real processing time when actually running DropBox on the cloud VM, and the prediction results using the naive replay mechanism. The prediction result of CloudProphet closely matches the real processing time. Moreover, with multiple threads the naive mechanism predicts almost ten-fold of the real processing time, suggesting that the workload collected on our local machine diverges significantly from the real workload in cloud. The result shows our approach is promising in predicting the performance of applications with non-deterministic workload.

4. REFERENCES

[1] Cloudharmony benchmark results. http://cloudharmony.com/benchmarks.
[2] Jong-Deok Choi and Harini Srinivasan. Deterministic replay of Java multithreaded applications. In *Proceedings of the SIGMETRICS symposium on Parallel and distributed tools - SPDT '98*, pages 48–59, New York, New York, USA, 1998. ACM Press.
[3] Ang Li, Xiaowei Yang, Srikanth Kandula, and Ming Zhang. CloudCmp: Comparing Public Cloud Providers. In *ACM IMC*, 2010.
[4] Michael P. Mesnier, Matthew Wachs, Raja R. Sambasivan, Julio Lopez, James Hendricks, Gregory R. Ganger, and David O'Hallaron. //trace: parallel trace replay with approximate causal events. In *USENIX FAST*, 2007.
[5] Mengzhi Wang, Kinman Au, Anastassia Ailamaki, Anthony Brockwell, Christos Faloutsos, and Gregory R. Ganger. Storage device performance prediction with cart models. In *MASCOTS*, pages 588–595, Washington, DC, USA, 2004.
[6] Steven Cameron Woo, Moriyoshi Ohara, Evan Torrie, Jaswinder Pal Singh, and Anoop Gupta. The SPLASH-2 programs: characterization and methodological considerations. In *ACM ISCA*, 1995.

A Novel Approach for Making Energy Efficient PON

[1]S.H. Shah Newaz
[2]JunKyun Choi
Dept. of Electrical Engineering (EE)
Korea Advanced Institute of Science and Technology
(KAIST)
Daejeon, South Korea
[1]newaz@kaist.ac.kr, [2]jkchoi59@kaist.edu

[1]Ángel Cuevas
[2]Gyu Myoung Lee
[3]Noël Crespi
Dept. of Wireless Networks and Multimedia Services
Institut Telecom, Telecom SudParis
Evry, France
[1]angel.cuevas_rumin@it-sudparis.eu, [2]gm.lee@it-sudparis.eu, [3]noel.crespi@it-sudparis.eu

ABSTRACT

Nowadays Passive Optical Network (PON) requires that Optical Network Units (ONUs) wake up periodically to check if the Optical Line Terminal (OLT) has any message directed to them. This implies that ONUs change from sleeping mode in which they just consume 1 W to active mode in which the consumption goes up to 10 W. In many cases, the OLT does not have any packets for the ONU and it goes to sleep again, what supposes a waste of energy. In this paper, we propose a novel Hybrid ONU that relies on a low-cost and low-energy technology, IEEE 802.15.4, to wake up those ONUs that are going to receive a packet. Our first estimations demonstrates that our solution would save around 25000$ per year and OLT.

Categories and Subject Descriptors: C.2.1
[Computer Communication Networks]: Network Architecture and Design

General Terms: Algorithms, Design, Management

Keywords: Energy saving, PON, Sleep mode, converged.

1. INTRODUCTION

In a Passive Optical Network (PON), an Optical Line Terminal (OLT) is the centralized intelligence. It receives the packets from the core network and then delivers them to the destination Optical Network Unit (ONU) through optical fiber. On the other hand, the OLT assigns fixed time slots to the ONUs for the upstream transmission. In a typical PON architecture, in the downstream direction signal is broadcasted using a passive splitter, while in the uplink an ONU uses unicast transmissions. Under one OLT there can be 16, 32, or 64 ONUs.

According to the existing solutions [1, 2], an ONU goes to sleep mode when it does not have anything to send or receive. Then, the OLT sends a message to the ONU informing the next listening interval. ONU needs to wake up before that listening interval in order to receive the OLT's feedback. If there is any packet destined for that ONU, the OLT forwards it to the ONU. Otherwise, the OLT notifies the ONU when the next listening interval will take place and asks to switch into sleep state. Conversely, if an ONU receives any packets from the customer premises to the network, it stores the packet and transmits to the OLT during the assigned uplink transmission slot.

When the packet arrival rate is low, an ONU can take long sleep [1, 2] to save more energy. In such case, any arrived packet at the OLT might experience delay. As shown in Figure 1 the first packet destined to ONU 1 experiences delay $D = t_1-t_0$. Furthermore, in the existing approaches an ONU needs to wake up periodically and listen, even though it may not have any downstream packets to receive (see Figure 1). During these listening intervals an ONU approximately consumes 10 W of power, whereas the sleeping mode just requires 1 W consumption. Indeed, it is a waste of energy.

In this paper, we address those aforementioned issues. To mitigate such problems, we introduce a new ONU module, named as Hybrid OUN (HONU), and a novel protocol procedures. Using our approach, a significant amount of energy can be saved.

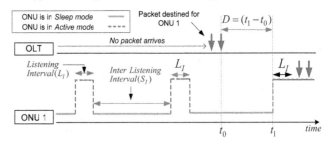

Figure 1. Listening procedure in the existing ONUs.

2. SOLUTION

The new ONU architecture (i.e., HONU) integrates the existing ONU module and an IEEE 802.15.4 module. In this approach, when the ONU module needs to go to sleep state the IEEE 802.15.4 module takes over the responsibility of periodic listening through its wireless interface, and after a packet arrival at the OLT, it is invoked to make the ONU module waking up. We design the protocol procedure in such a way that IEEE 802.15.4 module of a sleeping HONU can be invoked from the OLT through other active HONUs' IEEE 802.15.4 module using its wireless interface. It must be noted that IEEE 802.15.4 is a low-cost technology whose installation will just be a minor part of the budget required to deploy a PON network. Therefore, at a very low cost, we will be able to reduce a lot the energy consumption by extending the time in which an ONU uses the sleeping mode.

Basically, an ONU is composed of two parts: analog and digital as shown in Figure 2 (a). In absence of packet arrival, ONU goes to sleep mode by switching off most of the components (e.g., laser driver circuit, Tx, Rx [2]) of its Analog part. After switching off those components, the sleep coordinator notifies Interrupter (i.e., IEEE 802.15.4) module to wake up periodically to check whether there is any downstream packet arrival notification arrives or not.

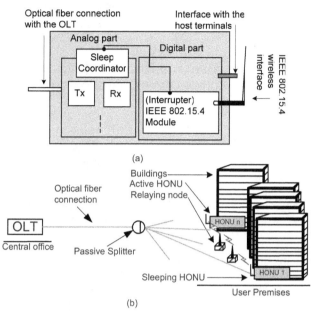

Figure 2. (a) Functional block diagram of a HOUN. (b) HONU deployment scenario in a customer premises.

We assume that at a given time at least one of the HOUNs is in active mode under the OLT. The OLT needs to notify a HONU on downstream packet arrival. Hence, even if there is no incoming downstream traffic, OLT invokes one of the HONUs to stay in active mode. As a result, the OLT can reach any Interrupter and make a HONU's analog part active on packet arrival. Furthermore, we assume that in the customer premises all the Interrupters can communicate among themselves through their wireless interfaces. Figure 2 (b) states a scenario where OLT requests the HONU 1 to be waked up through the HONU n, which is in active mode.

As the number of PON hosts is exponentially increasing, there would not be much distance between two HOUNs (e.g., the distance can be two consecutive buildings in an urban area). Then PON operators should deploy an IEEE 802.15.4 network that allows the interconnection of the different HONUs satisfying reliability and delay requirements. We consider that all these Interrupters and the intermediate relaying nodes sleep and wakeup synchronously. When a new packet arrives for a sleeping HONU, the OLT notifies the Interrupter of that HONU through any active HONU. After getting the notification from the OLT, the Interrupter of that HONU invokes the sleep coordinator. Sleep coordinator makes the analog part of the sleeping HONU active. Figure 3 states how HONU's ONU module switches to Active state. After being active, that ONU module synchronizes with the OLT's downstream clock and then start receiving the packets.

3. INITIAL RESULTS AND DISCUSSION

We perform some initial analysis in order to compute the energy saved when a PON network utilizes the proposed HONUs instead of the standard one. Figure 3 depicts that while an ONU of a 10 G Ethernet PON consumes 10 W, the Interrupters of our HONUs just need to use 30 mw [3] in the listening state. Then we roughly estimate that in a PON network with 32 ONUs our solution saves 450 kW/day. Then, assuming an average kW price of 0.15$, our solution would save 67.5$ per day. If we extend that saving to a complete year, the saving per OLT and year goes up to $25000. Then, in case an operator decides to widely deploy PON technology in a big and dense city (e.g. Seoul) thousands of OLTs would be required, and our solution would reduce electricity bill in millions of dollars. Besides, as all the HOUNs are reachable from the OLT, downstream packets experience reduced amount of delay. Future work will present this idea in more detailed.

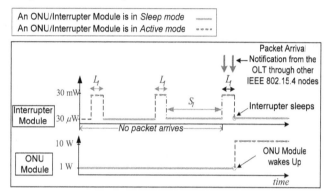

Figure 3. Proposed periodic listening procedure for an interrupter and on packet arrival wake up procedure for an ONU module.

4. REFERENCES

[1] R. Kubo, J.-i. Kani, H. Ujikawa, T. Sakamoto, Y. Fujimoto, N. Yoshimoto, H. Hadama, "Study and Demonstration of Sleep and Adaptive Link Rate Control Mechanisms for Energy Efficient 10G-EPON," *Journal of Optical Communications and Networking*, IEEE/OSA, vol.2, pp.716-729, Sep. 2010.

[2] Z. Jingjing, N. Ansari, "Toward energy-efficient 1G-EPON and 10G-EPON with sleep-aware MAC control and scheduling," *IEEE Communications Magazine* , vol.49, pp.s33-s38, February 2011.

[3] Dong-Hoon Cho, Jung-Hoon Song, Ki-Jun Han, "An Adaptive Energy Saving Mechanism for the IEEE 802.15.4 LR-WPAN, Wireless Algorithms, Systems, and Applications. Lecture Notes in Computer Science. Springer, Berlin, 2006.

On the Efficacy of Fine-Grained Traffic Splitting Protocols in Data Center Networks

Advait Dixit
dixit0@cs.purdue.edu

Pawan Prakash
pprakash@cs.purdue.edu

Ramana Rao Kompella
kompella@cs.purdue.edu

Department of Computer Science
Purdue University

ABSTRACT

Multi-rooted tree topologies are commonly used to construct high-bandwidth data center network fabrics. In these networks, switches typically rely on equal-cost multipath (ECMP) routing techniques to split traffic across multiple paths, such that packets within a flow traverse the same end-to-end path. Unfortunately, since ECMP splits traffic based on flow-granularity, it can cause load imbalance across paths resulting in poor utilization of network resources. More fine-grained traffic splitting techniques are typically not preferred because they can cause packet reordering that can, according to conventional wisdom, lead to severe TCP throughput degradation. In this work, we revisit this fact in the context of regular data center topologies such as fat-tree architectures. We argue that packet-level traffic splitting, where packets of a flow are sprayed through all available paths, would lead to a better load-balanced network, which in turn leads to significantly more balanced queues and much higher throughput compared to ECMP.

Categories and Subject Descriptors

C.2.2 [**Computer Communication Networks**]: Network Protocols

General Terms

Performance

Keywords

Data centers, traffic splitting

1. INTRODUCTION

To scale the data center network to provide the level of connectivity required, most data center network fabrics are organized in the form of a multi-rooted tree topology. Further, they use multipathing between servers so that load is balanced among several alternate paths and the chances of congestion are reduced. One popular multipathing mechanism used in data centers today is equal-cost multipath (ECMP). Many recent works have identified the load imbalance that can arise due to ECMP and suggested different approaches for making the load more balanced across the different available paths.

We revisit the conventional wisdom that packet-level traffic splitting (PLTS) is inherently harmful to TCP. Specifically, our observation is grounded on the fact that many popular data center network designs such as the fat tree, or more generally, multi-rooted tree topologies are symmetric in their architecture, and by spraying packets across different paths leads to a more balanced and predictable network architecture, that interacts well with TCP.

We propose different variants of the per-packet load balancing algorithms in this paper that exploit the basic idea, but vary depending on the amount of state each of the solution maintains in the routers. Using simulations, we compare these various strategies in terms of TCP throughput achieved. We also compare them against ECMP on various network parameters like latency, fairness etc. Specifically, we show that per-packet load balancing outperforms ECMP in all the dimensions—1.5× better throughput and 6× better latency at the 99th percentile.

2. PACKET-LEVEL TRAFFIC SPLITTING

We use three simple techniques—random, counter-based and round-robin—to demonstrate the power and limitations of PLTS. All these techniques essentially split a flow across all available paths, but differ based on the amount of state maintained at the switches. Random picks an arbitrary port at random (among the multiple next hops) to forward a packet, and hence requires no state to implement. At the other end of the spectrum, we discuss a per-flow round robin technique where packets within a flow are transmitted in a round robin fashion. However, it requires remembering the last port used on a per-flow basis making it more complicated than the random.

In addition to the above, we also propose a new algorithm that splits traffic based on local port counters. This reduces the amount of state required significantly, but also results in slightly worse load balancing in the network (as we shall see) and consequently, a slight loss in throughput. While this list of algorithms is not meant to be exhaustive, we chose these three schemes as potential candidates since they can be implemented in a rather straight-forward fashion.

3. EVALUATION

Most of our experiments in this paper are based on simulations using QualNet , a packet-level discrete event simulator. For evaluating PLTS, we focus mainly on fat-tree [1] architecture. However, the results shown should hold good in many topologies with multiple equal-cost paths between end hosts.

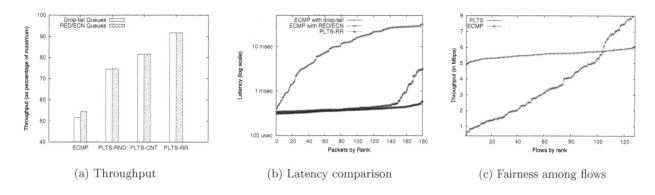

| (a) Throughput | (b) Latency comparison | (c) Fairness among flows |

Figure 1: Throughput, latencies and fairness achieved among flows.

For this evaluation, we simulate a 6-pod fat tree topology with 54 end-hosts and create 27 FTP applications which run for the entire duration of the simulation. The end hosts for each FTP application are chosen at random while ensuring that each end host executes either one FTP server or client. Since a fat tree topology offers full bisection bandwidth, ideally each FTP application should be able to transfer data at full link capacity.

Figure 1(a) shows the average throughput observed by FTP applications, under different schemes, as a percentage of the ideal throughput.

All the three PLTS techniques achieve better throughput than ECMP as shown in Figure 1(a). [4] reports that MP-TCP achieves almost 90% utilization for the same experimental setup, which is comparable to what the PLTS-RR achieves. Among packet-level traffic splitting, PLTS-RND attains the least throughput because skews in short sequences of random numbers increases variability in latencies across different path. PLTS-CNT attains around 81% of the ideal throughput. PLTS-RR ensures that all the paths between source and destinations are utilized. Figure 1(a) confirms this behavior and PLTS-RR is able to achieve almost 92% of the ideal throughput.

The latencies for the sampled packets are ranked and plotted in figure 1(b). PLTS with drop-tail policy shows significantly better packet latency values as compared to ECMP with RED/ECN. A packet in PLTS experiences only one-third of the packet latency of ECMP with RED/ECN at the 90th percentile and one-sixth of the packet latency at the 99th percentile. In PLTS, flows achieve better TCP throughput on an average as compared to flows with ECMP forwarding. Figure 1(c) shows the throughput observed by all flows. Flow throughputs for ECMP show a huge variability as compared to those of PLTS. There is an order of magnitude of difference between the highest and lowest throughput seen by ECMP.

4. RELATED WORK

The most related to our work are those mechanisms that rely on flow-level traffic splitting such as ECMP, Hedera [2] and Mahout [3]. Techniques like Hedera and Mahout, which select a path for a flow based on current network conditions suffer from a common problem: When network conditions change over time, the selected path may no longer be the optimal one. VL2[5] propose using Valiant Load Balancing

(VLB) at a per-flow granularity, but they too do not split an individual flow across multiple paths.

Two research efforts propose traffic splitting at a sub-flow granularity. MPTCP [4] splits a TCP flow into multiple flows at the end hosts. FLARE [6] exploits the inherent burstiness of TCP flows to break up a flow into bursts called flowlets. We did experiment with some simple variants of FLARE, such as forwarding a small number of consecutive packets of a flow along the same path. But we observed that, since bursts of packets may actually lead to disparity in queue lengths across different paths, they cause much more packet reordering and reduction in throughput.

5. CONCLUSION

We show that simple packet-level traffic splitting mechanisms can yield significant benefits in keeping the network load balanced resulting in better overall utilization, despite the well-known fact that TCP interacts poorly with reordered packets. These schemes are also readily implementable and are of low complexity making them an appealing alternative to ECMP and other complicated mechanisms like Hedera or MPTCP. While more work needs to be done, we believe that the myth that TCP interacts poorly with reordering, while may be true in more general settings, does not seem to hold true in regular data center topologies.

6. REFERENCES

[1] M. Al-Fares, A. Loukissas, and A. Vahdat, "A scalable, commodity data center network architecture," *SIGCOMM 08*.

[2] M. Al-fares, S. Radhakrishnan, B. Raghavan, N. Huang, and A. Vahdat, "Hedera: Dynamic flow scheduling for data center networks," in *NSDI*, 2010.

[3] A. Curtis, W. Kim, and P. Yalagandula, "Mahout: Low-overhead datacenter traffic management using end-host-based elephant detection," in *Infocom*, 2011.

[4] Alan Ford, Costin Raiciu, and Mark Handley, "Tcp extensions for multipath operation with multiple addresses," Internet-draft, IETF, Oct. 2009.

[5] A. Greenberg, J. R. Hamilton, N. Jain, S. Kandula, C. Kim, P. Lahiri, D. A. Maltz, P. Patel, and S. Sengupta, "Vl2: a scalable and flexible data center network," in *SIGCOMM '09*.

[6] Shan Sinha, Srikanth Kandula, and Dina Katabi, "Harnessing TCPs Burstiness using Flowlet Switching," in *3rd ACM SIGCOMM Workshop on Hot Topics in Networks (HotNets)*, San Diego, CA, November 2004.

Wide-area Routing Dynamics of Malicious Networks

Maria Konte, Nick Feamster
Georgia Tech
{mkonte, feamster}@cc.gatech.edu

ABSTRACT

This paper studies the routing dynamics of malicious networks. We characterize the routing behavior of malicious networks on both short and long timescales. We find that malicious networks more consistently advertise prefixes with short durations and long interarrival times; over longer timescales, we find that malicious ASes connect with more upstream providers than legitimate ASes, and they also change upstream providers more frequently.

Categories and Subject Descriptors: C.2.0 [Computer Communication Networks]: Security and protection.

General Terms: Measurement, Security, Management.

Keywords: Hostexploit, malicious networks, BGP, routing dynamics, security.

1. INTRODUCTION

Attackers use advanced techniques to launch spam campaigns or mount attacks; in particular, Ramchandran *et al.* [?] observed that some some attackers send spam from hijacked prefixes. Previous studies have studied different malicious activities in isolation such as worms, botnets, spam, and Internet scam infrastructure [?, ?] and proposed detection solutions for each of them. Unfortunately, observing just the nature of the attack itself is not sufficient, because any given network or host may mount different attacks on different days. Rather than attempting to detect any individual attack, we characterize the *routing behavior* of malicious networks that are primarily responsible for cybercriminal activities and identify features of this behavior that may be more stable across time. Although our initial goal is simply to characterize this behavior, our belief is that ultimately certain aspects of routing behavior may serve as invariants for detecting malicious infrastructure, even as the attacks themselves evolve. Specifically, we believe that routing behavior may ultimately be useful for identifying and monitoring the activity of networks that mount attacks, even as the attacks themselves change.

We perform the first systematic study of the wide area routing behavior of malicious networks. To understand the nature of malicious routing behavior with respect to legitimate domains, we compare the routing behavior from autonomous systems (ASes) listed in Hostexploit to the routing behavior of the ASes that host the top 500 Alexa domains. Hostexploit [?], an organization that correlates data from multiple sources such as spam, malware, spam bots, botnet C&C servers, and phishing servers from industry partners, has been publicizing lists of ASes that show the highest levels of cy-

bercriminal activity for the last three years. Hostexploit rates each AS with an index based on the activity of the AS weighted by the size of its allocated address space. There are examples of these networks that were detected and eventually disconnected including ATRIVO/Intercage on September 2008 and VolgaHost on January 2011.

We perform our analysis across two timescales. On short timescales, we study how malicious networks advertise their prefixes. For every prefix, we group the announcements into distinct events and study the duration and interarrival time of each event over the period of one month. We perform our analysis for two months, January and June, for four consecutive years (2008–2011). We show only the results for January 2011, but our results are qualitatively consistent for all time periods. We find that malicious ASes advertise a large portion of their prefixes (45%) over events that have both shorter duration *and* longer interarrival time than legitimate ASes. Over long timescales, we study the wiring trends of malicious ASes and find that malicious ASes connect with more providers than legitimate ASes; they also change their upstream providers more frequently.

2. DATA

We use the list of networks that are reported as top in Internet criminal activities according to Hostexploit from 2009–2011 to identify a set of malicious ASes. We augment this dataset with the following sources: (1) To study the behavior of malicious networks on *short timescales*, we collect the complete set of BGP updates from malicious networks, from all RouteViews monitors. We cluster the BGP updates we observe for each prefix into *prefix events*. A prefix event begins when a RouteViews monitor receives a new announcement for a prefix from some origin AS. A prefix event ends at the time when the same monitor receives the *first* withdrawal for the corresponding prefix. (2) To understand the behavior of malicious networks over *long timescales*, we obtain a publicly available dataset of customer-provider links formed among ASes over a ten-year period [?]. To understand how malicious behavior of malicious ASes differs from legitimate ASes, we perform the same analysis for the ASes that host the top 500 Alexa domains.

3. PRELIMINARY RESULTS

Malicious networks advertise their prefixes over events with shorter duration and longer interarrival time than legitimate networks. To study the behavior of malicious networks over short timescales, we proceed as follows: (1) We cluster all the announcements for all the prefixes that originate from malicious networks, as observed from all RouteViews monitors for one month into events as described in Section ??. (2) We *jointly* examine the duration and

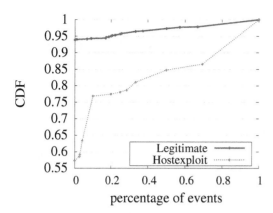

Figure 1: Malicious networks advertise their prefixes over events with shorter duration and longer interarrival time than legitimate networks.

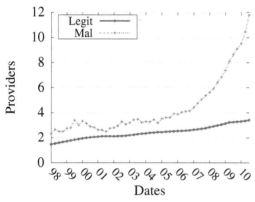

(a) Malicious ASes connect to more providers over time.

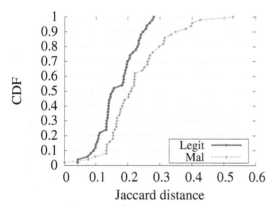

(b) Malicious ASes are more aggressive in connecting to new upstream providers.

Figure 2: Malicious ECs link with more providers through their lifetime and change their upstream connectivity more frequently than legitimate EC.

the interarrival time of these events. More specifically, for each prefix, we categorize its events into four types: a) long duration - short interarrival time, b) long duration - long interarrival time, c)

short duration - short interarrival time and d) short duration - long interarrival time. We consider the *duration* of a prefix event to be short if is less than five minutes, which is the median advertisement duration of about 40% of the prefixes. Similarly, we consider the *interarrival time* of a prefix event to be short if it is less than 100 seconds, which is the median interarrival value for about 40% of the prefixes for all of their events. (3) For every prefix, we compute the fraction of the events we observe for each event type. Figure **??** shows the distribution of events per prefix for each event type. The most striking finding is that about 80% of the prefixes advertised by malicious ASes are advertised mostly with events of short duration and long interarrival time for about 70% of prefix events, whereas roughly 85% of the legitimate prefixes have no events of this type at all.

Malicious networks link with more providers through their lifetime than legitimate networks. We examine the total number of providers that ASes connect to over their lifetime. Here, we focus on the ASes that are Enterprise Customers (EC) according to their AS classification [**?**]. Figure **??** shows the cumulative number of average providers that malicious and legitimate ASes connect to over time. We note that both the number of ASes and the cumulative number of providers increase as time progresses, but the rate at which the two increase is not always the same. For some snapshots we observe a small decrease in the average cumulative number of providers. We observe that malicious ASes link on average with a total of twelve providers over the course of twelve years, whereas the legitimate ASes connect to an average of four providers. AS23456 linked with a total of 183 providers from April 2007 through January 2010.

Malicious networks change their upstream connectivity more frequently than legitimate networks. To quantify the aggressiveness of an AS in changing its upstream connectivity, we consider the distance between the set of the AS's providers for two consecutive snapshots. We use the Jaccard distance as a metric of distance between the set of providers between two consecutive snapshots. For example, a Jaccard distance of 0.8 indicates that 80% of the links seen in the two snapshots are observed in one of the two snapshots but not in both. We calculated the Jaccard distance between two consecutive snapshots for each AS throughout its lifetime. Figure **??** shows the distribution of the Jaccard distance values. We observe that malicious ASes more frequently change their upstream connectivity than legitimate ASes.

Acknowledgements

This work is funded by the National Science Foundation under NSF CAREER Award CNS-0643974 and CNS-0831300, and the Department of Homeland Security under contract number FA8750-08-2-0141.

REFERENCES

[1] A. Dhamdhere and C. Dovrolis. Ten Years in the Evolution of the Internet Ecosystem. In *Proceedings of ACM SIGCOMM/USENIX Internet Measurement Conference (IMC).*, 2008.

[2] Hostexploit. http://www.hostexploit.com.

[3] H. A. Kim and B. Karp. Autograph: Toward automated, distributed worm signature detection. In *the 13th conference on USENIX Security Symposium*, 2004.

[4] C. Kreibich and J. Crowcroft. Honeycomb: Creating intrusion detection signatures using honeypots. In *2nd Workshop on Hot Topics in Networks (HotNets-II)*, 2003.

[5] A. Ramachandran and N. Feamster. Understanding the network-level behavior of spammers. In *Proceedings of Sigcomm*, 2006.

Online Testing of Federated and Heterogeneous Distributed Systems

Marco Canini, Vojin Jovanović, Daniele Venzano, Dejan Novaković, and Dejan Kostić

School of Computer and Communication Sciences, EPFL, Switzerland

{marco.canini,vojin.jovanovic,daniele.venzano,dejan.novakovic,dejan.kostic}@epfl.ch

ABSTRACT

DiCE is a system for online testing of federated and heterogeneous distributed systems. We have built a prototype of DiCE and integrated it with an open-source BGP router. DiCE quickly detects three important classes of faults, resulting from configuration mistakes, policy conflicts and programming errors.

The goal of this demo is to showcase our DiCE prototype while it executes an experiment that involves exploring BGP system behavior in a topology with 27 BGP routers and Internet-like conditions (Figure 1).

Categories and Subject Descriptors

C.2.4 [**Computer-Communication Networks**]: Distributed Systems

General Terms

Reliability

Keywords

Online testing, Fault detection, Federated and heterogeneous distributed systems

1. INTRODUCTION

The successfully deployed distributed systems typically use open interfaces, but often end up being heterogeneous due to the creation of multiple implementations. Moreover, the success drives deployment across the wide-area network, which then leads to the systems becoming federated to allow separate administrative domains to retain control over the local nodes' configuration. A prime example of such a system is the Internet's inter-domain routing, today based on BGP.

The important services these systems provide have to remain uninterrupted over long periods of time. However, the unanticipated interaction of nodes under seemingly valid configuration changes and local fault-handling can have a profound effect. For example, the Internet's routing has suffered from multiple IP prefix hijackings, as well as performance and reliability problems due to emergent behavior resulting from a local session reset.

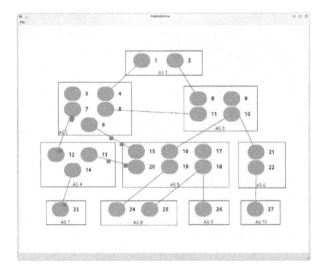

Figure 1: **A graphical interface showing the execution of DiCE over a topology with 27 BGP routers.**

In a position paper [3], we argued that making heterogeneous and federated distributed systems reliable is challenging because (*i*) the source code of every node may not be readily available for testing and (*ii*) competitive concerns are likely to induce individual providers to keep private much of their current state and configuration.

In an effort to increase distributed system reliability, our overarching vision is to harness the continuous increases in available computational power and bandwidth. Specifically, we argue that the system should proactively detect potential faults that can occur in it due to, for example, programming errors, policy conflicts, and operator mistakes. In this work, our goal is to explore system behavior so to find node actions that lead to faults.

The remainder of this paper is organized as follows. Section 2 provides an overview of our approach. Section 3 highlights certain prototype details and evaluation results. Finally, Section 4 discusses some related material.

2. APPROACH OVERVIEW

We propose DiCE, an approach that continuously and automatically explores the system behavior, to check whether the system deviates from its desired behavior. At a high-level, as illustrated in Figure 2, DiCE (*i*) creates a snapshot consisting of lightweight node checkpoints, (*ii*) orchestrates the exploration of relevant system behaviors across

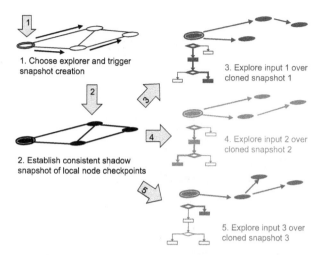

Figure 2: DiCE systematically explores and checks system behavior over isolated snapshots.

1. Choose explorer and trigger snapshot creation

2. Establish consistent shadow snapshot of local node checkpoints

3. Explore input 1 over cloned snapshot 1

4. Explore input 2 over cloned snapshot 2

5. Explore input 3 over cloned snapshot 3

the snapshot by subjecting system nodes to many possible inputs that exercise node actions, and (*iii*) checks for violations of properties that capture the desired system behavior. DiCE starts exploring from current system state, and operates alongside the deployed system but in isolation from it. In this way, testing can account for the current code, state and configuration of the system. DiCE reuses existing protocol messages to the extent possible for interoperability and ease of deployment.

DiCE drives exploration by using concolic execution [4] to produce inputs that systematically explore all possible paths at one node. Concolic execution[1] is an automated software testing technique that executes a program by treating the inputs to the program as symbolic. A concolic execution engine tracks the constraints of the code branches on symbolic inputs encountered during execution. For each constraint, it then queries a solver to find a value that negates the constraint and leads down to a different code path.

We face several difficult challenges in our work. Because of the federated nature and heterogeneity of the systems we target, we cannot drive system behavior from atop. DiCE explores system behavior by letting each node autonomously exercise its local actions and observe their system-wide consequences over a set of lightweight checkpoints. Second, approaches that systematically explore code paths easily run into the problem of exponential explosion of possible code paths. Three insights allow us to manage this problem: (*i*) we start exploring from current system state so that we avoid to replay a long history of inputs to explore deep in code behavior. (*ii*) We localize and focus on code that changes state (*e.g.*, message handlers). This decision allows us to quickly explore relevant code paths, whereas other code such as message parsers could be tested offline. (*iii*) We subject the node's code to small-sized inputs, and apply grammar-based fuzzing to produce a large number of valid inputs. Lastly, it is challenging to detect faults by checking for violations of properties while there cannot be unrestricted access to remote node states because the systems we target are federated. We define a narrow information-sharing interface that

allows nodes to communicate the result of local state checks while preserving confidential information.

3. DiCE PROTOTYPE AND EVALUATION

We have successfully integrated DiCE with the BGP implementation of the BIRD open-source router [1]. We use the Oasis concolic execution engine [4] as the basis for code path exploration. For integrating with BIRD, we first change its BGP implementation to mark certain inputs as symbolic. We choose to treat UPDATE messages as the basis to derive new inputs during exploration. For instance, the Network Layer Reachability Info (NLRI) region of the message contains the announced routes with their respective netmask lengths. We mark these as symbolic. An UPDATE message also typically carries multiple path attributes each of which is encoded as a type, length, and value fields that are also treated as symbolic. In practice, this choice allows DiCE to construct inputs that exercise BGP behavior in two dimensions: the first due to BIRD's code implementing BGP, the second as the result of the particular configuration currently in use. This is because the source code instrumentation encompasses the BIRD's configuration interpreter and so allows Oasis to record constraints for the interpreted configuration. Therefore, the explored execution paths are comprehensive of both code and configuration. Finally, we consider behaviors due to configuration changes. We treat as symbolic the condition that describes whether a route is the locally most preferred one. This allows us to systematically explore the outcome of BGP's route selection process.

Our evaluation using a set of BGP routers in a testbed with Internet-like conditions demonstrates DiCE's effectiveness, low overhead, and ease of integration with existing software written in C. Specifically, our prototype quickly detects faults that can occur due to programming errors, policy conflicts, and operator mistakes.

4. RELATED MATERIAL

Our work is on-going. We published a position paper in [3], and a paper describing our initial design and prototype is in [2]. A presentation of DiCE given at the RIPE62 meeting is available at `http://ripe62.ripe.net/archives/video/96`. A technical report in [4] fully describes Oasis, the concolic execution engine we use.

5. REFERENCES

[1] The BIRD Internet Routing Daemon. `http://bird.network.cz`.

[2] M. Canini, V. Jovanović, D. Venzano, B. Spasojević, O. Crameri, and D. Kostić. Toward Online Testing of Federated and Heterogeneous Distributed Systems. In *USENIX ATC*, June 2011.

[3] M. Canini, D. Novaković, V. Jovanović, and D. Kostić. Fault Prediction in Distributed Systems Gone Wild. In *LADIS*, July 2010.

[4] O. Crameri, R. Bachwani, T. Brecht, R. Bianchini, D. Kostić, and W. Zwaenepoel. Oasis: Concolic Execution Driven by Test Suites and Code Modifications. Technical Report LABOS-REPORT-2009-002, EPFL, 2009.

---

[1]A variant of symbolic execution. Concolic stands for CONCrete + symbOLIC.

Performance Based Traffic Control with IDIPS

Damien Saucez
Université catholique de Louvain
ICTEAM
2 Place Sainte-Barbe
B-1348 Louvain-la-Neuve, Belgium
damien.saucez@uclouvain.be

Olivier Bonaventure
Université catholique de Louvain
ICTEAM
2 Place Sainte-Barbe
B-1348 Louvain-la-Neuve, Belgium
olivier.bonaventure@uclouvain.be

ABSTRACT

Nowadays Internet is ubiquitous resulting in an increasing path diversity and content duplication. However, while content can be retrieved from many different places, the paths to those places are not equivalent. Indeed, some paths offer better bandwidth while others are less expensive or more stable. In addition, a new range of applications is sensitive to the performance of the paths that carry their traffic. To support this evolution of the Internet, we propose ISP-Driven Informed Path Selection (IDIPS). Any ISP can easily deploy IDIPS to help its customers to select the paths that best meet their requirements in order to reach their content. IDIPS helps in this selection through pro-active measurements and ISP-defined policies. IDIPS is scalable and can support thousands of clients. IDIPS is also flexible and can thus be used by the ISP to optimize its routing decisions to take the performance of its inter-domain links into account.

Categories and Subject Descriptors

C.2.1 [**Computer-Communication Networks**]: Network Architecture and Design

General Terms

Measurement, Performance

Keywords

route control, traffic engineering, XORP

1. INTRODUCTION

Content is often replicated and distributed with the help of efficient content distribution networks (CDN) [3, 5] or even end-user based replication with peer-to-peer applications. This creates several problems in Internet Service Provider (ISP) networks where client-server asymmetry does not hold anymore. In addition, due to the transition from IPv4 to IPv6 many hosts will be dual-stack for the foreseeable future. Furthermore, measurements show that IPv4 and IPv6 do not always provide the same performances, even for a single source-destination pair. To reach a destination supporting both IPv4 and IPv6, a source host can achieve better performance by selecting the stack that provides the best performance. In such a context, applications can improve their performance by selecting the most appropriate paths. For instance, bulk data transfer peer-to-peer clients will favor paths with the largest bandwidth so that the targeted file will be downloaded faster.

A way to enable efficient path selection for applications would be to allow the network to cooperate with them [2, 7, 8]. Such a cooperation would also give the opportunity to operators for managing incoming and outgoing traffic on their networks. Indeed, according to their traffic engineering needs, operators could balance traffic from one link to another.

We propose an informed path selection service called *ISP-Driven Informed Path Selection (IDIPS)*. IDIPS is generic and does not require fundamental changes in the current Internet architecture (only the clients need to implement a library for using the service).

IDIPS is designed as a request/response service. The network operators deploy servers that are configured with policies and that collect routing information (e.g., OSPF/ISIS, BGP) and pro-actively measure the performance of popular destinations. The clients that need to select a path send requests to a server. A request contains a list of sources and destinations and a ranking criterion. The server replies with an ordered list of <source,destination,rank > tuples to the client. This ranking is based on the current network state and policies. The client then uses the first pairs of the list and potentially switches to the next one(s) in case of problem.

An IDIPS client refers to any entity that has the possibility to select paths to reach a destination or retrieve some content. *Peer-to-peer* applications are clear candidate for such an informed path selection service. In Peer-to-peer, IDIPS can be used to select the peers that minimize the download completion time without harming the ISP by using costly links. The IDIPS related work in such a context is P4P, Oracle and ALTO [8, 2, 7]. However, unlike these related works, IDIPS is not limited to the peers selection in P2P and can measure path performances. Consequently, IDIPS can, for example, be used by *dual stack hosts* to determine when IPv6 is faster than IPv4. Moreover, an increasing number of networks are *multihomed* [1] and an important benefit of multihoming as shown by Akella et al. is that multihoming allows sites to choose better quality paths over the Internet [4]. In this context, BGP can be coupled with IDIPS to dynamically use the most qualitative links to send traffic to or to attract traffic from, instead of relying on static policies.

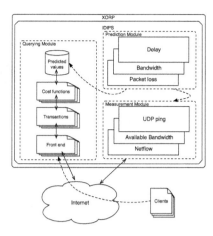

Figure 1: IDIPS architecture

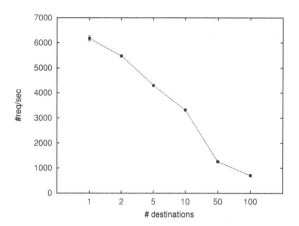

Figure 2: Load supported by the XORP implementation of IDIPS

2. IDIPS ARCHITECTURE

IDIPS is a service that can be used in many situations. This is why IDIPS presents a simple but powerful programming interface and is implemented in XORP.

As illustrated in Fig. 1 IDIPS is composed of three independent modules: the *Querying* module, the *Prediction* module, and the *Measurement* module. The Querying module is directly in relation with the client as it is in charge of receiving the requests, computing the path ranking based on the ranking criterion provided by the client and the ISP traffic engineering requirements, and replying with the ranked paths. The Measurement module is in charge of measuring path performance metrics if required. Finally, the Prediction module is used for predicting path performance (i.e., future performance metrics of a given path based on the past measurements).

The ranking criterion provided by clients in their requests might require measuring the network to obtain path performance metrics, such as delay or bandwidth estimation. The Measurement module pro-actively measures the most important destinations on behalf of the clients. Those measurements can be active (i.e., probes are sent in the network) or passive (i.e., no additional traffic is injected). The definition of important can be adapted to the needs (e.g., the destination that carry most of the traffic).

It is possible to predict the performance of a given path if it has been previously measured. This prediction task is achieved by the Prediction module. Note that a given measurement can be used in several different predictions. For instance, the previous delay measurements can serve for predicting the delay, the jitter, or for determining whether the path is reachable or not.

To enable flexibility, ease of implementation and performance, IDIPS clearly separates the Querying, Measurement and Prediction modules. Each module communicates with the other modules thanks to a standardized XRL interface. Therefore, the handling of requests from the clients is strictly separated from the prediction of path performance and path performance prediction is separated from path measurements.

The module interfaces are abstracted into XORP XRL interfaces such that anyone can add new measurement and prediction modules to IDIPS. The choice of implementing IDIPS in XORP makes the interaction between IDIPS, the control planes and the data plane easy.

Fig. 2 shows the achievable performance of our XORP implementation of IDIPS on a Intel Xeon E5430 at 2.66GHz processor with 4GB of RAM. To determine the achievable performance of our implementation, we repeated, for various size of random destination lists, ten times a run of 1,000,000 ranking requests. Fig 2 shows the mean (and its 95th confidence interval) rate supported by IDIPS. We can see that IDIPS can handle more than one thousands of requests per second for reasonable destination list sizes which should be sufficient to support a few tens of thousands clients. The degradation of performance with the size of the destination list is mostly due to the marshaling and unmarshaling events inside XORP. A detailed description and evaluation of IDIPS can be found in [6].[1]

3. ACKNOWLEDGMENTS

This work is supported by the ECODE European Project.

4. REFERENCES

[1] S. Agarwal, C.-N. Chuah, and R. H. Katz. OPCA: Robust interdomain policy routing and traffic control. In *Proc. IEEE OPENARCH*, April 2003.

[2] V. Aggarwal, A. Feldmann, and C. Scheideler. Can ISPs and P2P users cooperate for improved performance. *ACM SIGCOMM CCR*, 37(3):29–40, July 2007.

[3] Akamai. Akamai. http://www.akamai.com.

[4] A. Akella, B. Maggs, S. Seshan, A. Shaikh, and R. Sitaraman. On the performance benefits of multihoming route control. *IEEE Transactions on Networking*, 16(1):96–104, February 2008.

[5] Limelight Networks. Limelight. http://www.limelightnetworks.com/.

[6] D. Saucez, B. Donnet, and O. Bonaventure. ISP-Driven Informed Path Selection. Technical report, 2011. http://inl.info.ucl.ac.be/idips.

[7] J. Seedorf and E. Burger. Application-Layer Traffic Optimization (ALTO) Problem Statement. RFC 5693 (Informational), 2009.

[8] H. Xie, Y. Yang, A. Krishnamurthy, Y. Liu, and A. Silberschatz. P4P: Provider portal for applications. In *Proc. ACM SIGCOMM*, Agust 2008.

[1]IDIPS code on http://inl.info.ucl.ac.be/idips

Eco-Sign: A Load-Based Traffic Light Control System for Environmental Protection with Vehicular Communications

Lien-Wu Chen
Department of Computer
Science, National Chiao-Tung
University, Hsin-Chu, Taiwan
lwchen@cs.nctu.edu.tw

Pranay Sharma
Department of Computer
Science, National Chiao-Tung
University, Hsin-Chu, Taiwan
pranay@cs.nctu.edu.tw

Yu-Chee Tseng
Department of Computer
Science, National Chiao-Tung
University, Hsin-Chu, Taiwan
yctseng@cs.nctu.edu.tw

ABSTRACT

The Eco-Sign system is a traffic light control system for minimizing greenhouse gases emitted by idling vehicles at intersections. Eco-Sign provides the following features: (i) it can notify vehicles to turn on/off their engines based on expected waiting time for green lights at intersections, (ii) it can dynamically adjust traffic light timing to minimize the number of vehicles stopping at an intersection based on vehicle arrival and departure rates, and (iii) it is a fully distributed system in the sense that each intersection can learn its local traffic condition and optimize its traffic sign setting to prevent congestions and thus traffic jams. Eco-Sign thus demonstrates a new traffic light control system for environmental protection.

Categories and Subject Descriptors: C.2.1 [Network Architecture and Design]: Network communications

General Terms: Algorithms, Design, Management

Keywords: Dynamic Traffic Light Control, Environmental Protection, Ignition Control, Vehicular Communications

1. INTRODUCTION

Traffic congestion in modern cities seriously affects the living quality and environments. Vehicles on the roads produce mass air pollution that emits greenhouse gases such as carbon dioxide, hydrocarbons, and nitrogen oxides. Idling vehicles caused by traffic jams and red lights at intersections waste a large amount of fuel and seriously pollute the air. Studies show that the ratio of man-made dioxide emissions from transportation systems is about 30% [1]. Efforts have been made to increase the traffic flows in urban arterial roads [2], to reduce the waiting time at intersections [3], and to navigate vehicles in congested roads [4].

In this paper, we propose a load-based traffic light control system called Eco-Sign, which can help determine the timing of engine ignition at intersections and thus minimize greenhouse gases emitted by idling vehicles at intersections. At an intersection, a *localization unit (LU)* is placed on each road segment before the intersection to help vehicles know where they are. In addition, a *traffic control unit (TCU)* is connected to traffic lights to control their timing. Each vehicle equips with a *vehicle unit (VU)* to receive from LU the IDs of its road segment and TCU. It then controls its engine ignition based on the traffic light timing from TCU.

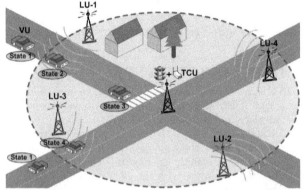

Figure 1: System architecture of Eco-Sign.

In Eco-Sign, a vehicle can get the intersection information from the first passed LU and register itself to TCU as stoping at the intersection. During the registration process, the vehicle will receive the traffic light timing from TCU and its onboard VU can automatically turn off its engine as the remaining waiting time is larger than or equal to a predefined time threshold α. If the engine is turned off by VU, it will be automatically turned on to pass the intersection at the next green light as the remaining waiting time is smaller than or equal to another time threshold β. As passing the second LU at the intersection, VU will deregister itself from TCU. According to vehicle registration and deregistration frequencies, TCU can estimate vehicle arrival and departure rates to achieve dynamic traffic light control.

Eco-Sign can thus help turn on/off engines of vehicles to reduce air pollution as they are waiting at intersections. On the other hand, TCU can dynamically adjust the traffic light timing to minimize the number of vehicles stopping at an intersection based on the observed vehicle arrival and departure rates. It is a fully distributed system in that each intersection can learn its local traffic condition and optimize the traffic sign setting to prevent road congestions. Eco-Sign thus demonstrates a new traffic light control system for environmental protection.

2. SYSTEM DESIGN

Fig. 1 shows the system architecture and vehicles' states at different locations nearby an intersection. On the intersection side, it consists of a LU on each road segment, which provides the location information to vehicles, and a TCU, which decides and transmits the traffic light timing. On the vehicle side, a VU is equipped onboard to receive the traffic light timing from TCU and control the engine ignition timing.

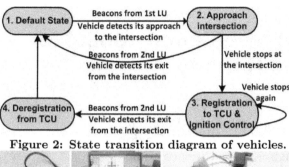

Figure 2: State transition diagram of vehicles.

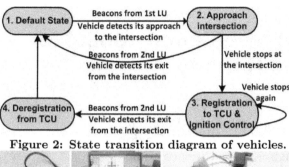

Figure 3: Eco-Sign hardware components.

VU consists of a network interface, an On Board Diagnostics (OBD) interface [5], an ignition control circuit, and a microprocessor. The network interface is to communicate with LU and TCU. The OBD interface is to capture the current vehicle status. The ignition control circuit is responsible for turning on/off the engine at intersections as its speed is 0 (Alternatively, this can serve as a recommendation service only.). The microprocessor collects information from all other components and issues commands to them. LU is equipped with a directional antenna and is placed at a road segment with a certain distance from the intersection. It periodically broadcasts location beacons on a dedicated channel, which contain IDs of the road segment and TCU, to vehicles entering or exiting the intersection. TCU consists of a microprocessor and two omnidirectional antennas operating in distinct channels, one for vehicle registration and the other for deregistration.

Fig. 2 shows the state transition diagram of vehicles. Initially, a vehicle is in state 1 (Default State). When the vehicle approaches an intersection, it will receive beacons from the first passed LU and then enter state 2 (Approach Intersection). If it passes the intersection without stopping, it will receive beacons from the second passed LU and then switch back to state 1. On the contrary, if it stops at the intersection due to red lights, it will enter state 3 (Registration to TCU & Ignition Control), register itself to TCU, and decide if its engine should be turned off. Note that if it stops at the intersection more than once, it will register itself again and turn off its engine for each stop. When it exits the intersection, it will receive beacons from the second passed LU and then enter state 4 (Deregistration from TCU). After it deregisters itself from TCU, it will go back to state 1.

3. PROTOTYPE IMPLEMENTATION

We have developed a prototype of Eco-Sign. The microprocessor and network interface used in VU, LU, and TCU is Jennic JN5139 [6], which has a 16MIPs 32-bit RISC processor, a 2.4GHz IEEE 802.15.4-compliant transceiver, 192kB of ROM, and 96kB of RAM. As shown in Fig. 3(a), LU is implemented by JN5139 development board powered by four AA batteries. TCU is implemented by integrating two JN5139 development boards connected with a notebook via USB ports, which is running on Windows XP operating system, as shown in Fig. 3(b).

Figure 4: Prototype demonstration.

VU is implemented by JN5139 development board integrated with the ignition control circuit, as shown in Fig. 3(c). The interfacing circuit for ignition control is using ULN2003 [7] Darlington transistor arrays, which takes the signal from Jennic I/O pins and controls 12 V, 40 A automotive relays. A Y-type connector is provided to avoid cutting the original wires inside the car. The power of VU is supplied by the 12 V in-vehicle battery.

Fig. 4 shows the prototype demonstration of Eco-Sign. TCU and LU are installed at the intersection and the roadside lamppost on each direction leading to the intersection, as shown in Fig. 4(a) and Fig. 4(b), respectively. They are operating on 3 different channels. VU is set up in Maruti Suzuki 800 [8], as shown in Fig. 4(c). On one hand, the vehicle is driven from each road segment of the intersection to register/deregister itself to/from TCU. On the other hand, the traffic light timing is varied in road segments of the intersection and the vehicle can receive the correct timing value from TCU. In addition, automatic ignition control is activated as the vehicle speed is 0 km/hr and the remaining waiting time is larger than 30 seconds.

For indoor demonstration, we use a projector to simulate traffic conditions on road segments at an intersection, as shown in Fig. 4(d). A remote control car with VU is used to approach the intersection and trigger operations of Eco-Sign. Fig. 4(e) shows the car status including motion status, approaching side, remaining waiting time, and ignition advice.

4. ACKNOWLEDGMENTS

Y.-C. Tseng's research is co-sponsored by MoE ATU Plan, by NSC grants, 97-3114-E-009-001, 97-2221-E-009-142-MY3, 98-2219-E-009-019, 98-2219-E-009-005, and 99-2218-E-009-005, by ITRI, Taiwan, by III, Taiwan, by D-Link, and by Intel.

5. REFERENCES

[1] eSafety Forum. ICT for Clean and Efficient Mobility. *Working Group Final Report*, Nov. 2008.
[2] Y. Li, W. Wei, and S. Chen. Optimal Traffic Signal Control for an Urban Arterial Road. In *2nd Int'l Symp. on Intelligence Information Technology Application*, pages 570-574, Dec. 2008.
[3] E. Azimirad, N. Pariz, and M.B.N. Sistani. A Novel Fuzzy Model and Control of Single Intersection at Urban Traffic Network. *IEEE Systems Journal*, 4(1):107-111, Mar. 2010.
[4] V. Verroios, K. Kollias, P. K. Chrysanthis, and A. Delis. Adaptive Navigation of Vehicles in Congested Road Networks. In *5th Int'l Conf. on Pervasive Services*, pages 47-56, July 2008.
[5] On Board Diagnostics. http://www.obdii.com/background.html.
[6] Jennic, JN5139. http://www.jennic.com.
[7] ULN2003, High Voltage and Current Darlington Transistor Array. http://www.datasheetcatalog.org/datasheets/120/489337_DS.pdf
[8] Maruti Suzuki 800. http://www.maruti800.com/.

FSR: Formal Analysis and Implementation Toolkit for Safe Inter-domain Routing

Yiqing Ren*   Wenchao Zhou*   Anduo Wang*   Limin Jia†
Alexander J.T. Gurney*   Boon Thau Loo*   Jennifer Rexford‡
*University of Pennsylvania   †Carnegie-Mellon University   ‡Princeton University
{yiqingr, wenchaoz, anduo, agurney, boonloo}@cis.upenn.edu,
liminjia@cmu.edu, jrex@cs.princeton.edu

ABSTRACT

We present the demonstration of a comprehensive toolkit for analyzing and implementing routing policies, ranging from high-level guidelines to specific router configurations. Our Formally Safe Routing (*FSR*) toolkit performs all of these functions from the same algebraic representation of routing policy. We show that routing algebra has a very natural translation to both *integer constraints* (to perform safety analysis using SMT solvers) and *declarative programs* (to generate distributed implementations). Our demonstration with realistic topologies and policies shows how *FSR* can detect problems in an AS's iBGP configuration, prove sufficient conditions for BGP safety, and empirically evaluate convergence time.

Categories and Subject Descriptors

C.2.1 [**Computer-Communication Networks**]: Network Architecture and Design

General Terms

Design, Languages, Experimentation

1. OVERVIEW

The Internet's global routing system does not necessarily converge, depending on how individual networks configure their Border Gateway Protocol (BGP) policies. Since protocol oscillations cause serious performance disruptions and router overhead, researchers devote significant attention to BGP stability (or "safety").

To aid the design, analysis, and evaluation of safe interdomain routing, we propose the *Formally Safe Routing* (*FSR*) analysis and implementation toolkit. *FSR* serves two important communities. For researchers, *FSR* automates important parts of the design process and provides a common framework for describing, evaluating, and comparing new safety guidelines. For network operators, *FSR* automates the analysis of internal router (iBGP) and border gateway (eBGP) configurations for safety violations. For both communities, *FSR* automatically generates realistic protocol implementations to evaluate real network configurations (e.g., to study convergence time) prior to actual deployment.

FSR bridges analysis and implementation, by combining *routing algebras* [3, 7] with recent advances in *declarative networking* [4] to produce provably-correct implementations of safe interdomain routing. Given policy configurations as input, *FSR* produces an analysis of safety properties and a distributed protocol implementation, as shown in Figure 1. In this section, we briefly summarize its main underlying technologies. Our technical report [8] provides details of the toolkit, including several examples and use cases.

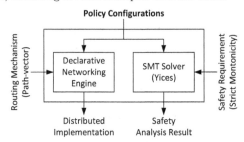

Figure 1: *FSR* Architecture.

Policy Configuration as Routing Algebra. *FSR* uses routing algebra [3, 7] to allow researchers and network operators to express policy configurations in an abstract algebraic form. A routing algebra is an abstract structure that describes how network nodes calculate routes, and the preference for one route over another. *FSR* uses our extensions to routing algebra for distinguishing import and export filtering policies, to enable automated translation from a policy configuration to a distributed protocol implementation. We support a wide range of policy configurations, ranging from high-level *guidelines* (e.g., the Gao-Rexford guideline [1]) to specific network configurations expressed as an instance of the Stable Paths Problem (SPP) [2].

Safety Analysis. Given any algebra, *FSR* fully automates the process of safety analysis, relieving users from the manual and error-prone process of proving safety for each new guideline or router configuration. The key insight is that the safety analysis can be translated automatically into integer constraints checkable by a standard SMT (Satisfiability Modulo Theories) solver. In a nutshell, a SMT solver determines whether a set of constraints (i.e., first-order logic formulas) are satisfiable with respect to a given background theory (e.g., integer theory).

Given a policy configuration written in routing algebra, *FSR* automatically generates integer constraints for safety analysis recognizable by the Yices SMT solver [9]. The solver determines whether it is possible to jointly satisfy the policy configuration and the safety requirement of "strict monotonicity" (the rightmost input in Figure 1, drawn from previous work [7] on sufficient conditions for safety). If all constraints can be satisfied, the routing system is provably safe; otherwise, the solver outputs the minimal subset of the constraints that are not satisfiable to aid in identifying the problem and fine-tuning the configuration.

Provably Safe Implementations. To enable an evaluation of protocol dynamics and convergence time, *FSR* uses our extended routing algebra to automatically generate a distributed routing-protocol implementation that matches the policy configuration—avoiding the time-consuming and error-prone task of manually creating an implementation. Given the policy configuration and a formal description of the path-vector mechanism (the leftmost input in Figure 1), *FSR* generates a correct translation to a *Network Datalog (NDlog)* specification, which is then executed using the RapidNet declarative networking engine [5]. In practice, *FSR*'s safe implementation can be used as an emulation platform for studying BGP performance. (By changing the left input in Figure 1, researchers can also experiment with alternative routing mechanisms, as in Scenario Set D below.)

Our choice of *NDlog* is motivated by the following. First, the declarative features of *NDlog* allow for straightforward translation from the algebra to *NDlog* programs. Second, *NDlog* results in compact specifications that have orders of magnitude less code than imperative implementations. This makes possible a clean and concise proof (via logical inductions) of the correctness of the generated *NDlog* programs with regard to the algebra. The compact specifications also make it easy to incorporate alternative routing mechanisms to the basic path-vector protocol. Third, *NDlog*'s roots in logic and Datalog makes it amenable to the use of theorem provers to verify correctness properties. Finally, prior work [4] has shown that these declarative networks perform efficiently relative to imperative implementations.

2. DEMONSTRATION PLAN

FSR provides a graphical user-interface for users to specify policy configurations using algebraic specifications, which are compiled into *NDlog* programs and executed on Rapid-Net. This engine allows for a *simulation mode* in ns-3 [6], enabling comprehensive examination under various network topologies and conditions, as well as a *deployment mode* where different hosts in a testbed environment execute the deployed system over a real network.

In our demonstration, network traces obtained from actual *NDlog* execution runs are directed to the RapidNet visualizer. The visualizer displays the network topology, routing state, alongside actual performance statistics such as bandwidth utilization. Our demonstration showcases the following four scenario sets:

Scenario Set A: Provably Safe Guidelines. Our first case study presents scenarios where a researcher empirically evaluates policy guidelines using the distributed *NDlog* implementation automatically generated from the algebraic specifications. The researcher uses the *FSR* tool to analyze policy guidelines for safety properties using Yices. In addition, the researcher can use the declarative *NDlog* implementation generated by *FSR* to study the actual behavior of the protocol when executed under the guideline constraints,

for instance, to measure the convergence time with respect to the depth of the AS hierarchy.

Scenario Set B: Pinpoint iBGP Configuration Errors. We also emulate scenarios where a network operator uses our *FSR* toolkit to study the safety properties of existing iBGP network configurations. We use the intradomain topology from the Rocketfuel dataset as a basis. To experiment with *FSR*'s ability to detect configuration errors in large network instances, we embed gadgets that are known to cause oscillation in an iBGP setting. *FSR* detects the errors in both its analysis and actual execution runs. In our demonstration, we fix these configuration errors pointed out by Yices, and demonstrate that the resulting iBGP configuration is safe, both in analysis and implementation.

Scenario Set C: eBGP Gadget Analysis. *FSR*'s applicability extends beyond high-level guidelines and iBGP configurations. Our third scenario is to use *FSR* to analyze well-known eBGP gadgets, such as GOODGADGET, BADGADGET and DISAGREE [2] when embedded into large network instances. We execute these embedded gadgets using the automatically-generated *NDlog* implementation, to visually study their behavior in actual execution.

Scenario Set D: Alternative Routing Mechanisms. In our final scenario set, we demonstrate the flexibility of the *FSR* toolkit to support alternative routing mechanisms beyond the basic path-vector protocol, for instance, the *Hybrid Link-State and Path-Vector Protocol* (HLP).

Acknowledgments. This research was supported by NSF grants IIS-0812270, CCF-0820208, CNS-0830949, CNS-0845552, CNS-1040672, AFOSR Grant No: FA9550-08-1-0352, ONR Grant No: N00014-09-1-0770, and a gift from Cisco Systems.

3. REFERENCES

[1] GAO, L., AND REXFORD, J. Stable Internet routing without global coordination. In *ACM SIGMETRICS* (2000).

[2] GRIFFIN, T. G., SHEPHERD, F. B., AND WILFONG, G. The stable paths problem and interdomain routing. *IEEE/ACM Trans. on Networking 10* (2002).

[3] GRIFFIN, T. G., AND SOBRINHO, J. L. Metarouting. In *ACM SIGCOMM* (2005).

[4] LOO, B. T., CONDIE, T., GAROFALAKIS, M., GAY, D. E., HELLERSTEIN, J. M., MANIATIS, P., RAMAKRISHNAN, R., ROSCOE, T., AND STOICA, I. Declarative networking. In *Communications of the ACM 52* (2009).

[5] MUTHUKUMAR, S. C., LI, X., LIU, C., KOPENA, J. B., OPREA, M., AND LOO, B. T. Declarative toolkit for rapid network protocol simulation and experimentation. In *ACM SIGCOMM (demo)* (2009).

[6] NETWORK SIMULATOR 3. http://www.nsnam.org/.

[7] SOBRINHO, J. An algebraic theory of dynamic network routing. *IEEE/ACM Trans. on Networking 13* (2005).

[8] WANG, A., JIA, L., ZHOU, W., REN, Y., LOO, B. T., REXFORD, J., NIGAM, V., SCEDROV, A., AND TALCOTT, C. FSR: Formal analysis and implementation toolkit for safe inter-domain routing. University of Pennsylvania Tech. Report MS-CIS-11-10 (2011), http://repository.upenn.edu/cis_reports/954/.

[9] YICES. http://yices.csl.sri.com/.

PANDAA: A Physical Arrangement Detection Technique for Networked Devices through Ambient-Sound Awareness

Zheng Sun, Aveek Purohit, Philippe De Wagter, Irina Brinster, Chorom Hamm,
Pei Zhang
Department of Electrical and Computer Engineering
Carnegie Mellon University
5000 Forbes Avenue, Pittsburgh, PA, USA
{zheng.sun, aveek.purohit, philippe.dewagter, irina.brinster, chorom.hamm, pei.zhang}@west.cmu.edu

ABSTRACT

This demo presents PANDAA, a zero-configuration automatic spatial localization technique for networked devices based on ambient sound sensing. We will demonstrate that after initial placement of the devices, ambient sounds, such as human speech, music, footsteps, finger snaps, hand claps, or coughs and sneezes, can be used to autonomously resolve the spatial relative arrangement of devices, such as mobile phones, using trigonometric bounds and successive approximation.

Categories and Subject Descriptors

C.3 [**Special-purpose and application-based systems**]: Signal processing systems.

General Terms

Algorithms, Design, Experimentation.

Keywords

Arrangement detection, networked devices, localization.

1. INTRODUCTION

Future ubiquitous home or office environments can contain 10s or 100s of consumer devices connected through wireless networks, such as mobile phones, laptops, smart TVs, printers, etc. Ubiquitous services running on these devices (i.e. localizing users, routing, security algorithms) will commonly require an accurate location of each device. PANDAA (Physical Arrangement Detection of Networked Devices through Ambient-Sound Awareness) is a spatial localization technique for networked devices in office and home environments. Different from previous work that uses special-purpose hardware (e.g. ultrasonic transmitters [2]) or intrusive audible chirp sound [3], PANDAA leverages ambient sound randomly and passively generated in indoor environments to automatically determine the physical arrangement of devices without prior calibration of their location. To the best of our knowledge, PANDAA is the first indoor arrangement detection technique that relies purely on the use of ambient sounds and achieves high accuracy.

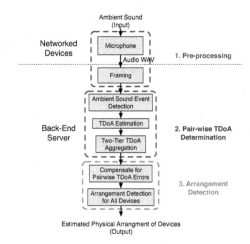

Figure 1: The system architecture of PANDAA.

In this demo, we will show how the system operates, how the algorithms in PANDAA manage to compensate for various ambient noises, and highlight the system's high accuracy of location estimation (about 0.17m precision in a 50m^2 indoor space).

2. THE PANDAA TECHNIQUE

PANDAA leverages microphones that already exist in various consumer devices, such as mobile phones, laptops, smart TVs, and context-aware systems (e.g. indoor acoustic sensing systems [1, 4]), to detect usable segments of ambient sound generated in a room. The time difference of sound arrival (TDoA) between devices is calculated and used to iteratively estimate inter-device distances. These distances are then used to determine the overall arrangement of devices. Finally, multiple TDoA measurements are combined to improve arrangement detection accuracy over time. The system architecture of PANDAA is shown in Figure 1.

The PANDAA system addresses several major challenges of ambient sound-based arrangement detection as follows.

Challenge 1: Choosing Usable Ambient Sound Segments. Ambient sounds, such as music played on a radio, human speech, noise from a working vacuum cleaner or a barking dog, may vary significantly in signal-to-noise ratio (SNR). Low SNR sound may lead to poor TDoA estimation accuracy. PANDAA addresses this challenge using an algo-

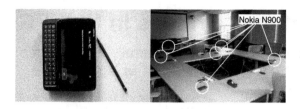

Figure 2: Left: A Nokia N900 phone that is used in the demo. Right: A meeting room where previous experiments were conducted.

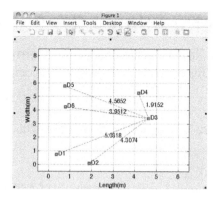

Figure 3: GUI that shows the estimated physical arrangement of devices (represented by blue squares) in the demo.

rithm that detects *impulsive sounds*. Impulsive sounds are short duration sounds with relatively higher amplitude, such as human cough, finger snaps, or beats in a song. Using this approach, PANDAA can automatically extract high SNR sound events from a variety of ambient sound types, and compute time difference of sound arrivals (TDoA) between devices.

Challenge 2: Correcting Inaccurate TDoA Measurements. In indoor environments, TDoA measurements can be affected by environmental factors, such as reflections, non-line-of-sight path, or ambient noise. To compensate for TDoA errors, PANDAA uses a novel two-tier TDoA aggregation algorithm. The lower tier aggregates cross-spectrums over successive audio frames in the same sound event to suppress any uncorrelated frame-to-frame effects. To handle longer lasting ambient effects, such as a moving person blocking acoustic line-of-sight of several nodes, the upper-tier aggregation averages TDoA estimates over multiple consecutive sound events belonging to the same sound source.

Challenge 3: Localizing Devices From TDoA Measurements. TDoA measurements from one single sound source are insufficient for estimating distance between two devices. PANDAA addresses this challenge by considering TDoA measurements from multiple ambient sound sources over time, to obtain pairwise TDoA measurements as an estimate of the lower bounds of the inter-device distances, and use the distribution of TDoA measurements to estimate the true inter-device distances, from which device arrangement is derived.

3. IMPLEMENTATION

We have implemented the PANDAA system on Nokia N900 mobile phones. The software on the phones was written in C++, including the sound event detection, the device synchronization, and the audio transmission modules. The code on the server was written in MATLAB, including the TDoA aggregation and the location estimation module, as well as a graphical user interface (GUI) for displaying the actual and estimated device arrangement. Figure 2 (left) shows a Nokia N900 phone displaying client-end GUI during an experiment. Figure 2 (right) shows a typical meeting room where we did our previous experiments.

The mobile phones are synchronized between each other using well developed synchronization techniques. To achieve required precision, we used the Network Time Protocol (NTP) to synchronize the devices to a laptop and modified the standard QT libraries to timestamp the audio recording with high precision.

4. DEMO DESCRIPTION

We will demonstrate the PANDAA technique that comprises a number of mobile devices connected through wireless networks. Several mobile phones and laptops will be randomly placed in the demo area, without calibrating their locations. Then, attendees will be encouraged to generate a number of ambient sounds at different and arbitrary locations in the demo area, such as human speech, coughs, finger snaps, hand claps or by singing a song. We will then use our laptop that runs the server-end program to show the detected impulsive sound segments (events) in real time, as well as the estimated device arrangement on a GUI. Figure 3 shows the GUI that will be used in the demo. As ambient sounds are generated in the demonstration area, the estimated device arrangement will be updated in real time.

We also develop software packages of PANDAA's client-end code, and provide the packages in terms of Android apps or iPhone apps on the Web. Attendees will also be encouraged to download these apps to their own mobile devices, and use the PANDAA technique to localize their devices during the demo.

5. REFERENCES

[1] X. Bian, G. Abowd, and J. Rehg. Using sound source localization to monitor and infer activities in the Home. In *Proc. Pervasive*, 2005.

[2] M. Hazas, C. Kray, H. Gellersen, H. Agbota, G. Kortuem, and A. Krohn. A Relative Positioning System for Co-located Mobile Devices. In *Proc. the 3rd International Conference on Mobile Systems, Applications, and Services*, pages 177–190, New York, New York, USA, 2005. ACM.

[3] C. Peng, G. Shen, Y. Zhang, Y. Li, and K. Tan. BeepBeep: A High Accuracy Acoustic Ranging System Using COTS Mobile Devices. In *Proc. the 5th International Conference on Embedded Networked Sensor Systems*, pages 1–14. ACM, 2007.

[4] Z. Sun, A. Purohit, K. Yang, N. Pattan, D. Siewiorek, I. Lane, and P. Zhang. CoughLoc : Location-Aware Indoor Acoustic Sensing for Non-Intrusive Cough Detection. In *Proc. International Workshop on Emerging Mobile Sensing Technologies, Systems, and Applications*, pages 1–6, 2011.

Implementing ARP-Path Low Latency Bridges in NetFPGA

Elisa Rojas[1], Jad Naous[2], Guillermo Ibañez[1], Diego Rivera[1], Juan A. Carral[1], Jose M. Arco[1]

elisa.rojas@uah.es, jnaous@gmail.com, guillermo.ibanez@uah.es, diego.rivera@uah.es, jac@aut.uah.es,
josem.arco@uah.es

[1]University of Alcala
Campus Externo, Alcalá de Henares 28805, Spain

[2]Stanford University
Stanford, California 94305, USA

ABSTRACT

The demo is focused on the implementation of ARP-Path (a.k.a. FastPath) bridges, a recently proposed concept for low latency bridges. ARP-Path Bridges rely on the race between broadcast ARP Request packets, to discover the minimum latency path to the destination host. Several implementations (in Omnet++, Linux, OpenFlow, NetFPGA) have shown that ARP-Path exhibits loop-freedom, does not block links, is fully transparent to hosts and neither needs a spanning tree protocol to prevent loops nor a link state protocol to obtain low latency paths. This demo compares our hardware implementation on NetFPGA to bridges running STP, showing that ARP-Path finds lower latency paths than STP.

Categories and Subject Descriptors

C.2.5. [**Computer-Communication Networks**]: Local and Wide-Area Networks – *Ethernet*.

General Terms

Performance, Design, Experimentation, Verification.

Keywords: Ethernet, Routing bridges, NetFPGA, Shortest Path Bridges, Spanning Tree.

1. INTRODUCTION

Ethernet switched networks offer important advantages in terms of price/performance ratio, compatibility, and simple configuration without the need for IP address administration. But the spanning tree protocol (STP) [1] limits the performance and size of Ethernet networks. Current standards proposals, such as Shortest Path Bridges (SPB) [2] and Routing Bridges [3] rely on a link-state routing protocol, which operates at layer two, to obtain shortest path routes and build trees rooted at bridges. However, they have significant complexity both in terms of computation and control message exchange and need additional loop control mechanisms.

2. ARP-PATH PROTOCOL
2.1 ARP-Path Path setup

The ARP-Path protocol relies on the race between flooded ARP requests to establish the fastest path. Note that only ARP frames (or special broadcast frames in failure cases) discover or create new paths. [4]

2.1.1 ARP-Path Broadcast Discovery (ARP Request)

When host S wants to send an IP packet over Ethernet to host D over IP, it needs D's MAC address. If the mapping of D's IP

address to D's MAC address is not in S's ARP cache, S broadcasts an ARP Request, B, for D's MAC address (Figure 1-a). Ingress bridge 2 receives the frame from S and temporarily associates (locks) S's MAC address to the ingress port. Unlike traditional learning switches, further broadcast frames from S arriving to other input ports of bridge 2 will be discarded because they arrived over slower paths. S's address is now in a locked state and bridge 2 broadcasts B on all other ports (Figure 1-b). Bridges 1 and 3 behave similarly, locking S's address to B's ingress port and broadcasting B over all other ports, thus sending duplicate copies to each other. Because these frames arrive at a different port from the one already locked to S's MAC address, they are discarded (Figure 1-c). In turn, bridges 4 and 5 process B the same way, finally delivering B to the destination host D. There is now a chain of bridges, each with a port locked to S's MAC address forming a temporary reverse path from D to S (Figure 1-c).

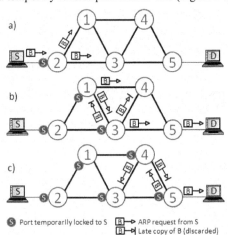

Figure 1: ARP-Path discovery from host S to host D. The small bubbles on the links show which bridge port locked S's address

2.1.2 ARP-Path Unicast Discovery (ARP Reply)

The next step is in the reverse direction (i.e. from D to S) when host D sends the ARP Reply to host S in a unicast frame U, with S's MAC address as destination address. Given the temporary reverse path back to S that was established by the ARP Request frame, U can be delivered with no further broadcasts. Like the ARP Request frame, U establishes a path from S to D for other unicast packets from S to D. Note that ARP-Path only establishes symmetric paths.

2.1.3 Unicast/Multicast/Broadcast communication

Once a bidirectional path is established (such as the one between S and D), all unicast frames between the two endpoints use that path. Multicast and broadcast frames use a loop-free broadcasting mechanism similar to that described for ARP Requests above.

ARP-Path bridges only accept frames from a particular source at the port that receives the first multicast or broadcast frame from that source. Unlike ARP Requests, other multicast and broadcast frames do not establish new paths.

2.1.4 Path Repair

When a unicast frame arrives at a bridge, the bridge may not know the output port for the frame's destination MAC address. The entry could have expired, or a link or a bridge might have failed. The Path Repair protocol emulates an ARP exchange to establish a new path, using PathFail, PathRequest, and PathReply messages. PathRequest messages are similar to ARP Request frames and establish the new path to the unknown destination. Thus a full path from to the destination end-host is restored.

2.2 Advantages

The protocol has several important advantages over other protocols that build routes *a priori* before any packet transmissions.

- *Minimum Latency*: The selected path is the minimum latency path as found by the ARP Request message.
- *Zero configuration*: There is no need to configure hosts and bridges.
- *Simplicity*: Bridges mainly behave as learning switches with optional ARP proxying to reduce broadcasts.
- *Load distribution and path diversity*
- *Scalability*: ARP broadcast traffic can be reduced dramatically by implementing ARP Proxy function inside the switches as shown in [5].

3. ARP-PATH OVER NETFPGA DEMO

The objective of the NetFPGA [6] implementation is to understand the robustness and throughput of ARP-Path transparent bridges in 1 Gbit/s wired networks, without the spanning tree protocol or any ancillary routing protocol operating at layers two or three.

To test the implementation we will use a PC with four NetFPGAs installed, that will behave as separated switches, connected between them and to external hosts. A user interface was created to visualize results that will launch the scripts that run the demonstration, and will build graphs to show the latencies obtained.

3.1 ARP-Path vs. STP

The main goal is to compare ARP-Path's behaviour with that of STP. The setup will consist of one desktop with 4 NetFPGAs and 2 NICs. The connections are to be physically as indicated in Figure 2.

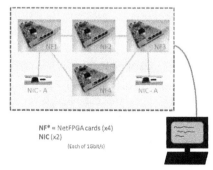

Figure 2: 4 NetFPGAs and 2 NICs connection, for the test.

The four NetFPGAs (NF1, NF2, NF3 and NF4) operate as ARP-Path bridges in one part of the demo and as STP bridges (NICs operating as separate STP bridges managed using Linux's bridge_utils) in another. We will show that ARP-Path chooses lower latency paths as opposed to STP that builds a routing tree rooted at an arbitrary switch.

3.2 ARP-Path switches Path repair

The second goal is to show that the protocol path repair is fast. Hosts *A* and *B* will start a video streaming communication. Host *A* will act as a HTTP server and *B* will connect to it and start streaming a video. We show ARP-Path's Path Repair's effectiveness after sucessive link failures and its minimal effect on the streamed video. See Figure 3.

Figure 3: Two hosts connected to a PC with four NetFPGA installed

4. ACKNOWLEDGMENTS

This work was supported in part by grants from Comunidad de Madrid and Comunidad de Castilla la Mancha through Projects MEDIANET-CM (S-2009/TIC-1468) and EMARECE (PII1I09-0204-4319).

5. REFERENCES

[1] 802.1D-2004 IEEE standard for local and metropolitan area networks – Media access control (MAC) Bridges. http://standards.ieee.org/getieee802/802.1.html.

[2] Allan, D., Ashwood-Smith, P., Bragg, N., Farkas, J., Fedyk, D., Ouellete, M., Seaman, M., and Unbehagen, P. Shortest path bridging: Efficient control of large Ethernet networks. *Communications Magazine, IEEE*, 48(10):128-135, October 2010.

[3] Transparent interconnection of lots of links (TRILL) WG. https://datatracker.ietf.org/wg/trill/charter/.

[4] Ibañez, G., Carral, J. A., Martinez, A. G., Arco J. M., Rivera, D. and Azrorra, A. Fastpath Ethernet switching: On-demand efficient transparent bridges for data center and campus networks. LANMAN, May 2010. Available on-line at: hdl.handle.net/10017/6298.

[5] Elmeleegy, K. and Cox, A. EtherProxy: Scaling the Ethernet by suppressing broadcast traffic. *Proceedings of IEEE INFOCOM*, 2009, Rio de Janeiro, Brazil.

[6] NetFPGA: http://www.netfpga.org

LifeNet: A Flexible Ad hoc Networking Solution for Transient Environments

Hrushikesh Mehendale, Ashwin Paranjpe, and Santosh Vempala
hrushi@gatech.edu, ashwin.p@gatech.edu, and vempala@cc.gatech.edu
College of Computing, Georgia Institute of Technology, Atlanta, GA, USA

ABSTRACT

We demonstrate a new ad hoc routing method that can handle transience such as node-mobility, obstructions and node failures. It has controlled management overhead, and is platform-independent (our demo includes phones, routers, and laptops running different operating systems). It achieves reliability and flexibility at the expense of throughput. It is ideal for scenarios where the reliability of connectivity is critical and bandwidth requirements are low. For e.g., disaster relief operations and sensor networks. Along with applications, we exhibit measurements to illustrate the advantages of our approach in dealing with transience.

Categories and Subject Descriptors:
C.1.1 Computer-Communication Networks: Network Architecture and Design - Wireless Communication
C.2.2 Computer-Communication Networks: Network Protocols - Routing Protocols
General Terms: Design, Experimentation, Measurement, Reliability.
Keywords: MANETs, Reliable routing, Minimum infrastructure.

1. INTRODUCTION

Multihop ad hoc wireless networks have not delivered on their promise, especially for bandwidth-intensive applications. This is in part due to the inherent capacity limitations of multihop TCP communication ([5]). Recent implementation efforts have achieved substantial throughput improvements at the expense of flexibility and reliability ([2, 4]). However, the improvements are still not good enough to warrant real-life use, especially with mobile nodes. The goal of this demo is to suggest that if the constraint of high throughput is relaxed, it is possible to realize ad hoc networks that are flexible and reliable under transience. Moreover, such networks have natural use cases for e.g. communication in disaster relief operations, wireless sensor networks such as forest fire detection networks, smart-home networks, etc. By transience, we refer to the changing state of a network along the following dimensions: (1) changing network topology due to mobility, (2) changing physical obstructions, (3) node failures and new nodes joining the network and (4) interference.

In this demo, we propose to present a new routing metric called 'Reachability' and a new routing protocol based on it, called 'Flexible Routing'. Reachability is suitable for transient environments because it accurately captures transience, is easy to compute and maintain, enables a compact representation of the entire network graph at individual nodes, and facilitates routing. Flexible Routing is a multipath routing protocol that uses pairwise-reachabilities to reliably deliver packets under varying degrees of transience. It trades throughput for availability and reliability.

2. REACHABILITY

Our routing method is based on the notion of *reachability*, a directional metric, which captures the effects of transience in a single numerical value. Roughly speaking, it measures the end-to-end, multipath probability that a packet transmitted by a source node reaches the destination node. It is important to note that this probability should be over all possible paths and not any single path (unlike previous routing metrics, e.g., [3]).

Definition. Reachability(A,B,T,L) of node B from node A is defined as the expected number of packet copies received by B for every packet originated at A and diffused in the network for at most L hops in time interval T.

Reachability can be efficiently measured by exploiting the broadcast nature of the wireless channel. To measure reachabilities of all other nodes, a node SRC transmits a packet to the broadcast MAC address with a pre-defined Time-to-Live (TTL) value. Nodes receiving this packet diffuse it further into the network until the TTL field of all the packet copies reaches zero. Thus, a node that is well-connected or highly reachable from SRC receives more packet copies than a node which is not. We map reachability to a finite value, roughly its inverse, and call it *Effective Distance*.

$$ED = \begin{cases} 100/R & \text{if } R > 1 \\ 255 - (155R) & otherwise \end{cases}$$

3. FLEXIBLE ROUTING

Idea. Maintaining paths explicitly is not practical under transience. Hence the core routing decision for flexible routing is *"Whether or not to forward?"* instead of *"Which node to forward the packet to?"*. Each node maintains a compact table ($O(n)$ size) of pairwise effective distance values computed from receiving control packets, and uses these to selectively forward data packets, effectively pruning a flooding tree. Although paths are not being created or maintained, this opportunistic approach ensures that the packets end

SIGCOMM'11, August 15–19, 2011, Toronto, Ontario, Canada.
ACM 978-1-4503-0797-0/11/08.

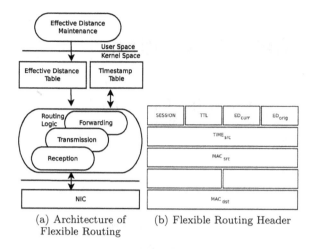

(a) Architecture of Flexible Routing

(b) Flexible Routing Header

Figure 1: Flexible Routing Layer 2.5 Architecture and Header

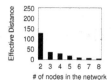
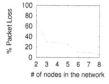

(a) Reachability captures increased connectivity as the network grows

(b) Flexible routing utilizes reachability to improve packet loss as the network grows

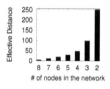
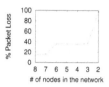

(c) Reachability captures node failures

(d) Flexible routing gracefully degrades under node failures

Figure 2: Evaluation Results

up traveling along multiple available paths towards the destination. This approach is network-aware and hence different from controlled flooding, directed diffusion, probabilistic flooding or broadcast-storm techniques. In other words, the routing algorithm ensures that packets on the network are forwarded by only those nodes that are likely to increase the chances of the packets reaching their destination.

Design and Implementation. We extend the mobile ad hoc networking framework proposed in ([6]). Packets on the network carry an additional header (Figure 1(b)). The routing functionality can be broadly divided into two categories - *ED Table Maintenance (EDM)* and *Routing*. ED Table (*EDT*) is implemented in user space. Routing uses data from *EDT* to make routing and forwarding decisions (Figure 1(a)). Nodes make the forwarding decision by comparing the effective distance in the received packet (ED_{curr}, Figure 1(b)) with the effective distance to their final destination. A non-duplicate packet is forwarded only if the *EDT* distance is within a threshold of the packet distance. Duplicate packets require a second stricter check. Broadcast storms in dense network zones are avoided by probabilistic forwarding rules based on the *EDT*. Layer 2.5 approach allows interoperability with different MAC technologies. The current implementation uses 802.11 a/b/g in ad hoc mode.

4. CONCLUSION

A preliminary evaluation of reachability and flexible routing was conducted in a university building environment on a network of eight nodes. Results (Figure 2) show that reachability captures (1) the phenomenon of increased connectivity as network scales (Figure 2(a)), (2) the effect of degraded connectivity after node failures (Figure 2(c)) and (3) node mobility. Moreover, flexible routing utilizes reachability to (i) strengthen routing as the network scales (Figure 2(b)), (ii) gracefully degrade its performance as node failures happen (Figure 2(d)) and (iii) maintain performance for changing node positions.

Scaling flexible routing to larger sized networks would require addressing challenges such as achieving desired consistency in topology information (*EDT*) and energy conservation. By focusing on availability under eventual consistency,

our approach aims to achieve a practical trade-off between the mutually conflicting goals of reliability, efficiency and usability. Our technology, packaged as LifeNet [1], is currently being field-evaluated for disaster communication applications.

Acknowledgment. We are grateful to Mike Best, Ashok Jhunjhunwala and Shibu Mani for helpful discussions, to Sanjit Biswas for 50 Meraki nodes, and to the NCIIA for a sustainable vision grant supporting this work.

5. REFERENCES

[1] Lifenet website: "http://www.thelifenetwork.org".

[2] S. Biswas and R. Morris. Exor: Opportunistic multi-hop routing for wireless networks. In *Proc. SIGCOMM*, pages 133–144, 2005.

[3] Douglas S. J. De Couto, Daniel Aguayo, John Bicket, and Robert Morris. A high-throughput path metric for multi-hop wireless routing. In *Proceedings of the 9th annual international conference on Mobile computing and networking*, MobiCom '03, pages 134–146, New York, NY, USA, 2003. ACM.

[4] R. Draves, J. Padhye, and B. Zill. Routing in multi-radio, multi-hop wireless mesh networks. In *MobiCom '04: Proceedings of the 10th annual international conference on Mobile computing and networking*, pages 114–128, New York, NY, USA, 2004. ACM.

[5] Jinyang Li, Charles Blake, Douglas S. J. De Couto, Hu I. Lee, and Robert Morris. Capacity of Ad Hoc wireless networks. In *MobiCom '01: Proceedings of the 7th annual international conference on Mobile computing and networking*, pages 61–69, New York, NY, USA, 2001. ACM.

[6] Ashwin Paranjpe and Santosh Vempala. Mymanet: A customizable mobile ad hoc network. In *NSDR '09*, Big Sky, Montana, USA, 2009. ACM.

A Protocol for Disaster Data Evacuation

Tilmann Rabl, Florian Stegmaier, Mario Döller, and The Tong Vang
Chair of Distributed Information Systems, University of Passau
Passau, Germany
{rabl,stegmai,doeller,vang}@fim.uni-passau.de

ABSTRACT

Data is the basis of the modern information society. However, recent natural catastrophes have shown that it is not possible to definitively secure a data storage location. Even if the storage location is not destroyed itself the access may quickly become impossible, due to the breakdown of connections or power supply. However, this rarely happens without any warning. While floods have hours or days of warning time, tsunamis usually leave only minutes for reaction and for earthquakes there are only seconds. In such situations, timely evacuation of important data is the key challenge. Consequently, the focus lies on minimizing the time to move away all data from the storage location whereas the actual time to arrival remains less (but still) important. This demonstration presents the dynamic fast send protocol (DFSP), a new bulk data transfer protocol. It employs striping to dynamic intermediate nodes in order to minimize sending time and to utilize the sender's resources to a high extent.

Categories and Subject Descriptors

C.2.2 [**Computer-Communication Networks**]: Protocols

General Terms

Reliability, Security

1. INTRODUCTION

To enable a fast data evacuation solution, we developed the Fast Send Protocol (FSP) which aims at overcoming the weakest link by introducing intermediate nodes [1]. The central idea of the protocol is to partition the data into smaller blocks and start a striped transfer to intermediate nodes. As soon as all blocks are distributed, the server can retreat from the transfer, while the receiver collects the blocks from the intermediate nodes. Although the protocol shows excellent results in terms of data distribution speed, there are limitations related to security, reliability and the choice of the intermediate nodes (which are fixed beforehand). Especially, the selection process of intermediate nodes is important. Therefore, an enhanced version, the *Dynamic Fast Send Protocol* (DFSP), has been implemented which overcomes the identified weaknesses. DFSP comprises a novel

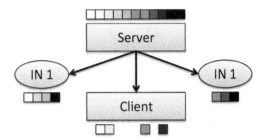

Figure 1: Striping Phase of the DFSP Protocol

approach for selecting the number and set of intermediate nodes. Reliability is guaranteed in the enhanced protocol by a concept similar to RAID-1 which ensures *k-safety*. Security has been enhanced by integrating a challenge response approach based on an asymmetric cryptosystem.

The demonstration of the *Dynamic Fast Send Protocol* will present the benefits of DFSP for large data transfers in contrast to the predecessor protocol FSP.

2. DYNAMIC FAST SEND PROTOCOL

DFSP is an application layer protocol. It extends the well-known File Transfer Protocol (FTP) and is fully compatible with it. DFSP is designed to fully exploit available bandwidth at a server to evacuate its data. To maximize the throughput the following issues have been addressed in DFSP: (i) slow network link between a sender and a receiver, (ii) slow receivers due to other transfers and (iii) transport protocol limitations.

A DFSP file transfer is divided into two main phases: a distribution phase and a collection phase. After a *client request* the server sends the data at maximum speed to the client and multiple intermediate nodes as shown in figure 1 (*striping phase*). When it has sent all blocks it can retreat from the transfer. The client then collects the missing blocks from the intermediate nodes.

As indicated in figure 1, the DFSP server performs a *block partitioning* of the data. The block size is configurable and to ensure security and fault tolerance of the data, the blocks can be encrypted and checksums can be computed. The intermediate nodes can be chosen from a list or are provided dynamically by a Meridian based peer-to-peer overlay [2]. The overlay allows to dynamically build the list of possible intermediate nodes and to choose nodes which have a network location between sender and receiver. This improves the reliability of the protocol, since Meridian pro-

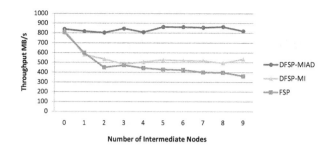

Figure 2: Effective Throughput of DFSP vs. FSP

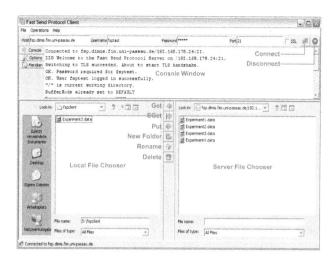

Figure 3: Screenshot of the DFSP GUI

vides a bootstrap procedure and gossip protocol that make the protocol tolerant to node outages. Depending on the throughput, the DFSP increases or decreases the number of intermediate nodes. The heuristic for the number of nodes increases the number of nodes by a multiplicative factor and decreases it one by one. The number of intermediate nodes is increased until the throughput of the sender is maximized. If the throughput decreases after new nodes were added, the number of nodes is decreased again. Furthermore, nodes with bad throughput will be replaced. The dynamic adaption improves the sending time, but it also improves the receiving time.

FSP uses user name and password to connect to the intermediate nodes. This is insecure, since the passwords have to be stored on all clients. Therefore, DFSP additionally provides challenge response authentication with certificates. To increase the scalability and speed of authentication a trust server is used as authority.

The distribution of the data increases the possibility that parts of the data are lost due to failures. The more nodes are involved in the data transfer, the higher are the chances for that one of the nodes fails. As long as the sender is still online this is no problem since it will transfer the data to another node. However, if the sending phase is finished, the server is not part of the transfer any more. Hence, a failure in the collection phase results in an abort of the transfer in FSP. Since the goal of the protocol is fast data evacuation this is not acceptable. Therefore, DFSP provides a k-safe transfer. In this mode, it is ensured that each block of the data which is not sent to the client directly is replicated at least $k + 1$ times. Therefore, the transfer can tolerate the loss of k intermediate nodes and still succeeds.

Due to the dynamic approach DFSP is usually faster than FSP. FSP has an optimal sending throughput if the number and choice of intermediate nodes is optimal. However, this is hard to determine beforehand. Furthermore, a slow intermediate node will degrade the sending time and especially the overall transfer time. If the number of intermediate nodes is too small the sending time suffers, since the servers capabilities are not exploited. If the number of intermediate nodes is too large, the additional overhead during collection reduces the total throughput noticeable. This can be seen in the following evaluation.

3. EVALUATION

In contrast to the fixed selection of intermediate nodes in FSP, DFSP features a *Multiplicative Increase* (MI) and a *Multiplicative Inscrease, Additive Decrease* (MIAD) strategy. The first method (MI) starts with a fixed set of nodes

which is multiplicative increased if the effective throughput is higher than the previous one. The second approach (MIAD) is similar to the MI-method except that the amount of intermediate nodes is decreased if the current effective throughput is smaller or equal to the previous one. To demonstrate the advantage of the two different methods in contrast to FSP, figure 2 presents the results of our evaluation.

The evaluation was executed at our cluster with one server and 16 nodes. The server is connected by a 1 Gbit switch and all nodes by 100 MBit switches. The x-axis presents the variable amount of intermediate nodes (0-9). The y-axis shows the effective throughput (MBit/s), where detailed numbers are given in the table. The evaluation verifies that both strategies (MI and MIAD) improve the throughput over FSP by any configuration, whereas MIAD demonstrates a more stable behavior.

4. DEMONSTRATION

In the demonstration we will show the functionality of the protocol which is administrated by the DFSP graphical user interface (see figure 3). Apart from standard file manager functionality, like moving files, creating folders and deleting files or folders, the GUI shows the status of the connection and makes it possible to configure the data transfer and the Meridian overlay.

In order to demonstrate a data evacuation scenario, we will initiate a third party transfer. For the demonstration we will use a laptop connected to the Internet that can issue the third party transfer. The transfer itself will be issued in our lab at the University of Passau. For the test, we will transfer a 1 Gbyte sized file.

5. REFERENCES

[1] T. Rabl, C. Koch, G. Hölbling, and H. Kosch. Design and implementation of the fast send protocol. *Journal of Digital Information Management*, 7(2):120–127, 2009.

[2] B. Wong, A. Slivkins, and E. G. Sirer. Meridian: A Lightweight Network Location Service without Virtual Coordinates. *ACM SIGCOMM Computer Communication Review*, 35(4):85–96, 2005.

Towards Energy-Efficient Streaming System for Mobile Hotspots

Ming-Hung Chen, Chun-Yu Yang, Chun-Yun Chang, Ming-Yuan Hsu, Ke-Han Lee,
Cheng-Fu Chou
National Taiwan University
{mhchen, left, ccf}@cmlab.csie.ntu.edu.tw

ABSTRACT

Modern mobile devices have become an important part of our daily life but the performance of multimedia applications still suffers from the constrained energy supply and communication bandwidth of the mobile devices. In this work, we develop an energy-efficient streaming system for mobile hotspots to achieve better Quality-of-Experience. Our main idea is (a) to avoid redundant 3G transmissions as well as reduce the usage of 3G links for those low residual-energy users, and (b) to enable nearby mobile users cooperatively to share the downloaded data via short-range interfaces. The experiment results shows our scheme can improve the system lifetime by 27%, and provide better throughput as well as lower loss rate than conversional 3G systems do.

Categories and Subject Descriptors: C.2.1 [Computer-Communication Networks]: Network Architecture and Design

General Terms: Design, Performance

Keywords: Composite networks, Cooperative networks, Energy efficiency, Mobile hotspots, Streaming, Wireless networks

1. INTRODUCTION

The proliferation of modern mobile devices such as iPad, iPhone, and other PDA Phones, which are equipped with high performance CPU, large-size displayer, and multiple communication interfaces, has changed the users' behavior on portable handhold devices. For example, in many cities, we always see people use those devices to access Facebook, play games, access their e-mails or watch TV programs, etc, via 3G access link. Despite the popularity of these applications, those mobile devices still suffer from limited energy supply and 3G bandwidth. Therefore, how to leverage limited energy and 3G bandwidth to achieve better Quality-of-Experience becomes a challenging issue. In this work, we focus on the streaming applications and develop an energy-efficient cooperative streaming system for mobile devices.

We investigate the energy consumption of an Apple's iPad device. A key observation is the 3G interface consumes 83 times energy than Bluetooth interfaces, and 18 times than 802.11 wireless interface when transmitting the same amount of data. This indicates that if we properly replace 3G interface with other interfaces, e.g. Bluetooth, we may extend the lifetime of the devices. We also notice that people are used to gather in the same area, i.e., hotspots, where

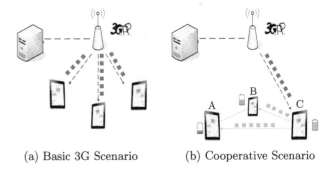

(a) Basic 3G Scenario   (b) Cooperative Scenario

Figure 1: Different download scenarios for mobile devices

they enjoy the mobile multimedia applications. This may induce high device density in some particular places at certain time periods, e.g. hotspots in the airports, cafes, malls for the day time, or subway stations during the rush hour. For such mobile hotspots, two important observations are (a) the high device density by natural, and (b) the discrepancy of energy consumption between those communication interfaces; so, these observations motivate us to design an energy-efficient cooperative streaming system for extending the lifetime of the devices and dealing with the potential insufficient shared 3G bandwidth.

2. METHODOLOGY

Our objective is to maximize the system lifetime, which is to maximize the minimal watching time of the users in a connected group. We can fulfill the goal via following two design philosophies: 1) The data chunk should be downloaded as few times as possible to avoid redundant 3G transmissions, and 2) The data chunk should not be relayed to other users by those with less residual energy.

We give a overview of our distributed algorithm here. Each mobile device periodically broadcasts its energy status to others via short-range interface. When a mobile device needs a certain chunk, it checks if there exists a device with most residual energy in the local area. If so, it will send an entrustment, i.e. a download task assignment, to the device. When the device receives the entrustment, it will start the same procedure to check if the entrustment can be forward. If so, it will forward the entrustment and rebroadcast the chunk to the original requestor when the chunk is received. If a mobile device is unable to find other devices with higher energy and it has sufficient bandwidth

| (a) Basic 3G Scheme | (b) CPR Scheme | (c) Our Scheme |

Figure 2: Comparison of visual quality (average source streaming rate: 700kbps)

to download the chunk, it will download the chunk via 3G interface and broadcast the chunk. Otherwise, it will tell others that its bandwidth is insufficient at this time slot, and the entrustment will be forwarded to those devices with higher energy.

For example, as shown in Figure 1(b), when the device A requires a chunk X, it looks up its neighbor list for the device with highest energy to entrust. Then the device A sends an entrustment to the device C. When the device C receives the entrustment, it downloads the chunk X via 3G interface, because it finds that no other devices have higher energy than itself and it has sufficient 3G bandwidth. After the device C receives the chunk X, it will broadcast the chunk via short-range interface, so that the device A and B will get the chunk with less energy cost.

With the proposed mechanism, we download each chunk only once in a well-connected group to reduce the total use of the 3G interface and extend the system lifetime.

3. DEMONSTRATION

We develop our energy-efficient cooperative streaming system on Apple iOS version 4.2. The system is based on a pull-based peer-to-peer live streaming system. For more detail, please refer to our website [3]. We deploy our system to three Apple iPad devices to collect the results as shown in Figure 1(b). They connect to the Internet via 3G interface, and the Bluetooth interface is used for point-to-point short-range communication. We also implement the conventional 3G approach as mentioned in Figure 1(a), and the Cooperative Peer-to-Peer Repair (CPR) [2] scheme as mentioned in the related works section to be compared with our scheme.

- **Lower energy consumption:** We set average source streaming rate to 350kbps and plot the energy cost of different schemes over time. Our scheme, which benefits from the less use of the 3G interface, can *improve about 27% lifetime*, compared with the conventional 3G approach. The CPR costs more energy than the conventional 3G approach. This is because the devices need to download all chunks by themselves and cost some extra energy to recover the loss chunks. On the other hand, the CPR can achieve better visual quality than the conventional 3G approach does.

- **Lower loss rate and higher throughput:** As shown in the Figure 2, the perceived video distortion of the conventional 3G approach or CPR scheme is large when the streaming rate is 700kbps on average but our scheme can still provide higher visual quality than other schemes

do. The primary reason is that our scheme can support higher throughput via cooperative downloading and this results in lower packet loss rate. Note that with the popularity of 3G devices, insufficient bandwidth could become a common problem during the busy hours, since the bandwidth is limited and shared by all devices connected to the same base station.

4. DISCUSSION

In this section, we point out several issues based on our experiences during developing the system.

- **Fairness and freeriders:** Our current implementation does not take account of the fairness. For the users nearby, the device with the most residual energy always costs more energy than others. How to attract those devices join the group,i.e. maintain the fairness, and avoid freeriders will become another challenging issue. We are currently working on this issue and will have some outcomes in the near future.

- **Privacy-preserving:** The privacy-preserving issues have came into the spotlight. The cooperative scheme needs to release the user's interests and device profiles. However, it will be effective only when the users team up with those watching the same channel, which means it could mostly happen on the popular public live channels. This also means collecting the users' interests should be futile. Moreover, the users could always turn off the function to keep them secretly.

5. RELATED WORKS

The authors of CPR [2, 1] well use the communication interfaces on the mobile devices to cooperatively repair corruption multimedia broadcast/multimedia service (MBMS) data chunks. However, CPR still suffers from the limited energy supply, and requires Internet service provider (ISP)'s support. Expectably, our scheme is more flexible than CPR approach.

6. REFERENCES

[1] X. Liu, G. Cheung, and C. Chuah. Structured network coding and cooperative wireless ad-hoc peer-to-peer repair for wwan video broadcast. *Multimedia, IEEE Transactions on*, 11(4):730–741, 2009.

[2] S. Raza, D. Li, C. Chuah, and G. Cheung. Cooperative peer-to-peer repair for wireless multimedia broadcast. In *Multimedia and Expo, 2007 IEEE International Conference on*, pages 1075–1078. IEEE, 2007.

[3] http://www.cmlab.csie.ntu.edu.tw/c̃mlpp/eeps.

MPLS-TE and MPLS VPNs with OpenFlow

Ali Reza Sharafat, Saurav Das, Guru Parulkar, and Nick McKeown

Department of Electrical Engineering, Stanford University, Stanford, California 94305, USA

sharafat, sd2, parulkar, nickm@stanford.edu

ABSTRACT

We demonstrate MPLS Traffic Engineering (MPLS-TE) and MPLS-based Virtual Private Networks (MPLS VPNs) using OpenFlow [1] and NOX [6]. The demonstration is the outcome of an engineering experiment to answer the following questions: How hard is it to implement a complex control plane on top of a network controller such as NOX? Does the global vantage point in NOX make the implementation easier than the traditional method of implementing it on every switch, embedded in the data plane?

We implemented every major feature of MPLS-TE and MPLS-VPN in just 2,000 lines of code, compared to much larger lines of code in the more traditional approach, such as Quagga-MPLS. Because NOX maintains a consistent, up-to-date topology map, the MPLS control plane features are quite simple to implement. And its simplicity makes it easy to extend: We have easily added several new features; something a network operator could do to customize their network to meet their customers' needs.

The demo consists of two parts: MPLS-TE services and then MPLS VPN driven by a GUI.

Categories and Subject Descriptors: C.2.1 – Computer Systems Organization [**Computer-Communication Networks**]: Network Architecture and Design

General Terms: Management, Design, Experimentation

Keywords: MPLS, MPLS-TE, VPN, Traffic Engineering, OpenFlow

1. SCIENTIFIC RATIONALE

We claim that while the MPLS data plane is fairly simple, the control planes associated with MPLS-TE and MPLS VPNs are rather complicated. For instance, in a typical traffic engineered MPLS network, one needs to run OSPF, LDP, RSVP-TE, I-BGP, and MP-BGP to name a few protocols. The distributed nature of these protocols results in excessive traffic of update messages when there are frequent changes in the network. This, in turn causes the routers to spend a lot of CPU time recalculating routing information. Hence, CPU message queues may get filled leading to incoming hello messages getting dropped. This leads to false link-state information being distributed throughout the network. The described vicious cycle causes large convergence times for the above protocols, meaning excessive control traffic on the network and stale information on the routers.

In SDN, the Network Operating System (NOS) is responsible for constructing and presenting a logically centralized map of the network. Instead of a set of distributed protocols implemented on each router, we implement these functionalities as simple software modules that work on the network map in NOS. Implementation of these functions on a logical map of the network is very simple. Hence, by pushing the control plane functionality to NOS, we benefit from not only simplicity of implementation, but also the fact that maintaining and updating applications are easy as well. This is because new features are no longer tied to multiple protocols that would normally have to be changed. In fact, with the controller in charge of the control plane, there is no need for any distributed protocol running in the routers as the NOS has complete knowledge of the network.

2. ARCHITECTURE

The architecture of our system is given in Figure 1. Our test-bed consists of several software and physical switches. The software switches are instances of Open vSwitch [2] which are hosted within the Mininet environment [3]. These switches are connected to a network of physical switches. Both software and physical switches support the OpenFlow 1.0 specifications [4] as well as the MPLS related section of the OpenFlow 1.1 specifications [5]. The switches are designed so that they handle the data plane, and not the control plane functionality of MPLS.

With the abovementioned network, we emulate a wide area network for the purpose of our demonstration. All switches are controlled by a single instance of the NOX [6] controller. The MPLS-TE and VPN services are managed via an application that runs in NOX. The control plane and the MPLS features are exclusively handled by NOX. The data plane simply supports the push swap and pop actions. When changes are needed in the data plane, NOX modifies the flow tables in the appropriate switches.

We use multiple GUIs to show the workings of the network and to dynamically interact and modify the TE-LSPs and/or VPNs.

3. DEMO SCENARIOS

The demonstration consists of two parts, the first pertaining to MPLS-TE [7] and the second pertaining to MPLS VPNs.

3.1. MPLS-TE

The first part of the demo is visualized via two GUIs, both showing the topology of the entire physical network. The first GUI displays the IP flows in the network and the second GUI displays the LSPs and the flows routed through them. All the flows and LSPs are color-coded to distinguish between various

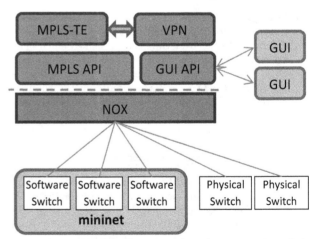

Figure 1. The architecture of the physical network and the controller used in our demonstration.

SIGCOMM'11, August 15–19, 2011, Toronto, Ontario, Canada.
ACM 978-1-4503-0797-0/11/08.

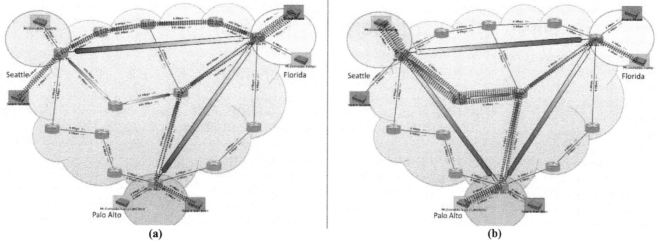

Figure 2. Sample GUIs corresponding to the MPLS VPN demonstration. Two VPNs with their corresponding flows and LSPs are shown in (a) and (b)

types. The demonstration starts with all the flows in the IP plane, and as we step through the demo, we create TE-LSPs and reroute some of the IP flows through the LSPs. By creating TE-LSPs of different characteristics, we demonstrate the following features:

Constrained Shortest Path First (CSPF) The CSPF algorithm allows us to find the shortest path for a TE-LSP that satisfy its bandwidth and priority requirements.

Auto-route When a TE-LSP is created, we automatically reroute any flow whose path goes through the head-end and the tail-end router of the created LSP onto the LSP.

Traffic Aware LSPs We can create TE-LSPs that carry a specific type of traffic. These can include VOIP, HTTP, etc.

Priority LSPs can have different levels of priority. When the reservable bandwidth of a link is fully allocated, we reroute LSPs of lower priority to alternative paths.

Auto-bandwidth The auto-bandwidth feature allows for the bandwidth reservation of a TE-LSP to dynamically adjust to its actual bandwidth usage (as opposed to the bandwidth being statically set at the creation of the LSP).

Interactive Management Users can create custom TE-LSPs from the GUI. That is, the user specifies the head-end and tail-end routers and the characteristics of the desired TE-LSP, which is then created in the network and shown in the GUI.

3.2. MPLS VPNs

The second part of the demo is visualized using multiple GUIs as well. In this case, all GUIs show the physical network, and each GUI pertains to a VPN and its associated flows and LSPs. Screenshots of working versions of this part of the demo are given in Figure 2. Our MPLS-VPN network has a simpler backbone topology compared to the previous section, but with some customer nodes added to the edge of the backbone network.

The backbone network is MPLS-TE enabled and so when LSPs are created to support a VPN, they are accompanied with all the TE features mentioned in Section 3.1.

We configure multiple VPNs with overlapping private IP address spaces. Each VPN comes with different characteristics which enables us to demonstrate the following:

Isolation of VPNs We demonstrate that multiple VPNs can coexist in a single backbone network where different VPNs may have overlapping address spaces. The flows associated with different VPNs are routed through their respective LSPs and do not aggregate with each other.

Custom Topologies The logical topology of each VPN can be specified by the customer. The topology can be anything from the traditional hub-and-spokes to full-mesh.

TE Services Since the backbone network is MPLS-TE enabled, we can readily offer TE services to the customers. We demonstrate the Priority and Auto-bandwidth features of TE. This allows for a high priority VPN to force others to reroute when it requires more bandwidth along its LSPs.

Interactive Management Users can create a new VPN by specifying the connection between the customer and provider routers as well as the topology and other characteristics of the network. After the specifications are given, we create the desired VPN network and display the results in the GUI.

4. REFERENCES

[1] N. McKeown, T. Anderson, H. Balakrishnan, G. Parulkar, L. Peterson, J. Rexford, S. Shenker, and J. Turner. OpenFlow: enabling innovation in campus networks. *ACM SIGCOMM Computer Communication Review*, 38(2):69–74, April 2008.

[2] Open vSwitch [Online]. Available: http://openvswitch.org/

[3] B. Lantz, B. Heller, and N. McKeown. A Network in a Laptop: Rapid Prototyping for Software-Defined Networks. In *ACM SIGCOMM HotNets Workshop*, 2010.

[4] OpenFlow Switch Specification: Version 1.0.0 [Online]. Available: http://www.openflow.org/documents/openflow-spec-v1.0.0.pdf

[5] OpenFlow Switch Specification: Version 1.1.0 Implemented [Online]. Available: http://www.openflow.org/documents/openflow-spec-v1.1.0.pdf

[6] N. Gude, T. Koponen, J. Pettit, B. Pfaff, M. Casado, N. McKeown, and S. Shenker. NOX: Towards and operating system for networks. In *ACM SIGCOMM Computer Communication Review*, July 2008.

[7] S. Das, A. R. Sharafat, G. Parulkar, and N. McKeown MPLS with a Simple OPEN Control Plane. In *Optical Fiber Communication Conference*, March 2011.

Dasu - ISP Characterization from the Edge

A BitTorrent Implementation

Mario A. Sánchez
Northwestern University

John S. Otto
Northwestern University

Zachary S. Bischof
Northwestern University

Fabián E. Bustamante
Northwestern University

ABSTRACT

Evaluating and characterizing access ISPs is critical to consumers shopping for alternative services and governments surveying the availability of broadband services to their citizens. We present *Dasu*, a service for crowdsourcing ISP characterization to the edge of the network. *Dasu* is implemented as an extension to a popular BitTorrent client [5] and has been available since July 2010. While the prototype uses BitTorrent as its host application, its design is agnostic to the particular host application. The demo showcases our current implementation using both a prerecorded execution trace and a live run.

Categories and Subject Descriptors

C.2.3 [**Computer Systems Organization**]: Computer Communication Networks—*Network Operations*; C.2.5 [**Computer Communication Networks**]: Local and Wide-Area Networks—*Internet*; C.4 [**Performance of Systems**]: Measurement techniques

General Terms

Experimentation, Performance, Measurement

Keywords

Broadband access networks, ISP, Characterization

1. INTRODUCTION

Evaluating and characterizing access ISPs is critical to subscribers shopping for alternative ISPs, companies providing reliable Internet services, and governments surveying the availability of high-speed Internet services to their citizens [3, 4].

Given its importance and the lack of publicly available information, several recent projects have started to evaluate alternative approaches for profiling edge network services. The approaches being explored range from using Web-based technologies to run tests against centralized or cloud servers, to actively measuring end hosts from a set of dedicated servers, to installing special networking devices for active monitoring from inside PoPs or home networks. While these efforts have begun to shed some much needed clarity on network conditions at the edge, their approaches present an apparently unavoidable tradeoff between extensibility, vantage point coverage and continuous monitoring.

Measurement from dedicated servers in the core of the network, including platforms such as Archipelago and PlanetLab, can be done at scale, but cannot capture the view of end users, typically located behind middle boxes and not welcoming unsolicited active measurements. Web-based approaches can capture the user's perspective and have low barriers to adoption, but are susceptible to white-listing from ISPs and limited by infrastructure and bandwidth costs that scale with the number of adopters. In addition, both of these approaches capture performance *only* when the test is run, missing dynamic changes to service levels. Last, while deploying devices inside home networks provides continuous monitoring at the network edge, the dependence on hardware devices severely limits these approaches' geographic coverage and flexibility, hampering the representativeness of the captured view.

We have argued [1] that hosting ISP characterization on end systems running network-intensive applications can avoid these tradeoffs. We have presented a new approach for crowdsourced ISP characterization that leverages the detailed views of Internet-wide ISP performance offered by these applications and evaluate its feasibility through a large-scale study of data gathered from BitTorrent users. By passively monitoring user-generated traffic within these applications, our approach is able to capture the end user's view in a scalable manner. By extending existing applications, it has the flexibility and low-barrier to adoption of other software-based models. By combining passive monitoring with dynamically extensible active measurements, it can achieve the effectiveness of hardware-based solutions without their associated costs.

In this demo, we present a prototype implementation of these ideas as an extension to a popular BitTorrent client [5]. Our extension – *Dasu* – was first released to Beta testers in June 2010. At the time of submission and *without any advertisement*, Dasu has been adopted by more than 37,000 users in over 100 countries. While the prototype uses BitTorrent as its host application, its design is agnostic to the particular host application.

Additional information about the project and the current Dasu implementation can be found at: http://www.aqualab.cs.northwestern.edu/projects/Dasu.html.

2. DASU

Dasu is implemented as an extension to a popular BitTorrent client [5]. The extension passively monitors user-generated BitTorrent traffic, which allows it to scale while monitoring the performance experienced by end users, as well as relevant signals from the host application and OS in real time. Examples of the collected information include per torrent statistics (such as the number of RSTs received, upload rate and download rate), application-wide statistics (such as total upload and download rates, number of active

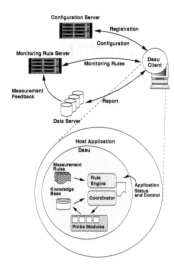

Figure 1: Dasu System components.

torrents) and system-wide statistics (including connection-related statistics reported by the operating system such as number of active, current and passive connections, number of connections torn by TCP RST, and number of failed connections).

In addition, each Dasu client (Fig.1) includes an easy to extend set of *Probe Modules* for active measurements such as traceroute, ping, and the MLab's Network Diagnostic Tool (NDT).

Launched probe modules add measurement results to the client's *Working memory* or *Knowledge Base* – a repository of objects known as *facts*. The set of facts in the working memory drives the firing of monitoring rules by the *Rule Engine*. As new facts are added to the working memory and new monitoring rules are added to the rule base, the rule engine fires rules whose actions can result on the launching of new monitoring probes. The *Measurement Coordinator* is responsible for launching the necessary active probes as required by the rule engine. The coordinator receives measurement requests and schedules them in such a way as to guarantee maximum responsiveness (in terms of time taken to launch the requested probe) while minimizing overhead and interference between probes and the host's application activity. The coordinator is also responsible for limiting the number of active probes that can be executed on the system over a period of time.

2.1 Dasu System

Each client, upon initialization, contacts the *Dasu Configuration Server* to register itself and retrieve a configuration file. Each client's configuration file specifies the set of servers to use (to report collected measurements or retrieve new monitoring rules, for instance), and the frequency with which it should contact them. Other parameters in the configuration file include the size of measurement logs and the maximum frequency of periodic events, for instance. After registering, clients contact the *Monitoring Rule Servers* to retrieve the measurement rules they would run for both passive and active monitoring. Clients submit their collected results to the *Database* server, at a given rate specified by the configuration file, and can access experiment descriptions from the *Web Server* as needed.

All monitoring rule files served by the active or continuous monitoring rule servers are digitally signed for authenticity. The servers use public-key cryptography to sign every rule file served to clients. Clients verify the authenticity of the file using the public-key distributed as part of the Dasu client.

Limits on the number, type and rate of measurements that a client can issue together with the secure assignments of tasks ensure the fail-safe property of the platform.

Rules Specification. The basic structure of monitoring rules include a rule name followed by the condition and consequence sections. Rules have the following general form:

```
rule <name>
when {<condition>}
then {<consequence>}
```

Actions can result in the inclusion or removal of facts to/from the knowledge base, and the launching of new monitoring probes.

As a concrete example, the following simple rule triggers the Vuze BitTorrent Speed Test when this has been requested to validate potential interference. The request appears as a fact `FactFireAction( action == "launchBTSpeedTest")` in the client knowledge base. The consequence section issues a request for the probe and retracts the triggering fact from the knowledge base.

```
rule "Launch BT speed test to
       corroborate interference"
   when
      $fact : FactFireAction( action ==
              "launchBTSpeedTest");
   then
      addPriorityProbe("download_non_encrypted",
         ProbeType.BTTest);
      sendToLog("Launching BT download Test");
      retract($fact);
end
```

Monitoring rules support a straightforward implementation of a number of useful functions for ISP characterization including interference detection (as in [2]), and evaluation of the users' DNS resolver.

2.2 Demonstration

Our demonstration will showcase our current implementation of *Dasu* using both a prerecorded execution trace and a live run. We will show the information available to users through the plugin interface and demonstrate the behind the scenes execution of monitoring rules.

3. REFERENCES

[1] BISCHOF, Z. S., OTTO, J. S., SÁNCHEZ, M. A., RULA, J. P., CHOFFNES, D. R., AND BUSTAMANTE, F. E. Crowdsourcing ISP characterization to the network edge. In *Proc. of ACM SIGCOMM W-MUST* (August 2011).

[2] DISCHINGER, M., MARCON, M., GUHA, S., GUMMADI, K. P., MAHAJAN, R., AND SAROIU, S. Glasnost: Enabling end users to detect traffic differentiation. In *Proc. of USENIX NSDI* (2010).

[3] SAMKNOWS. Samknows & Ofcom UK broadband performance testing. http://www.samknows.com/broadband/ofcom_and_samknows, June 2009.

[4] SAMKNOWS. Samknows & the FCC American broadband performance measurement. http://www.samknows.com/broadband/fcc_and_samknows, June 2009.

[5] VUZE, INC. Vuze. http://www.vuze.com/.

WiFire: A Firewall for Wireless Networks

Matthias Wilhelm*   Ivan Martinovic¶   Jens B. Schmitt*   Vincent Lenders‡

*Disco Labs, TU Kaiserslautern
{wilhelm,jschmitt}@cs.uni-kl.de

¶EECS, UC Berkeley
martinov@eecs.berkeley.edu

‡Armasuisse, Switzerland
vincent.lenders@armasuisse.ch

ABSTRACT

Firewalls are extremely effective at enforcing security policies in wired networks. Perhaps surprisingly, firewalls are entirely nonexistent in the wireless domain. Yet, the need to selectively control and block radio communication is particularly high in a broadcast environment since any node may receive and send packets. In this demo, we present WiFire, a system that brings the firewall concept to wireless networks. First, WiFire detects and analyzes packets during their transmission, checking their content against a set of rules. It then relies on reactive jamming techniques to selectively block undesired communication. We show the feasibility and performance of WiFire, which is implemented on the USRP2 software-defined radio platform, in several scenarios with IEEE 802.15.4 radios. WiFire is able to classify and effectively block undesired communication without interfering with desired communication.

Categories and Subject Descriptors

C.2.0 [**Computer Communication Networks**]: General—*Security and protection (e.g., firewalls)*

General Terms

Security, Design, Experimentation

1. INTRODUCTION

Access to the wireless medium is hard to regulate and control as any device in the transmission range can eavesdrop and inject packets into a network with low effort. In this demonstration, we showcase WiFire, a system that helps regaining control over the RF spectrum by *enforcing* security policies at the physical layer. The idea is simple: WiFire scans the RF spectrum for packets that might reach the protected network, analyzes whether they comply to a given ruleset or not, and blocks them if necessary. WiFire achieves this by demodulating and decoding packets sequentially *during* their transmission, classifying each individual packet with a set of rules based on its content (such as the source or destination addresses, frame type or even parts of the payload) and jamming it before it reaches the receiver. This approach has many system challenges because of the real-time constraints of detection and subsequent jamming of packets. On the other hand, this approach enables WiFire

to offer the service of a wireless firewall, i.e., enforcing a security policy from a single point of administration and control, without the need to make WiFire explicitly participate in the network. We show the feasibility and applicability of this concept with a demonstration of WiFire protecting an IEEE 802.15.4 network in several attack scenarios.

The system runs on the software-defined radio platform USRP2 and is implemented both in FPGA logic and firmware code to satisfy the hard timing constraints; a host PC is used to configure the operational parameters and collect firewall statistics and logging messages. In previous work [2], a predecessor of WiFire is described and its performance of selective jamming in 802.15.4 networks is evaluated. With the added rule checker, we aim to promote the idea of "friendly jamming" that can help to reach security goals in wireless networks [1].

2. WIFIRE'S OPERATION

WiFire proceeds in three steps in its operation: *(i)* spotting packets, *(ii)* distinguishing friends from foes, and *(iii)* destroying malicious packets.

Detecting packets. WiFire continuously monitors the wireless medium, spotting packets for analysis. WiFire exploits the fact that an attacker must be constructive to inject packets, it must comply to the correct frame format to ensure that its packets have a chance to be received. WiFire scans the medium for the physical layer header of 802.15.4, consisting of a preamble and start-of-frame delimiter (SFD).

Identifying malicious packets. When a packet transmission is detected, WiFire analyzes the signal and checks whether a rule in the stored ruleset matches. We have implemented an O-QPSK demodulator and an 802.15.4 frame decoder to access link layer fields or payload bytes while the packet is on the air, one byte at a time. This output stream is fed into an `iptables`-style rule checker that supports chains of rules consisting of an arbitrary combination of matches, i.e., functions that check for packet features. An example chain that can directly be interpreted by WiFire's rule checker is

```
wftables -A -m dot15.4-ftype --data
        -m dot15.4-dst --mode 2 --pan 0x11 --addr 10
        -j JAM                    # Rule 1
wftables -A -m dot15.4-ftype --ctrl
        -m ! dot15.4-src --mode 2 --pan 0x11 --addr 1
        -j JAM                    # Rule 2
wftables -A -j ACCEPT             # Default policy
```

This ruleset specifies that all transmissions are allowed (the default policy), except for ...

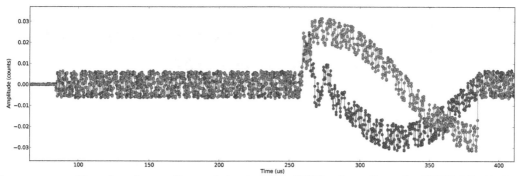

Figure 1: A sequence of baseband sampling points showing WiFire in action. An IEEE 802.15.4 transmission begins (with constant amplitude), and WiFire detects and analyzes the signal and decides whether the packet must be jammed or not. It then emits a short jamming burst (the sinusoidal signal) to distort the signal, destroying the packet at the receiver.

1. data frames coming from node 10 in the current networks (with the identifying PAN ID), and

2. control frames that are sent from other source addresses than 1.

Rule 1 is used to block all data traffic from a node of choice, virtually separating it from the network. This can be used to enforce a fast *node revocation*, e.g., when the keying material of this node is leaked. Rule 2 enforces that only node 1 (e.g., the PAN coordinator) can send control messages on the current channel to protect other nodes from being hijacked.

Preventing packet reception. WiFire prevents packet receptions by jamming. The intended receiver then either misses the packet completely or detects a corrupted frame with a failed integrity check. This approach to prevent receptions gives WiFire the *transparency* property: protected devices do not need to know about WiFire's presence, no protocol adaptations or control messages from the firewall are necessary. Therefore, WiFire can be added to existing legacy networks to "patch" their security problems, filtering out malicious packets. At the same time, WiFire is friendly to co-existing networks despite its active nature: *(i)* it uses efficient jamming waveforms and short jamming durations (down to $32\,\mu s$ for 802.15.4), *(ii)* it limits its activity to times of attack, and *(iii)* it can be restricted to selected regions with physical layer means such as directional antennas. During normal operation, WiFire monitors the channel passively and reacts to immediate threats only. Fig. 1 shows WiFire in action: it has analyzed an incoming packet, detected a policy violation, and, thus, interferes with a part of the packet to prevent its reception.

3. THE DEMONSTRATION

In the demo we show that the concept of a wireless firewall based on real-time detection and selective jamming is technically feasible and provides interesting perspectives in securing wireless networks.

3.1 Scenarios

We use an 802.15.4-based wireless sensor network and an attacker using the KillerBee framework [3] to show several usage scenarios for WiFire. With its rule-based system, WiFire can be easily adapted to specify and block adversarial flows while leaving the legitimate flows intact. We show that WiFire protects effectively from flooding attacks, node capturing and injection attacks.

We offer several ways to observe WiFire's operation: *(i)* packet reception rate measurements on the sensor motes to show that selected flows can be effectively blocked, and *(ii)* a GNU Radio-based monitor application that provides visualizations such as in Fig. 1 in real-time.

3.2 Interaction

We want to offer an interactive demo to the attendees, e.g., to let them choose the network topology, and the placement of the firewalls antennas and sensor motes. Additionally, the set of active rules for WiFire to enforce are adaptable on the fly, enabling attendees to evaluate the performance of our implementation in settings of their choice.

3.3 Discussion

We are aware that the idea of active protection measures such as jamming is a rather controversial one, so we also like to hear the opinions of the attendees of SIGCOMM '11 and discuss with them about possible problems and limitations of this idea, especially attacks against WiFire on the physical layer. On the other hand, as this concept is applicable to a variety of wireless technologies and scenarios, we expect that a number of additional ideas will come up on applications and uses for WiFire.

3.4 Experimental Platform

While the main theme of the demo is the wireless firewall, WiFire itself can also be used as an experimental platform to generate finely controllable interference for repeatable testbed experiments. We are able to present further uses that the platform may find in wireless network testbeds, and how researchers can employ WiFire in their experimentation work. We will provide all necessary resources of WiFire online to interested researchers after the conference.

4. REFERENCES

[1] I. Martinovic, P. Pichota, and J. B. Schmitt. Jamming for good: a fresh approach to authentic communication in WSNs. In *Proc. of ACM WiSec '09*, pages 161–168. ACM, Mar. 2009.

[2] M. Wilhelm, I. Martinovic, J. B. Schmitt, and V. Lenders. Reactive jamming in wireless networks: how realistic is the threat? In *Proc. of ACM WiSec '11*, pages 47–52. ACM, June 2011.

[3] J. Wright. KillerBee—practical ZigBee exploitation framework (presented at ToorCon '10), Oct. 2010. Available at http://code.google.com/p/killerbee.

Demonstrating Generalized Virtual Topologies in an OpenFlow Network

Elio Salvadori, Roberto Doriguzzi Corin, Matteo Gerola,
Attilio Broglio, Francesco De Pellegrini
CREATE-NET
Via alla Cascata 56/D Povo, 38123 Trento - Italy
{esalvadori, rdoriguzzi, mgerola, abroglio, fdepellegrini}@create-net.org

1. INTRODUCTION

Network Virtualization (NV) is one of the most promising approaches to enable innovation in today's network. Generally speaking, NV refers to the possibility of pooling together low–level hardware and software resources belonging to a networked system into a single administrative entity. In such a way network resources could be effectively shared in a transparent way among different logical network instances corresponding to different virtual network topologies.

A recent approach toward Network Virtualization has been proposed through FlowVisor [1], whose aim is to leverage on the specific features of an OpenFlow–controlled network [2] to share the same hardware forwarding plane among multiple logical networks.

As highlighted by the authors in [1], one of the major limitations of FlowVisor is the inability to establish virtual topologies not restricted by the underpinning physical topology. As a consequence, FlowVisor is unable to provide researchers flexibility in designing their experiments with arbitrary network topologies on a defined physical infrastructure.

The architecture presented in Chapter 2 of this paper, called ADVisor (ADvanced FlowVisor), provides the functionalities to overcome the above-mentioned FlowVisor's limitation by allowing the instantiation of generalized virtual topologies in a OpenFlow network through the implementation of virtual links as aggregation of multiple physical links and OpenFlow-enabled switches.

In this demo we will show the configuration of a simple virtual topology performed through a Web-based control framework which allows the reservation of network resources (nodes, links and bandwidth) and the management of virtual resources (virtual links and virtual ports). We will also demonstrate the effective instantiation of the virtual topology by running a synthetic traffic generator application.

Categories and Subject Descriptors

D.2.8 [**Computer Communication Networks**]: Network Architecture and Design

General Terms

Experimentation

Keywords

Network Virtualization, OpenFlow

2. PROPOSED ARCHITECTURE

Like FlowVisor, ADVisor sits between the physical hardware and the guest OpenFlow controllers and enables the implementation of logical topologies and, like FlowVisor, ADVisor can recursively "slice" a virtual topology (see Fig. 1). Differently from FlowVisor, ADVisor does not act as a transparent proxy but can directly reply to the OpenFlow network with the purpose of enabling the instantiation of logical topologies completely decoupled from the underlying physical network.

In ADVisor, Virtual Topologies (VT) are identified through a set of tuples included in configuration files and specifying each component of a Virtual Topology (virtual nodes, virtual links and virtual ports). Furthermore, the flow space of each switch in the network is partitioned among Virtual Topologies through combinations of bits involving only the OSI-Layer 2 fields of the packet header such as the *VLAN ID*, the *MPLS labels* or *IEEE 802.1ad*–based multiple vlan tagging. These last two options are giving higher flexibility since they both allow the experimentation to be performed up to L2, however they are not available yet on any switch hardware being the OpenFlow specification version 1.1.0 [3] recently released.

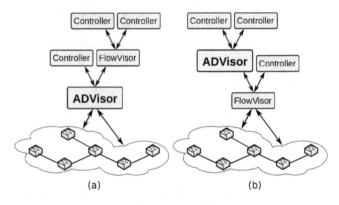

(a)   (b)

Figure 1: (a) ADVisor can be placed between the OpenFlow switches and the physical network or (b) between an instance of FlowVisor and the controllers to recursively "slice" a virtual topology.

In order to provide a full overview of the system, we will give a description of the modules composing ADVisor:

Topology Monitor. This module checks the Virtual Topology configuration in order to determine whether the switch that generated the OpenFlow protocol message is an

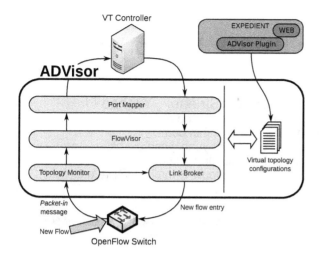

Figure 2: ADVisor software architecture.

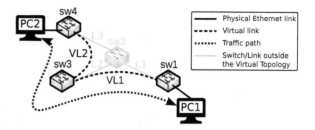

Figure 3: The Virtual Topology used in the demonstration.

end-point of a link or is part of a virtual link (e.g. switch sw2 in Fig. 3). In the first case the message is forwarded to the controller, in the second case the message is managed directly by the Link Broker.

Port Mapper. This module edits the *in_port* and *actions* fields of the OpenFlow protocol messages by replacing their values with ones consistent with the virtual links configuration. For instance, switch sw3 in Fig. 3 is connected to the physical network through a single link while to the Virtual Topology through two different virtual links. Port Mapper remaps the in_port value contained in the Packet_in messages generated by the switch with a virtual value dependent on the virtual link.

Link Broker. The Link Broker creates or modifies OpenFlow protocol messages directed to the switches. Its main objective is to control switches composing virtual links and that should not be managed by controllers. For instance, switch sw2 in Fig. 3 is a component of virtual links between switches sw1 and sw3 and between switches sw3 and sw4. OpenFlow protocol messages sent by sw2 to the controller of this topology are always managed by the Link Broker that directly replies to the switch hiding sw2 to the controller.

FlowVisor. Provides the basic slicing mechanism based on the OpenFlow protocol and manages the TLS secure connections with OpenFlow switches and controllers.

SFA-based control framework. The Expedient-based framework [4] provides an intuitive web user interface for the ADVisor managers to configure the resources for the experimenters. Expedient includes the ADVisor plugin, an extension of the original OpenFlow plugin, which allows the selection of network resources (OpenFlow switches, virtual links, bandwidth etc.) for each Virtual Topology assigned to experimenters.

3. DEMONSTRATION

The primary goal of the demonstration is to show the effective instantiation of a virtual topology and the management of virtual links and virtual ports with this initial prototype of ADVisor. The demonstration is performed on a remote testbed at the CREATE-NET premises composed of four NetFPGA-based OpenFlow switches (interconnected as shown in Fig. 3) and one central unit running ADVisor and

an instance of the NOX controller. All testbed devices are connected through Ethernet cables and are compliant with OpenFlow specification 1.0.0. The virtual topology instantiated for the demonstration includes three switches sw1, sw3 and sw4 plus two virtual links: VL1, formed with the aggregation of physical links L1 and L2 plus switch sw2; VL2 formed with the aggregation of L2, L3 and sw2.

During the demonstration, the Expedient-based user interface (see Fig. 4) is used to configure the virtual topology depicted in Fig. 3 including virtual links VL1 and VL2; once configured, some synthetic traffic is transmitted from *PC1* to *PC2*.

Through the output of the NOX controller, the experiment demonstrates the ability of ADVisor to correctly control switch sw2 (i.e keeping sw2 out of the view of the NOX controller) and to properly manage virtual links and virtual ports on sw3. Of course being the system fully reconfigurable, other virtual topologies "carved" from the physical topology will be shown as well.

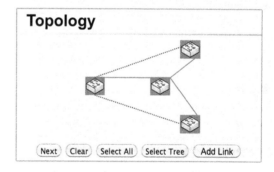

Figure 4: Screenshot of Expedient showing the topology configuration page.

4. REFERENCES

[1] R. Sherwood, G. Gibb, K. Yap, G. Appenzeller, M. Casado, N. McKeown, and G. Parulkar, "FlowVisor: A Network Virtualization Layer," OpenFlow Switch Consortium, Tech. Rep., October 2009.

[2] N. McKeown, T. Anderson, H. Balakrishnan, G. Parulkar, L. Peterson, J. Rexford, S. Shenker, and J. Turner, "OpenFlow: enabling innovation in campus networks," *ACM SIGCOMM Computer Communication Review*, vol. 32, no. 2, pp. 69–74, April 2008.

[3] OpenFlow Switch Consortium, "OpenFlow Switch Specification Version 1.1.0," Tech. Rep., February 2011.

[4] Expedient: A Pluggable Platform for GENI Control Frameworks. [Online]. Available: http://yuba.stanford.edu/~jnaous/expedient/

Visualizing Anomalies in Sensor Networks

Qi Liao*, Lei Shi†, Yuan He‡, Rui Li§, Zhong Su†, Aaron Striegel*, Yunhao Liu◇
*University of Notre Dame, USA. E-mail: {qliao,striegel}@nd.edu.
†IBM Research, China. E-mail:{shllsh,suzhong}@cn.ibm.com.
‡Hong Kong University of Science and Technology. E-mail: heyuan@cse.ust.hk.
§Xi'an Jiao Tong University, China. E-mail:rli@mail.xjtu.edu.cn.
◇Tsinghua University & Hong Kong University of Science and Technology. E-mail: liu@cse.ust.hk.

ABSTRACT

Diagnosing a large-scale sensor network is a crucial but challenging task due to the spatiotemporally dynamic network behaviors of sensor nodes. In this demo, we present Sensor Anomaly Visualization Engine (SAVE), an integrated system that tackles the sensor network diagnosis problem using both visualization and anomaly detection analytics to guide the user quickly and accurately diagnose sensor network failures. Temporal expansion model, correlation graphs and dynamic projection views are proposed to effectively interpret the topological, correlational and dimensional sensor data dynamics and their anomalies. Through a real-world large-scale wireless sensor network deployment (GreenOrbs), we demonstrate that SAVE is able to help better locate the problem and further identify the root cause of major sensor network failures.

Categories and Subject Descriptors

C.2.3 [**Computer Systems Organization**]: Computer-Communication Networks—*Network Management*; H.5.2 [**Information Interfaces and Presentations**]: User Interfaces

General Terms

Management

Keywords

Wireless sensor networks, diagnosing, anomaly detection and analysis, visualization

1. INTRODUCTION

Sensor networks play a pivotal role in numerous modern and future industries such as smart grid, logistics and healthcare. However, diagnosing sensor networks can be tremendously challenging when faced with the issues in full scale deployments: First, sensor networks consisting of numerous low-end embedded devices are resource-constrained, especially its non-rechargeable batteries, making it hard to deploy the approaches of traditional networks (e.g. SNMP). Second, most sensor networks are deployed in outdoor or even hostile environments, thus greatly affects the performance and reliability of sensor networks. For example, the changes in temperature and humidity, the wind and rain, and the physical damages by human and wild animals, may all cause performance degradation or even system failures in sensor networks. Third, the low-power wireless communication of sensor networks is likely to

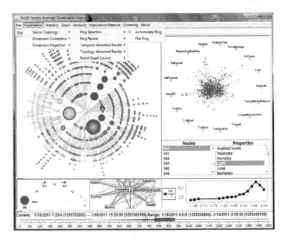

Figure 1: SAVE: Analyzing spatiotemporal anomalies for wireless sensor networks.

be lossy in certain environments and hence cannot guarantee perfect data collection.

The current algorithms to diagnose sensor networks from the collected data mainly rely on certain inference models which link symptoms to the underlying root causes. They depend on the evidence-based sensor data fault taxonomy [1] to characterize the symptom. However, due to the resource constraints and the existence of salient failures, such inference models could only focus on a portion of symptoms, restricting their applicability and efficiency in real usage.

In this work, we present Sensor Anomaly Visualization Engine (SAVE) (Figure 1), an integrated system that tackles the sensor network diagnosis problem using both visual analytics technologies. Compared to simple algorithmic approaches, our method has the following advantages:

- The visualization of sensor network data from multiple perspectives, at large scale and in long term helps the administrator collect evidence in a more comprehensive manner. In our system, we introduce several novel visualizations to illustrate all the three time-varying high-dimensional sensor data facets – routing topology, sensor networking status and physical sensor readings.

- Rather than derive hypothesis directly with the inference model, visual analytics solution focuses on collecting better evidence for the human to improve the decision-making process. This extra robustness makes it a better choice in diagnosing salient sensor network failures, whose symptoms and root causes are previously unknown to network operators and researchers.

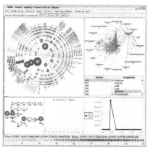

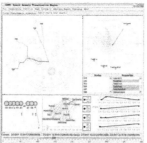
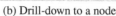
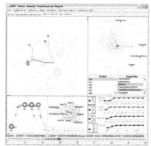
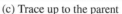
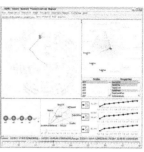

(a) Locate *NoParent* anomaly   (b) Drill-down to a node   (c) Trace up to the parent   (d) Check the parent's health.

Figure 2: Case studies on sensor network link failure diagnosis.

- The visual interface provides more intuitive and interactive display of data. It is also easier to incorporate human domain knowledge, and furthermore, save significant amount of time by working on the machine-generated insights directly, rather than executing the algorithms and putting them together manually.

2. SYSTEM

2.1 GreenOrbs and Data Collection

GreenOrbs [2] is a long-term large-scale wireless sensor network system in the forest located on the campus of Zhejiang Forestry University. The system realizes all-year-round forest ecological surveillance and supports various forestry applications. The current deployment includes approximately 500 nodes in total. A portion of the sensor nodes have been in continuous operation for over one year. Each sensor node in GreenOrbs collects four categories of data: the first is sensor readings such as temperature, humidity, etc. The second is the routing path to the sink. The third is link status, including the RSSI/LQI/ETX value of all the neighbors. The fourth is a large collection of statistical information on each sensor node, including the cumulative time of radio power on, the cumulative number of packets (received, transmitted, dropped, etc.).

2.2 SAVE System Framework

SAVE system is designed as a three-stage pipeline: data preprocessing, anomaly detection and multi-view visualization. In GreenOrbs case, the data collected are streamed to a central database in real time. In the first stage, the multi-facet raw data is preprocessed, including cleansing, structuring and normalization. Next, anomalies are detected online by the analytics components of SAVE. Results such as outliers and correlation changes are computed and cached. Then as a core stage, all these data facets and the prepared analytics results are brought together and consumed by the visualization components integrated with SAVE.

2.3 Anomaly Detection and Visualization

By nature, the sensor routing topology is a large-scale time-varying graph, analytics-unfriendly due to the extremely random routing changes over time. Such a graph is quite messy drawn in normal methods either with geographical or logical layouts. We propose the Temporal Expansion Model (TEM) graph in this work to prepare a more intuitive graph for the following visualization stage. TEM leverages the key feature of the sensor network studied here – all the sensor nodes only send packets to the central sink node for information fusion. The basic idea is to split one physical sensor node into multiple logical nodes according to the separate routing paths to the sink. A snapshot of the TEM graph is shown

in the top-left part of Figure 1. To visualize this packet sending pattern, a temporal ring is composed for each node. The color of each ring is selected by interpolating between two boundary colors using the normalized value, i.e., orange to indicate the earliest time and blue to indicate the latest time. The advantages of TEM are two-fold: first, the graphs generated are directed trees, much better for visualization and navigation; second, temporal changes to the network are surfaced to the graph, providing input for further analytics.

Another temporal dynamic occurs at the various dimensions of sensor data. One question is to ask how one dimension changes in relation to another. For example, should the number of packet in transmission increase in the same proportion of sensor voltage decrease? We introduce the correlation graph to address such questions to the data. Two time-series data sets of property value vectors (i.e., one for sensor readings and one for sensor counters) are extracted from the raw reported sensor data in real time based on the selection of the node, start and end timestamps in the system. SAVE computes the correlation scores according to the Pearson's product-moment coefficient and construct a graph representing the correlations among dimensions, An example is given in the bottom-center of Figure 1.

The data reported from sensor nodes is also high-dimensional (up to 30 dimensions). Since the wireless sensors deployed in wild environment are quite dynamic, how to detect and analyze the anomalies in high-dimensional space becomes a challenging task. Specifically, we want to know both the spatial and temporal anomalies of high-dimensional sensor nodes. To achieve such goal, we introduce a dynamic projection graph to represent the distribution of multi-dimensional data in 2D space, as shown in the top-right of Figure 1. Each high-dimensional sensor node measurement in a given time is mapped as a data point onto the space using a concept similar to Star Coordinates. Figure 2 shows a series of interactive visual exploration steps guided by built-in spatiotemporal anomaly analytic algorithms. With SAVE, the underlying causes for these hard-to-detect silent failures in the complex yet dynamic sensor networks may be efficiently identified.

3. REFERENCES

[1] K. Ni, N. Ramanathan, M. N. H. Chehade, S. Nair, S. Z. E. Kohler, G. Pottie, M. Hansen, and M. Srivastava, "Sensor network data fault types," *ACM Transactions on Sensor Networks (TOSN)*, vol. 5, pp. 25:1–29, May 2009.

[2] Y. Liu, Y. He, M. Li, J. Wang, K. Liu, L. Mo, W. Dong, Z. Yang, M. Xi, J. Zhao, and X.-Y. Li, "Does wireless sensor network scale? A measurement study on GreenOrbs," *IEEE INFOCOM*, April 10-15 2011.

WiRE: A New Rural Connectivity Paradigm

Aditya Dhananjay, Matt Tierney, Jinyang Li, and Lakshminarayanan Subramanian
New York University
{aditya, tierney, jinyang, lakshmi}@cs.nyu.edu

ABSTRACT

Many rural areas in developing regions remain largely disconnected from the rest of the world due to low purchasing power and the exorbitant cost of existing connectivity solutions. Wireless Rural Extensions (WiRE) is a low-power rural wireless network architecture that provides inexpensive, self-sustainable, and high-bandwidth connectivity. WiRE relies on a high-bandwidth directional wireless backbone with local distribution networks to provide focused IP coverage. WiRE also provides cellular connectivity using OpenBTS-based GSM microcells. It supports a naming and addressing framework that inter-operates with traditional telecom networks and enables a wide range of mobile services on a common IP framework. The entire WiRE network can be built by integrating a range of off-the-shelf components and existing open source tools.

Categories and Subject Descriptors

C.2.1 [**Network Architecture and Design**]: Wireless communications

General Terms

Design, Economics, Reliability

1. INTRODUCTION

The existing cellular connectivity model is not economically viable in rural settings due to two fundamental challenges: a) rural regions lack stable grid-based power sources, and b) low density and purchasing power of the users leads to insufficient revenue to cover the high capital and operationsl expenses.

Wireless Rural Extensions (WiRE) is a low-cost and low-power rural network architecture that extends data and voice connectivity from the closest city/town to nearby rural regions. Unlike cellular networks which provide universal coverage at high power consumption, WiRE provides focused coverage at low power consumption using a highly directional wireless backhaul network to efficiently reach out to sparsely spread out rural regions. WiRE uses OpenBTS-based GSM microcells (1–2km radius) and small-scale wireless mesh networks to provide cellular and Internet services within each rural region. The low-power consumption allows the entire WiRE network to be completely solar-powered

with no dependence on the grid or oil. WiRE leverages and integrates a large-body of prior work into a unified rural network connectivity solution for extending cellular and Internet services. Achieving this objective requires us to address several non-trivial challenges, the following of which are illustrated in this demo: a) builing a back-haul network using low-cost and low-power hardware, b) using the naming and addressing layer to manage end-user identities in the face of network partition and churn, c) enabling low-power cellular base stations using OpenBTS, and d) end-to-end system integration.

2. WiRE NETWORK

There are two main components of a WiRE network: a) local distribution mesh networks that cover small regions (ROMA [1]), and b) long distance point-to-point links (WiLD-Net [3]) that form the backbone that connects the regions together. Each region has an *egress point* through which it connects to the back-haul. A region may also leverage OpenBTS, a software-based GSM base station that operates over USRP radio boards. It allows GSM phones to make calls and terminates calls on the same box, and forwards the voice data to the open-source Asterisk PBX system via Inter-Asterisk eXchange (IAX). The advantages are: a) end-users can use their existing cellular phones, b) it can be made to inter-operate with existing telephony networks (§3.2), and c) the power required to run the entire setup is less than 100W, which is more than an order of magnitude lower than traditional GSM base stations, though the coverage area is restricted to $1 - 2$ kms in outdoor settings. In order to enable telephony, there are PBX servers at the egress point of each region and at the main gateway to the city, where the WiRE network connects with the outside world.

3. NAMING AND ADDRESSING

End-users have unique identities; we need to discover and locate identities, for telephony and other applications. Let us say that the network is trying to route a call to an identity *John*, and therefore first needs to *find* John.

When a client m associates with an infrastructure node p (the publisher), the information pertaining this client needs to be disseminated. Inspired by SEATTLE[2], address resolution in WiRE works through a DHT mechanism, with consistent hashing. The underlying routing layer provides the address resolution layer with the current list of infrastructure nodes K that are alive and reachable in the network. For every node $k \in K$, the publisher calculates $H(k)$, where

H is a standard hash function. It then calculates $H(m)$, and the resolver $\hat{k}$ is chosen as that node k that minimizes $H(k) - H(m)$. The publisher p then sends a message (over TCP) to the resolver $\hat{k}$, telling it that m is now reachable through publisher p. The querier uses the identical hashing mechanism to find m. If the publisher p and the querier x are in the same connected component, we are guaranteed that they will hit the same resolver node.

3.1 Partitions and Recovery

Say an identity m published by p has been stored at resolver r. At some point of time, the network becomes partitioned into P_1 and P_2, such that $p \in P_1$ and $r \in P_2$. If any node in P_1 now tries to find m, the query will fail because the querier will choose a different resolver s. This resolver s knows nothing about m because p has not registered m with it. To overcome this issue, each publisher keeps a local list of identities that it is the publisher of, along with the resolver at which this entry is stored. The publisher p periodically monitors the network topology for changes. Suppose it is the publisher for identity m and the entry was stored at resolver r. If r is unreachable from p, it immediately re-hashes m by choosing a new resolver s (from its present partition) and stores the entry there. The old resolver r similarly ensures that it does not store values published by nodes that are not in its present partition. Finally, when two or more partitions become reconnected, re-hashing takes place to maintain consistency.

3.2 Voice Calls and Interoperability

We now describe how WiRE enables telephony and integrates with existing telephony providers.

WiRE to WiRE: Assume that an identity m is trying to call another identity n. Suppose the PBX servers (publishers) of the region containing m and n are $PBX(m)$ and $PBX(n)$ respectively. First, m contacts $PBX(m)$ stating its intention to call n. $PBX(m)$ then uses the address resolution layer and queries for n, whereupon it learns that it needs to tunnel the call to $PBX(n)$. Finally at $PBX(n)$, the call is again tunnelled through to n.

Outside World to WiRE: An existing cellular network user who wants to also use the WiRE network sets up call forwarding to a WiRE specific phone number $N_{gateway}$, which is associated with the PBX gateway. When this user receives a call on the cellular network but is not reachable, the cellular network forwards to $N_{gateway}$. Once the call reaches the WiRE PBX gateway, the destination phone number is resolved to the particular WiRE identifier (say, m). This registration (phone number to IMSI number pairing) is done one-time, when the user signs up for WiRE service. The network then needs to find the location of m, which is done using the techniques discussed above.

WiRE to Outside World: When a WiRE user wants to make a call to the outside world, the call is simply forwarded to the PBX gateway at the main gateway of the WiRE network. This gateway then routes the call through to the existing telephone service provider.

4. EVALUATION

We expect a WiRE deployment to experience churn; end-users will enter and exit the network. On our 12-node testbed, we measure how long it takes for a user identity to be discoverable by all other users in the network, after it has joined

| | | Num. of Identities | | |
		100	300	500
Num. of Failures	1	2	3	4
	3	4	4	21
	5	7	22	24

Table 1: Recovery (reconvergence) time measured in seconds, as a function of the number of node failures, and the number of identities at each publisher.

the network. Figure 1 is a box-and-whisker plot of the convergence times, as a function of the number of identities at each of the 12 publishers.

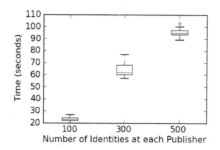

Figure 1: Convergence time varies linearly with the number of identities published at each node.

Due to many failure scenarios, we would like the network to be partition tolerant. We artificially kill nodes to create partitions, and then measure how long it takes the naming and addressing layer to re-hash and recover. From Table 1, we see that in all cases, the convergence time is within acceptable limits.

In order to study the quality of voice calls, we plot the PESQ scores over different backbone path lengths in Figure 2. A reference point is given by hop-count 0, which shows the PESQ score through a wired ethernet connection is 2.95. Even over long multi-hop wireless paths, the PESQ scores remain comparable with that of a wired connection.

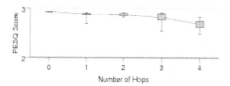

Figure 2: PESQ scores indicate that the speech quality is good, even with longer path lengths.

5. REFERENCES

[1] A. Dhananjay, H. Zhang, J. Li, and L. Subramanian. Practical, distributed channel assignment and routing in dual-radio mesh networks. In *SIGCOMM '09*.

[2] C. Kim, M. Caesar, and J. Rexford. Floodless in SEATTLE: A Scalable Ethernet Architecture for Large Enterprises. In *SIGCOMM '08*.

[3] R. Patra, S. Nedevschi, S. Surana, A. Sheth, L. Subramanian, and E. Brewer. WiLDNet: Design and Implementation of High Performance WiFi Based Long Distance Networks. *Proceedings of NSDI 2007*, 2007.

Supporting Novel Home Network Management Interfaces with Openflow and NOX

Richard Mortier,
Ben Bedwell,
Kevin Glover, Tom Lodge,
Tom Rodden
University of Nottingham, UK
first.last@nottingham.ac.uk

Charalampos Rotsos,
Andrew W. Moore
University of Cambridge, UK
first.last@cl.cam.ac.uk

Alexandros Koliousis,
Joseph Sventek
University of Glasgow, UK
first.last@glasgow.ac.uk

ABSTRACT

The Homework project[1] has examined redesign of existing home network infrastructures to better support the needs and requirements of actual home users. Integrating results from several ethnographic studies, we have designed and built a home networking platform providing detailed per-flow measurement and management capabilities supporting several novel management interfaces. This demo specifically shows these new visualization and control interfaces (§1), and describes the broader benefits of taking an integrated view of the networking infrastructure, realised through our router's augmented measurement and control APIs (§2).

Aspects of this work have been published: the Homework Database in Internet Management (IM) 2011 [3] and implications of the ethnographic results are to appear at the SIGCOMM W-MUST workshop 2011 [2]. Separate, more detailed expositions of the interface elements and system performance and implications are currently under submission at other venues. A partial code release is already available[2] and we anticipate fuller public beta release by Q4 2011.

Categories and Subject Descriptors:
C.2.6 [**Computer-Communication Networks**]: Routers

General Terms:
Management, Design, Security, Human Factors

Keywords: Home networks; Network management; DHCP; NOX; OpenFlow

1. USER INTERFACES

The first two interfaces make use of the *hwdb* streaming database for visualization. The first, Figure 1, runs on an iPhone/iTouch device and simply displays the per-device per-protocol bandwidth consumption. This allows users to focus on how their devices and their applications, to the extent permitted by the imperfect application–protocol mapping, are using the network.

The second, Figure 2, is a custom hardware interface based on the Arduino platform[3] enabling awareness of the *network as a whole* rather than specific devices. Via its LEDs, It

---

[1]http://www.homenetworks.ac.uk/

[2]https://github.com/homework/

[3]http://www.arduino.cc/

Figure 1: Per-device bandwidth consumption.

Figure 2: Network artefact as physical interface.

displays one of (*i*) wireless signal strength (RSSI) based on number lit; (*ii*) current total bandwidth use mapped to the speed of animation across the device; and (*iii*) DHCP lease grant activity indicated by the colour of flashes.

The next two interfaces demonstrate two control mechanisms available in our platform. The first, Figure 3, is a simple control interface that exercises the control API to manage DHCP allocations, accessed via a situated display in the home. This allows non-expert users to detect, interrogate and supply metadata for devices requesting access, and to control the DHCP server on a case-by-case basis by dragging the device's tab into the appropriate permitted/denied category.

The final interface, Figure 4, integrates physical mediation of control into a simple visual policy language. When the user plugs a USB storage device with appropriate filesystem layout into the router, it enables specific devices to

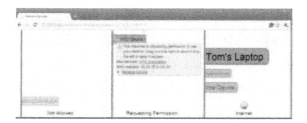

Figure 3: Simple control interface.

Figure 4: Novel interactive policy interface.

connect to the network as well as limiting access to specified web-hosted services, e.g., Facebook. By selecting appropriate options for each panel in the cartoon, non-expert users can implement simple policies such as "the kids can only use Facebook on weekdays after they've finished their homework." This is mapped to per-device network and DNS access restrictions which are only lifted once a suitably responsible adult inserts the appropriate USB storage key.

2. TECHNICAL DETAILS

Our platform takes the form of a small form-factor PC acting as the home router, exposing various APIs used by satellite interrogation and control devices. Providing those APIs, our software sits atop a standard Linux Ubuntu distribution running Open vSwitch[4] and NOX,[5] depicted in Figure 5 with our code shown as the shaded components.

The Homework Database, *hwdb*, provides measurement support as an active ephemeral stream database which stores ephemeral events into a fixed size memory buffer. It links events into tables and supports queries via a CQL [1] variant able to express temporal and relational operations on data. The database supports a simple UDP-based RPC interface enabling applications to subscribe to query results, persisting output as desired. Tables used are *Flows*, periodically observed active five-tuples; *Links*, link-layer information, e.g., MAC address and received signal strength (RSSI); and *Leases*, mapping Ethernet to IP address.

The *control API* NOX module provides a simple RESTful web interface to the router, invoked to exercise control over connected devices: by the Linux *udev* subsystem when a suitably formatted USB storage device is inserted; and directly by the various graphical control interfaces. The con-

---

[4] http://openvswitch.org/
[5] http://noxrepo.org/

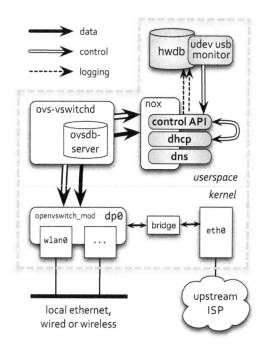

Figure 5: Software architecture of the Homework home router.

trol API configures the behaviour of our DHCP server and DNS proxy NOX modules. The first manages DHCP allocations to ensure that *all* traffic flows are visible to software running on the router, avoiding direct Ethernet-layer communication between devices. The second intercepts outgoing DNS requests, performing reverse lookups on flows not matching previously requested names, to ensure that upstream communication is only allowed between permitted devices and sites.

ACKNOWLEDGEMENTS

The research on which this paper is based was funded by the RCUK supported Horizon Hub, EP/G065802/1, and EPSRC Wired and Wireless Intelligent Networked Systems Initiative "Homework", EP/F064276/1.

3. REFERENCES

[1] A. Arasu, S. Babu, and J. Widom. The CQL continuous query language: semantic foundations and query execution. *The VLDB Journal*, 15:121–142, June 2006.

[2] P. Brundell, A. Crabtree, R. Mortier, T. Rodden, P. Tennent, and P. Tolmie. The network from above and below. In *Proc. ACM SIGCOMM Workshop on Measurements Up the STack (W-MUST)*, Toronto, Canada, Aug. 2011. To appear.

[3] J. Sventek, A. Koliousis, O. Sharma, N. Dulay, D. Pediatitakis, M. Sloman, T. Rodden, T. Lodge, B. Bedwell, K. Glover, and R. Mortier. An information plane architecture supporting home network management. In *Proc. IFIP/IEEE International Symposium on Integrated Network Management (IM)*, Dublin, Ireland, May 2011.

Using NetMagic to Observe Fine-Grained Per-Flow Latency Measurements

Tao Li
School of Computer
National University of Defense
Technology
Changsha, Hunan, China
taoli.nudt@gmail.com

Zhigang Sun
School of Computer
National University of Defense
Technology
Changsha, Hunan, China
sunzhigang@263.net

Chunbo Jia
School of Computer
National University of Defense
Technology
Changsha, Hunan, China
jiachunbo1988@sina.com

Qi Su
School of Computer
National University of Defense
Technology
Changsha, Hunan, China
suqi1115@163.com

Myungjin Lee
School of Electrical and
Computer Engineering
Purdue University
West Lafayette, USA
mjlee@purdue.edu

ABSTRACT

We introduce NetMagic [1] to demonstrate the efficacy of RLI architecture [2] for the fine-grained per-flow latency measurements. In this demo, the main function of RLI is implemented in NetMagic, which is the key component of our experimental network comprising several computers and switches. We are going to show how NetMagic can provide rapid implementation and evaluation of RLI architecture that is difficult with commercial switch or router platforms. In the demo, the estimated fine-grained per-flow latency by RLI is monitored and dynamically presented. Further, the true latency with a resolution of 8ns is also provided by NetMagic for the evaluation. The efficacy of RLI architecture can be observed in a real-time fashion by the difference between estimated latencies and true ones.

Categories and Subject Descriptors

C.2.1 [**Computer Communication Networks**]: Network Architecture and Design; C.2.3 [**Computer Communication Networks**]: Network Operations—*Network monitoring*

General Terms

Design, Experimentation, Measurement

Keywords

NetMagic Platform, Per-Flow Latency, Measurement, RLI Architecture

1. INTRODUCTION

Reference Latency Interpolation (RLI) architecture [2] is proposed for accurately detecting per-flow latencies in the order of a few 10s to 100s microseconds. It can be implemented in a router by integrating the adaptive refer-

ence packet generation component at a sender side (e.g., an ingress interface) and the measurement component at a receiver (e.g., an egress interface). However, the implementation involves software/hardware modification or upgrade of the router, which may be difficult for router vendors to accept due to reliability and security. Mirroring all the packets from the receiver to a PC, or to a network appliance capable of processing them (such as NetFPGA [3] or high-speed network processor dedicated for these fine-grained measurements) is a way for deploying the RLI. However, the ingress and egress timestamps of the packets are hardly obtained by mirroring way for calculating *true* latencies of the flows under measurement. In fact, these timestamps are essential for the demo to show the efficacy of the RLI architecture.

To address the above problems, we use an open reconfigurable switching platform - NetMagic [1] to implement a RLI experimental prototype. NetMagic is designed to enable researchers and students to build high-performance networking systems and verify their new ideas and methods for network innovation. Different from the NetFPGA [3], the NetMagic is designed with a novel architecture, where a common high-density FPGA is combined with a commercial Ethernet switching chip. The high-speed Gigabit Ethernet switching capacity, as well as reconfigurable user-defined packet processing function, can be obtained from the NetMagic platform. Secondly, the NetMagic is a standalone network device which is loosely coupled with controller. Standard Ethernet ports and socket interface are utilized for the communication between the remote controller and the NetMagic platform. The NetMagic does not need to be plugged into a specific host machine with related drivers, which simplifies the construction of network experimental systems. Thirdly, the NetMagic provides 2x reconfigurable ports than the NetFPGA, which is essential for a larger network experimental systems such as this demo.

ServerSwitch [4] is proposed for implementing and evaluating the design of data center networks, which utilizes an ASIC commodity switching chip for data plane and the server CPU for control plane. It thus provides full programmability in the control plane. However, the reconfigurability in data-plane is limited, which can not support some specific packet processing functions such as timestamping, digest extraction and arbitrary field modification. For more comparison among the NetMagic, the NetFPGA and the ServerSwitch, see [1].

Like the NetFPGA, to ease the development effort of beginners, the NetMagic platform provides simple and rapid development model, clear module interface and several standard reference designs, which allows users to focus on the implementation of self-defined functional modules. Verified functional components are also provided, including hardware modules, physical interfaces, and software functions. The RLI demo system was developed rapidly by utilizing these reusable functional components of NetMagic.

2. DEMO OVERVIEW

Fig. 1 shows the deployment of our demonstration. The demo consists of a NetMagic platform, two Ethernet switches and several PCs or laptops. The device under measurement (DUM) is composed of two 10/100/1000M adaptive Ethernet switches connected by a 100M link (In fact, only one standalone 10/100/1000M Ethernet switch is used in the demo, because the Ethernet switching chip integrated in the NetMagic functions the same as commercial switches.). PC1, PC2,..., PC5 are computers with 1000M Ethernet interface adaptor. NetMagic connects PC1 and PC2 to the DUM through its 1000M ports linking to the integrated FPGA. PC3 and PC4 connect with the two Ethernet switches respectively. PC5 connects with NetMagic for receiving, processing and displaying packet latency information.

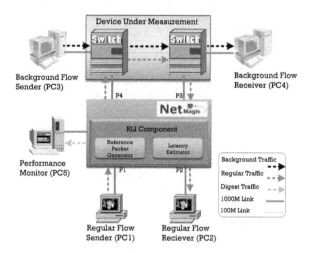

Figure 1: The topology of RLI demonstration.

RLI component is implemented with NetMagic platform for the functions of reference packet generation and latency estimation. The reference packet generator injects reference packets with egress timestamps periodically into the regular packet stream at the egress interface (P4) of NetMagic. It also extracts and sends the digest information (e.g., egress timestamp) of the regular packets to the performance monitor. The ingress timestamps of the reference and regular packets are recorded by NetMagic when the packets return from the DUM (P3). The latency estimator calculates the delay of the reference packets based on their ingress and egress timestamps. It also extracts and sends the digest

information with ingress timestamps of the regular packets to the performance monitor. Based on the received information, the performance monitor calculates the estimated delay and the true delay of each regular packet. It then dynamically displays the true delay versus the estimated delay values of every sample packet, as well as the average delay values of the flows. Because all the interfaces of the NetMagic operates within the same time-domain (125MHz Clock), we do not need extra time synchronization for timestamping and the timestamps are with a resolution of 8ns.

In the demo, we will adopt delay-sensitive streaming media applications to generate regular flows for measurements. PC1 will send several standard-definition video flows to PC2. After the packets of the video streams traverse the NetMagic platform and the DUM, PC2 displays them on its screen.

The PC3 and PC4 (with 1000M Ethernet interface) will run Iperf applications [5], where PC3 is set to the UDP client and PC4 is set to UDP server. By changing the parameters of Iperf at the client side, the utilization rate of the 100M link between the two switches can be adjusted. The 100M link of DUM can be made congested, as PC3 can send UDP packets to PC4 at the speed of up to 1000Mbps.

From PC5, attendees will observe the real-time curves of the true and estimated latency values of the sample packets and the corresponding average values of the buffered packets. They can also watch the videos on the screen of PC2 for the intuitive experience of video quality. By adjusting the parameters of Iperf application, the attendees can vary the sending rate of background traffic. As a consequence, they will observe the changes of the quality of the video (e.g. smooth, distortion or frequent pauses) from PC2. Correspondingly, the changes of the latency values will be shown on PC5. The accuracy of the RLI architecture is illustrated by the positions and the shapes of the curves indicating the true and estimated latency values. This demo will prove that RLI achieves a high accuracy for the fine-grained per-flow latency measurement if the two dynamic curves fit well.

3. ACKNOWLEDGMENTS

The work was supported by China National Basic Research (973) Program (No. 2009CB320503) and China State High-Tech Development (863) Plan (No. 2009aa01a334).

4. REFERENCES

[1] NetMagic Research Group. http://www.netmagic.org.
[2] Myungjin Lee, Nick G. Duffield, and Ramana Rao Kompella. Not all microseconds are equal: fine-grained per-flow measurements with reference latency interpolation. In *SIGCOMM*, pages 27–38, 2010.
[3] John W. Lockwood, Nick McKeown, Greg Watson, and etc. NetFPGA–an open platform for gigabit-rate network switching and routing. In *MSE '07*, 2007.
[4] Guohan Lu, Chuanxiong Guo, Yulong Li, Zhiqiang Zhou, Tong Yuan, Haitao Wu, Yongqiang Xiong, Rui Gao, and Yongguang Zhang. Serverswitch: a programmable and high performance platform for data center networks. NSDI'11, pages 2–2, Berkeley, CA, USA, 2011.
[5] A. Tirumala, M. Gates, F. Qin, J. Dugan, and J. Ferguson. Iperf - the tcp/udp band- width measurement tool. http://dast.nlanr.net/Projects/Iperf.

OSPF failure reconvergence through SRG inference and prediction of link state advertisements

Bart Puype
Dept. of Information
Technology (IBCN)
Ghent University - IBBT
Ghent, Belgium
bpuype@intec.ugent.be

Dimitri Papadimitriou
Alcatel-Lucent Bell
Antwerp, Belgium
dimitri.papadimitriou@alcatel-lucent.com

Goutam Das
Dept. of Information
Technology (IBCN)
Ghent University - IBBT
Ghent, Belgium
gdas@intec.ugent.be

Didier Colle
Dept. of Information
Technology (IBCN)
Ghent University - IBBT
Ghent, Belgium
dcolle@intec.ugent.be

Mario Pickavet
Dept. of Information
Technology (IBCN)
Ghent University - IBBT
Ghent, Belgium
mpick@intec.ugent.be

Piet Demeester
Dept. of Information
Technology (IBCN)
Ghent University - IBBT
Ghent, Belgium
demeester@intec.ugent.be

ABSTRACT

We demonstrate machine learning augmented Open Shortest Path First (OSPF) routing which infers Shared Risk Groups (SRG) from link failure history. For an initial link failure matching an SRG, it predicts subsequent link state advertisements corresponding with that SRG, improving convergence and recovery times during multiple network failures.

Categories and Subject Descriptors

C.2.2 [**Computer Systems Organization**]: Computer-communication Networks—*Network Protocols*; I.2.6 [**Computing Methodologies**]: Artificial Intelligence—*Learning*

General Terms

Experimentation

Keywords

OSPF, machine learning, cognitive routing, network recovery, shared risk group

1. INTRODUCTION

As part of the Future Internet Research and Experimentation (FIRE) initiative within the European Seventh Framework Programme, the ECODE (Experimental COgnitive Distributed Engine) project [1] designs, evaluates and experiments cognitive routing system functionality using online distributed machine learning techniques.

In this demonstration, concurrent failures under Open Shortest Path First (OSPF [2]) link state routing are considered. A machine learning engine (MLE) was developed and implemented, which clusters and data-mines multiple network failures from locally received OSPF routing information sequences. From these, it predicts link state advertisements (LSA) for future concurrent failures and coordinates

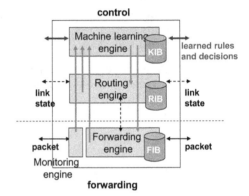

Figure 1: Routing system functional overview

with OSPF to speed-up convergence connectivity recovery. The MLE is inserted in the router architecture as part of the control plane (Fig. 1). This experiment uses the ECODE cognitive routing platform, based on the eXtensible Open Routing Platform (XORP) [3].

2. SRG INFERENCE

Layered networks often suffer from concurrent upper layer failures of multiple links (the shared risk group or SRG) caused by failure of a single lower layer resource. It might seem SRG information may be derived from the current network configuration. In reality, IP link topology is often constructed on top of different network layers and domains, e.g., IP links carried over optical channels provided by different operators leasing fibers in the same physical duct. This makes SRG disjointness a hard problem. Furthermore, simultaneous failures can trigger multiple successive routing table re-computations. In this work, machine learning is used to identify and predict SRGs from statistical information embedded in LSAs, without a-priori SRG knowledge.

The XORP OSPF module's process-flow in-between LSA reception and routing table re-computation was modified, to allow interaction with the MLE module (Fig. 2), which

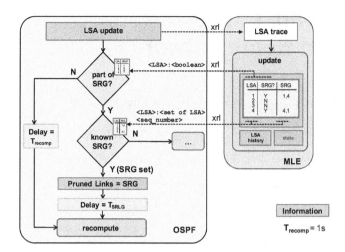

Figure 2: Flow model of OSPF and SRG inference interactions

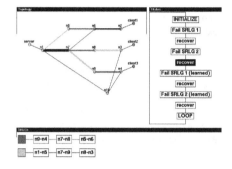

Figure 3: Network and SRG information screenshot

runs the SRG inference algorithm receiving link failure event data from OSPF running in the local routing engine. The algorithm learns SRGs from this data using techniques developed in [4][5], and passes the SRG prediction information on to OSPF.

3. DEMONSTRATION

SRG inference is demonstrated on an emulated OSPF area which is augmented with the machine learning component. The setup visualizes network connectivity by displaying a graph model of the network and SRG information on one screen (Fig. 3), as well as showing output of several video streams transported over the network on a second screen, allowing spectators to verify the impact on network connectivity of multiple link failures. We compare standard OSPF which offers slow, piece-wise recovery of connectivity, versus SRG inference augmented OSPF operation which reroutes and recovers for all links in an entire SRG at once. A video of the demonstration is available [6].

4. RESULTS

Fig. 4 shows packet traces obtained when applying the proposed technique to recover three video streams. The streams are routed over different paths, visiting a set of spread-out links in two SRGs. Recovery times for normal OSPF (top three traces) and SRG inference augmented OSPF (bottom three traces) are shown.

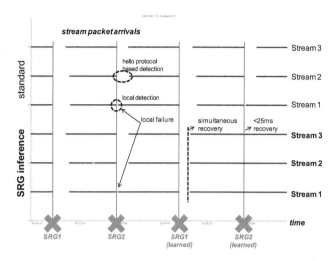

Figure 4: Video stream traces showing recovery times

First, both SRGs are failed and recovered (i.e., the OSPF adjacencies are interrupted and then re-established) once. This allows the SRG inference algorithm to learn the existence of these SRGs. Initially, both cases show normal OSPF reconvergence — the three streams are recovered one by one as the failures in each of the paths links are detected. Note that the SRG2 link corresponding with end-to-end connectivity for stream 1 is detected locally through a hardware alarm, yielding faster detection than normal Hello protocol based neighbor discovery seen for the other streams. Next, the SRGs are both failed again, to show the improvement offered by the SRG inference. For the SRG inference scenario the streams are now recovered simultaneously as the first LSA arrives. When one of the failing links in a SRG is detected locally, all SRG links and thus all streams benefit from this fast detection, which allows for sub 25 ms recovery in the demonstration setup.

5. ACKNOWLEDGMENTS

This research work is (partially) funded by the European Commission (EC) through the ECODE project (INFSO-ICT-223936), part of the European Seventh Framework Programme (FP7).

6. REFERENCES

[1] ECODE project. http://www.ecode-project.eu/.
[2] J. Moy. OSPF Version 2. RFC 2328, IETF, April 1998.
[3] XORP, eXtensible Open Router Platform, http://www.xorp.org/.
[4] G. Das et al. Link state protocol data mining for shared risk link group detection. In *19th Int. Conf. on Computer Communications and Networks (ICCCN 2010)*, Zurich, Switzerland, August 2010.
[5] G. Das et al. SRLG identification from time series analysis of link state data. In *3rd Int. Conf. on Communication Systems and Networks (COMSNET 2011)*, Bangalore, India, January 2011.
[6] Demonstration video. http://users.ugent.be/~bpuype/pub/sigcomm2011/.

Communicating with Caps:
Managing Usage Caps in Home Networks

Hyojoon Kim
Georgia Tech
joonk@gatech.edu

Srikanth Sundaresan
Georgia Tech
srikanth@gatech.edu

Marshini Chetty
Georgia Tech
marshini@cc.gatech.edu

Nick Feamster
Georgia Tech
feamster@cc.gatech.edu

W. Keith Edwards
Georgia Tech
keith@cc.gatech.edu

ABSTRACT

As Internet service providers increasingly implement and impose "usage caps", consumers need better ways to help them understand and control how devices in the home use up the available network resources or available capacity. Towards this goal, we will demonstrate a system that allows users to monitor and manage their usage caps. The system uses the BISMark firmware running on network gateways to collect usage statistics and report them to a logically centralized controller, which displays usage information. The controller allows users to specify policies about how different people, devices, and applications should consume the usage cap; it implements and enforces these policies via a secure OpenFlow control channel to each gateway device. The demonstration will show various use cases, such as limiting the usage of a particular application, visualizing usage statistics, and allowing users within a single household to "trade" caps with one another.

Categories and Subject Descriptors

C.2.3 [**Computer-Communication Networks**]: Network Operations—*network management, network monitoring*; H.1.2 [**Models and Principles**]: User/Machine Systems—*human factors*

General Terms

Design, Human Factors, Management, Measurement

Keywords

OpenFlow, usage cap, home network

1. MOTIVATION AND SUMMARY

Internet service providers in the United States are beginning to deploy monthly "usage caps", which limit the amount of traffic that any particular subscriber can transfer within a billing cycle. For example, Comcast has deployed a monthly usage cap of 250 gigabytes, and AT&T DSL and U-Verse users are subject to a 150-gigabyte usage cap. Users in other countries already experience much more constrained usage caps [1]. Given the growing diversity of applications, the increasing demands of certain applications (*e.g.*, a high-definition NetFlix movies) and the relative opacity of usage information to individual users [3], consumers need better ways of managing these caps.

Unfortunately, intuitive tools for helping users monitor and manage their usage caps effectively do not exist today. To fill the need

for such a tool, we are developing a system to help consumers perform flexible and fine-grained monitoring and management of their usage caps. Based on our user studies, we have identified that consumers want information to help them manage the usage cap to ensure all household members enjoy good performance for their activities, while also avoiding overage charges or service interruptions if the cap is exceeded [3]. Our demonstration will show a framework that allows users to perform some of the following management functions:

- *Provide visibility about how different activities and applications use network resources.* Users need better interfaces to show them how activities and applications consume their usage caps, both for intentional applications (*e.g.*, Web browsing, streaming video) and for automated or "background" applications like software updates. Better tools can allow users to manage what and who is consuming the most capacity and take actions accordingly.

- *Allocating portions of the usage cap to a specific user, group of users, device, application, or time of day.* Users may wish to restrict particular applications or activities (*e.g.*, ensure that streaming video does not consume more than 50% of the allocated data for the month). Our previous work has shown that a household might wish to allocate portions of the usage cap to each occupant, to ensure that no one occupant uses more than his or her fair share of the usage cap. Users may also wish to limit traffic usage based on time of day or day of the week (*e.g.*, parents may wish to limit or throttle usage in the evening [4]).

- *Allowing users to "swap" micro-caps with one another.* Provisioning allocations from an overall monthly usage cap to individual users in a household might result in inefficiencies where one user has not fully utilized his or her allocation but another user has exhausted his or her allocation. We found that users might want to trade and bargain to ensure the maximum allocation is used, while still allowing each user to carry on activities as needed.

Despite the appeal of a system to help users track and manage data caps, developing such a system has many challenges. First, the desire to allocate data caps to each user within a household requires a system that can *associate traffic flows to specific users*. Typically, traffic flows are associated with individual devices, where a device might be identified by its MAC address. In reality, however, multiple users may share the same device; as such, the system requires a usable captive portal interface to allow users to log in to a device. We have implemented an OpenFlow-based captive portal for associating flows to users, Resonance [5], which we will use for this purpose. Second, the system must support a diverse set

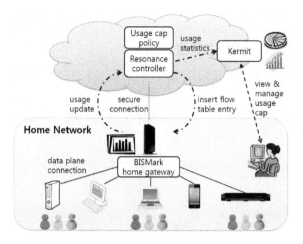

Figure 1: **Proposed demo system.** The demo system comprises a front-end interface (Kermit), OpenFlow controller (Resonance), and a home gateway router (BISMark).

of requirements and policies involving provisioning and enforcing data-cap allocations across users, applications, and devices. To address this challenge, we propose to manage and implement policies regarding usage caps from a network controller "in the cloud" that runs an OpenFlow controller. Third, users may want access to both historical and real-time usage patterns in ways that allow them to understand what is contributing to their usage.

Our demonstration will essentially be a canonical home network, with an access point and several machines and consumer devices connecting to it through wired and wireless interfaces. The setup will have the following components: (1) the BISMark gateway platform and supporting software [6]; (2) a front-end on `networkdashboard.org` that shows traffic utilization over different time intervals, and also help users understand their Internet usage; (3) an interface to help users manage their caps, by performing allocations and setting policies; (4) an OpenFlow-based framework for implementing and enforcing these policies on the BISMark gateway.

2. SYSTEM

We describe the system that we will demonstrate to help users manage data usage caps in their homes. Figure 1 shows the system we plan to demonstrate and how the components fit together.

2.1 Front-end Interface: Kermit

Our front-end system, Kermit [4], will create a user-friendly interface to the underlying networking monitoring and control infrastructure. Kermit will show users three views to help them identify which people, devices, and applications are contributing to the cap in real-time. Kermit will also allow users to track usage over time per each calendar month to see if the cap will run out before the end of the month, if there will be remaining cap, if overage charges may be incurred, or whether additional capacity should be purchased. Kermit will also allow users to easily divide up their usage cap by people, devices or applications at the beginning of the month, and to allow users to trade capacity with each other. In our demonstration, we will showcase this user interface to the functionality described below.

2.2 Network Gateway: BISMark

A cornerstone of our system for managing caps is the *BISMark* custom router firmware, built on top of OpenWRT. BISMark

("Broadband Internet Service BenchMARK") has three separate packages: (1) an active measurement package, which initiates periodic measurement probes to measure properties of the access link; (2) a passive measurement package, which records the traffic flows that pass through the gateway device; (3) a management package, which facilitates remote management, such as software upgrades, as well as pushing traffic logs to a central server. This demonstration will primarily use the latter two packages. BISMark is under active development with many regular contributors and developers [2], and the current version of the firmware is thoroughly tested on the NetGear WNDR 3700v2 router.

2.3 Tracking and Managing Caps: Resonance

Resonance is a network management system that can apply different policies to network traffic flows, depending on the user that originates the traffic flow and that user's state in the system [5]. Resonance uses OpenFlow to centralize management, define policies, make decisions, and enforce policy by installing flow table entries at OpenFlow-enabled switches. Resonance has the following properties that we will use in the demonstration: (i) *Fine-grained:* Resonance allows the network to express policies based on a variety of parameters, ranging from a user's identity to the type of application traffic. (ii) *Event-based:* Resonance reacts to events (*e.g.*, time of day, cap limit reached, a detected attack) and modifies the flow table according to the specified policy. A cornerstone of Resonance is a central network controller that is coupled with a dynamic *listener* that tracks the state of each user and forwards traffic for the user's flows depending on the the state of the user (*e.g.*, whether the user is capped).

3. DEMONSTRATION

- **Login-based accounting:** To access the Internet, users must login through a Web portal. This login process triggers functionality that associates traffic flows from a device to the user logged in on that device. We will show how the system can enable accounting based on device or application, and how the system can rate-limit or quarantine a user who has exceeded a cap.

- **Exchanging caps:** After showing basic functionality, we will show how users with extra available capacity can swap their cap with a user that has exhausted their allocation.

- **Front-end visualization and management:** We also show how ordinary users interact with the management system to see how different applications are spending their caps. We also demonstrate how an administrator can visualize the network and allocate caps to users.

REFERENCES

[1] Next generation connectivity: A review of broadband internet transitions and policy from around the world, 2010. The Berkman Center for Internet & Society.
[2] Project BISMark (Broadband Internet Service BenchMARK). http://projectbismark.net/.
[3] M. Chetty, R. Banks, A. J. Bernheim Brush, J. Donner, and R. E. Grinter. Under development: While the meter is running: computing in a capped world. *Interactions*, 18:72–75, Mar. 2011.
[4] M. Chetty, D. Haslem, A. Baird, U. Ofoha, B. Sumner, and R. Grinter. Why is my internet slow?: Making network speeds visible. In *CHI*, Vancouver, Canada, 2011.
[5] A. Nayak, A. Reimers, N. Feamster, and R. Clark. Resonance: Dynamic access control in enterprise networks. In *Proc. Workshop: Research on Enterprise Networking*, Barcelona, Spain, Aug. 2009.
[6] S. Sundaresan, W. de Donato, N. Feamster, R. Teixeira, S. Crawford, and A. Pescapè. Broadband internet performance: A view from the gateway. In *Proc. ACM SIGCOMM*, Toronto, Ontario, Canada, Aug. 2011.

Cyber-Physical Handshake

Fang-Jing Wu
Department of Computer
Science, National Chiao Tung
University, Hsin-Chu, Taiwan
fangjing@cs.nctu.edu.tw

Feng-I Chu
Department of Computer
Science, National Chiao Tung
University, Hsin-Chu, Taiwan
fychu@cs.nctu.edu.tw

Yu-Chee Tseng*
Department of Computer
Science, National Chiao Tung
University, Hsin-Chu, Taiwan
yctseng@cs.nctu.edu.tw

ABSTRACT

While sensor-enabled devices have greatly enriched human interactions in our daily life, discovering the essential knowledge behind sensing data is a critical issue to connect the cyber world and the physical world. This motivates us to design an innovative sensor-aided social network system, termed *cyber-physical handshake*. It allows two users to naturally exchange personal information with each other after detecting and authenticating the handshaking patterns between them. This work describes our design of detection and authentication mechanisms to achieve this purpose and our prototype system to facilitate handshake social behavior.

Categories and Subject Descriptors: C.2.1 [Network Architecture and Design]: Wireless communication

General Terms: Algorithms, Design, Experimentation

Keywords: cyber-physical system, participatory sensing, pervasive computing, social network, wireless sensor network

1. INTRODUCTION

Recently, sensor-enabled mobile phones have become essential tools in the study of cyber-physical systems (CPSs) [1]. CPSs enrich the interactions between the virtual and the physical worlds and sensor-aided social networking has been recognized as one of the main CPS applications [2, 3].

This work designs an innovative sensor-aided social network system, termed *cyber-physical handshake*, to enable natural information exchange after detecting and authenticating the handshaking patterns between two persons. In the physical world, the *handshake* behavior between two people implies that a social link will be authenticated between them before they exchange personal information (e.g., exchanges of business cards). On the other hand, in the cyber world, a handshake procedure is adopted by two nodes to authenticate each other before they start data exchanges. The work follows the concept of "handshakes" to design an authentication mechanism based on sensing patterns to facilitate automatic data exchanges between two users after they have a handshake, as shown in Fig. 1. Instead of generating and authenticating shared keys [4, 5], our system is

*Y.-C. Tseng's research is co-sponsored by MoE ATU Plan, by NSC grants 97-3114-E-009-001, 97-2221-E-009-142-MY3, 98-2219-E-009-019, and 98-2219-E-009-005, 99-2218-E-009-005, by ITRI, Taiwan, by III, Taiwan, by D-Link, and by Intel.

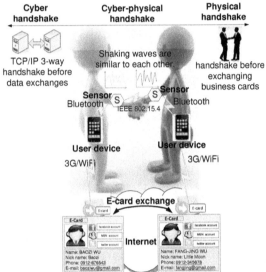

Figure 1: Architecture of our cyber-physical handshake system.

a light-weight approach which incurs less computation overhead and is more suitable for simple sensor devices (e.g., a watch).

2. SYSTEM ARCHITECTURE

The basic idea of the cyber-physical handshake system is to allow two users to exchange data if they have a handshake with each other. When two users make friends with a handshake in the physical world, the shaking waves perceived by the two users' sensor nodes will have high degree of similarity in both frequency and time domains. We then use the similarities to authenticate a handshake behavior. Fig. 1 shows our system architecture. Each user is equipped with a smart phone and wears a watch-like sensor node with an accelerometer on his/her wrists. Sensor nodes follow IEEE 802.15.4 to communicate with each other. Each sensor node is associated with its user's smart phone through bluetooth. Each sensor node is responsible for detecting and reporting handshaking samples to its user's smart phone. The smart phone will compute a value of similarity between the two users' samples. If the value of similarity is greater than a predefined threshold, it will exchange the user's E-card with the other user over the Internet.

2.1 Software Design

Our software design is composed of four phases, as shown in Fig. 2.

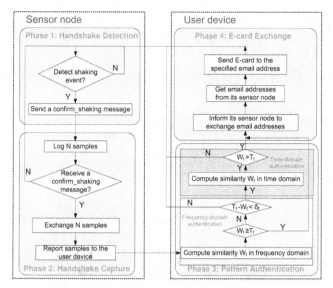

Figure 2: Software design of our system.

Phase 1: handshake detection. In this phase, we use each sensor node to detect shaking events. We sample data at a rate of R_s. For each sample ν, we check if the shaking condition $|\nu - 1g| > \tau_s$ holds, where g is the gravity and τ_s is a predefined threshold. If the number of shaking samples per second detected is greater than $R_s/2$, the sensor node will broadcast a *confirm_shaking* message and enter the next phase.

Phase 2: handshake capture. In this phase, the sensor node logs the upcoming N samples and checks if it has received a *confirm_shaking* message recently. If so, it exchanges these N samples with that sensor node and then reports all these samples to its smart phone.

Phase 3: pattern authentication. In this phase, each smart phone will compute the values of similarity in both frequency and time domains to decide whether the two samples are resulted from the same handshake in the physical world. First, we compute the value of similarity in the frequency domain between two samples, say a and b, by $W_f = \frac{1}{5}\int_{f=0}^{5} C_{ab}(f)$, where $C_{ab}(f) = \frac{|P_{ab}(f)|^2}{P_{aa}(f) \times P_{bb}(f)}$ is the *magnitude squared coherence* of the two samples. Here, we only consider the coherence between $0 \sim 5\,Hz$ because the handshake frequency of a human can hardly exceed this range. If $W_f \geq T_f$, we have a handshake match and enter the next phase, where T_f is a predefined threshold. Otherwise, if $T_f - W_f < \delta_f$, where δ_f is a small value, then the value of similarity in the time domain will be computed by the Pearson's correlation coefficient $W_t = |\frac{1}{(N-1)}\frac{\Sigma_{i=1}^{N}(A_i-\overline{A})\times(B_i-\overline{B})}{\sigma_a \times \sigma_b}|$, where σ_a and σ_b are the standard deviations of a and b, respectively. Here, A_i (resp., B_i) and $\overline{A}$ (resp., $\overline{B}$) denote the i-th reading and the mean of the a's (resp., b's) samples. Here, δ_f is a guard parameter to involve the time-domain handshake detection. If $W_t > T_t$, a handshake is detected and we enter phase 4, where T_t is a predefined threshold.

Phase 4: E-card exchange. In this phase, the user device will inform its sensor node to exchange user's email address with the other sensor. Then it sends a personal E-card to that address over the Internet for further social networking behaviors.

2.2 Demonstrations

Each sensor node is a two-layer sensor board including a

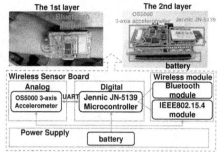

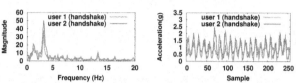

Figure 3: Hardware design of our system.

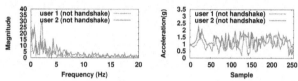

(a) The frequency distribution of a handshake event.

(b) The time-domain samples of a handshake event.

(c) The frequency distribution of a non-handshake event.

(d) The time-domain samples of a non-handshake event.

Figure 4: Experiments of a handshake and a non-handshake events.

bluetooth module, an OS5000 sensor [6], a Jennic JN5139 [7], and a battery, as shown in Fig. 3. Each OS5000 has a 3-axes accelerometer. We set $R_s=40$Hz. Jennic JN5139 has a micro-controller and a built-in 2.4GHz/IEEE802.15.4 wireless module. The user device is a smart phone (HTC Touch 2 [8]) with a bluetooth and a WiFi/3G wireless modules.

We also conduct experiments to log shaking waves of a handshake event and a non-handshake event for 7 seconds. Fig. 4 shows the experimental results, where the two users' sensing data have high degree of similarity in a handshake event in both frequency distribution and time domain samples.

3. REFERENCES

[1] F.-J. Wu, Y.-F. Kao, and Y.-C. Tseng, "From wireless sensor networks towards cyber physical systems," *Pervasive and Mobile Computing*, to appear.

[2] S. Gaonkar, J. Li, and R. R. Choudhury, "Micro-Blog: Sharing and querying content through mobile phones and social participation," in *Proc. ACM Int'l Conf. on Mobile Systems, Applications, and Services*, 2008, pp. 174–186.

[3] M.-C. Chiu, S.-P. Chang, Y.-C. Chang, H.-H. Chu, C. C.-H. Chen, F.-H. Hsiao, and J.-C. Ko, "Playful bottle: a mobile social persuasion system to motivate healthy water intake," in *Int'l Conf. Ubiquitous Computing*, 2009, pp. 185–194.

[4] R. Mayrhofer and H. Gellersen, "Shake well before use: Intuitive and secure pairing of mobile devices," *IEEE Trans. Mobile Computing*, vol. 8, no. 6, pp. 792–806, 2009.

[5] D. Bichler, G. Stromberg, M. Huemer, and M. Löw, "Key generation based on acceleration data of shaking processes," in *Int'l Conf. Ubiquitous Computing*, 2007, pp. 304–317.

[6] "Os5000," http://www.ocean-server.com.

[7] "Jennic JN5139," http://www.jennic.com.

[8] "HTC Touch 2," http://www.htc.com/tw/product/touch2/overview.html.

An Online Gaming Testbed for Peer-to-Peer Architectures

Max Lehn   Christof Leng   Robert Rehner   Tonio Triebel   Alejandro Buchmann
Databases and Distributed Systems   Praktische Informatik IV
Technische Universität Darmstadt, Germany   Universität Mannheim, Germany
{mlehn,cleng,rehner,buchmann}@dvs.tu-darmstadt.de   triebel@pi4.informatik.uni-mannheim.de

ABSTRACT

In this demo we present a testbed environment for Peer-to-Peer (P2P) game architectures. It is based on Planet PI4, an online multiplayer game whose gameplay provides a standard workload for a set of gaming-specific network interfaces. Its pluggable architecture allows for the evaluation and comparison of existing and new P2P networking approaches. Planet PI4 can run on a real network for prototypical evaluation as well as in a discrete-event simulator providing a reproducible environment.

Categories and Subject Descriptors

C.2.4 [**Distributed Systems**]: Distributed Applications;
C.4 [**Performance of Systems**]: Design studies

General Terms

Experimentation, Performance, Measurement

1. INTRODUCTION

Massively multiplayer online games (MMOGs) have become very popular in the recent years. Well-known examples are *World of Warcraft* and *Eve Online*, which support up to several ten thousand players simultaneously online in one virtual world. Today, these MMOG use server-based network architectures for the synchronization of the game content among the players. However, the permanent (inter-) activity of the players puts a high demand on the servers' resources, making the operation of an MMOG expensive.

This is why peer-to-peer architectures are an appealing approach to saving server resources. P2P research has already brought up a plethora of P2P systems designed specifically for networked games or networked virtual environments (NVE). But until now, only very few P2P systems have made it to real games. (One example for the latter is Badumna [6].) Many of the academic approaches are evaluated using an oversimplified model of the game and the players' behavior. Round-based simulation and random walk or random waypoint mobility models are simple to use; however, they cover only a small part of the issues of a real game on a real network. Deploying a real game equipped with a new P2P mechanism, on the other hand, is a hard piece of work. Furthermore, measurements may be hardly reproducible in real-world Internet setups.

Figure 1: A screenshot of the game Planet PI4

2. GOALS

We are developing the 3D real-time massively multiplayer online game *Planet PI4* [10, 7], which serves as a benchmark for various P2P networking components. For an effective evaluation we have identified the following objectives:

- The gameplay must be complex enough to represent a real game and cover all relevant aspects.
- It should be attractive to real players, which provide the reference player behavior.
- At the same time it should be as simple as possible to allow focusing on the important aspects and to be successfully played by bots.
- It should be able to run in a real network as well as in a deterministic emulated network environment.
- It should be resource-efficient for a good simulation scalability.
- The networking components must have well-defined and flexible interfaces to facilitate the replacement of the network architecture.

We believe that with these features we can provide a testbed for a realistic comparison of P2P network architectures. Supporting execution on a real network ensures that the tested systems do not use any shortcuts available only in a simulation, while network emulation is the only way to achieve a reproducible network environment. A realistic user model for a game can only be obtained by analyzing the behavior of human players, but again, a reproducible workload has to be generated synthetically. Our approach is to collect traces from human players, e.g., by running a client-server game session, from which we derive an abstract user model. This model will be fed in a bot implementation to reproduce human behavior. Using player traces directly as a game workload is infeasible, because the traces are not parameterizable for scaling the workload. Moreover, traces cannot reproduce the interactivity between players, which is in turn influenced by the network environment.

3. GAMEPLAY

In Planet PI4 each player joins a team to play against other teams. The game set is in an asteroid field, and each player navigates his spaceship and shoots at other ships. Once a ship is destroyed, the player respawns at the team's initial position. The goals are to destroy the other teams' players and to capture bases. Bases are strategic points of interest providing certain improvements (energy, points, etc.) to the possessing team. To capture a base, it is necessary to stay within the range of the base while keeping players of other teams out. Figure 1 shows a screenshot of the game.

The asteroid field defines the three-dimensional gameplay region. Bases particularly attract players, causing hotspots in player density. To evaluate scalability, the game map size and player density must be variable. Therefore, the map is generated algorithmically, based on a common random seed.

4. ARCHITECTURE

The testbed architecture has been consequently designed to fulfill the above defined requirements. Figure 2 shows its high-level components. The interfaces allow for an exchangeability of the components on the different layers. PlanetPI4's game core provides a player control interface which can be used either by the GUI or by bot implementations. The network interfaces connect the exchangeable network parts, and the system interfaces abstract the run-time.

4.1 Network Components

Different networking issues are split into separate interfaces, allowing independent implementations for each.

Spatial Multicast The most important functional requirement for the networking component of a massively multiplayer online game is the dissemination of position updates. In fact, position updates cause most traffic in MMOG [3]. This is also why a large fraction of publications of P2P systems for games focus on this topic, e.g., VON [5], pSense [8], and Donnybrook [1].

Object Management Another important issue is the management of persistent game objects that can be manipulated by players. Exemplary systems in this category have been presented by Hu et al. [4] and Bharambe et al. [2]. We define *active objects* as objects which have an associated 'think function' for object-specific processing.

Channel-based publish/subscribe For team communication as well as object-specific updates we have defined an interface for channel-based publish/subscribe.

Global statistics Player and team scores that are globally available are stored using the global statistics interface.

At the present time we have an implementation of pSense and an approach based on BubbleStorm [9] for position updates. A client-server implementation, which serves as a reference, supports the full set of network interfaces, including object management and publish/subscribe communication.

4.2 System Runtime

To be able run in a simulated network environment, the whole game code uses an event-based design. All components which have to regularly execute a certain task register at the central task scheduler. The task scheduler implementation is exchanged for different runtime environments.

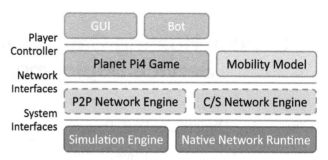

Figure 2: High-level testbed architecture

To run in a discrete-event simulator, the scheduler creates simulator events for each task, while the native-network implementation runs a real-time event loop.

5. CONCLUSION AND OUTLOOK

Our modular testbed provides powerful means for a realistic evaluation and comparison of P2P gaming architectures. Evaluation in both a real environment and an emulated network promotes valuable insights into the properties of the tested systems. Being able to run a real game does not only increase the confidence in the obtained results of a P2P system, but also gives a feeling of its real-world applicability.

As next step we will conduct user studies to obtain player behavior data. From these, we want to derive user models and build bot implementations with a calibrated behavior.

This work was partially funded by the DFG research group FOR 733 and the DFG research training group GRK 1343.

6. REFERENCES

[1] A. Bharambe, J. R. Douceur, J. R. Lorch, T. Moscibroda, J. Pang, S. Seshan, and X. Zhuang. Donnybrook: Enabling Large-Scale, High-Speed, Peer-to-Peer Games. *ACM SIGCOMM Computer Communication Review*, 38(4):389–400, 2008.

[2] A. Bharambe, J. Pang, and S. Seshan. Colyseus: A Distributed Architecture for Online Multiplayer Games. In *NSDI '06*, Berkeley, CA, USA, 2006. USENIX Association.

[3] K. Chen, P. Huang, C. Huang, and C. Lei. Game traffic analysis: an MMORPG perspective. In *NOSSDAV'05*, pages 19–24. ACM, 2005.

[4] S. Hu, S. Chang, and J. Jiang. Voronoi State Management for Peer-to-Peer Massively Multiplayer Online Games. In *CCNC '08*, pages 1134–1138, 2008.

[5] S.-Y. Hu and G.-M. Liao. Scalable Peer-to-Peer Networked Virtual Environment. In *NetGames '04*, pages 129–133, 2004.

[6] S. Kulkarni, S. Douglas, and D. Churchill. Badumna: A decentralised network engine for virtual environments. *Computer Networks*, 54(12):1953–1967, 2010.

[7] M. Lehn, T. Triebel, C. Leng, A. Buchmann, and W. Effelsberg. Performance Evaluation of Peer-to-Peer Gaming Overlays. In *IEEE P2P '10*, 2010.

[8] A. Schmieg, M. Stieler, S. Jeckel, P. Kabus, B. Kemme, and A. Buchmann. pSense - Maintaining a Dynamic Localized Peer-to-Peer Structure for Position Based Multicast in Games. In *IEEE P2P '08*, pages 247–256, 2008.

[9] W. Terpstra, J. Kangasharju, C. Leng, and A. Buchmann. BubbleStorm: Resilient, Probabilistic, and Exhaustive Peer-to-Peer Search. In *ACM SIGCOMM '07*, pages 49–60, 2007.

[10] T. Triebel, B. Guthier, R. Süselbeck, G. Schiele, and W. Effelsberg. Peer-to-Peer Infrastructures for Games. In *NOSSDAV '08*, pages 123–124, 2008.

Service Hosting Gateways - a Platform for Distributed Service Deployment in End User Homes

Martin May, Christophe Diot, Pascal Le Guyadec, Fabio Picconi, Joris Roussel, Augustin Soule
Technicolor, Paris Research Lab
1 Rue Jeanne d'Arc, 92443 Issy-les-Moulineaux, France
firstname.lastname@technicolor.com

ABSTRACT

The success of broadband residential Internet access is changing the way home users consume digital content and services. Currently, each home service requires the installation of a separate physical box (for instance, the NetFlix box or IPTV set-top-boxes). Instead, we argue for deploying a single box in the home that is powerful and flexible enough to host a variety of home services. In addition, this box is managed by the Internet Service provider and is able to provide service guarantees. We call such a box a service-hosting gateway (*SHG*), as it combines the functionalities of the home gateway managed by the network service provider with the capability of hosting services. Isolation between such services is ensured by virtualization.

We demonstrate a prototype of our (*SHG*). It is based on the hardware platform that will be used for future home gateways. We illustrate the features of the *SHG* with multiple use cases ranging from simple service deployment scenarios to complex media distribution services and home automation features.

Categories and Subject Descriptors

C.2.1 [**Computer Systems Organization**]: Network Architecture and Design—*Distributed networks*

General Terms

Experimentation

1. INTRODUCTION

Hundreds of millions of homes today connect to the Internet using broadband access, and the penetration of fiber to the home is growing quickly in developed areas. Such high-speed, always-on connectivity is changing the way home-users access media services and consume content. For instance, many Internet Service Providers (ISPs) offer "triple-play" services, which bundle Internet, telephony, and TV. The success of over-the-top (OTT) services (*i.e.*, services that utilize the existing Internet connectivity to deliver media services outside the ISP service bundle, and that require the deployment of a specific box at home) suggests that the demand for personalized services will increase quickly with bandwidth availability.

In the current model, the home network is connected to the Internet using a home gateway, which is generally provided by the Network Access Provider (NAP). Services managed by the NAP rely on the deployment of set-top-boxes (and sometimes IP phones).

All other services are OTT, including online multiplayer gaming networks, video-on-demand, and home automation to mention just a few. These services are unmanaged and their quality relies heavily on the available bandwidth provided by the NAP. As the number of offered services increases, the model of dedicated boxes per service is difficult to maintain. as it culminates in a "box explosion" phenomenon in the home with the consequent complexity to utilize and manage these boxes.

In this demonstration, we show a prototype of a home gateway that is able to deploy digital services to the homes in a flexible and managed way. A single physical box will combine the functions of a home gateway with the capability of hosting an open portfolio of services. We call this box a service-hosting gateway (*SHG*). The *SHG* will be deployed and managed by the NAP and is able to provide service guarantees. *SHGs* give users the flexibility to compose their service portfolio from different service providers without the need for new boxes, while allowing NAPs to make revenue by guaranteeing a minimum SLA per service delivered. Note that functionalities that are specific to a device (*e.g.*, rendering for a TV or gaming console) are either integrated in the end device or in a set-top-box per end device.

We implemented the *SHG* using a classic virtualization technique as it is the mechanism of choice to provide strong isolation between the services running simultaneously, *i.e.*, each deployed service is running in its own host OS. Virtualization introduces some performance overhead [6, 1, 7], but it also provides isolation and a flexible environment for service developers. There are a number of virtualization techniques to choose from, with different performance overhead and different levels of flexibility. We have installed and tested different virtualization solutions including Xen [8], Linux Containers [4], and KVM ğ[2]. Based on the requirements for this demo and the overhead induced by each of the mentioned solutions, we decided to base the prototype on the Linux Containers (LXC) solution.

We demonstrate the *SHG* concept with two physical gateways combined with multiple emulated gateways running on a server. This distributed infrastructure will be used to showcase how new services can be deployed on an ISP infrastructure, how the new services are monitored on the gateways. The *SHGs* are then used to illustrate this distributed infrastructure is able to host and run services in a combined manner. We show how his distributed datacenter infrastructure is able to distribute media content using peer-to-peer technology and with that to save investments on the centralized datacenter infrastructure used today (see also [5] for more details).

2. SHG HARDWARE DESCRIPTION

The *SHG* used in this demo is based on an Intel SoC platform

SIGCOMM'11, August 15–19, 2011, Toronto, Ontario, Canada.
ACM 978-1-4503-0797-0/11/08.

Figure 1: Service Hosting Gateway running three services: gaming, social networking and streaming

CE4200. The CE4200 has an 1.2GHz dual core processor integrated, together with an additional CPU for transcoding (not used for this demo). The system has 1GByte of RAM and no onboard hard disk, but we added USB-attached storage. The boards also provide two 1GBit/s Ethernet interfaces. We run a modified Linux (provided together with the Intel development kit) on this platform and managed to installed Linux Containers [4].

The gateways and the server are connected via a switch; to emulate realistic bandwidth for the connection between the gateways and the server, we added a dummynet module and limit the bandwidth to typical DSL settings and also delay and jitter.

3. SHG DEMONSTRATION

We will demonstrate how the three players (the NSP, the hosting service provider, and the end user) interact. A new SHG only runs classic triple play: voice, Internet, IPTV). Then, we let the NSP deploy new services to all or a subset of all devices. Aside, the NSP will be able to monitor where and how the service is used. Finally, the user will select the applications he subscribes to and runs them on its local *SHG*.

We show the deployment and use of the platform with the following examples:

- Gaming A network gaming service provider is deploying a distributed game platform. Each gateway is gunning a part of the gaming service, *i.e.*, hosting a portion of the map played by the end users. We will showcase such a game using a distributed but simple PacMan implementation.

- Home Automation The energy provider is renting a slice of the distributed hosting platform and is deploying a software suite to monitor and control the devices connected to the home automation system.

- Peer-assisted Video on Demand Distribution We demonstrate how a video streaming provider is able to use the SHGs to deliver video content from a centralized streaming source (CDN) but also from the distributed storage system provided by the SHGs. The service implemented is building on a modified BitTorrent implementation that downloads the media chunks from the closest gateways instead of the data centers (see [3] and [5] for details).

- Remote Surveillance The SHG is finally used to host a network surveillance service. For this service, the gateway hosts a solution that captures images form a video camera and makes the images available on the TV screen of the end user. The same video information can also sent over the Internet and the stream can be retrieved remotely through a web page also hosted on the SHG.

With these set of applications, we illustrate how a low power and always on home gateway is able to host and run multiple applications simultaneously. The hardware used for our prototype is realistic as this is the platform will be used by NSPs for their future home gateways or set top boxes. We show how virtualization is able to isolate the services and how access can be controlled and how dedicated resources can be guaranteed to the service provider. The management framework illustrates how such a distributed platform is used and how the services and applications are deployed and monitored.

4. CONCLUSION

The success of the service hosting platform deployed in home networks will result from a complex mixture of ingredients. The service running on the SHG needs to be able to guarantee a similar Quality of Experience for the end user to the QoE provided by a dedicated device running the same service. At the same time, the NSP has to maintain the cost for the SHG as low as possible to increase the margins for each deployed gateway. These conflicting results require a careful selection of the underlying hardware for the SHG.

We have selected a platform that is foreseen to be used for future home gateway products. This Intel_SoC platform offers an interesting tradeoff between cost and performance providing enough performance for standard applications and services. In the prototype implementation used for this demo, we are able to showcase multiple applications and service running simultaneously on the system. Even when all services are used at then same time, none is encountering service interruptions or degradation.

Key for success however will be the management of the platform. We will demonstrate a simple management tool used by the NSP to deploy and monitor services on the SHGs. On top, we demonstrate how service providers are able to develop their applications and services for the proposed platform and how service monitoring is implemented. Finally, the demo illustrated how the end user can run multiple service without the need of deploying and configuring multiple devices.

5. REFERENCES

[1] N. Egi, A. Greenhalgh, M. Handley, M. Hoerdt, L. Mathy, and T. Schooley. Evaluating xen for router virtualization. In *Proceedings of ICCCN*, pages 1256–1261, 2007.

[2] KVM. http://www.linux-kvm.org/.

[3] N. Laoutaris, P. Rodriguez, and L. Massoulie. ECHOS: Edge Capacity Hosting Overlays of Nano Data Centers. *ACM SIGCOMM Computer Communication Review*, Jan. 2008.

[4] LXC: Linux Containers. http://lxc.sourceforge.net/.

[5] V. Valancius, L. Masoulie, N. Laoutaris, C. Diot, and P. Rodriquez. Greening the internet with nano data centers. In *ACM CoNEXT 2009*, December 2009.

[6] G. Wang and T. S. E. Ng. The impact of virtualization on network performance of amazon EC2 data center. In *INFOCOM*, 2010.

[7] J. Whiteaker, F. Schneider, and R. Teixeira. Explaining packet delays under vitualization. *SIGCOMM Comput. Commun. Rev.*, 2010.

[8] Xen. http://www.xen.org/.

Optimizing a Virtualized Data Center

David Erickson, Brandon Heller,
Shuang Yang, Jonathan Chu,
Jonathan Ellithorpe, Nick McKeown,
Guru Parulkar, Mendel Rosenblum
Stanford University

Scott Whyte, Stephen Stuart
Google

ABSTRACT

Many data centers extensively use virtual machines (VMs), which provide the flexibility to move workload among physical servers. VMs can be placed to maximize application performance, power efficiency, or even fault tolerance. However, VMs are typically repositioned without considering network topology, congestion, or traffic routes.

In this demo, we show a system, Virtue, which enables the comparison of different algorithms for VM placement and network routing at the scale of an entire data center. Our goal is to understand how placement and routing affect overall application performance by varying the types and mix of workloads, network topologies, and compute resources; these parameters will be available for demo attendees to explore.

Categories and Subject Descriptors: C.2.3 [Computer-Communication Networks]: Network Operations

General Terms: Experimentation, Measurement, Performance

Keywords: Data center network, OpenFlow, Virtualization, Virtue

1. INTRODUCTION

Over the past decade, virtual machines have grown in popularity as application containers, since they improve server utilization and support fast provisioning for scale-out services. Increasingly, VMs are hosted in "clouds", large data centers that host thousands of customer VMs. Amazon EC2, the leading cloud provider, has approximately 40,000 servers [2], launches 80,000 VMs each day, and has launched 23 million VMs since its inception [7].

Equipment and energy costs provide a strong motivation for cloud owners to maximize operational efficiency. One way to improve operational efficiency is through workload placement algorithms, which map VMs onto physical machines (PMs). A placement algorithm might squeeze VMs onto as few servers as possible, then power down the unneeded servers or sell access to them on a spot market. Alternately, it might spread the VMs as evenly as possible, to maximize headroom for new VMs or avoid bandwidth bottlenecks. The placement algorithm could even maximize the performance of individual services, by co-locating their VMs or considering policy requests from customers.

Currently published workload placement algorithms en-

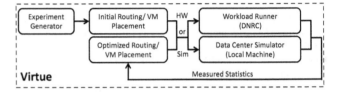

Figure 1: Experimenter's workflow using Virtue

force CPU, RAM, and NIC sharing policies [8, 9]; notably absent from this list is the network fabric interconnecting PMs in the infrastructure. Given the obvious operational impact of the network, it is natural to ask the question: *Can a virtualized data center be more efficient if the operator has visibility into network traffic, as well as control over packet routing?* Answering this question demands a number of prerequisites: representative workloads, a way to run those workloads at data center scale, an algorithm to place VMs and find routes, and a way to evaluate each algorithm's optimization metric. Perhaps most importantly, it requires a way to measure and control network traffic.

The purpose of our demo is to show such a system, named *Virtue*. Virtue enables a researcher to run synthetic data center workloads on both a simulator and a real data center. To provide flexibility in VM placement, Virtue offers an interface to XenServer. To provide network traffic flexibility, Virtue leverages OpenFlow [5]. On this platform, we can investigate the scalability tradeoffs (state and computation) between coarse-grained traffic aggregation and fine-grained, low-level traffic routing. We can try approaches to VM placement that ignore the network, staged approaches that optimize for placement first then do routing, or even a joint optimization with a mixed integer linear program.

Our hope is that this investment in infrastructure and software will enable realistic comparisons of workloads and placement algorithms, resulting in both an understanding of the potential benefits of joint placement, as well as practical algorithms to achieve them.

2. SYSTEM

Virtue supports experiments targeted to either hardware or simulation, at the scale of an entire data center; its components are shown in Figure 1. The demo will show the entire Virtue system running live on a remote data center. Demo attendees can choose a workload and a placement algorithm, then explore the effects on VM placement, network communication, and service-level performance.

2.1 Generating an Experiment

There are many workloads, such as Facebook or Amazon, which we would love to test, but for which we will never have equivalent hardware or software. However researchers will likely have access to some hardware, and the ability to simulate other environments. These observations motivated the creation of a software abstraction layer for rapidly developing synthetic workloads that can run without modification on both real hardware and in a software simulator. The abstraction layer gives applications an API to send and receive network traffic, consume CPU cycles, access timers, and perform other utility methods. For example, an experimenter could create a 3-tier web workload by creating a simple application for each tier plus a client request application. The experimenter could then easily vary the number of VMs per tier, the distribution of request/response sizes between tiers, fan-out and fan-in of network messages, and network bisection bandwidth. More advanced experiments could introduce clusters of applications using varying numbers of VMs, similar to what might be seen in a cloud provider such as Amazon.

2.2 Routing and VM Placement

After defining the workload specifics of an experiment, the "algorithm" stage must define the physical locations on which to run virtual machines, as well as the physical path of flows between virtual machines. Here, a range of placement algorithms are possible, from naive (random placement) to intelligent (constraint satisfaction), for a range of optimization metrics. We have initially created mixed integer programming model algorithms that will optimize for performance (spread workload and network traffic as evenly as possible) or energy (collapse workload onto as few machines and network links as possible). Due to the complexity of the problem, we expect to also create and evaluate other approximation algorithms.

2.3 Hardware

To run a workload on hardware, Virtue requires physical servers running the Xen hypervisor and switches supporting the OpenFlow protocol. The demo will run on the Data center Network Research Cluster (DNRC), a 200-node cluster developed in a collaboration with Google for research use. The switches in the DNRC are wired together to provide three distinct topologies, two different fat-trees and a multi-rooted tree, while the nodes are virtualized by XenServer.

To run an experiment, the *workload runner* coordinates with the XenServer pool master to start the VMs, then passes the routing table to Beacon, the OpenFlow controller managing all aspects of the DNRC network. While the workload is running, Virtue records utilizations for the CPU, RAM, NIC, network links, and network traffic matrix, plus application-level measurements such as responses per second and completion time. After the workload completes, the experiment description and measurement data are passed back to the Optimized Routing/VM Placement stage, which can modify the virtual machine placement and network routes. The modified experiment can then be run to look for changes in any metrics of interest.

2.4 Simulation

To explore other network topologies, hardware configurations, and scales, we created a software data center simulator. The simulator is a simple discrete event-driven simulation based on the DESMO-J framework. It tracks all the resources available via the application abstraction layer, namely CPU cycles, network traffic at flow granularity, and scheduled timers. Although the simulator provides the same measurements and workflow as the hardware path, we don't expect both platforms to provide identical results. Still, the simulator allows us to explore and characterize unavailable hardware configurations within a reasonable error margin.

3. RELATED WORK

Several authors have analyzed data center workload placement optimization, focusing on shared resources such as the CPU, RAM, and NIC. Wood et al. explore hotspot detection and mitigation in a virtualized data center [9]. A system by Ruth et al. migrates VMs in clusters to achieve higher performance [8]. Commercial products are also available from VMware and Citrix; our work expands on all of these techniques by also monitoring and controlling the network.

Prior work on data center networks focuses on routing algorithms that spread traffic over all available paths, often via the introduction of scalable topologies [3, 6]. These papers generally assume traffic follows a path picked by a routing protocol or by oblivious load balancing. Hedera [1] uses OpenFlow (alongside ECMP) to detect and re-route long-lived, high data-rate flows, to achieve higher bi-section bandwidth than possible with ECMP alone. We make no assumptions about the network topology or hardware, other than OpenFlow support. Another example in this vein, ElasticTree, routes traffic through a minimum of switches and links to save energy by turning off unneeded switches [4].

Acknowledgments

David Erickson is funded by a Microsoft Research PhD fellowship.

References

[1] M. Al-Fares, S. Radhakrishnan, B. Raghavan, N. Huang, and A. Vahdat. Hedera: Dynamic flow scheduling for data center networks. In *NSDI*, San Jose, CA, April 2010. USENIX.

[2] R. Bias. Amazon's EC2 generating 220M+ annually. http://cloudscaling.com/blog/cloud-computing/amazons-ec2-generating-220m-annually, Oct 2009.

[3] A. Greenberg, J. R. Hamilton, N. Jain, S. Kandula, C. Kim, P. Lahiri, D. A. Maltz, P. Patel, and S. Sengupta. VL2: a scalable and flexible data center network. In *SIGCOMM*, pages 51–62, New York, NY, 2009. ACM.

[4] B. Heller, S. Seetharaman, P. Mahadevan, Y. Yiakoumis, P. Sharma, S. Banerjee, and N. McKeown. ElasticTree: Saving Energy in Data Center Networks. In *NSDI*, San Jose, CA, April 2010. USENIX.

[5] N. McKeown, T. Anderson, H. Balakrishnan, G. Parulkar, L. Peterson, J. Rexford, S. Shenker, and J. Turner. OpenFlow: enabling innovation in campus networks. *ACMCCR*, 38(2):69–74, April 2008.

[6] R. Niranjan Mysore, A. Pamboris, N. Farrington, N. Huang, P. Miri, S. Radhakrishnan, V. Subramanya, and A. Vahdat. PortLand: a scalable fault-tolerant layer 2 data center network fabric. 39(4):39–50, 2009.

[7] G. Rosen. Presentation at CloudConnect. http://www.jackofallclouds.com/2010/04/presentation-at-cloudconnect/, April 2010.

[8] P. Ruth, J. Rhee, D. Xu, R. Kennell, and S. Goasguen. Autonomic live adaptation of virtual computational environments in a multi-domain infrastructure. In *ICAC*, pages 5–14, Washington, DC, 2006. IEEE.

[9] T. Wood, P. Shenoy, A. Venkataramani, and M. Yousif. Black-box and Gray-box Strategies for Virtual Machine Migration. In *NSDI*, Cambridge, MA, April 2007. USENIX.

Efficient Content Dissemination in Heterogeneous Networks Prone to Episodic Connectivity

Amir Krifa
Planète Project-team
INRIA Sophia Antipolis
akrifa@sophia.inria.fr

Marc Mendonca
University of California
Santa Cruz, CA, USA
msm@soe.ucsc.edu

Rao Naveed Bin Rais
Planète Project-team
INRIA Sophia Antipolis
nbrais@sophia.inria.fr

Chadi Barakat
Planète Project-team
INRIA Sophia Antipolis
cbarakat@sophia.inria.fr

Thierry Turletti
Planète Project-team
INRIA Sophia Antipolis
turletti@sophia.inria.fr

Katia Obraczka
University of California
Santa Cruz, CA, USA
katia@soe.ucsc.edu

Categories and Subject Descriptors

C.2.1 [**Computer-Communication Networks**]: Network Architecture and Design—*network communications*

General Terms

Design, Experimentation

1. INTRODUCTION

Ubiquity of portable computing devices coupled with wide availability of wireless communication present new important opportunities for applications involving media-rich content dissemination. However, as access networks become increasingly more heterogeneous, seamless data delivery across internets consisting of a variety of network technology becomes a real challenge. In this demonstration, we showcase a system that enables content dissemination over heterogeneous internets consisting of wired–, infrastructure-based and infrastructure-less wireless networks that may be prone to intermittent connectivity. Using an efficient, yet flexible buffer management scheme, we are able to address application-specific performance requirements such as average delay, delivery probability, energy efficiency, etc.

Our system uses the Message Delivery in Heterogeneous, Disruption-prone Networks (MeDeHa [2]) framework to deliver messages across a heterogeneous internet coupled with History-Based Scheduling and Drop (HBSD) buffer management [1] as a way to optimize resources provided by opportunistic networks. MeDeHa, which is described in detail in [2], provides seamless data delivery over interconnecting networks of different types, i.e., infrastructure-based and infrastructure-less networks. MeDeHa's comprehensive approach to bridging infrastructure-based and infrastructure-less networks also copes with intermittent connectivity. For this demonstration, we showcase a "complete stack" solution featuring, from to top to bottom, the DTN2 "bundle" layer, HBSD as an "external router" to DTN2, and MeDeHa, which handles message delivery. We have implemented, on a Linux-based testbed, *(i)* the MeDeHa framework, *(ii)* the HBSD [3] external router for the DTN2 [4] architecture.

2. ARCHITECTURE OVERVIEW AND IMPLEMENTATION

Our main goal is to cope with heterogeneous networks and to take advantage of content relaying over DTNs in order to reduce communication costs and network resource consumption. In this context, Figure 1 depicts an example scenario targeted by our framework, where we have two infrastructure networks (Ethernet and 802.11) connected to a MANET (nodes running OLSR) and a DTN network (nodes running HBSD and DTN2). Gateway nodes with the MeDeHa framework will interconnect the diverse networks. In the following, we detail the main building blocks of our framework with respect to Figure 1.

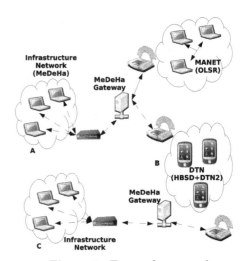

Figure 1: Example scenario.

MeDeHa nodes deployed within the infrastructure network (running the MeDeHa protocol [2]) have several responsibilities, including finding paths (or a suitable relay, gateways in this case) to a destination across all connected networks (even MANET or DTN) and exchanging topological and routing information to aid in relay selection. MeDeHa nodes also store data for other unavailable nodes, or transfer custody to better suited relay (based on some utility metric).

MeDeHa gateways [2] are simply MeDeHa nodes that are connected to and forward content between multiple networks. With respect to the scenario presented in Figure 1, MeDeHa gateways provide interface for communication with two opportunistic networks, *(i)* A MANET network running the OLSR protocol, and *(ii)* An Epidemic DTN Network running the optimal HBSD scheduling and drop policy on top of DTN2. We define the former interface as a MeDeHa-MANET gateway, as shown in Figure 3, and the latter as a MeDeHa-DTN gateway, as shown in Figure 2.

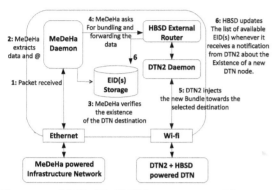

Figure 2: MeDeHa-DTN gateway architecture.

Whenever a new packet is received through the Ethernet interface of a MeDeHa-DTN gateway, the MeDeHa daemon extracts the packet data and IP addresses, and verifies whether this packet is destined to a node within the adjacent DTN network or to another Internet node beyond the DTN network. If the packet needs to be forwarded to the DTN network, the MeDeHa daemon asks the HBSD external router to create a *bundle* that encapsulates the required packet fields and data. In a last step, the HBSD external router forwards the created bundle towards another MeDeHa gateway beyond the DTN network or towards a DTN node. Thanks to the HBSD external router running on both the gateway and DTN nodes, bundles forwarding within the DTN network are optimized towards either decreasing the bundles average delivery delay or increasing their average delivery rate.

The same control flow is reproduced for the MeDeHa-MANET gateway described in Figure 3. However, unlike the DTN gateway, there is no need for a mapping process between different data types or between different naming schemes. The MeDeHa daemon takes the responsibility of interfacing with the MANET underlaying routing protocol (OLSR in this case) in order to identify the packet's next hop which can either be a local MANET node or a MeDeHa gateway if the packet needs to traverse the MANET network.

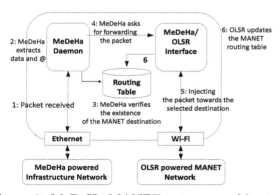

Figure 3: MeDeHa-MANET gateway architecture.

2.1 Hybrid Simulator Integration

We integrate our MeDeHa ns-3 simulator implementation with the testbed through ns-3 emulation and real-time scheduling capabilities, as shown in Figure 4. Specifically, we use ns-3 TAP to bridge part of the simulated network to the testbed network. This works by creating a "ghost" node on the ns-3 network that passes all Ethernet frames between a Linux TAP device on the real node and the simulated links to which the ghost node is connected. Packets can then be routed between the simulated network and the networks to which the real node is connected.

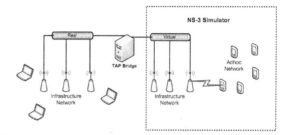

Figure 4: A sample hybrid network with both real and virtual ns-3 nodes

3. DEMONSTRATION

The demonstration will showcase our implementation of the MeDeHa protocol and the HBSD external router as well as their joint ability to perform optimized message delivery over heterogeneous networks. Our target scenario consists of two infrastructure networks bridged via opportunistic networks (highlighted with dash arrows in Figure 1).

Our demonstration testbed will consist of Linux laptops and Android Smartphones: some laptops will be connected to two different infrastructure networks and will run our MeDeHa gateway while the other nodes communicate opportunistically on an epidemic DTN network. The intermittently-connected DTN stations will run our HBSD external router on top of DTN2. Additionally, a portion of the infrastructure network as well as an OLSR MANET will be be simulated (Figure 4) to extend the scenario beyond what would be available given limited equipment.

4. ACKNOWLEDGMENTS

This work has been supported in part by an "Associated Team" grant from INRIA, NSF grant CCF-091694, and a Center for the Dynamics and Evolution of the Land-Sea Interface (CDELSI) fellowship.

5. REFERENCES

[1] A. Krifa, C. Barakat, and T. Spyropoulos, *Optimal Buffer Management Policy for Delay Tolerant Networks*, in proceedings of SECON, San Francisco, June 2008, CA.

[2] R. N. Bin Rais, M. Mendonca, T. Turletti, and K. Obraczka, *Towards Truly Heterogeneous Networks: Bridging Infrastructure-based and Infrastructure-less Networks*, in Proceedings of IEEE/ACM COMSNETS Conference, Bangalore, India, 2011.

[3] HBSD, an external router for DTN2, http://planete.inria.fr/HBSD_DTN2

[4] DTN2 architecture, http://www.dtnrg.org/wiki/Code

Networking in the Long Emergency

Barath Raghavan and Justin Ma
ICSI and UC Berkeley

ABSTRACT

We explore responses to a scenario in which the severity of a permanent energy crisis fundamentally limits our ability to maintain the current-day Internet architecture. In this paper, we review why this scenario—whose vague outline is known to many but whose consequences are generally understood only by the scientists who study it—is likely, and articulate the specific impacts that it would have on network infrastructure and networking research. In light of this, we propose a concrete research agenda to address the networking needs of an energy-deprived society.

Categories and Subject Descriptors

C.2.1 [**Computer-Communication Networks**]: Network Architecture and Design

General Terms

Design, Economics, Management

Keywords

Internet Architecture, Energy, Resource Limits

1. INTRODUCTION

"If I had my finger on the switch, I'd keep the juice flowing to the Internet even if I had to turn off everything else...The Net is the one solvent we can still afford; jet travel can't be our salvation in an age of climate shock and dwindling oil, so the kind of trip you can take with the click of a mouse will have to substitute." And thus eminent science journalist Bill McKibben sums up his sobering survey of our current energy and climate predicament and identifies the importance of the Internet to our future [29]. We think he's right, and present in this paper a challenge to the research community that may be among the hardest we have faced.

Computer networking is rightly a linchpin of modern society—it has given us the ability to exchange information at a speed and

Reprinted from the proceedings of GreenNet'11 with permission.

scale that is unprecedented in human history. However, networking is the product of an energy-intensive economy and industrial system, and if that economic system faces a sudden and permanent energy shock, then networking must change to adapt. If we wish to preserve the benefits of the Internet, then a crucial opportunity emerges for networking researchers to reevaluate the overall research agenda to address the needs of an energy-deprived society. Due to the near-term depletion of oil this scenario is not hypothetical; it marks the beginning of an era of contraction.

Oil is the foundation of our industrial system—its energy enables the creation and transportation of goods and services that were unimaginable a century ago. Unfortunately, we face worldwide oil depletion—an era when oil production declines. Although it is unknown precisely when this era will begin, recent studies suggest it will be underway soon, as we survey later. A study commissioned in 2005 by the U.S. Department of Energy on the peaking of world oil production found the following [23]:

> "The problems associated with world oil production peaking will not be temporary, and past 'energy crisis' experience will provide relatively little guidance. The challenge of oil peaking deserves immediate, serious attention, if risks are to be fully understood and mitigation begun on a timely basis."

A severe, permanent energy crisis would have far-reaching consequences.[1] Though we are far from the first to consider such a scenario, we are unaware of prior work that considers the implications that this challenge will have for networking or computing generally. In this paper we issue a call to re-evaluate the broader networking research agenda to face this unprecedented predicament.

At first glance, the connection between the global energy system—oil in particular—and networking research may be unclear. However, our oil-depleted, post-peak future will bring about energy and financial pressures that will make developing and maintaining network infrastructure much more difficult. We explore this connection and touch on the direct and indirect impacts on networking infrastructure and networking research as this foundation of oil crumbles, consider practical constraints that we are likely to face, suggest design principles that might aid in future research, and propose a small list of research questions for the community to tackle. We begin our discussion with a brief overview of near-term global energy constraints.

---

[1] In this paper we primarily consider impacts on industrial nations, though any society that uses oil, or interacts with those that do, will be affected in some way.

2. BACKGROUND

Our society faces long-term energy scarcity. Although the exact timing is uncertain, the emerging consensus is that this transition will begin soon. This section provides a brief overview of the coming energy challenges, of why existing alternatives are inadequate substitutes, and of economic impacts. While modern networking exists in the zeitgeist as the seemingly abstract movement of information, we cannot ignore the depletion of physical and financial resources that make it possible. Although we focus on oil and energy due to Liebig's Law[2], the global limits we face are all-encompassing [30] and thus our survey of these issues, and of the post-peak era sometimes called the Long Emergency, is necessarily truncated; we refer interested readers to the many works on the subject [10, 12, 13, 18, 19, 21, 23, 26, 29, 30, 35, 36, 38].

2.1 Fossil Fuel Dependence

Industrialized economies require oil for vital functions such as transportation, manufacturing, and agriculture; they similarly depend on coal and natural gas for the production of electricity.[3] Combined, these three fossil fuels account for 81% of global energy consumption [1], and oil is the plurality of that share. Since oil is the most malleable and energy-dense of these fossil fuels, it is also the most highly prized (especially for transportation, which consumes 61% of global oil production). Oil is also an essential input in the extraction, production, and transportation of other energy resources, from coal to natural gas to alternative technologies.

Because fossil fuels are non-renewable, there is a point at which the rate of resource extraction reaches a peak and begins to decline. A persistent decline in annual energy yields can significantly disrupt the economy. Thus a pressing matter is the question of timing—when do we expect to face energy constraints?

2.2 Near-Term Energy Shortage

In 2005 the U.S. Department of Energy commissioned a study known as the Hirsch report, which analyzed the timing, consequences, and mitigation of a peak and subsequent decline in world oil production [23]. Nine out of twelve of its forecasts predicted the date of peak oil production to occur by 2016. Similar studies were commissioned last year, projecting peak production by 2015: a consortium of British corporations (peak: 2014–15) [38], the German military (peak: 2010) [36], Kuwait University (peak: 2014) [31], the U.S. Defense Department (peak: 2012) [2], and Lloyd's of London (peak: 2013) [12]. The peak may even be behind us—the International Energy Agency suggests that conventional oil production may have peaked in 2006, though they anticipate no peak in all-liquids production [3].

None of these studies claims to be or can in fact be definitive—oil reserves and production capacity are closely guarded secrets in many countries, and a production peak can only be confirmed years after the fact because of year-to-year production variability. Also, as Heinberg notes, disagreement regarding the date of peak production is due to varied definitions of "oil", ranging from solely conventional crude to all liquid fuels; his study in 2003 concluded that an all-liquids peak would occur between 2006–2015 [18]. These studies represent a wide range of expert analysis that suggests that we will soon live in a world that has less oil available each year than the year before.

[2]Liebig's Law of the Minimum states that growth is limited not by total resources but by the most constrained resource [8].
[3]Nuclear provides a select few nations most of their electricity.

2.3 Inadequate Alternatives

Replacing oil is extremely difficult. Industrially feasible alternatives are environmentally-unfriendly whereas environmentally-friendly alternatives are industrially infeasible. Also, the scale of the transition requires a multi-decade effort, yet energy companies may be reluctant to immediately convert their current fossil-fuel infrastructure, which represents a $10 trillion investment that will require 10–50 years of continued operation to recover [29].

The Hirsch report surveyed a number of responses to the challenge of oil depletion: enhanced oil recovery, heavy oil / tar sands production, coal liquefaction, gas-to-liquids, and fuel-efficient vehicles; the report shows that such a successful mitigation response would not only have to begin at least *20 years before* the peak date, but also would have to be a *crash program*—one that takes on singular national importance and focus. Moreover, the report did not consider the environmental or climate impact of the above mitigation approaches. Because coal, heavy oil, and tar sands are highly polluting sources, increasing their use would have significant, negative consequences [16].

In a broader analysis, Heinberg evaluates the full spectrum of energy alternatives: he concludes that while it is possible that some alternatives may be viable in the future, they cannot easily replace oil in its role in transportation or agriculture [18]. Ignoring substitutability, Griffith constructs a hypothetical global energy profile (for the 2030s) using an array of alternatives [14]; however, for these alternatives (solar, wind, nuclear, etc.) current industrial capacity is inadequate and would require a WWII-like manufacturing effort. For example, we would have to construct nuclear power plants at roughly *5 times* the peak rate ever achieved globally—and sustain it for 20 years—to supply just the nuclear contribution to the alternative energy profile [14, 28].

While we can imagine optimistic future energy profiles, there exist no practical (i.e., within even generous assumptions about industrial capacity) and acceptable (i.e., no worse than oil environmentally) energy alternatives to address a *near-term peak* in oil production. While we believe a multi-decade transition to alternatives may be achievable, we expect that it will be extraordinarily difficult in the face of the economic consequences of peak oil.

2.4 Economic Consequences

The predominant way that oil depletion is expected to impact developed nations is via oil price shocks and consequent economic hardship. We omit a detailed survey of possible economic impacts in this paper, but note that most conventional economic analyses ignore the issue of oil depletion. It is however well established that high oil prices have been a factor in most recent recessions in the United States [15]. In addition, the Hirsch report provides a warning of the economic consequences of peak oil production, and that only via timely mitigation (at least 20 years before peak in a crash program) can these consequences be avoided [23]:

> "The long-run impact of sustained, significantly increased oil prices associated with oil peaking will be severe. Virtually certain are increases in inflation and unemployment, declines in the output of goods and services, and a degradation of living standards. Without timely mitigation, the long-run impact on the developed economies will almost certainly be extremely damaging, while many developing nations will likely be even worse off."

Said another way [18]:

> "Energy scarcity will cause a recession of a new kind—one from which anything other than a temporary, partial recovery will be impossible."

This will mark a new era for industrial society, and we believe computer networking may be eclipsed by more pressing needs such as food and transportation. Nevertheless, like McKibben we believe that the Internet is a key resource for the post-peak future, and therefore it is important for us to consider how to respond to this predicament.

3. NETWORKING RECONSIDERED

Although the challenges we face are dire, they also offer tremendous intellectual and practical prospects. In this section we consider what the future of networking might look like and how an energy descent will change the way we navigate systems constraints. After establishing this baseline panorama, we propose a set of guiding principles that may be valuable when developing research responses to these new challenges. Finally, we pose a series of concrete open questions on research challenges in post-peak networking that we believe are well worth answering. We hope this provides a starting point for discussion so that our community will consider future scenarios that differ markedly from conventional, optimistic projections of increasingly plentiful bandwidth, powerful cloud platforms, and rapid development and adoption of new technology. We begin by establishing several key premises.

3.1 Premises

Non-uniform / volatile descent. We expect that energy and financial constraints will affect different regions and nations at different times and with different degrees of severity, and we expect that both resource availability and prices are likely to exhibit dramatic volatility in the years ahead. As part of this variability, we expect the economy to proceed in cycles of contraction and partial recovery, with an overall downward trajectory [13, 18, 22, 23].

Economic impacts. We expect that economic decline (rather than direct impacts of energy scarcity) will be the primary challenge for networking in the initial post-peak years [18, 22, 23].

Liquid fuels, then electricity. We expect that the initial true energy constraint will be in liquid fuels and not in electricity [23], but that over time constraints and challenges will become more apparent with electricity and the grid [18].

Stalling trends. Much of systems and networking research depends upon the ability to project into the future and meet that future with a research solution. These projections often depend on a) the extension of current trends into the future, b) the expectation that the future will resemble the present, c) the analysis of technology stair-steps that are expected, or some combination of these approaches. We expect that such conventional projections are likely to be overly optimistic in a post-peak world; we expect current technology trends to slow or stall [30].

Relocalization. Those who have studied this predicament have by and large concluded that societal relocalization is a crucial (though imperfect) response [18, 26, 29, 35], since the cost of moving goods long distances will become prohibitive. We expect that relocalization of social and governing structures will begin to occur, though it may be slow at first.

Shrinking user bases. We expect the societal discontinuity we face—from growth to contraction—to eventually cause a decrease in the overall use of computing to meet societal needs. That is, low-energy or low-complexity alternatives may come to replace current technology [13, 18, 26, 29], though this process may take decades to even begin. Thus Metcalfe's Law will be forced to run in reverse: as user bases shrink, the value of certain technologies or systems may fall quite quickly.

3.2 A Future Scenario

To provide a concrete basis for discussion, we begin with a possible glimpse into our collective future. To ground this forecast, we first look to oil production. In the coming years, it appears that the best case for annual post-peak oil production decline is as follows: 1% for all-liquids production, 2% for crude production, and 4% for available net exports of crude [5, 9, 22]. Using Hirsch's estimate of a one-to-one correspondence between production decline and GDP decline, this roughly yields a *best-case* of *1-4% annual global economic decline* as long as no crash program is pursued [22].[4] A decline of 1-4% may not seem significant—it is on the order of an ordinary recession—but a consistent, long term decline in that range yields a best-case 5-19% decline over 5 years, 10-34% decline over 10 years, and 19-56% decline over 20 years.

Given the number of different complicating factors that will interact in the coming post-peak years—from agriculture to climate to finance to geopolitics—it is extremely difficult to make projections of any sort. Nevertheless, we attempt to provide one here based upon simple analyses of the impacts of past declines or shortfalls in oil production and compounding factors [15, 22]. In Table 1 we translate the decline rate into quantitative guesstimates of costs and other constraints for dates 5, 10, and 20 years post-peak.[5]

Since small decreases in the supply of commodities such as oil can yield large increases in prices, we expect that prices for transportation and shipping will go up significantly. Eventually we expect that electricity prices will follow due to the falling net energy of present and future sources and the increased input cost of oil in their production.[6] We present our projections as ranges since we expect there to be significant variation between regions and over time. Thus in our view, the challenge for systems and networking researchers is in coping with the full range of these radically new constraints, though in the near term they will first be felt by those who operate today's networks.

The constant upgrading and maintenance of the Internet and network infrastructure today is not a cheap undertaking: telecoms spent about $3 trillion over the last decade on capital expenditures [24]. Thus some operations may be downscaled or canceled for lack of funds; we suspect that R&D and maintenance may be the first to go, as the former requires the promise of future financial growth and the latter requires the constant use of expensive

---

[4]Hirsch's best-case scenario projection is a slightly more pessimistic 2-5% annual decline [22]. Also, as we stated earlier, we expect the decline to be uneven across regions and time, with periods of partial recovery.

[5]Our guesstimates are roughly in line with similar analyses such as that of the recent IMF World Economic Outlook, which projects that a 2% annual decline in oil production would result in a price increase of 8x over 20 years (not considering declining purchasing power or other factors) [4].

[6]For example, we may be at peak energy from coal [34] or soon at peak cheap coal [20]; also, other analyses put all future potential sources at far below the net energy of past sources [19].

Category	Years Post-Peak		
	5	10	20
Transportation	3-5x	5-15x	10-25x
Electricity	2-4x	2-10x	5-20x
Grid Reliability	98-99%	95-99%	75-98%
Discretionary Income	5-15%	2-10%	1-5%

Table 1: A set of possible post-peak constraints for industrial nations given a 1-4% annual decline and no crash program. Transportation and electricity are expressed as costs relative to peak in terms of purchasing power, grid reliability is in uptime, and discretionary income is in % of median household budget.

resources. Just as recent studies have indicated that the aviation industry is likely to discontinue service to smaller, rural airports in response to energy descent [29], we expect telecoms will have a financial incentive to focus on their networks in major cities at the expense of less populated regions. This will likely have a downstream effect on hardware vendors, who rely on network infrastructure operators to regularly purchase new equipment and service contracts. Since we expect end users to have less discretionary income, network services and device vendors that depend upon consumer spending will face threats to their existence as the ubiquity of networking declines.

3.3 Principles

To design for a post-peak world, we will have to revisit the doctrines that guide present-day networking. Below, we discuss six principles that we believe are worth considering, all of which are already known and applied in specific contexts.

P1. Target Absolute (not Relative) Consumption. For an energy descent to be controlled and intelligent rather than uncontrolled and haphazard, our energy constraint must be self-imposed rather than exogenous [13, 19, 29]. Thus rather than aiming to improve status quo energy consumption by some relative fraction, resource-efficient networking should aim to work within a specific energy and resource budget. By targeting an absolute consumption goal—which may be orders of magnitude lower than current-day consumption—it may be necessary to discard components, services, etc. that cannot be sustained within that constraint.

P2. Account for All Energy Inputs. A common myth is that technological innovation alone can solve our energy challenges—this ignores that all technology depends upon and is distinct from energy. Fundamentally, any energy technology must derive its energy from one of the sources available on Earth. All new energy technologies require some resources and some energy expenditure to construct (e.g. the energy and resources to build a power plant or a solar panel), and quantifying this expenditure is crucial—this is captured in the well-known concepts of Energy Returned on Investment (EROI) and net energy [19]. Embodied energy (*emergy*) or life-cycle energy—the amount of energy used to mine, assemble, transport, use, dispose, etc. a system or device—is similar to EROI and applies to all systems, including networking technology [32].[7] In particular, we should not focus exclusively on the operational power cost of a networked system. There is no doubt

[7]As Odum noted in his classic work, "The natural conversion of sunlight to electric charge that occurs in all green-plant photosynthesis after 1 billion years of natural selection may already be the highest net emergy possible." [32]

that recursively accounting for all energy inputs for a system (from manufacture, to installation, to operation, to disposal, etc.) will be challenging. However, accounting for these inputs will be important for determining whether existing and future networking and energy technologies are truly "green" or whether they use more energy to create than they will save.

P3. Reuse Hardware and Software. In a scenario where energy and other resources are scarce, creating new energy-efficient network devices to replace old network devices and/or their software potentially increases the energy deficit—the embodied energy costs of new devices would accumulate quickly. Thus we must be willing to reuse existing hardware and software. A future Internet may consist of partially-disconnected networks cobbled together using a range of different protocol stacks that suit each local region. As a result, we may have to account for a higher degree of hardware and software diversity than for present-day standards, which assume that perpetual, periodic upgrades are the norm.

P4. Design Resilient Systems. An old urban legend is that the Internet was designed to survive a nuclear war. However, the story is apocryphal and we have in fact a limited understanding about the resilience of the Internet. Today's Internet has grown organically; the evolution of its interconnection has been a disorderly process and the complete topology is unknown. Beyond the basic structure of the network, years of research have suggested that it is important to design robust and resilient network protocols [6]. Designing and studying resilient protocols and systems will be especially important since economic decline, energy shortages, and an erratic climate can only make network infrastructure less reliable.

P5. Become Multidisciplinary. To conduct networking research in the context of an energy-deprived society, we must gain a deeper understanding of the environment and the constraints. For example, if we want to assess the energy inputs and resilience of a networked system (including its materials, assembly, transportation, maintenance, impacts, etc.), then collaborating with geologists, mechanical and civil engineers, ecologists, and others will be crucial. It will become increasingly difficult to think about networking in isolation because the multi-faceted nature of the post-peak scenario will no doubt impact networking.

P6. Build Self-Sustaining Systems. Current networks are composed of a complex array of hardware and software assembled around the world with materials, energy, skills, and designs also from a global resource base. We expect that today's approach to the design, creation, and deployment of networking technology is likely, in time, to become too costly or simply physically infeasible. Thus networking technology should follow the principles of Appropriate Technology [17, 37]: be designed to be a) simple, b) locally reproducible, c) composed of local materials / resources, d) easily repairable, e) affordable, and f) easily recyclable.

3.4 A Research Agenda

Next we propose a research agenda of open questions that range in flavor from specific to broad. The list of questions is far from exhaustive, and the questions themselves may require significant refinement; we offer them as concrete starting points.

3.4.1 Network Structure

While today's networks and services are generally oligarchic in nature, we expect that a post-peak Internet will need to distribute all of its functions in the service of relocalization. The "core" may cease to be a clear group of providers, and the hierarchy might break down. In this model, services and control might be pushed further to what we think of today as the edge of the network.

Open Question 1. *As networks become more localized, the cost and latency of communicating with far away nodes will be higher than it is today. How will we cope with this?*

Open Question 2. *How might we carefully guide this structural transition (transferring management from the core to the edges), instead of allowing it to descend haphazardly?*

Open Question 3. *What do standards look like post-peak? What role do standards bodies such as ICANN and IETF play?*

Open Question 4. *What cost sharing mechanisms can be feasibly deployed to offload a substantial portion of the true cost of a network service onto its user?*

Open Question 5. *What does the programming model for a fully-distributed datacenter-less cloud look like?*

3.4.2 Reevaluation

We are moving into the post-peak future with a huge existing base of networking hardware, software, protocols, and metrics. We must begin to reevaluate networks, networking components, and network research in a new light, with changed constraints, goals, metrics, and circumstances—in particular, accounting for the emergy of devices, as well as coping with greater network volatility. In doing so, we might find that some protocols and systems can readily be adapted or salvaged, while others must be discarded.

Open Question 6. *Can we develop a common methodology for calculating the emergy of a network device? Can hardware vendors develop a standard for describing how much energy went into producing a device?*

Open Question 7. *Can we measure which existing projects in energy-efficient networking are well-suited to the post-peak world and which are not?*

Open Question 8. *When do free network services become infeasible due to energy costs? In other words, at what price per KWh (and auxiliary costs in real terms) will Google no longer be able to offer free searches?*

Open Question 9. *How can network protocols be best redesigned to cope with post-peak volatility?*

Open Question 10. *How can existing software implementations of network protocols be re-purposed without modification?*

Open Question 11. *When is it the case that software upgrades—while using old hardware—are preferable to upgrading to a more resource-efficient hardware platform?*

Open Question 12. *Will wireless deployments continue to be a good bet? Or will the emergy and power cost of wireless devices and infrastructure eventually make them cost prohibitive vs. reusing old wire-line infrastructure?*

Open Question 13. *Which services provided by the Internet are least essential to its continued value and operation? Which are most essential?*

3.4.3 Integration

Coping with the complexities and vicissitudes of a post-peak world is likely to require knowledge from more than one domain or field of study. Old models and expertise in one area may apply to the new circumstances in another. Systems may need to be more than the sum of their parts for their continued survival.

Open Question 14. *Can we encourage more video conferencing adoption by incorporating computer vision or similar techniques into video streaming protocols to augment the video?*

Open Question 15. *Can computer network protocols and algorithms be applied to transportation networks (or vice versa) so as to improve their overall efficiency?*

Open Question 16. *Using today's architecture, how can we enable and promote a systematic way of leveraging cross-layer and network-internal knowledge at end points?*

Open Question 17. *What are the economic models for a demand-based pricing system for a post-peak Internet?*

Open Question 18. *How will the economics of network misbehavior (spam, DoS, malware, etc.) change post-peak?*

Open Question 19. *How can a secure, peer-to-peer localized microlending system be built?*

3.4.4 Components and Tools

Ultimately, the network is only going to be of value to post-peak society if it meets basic needs. For this reason, specifically engineering components and tools for new constraints will be of great value.

Open Question 20. *What is the minimal set of mining facilities, hardware manufacturing, software tools, etc., all capable of self-bootstrapping, that can provide all the needed components of the Internet? How small and cheaply can it be made?*

Open Question 21. *How can network switches and routers be built to passively perform forwarding?*

Open Question 22. *How might technology costs and energy trends change with respect to in-network storage, and when will it become unviable?*

Open Question 23. *How can a long-term network-attached data archival service be designed to provide persistence and proof of storage?*

Open Question 24. *Can we develop a "currency" for local network bandwidth sharing?*

Open Question 25. *How might networks leverage older, simpler technologies such as packet radio?*

4. RELATED WORK

In the last decade, and especially in the last few years, networking researchers have turned their attention to improving the energy efficiency of network devices, protocols, and systems and to reevaluating and integrating prior approaches. Some recent efforts have looked at large-scale challenges, such as applying networking ideas to the design of smart grids [25, 27]. We believe that these strands of research are valuable—and too broad to itemize here—and can be repurposed to target the future we describe in this paper.

The work that may in fact be closest in spirit to what we describe herein is networking research for developing regions [7, 33]. This body of work has typically encompassed low-cost, low-energy, and low-infrastructure solutions to networking problems. While the constraints in developing-regions research are somewhat different—the regions in question typically have little existing infrastructure or computing resources and likewise have little dependence upon them—once again its techniques can likely be repurposed to meet these new challenges. However, for bootstrapping—manufacturing, deployment, and repair—such work typically relies upon the globalized, fossil-fuel based industrial system.

More broadly, research into resilient network models such as delay-tolerant networking [11] and older network technologies such as packet radio are highly appropriate for further exploration as approaches for post-peak networking. The key properties that these and similar approaches possess is a key ability to function in a wide range of operating conditions during an irregular post-peak decline over time and across space.

5. CONCLUSIONS

"And so we turn to the essentials of our future. In order: food, energy, and—yes—the Internet" says McKibben [29]. Modern society has never before faced a predicament like this. Experts in food and energy and myriad other areas are beginning to take appropriate action and we believe that it is incumbent upon us, as researchers in one of these most crucial areas of study, to do our part.

6. ACKNOWLEDGEMENTS

We thank Scott Shenker, John Michael Greer, Harsha Madhyastha, Stuart Staniford, Jenny Trujillo, and the anonymous reviewers for their encouragement and thoughtful feedback.

7. REFERENCES

[1] Key world energy statistics. *International Energy Agency*, 2010.

[2] The Joint Operating Environment. *U.S. Joint Forces Command*, 2010.

[3] World energy outlook. *International Energy Agency*, 2010.

[4] World economic outlook. *International Monetary Fund*, 2011.

[5] K. Aleklett, M. Höök, K. Jakobsson, M. Lardelli, S. Snowden, and B. Söderbergh. The Peak of the Oil Age-Analyzing the world oil production Reference Scenario in World Energy Outlook 2008. *Energy Policy*, 38(3), 2010.

[6] T. Anderson, S. Shenker, I. Stoica, and D. Wetherall. Design guidelines for robust Internet protocols. In *Proceedings of HotNets*, 2002.

[7] E. Brewer, M. Demmer, B. Du, M. Ho, M. Kam, S. Nedevschi, J. Pal, R. Patra, S. Surana, and K. Fall. The case for technology in developing regions. *IEEE Computer*, 38(6), 2005.

[8] R. Brewer. *Principles of ecology*. Saunders, 1979.

[9] J. J. Brown and S. Foucher. Egypt, a Classic Case of Rapid Net-Export Decline and a Look at Global Net Exports. *ASPO-USA*, Feb. 2011.

[10] K. Deffeyes. *Beyond oil: The view from Hubbert's Peak*. Farrar, Straus, and Giroux, 2005.

[11] K. Fall. A delay-tolerant network architecture for challenged internets. In *Proceedings of ACM SIGCOMM*, 2003.

[12] A. Froggatt and G. Lahn. Sustainable energy security: Strategic risks and opportunities for business. *Chatham House-Lloyd's 360 Risk Insight White Paper*, 2010.

[13] J. M. Greer. *The Long Descent*. New Society Publishers, 2008.

[14] S. Griffith. Climate change recalculated. In *The Long Now Foundation Seminars*, 2009.

[15] J. Hamilton. Causes and Consequences of the Oil Shock of 2007–08. *Brookings Papers on Economic Activity*, 2009.

[16] J. Hansen. The threat to the planet. *The New York Review of Books*, Jul. 13, 2006.

[17] B. Hazeltine and C. Bull. *Appropriate Technology; Tools, Choices, and Implications*. Academic Press, 1998.

[18] R. Heinberg. *The Party's Over*. New Society Publishers, 2003.

[19] R. Heinberg. Searching for a Miracle:"Net Energy" Limits and the Fate of Industrial Society. *The International Forum on Globalization and the Post Carbon Institute*, 2009.

[20] R. Heinberg and D. Fridley. The end of cheap coal. *Nature*, 468(7322), 2010.

[21] R. Heinberg and D. Lerch. *The Post Carbon Reader: Managing the 21st Century's Sustainability Crises*. University of California Press, 2010.

[22] R. Hirsch. Mitigation of maximum world oil production: Shortage scenarios. *Energy Policy*, 36(2), 2008.

[23] R. Hirsch, R. Bezdek, and R. Wendling. Peaking of World Oil Production: Impacts, Mitigation, & Risk Management. *U.S. Department of Energy NETL*, 2005.

[24] Infonetics Research. http://www.infonetics.com/.

[25] S. Keshav and C. Rosenberg. How internet concepts and technologies can help green and smarten the electrical grid. In *Proceedings of the ACM SIGCOMM Workshop on Green Networking*, 2010.

[26] J. Kunstler. *The Long Emergency*. Grove Press, 2005.

[27] LoCal Project. http://local.cs.berkeley.edu/.

[28] D. MacKay. *Sustainable Energy — without the hot air*. UIT, 2009.

[29] B. McKibben. *Eaarth: Making a life on a tough new planet*. Henry Holt and Company, 2010.

[30] D. Meadows, J. Randers, and D. Meadows. *The limits to growth: the 30-year update*. Chelsea Green, 2004.

[31] I. Nashawi, A. Malallah, and M. Al-Bisharah. Forecasting world crude oil production using multicyclic Hubbert model. *Energy & Fuels*, 24(3), 2010.

[32] H. Odum. *Environmental accounting: emergy and environmental decision making*. John Wiley and Sons, 1996.

[33] T. Parikh and E. Lazowska. Designing an architecture for delivering mobile information services to the rural developing world. In *Proceedings of ACM WWW*, 2006.

[34] T. Patzek and G. Croft. A global coal production forecast with multi-Hubbert cycle analysis. *Energy*, 35(8), 2010.

[35] J. Rubin. *Why your world is about to get a whole lot smaller*. Random House of Canada, 2009.

[36] S. Schultz. Military study warns of a potentially drastic oil crisis. *Der Spiegel*, Sep. 1, 2010.

[37] E. Schumacher. *Small is Beautiful: A study of economics as if people mattered*. Abacus, 1974.

[38] W. Whitehorn, S. Roberts, J. Miles, S. Behling, I. Marchant, J. Chandler, S. Leggett, S. Stewart, N. Fox, and A. Knight. The Oil Crunch - a wake-up call for the UK economy. *Second report of the UK Industry Taskforce on Peak Oil and Energy Security*, 2010.

Towards Continuous Policy-driven Demand Response in Data Centers

David Irwin, Navin Sharma, and Prashant Shenoy
University of Massachusetts, Amherst
{irwin,nksharma,shenoy}@cs.umass.edu

ABSTRACT

Demand response (DR) is a technique for balancing electricity supply and demand by regulating power consumption instead of generation. DR is a key technology for emerging smart electric grids that aim to increase grid efficiency, while incorporating significant amounts of clean renewable energy sources. In today's grid, DR is a rare event that only occurs when actual peak demands exceed the expected peak. In contrast, smart electric grids incentivize consumers to engage in continuous policy-driven DR to 1) optimize power consumption for time-of-use pricing and 2) deal with power variations from non-dispatchable renewable energy sources. While data centers are well-positioned to exploit DR, applications must cope with significant, frequent, and unpredictable changes in available power by regulating their energy footprint.

The problem is challenging since data centers often use distributed storage systems that co-locate computation and storage, and serve as a foundation for a variety of stateful distributed applications. As a result, existing approaches that deactivate servers as power decreases do not translate well to DR, since important application-level state may become completely unavailable. In this paper, we propose a DR-compatible storage system that uses staggered node blinking patterns combined with a balanced data layout and popularity-based replication to optimize I/O throughput, data availability, and energy-efficiency as power varies. Initial simulation results show the promise of our approach, which increases I/O throughput by at least 25% compared to an activation approach when adjusting to real-world wind and price fluctuations.

Categories and Subject Descriptors

C.5.0 [**Computer System Implementation**]: General

General Terms

Design, Management, Performance

1. INTRODUCTION

Data centers are rapidly expanding to accommodate the growth of online cloud-based services—facilities with hundreds of thousands of servers and up to a million cores are on the horizon. As is now well-known, larger data centers require more energy to power and cool their servers. The most recent estimates attribute 0.3%

Reprinted from the proceedings of GreenNet'11 with permission.

of *all* U.S. energy consumption specifically to data centers [11], with consumption estimated to double every 5 years [1]. Since over 83% of electrical energy in the U.S. derives from burning dirty fossil fuels, this rising energy demand has serious environmental ramifications [17]. Additionally, since the growth in society's energy demand is beginning to outpace its ability to locate, extract, and burn fossil fuels, energy prices are on a long-term upward trend [12]. Even using the "cheap" power available today, the energy-related costs of data centers already represent a significant fraction (~31% [10]) of their total cost of ownership. Thus, designing techniques to reduce the financial and environmental impact of data center energy consumption is an important problem. Energy price trends have already led data centers to experiment with alternative energy sources, such as wind [9], solar [20], and tidal [21].

Prior research focuses largely on increasing overall energy-efficiency by reducing data center energy consumption. For example, power-proportional data centers and servers that consume power in proportion to workload demands, e.g., by deactivating idle servers, increase efficiency by significantly reducing wasted power from idle servers [6, 26]. Likewise, balanced systems increase efficiency by reducing wasted power from idle server components [5, 23]. However, little prior research focuses on optimizing *when* data centers consume power. The timing of data center power consumption has a disproportionate affect on both the monetary cost and carbon footprint of power generation for at least two reasons.

Heterogenous Generators. Utilities operate a variety of generators that vary in their carbon emissions and fuel costs. For instance, the "peaking" generators that satisfy transient demand peaks have significantly higher emissions and fuel costs than the baseload generators that operate continuously. Thus, electricity generated during peak hours is more expensive and "dirty" than off-peak hours.

Intermittent Renewables. Both data centers and utilities are beginning to harvest energy from intermittent renewable power sources, such as wind and solar, which have no carbon footprint or fuel costs. As a result, data centers have an opportunity to decrease their carbon footprint by aligning when they consume power with when these clean energy sources are producing it.

The economics of power generation is also motivating utilities to adopt a variety of pricing structures that better reflect generation costs. As one example, utilities often add surcharges to electricity bills based on peak electricity usage over a billing cycle to incentivize consumers to "flatten" their electricity demand. As another example, many utilities are shifting from flat-rate pricing models for consumers to time-of-use pricing models that allow electricity prices to rise and fall with demand. Such market-based pricing, which is already common in wholesale electricity markets, incentivizes consumers to shift their usage to off-peak hours. Additionally, to further encourage the use of intermittent renewables, governments are beginning to impose cap-and-trade policies that artificially increase the cost of energy from fossil fuels. For example, a cap-and-trade policy went into effect in the U.K. in April 2010 for businesses consuming more than 6GWh per year [14]. Each of the examples above represent strong monetary incentives for consumers, including data centers, to regulate not only how much power they consume, but also when they consume power. These incentives are an integral part of recent smart grid efforts.

Demand response (DR) is a general term for dynamically regulating energy consumption over time. In today's electric grid, utilities typically implement DR by manually signaling large consumers, e.g., via phone or email, to request reductions in their electricity usage during times of grid congestion or capacity constraints. Since the grid has the generation capacity to meet estimated peak demands, it uses DR rarely to prevent unexpected outages or "brownout" scenarios. As smart grid efforts expand, we envision consumers engaging in *continuous policy-driven DR* to optimize power consumption for time-of-use market-based pricing or to deal with power variations from non-dispatchable renewable energy sources. In this case, rather than the utility directing consumer DR on rare occasions, consumers will automatically decide when and how to consume power based on automated policies that precisely control their cost and carbon footprint.

Data centers are particularly well-positioned to adopt and benefit from continuous policy-driven DR for at least three reasons.

- First, servers already include sophisticated power management mechanisms that are remotely programmable. As a result, data centers are capable of programmatically varying their power consumption over a wide dynamic power range.

- Second, many workloads are tolerant to delays or performance degradation, enabling data centers to adjust their power consumption over time. The price elasticity of demand is higher for these flexible workloads than many household and industrial loads, which are not highly responsive to price fluctuations.

- Finally, data centers are large industrial power consumers that have a substantial impact on grid conditions—utilities typically target these large consumers for DR first.

Due to the explosive growth of data center size and energy consumption, a 2007 EPA report to Congress on data center energy efficiency encourages them to adopt DR to reduce their strain on the electric grid [1]. However, *to exploit DR, the key challenge that systems researchers must address is designing applications that perform well in the face of significant, frequent, and potentially unpredictable variations in power.* Thus, designing for DR differs significantly from past research efforts on designing for energy-efficiency or proportionality. Rather than optimizing the energy required to satisfy a given workload, designing for DR requires systems to optimize application performance as power varies. The problem is particularly challenging *since power fluctuations may occur independently of workload demands.*

2. BLINKING: A GENERAL DR ABSTRACTION FOR DATA CENTERS

There are multiple possible approaches to handling power variations in data centers. One option is to migrate workload, in the form of virtual machines (VMs), from locations with power shortages to those with power surpluses [3]. For example, solar-powered data centers may migrate VMs to daytime locations to handle nighttime power shortages. Power costs for geographically-disparate data centers may differ for a variety of other reasons as well [22], motivating migrations to data centers with cheap power. However, despite recent advances in optimizing live VM migration for the wide-area network links between data centers [28], the approach is not

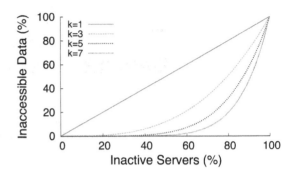

Figure 1: Inactive servers result in inaccessible data. Replication mitigates, but does not eliminate, the problem, especially for high percentages (>50%) of inactive servers.

suitable for data-intensive workloads that access vast amounts of storage. Even with dedicated high-bandwidth network links, daily transfers of multi-petabyte storage volumes is infeasible. Further, while solar power may vary somewhat slowly and predictably on a daily basis, in general, data centers may wish to optimize for power variations that are much more rapid and unpredictable, e.g., from changing spot prices or wind power.

We recently proposed a new technique, called blinking [24], to regulate a data center's energy footprint in response to power variations. Blinking rapidly transitions servers between a high-power active state and a low-power inactive sleep state. Since power consumption in the inactive state, e.g., ACPI's S3 state, is minimal, it is possible to regulate cluster energy consumption over small time scales by changing the relative duration of each server's active and inactive modes. We briefly outline our implementation of a prototype blinking cluster in Section 4. In prior work, we demonstrate how to enable blinking in memcached, a stateless distributed memory cache [24]. However, we intend blinking to be a *general abstraction for implementing DR for a wide range of data center applications.* In this paper, we examine how blinking might enable DR for the distributed storage systems now common in data centers. Since power variations result in servers becoming periodically unavailable, distributed storage represents one of the most challenging problems for implementing DR in data centers.

The blinking abstraction supports a variety of *blinking policies.* For instance, an *activation* policy is any blinking policy that only varies the fraction of inactive servers to vary power consumption. Activation policies are commonly used to ensure data centers are energy-proportional by varying the fraction of active servers to match demand [4, 16, 26]. Prior research has also used activation policies to address power variations from renewable energy sources, although the primary focus is on simple computationally-intensive workloads using always-accessible storage [15]. The blinking abstraction permits other more sophisticated policies as well, including *synchronous* policies that transition servers between the active and inactive states in tandem, *asynchronous* policies that stagger server active periods over time, and various *asymmetric* policies that blink servers at different rates based on application-specific performance metrics. In the next section, we focus on issues with enabling DR for distributed storage, and discuss the disadvantages of commonly-used activation policies.

3. PROBLEMS WITH ACTIVATION

Distributed storage layers, such as HDFS [25], distribute data across compute servers in data centers, and serve as the foundation for many higher-level distributed data center applications. An activation policy that naïvely deactivates servers to save energy or match a given level of available power is capable of making the data on inactive servers inaccessible. One way to prevent data on inactive servers from becoming inaccessible is by storing replicas on active servers. Replication is already used to improve the performance and reliability of distributed storage, and works well for an activation policy if the number of inactive servers is small. For example, with HDFS's random replica placement policy, the probability that any block is unavailable is $\frac{m!(n-k)!}{n!(m-k)!}$ for n servers, m inactive servers, and k replicas per block. Figure 1 plots the expected percentage of inaccessible data as a function of the percentage of inactive servers, and shows that nearly all data is accessible for small percentages of inactive servers.

However, the amount of inaccessible data rises dramatically once 50% of servers are inactive, even for aggressive replication factors, e.g., $k = 7$. Frequent periods of low power and many inactive servers is a common case for many DR scenarios. Further, even a few inactive servers, where the expected percentage of inaccessible data is small, have the potential to cause significant performance issues, e.g., by stalling large batch jobs that are dependent on some inaccessible data. One way to address the problem is through careful placement of data and replicas. For instance, prior work on energy-efficient distributed storage proposes data layouts that enable servers to be deactivated without causing any data to become unavailable [4, 13, 18]. In general, the proposed layouts store primary replicas on one subset of servers, secondary replicas on another mutually-exclusive subset, tertiary replicas on yet another subset, etc. However, these *concentrated data layouts* introduce at least three issues if available power varies frequently and significantly, and is independent of workload demands.

Wasteful Thrashing. Power variations may trigger frequent changes to the number of the active servers storing primary, secondary, tertiary, etc. replicas that require migrations to either 1) spread data out to provide higher I/O throughput or 2) concentrate data to keep it accessible. Minimizing these migration overheads is a focus of prior work on energy-efficient storage [29].

Wasted Capacity. Recent work on energy-proportional distributed storage reduces migration-related thrashing by making replica sets progressively larger, e.g., more servers store secondary replicas than primary replicas [4]. Assuming servers have similar storage capacity, the approach wastes progressively more capacity on the servers storing secondary, tertiary, etc. replicas.

Inaccessible Data. Regardless of the data layout, if there is not enough power to activate the necessary servers to store a complete data set, then some data will be inaccessible. Thus, even data layouts that ensure a small "covering" subset of servers store all primary replicas has the potential to make data inaccessible [18].

To highlight the problems of wasteful thrashing and inaccessible data, consider a simple example where there is enough power to currently operate $2N$ servers storing a data set's primary replicas. Also assume that the data set fills the storage capacity of N servers. Now consider the consequences of a sudden and unexpected drop in power by a factor 2, which leaves only N servers active. To ensure that the data is available, we must migrate to a new concentrated data layout that spreads data across the N active servers. However, if we did not expect the drop, there may not have been enough time to migrate to the more concentrated data layout. In this case, 50% of the data may be inaccessible even if we have enough capacity to store it on N active servers. Now consider what happens if available power drops again by a factor of 2, which leaves only $0.5N$ remaining active servers. Since the data set fills the storage capacity of N servers, migration is not even possible and 50%

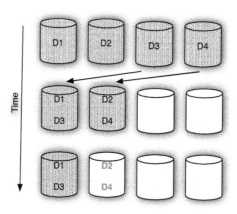

Figure 2: Power variations may cause the subset of active servers storing a data set's primary replicas to decrease, which triggers costly migrations to keep data accessible. At low power levels, some data is certain to be inaccessible.

of the data set is inaccessible at best. Figure 2 graphically depicts our example for $N = 4$. Note that power increases also require time-consuming data migrations to spread data out and increase aggregate I/O throughput. In the next section we discuss a blinking approach that addresses the problems above, while providing better I/O throughput, data availability, and energy-efficiency.

4. BLINKING DISTRIBUTED STORAGE

We first provide a brief summary of blinking. Our prior work includes a complete description, and applies the concept to a simple distributed memory cache that does not persist data [24]. Blinking is a simple mechanism that enables an external controller to remotely set a blink interval t and an active interval t_{active} on a server, such that for every interval t a server is active for time t_{active} and inactive for time $t - t_{active}$. ACPI's S3 state is a good choice for the inactive state, since it combines the capability for fast millisecond-scale transitions with low power consumption (<5% peak power). In contrast, component-level techniques, such as DVFS, are much less effective at satisfying steep drops in available power, since they are often unable to reduce consumption below 50% peak power [27]. To control inter-server blinking patterns, the blinking abstraction also enables a controller to specify when a blink interval starts, as well as when within a blink interval the active interval starts.

To illustrate the advantages of blinking distributed storage for DR, we consider our example from the previous section and discuss how blinking affects I/O throughput, data availability and request latency, and energy-efficiency. We assume the use of flash-based SSDs, which have already been shown to be more energy-efficient than disks for a range of both seek- and scan-intensive workloads [5, 23, 27]. As a result, flash-based SSDs are becoming increasingly popular for data-intensive workloads. Flash-based SSDs are also compatible with blinking, which relies on frequent and rapid transitions between power states. Blinking could also be applicable to mechanical disks, but would require a new low-power state that is similar to ACPI's S3 state but permits disks to remain spun-up. Frequent disk spin-up and spin-down transitions have been shown to degrade their reliability [29].

4.1 I/O Throughput

Recall that in our example there is initially enough power to operate $2N$ servers that each provide storage for a fraction of our

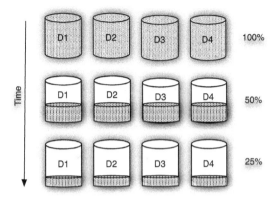

Figure 3: Power variations decrease the fraction of time each server is active during a blink interval. No migrations are necessary to adjust to power variations, since all blocks are accessible for a fraction of each blink interval.

data set. If the available power decreases by a factor of 2, with blinking we have the option of keeping $2N$ servers active for time $t_{active} = \frac{t}{2}$ every blink interval t. In this case, instead of migrating data and concentrating it on N active servers, we are able to keep the same data layout as before without changing our maximum I/O throughput over each blink interval, assuming negligible transition overheads. To see why, consider that a layout that concentrates data storage on N servers is capable of NM MB/sec, assuming a maximum I/O throughput per server of M MB/sec, while a distributed layout on $2N$ servers with blinking is capable of $2NM$ MB/sec for half of every blink interval (or NM MB/sec on average).

Our example highlights that at any fixed power level, blinking is able to provide the same maximum I/O throughput, assuming negligible transition overheads, as an activation approach. Blinking, however, has a distinct advantage over activation if the available power changes, since it is possible to alter server active intervals nearly instantly to match the available power. In contrast to an activation approach, a blinking approach need not waste time and bandwidth by migrating data to 1) keep it accessible or 2) increase the maximum I/O throughput. If power suddenly drops again by another factor of 2, blinking is able to nearly instantly reduce each server's active interval by another 2x ($t_{active} = \frac{t}{4}$). Whereas with activation 50% of the data is completely inaccessible after the drop, blinking gracefully handles the drop by ensuring that 100% of the data is accessible for 25% of every blink interval. The average drop in aggregate I/O throughput per block is also proportional to the power drop (a factor of 2 to $0.5NM$ MB/sec). Since no migrations are necessary to gracefully handle the sudden power drop, there is no risk of inaccessible data due to unfinished migrations. Figure 3 graphically depicts our simple example with $N = 4$.

4.2 Data Availability and Latency

Blinking's primary drawback is a significant increase in average latency to retrieve data, since any request for data to an inactive server stalls until the server becomes active. If we assume that data access latency is negligible for data stored on active servers, then average latency increases from near 0 with a concentrated data layout in an activation approach (assuming all data is accessible) to $\frac{t-t_{active}}{2}$ with blinking, assuming request interarrival times are randomly distributed. Since blink intervals are on the order of 10s of seconds for platforms with transition latencies of a few hundred milliseconds, the latency penalty of our naïve blinking policy is

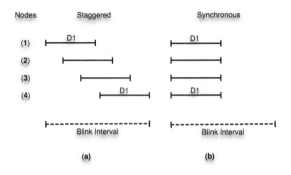

Figure 4: A staggered server blinking pattern is able to use replication to maximize the availability of data and decrease average I/O latency as power varies.

high. While a long average request latency is not important for long-running batch jobs that take many blink intervals to complete, it is important for shorter jobs or more interactive workloads.

One way to increase data availability and reduce average I/O latency with blinking is using replication. Staggering server active intervals equally over each blink interval, by 1) ordering servers n_i for $i = 1, 2, 3, ...N$, 2) starting their active intervals in order, and 3) pausing for time t_{pause} after each activation, enables a simple replica placement policy that maximizes a block's availability over each blink interval, regardless of the available power. In this case, the size of t_{pause} varies according to available power. The placement policy spaces out block replicas among servers with active intervals that start as far apart as possible within each blink interval to minimize overlap in the active intervals. We contrast a staggered blinking schedule with a synchronous blinking schedule in Figure 4. While both blinking schedules provide the same I/O throughput, our staggered schedule reduces the average latency to access $D1$ by ensuring it is available for the entire blink interval.

As we discuss in our preliminary analysis, significantly reducing average latency may require aggressive replication. However, aggressively replicating all blocks significantly reduces storage capacity. Thus, *popularity-based replication and reclamation* of individual blocks is an important optimization for maintaining both low access latency and ample storage capacity. In this case, as blocks become more popular more replicas are deployed to increase availability, and as blocks become less popular more replicas are reclaimed to increase capacity. Additionally, data centers could use small amounts of stored power from battery arrays to power additional servers and accelerate replication for blocks that gain popularity rapidly under low-power situations. While recent work demonstrates how to leverage stored power for multi-tier web applications [8], DR for distributed storage represents another opportunity for leveraging local energy storage.

Further, unlike data layouts that concentrate replicas on mutually-exclusive subsets of servers, blinking enables replica placement of blocks on servers to *balance* I/O throughput among servers. Load balancing to ensure each server stores equally popular data is a worthy goal at both high power—with all servers active—and low power—with a staggered blinking pattern. In contrast, the appropriate size of a server subset in a concentrated data layout changes with available power. One advantage of blinking is that data layout decisions, which are costly to change, need not be based on the available power level: replication combined with equally-sized, staggered active intervals reduces average latency under low power, while improving I/O throughput and reliability

Figure 5: Wind turbine and solar panel deployment on the roof of the Computer Science Building at the University of Massachusetts Amherst.

under high power. Finally, recent work [19] has demonstrated the difficulty of making online data-intensive services energy-proportional while maintaining low latency data access using conventional per-server power modes. Our DR-motivated techniques may also prove useful in this context.

4.3 Energy-efficiency

Blinking also improves energy-efficiency. Recent research points out the contradiction between deactivating servers to save energy and load balancing to decrease cooling costs, since fully active servers introduce hotspots that increase the energy consumption of cooling [2]. In contrast, staggering active intervals saves the same energy as deactivating servers, while eliminating hotspots by load balancing heat generation across all servers. Balancing power equally across servers is also useful under 3-phase power, since unequal consumption across phases wastes power and generates heat that requires additional energy to cool. Finally, since a staggered blinking policy minimizes the set of servers that is concurrently active, it reduces peak power. Both operational and capital costs are disproportionately affected by peak, rather than average, power [7].

5. PRELIMINARY ANALYSIS

To gain insight into DR's potential benefits for data centers, we simulated two DR scenarios for a small-scale 15-server prototype we are building, which uses SSD-enabled Mac minis connected to programmable power supplies that drive variable power traces. While DR is applicable in many scenarios, our analysis focuses on 1) powering our prototype using wind energy and 2) adhering to a fixed power budget despite variable energy prices. Both scenarios generate a variable supply of available power. For wind energy, we scale a power signal collected from our own small-scale wind turbine deployment [24], such that its average power is equal to the power our cluster requires. Figure 5 is a photograph of our wind turbine and solar panel deployment on the roof of the Computer Science Building. Since wind often generates no power for long time periods, we assume a base power level of 5% peak cluster power (18.75W). For variable prices, we use the New England ISO's 5-minute spot price of energy for the last 3 months of 2010.

Each Mac mini consumes a maximum of 25W for a total cluster power consumption of 375W. For our simulation, we assume each SSD stores 10GB of data and has infinite capacity to prevent inaccessible data due to a lack of storage space. Since the S3 transition latency is roughly 1 second, we assume a 60 second blink interval.

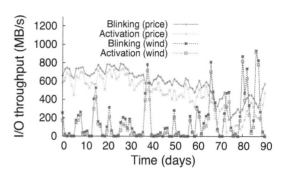

Figure 6: The maximum aggregate I/O throughput for blinking is greater than for activation for both our wind energy and variable price scenarios.

Our analysis assumes a maximum I/O throughput of 65 MB/sec per server, which represents roughly an equal mix of (fast) reads and (slow) writes to the SSD. We also assume that the migration speed between servers is equal to the maximum per-server I/O throughput. We then compare the maximum I/O throughput possible over a 3-month period for activation and blinking in both scenarios, where the activation approach must finish migrating data before accessing it and the blinking approach incurs 1 second of downtime every 60 seconds. The maximum aggregate I/O throughput is one important measure of the performance of a distributed storage system.

Figure 6 shows that blinking's I/O throughput is higher than activation in both scenarios. For wind, the average I/O throughput over the 3 month period is 174 MB/sec for blinking and 136 MB/sec for activation, yielding an improvement of nearly 28%. For variable prices, we use a budget of 2.67¢/kWh, which for our small-scale cluster, which translates to paying 1¢/hour for energy over the 3-month period. By comparison, the average price in our trace is 4.55¢/kWh, the peak price is 33.16¢/kWh, and the minimum price is 0.97¢/kWh. In this case, the average I/O throughput over the 3 month period is 575 MB/sec with blinking and 457 MB/sec with activation, yielding an improvement of over 25%. Thus, blinking enables either 25% more work to be done for the same budget, or the same work to be done for 25% less money.

Figure 7 shows that replication reduces average latency with blinking significantly, assuming a 20ms latency to access data on active servers. Since wind requires aggressive replication (10x) to reduce average latency below 1 second, due to many periods of no power, per-block popularity-based replication is an important optimization. Note that we are not advocating permanent 10x replication for every data object to decrease the latency penalty of intermittent power. Rather, we propose aggressive per-object popularity-based replication as objects become more popular, and aggressive replica reclamation as objects become less popular. Our premise is that the average latency for data-intensive workloads that exhibit high degrees of temporal locality should decrease significantly with per-object popularity-based replication, without a significant decrease in the aggregate storage capacity.

We view our simulation results, while admittedly rough, as a conservative estimate of blinking's benefits. In reality, network transfers will likely not be as fast as I/O, especially since the cluster will be using network bandwidth to do useful work, which will reduce activation's I/O throughput. Additionally, we assume only enough energy storage for 60 seconds. For wind energy, there are periods where our cluster is unable to consume 100% of the available wind energy. Thus, slightly more energy storage could provide significant benefits. Interestingly, with renewables, it is possible to

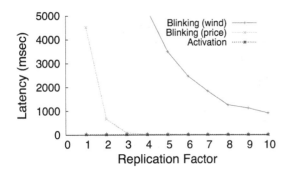

Figure 7: A small amount of replication is capable of significantly improving data access latency with blinking.

waste energy by not consuming more of it. We also do not quantify any of the potential indirect benefits to energy-efficiency discussed in Section 4.3. Finally, we assume data is never inaccessible with activation, which is not likely for significant power fluctuations.

6. CONCLUSION AND FUTURE WORK

While we focus on two examples—renewable energy and variable pricing—DR is applicable in other scenarios. For instance, DR is useful during grid power outages or when data center PDUs fail. Another compelling example is continuously running background workloads that always consume the excess power PDUs are capable of delivering. Since data center capital costs are enormous, maximizing the power delivery infrastructure's utilization by operating as many servers as possible is important. However, data centers provision power for peak demands, resulting in low utilization [7].

We are currently designing a distributed storage layer for DR. There are numerous challenges to address in a real system, although space limitations afford only a brief summary of them here. We are studying specific policies for deciding when and where to spawn or destroy replicas based on data popularity and application-specific performance goals. Additionally, applications that co-locate computation and data require a new mechanism to transfer data between servers if they are never concurrently active. Another challenge is ensuring consistency between replicas, while maintaining high throughput. In the worst case, an entire blink interval is necessary to ensure consistency. Performing well for write-intensive workloads is related, since writes apply to replicas on both active and inactive servers. We are exploring using a small set of always-active proxies to address these issues. Proxies absorb writes for an entire blink interval, and then apply them in order as servers become active in the next interval. Proxies may also act as routers, to transfer data between servers that are not concurrently active, or caches to store newly popular data during the replication process.

In conclusion, in this paper, we motivate DR for data centers, discuss the issues with enabling DR for distributed storage, and propose a DR-compatible blinking-based approach. While more work is necessary to validate our ideas, given current trends in energy consumption and pricing, we believe that DR is worth exploring in future data centers.

Acknowledgements. This work was supported by the National Science Foundation under grants CNS-0855128, CNS-0834243, CNS-0916577, and EEC-0313747.

7. REFERENCES

[1] U.S. Environmental Protection Agency. Report to Congress on Server and Data Center Energy Efficiency. August 2007.

[2] F. Ahmad and T. Vijaykumar. Joint Optimization of Idle and Cooling Power in Data Centers while Maintaining Response Time. In *ASPLOS*, March 2010.

[3] S. Akoush, R. Sohan, A. Rice, A. Moore, and A. Hopper. Free Lunch: Exploiting Renewable Energy for Computing. In *HotOS*, May 2011.

[4] H. Amur, J. Cipar, V. Gupta, M. Kozuch, G. Ganger, and K. Schwan. Robust and Flexible Power-Proportional Storage. In *SoCC*, June 2010.

[5] D. Andersen, J. Franklin, M. Kaminsky, A. Phanishayee, L. Tan, and V. Vasudevan. FAWN: A Fast Array of Wimpy Nodes. In *SOSP*, October 2009.

[6] L. Barroso and U. Hölzle. The Case for Energy-Proportional Computing. *Computer*, 40(12):33–37, December 2007.

[7] X. Fan, W. Weber, and L. Barroso. Power Provisioning for a Warehouse-Sized Computer. In *ISCA*, June 2007.

[8] S. Govindan, A. Sivasubramaniam, and B. Urgaonkar. Benefits and Limitations of Tapping into Stored Energy for Datacenters. In *ISCA*, June 2011.

[9] P. Gupta. Google to use Wind Energy to Power Data Centers. In *New York Times*, July 20th 2010.

[10] J. Hamilton. Overall Data Center Costs. In *Perspectives*. *http://perspectives.mvdirona.com/*, September 18, 2010.

[11] J. Hamilton. 2011 European Data Center Summit. http://perspectives.mvdirona.com/, May 25, 2011.

[12] R. Hirsch, R. Bezdek, and R. Wendling. Peaking of World Oil Production: Impacts, Mitigation, and Risk Management. In *U.S. Department of Energy*, February 2005.

[13] R. Kaushik and M. Bhandarkar. GreenHDFS: Towards an Energy-Conserving Storage-Efficient, Hybrid Hadoop Compute Cluster. In *USENIX Annual Technical Conference*, June 2010.

[14] United Kingdom. CRC Energy Efficiency Scheme. http://www.decc.gov.uk/, June 2011.

[15] A. Krioukov, C. Goebel, S. Alspaugh, Y. Chen, D. Culler, and R. Katz. Integrating Renewable Energy Using Data Analytics Systems: Challenges and Opportunities. In *Bulletin of the IEEE Computer Society Technical Committee*, March 2011.

[16] A. Krioukov, P. Mohan, S. Alspaugh, L. Keys, D. Culler, and R. Katz. NapSAC: Design and Implementation of a Power-Proportional Web Cluster. In *GreenNet*, August 2010.

[17] Lawrence Livermore National Laboratory. U.S. Energy Flowchart 2008. https://flowcharts.llnl.gov/, June 2011.

[18] J. Leverich and C. Kozyrakis. On the Energy (In)efficiency of Hadoop Clusters. In *HotPower*, October 2009.

[19] D. Meisner, C. Sadler, L. Barroso, W. Weber, and T. Wenisch. Power Management of Online Data-Intensive Services. In *ISCA*, June 2011.

[20] R. Miller. Microsoft to use Solar Panels in New Data Center. In *Data Center Knowledge*, September 24th 2008.

[21] R. Miller. Morgan Stanley Plans Tide-Powered Data Center. In *Data Center Knowledge*, October 17th 2008.

[22] A. Qureshi, R. Weber, H. Balakrishnan, J. Guttag, and B. Maggs. Cutting the Electric Bill for Internet-Scale Systems. In *SIGCOMM*, August 2009.

[23] S. Rivoire, M. Shah, , and P. Ranganathan. JouleSort: A Balanced Energy-Efficient Benchmark. In *SIGMOD*, June 2007.

[24] N. Sharma, S. Barker, D. Irwin, and P. Shenoy. Blink: Managing Server Clusters on Intermittent Power. In *ASPLOS*, March 2011.

[25] K. Shvachko, H. Kuang, S. Radia, and R. Chansler. The Hadoop Distributed File System. In *MSST*, May 2010.

[26] N. Tolia, Z. Wang, M. Marwah, C. Bash, P. Ranganathan, and X. Zhu. Delivering Energy Proportionality with Non-Energy-Proportional Systems: Optimizing the Ensemble. In *HotPower*, December 2008.

[27] V. Vasudevan, D. Andersen, M. Kaminsky, L. Tan, J. Franklin, and I. Moraru. Energy-efficient Cluster Computing with FAWN: Workloads and Implications. In *e-Energy*, April 2010.

[28] T. Wood, K. Ramakrishnan, P. Shenoy, and J. Van der Merwe. CloudNet: Dynamic Pooling of Cloud Resources by Live WAN Migration of Virtual Machines. In *VEE*, March 2011.

[29] Q. Zhu, Z. Chen, L. Tan, Y. Zhou, K. Keeton, and J. Wilkes. Hibernator: Helping Disk Arrays Sleep Through the Winter. In *SOSP*, October 2005.

Slicing Home Networks

Yiannis Yiakoumis   Kok-Kiong Yap   Sachin Katti   Guru Parulkar   Nick McKeown
Stanford University
{yiannisy,yapkke,skatti,parulkar,nickm}@stanford.edu

ABSTRACT

Despite the popularity of home networks, they face a number of systemic problems: (i) Broadband networks are expensive to deploy; and it is not clear how the cost can be shared by several service providers; (ii) Home networks are getting harder to manage as we connect more devices, use new applications, and rely on them for entertainment, communication and work—it is common for home networks to be poorly managed, insecure or just plain broken; and (iii) It is not clear how home networks will steadily improve, after they have been deployed, to provide steadily better service to home users.

In this paper we propose *slicing* home networks as a way to overcome these problems. As a mechanism, slicing allows multiple service providers to share a common infrastructure; and supports many policies and business models for cost sharing. We propose four requirements for slicing home networks: bandwidth and traffic isolation between slices, independent control of each slice, and the ability to modify and improve the behavior of a slice. We explore how these requirements allow cost-sharing, out-sourced management of home networks, and the ability to customize a slice to provide higher-quality service. Finally, we describe an initial prototype that we are deploying in homes.

Categories and Subject Descriptors

C2.1 [**Computer Systems Organization**]: COMPUTER-COMMUNICATION NETWORKS—*Network Architecture and Design*

General Terms

Design, Experimentation, Management

Keywords

Home Networks, Software-Defined Networks, Network Slicing, OpenFlow

Reprinted from the proceedings of HomeNets'11 with permission.

1. INTRODUCTION

Broadband connectivity, and a network inside the home, are essential ingredients of a modern household. A large variety of home devices connect to the Internet, and high bandwidth Internet applications such as video and audio streaming, high quality video conferencing, file sharing and backup are now commonplace. But despite huge investments in broadband, and over a decade of experience with home WiFi, home networks still face a number of systemic challenges:

Expensive to deploy: Broadband connections to the home require huge investment for initial buildout, and continued high investment to improve data rates. Governments and industry are investing many billions of dollars in broadband connectivity [2, 6]. Yet in almost every case, the cost is borne by a single investor—there are no effective ways to amortize the cost and share the burden among several providers. Almost everyone loses: Investors must take on enormous risk; service providers fear becoming "dumb bit pipes", unable to reap the rewards of their huge investment (and hence fueling concerns about network neutrality); most home owners can only choose between one or two providers, giving users little choice. Even if several providers would like to share the cost of the broadband connection (e.g. an Internet provider such as Verizon, and a utility provider for reading meters), there are no mechanisms to isolate the traffic and bandwidth between providers.

Hard to manage: Most home users lack the technical know-how (or the desire) to manage their home network. Networks typically operate with the default settings shipped with the access router. Worse, a large number of access routers are returned because users could not get them to function[1]. While there has been plenty of discussion of outsourcing the management of networks inside the home, it is not widespread. There is no common interface to home networking equipment to allow it to be remotely controlled.

Prone to failure: Networks in the home often suffer unpredictable failures (e.g high packet-loss and disconnection). Reasons for failures are numerous, ranging from poor AP placement, to interference with neighboring WiFi APs, to misconfigured APs and network settings. Presumably a service provider with access to more expert resources and technical know-how can better diagnose these failures and manage the network to deliver predictable and good performance. However, in spite of the strong incentives (e.g. Net-

---

[1]25% of wireless networking equipment is returned (of which 90% is fully functional)—one of the highest return rates among consumer electronics [3].

flix would be motivated to carefully manage the home network to deliver good streaming quality), current home networks lack the affordable mechanisms for the service provider to innovate and improve the behavior of the home network to increase the quality of the product they deliver.

Motivated by these challenges, we argue that future home networks should provide two capabilities. First, the capability to virtually split a physical network into multiple *slices*, and second, the capability to allow independent programmatic control of each slice. We believe such home network *slicing* can help solve the problems described above. Slicing can help reduce the cost of deployment, because it allows multiple providers to share the cost of deploying the physical network, and then co-exist on the deployed network substrate. For example, an internet service provider and a utility company might share the cost of deploying broadband to the home, and simultaneously use the network for providing broadband connectivity and smart metering, respectively. In the particular sliced networks we propose, the control plane is separated from the dataplane, and therefore users can out-source network configuration and management. Trusted third parties can programmatically control slices to better manage WiFi configuration, improve routing and implement access control (e.g. configure WiFi channel and power to minimize interference and/or set parental controls). We can take it one step further, and allow an application provider (e.g. Netflix) to control their own slice, and customize it to provide higher quality user experience.

Our proposed approach poses several new challenging requirements for the home network; this paper merely raises these concerns and suggests initial ideas on how to tackle them:

- *Isolation of traffic:* To safely share a network among multiple slices, the slicing mechanism has to ensure that data should not leak from one slice to another.

- *Isolation of bandwidth:* A slice should not be able to "starve" another slice of its bandwidth. This may include bandwidth on links, or in network processing elements, such as routers and access points.

- *Independent control:* Each provider should be able to control and manage its own slice as if it owns the underlying physical network. Separation of control gives each provider the opportunity to impove reliability, while allowing clear accountability.

- *Ability to customize and modify:* A provider should be able to modify and customize a slice to optimize the application according to its specific needs. For example it should decide which packets are blocked, how packets are routed, the power level of a wireless channel, and so on.

Our focus in this paper is on the design of the slicing mechanism itself, and not on the policies that govern how slicing is used or the individual services within a slice. As discussed above, the capability to slice enables a number of interesting economic models, from network sharing to outsourced network management to guaranteed QoS for specific content providers. Some of these models also have implications for regulatory policies such as network neutrality. Our goal however is modest: specifically, we aim to separate mechanism from policy, and design a mechanism that supports a number of policies and enables their independent evolution.

In the following section, we discuss in some detail a few representative applications of slicing. In particular, we will examine sharing the investment in broadband connections between Internet providers, smart-grid utilities and cellular companies; outsourcing network management and guest WiFi; and dedicated slices for video streaming. In §3 we describe one possible design for a sliced home network; in §4 we report on a prototype we are building and deploying to experiment with slicing in home networks. We refer to related work and conclude in §5 and §6.

2. APPLICATIONS

We pick three classes of application to motivate our exploration of slicing home networks. For each, we consider the importance of our four requirements: traffic isolation, bandwidth isolation, individual control, and the ability to modify network behavior.

2.1 Sharing the Physical Network

Slicing would allow multiple providers to share one physical network and amortize their deployment costs. For example, consider smart metering for "smart grids". Electricity and gas suppliers are rolling out a parallel network to the home to enable measurement and metering, and in some cases control of home devices to improve energy efficiency and load prediction. Deploying, managing, and maintaining a separate physical infrastructure is expensive. Instead, if the broadband connection and the home network are sliced, the utility provider can share the cost, or rent a slice from the broadband provider. If the network is sliced inside the home, the slice could extend right to the home devices.

Such a slice would have strict requirements. First, to guarantee reliable billing, and clear accountability, the slice must be tamper-proof. Billing and accounting traffic should be isolated to stay private within the slice, and should keep out traffic from other slices. Second, if devices are to be remotely controlled, then the slice may need bandwidth and latency guarantees. There needs to be a way for the utility to express the bandwidth and latency requirements of a slice (or subset of the slice's traffic), and for the slicing mechanism to enforce it. If the utility wishes to enhance the behavior of the slice—e.g. to make it more secure or more reliable over time—then the utility should be able to provide and modify the control plane of its slice.

Cellular providers are already expanding their coverage by placing micro- and pico-cells in homes, and offloading cellular traffic to their customers' home and broadband networks. Today, the traffic is carried best-effort by the broadband network. If instead the cellular providers could rent a slice (or share the broadband deployment cost), they could potentially control the slice all the way to the micro-cell basestation. As before, traffic isolation is important for privacy and billing; and bandwidth isolation is important to guarantee good user experience. If the cellular providers can provide their own control plane for their slice, they can control routing and handoff, and could even support and route between multiple micro-cells per property, or use one micro-cell to serve multiple customers. In the extreme, in an urban setting, the cellular operator could obtain multiple slices and aggregate them to create (or augment) a city-wide wireless network from home WiFi deployments. A standardized slicing mechanism would allow multiple ways for such a network to be built and paid for. Deploying an open mechanism today, would allow new policies and business models to evolve over time.

A related, but simpler scenario is to create an isolated "Guest WiFi" slice in the home network, to allow friends and guests to share Internet access, or enable a community WiFi network. The slice could be managed by a local or remote control plane—perhaps managed remotely by a third party—for AAA service (association, authentication and accounting). The slice would need bandwidth isolation to prevent hogging of the WiFi or uplink bandwidth, and traffic isolation would be needed to protect the home network from attack. The home owner could choose to create multiple slices, one for friends, and rent others to 3rd party service providers. Again, one slicing mechanism could support a variety of business models and policies.

2.2 Outsourcing Network Management

Home networks are getting more complicated. In our homes, we attach a growing variety of devices (smartphones, laptops, TVs, heating controllers, loudspeakers, sensors etc), use applications with diverse needs (video streaming, browsing, VoIP, etc), and then operate them over unreliable WiFi networks. It is hardly surprising that many consumers are confused and frustrated when trying to manage their home network, and trying to make it secure. While managing such a network is not inherently difficult for a sophisticated network administrator, the typical home user lacks the technical know-how and desire to do so. It seems likely that – if they could – many would opt to delegate and out-source the configuration and management to a trusted third-party expert. Inspired by recent work on outsourcing home network security [10], we envision users delegating control of a slice of their home network, or even the entire physical network. A network management company might remotely set power levels and channels to reduce interference, suggest AP location, provide parental controls, set firewall rules, set the right priorities and QoS levels for a TV set or VoIP call, and so on.

A "one-stop-shop" management company might offer to manage the entire physical home network, including configuring network devices inside the home, controlling their day-to-day operation, and managing upgrades. The management company might manage slicing, too. For example, they could slice the network for the home-owner, creating slices for different applications, such as cellular offload and guest WiFi. They might also manage, and collect revenue from a utility company that was sharing the cost of the network. Alternatively, some home-owners will choose to manage the physical network themselves, and create slices for different applications. The home-owner then cedes control of a slice to an application provider, who then provides a dedicated control plane to manage traffic and bandwidth within its slice. By outsourcing control we can decouple high level, user-defined policies from the actual implementation, hiding technical details from the user.

2.3 Customizing Slices for Applications

Slicing can enable a new model of application delivery to the home, where an application provider can obtain a slice of the home network with certain resource reservations and the ability to modify it to meet an application's requirements. For example, an application provider such as Netflix could obtain a slice with sufficient bandwidth guarantees to

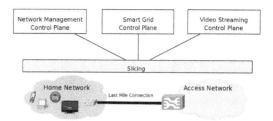

Figure 1: Slicing on a Home Network : Multiple service providers share the same infrastructure. Each provider controls a given slice, and a slicing layer enforces isolation between different slices.

support the high datarates of the video stream. Further, Netflix could customize the slice to handle packet loss and caching in a way that is optimized for video delivery, to ensure a smooth and high quality user experience. Such a model is in contrast to the current model, where applications are passive participants and are at the mercy of the network. Infrastructure owners can leverage this capability to further subsidize the cost of network deployment and operation from application providers.

Extending the slice within the home network, the content provider can now provision video delivery in an end-to-end manner, i.e through the last-mile link and up to the end-device playing-back the video. Given the ability to modify how forwarding takes place, the application provider can implement his own routing mechanism, use replication and retransmission methods to optimize video streaming over wireless, minimize latency for user interaction (streaming control operations like video seeking and rewind), or even use special congestion control protocols like WCP to improve the user experience [18].

To enable such new models of application delivery, the slicing mechanism has to support both bandwidth and traffic isolation, as well as allow the slice to be modified and customized independently by each provider.

3. DESIGN

3.1 Overview

Motivated by our requirements for slicing, we sketch out a potential design for slicing home networks. We leverage recent work on FlowVisor, a slicing mechanism for OpenFlow-based networks [17].

Fig. 1 shows the basic architecture of our sliced system. The network substrate consists of network elements (e.g. Wireless Access Point at home, Ethernet switch in the Access Network). The network elements are *programmable*, in the sense that they can be remotely controlled, allowing us to modify and customize the network behavior. The network elements connect to multiple providers through a slicing layer. Each slice is independent of the rest, and defined by (1) reserved network resources (e.g. bandwidth, forwarding table entries, router CPU), (2) the traffic it can carry, and (3) control logic that defines how packets are controlled and routed in the network.

3.2 Programmable Network Elements

Programmable network elements are needed both for building the slicing mechanism itself, as well as providing the flexibility on top. Ability to *control and modify* a slice should include arbitrary forwarding policies, mapping flows to queues, configuration of wireless parameters etc. In our example of outsourcing network management, the provider needs to block malicious traffic, or give VoIP calls priority over P2P traffic. Similarly, a smart-grid provider might need to connect metered equipment to an encrypted wireless network. And a video content provider might want to mark data to implement a customized congestion control mechanism. A *low-level network API* is therefore essential for our design.

The control logic that specifies a slice's behavior can be flexibly placed within the network equipment, or in a controller either at home or at the provider's premises. The decoupling allows different slicing models as we describe next.

3.3 Slicing Layer

The slicing layer enforces isolation between different slices so they can safely coexist. The slicing layer sits on top of the programmable network elements, and orchestrates the independent control of each slice by a slice-specific control plane. Our current design provides the four different isolation guarantees we sketched out earlier, namely (i) *isolation of bandwidth*, (ii) *isolation of traffic*, (iii) *isolation of control* and (iv) *ability to independently modify*. However, in practice different applications may need only a particular subset of the four isolation guarantees above.

To isolate traffic, a subset of all traffic is allocated to each slice. For example, all video traffic from Amazon might be under the control of one slice; all smart-meter traffic part of another; and all remaining traffic may be part of a default slice. The slicing mechanism must ensure that a slice's control plane can only control traffic belonging to its slice.

To isolate bandwidth between slices, every networking component must provide the means for bandwidth isolation. A guest WiFi user should not be able to affect the home user's experience by exhausting the available bandwidth. In the packet world this implies queueing, scheduling or policing; or using wavelengths or frequency bands, if the last-mile sharing takes place at a lower layer. Other network resources (e.g. router CPU and forwarding table entries) should also be divided and isolated.

To isolate control, the slicing layer intercepts messages between the control logic of each slice and the underlying network substrate. Each slice should be able to control only its related traffic, using its available network resources.

Note that we have intentionally left the definition of what a slice is unspecified. In our architecture, a slice may consist of a single slice, a combination of multiple slices, or even a subdivision (or delegation) of an existing slice. Such flexibility is needed to accommodate different policies with regards to privacy, ownership and control of the infrastructure. Fig. 2 highlights an instance of the suggested design where a home network subscribes to multiple providers using different policies.

Finally, while the slicing layer provides the basic scaffold on top of which several providers can coexist, additional application specific functional blocks may be needed. For example, to enable "advertisement" of and subscription to available services, a service broker may translate high-level policies to lower-level network semantics, define the division of duty among slices and detect potential conflicts. To address privacy concerns while outsourcing control of the network, it might be necessary to aggregate and/or anonymize

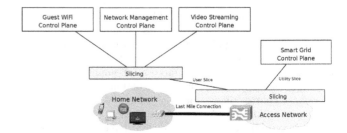

Figure 2: Multiple Service Providers on a Sliced Home Network: The access network owner gives a slice of the last-mile infrastructure to the user, and rents another one to a utility company. The user trusts a network management company to operate his network for security, configuration, and basic QoS management. He delegates resources and control for video traffic to a content provider. He shares a small portion of his network with guests and neighbors, outsourcing AAA to a GuestWiFi service.

data before we send them to the controller without hindering its usefulness. We believe our slicing design is sufficiently extensible to accommodate such additions.

4. PROTOTYPE AND DEPLOYMENT

To better understand how to slice home networks, and to gain practical experience, we created a prototype sliced home network, and deployed it in several homes. To date, we manage seven home networks, but are steadily increasing the population of users. In this section, we describe our prototype. An immediate goal is to implement and experiment with interesting applications on top–allowing us to present practical functional examples on top of slicing.

Our prototype exploits prior work on OpenFlow [15]—an open API to remotely control forwarding in network elements, and FlowVisor [17], a slicing mechanism for OpenFlow networks. OpenFlow separates control logic from the datapath of the network. A remote controller defines the forwarding logic of a network switch (data plane) by installing flow entries. A flow entry consists of a match, a set of actions, and a set of counters. The switch looks-up incoming packets against installed flow entries, and performs the corresponding actions. If no match is found, an event is sent to the controller, which in turn decides how to forward the packet and caches this decision as a flow entry into the switch. FlowVisor slices an OpenFlow network by policing and proxying OpenFlow control messages, allowing it to *isolate traffic and bandwidth* (together with queuing in the datapath).

Each OpenFlow controller (e.g., NOX [12]) runs on top of the FlowVisor, and is given *independent, programmatic control* of its slice. OpenFlow provides the low-level control so that slices can *be customized*, to some extent. We use SNMP to configure the wireless access-points (SSID, WiFi encryption, queues, etc) [13]. To interoperate with NATs and firewalls typical in the home environment, we run SNMP over a TCP tunnel (i.e., UDP-in-TCP tunneling).

For our prototype we ported OpenFlow 1.0 to OpenWrt, a Linux distribution for low-cost home WiFi routers. Using low-cost home routers allows us to deploy more of them; and allows us to explore how a simple AP can be controlled

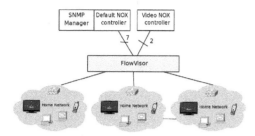

Figure 3: Prototype Deployment. Seven homes connect to a default controller through FlowVisor. A separate controller manages traffic from video settop boxes.

by a sophisticated control plane. This is in contrast to the more capable, and more expensive boxes used in other deployments [7]—for which slicing would work just as well.

In our initial deployments, we make use of the TP-Link WR1043ND AP, with 400 MHz CPU, 16 MB flash memory, 4 Ethernet ports and an Atheros 802.11n WiFi chipset. The OpenWrt driver for the Atheros chipset supports multiple SSID on a single radio interface. The APs are deployed in seven homes (three on campus and four off campus), with different broadband providers (campus Ethernet, DSL, cable and WiMAX). Inside the homes are a variety of laptops, desktops, smart-phones, game consoles, and video setupboxes. All homes have a default slice which is managed by a controller that runs at Stanford. The controller is implemented using NOX, and an SNMP manager to configure the APs, and each slice connects to the controller through FlowVisor (Fig. 3).

To experiment with slicing, we create a "video slice" for all video devices. In our deployment, these include GoogleTV and Netflix boxes. All of the traffic in the video slice (defined as all the traffic to and from the MAC addresses of these devices) is controlled by a separate controller. To control the video slice, we run a dedicated video controller at Stanford, also based on NOX. Currently this slice is configured manually, but we plan to create a web-based platform—to configure the FlowVisor via XML-RPC—so that home owners can configure their slices more easily.

At the time of writing, our deployment is in its infancy, and we have run it for one month. Over time, we aim to build practical experience slicing and controling home networks. Moving forward, we will enhance the slice controllers (video and network management), integrate an existing GuestWiFi application, and expand our population of users. So far, our deployments do not allow us to control the last-mile infrastructure. However, we are exploring several alternatives that would allow slicing back into the broadband network.

4.1 The Cost of Slicing

A natural question about slicing is "what is its overhead"? While this has been previously quantified for the campus network [17], we iterate and interpret the results in the context of home networks.

From the user's experience perspective, remote control of the network and more specifically RTT between the home router and the FlowVisor/controller seems to dominate performance penalties. In our deployment, the median RTT between the controller and the homes is 16 ms (with CDF

of latency shown in Fig. 4(b)). It's expected that "proximity" between the home and FlowVisor/Controller should be considered through slicing and control delegation.

A significant portion of the traffic in home networks can be proactively managed ((Fig. 4(a))—with about 20% being DNS and ARP, reducing both the initial delay a new flow suffers and the load on FlowVisor and controllers.

In terms of scalability, FlowVisor scales linearly to the network of switches and number of flows. In our deployment of 7 homes where a single slicing layer exists, FlowVisor is running with an average load of 4.07 flows per second with a maximum load of 331 flows per second (and CDF is shown in Fig. 4(c)). This means we can expect to scale up our deployments by over 200 times with our current setup. In the context of home networks, both FlowVisor and OpenFlow controllers can easily perform better by demultiplexing matching of slice rules and network state based on the individual residency—which will allow for efficient load-balancing.

A detailed description of how to optimize slicing and control for the home networks is beyond the scope of this paper.

5. RELATED WORK

Slicing has been proposed by Sherwood et al [17] to enable networking experiments on a production network. In our prototype we heavily borrow ideas and implementation efforts from this prior work.

Others have previously identified the need for applications and services within the home to cope with increasing complexity and heterogeneity. Dixon et al suggested an operating system for the home (HomeOS and app store) in which users deal with applications and high-level policies to deal with integration and management of their network [9]. In [19] the authors use an OSGI-based framework to install applications on a residential gateway.

Feamster proposed outsourcing of network security to an offsite controller that can both detect Internet-wide coordinated activity coming from homes and automatically take corrective action on behalf of unskilled home users. The architecture suggested in this paper is the closest to a slice of our design. Other applications such as 3G/WiFi offloading [5, 14] and video streaming over wireless [20] have been explored in their own context.

Sharing of the last-mile infrastructure has been mostly discussed under the terms of multiple ISPs [1]. The most popular way today is to terminate the link on ISP-specific data-link layer equipment (e.g. DSLAM, OLT), while others suggest to share the physical medium or enforce separation in the network layer [6, 16]. This gives users more options, but there is still a single provider present at the home.

Significant work has been done to automate detection and diagnosis of faults in home networks, and to define the appropriate interaction and interfaces between the users and tools to manage and configure the home network [4, 7, 8, 11]. We seek to build intuitive and meaningful interfaces for the user to subscribe and configure new services, and we plan to leverage on existing work in this field.

6. CONCLUSION

The home network faces growing challenges. It is the meeting point for home automation, smart-grid, seamless connectivity, online entertainment, ubiquitous access to data; all of which require a working home network, customized for

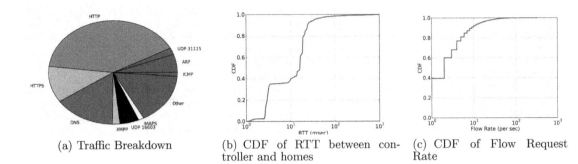

(a) Traffic Breakdown   (b) CDF of RTT between controller and homes   (c) CDF of Flow Request Rate

Figure 4: Measurements from current deployments in seven homes

their needs. Our long-term goal is the architecture of home networks to allow all of these new applications; plus the ability to evolve and improve the home network to support new applications as-yet unthought of. We propose slicing as a starting point, and our prototype allows us to experiment with different policies and applications. Through this exercise, we hope to gain a better understanding of the needs and trade-offs between performance, privacy, security and flexibility. Moving forward we want to make our prototype platform available to the community and so others can build upon our work.

Acknowledgment

The authors would like to thank Julius Schulz-Zander, Jiang Zhu and Bobby Holley for their initial port of OpenFlow to OpenWrt. We would also like to thank Te-Yuan Huang, Rob Sherwood and the anonymous reviewers for comments and suggestions.

7. REFERENCES

[1] Telecommunications act of 1996, pub. la. no. 104-104, 110 stat. 56 (1996).

[2] Verizon Fios Press Release. http://investor.verizon.com/news/view.aspx?NewsID=773.

[3] Accenture. Big trouble with no trouble found: How consumer electronics firms confront the high cost of customer returns, 2008.

[4] B. Aggarwal, R. Bhagwan, T. Das, S. Eswaran, V. N. Padmanabhan, and G. M. Voelker. Netprints: diagnosing home network misconfigurations using shared knowledge. In *NSDI '09*, pages 349–364, Berkeley, CA, USA, 2009. USENIX Association.

[5] A. Balasubramanian, R. Mahajan, and A. Venkataramani. Augmenting mobile 3g using wifi. In *MobiSys '10*, pages 209–222, New York, NY, USA, 2010. ACM.

[6] A. Banerjee and M. Sirbu. *Towards a Technologically and Competitively Neutral Fiber-to-the-Home (FTTH) Infrastructure*, pages 119–139. John Wiley & Sons, Ltd, 2005.

[7] K. L. Calvert, W. K. Edwards, N. Feamster, R. E. Grinter, Y. Deng, and X. Zhou. Instrumenting home networks. *SIGCOMM CCR*, 41:84–89, January 2011.

[8] M. Chetty, R. Banks, R. Harper, T. Regan, A. Sellen, C. Gkantsidis, T. Karagiannis, and P. Key. Who's hogging the bandwidth: the consequences of revealing

the invisible in the home. In *CHI '10*, pages 659–668, New York, NY, USA, 2010. ACM.

[9] C. Dixon, R. Mahajan, S. Agarwal, A. J. Brush, B. Lee, S. Saroiu, and V. Bahl. The home needs an operating system (and an app store). In *Hotnets '10*, pages 18:1–18:6, New York, NY, USA, 2010. ACM.

[10] N. Feamster. Outsourcing home network security. In *HomeNets '10*, pages 37–42, New York, NY, USA, 2010. ACM.

[11] R. E. Grinter, W. K. Edwards, M. W. Newman, and N. Ducheneaut. The work to make a home network work. In H. Gellersen, K. Schmidt, M. Beaudouin-Lafon, and W. Mackay, editors, *ECSCW 2005*, pages 469–488. Springer Netherlands, 2005.

[12] N. Gude, T. Koponen, J. Pettit, B. Pfaff, M. Casado, N. McKeown, and S. Shenker. NOX: Towards and operating system for networks. In *ACM SIGCOMM CCR*, July 2008.

[13] K.-K. Yap, et. al. Blueprint for introducing innovation into wireless mobile networks. In *VISA '10*, pages 25–32, New York, NY, USA, 2010. ACM.

[14] K. Lee, I. Rhee, J. Lee, S. Chong, and Y. Yi. Mobile data offloading: how much can wifi deliver? In *Co-NEXT '10*, pages 26:1–26:12, New York, NY, USA, 2010. ACM.

[15] N. McKeown, T. Anderson, H. Balakrishnan, G. Parulkar, L. Peterson, J. Rexford, S. Shenker, and J. Turner. OpenFlow: enabling innovation in campus networks. *SIGCOMM CCR*, 38(2):69–74, April 2008.

[16] O'Donnell, Shawn. Broadband Architectures, ISP Business Plans, and Open Access. http://dspace.mit.edu/handle/1721.1/1513.

[17] R. Sherwood, et. al. Can the production network be the testbed? In *OSDI'10*, pages 1–6, Berkeley, CA, USA, 2010. USENIX Association.

[18] S. Rangwala, A. Jindal, K.-Y. Jang, K. Psounis, and R. Govindan. Understanding congestion control in multi-hop wireless mesh networks. In *MobiCom '08*, pages 291–302, New York, NY, USA, 2008. ACM.

[19] D. Valtchev and I. Frankov. Service gateway architecture for a smart home. *Communications Magazine, IEEE*, 40(4):126 –132, Apr. 2002.

[20] X. Zhu and B. Girod. Distributed media-aware rate allocation for wireless video streaming. *IEEE TCSVT*, 20(11):1462 –1474, 2010.

Automating Energy Management in Green Homes

Nilanjan Banerjee*
University of Arkansas
Fayetteville, AR, USA
nilanb@uark.edu

Sami Rollins*
University of San Francisco
San Francisco, CA, USA
srollins@cs.usfca.edu

Kevin Moran
University of San Francisco
San Francisco, CA, USA
ksmoran@cs.usfca.edu

ABSTRACT

Homes powered fully or partially by renewable sources such as solar are becoming more widely adopted, however energy management strategies in these environments are lacking. This paper presents the first results of a study that explores home automation techniques for achieving better utilization of energy generated by renewable technologies. First, using a network of off-the-shelf sensing devices, we observe that energy generation and consumption in an *off-grid* home is both variable and predictable. Moreover, we find that reactive energy management techniques are insufficient to prevent critical battery situations. We then present a recommendation based system for helping users to achieve better utilization of resources. Our study demonstrates the feasibility of three recommendation components: an early warning system that allows users of renewable technologies to make more conservative decisions when energy harvested is predicted to be low; a task rescheduling system that advises users when high-power appliances such as clothes dryers should be run to optimize overall energy utilization; and an energy conservation system that identifies sources of energy waste and recommends more conservative usage.

Categories and Subject Descriptors

H.1.2 [**Models and Principles**]: User/Machine Systems—*human factors*

General Terms

Human Factors

1. INTRODUCTION

Homes that derive part or all of their energy from renewable sources, such as solar and wind, are becoming more widely adopted. Though early adopters of renewable technologies

*lead co-authors listed in alphabetical order

often report that their motivation for adoption was a desire to be more environmentally responsible, new pricing models such as leases have made renewables more affordable. As a result, renewables have become an alternative for people interested in reducing their energy costs. In the US, the number of *grid-tied* homes with photovoltaic installations grew by 40% in 2009 [8, 16]. The growth was largely fueled by decreasing cost of solar technologies and increase in incentives offered to consumers who install the technology. These trends are unlikely to reverse [16].

Technology and services that help consumers to manage the energy generated by their renewables have improved in recent years. We spoke to one user who installed solar panels at his home in 2002 and who, in order to log the performance of the system, manually recorded readings from a control panel on a daily basis over a period of several months. Another user, however, who is in the process of installing solar panels, reports that he will have access to a web-based service that reports overall energy generation and consumption at his home. There has also been a significant increase in technologies, such as the WattsUpMeter [12] and Android@Home [1], that allow users to monitor the fine-grained power consumption of individual appliances, as well as services, such as Google PowerMeter [4, 7, 10], that provide users with convenient access to such information. These technologies, however, do little more than provide access to raw data. The user must still attentively monitor readings, aggregate the information collected by a diverse set of sensing devices, and decide how to use the information to make smart decisions about energy consumption.

This paper presents the first results of a study that explores automated techniques for changing energy consumption patterns to achieve better utilization of available resources in green homes. Through an empirical case study, we derive four key insights that demonstrate the need for and the feasibility of automated energy management in green homes. First, we explore how energy is both generated and consumed in an *off-grid* home entirely powered by solar panels. Using a network of off-the-shelf sensing devices, we observe that energy generation and consumption in the home is both variable and predictable. Moreover, we observe that the residents in the home use *reactive* energy management techniques—they wait until the energy supply is low before taking action to reduce overall energy consumption. This approach, we find, is not sufficient to prevent the critical situation in which a generator must be used to power the home. Based on our observations, we propose a recommendation-based system that monitors energy harvested and consumed and provides

Figure 1: The monitoring setup at the off-grid, solar-powered home. The primary monitoring device is a FitPC tethered to a Mate remote control that profiles the inverter. It is possible to access the solar charging and energy expended data over a standard RS232 interface using custom software.

users with feedback and advice on how to adjust energy consumption patterns via a smartphone application. Our study demonstrates the feasibility of three recommendation components: an early warning system that allows users of renewable technologies to make more conservative decisions when energy harvested is predicted to be low; a task rescheduling system that advises users when high-power appliances such as clothes dryers should be run to optimize overall energy utilization; and an energy conservation system that identifies sources of energy waste and recommends more conservative usage.

This exploratory study focuses on an off-grid, solar home in Arkansas. We recognize that off-grid users are an extremely small segment of the population, and our goal is not to develop technology that will only be useful in an off-grid home. There are two significant benefits to working in this space, however. First, these users are at the extreme end of the spectrum when it comes to conservation. Understanding and classifying the manual techniques they have developed for demand-response can inform the recommendations we can make to other grid-tied, or even standard grid users. Second, off-grid users are likely to be enthusiastic early adopters of our technology, helping us to validate and improve our techniques without a significant barrier to adoption.

2. AN OFF-GRID SOLAR HOME

To understand the semantics governing energy utilization in green homes, we have deployed a suite of monitoring tools in a solar-powered home in Fayetteville, Arkansas. The goal of the monitoring infrastructure is to drive measurement-driven analysis to understand how users in solar-powered houses interact with energy. The house is occupied by a couple; one occupant works for the University of Arkansas and the other occupies the house most of the day.

Our deployment is shown in Figure 1. The house is located several kilometers from the city and is powered by 8 Kyocera 120 W solar panels [11]. The solar panels drive 24 2V 840 Ah Lead Acid batteries (two banks of 12 batteries = 24V) through a FlexMax 60 charge controller [13]. A VFX3524 Power Inverter is used to transform DC current to AC, which powers the appliances at home. We have augmented the above setup with a monitoring station that consists of a low-power FitPC [6]. A custom software tool on the FitPC periodically collects data from a controller device (called the MATE remote [14]) that collects data from the inverter.

Data at the rate of one sample per minute is captured over the RS232 interface and written to an append-only log. Each sample consists of the instantaneous residual battery voltage (in Volts) and the energy consumed by the house (in KWh). The amount of energy scavenged from the panels can be calculated using these values and the maximum battery capacity. At this time the log files are manually transferred by the house occupants. In addition to monitoring the cumulative energy consumption for the home, we have deployed networked WattsUpMeters to monitor individual appliances. We currently monitor a television and a refrigerator. We have collected data over a period of 55 days (14 days during the summer of 2010 and 41 days in Nov-Dec 2010) and plan to continue collecting data over the next two years.

3. DATA ANALYSIS

Analysis of the data collected by our monitoring infrastructure highlights four key findings that have informed the design of our automated energy management system.

Traditional energy management techniques are insufficient in off-grid homes.

First, we consider whether established norms of energy management, for example the 7PM-7AM policy that recommends users run important household appliances between 7PM and 7AM when the demand for power is low, are appropriate for green homes. Figure 2 shows the total energy consumption in the off-grid house at different times of the day over 41 winter days. While the energy consumption varies considerably over 24 hours, we find that a large portion of energy is consumed between 10AM-8PM (10-20 on the x-axis). Conversations with our subject indicate that consumption is primarily driven by residual energy in their batteries. During the day when the batteries are close to full, the users maximally use their household appliances like washers and water heater. This is, in fact, the opposite of the 7PM-7AM strategy. These findings demonstrate a need to develop new energy management techniques that consider the unique energy harvesting conditions in homes powered by renewable technologies.

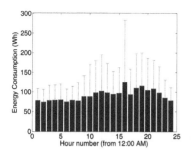

Figure 2: Energy consumption during different hours of the day averaged over 41 winter days. The errorbars indicate the standard deviation across 41 days.

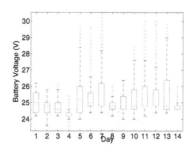

Figure 3: Variability in battery voltage in the off-grid home across a single day over 14 summer days in 2010.

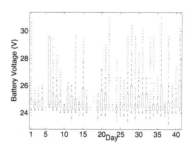

Figure 4: Variability in battery voltage in the off-grid home across a single day over 41 winter days in 2010.

Variability in energy generation and consumption suggests the need for adaptive management strategies.

We next consider whether a simple, fixed strategy for energy management would be appropriate for off-grid homes. Figure 3 and Figure 4 are box-plots of the battery voltage (in the lead-acid batteries in the off-grid home) over 14 summer and 41 winter days in 2010. Each point on the x-axis corresponds to data collected over a single day. The battery voltage is a function of the energy harvested from the panels and energy consumed by the house. Although the overall energy consumed per day, shown in Figure 5 varies, a large proportion of the variability in the battery voltage can be attributed to the energy harvested from the panels. From the figure, we conclude that energy harvested from the panels and energy consumed by the house are both highly variable. There is variance across a single day, across several days, and across seasons. This suggests that fixed energy management strategies are insufficient and adapting to variability is a key element for green homes.

Reactive techniques do not prevent critical battery situations.

We further analyze whether manual techniques employed by our green home user are sufficient. Our user reports that he is extremely conservative; he monitors the voltage of his batteries and reduces consumption, for example by switching off lights, when the voltage drops below 90%. Even so, there are periods of time when he must use a generator to power his home. We observed that he used the generator on 10 days during the 41-day winter data collection period—approximately 25% of the time. To understand what influenced the use of the generator, in Figure 10 we plot the battery voltage over 24 hours for three instances before the generator was used. It is clear that the period saw a gradual decrease in the voltage and the AC generator was used when the residual battery voltage was close to 24V. Our conversation with our subject further ratified the above observation. While he agreed that most of the time the AC generator was used when the battery capacity was low, on one occasion he had used the generator to "equalize" the batteries—a process of overcharging the batteries for a few hours which causes boiling of the electrolyte (acid) and helps breakup any calcification on the lead

plates and stratification of the acid[1]. To understand whether our subject used any techniques to prevent the use of the generator, we plot the total energy consumption of the house over 24 hours before the generator was used in Figure 6. Although there is a decrease in energy consumption in the last 10 hours, it did not circumvent the use of the generator. Hence, manual *reactive* techniques to prevent energy outages are not sufficient to prevent the system from running out of charge.

Energy generation and consumption exhibit predictability.

Finally, we consider whether energy generation and consumption patterns in green homes can be predicted in order to inform optimal energy management decisions. To quantify the predictability of the harvester source and energy consumed by appliances, in Figure 7 we calculate correlograms (autocorrelation at different lags) from the battery voltage data and energy consumed by the television set in our solar home. A lag corresponds to one hour. Hence, if the autocorrelation at lag k is a_k, it implies that the correlation between data at time t and $t + k$ hours is a_k. For battery voltage, the autocorrelation decreases with increasing lag, hence the battery capacity is predictable at short time spans—for example, around every 5-10 hours. However, the television data shows high correlation at short lags and lags around 20 hours. The higher correlation at 20 hours is due to the periodic use of the TV set. Our subject watches the television (located in his kitchen) when he cooks in the evening. Therefore, while there is variability in energy consumed and generated, there is considerable predictability in the data, pointing to the feasibility of automated and *proactive* energy management schemes.

4. SYSTEM DESIGN

Our measurement analysis demonstrates both the need for and the viability of energy management techniques that consider the unique properties of renewable energy sources. We propose a system that exploits these properties and offers the following contributions:

---

[1]We found that on one instance (not shown in the figure) the generator was used when the voltage was close to 29V

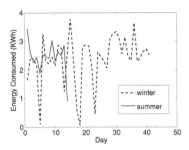

Figure 5: Total energy consumption of the off-grid home during 14 summer and 41 winter days.

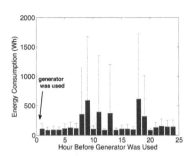

Figure 6: Energy consumption during 24 hours before the AC generator was used. The errorbars indicate the standard deviation over 10 different instances.

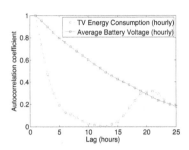

Figure 7: Autocorrelation at different lags (a lag equal to an hour) for the battery voltage data and energy consumed by a TV set.

- **Early Warning:** By predicting times when a home's energy store is likely to be critically low, the user can be notified in advance and take proactive measures for reducing energy consumption. This both saves the user from the manual task of monitoring the state of the home's batteries and it also allows for earlier and more accurate detection of critical situations.

- **Task Rescheduling:** By predicting when energy harvesting is at its peak or when energy storage is full, the user can be advised of the best times to execute high-power tasks such as running a dishwasher or clothes washer.

- **Energy Conservation:** Even the manual energy conservation techniques employed by our extremely conservative off-grid user can be improved. For each device from which we collect power measurements, we identify a *risk* [9]—the margin of error that is tolerable by the user. We use this information to suggest more conservative power states, for example adjusting the temperature of a refrigerator up one or two degrees, that will not have a noticeable impact for the user.

Though our data demonstrates the utility of these recommendations in an off-grid environment, our goal is to design a system that will meet the needs of green home users in both off-grid and grid-tied homes. While an off-grid user may want to maximally use power during peak generation times, a grid-tied user may actually want to minimize power use and maximize revenue by selling power back to the grid during peak times. By identifying peak and low generation times in advance, our system allows a user to decide to maximally or minimally use available energy to meet the desired objective.

We present a recommendation-based system that monitors energy generation and consumption and provides users with advice, including warnings in advance of critical battery situations, recommendations for the best times to execute high-power tasks, and opportunities to adjust the power states of devices to reduce energy consumption. We have chosen a recommendation-based model to minimize user irritation and ensure that control of household appliances ultimately resides with the user. A smartphone application notifies the user when the system suggests changes to the power states of

devices, for example suggests that the user turn an appliance on. The user is responsible for implementing the suggestion, and control of the devices is supported via the smartphone application. Figure 8 illustrates the primary components of the system.

Monitoring Infrastructure: The monitoring infrastructure collects raw data on energy generation and consumption. Minimally, the system requires measurements of the energy generated by a renewable source and the overall energy consumption of the house. Our system, however, can be improved by integrating fine-grained power measurements of individual appliances.

Web Application and Scheduling Logic: A central server implements the logic of an optimization algorithm and exposes recommendations via a web service accessed by a smartphone application. A *profiler* aggregates data collected by all components of the monitoring infrastructure and provides the data to a *scheduler*. The scheduler implements an optimization framework that determines appropriate recommendations. Our present optimization framework (work-in-progress) allocates energy from batteries to appliances proportional to their consumption in the past and their associated *risk*. When a new recommendation is available, the scheduler notifies the web service, which pushes a notification to an iPhone application. The iPhone application can then retrieve further information, including specifics about the recommendation or raw data produced by the monitoring infrastructure, for example the current power draw of a specific appliance.

Control System: The smartphone application, shown in Figure 9, both displays the recommendations and other information about the status of devices in the home and provides the user with the ability to control supported devices from the phone itself. Commands issued in the application, for example adjusting the brightness of a lamp, generate requests to the web service. The web service forwards requests to a control infrastructure that can directly control individual devices. The control infrastructure is an application built on top of the HomeOS [3, 5] framework that provides the necessary drivers and API to control appliances remotely.

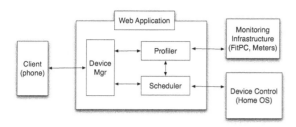

Figure 8: The design of a recommendation-based system for improving energy utilization in a green home.

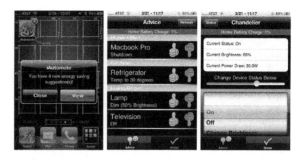

Figure 9: A smartphone application that displays system recommendations, collects user feedback, and allows control of selected appliances.

5. FEASIBILITY ANALYSIS

We are currently in the process of testing our components and deploying our recommendation system in the off-grid home. In this section, we demonstrate the feasibility of generating useful recommendations.

Battery voltage can be used to predict when the generator will be necessary.

The *early warning system* requires accurate predictions of when the AC generator is likely to be used. Moreover, it is critical that the prediction occurs long before the actual event so that remedial actions can be taken. Figure 10 shows the battery voltage over 24 hours for three instances before the generator was used. The trend shows that the generator is used when the voltage either remains close to 24V for a long time, or has a gradual decrease from a higher voltage to 24V. Such a trend can be captured using simple autoregressive or moving average models [2], demonstrating the feasibility of predicting energy outages long before they occur.

There are instances when the battery voltage is high and overall energy consumption is low.

To demonstrate that *task rescheduling* can help conserve energy in green homes, we present a scatter plot of battery voltage and overall energy consumption of the house in Figure 11. Each point in the plot corresponds to the energy consumed and the average battery voltage during a particular hour. The figure shows that there are several instances when the battery voltage is low (the AC generator is likely to be used) and the energy consumption is high. It also demonstrates that it is frequently the case that the voltage is high and energy consumption is low. Such a mismatch points to the potential for rescheduling delay-tolerant tasks, such as running a clothes washer, such that they occur when there is significant capacity in the batteries that is not being used for other critical tasks.

Even our conservative off-grid user could reduce energy usage.

Finally to corroborate the feasibility of energy conservation using *risk* associated with appliances, we present results from an experiment using a television set in our solar house in Arkansas. Figure 12 shows the power draw of the TV set during two instances of its use. We observe that on both

occasions, the power draw can be reduced by 3W (quantified as *risk*) without affecting the user.

6. FUTURE WORK

This paper explores the feasibility of using automated techniques for energy management in homes powered by renewable technologies. The data collected by a network of off-the-shelf components deployed in a single off-grid home demonstrates the potential for a system that changes energy consumption patterns to achieve better utilization of available resources. Our current work focuses on the following areas:

- **Improved Monitoring**: We are developing *auxiliary* monitoring devices that will supplement the data collected by the off-the-shelf components with information about environmental conditions, such as ambient light, temperature, and humidity, that have a causal relationship with energy consumption (similar to [15, 17]). This will help us to derive correlations between energy consumed and ambient environmental conditions and will provide insight on how humans duty cycle appliances based on environmental conditions. There are several challenges to overcome, however, including how to collect data in a *non-intrusive* way.

- ***Holistic* System**: We are building a general-purpose optimization framework that will adaptively balance the amount of energy harvested with energy expended such that usability needs are met. This requires identifying the importance of individual devices and allocating the energy predicted to be harvested accordingly.

- **User Evaluation**: We plan to deploy the web and iPhone application to collect information about the utility of the recommendations generated by the scheduling algorithm. The system will collect in situ feedback about whether recommendations are useful and correlate the recommendations with the power readings from individual devices.

- **Wider Deployment**: We are in the process of identifying other users, in off-grid and grid-tied homes that are only partially powered by renewable sources, who are willing to participate in our study.

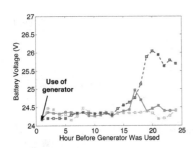

Figure 10: Battery voltage over 24 hours for three instances before the AC generator was used. Voltages drop from a high or are consistently low before the generator is used.

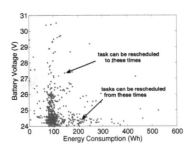

Figure 11: Scatter plot showing instances when the energy consumption and battery voltage are inversely correlated. Rescheduling tasks can help conservation.

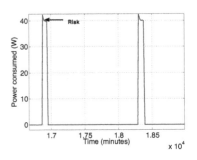

Figure 12: Risk associated with a television set—3W of power can be reduced without affecting the user.

Acknowledgments

We are thankful to the anonymous reviewers for their insightful comments and suggestions. We would also like to thank Ratul Mahajan for sharing the HomeOS platform executables with us and our off-grid house subject for volunteering to have his home monitored. This work was partially funded by National Science Foundation grants CNS-1018112 and CNS-1055061. Any opinions, findings, and conclusions or recommendations expressed in this material are those of the authors and do not necessarily reflect the views of the National Science Foundation.

7. REFERENCES

[1] Android @ Home. http://developer.android.com/guide/topics/usb/adk.html.

[2] Autoregressive moving-average models. http://en.wikipedia.org/wiki/Autoregressive_moving_average_model.

[3] A. B. Brush, B. Lee, R. Mahajan, S. Agarwal, S. Saroiu, and C. Dixon. Home Automation in the Wild: Challenges and Opportunities. In *ACM CHI*, 2011.

[4] Cisco Home Energy Management. http://www.cisco.com/web/consumer/products/hem.html.

[5] C. Dixon, R. Mahajan, S. Agarwal, A. Brush, B. Lee, S. Saroiu, and V. Bahl. The Home Needs an Operating System (and an App Store). In *ACM Hotnets IX*, 2010.

[6] FitPC2. http://www.fit-pc.com/web/.

[7] Google Power Meter. http://www.google.com/powermeter/about/.

[8] Google Trend: Solar Homes. http://www.google.com/trends?q=+solar+homes&ctab=0&geo=all&date=all.

[9] H. Hu. *Risk-Conscious Design of Off-Grid Solar Energy Houses*. PhD dissertation, The Georgia Institute of Technology, Department of Architecture, Nov. 2009.

[10] Intel Home Energy Meter. http://edc.intel.com/embedded/homeenergy/323157-001US.pdf.

[11] Kyocera Solar Panels. http://www.altersystems.com/catalog/kyocera-kc120-120-watt-solar-panel-p-569.html.

[12] W. meters. https://www.wattsupmeters.com/secure/index.php.

[13] Outback FlexMax 60 Solar Charge Controller. http://www.altestore.com/store/Charge-Controllers/Solar-Charge-Controllers/MPPT-Solar-Charge-Controllers/Outback-Solar-Charge-Controllers-MPPT/Outback-Flexmax-60-Solar-Charge-Controller/p6875/.

[14] Outback Mate Remote. http://www.altestore.com/store/Inverters/Inverter-Accessories/Remote-Controls/Outback-Mate-Remote-Monitor-And-Control/p857/.

[15] T. Schmid, D. Culler, and P. Dutta. Meter any wire, anywhere by virtualizing the voltage channel. In *BuildSys*, 2010.

[16] L. Sherwood. US Solar Market. 2010.

[17] J. Taneja, D. Culler, and P. Dutta. Towards cooperative grids: Sensor/actuator networks for promoting renewables. In *SmarGridComm*, 2010.

Naming in Content-Oriented Architectures

Ali Ghodsi
UC Berkeley
alig@eecs.berkeley.edu

Teemu Koponen
Nicira Networks
koponen@nicira.com

Jarno Rajahalme
Nokia Siemens Networks
jarno.rajahalme@nsn.com

Pasi Sarolahti
Aalto University
pasi.sarolahti@iki.fi

Scott Shenker
UC Berkeley & ICSI
shenker@icsi.berkeley.edu

ABSTRACT

There have been several recent proposals for content-oriented network architectures whose underlying mechanisms are surprisingly similar in spirit, but which differ in many details. In this paper we step back from the mechanistic details and focus only on the area where the these approaches have a fundamental difference: naming. In particular, some designs adopt a hierarchical, human-readable names, whereas others use self-certifying names. When discussing a network architecture, three of the most important requirements are security, scalability, and flexibility. In this paper we examine the two different naming approaches in terms of these three basic goals.

Categories and Subject Descriptors

C.2.1 [**Computer-Communication Networks**]: Network Architecture and Design

General Terms

Design, Documentation, Security

Keywords

content, naming, scalability, and security.

1. INTRODUCTION

There have been several recent proposals for content-oriented network architectures[1] whose underlying protocols are surprisingly similar in spirit, but which differ in many details. In this paper we step back from the minor mechanistic differences and focus only on the one area where these proposals have a fundamental difference: naming. In particular, some designs adopt hierarchical, human-readable names, whereas others use flat, self-certifying names. There is an ongoing debate in the community (see [10]) about which approach is most appropriate, but this debate has produced more heat than light. To help clarify the issues around naming, and

[1]See [1, 2, 4–6, 8, 13] for a small sampling of the recent literature, which is too large to provide a comprehensive overview of here.

Reprinted from the proceedings of ICN'11 with permission.

thereby move this debate forward, in this paper we examine the two different naming approaches in terms of three basic architectural goals: security, scalability, and flexibility.

Content-oriented architectures differ from today's architecture in several fundamental ways, and it is useful to review the relevant differences before plunging into the main content of this paper. Data retrieval in today's architecture is typically done through HTTP, which uses URLs as names for content; to fetch data a client sends a request to the host associated with the URL. The requester is assured the data is valid by using protocols that ensure that they are talking to the host named in the URL. Scalability follows from the hierarchical structure of DNS names (and, at the IP layer, the aggregation of prefixes). The design is flexible in that the data path makes no assumptions about the naming model.

In content-oriented architectures, content is named directly, placed in the network by "publishers", replicated in caches by the network, and requested by name through a find or fetch primitive. Finding a copy of the desired data object is accomplished through the equivalent of a name-based anycast distribution of the request, and the object can be returned from any host (or network element) holding a copy. The validity of the object must therefore be ascertained directly, not by verifying which host supplied the object. This need for direct object verification was the original motivation for using self-certifying names in content-oriented architectures.[2] By "self-certifying name" we mean a name that (together with some signed metadata) allows direct verification of the binding between the name and an associated object, as will be described in more detail in Section 2.

However, the use of self-certifying names has been recently criticized on two grounds in particular (see [10] for a critique of this approach and [12] for a response). These objections can be roughly summarized as follows:

- Scalability: because these names are not hierarchical, they cannot handle the necessary scales.

- Security: self-certifying names require another service to translate between human-friendly and self-certifying names, so any security benefits are nullified by weaknesses in such a translation service.

In this paper we respond to these objections. We argue that, in fact, self-certifying names (i) have better security properties than human-readable names because they can deal with denial of service without greatly limiting the nature of trust mechanisms and (ii) can have better scalability properties than hierarchical names by allowing more flexible aggregation. Thus, based on the

[2]See [14] for an early discussion of self-certification in "named data".

architectural goals of security, scalability, and flexibility, we believe that self-certifying names are the correct choice. However, we also observe that the two naming schemes are not as different as commonly believed, and can be combined quite easily.

This paper is structured as follows. We discuss the relationship between naming and security in Section 2, and analyze scalability in Section 3. We review approaches to trust management in Section 4 and we conclude in Section 5.

2. NAMING AND SECURITY

Network security is often broken down into four components: integrity, confidentiality, provenance, and availability. That is, the security measures in the network infrastructure and end-host network stacks must ensure that data is delivered reliably (availability), comes from the appropriate original source (provenance), and has not been tampered with (integrity) or read by others (confidentiality).

The latter three of these can be handled on an end-to-end basis using basic cryptography, once cryptographic keys are properly bound to the appropriate entities (as discussed below). In contrast, availability is the responsibility of the network itself and must be addressed on two different levels. First, the underlying network infrastructure must reliably deliver bits, which requires that its components cannot be easily compromised and data delivery cannot be overwhelmed by denial-of-service attacks; this is completely independent of the naming system, so we do not consider it further here. Second, the infrastructure must provide protection against content-level denial-of-service attacks; *i.e.*, even if bits are delivered reliably, the network must ensure that the delivered object has the correct name and provenance, or else requesters could be denied the object they desire. Naming does play a critical role here, and our subsequent discussion of availability will focus only on this aspect of denial of service.

2.1 The Basic Bindings

As in the SDSI/SPKI framework [3, 9], in content-oriented networks each piece of mutable data is associated with a "principal" who is responsible for its content (either because the principal created it, verified it, or merely because the principal vouches for it). When we talk about the provenance of an object, we are referring to this principal.[3] To effectively use cryptography to achieve our security goals, for each object we must establish bindings between three different entities:

- *Real-World Identity (RWI)*: This is the real-world entity who is the principal for the data. For example, a real-world identity may refer to a person or organization.

- *Name*: This is the name handed to the network in the fetch-by-name primitive, and must be sufficient to identify the object within the network. Principals are responsible for naming their content.

- *Public Key*: Each principal is associated with a public-private key pair. This is the cryptographic key that can be used by the receiver to verify that the RWI did indeed sign the content.[4]

All the three potential bindings between the above entities (RWI–name, RWI–public key, and public key–name) have an essential role in verifying the provenance of data.[5] If the public key is not bound (directly or indirectly, as we discuss below) with the corresponding RWI, then anyone could claim to be the principal associated with the data; that is, principals with keys k_1 and k_2 could both claim to be CNN, and without a key–RWI binding a user cannot know which claim to believe. If the name is not bound to the RWI, then it is impossible to identify the principal of the object; if someone claims that fetching foobar will return CNN headlines, but there is no cryptographic connection between foobar and CNN, then there is no way to validate that assertion. Finally, if the name is not bound to the public key, then the receiver doesn't know which public key to use to verify the provenance of the data: that is, if a user fetches the object named foobar, but the name foobar is not bound to any cryptographic key, then the user has no way of cryptographically verifying anything about the returned object (in particular, the user cannot verify that the object is indeed named foobar).

Because bindings are transitive, one does not need to directly ensure all three bindings: providing any two of them implies the third. The question, then, is how are these two basic bindings established, and it turns out that the two naming schemes we have discussed establish the bindings in rather different ways.

2.2 Binding in Naming Schemes

With human-readable, hierarchical naming (as used in *e.g.*, [5]), the entire name is specified as free-form hierarchy and the name (much like DNS names) is a sequence of human-readable strings. The purpose of human-readability is to establish an intrinsic binding between the name and the RWI. The second binding (between the name and key) can be established using an external authority such as a Certificate Authority (CA). In other words, in our example above, the string "CNN" in the name would be sufficient for the user to determine that the RWI associated with the name is CNN, and a CA will verify that a key belongs to the name containing CNN.

For convenience, we will assume that self-certifying names for *mutable* data consist of a cryptographic hash of a public key (principal identifier) and a globally unique label determined by the RWI, and both are of fixed size.[6] That is, names have the form **P:L**, where P is a cryptographic hash of the principal's public key and L is the label. The use of cryptographic hash function for computing P provides the binding between the name and the key, by enabling the receiver to check that the key indeed hashed to P. That is, if someone claims that a key is associated with a name P, then simply taking the hash confirms it; the existence of a binding does not mean that knowing P is enough to derive the key, it is merely enough to verify a key.[7] However, the use of such hash functions renders the name unreadable to humans, so the binding between the RWI and key must be established by an external authority.

Note that in both naming approaches, one binding is intrinsic to the naming system, while the other must be supplied by an

---

[3]Immutable data can be checked against a cryptographic hash of the content, and is therefore easier to deal with, so we ignore it in the following discussion.

[4]We do not consider the particular cryptographic algorithms used, how agreement on them is reached, or how they can be changed over time; suffice it to say here that these are not insurmountable barriers, but do require careful thought.

[5]The other two properties, integrity and confidentiality, do not require all three, so we do not discuss these properties further.

[6]There are other ways to construct self-certifying names, but they are logically equivalent. Also, note again how the naming of *immutable* data may simply rely on cryptographic content hashes.

[7]Each object consists of the following: <data, public key, L, metadata, signature>. This is enough information to verify the name-object binding, so the receiver can know that a delivered object does indeed have the appropriate name. By omitting the label L inside the signature, the text in [6] is in error on this point.

outside authority. See Figure 1 for a depiction of the bindings. Because these externally provided bindings are similar in spirit (whether they be for RWI–key, for self-certifying names, or name–key for human-readable names), the need for, and the nature of, these external mechanisms is not a deciding factor between these two naming systems. We will call systems that bind keys to RWIs or names *trust mechanisms*. These mechanisms don't mean you actually trust the entity or person to be honest, only that you trust that they are who they say they are.

There are obvious and well-known drawbacks with both naming schemes. Self-certifying names pose a challenge to usability, since humans cannot understand or remember them.[8] In addition, any move to such names would require significant reworking of the architecture (which, because this is a clean-slate discussion, is not seen as disqualifying them, but it is a serious drawback).[9] Finally, cryptographic algorithm upgrades will result in name changes, and careful engineering is required to manage their usability implications.

In contrast, human-readable, hierarchical names are more usable, more backwards-compatible, and remain unchanged while cryptographic algorithms evolve, but they provide a much weaker intrinsic binding. While the intrinsic name-key binding is cryptographically tight in self-certifying names, the intrinsic binding between name and RWI in human-readable names is far from perfect because it relies on the name being well-understood and unambiguous. This clearly does not always hold; as an example of a potentially ambiguous name, "ICSI" simultaneously refers to the Institute for Clinical Systems Improvement, the Institute of Company Secretaries in India, and the International Computer Science Institute. There is no way for a reader encountering this acronym in an object name to make this distinction without some external guidance. Even worse, phishing attacks try to confuse users with names similar to real ones; users frequently make mistakes in separating misspelled or names in different character sets from real names. Moreover, tiny URLs completely obliterate the name–RWI binding. In addition, human-readability creates contention in the namespace; when names are meaningful to users, some names become more desirable than the others.

Thus, both systems have serious disadvantages, but none of these flaws are fatal. However, the two naming systems have very different ways of dealing with denial of service, and this represents a more fundamental difference between the two.

Denial of Service

If the network cannot determine which objects are legitimately associated with a given name, then attackers can launch a denial of service attack by having many hosts claim to have data associated with that name. Thus, to protect the receiver from receiving[10] (possibly large amounts of) false content, the network needs to know the binding between the name and the key so it can verify that a given object is associated with a given name. However, the network does not need to know the RWI; all the network needs to do is reliably map names into objects associated with that name, while the receiver is left with a responsibility to use a name that corresponds to the RWI it finds trustworthy (and not trust to

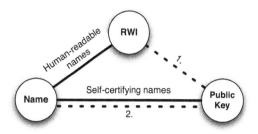

Figure 1: A depiction of the three entities and the different bindings between them. Two naming schemes provide different intrinsic bindings (solid lines) but require both an external authority to provide one additional binding (dashed line): with self-certifying names it's the binding (1), whereas with human-readable names it's the binding (2).

content referals from questionable sources). We'll return to the trustworthiness in Section 4.

In self-certifying names, the binding between the name and key is intrinsic and strong: given a key, one can reliably (within the certainty of modern cryptography) determine if a name is associated with that key. On the other hand, in human-readable names, the binding between the key and name is not inherent in the name itself, so the network must obtain that binding somehow. How this occurs depends on when in the retrieval process the validation occurs; there are two possibilities.

First, the data can be validated when it is first published.[11] With self-certifying names, the network has the necessary verification tools to do this; it can require any publisher of data to provide the necessary signatures that associate the object with the name, as the key and name are intrinsically bound. For human-readable names, the network needs to use an external mechanism to bind the name to a key (which can then be used to check the signatures provided by publishers). For this, the network needs to know about and understand the external trust mechanisms relevant for that particular principal. This greatly limits the nature of the external trust mechanisms that can be employed. In practice, we argue this translates to a requirement of deploying a global PKI, which has its known issues that range between practical management challenges to almost Orwellian concerns [11].

Second, the data can be validated at fetch time, with the key provided within the request itself; that is, the binding between name and key is provided by the requester (who presumably could know about and understand the relevant trust mechanisms). In this case, the requester supplies the key (or its hash) along with the name in her request (and can sign them, so that this binding can't be tampered with). For this to work, content-oriented routing must be done on a name-key basis, not just on the name, in order for routing requests to reach objects associated with the appropriate key. This makes the key an essential part of the name (because it is used for routing); the name is no longer a pure human-readable string but includes a cryptographic part. The name has now become self-certifying, taking the form of P:L, with P being (as before) the hash of the public key and the label L being the hierarchical, human-readable name. The debate, then, is not about

---

[8]However, see [14] for a discussion of usability.

[9]The DOI project is an interesting experiment in incremental deployment of a flat naming structure.

[10]Here we assume that the receiver can tell that the delivered object is false, but our concern is that the network never delivers the correct data because it has responded to the request with a false object; this can be used as a denial of service attack.

---

[11]A host can "publish" content by telling the network that it is willing to provide copies of an object with a certain name. The question we are discussing here is what kinds of cryptographic checks are used to verify that the object is indeed associated with that name.

Figure 2: In deepest match, an exact match for each part of the name is looked for. The matching begins from the end of the name (above D) and proceeds a part by part to the beginning (A), until a match or there's nothing to look for.

human readable versus self-certifying, it is about what kinds of self-certifying names should be used. This hybrid choice merely requires that the labels in the P:L format for self-certifying names be human readable and hierarchical.

It is worthwhile to note that delaying the validation of the data until after the data is delivered is not an option: validation *after* fetching results in denial of service, as the requester may never receive a valid copy.

This completes our discussion of the security concerns, which we feel drives us towards self-certifying names. We now must confront two remaining issues: scalability and flexibility. We do so in the next two sections.

3. NAMING AND SCALABILITY

In this section, we examine the scalability of naming.

3.1 Explicit Aggregation

Hierarchical names help scalability by reducing the size and update-rate of the routing tables. While this is well-known, it is instructive to walk through the semantics of hierarchical routing in more detail. Consider a name of the form com.CNN.headlines. In terms of routing semantics, this name means that if you follow routing entries to com, you are guaranteed to find an entry for com.CNN somewhere along your path, and similarly if you follow routing entries to com.CNN you will eventually find an entry for com.CNN.headlines. These semantics, not any other details about hierarchies, are what enable scaling.

In terms of global uniqueness, each entry in the hierarchy is not guaranteed to be unique, but each prefix is (*i.e.*, com, com.CNN, and com.CNN.headlines are all globally unique). Because of this, one cannot route to arbitrary fragments (*i.e.*, headlines, or CNN.headlines) but must look for prefixes to be assured you are routing towards the right entity. It is the lack of global uniqueness of fragments, not the need for aggregation, that drives the use of longest-prefix-match.

The common assumption is that aggregation is impossible with flat naming.[12] It is true that names do not build in hierarchy, so aggregation does not simply fall out of the naming structure itself, but it turns out that this lack of inherent hierarchy provides greater flexibility in aggregation.

Given a set of globally unique names (say, A, B, C, etc., each of the form P:L), one can construct "explicit aggregation" by using concatenations of the form A.B.C.[13] The semantics of such concatenations are that when following routing entries for A, you

will eventually find one for B; and that when following routing entries for B, you will eventually find an entry for C. We will call this the *aggregation invariant*. There are two questions to address:

How do you route using concatenations? The routing table consists of individual names A, B, etc., and when confronted with concatenated name A.B.C.D, the router searches for the *deepest match* (as depicted in Figure 2) and forwards the message accordingly. There are two advantages over longest-prefix match: the algorithm has the potential to be simpler to implement, and the aggregation does not affect the structure of the routing table (which is just a set of flat names and their associated outgoing port).[14] Instead, all of the aggregation occurs on the naming side, not on the routing side.[15]

How do you know when you can use a concatenation? When naming an object, one thinks about two things: the identifier (which is the name itself) and one or more fetch-terms which we can use to retrieve the object (which, in our case, consist of various concatenated names). These fetch-terms can be included in metadata associated with the name (and signed by the principal of the object) and when asking for the object the request can use these fetch-terms (rather than just the name); the fetch-terms enable the routing system to more easily find the object. It is the responsibility of the principal of an object to not sign any concatenation unless the aggregation invariant holds. This invariant might hold because of administrative relationships (as in DNS names), because of economic relationships (contracts with a CDN), or the organization of a particular piece of content (such as chunks of a large file). This form of aggregation is far more flexible than a strict hierarchy, and several forms of aggregation involving the same object can coexist simultaneously.

This last point is important. Note that in in hierarchies, the object com.CNN.headlines can only fall under the aggregates com and com.CNN. In contrast, with explicit aggregation an object A can fall under an arbitrarily large number of concatenations, say C.B.A and D.F.A.

3.2 Building on Deepest Match

We now discuss several use cases for deepest match.

Structured Content

Consider the concatenation A.B.C, where A represents an aggregate for all of the principal's content, B is the name of a large file belonging to A, and C is an individual chunk in that file. Then, while the network elements will try to forward the fetch towards the chunk (C) if there's a known route, they will fall back to routing towards the aggregate of chunks (B) and eventually to forwarding towards the principal (A), if no more specific routes are known.

In addition, nothing prevents the chunk C to be part of two aggregates B_1 and B_2, in which case the chunk could be fetched using either of the two possible aggregated names (A.B_1.C or A.B_2.C), with the deepest match preferring routing entries towards the individual chunk C or the aggregates B_1 and B_2 before defaulting back to the routes towards A.

Because most content-oriented network architectures rely heavily on caching, a request might well encounter a detailed entry

---

[12]Simple scaling estimates in [6] suggest that routing on flat names without aggregation is easily within reach of today's technologies, so the entire question of aggregation may be moot. However, for the purposes of this paper we will assume aggregation is necessary.

[13]There is nothing special in self-certifying names that allows this to happen; explicit aggregation can be applied to any naming system. Our only point is that explicit aggregation is more flexible than inherent aggregation.

[14]The deepest match seems intuitively simpler than the longest prefix match, but how much the *implementation* complexities actually differ remains unclear without a detailed comparison of their (hardware and software) implementations. However, since longest prefix matching often transforms into a sequence of exact matching, the differences may be negligible in the end.

[15]See [7] for various anomalies that can occur when routers aggregate entries.

in a routing table (for, say, the individual chunk). Thus, one can limit proactive publishing to higher-level aggregates, but realize the benefits when finer-grain objects are cached nearby.

Content Aggregators

Another form of aggregation arises when third-parties assist in content publishing. With explicit aggregation the principal can use names indicating that it can be found by routing towards a third-party aggregate. We emphasize this sort of outsourcing of content dissemination doesn't imply anything about binding the content to a *topological* location, but only to a third-party service for which the principal might have technical or non-technical reasons to do.[16]

This resembles the use of CDNs today: the principal attaches the name of the content aggregator, say C, to the (beginning) of the name of the object, say A, and then uses this concatenation C.A as a fetch-term. If the principal wants to publish A on its own, in addition to using a content aggregator, it can do so by publishing the object with the fetch-term A. With deepest match, using either fetch-term C.A or A would match routing entries for A; this does not work with longest prefix matching. Moreover, this can be done with multiple third-parties simultaneously, so the principal could use C.A and D.A as fetch-terms, with C and D being different CDNs.

Binding Namespaces

In addition to providing the foundation for route aggregation, the deepest match can assist in mapping between different namespaces.

For instance, assume that we wanted to provide a mapping between a human-readable namespace and a self-certifying namespace. Consider a name "com.CNN.headlines". By representing it as a sequence of hashes, each part representing a longer prefix, we can construct a name A.B.C appropriate for deepest matching. We can make this name self-certifying by using the public key of com as the principal for each of the component names:

A $\quad$ HASH($com_{public\ key}$) : *
B $\quad$ HASH($com_{public\ key}$) : HASH(CNN)
C $\quad$ HASH($com_{public\ key}$) : HASH(CNN.headlines)

The principal of the content could publish the content directly under the name C, and use A.B.C as a fetch-term – and as long as the principal has a certificate from the root principal of the com namespace binding "CNN" to its key, by including the certificate in the object the content principal can continue to use its key to sign the content. This would allow human-readable names to have counterparts in the self-certifying namespace.

The publisher could also opt for a more indirect approach as well: fetching C (either directly, or using the fetch-term A.B.C) could result in a (signed) pointer to a pure self-certifying name without human-readable semantics embedded.[17] As long as the mappings between these two namespaces are relatively static, their dissemination and caching throughout the network could be made more pervasive than the actual content.

---

[16]Hence, the aggregated name changes only if the used content aggregator is replaced, not if the aggregator's location changes.

[17]An advantage of a pure self-certifying name is that it is semantic free and therefore persistent; for example if the human-readable name points to a home page, and that page changes domains — because the person changed universities — a pure self-certifying name need not change while a human-readable name does; see [14].

4. NAMING AND FLEXIBILITY

No matter what naming scheme is used, external trust mechanisms will be needed to bind keys to RWIs (for self-certifying names) or keys to names (for human-readable). We consider these two cases separately.

A Public-key Infrastructure (PKI) is the most well-known technique for binding keys to names, but has the well-known drawback of requiring universal agreement on the root trust authority and its policies. Decentralized trust mechanisms such as SDSI/SPKI provide an alternative not requiring a universal root of trust. Recall, however, that the network must understand the key–name binding (in order to prevent denial of service), and if the names themselves don't provide this binding then the network must get this binding from the trust mechanism. This precludes the use of a decentralized solution without a global root (as it would be untenable to have different portions of the network invoking different bindings), and forces the use of a PKI. Thus, human-readable names require the use of a PKI.

Not only do human-readable names reduce the flexibility in trust mechanisms, their name–RWI binding is imperfect (*e.g.*, which RWI does the name icsi.org refer to?), so an external mechanism must be used to provide more secure bindings between names and RWIs (in addition to the PKI used to bind keys to names).

Any binding to RWIs (whether key–RWI or name–RWI) involves human-level notions of identity so the binding cannot be completely reduced to cryptographic mechanisms. In particular, we imagine that search engines and social networks will play an important role in future trust mechanisms involving RWIs. In fact, the whole purpose of search engines is to map real-world identities (based on given keywords) to their relevant network names (URLs).[18]

Social networking platforms have the opportunity to provide trust on a more personal level. The networks of friendship could map directly to the use of webs of trust, facilitating decentralized trust management: in this model, establishing a trust in a name becomes a matter of traversing your social network and finding the certificate chain(s) from yourself to the name via your friends.

These and other RWI-based trust mechanisms are imperfect, but they are the best we have, regardless of what naming scheme is used. Moreover, the diversity of these mechanisms requires that they be completely separate from the network.

Self-certifying names provide a clean, algorithmic binding between names and keys that is understandable by the network, and leave the more amorphous RWI bindings to a collection of trust mechanisms external to the network that can evolve over time as new sources of trust arise (*e.g.*, search engines and social networks are relatively recent developments, and they will undoubtedly be augmented by future innovations).

Human-readable names provide an imperfect binding between names and RWIs, and thus require external mechanisms for both bindings; moreover, they dictate the use of a PKI-like infrastructure for the network because the network must understand the key–name bindings.

5. DISCUSSION

The intuition underlying this paper is summarized by the following design maxim: *You should architect for security and flexibility*

---

[18]Having the search engine to return a key (and/or self-certifying name) for given a real-word identity description would be straightforward, and at least one large search engine company is planning to do so.

511

but engineer for performance. We now review the findings of this paper with this maxim in mind.

There are essentially three options for the names used to route requests:

Intrinsically bound to RWIs but not to keys. In this case, to prevent denial of service the network must be able to determine the keys itself, which means that the network must understand the trust mechanism for key–name binding. This leads to the use of a PKI, which reduces flexibility in trust management.

Intrinsically bound to both keys and RWIs. In this subcategory of self-certifying names (motivated by the need to include keys when fetching content to prevent denial of service), the self-certifying component binds the key to the name and human-readable component binds the RWI to the name. While superficially attractive, this approach is suboptimal because the name–RWI binding provided by human-readable names is not reliable. This would then leave a security hole unless replaced or augmented by an external mechanism for name–RWI binding, which brings us to the next option.

Intrinsically bound only to keys. This is the canonical self-certifying naming paradigm, where key is bound to name through self-certification and the RWI–key binding is provided externally through a variety of mechanisms. While the RWI–key binding will never be perfect, at least it can continue to evolve and improve. This approach provides maximal flexibility in trust mechanisms, cryptographically secure name–key binding, and still allows one (though various forms of aggregation) to engineer for better performance.

This is our rationale for promoting the use of self-certifying names. We view this not as the final word on the subject, but hopefully the beginning of a reasonable exchange of viewpoints that can help lead the community to a deeper understanding of the issues.

Acknowledgments

This work was supported by TEKES as part of the Future Internet program of TIVIT (Finnish Strategic Centre for Science, Technology and Innovation in the field of ICT).

6. REFERENCES

[1] B. Ahlgren et al. Second NetInf Architecture Description. Technical Report D-6.2 v2.0, 4WARD EU FP7 Project, 2010.

[2] C. Dannewitz, J. Golić, B. Ohlman, and B. Ahlgren. Secure Naming for a Network of Information. In *Proc. of Global Internet Symposium*, March 2010.

[3] C. Ellison, B. Frantz, B. Lampson, R. Rivest, B. Thomas, and T. Ylönen. SPKI Certificate Theory. RFC 2693, IETF, September 1999.

[4] M. J. Freedman, M. Arye, P. Gopalan, S. Y. Ko, E. Nordstrom, J. Rexford, and D. Shue. Service-Centric Networking with SCAFFOLD. Technical Report TR-885-10, Princeton University, CS, September 2010.

[5] V. Jacobson, D. K. Smetters, J. D. Thornton, M. F. Plass, N. H. Briggs, and R. L. Braynard. Networking Named Content. In *Proc. of CoNEXT*, December 2009.

[6] T. Koponen, M. Chawla, B.-G. Chun, A. Ermolinskiy, K. H. Kim, S. Shenker, and I. Stoica. A Data-Oriented (and Beyond) Network Architecture. In *Proc. of SIGCOMM*, August 2007.

[7] A. R. R. White, D. Slice. *Optimal Routing Design*. Cisco Press, 2005.

[8] J. Rajahalme, M. Särelä, K. Visala, and J. Riihijärvi. On Name-based Inter-domain Routing. *Comput. Netw.*, December 2010.

[9] R. L. Rivest and B. Lampson. SDSI – A Simple Distributed Security Infrastructure. Technical report, MIT, 1996.

[10] D. Smetters and V. Jacobson. Securing Network Content. Technical report, PARC, October 2009.

[11] C. Soghoian and S. Stamm. Certified Lies: Detecting and Defeating Government Interception Attacks Against SSL. In *Proc. of HotPETS*, July 2010.

[12] D. Trossen. On long-lived routing identifiers. http://www.fp7-pursuit.eu/PursuitWeb/?p=244, October 2010.

[13] D. Trossen, M. Särelä, and K. Sollins. Arguments for an Information-centric Internetworking Architecture. *SIGCOMM CCR*, 40, April 2010.

[14] M. Walfish, H. Balakrishnan, and S. Shenker. Untangling the Web from DNS. In *Proc. of NSDI*, March 2004.

A Reality Check for Content Centric Networking

Diego Perino
Bell Labs, Alcatel-Lucent, Villarceaux, France
diego.perino@alcatel-lucent.com

Matteo Varvello
Bell Labs, Alcatel-Lucent, Holmdel, USA
matteo.varvello@alcatel-lucent.com

ABSTRACT

Content-Centric Networking (CCN) is a novel networking paradigm centered around content distribution rather than host-to-host connectivity. This change from *host-centric* to *content-centric* has several attractive advantages, such as network load reduction, low dissemination latency, and energy efficiency. However, it is unclear whether today's technology is ready for the CCN (r)evolution. The major contribution of this paper is a systematic evaluation of the suitability of existing software and hardware components in today's routers for the support of CCN. Our main conclusion is that a CCN deployment is feasible at a Content Distribution Network (CDN) and ISP scale, whereas today's technology is not yet ready to support an Internet scale deployment.

Categories and Subject Descriptors

B.3.2 [**Design Styles**]: Cache memories, Mass storage; C.2.1 [**Network Architecture and Designs**]: Network communications

General Terms

Design, Verification

Keywords

CCN, Router, Architecture

1. INTRODUCTION

The Internet is founded on a host-centric principle: machines are uniquely identified with an IP address and communication is possible between any pair of machines. Content dissemination, i.e., the distribution of a piece of information from one source to multiple consumers, is not a feature of today's communication model, but it can be easily supported because of its flexibility. For example, CDNs efficiently tackle the content distribution problem by redirecting user requests for content located at a given host to a closeby data center.

Recently, we have observed an explosion of traffic associated with content production and dissemination.This traffic is mostly

Reprinted from the proceedings of ICN'11 with permission.

generated by popular applications, such as Netflix, Facebook, and YouTube. This new trend has two main consequences: (1) from a business perspective, there is clear increase in the number of CDN providers and offers, (2) from a research perspective, a novel communication paradigm is envisaged: *Content-Centric Networking*.

Content-Centric Networking (CCN) aims to replace *machines* with *content* in the networking communication model. The fundamental principles of CCN have been investigated by a number of researchers over the last decade. Populard esigns are TRIAD [15], ROFL [11], DONA [17], and more recently NDN [3, 16]. Key CCN features are: (1) content items have an identifier and not content hosts, (2) routing leverages content identifiers and not host identifiers for forwarding operations, (3) content packets can be transparently cached, and (4) native support for multicast.

The CCN (r)evolution requires severe changes to today's routers. For example, high speed hardware and software are required to support name-based data forwarding and packet-level caching. Moreover, shifting the address space from one billion IPs to at least one trillion content names [7] causes a neat increase of the routing state to be stored at content routers. However, allowing routers to serve content from a local cache can potentially alleviate the frequency of forwarding operations. Generally, the interaction between caching and forwarding is still poorly understood, and it is not clear whether today's technology can sustain the described additional operations.

Arianfar et al. [9] are the first to explore some practical considerations in the design of content routers. Specifically, they analyze how to extend today's routers to support packet-level caching. Our work is the logical continuation of this work. Accordingly, we aim to answer the following question: *is today's router technology (both hardware and software) ready to support the CCN (r)evolution?* In order to answer this question, we leverage NDN as a design example. Our motivations are as follows: (1) NDN is founded on conventional routing and it is so largely compatible with IP routing, (2) NDN is a complete CCN proposal including naming, routing, transport and caching, and (3) a full-fledged prototype is publicly available. Nevertheless, we plan to extend our analysis to other designs as future work.

In this work, we provide an abstract model of a generic content router component. Then, we detail the processing performed by each content router component as well as their interconnections. Our analysis indicates that the additional cost and operations to support content caching and data forwarding, can be afforded by today's technology. However, today's hardware and software can only support a fraction of the routing state required for forwarding operations at Internet scale. Nevertheless, by reducing the scope of a CCN deployment, i.e., from Internet scale to CDN or ISP scale, today's routers could be easily extended to become content routers.

Technology	Access time [ns]	Max. size	Cost [$/MB]	Power [W/MB]
TCAM	4	~20 Mb	200	15
SRAM	0.45	~210 Mb	27	0.12
RLDRAM	15	~2 Gb	0.27	0.027
DRAM	55	~10 GB	0.016	0.023
High-speed SSD	1,000	~10 TB	0.03	0.00005
SSD	10,000	~1 TB	0.003	0.00001

Table 1: Summary of memory technologies.

Policy	Bits/packet	Random Read	Random Write
HC-basic	40	1	1
HC-log	72	1	0
HC-log + LRU	136	1	0

Table 2: Summary of caching designs ; H-bit=40.

2. BACKGROUND

This section serves as a background for a clear understanding of the paper. We start by overviewing the NDN design. Then, we focus on hardware and software technologies that we leverage for the content router design.

2.1 Named Data Networking

NDN uses hierarchical human-readable names to address content items. A content name has several *components* delimited by a character, e.g., /ICN/PAPERS/PaperA.pdf. Content is requested using an *Interest* packet that contains the name of the desired component-wise content. An Interest packet propagates toward potential data using longest prefix match. The Interest propagation leaves a trail of "bread crumbs" that a matching *Data* packet follows to reach back the original requester(s), naturally realizing multicast. Content routers cache Data packets for later transmission.

2.2 Hardware

We now provide an overview of current memory technologies that may be employed for the deployment of a content router (Tab. 1). Note that memory access is the main bottleneck of today's hardware router design, while packet processing takes only few clock cycles.

Ternary Content Addressable Memories (TCAMs) minimize the memory accesses required to locate an entry by comparing it against all memory words in one clock cycle. Today's largest commercially available single-chip CAMs have a size of 18 Mbits [19].

Static Random-Access Memories (SRAMs) are volatile semi-conductor memories that do not need to be periodically refreshed. SRAMs are typically implemented on-chip. Modern SRAMs can transfer up to 4 words of data in a single access. The largest single-chip SRAM has a size of 72 Mbits, and word size ranges from 9 to 36 bits [6].

Dynamic Random-Access Memories (DRAMs) are volatile memories that need to be periodically refreshed. In today's routers, DRAMs are typically installed off-chip. The most recent DRAM can read up to 8 words of data in a single access. The largest single chip DRAM implementation has a size of 4 Gbits, and word size ranges from 4 to 16 bits. *Reduced Latency DRAMs (RLDRAMs)* provide faster access time than DRAMs but can only read up to 4 words of data in a single access. The largest single chip RLDRAM has a size of 576 Mbits, and word size ranges from 8 to 32 bit.

Flash-based Solid-State Drives (SSDs) provide persistent data storage similarly to traditional hard disks. However, SSDs are based on microchips, and have lower access time compared to hard disks. SSDs have limited lifetime and their reliability largely decreases over time. SSD size ranges from hundreds of GBytes to TBytes [2, 5, 6].

2.3 Software

We now focus on software solutions for caching and forwarding functionalities in a content router. Our terminology relates to a NDN-like environment.

Caching – Several designs have been recently proposed for cache storage systems (Tab. 2), which consist of a *packet store*, where Data packets are contained, and of an *index table*, that keeps track of Data packets in the packet store. We now describe each design in detail.

HC-basic [10] treats the packet store as a fixed size hash-table. A Data packet name is hashed and the packet is inserted in the location corresponding to the hash value modulo the number of *bins*, i.e., the addressable elements of an hash-table. Differently from the original HC-basic design, we consider an index table which is addressed similarly and stores H-bit hash value for each Data packet name[1]. In the following we simply refer to this approach as HC-basic. It follows that a request generates a read operation from the packet store only in case of index hit or false positive (2^{-H}). A write operation to the packet store is random because of the hash function. To reduce the probability of conflicting packets, a bin could store multiple items (*HC-SetMem* [10]), or multiple hash functions could be employed.

HC-log [10] allows sequential packet writing to the packet store similarly to high performance caches. The index table stores H bits per Data packet plus four additional bytes to address the packets in the content store. A similar approach is proposed in *FAWN* [8]. The deployment of simple replacement policies, such as LRU, requires additional 64 bits for pointers, and extra accesses to index for pointer update.

Packet Forwarding – Content routers use Longest Prefix Match (LPM) for Interest packet forwarding. LPM can be implemented either in hardware using a TCAM or in software using a multi-bit trie [13, 14] or Bloom filters [12]. Solutions based on software are preferred because of TCAM's excessive cost and power consumption. We only focus on LPM using Bloom filters as it is the most promising approach [3].

Dharmapurikar et al. [12] propose to perform IPv4 LPM by using a combination of Bloom filters and an hash-table. A Bloom filter is a data structure for membership queries with no false negatives probability and tunable false positive probability of about $(1 - e^{\frac{-NK}{M}})^k$, where M is the Bloom filter size, N is the number of indexed elements and K is the number of hash functions used. The false positive probability at its optimal point implies $K = \frac{M}{N} \cdot ln2$ with $\frac{M}{N} \simeq [5 - 20]$ [12, 14]. In the following, we describe how this approach works assuming LPM over content names.

Assuming content names formed by B components, B Bloom filters are stored on on-chip memory, each corresponding to a unique prefix length. Each Bloom filter is populated with prefixes having the same length. A off-chip hash-table is used to store for each prefix the next hop information, i.e., the interface where to forward an Interest packet. Upon reception of an Interest packet whose content name has B components, we query the B Bloom filters associated to each possible prefix length. Given Bloom filters are stored on-chip all Bloom filters can be looked up in a single clock cycle. As a result, we obtain a vector of possible prefix matches. We then query the hash-table starting from the longest prefix match in order to verify eventual false positives, and retrieve the interface associated to the longest prefix match. The average number of off-chip

---
[1]The index table and the packet store can also be considered as arrays and addressed using a substring of the Data packet name [9].

memory accesses, E_{avg}^{FIB}, along with the access time, L_{avg}^{FIB}, are formulated as follows:

$$E_{avg}^{FIB} = B \times \left(\frac{1}{2}\right)^{\frac{M ln2}{N}} + 1$$

$$L_{avg}^{FIB} = 1 \cdot L_{on} + E_{avg}^{FIB} \cdot L_{off} \simeq E_{avg}^{FIB} \cdot L_{off}$$

(1)

where L_{on} and L_{off} are on-chip and off-chip memory access time, respectively. Note that the access time for the on chip memory is negligible as it is two orders of magnitude shorter than the off chip memory (Tab. 1).

3. CONTENT ROUTER MODELING

This section focuses on the modeling of a content router. We only consider the *data plane*, i.e., the part of the content router that deals with Data and Interest packets. We do not consider the *control plane*, i.e., the part of the content router responsible to populate the routing state across the network, but we plan to address this limitation as a future work.

Three main components form a content router: *Forwarding Information Base (FIB)*, *Content Store (CS)* and *Pending Interest Table (PIT)*. The FIB is a table that associates prefixes of content names to one or multiple next hop routers. The CS plays the same role of a buffer in an IP router. However, it also stores Data packets after they have been forwarded so that they can serve future requests. The PIT keeps track of the content items that have recently been requested and not yet served. Requests for the same content are aggregated within a single PIT entry.

Upon reception of an Interest packet on an interface I, a content router checks for content availability in its CS; if the content is available, the CS sends the requested data back on I. Otherwise, the content router checks in the PIT whether this content has been already requested upward; if an entry is found in the PIT, this is updated in order to track that interface I is waiting for this content. If no PIT entry is found, a new entry is created and the Interest packet is forwarded to one or multiple interfaces determined via longest prefix match on the content name prefixes stored in the FIB.

When a Data packet is received, a content router checks for pending requests in its PIT. If a pending request is found, the Data packet is stored in the CS and forwarded towards all requesting interfaces as listed in the PIT. If no matching PIT entry is found, the Data packet is discarded. In fact, either another Data packet already consumed the PIT entry or an "unsolicited" Data packet was received.

We model each component of a content router as described in Fig. 1. λ_f^{in} denotes the average packet arrival rate at component f; μ_f denotes the average rate of packets that do not require further processing after component f; λ_f^{out} denotes the rate of packets that are forwarded to the next component. A component may not be able to process all λ_f^{in} incoming packets, as a consequence only a fraction p_f is served.

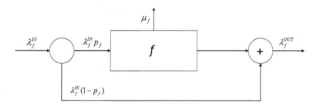

Figure 1: Generic model of a content router component.

3.1 Content Store

The CS can be implemented using one of the caching designs presented in Sec. 2. The CS is the first content router component being accessed when an Interest packet is received. The following operations are performed: (1) exact match on content name in the index table, and (2) update of the index table in case of match; this operation is not always performed as it depends on the replacement policy adopted, e.g., RANDOM, LRU and LFU.

We call *CS hit probability*, denoted by p_{CS}^{hit}, the fraction of Interest packets that are satisfied by a Data packet stocked in the content store and thus not forwarded to the PIT. The rate of Interest packets that do not require further processing within a content router is $\mu_{CS} = p_{CS}^{hit} \cdot \lambda_{CS} \cdot p_{CS}$; whereas, the rate of Interest packets forwarded to the PIT is $\lambda_{CS}^{out} = (1 - p_{CS}^{hit}) \cdot \lambda_{CS}^{in} \cdot p_{CS} + \lambda_{CS}^{in} \cdot (1 - p_{CS})$.

The CS is the last content router component to be accessed (right after the PIT) when a Data packet is received. It follows that $\lambda_{CS}^{in} = \lambda_{PIT}^{out}$. The following operations are performed: (1) exact match on full name lookup in the index table, (2) storage of the Data packet in the packet store and update of the index table if the Data packet is not yet stocked. λ_{CS}^{out} packets are not added to the packet store: a fraction of them is already present in the CS, while $\lambda_{CS}^{in}(1 - p_{CS})$ are not processed by the component. These packets are not moved to any other component.

When a content router interface sends out a Data packet, it reads it from the content store. For this purpose, we assume each interface keeps a queue of pointers to Data packets in the packet store that are waiting for transmission. The overall access rate to the packet store is therefore determined by the sum of Data packet reception and transmission rate.

3.2 Pending Interest Table

The PIT can be implemented using an indexing scheme à la HC-basic (Tab. 2). However, the PIT does not include a store and the index contains two additional bytes per router interface which has requested a given packet[2].

An *Interest* packet is forwarded to the PIT if not satisfied by the CS, i.e., $\lambda_{PIT}^{in} = \lambda_{CS}^{out}$. Then, the following operations are performed: (1) exact match on content name lookup in the index table, (2) update of the index table in case of positive exact match, or creation of a new entry otherwise.

We call *PIT hit probability*, denoted by p_{PIT}^{hit}, the fraction of Interest packets for which a request for the same content has already been issued. In this case, the Interest packet is not forwarded to the FIB. It follows that the rate of Interest packets that do not require further processing within a content router is $\mu_{PIT} = p_{PIT}^{hit} \cdot \lambda_{PIT} \cdot p_{PIT}$. Conversely, the rate of Interest packets forwarded to the FIB is $\lambda_{PIT}^{out} = (1 - p_{PIT}^{hit}) \cdot \lambda_{PIT}^{in} \cdot p_{PIT} + \lambda_{PIT}^{in} \cdot (1 - p_{PIT})$.

When a *Data* packet is received at a content router the PIT is the first component to be accessed and the following operations are performed: (1) exact match on content name lookup in the index table, and (2) removal of the entry from the index table in case of positive match.

We call PIT unsolicited probability, denoted by p_{PIT}^u, the fraction of incoming Data packets for which a PIT entry does not exist. It follows that the rate of Data packets that are not forwarded to the CS is $\mu_{PIT} = p_{PIT}^u \cdot \lambda_{PIT} \cdot p_{PIT}$. Note that μ_{PIT} also corresponds to the rate of incoming Data packets that are dropped by the content router because "unsolicited". Conversely, the rate of Data packets forwarded to the CS is $\lambda_{PIT}^{out} = (1 - p_{PIT}^{hit}) \cdot \lambda_{PIT}^{in} \cdot p_{PIT} + \lambda_{PIT}^{in} \cdot (1 - p_{PIT})$. λ_{PIT}^{out} also corresponds to the rate of incoming Data packets that are forwarded towards requesting interfaces.

---

[2]As in [14], we use 16 bits for next hop information.

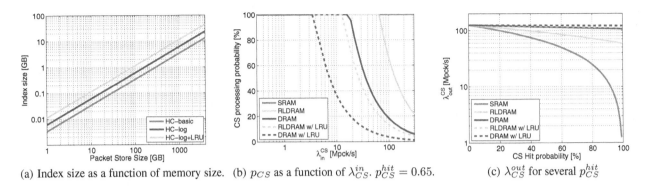

(a) Index size as a function of memory size.   (b) p_{CS} as a function of λ_{CS}^{in}. $p_{CS}^{hit} = 0.65$.   (c) λ_{CS}^{out} for several p_{CS}^{hit}

Figure 2: CS Analysis ; Interest packet size = 40 Bytes ; Data packet size = 1,500 Bytes.

We call RTT_{avg} the average amount of time a request remains in the PIT, i.e., the time between the creation of an entry and the arrival of the corresponding Data packet. In the worst case where Interest packets cannot be aggregated, i.e. every Interest packet carries a request for a different Data packet, the average number of PIT entries can be easily derived as $\lambda_{PIT}^{in} \cdot RTT_{avg}$. In a real deployment, a timeout would be associated to every PIT entry in order to bound the maximum time-frame a request is pending and consequently the PIT size.

3.3 Forwarding Information Base

The FIB consists of bloom filters stored on on-chip memory, as described in Sec. 2, and of an off-chip hash-table that can be designed using an indexing scheme à la HC-basic (Tab. 2) plus two additional bytes for next hop information[2].

The FIB is the last content router component reached by an Interest packet, i.e., $\lambda_{FIB}^{in} = \lambda_{PIT}^{out}$. When an interest packet reaches the FIB, a longest prefix match (LPM) on the content name prefixes stored in the FIB is performed. Although the FIB is the last component of a content router, i.e., $p_{FIB} = 1$, we anticipate a possibility to skip LPM operations by flooding all the interfaces or a subset of them. Thus, $\lambda_{FIB}^{out} = \lambda_{FIB}^{in} \cdot (1 - p_{FIB})$ is the rate of flood operations to be performed and $\mu_{FIB} = \lambda_{FIB}^{in} \cdot p_{FIB}$ is the fraction of Interest packets forwarded upward.

4. EVALUATION

This section focuses on content router performance evaluation. For every component, we analyze storage requirements and access latency constraints related to the processing of incoming Interest and Data packets. We then discuss the design of edge and core content routers along with an estimation of their cost and energy consumption.

We consider routers with up to 64,000 interfaces[2] with line-speed in the range 100 Mbps - 100 Gbps, i.e., from PC to high-speed router line cards. As in [9], we assume 40-Byte Interest packets and 1500-Byte Data packets. For CS and PIT indexing we use an H-bit value of 40 bits, i.e., the false positive probability is lower than 1% even for large tables (10^{10} entries).

Content names can potentially be formed by an infinite number of components B. In order to derive a reasonable value of B for our analysis, we analyze 10 hours web traffic collected at a wireless service provider [18]. This trace spans 10,000 unique users and 15,000 unique URLs. We find that 99.9% of the URLs are composed by less than 30 components, whereas the longest URL has about 70 components. For this reason, unless otherwise specified, we set $B = 30$.

We also need some indications about the size of the content name space along with how much aggregation is possible. Google reports that the web contains more than 1 trillion webpages [7]; as for January 2011, these webpages are mapped to about 280 million globally unique and routable hostnames, although only 86 million are active [4]. In case, of maximum aggregation, a high-end router would only be aware of the hostname component of content name, i.e., about 280 million prefixes.

4.1 Content Store

We first analyze the memory required to store the index table as a function of the packet store size assuming indexing techniques à la HC-log, HC-basic and HC-log+LRU (Fig. 2(a)). Fig. 2(a) shows that a packet store of 10 GBytes, which can easily be implemented using a DRAM (Tab. 2), requires an index table with size between 30 and 100 MBytes according to the indexing scheme used. Such small amounts of memory can easily be stored on SRAM or RL-DRAM. However, as the packet store size grows over 1 Terabyte, which requires an SSD-based implementation, the index table associated grows over several GBytes and thus requires to be stored on a DRAM memory.

We now analyze the impact of the average Interest packet arrival rate at the CS, λ_{CS}^{in}, on the fraction of Interest packets that can be processed (Fig. 2(b)). We consider different memories (SRAM, DRAM and RLDRAM) along with random and LRU replacement strategies. We only focus on the Interest packets as the operations performed by the CS on the Data packets are negligible, e.g., they account for less than 5% of the total operations in the worst case. Fig. 2(b) shows that an SRAM-based index table implementation ensures that all incoming Interest packets are correctly processed even for the highest value of λ_{CS}^{in}, i.e., 300 Mpck/s or 100 Gbps, with LRU replacement. Conversely, RLDRAM and DRAM-based index table implementations can only sustain a maximum rate of 75 and 18 Mpck/s respectively, that reduces to 15 and 3.5 Mpck/s with LRU replacement, without skipping any Interest packet processing. Then, as λ_{CS}^{in} increases, the fraction of Interest packets that can be served decreases and gets close to 0 for most technologies.

Finally, we analyze the impact of the CS hit probability, p_{CS}^{hit}, on the rate of packets forwarded to the PIT, $\lambda_{CS}^{out} = \lambda_{PIT}^{in}$, assuming $\lambda_{CS}^{in} = 125$ Mpck/s (Fig. 2(c)). Intuitively, as the probability to find a requested content item in the CS increases, λ_{CS}^{out} decreases. However, this holds only when the memory used for the index table is fast enough to process all incoming packets. Fig. 2(c) shows that when the CS hit probability is very low, even a DRAM-based index table implementation ensures a reduction on λ_{CS}^{out}. However, as the CS hit probability increases there is a clear need to move

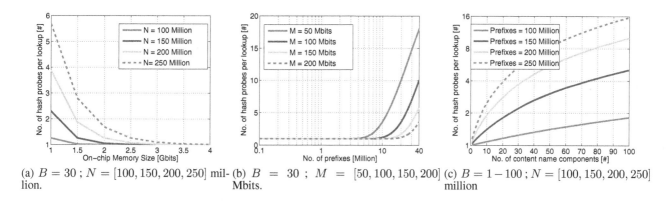

(a) $B = 30$; $N = [100, 150, 200, 250]$ million.

(b) $B = 30$; $M = [50, 100, 150, 200]$ Mbits.

(c) $B = 1 - 100$; $N = [100, 150, 200, 250]$ million

Figure 3: FIB Analysis ; Avg. number of hash probes per lookup.

towards faster memories, e.g., RLDRAM or SRAM. For example, if we consider a CS hit probability of 90%, e.g., similar to what we observe in today's CDNs, an SRAM reduces λ_{CS}^{out} seven times more than an RLDRAM.

4.2 Pending Interest Table

The PIT is implemented using an indexing à la HC-basic whose performance has been previously analyzed. Here, we evaluate the memory size required to store the PIT. Although not shown due to space limitations, we find that even in the worst case, i.e., each request generates a new PIT entry and $\lambda_{PIT}^{in} = \lambda_{CS}^{in}$, if we consider $RTT_{avg} = 80$ ms [1] and a line-speed of 1-100 Gbps the average PIT size is 14 Mbits to 1.4 Gbits. The PIT can therefore be easily stored on RLDRAM chips but is too large for SRAM memory.

4.3 Forwarding Information Base

To start with, we analyze the evolution of the average number of lookups in the off-chip memory (DRAM or RLDRAM) as a function of the on-chip memory (SRAM) size M (Fig. 3(a)). We assume Internet scale values for total content name prefixes, i.e, $N = [100, 150, 200, 250]$ million. Given for Bloom filters it holds $\frac{M}{N} \simeq [5 - 20]$ (Sec. 3), we vary M in the range 1-4 Gbits. Fig. 3(a) shows that as M increases, the number of hash probes per lookup tends to one. For example, if we consider 100 million prefixes, i.e., the number of active prefixes in today's Internet, about 1 Gbit of on-chip memory is required to achieve a single lookup on the off-chip memory. Unfortunately, this value is too high for today's standard; 200 Mbits is a reasonable value, e.g., the amount available in current NetFPGA.

We now analyze the impact of the prefix set size N on the average number of lookups in the off-chip memory; we assume standard on-chip memory in the range from 50 to 200 Mbits. Fig. 3(b) shows that 40 million prefixes can be sustained at maximum; when $N = 40$ million, the average number of lookups in the off-chip memory varies between 4 and 18 as the memory size grows from 50 to 200 Mbits. In order to achieve a single lookup in the off-chip memory, a maximum of 20 million prefixes can be supported assuming 200 Mbits on-chip memory. Note that 20 million prefixes equals 10% of today's hostnames and 25% of the active ones.

Figure 3(c) shows the impact of the content name lenght B on the average number of lookups in the off-chip hash-table. We vary B in the range 1-100 and consider $N = [100, 150, 200, 250]$ million. We assume an on-chip SRAM of 1 Gbps. Fig. 3(c) shows that as B increases, the number of hash probes per lookup becomes very large. This can reduce the fraction of packets that are processed by the FIB, increasing the rate of flood operation. On the contrary, if

we consider short content names, e.g., $B < 10$, the number of hash probes per Interest packet gets close to 1. This result indicates that a regulation on the content name length would be very beneficial to CCN.

Finally, we analyze the impact of the average Interest packet arrival rate at the FIB, λ_{in}^{FIB}, on the memory size M. Fig. 4 plots M as a function of λ_{in}^{FIB} when N equals 5 and 20 million and the off-chip memory is implemented using a DRAM and a RLDRAM. Fig. 4 shows that a DRAM-based implementation of the off-chip memory allows the FIB to sustain a maximum λ_{in}^{FIB} of about 18 Mpck/s; this value goes up to 54 Mpck/s when using a RLDRAM. Fig. 4 also shows that M increases with λ_{in}^{FIB}; for example, when $N = 20$ million 300 and 450 Mbits of on-chip memory are required to support 18 and 54 Mpck/s, respectively.

Finally, we discuss the off-chip memory dimensioning. In a realistic scenario, we have M=200 Mbits, N=20 million and a maximum tolerable λ_{in}^{FIB} of 50 Mpck/s, assuming RLDRAM for the off-chip memory. In a classic HC-basic implementation, the off-chip memory occupies just 140 MBytes.

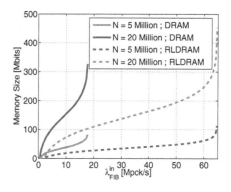

Figure 4: FIB Analysis ; Memory size ; $N = [5, 20]$ million ; DRAM and RLDRAM.

4.4 Global Content Router

We now discuss the design of a backbone and edge content routers. Given multiple designs are possible, we present two solutions that minimize cost and power consumption.

As an edge router, we consider a Cisco 7507; this router has five Gigabit Ethernet line cards and a peak power consumption of 400 W. Under CCN premise, the five line cards generate an overall Interest rate of 15 Mpck/s. The packet store can be implemented using a 1-TByte high speed SSD (similarly to today caches) as the overall access rate is of 0.417 Mpck/s. It follows that the index table with HC-log indexing can be implemented on a 6-Gbyte DRAM, which easily sustains an Interest rate of 15 Mpck/s (Fig. 2(b)). The average PIT size is 70 Mbits and the table should be implemented in a RLDRAM chip to sustain a rate of $\lambda_{PIT}^{in} = 15$ Mpcks/s. Finally, we use 200-Mbit SRAM for the on-chip FIB memory, i.e., the amount available in current NetFPGA. It follows the FIB off-chip memory requires 140 MBytes and can be implemented using a single DRAM chip. Such a configuration allows to perform LPM on about 20 million prefixes at a maximum speed of 15 Mpck/s (Fig. 4). A rough estimate of the additional cost and energy consumption to extend an edge router to CCN functionalities would be of 195 W and 31,000 $, respectively. Remark that, 30,000 $ of this additional cost are due to high-speed SSD; reducing the Data packet rate by a factor of ten would cut the SSD price by the same factor, i.e., more reasonable 3,000 $.

As a backbone router, we consider a Cisco CRS 1 series router with eight line cards at 40 Gbps with peak power consumption of 4,834 W. Under the CCN premise, eight line cards at 40 Gbps each would generate an overall Interest packet rate of about 1 Gpck/s, while the overall access rate to the packet store would be of 0.026 Gpck/s. Thus, we need to deploy a packet store per line card and to use 10-GByte DRAM memory (Fig. 2(a)). Each 10-GByte packet store requires an index table of 266 Mbits duplicated in two RL-DRAM chips in order to sustain 40 Gbps or 120 Mpck/s (Fig. 2(b)). 560 Mbits of PIT per line card are required implemented using SRAM memory. At a core router, about 250 million content name prefixes should be stored (Sec. 4.3); it follows that a 4 Gbits on-chip SRAM[3] (Fig. 3(a)) and about 1.5 GBytes off-chip RLDRAM memory should be employed. Under this configuration the FIB can support up to $\lambda_{FIB}^{in} = 66$ Mpck/s; in order to support the peak Interest rate of 120 Mpck/s the CS and the PIT should serve half of the incoming Interests, or the off-chip FIB should be duplicated. A rough estimate of the additional cost and energy consumption to extend a core router to CCN functionalities would be of 3,302 W and 130,000 $.

5. CONCLUSIONS AND FUTURE WORK

Content-centric networking (CCN) is a novel networking paradigm that centers around content dissemination. In the past, CCN concepts have been extensively analyzed, and many interesting designs have been proposed. However, the practical impact of a CCN (r)evolution on today's routers is an area that has not been fully explored yet. The major contribution of this paper is a reality check for CCN.

We provide models that describe the design of each content router component. Then, we analyze candidate hardware and software solutions for each component. We find that today's technology is not ready to support an Internet scale CCN deployment, whereas a CDN or ISP scale can be easily afforded.

As a future work, we aim to derive a better understanding of how the described results would change when considering the interconnection of multiple routers as well as a real traffic component. Another interesting avenue of future work consists of leveraging the tools introduced in this paper to compare several CCN designs. The final goal would be to give recommendations on CCN designs at different networking scales, e.g., Internet, ISP and CDN.

---

[3]Note that this value is too high for today's standard.

Acknowledgments

This work has been partially funded by the French national research agency (ANR), CONNECT project, under grant number ANR-10-VERS-001.

6. REFERENCES

[1] Meridian. http://www.cs.cornell.edu/.
[2] Micron. http://www.micron.com.
[3] Named data networking. http://www.named-data.net/.
[4] Netcraft web server survey. Website. http://news.netcraft.com/archives/category/web-server-survey/.
[5] Ramsan. http://www.ramsan.com.
[6] Samsung. http://www.samsung.com/.
[7] We knew the web was big... Blog. http://googleblog.blogspot.com/2008/07/we-knew-web-was-big.html.
[8] D. G. Andersen, J. Franklin, M. Kaminsky, A. Phanishayee, L. Tan, and V. Vasudevan. Fawn: a fast array of wimpy nodes. In *SIGOPS'09*, Big Sky, Montana, USA, Oct. 2009.
[9] S. Arianfar, P. Nikander, and J. Ott. On content-centric router design and implications. In *ReARCH'10*, Philadelphia, PA, USA, Dec. 2010.
[10] A. Badam, K. Park, V. S. Pai, and L. L. Peterson. Hashcache: cache storage for the next billion. In *NSDI'09*, Boston, Apr. 2009.
[11] M. Caesar, T. Condie, J. Kannan, K. Lakshminarayanan, I. Stoica, and S. Shenker. ROFL: Routing on Flat Labels. In *SIGCOMM'06*, Pisa, Italy, Sept. 2006.
[12] S. Dharmapurikar, P. Krishnamurthy, and D. E. Taylor. Longest prefix matching using bloom filters. In *SIGCOMM '03*, Karlsruhe, Germany, Aug. 2003.
[13] W. Eatherton, G. Varghese, and Z. Dittia. Tree bitmap: hardware/software ip lookups with incremental updates. *CCR*, 34:97–122, Apr. 2004.
[14] K. Fall, G. Iannaccone, and S. Ratnasamy. Routing tables: Is smaller really much better? In *HOTNETS '09*, NY, USA, Oct. 2009.
[15] M. Gritter and D. Cheriton. An Architecture for Content Routing Support in the Internet. In *USITS'01*, SFO, CA, USA, Mar. 2001.
[16] V. Jacobson, D. K. Smetters, J. D. Thronton, M. F. Plass, N. H. Briggs, and R. L. Braynard. Network Named Content. In *CoNEXT '09*, Rome, Italy, Dec. 2009.
[17] T. Koponen, M. Chawla, B.-G. Chun, A. Ermolinskiy, K. Kim, S. Shenker, and I. Stoica. A Data-Oriented (and Beyond) Network Architecture. In *SIGCOMM '07*, Kyoto, Japan, Aug. 2007.
[18] C. Lumezanu, K. Guo, N. Spring, and B. Bhattacharjee. The effect of packet loss on redundancy elimination in cellular wireless networks. In *IMC'10*, Melbourne, Australia, Nov. 2010.
[19] K. Pagiamtzis and A. Sheikholeslami. Content-addressable memory (CAM) circuits and architectures: A tutorial and survey. *IEEE Journal of Solid-State Circuits*, 41(3):712–727, March 2006.

The Network from Above and Below

Pat Brundell, Andy Crabtree, Richard Mortier, Tom Rodden, Paul Tennent, Peter Tolmie

School of Computer Science
University of Nottingham
Nottingham NG8 1BB, UK

+44 115 951 4251
firstname.lastname@nottingham.ac.uk

ABSTRACT

Recently, the HCI community has taken a strong interest in problems associated with networking. Many of those problems have also been the focus of much recent networking research, e.g., traffic identification, network management, access control. In this paper we consider these two quite different viewpoints of the problems specifically associated with home networking. Focusing on traffic identification as a core capability required by much recent HCI work, we explore the mismatch between the approaches the two communities have taken, and suggest some resulting challenges and directions for future work.

Categories and Subject Descriptors

C.2.3 [**Network Operations**]: Network monitoring.

General Terms

Measurement, Design, Human Factors.

Keywords

Home networks; Application identification; Ethnographic fieldwork.

1. INTRODUCTION

The network has become a major empirical focus in HCI. Recent studies have provided empirical insights into the ways in which network technologies are being incorporated into everyday life, e.g., [6][15][18]. Empirical studies have focused on network infrastructure and the work implicated in setting up and maintaining home networks [6], the work of weaving the home network into domestic routines [18], and user understandings of the home network [15]. Many have made the point that the design and construction of these domestic networks are opaque to users, stressing the need to enhance the network's transparency and local accountability, e.g., [3][16].

Studying network use has a tradition within the systems community that significantly predates recent interest by HCI

Reprinted from the proceedings of W-MUST'11 with permission.

researchers. Network traffic modeling and analysis is a key cornerstone of how the systems and networking communities seek to understand and manage increasingly complex networks. Elaborate models of the nature of different forms of traffic and the temporal characteristics of this traffic have been developed to characterize and explain network behavior e.g., [4][8][12][13].

We suggest that a gulf exists between the ways in which the network is perceived by those who study and understand it from the perspective of users, and by those who analyze and understand traffic from the perspective of the network. Although both seek to understand and characterize the forms of network use and the temporal nature of the network, the characterizations of network traffic and use are markedly different. Mapping between these different perspectives represents a fundamental research challenge.

In this paper we briefly explore these two perspectives before discussing the ways in which they need to be reconciled, and the research agenda that doing so raises for both the HCI and the Systems and Networking communities.

2. THE VIEW FROM ABOVE

We wish to begin by considering how the domestic network is seen from the perspective of those who use it, and how they make use of it. Researchers have exploited field studies and human-centered design techniques to develop the community's understanding of home networks. In a seminal paper, *The Work To Make The Home Network Work*, Grinter *et al.* [6] subjected the home network to the same kind of careful empirical scrutiny that HCI and CSCW researchers had previously accorded the introduction of networks into the workplace [2]. The study revealed that home networks are characterized by 'coordination challenges' implicated in the management of shared resources, troubleshooting, and network administration.

Tolmie *et al.* picked up where Grinter *et al.* left off, carrying out field studies to articulate the cooperative work implicated in the 'domestication' of home networks [17][18]. These studies revealed that home networks are characterized by 'digital plumbing' and 'digital housekeeping', i.e., the cooperative work involved in situating network technologies in the home and the recurrent and ongoing work of maintaining home networks as part of the broader round of domestic routines.

We illustrate the nature of this relationship between the network and those who use it by considering a network day drawn from one of our recent studies exploring both network usage in a domestic setting, and how people reason about the activities of the network.

3. A NETWORK DAY

To gain an understanding of domestic network use we undertook a series of studies that combined fieldwork with a bespoke HTTP proxy logger to record network activities. The studies formed part of a broader ongoing enterprise to understand the impact of the home network on everyday life, involving 8 households located largely in the Midlands area of the UK. The logging tool ran on an *Acer eeePC* with a solid state hard drive, which was given a static IP address and connected directly to the household's wireless access point via a wired Ethernet connection. Written in Java, the software consisted of a simple multithreaded logging HTTP proxy.

Logging was complemented by fieldwork, which prefaced installation of the proxies and continued intermittently throughout their deployment, which varied according to household permission. Fieldwork focuses on exploiting situated observation of action in context and informal interviews to account for the organization of technology use in the home and to elaborate the nature of the logged activities. The logs *informed and directed* fieldwork, providing a focus for empirical study and a starting point for considering the use of the network with users.

To illustrate our broader points we focus on the results to emerge from one particular home network. The household in question consisted of two adults, one male '*Andy*' aged 43, one female '*Tina*' aged 42, and two teenage girls, '*Orla*' who is 14 and '*Amy*' 16.[1] The girls are in full time secondary education. Andy is a teacher. Tina is a health worker. Each family member has irregular working hours, as well as a range of commitments and interests outside the home.

3.1 The Temporal Rhythms of Use

A striking characteristic of all our households was the extent to which domestic network use is *organized in terms of temporal rhythms and routines that exhibit differences between weekdays and weekends*. In the particular household in question, almost all network use on a weekday occurs between 3pm and midnight, with activity peaking between 7pm and 10pm. Internet access by adults is primarily concentrated into the hours between 8pm and 10pm. These distinctive rhythms and routines are driven by the exigencies of everyday life: during the week the girls go to school, the adults to work. As Andy puts it,

> "The girls get home at quarter to 4. I get back 6-ish, Tina gets back similar time, sometimes later. In terms of Tina and me it's getting back, pottering about, doing things, cooking food, sorting bits and bobs out, so if we then use the computer it will tend to be after that; kind of 7, half 7, 8 o'clock onwards."

---

[1] Not their real names.

Evidently, the exigencies of everyday life extend beyond going to school and work to "pottering about, doing things, cooking food, sorting bits and bobs out"; in other words, that gamut of contingent and routine activities that animate everyday life at home and take priority over Internet use. As Tolmie *et al.* [18] note with reference to digital housekeeping,

> "Many routine activities in the home are given priority: access to the bathroom before going to work, children's bedtime, and so on ... [Consequently, digital housekeeping] becomes something that will **fit in, around and with** other routines."

The rhythms and routines that might be evident in any network are shaped by other household routines and the priority they have on members' activities. This means that for the adults, network activities are concentrated into short time frames, often during the evening after domestic chores are completed, whereas the teenagers have a period after arriving home from school and before the adults come home when they are relatively unconstrained in their activities. As Andy describes it,

> "The girls get home from school an hour, an hour and a half, before we do and then they're installed in there [the living room] with their laptops and TV on."

It is important to appreciate that routines can be quite subtle: they are not necessarily manifest everyday but may be more occasional in their frequency. For example, Amy's weekend network activity occasionally dropped to a much lower level. It turns out that she has an irregular weekend job at a local restaurant, where she works variable shifts, sometimes Friday and Saturday evenings, sometimes also during the day, and occasionally she is not required at all. Furthermore, when not working at the restaurant, Amy is often engaged in extended periods of sporting activity. School, work and play all combine to shape Amy's use of the home network and result in routine periods of intense Internet activity that are fitted around outside commitments.

Understanding the inner life of the network requires that we understand the outer lives of its users as well. Rhythms and routines of use are rooted in and shaped by the social organization of everyday life: in going to school, going to work, playing sports, doing domestic chores, and all the other 'bits and bobs' that need 'sorting'. Network activities reflect the social organization of everyday life; they get their sense and reference from it, as can be seen when we consider service access routines in more detail.

3.2 The Difference Between Access and Use

It is worth reflecting on the distinction between network access and the actual use of network services by users. For example, websites increasingly consist of portal services, which are often used in a variety of ways. For example, Facebook may be used for various purposes, from chat to gaming to photo and media sharing. For the majority of the time they are online, Amy and Orla's machines are accessing Facebook. This is not the case for the adults' shared machine, which shows *regular* but not *continuous* Facebook access. Similarly, Amy's laptop shows almost continuous access to MSN Messenger, Windows Live, and

Hotmail services unlike the other machines, which showed regular but intermittent access.

Fieldwork revealed that Amy routinely boots up her machine, signs into MSN, and then clicks on the Hotmail inbox icon. Amy accounts for the procedure in saying,

> " ... it's like stuff that I've emailed from my school account to my home account, like documents and stuff."

Given this style of work it is unsurprising that Messenger, Live, and Hotmail services appear to be accessed to a high degree. However, the *use* Amy to which puts these services is not immediately apparent from any logging or measurement. Interaction between her school network account, which leaves a small trace in the logs, and other communication services is hard to infer from the logs alone.

The moral of the story is that inferring continuous service use by household members on the basis of measurement of access by a machine is unwarranted. What is warranted though, is the inference that household members have different work-practices of service use: for example, the adults frequently log in and out of MSN services, pulling data to them on demand; whereas the children adopted an always on practice with data continuously pushed to them.

3.3 The Diversity of Network Activities

Our studies also suggest stability about network use that allows people to speak about and characterize the ways in which they use the network. These characterizations are reflected in how they talk about and describe their network use. The characterizations at play tend to focus not on forms of traffic or the application being used but on the activities the network enables and allows. As Tina put it when discussing her use of the web during the logging period,

> "I used it like I normally do: the bank, Hotmail and John Lewis [laughs]"

John Lewis is a large department store in the UK. Tina uses John Lewis on a regular basis for her shopping needs. What is interesting here is the everyday language used to characterize different sorts of use. These separations are not technical – for Tina they are based on activity and purpose. Thus she does not use the web, transfer files, fetch email, or stream media; instead, she shops, banks, watches films and sends messages.

Users often use these characterizations of the network to describe how the network is used. For example, Andy offered the following account of Orla's activities during a fieldsite visit in which Orla was quite visibly 'otherwise engaged',

> "A lot of it will be headphones, you know, music on the laptop – she listens to Grooveshark – there'll be Facebook, Messenger, one or two other things on at the same time."

Users characterizations' are practical understandings of the network. They may have a loose association with the types of traffic and application in play, but fundamentally what they convey are the different things done with the network. From our

broad range of studies we suggest a number of common distinct categories emerge from our work.

Email is often talked about as a particular form of network use. People talk of *"getting their email"* or *"catching up with email"* but use a range of applications and protocols for email. These include Outlook/Exchange on Windows, as well as clients using POP3 and IMAP, as well as significant use of various webmail systems from Microsoft, Google, Yahoo and others.

Gaming was a particular class of activity spoken about by users. This was often in terms of the impact of this form of activity on the network. People would talk about *"gaming slowing the network"* or complaints of others slowing the network stopping gaming.

Skype audio and video calling has grown dramatically over recent years, in both domestic and work settings.[2] Users often speak of regular video communication and conversations and the impact this has on the overall network performance.

Social media such as Facebook, MSN and Twitter are often referred to as a part of the overall activity of the network. Often this is presented and talked about in terms of access: *"you're not allowed on Facebook until you've done your homework."* Given the growing popularity of social games, the inter-relationship between this categorization and gaming needs further study.

Streaming media has a growing presence in homes, with services such as BBC iPlayer and Last.fm becoming the normal means of media consumption. For video services, people coordinate with others to ensure video watching is not impacted due to network congestion.

Downloads are a specific set of network activities having a dramatic effect on domestic networks, and were often talked about negatively due to their perceived impact on the home network. People were often asked to schedule any downloads considerately, e.g., asking others to *"do your downloads at night time."*

Shopping was a specific online activity for many users, spanning a number of websites including both traditional and specifically online retailers, e.g., John Lewis, Amazon. People were concerned that shopping activities would not be impacted by network variations. This was particularly critical when processing final payments or undertaking activities such as comparative browsing of products.

3.4 Where the Network is Used

Network use is highly situated, with network activities taking place in particular settings and situations. People routinely reason about and account for what one another are up to on the network, according to their local understanding of those settings and situations; this includes how they understand those activities to be *embedded in and exploiting space and place.*

Thus, fieldwork makes it perspicuous that the use of network services by the girls is exclusively confined to the family living

---

2 http://www.techtified.com/2010/05/13-percent-of-international-calls-now-go-via-skype/

room. On the other hand, adult access occurred exclusively in the kitchen. Though there was regular visual and verbal contact between the girls in the living room and the adults in the kitchen, there was a definite spatial or *ecological separation* of network service access between adults and teenagers. Typically, this separation maintains until around 9pm when domestic chores have usually been completed and eating has finished. However, when the adults have addressed the day's priorities, they deliberately try to claim the living room space to watch TV, often the BBC's online iPlayer service. As Andy puts it,

> *"When things settle down for us we'll ask the girls 'what have you got to do?' Orla often goes off to her room to do her homework, Amy normally stays about; she's more sociable."*

We are *not* suggesting that this particular arrangement is of any general significance. We *are* suggesting that use of network services is intimately connected to the organization of space and place and the ways in which that organization is locally *designed to meet social need* [6][18]. As Tina puts it,

> *"We had discussion before we moved in that we wouldn't have television points in the girls' bedrooms because they escaped to their bedrooms too much and I wasn't happy about the amount of time they spent on their own. The laptops don't work in their bedrooms – fantastic! – so they have to be in the sitting room which is where I'd rather it be: a communal thing so there's people about, more social interaction, we get to share more"*

In this case what could be viewed as poor performance of the wireless network becomes a concrete benefit! Previous empirical studies have highlighted that household members organize space to cater for network technology, e.g., [6][18]. When we move beyond infrastructure it is also the case that household members organize the spatially embedded use of technology around the social dynamics, expectancies and routines that hold sway in the home. Not only is the positioning of network technology "accountable to the broader issues in the household" [6], its situated use is shot through with them.

This section has explored how network users understand home networks in terms of *when* they are used, *what* use is made of them, and *where* this use takes place. In the following section we consider the understanding of network use "from below", i.e., how this use might be understood from the perspective of the traffic visible on the network.

4. THE VIEW FROM BELOW

Traditional network measurement and management techniques arose in large backbone and later enterprise networks. Using extensive and distributed measurement techniques, statistical models are constructed primarily for purposes such as attack detection and capacity planning, but also to describe network behavior to enable simulation of network traffic. These models typically take account of time-of-day, day-of-week, seasonal, and other macroscopic factors leading to temporal variation. They describe traffic in terms of volume (byte and packet counts) and generating application, often aggregated into coarser categories.

Models for attack detection often also consider communication patterns between hosts as identified by IP address.

The application classes and categories into which network engineers classify traffic are based on factors with network-wide significance. For example, large shifts in traffic volume signifying rerouting events due to, e.g., link failure; changes in the applications generating the bulk of traffic indicating trends pertinent to capacity planning, e.g., the changing significance of email, web and peer-to-peer file sharing traffic over the past decade; and communication patterns indicative of security scans, attacks and breaches whether low-volume port-scanning or high volume targeted distributed denial-of-service.

Unfortunately, these traditional categorizations are of limited use in the home network context. Not only do the events of significance change when considered from a home network point of view, even from a network point-of-view these categories are not always cleanly separated. For example, others have noted the rise of HTTP as a universal transport protocol, used for web browsing, social communications, video access and email, often muddies the waters [10][14].

Additionally, applications that generate low volumes of traffic across a backbone network might be considered highly significant by the homeowner when carried on their home network. For example, Skype traffic is not typically such high volume that it is of particular importance to the network operator. However, as noted above, to the homeowner, how Skype traffic is treated may well be critical to their work and social lives.

4.1 Categorizations

There is no explicit consensus in the networking community as to how to categorize traffic by application, with a range of ad hoc categorizations and many authors even using the terms "application" and "protocol" interchangeably, e.g., [1][4][8]. The nearest to a consensus view appears to be that of Moore et al. [12][13], recently updated by Kim et al. [9]. The resulting categorization is given in Table 1, with some less widely used extensions given in Table 2.

Comparing these to the categories from users (§3.3) we see limited overlap, e.g., gaming, streaming, email, downloads (P2P). As other authors have noted however, some of these categories are misleading, e.g., email now really must include some web traffic due to widespread use of Hotmail, Gmail and others. One category beloved of network engineers that is notably absent from the user categorization is that of the Web (WWW). It seems that, perhaps unsurprisingly, users categorize their network behavior by activity not by protocol or even service. Thus the network engineer's "www" becomes a mixture of (in this case) "social media", "streaming media", "email", and "shopping". It is quite possible that a broader sample of users would further extend that category.

Skype deserves special mention as a category important to users: it is difficult to identify, designed to evade firewalls and NATs, and to obfuscate its traffic patterns. Furthermore, it uses both TCP and UDP, and in some cases uses well-known ports (80, 443).

Considerable effort has been expended to identify Skype nonetheless, perhaps because its presence often poses a threat to traditional network operator profit models. A variety of techniques have been used; perhaps the most thorough approach is that of Molnár [11] which makes use of observed signaling traffic on a range of ports, timing characteristics of UDP keepalive messages, and a range of call connection properties (bandwidth, packet rate, average packet size, main mode of packet inter-arrival time).

Table 1. Consensus network traffic categorization [9].

Application	Protocols
WEB	HTTP, HTTPS
P2P	FastTrack, eDonkey, BitTorrent, Ares, Gnutella, WinMX, OpenNap, SoulSeek, MP2P, Direct Connect, GoBoogy, Soribada, PeerEnabler
FTP	FTP
DNS	DNS
Mail/News	SMTP, POP2/3, IMAP, identd, NNTP
Streaming	MMS (Windows Media Player), Real, Quicktime, Shoutcast, VBrick streaming, Logitech Video IM
Network operations	NetBIOS, SMB, SNMP, NTP, SpamAssassin GoToMyPc
Encryption	SSH, SSL
Games	Quake, HalfLife, Age of Empires, Battlefield Vietnam
Chat	AIM, IRC, MSN Messenger, Yahoo messenger
Attack	Address scans, Port scans
Unknown	

Table 2. Additional commonly used categories [5][7].

Application	Protocols
VoIP	SIP, RTP, Cisco Callmanager, SCCP, Vocera, Skype
Filesystems	SMB, CIFS, NetBIOS, Appleshare, NFS, AFS
Services	X11, DNS, finger, identd, DND, Kerberos, LDAP, NTP, printer

5. IMPLICATIONS & CHALLENGES

Having discussed these two rather disparate views of network traffic classification, the question arises: so what? In this section we present and discuss some of the implications and challenges that arise in reconciling them.

Legibility. As network connectivity becomes more ubiquitous in household devices, e.g., TVs and fridges, network management becomes a required everyday activity. However, those that must carry it out are unlikely to want to become professional network managers, thus it behooves the networking community to provide better, more accessible tools to give greater insight into the network to non-experts, who do have no desire to concern themselves with details such as protocols. Traffic classification

for presentation in user interfaces must take account of the categories that are important to users.

Quality of service (QoS). The major sites of congestion are currently believed to be the home and edge networks. QoS mechanisms can be used to make better use of available resource, but must be applied to the *service* not the protocol. Thus it might be video (not RTMP), or Skype (not VoIP), or shopping (not HTTP) that needs protection. Doing so relies on both accurate identification of traffic with useful categories, and automatic techniques for determining the bandwidth requirements and impact of any given QoS mechanism.

Temporality. The high degree of temporal variation in both traffic volume and type, coupled with the fuzziness and complexity with which related policies are expressed, e.g., "no Facebook until after dinner", "no gaming except at weekends", gives rise to and scope for mechanisms to timeshift different types of traffic. Taking these factors into account might inform operators' capacity planning, as well as prove useful in alleviating particular hotspots. The presence of activity from certain applications, devices or even users on the network might be used to indicate the temporal rhythm of the setting allowing different policies should come into play at key times.

Flexibility. Home networks evolve the types of traffic carried and the demands placed upon them more quickly and more radically than core networks. The simple addition of a new device such as the latest games console can significantly alter the traffic patterns observed on a home network, as well as radically change the relative desired treatment of traffic by the network. Classification or management tools for home networks *must* be sufficiently flexible to cope with these step changes.

Geography. Home network access and use is socially mediated, to a far greater degree than in the enterprise network. Even given the reliance on wireless networking technologies, the geography of the home still plays an important part in this. How well signals propagate through the physical building has an important impact on network use from different points: how public or private the situation will change both permitted and actual behavior.

6. ACKNOWLEDGMENTS

The research on which this paper is based was funded by the RCUK supported Horizon Hub, EP/G065802/1, and EPSRC Wired and Wireless Intelligent Networked Systems Initiative 'Homework', EP/F064276/1.

7. REFERENCES

[1] Bernaille, L., Teixeira, R., and Salamatian, K. "Early application identification", *Proceedings of ACM CoNEXT, '06*.

[2] Bowers, J. and Rodden, T. (1994) "The work to make a network work: studying CSCW in action", *Proceedings of CSCW '04*, pp. 287–298, Chapel Hill, ACM.

[3] Chetty, M., Banks, R., Harper, R., Regan, T., Sellen, A., Gkantsidis, C., Karagiannis, T. and Key, P. (2010) "Who's hogging the bandwidth? The consequences of revealing the

invisible home", *Proceedings of CHI '10*, pp. 659–668, Atlanta, ACM.

[4] Crotti, M., Dusi, M., Gringoli, F., and Salgarelli, L. "Traffic Classification Through Simple Statistical Fingerprinting", *ACM SIGCOMM Computer Communications Review* 37(1) January 2007.

[5] Erman, J., Gerber, A., Hajiaghayi, M.T., Pei, D., and Spatscheck, O. "Network-aware forward caching", *Proceedings of ACM WWW '09*.

[6] Grinter, R., Edwards, K., Newman, M. and Duchenaut, N. (2005) "The work to make the home network work", *Proceedings of ECSCW '05*, pp. 469–488, Paris, Springer.

[7] Henderson, T., Kotz, D., and Abyzov, I. "The Changing Usage of a Mature Campus-wide Wireless Network", *Proceedings of ACM MOBICOM '04*.

[8] Iliofotou, M., Pappu, P., Faloutsos, M., Mitzenmacher, M., and Varghese, G. "Network Monitoring Using Traffic Dispersion Graphs", *Proceedings of IMC '07*. ACM.

[9] Kim, H-C., Claffy, kc., Fomenkov, M., Barman, D., Faloutsos, M., and Lee, K.-Y. "Internet Traffic Classification Demystified: Myths, Caveats and the Best Practices", *Proceedings of ACM CoNEXT '08*.

[10] Maier, G., Feldmann, A., Paxson, V., and Allman, M. (2009) "On Dominant Characteristics of Residential Broadband Internet Traffic", *Proceedings of IMC '09*. Chicago, Illinois, USA. ACM.

[11] Molnár, S. and Perényi, M. "On the identification and analysis of Skype traffic", *International Journal of Communication Systems*, 24(1):94–117, January 2011.

[12] Moore, A.W., and Konstantina, P. "Toward the Accurate Identification of Network Applications", *Proceedings of PAM '05*. LNCS 3431, 2005.

[13] Moore, A. and Zuev, D. "Internet Traffic Classification Using Bayesian Analysis Techniques", *Proceedings of ACM SIGMETRICS '05*.

[14] Schneider, F., Agarwal S., Alpcan T., and Feldmann A. (2008) "The New Web: Characterizing AJAX Traffic", *Proceedings of PAM '08*.

[15] Shehan Poole, E., Chetty, M., Grinter, R., Edwards, K. (2008) "More than meets the eye: transforming the user experience of home network management", *Proceedings of DIS '08*, pp. 455–464, Cape Town, ACM.

[16] Tolmie, P. (2010) "Making the home network accountable", *2010 Multi-Service Networks Workshop*, July 8-9, Cosener's House, Abingdon, UK.

[17] Tolmie, P., Crabtree, A., Egglestone, S., Humble, J., Greenhalgh, C. and Rodden, T. (2010) "Digital plumbing: the mundane work of deploying ubicomp in the home", *Personal and Ubiquitous Computing*, vol. 14 (3), pp. 181–196.

[18] Tolmie, P., Crabtree, A., Rodden, T., Greenhalgh, C. and Benford, S. (2007) "Making the home network at home: digital housekeeping", *Proceedings of ECSCW '07*, pp, 331–350, Springer.

Large-scale App-based Reporting of Customer Problems in Cellular Networks: Potential and Limitations

Yu Jin*, Nick Duffield*, Alexandre Gerber*, Patrick Haffner*, Wen-Ling Hsu*, Guy Jacobson*, Subhabrata Sen*, Shobha Venkataraman*, Zhi-Li Zhang†

*AT&T Labs - Research, Florham Park, New Jersey, USA
†Computer Science Dept., University of Minnesota, Minneapolis, Minnesota, USA
*{yjin,duffield,haffner,hsu,guy,sen,shvenk}@research.att.com   †zhzhang@cs.umn.edu

ABSTRACT

In this paper, we study the *Location-based Reporting Tool (LRT)*, a smartphone application for collecting large-scale feedback from mobile customers. Using one-year data collected from one of the largest cellular networks in the US, we compare LRT feedback to the traditional customer feedback channel – customer care tickets. Our analysis shows that, due to the light-weight design, LRT encourages customers to report more problems from anywhere and at any time. In addition, we find LRT users access network services more intensively than other mobile users, and hence are more likely to experience and are more sensitive to network problems. All these render LRT feedback a valuable information source for early detection of emerging network problems.

Categories and Subject Descriptors

C.2.3 [**Computer-Communication Networks**]: Network Operations

General Terms

Measurement, Management

Keywords

Cellular network, Troubleshooting, App-based reporting tool

1. INTRODUCTION

With the rapid growth in mobile voice and data services, effective management of large-scale cellular data networks is critical to meet customer demands and expectations. Due to the vast complexity involved, problems may occur in a number of different places, e.g., mobile handsets, software and apps running on the handsets, or within the cellular network infrastructure – the latter itself spans large geographical regions, consisting of thousands of cell towers, radio spectrum access controllers, and a whole gamut of other network elements and servers, supporting millions of users. Identifying and pinpointing – not to mention troubleshooting – these problems can be an extremely challenging task.

Traditional troubleshooting approaches utilize network measurements, e.g., RTT, loss rate, collected by cellular service providers either at various locations in the network [1, 2] or at mobile handsets [3, 4]. However, such measurements do not necessarily reflect customers' experience on the network. Due to this reason, direct customer feedback through the traditional customer problem report channel – customer care tickets – as a valuable source of information for troubleshooting problems in cellular networks has recently attracted more attention [5, 6]. A customer ticket is issued when a customer calls the technical support line and reports the problem to a customer agent, and it records the whole conversation between the two parties. Despite their usefulness, customer tickets involve high overhead. A customer needs to call in and wait on the line for a customer agent to speak to and spends time diagnosing the problem with the agent. Hence customer tickets depend heavily on the availability of customer agents. Because of this, a light-weight channel is demanded for real-time customer problem reporting and troubleshooting.

The increasing popularity of smartphone devices and the roll-out of more complex software and apps make possible a new channel of large-scale location-based customer trouble-reporting in cellular networks. Users can launch performance tests on their mobile handsets and inform service providers of any problems through smartphone apps. The *Location-based Reporting Tool* (LRT) is an example of such apps[1]. LRT enables customers to report any performance problem by simply pressing a button, and the report sent via LRT, which we refer to as a *LRT message*, contains important information regarding the user's location in the network (see an overview of LRT in Section 3). Since its debut in one of the largest cellular networks in the US, LRT has received more than 1 million downloads and millions of LRT messages have been collected in the past year. In this paper, we focus on making sense of these LRT messages. *How different are they from the traditional customer care tickets? What are the advantages and limitations of this new channel for detecting emerging network problems?* In addition, since LRT users are self-selected – the user needs to actively choose to download and use LRT, *are they a good representative sample of the entire mobile user population, especially, in terms of troubleshooting network issues?*

To answer these questions, in this paper we study the unique characteristics of LRT feedback compared to customer care tickets (see Section 4). Our study demonstrates that the light-weight and simple design of LRT encourage customers to report more problems from *anywhere* and at *any time*. Because of this, LRT mes-

---

[1]For proprietary reasons, we cannot use the actual name of the app.

sages can indeed help detect emerging network issues much earlier than customer tickets, especially during nights and weekends, when the number of customer tickets are constrained by the limited number of customer agents. Moreover, the location information contained in LRT messages makes isolating problematic components in the cellular network easier.

We further conduct a comprehensive analysis of LRT users. Our study shows that the LRT users represent a self-selected non-uniform sample of the entire mobile user population. Compared to other users, LRT users tend to access network services, both voice and data services, more intensively and at more network locations (see Section 5). Furthermore, due to their preference of applications with stringent performance requirements, e.g., voice-over-IP and media streaming, LRT users are more sensitive to network performance variations. Both properties are desirable from the perspective of troubleshooting network problems, which enables LRT users to sense and report problems in the cellular network much earlier. Our analysis also points out several limitations of LRT, such as the small population size and the bias towards certain kinds of applications, and suggests remedies to make LRT a more practical network troubleshooting solution.

2. BACKGROUND AND DATASETS

Cellular Network Overview. The cellular network under study uses primarily UMTS (Universal Mobile Telecommunication System), a popular 3G mobile communication technology supporting both voice and data services. Fig. 1 depicts the key components in a typical UMTS network. When making a voice call or accessing a data service, a mobile device directly communicates with a cell tower or node-B, which forwards the voice/data traffic to a Radio Network Controller (RNC). In case of mobile voice, the RNC delivers the voice traffic toward the PSTN or ISDN (Public Switched Telephone Network) or ISDN (Integrated Services Digital Network) telephone network, through a Mobile Switching Center (MSC) server. In case of mobile data, the RNC delivers the data service request to a Serving GPRS Support Node (SGSN), which establishes a tunnel with a Gateway GPRS Support Node (GGSN) using GPRS Tunneling Protocol (GTP), through which the data enters the IP network (and the public Internet) The UMTS network has a hierarchical structure: where each *Radio Network Controller* (RNC) controls multiple node-Bs, and one *Serving GPRS Support Node* (SGSN) serves multiple RNCs (see [6] for details of the UMTS network).

Datasets. Our study uses LRT messages collected in the UMTS network for a one-year time period. To assist our analyses, we utilize additional datasets collected at various locations inside the UMTS network over the same time period, such as voice usage, data usage, Short Message Service (SMS) usage and so forth. We emphasize here that no customer private information is used in our analysis and all customer identities are *anonymized* before any analysis is conducted. Similarly, to adhere to the confidentiality under which we had access to the data, at places, we present normalized views of our results while retaining the scientifically relevant magnitudes.

Customer Tickets. To study the difference of LRT from the traditional customer report channel – customer tickets, we collect all customer tickets during the same time period. Customer ticket is the default way for *all the mobility customers* to inform the service provider regarding any problem by calling in a customer support line. A customer ticket contains the time of the call and a summary of the entire conversation between the customer and the customer

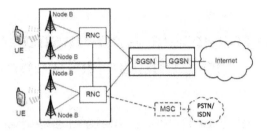

Figure 1: UMTS network architecture.

agent during the call. We note that customers may call for a variety of reasons. A large majority of calls are *non-technical* related, e.g., questions about billing, service contracts, etc. Sometimes customers call when experiencing certain *technical* problems, e.g., unable to connect to the network, etc. Similar to [6], in this paper, we refer to customer tickets as these *technical tickets*, which contain none of the following keywords: bill, account, plan and feature.

Mapping Users to Network Locations. One of the key advantages of LRT is that it is a location-based report tool. Each LRT message contains the cell tower name that the customer is connected to. With this, we can easily correlate LRT messages at each level of the cellular network hierarchy (see Section 4.2). However, for other data sources, e.g., customer tickets, this information is not readily available. We infer such information from *GPRS Tunnelling Protocol Control* (GTP-C) messages as follows.

When a customer wants to access the cellular network data service, a *GTP Create* message is sent to the GGSN (recall Fig. 1) to establish a GTP tunnel for the current GTP session, which contains the Location Area Code (LAC) and Cell ID (CID) of the node-B that is currently serving the customer. A *GTP Update* message will be sent to the GGSN to update the latest LAC and CID when the customer travels beyond a certain distance and a RNC handover happens. When the customer finishes using the data service, the GGSN is informed by a *GTP Delete* message to remove the GTP tunnel and hence terminate the GTP session. By tracking GTP-C messages, we are able to associate customers with network locations with a good accuracy at RNCs or higher level network locations, e.g., SGSNs or cities [7].

3. OVERVIEW OF LRT

LRT is a smartphone application that provides customers a means to submit feedback on their network experience to their cellular service provider. LRT has a simple design, allowing users to report problems by simply pressing a button.

Three major problem categories and five subcategories are predefined, see Table 1. We note that the five subcategories may change along with different versions of the application. However, the three major categories – coverage, voice and data – remain the same. Today, LRT can be installed on a selected number of smartphone devices and requires access to the data service[2]. We expect more mobile devices will support running LRT in the near future.

Table 1: Predefined LRT problem categories.

Major	Subcategory
Coverage	No Coverage
Voice related	Dropped Call *and* Failed Call Attempt
Data related	Data - Can't Connect *and* Data - Too Slow

[2]When data service is not accessible, LRT messages will be buffered and then delivered after the connection has been re-established.

Figure 2: LRT message categories.

In addition to these predefined problem categories, a user can also submit free-text comments about the event. Other additional features, such as viewing nearby free Wi-Fi locations, etc., are also provided. In our dataset, the free-text comments are empty in most cases. Therefore, in this paper, we rely on the predefined categories to classify reported problems. Fig. 2 illustrates the breakdown of different reported problems in four quarters during our observation period, one calendar year (denoted as T1 to T4, in chronological order). Though the number of LRT messages received are different in the four quarters, voice-related problems always constitute the largest fraction (more than 40%) and the coverage problems account for approximately 30% of the problems reported. We find also that data-related problems become more significant over the calendar year, increasing from 18% to 32%, and this is consistent with our observations with respect to the growth of usage and expectation from mobile customers on data services.

4. COMPARING LRT MESSAGES TO CUSTOMER TICKETS

As LRT is a new approach for mobile customers to report network problems, the LRT messages have characteristics distinct from more traditional ways of reporting problems, i.e., customer care tickets. In this section, we compare these two channels of customer feedback, and our analysis highlights opportunities and limitations in detecting emerging network issues using LRT.

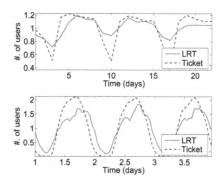

Figure 3: Number of ticket callers or LRT senders across time

4.1 LRT: Opportunities and Limitations

Any time reporting. Customer care tickets require phone interviews between the customers and the agents and thus are limited by the availability of the customer agent resource. In comparison, *the flexibility of LRT enables users to report problems at any time*. This difference is reflected in the statistics of the tickets or messages generated across the day that we now describe.

Fig. 3 displays the number of users who send LRT messages and customer tickets over a two-week time period (For proprietary reasons, we normalize the actual numbers of tickets or messages by their respective means.). For ease of visualization, we show two graphs; the top graph plots a single point for each day, while the bottom graph plots one point per hour. Clearly, there is a strong

time-of-day effect and day-of-week effect in both channels. In both graphs, LRT messages exhibit a lower variability across time, especially during nights and weekends, when there are limited customer agent resources and so much fewer customer tickets can be generated. As we show in Section 4.2, using LRT messages, we can quickly detect network performance issues that happen during times when few customer tickets are available.

A second observation from Fig. 3 is that customer tickets peak in the late morning, while LRT messages peak mostly in the late afternoon. This is most likely due to the lag between the time when problems occur and when the user reports them. Indeed, detailed notes in customer tickets indicate that many customers report problems that happened a day before (or sometimes, even earlier). This reporting lag causes the the highest customer care call volume to occur around the beginning of the day. In contrast, LRT messages, due to their low cost, are sent more promptly. The peak of LRT messages in the afternoon coincides with daily periods of heavy traffic load; as network load increases (and especially when subscribers use demanding applications such as video streaming), the overall performance may degrade, and this causes users to send more LRT messages. We describe in Section 4.2 how LRT messages enables us to detect emerging network issues earlier than with customer tickets.

Anywhere reporting. Generating a ticket typically involves a substantial overhead on the part of the customer, e.g., he needs to wait on the phone until an agent is available to discuss his problem, and then spend time diagnosing with the agent. This overhead tends to discourage users from reporting every problem that they encounter; instead, most customer tickets are reported when users persistently encounter the problem. Thus from a location perspective, most tickets concern a user's *primary usage locations* (i.e. where he stays most of the time), such as home or work place [6]. In contrast, sending an LRT message involves little overhead beyond pressing a button. Because of this, *LRT messages encourage reporting problems that occur anywhere the customer goes*, and we now show that this does indeed make a difference in terms of locations where customers provide feedback.

Recall that we use GTP-C messages to obtain the trajectory of a user's physical path. We can estimate the *primary usage location* for the user at the RNC level. Similarly, we define the *primary LRT location* as the RNC that a user is mapped to when most of the LRT messages are sent[3]. Comparing these two metrics lets us see which network locations a user complains about most in LRT messages.

Fig. 4 shows the percentage of LRT users whose primary usage location differs from their primary LRT location, as a fraction of the LRT users who sent at least x LRT messages in September 2010. We present this analysis for both data-related LRT messages and all LRT messages separately in Fig. 4. We observe that, unlike customer tickets, in most of the cases (more than 72% for all LRT messages and more than 60% for data related LRT messages), LRT users complain about places different from their primary usage locations. One explanation for this behavior may be that customers prefer using customer tickets to report problems at their primary usage locations, in order to ensure that they can interact with a live customer agent and hence the problems can be resolved appropriately. In comparison, at the other locations (e.g., places that they pass through), customers tend to report problems via LRT, since these problems are less disruptive to users' normal activities. In Fig. 5, we show the number of users observed (averaged on an

---

[3]Our designation of a user's primary usage location can be affected if they use Wi-Fi for data usage. We shall address such measurement bias in our future work.

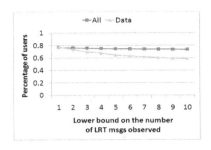 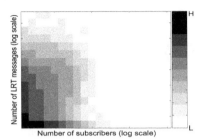 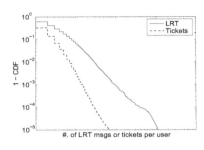

Figure 4: Proportion of LRT users whose primary LRT locations do not match their primary usage location.

Figure 5: # of users vs. # of LRT msgs associated with each RNC

Figure 6: CCDF of the Number of tickets or LRT msgs per user

hourly basis) at each RNC vs. the number of LRT messages received complaining about that RNC during one week in August 2010. Note that many RNCs associated with more LRT complaints only have a small population (note both the x-axis and the y-axis are in log scale). This suggests that at locations with a small stable user population, LRT can be a good complement to customer tickets for detecting network issues.

Increased Reporting. We find that *the low cost of LRT also encourages users to send more LRT messages.* Fig. 6 shows the number of LRT messages from each LRT user (who have sent at least one LRT message) compared to the number of customer tickets from each mobile user (who have initiated at least one ticket) in a whole month. We observe that more LRT messages are observed from LRT users than the number of customer tickets submitted by the mobile users. In particular, more than 20% of the LRT users send more than 5 LRT messages in a month, where only less than 3% of the users generate more than 5 customer tickets.

Limitations: Despite these advantages of LRT, LRT has a number of limitations. First, in most cases, an LRT message provides limited information, as it only contains a label from one of the five predefined problem categories. In comparison, customer tickets typically record detailed descriptions of the problems that the user has encountered. Second, the uni-directional nature of LRT reporting (i.e., lack of interaction between users and the service provider) is likely add some noise to customer feedback. For example, a user may report a connectivity problem with an LRT message, that in fact is due to a software issue or a problem with the mobile device. Such issues can often be eliminated by interaction with a live agent, as the agent steps through standard trouble-shooting when generating customer tickets.

Because of the limited information and added noise in LRT, diagnosing each individual LRT message may be difficult. Instead, a better way to use LRT messages may be to pinpoint emerging network issues, by analyzing the temporal and spatial correlations in them – intuitively, when a network problem occurs at a particular location, we expect a corresponding burst in LRT messages at that location. A similar approach has been used in detecting network problems using customer tickets [5, 8] with promising results. In the following, using this method, we compare the detection results using customer tickets and using LRT messages.

4.2 Detecting Network Problems using LRT Messages

In our study, we focus on one large city in the US. Fig. 7 compares the time-series of the number of LRT senders (top plot) vs. the number of ticket callers (bottom plot) per hour for a four month time period. We observe two bursts in the LRT time-series. The first one appeared at 2pm-6pm on the 75th day of observation.

The ticket time-series shows a burst at 3pm-7pm on the same day. "No coverage" is the dominant complaint associated with both LRT bursts. We also validated that this incident reflected a problem in the network – the network operators confirmed that in fact, the associated MSC was not processing incoming or outgoing calls, resulting in no or very degraded service to a very substantial number of users in the city.

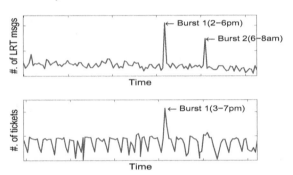

Figure 7: Correlation of LRT bursts with ticket bursts.

Interestingly, the second burst on the LRT time-series has no counterpart burst of customer tickets. Such a LRT burst has been confirmed to be associated with a network outage that happened at a particular RNC. Investigation shows that this LRT burst happened between 6am-8am, and it is possible that during this time period, people may not notice the problem or do not bother to report problems (perhaps if they are busy commuting). Another reason may be the limited customer care resources that handle complaints in early mornings. LRT, on the other hand, has no such constraints, and hence can detect such network problems missed by using customer tickets alone.

Further, LRT messages also report the node-B to which the user is currently connected, and this can help easily isolate problematic components in the cellular network. For instance, the first LRT burst in Fig. 7 can be isolated to a failed MSC, since most of the LRT messages are associated with one particular MSC. Likewise, we can attribute the second burst to an RNC failure. In contrast, customer tickets do not contain this information, and inferring this information with GTP-C messages may not be sufficiently accurate at node-Bs and cell towers (see [7]).

Despite many advantages of LRT messages over customer tickets in detecting emerging network issues, LRT-based detection may not be applicable at network locations where the LRT user population is small. Although LRT has received millions of downloads, the *LRT users still only account for a very small percentage of the mobile users in the network* and hence at many locations there are not enough LRT users to generate statistically significant bursts

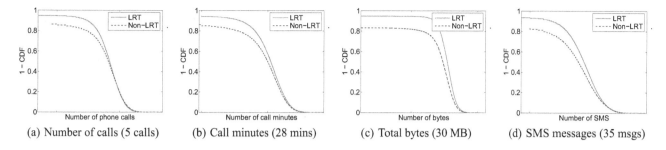

| (a) Number of calls (5 calls) | (b) Call minutes (28 mins) | (c) Total bytes (30 MB) | (d) SMS messages (35 msgs) |

Figure 8: Comparing LRT users to Non-LRT users

when problems occur. Moreover, LRT users are self-selected – the user needs to actively choose to download and use LRT. This naturally leads to questions about *whether LRT users are good representatives of the whole user population. Do the problems reported by LRT users indeed affect other users?* To answer these questions, we compare from various aspects between LRT users and non-LRT users in the next Section.

5. ANALYSIS OF LRT USERS

We now compare the network usage patterns of LRT users with other mobile users, in order to analyze whether they are a representative sample of the entire set of users. For this analysis, we select two popular smartphone devices which support LRT. Let U denote the mobile customers who use one of the above two smartphone devices exclusively during the whole calendar year of observation. We denote $U_p \in U$ as the set of users who have sent at least one LRT message, which we refer to as the LRT user group; the rest of the users (denoted as $U_n := U - U_p$) comprise the non-LRT user group[4]. We find that U_p only accounts for a small percentage of U.

Data/Voice/SMS Usage. We first compare how these two groups of users access mobile services over a one-week time period in August 2010, including their voice usage (the number of calls made in Fig. 8[a] and the total call minutes in Fig. 8[b]), data service (the total bytes – both uploading and downloading – in Fig. 8[c]) and SMS usage (the number of SMS messages sent in Fig. 8[d]). We note that, in each plot, the x-axis is in log scale, therefore the difference between two CCDF curves is much larger than it appears to be. We also include inside the parentheses the difference between the median values of the two CCDF curves.

We observe that *LRT users typically use the network services much more intensively than non-LRT users.* This intensive usage of many different network services over a long period of time makes them more likely to experience network performance problems. We also observe that *LRT users use the network in more locations.* In particular, we find that the activities of LRT users span 2.2 miles (difference between the medians) more than that of non-LRT users during a week-long observation period. This also makes them more likely to experience a performance degradation.

We can also use customer tickets as another measure of whether LRT users indeed experience more problems. We compared customer (technical) ticket rates of LRT users and non-LRT users from August to October 2010, and we found that LRT users consistently report more tickets over time (persistently around 30% higher than non-LRT users). This also suggests their increased exposure and higher sensitivity to different network problems, all of which leads them to generate more customer tickets. These LRT users are also

likely to seek additional tools (e.g., LRT) for reporting problems when the customer ticket channel is unreachable or inconvenient to use.

Application preference. In addition to differences in network usage, LRT and non-LRT users also favor different applications[5]. We show the ratio $P(app|u_p)/P(app|u_n)$ in Fig. 9, where $u_p \in U_p$ and $u_n \in U_n$. The dotted horizontal line represents $y = 1$ [6]. A higher value of the ratio (greater than 1) indicates a higher chance that a LRT user will participate in that particular class of applications. We see that LRT users use more kinds of applications, especially smartphone *app* applications, than non-LRT users. This makes them more likely to be aware of the LRT application and try it out. We note also LRT users are also much more likely to use voice-over-IP and streaming, which are sensitive to variations in network performance.

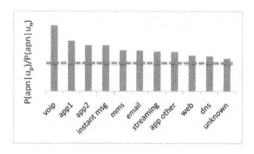

Figure 9: Application preference.

We further break down web traffic according to the content providers. Table 2 displays the top 100 content providers ranked by the ratio $P(apn|u_p)/P(apn|u_n)$ (the ratios associated with these 100 content providers are all above 1). Even though the difference between these two groups of users in terms of web usage is not as significant, they access very different sets of content providers. Interestingly, LRT users visit a lot of e-commerce, popular media, social networking and blog sites. Extensive activity on these sites will again make them more sensitive to network performance changes.

In summary, LRT users are a self-selected group that are quite different from most users in a number of dimensions – how intensive their network usage is, how many network locations they access, how diverse their applications are, how demanding the requirements of their applications are. Thus, LRT users are a little like canaries in a coal mine, since they are very sensitive to the problems and potentially exposed to more of them than typical

---

[4]Of course, only considering these two smartphone devices introduces bias to our analysis. However, due to their predominance in the network, we believe such bias is negligible.

[5]We match level 4 and level 7 headers in packets with predefined manual rules, we classify traffic into 12 application classes. The details are in [9].

[6]*app*1 and *app*2 are the most dominant smartphone apps in the network.

Table 2: Popular content providers for the LRT users

Category	Count	Examples
E-commerce	17	ebay, amazon, groupon, slickdeals, etc.
Ads	17	adbrite, tapjoyads, admarvel, adsonar, etc.
Media	16	tv.com, shazamid, transpera, turner.com
Tool	14	bit.ly, sitemeter, flurry, recaptcha, etc.
News	10	localwireless, cnn.com, nytimes, go.com
Social Network	7	digg, linkedin, twitter, plusplus, etc.
Blogs	6	wordpress, sharethis, blogspot, blogger, etc.
Weather	4	accuweather, weather.com, etc.
Photo	4	Picasa, flickr, imageshack.us, gravatar
Other	5	secureserver.net, gmail, etc.

users[7]. On one hand, this is advantageous as these LRT users may help alert us the emerging network issues much earlier before most users notice a performance degradation. On the other hand, since LRT users use applications (e.g., VoIP, streaming) that are much more sensitive to performance variations, the issues detected by LRT users may not necessarily affect other mobile users. For example, an abnormally high latency may affect an LRT user watching video but is tolerable to a mobile user only sending e-mails. In addition, as we have seen in Section 4, LRT users report many problems happening at the network locations with a small number of users. Troubleshooting based on LRT messages alone may therefore not be cost-effective from a service provider's perspective. One way to address this may be to prioritize those problems detected from LRT messages according to the potential number of customers affected by each problem, i.e., the stable customers at that location. Furthermore, expanding the LRT population (e.g., through advertisements on popular content providers, or pre-installing LRT on user devices) can help create a more representative sample and potentially detect more network problems. We leave these as our future work.

6. RELATED WORK

There is a rich literature in detecting and troubleshooting network problems in large networks. A majority of work focus on detecting, locating or trouble-shooting wired/wireless IP data network problems using passive or active network measurement data, e.g., via expert rule-based inference [10] or machine-learning techniques [11,12], or via inference of dependency among network elements, entities and events [13,14], or correlating bursts of customer tickets with other network events [5]. Our work differs in that we focus on studying a new channel of large-scale customer feedback to cellular service providers. We demonstrate unique characteristics that distinguish this new channel to traditional customer care tickets. Our work sheds light on how to make sense of this new channel and how to apply it for detecting emerging network related issues.

7. CONCLUSION AND FUTURE WORK

In this paper, we presented comprehensive analyses of a smartphone application LRT, a new channel for collecting large-scale customer feedback. We showed that LRT is a valuable light-weight channel that enables customers to report problems without temporal/spatial constraints. In addition, we found that LRT users access network services more intensively, making them good candidates to sense emerging network problems. Our future work will focus on

conducting detailed analysis of different problems reported from various channels, designing more advanced apps that are able to collect real-time performance metrics while a problem is reported. All these will lead to the development of a model for automatic detection and isolation of network problems by combing different customer report channels.

Acknowledgement

Zhi-Li Zhang is supported in part by the NSF grants CNS-0905037 and CNS-1017647, and an AT&T VURI gift grant.

8. REFERENCES

[1] M. Chan and R. Ramjee. Tcp/ip performance over 3g wireless links with rate and delay variation. In *MobiCom '02*, pages 71–82, 2002.

[2] X. Liu, A. Sridharan, S. Machiraju, M. Seshadri, and H. Zang. Experiences in a 3g network: interplay between the wireless channel and applications. In *MobiCom '08*, pages 211–222, 2008.

[3] H. Falaki, R. Mahajan, S. Kandula, D. Lymberopoulos, R. Govindan, and D. Estrin. Diversity in smartphone usage. In *MobiSys '10*, pages 179–194, 2010.

[4] J. Huang, Q. Xu, B. Tiwana, M. Mao, M. Zhang, and P. Bahl. Anatomizing application performance differences on smartphones. In *MobiSys '10*, 2010.

[5] A. Mahimkar, Z. Ge, A. Shaikh, J. Wang, J. Yates, Y. Zhang, and Q. Zhao. Towards automated performance diagnosis in a large iptv network. In *SIGCOMM'09*, pages 231–242, 2009.

[6] Y. Jin, N. Duffield, A. Gerber, P. Haffner, W.-L. Hsu, G. Jacobson, S. Sen, S. Venkataraman, and Z.-L. Zhang. Making sense of customer tickets in cellular networks. In *INFOCOM'11 Mini-Conference*, 2011.

[7] Q. Xu, A. Gerber, M. Mao, and J. Pang. Acculoc: practical localization of peformance measurement in 3g networks. In *MobiSys '11*, 2011.

[8] T. Qiu, J. Feng, Z. Ge, J. Wang, J. Xu, and J. Yates. Listen to me if you can: tracking user experience of mobile network on social media. In *IMC'10*, 2010.

[9] J. Erman, A. Gerber, M. Hajiaghayi, D. Pei, and O. Spatscheck. Network-aware forward caching. In *WWW '09*, 2009.

[10] G. Khanna, M. Yu Cheng, P. Varadharajan, S. Bagchi, M. P. Correia, and P. J. Veríssimo. Automated rule-based diagnosis through a distributed monitor system. *IEEE Trans. Dependable Secur. Comput.*, 2007.

[11] I. Cohen, M. Goldszmidt, T. Kelly, J. Symons, and J. S. Chase. Correlating instrumentation data to system states: a building block for automated diagnosis and control. In *OSDI'04*, 2004.

[12] B. Aggarwal, R. Bhagwan, T. Das, S. Eswaran, V. N. Padmanabhan, and G. M. Voelker. Netprints: diagnosing home network misconfigurations using shared knowledge. In *NSDI'09*, 2009.

[13] P. Bahl, R. Chandra, A. Greenberg, S. Kandula, D. A. Maltz, and M. Zhang. Towards highly reliable enterprise network services via inference of multi-level dependencies. In *SIGCOMM'07*, 2007.

[14] S. Kandula, R. Mahajan, P. Verkaik, S. Agarwal, J. Padhye, and P. Bahl. Detailed diagnosis in enterprise networks. In *SIGCOMM'09*, 2009.

---

[7]We can see LRT users as precursors of how users will be in a couple of years. Therefore, understanding their issues now can help improve the network for a near future when most users will use more sensitive apps.

Getting Students' Hands Dirty with Clean-Slate Networking

Nick Feamster
Georgia Tech

Jennifer Rexford
Princeton University

ABSTRACT

Conventional networking courses treat today's protocols and mechanisms as fixed artifacts, rather than as part of a continually evolving system. To prepare students to think critically about Internet architecture, we created a graduate networking course that combines "clean slate" networking research with hands-on experience in analyzing, building, and extending real networks. Our goal was to prepare students to create and explore new architectural ideas, while teaching them the platforms and tools needed to evaluate their designs in practice. The course, with offerings at both Georgia Tech and Princeton, focused on network management as a concrete way to explore different ways to split functionality across the end hosts, network elements, and management systems. The programming assignments exposed students to a range of systems, including Click, Quagga, Emulab, OpenFlow/NOX, Mininet, the Transit Portal, and publicly-available Netflow and BGP measurement data.

Categories and Subject Descriptors

C.2.1 [**Network Architecture and Design**]: Network communications

General Terms

Experimentation

Keywords

Education, curriculum

1. INTRODUCTION

Most networking courses are organized around the layers of the network protocol stack, implicitly assuming that the Internet architecture is set in stone. Network architect John Day argues that we teach the design of the Internet as a "paragon of engineering, rather than a snapshot of our understanding at the time". Historically, this mode of instruction was a natural reaction to the difficulty in changing

the form and function of existing protocols and networking equipment. Recent trends in networking research—notably, the "clean slate" networking philosophy and the increasing availability of programmable network elements—create new opportunities to re-think the Internet architecture. Changes to the Internet could range from minor tweaks to a major refactoring of network functionality.

These trends suggest to us that networking should be taught in a fundamentally different way, but they also raise questions about how to structure a course without the familiar scaffolding of the network protocol stack. Because so many networking concepts are abstract, so we want to present these concepts in a real, practical context and equip students to go beyond high-level architectural ideas to specific designs and implementations. In other words, the course should both train students in clean-slate design *and* get their hands dirty with the details of network protocols and systems. Our new course design aims to achieve these goals through a combination of lectures, selected readings, and programming assignments that focus on specific networking *problems*, rather than any particular protocol, layer, or application.

Organizing around problems rather than layers avoids redundant material while stressing concepts that appear at multiple layers of the protocol stack. For example, the Ethernet back-off mechanism and TCP congestion control are both examples of distributed resource-allocation algorithms running on the end hosts. This organization also allows us to compare and contrast multiple approaches to the same problem. For example, should load balancing over network paths happen through central optimization of the routing-protocol configuration or distributed control where hosts shift traffic to less-congested paths? To scope the material, our first offering of the course focused on problems that arise in *network management*, covering both how to manage today's networks and how to design future networks that are easier to manage. We explore a range of settings, including home, enterprise, data-center, and backbone networks.

A cornerstone of the course is the set of hands-on programming assignments and laboratories that teach students the platforms, tools, and data sets commonly used in networking research. Our goal is to train students to take their architectural ideas beyond paper designs by building and deploying real systems. We also believe that hands-on experience is a better way to learn the considerable domain details in today's networking protocols than marching through the individual protocols in lecture. In the first offering of the course, the assignments covered programmable network elements (*e.g.*, Click [7], Quagga [11], and OpenFlow/NOX [3]), experimental platforms (*e.g.*, Emulab [2], Mininet [8], and the Transit Portal [13]), and measurement data (*e.g.*, Net-Flow traffic traces and BGP routing data). Using multiple platforms, each with its own scripting languages and parsing tools, also gave the students the confidence to learn new systems for their own research.

We have taught two instantiations of graduate-level networking courses following the philosophy outlined above, at both Princeton and Georgia Tech, and course reviews have shown that students find this new course design provides them both relevant practical experience and teaches them critical thinking skills that apply both within the context of networking and beyond. As a service to the community, we have made our course materials available on the SIGCOMM education portal Web site.

2. COURSE ORGANIZATION

The course focused on clean-slate network architecture, from the vantage point of the challenges facing the operators of enterprise, data center, and backbone networks. The emphasis on the definition and placement of function is in sharp contrast to the traditional organization of networking courses by protocol layer. We also selected a diverse mix of research papers emphasizing both old and new work, and clean-slate and evolutionary approaches.

2.1 Network Management Tasks

A course on clean-slate network architecture can quickly devolve into high-level discussions of paper designs without any clear way to argue if one architecture is "better" than another. To make the discussion concrete, we need some sort of user in mind to see if some particular architectural decisions benefits or harms the user in some way. Some users, like end users who run applications or developers who write applications, are somewhat removed from the underlying architectural decisions. The protocol designer has a lower-level view, but typically presupposes some overall design of the system by focusing mainly on a single protocol that fits in a larger framework.

Instead, we chose to focus on the network operator who designs and manages a network. The network operator is responsible for composing many protocols and component together to achieve a variety of relatively concrete goals. As such, focusing on the network operators gives us a frame of reference with well-defined problems. In addition, today's Internet architecture was not designed with network management in mind. This gives us a great opportunity to reflect on how early architectural decisions inadvertently induced difficult network-management challenges that new designs could remedy. As such, we organized our course around the primary tasks network operators perform, with a balance of discussion of how to manage today's protocols and mechanisms and how to design future networks that are inherently easier to manage.

Network configuration: Configuring the underlying network elements is the main challenge in network management. In this segment of the course, we explored how enterprise administrators use Virtual Local Area Networks (VLANs [4]) and backbone operators detect configuration mistakes and express local policies using the Border Gateway Protocol (BGP [12]). We also stepped back to explore the recent trend toward logically-centralized control of networks (culminating in the recent OpenFlow initiative), as a possible way to make network configuration simpler and more flexible.

Traffic engineering: Traffic engineering involves adapting routing to the prevailing traffic to balance load and improve performance. This segment of the course explored several approaches to traffic engineering, such as tuning the configurable parameters in conventional routing protocols, distributed load balancing over multiple paths, and oblivious spreading of traffic over multiple intermediate nodes.

Network security: Network administrators devote significant effort to protecting their users and their own infrastructure from attack. In this section of the course, we covered techniques for preventing attacks (*e.g.*, access control and secure routing protocols) and detecting attacks (*e.g.*, intrusion detection systems and anomaly detection). Discussions of security lead to useful discussion about the need for verifiable notions of identity, something missing in today's Internet.

Network troubleshooting: Network operators rely on measurement data to detect and diagnose problems affecting their users. This section of the course gave an overview of network measurement and effective techniques (such as sampling, filtering, and aggregation) for reducing the volume of measurement data. We also covered techniques for inferring network performance and load from limited measurement data, including a rich body of related work on network tomography.

Emerging topics: Inevitably, some topics don't fit naturally into a simple taxonomy, and this is especially true for active areas of research. In this section of the course, we focused on emerging topics, such as energy-efficient networks and network support for online services (such as geo-replicated servers and IPTV). Then, the course ended with a look at programmable and virtualized networks, allowing us to reflect on the ongoing debate in the research community on the merits of rethinking the Internet architecture.

2.2 Rethinking the Division of Labor

The course focused on network *architecture*—the definition and placement of function in the network—rather than the existing protocol stack. How to divide functionality between the end hosts, the network elements, and the management systems was a recurring theme in the lectures, papers, and discussions.

Overview of today's division of labor: To set the stage for the course, we had three lectures—on the end host, the data plane, and the control plane—that reviewed computer networking, with an emphasis on today's Internet architecture. The lecture on the end host focused on how the bootstrapping the end host, network identifiers (*e.g.*, domain names, IP addresses and MAC addresses), the socket abstraction, and distributed resource-allocation techniques like TCP congestion control and the Ethernet back-off mechanism. The lecture on the data plane focused broadly on packet-streaming algorithms that perform simple actions on incoming packets based on previously-installed rules, providing a common framework for thinking about routers, switches, firewalls, network address translators, and so on.

The lecture on the control plane discussed routing protocols, with a clear separation between what state the protocol computes (*e.g.*, spanning tree vs. shortest-path graph), the distributed algorithms that compute these paths, and how the routers learn where end hosts connect to the network.

Revisiting the division of labor: The course frequently returned to the theme of rethinking the division of labor. For example, the section on traffic engineering fostered discussion of whether traffic engineering should be handled by the management system (*e.g.*, tuning OSPF link weights), the network elements (*e.g.*, load balancing in TeXCP [5]), or the end hosts (*e.g.*, by switching paths in response to performance problems). Similarly, the section on configuration in enterprise networks lead to discussion over whether switches should learn end-host locations through MAC learning in the data plane (as in today's Ethernet) or by querying a distributed directory in the control plane (as in SEATTLE [6]).

Multiple types of networks: To give the students broad exposure, we covered a mix of enterprise, data-center, backbone, and home networks; ideally, the course would have also covered wireless networks as well. Considering different kinds of networks fostered good discussions of the unique opportunities and constraints in each network setting. For example, while traffic engineering in data-center networks must handle volatile traffic patterns, greater path diversity and the opportunity to modify the end host lead to different solutions than earlier work in backbone networks. Similarly, in the discussion of security, enterprise network operators place greater emphasis on access control and intrusion detection, whereas backbone operators focus on routing-protocol security and network-wide anomaly detection.

2.3 Diverse Collection of Research Papers

In organizing the course, we intentionally exposed students to a wide range of research papers, including a mix of classic and recent papers, evolutionary and clean-slate research, and interdisciplinary work incorporating relevant theoretical techniques.

Mix of classic and recent papers: As with many graduate courses, we wanted to have a healthy mix of classic papers in computer networking and newer papers reflecting the current activity in the field. The classic papers fit naturally at the beginning of the course (in conjunction with a brief overview of the current Internet architecture) and at the end of the course (as a way to look forward toward a future Internet). Several of the classic papers, written well before the Internet's success was a forgone conclusion, offered refreshing examples of clean-slate design in action, while ironically also providing background on the legacy Internet. Others, such as the early work on active networks, gave the student an opportunity to see how certain themes in network research recur, as witnessed by the renewed interest in programmable networks.

Evolutionary vs. clean-slate solutions: For most classes, we intentionally paired a paper proposing a clean-slate solution with a corresponding evolutionary approach to the same problem For example, the class on access control included one paper describing a formal tool for configuring existing firewalls (Firmato [1]) and another on a dynamic access control system built on top of OpenFlow (Reso-

nance [10]). Similarly, the class on interdomain routing security included incrementally-deployable techniques for detecting and avoiding anomalous BGP routes, as well as clean-slate cryptographic solutions like S-BGP and soBGP. Comparing these kinds of papers fostered to good discussions of the challenges (and successes) of working within today's network architecture, as well as the opportunities for entirely new approaches to network-management problems.

Interdisciplinary research: The course stressed that practical problems in networking often lead to interesting interdisciplinary work that applies theoretical techniques from other fields. For example, the treatment of traffic engineering naturally emphasized connections to optimization theory and control theory, whereas the discussion of network troubleshooting led to discussions about tomographic techniques for inferring network properties from limited measurement data. While we could not cover the many theoretical topics in great depth, the course stressed the value of applying techniques from other fields or collaborating with colleagues in theoretical fields.

3. PROGRAMMING ASSIGNMENTS

While many graduate courses focus primarily on reading and discussing research papers, we believe that programming assignments are crucial for teaching students tools for use in research and helping them understand the material. In this section, we survey the goals of the assignments and summarize the specific assignments used in our two offerings of the course.

3.1 Goals of the Assignments

Our main goal for the assignments was to *help students develop an arsenal of tools* that they could apply to implement and evaluate their own research ideas. To achieve this goal, the assignments require students to become familiar with a variety of platforms, including development platforms such as Emulab, OpenFlow, and the Transit Portal, but also with tools and techniques for analyzing network measurement data. Each assignment focused on a different platform; our introduction of many different platforms and tools served not only familiarize the students with a variety of tools, but also to improve their confidence in quickly learning new environments for development, testing, and experimentation..

Many networking courses aim to *teach domain details*. Learning the details of various networking protocols is essential, but we believe that the best way for students to learn these details is *by doing*: students learn the details of these protocols best when they can gain exposure to these protocols through hands-on tasks and activities. For example, the abstract details of the Border Gateway Protocol can be made much more concrete if students are asked to establish a live BGP session and direct traffic over that session; similarly, various network operations tasks such as billing and provisioning can be made more concrete if students are given network data and asked to perform the tasks themselves.

Many networking courses teach students networking by presenting the details of each layer of the network stack. In contrast, one of our goals in the assignments is to *teach students to think across traditional layer boundaries*. We believe that many important network concepts and network management tasks transcend layers, and that some network management problems may actually result from interactions across layers. In one of our assignments, we ask students to implement the the same set of network functions at different layers of the protocol stack, effectively demonstrating that the concepts are largely the same with only subtle differences in the details (*e.g.*, the format of forwarding-table entries in a switch vs. a router).

In each of the assignments, we encourage students to think critically about network design—and the design of experimental platforms themselves—with an eye toward redesigning systems to make them easier to use and extend. Admittedly, the assignments could go much further in helping students think critically about design: the current versions of the assignments still focus largely on familiarizing students with the mechanics of existing platforms and protocols. For each assignment below, we describe possible ways to extend it to encourage students to think more critically about network design.

3.2 Summary of Assignments

We now summarize the assignments we developed and describes the conceptual themes, the skills that students develop, and the domain details that students learn when doing the assignment. To expose students to problems in different environments, we have students study problems in both enterprise networks and wide-area networks. We are also in the process of developing an additional assignment for familiarizing students with home networks, which we will discuss in Section 4.

3.2.1 Enterprise Networks

Layer-Two Configuration (using Emulab, Click, and Quagga) To familiarize students with layer-two networking concepts, as well as with Emulab and Click, we provided students with a sample network topology and asked them to set up the topology as a single, switched local area network. First, to familiarize students with the capabilities of Emulab, we asked them to use the scripting language embedded in Emulab's configuration to automatically configure a large network topology. We then asked the students to use Emulab capabilities to place all of these nodes in a single local area network. To familiarize students with layer-two networking concepts, as well as the Click software router, we then asked students to implement the same layer-two connectivity, but using a Click configuration, rather than relying on the Emulab infrastructure to provide the layer-two topology. This part of the assignment taught students the details of how learning bridges work and familiarized them with the capabilities and configuration of Click elements. The students also experimented with intradomain routing protocols by running OSPF on the Quagga routing software. This gave the students experience with using and configuring Quagga, and measuring the time required to detect and recover from a link failure.

The current version of this assignment familiarizes students with existing layer two protocols; we intend to extend the current assignment to also encourage students to think more about new and emerging layer-two protocols, such as various emerging scalable Ethernet protocols (*e.g.*, SEAT-TLE [6], Portland [9]). Although our current course offerings teach many of these designs in lecture, we believe that students may be able to reason about the tradeoffs associated with each of these designs.

Hubs, Switches, and Routers (using Mininet and OpenFlow/NOX) The next assignment illustrates how many kinds of network elements ultimately perform similar rules on streams of packets that involve matching on attributes and performing actions, and exposed students to OpenFlow switches and the Mininet environment. The students downloaded a VirtualBox [14] image that runs Mininet to emulate a network of hosts, switches, and controllers. After constructing a simple topology, the students write a series of small applications that run on the NOX controller. In the first two applications, all packets go to the controller which acts either as a hub or a learning switch. In the next two applications, the controller applications install either microflow rules or wildcard rules in the underlying switches, so the switches act either as a layer-two MAC-learning switch or an IP router. In all four cases, the students perform ping measurements between various pairs of hosts and analyze the sources of delay in delivering traffic.

The assignment intentionally uses the same platform to study hubs, switches, and routers, to stress the inherent similarities between these components and the value of a general data-plane model in network elements. Still, the current assignment primarily focuses on the mechanics of using OpenFlow, NOX, and Mininet. In a future version of the assignment, we could have the students design and implement fundamentally new network functionality on top of the OpenFlow switches.

3.2.2 Wide-Area Networks

We have developed two assignments to expose students to problems in wide-area networking. The first assignment asks students to set up a virtual network and connect that network to the Internet via BGP, using the Transit Portal. The second assignment asks students to analyze different network traces, asking them to perform various network management tasks.

Connecting a Virtual Network to the Internet (using Transit Portal) In this assignment, we give students a simple network topology and ask them to set up the topology in a virtual network environment of their choice. We gave students the option of selecting their own virtual network environment to allow students to focus on the networking-related aspects of the assignment, rather than on the minutia of any particular virtual network environment. Most students opted to use either VirtualBox or Qemu to set up their virtual network. After setting up the network topology, students were asked to run an intradomain routing protocol between the nodes (*e.g.*, by configuring a software router on each of the nodes). All students elected to use Quagga for this part of the assignment. Once students set up an intradomain routing protocol on the nodes, we asked them to connect their network to the Internet via BGP (using the Transit Portal as an upstream provider) and announce an IP prefix corresponding to their virtual network over the BGP session that they established.

Once the students established interdomain connectivity, we asked them to perform or demonstrate a few simple network management tasks. First, we asked them to establish an HTTP server on one of the nodes in the topology and demonstrate that the server was reachable from the Internet. We then asked them to introduce a link failure in the intradomain topology and demonstrate intradomain route convergence. By performing this experiment, students were able to understand interdomain routing configuration and understand how intradomain routing protocol convergence works. Finally, we asked them to rate-limit the HTTP traffic on the link between the virtual network and the rest of the Internet. Most students used the Linux `tc` tool for this part of the assignment.

A future version of this assignment might ask students to perform more network management-related tasks with the network that they set up (*e.g.*, experimenting with different traffic load balancing schemes).

Analyzing Measurement Data (using Netflow and BGP Traces) We gave students both routing and traffic traces from several real-world networks and asked them to perform several management-related traffic analysis tasks using the data. The assignment included a BGP routing table dump, as well as NetFlow traces from the Georgia Tech and Internet2 networks. In the traffic measurement portion of the assignment, we asked students to analyze network flow traces. We asked students to address various network management-related questions, such as determining the heavy-hitter applications and users for both inbound and outbound traffic. We also asked them to propose methods for balancing traffic load across the available links. In the BGP portion of the assignment, we asked students various questions about the BGP routing table, ranging from which ISPs served as the upstream provider for various edge networks to how various networks perform inbound and outbound route control. We also asked the students to analyze streams of BGP update messages to under BGP convergence behavior, such as the frequency of updates across different prefixes, the interarrival times between messages during BGP path exploration, and typical convergence delays.

In future offerings of the course, we aim to better integrate this assignment with the experimental tools and platforms that students use for other assignments. One possibility might be to integrate the BGP-related questions with the assignment that uses Transit Portal, and perhaps even have students set up traffic monitoring tools on the virtual network that they establish.

4. DISCUSSION AND LESSONS LEARNED

In this section, we briefly discuss the lessons we have learned from our course offerings, and what we plan to do differently when the course is offered in the future. Many of the discussion points below reflect the feedback that we received on course feedback forms collected at the end of the semester at both Princeton and Georgia Tech. Most students expressed excitement at the new course organization; one even told us that the course modules on OpenFlow helped him better prepare for a job interview for a job that he ultimately landed.

Alternate Course Organization In the first offerings of the course, we organized lectures around network management tasks, in an attempt to eliminate the redundancy in instruction that can occur when networking is taught layer-by-layer. Still, the existing organization also had problems, since different network domains (*e.g.*, data-center networks)

were spread throughout the course, rather than consolidated in a single module. This organization made it more difficult to align the assignments thematically with lecture topics, since each assignment naturally focused on one particular domain. It also introduced some abruptness into the flow of lectures, since some lecture topics naturally required introducing more background material before an in-depth discussion of the research problems could take place. In the next offering of the course, we will attempt to organize the lectures around different types of networks (*i.e.*, enterprise networks, data-center networks, transit networks, home networks, and wireless networks) in an attempt to streamline the lectures and align them more closely with assignments.

More Novelty, Less Grunt Work In course surveys, many of the students complained that many of the assignments involved a substantial amount of "grunt work" to set up the infrastructure required to do the assignments. Some of this grunt work entailed setting up the platforms and infrastructure associated with the assignments and is, in some sense, the nature of becoming familiar with the ins and outs of new tools and platforms for networking research.

Nevertheless, we believe that some aspects of assignment setup could be better streamlined, to help students focus on the more interesting aspects of each assignment. For example, in the assignment that requires students to build a learning switch with Click on the Emulab testbed, students spent a considerable amount of time finding and compiling a version of Click that would run on the default Emulab image. One way to streamline this process might be to create an Emulab image that students can install on the Emulab nodes that already has some of the working software for the course (*e.g.*, Click, Quagga). In the absence of teaching assistant support, another possibility will be to openly encourage students to work together on the aspects of the assignment that involve experiment setup. For example, one idea we may explore in the future is to use a course wiki to allow students to collaborate and troubleshoot certain parts of the assignment (*e.g.*, the initial platform setup) together as a class.

Another possibility that we are exploring is to design assignments that build on one another. This approach may not be possible as a general rule, because, by their nature, the assignments are intended to teach students about a variety of platforms for networking research, but there may be some cases where tools or concepts learned in one assignment might be re-used in another. For example, after students learn about Click elements and configuration in the initial assignment on layer-two networking, we might ask them to re-use Click in the assignment on building a virtual network to perform specific network management tasks (*e.g.*, to implement the rate-limiting function, or some other traffic classification function, in Click, rather than with `tc`).

New Course Modules In keeping with a new organization of course material around different types of networks, we plan to augment the course with material on an emerging fourth type of network: home networks. In the additional module and planned assignment, we intend to explore the theme of network-management problems that occur in this new increasingly important type of network. To help students develop hands-on experience with networking problems in the home, we have developed a home networking laboratory where students can install customized (and

OpenFlow-enabled) programmable gateways and also create network configurations that include a variety of consumer devices, ranging from game consoles to networked television sets. We are still in the process of developing the assignment for this part of the course, but possibilities including developing an automated network management tool for certain home network configuration scenarios, or possibly a remote troubleshooting module.

On a related note, many of the students asked for coverage of wireless networks. Given the growing prevalence of wireless and cellular networks, future offerings of the course will incorporate a module on these topics, with a course assignment devoted to these topics, as well.

5. CONCLUSION

The emergence of many new networking technologies in recent years has enabled researchers, developers, and network operators to solve conventional networking problems in radically different ways. Rather than teaching students about network protocols and layers as fixed artifacts, we believe that networking courses should instead focus on the most pressing problems that network users and operators face today, as well as the tools that we, as researchers, can apply to tackle these problems. Towards this goal, we have designed a networking course to help students take advantage of these new opportunities by allowing them to solve problems in networking by completely re-thinking network design and providing them with the tools that they need to implement their designs.

We have found that such a course can better help students appreciate the problems and solutions in today's communications networks, while still teaching students fundamental skills and concepts that will persist in communications networks well beyond today's problems. Indeed, although layering is a fundamental design principle for today's networks, we believe that it need not and should not form the basis of course organization. In fact, many emerging network designs make layers of the protocol stack less distinct, and interaction across layers is also becoming more commonplace. Ultimately, we may find that the network management problems around which we center our course are much more persistent than even the layers of the protocol stack.

Acknowledgments

We thank Yogesh Mundada, Vytautas Valancius, and Richard Wang for their help developing several course modules and assignments.

6. REFERENCES

[1] Y. Bartal, A. Mayer, K. Nissim, and A. Wool. Firmato: A novel firewall management toolkit. In *Proc. IEEE Symposium on Security and Privacy*, pages 17–31, Oakland, CA, 1999.

[2] Emulab. http://www.emulab.net/.

[3] N. Gude, T. Koponen, J. Pettit, B. Pfaff, M. Casado, N. McKeown, and S. Shenker. NOX: towards an operating system for networks. *ACM SIGCOMM Computer Communication Review*, 38(3):105–110, July 2008.

[4] IEEE 802.1Q - Virtual LANs. http://www.ieee802.org/1/pages/802.1Q.html, 2006.

[5] S. Kandula, D. Katabi, B. Davie, and A. Charny. Walking the tightrope: Responsive yet stable traffic engineering. In *Proc. ACM SIGCOMM*, Philadelphia, PA, Aug. 2005.

[6] C. Kim, M. Caesar, and J. Rexford. Floodless in SEATTLE: A scalable ethernet architecture for large enterprises. In *Proc. ACM SIGCOMM*, Seattle, WA, Aug. 2008.

[7] E. Kohler, R. Morris, B. Chen, J. Jannotti, and M. F. Kaashoek. The Click modular router. *ACM Transactions on Computer Systems*, 18(3):263–297, Aug. 2000.

[8] B. Lantz, B. Heller, and N. McKeown. A network in a laptop: Rapid prototyping for software-defined networks (at scale!). In *Proc. HotNets*, Oct. 2010.

[9] R. N. Mysore, A. Pamboris, N. Farrington, N. Huang, P. Miri, S. Radhakrishnan, V. Subramanya, and A. Vahdat. Portland: A scalable fault-tolerant layer2 data center network fabric. In *Proc. ACM SIGCOMM*, Barcelona, Spain, Aug. 2009.

[10] A. Nayak, A. Reimers, N. Feamster, and R. Clark. Resonance: Dynamic access control in enterprise networks. In *Proc. Workshop: Research on Enterprise Networking*, Barcelona, Spain, Aug. 2009.

[11] Quagga software routing suite. http://www.quagga.net/.

[12] Y. Rekhter, T. Li, and S. Hares. *A Border Gateway Protocol 4 (BGP-4)*. Internet Engineering Task Force, Jan. 2006. RFC 4271.

[13] V. Valancius, N. Feamster, J. Rexford, and A. Nakao. Wide-Area Route Control for Distributed Services. In *Proc. USENIX Annual Technical Conference*, Boston, MA, June 2010.

[14] VirtualBox. http://www.virtualbox.org.

Author Index

www.ingramcontent.com/pod-product-compliance
Lightning Source LLC
Chambersburg PA
CBHW080132060326
40689CB00018B/3754